Romanticism
An Anthology

BLACKWELL ANTHOLOGIES

Editorial Advisers

Rosemary Ashton, University of London; Gordon Campbell, University of Leicester; Terry Castle, Stanford University; Margaret Ann Doody, Vanderbilt University; Richard Gray, University of Essex; Joseph Harris, Harvard University; Jerome J. McGann, University of Virginia; David Norbrook, University of Oxford; Tom Paulin, University of Oxford; Michael Payne, Bucknell University; Elaine Showalter, Princeton University; John Sutherland, University of London; Jonathan Wordsworth, University of Oxford.

Blackwell Anthologies are a series of extensive and comprehensive volumes designed to address the numerous issues raised by recent debates regarding the literary canon, value, text, context, gender, genre and period. While providing the reader with key canonical writings in their entirety, the series is also ambitious in its coverage of hitherto marginalized texts, and flexible in the overall variety of its approaches to periods and movements. Each volume has been thoroughly researched to meet the current needs of teachers and students.

ROMANTICISM

AN ANTHOLOGY

Second Edition

EDITED BY **DUNCAN WU**

Copyright © Blackwell Publishers Ltd 1994, 1998
Introduction, notes, selection and arrangement copyright © Duncan Wu 1994, 1998

First published 1994
Second edition 1998
2 4 6 8 10 9 7 5 3 1

Blackwell Publishers Ltd
108 Cowley Road
Oxford OX4 1JF
UK

Blackwell Publishers Inc.
350 Main Street
Malden, Massachusetts 02148
USA

British Library Cataloguing-in-Publication Data

A CIP catalogue record for this book is available from the
British Library.

Library of Congress Cataloging in Publication Data

Romanticism: an anthology / edited by Duncan Wu. – 2d ed.
p.   cm.—(Blackwell anthologies)
Includes indexes.
ISBN 0–631–20481–4 (pbk.)
1. English literature—19th century.   2. English literature—18th
century.   3. Romanticism—Great Britain.   I. Wu, Duncan.
II. Series.
PR1139.R66   1998
820.8'0145—dc21   97–22672
CIP

Typeset in 9½ on 11 pt Garamond
by Wearset, Boldon, Tyne and Wear.
Printed in Great Britain by T. J. International, Padstow, Cornwall

This book is printed on acid-free paper

Contents

Selected Contents by Theme

REVOLUTION AND REPUBLICANISM

LANGUAGE AND RHETORIC

ABOUT THE ROMANTICS

THE NATURAL WORLD

THE LAKE DISTRICT

EDUCATION

Transcendence

Imagination

Religion

Anti-War

Selected Contents by Version (Coleridge)

Recent critical commentary has highlighted the need to consider Coleridge's poems in their different versions (see, most notably, Jack Stillinger, *Coleridge and Textual Instability* (New York, 1994)). This anthology includes both the canonical texts (usually the later versions) as well as earlier ones; the supplementary table below lists all multiple Coleridge texts under poem title.

Alphabetical List of Authors

Introduction

I perceive that in Germany as well as in Italy there is a great struggle about what they call 'Classical and Romantic' terms which were not subjects of Classification in England - at least when I left it four or five years ago.

Byron, in the rejected Dedication to Marino Faliero,
dated 14 August 1820; McGann iv 546

I

When *Lyrical Ballads* first appeared in 1798 the word 'romantic' was no compliment. It meant 'fanciful', 'light', even 'inconsequential'.[1] Wordsworth and Coleridge would have resisted its application, and, twenty years later, the second generation of romantic writers would recognize it only as an element in a debate conducted among European intellectuals, barely relevant to what they were doing. On one level, of course, that's the way of literary discourse: critical debates, even when conducted by practitioners, don't always bear much on the practical business of writing. A number of critics have observed that Shelley's Preface to *Alastor* misrepresents the poem it pretends to illuminate, just as Wordsworth's Fenwick Notes aren't invariably accurate in their recollections of the poems they discuss.

'Romance' was originally a descriptive term, used to refer to the verse epics of Tasso and Ariosto. Later, eighteenth-century critics like Thomas Warton used it in relation to fiction, often European, and it was in that context that Novalis applied it to German literature. The idea didn't take flight until August Wilhelm Schlegel exploited it in a lecture course at Berlin, 1801–4, when he made the distinction mentioned by Byron. Romantic literature, he argued, first appeared in the middle ages with the work of Dante, Petrarch and Boccaccio; in reaction to classicism it was identified with progressive and Christian views. In another course of lectures in Vienna, 1808–9, he went further: romanticism was 'organic' and 'plastic', as against the 'mechanical' tendencies of classicism. By the time Byron dedicated *Marino Faliero* to Goethe (1821), the debate was in full flood: Schlegel's ideas had been picked up and extrapolated by Madame de Staël, and in 1818 Stendhal became the first Frenchman to claim himself as *un romantique* – for Shakespeare and against Racine; for Byron and against Boileau. Within a year even Spanish and Portuguese critics were wading in.

It could hardly be expected that a concept that grew out of disagreement should aspire to consensus, and it never has. When the Pre-Raphaelite Brotherhood turned themselves into a school, they knew exactly how they wanted to challenge received notions about pictorial representation; the imag-

---

[1] It is in this sense that Thomas Paine uses it in his comments 'On Revolution', p. 16, below.

ists published a manifesto of sorts in *Blast* that represented an agreed line of attack. But the romantics could never have done this. The 'big six' male poets – Blake, Wordsworth, Coleridge, Byron, Shelley and Keats – never met together and, if they had done, would probably have fallen out immediately.[2] By temperament, preoccupation and sensibility they were diverse. One factor was the generation gap. Byron, Shelley and Keats might have enjoyed the company of Wordsworth as he had been in his later twenties and early thirties, for they regarded his greatest work as *Tintern Abbey* and the *Ode*. By the time they had reached artistic maturity – *c*.1816 for Shelley and Byron, 1819 for Keats – he was the lost leader who had accepted the job of Distributor of Stamps for Westmoreland, and abandoned the unconventional religious and political views of his youth. As far as they were concerned, he had betrayed the promise of *Tintern Abbey* in return for the respectability of a sinecure. Little did they realize that, years before, his promise had culminated in the composition of *The Prelude*, which would remain unpublished until after his death in 1850.

Byron caught up with the critical debate surrounding the new concept of romanticism in 1821, but Coleridge beat him to it by a year. In 1820 the sage of Highgate compiled a list of 'romantic' writers in which the only English poets of the day were Southey, Scott and Byron.[3] That odd choice serves only to underline the inbuilt resistance of the concept to satisfactory definition – a factor that has guaranteed its usefulness as a critical and pedagogical tool. Critics have not hesitated to adapt it to their various concerns, while teachers have found it a good means of making connections between disparate writers of roughly the same period. The increasing tendency to argue against its usefulness is, therefore, consistent with its history, and the titles of several collections of essays published in recent years attest to the growing urge to demolish the 'monolith': *At the Limits of Romanticism, Re-Visioning Romanticism, Questioning Romanticism*.

The pre-eminence of Blake, Wordsworth, Coleridge, Byron, Shelley and Keats is largely the invention of the twentieth century, and has depended on two factors. The first is the publication of works not available to readers of the day: Blake's were unknown to most of his contemporaries; Wordsworth's *Prelude* was known only to a handful of people; Keats's poems gained popularity only during the Victorian period, and Shelley's were published in full only in 1839. The second factor is the tide of literary opinion, which has favoured these six writers as a group only in the twentieth century. Blake, for instance, though appreciated by some Victorian critics, found widespread critical favour only during and after the Second World War, with the appearance of such books as Jacob Bronowski's *A Man Without A Mask* (1944), and Bernard Blackstone's *English Blake* (1949). The almost mythic resonance of Coleridge's *The Ancient Mariner, Kubla Khan* and *Christabel* gained general acceptance only in the wake of John Livingston Lowes's *The Road to Xanadu* (1927). By the post-war period this had produced a consensus as to the nature of romanticism, but the recent 'discovery' of female writers has led to widespread dissatisfaction with it.

Before turning to the issue of gender – doubtless a factor pertinent to the formation of an artist's identity – I want to ask in what sense the writers of the period, male and female, might be regarded as comprising a community, and to what extent the term 'romantic' may be depended on for an understanding of their work, and the context in which it was created.

II

To some extent all writers, at any given moment in time, are part of a community. Critics, especially in this conference-going age, should know that better than most. In literary centres, such as Bristol, London and Edinburgh, those engaged in the business of writing are likely to be aware of the work of colleagues working locally. Contact is often informal, and therefore largely undocumented. Accounts may exist of meetings between distinguished writers, but they are usually anecdotal in nature, provid-

---

[2] For more on this, see George Whalley, 'England/Romantic-Romanticism', *'Romantic' and Its Cognates: The European History of a Word* ed. Hans Eichner (Toronto, 1972), pp. 157–262.

[3] He includes Goethe, Tieck, Southey, Scott and Byron among poets, and himself, Schlegel and Campbell among critics; see CC *Shorter Works* ii 858.

ing little more than a general notion of what took place. Nor can they represent more than a small proportion of the significant encounters of this kind.

There is a large volume of evidence to show that writers of the romantic period, even if they did not form movements or schools, met frequently, often at social events such as gatherings of the Holland House set. It was there that Charles James Fox, who had been sent a copy of *Lyrical Ballads* (1800) by its authors, told Wordsworth, 'I am very glad to see you, Mr Wordsworth, though I am not of your faction.'[4] And throughout the period it is possible to trace a multitude of connections between authors of both sexes: Anna Laetitia Barbauld helped promote Ann Batten Cristall and Isabella Lickbarrow; Southey, De Quincey and Wordsworth were among the subscribers to Lickbarrow's first volume of poems; Felicia Hemans was a 'tyger' to the young Shelley; Mary Tighe's *Psyche* was a formative influence on Keats; Charlotte Dacre's father lent money to Shelley, and Dacre's *Zofloya* was one of Shelley's favourite novels. It would be possible to cite numerous connections of this kind that confirm that, although they did not consolidate themselves as a movement, writers kept abreast of contemporary literature, and were part of a larger community that mixed widely, both formally and informally.

What really bound them together was the fact that they inhabited the same troubled world. The literature had its roots in an age of revolution. For Pitt's Tory administration, events in Paris from 1789 onwards were much too close to home. It may almost have been a relief when, with the execution of Louis XVI in January 1793, they were able to declare war on France. The Revolution had as its ideal the notion that society could be made fairer and more just for everyone – liberté, fraternité, egalité. Of these objectives, that of brotherhood was central to the concerns of the romantics. It is actually invoked by Coleridge in his *Religious Musings*, and most of the six 'canonical' poets believed that a better world was in prospect. Wordsworth crossed the Channel in 1791–2 to witness the Revolution for himself, Coleridge lectured on the subject, and Blake wore his *bonnet rouge* in sympathy with the revolutionaries. And with good reason. The vast majority of British citizens were impoverished, working-class labourers; thanks largely to the war, and the repressive policies of Pitt's Tory administration, they suffered severely from the effects of high inflation, high taxation, and high unemployment. Britain's laws were among the most savage in Europe; the poor were hung for no more than poaching rabbits.[5] Writers of the period were outraged by the world in which they lived, and that outrage fed directly into the culture.

From 1793 to 1815 Britain was at war with France on all fronts, from Europe to the West Indies, and often under direct threat of invasion. This placed enormous pressure on those determined to declare themselves atheists (in line with some French revolutionary thinking), and politically radical. Those brave enough publicly to side with the French were often persecuted by the government. Helen Maria Williams remained in France even after being imprisoned by Robespierre; Shelley and Byron left England partly out of disillusionment with the British political system; John Thelwall was followed wherever he went by government agitators (à la *Caleb Williams*).[6] Even after the end of the war, the government did not relax its grip. The Ely and Littleport bread riots of 1816 resulted in the execution of five ringleaders; when, in March 1817, six hundred starving weavers set out from Manchester, to petition the Prince Regent to remedy the ailing cotton trade, they were rounded up by government forces as they crossed from Staffordshire into Derbyshire; and in August 1819, armed militiamen cut down hundreds of men, women and children, who were demonstrating peacefully at St Peter's Fields, Manchester.

The six canonical male writers believed that a better world was possible – and, moreover, that it could be attained not in the afterlife, but in the real, material world that they inhabited. Blake's

4 *The Table-Talk of Samuel Rogers* (London, 1856), p. 88.
5 For a plea against this injustice, see George Dyer, *The Complaints of the Poor People of England* (p. 45). See also Godwin's novel, *Caleb Williams* (1794).
6 When Thelwall proposed settling near Wordsworth and Coleridge in Somerset in August 1797, Coleridge told him that they would be accused of 'plot and damned conspiracy – a

school for the propagation of demagogy and atheism' (Griggs i 344). Indeed, it is a fact that, as Coleridge reported, 'The aristocrats seem determined to persecute even Wordsworth' (Griggs i 341). Both Wordsworth and Coleridge were spied on as 'a set of violent democrats' (see Nicholas Roe, *Wordsworth and Coleridge: The Radical Years* (Oxford, 1988), pp. 260–1).

poetry envisioned that transcendent realm as a reality; Wordsworth aimed to describe how it would evolve in *The Recluse*, just as Shelley would do in *Prometheus Unbound*. They believed in a promised land that could be reclaimed from the fallen world, here and now – or at least in the very near future. To that extent there is something very unconventional about their poetry; it shortcircuits the central tenets of Christian theism in the hope that we need not wait until the dead are raised uncorrupted from the grave. Nor need we await the offices of a benevolent deity; even the concept of God is abridged in favour of something much closer to home:

> A presence that disturbs me with the joy
> Of elevated thoughts, a sense sublime
> Of something far more deeply interfused,
> Whose dwelling is the light of setting suns,
> And the round ocean, and the living air,
> And the blue sky, and in the mind of man –
> A motion and a spirit that impels
> All thinking things, all objects of all thought,
> And rolls through all things.
>
> *Tintern Abbey* 95–103

Wordsworth's claim is astonishing: the feeling he has as he stands on the banks of the Wye is in itself divine. It is evidence of the inner powers that will redeem humanity from the post-lapsarian 'weariness' encountered earlier in the poem. Wordsworth is famous for having said that he had no need of a redeemer;[7] the fact is, when he wrote *Tintern Abbey*, he had little need for God, at least in the generally accepted sense.[8] In *Tintern Abbey* mankind is seen to be inherently capable of redemption through an act of self-realization. It is this aspect of the poem – its inherent religious scepticism – to which Byron, Shelley and Keats constantly returned. You can write like this only if you believe, as Wordsworth and Coleridge did, in the redemptive potential of the human mind – a conviction that can be traced directly to *The Eolian Harp* (1795), in which Coleridge had asked whether all living things were

> but organic harps diversely framed,
> That tremble into thought, as o'er them sweeps,
> Plastic and vast, one intellectual breeze,
> At once the soul of each, and God of all? (ll. 37–40)

The answer Coleridge gets from his wife-to-be, Sara Fricker, is 'no'. But she merely embodies his own awareness of the radical nature of his proposition. Coleridge affirms the existence of God – essential to his understanding of what he describes – while remaining thoroughly innovatory in believing that the divine afflatus might fill all living beings with its spiritual ('intellectual') inspiration. It is an essentially pantheistic notion, and comprises Coleridge's vision of universal brotherhood – the millennium predicted in the Bible,[9] which he later believed Wordsworth would play his part in bringing about through the composition of *The Recluse*, that epic, never-completed monument to human optimism.[10]

There was nothing escapist about this, but it would take *Tintern Abbey* to contextualize the transcendent possibilities of the imagination within the real hopelessness and misery that was the lot of ordinary people in Pitt's Britain. One reason why Wordsworth's poem works so well is because, as the author of *The Ruined Cottage*, he knew that the aspirations he shared with Coleridge for human salvation must be rooted firmly in human suffering – the 'heavy and the weary weight / Of all this unintel-

---

7 'I recollect Wordsworth saying to me: "I have no need of a Redeemer"; but I believe his religion to be like [that] of the German metaphysicians, a sentimental and metaphysical mysticism in which the language of Christianity is used, which is a sort of analogy to this poetical and philosophical religion' (*Henry Crabb Robinson on Books and their Writers* ed. Edith J. Morley (3 vols, London, 1938), i 158).

8 In May 1796 Coleridge told Thelwall that Wordsworth 'is a republican, and at least a semi-atheist' (Griggs i 216).

9 Christ's thousand-year rule on earth is described by St John the Divine: 'And I saw thrones, and they sat upon them: and I saw the souls of them that were beheaded for the witness of Jesus, and for the word of God, and which had not worshipped the beast, neither his image, neither had received his mark upon their foreheads, or in their hands; and they lived and reigned with Christ a thousand years' (Revelation 20:4).

10 For more on *The Recluse*, see p. 271.

ligible world' (ll. 40–1). These were the elements of the early poetry of the romantics to which Shelley, Keats and Byron returned time and again. When Keats wrote to John Hamilton Reynolds about Wordsworth in May 1818, it was to commend his ability to sharpen 'one's vision into the heart and nature of man, of convincing one's nerves that the world is full of misery and heartbreak, pain, sickness, and oppression'.[10] In that respect, Wordsworth proved a crucial influence on how Keats conceived *Hyperion* – a poem about the aspirations that sprang out of failure and sorrow. Similarly, Shelley predicts universal brotherhood in terms that would have won the admiration of Wordsworth and Coleridge in 1798:

> Man, oh not men! a chain of linked thought,
> Of love and might to be divided not . . .
> Man, one harmonious soul of many a soul,
> Whose nature is its own divine control,
> Where all things flow to all, as rivers to the sea . . .
>
> *Prometheus Unbound* IV 394–5, 400–2

Shelley draws his inspiration from the same neo-Platonic tradition as Wordsworth and Coleridge; for him, humanity is a unity, a 'harmonious soul' redeemed from hatred and hostility by the Christlike quality of pity and forgiveness. The difference is that where Coleridge needed a Unitarian God, and Wordsworth demanded only an unspecific 'presence', Shelley goes one step further, reducing the deity to the 'divine control' within.

Byron always shared the radical aspirations expressed by Wordsworth and Coleridge in their youth, but was less sympathetic to the philosophy. Metaphysics, he believed, never achieved anything; he was more practical, and became the only one of these writers to die fighting for a better world – in the Greek War of Independence. (Today he remains a national hero in Greece, with streets and squares named after him.) But even he is capable of expressing, in a poem such as *Childe Harold's Pilgrimage*, Canto III, something of Wordsworth's pantheist conviction in the redemptive power of nature:

> I live not in myself, but I become
> Portion of that around me; and to me
> High mountains are a feeling, but the hum
> Of human cities torture . . . (ll. 680–3)

Lines like this are pure Wordsworth; if they sound imitative and unpersuasive, Byron remained true to himself insofar as he saw that the Wordsworthian response to nature affirmed something he took very seriously – the sense of an unrealized inner power. Frustration with the limitations and restrictions imposed by our earthly state permeates Byron's poetry, and compels him to aspire to a level of existence beyond the merely human. Hence his ambiguous praise for that arch-overreacher Napoleon,[11] the divinations of his anti-hero Manfred, who can command the spirits, and Byron's enduring admiration for Prometheus, who is in some sense the archetype of the Byronic protagonist. In all this he was, of course, deeply Wordsworthian, for the Byronic dilemma is encapsulated by one of Wordsworth's greatest lines: 'We feel that we are greater than we know'.[12]

Blake is often considered the exception to virtually anything one might want to say about other writers of the time – and so, in a sense, he is. He was born in 1757 – and thus is technically as much an eighteenth-century writer as a romantic. And if, like the other writers I have been discussing, he read Wordsworth, it was late in life, and without much pleasure.[13] However, it was he who, in 1789, on the brink of tumult in France, described the 'son of fire':

---

[11]   See pp. 1017–18.
[12]   See pp. 678–9.
[13]   'Afterthought' to *The River Duddon*, l. 14. Peter Manning has written on the similarities between Byron and Wordsworth in '*Don Juan* and Byron's Imperceptiveness to the English Word', *Romanticism: A Critical Reader* 217–42.

[14]   A particularly memorable marginal note in Blake's copy of Wordsworth's *Poems* (1815) reads: 'I see in Wordsworth the natural man rising up against the spiritual man continually – and then he is no poet but a heathen philosopher at enmity against all true poetry or inspiration' (see *The Complete Poetry and Prose of William Blake* ed. David V. Erdman, commentary by Harold Bloom (2nd edn, New York, 1982), p. 665).

... Spurning the clouds written with curses, stamps the stony law to dust, loosing the eternal
horses from the dens of night, crying,
    'Empire is no more! And now the lion and wolf shall cease.' (See p. 94 below.)

Revolution as apocalypse: to him, events in France were the harbinger not just of political liberation,
but of the millennium. And in this Blake was no less a romantic than the writers who were to follow.
For him, as for the rest, the fallen world was a conundrum the resolution of which led back to par-
adise. And he would spend most of his creative life explaining to the world, in his own distinctive
manner, how paradise had been lost, and how it could be reclaimed.

Who, in view of what I have already said, would want to define romanticism? In any case, the liter-
ature comprises its own definition. But were one to point to what might be considered distinctive of
the moment, it would be this: that unquenchable aspiration for universal betterment, the reclaiming
of paradise. Today, when the world seems so inexorably drawn to global destruction of various kinds,
such hopes may seem ludicrous. But two hundred years ago, when the world was gripped, for what
seemed like the first time, by successive revolutions in America, France, and even South America, it
was possible to believe, just for a brief period, that improvement, both on the physical and spiritual
planes, could be made real, and that humanity was about to be transformed.

III

Women of the romantic period (say, 1789–1834), like those of any other, had a good deal to say
about experiences peculiar to their social and political situation. To take a prime example, *Records of
Woman* is a serious attempt to explore the experience of women in history and literature within a
male-dominated society. Emphatically, for Felicia Hemans, these poems investigate women's relation
to the men with whom they are closest. Some critics have suggested that her concerns are primarily
'domestic', but that strategy fails as conclusively to establish the terms of a 'female romanticism' as it
belittles her achievement. Many of the *Records of Woman* are concerned with the plight of those lum-
bered with feckless, unreliable, weak or ineffectual men: Seymour saves himself, but fails to save Ara-
bella Stuart; Werner Stauffacher is saved only by 'the entreaties of his wife, a woman who seems to
have been of an heroic spirit'; Properzia Rossi lavishes her love and art on a man unworthy of her; the
Indian Woman is deserted by her husband for another woman, and so forth. But it would be a mis-
take to describe Felicia as having feminist designs; the other side to these poems is the high value
their author places on the relationship between the sexes. *Gertrude, or Fidelity till Death* is about pre-
cisely that: Gertrude nurses her husband in his final tormented hours with what Felicia calls 'the most
heroic devotedness'. In so doing, she becomes an exemplar for a mode of behaviour that, in spite of
her own sad experience, Felicia valorized. Even Juana, despite the neglect which her husband has
shown her, is praised for wifely devotion after his death: 'Surely that humble, patient love *must* win
back at last!'[14] These highly moral poems stand as models of heroic conduct. Felicia is concerned
essentially with the limits of human endeavour, and in that respect embodies aspects of the influence
of both Wordsworth and Byron. What is so remarkable about her is that, in doing so, she is never less
than herself – a distinctive, powerful voice, with her own preoccupations and beliefs.

What does this tell us? That to categorize Felicia, or any of her female contemporaries as 'female',
and to use gender as a governing factor in our assessment of her work, is necessarily to trivialize it.
That is not to deny the significance of gender, which is doubtless a noteworthy factor in the work of
any writer – but it can be only one of many in the formation of the literary sensibility. Were one to
argue that it determines the selection of subject-matter, genre, and poetic form, it would be necessary
also to prove that certain subjects, genres, and forms were chosen only, or at least predominantly, by
women. That is palpably not the case, and why should it have been? Felicia and her female contempo-
raries saw themselves as participating in a literary forum with male writers against whose talents they

---

[15] *Juana* 32.

sought to prove their own. Thus, Lady Caroline Lamb deliberately sets out to mimic – and excel – *Don Juan* in her own *A New Canto*, appropriating both Byron's personality and his *ottava rima*, proving that she can handle both as deftly as he. Mary Tighe unabashedly uses the Spenserian stanza to tell the story of her Psyche. Charlotte Smith brilliantly outperforms Petrarch in her use of his sonnet in her *Elegiac Sonnets*. It is that assumption of centrality within the cultural life of society that distinguishes these writers – whether Anna Seward in Lichfield society, or Mary Robinson, who first found her public through association with the Della Cruscans. It is not, in other words, as 'women writers' that they saw themselves, but as participants in the cultural mainstream.

Some critics have argued that 'male' romanticism is characterized by its preoccupation with the sublime, but female writers were just as persuasive in their understanding of sublimity – as, for instance, in Felicia Hemans's *Second Sight* and *The Spirit's Mysteries*, or Elizabeth Barrett Browning's *Sonnet on Mr Haydon's Portrait of Mr Wordsworth*. No doubt women brought to their art insights deriving from gendered experience, but those distinctive elements need to be seen in their larger context as vectors in the personality of each writer. And they were not without influence themselves. At school and university, Wordsworth and Coleridge were fervent admirers of Charlotte Smith, Helen Maria Williams and Anna Laetitia Barbauld: when he began composing sonnets at Cambridge in 1788, it was Smith whose work Wordsworth was most anxious to emulate. It was they whom he sought when first he visited London, Brighton and Paris, and to Barbauld (and Georgiana Cavendish, Duchess of Devonshire) that he and Coleridge sent an early copy of *Lyrical Ballads* (1800).

The literature is too complex to permit simplistic judgements about what 'male' or 'female' romanticism might be. Rounded literary personalities cut across such distinctions, as they always have; the fifty-year period covered by this anthology is one in which male and female writers contributed to the same vigorous and evolving culture – gender was always a factor, but never as all-embracing as late twentieth-century critics have sometimes claimed.

IV

The bias in this anthology is towards the six canonical poets, although most of the major female poets of the day are represented here – Anna Laetitia Barbauld by some of her most important early works, Mary Robinson by *The Haunted Beach*, Lady Caroline Lamb by a complete text of *A New Canto*, and Ann Batten Cristall by a generous selection from her *Poetical Sketches*. Readers desiring a fuller treatment of female writers, including complete texts of Hemans's *Records of Woman*, Smith's *Elegiac Sonnets*, *The Emigrants* and *Beachy Head*, Mary Tighe's *Psyche*, Barbauld's *Eighteen Hundred and Eleven*, Robinson's *Sappho and Phaon*, and Cristall's *Poetical Sketches*, should turn to the companion volume, *Romantic Women Poets: An Anthology* (1997).

Texts in this volume are freshly edited from manuscripts and early printed sources. Characteristically, readers are not restricted to highlights (as in comparable anthologies), but have access to entire works, with all their fluctuations of tone, mood, and rhythm. Contents include complete texts of Blake, *Songs of Innocence and of Experience*, *The Marriage of Heaven and Hell* and *The Book of Urizen*; Wordsworth and Coleridge, *Lyrical Ballads* (1798); Wordsworth, *The Two-Part Prelude*, *Michael*, and *The Brothers*; Byron, *Childe Harold's Pilgrimage* Canto III, *Don Juan* Dedication and Cantos I and II; Shelley, *Alastor*, *Prometheus Unbound*, *Adonais*; and Keats, *Hyperion* and *Lamia*. Coleridge's poetry is more comprehensively selected than in other anthologies of this kind, including early and late versions of *The Eolian Harp*, *This Lime-Tree Bower My Prison*, *Frost at Midnight*, *The Ancient Mariner*, *Kubla Khan*, as well as *Letter to Sara Hutchinson* and 1802 and 1817 texts of *Dejection: An Ode*.

Essays are generally presented in full. The selection contains complete texts of Lamb's 'Imperfect Sympathies' and 'Witches, and Other Night-Fears', Hazlitt's 'On Gusto', 'My First Acquaintance with Poets', and 'Mr Coleridge', Leigh Hunt's 'A Now, Descriptive of a Hot Day', and De Quincey's 'On the Knocking at the Gate in *Macbeth*'. Reasons of space leave me with no option but to extract from longer prose works. It is not practicable to represent works of fiction here, and in any case those wishing to cover novels of the period are best advised to use complete texts.

In this second edition I have responded to the comments of readers by increasing the volume of pedagogical material. Author headnotes are expanded to provide biographies and brief critical introductions to the selected texts, as well as lists of further reading. These lists aim to provide a representative list of critical works of use to students, bearing on the author concerned. Footnotes are augmented, providing many new points of information and interpretive comment. The contents, too, have been altered, the most obvious being the omission of Wordsworth's *Thirteen-Book Prelude*. As it is widely available in a number of fine student editions, I have replaced it with the shorter *Two-Part Prelude*, and added other works by Wordsworth, such as *The Ruined Cottage* and *The Pedlar*, and extended coverage of his mature poetry, including extracts from *The Excursion* and the *Fourteen-Book Prelude*. I hope that this second edition, which has been completely rewritten, will provide its readers with a comprehensive guide to one of the richest periods in literary history, from its eighteenth-century beginnings to the point at which younger writers like Elizabeth Barrett and Letitia Landon reconceived the romantic aesthetic for the new, Victorian age.

Further reading

M. H. Abrams, *The Mirror and the Lamp: Romantic Theory and the Critical Tradition* (New York, 1953)
John Bayley, 'Romantic or Classic?', *The Romantic Survival: A Study in Poetic Evolution* (London, 1957), pp. 49–58
Walter Jackson Bate, *From Classic to Romantic: Premises of taste in Eighteenth-Century England* (New York, 1961)
R. J. White, *The Age of George III* (London, 1968)
M. H. Abrams, *Natural Supernaturalism: Tradition and Revolution in Romantic Literature* (New York, 1971)
Harold Bloom, *The Visionary Company: A Reading of English Romantic Poetry* (2nd edn, Ithaca and London, 1971)
M. H. Abrams ed., *English Romantic Poets* (Oxford, 1975)
Jerome J. McGann, *The Romantic Ideology: A Critical Investigation* (Chicago, 1983)
M. H. Abrams, *The Correspondent Breeze: Essays on English Romanticism* (New York, 1984)
Jonathan Wordsworth, Michael C. Jaye, and Robert Woof, *William Wordsworth and the Age of English Romanticism* (New Brunswick, 1987)
Aidan Day, *Romanticism* (London, 1996)
A Companion to Romanticism, ed. Duncan Wu (Oxford, 1998)

Acknowledgements

First Edition (1994)

Work on the this volume began with consultation of numerous colleagues, who kindly offered advice on the anthology they wished to use. For that and help of various kinds it is a pleasure to thank Jonathan Bate, Shahin Bekhradnia, J. Drummond Bone, Geoffrey Brackett, Richard W. Clancey, David Fairer, Richard Gravil, Jack Haeger, Keith Hanley, Anthony Harding, Brooke Hopkins, M. C. Howatson, Kenneth Johnston, Grevel Lindop, Jerome J. McGann, Philip Martin, Michael O'Neill, Roy Park, Janice Patten, Tom Paulin, Cecilia Powell, Roger Robinson, Nicholas Roe, the late William Ruddick, Charles Rzepka, William S. Smith, Jane Stabler, David Stewart, Tim Trengove-Jones, J. R. Watson, Mary Wedd, Pamela Woof and Jonathan Wordsworth. I wish also to thank the advisers consulted by Blackwell for comments and advice.

This anthology is more dependent than most on original research for its texts, and in the course of editing I have incurred debts of many kinds to various librarians and archivists whom it is a pleasure to thank here: B. C. Barker-Benfield and the staff of the Upper Reading Room, Bodleian Library, Oxford; Elaine Scoble of the Wolfson Library, St Catherine's College, Oxford; the staff of the English Faculty Library, Oxford; Deborah Hedgecock of the Guildhall Library, London; and Jeff Cowton of the Wordsworth Library, Grasmere. It was my good fortune to have been a Fellow of St Catherine's College, Oxford, during work on this book, and among friends and colleagues there I acknowledge the generous help of Richard Parish, J. Ch. Simopoulos, and J. B. McLaughlin. Nicola Trott was my collaborator at an early stage of work, and played a crucial part in formulating its aims and procedures, and in seeking advice from colleagues. My work has been expedited by the rapid and accurate typing of Pat Wallace; James Price of Woodstock Books kindly provided me with early printed texts of a number of works included; and Andrew McNeillie, my editor, offered enthusiastic help and advice throughout. For a retreat in the Cotswolds where much of the editing was completed during the summer of 1993, and for assistance of many kinds, I thank Caroline Cochrane.

This book was produced during tenure of a British Academy postdoctoral Fellowship, 1991–4; I am deeply grateful to the Academy for its kind support.

Second Edition (1998)

Since this anthology was first published, I have received suggestions for revision from many people; I thank them all. I owe a particular debt to those students with whom I have used it as a course text, and who have helped determine the various ways in which revision might be implemented.

For expert advice and information I thank Douglas Gifford, Bonnie Woodbery, Nicholas Roe, Jane Stabler, Edwin Moïse, Nelson Hilton, Suzanne Gilbert, Bob Cummings, Richard W. Clancey, David Pirie, Roger Robinson, R. E. Cavaliero, Zachary Leader, David Fairer, David Birkett, Peter Cochran, J. B. McLaughlin Richard Cronin, Charles Branchini, Susan Castillo, E. A. Moignard, Michael O'Neill, Jonathan Wordsworth and Constance Parrish.

In researching many of the new texts for this anthology, I am grateful once again to Jeff Cowton of the Wordsworth Library, Grasmere, and the staffs of the Upper Reading Room, Bodleian Library, Oxford, and the British Library, London. I am particularly indebted to my proof-reader, Henry Maas, and Alison Truefitt, my copy-editor, for the care they have taken over a challenging typescript. Once again, Andrew McNeillie has proved a patient and supportive editor, and Caroline Cochrane has provided much encouragement along the way. I thank them both.

The editor and publishers wish to thank the following for permission to quote material in copyright: Curtis Brown on behalf of Eric Robinson for material from John Clare, *The Shepherd's Calendar* ed. Eric Robinson and Geoffrey Summerfield, Oxford University Press, 1967; *John Clare* ed. Eric Robinson and David Powell, The Oxford Authors, Oxford University Press, 1984, copyright © 1967 and 1984 Eric Robinson; Harvard University Press for material from John Keats, *The Letters of John Keats* ed. Hyder Edward Rollins, vols 1–2, copyright © 1958 by the President and Fellows of Harvard College; the Houghton Library, Harvard University, for material from texts of John Keats MS transcripts; and manuscript material by Mary Shelley, fMS Eng. 822, 2r–2v, and Percy Bysshe Shelley, MS Eng. 258.3, 2r–3r; the London Borough of Camden for the Collections at Keats House, Hampstead, for John Keats's holograph texts, *On Sitting Down to Read King Lear Once Again* and 'Bright star, would I were steadfast as thou art'; John Murray Publishers, Ltd., for material from Lord Byron's letters from *Byron's Letters and Journals* ed. Leslie A. Marchand; Oxford University Press for material from William Blake, *The Letters of William Blake* ed. Geoffrey Keynes, 3rd edn, Clarendon Press, 1980; Robert Burns, *The Letters of Robert Burns* ed. J. De Lancey Ferguson, 2nd edn, ed. G. Ross Roy, vols 1–2, Clarendon Press, 1985; Dorothy Wordsworth, *The Grasmere Journals* ed. Pamela Woof, Clarendon Press, 1991; Samuel Taylor Coleridge, *The Letters of Samuel Taylor Coleridge* ed. Earl Leslie Griggs, vols 1–6, Clarendon Press, 1956–71; George Gordon Byron, 6th Baron Byron, *The Complete Poetical Works of Lord Byron* ed. Jerome J. McGann and Barry Weller, vols 1–7, Clarendon Press, 1980–93; and Percy Bysshe Shelley, *The Letters of Percy Bysshe Shelley* ed. Frederick L. Jones, vols 1–2, Clarendon Press, 1964; Routledge for material from Samuel Taylor Coleridge, *Table Talk* ed. Carl Woodring, vols 1–2, 1990; the Bodleian Library, Oxford, for material from MS texts of John Clare, George Dyer, Mary Shelley and Percy Bysshe Shelley; the Wordsworth Trust, Grasmere, for material from MS texts of Samuel Taylor Coleridge, Dorothy Wordsworth and William Wordsworth; the British Library, for material from MS texts of Samuel Taylor Coleridge and John Thelwall; Lord Abinger, for material from MS texts of Mary Shelley.

Every effort has been made to trace copyright holders; if any have been inadvertently overlooked the publishers will be pleased to make the necessary arrangement at the first opportunity.

Editorial Principles

This edition adopts the general policy advocated by Coleridge on New Year's Day 1834, widely accepted as the basis for most contemporary scholarly editions: 'After all you can say, I think the chronological order is the best for arranging a poet's works. All your divisions are in particular instances inadequate, and they destroy the interest which arises from watching the progress, maturity, and even the decay of genius.'[1] This anthology is arranged chronologically, in that authors are introduced successively by date of birth. Works are placed in order of composition, where known; when not known, by date of publication. As a rule, they are presented in their earliest complete recoverable form, whether it be early printed source or manuscript. In a number of cases, where later versions have acquired the status of received text, those versions are presented as well, in their correct chronological place. The 1834 text of *The Eolian Harp* is thus presented as work of that year, and *Effusion XXXV* under 1796, when it was published. In those cases where it has been necessary to present extracts from larger works, editorial titles are usually added, placed within square brackets.

The edition is designed for the use of students and the general reader, and textual procedures are geared accordingly. Except for poems in dialect or in which archaic effects were deliberately sought, punctuation and orthography are normalized, pervasive initial capitals and italics removed, and contractions expanded except where of metrical significance (for instance, Keats's 'charact'ry' in his *Sonnet*, p. 1016, is demanded by the exigencies of metre, but 'thro'' is expanded to 'through'). Although the punctuation, capitalization and other stylistic features of late eighteenth- and early nineteenth-century printed texts have their own intrinsic interest, and are of importance in considering the evolution of any given work, it should be noted that most poets were content to leave such matters to the printer or collaborators.[2] In most cases, therefore, stylistic features of the text cannot be assumed to be disposed according to the author's wishes. Conversely, I have taken the view that, on those occasions when capitalization is demonstrably authorial, and consistently applied, it is allowed to stand – as in the case of Shelley's *Adonais* and *The Mask of Anarchy*. The punctuation applied by writers to their own works is another matter, as styles differ from one author to another, are sometimes eccentric, and can often be misleading to the modern reader. I have treated authorial punctuation as a good (though not infallible) guide as to emphasis, meaning and sentence structure, but have not followed it with unquestioning obedience. I have not attempted to correct or update authors' spelling of foreign languages or of proper names, including place names.

Many of the texts included here have been edited for this anthology, some for the first time, from

---

[1] CC *Table Talk* i 453.
[2] The numerous errors in *Lyrical Ballads* (1800) were due in part to Wordsworth's reliance on Humphry Davy, whom he had not met, as punctuator and proofreader. Similarly, the notoriously unsatisfactory state of many of Byron's and Shelley's printed texts can be traced to the fact that they were out of the country when publication took place, and were unable to supervise production.

manuscript (see pp. xlii–iv). I have followed procedures designed to produce a clear reading text for the student. In editing from manuscript, I have aimed to present each draft as it stood on completion. Deletions are accepted only when alternative readings are provided; where they are not, the original is retained. Alternative readings are accepted only when the original has been deleted; where they are not, the original is retained. Where the original reading is deleted but legible, and the alternative is either fragmentary, illegible, or inchoate, the original has been retained. Where, in the rush of composition, words are omitted from a draft – as is not infrequently the case in Wordsworth's manuscripts – they are supplied from adjacent drafts or manuscripts. As a rule, I have silently corrected all scribal errors. Ampersands are expanded to 'and' throughout.

There is, perhaps inevitably, an exception to all this: John Clare, who famously told his publisher, John Taylor, that 'grammer in learning is like Tyranny in government'.[3] In editing the poet's manuscripts, Eric Robinson, his longest-serving textual critic, has consistently defended the practice of transcribing 'exactly what Clare wrote' with minimal intervention from the editor, leaving his spelling and punctuation as they are, scribal errors intact. This is a policy that has won the support of many critics, including John Barrell, who writes persuasively on the significance of the fact that, although Clare could punctuate, he chose not to, as he saw it as 'an imprisonment of the words of the poem, an imposition on them of a sort of *military* discipline'.[4] But there are dissenting voices. Greg Crossan suggests that 'Robinson's insistence on transcribing obvious mistakes may be an inverted pedantry no more congenial to the poet than the over-fussy "improvement" of his texts by John Taylor in the 1820s',[5] and this argument is supported by Zachary Leader's eloquent defence of Taylor's 'versions' of Clare.[6] Nor, I think, should a literal transcription of the manuscripts, with their errors (not all attributable to the poet), be justified purely on the grounds of 'intention'.[7] However, Robinson's procedures have governed most contemporary editions of Clare's works, and it would be inappropriate to challenge them here. In this exceptional case I have therefore followed him in reproducing the punctuation, capitalization, and grammar of the manuscripts of Clare and his copyists. (*To Elia*, which derives from a printed source, is edited according to the standards applied to other printed sources in this volume.)

Dates of composition, where they can be verified, are indicated alongside the title of each work, with details of publication. Copy-text details are provided alongside titles, whether early printed sources (usually presented in small capitals under the title of the work), or manuscript. Titles in square brackets are editorial, that is, they cannot reliably be attributed to the author's intention, either from MS sources or from publications approved by the author during his or her lifetime.

Headnotes are provided for each author, giving biographical materials, critical comments on the selection, and useful secondary reading. Annotations gloss archaisms, difficult constructions, allusions, echoes, other verbal borrowings, and provide points of information where necessary. On occasion they direct the reader to secondary materials with a particular bearing on the work in question.

---

[3] *The Letters of John Clare* ed. Mark Storey (Oxford, 1985), p. 231.

[4] *Poetry, Language, and Politics* (Manchester, 1988), p. 120.

[5] 'John Clare's Poetry: An Examination of the Textual Accuracy of Some Recent Editions', *Studies in Romanticism* 24 (1985) 581–98, p. 581.

[6] 'John Taylor and the Poems of Clare', *Revision and Romantic Authorship* (Oxford, 1996), pp. 206–61.

[7] 'That is why to adhere faithfully to his own way of writing is not, as some have suggested, to condescend to him but to respect him, except, paradoxically, that to retain all his redundant punctuation when he was first trying to conform to the educated world or to preserve the proprieties thrust upon him by his publishers and patrons is to misrepresent his intentions, better reflected in his manuscripts' (*John Clare* ed. Eric Robinson and David Powell (Oxford, 1984), p. xxii). While stylistic features of the text attributable to the author must have their significance within the history of a poet's works, it would be wrong to impose them as immutable features on all subsequent texts.

List of Manuscripts

Texts in this volume are edited from the following manuscripts:

JOHN CLARE

Sonnet ('Ere I had known the world and understood'): copy-text is Clare's letter to Taylor and Hessey of 18 July 1822 (Bodleian Library MS Montagu d.4, 97r), which served as press-copy for the printed text published in September.

SAMUEL TAYLOR COLERIDGE

To William Wordsworth: fair copy in Coleridge's hand at the Wordsworth Library MS 14/7.

On Donne's First Poem: draft in Coleridge's hand, BL Add MS 47515, 145v–147v, 149r. The later, revised readings of the draft have been preferred, even where there are no crossings-out.

Letter to William Wordsworth, 30 May 1815, Wordsworth Library MS 14/9.

GEORGE DYER

In deep distress, I cried to God: from Dyer's fair copy notebook bearing the title, *The Blind Man's Legacy*, 1836, Bodleian Library MS Eng. poet. c.21, pp. 73–4. Hitherto unpublished.

LEIGH HUNT

To Hampstead: copy-text from *The Examiner*; draft of the poem in Hunt's hand at Bodleian Library MS Eng. poet. e.38, 46v.

JOHN KEATS

On Sitting Down to Read King Lear Once Again: edited from Keats's fair copy holograph in his 1808 facsimile of Shakespeare's first folio, Keats House, Hampstead.

Sonnet ('When I have fears that I may cease to be'): edited from Charles Brown's fair copy MS transcript at Harvard, 20r.

La Belle Dame Sans Merci: A Ballad: edited from Charles Brown's fair copy MS transcript at Harvard, 7r.

Ode on Indolence: edited from Charles Brown's fair copy MS transcript at Harvard, 112r.

The Fall of Hyperion: from Richard Woodhouse's fair copy MS transcript at Harvard, 165r–181r.

'Bright star, would I were steadfast as thou art': edited from Keats's holograph fair copy on a blank page of the 1806 *Poetical Works* of William Shakespeare at Keats House, Hampstead.

MARY WOLLSTONECRAFT SHELLEY

Journals: 28 May 1817, Bodleian Library, Abinger Deposit, Dep.d.311(2), 52v–53r. 15 May 1824, Bodleian Library, Abinger Deposit, Dep.d.311(4), 38v–39r.

On Reading Wordsworth's Lines on Peele Castle: fair copy in Mary Shelley's hand, Bodleian Library, Abinger Deposit, Dep. c.516/12.

A Dirge: edited from Mary Shelley's press-copy, now at Harvard, fMS Eng.822, 2r–2v. Collated with the printed text in *The Keepsake* (1831), p. 35.

Oh listen while I sing to thee: fair copy in Mary Shelley's hand, Bodleian Library MS Shelley adds. c.5, 111r. Hitherto unpublished.

PERCY BYSSHE SHELLEY

Hymn to Intellectual Beauty: copy-text from *The Examiner* No. 473 (19 January 1817, p. 41), as corrected by Shelley, Harvard MS Eng.258.3, 2r–3r.

On Love: copy-text is Shelley's draft at Bodleian Library MS Shelley adds. e.11, pp. 1–9.

England in 1819: copy-text is Shelley's fair copy at Bodleian Library MS Shelley adds. e.12, p. 182, entered December 1819.

Prometheus Unbound: copy-text is the flawed printed text of 1820 corrected and emended from Shelley's fair copy, Bodleian Library MSS Shelley e.1, e.2, and e.3. Where Mary Shelley's edition of 1839 returns to the readings of the MSS, the MSS readings have been preferred over those of 1820. Errors and emendations introduced by hands other than Shelley's have been corrected from the MSS; and where the MSS provide clearer or more trustworthy readings, they have been given priority over printed sources. Shelley's capitals have been regularized, and the primary authority for punctuation is 1820, corrected by reference to the MSS.

The Mask of Anarchy: text from Mary Shelley's press copy, corrected by Percy Bysshe Shelley, complete by 23 September 1819, Library of Congress MMC 1399.

A Defence of Poetry: first extract from Mary Shelley's press copy, corrected by Percy Bysshe Shelley, March 1821, Bodleian Library MS Shelley e.6; second extract from Shelley's fair copy, Bodleian Library MS Shelley adds. c.4, ff.221v–230r, 232r–241r.

JOHN THELWALL

Letter to S. T. Coleridge, 10 May 1796: BL MS Adds. 35,344, f.183.

DOROTHY WORDSWORTH

Poems edited from her Commonplace Book, Wordsworth Library MS 120: *A Sketch* (19r); *A Cottage in Grasmere Vale* (19r–20r); *After-recollection* (20r); *A Winter's Ramble* (20v–21r); *Floating Island* (29v–30r); *Thoughts* (30v–31r); '*When shall I tread*' (51r).

WILLIAM WORDSWORTH

A Night-Piece, headed 'A Fragment' in Wordsworth Library MS 16, 69v.

The Discharged Soldier, Wordsworth Library MS 16, 74r–77r.

The Ruined Cottage MS D, Wordsworth Library MS 16.

The Pedlar, Wordsworth Library MS 16.

'*There is an active principle*', Wordsworth Library MS 16.

'*Not useless do I deem*', Wordsworth Library MS 16, 67v, 68r, 68v, 69r.

The Two-Part Prelude, Wordsworth Library MSS 22–3.

The Five-Book Prelude, Wordsworth Library MS 38.

The Thirteen-Book Prelude, Wordsworth Library, fair copies, MSS 52–3. Like Mark L. Reed in his Cornell Wordsworth Series edition, I present an AB-stage text, designed to reveal the 'poet's latest preference' for his work as it stood at the end of composition in early 1806. Gaps are filled from draft MSS.

Prospectus to 'The Recluse': fair copy in Wordsworth's hand, Wordsworth Library MS 45, 2r–4r. Gaps in the MS filled from Wordsworth Library MS 59.

'These chairs they have no words to utter': draft at Wordsworth Library MS 41, 17v.

Abbreviations

Blake, *Early Illuminated Books*	William Blake, *The Early Illuminated Books* ed. Morris Eaves, Robert N. Essick, and Joseph Viscomi (London, 1993)
Blake, *Urizen Books*	William Blake, *The Urizen Books* ed. David Worrall (London, 1995)
CC *Biographia*	Samuel Taylor Coleridge, *Biographia Literaria*, ed. James Engell and Walter Jackson Bate (2 vols, Princeton, NJ, 1983)
CC *Shorter Works*	Samuel Taylor Coleridge, *Shorter Works and Fragments* ed. H. J. Jackson and J. R. de J. Jackson (2 vols, Princeton, NJ, 1995)
CC *Table Talk*	Samuel Taylor Coleridge, *Table Talk* ed. Carl Woodring (2 vols, Princeton, NJ, 1990)
Cornell *Lyrical Ballads*	William Wordsworth, *Lyrical Ballads and Other Poems, 1797–1800* ed. James A. Butler and Karen Green (Ithaca, NY, 1992)
DWJ	*The Journals of Dorothy Wordsworth* ed. Ernest de Selincourt (2 vols, London, 1941)
EHC	*The Poetical Works of Samuel Taylor Coleridge* ed. E. H. Coleridge (2 vols, Oxford, 1912)
EY	*The Letters of William and Dorothy Wordsworth: The Early Years 1787–1805* ed. Ernest de Selincourt, revised Chester L. Shaver (Oxford, 1967)
FN	*The Fenwick Notes of William Wordsworth* ed. Jared Curtis (London, 1993)
Grasmere Journals	Dorothy Wordsworth, *The Grasmere Journals* ed. Pamela Woof (Oxford, 1991)
Griggs	*The Collected Letters of Samuel Taylor Coleridge* ed. E. L. Griggs (6 vols, Oxford, 1956–71)
Howe	*The Works of William Hazlitt*, ed. P. P. Howe (21 vols, London, 1930–4)
Jones	*The Letters of Percy Bysshe Shelley* ed. F. L. Jones (2 vols, Oxford, 1964)
Keats Circle	*The Keats Circle: Letters and Papers 1816–1878* ed. Hyder E. Rollins (2 vols, Cambridge, Mass., 1948)
Lucas	*The Letters of Charles and Mary Lamb* ed. E. V. Lucas (3 vols, London, 1935)
LY	*The Letters of William and Dorothy Wordsworth: The Later Years 1821–53* ed. Ernest de Selincourt, revised Alan G. Hill (4 vols, Oxford, 1978–88)

Marchand	*Byron's Letters and Journals* ed. Leslie A. Marchand (12 vols, London, 1973–82)
Marrs	*The Letters of Charles and Mary Anne Lamb* ed. Edwin W. Marrs, Jr (3 vols, Ithaca, NY, 1975–8)
Masson	*The Collected Writings of Thomas De Quincey* ed. David Masson (14 vols, Edinburgh, 1889–90)
Medwin	Thomas Medwin, *Conversations of Lord Byron* (London, 1824)
MLR	*Modern Language Review*
Morley (1927)	*The Correspondence of Crabb Robinson with the Wordsworth Circle* ed. Edith J. Morley (2 vols, Oxford, 1927)
Morley (1938)	*Henry Crabb Robinson on Books and Their Writers* ed. Edith J. Morley (3 vols, London, 1938)
MY	*The Letters of William and Dorothy Wordsworth: The Middle Years*, ed. Ernest de Selincourt, *i: 1806–11*, rev. Mary Moorman (Oxford, 1969); *ii: 1812–20*, rev. Mary Moorman and Alan G. Hill (Oxford, 1970)
N&Q	*Notes and Queries*
Notebooks	*The Notebooks of Samuel Taylor Coleridge* ed. Kathleen Coburn et al. (5 vols, New York, 1957–)
Owen and Smyser	*The Prose Works of William Wordsworth* ed. W. J. B. Owen and Jane Worthington Smyser (3 vols, Oxford, 1974)
PMLA	*Publications of the Modern Language Association of America*
RES	*Review of English Studies*
Rollins	*The Letters of John Keats, 1814–1821* ed. Hyder E. Rollins (2 vols, Cambridge, Mass., 1958)
Romanticism: A Critical Reader	*Romanticism: A Critical Reader* ed. Duncan Wu (Oxford, 1995)
RR	*Re-Visioning Romanticism: British Women Writers, 1776–1837* ed. Carol Shiner Wilson and Joel Haefner (Philadelphia, 1994)
RWW	*Romantic Women Writers: Voices and Countervoices* ed. Paula R. Feldman and Theresa M. Kelley (Hanover, NH, 1995)
SC	*Shelley and his Circle 1773–1822* ed. K. N. Cameron and D. H. Reiman (8 vols, Cambridge, Mass., 1961–86)
Shelley Journals	*The Journals of Mary Shelley 1814–1844* ed. Paula R. Feldman and Diana Scott-Kilvert (2 vols, Oxford, 1987)
Shelley's Prose	*Shelley's Prose* ed. David Lee Clark (London, 1988)
SIR	*Studies in Romanticism*
The Brownings' Correspondence	*The Brownings' Correspondence* ed. Philip Kelley, Ronald Hudson and Scott Lewis (9 vols, Winfield, Kansas, 1984–91)
TWC	*The Wordsworth Circle*
WPW	*The Poetical Works of William Wordsworth* ed. Ernest de Selincourt and Helen Darbishire (5 vols, Oxford, 1940–9)

A Note for Teachers

Those adopting this book as a teaching text may appreciate a brief note as to ways in which it may be used. As in most anthologies of this kind, works are grouped under author, and that provides one way in which the teacher may readily cover the period. Another, equally effective method, is to deal with the literature by subject. For this reason I provided a subject index to the first edition, in addition to which this second edition contains a table of contents listed by theme. My own teaching syllabus, which covers a nine-week teaching term at the University of Glasgow, is organized by subject. Each week, a topic relevant to the period is covered through both canonical and non-canonical writers. Although seminars tend to concentrate on one or two major works, thematic connections are made across the entire range of items listed for reading. Depending on student response, class discussion can gravitate toward any of the prescribed works. This is admittedly a different way of approaching the subject from those biased towards authors and the chronology of the period, but it has the advantage of ensuring that students read a wide range of works – by both male and female writers. My own teaching syllabus (geared to the first edition of this book) is reproduced below.

WEEK 1: TRANSCENDENCE

Edmund Burke, *Obscurity*; Ann Radcliffe, extracts from *A Journey Made in the Summer of 1794*; Wordsworth, *Tintern Abbey*, *Prospectus to 'The Recluse'*, *Ode*, *On the 'Ode'*; Coleridge, *The Eolian Harp*, *This Lime-Tree Bower My Prison*, *Frost at Midnight*

WEEK 2: PERCEPTIONS OF NATURE

Thomas Warton, *To the River Lodon*; Cowper, *The Winter Evening*; Charlotte Smith, *To the South Downs*; William Lisle Bowles, *To the River Itchin*; Wordsworth, *Daffodils*; Dorothy Wordsworth, Grasmere Journals 15 April 1802; Coleridge, *To the River Otter*; *Chamouny; the Hour before Sunrise*; Southey, *Natural Religion*; Shelley, *Mont Blanc*; Byron, *Childe Harold's Pilgrimage* III

WEEK 3: REVOLUTION AND REACTION

Richard Price, extracts from *A Discourse on the Love of our Country*; Edmund Burke, extracts from *Reflections on the Revolution*; Thomas Paine, extracts from *The Rights of Man*; George Dyer, *The Injustice of the Law*; William Godwin, extracts from *Political Justice*; Mary Wollstonecraft, extract from *A Vindication of the Rights of Men*; extracts from *A Vindication of the Rights of Woman*; Helen Maria Williams, *Letters Written in France*; John Thelwall, *The Old Peasant*; Wordsworth, *London 1802*; Shelley, *The Mask of Anarchy*

WEEK 4: LANGUAGE AND THE NEW POETIC

Robert Burns, *Epistle to J. L*****k*, *To a Mouse*; Joanna Baillie, *On Passion*; John Thelwall, Letter to Coleridge; Wordsworth, *The Thorn*, *Note to 'The Thorn'*, *Preface to Lyrical Ballads*; Coleridge, extract from *Religious Musings*, *On 'The Recluse'*; William Hazlitt, *On Gusto*; Shelley, *A Defence of Poetry*

WEEK 5: IMAGINATION (I)

William Blake, *The Marriage of Heaven and Hell*, Letter to Trusler; Wordsworth, *Resolution and Independence*, *Preface to Poems* (1815); Dorothy Wordsworth, *Grasmere Journal 3 October 1800*; Coleridge, *Kubla Khan*, *The Picture*, *Of the Fragment of 'Kubla Khan'*, extracts from *Biographia Literaria*

WEEK 6: IMAGINATION (II)

Richard Woodhouse, Letter to John Taylor; John Keats, Letter to Bailey, Letter to George and Tom Keats, Letter to Woodhouse, *The Eve of St Agnes*, *Ode to a Nightingale*, *Ode on a Grecian Urn*

WEEK 7: PSYCHOLOGY

Wordsworth, *Strange fits of passion I have known*, 'Spots of Time' passage from *The Two-Part Prelude*; Thomas De Quincey, *The Pains of Opium*, *Oriental Dreams*, *Easter Sunday*, *On the Knocking at the Gate in Macbeth*, *On Wordsworth's 'There was a boy'*, extracts from *Suspiria De Profundis*

WEEK 8: THE CITY

William Blake, *London*; Wordsworth, *Tintern Abbey*; *Composed upon Westminster Bridge*; Coleridge, *Frost at Midnight*; Charles Lamb, Letter to Wordsworth; Charles Lloyd, *London*; Thomas De Quincey, *Ann of Oxford Street*

WEEK 9: RELIGION

William Blake, *All Religions Are One*, *There is no Natural Religion*, *The Garden of Love*; Coleridge, extract from *Religious Musings*; Byron, *Manfred*; Shelley, *Hymn to Intellectual Beauty*, *Mont Blanc*, *On Love*, *On Life*; Mary Shelley, *Note on the 'Prometheus Unbound'*

Richard Price (1723–1791)

No man was more thoroughly a product of enlightenment ideals than Dr Richard Price – except, perhaps, his friend, Thomas Jefferson. Philosopher, theologian, mathematician, [1] became an expert on insurance and advised the newly founded Society for Equitable Assurances on Lives and Survivorships on actuarial matters. He also advised the Prime Minister, William Pitt, on how to reduce the national debt. A leading Dissenter, he campaigned vigorously for legal recognition of the right to freedom of worship.

But it is as a pamphleteer that Price is best known today. Always a believer in liberty and representative government, he had supported the American Revolution without reservation, and told John Adams and Thomas Jefferson how to consolidate its achievements. He found the French Revolution equally inspiring and, shortly after the fall of the Bastille (14 July 1789), described it as 'the commencement of a general reformation in the governments of the world which hitherto have been little better than usurpations on the rights of mankind, impediments to the progress of human improvement, and contrivances for enabling a few grandees to oppress and enslave the rest of mankind'.[1]

Price's famous *Discourse* was delivered as a sermon to the London Revolution Society, 4 November 1789, founded in honour not of the recent uprisings in France or America, but of the Glorious Revolution of 1688 (the expulsion of the Stuarts from England, and transfer of sovereignty to the Protestant William and Mary). The Society contained members of the established church, and 'many persons of rank and consequence from different parts of the kingdom'. At annual anniversary meetings it held a religious service in the morning, followed by a more festive gathering at a tavern; it was at the religious service that Price delivered his famous *Discourse*. For Price, the Glorious Revolution had established the principles of just and stable government: the right to liberty of conscience in religious matters; the right to resist power when abused; and the right of the people to choose their own governors. His *Discourse*, with its fulsome praise for the French, was received with acclaim by the Society, whose members voted immediately to encourage the establishment of similar groups throughout the country, and to congratulate the National Assembly in Paris on the Revolution. This, and the applause which greeted the *Discourse* when read out in the National Assembly on 25 November, was incendiary: Price became the subject of scurrilous caricatures,[2] and, more importantly, the *Discourse* sparked off a pamphlet war that inspired some of the most important political works ever written, including Burke's *Reflections on the Revolution in France*, Paine's *The Rights of Man*, and Wollstonecraft's two *Vindications*. A compelling barometer of conservative anxiety, this flurry of publications was followed by readers of all classes, including the young Wordsworth, who in *The Thirteen-Book Prelude* recalls having read 'the master pamphlets of the day' (ix 97).

Price was treading on thin ice; a few years later, and he would probably have been tried for treason. You have to remind yourself, as you read his *Discourse*, that the storming of the Bastille was still news; and that less than a month before he spoke these words, 20,000 people had stormed Versailles and 'escorted' the King and Queen to Paris in what many saw as one of the most sinister developments in the Revolution so far. Louis's execution would wait until January 1793, but for many it was prefigured in the events of the summer and autumn of 1789.

Further reading

D. O. Thomas, *The Honest Mind: The Thought and Work of Richard Price* (Oxford, 1977)

Richard Price, *A Discourse on the Love of our Country 1789* (Spelsbury, 1992)

P. M. Zall, 'The Cool World of Samuel Taylor Coleridge: The American Connection: Dr Richard Price (1723–91)', *TWC* 7 (1976) 95–100

RICHARD PRICE
[1] D. O. Thomas, *The Honest Mind: The Thought and Work of Richard Price* (Oxford, 1977), p. 295.
[2] Most notably, James Gillray's *Smelling Out a Rat* (3 December 1790), reproduced Jonathan Wordsworth, Michael C. Jaye, and Robert Woof, *William Wordsworth and the Age of English Romanticism* (New Brunswick, 1987), p. 16.

[On Representation]

From A DISCOURSE ON THE LOVE OF OUR COUNTRY (1789) (pp. 40–2)

When the representation is fair and equal, and at the same time vested with such powers as our House of Commons possesses, a kingdom may be said to govern itself, and consequently to possess true liberty. When the representation is partial, a kingdom possesses liberty only partially; and if extremely partial, it only gives a *semblance* of liberty. But if not only extremely partial, but corruptly chosen, and under corrupt influence after being chosen, it becomes a *nuisance*, and produces the worst of all forms of government: a government by corruption, a government carried on and supported by spreading venality and profligacy through a kingdom.

May heaven preserve this kingdom from a calamity so dreadful! It is the point of depravity to which abuses under such a government as ours naturally tend, and the last stage of national unhappiness. We are at present, I hope, at a great distance from it. But it cannot be pretended that there are no advances towards it, or that there is no reason for apprehension and alarm.

The inadequateness of our representation has been long a subject of complaint.[1] This is, in truth, our fundamental grievance, and I do not think that anything is much more our duty (as men who love their country and are grateful for the Revolution)[2] than to unite our zeal in endeavouring to get it redressed. At the time of the American war, associations were formed for this purpose in London and other parts of the kingdom, and our present Minister himself has, since that war, directed to it an effort which made him a favourite with many of us.[3] But all attention to it seems now lost, and the probability is that this inattention will continue and that nothing will be done towards gaining for us this essential blessing till some great calamity again alarms our fears, or till some great abuse of power again provokes our resentment – or perhaps till the acquisition of a pure and equal representation by other countries (while we are mocked with the shadow)[4] kindles our shame.

[Prospects for Reform]

From A DISCOURSE ON THE LOVE OF OUR COUNTRY (1789) (pp. 49–51)

What an eventful period is this! I am thankful that I have lived to it, and I could almost say, 'Lord, now lettest thou thy servant depart in peace, for mine eyes have seen thy salvation.'[1] I have lived to see a diffusion of knowledge which has undermined superstition and error; I have lived to see the rights of men better understood than ever, and nations panting for liberty which seemed to have lost the idea of it. I have lived to see *thirty millions* of people,[2] indignant and resolute, spurning at slavery, and demanding liberty with an irresistible voice, their King led in triumph, and an arbitrary monarch surrendering himself to his subjects.[3]

After sharing in the benefits of one revolution, I have been spared to be a witness to two other revolutions, both glorious.[4] And now, methinks, I see the ardour for liberty catching and spreading; a

---

ON REPRESENTATION

[1] *The inadequateness . . . complaint* few working people, and no women, had the vote.

[2] *Revolution* the Glorious Revolution of 1688.

[3] *At the time . . . us* In the early 1780s William Pitt the Younger advocated peace with the American colonies, economic reform, and reform of parliamentary representation. Such organizations as the Constitutional Society (established 1780) lobbied for Parliamentary reform.

[4] 'A representation chosen principally by the Treasury, and a few thousands of the dregs of the people, who are generally paid for their votes' (Price's footnote). Price was an enthusiastic advocate of parliamentary reform.

PROSPECTS FOR REFORM

[1] Luke 2:29–30.

[2] *thirty millions of people* the population of France.

[3] *their King . . . subjects* See headnote p. 1.

[4] *After sharing . . . glorious* Price sees himself as a beneficiary of the Glorious Revolution; he also witnessed the American Revolution, which resulted in independence from Britain in 1776 and, of course, the start of the French Revolution.

general amendment beginning in human affairs; the dominion of kings changed for the dominion of laws, and the dominion of priests giving way to the dominion of reason and conscience.

Be encouraged, all ye friends of freedom, and writers in its defence! The times are auspicious. Your labours have not been in vain. Behold kingdoms admonished by you, starting from sleep, breaking their fetters, and claiming justice from their oppressors! Behold the light you have struck out, after setting America free, reflected to France and there kindled into a blaze that lays despotism in ashes, and warms and illuminates Europe!

Tremble all ye oppressors of the world! Take warning all ye supporters of slavish governments and slavish hierarchies! Call no more (absurdly and wickedly) reformation, innovation. You cannot now hold the world in darkness. Struggle no longer against increasing light and liberality. Restore to mankind their rights, and consent to the correction of abuses, before they and you are destroyed together.

Thomas Warton (1728–1790)

'Thomas Warton was a man of taste and genius', Hazlitt wrote: 'His sonnets I cannot help preferring to any in the language.'[1] The son of Thomas Warton the elder (c.1688–1745), Warton the Younger grew up to be one of the foremost poets and historians of his time. He studied at Trinity College, Oxford, where he remained as fellow and tutor (1751 onwards), Professor of Poetry (1757–67), and Camden Professor of History (1785). By the time he was appointed Poet Laureate in 1785 most of his best verse was behind him. In many ways his most enduring achievement turned out to be his *History of Poetry* (1774–81). He was still writing it when he died, and in succeeding years it was 'completed' by a number of acolytes. It remained the standard history of the subject until the early twentieth century.

Wordsworth and Coleridge were not twenty-one at his death (Wordsworth was at Cambridge, Coleridge at Christ's Hospital), but they knew his poetry well, and would have recognized the influence of *To the River Lodon* on Bowles's *To the Itchin* (p. 155). It is in his use of the river as the image of a man's life – one that enables him to trace his way back to childhood memories – that Warton's sonnet was exemplary, and it became the model for almost every romantic apostrophe to a stream, fountain, or river, including Coleridge's *To the River Otter* (p. 450), and the address to the Derwent in Wordsworth's *Two-Part Prelude* (p. 300).

Further reading

David Fairer, 'Thomas Warton, Thomas Gray, and the Recovery of the Past', in *Thomas Gray: Contemporary Essays* ed. W. B. Hutchings and William Ruddick (Liverpool, 1993), pp. 146–70

The Correspondence of Thomas Warton ed. David Fairer (Athens, Georgia, 1995)

Robert J. Griffin, *Wordsworth's Pope: A Study in Literary Historiography* (Cambridge, 1995), pp. 28–38

A. Harris Fairbanks, ' "Dear Native Brook": Coleridge, Bowles, and Thomas Warton the Younger', *TWC* 6 (1975) 313–15

Sonnet IX. To the River Lodon[1]

From POEMS (1777)

Ah! what a weary race my feet have run
    Since first I trod thy banks with alders crowned,
    And thought my way was all through fairy ground
    Beneath thy azure sky and golden sun,

THOMAS WARTON
[1] Howe ix 242.

TO THE RIVER LODON
[1] The River Loddon runs through Basingstoke, where Warton was born, and where his father was vicar and headmaster of the Grammar School.

Where first my muse to lisp her notes begun.[2]
    While pensive memory traces back the round
    Which fills the varied interval between,
    Much pleasure, more of sorrow, marks the scene.
Sweet native stream, those skies and suns so pure
No more return to cheer my evening road;   10
    Yet still one joy remains – that not obscure,
Nor useless, all my vacant days have flowed,
    From youth's gay dawn to manhood's prime mature,
    Nor with the muse's laurel[3] unbestowed.

Edmund Burke   (1729–1797)

One of the most powerful intellects of the eighteenth century, Burke was raised in an atmosphere of toleration; his father was a Protestant, his mother a Catholic. A native of Dublin, he graduated from Trinity College (1747–8) and moved to London to read law. He was never called to the bar partly because he spent more time writing than studying. He was nineteen when he composed the *Philosophical Enquiry into the Origin of our Ideas of the Sublime and Beautiful* (1757), which explores the nature of 'negative' pleasures – the mixed experience of pleasure and pain, attraction and terror. It marked the point at which the classical formalism of the eighteenth century gave way to the aesthetic of romanticism. His central innovation was to question the classical ideal of clarity, arguing that vagueness and obscurity were far more evocative of the infinite. Fear (a desirable sensation for Burke) is diminished by knowledge, but heightened by veiled intimations. It was nothing short of a revolution in aesthetic theory, and shaped the thinking behind much of the poetry in this volume, including, for instance, Wordsworth's climbing of Snowdon (pp. 401–5), De Quincey's account of opium addiction (pp. 633–5), Byron's *Childe Harold* Canto III (pp. 671–96), and Shelley's *Hymn to Intellectual Beauty*.

By 1765, when he worked for Lord Rockingham, First Lord of the Treasury, he was involved in politics at the highest level. A Whig, Burke favoured liberty of commerce and defended the rights of the colonies, especially America – which made his outspoken, and eloquent, opposition to the French Revolution all the more shocking. He was sixty by the time the Bastille fell in July 1789. The storming of Versailles in October, and Price's *Discourse*, celebrating what many in England regarded as the prelude to tyranny and blood-

shed (see pp. 1–3, above), led him to compose *Reflections on the Revolution in France* (1790). Unlike such thinkers as Rousseau (whom he detested), Burke saw man as unavoidably and essentially prone to evil – in view of which the only hope lay in safeguards which had stood the test of time; hence his support of Englishness, and the view that the English form of government, for all its faults, was divinely sanctioned. If all this seems eccentric now, it is worth remembering that the *Reflections* has been an enduringly popular work. Priced at three shillings, it sold 30,000 copies in the first two years of publication, and exercised a continuing influence on conservative thought, including some of Coleridge's political writings in the *Lay Sermons* (1816–17) and *On the Constitution of the Church and State* (1830).

Further reading

Alfred Cobban, *Edmund Burke and the Revolt Against the Eighteenth Century: A Study of the Political and Social Thinking of Burke, Wordsworth, Coleridge, and Southey* (New York, 1961)

Isaac Kramnick, *The Rage of Edmund Burke: Portrait of an Ambivalent Conservative* (New York, 1977)

D. O. Thomas, *The Honest Mind: The Thought and Work of Richard Price* (Oxford, 1977), chapter 15

Edmund Burke, *A Philosophical Enquiry into the Origin of our Ideas of the Sublime and Beautiful* ed. James T. Boulton (2nd edn, Oxford, 1987)

Conor Cruise O'Brien, *The Great Melody: A Thematic Biography and Commented Anthology of Edmund Burke* (London, 1992)

Tom Furniss, *Edmund Burke's Aesthetic Ideology: Language, Gender, and Political Economy in Revolution* (Cambridge, 1993)

---

[2]   *Where first ... begun* Warton lived in Basingstoke until 1744, when he matriculated at Trinity College, Oxford, and his earliest poems were certainly composed there. His earliest known poem is *Birds nesting in Dunsfold Orchard*, written when

he was seven or eight.
[3]   *muse's laurel* i.e. poetic fame. He was well established as a major poet of the time by 1757 when he became Professor of Poetry at Oxford.

Obscurity

From A PHILOSOPHICAL ENQUIRY INTO THE ORIGINS OF OUR IDEAS OF THE SUBLIME
AND BEAUTIFUL (1757) (Part II, Section III, pp. 43–5)

To make anything very terrible,[1] obscurity seems in general to be necessary. When we know the full extent of any danger, when we can accustom our eyes to it, a great deal of the apprehension vanishes. Everyone will be sensible of this who considers how greatly night adds to our dread in all cases of danger, and how much the notions of ghosts and goblins (of which none can form clear ideas) affect minds, which give credit[2] to the popular tales concerning such sorts of beings.

Those despotic governments which are founded on the passions of men – and principally upon the passion of fear – keep their chief as much as may be from the public eye. The policy has been the same in many cases of religion; almost all the heathen temples were dark. Even in the barbarous temples of the Americans[3] at this day, they keep their idol in a dark part of the hut, which is consecrated to his worship. For this purpose too the druids performed all their ceremonies in the bosom of the darkest woods, and in the shade of the oldest and most spreading oaks.

No person seems better to have understood the secret of heightening, or of setting terrible things (if I may use the expression) in their strongest light by the force of a judicious obscurity, than Milton. His description of Death in the second Book is admirably studied; it is astonishing with what a gloomy pomp, with what a significant and expressive uncertainty of strokes and colouring he has finished the portrait of the king of terrors.

> The other shape
> (If shape it might be called) that shape had none
> Distinguishable in member, joint, or limb;
> Or substance might be called that shadow seemed,
> For each seemed either. Black he stood as night,
> Fierce as ten furies, terrible as hell,
> And shook a deadly dart. What seemed his head
> The likeness of a kingly crown had on.[4]

In this description all is dark, uncertain, confused, terrible and sublime to the last degree.

[On Englishness]

From REFLECTIONS ON THE REVOLUTION IN FRANCE (1790) (pp. 127–30)

I almost venture to affirm that not one in a hundred amongst us participates in the 'triumph' of the Revolution Society.[1] If the King and Queen of France and their children were to fall into our hands by the chance of war in the most acrimonious of all hostilities (I deprecate such an event, I deprecate such hostility), they would be treated with another sort of triumphal entry into London. We formerly have had a king of France in that situation;[2] you have read how he was treated by the victor in the field, and in what manner he was afterwards received in England. Four hundred years have gone over us, but I believe we are not materially changed since that period.

OBSCURITY
[1] *terrible* terrifying.
[2] *credit* credibility.
[3] *the Americans* i.e. the American Indians.
[4] *Paradise Lost* ii 666–73.

ON ENGLISHNESS
[1] Price delivered his famous *Discourse* to the London Revolution Society on 4 November 1789 (see pp. 1–3).
[2] *We formerly have had ... situation* John II of France, captured by the Black Prince at the Battle of Poitiers 1356, died in captivity, London, 1364.

Thanks to our sullen resistance to innovation, thanks to the cold sluggishness of our national character, we still bear the stamp of our forefathers. We have not (as I conceive) lost the generosity and dignity of thinking of the fourteenth century, nor as yet have we subtilized[3] ourselves into savages.[4] We are not the converts of Rousseau; we are not the disciples of Voltaire; Helvetius has made no progress amongst us.[5] Atheists are not our preachers; madmen are not our lawgivers. We know that *we* have made no discoveries, and we think that no discoveries are to be made in morality – nor many in the great principles of government, nor in the ideas of liberty which were understood long before we were born, altogether as well as they will be after the grave has heaped its mould upon our presumption, and the silent tomb shall have imposed its law on our pert loquacity.[6]

In England we have not yet been completely embowelled of our natural entrails; we still feel within us, and we cherish and cultivate, those inbred sentiments[7] which are the faithful guardians, the active monitors[8] of our duty, the true supporters of all liberal and manly[9] morals. We have not been drawn and trussed[10] in order that we may be filled, like stuffed birds in a museum, with chaff and rags and paltry blurred shreds of paper about the rights of man. We preserve the whole of our feelings still native and entire, unsophisticated[11] by pedantry and infidelity. We have real hearts of flesh and blood beating in our bosoms. We fear God. We look up with awe to kings, with affection to parliaments, with duty to magistrates, with reverence to priests, and with respect to nobility. Why? Because when such ideas are brought before our minds, it is *natural* to be so affected; because all other feelings are false and spurious, and tend to corrupt our minds, to vitiate our primary morals, to render us unfit for rational liberty, and (by teaching us a servile, licentious, and abandoned insolence) to be our low sport for a few holidays, to make us perfectly fit for, and justly deserving of slavery, through the whole course of our lives.

You see, sir,[12] that in this enlightened age I am bold enough to confess that we are generally men of untaught[13] feelings, that instead of casting away all our old prejudices, we cherish them to a very considerable degree and, to take more shame to ourselves, we cherish them because they *are* prejudices. And the longer they have lasted, and the more generally they have prevailed, the more we cherish them.

We are afraid to put men to live and trade each on his own private stock of reason,[14] because we suspect that this stock in each man is small, and that the individuals would do better to avail themselves of the general bank and capital of nations and of ages. Many of our men of speculation,[15] instead of exploding general prejudices, employ their sagacity to discover the latent wisdom which prevails in them. If they find what they seek (and they seldom fail), they think it more wise to continue the prejudice, with the reason involved, than to cast away the coat of prejudice, and to leave nothing but the naked reason – because prejudice, with its reason, has a motive to give action to that reason, and an affection which will give it permanence. Prejudice is of ready application in the emergency; it previously engages the mind in a steady course of wisdom and virtue, and does not leave the man hesitating in the moment of decision – sceptical, puzzled and unresolved. Prejudice renders a man's virtue his habit, and not a series of unconnected acts. Through just prejudice, his duty becomes a part of his nature.

---

3   *subtilized* refined (an ironic usage).
4   *savages* Jean-Jacques Rousseau (1712–78) had written admiringly of primitive man for his ability to live in accordance with his own innate needs, as opposed to the inequality and over-refinement found in 'civilized' societies.
5   The writings of Rousseau, François-Marie Arouet de Voltaire (1694–78), and Claude-Adrien Helvétius (1715–71) strongly influenced revolutionary thought and action in the eighteenth century.
6   *pert loquacity* impudent talk.
7   *inbred sentiments* innate feelings.

8   *monitors* reminders.
9   *manly* humane.
10   *drawn and trussed* after disembowelling (drawing) a bird, its wings were pinned to its sides with skewers (trussing).
11   *unsophisticated* uncontaminated.
12   *sir* Richard Price.
13   *untaught* natural, spontaneous.
14   *reason* leading radicals placed their faith in the redemptive power of reason.
15   *speculation* intelligence, wisdom.

[*Society is a Contract*]

From REFLECTIONS ON THE REVOLUTION IN FRANCE (1790) (pp. 143–7)

Society is indeed a contract.[1] Subordinate contracts for objects of mere occasional interest may be dissolved at pleasure, but the state ought not to be considered as nothing better than a partnership agreement in a trade of pepper and coffee, calico or tobacco, or some other such low concern, to be taken up for a little temporary interest, and to be dissolved by the fancy of the parties. It is to be looked on with other reverence because it is not a partnership in things subservient only to the gross animal existence of a temporary and perishable nature.

It is a partnership in all science,[2] a partnership in all art,[3] a partnership in every virtue and in all perfection. As the ends[4] of such a partnership cannot be obtained in many generations,[5] it becomes a partnership not only between those who are living, but between those who are living, those who are dead, and those who are to be born. Each contract of each particular state is but a clause in the great primeval contract of eternal society, linking the lower with the higher natures, connecting the visible and invisible world[6] according to a fixed compact sanctioned by the inviolable oath which holds all physical and all moral natures each in their appointed place. This law is not subject to the will of those who, by an obligation above them and infinitely superior, are bound to submit their will to that law. The municipal corporations of that universal kingdom[7] are not morally at liberty at their pleasure, and on their speculations of a contingent improvement wholly to separate and tear asunder the bands of their subordinate community, and to dissolve it into an unsocial, uncivil, unconnected chaos of elementary principles.

It is the first and supreme necessity only, a necessity that is not chosen but chooses, a necessity paramount to deliberation, that admits no discussion and demands no evidence, which alone can justify a resort to anarchy. This necessity is no exception to the rule because this necessity itself is a part too of that moral and physical disposition of things to which man must be obedient by consent or force. But if that which is only submission to necessity should be made the object of choice, the law is broken, nature is disobeyed, and the rebellious are outlawed, cast forth, and exiled from this world[8] of reason, and order, and peace, and virtue, and fruitful penitence, into the antagonist world of madness, discord, vice, confusion, and unavailing sorrow.

These, my dear sir, are, were, and I think long will be the sentiments of not the least learned and reflecting part of this kingdom. They who are included in this description form their opinions on such grounds as such persons ought to form them; the less enquiring receive them from an authority which those whom providence dooms to live on trust need not be ashamed to rely on. These two sorts of men move in the same direction, though in a different place. They both move with the order of the universe. They all know or feel this great ancient truth: 'Quod illi principi et praepotenti deo qui omnem hunc mundum regit, nihil eorum quae quidem fiant in terris acceptius quam concilia et caetus hominum jure sociati quae civitates appellantur.'[9] They take this tenet of the head and heart not from the great name which it immediately bears, nor from the greater from whence it is derived, but from that which alone can give true weight and sanction to any learned opinion: the common nature and common relation of men.

Persuaded that all things ought to be done with reference, and referring all to the point of reference

---

SOCIETY IS A CONTRACT
[1] *Society is indeed a contract* In his *Contrat social* (1762), Rousseau had argued that genuine political society could only be formed through a social pact, or free association of intelligent human beings who deliberately choose to form the kind of government to which they will owe allegiance. Burke invokes Rousseau's notion so as to revise it.
[2] *science* knowledge.
[3] *art* skill.
[4] *ends* aims, objectives.
[5] *in many generations* i.e. it takes many generations.

[6] *the visible and invisible world* i.e. earth and heaven.
[7] *The municipal corporations of that universal kingdom* i.e. the universe (heaven as well as earth).
[8] *nature is disobeyed . . . world* Burke is thinking of Adam and Eve, cast out of Eden for eating the fruit of the tree of knowledge.
[9] 'To the great and all-powerful God who rules this entire universe, nothing is more pleasing than the unions and gatherings of men bound together by laws that are called states' (Cicero, *Dream of Scipio* III:5 [13]).

to which all should be directed,[10] they think themselves bound (not only as individuals in the sanctuary of the heart, or as congregated in that personal capacity) to renew the memory of their high origin and caste; but also in their corporate character to perform their national homage to the institutor and author and protector of civil society, without which civil society man could not by any possibility arrive at the perfection of which his nature is capable, nor even make a remote and faint approach to it.

They conceive that He who gave our nature to be perfected by our virtue willed also the necessary means of its perfection. He willed therefore the state; He willed its connection with the source and original archetype of all perfection. They who are convinced of this His will (which is the law of laws and the sovereign of sovereigns) cannot think it reprehensible that this our corporate fealty and homage, that this our recognition of a signiory paramount[11] (I had almost said this oblation[12] of the state itself), as a worthy offering on the high altar of universal praise, should be performed as all public solemn acts are performed – in buildings, in music, in decoration, in speech, in the dignity of persons, according to the customs of mankind, taught by their nature; that is, with modest splendour, with unassuming state, with mild majesty and sober pomp.

For those purposes they think some part of the wealth of the country is as usefully employed as it can be, in fomenting[13] the luxury of individuals. It is the public ornament; it is the public consolation; it nourishes the public hope. The poorest man finds his own importance and dignity in it, whilst the wealth and pride of individuals at every moment makes the man of humble rank and fortune sensible of his inferiority, and degrades and vilifies his condition. It is for the man in humble life – and to raise his nature, and to put him in mind of a state[14] in which the privileges of opulence will cease, when he will be equal by nature, and may be more than equal by virtue – that this portion of the general wealth of his country is employed and sanctified.

I assure you I do not aim at singularity.[15] I give you opinions which have been accepted amongst us from very early times to this moment, with a continued and general approbation, and which indeed are so worked into my mind that I am unable to distinguish what I have learned from others from the results of my own meditation.

William Cowper   (1731–1800)

The loss of his mother when he was six, and persecution by an older boy at school, led to a mental imbalance from which Cowper was to suffer for the rest of his life. For a while in early manhood he looked set for a successful career as a lawyer or politician, but the prospect of a formal examination for the post of clerk of journals in the House of Lords led to near suicide in 1763. After a religious conversion while at Dr Cotton's St Albans asylum in 1765, he lived in retirement, and in 1767 came under the influence of the former slave trader turned evangelist John Newton.[1] An abortive engagement to Mrs Unwin, the widow of his local clergyman, led to another bout of depression in 1773, which now entailed a belief that he was eternally damned.

Cowper's most impressive work, *The Task* (1785), was originally conceived as a sort of a joke, when an acquaintance suggested he write a mock-heroic poem in blank verse on the subject of 'the sofa'. Its conversational, self-deprecatory manner suited him, and it grew into a work of six books and 5000 lines. What made it innovatory was a concentration on man, nature and society (the future subject of Wordsworth's proposed epic, *The Recluse*), and its unabashed preoccupation with the self. Cowper explained its purpose as being 'to discountenance the modern enthusiasm after a London life, and to recommend rural ease and leisure as friendly to piety and virtue'. It attacks corruption in the city, the slave trade, and contemporary education. But its primary significance for Wordsworth and

---

[10]   *the point of reference to which all should be directed* God.
[11]   *signiory paramount* executive authority.
[12]   *oblation* devotional offering.
[13]   *fomenting* encouraging.
[14]   *a state* heaven.

[15]   *singularity* eccentricity.

WILLIAM COWPER
[1]   For more on this interesting character, see Bernard Martin, *John Newton: A Biography* (London, 1950).

Coleridge, both of whom read it shortly after publication, was its overtly confessional manner. No one had written like this before. In stylistic terms alone it was a revelation – it gave rise to a comparatively relaxed style that Wordsworth may have been recalling when, in the Preface to *Lyrical Ballads*, he described the poet as 'a man speaking to men – a man (it is true) endued with more lively sensibility, more enthusiasm and tenderness, who has a greater knowledge of human nature, and a more comprehensive soul, than are supposed to be common among mankind' (p. 360). The passage describing the winter evening in *Task* Book IV (pp.

11–12) is Coleridge's source for *Frost at Midnight*, providing a setting, a state of mind, and an account of the fancy that would influence *Biographia Literaria* (pp. 525–6); crazy Kate, in the first of the extracts, provided the model for the despairing Margaret in Wordsworth's *The Ruined Cottage* (pp. 277–89).

Further reading

Vincent Newey, *Cowper's Poetry: A Critical Study and Reassessment* (Liverpool, 1982)

Martin Priestman, *Cowper's Task: Structure and Influence* (Cambridge, 1983)

[Crazy Kate]

From THE TASK (1785) (Book I)

There often wanders one whom better days
Saw better clad, in cloak of satin trimmed   535
With lace, and hat with splendid ribbon bound.
A serving-maid was she, and fell in love
With one who left her, went to sea, and died.
Her fancy followed him through foaming waves
To distant shores, and she would sit and weep   540
At what a sailor suffers; fancy too
(Delusive most where warmest wishes are)
Would oft anticipate his glad return
And dream of transports she was not to know.
She heard the doleful tidings of his death   545
And never smiled again. And now she roams
The dreary waste, there spends the livelong day,
And there, unless when Charity forbids,[1]
The livelong night. A tattered apron hides,
Worn as a cloak, and hardly hides a gown   550
More tattered still, and both but ill conceal
A bosom heaved with never-ceasing sighs.
She begs an idle pin of all she meets
And hoards them in her sleeve, but needful food,
Though pressed with hunger oft, or comelier clothes, 555
Though pinched with cold, asks never. Kate is crazed.

[On Slavery]

From THE TASK (Book II)

Oh for a lodge in some vast wilderness,
Some boundless contiguity[1] of shade,

CRAZY KATE
[1] *unless ... forbids* Charity (in the form of a householder) might forbid Kate from wandering at night and provide her with accommodation.

ON SLAVERY
[1] *contiguity* proximity.

Where rumour of oppression and deceit,
Of unsuccessful or successful war
Might never reach me more! My ear is pained,   5
My soul is sick with ev'ry day's report
Of wrong and outrage with which earth is filled.
There is no flesh in man's obdurate heart –
It does not feel for man. The nat'ral bond
Of brotherhood is fevered as the flax   10
That falls asunder at the touch of fire.
He finds his fellow guilty of a skin
Not coloured like his own, and having pow'r
T' enforce the wrong, for such a worthy cause[2]
Dooms and devotes[3] him as his lawful prey.   15
Lands intersected by a narrow frith[4]
Abhor each other. Mountains interposed
Make enemies of nations who had else
Like kindred drops been mingled into one.
Thus man devotes his brother, and destroys;   20
And worse than all, and most to be deplored
As human nature's broadest, foulest blot,
Chains him, and tasks him, and exacts his sweat
With stripes that Mercy with a bleeding heart
Weeps when she sees inflicted on a beast.   25
    Then what is man? And what man seeing this,
And having human feelings, does not blush
And hang his head to think himself a man?
I would not have a slave to till my ground,
To carry me, to fan me while I sleep   30
And tremble when I wake, for all the wealth
That sinews bought and sold have ever earned.
No, dear as freedom is, and in my heart's
Just estimation prized above all price,
I had much rather be myself the slave   35
And wear the bonds, than fasten them on him.
We have no slaves at home – then why abroad?
And they themselves, once ferried o'er the wave
That parts us, are emancipate and loosed.[5]
Slaves cannot breathe in England; if their lungs   40
Receive our air, that moment they are free,
They touch our country and their shackles fall.
That's noble, and bespeaks a nation proud
And jealous of the blessing. Spread it then,
And let it circulate through ev'ry vein   45
Of all your Empire, that where Britain's power
Is felt, mankind may feel her mercy too.

---

[2] *a worthy cause* ironic; the cause is completely unworthy.
[3] *devotes* curses.
[4] *frith* wood.
[5] *And they . . . loosed* At the trial of the slave James Somerset
in 1772 it was deemed that, 'as soon as any slave sets his foot

upon English territory, he becomes free'. This did not imply
abolition of the slave trade; it merely meant that a former
slave who arrived in England could not be forcibly removed
and returned to slavery elsewhere. This gave hope to those
who, like Cowper, hoped for abolition.

[*The Winter Evening*]

From THE TASK (Book IV)

Just when our drawing-rooms begin to blaze
With lights by clear reflection multiplied
From many a mirror (in which he of Gath,
Goliath,[1] might have seen his giant bulk   270
Whole without stooping, tow'ring crest and all),
My pleasures too begin. But me perhaps
The glowing hearth may satisfy awhile
With faint illumination that uplifts
The shadow to the ceiling, there by fits   275
Dancing uncouthly[2] to the quiv'ring flame.
 Not undelightful is an hour to me
So spent in parlour twilight; such a gloom
Suits well the thoughtful or unthinking mind,
The mind contemplative, with some new theme 280
Pregnant,[3] or indisposed alike to all.
Laugh ye, who boast your more mercurial pow'rs
That never feel a stupor, know no pause
Nor need one. I am conscious, and confess
Fearless, a soul that does not always think.   285
Me oft has fancy ludicrous and wild
Soothed with a waking dream of houses, tow'rs,
Trees, churches, and strange visages expressed
In the red cinders, while with poring eye
I gazed, myself creating what I saw.   290
Nor less amused have I quiescent watched
The sooty films that play upon the bars –
Pendulous, and foreboding in the view
Of superstition, prophesying still,
Though still deceived, some stranger's near approach. 295
 'Tis thus the understanding takes repose
In indolent vacuity of thought,
And sleeps and is refreshed. Meanwhile the face
Conceals the mood lethargic with a mask
Of deep deliberation, as[4] the man   300
Were tasked to his full strength, absorbed and lost.
Thus oft reclined at ease, I lose an hour
At evening, till at length the freezing blast
That sweeps the bolted shutter, summons home
The recollected powers and, snapping short   305
The glassy threads with which the fancy weaves
Her brittle toys, restores me to myself.
How calm is my recess, and how the frost
Raging abroad, and the rough wind, endear
The silence and the warmth enjoyed within.   310
 I saw the woods and fields at close of day,

THE WINTER EVENING
[1] *he of Gath, / Goliath* The story of how young David slew
the giant Goliath of Gath is told at I Samuel 17.

[2] *uncouthly* strangely.
[3] *pregnant* inspired.
[4] *as* i.e. as if.

A variegated show; the meadows green
Though faded, and the lands where lately waved
The golden harvest, of a mellow brown,
Upturned so lately by the forceful share.[5]   315
I saw far off the weedy fallows[6] smile
With verdure not unprofitable, grazed
By flocks fast-feeding and selecting each
His fav'rite herb; while all the leafless groves
That skirt th' horizon wore a sable hue   320
Scarce noticed in the kindred dusk of eve.
Tomorrow brings a change, a total change
Which even now – though silently performed,[7]
And slowly, and by most unfelt – the face
Of universal nature undergoes.   325
        Fast falls a fleecy show'r. The downy flakes
Descending, and with never-ceasing lapse
Softly alighting upon all below,
Assimilate all objects. Earth receives
Gladly the thick'ning mantle, and the green   330
And tender blade that feared the chilling blast
Escapes unhurt beneath so warm a veil.

Sweet Meat has Sour Sauce, or The Slave-Trader in the Dumps (composed 1788)[1]

From WORKS ed. Robert Southey (15 vols, 1835–7) (vol. x p. 10)

A trader I am to the African shore,
But since that my trading is like to be o'er,[2]
I'll sing you a song that you ne'er heard before,
        Which nobody can deny, deny,
        Which nobody can deny.   5

When I first heard the news it gave me a shock,
Much like what they call an electrical knock,
And now I am going to sell off my stock,
        Which nobody can deny.

'Tis a curious assortment of dainty regales,[3]   10
To tickle the Negroes with when the ship sails –
Fine chains for the neck, and a cat with nine tails,
        Which nobody can deny.

---

[5]   *share* ploughshare.
[6]   *weedy fallows* fields lying fallow, full of weeds.
[7]   *silently performed* Coleridge had this phrase in mind when he composed the opening line of *Frost at Midnight*: 'The frost performs its secret ministry / Unhelped by any wind.'

THE SLAVE-TRADER
[1]   This poem was inspired by the passing of a Bill proposed in the House of Commons on 21 May 1788 by Sir William Dolben, MP for the University of Oxford. It aimed to limit the number of slaves which could be transported from Africa to British colonies in the West Indies. On 26 May merchants and inhabitants of Liverpool presented a petition to the House, saying that the Bill would cause them financial ruin. And there was a good deal of argument from those MPs with slave-owning interests. Fortunately, the Bill was passed in both Houses: the move towards abolition had begun.
[2]   *is like to be o'er* a reference to the Bill restricting the slave trade (see preceding note).
[3]   *dainty regales* choice gifts (ironic).

Here's supple-jack plenty, and store of rattan[4]
That will wind itself round the sides of a man   15
As close as a hoop round a bucket or can,
    Which nobody can deny.

Here's padlocks and bolts, and screws for the thumbs
That squeeze them so lovingly till the blood comes;
They sweeten the temper like comfits[5] or plums,   20
    Which nobody can deny.

When a Negro his head from his victuals withdraws
And clenches his teeth and thrusts out his paws,
Here's a notable engine to open his jaws,[6]
    Which nobody can deny.   25

Thus going to market, we kindly prepare
A pretty black cargo of African ware,
For what they must meet with when they get there,
    Which nobody can deny.

'Twould do your heart good to see 'em below   30
Lie flat on their backs all the way as we go,
Like sprats[7] on a gridiron, scores in a row,[8]
    Which nobody can deny.

But ah! if in vain I have studied an art
So gainful to me, all boasting apart,   35
I think it will break my compassionate heart,[9]
    Which nobody can deny.

For oh, how it enters my soul like an awl;[10]
This pity, which some people self-pity call,
Is sure the most heart-piercing pity of all,   40
    Which nobody can deny.

So this is my song, as I told you before;
Come buy off my stock, for I must no more
Carry Caesars and Pompeys to sugar-cane shore,
    Which nobody can deny, deny,   45
    Which nobody can deny.

---

[4] *Here's supple-jack plenty ... rattan* Canes, switches, and ropes were made out of supple-jack (stems of creeping or twining shrubs found in the West Indies) and rattan.

[5] *comfits* sweetmeat made of some fruit, root, etc., preserved with sugar.

[6] *to open his jaws* for force-feeding; many slaves attempted to starve themselves to death.

[7] *sprats* small sea-fish.

[8] *scores in a row* Plans showing how slaves were crammed into slave ships were a powerful weapon in the abolitionist campaign. Hannah More carried one with her, showing it to horrified guests at dinner parties.

[9] *my compassionate heart* ironic.

[10] *awl* small tool for making holes in leather.

Thomas Paine   (1737–1809)

Writer, deist, and American revolutionary leader, Tom Paine was one of the foremost political thinkers of the time. A former corset maker and customs officer, he emigrated to America at the age of thirty-seven in 1774 to be swept up in what was to become the American War of Independence. Two years later he published *Common Sense*, the first appeal for independence, to popular acclaim, selling 120,000 copies within three months. His forthright account of British government as a 'monarchical tyranny' marked him out as a republican: 'it is the pride of kings which throws mankind into confusion', he wrote.[1]

After America won the war, he returned briefly to England (May–September 1789), and went from there to France, seeking finance for an iron bridge of his own design. He became involved, once again, in pamphleteering. *The Rights of Man* (1791–2) was one of the most effective and distinguished replies to Burke's *Reflections on the Revolution in France*. Beginning with the idea that good government is founded on reason (that radical signifier so heartily despised by Burke, see p. 6), Paine argued that democracy – a society in which all men have equal rights and in which leadership depends on talent and wisdom – is better than aristocracy. Even today, his attack on the monarchy and defence of republicanism seems controversial to the English. The work sold 200,000 copies in 1791–3, many in cheap editions designed for working people, and earned him the hatred of the government. Back in England, he narrowly escaped arrest prior to being charged with sedition and sentenced to death in December 1792. (*The Rights of Man* had been banned in September.)

Paine fled to Paris where, for a time, he enjoyed his privileges as a member of the National Assembly. Significantly, he voted against the execution of Louis in January 1793, an act that earned him no friends among those responsible for the Reign of Terror. In December he was imprisoned in the Luxembourg gaol, where his health declined drastically. Avoiding execution only by an oversight, he was eventually released in November 1794. He remained in France for some years before returning to America in 1802. He died at his home in New Rochelle in 1809 from the fever he had contracted in prison; the whereabouts of his remains is unknown.

Further reading

Thomas Paine, *Common Sense* ed. Isaac Kramnick (2nd edn, Harmondsworth, 1976)

Thomas Paine, *Rights of Man* introduced by Eric Foner (Harmondsworth, 1984)

A. J. Ayer, *Thomas Paine* (New York, 1988)

David Bindman, ' "My own mind is my own church": Blake, Paine and the French Revolution', *Reflections of Revolution: Images of Romanticism* ed. Alison Yarrington and Kelvin Everest (London and New York, 1993), pp. 112–33

Of the Origin and Design of Government in General

From COMMON SENSE (Philadelphia, 1776) (pp. 1–2)

Some writers have so confounded[1] society with government as to leave little or no distinction between them – whereas they are not only different, but have different origins. Society is produced by our wants, and government by our wickedness; the former promotes our happiness positively by uniting our affections, the latter negatively by restraining our vices. The one encourages intercourse, the other creates distinctions.[2] The first is a patron, the last a punisher.

Society in every state is a blessing, but government even in its best state is but a necessary evil – in its worst state an intolerable one. For when we suffer, or are exposed to the same miseries by a government which we expect in a country without government, our calamity is heightened by reflecting that we furnish the means by which we suffer.

Government, like dress, is the badge of lost innocence; the palaces of kings are built on the ruins of

---

THOMAS PAINE
1   Thomas Paine, *Common Sense* ed. Isaac Kramnick (2nd edn, Harmondsworth, 1976), p. 72.

GOVERNMENT IN GENERAL
1   *confounded* confused.
2   *The one . . . distinctions* society encourages social intercourse; government promotes the social hierarchy.

the bowers of paradise.[3] For were the impulses of conscience clear, uniform, and irresistibly obeyed, man would need no other lawgiver. But that not being the case, he finds it necessary to surrender up a part of his property[4] to furnish means for the protection of the rest – and this he is induced to do by the same prudence which in every other case advises him out of two evils to choose the least. Wherefore, security being the true design and end of government, it unanswerably follows that whatever form thereof appears most likely to ensure it to us, with the least expense and greatest benefit, is preferable to all others.

[Freedom of Posterity]

From THE RIGHTS OF MAN Part I (1791) (pp. 8–10)

The English Parliament of 1688 did a certain thing[1] which, for themselves and their constituents, they had a right to do, and which it appeared right should be done. But, in addition to this right (which they possessed by delegation), they set up another right by assumption: that of binding and controlling posterity to the end of time. The case, therefore, divides itself into two parts – the right which they possessed by delegation, and the right which they set up by assumption. The first is admitted but with respect to the second I reply:

There never did, there never will, and there never can, exist a parliament, or any description of men, or any generation of men, in any country, possessed of the right or the power of binding and controlling posterity to the 'end of time', or of commanding for ever how the world shall be governed, or who shall govern it. And therefore all such clauses, acts or declarations by which the makers of them attempt to do what they have neither the right nor the power to do – nor the power to execute – are in themselves null and void. Every age and generation must be as free to act for itself, in all cases, as the ages and generations which preceded it.

The vanity and presumption of governing beyond the grave is the most ridiculous and insolent of all tyrannies. Man has no property in man, neither has any generation a property in the generations which are to follow. The parliament or the people of 1688, or of any other period, had no more right to dispose of the people of the present day, or to bind or to control them *in any shape whatever*, than the parliament or the people of the present day have to dispose of, bind or control those who are to live a hundred or a thousand years hence. Every generation is and must be competent to all the purposes which its occasions require. It is the living, and not the dead, that are to be accommodated. When man ceases to be, his power and his wants cease with him, and having no longer any participation in the concerns of this world, he has no longer any authority in directing who shall be its governors, or how its government shall be organized, or how administered.

[On Revolution]

From THE RIGHTS OF MAN Part I (1791) (pp. 156–9)

When we survey the wretched condition of man under the monarchical and hereditary systems of government, dragged from his home by one power, or driven by another, and impoverished by taxes more than by enemies, it becomes evident that those systems are bad, and that a general revolution in the principle and construction of governments is necessary.

---

[3] *the palaces of kings ... paradise* an idea deriving from Rousseau's concept of the noble savage, outlined in his *Discourse on Inequality*.

[4] *surrender up a part of his property* in taxes – one cause of the American Revolution.

FREEDOM OF POSTERITY
[1] *a certain thing* i.e. replace the Catholic James II with the Protestant William of Orange. The Glorious Revolution was seen by English radicals as the forerunner of the revolutions in America and, subsequently, France.

What is government more than the management of the affairs of a nation? It is not, and from its nature cannot be, the property of any particular man or family, but of the whole community at whose expense it is supported. And though by force or contrivance it has been usurped into an inheritance, the usurpation cannot alter the right of things. Sovereignty, as a matter of right, appertains to the nation only, and not to any individual; and a nation has at all times an inherent indefeasible[1] right to abolish any form of government it finds inconvenient, and establish such as accords with its interest, disposition and happiness. The romantic[2] and barbarous distinction of men into kings and subjects, though it may suit the condition of courtiers, cannot that of citizens – and is exploded by the principle upon which governments are now founded. Every citizen is a member of the sovereignty, and as such can acknowledge no personal subjection, and his obedience can be only to the laws.

When men think of what government is, they must necessarily suppose it to possess a knowledge of all the objects and matters upon which its authority is to be exercised. In this view of government, the republican system as established by America and France operates to embrace the whole of a nation, and the knowledge necessary to the interest of all the parts is to be found in the centre, which the parts by representation form. But the old governments are on a construction that excludes knowledge as well as happiness – government by monks who know nothing of the world beyond the walls of a convent is as consistent as government by kings.

What were formerly called revolutions were little more than a change of persons or an alteration of local circumstances. They rose and fell like things of course,[3] and had nothing in their existence or their fate that could influence beyond the spot that produced them. But what we now see in the world, from the revolutions of America and France, are a renovation of the natural order of things, a system of principles as universal as truth and the existence of man, and combining moral with political happiness and national prosperity.

I. Men are born and always continue free and equal in respect of their rights. Civil distinctions, therefore, can be founded only on public utility.

II. The end[4] of all political associations is the preservation of the natural and imprescriptible rights of man; and these rights are liberty, property, security, and resistance of oppression.

III. The nation is essentially the source of all sovereignty; nor can any individual or any body of men be entitled to any authority which is not expressly derived from it.

In these principles there is nothing to throw a nation into confusion by inflaming ambition. They are calculated to call forth wisdom and abilities, and to exercise them for the public good, and not for the emolument[5] or aggrandizement of particular descriptions of men or families. Monarchical sovereignty – the enemy of mankind and the source of misery – is abolished, and sovereignty itself is restored to its natural and original place: the nation. Were this the case throughout Europe, the cause of wars would be taken away.

[*Republicanism*]

From THE RIGHTS OF MAN Part II (1792) (pp. 22–3, 24)

What is called a republic is not any particular form of government. It is wholly characteristical of the purport,[1] matter or object for which government ought to be instituted, and on which it is to be employed: 'res-publica' (the public affairs, or the public good – or, literally translated, the public thing). It is a word of a good original,[2] referring to what ought to be the character and business of

---

ON REVOLUTION
[1]   *indefeasible* undeniable.
[2]   *romantic* impractical, fanciful.
[3]   *of course* i.e. of succession, over a course of time.
[4]   *end* aim.

[5]   *emolument* profit.

REPUBLICANISM
[1]   *purport* purpose, intention.
[2]   *original* meaning, referent.

government, and in this sense it is naturally opposed to the word 'monarchy', which has a base original signification – it means arbitrary power in an individual person, in the exercise of which *himself* (and not the 'res-publica') is the object.

Every government that does not act on the principle of a republic – or, in other words, that does not make the res-publica its whole and sole object – is not a good government. Republican government is no other than government established and conducted for the interest of the public, as well individually as collectively. It is not necessarily connected with any particular form, but it most naturally associates with the representative form, as being best calculated to secure the end for which a nation is at the expense of supporting it.

Various forms of government have affected to style themselves a republic. Poland calls itself a republic, which is an hereditary aristocracy with what is called an elective[3] monarchy. Holland calls itself a republic, which is chiefly aristocratical with an hereditary stadtholdership.[4] But the government of America, which is wholly on the system of representation, is the only real republic in character and in practice that now exists. Its government has no other object than the public business of the nation, and therefore it is properly a republic; and the Americans have taken care that *this* and no other shall always be the object of their government, by their rejecting everything hereditary, and establishing government on the system of representation only.... . What Athens was in miniature, America will be in magnitude: the one was the wonder of the ancient world, the other is becoming the admiration, the model of the present. It is the easiest of all the forms of government to be understood, and the most eligible in practice – and excludes at once the ignorance and insecurity of the hereditary mode, and the inconvenience of the simple democracy.

Anna Seward (1742–1809)

Anna was born in Eyam, Derbyshire, the daughter of Thomas Seward and Elizabeth Hunter, of Lichfield. Her father was headmaster of Lichfield Grammar School, and had taught Samuel Johnson. Under his tutelage she was reading Milton at two, and composing religious verse by the age of ten. An accident lamed her in childhood. In 1750 her father became Canon of Lichfield Cathedral, and from 1754 the family resided in the Bishop's Palace. Partly, no doubt, because her brother and two sisters died in infancy, Anna enjoyed an intensely close relationship with Honora Sneyd, adopted by the Sewards as a child; Honora's marriage to Richard Lovell Edgeworth in 1773 caused Anna profound unhappiness, and their affection is the subject of some of her finest verse.

To Time Past, composed in 1788, is one of her finest love poems to Honora Sneyd. Written in anticipation of Honora's impending marriage to Edgeworth, it brings her anxiety at her own future into painfully

sharp focus; the prospect before her is one of loneliness among the 'bare bleak fields' of winter. In the event, Anna had a remarkably comfortable life; unlike many other women writers of the time, she enjoyed financial security. After her father's death in 1790 she lived comfortably on £400 per annum until her death, dispensing advice to other writers (not always soliticited), and enjoying the honoured status of literary icon – 'the swan of Lichfield'.

A complete text of Anna's other important poem of this moment, *Eyam*, is to be found in my *Romantic Women Poets: An Anthology* (1997) pp. 5–6.

Further Reading

Margaret Eliza Ashmun, *The Singing Swan* (London, 1931)

Anna Seward, *Llangollen Vale 1796* introduced by Jonathan Wordsworth (Oxford and New York, 1994)

---

[3] *elective* elected.

[4] *stadtholdership* magistrate-general (abolished 1802).

To Time Past. Written Dec. 1772

From LLANGOLLEN VALE, WITH OTHER POEMS (1796)

Return, blessed years, when not the jocund spring,
Luxuriant summer, nor the amber hours
Calm autumn gives, my heart invoked to bring
Joys whose rich balm o'er all the bosom pours! –
When ne'er I wished might grace the closing day   5
One tint purpureal[1] or one golden ray;
When the loud storms that desolate the bowers
Found dearer welcome than favonian[2] gales,
And winter's bare bleak fields, than summer's flowery vales!

Yet not to deck pale hours with vain parade   10
Beneath the blaze of wide-illumined dome;
Not for the bounding dance; not to pervade
And charm the sense with music; nor, as roam
The mimic passions o'er theatric scene,
To laugh or weep – oh not for these, I ween,   15
But for delights that made the *heart* their home
Was the grey night-frost on the sounding plain
More than the sun invoked, that gilds the grassy lane.

Yes, for the joys that trivial joys excel,
My loved Honora,[3] did we hail the gloom   20
Of dim November's eve; and, as it fell,
And the bright fires shone cheerful round the room,
Dropped the warm curtains with no tardy hand,
And felt our spirits and our hearts expand,
Listening their steps, who still, where'er they come,   25
Make the keen stars that glaze the settled snows,
More than the sun invoked, when first he tints the rose.

Affection, friendship, sympathy – your throne
Is winter's glowing hearth, and ye were ours;
Thy smile, Honora, made them all our own.   30
Where are they *now*? Alas, their choicest powers
Faded at thy retreat, for thou art gone!
And many a dark long eve I sigh alone
In thrilled remembrance of the vanished hours,
When storms were dearer than the balmy gales,   35
And winter's bare bleak fields than green luxuriant vales.

TO TIME PAST
[1] *purpureal* purple.

[2] *favonian* of the west wind, and therefore favourable, gentle.
[3] Honora Sneyd, see headnote.

Anna Laetitia Barbauld (*née* Aikin) (1743–1825)

Anna Laetitia Aikin was born at Kibworth, Leicester, the elder child of Dr John Aikin, a schoolmaster, and Jane Jennings. In 1758 her father became a teacher at the Warrington Academy for Dissenters, where one of his colleagues, Joseph Priestley (discoverer of oxygen and founder of modern Unitarianism), encouraged her poetic talents, one of her earliest works being *A Summer Evening's Meditation*. Her brother John (1747–1822), a physician and accomplished author, worked with her, and together they published *Miscellaneous Pieces in Prose* in 1773, the same year which saw publication of her *Poems*. The latter volume was a success, running to a fifth edition by 1777. In 1774, despite well-founded doubts, she married Rochemont Barbauld, a Dissenting minister who had been educated at the Warrington Academy; together they ran a successful boys' school in Palgrave, Suffolk, until 1785. Visits to London brought her into contact with the bluestockings, among whom she is celebrated in Hannah More's *Sensibility* (1782).

She and her husband settled in Hampstead, where she devoted herself to pamphleteering, most notably in defence of Dissenters (1790), democratic government and popular education (1792), and the newly-declared war with France. Political concerns were never far from her mind, and her *Epistle to William Wilberforce* (1791) ranks as one of the most eloquent anti-slavery poems of the day. It was composed at a moment when the campaign against slavery faltered: on 17 April 1791 Wilberforce (1759–1833) proposed his first Bill urging abolition, but it was defeated two days later. He tried again in April 1792, and although that Bill was passed by the House of Commons, it was thrown out by the Lords the following year; this is the struggle recalled by Wordsworth at *Thirteen-Book Prelude* x 201–10. The slave trade was not outlawed until February 1807.

From 1796 Anna's brother was editor of the *Monthly Magazine*, an important periodical published by the radical sympathizer, Joseph Johnson, and read enthusiastically by Wordsworth and Coleridge. She contributed poetry, including *To Mr Coleridge*. Composed shortly after their meeting in Bristol, August 1797, it is distinguished by her early recognition of his talents, and her shrewd warning against the 'metaphysic lore' which was to preoccupy him in later years. Such was her importance in literary circles that in 1800 Wordsworth ordered his publisher to send her a complimentary copy of the new two-volume *Lyrical Ballads*, and George Dyer included three of her poems in an anthology of *Odes*.[1]

In 1802 the Barbaulds moved to Stoke Newington; by this time her husband's mental health was increasingly fragile, and in 1808, after several fits of violence against her, he drowned himself. She was tremendously productive in subsequent years, editing Akenside and Collins, the *Letters* of Richardson, *The British Novelists* (50 vols, 1810), and reviewing fiction and verse for the *Monthly Review* (1809–15). But her most important piece of work was the last to be published: *Eighteen Hundred and Eleven* (1812), a passionate, shrewd poem about the disastrous state in which the country found itself. A complete text may be found in my *Romantic Women Poets: An Anthology* (1997) pp. 10–18.

Further reading

Julie Ellison, 'The Politics of Fancy in the Age of Sensibility', *RR* 228–55

The Poems of Anna Laetitia Barbauld ed. William McCarthy and Elizabeth Kraft (Athens, Georgia, 1994)

William McCarthy, ' "We hoped the Woman was Going to Appear": Repression, Desire, and Gender in Anna Laetitia Barbauld's Early Poems', *RWW* 113–37

A Summer Evening's Meditation

From POEMS (1773)

One sun by day, by night ten thousand shine.

(Young)[1]

'Tis passed! – the sultry tyrant of the south[2]
Has spent his short-lived rage. More grateful hours

ANNA LAETITIA BARBAULD
[1]   *Odes* ed. George Dyer (Ludlow, 1800), includes her poems *To Content*, *To Wisdom*, and *To Spring*.

A SUMMER EVENING'S MEDITATION
[1]   Edward Young, *Night Thoughts* ix 748. Though little read today, Young was tremendously influential in the late eighteenth century.
[2]   *the sultry tyrant of the south* the sun.

Move silent on; the skies no more repel
The dazzled sight, but with mild maiden beams
Of tempered light invite the cherished eye   5
To wander o'er their sphere, where, hung aloft,
Dian's bright crescent,[3] like a silver bow
New-strung in heaven, lifts high its beamy horns
Impatient for the night, and seems to push
Her brother down the sky. Fair Venus shines   10
Even in the eye of day – with sweetest beam
Propitious shines, and shakes a trembling flood
Of softened radiance from her dewy locks.
The shadows spread apace, while meekened Eve,
Her cheek yet warm with blushes, slow retires   15
Through the Hesperian gardens of the west,[4]
And shuts the gates of day.
                                    'Tis now the hour
When Contemplation from her sunless haunts
(The cool damp grotto or the lonely depth
Of unpierced woods, where, wrapped in solid shade,   20
She mused away the gaudy hours of noon
And fed on thoughts unripened by the sun)[5]
Moves forward, and with radiant finger points
To yon blue concave swelled by breath divine,
Where, one by one, the living eyes of heaven[6]   25
Awake, quick kindling o'er the face of ether[7]
One boundless blaze – ten thousand trembling fires
And dancing lustres – where th' unsteady eye,
Restless and dazzled, wanders unconfined
O'er all this field of glories: spacious field,   30
And worthy of the Master![8] – He whose hand
With hieroglyphics older than the Nile
Inscribed the mystic tablet[9] hung on high
To public gaze, and said, 'Adore, oh man,
The finger of thy God!' From what pure wells   35
Of milky light, what soft o'erflowing urn
Are all these lamps so filled – these friendly lamps
For ever streaming o'er the azure deep
To point our path and light us to our home?
How soft they slide along their lucid spheres,   40
And, silent as the foot of time, fulfil
Their destined courses! Nature's self is hushed
And, but[10] a scattered leaf which rustles through
The thick-wove foliage, not a sound is heard
To break the midnight air – though the raised ear,   45
Intensely listening, drinks in every breath.

---

[3] *Dian's bright crescent* the moon, of which Diana was god-
dess.
[4] *the Hesperian gardens of the west* In Greek myth, the daugh-
ters of Hesperus (the evening star) guarded the garden in
which golden apples grew in the Isles of the Blessed, at the
western extremity of the earth.
[5] *fed on thoughts unripened by the sun* cf. Wordsworth, *These
chairs they have no words to utter* 13: 'I have thoughts that are

fed by the sun'.
[6] *the living eyes of heaven* the stars.
[7] *ether* heaven, the sky.
[8] *the Master* God.
[9] *the mystic tablet* on which were written the Ten Command-
ments.
[10] *but* except.

How deep the silence, yet how loud the praise!
But are they silent all, or is there not
A tongue in every star that talks with man
And woos him to be wise – nor woos in vain?   50
    This dead of midnight is the noon of thought,
And wisdom mounts her zenith with the stars.
At this still hour the self-collected soul
Turns inward, and beholds a stranger there
Of high descent, and more than mortal rank: 55
An embryo God, a spark of fire divine
Which must burn on for ages, when the sun
(Fair transitory creature of a day!)
Has closed his golden eye and, wrapped in shades,
Forgets his wonted journey through the east.   60
    Ye citadels of light and seats of gods!
Perhaps my future home from whence the soul,
Revolving periods past, may oft look back
With recollected tenderness on all
The various busy scenes she left below,   65
Its deep-laid projects and its strange events,
As on some fond and doting tale that soothed
Her infant hours. Oh be it lawful now
To tread the hallowed circle of your courts,
And with mute wonder and delighted awe   70
Approach your burning confines!
                              Seized in thought,
On fancy's wild and roving wing I sail,[11]
From the green borders of the peopled earth
And the pale moon, her duteous fair attendant;
From solitary Mars; from the vast orb   75
Of Jupiter, whose huge gigantic bulk
Dances in ether like the lightest leaf;
To the dim verge, the suburbs of the system[12]
Where cheerless Saturn midst her wat'ry moons,
Girt with a lucid zone,[13] majestic sits   80
In gloomy grandeur, like an exiled queen
Amongst her weeping handmaids. Fearless thence
I launch into the trackless deeps of space
Where, burning round, ten thousand suns appear
Of elder beam, which ask no leave to shine   85
Of our terrestrial star, nor borrow light
From the proud regent of our scanty day[14] –
Sons of the morning, first-born of creation,
And only less than Him who marks their track
And guides their fiery wheels. Here must I stop,   90
Or is there aught beyond? What hand unseen
Impels me onward through the glowing orbs
Of habitable nature far remote,

---

[11]   McCarthy and Kraft (*The Poems of Anna Laetitia Barbauld*, Athens, Georgia, 1994) suggest an antecedent in Hume, *Enquiry Concerning Human Understanding*: 'the thought can in an instant transport us into the most distant regions of the universe; or even beyond the universe, into the unbounded chaos, where nature is supposed to lie in total confusion'.
[12]   *suburbs of the system* outskirts of the solar system.
[13]   *zone* belt; a reference to the rings around Saturn.
[14]   *the proud regent of our scanty day* the sun.

To the dread confines of eternal night,
To solitudes of vast unpeopled space,   95
The deserts of creation, wide and wild,
Where embryo systems and unkindled suns
Sleep in the womb of chaos?

                            Fancy droops,
And thought astonished stops her bold career;
But oh, thou mighty mind, whose powerful word   100
Said, 'Thus let all things be', and thus they were –
Where shall I seek thy presence? How unblamed[15]
Invoke thy dread perfection?[16]
Have the broad eyelids of the morn[17] beheld thee,
Or does the beamy shoulder of Orion[18]   105
Support thy throne? Oh, look with pity down
On erring, guilty man – not in thy names
Of terror clad; not with those thunders armed
That conscious Sinai felt,[19] when fear appalled
The scattered tribes: Thou hast a gentler voice   110
That whispers comfort to the swelling heart
Abashed, yet longing to behold her maker.
    But now my soul, unused to stretch her powers
In flight so daring, drops her weary wing
And seeks again the known accustomed spot   115
Dressed up with sun and shade, and lawns and streams,
A mansion fair and spacious for its guest,
And full replete with wonders. Let me here,
Content and grateful, wait th' appointed time
And ripen for the skies: the hour will come   120
When all these splendours bursting on my sight
Shall stand unveiled, and to my ravished sense
Unlock the glories of the world unknown.

Epistle to William Wilberforce, Esq.,[1] *on the Rejection of the Bill for Abolishing the Slave Trade*[2]

From POEMS (1792)

Cease, Wilberforce, to urge thy generous aim –
Thy country knows the sin and stands the shame!
The preacher, poet, senator,[3] in vain

---

[15]   *unblamed* uncensured (i.e. without doing God an injustice).
[16]   *How unblamed . . . perfection* McCarthy and Kraft note the allusion to *Paradise Lost* iii 3: 'May I express thee unblamed?'
[17]   *eyelids of the morn* a biblical expression, as McCarthy and Kraft note; cf. Job 41:18.
[18]   *Orion* giant hunter who sprang from the urine of Jupiter, Neptune and Mercury. Anna refers to the constellation of Orion into which he was turned at his death.
[19]   *those thunders . . . felt* Jehovah delivered the Ten Commandments to Moses on Mount Sinai in a cloud of 'thunders and lightnings', Exodus 19.

EPISTLE TO WILLIAM WILBERFORCE
[1]   William Wilberforce (1759–1833), leader of the movement for the abolition of the slave trade in Parliament.
[2]   The Society for the Abolition of the Slave Trade was founded by Thomas Clarkson and a group of Quakers in 1787; Wilberforce was its representative in the House of Commons, and the cause was taken up by a number of bluestockings, including Hannah More and Barbauld. Wilberforce proposed abolition of the slave trade in the House in April 1791, but despite support from Edmund Burke, Charles James Fox, and the Prime Minister, the motion was rejected. This poem was composed soon after, and certainly by 17 June.
[3]   *senator* politician.

Has rattled in her sight the Negro's chain,
With his deep groans assailed her startled ear   5
And rent the veil that hid his constant tear,
Forced her averted eyes his stripes to scan,
Beneath the bloody scourge laid bare the man,
Claimed pity's tear, urged conscience' strong control
And flashed conviction on her shrinking soul.   10
The muse, too soon awaked, with ready tongue
At mercy's shrine applausive[4] paeans rung,
And freedom's eager sons in vain foretold
A new Astrean[5] reign, an age of gold!
She knows and she persists – still Afric bleeds;   15
Unchecked, the human traffic still proceeds;
She stamps her infamy to future time
And on her hardened forehead seals the crime.
    In vain, to thy white standard gathering round,
Wit, worth, and parts and eloquence are found;[6]   20
In vain to push to birth thy great design
Contending chiefs and hostile virtues join;
All from conflicting ranks, of power possessed
To rouse, to melt, or to inform the breast.
Where seasoned tools of avarice prevail,   25
A nation's eloquence, combined, must fail.
Each flimsy sophistry by turns they try –
The plausive[7] argument, the daring lie,
The artful gloss that moral sense confounds,
Th' acknowledged thirst of gain[8] that honour wounds   30
(Bane of ingenuous minds!), th' unfeeling sneer
Which sudden turns to stone the falling tear.
They search assiduous with inverted skill
For forms of wrong, and precedents of ill;
With impious mockery wrest the sacred page,   35
And glean up crimes from each remoter age;
Wrung nature's tortures, shuddering, while you tell,
From scoffing fiends bursts forth the laugh of hell;[9]
In Britain's senate,[10] misery's pangs give birth
To jests unseemly, and to horrid mirth –   40
Forbear! thy virtues but provoke our doom
And swell th' account of vengeance yet to come.
For (not unmarked in Heaven's impartial plan)
Shall man, proud worm, contemn his fellow man?
And injured Afric, by herself redressed,   45
Darts her own serpents at her tyrant's breast.

---

[4]   *applausive* applauding.
[5]   *Astrean* Astrea, goddess of justice in the Golden Age,
abandoned the earth in disgust at the crimes of humanity. Her
reign will be just.
[6]   *Wit, worth, and parts and eloquence are found* a reference to
the talented orators in the House of Commons who supported
the Abolitionist cause.
[7]   *plausive* specious.

[8]   *thirst of gain* as in the debate of 1788 (see p. 000), a central
argument of those opposed to Abolition was that the slave trade
was a highly lucrative national industry.
[9]   *From scoffing fiends … hell* McCarthy and Kraft note
that when William Smith, one of the Abolitionist MPs,
described how an African woman had been forced to throw
her murdered child from a ship, some members had
laughed.
[10]   *Britain's senate* the Houses of Parliament.

Each vice, to minds depraved by bondage known,
With sure contagion fastens on his own;[11]
In sickly languors melts his nerveless frame,
And blows to rage impetuous passion's flame;   50
Fermenting swift, the fiery venom gains
The milky innocence of infant veins;
There swells the stubborn will, damps learning's fire,
The whirlwind wakes[12] of uncontrolled desire,
Sears the young heart to images of woe   55
And blasts the buds of virtue as they blow.
    Lo! where reclined, pale Beauty courts the breeze,
Diffused on sofas of voluptuous ease;
With anxious awe, her menial train around
Catch her faint whispers of half-uttered sound.   60
See her, in monstrous fellowship, unite
At once the Scythian and the Sybarite;[13]
Blending repugnant vices, misallied,
Which frugal nature purposed to divide;
See her, with indolence to fierceness joined,   65
Of body delicate, infirm of mind,
With languid tones imperious mandates urge,
With arm recumbent wield the household scourge,[14]
And with unruffled mien, and placid sounds,
Contriving torture and inflicting wounds.   70
    Nor in their palmy walks and spicy groves
The form benign of rural pleasure roves;
No milkmaid's song or hum of village talk
Soothes the lone poet in his evening walk;
No willing arm the flail unwearied plies   75
Where the mixed sounds of cheerful labour rise;
No blooming maids and frolic swains are seen
To pay gay homage to their harvest queen;
No heart-expanding scenes their eyes must prove[15]
Of thriving industry and faithful love: 80
But shrieks and yells disturb the balmy air,
Dumb sullen looks of woe announce despair
And angry eyes through dusky features glare.
Far from the sounding lash the muses fly
And sensual riot drowns each finer joy.   85
    Nor less from the gay east[16] on essenced wings,
Breathing unnamed perfumes, contagion springs;[17]
The soft luxurious plague alike pervades
The marble palaces and rural shades;
Hence thronged Augusta[18] builds her rosy bowers   90

---

[11]   *Darts her own serpents ... breast* a reference, as McCarthy
and Kraft suggest, to the argument that Britons degraded
themselves by their participation in the slave trade.
[12]   *wakes* trails.
[13]   *The Scythian and the Sybarite* the pagan and the sensualist.
The ancient Scythians were notorious for savagery; the citizens
of Sybaris, an ancient Greek city of southern Italy, were
renowned for effeminacy and luxury.

[14]   *pale Beauty ... scourge* the pale, beautiful mistress of the
house lies down ('recumbent') as she whips (scourges) her ser-
vants into action.
[15]   *prove* experience, witness.
[16]   *east* the East Indies, or India.
[17]   *contagion springs* it was believed that disease was carried by
the wind.
[18]   *Augusta* London.

And decks in summer wreaths her smoky towers;[19]
And hence in summer bow'rs Art's costly hand
Pours courtly splendours o'er the dazzled land.
The manners melt, one undistinguished blaze
O'erwhelms the sober pomp of elder days;   95
Corruption follows with gigantic stride
And scarce vouchsafes his shameless front to hide;
The spreading leprosy taints ev'ry part,
Infects each limb, and sickens at the heart.
Simplicity, most dear of rural maids,   100
Weeping resigns her violated shades;
Stern Independence from his glebe[20] retires
And anxious Freedom eyes her drooping fires;
By foreign wealth are British morals changed,
And Afric's sons, and India's, smile avenged.   105
      For you whose tempered ardour long has borne
Untired the labour, and unmoved the scorn,
In virtue's fasti[21] be inscribed your fame,
And uttered yours with Howard's honoured name.[22]
      Friends of the friendless – hail, ye generous band   110
Whose efforts yet arrest Heaven's lifted hand,
Around whose steady brows in union bright
The civic wreath and Christian's palm unite!
Your merit stands, no greater and no less,
Without or with the varnish of success;   115
But seek no more to break a nation's fall,
For ye have saved yourselves, and that is all.
Succeeding times your struggles, and their fate,
With mingled shame and triumph shall relate,
While faithful history in her various page,   120
Marking the features of this motley age,
To shed a glory, and to fix a stain,
Tells how you strove, and that you strove in vain.

The Rights of Woman (composed c.1795)[1]

From WORKS (1825)

Yes, injured woman, rise, assert thy right!
Woman! too long degraded, scorned, oppressed;
Oh born to rule in partial law's despite,
Resume thy native empire o'er the breast!

Go forth arrayed in panoply[2] divine,   5
That angel pureness which admits no stain;
Go bid proud man his boasted rule resign
And kiss the golden sceptre of thy reign.

---

[19] *decks . . . towers* pollution, generated by the burning of fossil fuels, was already a problem in eighteenth-century London.
[20] *glebe* field.
[21] *fasti* annals.
[22] John Howard (1726–90), prison reformer and philanthropist.

THE RIGHTS OF WOMAN
[1] This was an angry response to Wollstonecraft's criticism of Anna's *To a Lady, with some painted Flowers* as being an 'ignoble' poem (because patronizing to women), in *Vindication of the Rights of Woman* (1792), chapter 4.
[2] *panoply* armour for spiritual warfare.

Go gird thyself with grace, collect thy store
Of bright artillery glancing from afar –   10
Soft melting tones thy thundering cannon's roar,
Blushes and fears thy magazine[3] of war.

Thy rights are empire: urge no meaner claim –
Felt, not defined, and, if debated, lost;
Like sacred mysteries which, withheld from fame,   15
Shunning discussion, are revered the most.

Try all that wit and art suggest to bend
Of thy imperial foe the stubborn knee;
Make treacherous man thy subject, not thy friend –
Thou mayst command, but never canst be free.   20

Awe the licentious and restrain the rude;
Soften the sullen, clear the cloudy brow;
Be more than princes' gifts, thy favours sued –
She hazards all, who will the least allow.

But hope not, courted idol of mankind,   25
On this proud eminence secure to stay;
Subduing and subdued, thou soon shalt find
Thy coldness soften, and thy pride give way.

Then, then, abandon each ambitious thought,
Conquest or rule thy heart shall feebly move,   30
In Nature's school, by her soft maxims taught
That separate rights are lost in mutual love.

To Mr Coleridge[1] (composed c.1797)

From THE MONTHLY MAGAZINE 7 (1799, pp. 231–2)

Midway the hill of science,[2] after steep
And rugged paths that tire the unpractised feet,
A grove extends, in tangled mazes wrought,
And filled with strange enchantment: dubious shapes
Flit through dim glades, and lure the eager foot   5
Of youthful ardour to eternal chase;
Dreams hang on every leaf; unearthly forms
Glide through the gloom, and mystic visions swim
Before the cheated sense.[3] Athwart the mists,

---

3   *magazine* munitions.

TO MR COLERIDGE
1   Barbauld met Coleridge in August 1797, on a visit to
their mutual friend John Prior Estlin, a fellow Unitarian, in
Bristol.
2   *science* knowledge.

3   *A grove extends . . . sense* Barbauld correctly discerned in the
young Coleridge a tendency to abstraction and sophistry; as
late as 1800 he concurred with her judgement in a letter to
Estlin: 'The more I see of Mrs Barbauld the more I admire her
– that wonderful propriety of mind! She has great acuteness,
very great . . . . My own subtleties too often lead me into
strange (though, God be praised) transient out-of-the-way-
nesses' (Griggs i 578).

Far into vacant space, huge shadows stretch   10
And seem realities; while things of life,
Obvious to sight and touch, all glowing round,
Fade to the hue of shadows. Scruples[4] here,
With filmy net, most like the autumnal webs
Of floating gossamer, arrest the foot   15
Of generous enterprise, and palsy[5] hope
And fair ambition with the chilling touch
Of sickly hesitation and blank fear.
Nor seldom Indolence these lawns among
Fixes her turf-built seat, and wears the garb   20
Of deep philosophy, and museful sits
In dreamy twilight of the vacant mind,
Soothed by the whispering shade – for soothing soft
The shades, and vistas lengthening into air
With moonbeam rainbows tinted. Here each mind   25
Of finer mould,[6] acute and delicate,
In its high progress to eternal truth[7]
Rests for a space in fairy bowers entranced,
And loves the softened light and tender gloom,
And, pampered with most unsubstantial food,   30
Looks down indignant on the grosser world
And matter's cumbrous shapings.
                              Youth beloved
Of science, of the muse beloved: not here,
Not in the maze of metaphysic lore
Build thou thy place of resting! Lightly tread   35
The dangerous ground, on noble aims intent;
And be this Circe[8] of the studious cell
Enjoyed but still subservient. Active scenes
Shall soon with healthful spirit brace thy mind,
And fair exertion, for bright fame sustained,   40
For friends, for country, chase each spleen-fed fog
That blots the wide creation:
Now Heaven conduct thee with a parent's love!

Hannah More   (1745–1833)

For Dr Johnson, she was 'the most powerful versifica-trix in the English language';[1] in purely financial terms, Hannah More was one of the most successful writers of her day, having made £30,000 by her publications by 1825. She was born at Fishponds in the parish of Stapleton, near Bristol, 2 February 1745, the fourth of five daughters of Mary Grace and Jacob More (d. 1783), a teacher at the Free School, who was determined to ensure that his five daughters were capable of making a useful independent living in the same profession. By the age of four she had learnt to read so well as to astonish the local clergyman with her recital of

---

4   *Scruples* intellectual conundrums.
5   *palsy* paralyse.
6   *mould* substance.
7   *its high progress . . . truth* Coleridge believed that mankind was 'progressive', i.e. that mankind was constantly improving.
8   *Circe* Greek enchantress who changed all who drank of her cup into swine. Anna is warning Coleridge not to become a slave of 'metaphysic lore', but to keep it subservient to his quest for knowledge and poetic talent.

HANNAH MORE
1   Sir William Forbes, *An Account of the Life and Writings of James Beattie, LL.D.* (2 vols, Edinburgh, 1806), ii 147.

the catechism. Her father was apparently 'frightened by his own success' at teaching her Latin and mathematics, but the entreaties of his family encouraged him to continue. Her eldest sister set up her own school in Bristol in 1757, and Hannah studied a wide range of subjects there, including Italian, Spanish and Latin.

An encounter with the poet John Langhorne in 1773 led her to publish *The Search after Happiness* later that year. Her tragedy *The Inflexible Captive* was performed at Bristol in 1774, with a prologue by Langhorne and an epilogue by Garrick. The meeting with Garrick was one of the most important in her life. He became her mentor, and introduced her to Burke, Johnson, Reynolds and, crucially, Elizabeth Montagu, queen of the bluestockings, who, with Mrs Vesey, was already bringing together the various participants of that important salon. Like many such coteries, the bluestockings were never as close-knit and exclusive as they are assumed to have been. At various times they included Anna Laetitia Barbauld, Elizabeth Carter, Mrs Boscawen, the Duchess of Beaufort, Mrs Leveson, Mrs Walsingham, the Duchess of Portland, and occasionally entertained visits from Reynolds, Johnson, Walpole and Lord Lyttelton. Hannah More's best poems were written for, and inspired by, the blues. Of these, *Sensibility* is the best; it no doubt enshrines something of the good humour that made the bluestockings so intriguing. But it would be wrong to deduce that they aspired to no more than the occasional bunfight; they were famous partly for the moral and religious works that several of their number (notably Hester Chapone and Catherine Macaulay) had published, and for campaigning on behalf of universal education. Moreover, as Sylvia Harcstark Myers has pointed out, Elizabeth Carter argued that it was 'unfair to women to keep them from rational conversation with men because it kept them from developing their intellectual capacities':[2] this is the feminist subtext that underlies Hannah's portrayal of this group of unusually well-educated women who wished to rid society of card-playing in exchange for polite conversation. Only an extract is presented here, but a complete, annotated text may be found in my *Romantic Women Poets: An Anthology* (1997) pp. 24–34.

There was a pious streak in Hannah, and Garrick's death in January 1779 led her to reconsider the direction her writing had taken; in the late 1780s she retired to a cottage in Cowslip Green, Somerset, and devoted herself to didactic and educational works. Of these, one of the most notable must be the Cheap Repository tracts. It was late 1791 or early 1792, and the revolutionary fervour that gripped working people made the likes of Hannah and her friends uneasy. Bishop Porteus suggested to her that she 'write some little thing tending to open their eyes under their present wild impressions of liberty and equality'.[3] The secret agenda of the Cheap Repository was to teach the working class to be satisfied with their lot (it should be noted that, despite being an enormous success, few copies were actually sold to working people; most were purchased by committees and given away in charity schools, workhouses, hospitals, and prisons). The first was published on 3 March 1795; over 300,000 copies were sold by 18 April, and two million within the first year. *The Sorrows of Yamba* is typical, combining the desire to evangelize with Hannah's anti-slavery convictions. The series stopped in 1799, when, due to ill health, she was compelled to give it up. Another of the Cheap Repository poems, *The Story of Sinful Sally*, may be found in my *Romantic Women Poets: An Anthology* (1997), along with complete texts of *The Bas-Bleu* (1786) and *Slavery* (1788).

In later years she continued to enjoy literary success with such works as *Coelebs in Search of a Wife* (1809) which, though published anonymously, went into eleven editions within the year. The enduring popularity of her work during the nineteenth century drew many pilgrims to her door, and she was compelled to reserve two days a week for visitors so that she could spend the remainder in peace. She died peacefully on 7 September 1833, at the age of eighty-eight, leaving her fortune to a range of charitable institutions and religious societies.

Further reading

Elizabeth Kowaleski-Wallace, *Their Father's Daughters: Hannah More, Maria Edgeworth, and Patriarchal Complicity* (New York, 1991)

Julie Ellison, 'The Politics of Fancy in the Age of Sensibility', *RR* 228–55

Joel Haefner, 'The Romantic Scene(s) of Writing', *RR* 256–73

Selected Writings of Hannah More ed. Robert Hole (London, 1996)

G. H. Spinney, 'Cheap Repository Tracts: Hazard and Marshall Edition', *The Library* 4th series 20 (1940) 295–340

---

[2] *The Bluestocking Circle: Women, Friendship, and the Life of the Mind in Eighteenth-Century England* (Oxford, 1990), p. 262.

[3] William Roberts, *Memoirs of the Life and Correspondence of Mrs Hannah More* (3rd edn, 4 vols, London, 1835), ii 345.

Sensibility: A Poetical Epistle to the Hon. Mrs Boscawen[1] (extract)

From SACRED DRAMAS: CHIEFLY INTENDED FOR YOUNG PERSONS: THE SUBJECTS
TAKEN FROM THE BIBLE. TO WHICH IS ADDED, SENSIBILITY, A POEM (1782)

Sweet sensibility, thou soothing pow'r
Who shedd'st thy blessings on the natal hour   240
Like fairy favours! Art can never seize,
Nor affectation catch thy pow'r to please:
Thy subtle essence still eludes the chains
Of definition, and defeats her pains.
Sweet sensibility, thou keen delight!   245
Thou hasty moral, sudden sense of right!
Thou untaught goodness! Virtue's precious seed!
Thou sweet precursor of the gen'rous deed!
Beauty's quick relish! Reason's radiant morn,
Which dawns soft light before Reflection's born!   250
To those who know thee not, no words can paint,
And those who know thee, know all words are faint!
'Tis not to mourn because a sparrow dies,
To rave in artificial ecstasies;
'Tis not to melt in tender Otway's fires;   255
'Tis not to faint when injured Shore expires;
'Tis not because the ready eye o'erflows
At Clementina's or Clarissa's woes.[2]
    Forgive, oh Richardson, nor think I mean,
With cold contempt, to blast thy peerless scene;   260
If some faint love of virtue glow in me,
Pure spirit, I first caught that flame from thee.
    While soft Compassion silently relieves,
Loquacious Feeling hints how much she gives;
Laments how oft her wounded heart has bled,   265
And boasts of many a tear she never shed.
    As words are but th' external marks to tell
The fair ideas in the mind that dwell;
And only are of things the outward sign,
And not the things themselves they but define;   270
So exclamations, tender tones, fond tears,
And all the graceful drapery Pity wears;
These are not Pity's self, they but express
Her inward sufferings by their pictured dress;
And these fair marks, reluctant I relate,   275

SENSIBILITY

[1] Frances, daughter of William Evelyn Glanville, Esq., married Admiral Edward Boscawen, Viscount Falmouth, in 1742. He was a national hero, having thwarted a French invasion in an important battle in Lagos Bay in August 1759. He died of typhoid fever, 10 January 1761. In 1775, More told her sister that 'Mrs Boscawen's life has been a continued series of afflictions that may almost bear a parallel with those of the righteous man of Uz'.

[2] More refers to Catullus's poem in which Lesbia mourns her dead sparrow; Thomas Otway's Venice Preserved (1682); Nicholas Rowe's tragedy, Jane Shore (1714); Richardson's Clarissa (1747–8), and Sir Charles Grandison (1754), the heroine of which is called Clementina Porretta.

These lovely symbols may be counterfeit.
Celestial Pity, why must I deplore
Thy sacred image stamped on basest ore?
There are, who fill with brilliant plaints the page,
If a poor linnet meet the gunner's rage;   280
There are, who for a dying fawn display
The tend'rest anguish in the sweetest lay;[3]
Who for a wounded animal deplore,
As if friend, parent, country, were no more;
Who boast quick rapture trembling in their eye,   285
If from the spider's snare they save a fly;
Whose well-sung sorrows every breast inflame,
And break all hearts but his from whom they came;
Yet scorning life's *dull* duties to attend,
Will persecute a wife, or wrong a friend;   290
Alive to every woe by fiction dressed,
The innocent he wronged, the wretch distressed,
May plead in vain; their suff'rings come not near,
Or he relieves them cheaply with a tear.[4]
Not so the tender moralist of Tweed;   295
His Man of Feeling is a man indeed.[5]

The Sorrows of Yamba, or the Negro Woman's Lamentation

From CHEAP REPOSITORY (*c.*1795)

In St Lucie's distant isle
    Still with Afric's love I burn,
Parted many a thousand mile
    Never, never to return.

Come, kind death, and give me rest!   5
    Yamba has no friend but thee;
Thou canst ease my throbbing breast,
    Thou canst set the prisoner free.

Down my cheeks the tears are dripping,
    Broken is my heart with grief,   10
Mangled my poor flesh with whipping;
    Come, kind death, and bring relief!

Born on Afric's golden coast,
    Once I was as blessed as you;
Parents tender I could boast,   15
    Husband dear, and children too.

---

3   More apparently disapproved of Marvell's *The Nymph Complaining for the Death of her Faun*.
4   More attacks a kind of sensibility that she and the other bluestockings regarded as debased. In 1782, shortly after *Sensibility* had been published, she told her sister: 'Mrs Montagu, Mrs Chapone, and Mrs Carter, are mightily pleased that I have attacked that mock feeling and sensibility which is at once the boast and disgrace of these times, and which is equally deficient in taste and truth' (William Roberts, *Memoirs of the Life and Correspondence of Mrs Hannah More* (3rd edn, 4 vols, London, 1835), i 236).
5   Henry Mackenzie (1745–1831), native of Edinburgh, published his sentimental novel, *The Man of Feeling*, in 1771.

Whity man he came from far,
    Sailing o'er the briny flood,
Who, with help of British tar,
    Buys up human flesh and blood.   20

With the baby at my breast
    (Other two were sleeping by),
In my hut I sat at rest
    With no thought of danger nigh.

From the bush at eventide   25
    Rushed the fierce man-stealing crew,
Seized the children by my side,
    Seized the wretched Yamba too.

Then for love of filthy gold,
    Straight they bore me to the sea,   30
Crammed me down a slave-ship's hold
    Where were hundreds stowed like me.

Naked on the platform lying,
    Now we cross the tumbling wave –
Shrieking, sickening, fainting, dying,   35
    Dead of shame for Britons brave.

At the savage Captain's beck
    Now like brutes they make us prance;
Smack the cat[1] about the deck,
    And in scorn they bid us dance.   40

I in groaning passed the night,
    And did roll my aching head:
At the break of morning light
    My poor child was cold and dead.

Happy, happy, there she lies!   45
    Thou shalt feel the lash no more;
Thus full many a Negro dies
    Ere we reach the destined shore.

Driven like cattle to a fair,
    See they sell us, young and old;   50
Child from mother too they tear,
    All for love of filthy gold.

I was sold to massa hard –
    Some have massas kind and good;
And again my back was scarred,   55
    Bad and stinted was my food.

THE SORROWS OF YAMBA
[1]   *cat* cat-o'-nine-tails, a whip with nine knotted lashes.

Poor and wounded, faint and sick,
    All exposed to burning sky,
Massa bids me grass to pick,
    And I now am near to die.   60

What and if to death he send me,
    Savage murder though it be?
British laws shall ne'er befriend me;
    They protect not slaves like me!

Mourning thus my wretched state   65
    (Ne'er may I forget the day),
Once in dusk of evening late,
    Far from home I dared to stray –

Dared, alas, with impious haste
    Tow'rds the roaring sea to fly;   70
Death itself I longed to taste,
    Longed to cast me in and die.

There I met upon the strand
    English missionary good;
He had Bible book in hand   75
    Which poor me no understood.

Then he led me to his cot,
    Soothed and pitied all my woe,
Told me 'twas the Christian's lot
    Much to suffer here below.   80

Told me then of God's dear son
    (Strange and wondrous is the story),
What sad wrong to him was done
    Though he was the Lord of Glory.

Told me too, like one who knew him   85
    (Can such love as this be true?),
How he died for them that slew him,
    Died for wretched Yamba too.

Freely he his mercy proffered
    And to sinners he was sent,   90
E'en to massa pardons offered –
    Oh, if massa would repent!

Wicked deed full many a time
    Sinful Yamba too hath done,
But she wails to God her crime;   95
    But she trusts his only son.

Oh ye slaves whom massas beat,
    Ye are stained with guilt within;
As ye hope for mercy sweet,
    So forgive your massas' sin.   100

And with grief when sinking low,
 Mark the road that Yamba trod,
Think how all her pain and woe
 Brought the captive home to God.

Now let Yamba too adore   105
 Gracious Heaven's mysterious plan;
Now I'll count thy mercies o'er
 Flowing through the guilt of man.

Now I'll bless my cruel capture
 (Hence I've known a Saviour's name),   110
Till my grief is turned to rapture
 And I half forget the blame.

But though here a convert rare
 Thanks her God for grace divine,
Let not man the glory share –   115
 Sinner, still the guilt is thine.

Duly now baptized am I
 By good missionary man;
Lord my nature purify
 As no outward water can!   120

All my former thoughts abhorred,
 Teach me now to pray and praise;
Joy and glory in my Lord,
 Trust and serve him all my days.

But though death this hour may find me,   125
 Still with Afric's love I burn
(There I've left a spouse behind me),
 Still to native land I turn.

And when Yamba sinks in death,
 This my latest prayer shall be   130
While I yield my parting breath:
 'Oh that Afric might be free!'

Cease, ye British sons of murder!
 Cease from forging Afric's chain;
Mock your Saviour's name no further,   135
 Cease your savage lust of gain.

Ye that boast ye 'rule the waves',[2]
 Bid no slave-ship soil the sea;
Ye that 'Never will be slaves',
 Bid poor Afric's land be free.   140

---

[2] *rule the waves* an allusion to '*Rule Britannia*', England's unofficial national anthem.

Where ye gave to war its birth,
   Where your traders fixed their den,
There go publish 'Peace on earth',
   Go proclaim 'Good will to men.'[3]

Where ye once have carried slaughter,   145
   Vice and slavery and sin,
Seized on husband, wife and daughter,
   Let the gospel enter in.

Thus where Yamba's native home,
   Humble hut of rushes stood –   150
Oh! if there should chance to roam
   Some dear missionary good,

Thou in Afric's distant land
   Still shalt see the man I love,
Join him to the Christian band,   155
   Guide his soul to realms above.

There no fiend again shall sever
   Those whom God hath joined and blessed;
There they dwell with Him for ever,
   There 'the weary are at rest'.[4]   160

Charlotte Smith (*née* Turner)   (1749–1806)

Charlotte was born in London, the elder daughter of Nicholas Turner of Stoke House, Guildford, and Bignor Park, Sussex, and Anna Towers. She and her sister were brought up by an aunt after their mother's death when she was three. After her father's second marriage in 1764, he arranged for her to marry Benjamin Smith, the son of a wealthy West Indian merchant and director of the East India Company. This might have seemed like a good idea at the time, but litigation over the will of Smith's father, and his own extravagance, led to his imprisonment for seven months from December 1783. Some of this punishment Charlotte shared with him; by this time they had a large and growing family. She began to publish sonnets in the *European Magazine* in 1782, and published her *Elegiac Sonnets* for the first time in 1784. It was an immediate success. Wordsworth and Coleridge both read it shortly after publication, and were profoundly influenced: Wordsworth footnoted an allusion to her work in his first published volume, *An Evening Walk*

(1793), and Coleridge included her in his *Sonnets from Various Authors* (1796). She enlarged her *Elegiac Sonnets* in successive editions, so that it became a two-volume work in 1797, with no less than 827 subscribers. What made her sonnets distinctive was the way in which the various hardships she had faced, though never explicitly outlined, coloured her close natural observations, producing a blend of the confessional and the sentimental.

During the late 1780s, in dire need of money to support her family, she wrote novels: *Emmeline* (1788), *Ethelinde* (1789), *Celestina* (1791), *Desmond* (1792), and *The Old Manor House* (1793). Their composition took a heavy toll on her health, and they never generated sufficient income for the needs of her family. Her literary reputation was assured by this time, as Andrew Bechet remarked in his review of *Ethelinde*: 'The character of Mrs Smith, both as a poet and as a novelist, is so firmly established, that our commendation at the present time may be thought unnecessary.'[1]

---

[3] *Peace on earth . . . Good will to men* Luke 2:14: 'Glory to God in the highest, and on earth peace, good will toward men'.
[4] *the weary are at rest* Job 3:17: 'There the wicked cease from troubling; and there the weary be at rest.'

CHARLOTTE SMITH
[1] *Monthly Review* 2 (1791) 161.

She died in 1806 at Tilford near Farnham, and was buried at Stoke Church, Guildford, close to her family home. She left behind a mass of manuscripts, many of which were destroyed on the spot. Of those which survived, most seemed to have provided copy for *Beachy Head, and Other Poems* (1807). *Beachy Head* is in many respects her greatest achievement in verse, and it may be found in my *Romantic Women Poets: An Anthology* (1997), along with complete texts of *Elegiac Sonnets* (1786), and *The Emigrants* (1793).

Further reading

Florence Anna May Hilbish, *Charlotte Smith, Poet and Novelist, 1749–1806* (Philadelphia, 1941)

Charlotte Smith, *Elegiac Sonnets 1789* introduced by Jonathan Wordsworth (Oxford and New York, 1992)

The Poems of Charlotte Smith ed. Stuart Curran (New York, 1993)

Jacqueline Labbe, 'Selling One's Sorrows: Charlotte Smith, Mary Robinson, and the Marketing of Poetry', *TWC* 25 (1994) 68–71

Daniel Robinson, 'Reviving the Sonnet: Women Romantic Poets and the Sonnet Claim', *European Romantic Review* 6 (1995) 98–127

Sonnet V. To the South Downs[1]

From ELEGIAC SONNETS (1784)

Ah, hills beloved! – where once, an happy child,
    Your beechen shades, 'your turf, your flowers among',[2]
I wove your bluebells into garlands wild,
    And woke your echoes with my artless song.
Ah, hills beloved! your turf, your flowers remain;   5
    But can they peace to this sad breast restore,
For one poor moment soothe the sense of pain,
    And teach a breaking heart to throb no more?
And you, Aruna,[3] in the vale below,
    As to the sea your limpid waves you bear,   10
Can you one kind Lethean[4] cup bestow
    To drink a long oblivion to my care?
Ah no! When all, e'en hope's last ray, is gone,
There's no oblivion but in death alone!

Sonnet XXXII. To Melancholy. Written on the Banks of the Arun, October 1785

From ELEGIAC SONNETS: THE THIRD EDITION. WITH TWENTY ADDITIONAL SONNETS (1786)

When latest autumn spreads her evening veil,
    And the grey mists from these dim waves arise,
I love to listen to the hollow sighs
    Through the half leafless wood that breathes the gale.

SONNET V. TO THE SOUTH DOWNS
[1] *South Downs* Smith apparently composed this important sonnet in Woolbeding, on the South Downs, in West Sussex, which is served by the River Rother, a tributary of the River Arun.
[2] Smith notes a borrowing from Gray's *Ode on a Distant*

Prospect of Eton College 8: 'Whose turf, whose shades, whose flowers among'.
[3] 'The River Arun' (Smith's note).
[4] *Lethean* water from the River Lethe, river of forgetfulness in Hades, which enabled souls to forget their previous existence.

For at such hours the shadowy phantom, pale,   5
   Oft seems to fleet before the poet's eyes;
Strange sounds are heard, and mournful melodies,
As of night-wanderers who their woes bewail;
Here, by his native stream, at such an hour,
   Pity's own Otway[1] I methinks could meet,   10
   And hear his deep sighs swell the saddened wind.
Oh melancholy, such thy magic power,
   That to the soul these dreams are often sweet,
   And soothe the pensive visionary mind!

George Crabbe   (1754–1832)

A native of Aldeburgh in Suffolk, George Crabbe set up in practice as a surgeon in 1775. He decided to try his fortunes as a writer in 1780 and went to London, where he secured the patronage of Edmund Burke. Returning to Aldeburgh as a curate after the publication of his poem, *The Library* (1781), he became chaplain to the Duke of Rutland in 1782. He published *The Village* in 1783 and *The Newspaper* in 1785. Then, for twenty-two years, he published nothing until *Poems* (1807), *The Borough* (1810), *Tales* (1812), and *Tales of the Hall* (1819). These works won him the admiration and friendship of a new generation: Jeffrey, Byron, Scott, Rogers, Moore and Campbell. As Byron told Murray in 1817, 'Crabbe's the man' (Marchand v 266). One reason for this was Crabbe's mastery of the post-Popean manner so popular towards the end of the eighteenth century; Byron and like-minded readers regarded Crabbe as free of what they saw as the misguided notions advocated by Wordsworth and Coleridge. That very quality helps explain his comparative unpopularity today. All the same, Crabbe's style should not hinder our appreciation of his imaginative genius, seen at its most striking in *Peter Grimes*, a complete text of which appears below. *Peter Grimes* merits comparison with *The Ancient Mariner* for its psychological insight, particularly its handling of guilt. It is best known today through Benjamin Britten's opera (1945).

Crabbe's most perceptive critic remains Hazlitt who, in *The Spirit of the Age*, summarized his technique as follows:

He takes the most trite, the most gross and obvious and revolting part of nature, for the subject of his elaborate descriptions; but it is Nature still, and Nature is a great and mighty Goddess! It is well for the Reverend Author that it is so. . . . Whoever makes an exact image of any thing on the earth, however deformed or insignificant, according to him, must succeed – and he himself has succeeded.[1]

Wordsworth concurred, observing in a letter to Rogers of 1808 that 'nineteen out of 20 of Crabbe's pictures are mere matters of fact; with which the Muses have just about as much to do as they have with a Collection of medical reports, or of law cases' (*MY* i 268). Coleridge accused Crabbe of 'an absolute defect of the high imagination; he gives me little or no pleasure: yet, no doubt, he has much power of a certain kind' (CC *Table Talk* ii 278).

Further reading

William Hazlitt, 'Mr Campbell – Mr Crabbe', *The Spirit of the Age* (London, 1825), pp. 183–205
Jerome J. McGann, 'The Anachronism of George Crabbe', *The Beauty of Inflections: Literary Investigations in Historical Method and Theory* (Oxford, 1985), pp. 294–312
George Crabbe: The Complete Poetical Works ed. Nora Dalrymple-Champneys and Arthur Pollard (3 vols, Oxford, 1988)
Frank Whitehead, *George Crabbe: A Reappraisal* (Selinsgrove and London, 1995)

SONNET XXXII. TO MELANCHOLY
[1] 'Otway was born at Trotten, a village in Sussex. Of Woolbeding, another village on the banks of the Arun (which runs through them both), his father was rector. Here it was, therefore, that he probably passed many of his early years. The Arun is here an inconsiderable stream, winding in a channel deeply worn, among meadow, heath and wood' (Smith's note).

Thomas Otway (1652–85), dramatist, was known chiefly for his tragedy, *Venice Preserved* (1681). He died in extreme poverty.

GEORGE CRABBE
[1] William Hazlitt, *The Spirit of the Age* (London, 1825), pp. 195–6.

Peter Grimes[1]

From THE BOROUGH (1810) Letter XXII: *The Poor of the Borough*

Old Peter Grimes made fishing his employ;
His wife he cabined with him and his boy,
And seemed that life laborious to enjoy:
To town came quiet Peter with his fish,
And had of all a civil word and wish.   5
He left his trade upon the Sabbath-day
And took young Peter in his hand to pray;
But soon the stubborn boy from care broke loose –
At first refused, then added his abuse.
His father's love he scorned, his power defied,   10
But being drunk, wept sorely when he died.

    Yes, then he wept, and to his mind there came
Much of his conduct, and he felt the shame!
How he had oft the good old man reviled,
And never paid the duty of a child;   15
How when the father in his Bible read,
He in contempt and anger left the shed:
'It is the Word of life!' the parent cried –
'This is the life itself!' the boy replied;
And while old Peter in amazement stood,   20
Gave the hot spirit to his boiling blood:
How he, with oath and furious speech, began
To prove his freedom and assert the man;
And when the parent checked his impious rage
How he had cursed the tyranny of age –   25
Nay, once had dealt the sacrilegious[2] blow
On his bare head and laid his parent low!
The father groaned – 'If thou art old', said he,
'And hast a son, thou wilt remember me:
Thy mother left me in an happy time,   30
Thou kill'dst not her – Heav'n spares the double crime.'
On an inn settle[3] in his maudlin grief,
This he revolved and drank for his relief.

    Now lived the youth in freedom, but debarred
From constant pleasure, and he thought it hard –   35
Hard that he could not every wish obey,
But must awhile relinquish ale and play –
Hard that he could not to his cards attend,
But must acquire the money he would spend.
With greedy eye he looked on all he saw,   40
He knew not justice, and he laughed at law;
On all he marked, he stretched his ready hand –

PETER GRIMES
[1] 'The original of Peter Grimes was an old fisherman of Aldborough while Mr. Crabbe was practising there as a surgeon. He had a succession of apprentices from London, and a certain sum with each. As the boys all disappeared under circumstances of strong suspicion, the man was warned that if another followed in like manner he should certainly be charged with murder' (note in 1834 edition of Crabbe's *Works*).
[2] *sacrilegious* because he was disobeying the fifth commandment, to honour thy father and mother.
[3] *settle* bench.

He fished by water and he filched by land.
Oft in the night has Peter dropped his oar,
Fled from his boat and sought for prey on shore;   45
Oft up the hedgerow glided, on his back
Bearing the orchard's produce in a sack,
Or farmyard load tugged fiercely from the stack.
And as these wrongs to greater numbers rose,
The more he looked on all men as his foes.   50
    He built a mud-walled hovel where he kept
His various wealth, and there he oft-times slept;
But no success could please his cruel soul –
He wished for one to trouble and control;
He wanted some obedient boy to stand   55
And bear the blow of his outrageous hand,
And hoped to find in some propitious hour
A feeling creature subject to his power.
Peter had heard there were in London then
(Still have they being?) workhouse-clearing men   60
Who, undisturbed by feelings just or kind,
Would parish-boys to needy tradesmen bind.
They in their want a trifling sum would take,
And toiling slaves of piteous orphans make.[4]
    Such Peter sought, and when a lad was found,   65
The sum was dealt him and the slave was bound.
Some few in town observed in Peter's trap
A boy, with jacket blue and woollen cap;
But none enquired how Peter used the rope,
Or what the bruise that made the stripling stoop;   70
None could the ridges on his back behold,
None sought him shiv'ring in the winter's cold,
None put the question, 'Peter, dost thou give
The boy his food? – What, man? The lad must live!
Consider, Peter, let the child have bread,   75
He'll serve thee better if he's stroked and fed.'
None reasoned thus – and some, on hearing cries,
Said calmly, 'Grimes is at his exercise.'
    Pinned,[5] beaten, cold, pinched, threatened and abused,
His efforts punished and his food refused,   80
Awake tormented, soon aroused from sleep,
Struck if he wept, and yet compelled to weep,
The trembling boy dropped down and strove to pray,
Received a blow and trembling turned away,
Or sobbed and hid his piteous face, while he,   85
The savage master, grinned in horrid glee!
He'd now the power he ever loved to show,
A feeling being subject to his blow.
    Thus lived the lad in hunger, peril, pain,
His tears despised, his supplications vain;   90
Compelled by fear to lie, by need to steal,

---

4   In order to reduce the poor-rate in London, it was custom-
ary towards the end of the eighteenth century to farm out
children of paupers to 'masters' in other parishes, who would
be given about £5 in return for maintaining them and teach-
ing them a trade.
5   *Pinned* pinned down by force.

His bed uneasy and unblessed his meal.
For three sad years the boy his tortures bore,
And then his pains and trials were no more.
    'How died he, Peter?' – when the people said, 95
He growled, 'I found him lifeless in his bed';
Then tried for softer tone, and sighed, 'Poor Sam is dead.'
Yet murmurs were there and some questions asked –
How he was fed, how punished and how tasked?
Much they suspected but they little proved, 100
And Peter passed untroubled and unmoved.
    Another boy with equal ease was found,
The money granted and the victim bound;
And what his fate? One night it chanced he fell
From the boat's mast and perished in her well 105
Where fish were living kept, and where the boy
(So reasoned men) could not himself destroy.
'Yes, so it was!', said Peter, 'in his play;
For he was idle both by night and day!
He climbed the main mast and then fell below' – 110
Then showed his corpse and pointed to the blow.
What said the jury? They were long in doubt,
But sturdy Peter faced the matter out.
So they dismissed him, saying at the time,
'Keep fast your hatchway when you've boys who climb.' 115
This hit the conscience, and he coloured more
Than for the closest questions put before.
Thus all his fears the verdict set aside,
And at the slave-shop Peter still applied.
    Then came a boy, of manners soft and mild – 120
Our seamen's wives with grief beheld the child;
All thought (though poor themselves) that he was one
Of gentle blood, some noble sinner's son
Who had, belike, deceived some humble maid
Whom he had first seduced and then betrayed. 125
However this, he seemed a gracious lad,
In grief submissive and with patience sad.
Passive he laboured, till his slender frame
Bent with his loads, and he at length was lame;
Strange that a frame so weak could bear so long 130
The grossest insult and the foulest wrong.
But there were causes – in the town they gave
Fire, food and comfort to the gentle slave;
And though stern Peter, with a cruel hand
And knotted rope, enforced the rude command, 135
Yet he considered what he'd lately felt,
And his vile blows with selfish pity dealt.
    One day such draughts the cruel fisher made,
He could not vend them in his borough trade
But sailed for London mart: the boy was ill, 140
But ever humbled to his master's will.
And on the river, where they smoothly sailed,
He strove with terror and awhile prevailed;
But new to danger on the angry sea,

He clung affrightened to his master's knee;   145
The boat grew leaky and the wind was strong,
Rough was the passage and the time was long;
His liquor failed, and Peter's wrath arose . . . .
No more is known – the rest we must suppose
Or learn of Peter. Peter, says he, spied   150
The stripling's danger and for harbour tried;
Meantime the fish and then th' apprentice died.
    The pitying women raised a clamour round,
And weeping said, 'Thou hast thy 'prentice drowned!'
Now the stern man was summoned to the hall,   155
To tell his tale before the burghers all:
He gave th' account, professed the lad he loved,
And kept his brazen features all unmoved.
The Mayor himself with tone severe replied,
'Henceforth with thee shall never boy abide;   160
Hire thee a freeman whom thou durst not beat,
But who, in thy despite, will sleep and eat.
Free thou art now! – again shouldst thou appear,
Thou'lt find thy sentence, like thy soul, severe.'
    Alas for Peter! not an helping hand,   165
So was he hated, could he now command;
Alone he rowed his boat, alone he cast
His nets beside, or made his anchor fast;
To hold a rope or hear a curse was none –
He toiled and railed, he groaned and swore alone.   170
Thus by himself compelled to live each day,
To wait for certain hours the tide's delay;
At the same times the same dull views to see,
The bounding marsh-bank and the blighted tree;
The water only, when the tides were high,   175
When low, the mud half-covered and half-dry;
The sunburnt tar that blisters on the planks,
And bankside stakes in their uneven ranks;
Heaps of entangled weeds that slowly float
As the tide rolls by the impeded boat.   180
    When tides were neap, and in the sultry day,
Through the tall bounding mud-banks made their way,[6]
Which on each side rose swelling, and below
The dark warm flood ran silently and slow;
There anchoring, Peter chose from man to hide,   185
There hang his head, and view the lazy tide
In its hot slimy channel slowly glide –
Where the small eels that left the deeper way
For the warm shore, within the shallows play;
Where gaping mussels, left upon the mud,   190
Slope their slow passage to the fallen flood.
Here dull and hopeless he'd lie down and trace
How sidelong crabs had scrawled their crooked race,
Or sadly listen to the tuneless cry

---

[6]   *When tides . . . way* When the tide is neap, the high-water
level is at its lowest point, leaving a larger area of mud
exposed than at other times.

Of fishing gull or clanging golden-eye;[7]   195
What time the seabirds to the marsh would come,
And the loud bittern, from the bullrush home,
Gave from the salt-ditch side the bellowing boom.
He nursed the feelings these dull scenes produce,
And loved to stop beside the opening sluice,   200
Where the small stream, confined in narrow bound,
Ran with a dull, unvaried, sad'ning sound –
Where all presented to the eye or ear
Oppressed the soul with misery, grief and fear.
    Besides these objects there were places three   205
Which Peter seemed with certain dread to see;
When he drew near them he would turn from each,
And loudly whistle till he passed the reach.[8]
    A change of scene to him brought no relief:
In town, 'twas plain, men took him for a thief;   210
The sailors' wives would stop him in the street
And say, 'Now, Peter, thou'st no boy to beat!'
Infants at play, when they perceived him, ran,
Warning each other, 'That's the wicked man!'
He growled an oath, and in an angry tone   215
Cursed the whole place and wished to be alone.
Alone he was, the same dull scenes in view,
And still more gloomy in his sight they grew.
Though man he hated, yet employed alone
At bootless labour, he would swear and groan,   220
Cursing the shoals that glided by the spot,
And gulls that caught them when his arts could not.
    Cold nervous tremblings shook his sturdy frame,
And strange disease (he couldn't say the name);
Wild were his dreams, and oft he rose in fright,   225
Waked by his view of horrors in the night –
Horrors that would the sternest minds amaze,
Horrors that demons might be proud to raise.
And though he felt forsaken, grieved at heart
To think he lived from all mankind apart,   230
Yet if a man approached, in terrors he would start.
    A winter passed since Peter saw the town,
And summer lodgers were again come down;
These, idly curious, with their glasses spied
The ships in bay as anchored for the tide –   235
The river's craft, the bustle of the quay,
And sea-port views which landmen love to see.
One, up the river, had a man and boat
Seen day by day – now anchored, now afloat.
Fisher he seemed, yet used no net nor hook;   240
Of sea fowl swimming by no heed he took,
But on the gliding waves still fixed his lazy look.
At certain stations he would view the stream
As if he stood bewildered in a dream,

---

[7] *golden-eye* a sea duck.   [8] *reach* portion of the river between two bends.

Or that some power had chained him for a time   245
To feel a curse or meditate on crime.
    This known, some curious, some in pity went,
And others questioned, 'Wretch, dost thou repent?'
He heard, he trembled, and in fear resigned
His boat: new terror filled his restless mind.   250
Furious he grew and up the country ran,
And there they seized him – a distempered man.
Him we received, and to a parish bed,
Followed and cursed, the groaning man was led.
Here when they saw him whom they used to shun –   255
A lost lone man, so harassed and undone –
Our gentle females (ever prompt to feel)
Perceived compassion on their anger steal;
His crimes they couldn't from their memories blot,
But they were grieved and trembled at his lot.   260
A priest too came to whom his words are told,
And all the signs they shuddered to behold.
    'Look, look!' they cried, 'his limbs with horror shake,
And as he grinds his teeth, what noise they make!
How glare his angry eyes, and yet he's not awake!   265
See what cold drops upon his forehead stand,
And how he clenches that broad bony hand!'
The priest attending found he spoke at times
As one alluding to his fears and crimes:
'It was the fall', he muttered, 'I can show   270
The manner how – I never struck a blow!'
And then aloud, 'Unhand me, free my chain!
On oath, he fell – it struck him to the brain!
Why ask my father? That old man will swear
Against my life – besides he wasn't there!   275
What, all agreed? Am I to die today?
My Lord, in mercy, give me time to pray!'
    Then as they watched him, calmer he became,
And grew so weak he couldn't move his frame,
But murmuring spake, while they could see and hear   280
The start of terror and the groan of fear;
See the large dew-beads on his forehead rise
And the cold death-drop glaze his sunken eyes.
Nor yet he died, but with unwonted force
Seemed with some fancied being to discourse.   285
He knew not us, or with accustomed art
He hid the knowledge, yet exposed his heart;
'Twas part confession and the rest defence –
A madman's tale, with gleams of waking sense.
    'I'll tell you all', he said, 'the very day   290
When the old man first placed them in my way –
My father's spirit (he who always tried
To give me trouble when he lived and died)!
When he was gone, he could not be content
To see my days in painful labour spent,   295
But would appoint his meetings, and he made
Me watch at these, and so neglect my trade.

'Twas one hot noon – all silent, still, serene;
No living being had I lately seen.
I paddled up and down and dipped my net   300
But (such his pleasure) I could nothing get;
A father's pleasure! – when his toil was done,
To plague and torture thus an only son.
And so I sat and looked upon the stream,
How it ran on – and felt as in a dream: 305
But dream it was not. No – I fixed my eyes
On the midstream and saw the spirits rise:
I saw my father on the water stand
And hold a thin pale boy in either hand,
And there they glided ghastly on the top   310
Of the salt flood, and never touched a drop.
I would have struck them, but they knew th' intent,
And smiled upon the oar, and down they went.
    Now from that day, whenever I began
To dip my net, there stood the hard old man,   315
He and those boys. I humbled me and prayed
They would be gone – they heeded not but stayed.
Nor could I turn, nor would the boat go by,
But gazing on the spirits, there was I;
They bade me leap to death, but I was loath to die. 320
And every day, as sure as day arose,
Would these three spirits meet me ere the close:
To hear and mark them daily was my doom,
And "Come", they said with weak sad voices, "come!"
To row away with all my strength I tried,   325
But there were they, hard by me in the tide,
The three unbodied forms – and "Come", still "come!", they cried.
    Fathers should pity, but this old man shook
His hoary locks and froze me by a look.
Thrice, when I struck them, through the water came   330
An hollow groan that weakened all my frame.
"Father", said I, "have mercy!" He replied
I know not what – the angry spirit lied:
"Didst thou not draw thy knife?" said he. 'Twas true,
But I had pity and my arm withdrew;   335
He cried for mercy, which I kindly gave,
But he has no compassion in his grave.
    There were three places where they ever rose –
The whole long river has not such as those –
Places accursed where, if a man remain,   340
He'll see the things which strike him to the brain.
And there they made me on my paddle lean
And look at them for hours – accursed scene!
When they would glide to that smooth eddy space,
Then bid me leap and join them in the place;   345
And at my groans each little villain sprite
Enjoyed my pains and vanished in delight.
    In one fierce summer day, when my poor brain
Was burning hot, and cruel was my pain,
Then came this father-foe, and there he stood   350

With his two boys again upon the flood.
There was more mischief in their eyes, more glee
In their pale faces when they glared at me.
Still did they force me on the oar to rest,
And when they saw me fainting and oppressed,   355
He with his hand (the old man) scooped the flood,
And there came flame about him mixed with blood;
He bade me stoop and look upon the place,
Then flung the hot red liquor in my face –
Burning it blazed, and then I roared for pain –   360
I thought the demons would have turned my brain!
    Still there they stood, and forced me to behold
A place of horrors – they cannot be told:
Where the flood opened, there I heard the shriek
Of tortured guilt no earthly tongue can speak.   365
"All days alike for ever!" did they say,
"And unremitted torments every day!"
Yes, so they said . . .'
                    But here he ceased and gazed
On all around, affrightened and amazed;
And still he tried to speak and looked in dread   370
Of frightened females gathering round his bed,
Then dropped exhausted and appeared at rest,
Till the strong foe the vital powers possessed.
Then with an inward, broken voice he cried,
'Again they come!' and muttered as he died.   375

George Dyer   (1755–1841)

He is famous for being the butt of one of Charles Lamb's most memorable anecdotes, in Elia's *Amicus Redivivus*:

> I do not know when I have experienced a stranger sensation, than on seeing my old friend G.D., who had been paying me a morning visit a few Sundays back, at my cottage at Islington, upon taking leave, instead of turning down the right hand path by which he had entered – with staff in hand, and at noon day, deliberately march right forwards into the midst of the stream that runs by us, and totally disappear.[1]

True or not (it was probably true, as the story turns up in at least three letters from Lamb to various correspondents in November 1823),[2] Dyer's reputation has suffered by having been turned into the holy fool of

the romantic period. In fact, he was a generation older than Lamb, Wordsworth and Coleridge, and in the early 1790s, when they were flirting with politics, he was respected in intellectual and Dissenting circles for such pamphlets as *The Complaints of the Poor People of England* (1793) and *A Dissertation on the Theory and Practice of Benevolence* (1795). In political terms he was as militant as Paine, and advocated social change along the lines suggested in the 'Ways and Means' chapter of *Rights of Man* Part II.

A Londoner by birth, Dyer attended Christ's Hospital and Emmanuel College, Cambridge, before becoming a tutor and then a radical pamphleteer. *The Complaints of the Poor People of England* was in many ways his most important work. In it, Dyer writes not just as a defender, but as a representative of the oppressed. He follows Paine in demanding wide-ranging reforms in taxation, the legal system, prisons, poor-rates, workhouses, schools, the army and navy.

GEORGE DYER
[1]   Charles Lamb, *Elia and The Last Essays of Elia* ed. Jonathan Bate (Oxford, 1987), pp. 237–8.

[2]   See *The Letters of Charles and Mary Lamb* ed. E. V. Lucas (3 vols, London, 1935), ii. 405, 407, 410.

'The Injustice of the Law' shows the *Complaints* at its best; beginning with an outline of the situation, Dyer finally allows his indignation to boil over in a statement of 'broad English'.

Though best known as a scholar and man of letters, Dyer was also the author of a moving confessional lyric: '*In deep distress*', inspired by depression at his failing sight, and published here for the first time, apparently draws on the prime confessional poem of the age, Coleridge's *Dejection: An Ode* (pp. 507–11).

Further reading

George Dyer, *Complaints of the Poor People of England 1793* introduced by Jonathan Wordsworth (Oxford and New York, 1990)

Nicholas Roe, *The Politics of Nature: Wordsworth and Some Contemporaries* (Houndmills, 1992), chapter 1

[*The Injustice of the Law*]

From THE COMPLAINTS OF THE POOR PEOPLE OF ENGLAND (1793) (pp. 55–8)

The air and the water, and the creatures that live in them, are the common gifts of providence.[1] And till a man has, by his own industry, acquired some right in what nature has left common, they are as much one man's as another's. How far society has a right to appropriate what nature has left common, I shall not stop to enquire. God has never said, the squire may shoot a partridge or a pheasant, but the labourer shall not. Or that Sir Robert may draw the fish out of the river, and that his poor tenant shall be imprisoned for the same action.

I do but just mention these among the many laws that oppress the poor, and not to insist that these are unjust – which, however, they certainly are. I affirm in general that the more injustice there is in the laws, the greater is the necessity for their being known, that a poor man may not be caught in a trap by his ignorance.

Considering the present complicated system of our laws, and the vast number of causes (the consequence of such a system) that are tried in our courts of law, frequent circumlocutions and the use of many technical expressions are useful for the profession and cannot be avoided. But this is only admitting that the smaller evil is tolerable that qualifies the greater. The greater evil should be removed.

I know it will be said that poor men need not be so ignorant of these laws as I seem to intimate. And I acknowledge that as the squire and lord of the manor are taught by our laws to consider the birds and the fish as their property, they are likely to let the poor man know who is master. And as they have time and money to procure the acts of parliament, and see occasion, may have them written out plain and get them pasted up in the village. This, however, is accidental; it may or it may not happen. But in a thousand instances in which the interest of the poor is concerned, it is literally true that a poor man has neither time nor money to know what our laws have made (in many instances unjustly) his duty, or to ascertain his just rights. In this country the consumption of time and money necessary to know what is law is more than poor men can afford to lose. And, after all, perhaps they may get ensnared, for if they should be able to spell out an act of parliament, they may probably get tricked by some dirty lawyer – if not directly to get money, in compliance at least with the wishes of some great person, and through fear of doing justice to a poor man.

Several poor men are now lingering in prison, when the men who have thrown them in are the criminals. But ignorance was the lot of the poor man, and their prosecutors and lawyers were, in broad English, KNOWING RASCALS.

THE INJUSTICE OF THE LAW
[1] *providence* i.e. God's grace.

[*In deep distress, I cried to God*] (edited from MS; not previously published)

In deep distress, I cried to God,
To God I cried, and told my grief;
He heard, and in my time of need
His goodness sent the wished relief.[1]

But still I mourned, for though relieved,   5
I felt my heart of secret sin,
And though relieved from foes without,
I felt a lurking foe within.

Body and mind, by night and day,
Pressed on me with their baneful powers;   10
My frailties had disturbed my days,
And frightful dreams my midnight hours.

And when in sleep my eyelids close,
Short is the sweet repose of sleep;
I wake, but ah! I wake in vain –   15
Alas, I only wake to weep.

My voice grows faint, my spirits droop,[2]
And all of life within me dies;
I strive to utter my complaint,
But I can only breathe in sighs.   20

Oh for that grace to sinners given,
That grace so ample, rich and free!
Shall that which is vouchsafed to all
Be, oh my God, denied to me?

Ah no! thy deeds of ancient times,   25
Thy works of love, unfold my will;
Thou art, Jehovah, still the same,
The same benignant Being still.

Thy firm decree is nature's law,
And worlds move as thy hand directs;   30
No eye can pierce the wondrous cause,
But all perceive the vast effects.

In heaven and earth, through seas and skies,
In all we see or feel or hear,
Each has a voice that speaks to man,   35
Each speaks a God for ever near.

IN DEEP DISTRESS I CRIED TO GOD
[1] Coleridge uses the grief/relief rhyme in *Dejection: An Ode*
22–3.

[2] *my spirits droop* compare both Milton, *Samson Agonistes* 594: 'my genial spirits droop', and Coleridge, *Dejection: An Ode* 40.

The seas, as by thy presence ruled,
Over the mountain-tops aspire,
Or troubled, as if seeing thee,
Into their inmost caves retire.

40

William Godwin   (1756–1836)

' "Throw aside your books of chemistry", said Wordsworth to a young man,[1] a student in the Temple, "and read Godwin on Necessity." '[2] Hazlitt had no reason to invent this story, which testifies to Godwin's intellectual status, for a brief period, in the 1790s; by the time Hazlitt published *The Spirit of the Age* in 1825 he was 'to all ordinary intents and purposes dead and buried'.[3] It is not so easy, two centuries later, to comprehend the importance granted political writers in the revolutionary period. When Godwin published *Political Justice* in February 1793, only days after England had declared war on France, the British government was as sensitive to radical dissent as America was to communism during the McCarthy era. For the next decade, he would be regarded as one of the main enemies of the state.

It was a curious fate for the son of a strict Calvinist minister. Only religious texts were read in his father's house, and when he was eleven he was boarded out to a violently puritanical Sandemanian minister, Samuel Newton, who whipped him for the slightest deviation from religious practice or thought. The followers of Robert Sandeman were more extreme than the Scottish Calvinists against whom they were reacting; two central tenets were that reason should not be 'sullied' by emotion or faith, and that wealth was inherently sinful, such that an individual's property should always be at the disposal of the church. Those two tenets were to feature prominently in Godwin's masterwork, *Political Justice* (1793).

By the time he graduated from the Hoxton Dissenting Academy in 1778, he was a staunch Tory Calvinist. But religion had made his childhood too unremittingly joyless, and he was too intelligent a freethinker, to refrain from questioning the assumptions of his teachers. After reading Holbach and Helvétius, the deist thinkers who influenced the French Revolution, Godwin abandoned the church, became an atheist, and went to London to earn his living as a writer. *Political Justice* was ostensibly a reply to

Burke, though it came out three years after the *Reflections*, and was considerably more ambitious as a work of philosophy. Godwin was remarkably fortunate in the timing of its publication: on 21 January 1793, Louis XVI was guillotined; on 1 February the French National Assembly declared war on Britain; Britain entered the war on the 11th; and *Political Justice* was published three days later. For radicals it was a welcome rallying cry just at the moment when they felt most embattled.

Godwin founded his vision of a better society on a belief in the perfectibility of mankind, attainable through the exercise of the reason. When all were governed by reason, human institutions, including that of marriage (which derived from property laws), would wither away. This was the 'dream' that, Wordsworth recalled years later,

Was flattering to the young ingenuous mind
Pleased with extremes, and not the least with that
Which makes the human reason's naked self
The object of its fervour.

Thirteen-Book Prelude x 815–18

Coleridge was always hostile to Godwinism, largely because, as a devout Unitarian, he could not accept its atheism,[4] but Wordsworth was for a time strongly attached to the ideas in *Political Justice*. He breakfasted with Godwin, who left his mark on such poems as *Adventures on Salisbury Plain* (1795) and *The Convict* (1796–8), but eventually tired of a creed that so emphatically denied the importance of the emotions. 'There was the rub that made philosophy of so short life', Hazlitt wrote, 'reason without passion'.[5]

Ten days after completing *Political Justice*, Godwin began writing a novel, *Caleb Williams* (1794), the plot of which effectively subverted the philosophy he had just elucidated. It was not surprising, therefore, that he revised *Political Justice* drastically for a second edi-

WILLIAM GODWIN
[1] Probably, William St Clair suggests, Basil Montagu; *The Godwins and the Shelleys* (1989), p. 95.
[2] William Hazlitt, *The Spirit of the Age* (London, 1825), p. 33.
[3] Ibid., p. 32.
[4] See Nicola Trott, 'The Coleridge Circle and the "Answer to Godwin"', *RES* 41 (1990) 212–29.
[5] *The Spirit of the Age* (London, 1825), p. 40.

tion in 1796 and a third in 1798. Their increased emphasis on psychology and toned-down criticism of institutions was responsible, De Quincey believed, for Godwin's obscurity in later years:

> The second edition, as regards principles, is not a re-cast, but absolutely a travesty of the first; nay, it is all but a palinode. In this collapse of a tense excitement I myself find the true reason for the utter extinction of the *Political Justice*, and of its author considered as a philosopher.
>
> Masson xi 328

The extracts below come from the first edition, which was the one best known to the romantics. 'On Property' provides Godwin's most concise account of the world he would ideally like to live in; 'Love of Justice' outlines his belief that humanity is motivated by an innate sense of moral good; 'On Marriage' observes that marriage is a branch of the property system, and suggests that in a rational society propagation would be motivated not by lust but 'by the dictates of reason and duty'.

Further reading

Don Locke, *A Fantasy of Reason: The Life and Thought of William Godwin* (London, 1980)

Nicholas Roe, *Wordsworth and Coleridge: The Radical Years* (Oxford, 1988)

William St Clair, *The Godwins and the Shelleys: The Biography of a Family* (London 1989)

William Godwin, *Political Justice 1793* introduced by Jonathan Wordsworth (2 vols, Oxford and New York, 1992)

The Political and Philosophical Writings of William Godwin ed. Mark Philp, Pamela Clemit, Austin Gee and William St Clair (7 vols, London, 1993)

[On Property]

From POLITICAL JUSTICE (2 vols, 1793) (vol. ii pp. 806–7)

Accumulated property treads the powers of thought in the dust, extinguishes the sparks of genius, and reduces the great mass of mankind to be immersed in sordid cares – beside depriving the rich (as we have already said) of the most salubrious and effectual motives to activity.

If superfluity were banished, the necessity for the greater part of the manual industry of mankind would be superseded, and the rest (being amicably shared among all the active and vigorous members of the community) would be burdensome to none. Every man would have a frugal yet wholesome diet; every man would go forth to that moderate exercise of his corporal functions that would give hilarity to the spirits – none would be made torpid with fatigue, but all would have leisure to cultivate the kindly and philanthropical[1] affections of the soul, and to let loose his faculties in the search of intellectual improvement.

What a contrast does this scene present us with the present state of human society, where the peasant and the labourer work till their understandings are benumbed with toil, their sinews contracted and made callous by being forever on the stretch, and their bodies invaded with infirmities and surrendered to an untimely grave! What is the fruit of this disproportioned and unceasing toil? At evening they return to a family, famished with hunger, exposed half-naked to the inclemencies of the sky, hardly sheltered, and denied the slenderest instruction (unless in a few instances, where it is dispensed by the hands of ostentatious charity, and the first lesson communicated is unprincipled servility). All this while their rich neighbour – but we visited him before.

[Love of Justice]

From POLITICAL JUSTICE (2 vols, 1793) (vol. ii p. 808)

All men love justice. All men are conscious that man is a being of one common nature, and feel the propriety of the treatment they receive from one another being measured by a common standard.

ON PROPERTY
[1] *philanthropical* benevolent.

Every man is desirous of assisting another, whether we should choose to ascribe this to an instinct implanted in his nature which renders this conduct a source of personal gratification, or to his perception of the reasonableness of such assistance. So necessary a part is this of the constitution of mind, that no man perpetrates any action, however criminal, without having first invented some sophistry, some palliation, by which he proves to himself that it is best to be done.

Hence it appears that offence, the invasion of one man upon the security of another, is a thought alien to mind, and which nothing could have reconciled to us but the sharp sting of necessity. To consider merely the present order of human society, it is evident that the first offence must have been his who began a monopoly, and took advantage of the weakness of his neighbours to secure certain exclusive privileges to himself. The man on the other hand who determined to put an end to this monopoly, and who peremptorily demanded what was superfluous to the possessor and would be of extreme benefit to himself, appeared to his own mind to be merely avenging the violated laws of justice. Were it not for the plausibleness of this apology, it is to be presumed that there would be no such thing as crime in the world.

[On Marriage]

From POLITICAL JUSTICE (2 vols, 1793) (vol. ii pp. 849–52)

It is absurd to expect that the inclinations and wishes of two human beings should coincide through any long period of time. To oblige them to act and to live together is to subject them to some inevitable portion of thwarting, bickering, and unhappiness. This cannot be otherwise so long as man has failed to reach the standard of absolute perfection. The supposition that I must have a companion for life is the result of a complication of vices. It is the dictate of cowardice, and not of fortitude. It flows from the desire of being loved and esteemed for something that is not desert.[1]

But the evil of marriage as it is practised in European countries lies deeper than this. The habit is for a thoughtless and romantic youth of each sex to come together, to see each other for a few times and under circumstances full of delusion, and then to vow to each other eternal attachment.

What is the consequence of this? In almost every instance they find themselves deceived. They are reduced to make the best of an irretrievable mistake. They are presented with the strongest imaginable temptation to become the dupes of falsehood. They are led to conceive it their wisest policy to shut their eyes upon realities, happy if by any perversion of intellect they can persuade themselves that they were right in their first crude opinion of their companion. The institution of marriage is a system of fraud – and men who carefully mislead their judgements in the daily affairs of their life must always have a crippled judgement in every other concern.

We ought to dismiss our mistake as soon as it is detected, but we are taught to cherish it. We ought to be incessant in our search after virtue and worth, but we are taught to check our enquiry and shut our eyes upon the most attractive and admirable objects. Marriage is law, and the worst of all laws. Whatever our understandings may tell us of the person from whose connection we should derive the greatest improvement – of the worth of one woman and the demerits of another – we are obliged to consider what is law, and not what is justice.

Add to this that marriage is an affair of property, and the worst of all properties. So long as two human beings are forbidden by positive institution to follow the dictates of their own mind, prejudice is alive and vigorous. So long as I seek to engross one woman to myself, and to prohibit my neighbour from proving his superior desert and reaping the fruits of it, I am guilty of the most odious of all monopolies. Over this imaginary prize men watch with perpetual jealousy, and one man will find his desires and his capacity to circumvent as much excited, as the other is excited to traverse his projects and frustrate his hopes. As long as this state of society continues, philanthropy will be crossed and checked in a thousand ways, and the still augmenting stream of abuse will continue to flow.

ON MARRIAGE
[1] *desert* deserving.

The abolition of marriage will be attended with no evils. We are apt to represent it to ourselves as the harbinger of brutal lust and depravity. But it really happens (in this as in other cases) that the positive laws which are made to restrain our vices, irritate and multiply them – not to say that the same sentiments of justice and happiness which in a state of equal property would destroy the relish for luxury, would decrease our inordinate appetites of every kind, and lead us universally to prefer the pleasures of intellect to the pleasures of sense.

The intercourse[2] of the sexes will in such a state fall under the same system as any other species of friendship. Exclusively of all groundless and obstinate attachments, it will be impossible for me to live in the world without finding one man of a worth superior to that of any other whom I have an opportunity of observing. To this man I shall feel a kindness in exact proportion to my apprehension of his worth. The case will be precisely the same with respect to the female sex. I shall assiduously cultivate the intercourse of that woman whose accomplishments shall strike me in the most powerful manner. 'But it may happen that other men will feel for her the same preference that I do': this will create no difficulty. We may all enjoy her conversation, and we shall all be wise enough to consider the sensual intercourse as a very trivial object. This, like every other affair in which two persons are concerned, must be regulated in each successive instance by the unforced consent of either party.

It is a mark of the extreme depravity of our present habits that we are inclined to suppose the sensual intercourse any wise material to the advantages arising from the purest affection. Reasonable men now eat and drink not from the love of pleasure, but because eating and drinking are essential to our healthful existence. Reasonable men then will propagate their species not because a certain sensible pleasure is annexed to this action, but because it is right the species should be propagated. And the manner in which they exercise this function will be regulated by the dictates of reason and duty.

Ann Yearsley (*née* Cromartie) (1756–1806)

Ann had no formal education, but her brother taught her to read, and her mother borrowed books on her behalf. She married John Yearsley in June 1774, by whom, within the space of six years, she had six children. During this time she managed to read and write poetry, some of which found its way to Hannah More, the leavings from whose table provided scraps for Ann's pig. In the Preface to Ann's first book, Hannah related her 'discovery', made after visiting Elizabeth Montagu in Berkshire:

> On my return from Sandleford, a copy of verses was shown me, said to be written by a poor illiterate woman in this neighbourhood, who sells milk from door to door. The story did not engage my faith, but the verses excited my attention; for, though incorrect, they breathed the genuine spirit of poetry and were rendered still more interesting by a certain natural and strong expression of misery which seemed to fill the heart and mind of the author.[1]

With Montagu, Hannah organized a subscription list for Ann's *Poems, on Several Occasions*. It was an extraor-

dinarily successful enterprise: over a thousand contributors were enrolled, including seven duchesses, sixteen countesses, Reynolds, Walpole, Burney, and most of the bluestockings.

Ann's first volume of poems was published in June 1785 to considerable acclaim, but strains quickly developed between poet and patronness. Hannah had placed the subscription money in a trust fund and appointed herself and Elizabeth Montagu as its trustees in order to prevent Ann's husband from gaining access to it. The scheme effectively made Ann and her children dependent on More for their income. Within a few months of the book's publication Ann's gratitude had turned to resentment. She agreed that she and her husband should not have access to the principal sum that had been collected, but thought they should get the interest, and wanted all the money divided among the children when they reached the age of twenty-one. She told her side of the story in an 'Autobiographical Narrative' added to the fourth edition of her *Poems* in 1786. The literary world was shocked, and reviewers made great play with the hostilities between the two poets. Hannah commented

---

2   *intercourse* i.e. social intercourse.

ANN YEARSLEY
1   Ann Yearsley, *Poems, on Several Occasions* (1785), p. iv.

that 'vanity, luxury, idleness, and pride, have entered the cottage the moment poverty vanished',[2] and told Mrs Montagu: 'Mrs Yearsley's conceit that you can envy her talents gives me comfort – for as it convinces me that she is mad, I build upon it a hope that she is not guilty in the all-seeing eye'.[3] She and Montagu hung on as trustees for a while but were eventually persuaded to resign, and the money passed to Ann through intermediaries.

By 1786 she had a new patron, Frederick Augustus Hervey, Bishop of Derry and Earl of Bristol, who contributed £50 towards the costs of the fourth edition of the *Poems*, and to whom she dedicated her *Poem on the Inhumanity of the Slave Trade* (1788). This was an important moment, as it marked the beginning of the numerous laws that led to abolition. On 21 May 1788, Sir William Dolben proposed a Bill to the House of Commons that limited the number of slaves which could be transported from Africa to British colonies in the West Indies; it was passed in both Houses. It is possible only to present an extract from the poem here; a complete, annotated text may be found in my *Romantic Women Poets: An Anthology* (1997), along with *On Mrs Montagu, Addressed to Sensibility*, and *Reflections on the Death of Louis XVI*.

Ann had a gift – what a reviewer of her first volume called 'a strong and fervid imagination'.[4] It enabled her to feel intensely the injustices that had been done both to her and others, and makes her poetry more than just the 'wild wood warblings' of a primitivist. As the reviewer of her second volume in the *Critical Review* admitted: 'In regard to modulation of numbers, particularly in blank verse, we know few authors superior to the Bristol milk-woman. Her sentiments are often equally just and original, her diction strong and animated, and her pauses judiciously varied'.[5]

Further reading

Moira Ferguson, 'The Unpublished Poems of Ann Yearsley', *Tulsa Studies in Women's Literature* 12 (1993) 13–46

—, *Eighteenth-Century Women Poets: Nation, Class, and Gender* (Albany, NY, 1995), chapters 4 and 5

Jerome J. McGann, *The Poetics of Sensibility: A Revolution in Literary Style* (Oxford, 1996), pp. 55–64

Alan Richardson, 'Darkness Visible: Race and Representation in Bristol Abolitionist Poetry, 1770–1810', *TWC* 27 (1996) 67–72

A Poem on the Inhumanity of the Slave Trade (1788) (extract)[1]

Luco is borne around the neighb'ring isles,
Losing the knowledge of his native shore
Amid the pathless wave, destined to plant   215
The sweet luxuriant cane.[2] He strives to please,
Nor once complains, but greatly smothers grief.
His hands are blistered, and his feet are worn,
Till ev'ry stroke dealt by his mattock[3] gives
Keen agony to life; while from his breast   220
The sigh arises, burdened with the name
Of Incilanda. Time inures the youth,
His limbs grow nervous, strained by willing toil,
And resignation, or a calm despair
(Most useful either) lulls him to repose.   225
    A Christian renegade that from his soul
Abjures the tenets of our schools, nor dreads
A future punishment, nor hopes for mercy,
Had fled from England to avoid those laws
Which must have made his life a retribution   230
To violated justice, and had gained,

[2] William Roberts, *Memoirs of the Life and Correspondence of Mrs Hannah More* (3rd edn, 4 vols, London, 1835), i 368–9.
[3] Ibid., i 374.
[4] *Critical Review* 60 (1785) 148–9, p. 148.
[5] *Critical Review* 64 (1787) 435–7, p. 436.

A POEM ON THE INHUMANITY OF THE SLAVE TRADE
[1] The extract describes the fate of a slave, Luco, when he is captured, separated from his beloved Incilanda, and put to work on a sugar plantation.
[2] *cane* sugar cane.
[3] *mattock* tool for loosening hard ground.

By fawning guile, the confidence (ill-placed)
Of Luco's master. O'er the slave he stands
With knotted whip, lest fainting nature shun
The task too arduous, while his cruel soul   235
Unnat'ral, ever feeds, with gross delight,
Upon his suff'rings. Many slaves there were,
But none who could suppress the sigh and bend
So quietly as Luco. Long he bore
The stripes that from his manly bosom drew   240
The sanguine stream (too little prized); at length
Hope fled his soul, giving her struggles o'er,
And he resolved to die. The sun had reached
His zenith; pausing faintly, Luco stood,
Leaning upon his hoe, while mem'ry brought,   245
In piteous imag'ry, his aged father,
His poor fond mother, and his faithful maid.
The mental group in wildest motion set
Fruitless imagination. Fury, grief,
Alternate shame, the sense of insult, all   250
Conspire to aid the inward storm – yet words
Were no relief; he stood in silent woe.

  Gorgon, remorseless Christian, saw the slave
Stand musing mid the ranks and, stealing soft
Behind the studious Luco, struck his cheek   255
With a too-heavy whip that reached his eye,
Making it dark for ever. Luco turned
In strongest agony, and with his hoe
Struck the rude Christian on the forehead. Pride,
With hateful malice, seized on Gorgon's soul,   260
By nature fierce, while Luco sought the beach
And plunged beneath the wave. But near him lay
A planter's barge, whose seamen grasped his hair,
Dragging to life a wretch who wished to die.

  Rumour now spreads the tale, while Gorgon's breath   265
Envenomed aids her blast. Imputed crimes
Oppose the plea of Luco, till he scorns
Even a just defence, and stands prepared.
The planters, conscious that to fear alone
They owe their cruel pow'r, resolve to blend   270
New torment with the pangs of death, and hold
Their victims high in dreadful view, to fright
The wretched number left. Luco is chained
To a huge tree, his fellow-slaves are ranged
To share the horrid sight; fuel is placed   275
In an increasing train, some paces back,
To kindle slowly, and approach the youth,
With more than native terror. See, it burns!
He gazes on the growing flame, and calls
For 'Water, water!' The small boon's denied.   280
E'en Christians throng each other to behold
The different alterations of his face
As the hot death approaches. (Oh shame, shame
Upon the followers of Jesus! Shame

On him that dares avow a God!) He writhes,   285
While down his breast glide the unpitied tears,
And in their sockets strain their scorched balls.
'Burn, burn me quick! I cannot die!' he cries,
'Bring fire more close!' The planters heed him not,
But still prolonging Luco's torture, threat   290
Their trembling slaves around. His lips are dry,
His senses seem to quiver ere they quit
His frame for ever, rallying strong, then driv'n
From the tremendous conflict. Sight no more
Is Luco's, his parched tongue is ever mute;   295
Yet in his soul his Incilanda stays,
Till both escape together. Turn, my muse,
From this sad scene; lead Bristol's[4] milder soul
To where the solitary spirit roves,
Wrapped in the robe of innocence, to shades   300
Where pity breathing in the gale dissolves
The mind, when fancy paints such real woe.

William Blake   (1757–1827)

'Blake is a real name, I assure you – and a most extraordinary man, if he be still living' (Lucas ii 424). When Charles Lamb made this remark to Bernard Barton in 1824 he was one of the few to have seen Blake's work, let alone regarded it highly. Blake's obscurity was partly his own doing; his books had a limited circulation partly because each was hand printed and hand illuminated. Only in the late nineteenth century did Alexander Gilchrist's biography (1863) prepare the ground for his subsequent popularity.

He was a native Londoner, one of seven children born to a London hosier, James Blake, and his wife, Catherine Hermitage. They were Dissenting Whigs (James Blake voted for Charles James Fox in elections), and seem to have given Blake and his siblings an unspectacularly pious and devout upbringing. All the same, the Blake children had some peculiar propensities. His older brother claimed to have seen Moses and Abraham, and Blake himself was almost beaten by his father for claiming to have seen angels in the treetops on Peckham Rye. Blake was not apparently educated until, at the age of ten, he was sent to Henry Pars's Drawing School, 101 the Strand, which gave him the best available training as a draughtsman. Four years later he was apprenticed to James Basire, engraver to the Society of Antiquaries. During this period he was inducted into the English Gothic tradition, partly by drawing the monuments in Westminster Abbey. There he apparently saw a vision of monks, priests, choristers and censer-bearers marching in procession.

For a few years after leaving Basire in 1779 he looked set for a career as a painter, but abandoned the formal training he began at the Royal Academy. Instead he married Catherine Boucher in 1782, and set up as an engraver. His principal employer from 1788 onwards was the Unitarian publisher Joseph Johnson.[1] Tom Paine, Mary Wollstonecraft, William Godwin and the young William Wordsworth were among those publishing with Johnson at this period; Blake may have met some of them, but he is known to have attended only one of Johnson's dinners at his rooms at 72 St Paul's Churchyard. Throughout the 1780s he experimented with verse forms and innovatory means of printing his work. His first volume of poems, *Poetical Sketches*, was printed in the usual manner in 1783, but *The Book of Thel* (1789) was executed using Blake's distinctive 'infernal' method. He would draw his design and text, in reverse, directly onto a copper plate using a varnish resistant to the corrosive effects of acid.[2] It is an inevitable consequence of his use of this technique that only sixteen copies of *Thel* survive today, only two of which date from 1789. It should be

---

4 *Bristol's milder soul* i.e. the more merciful among Bristol businessmen. Many slave traders operated from Bristol.

WILLIAM BLAKE
1 For more on whom see Gerald Tyson, *Joseph Johnson: A Liberal Publisher* (Iowa City, 1979).
2 The process is fully explained by Joseph Viscomi, *Blake and the Idea of the Book* (Princeton, NY, 1993), part III.

emphasized that Blake's illustrations are integral to the conception of each of his poems, and the serious student of his work cannot afford to ignore them; they are readily available in facsimile, all having been recently published in the Blake Trust/Tate Gallery series (see 'Further reading', p. 55).

Thel concerns the pre-existent soul and its unwilling 'fall' into the physical world and sexual experience. It contains a number of preoccupations that are to recur: (i) a parallel world; (ii) a fall from grace; (iii) sexual initiation. *Songs of Innocence* was completed in the same year. The fact that Blake varied the order of his *Songs of Innocence and of Experience*, sometimes placing some of the former (*The Schoolboy* and *The Voice of the Ancient Bard*, for instance) among the latter, suggests that he regarded the two groupings as being less in opposition than in dialogue with each other. Though intended for children, the *Songs of Innocence* nonetheless contained some highly sophisticated poetry. Innocence, in this volume, comprises a variety of qualities – unfettered energy, simplicity, love, spontaneity and freshness of vision. As in *Thel*, innocence is not sufficient on its own; it is necessary for the individual to make the journey toward experience; Blake certainly wished these poems to be considered alongside the *Songs of Experience* as he bound them together. No doubt the varying tone of the two volumes had something to do with the time in which they were written; where *Innocence* was composed at a time of optimism, when the French Revolution was just beginning, *Experience* was contemporaneous with the Reign of Terror.

Blake moved out of central London in 1790 and into the suburb of Lambeth. Three years before, perhaps inspired partly by grief at the death of his beloved brother Robert in 1787, he had studied the writings of Emanuel Swedenborg, the theologian and philosopher who had theorized that the spirits of the dead rise from the body and assume physical form in another world. Swedenborg was Swedish, but he died in London in 1772, when he was eighty-four and Blake fourteen. Such was the popularity of his work that, in the 1780s, his admirers formed Swedenborgian congregations of the New Church, or Church of the New Jerusalem – a forerunner of today's international New Church. In 1789 Blake and his wife had joined the Church of the New Jerusalem, but when, a year later, he learned that Swedenborg had argued in favour of predestination, he rejected his teachings, scribbling in his copy of Swedenborg's *Divine Providence*, 'Lies and Priestcraft' and 'Cursed Folly!'[3] He detested the systematizing tendencies of religious beliefs across the spectrum, and began

composing, as a kind of satire on Swedenborgianism, *The Marriage of Heaven and Hell*. It brings together a variety of literary forms, from proverbs to parables; as the title implies, it reflects Blake's faith in the interplay of 'contraries' such as heaven and hell. Blake's aim was to replace the dualistic way of thinking that dictated a rigid separation of opposite qualities with the view that good and evil were judgements dependent on one's point of view at any particular moment. This was an expression of his vision of opposites as part of a cosmic unity. The danger, as he saw it, was to use such concepts as static, unshifting poles that prevented us from thinking out our experiences for ourselves – 'man has closed himself up till he sees all things through narrow chinks of his cavern'. The characteristic trope of this belief is paradox: 'Opposition is true friendship'.

Visions of the Daughters of Albion was published in 1793 and takes us straight into Blake's mythical universe. On her way to her beloved Theotormon, Oothoon is raped by Bromion. Having impregnated her, he casts her off; they are nonetheless bound back to back. Theotormon refuses to marry her, and sits weeping on the threshold of Bromion's cave. The rest of the poem consists of their lamentations. 'The eye sees more than the heart knows': the poem is an attack on sexual and moral standards of the day as an element in the larger restriction of human consciousness. Between 1792 and 1795 Blake worked on engravings for John Gabriel Stedman's *Narrative of a Five Years' Expedition against the Revolted Negroes of Surinam* (1796), including the famous one of a negro hanging by the ribs from a gallows.[4] That work leaves its mark on the *Visions*: Bromion is a slave owner, and Theotormon hears the 'voice of slaves'. For Blake the plight of women and slaves was a component of the same failure in society to comprehend fully what the eye sees. Mary Wollstonecraft's *Vindication of the Rights of Woman* (1792) – and perhaps even the story of her rejected proposal to Henry Fuseli's wife to move into their home and form a platonic *ménage à trois* – provided inspiration for the *Visions*.[5]

Underlying these works is the nagging question: Why did God permit the Fall? Blake attempts an answer in *The Book of Urizen* (1794), which contains the kernel of the mythology developed in *Jerusalem* and *Milton*, and recapitulated in detail in *The Four Zoas*. *Urizen* was Blake's first effort in the larger project of rewriting the Scriptures, and it is, on one level, a parody of Genesis; in Blake's version, Creation and the Fall are a single event because, to Blake, Creation

---

3   *The Complete Poetry and Prose of William Blake* ed. David V. Erdman, commentary by Harold Bloom (2nd edn, Garden City, NY, 1982), pp. 609–10.

4   Reproduced Peter Ackroyd, *Blake* (London, 1995), p. 170.
5   Wollstonecraft probably met Blake when he engraved the illustrations for her *Original Stories from Real Life* in 1791.

means fragmentation of a primal unity, the God who rules over which must be a cruel demon. Time, formalized religion, and the human body itself are seen in this remarkable poem as different kinds of restriction imposed on mankind in the aftermath of the Fall. The plot concerns the promulgation of Urizen's tyrannic laws; the opposition of Los; the division of Los through Pity, which is created by Enitharmon; the birth of Orc; the travels of Urizen; the birth of his children, and the degeneration of the world under his religion. David Worrall, the most recent editor of the poem, describes it as one of Blake's 'most politically interventionist works of the 1790s' – for further details of which, see his useful introduction, Blake, *Urizen Books* 19–24.

Blake would go on to compose other visionary works, including *Vala, or the Four Zoas* (first version, 1797, revised 1802, 1807), *Milton* (1804–?8) and *Jerusalem* (1804–?20), but none has the clarity or simplicity of *Urizen*. His final years were revitalized by the friendship of artists such as John Linnell and John Varley. Linnell was an enthusiastic patron and commissioned Blake's *Illustrations of the Book of Job* and watercolours of *Paradise Lost* and *Paradise Regained*. He also introduced Blake to Samuel Palmer in 1824; Palmer was only nineteen, and the experience was enormously important to him. 'Do you work with fear and trembling?' Blake asked him. When he died, 12 August 1827, Blake was working on a series of designs illustrating Dante.

I am indebted, in my editing and annotation, to the labours of those responsible for the Blake Trust/Tate Gallery editions; their datings and bibliographical observations are accepted here as authoritative (though on occasion I have preferred my own readings of the various texts). This is the edition of choice for anyone wishing to get to grips with Blake's works, and full details of the relevant volumes are given under 'Further Reading', below. In particular, I would recommend the introductions to these editions, which give a much more detailed account of the intellectual context in which Blake was working than I am able to do here.

Further reading

Northrop Frye, *Fearful Symmetry: A Study of William Blake* (Princeton, NJ, 1947)

Harold Bloom, *Blake's Apocalypse: A Study in Poetic Argument* (New York, 1965)

David V. Erdman, *Blake: Prophet Against Empire* (Princeton, NJ, 1969)

Morton Paley, *Energy and the Imagination: A Study of the Development of Blake's Thought* (Oxford, 1970)

The Illustrated Blake annotated by David V. Erdman (London, 1975)

Zachary Leader, *Reading Blake's Songs* (London, 1981)

The Complete Poetry and Prose of William Blake ed. David V. Erdman, commentary by Harold Bloom (2nd edn, Garden City, NY, 1982)

Songs of Innocence and of Experience ed. Andrew Lincoln, The Blake Trust/Tate Gallery Editions (London, 1991)

William Keach, 'Blake, Violence, and Visionary Politics', *Representing the French Revolution* ed. James A. W. Heffernan (Hanover, NH, 1992), pp. 24–40

Jon Mee, *Dangerous Enthusiasm: William Blake and the Culture of Radicalism in the 1790s* (Oxford, 1992)

The Early Illuminated Books ed. Morris Eaves, Robert N. Essick, and Joseph Viscomi, The Blake Trust/Tate Gallery Editions (London, 1993)

E. P. Thompson, *Witness Against the Beast: William Blake and the Moral Law* (Cambridge, 1993)

Joseph Viscomi, *Blake and the Idea of the Book* (Princeton, NJ, 1993)

Peter Ackroyd, *Blake* (London, 1995)

The Urizen Books ed. David Worrall, The Blake Trust/Tate Gallery Editions (London, 1995)

Nelson Hilton, 'Blakean Zen', *Romanticism: A Critical Reader* 1–16

V. A. de Luca, 'Blake's Concept of the Sublime', *Romanticism: A Critical Reader* 17–54

All Religions Are One (composed c.1788)

The voice of one crying in the wilderness.[1]

The Argument. As the true method of knowledge is experiment, the true faculty of knowing must be the faculty which experiences: this faculty I treat of.

Principle 1. That the Poetic Genius is the true man, and that the body or outward form of man is derived from the Poetic Genius. Likewise that the forms of all things are derived from their genius which, by the ancients, was called an angel and spirit and demon.

ALL RELIGIONS ARE ONE

[1] Matthew 5:5; Mark 1:3; Luke 3:4; John 1:23. Blake's illustration shows John the Baptist, prophet of the coming of Christ; by implication, his situation – that of one crying in the wilderness – is one that Blake feels he shares.

Principle 2. As all men are alike in outward form, so (and with the same infinite variety) all are alike in the Poetic Genius.

Principle 3. No man can think, write or speak from his heart, but he must intend truth. Thus all sects of philosophy are from the Poetic Genius adapted to the weaknesses of every individual.

Principle 4. As none by travelling over known lands can find out the unknown, so, from already acquired knowledge, man could not acquire more. Therefore an universal Poetic Genius exists.

Principle 5. The religions of all nations are derived from each nation's different reception of the Poetic Genius, which is everywhere called the spirit of prophecy.

Principle 6. The Jewish and Christian Testaments are an original derivation from the Poetic Genius. This is necessary from the confined nature of bodily sensation.

Principle 7. As all men are alike (though infinitely various), so all religions and as all similars have one source.

The true man is the source, he being the Poetic Genius.

There is no Natural Religion (composed *c*.1788)[1]

The Argument. Man has no notion of moral fitness but from education. Naturally he is only a natural organ subject to sense.

I Man cannot naturally perceive, but through his natural or bodily organs.

II Man by his reasoning power can only compare and judge of what he has already perceived.

III From a perception of only three senses or three elements none could deduce a fourth or fifth.

IV None could have other than natural or organic thoughts if he had none but organic perceptions.

V Man's desires are limited by his perceptions; none can desire what he has not perceived.

VI The desires and perceptions of man, untaught by anything but organs of sense, must be limited to objects of sense.

I Man's perceptions are not bounded by organs of perception. He perceives more than sense (though ever so acute) can discover.

II Reason, or the ratio of all we have already known, is not the same that it shall be when we know more.

III [*missing*][2]

IV The bounded is loathed by its possessor. The same dull round, even of a universe, would soon become a mill with complicated wheels.

V If the many become the same as the few when possessed, 'More, more!' is the cry of a mistaken soul; less than all cannot satisfy man.

VI If any could desire what he is incapable of possessing, despair must be his eternal lot.

VII The desire of man being infinite, the possession is infinite, and himself infinite.

Conclusion. If it were not for the poetic or prophetic character, the philosophic and experimental would soon be at the ratio of all things, and stand still, unable to do other than repeat the same dull round over again.

Application. He who sees the infinite in all things, sees God. He who sees the ratio only, sees himself only.

Therefore God becomes as we are, that we may be as He is.

THERE IS NO NATURAL RELIGION
[1] This has traditionally been presented as two separate and distinct works, featuring the (a) and (b) series plates; however, recent editorial discoveries have led to its being regarded as one work consisting of two parts, the second answering the first: 'Unlike the *Songs of Innocence*, the "a" part cannot stand alone; without its second half, the irony would not be apparent and Blake would have appeared to contemporary readers as an advocate of the very position he is attacking' (Blake, *Early Illuminated Books*, Blake Trust Editions, 25). Accordingly, it is presented here as a single work. The first six principles present apparently straightforward statements of Lockean thought, only so that they can be refuted by the seven statements that follow.
[2] The plate etched for proposition III is lost.

The Book of Thel (1789)

[Plate 1]

Thel's Motto

Does the eagle know what is in the pit?
Or wilt thou go ask the mole:
Can wisdom be put in a silver rod
Or love in a golden bowl?[1]

[Plate 3]

Thel[2]

I

The daughters of Mne Seraphim[3] led round their sunny flocks,
All but the youngest; she in paleness sought the secret air,
To fade away like morning beauty from her mortal day.
Down by the river of Adona[4] her soft voice is heard,
And thus her gentle lamentation falls like morning dew: 5
  'Oh life of this our spring, why fades the lotus of the water?
Why fade these children of the spring, born but to smile and fall?
Ah, Thel is like a wat'ry bow and like a parting cloud,
Like a reflection in a glass, like shadows in the water,
Like dreams of infants, like a smile upon an infant's face,   10
Like the dove's voice, like transient day, like music in the air.
Ah, gentle may I lay me down, and gentle rest my head;
And gentle sleep the sleep of death, and gentle hear the voice
Of him that walketh in the garden in the evening time.'[5]
  The lily of the valley[6] breathing in the humble grass   15
Answered the lovely maid and said, 'I am a wat'ry weed,
And I am very small, and love to dwell in lowly vales –
So weak, the gilded butterfly scarce perches on my head.
Yet I am visited from heaven, and he that smiles on all
Walks in the valley, and each morn over me spreads his hand   20
Saying, "Rejoice, thou humble grass, thou new-born lily flower,
Thou gentle maid of silent valleys, and of modest brooks;
For thou shalt be clothed in light, and fed with morning manna[7]
Till summer's heat melts thee beside the fountains and the springs
To flourish in eternal vales!" Then why should Thel complain?   25

THE BOOK OF THEL
[1] The first two lines of the motto question the perspective from which knowledge can be gained; the second two question the containers of knowledge, either as verbal metaphor or the incarnation of spirit in body. *Silver rod ... golden bowl* in Ecclesiastes 12:6 a 'silver cord' and 'golden bowl' are images of mortality.
[2] *Thel* various meanings have been suggested, including 'will', 'wish', or 'desire' (from the Greek θέλω); and Thalia (from θάλλειν, 'blossoming'), the Greek muse of pastoral poetry.
[3] *Mne Seraphim* no one is sure of Blake's meaning. Some suggest that it is an error for 'Bne Seraphim', the sons of the

Seraphim. The Seraphim are the order of angels nearest to God whose duty is to love him.
[4] *Adona* related to Adonis, a figure in Greek myth associated with the cycles of the vegetable world.
[5] *hear the voice ... time* cf. Genesis 3:8: 'And they heard the voice of the Lord God walking in the garden in the cool of the day'.
[6] *lily of the valley* flower of innocence, symbol of Thel's virginity. Cf. Song of Solomon 2:1: 'the lily of the valleys'.
[7] *morning manna* God provided the Israelites with manna (food) in the wilderness, Exodus 16:14–26.

[Plate 4]
Why should the mistress of the vales of Har[8] utter a sigh?'
She ceased and smiled in tears, then sat down in her silver shrine.
    Thel answered: 'Oh thou little virgin of the peaceful valley,
Giving to those that cannot crave – the voiceless, the o'ertired;
Thy breath doth nourish the innocent lamb, he smells thy milky garments,   30
He crops[9] thy flowers while thou sittest smiling in his face,
Wiping his mild and meekin[10] mouth from all contagious taints.
Thy wine doth purify the golden honey; thy perfume,
Which thou dost scatter on every little blade of grass that springs,
Revives the milked cow, and tames the fire-breathing steed.   35
But Thel is like a faint cloud kindled at the rising sun:
I vanish from my pearly throne, and who shall find my place?'[11]
    'Queen of the vales', the lily answered, 'ask the tender cloud[12]
And it shall tell thee why it glitters in the morning sky,
And why it scatters its bright beauty through the humid air: 40
Descend, oh little cloud, and hover before the eyes of Thel.'
    The cloud descended, and the lily bowed her modest head
And went to mind her numerous charge among the verdant grass.

[Plate 5]
II

'Oh little cloud', the virgin said, 'I charge thee tell to me
Why thou complainest not when in one hour thou fade away;   45
Then we shall seek thee but not find. Ah, Thel is like to thee:
I pass away – yet I complain, and no one hears my voice.'
    The cloud then showed his golden head and his bright form emerged,
Hovering and glittering on the air before the face of Thel.
'Oh virgin, know'st thou not our steeds drink of the golden springs[13]   50
Where Luvah[14] doth renew his horses? Look'st thou on my youth,
And fearest thou because I vanish and am seen no more?
Nothing remains. Oh maid, I tell thee, when I pass away,
It is to tenfold life – to love, to peace, and raptures holy;
Unseen descending, weigh my light wings upon balmy flowers,   55
And court the fair-eyed dew to take me to her shining tent:
The weeping virgin trembling kneels before the risen sun
Till we arise linked in a golden band, and never part,
But walk united, bearing food to all our tender flowers.'
    'Dost thou, oh little cloud? I fear that I am not like thee;   60
For I walk through the vales of Har and smell the sweetest flowers,
But I feed not the little flowers; I hear the warbling birds,
But I feed not the warbling birds – they fly and seek their food.
But Thel delights in these no more because I fade away,
And all shall say, "Without a use this shining woman lived –   65
Or did she only live to be at death the food of worms?" '
    The cloud reclined upon his airy throne and answered thus:

---

[8]   *Har* another character of Blake's, the father of Tiriel.
[9]   *crops* eats.
[10]   *meekin* meek.
[11]   *But Thel . . . place* cf. Job 7:9: 'As the cloud is consumed and vanisheth away: so he that goeth down to the grave shall come up no more'.

[12]   *the tender cloud* the male principle, the fructifier.
[13]   *Oh virgin . . . springs* cf. Shakespeare, *Cymbeline* II iii 21–2: 'and Phoebus gins arise, / His steeds to water at those springs'.
[14]   *Luvah* god of desire, Prince of Love; one of Blake's Four Zoas (the four principles which rule human life).

'Then if thou art the food of worms, oh virgin of the skies,
How great thy use, how great thy blessing! Everything that lives
Lives not alone, nor for itself. Fear not, and I will call   70
The weak worm from its lowly bed, and thou shalt hear its voice.
Come forth, worm of the silent valley, to thy pensive queen!'
    The helpless worm arose and sat upon the lily's leaf,
And the bright cloud sailed on to find his partner in the vale.

[Plate 6]

III

Then Thel, astonished, viewed the worm upon its dewy bed.   75
'Art thou a worm? Image of weakness, art thou but a worm?
I see thee like an infant wrapped in the lily's leaf;
Ah, weep not, little voice, thou canst not speak[15] but thou canst weep.
Is this a worm? I see thee lay helpless and naked – weeping
And none to answer, none to cherish thee with mother's smiles.'   80
    The clod of clay[16] heard the worm's voice and raised her pitying head:
She bowed over the weeping infant, and her life exhaled
In milky fondness; then on Thel she fixed her humble eyes.
'Oh, beauty of the vales of Har, we live not for ourselves!
Thou seest me the meanest thing, and so I am indeed;   85
My bosom of itself is cold, and of itself is dark,
[Plate 7]
But he that loves the lowly pours his oil upon my head
And kisses me, and binds his nuptial bands around my breast,
And says, "Thou mother of my children, I have loved thee,
And I have given thee a crown that none can take away."[17]   90
But how this is, sweet maid, I know not and I cannot know;
I ponder and I cannot ponder – yet I live and love.'
    The daughter of beauty wiped her pitying tears with her white veil
And said, 'Alas, I knew not this, and therefore did I weep.
That God would love a worm, I knew, and punish the evil foot   95
That, wilful, bruised its helpless form. But that he cherished it
With milk and oil, I never knew. And therefore did I weep,
And I complained in the mild air because I fade away,
And lay me down in thy cold bed, and leave my shining lot.'
    'Queen of the vales', the matron clay answered, 'I heard thy sighs,   100
And all thy moans flew o'er my roof, but I have called them down.
Wilt thou, oh Queen, enter my house?[18] 'Tis given thee to enter
And to return. Fear nothing; enter with thy virgin feet.'

[Plate 8]

IV

The eternal gate's terrific porter lifted the northern bar;[19]
Thel entered in and saw the secrets of the land unknown.   105

---

[15] *thou canst not speak* a pun on the word 'infant', which means 'without speech' (*in-fans*).
[16] The worm and the clod are the baby and its mother.
[17] *a crown that none can take away* cf. I Peter 5:4: 'a crown of glory that fadeth not away'; see also Revelation 3:11.

[18] *my house* cf. Job 17:13: 'the grave is mine house: I have made my bed in the darkness'.
[19] *The eternal gate's ... bar* the exact meaning is unclear, although many interpretations have been offered. The porter is variously identified as Pluto, god of the underworld, or as Death, among others.

She saw the couches of the dead, and where the fibrous roots
Of every heart on earth infixes deep its restless twists –
A land of sorrows and of tears where never smile was seen.
She wandered in the land of clouds through valleys dark, list'ning
Dolours and lamentations; waiting oft beside a dewy grave 110
She stood in silence, list'ning to the voices of the ground,
Till to her own grave-plot she came, and there she sat down[20]
And heard this voice of sorrow breathed from the hollow pit:
    'Why cannot the ear be closed to its own destruction,
Or the glist'ning eye, to the poison of a smile? 115
Why are eyelids stored with arrows ready drawn
Where a thousand fighting men in ambush lie,
Or an eye of gifts and graces, show'ring fruits and coined gold?
Why a tongue impressed with honey from every wind?[21]
Why an ear, a whirlpool fierce to draw creations in? 120
Why a nostril wide inhaling terror, trembling and affright?
Why a tender curb upon the youthful burning boy?
Why a little curtain of flesh[22] on the bed of our desire?'
    The virgin started from her seat, and with a shriek
Fled back unhindered till she came into the vales of Har. 125

The End

Songs of Innocence (1789)

SONGS OF INNOCENCE AND OF EXPERIENCE (1789–93)

Introduction

Piping down the valleys wild,
Piping songs of pleasant glee,
On a cloud I saw a child
And he laughing said to me:

'Pipe a song about a lamb!' 5
So I piped with a merry cheer;
'Piper, pipe that song again!'
So I piped – he wept to hear.

'Drop thy pipe, thy happy pipe,
Sing thy songs of happy cheer!' 10
So I sung the same again
While he wept with joy to hear.

'Piper, sit thee down and write
In a book, that all may read.'
So he vanished from my sight 15
And I plucked a hollow reed.

---

[20] *there she sat down* cf. Psalm 137:1: 'By the rivers of Baby-
lon, there we sat down, yea, we wept'.
[21] *Why a tongue . . . wind* probably a recollection of Spenser,
Faerie Queene I ix stanza 31 l. 5: 'His subtill tongue, like drop-
ping honny'.

[22] *a little curtain of flesh* the hymen.

And I made a rural pen,
And I <u>stained</u> the water clear,
And I wrote my happy songs
Every child may joy to hear.   20

The Shepherd

How sweet is the shepherd's sweet lot!
From the morn to the evening he strays;
He shall follow his sheep all the day
And his tongue shall be filled with praise.

For he hears the lamb's innocent call,[1]   5
And he hears the ewe's tender reply;
He is watchful while they are in peace,
For they know when their shepherd is nigh.

The Echoing Green

The sun does arise
And make happy the skies;
The merry bells ring
To welcome the spring;
The skylark and thrush,   5
The birds of the bush,
Sing louder around
To the bells' cheerful sound,
While our sports shall be seen
On the echoing green.   10

Old John with white hair
Does laugh away care,
Sitting under the oak
Among the old folk.
They laugh at our play   15
And soon they all say,
'Such, such were the joys
When we all, girls and boys,
In our youth-time were seen
On the echoing green.'   20

Till the little ones weary
No more can be merry,
The sun does descend
And our sports have an end;
Round the laps of their mothers,   25
Many sisters and brothers
Like birds in their nest
Are ready for rest,
And sport no more seen
On the darkening green.   30

THE SHEPHERD
[1] *the lamb's innocent call* the stray sheep is a biblical symbol;
see, for instance, Psalm 119:176; Isaiah 53:6; Matthew 18:12.

The Lamb

Little lamb, who made thee?
Dost thou know who made thee?
Gave thee life and bid thee feed
By the stream and o'er the mead;
Gave thee clothing of delight –   5
Softest clothing, woolly, bright;
Gave thee such a tender voice,
Making all the vales rejoice?
Little lamb, who made thee?
Dost thou know who made thee?   10

Little lamb, I'll tell thee,
Little lamb, I'll tell thee;
He is called by thy name,
For he calls himself a lamb;
He is meek and he is mild,   15
He became a little child:
I a child and thou a lamb,
We are called by his name.[1]
Little lamb, God bless thee,
Little lamb, God bless thee.   20

The Little Black Boy[1]

My mother bore me in the southern wild
And I am black, but oh, my soul is white!
White as an angel is the English child,
But I am black, as if bereaved of light.

My mother taught me underneath a tree,   5
And sitting down before the heat of day,
She took me on her lap and kissed me,
And pointing to the east began to say,

'Look on the rising sun: there God does live,[2]
And gives his light, and gives his heat away;   10
And flowers and trees and beasts and men receive
Comfort in morning, joy in the noonday.

And we are put on earth a little space
That we may learn to bear the beams of love;
And these black bodies and this sunburnt face   15
Is but a cloud, and like a shady grove.

THE LAMB
[1] *I a child ... his name* Critics note the child's identification with Christ and the lamb.

THE LITTLE BLACK BOY
[1] This poem is a part of Blake's response to the slave trade; the society for its abolition had been founded in 1787, and he would have been aware of the passing of a Bill proposed in the House of Commons on 21 May 1788 by Sir William Dolben, MP for the University of Oxford. It limited the number of slaves which could be transported from Africa to British colonies in the West Indies.
[2] *Look on the rising sun ... live* The association of God with the rising sun echoes Isaiah 45:6; 59:19: 'So shall they fear the name of the Lord from the west, and his glory from the rising of the sun.'

For when our souls have learned the heat to bear
The cloud will vanish; we shall hear his voice
Saying, "Come out from the grove, my love and care,
And round my golden tent like lambs rejoice!" '   20

Thus did my mother say, and kissed me;
And thus I say to little English boy,
When I from black and he from white cloud free,
And round the tent of God like lambs we joy,

I'll shade him from the heat, till he can bear   25
To lean in joy upon our Father's knee;
And then I'll stand and stroke his silver hair,
And be like him, and he will then love me.

The Blossom

Merry merry sparrow
Under leaves so green!
A happy blossom
Sees you swift as arrow;
Seek your cradle narrow   5
Near my bosom.

Pretty pretty robin
Under leaves so green!
A happy blossom
Hears you sobbing, sobbing,   10
Pretty pretty robin,
Near my bosom.

The Chimney Sweeper[1]

When my mother died I was very young,
And my father sold me while yet my tongue
Could scarcely cry 'weep weep weep weep!'[2]
So your chimneys I sweep, and in soot I sleep.

There's little Tom Dacre, who cried when his head,   5
That curled like a lamb's back, was shaved; so I said,
'Hush, Tom! Never mind it, for when your head's bare
You know that the soot cannot spoil your white hair.'

And so he was quiet, and that very night,
As Tom was a-sleeping, he had such a sight!   10
That thousands of sweepers – Dick, Joe, Ned and Jack,
Were all of them locked up in coffins of black.

And by came an angel who had a bright key,

THE CHIMNEY SWEEPER
[1] Blake would have known that an attempt was made in 1788 to improve the conditions of child chimney-sweeps: eight was the proposed minimum age; hours of work would be limited; regulations were proposed to ensure that sweeps were properly washed every week; and a ban proposed on the use of children in chimneys on fire. In the event, the Porter's Act was not passed.
[2] *weep weep weep weep* suggestive of both the child's cry as he touts for work, as well as his grief.

And he opened the coffins and set them all free;
Then down a green plain leaping, laughing they run   15
And wash in a river, and shine in the sun.

Then naked and white, all their bags left behind,
They rise upon clouds and sport in the wind;
And the angel told Tom, if he'd be a good boy;
He'd have God for his father and never want joy.   20

And so Tom awoke, and we rose in the dark,
And got with our bags and our brushes to work;
Though the morning was cold, Tom was happy and warm –
So if all do their duty, they need not fear harm.

The Little Boy Lost

'Father, father, where are you going?
Oh do not walk so fast!
Speak, father, speak to your little boy
Or else I shall be lost.'

The night was dark, no father was there,   5
The child was wet with dew;
The mire was deep,[1] and the child did weep,
And away the vapour flew.

The Little Boy Found

The little boy lost in the lonely fen,
Led by the wand'ring light,[1]
Began to cry; but God, ever nigh,
Appeared like his father in white.[2]

He kissed the child, and by the hand led,   5
And to his mother brought,
Who in sorrow pale, through the lonely dale
Her little boy weeping sought.

Laughing Song

When the green woods laugh with the voice of joy,
And the dimpling stream runs laughing by;
When the air does laugh with our merry wit,
And the green hill laughs with the noise of it;

When the meadows laugh with lively green,   5
And the grasshopper laughs in the merry scene;
When Mary and Susan and Emily
With their sweet round mouths sing, 'Ha, ha, he!'

THE LITTLE BOY LOST
[1] *The mire was deep* a biblical image; e.g. Psalm 69:2: 'I sink
in deep mire'.

THE LITTLE BOY FOUND
[1] *the wand'ring light* will o' the wisp.
[2] *like his father in white* cf. the transfigured Christ; Matthew
17:2; Luke 9:29: 'And as he prayed, the fashion of his counte-
nance was altered, and his raiment was white and glistering'.

When the painted birds laugh in the shade,
Where our table with cherries and nuts is spread,　　　　　10
Come live and be merry, and join with me
To sing the sweet chorus of 'Ha, ha, he!'

A Cradle Song

Sweet dreams, form a shade
O'er my lovely infant's head;
Sweet dreams of pleasant streams
By happy, silent, moony beams.

Sweet sleep, with soft down　　　　　5
Weave thy brows an infant crown;
Sweet sleep, angel mild,
Hover o'er my happy child.

Sweet smiles in the night
Hover over my delight;　　　　　10
Sweet smiles, mother's smiles,
All the livelong night beguiles.

Sweet moans, dovelike sighs,
Chase not slumber from thy eyes;
Sweet moans, sweeter smiles,　　　　　15
All the dovelike moans beguiles.

Sleep, sleep, happy child,
All creation slept and smiled;
Sleep, sleep, happy sleep,
While o'er thee thy mother weep.　　　　　20

Sweet babe, in thy face
Holy image I can trace;
Sweet babe, once like thee,
Thy maker lay and wept for me,

Wept for me, for thee, for all,　　　　　25
When he was an infant small;
Thou his image ever see,
Heavenly face that smiles on thee –

Smiles on thee, on me, on all,
Who became an infant small:　　　　　30
Infant smiles are his own smiles;
Heaven and earth to peace beguiles.[1]

A CRADLE SONG
[1]   *Heaven and earth . . . beguiles* apparently an echo of Milton's
ode *On the Morning of Christ's Nativity*, where Christ's birth is
accompanied by a divine harmony which 'alone / Could hold
all heaven and earth in happier union' (ll. 107–8).

The Divine Image

To mercy, pity, peace and love
All pray in their distress;
And to these virtues of delight
Return their thankfulness.

For mercy, pity, peace and love   5
Is God our Father dear;
And mercy, pity, peace and love
Is man, his child and care.

For mercy has a human heart,
Pity, a human face,   10
And love, the human form divine,
And peace, the human dress.

Then every man of every clime
That prays in his distress,
Prays to the human form divine –   15
Love, mercy, pity, peace.

And all must love the human form
In heathen, Turk, or Jew;
Where mercy, love and pity dwell
There God is dwelling too.[1]   20

Holy Thursday[1]

'Twas on a Holy Thursday, their innocent faces clean,
The children walking two and two in red and blue and green,
Grey-headed beadles walked before, with wands as white as snow,
Till into the high dome of Paul's they like Thames' waters flow.

Oh what a multitude they seemed, these flowers of London town!   5
Seated in companies they sit, with radiance all their own;
The hum of multitudes was there, but multitudes of lambs –
Thousands of little boys and girls raising their innocent hands.

Now like a mighty wind they raise to heaven the voice of song,
Or like harmonious thunderings the seats of heaven among;   10
Beneath them sit the aged men, wise guardians of the poor;
Then cherish pity, lest you drive an angel from your door.

THE DIVINE IMAGE
[1] *Where mercy . . . dwelling too* cf. I John 4:16: 'God is love;
and he that dwelleth in love dwelleth in God, and God in
him'.

HOLY THURSDAY
[1] Blake describes the service for the poorest children in the
charity schools in London, of whom there were about 6,000,
held in St Paul's Cathedral, usually on the first Thursday in
May, from 1782 onwards. They would be marched there by
their Beadles (parish officers) for what Keynes called 'a com-
pulsory exhibition of their piety and gratitude to their
patrons'.

Night

The sun descending in the west,
The evening star does shine;
The birds are silent in their nest
And I must seek for mine.
The moon like a flower   5
In heaven's high bower,
With silent delight
Sits and smiles on the night.

Farewell, green fields and happy groves,
Where flocks have took delight;   10
Where lambs have nibbled, silent moves
The feet of angels bright;
Unseen they pour blessing
And joy without ceasing
On each bud and blossom   15
And each sleeping bosom.

They look in every thoughtless nest
Where birds are covered warm,
They visit caves of every beast
To keep them all from harm.   20
If they see any weeping
That should have been sleeping,
They pour sleep on their head
And sit down by their bed.

When wolves and tigers howl for prey   25
They pitying stand and weep,
Seeking to drive their thirst away
And keep them from the sheep;
But if they rush dreadful,
The angels most heedful   30
Receive each mild spirit,
New worlds to inherit.

And there the lion's ruddy eyes
Shall flow with tears of gold,
And pitying the tender cries,   35
And walking round the fold,
Saying, 'Wrath, by his meekness,
And by his health, sickness
Is driven away
From our immortal day.   40

And now beside thee, bleating lamb,
I can lie down and sleep,
Or think on him who bore thy name,
Graze after thee and weep.
For, washed in life's river,   45
My bright mane for ever
Shall shine like the gold
As I guard o'er the fold.'

Spring

Sound the flute!
Now it's mute.
Birds delight
Day and night;
Nightingale   5
In the dale,
Lark in sky,
Merrily
Merrily, merrily, to welcome in the year.

Little boy   10
Full of joy;
Little girl
Sweet and small;
Cock does crow,
So do you;   15
Merry voice,
Infant noise –
Merrily, merrily, to welcome in the year.

Little lamb
Here I am,[1]   20
Come and lick
My white neck!
Let me pull
Your soft wool,
Let me kiss   25
Your soft face;
Merrily, merrily, we welcome in the year.

Nurse's Song

When the voices of children are heard on the green
And laughing is heard on the hill,
My heart is at rest within my breast
And everything else is still.

'Then come home, my children, the sun is gone down   5
And the dews of night arise;
Come, come, leave off play, and let us away
Till the morning appears in the skies.'

'No, no! Let us play, for it is yet day
And we cannot go to sleep;   10
Besides, in the sky, the little birds fly
And the hills are all covered with sheep.'

SPRING
[1] *Here I am* frequently used in the Bible; see Genesis 22:1,
11; 31:11.

'Well, well, go and play till the light fades away
And then go home to bed.'
The little ones leaped and shouted and laughed   15
And all the hills echoed.

Infant Joy

'I have no name,
I am but two days old.'
What shall I call thee?
'I happy am,
Joy is my name.'   5
Sweet joy befall thee!

Pretty joy!
Sweet joy but two days old,
Sweet joy I call thee;
Thou dost smile,   10
I sing the while,
Sweet joy befall thee!

A Dream

Once a dream did weave a shade
O'er my angel-guarded bed,
That an emmet[1] lost its way
Where on grass methought I lay.

Troubled, wildered, and forlorn,   5
Dark, benighted, travel-worn,
Over many a tangled spray,
All heart-broke I heard her say,

'Oh my children! Do they cry?
Do they hear their father sigh?   10
Now they look abroad to see;
Now return and weep for me.'

Pitying, I dropped a tear;
But I saw a glow-worm near
Who replied, 'What wailing wight   15
Calls the watchman of the night?

I am set to light the ground
While the beetle goes his round;
Follow now the beetle's hum –
Little wanderer, hie thee home.'[2]   20

A DREAM
[1]   *emmet* ant.
[2]   The dor-beetle, which flies after sunset with a humming
sound, was known as 'the watchman'. The glow-worm was
said, in a folk-song, to light people 'home to bed' on moonless
nights.

On Another's Sorrow

Can I see another's woe
And not be in sorrow too?
Can I see another's grief
And not seek for kind relief?

Can I see a falling tear   5
And not feel my sorrow's share?
Can a father see his child
Weep, nor be with sorrow filled?

Can a mother sit and hear
An infant groan, an infant fear?   10
No, no! never can it be!
Never, never can it be!

And can He who smiles on all,
Hear the wren with sorrows small,
Hear the small bird's grief and care,   15
Hear the woes that infants bear —

And not sit beside the nest
Pouring pity in their breast?
And not sit the cradle near
Weeping tear on infant's tear?   20

And not sit both night and day
Wiping all our tears away?
Oh no! never can it be!
Never, never can it be!

He doth give his joy to all,   25
He becomes an infant small;
He becomes a man of woe,
He doth feel the sorrow too.

Think not thou canst sigh a sigh
And thy maker is not by;   30
Think not thou canst weep a tear
And thy maker is not near.

Oh! he gives to us his joy
That our grief he may destroy;
Till our grief is fled and gone   35
He doth sit by us and moan.

Songs of Experience (1793)

SONGS OF INNOCENCE AND OF EXPERIENCE (1789–93)

Introduction

Hear the voice of the bard!
Who present, past and future sees;
Whose ears have heard
The Holy Word
That walked among the ancient trees   5

Calling the lapsed soul,[1]
And weeping in the evening dew;
That might control
The starry pole,
And fallen, fallen light renew!   10

'Oh Earth, oh Earth, return!
Arise from out the dewy grass;
Night is worn,
And the morn
Rises from the slumberous mass.   15

Turn away no more!
Why wilt thou turn away?
The starry floor,
The wat'ry shore,
Is giv'n thee till the break of day.'   20

Earth's Answer

Earth raised up her head
From the darkness, dread and drear;
Her light fled,
Stony dread!
And her locks covered with grey despair.   5

'Prisoned on wat'ry shore,
Starry Jealousy[1] does keep my den;
Cold and hoar,
Weeping o'er,
I hear the father of the ancient men.   10

SONGS OF EXPERIENCE
1 *Whose ears have heard . . . soul* cf. Genesis 3:8, where Adam and Eve, now fallen, 'heard the voice of the Lord God walking in the garden in the cool of the day: and Adam and his wife hid themselves from the presence of the Lord God amongst the trees of the garden'.

EARTH'S ANSWER
1 *Starry Jealousy* the idea of God as jealous is biblical; see Exodus 20:5; 34:14, and Deuteronomy 4:24: 'For the Lord thy God is a consuming fire, even a jealous God'.

Selfish father of men!
Cruel, jealous, selfish fear!
Can delight
Chained in night
The virgins of youth and morning bear?   15

Does spring hide its joy
When buds and blossoms grow?
Does the sower
Sow by night,
Or the ploughman in darkness plough?   20

Break this heavy chain
That does freeze my bones around! –
Selfish, vain,
Eternal bane!
That free love with bondage bound.'   25

The Clod and the Pebble

'Love seeketh not itself to please,
Nor for itself hath any care;
But for another gives its ease
And builds a heaven in hell's despair.'

So sung a little clod of clay   5
Trodden with the cattle's feet,
But a pebble of the brook
Warbled out these metres meet:

'Love seeketh only self to please,
To bind another to its delight;   10
Joys in another's loss of ease,
And builds a hell in heaven's despite.'

Holy Thursday

Is this a holy thing to see
In a rich and fruitful land?
Babes reduced to misery,
Fed with cold and usurous hand?

Is that trembling cry a song?   5
Can it be a song of joy?
And so many children poor?
It is a land of poverty!

And their sun does never shine,
And their fields are bleak and bare,   10
And their ways are filled with thorns –
It is eternal winter there.

For where'er the sun does shine
And where'er the rain does fall,
Babe can never hunger there,   15
Nor poverty the mind appal.

The Little Girl Lost[1]

[handwritten margin note: Why did Blake include poem in 'Experience?']

In futurity
I prophetic see
That the earth from sleep
(Grave the sentence deep)

Shall arise and seek   5
For her maker meek,
And the desert wild
Become a garden mild.

In the southern clime,
Where the summer's prime   10
Never fades away,
Lovely Lyca lay.

Seven summers old
Lovely Lyca told;
She had wandered long   15
Hearing wild birds' song.

'Sweet sleep, come to me
Underneath this tree;
Do father, mother weep?
Where can Lyca sleep?   20

Lost in desert wild
Is your little child;
How can Lyca sleep
If her mother weep?

If her heart does ache   25
Then let Lyca wake;
If my mother sleep
Lyca shall not weep.

Frowning, frowning night,
O'er this desert bright,   30
Let thy moon arise
While I close my eyes.'

Sleeping Lyca lay
While the beasts of prey,
Come from caverns deep,   35
Viewed the maid asleep.

The kingly lion stood
And the virgin viewed,
Then he gambolled round
O'er the hallowed ground.   40

THE LITTLE GIRL LOST
[1] This poem, and *The Little Girl Found*, originally appeared in *Songs of Innocence*; in some respects they may be seen as counterparts of *The Little Boy Lost* and *The Little Boy Found*.

Leopards, tigers play
Round her as she lay,
While the lion old
Bowed his mane of gold

And her bosom lick,   45
And upon her neck
From his eyes of flame
Ruby tears there came;

While the lioness
Loosed her slender dress,   50
And naked they conveyed
To caves the sleeping maid.[2]

The Little Girl Found

All the night in woe
Lyca's parents go;
Over valleys deep,
While the deserts weep.

Tired and woe-begone,   5
Hoarse with making moan,
Arm in arm seven days
They traced the desert ways.

Seven nights they sleep
Among shadows deep,   10
And dream they see their child
Starved in desert wild.

Pale through pathless ways
The fancied image strays –
Famished, weeping, weak,   15
With hollow piteous shriek.

Rising from unrest,
The trembling woman pressed
With feet of weary woe;
She could no further go.   20

In his arms he bore
Her, armed with sorrow sore;
Till before their way
A couching lion lay.

Turning back was vain;   25
Soon his heavy mane
Bore them to the ground:
Then he stalked around

---

[2] The obvious parallel is with Daniel in the lions' den; cf. Daniel 6:16–22, though compare also Isaiah 11:6: 'The wolf also shall dwell with the lamb, and the leopard shall lie down with the kid; and the calf and the young lion and the fatling together; and a little child shall lead them'.

Smelling to his prey.
But their fears allay 30
When he licks their hands,
And silent by them stands.

They look upon his eyes
Filled with deep surprise,
And wondering behold 35
A spirit armed in gold.

On his head a crown,
On his shoulders down
Flowed his golden hair;
Gone was all their care. 40

'Follow me', he said,
'Weep not for the maid;
In my palace deep
Lyca lies asleep.'

Then they followed 45
Where the vision led,
And saw their sleeping child
Among tigers wild.

To this day they dwell
In a lonely dell; 50
Nor fear the wolvish howl,
Nor the lion's growl.

The Chimney Sweeper

A little black thing among the snow,
Crying 'weep weep' in notes of woe;
'Where are thy father and mother, say?'
'They are both gone up to the church to pray.

Because I was happy upon the heath 5
And smiled among the winter's snow,
They clothed me in the clothes of death,
And taught me to sing the notes of woe.

And because I am happy and dance and sing,[1]
They think they have done me no injury, 10
And are gone to praise God and his priest and king,
Who make up a heaven of our misery.'

THE CHIMNEY SWEEPER
[1]   *And because . . . sing* Erdman suggests a reference to May
Day, when sweeps and milkmaids danced in the streets of
London in return for alms.

Nurse's Song

When the voices of children are heard on the green
And whisp'rings are in the dale,
The days of my youth rise fresh in my mind,
My face turns green and pale.

Then come home, my children, the sun is gone down,   5
And the dews of night arise;
Your spring and your day are wasted in play,
And your winter and night in disguise.

The Sick Rose

Oh rose, thou art sick;
The invisible worm
That flies in the night
In the howling storm

Has found out thy bed   5
Of crimson joy,
And his dark secret love
Does thy life destroy.

The Fly

Little fly,
Thy summer's play
My thoughtless hand
Has brushed away.

Am not I   5
A fly like thee?
Or art not thou
A man like me?

For I dance
And drink and sing   10
Till some blind hand
Shall brush my wing.

If thought is life
And strength and breath,
And the want   15
Of thought is death,

Then am I
A happy fly,
If I live
Or if I die.   20

The Angel

I dreamt a dream! What can it mean?
And that I was a maiden queen
Guarded by an angel mild:
Witless woe was ne'er beguiled!

And I wept both night and day,   5
And he wiped my tears away,
And I wept both day and night,
And hid from him my heart's delight.

So he took his wings and fled,
Then the morn blushed rosy red;   10
I dried my tears, and armed my fears
With ten thousand shields and spears.

Soon my angel came again:
I was armed, he came in vain –
For the time of youth was fled,   15
And grey hairs were on my head.

The Tyger[1]

Tyger, tyger, burning bright
In the forests of the night,
What immortal hand or eye
Could frame thy fearful symmetry?

In what distant deeps or skies   5
Burnt the fire of thine eyes?
On what wings dare he aspire?
What the hand dare seize the fire?

And what shoulder and what art
Could twist the sinews of thy heart?   10
And when thy heart began to beat,
What dread hand and what dread feet?

What the hammer? What the chain?
In what furnace was thy brain?
What the anvil? What dread grasp   15
Dare its deadly terrors clasp?

When the stars threw down their spears
And watered heaven with their tears,
Did he smile his work to see?
Did he who made the lamb make thee?   20

[handwritten marginal notes: "Book of Judges, Song of Deborah"; "–allusion to Satan?"]

THE TYGER
[1] *Tyger* this spelling was already slightly archaic by Blake's time.

Tyger, tyger, burning bright
In the forests of the night,
What immortal hand or eye
Dare frame thy fearful symmetry?

My Pretty Rose-Tree

A flower was offered to me,
Such a flower as May never bore;
But I said, 'I've a pretty rose-tree',
And I passed the sweet flower o'er.

Then I went to my pretty rose-tree   5
To tend her by day and by night;
But my rose turned away with jealousy
And her thorns were my only delight.

Ah, Sunflower!

Ah, sunflower! weary of time,
Who countest the steps of the sun,
Seeking after that sweet golden clime
Where the traveller's journey is done;

Where the youth pined away with desire,   5
And the pale virgin shrouded in snow,
Arise from their graves and aspire
Where my sunflower wishes to go.

The Lily

The modest rose puts forth a thorn,
The humble sheep a threat'ning horn;
While the lily white shall in love delight,
Nor a thorn nor a threat stain her beauty bright.

The Garden of Love

I went to the Garden of Love
And saw what I never had seen:
A chapel was built in the midst
Where I used to play on the green.[1]

And the gates of this chapel were shut,   5
And 'Thou shalt not' writ over the door;
So I turned to the Garden of Love
That so many sweet flowers bore,

And I saw it was filled with graves
And tombstones where flowers should be;   10
And priests in black gowns were walking their rounds,
And binding with briars my joys and desires.

THE GARDEN OF LOVE
[1] A *chapel . . . green* possibly, though not necessarily, a reference to the building of a chapel on South Lambeth green in 1793. Members of the congregation were required to pay for their places.

The Little Vagabond

Dear mother, dear mother, the church is cold
But the alehouse is healthy and pleasant and warm;
Besides I can tell where I am used well –
Such usage in heaven will never do well.

But if at the church they would give us some ale,   5
And a pleasant fire our souls to regale,
We'd sing and we'd pray all the livelong day,
Nor ever once wish from the church to stray.

Then the parson might preach and drink and sing,
And we'd be as happy as birds in the spring;   10
And modest Dame Lurch, who is always at church,
Would not have bandy[1] children nor fasting nor birch.

And God, like a father rejoicing to see
His children as pleasant and happy as he,
Would have no more quarrel with the devil or the barrel,   15
But kiss him and give him both drink and apparel.

London

I wander through each chartered[1] street
Near where the chartered Thames does flow,
And mark in every face I meet
Marks of weakness, marks of woe.

In every cry of every man,   5
In every infant's cry of fear,
In every voice, in every ban,   *– curse*
The mind-forged manacles[2] I hear.   *handcuffs*

How the chimney-sweeper's cry
Every black'ning church appals,   10
And the hapless soldier's sigh
Runs in blood down palace walls.

But most through midnight streets I hear
How the youthful harlot's curse
Blasts the new born infant's tear,   15
And blights with plagues the marriage hearse.[3]

oxymoronic

THE LITTLE VAGABOND
[1] *bandy* bandy legs are a symptom of rickets, caused by vitamin deficiency.

LONDON
[1] *chartered* mapped, but also owned by corporations (by the terms of a charter).

[2] *mind-forged manacles* the original MS reading is 'German-forged links' – a reference to the House of Hanover, which provided Britain with its monarchs.
[3] *blights with plagues the marriage hearse* apparently a reference to the passing on of VD by mothers to their children. A feminist view might be that the profligate husband has passed VD to his wife.

The Human Abstract[1]

Pity would be no more
If we did not make somebody poor;
And mercy no more could be,
If all were as happy as we.

And mutual fear brings peace   5
Till the selfish loves increase;
Then Cruelty knits a snare
And spreads his baits with care.

He sits down with holy fears
And waters the ground with tears;   10
Then humility takes its root
Underneath his foot.

Soon spreads the dismal shade
Of mystery over his head,
And the caterpillar and fly   15
Feed on the mystery.

And it bears the fruit of deceit,
Ruddy and sweet to eat;
And the raven his nest has made
In its thickest shade.   20

The gods of the earth and sea
Sought through nature to find this tree,
But their search was all in vain –
There grows one in the human brain.

Infant Sorrow

My mother groaned, my father wept!
Into the dangerous world I leapt:
Helpless, naked, piping loud
Like a fiend hid in a cloud.

Struggling in my father's hands,   5
Striving against my swaddling bands,
Bound and weary I thought best
To sulk upon my mother's breast.

A Poison Tree

I was angry with my friend;
I told my wrath, my wrath did end.
I was angry with my foe;
I told it not, my wrath did grow.

THE HUMAN ABSTRACT
[1]   This song is a counterpart of *The Divine Image* in *Songs of Innocence*.

And I watered it in fears,   5
Night and morning with my tears;
And I sunned it with smiles,
And with soft deceitful wiles.

And it grew both day and night
Till it bore an apple bright;   10
And my foe beheld it shine,
And he knew that it was mine.

And into my garden stole
When the night had veiled the pole –
In the morning glad I see   15
My foe outstretched beneath the tree.

A Little Boy Lost

'Nought loves another as itself,
Nor venerates another so,
Nor is it possible to thought
A greater than itself to know.

idea on society?

And, father, how can I love you   5
Or any of my brothers more?
I love you like the little bird
That picks up crumbs around the door.'

The priest sat by and heard the child,
In trembling zeal he seized his hair;   10
He led him by his little coat
And all admired the priestly care.

And standing on the altar high,
'Lo, what a fiend is here!' said he,
'One who sets reason up for judge   15
Of our most holy mystery.'

The weeping child could not be heard,
The weeping parents wept in vain;
They stripped him to his little shirt
And bound him in an iron chain,   20

And burned him in a holy place
Where many had been burned before.
The weeping parents wept in vain –
Are such things done on Albion's shore?

A Little Girl Lost

Children of the future age
Reading this indignant page,
Know that in a former time
Love, sweet love, was thought a crime.

In the age of gold,   5
Free from winter's cold,
Youth and maiden bright
To the holy light,
Naked in the sunny beams delight.

Once a youthful pair   10
Filled with softest care
Met in garden bright
Where the holy light
Had just removed the curtains of the night.

There in rising day   15
On the grass they play;
Parents were afar,
Strangers came not near,
And the maiden soon forgot her fear.

Tired with kisses sweet,   20
They agree to meet
When the silent sleep
Waves o'er heavens deep,
And the weary tired wanderers weep.

To her father white   25
Came the maiden bright,
But his loving look,
Like the holy book
All her tender limbs with terror shook.

'Ona, pale and weak,   30
To thy father speak! –
Oh, the trembling fear!
Oh, the dismal care
That shakes the blossoms of my hoary hair!'

To Tirzah[1]

Whate'er is born of mortal birth
Must be consumed with the earth
To rise from generation free;
Then what have I to do with thee?

The sexes sprung from shame and pride –   5
Blowed in the morn, in evening died;
But mercy changed death into sleep –
The sexes rose to work and weep.

Thou mother of my mortal part,
With cruelty didst mould my heart   10

To TIRZAH
[1]   This poem does not appear in early copies of the *Songs*.
Tirzah was the first capital of the northern kingdom of Israel,
a counterpart of Jerusalem in the south; cf. Song of Solomon
6:4: 'Thou art beautiful, O my love, as Tirzah, comely as
Jerusalem, terrible as an army with banners'. See also Num-
bers 27:1–11; Blake associated Tirzah with the fallen realm of
the senses, a power that confines humanity within a vision of
the human body as finite and corrupt.

And with false self-deceiving tears
Didst bind my nostrils, eyes and ears;

Didst close my tongue in senseless clay
And me to mortal life betray:
The death of Jesus set me free –   15
Then what have I to do with thee?[2]
          It is raised
              a spiritual body[3]

The Schoolboy[1]

I love to rise in a summer morn
When the birds sing on every tree;
The distant huntsman winds his horn,
And the skylark sings with me –
Oh, what sweet company!   5

But to go to school in a summer morn,
Oh, it drives all joy away;
Under a cruel eye outworn,
The little ones spend the day
In sighing and dismay.   10

Ah! then at times I drooping sit
And spend many an anxious hour;
Nor in my book can I take delight,
Nor sit in learning's bower,
Worn through with the dreary shower.   15

How can the bird that is born for joy
Sit in a cage and sing?
How can a child, when fears annoy,
But droop his tender wing
And forget his youthful spring?   20

Oh, father and mother, if buds are nipped
And blossoms blown away,
And if the tender plants are stripped
Of their joy in the springing day
By sorrow and care's dismay,   25

How shall the summer arise in joy
Or the summer fruits appear?
Or how shall we gather what griefs destroy,
Or bless the mellowing year
When the blasts of winter appear?   30

---

[2] *Then what . . . thee* cf. Jesus to his mother, John 2:4: 'what have I to do with thee? Mine hour is not yet come'.
[3] *It is . . . body* On Blake's plate, these words appear on the garment of an old man ministering to a dead body; they come from I Corinthians 15:44: 'It is sown a natural body; it is raised a spiritual body.'

THE SCHOOLBOY
[1] This song was originally included in *Songs of Innocence.*

The Voice of the Ancient Bard[I]

Youth of delight, come hither
And see the opening morn –
Image of truth new-born;
Doubt is fled, and clouds of reason,
Dark disputes and artful teasing.   5
Folly is an endless maze,
Tangled roots perplex her ways –
How many have fallen there!
They stumble all night over bones of the dead,
And feel they know not what but care,   10
And wish to lead others, when they should be led.

A Divine Image[I]

Cruelty has a human heart
And jealousy a human face;
Terror the human form divine,
And secrecy the human dress.

The human dress is forged iron,   5
The human form a fiery forge,
The human face a furnace sealed,
The human heart its hungry gorge.

The Marriage of Heaven and Hell[I] (1790)[2]

[Plate 2]

The Argument

Rintrah[3] roars and shakes his fires in the burdened air;[4]
Hungry clouds swag[5] on the deep.

Once meek, and in a perilous path,
The just man kept his course along
The vale of death;   5
Roses are planted where thorns grow,
And on the barren heath
Sing the honey bees.

THE VOICE OF THE ANCIENT BARD
[I] This song was originally included in *Songs of Innocence*.

A DIVINE IMAGE
[I] This poem is known to us only through a print made after
Blake's death; it appears in one copy of the *Songs*, and was not
usually included in the volume. It was apparently composed as
a counterpart to *The Divine Image* in *Songs of Innocence*.

THE MARRIAGE OF HEAVEN AND HELL
[I] Blake's title alludes to two of Swedenborg's: *De coelo . . . et
de inferno* and *De amore conjugali* (*A Treatise Concerning Heaven
and Hell* and *Marital Love*). Emanuel Swedenborg

(1688–1772) was a Swedish mystic whose works prophesying
the end of the world Blake read, admired but, at the time of
writing, rejected (see headnote).
[2] Various datings have been suggested over the years, but
the editors of the Blake Trust/Tate Gallery edition settle on
1790; see Blake, *Early Illuminated Books*, Blake Trust Editions,
113–15.
[3] *Rintrah* the just wrath of the prophet, presaging revolu-
tion.
[4] *Rintrah . . . air* cf. Amos 1:2: 'The Lord will roar from
Zion, and utter his voice from Jerusalem'.
[5] *swag* sway, sag.

Then the perilous path was planted;
And a river, and a spring   10
On every cliff and tomb;
And on the bleached bones[6]
Red clay[7] brought forth.

Till the villain left the paths of ease
To walk in perilous paths, and drive   15
The just man into barren climes.

Now the sneaking serpent walks
In mild humility
And the just man rages in the wilds
Where lions roam.   20

Rintrah roars and shakes his fires in the burdened air;
Hungry clouds swag on the deep.

[Plate 3]

As a new heaven is begun, and it is now thirty-three years since its advent, the eternal hell revives.[8] And lo! Swedenborg[9] is the angel sitting at the tomb; his writings are the linen clothes folded up.[10] Now is the dominion of Edom[11] and the return of Adam into paradise (see Isaiah 34 and 35).[12]

Without contraries is no progression. Attraction and repulsion, reason and energy, love and hate, are necessary to human existence.[13]

From these contraries spring what the religious call good and evil. Good is the passive that obeys reason. Evil is the active springing from energy.[14]

Good is heaven; evil is hell.

[Plate 4]

The Voice of the Devil

All Bibles or sacred codes have been the causes of the following errors:
1. That man has two real existing principles, viz. a body and a soul.
2. That energy,[15] called evil, is alone from the body, and that reason, called good, is alone from the soul.
3. That God will torment man in eternity for following his energies.

But the following contraries to these are true:

---

[6] *bleached bones* a valley of dry bones symbolizes the exiled 'house of Israel', Ezekiel 37:3–4.

[7] *Red clay* sometimes taken to mean Adam, the first man, formed from the dust of the ground.

[8] *As a new heaven . . . revives* In 1790 it was thirty-three years since 1757, the year of the Swedenborgian Last Judgement, and, coincidentally, of Blake's birth. Christ was thirty-three at the time of his crucifixion and resurrection. Thus, Blake identifies his lifetime with Christ's and the eternal hell resurrected.

[9] See note 1 above.

[10] *his writings . . . folded up* Jesus's body was wrapped in a linen shroud, laid in a sepulchre, and closed with a rock (Mark 15:46). When three women came to anoint the body, they found the stone rolled aside, and the body gone.

[11] *Edom* Esau, cheated of his birthright by his brother Jacob (Genesis 25:29–34); his dominion is foreseen by his father,

Isaac (Genesis 27:40). The dominion of Edom is a time when the just man has restored to him what is his due – effectively, a time of revolution.

[12] *Isaiah 34 and 35* Isaiah 34 prophesies the 'day of the Lord's vengeance' against the enemies of Israel; Isaiah 35 concerns the restoration of power to Israel. Blake may have interpreted them as being about the French Revolution.

[13] *Without contraries . . . existence* a satire on Swedenborg's theory of correspondence and equilibrium. For detailed discussion see Blake, *Early Illuminated Books* 120–2.

[14] *Good is . . . energy* cf. Blake's marginalia in Lavater's *Aphorisms*: 'Active evil is better than passive good'.

[15] *energy* a term associated with revolutionary action, particularly in discussions of current events in revolutionary France; Burke commented on 'this dreadful and portentous energy' in 1790.

1. Man has no body distinct from his soul, for that called body is a portion of soul discerned by the five senses (the chief inlets of soul in this age).
2. Energy is the only life and is from the body, and reason is the bound or outward circumference of energy.
3. Energy is eternal delight.

[Plate 5]

Those who restrain desire do so because theirs is weak enough to be restrained; and the restrainer (or reason) usurps its place and governs the unwilling.

And, being restrained, it by degrees becomes passive, till it is only the shadow of desire.

The history of this is written in *Paradise Lost*, and the governor (or reason) is called Messiah.

And the original archangel, or possessor of the command of the heavenly host, is called the Devil, or Satan, and his children are called Sin and Death.[16]

But in the Book of Job, Milton's Messiah is called Satan.[17]

For this history has been adopted by both parties.

It indeed appeared to Reason as if Desire was cast out. But the Devil's account is that the Messi-
[Plate 6] -ah fell, and formed a heaven of what he stole from the abyss.

This is shown in the gospel, where he prays to the Father to send the comforter, or Desire,[18] that Reason may have ideas to build on, the Jehovah of the Bible being no other than he who dwells in flaming fire.

Know that after Christ's death he became Jehovah.

But in Milton the Father is destiny, the Son a ratio of the five senses, and the Holy Ghost vacuum!

Note: The reason Milton wrote in fetters when he wrote of angels and God, and at liberty when of devils and hell, is because he was a true poet and of the Devil's party without knowing it.

A Memorable Fancy[19] [The Five Senses]

As I was walking among the fires of hell,[20] delighted with the enjoyments of genius (which to angels look like torment and insanity), I collected some of their proverbs, thinking that as the sayings used in a nation mark its character, so the proverbs of hell show the nature of infernal wisdom better than any description of buildings or garments.

When I came home,[21] on the abyss of the five senses, where a flat-sided steep frowns over the present world,[22] I saw a mighty devil[23] folded in black clouds, hovering on the sides of the rock. With cor- [Plate 7] -roding fires[24] he wrote the following sentence, now perceived by the minds of men, and read by them on earth:

How do you know but ev'ry bird that cuts the airy way
Is an immense world of delight, closed by your senses five?[25]

---

[16]   *The history ... Death* a deliberate inversion of the plan of Milton's poem, by which it becomes the story of how desire and energy are usurped by restraint and reason. Blake casts Jesus as Reason, and Satan as the hero. Satan's daughter, Sin, is born from his head, and Death arises from their incest (*Paradise Lost* ii 745ff).

[17]   *But in the Book ... Satan* In Job, Satan accuses and torments Job (as God's agent); likewise, 'Milton's Messiah' accuses and torments Adam and Eve.

[18]   *This is shown ... Desire* a reference to John 14:16–17, 26, where Jesus tells his disciples that he will pray to the 'Father' to 'give you another Comforter', which is 'the Spirit of truth' and 'the Holy Ghost'.

[19]   The *Memorable Fancy* parodies Swedenborg's 'Memorable Relations', short tales used to underline particular ideas.

[20]   *As I was walking ... hell* parodic of Swedenborg's excursions in the spiritual world.

[21]   *home* various interpretations have been suggested: the world of daily business; Blake's workshop; or England.

[22]   *on the abyss ... world* In Blake's metaphor the abyss is the head, where all five senses are located, and the cliff is the face.

[23]   *a mighty devil* Blake himself, who has hell inside his head. He sees himself reflected in the copper plate.

[24]   *With corroding fires* acids; Blake etched sentences into copper plates with acids.

[25]   *How do you know ... five* an echo of Chatterton, *Bristowe Tragedie, or the Dethe of Syr Charles Bawdin* (1768): 'How dydd I knowe thatt ev'ry darte / That cutte the airie waie / Myghte nott fynde passage toe my harte / And close myne eyes for aie?'

Proverbs of Hell

In seed-time learn, in harvest teach, in winter enjoy.

Drive your cart and your plough over the bones of the dead.

The road of excess leads to the palace of wisdom.

Prudence is a rich ugly old maid courted by Incapacity.

He who desires but acts not breeds pestilence.

The cut worm forgives the plough.

Dip him in the river who loves water.

A fool sees not the same tree that a wise man sees.

He whose face gives no light shall never become a star.

Eternity is in love with the productions of time.

The busy bee has no time for sorrow.

The hours of folly are measured by the clock, but of wisdom no clock can measure.

All wholesome food is caught without a net or a trap.

Bring out number, weight and measure in a year of dearth.

No bird soars too high, if he soars with his own wings.

A dead body revenges not injuries.

The most sublime act is to set another before you.

If the fool would persist in his folly he would become wise.

Folly is the cloak of knavery.

Shame is pride's cloak.

[Plate 8]

Prisons are built with stones of Law, brothels with bricks of Religion.

The pride of the peacock is the glory of God.

The lust of the goat is the bounty of God.

The wrath of the lion is the wisdom of God.

The nakedness of woman is the work of God.

Excess of sorrow laughs; excess of joy weeps.

The roaring of lions, the howling of wolves, the raging of the stormy sea, and the destructive sword, are portions of eternity too great for the eye of man.

The fox condemns the trap, not himself.

Joys impregnate; sorrows bring forth.

Let man wear the fell[26] of the lion, woman the fleece of the sheep.

The bird a nest, the spider a web, man friendship.

The selfish smiling fool and the sullen frowning fool shall be both thought wise, that they may be a rod.

What is now proved, was once only imagined.

The rat, the mouse, the fox, the rabbit, watch the roots; the lion, the tiger, the horse, the elephant, watch the fruits.

The cistern contains; the fountain overflows.

One thought fills immensity.

Always be ready to speak your mind, and a base man will avoid you.

Everything possible to be believed is an image of truth.

The eagle never lost so much time as when he submitted to learn of the crow.

[Plate 9]

The fox provides for himself, but God provides for the lion.

Think in the morning, act in the noon, eat in the evening, sleep in the night.

He who has suffered you to impose on him knows you.

As the plough follows words, so God rewards prayers.

---

[26] *fell* skin.

The tigers of wrath are wiser than the horses of instruction.

Expect poison from the standing water.

You never know what is enough, unless you know what is more than enough.

Listen to the fool's reproach! It is a kingly title!

The eyes of fire, the nostrils of air, the mouth of water, the beard of earth.

The weak in courage is strong in cunning.

The apple tree never asks the beech how he shall grow; nor the lion, the horse how he shall take his prey.

The thankful receiver bears a plentiful harvest.

If others had not been foolish we should be so.

The soul of sweet delight can never be defiled.

When thou seest an eagle, thou seest a portion of genius – lift up thy head!

As the caterpillar chooses the fairest leaves to lay her eggs on, so the priest lays his curse on the fairest joys.

To create a little flower is the labour of ages.

'Damn!' braces; 'Bless!' relaxes.

The best wine is the oldest, the best water the newest.

Prayers plough not; praises reap not.

Joys laugh not; sorrows weep not.

[Plate 10]

The head sublime, the heart pathos, the genitals beauty, the hands and feet proportion.

As the air to a bird, or the sea to a fish, so is contempt to the contemptible.

The crow wished everything was black; the owl, that everything was white.

Exuberance is beauty.

If the lion was advised by the fox, he would be cunning.

Improvement makes straight roads, but the crooked roads without improvement are roads of genius.

Sooner murder an infant in its cradle than nurse unacted desires.

Where man is not, nature is barren.

Truth can never be told so as to be understood, and not be believed.

   Enough! or too much!

[Plate 11]

   The ancient poets animated all sensible objects with gods or geniuses, calling them by the names and adorning them with the properties of woods, rivers, mountains, lakes, cities, nations, and whatever their enlarged and numerous senses could perceive.

   And particularly they studied the genius of each city and country, placing it under its mental deity.

   Till a system was formed, which some took advantage of, and enslaved the vulgar by attempting to realize or abstract the mental deities from their objects: thus began priesthood.

   Choosing forms of worship from poetic tales.

   And at length they pronounced that the gods had ordered such things.

   Thus men forgot that all deities reside in the human breast.

[Plate 12]

A Memorable Fancy [Isiah and Ezekiel]

The prophets Isaiah and Ezekiel dined with me, and I asked them how they dared so roundly to assert that God spake to them, and whether they did not think at the time that they would be misunderstood, and so be the cause of imposition?

   Isaiah answered, 'I saw no god, nor heard any, in a finite organical perception.[27] But my senses

---

[27] *I saw no god ... perception* though appropriated for the priesthood by the religious, Isaiah is here reclaimed for the just man. The statement is highly subversive of the Bible, where Isaiah is inclined to say such things as 'Moreover the Lord said unto me' (Isaiah 8:1).

discovered the infinite in everything, and, as I was then persuaded, and remain confirmed, that the voice of honest indignation[28] is the voice of God, I cared not for consequences, but wrote.'

Then I asked, 'Does a firm persuasion that a thing is so, make it so?'

He replied, 'All poets believe that it does, and in ages of imagination this firm persuasion removed mountains;[29] but many are not capable of a firm persuasion of anything.'

Then Ezekiel said, 'The philosophy of the east taught the first principles of human perception. Some nations held one principle for the origin and some another. We of Israel taught that the Poetic Genius (as you now call it) was the first principle and all the others merely derivative, which was the cause of our despising the priests and philosophers of other countries, and prophesying that all gods would [Plate 13] at last be proved to originate in ours and to be the tributaries of the Poetic Genius. It was this that our great poet King David[30] desired so fervently, and invokes so pathetic'ly,[31] saying by this he conquers enemies and governs kingdoms. And we so loved our God that we cursed in his name all the deities of surrounding nations,[32] and asserted that they had rebelled. From these opinions the vulgar came to think that all nations would at last be subject to the Jews.

'This', said he, 'like all firm persuasions, is come to pass, for all nations believe the Jews' code and worship the Jews' God, and what greater subjection can be?'

I heard this with some wonder, and must confess my own conviction. After dinner I asked Isaiah to favour the world with his lost works; he said none of equal value was lost. Ezekiel said the same of his.

I also asked Isaiah what made him go naked and barefoot three years. He answered, 'The same that made our friend, Diogenes the Grecian.'[33]

I then asked Ezekiel why he ate dung, and lay so long on his right and left side.[34] He answered, 'The desire of raising other men into a perception of the infinite. This the North American tribes practise, and is he honest who resists his genius or conscience only for the sake of present ease or gratification?'

[Plate 14]

The ancient tradition that the world will be consumed in fire at the end of six thousand years is true,[35] as I have heard from hell.

For the cherub with his flaming sword is hereby commanded to leave his guard at the tree of life;[36] and when he does, the whole creation will be consumed and appear infinite and holy, whereas it now appears finite and corrupt.

This will come to pass by an improvement of sensual enjoyment.

But first the notion that man has a body distinct from his soul is to be expunged. This I shall do by printing in the infernal method, by corrosives[37] which in hell are salutary and medicinal, melting apparent surfaces away, and displaying the infinite which was hid.

If the doors of perception were cleansed, everything would appear to man as it is: infinite.

For man has closed himself up till he sees all things through narrow chinks of his cavern.

---

28 *honest indignation* at, for instance, social or political injustice. In the Bible indignation is attributed, by contrast, to God: 'his lips are full of indignation' (Isaiah 30:27).

29 *removed mountains* an allusion to Jesus, who withers a fig tree with his words, and tells his disciples, 'if ye have faith, and doubt not . . . if ye shall say unto this mountain, Be thou removed, and be thou cast into the sea; it shall be done' (Matthew 21:21).

30 *our great poet King David* second king of Judah and Israel, author of the Psalms.

31 *pathetic'ly* movingly.

32 *And we so loved . . . nations* ironic; Isaiah and Ezekiel curse the deities of other nations, and predict their destruction (Isaiah 19, Ezekiel 29–32).

33 *Diogenes the Grecian* Greek philosopher of the Cynic school (d. 320 BC), said to have wandered through Athens with a lantern searching for one honest person; also said to have lived in a barrel.

34 *I then asked Ezekiel . . . side* Ezekiel lay 390 days on his left side, 40 on his right. He did not eat dung but cooked with it (Ezekiel 4).

35 *The ancient tradition . . . true* In the fashion of Swedenborg, Blake predicts the end of the world. It was widely believed, at the end of the eighteenth century, that the 6,000-year lifespan of the world was about to end.

36 *For the cherub . . . life* at Genesis 3:22, 24, cherubims are commanded to guard the way of the tree of life with a flaming sword.

37 *corrosives* Blake's printing technique involved the use of acid.

[Plate 15]

A *Memorable Fancy*[38] [A Printing-House in Hell]

I was in a printing-house in hell and saw the method in which knowledge is transmitted from generation to generation.

In the first chamber was a dragon-man, clearing away the rubbish from a cave's mouth; within, a number of dragons were hollowing the cave.

In the second chamber was a viper[39] folding round the rock and the cave, and others adorning it with gold, silver, and precious stones.

In the third chamber was an eagle with wings and feathers of air[40] – he caused the inside of the cave to be infinite; around were numbers of eagle-like men, who built palaces in the immense cliffs.

In the fourth chamber were lions of flaming fire, raging around and melting the metals into living fluids.

In the fifth chamber were unnamed forms which cast the metals into the expanse.[41]

There they were received by men who occupied the sixth chamber, and took the forms of books and were arranged in libraries.

[Plate 16]

The giants who formed this world into its sensual existence and now seem to live in it in chains are, in truth, the causes of its life and the sources of all activity.[42] But the chains are the cunning of weak and tame minds, which have power to resist energy. According to the proverb, the weak in courage is strong in cunning.

Thus one portion of being is the prolific; the other, the devouring. To the devourer it seems as if the producer was in his chains, but it is not so: he only takes portions of existence and fancies that the whole.

But the prolific would cease to be prolific unless the devourer, as a sea, received the excess of his delights.

Some will say, 'Is not God alone the prolific?' I answer, 'God only acts and is in existing beings or men.'

These two classes of men are always upon earth, and they should be enemies; whoever tries [Plate 17] to reconcile them seeks to destroy existence.

Religion is an endeavour to reconcile the two.

Note: Jesus Christ did not wish to unite, but to separate them (as in the parable of sheep and goats),[43] and he says, 'I came not to send peace, but a sword.'[44]

Messiah or Satan or Tempter was formerly thought to be one of the antediluvians who are our energies.

A *Memorable Fancy*[45] [The Vanity of Angels]

An angel came to me and said, 'Oh, pitiable foolish young man! Oh, horrible! Oh, dreadful state! Consider the hot burning dungeon thou art preparing for thyself to all eternity, to which thou art going in such career.'

---

[38]   This memorable fancy picks up the metaphor of body as cave, in order to show how the 'doors of perception' can be cleansed by 'a printing-house in hell' with five chambers (one for each sense) and a sixth where men receive the products of the first five. The printing-house produces imaginative ('infernal') thoughts.

[39]   *viper* perhaps a brush or pen, or the lines made by such implements.

[40]   *feathers of air* Blake used feathers in his printing process, perhaps to stir the acid over his plates.

[41]   *cast the metals . . . expanse* probably copper plates 'cast . . . into the expanse' of paper, during the printing process.

[42]   *The giants . . . activity* By contrast, Swedenborg condemned the antediluvian giants at Genesis 6:4 for self-love and sensuality.

[43]   Matthew 25:32–3.

[44]   Matthew 10:34. See also Luke 12:51, where Jesus asks: 'Suppose ye that I am come to give peace on earth? I tell you, nay; but rather division'.

[45]   This memorable fancy is based on an episode in Swedenborg's *Conjugal Love* in which an angel shows a young man various contrary visions by alternately opening his internal, and closing his external sight. Blake satirizes Swedenborg by giving his narrator the energy and wisdom to challenge his angelic guide.

I said, 'Perhaps you will be willing to show me my eternal lot, and we will contemplate together upon it and see whether your lot or mine is most desirable.'

So he took me through a stable, and through a church, and down into the church-vault, at the end of which was a mill.[46] Through the mill we went, and came to a cave. Down the winding cavern we groped our tedious way, till a void, boundless as a nether sky, appeared beneath us, and we held by the roots of trees and hung over this immensity. But I said, 'If you please, we will commit ourselves to this void, and see whether providence is here also; if you will not, I will'. But he answered, 'Do not presume, oh young man; but as we here remain, behold thy lot which will soon appear when the darkness passes away.'

So I remained with him, sitting in the twisted [Plate 18] root of an oak. He was suspended in a fungus which hung with the head downward into the deep.

By degrees we beheld the infinite abyss,[47] fiery as the smoke of a burning city; beneath us, at an immense distance, was the sun, black but shining; round it were fiery tracks on which revolved vast spiders, crawling after their prey, which flew, or rather swum, in the infinite deep, in the most terrific shapes of animals sprung from corruption. And the air was full of them, and seemed composed of them. These are devils, and are called Powers of the Air. I now asked my companion which was my eternal lot. He said, 'Between the black and white spiders.'[48]

But now, from between the black and white spiders, a cloud and fire burst and rolled through the deep, black'ning all beneath so that the nether deep grew black as a sea, and rolled with a terrible noise. Beneath us was nothing now to be seen but a black tempest, till, looking east[49] between the clouds and the waves, we saw a cataract of blood mixed with fire; and, not many stones' throw from us, appeared and sunk again the scaly fold of a monstrous serpent. At last, to the east, distant about three degrees,[50] appeared a fiery crest above the waves. Slowly it reared, like a ridge of golden rocks, till we discovered two globes of crimson fire from which the sea fled away in clouds of smoke. And now we saw it was the head of Leviathan.[51] His forehead was divided into streaks of green and purple, like those on a tiger's forehead; soon we saw his mouth and red gills hang just above the raging foam, tinging the black deep with beams of blood, advancing toward us [Plate 19] with all the fury of a spiritual existence.

My friend the angel climbed up from his station into the mill; I remained alone, and then this appearance was no more, but I found myself sitting on a pleasant bank beside a river by moonlight, hearing a harper who sung to the harp.[52] And his theme was, 'The man who never alters his opinion is like standing water, and breeds reptiles of the mind.'

But I arose and sought for the mill, and there I found my angel, who, surprised, asked me how I escaped.

I answered, 'All that we saw was owing to your metaphysics. For when you ran away, I found myself on a bank by moonlight hearing a harper. But now we have seen my eternal lot, shall I show you yours?' He laughed at my proposal, but I by force suddenly caught him in my arms, and flew westerly through the night, till we were elevated above the earth's shadow.[53] Then I flung myself with him directly into the body of the sun; here I clothed myself in white, and, taking in my hand Swedenborg's volumes, sunk from the glorious clime, and passed all the planets till we came to Saturn. Here I stayed to rest, and then leaped into the void between Saturn and the fixed stars.[54]

---

46 *So he took me ... mill* The church is entered through a stable of rationalism and leads to the mill of mechanistic philosophy that Blake so thoroughly despised (see *All Religions are One* and *There is No Natural Religion*, pp. 55–6).

47 *the infinite abyss* presumably hell.

48 *Between the black and white spiders* In Swedenborgian terms, an existence between false reasoners, perhaps between false contraries such as good and evil.

49 *east* In Swedenborg the Lord is always 'to the east'.

50 *distant ... degrees* Paris, centre of the French Revolution, is three degrees in longitude from London.

51 *Leviathan* huge sea-dragon associated with eclipses of sun and moon, who threatens the natural order; see Isaiah 27:1

and Revelation 13:2, for instance. Blake probably has in mind the prophecy in Revelation that the Leviathan will be cast in a pit for a thousand years before being loosed – effectively turning him into a version of the just man whose time has come (Revelation 11:7; 20:1–3).

52 *and then this ... harp* the abrupt transition mimics, and to some extent parodies, that at Revelation 13–14, where the vision of the beast suddenly gives way to a vision of the Lamb where John hears 'the voice of harpers harping with their harps' (Revelation 14:2–3).

53 *I by force ... shadow* a parody of Swedenborgian space travel.

54 *into the void ... stars* i.e. into an intellectual vacuum.

'Here', said I, 'is your lot – in this space (if space it may be called).'[55] Soon we saw the stable and the church, and I took him to the altar, and opened the Bible, and lo! it was a deep pit, into which I descended, driving the angel before me. Soon we saw seven houses of brick.[56] One we entered; in it were a [Plate 20] number of monkeys, baboons, and all of that species, chained by the middle, grinning and snatching at one another, but withheld by the shortness of their chains. However, I saw that they sometimes grew numerous, and then the weak were caught by the strong, and, with a grinning aspect, first coupled with, and then devoured, by plucking off first one limb and then another, till the body was left a helpless trunk. This, after grinning and kissing it with seeming fondness, they devoured too. And here and there I saw one savourily picking the flesh off of his own tail. As the stench terribly annoyed us both, we went into the mill, and I in my hand brought the skeleton of a body, which in the mill was Aristotle's *Analytics*.[57]

So the angel said, 'Thy fantasy has imposed upon me and thou oughtest to be ashamed.'

I answered, 'We impose on one another, and it is but lost time to converse with you whose works are only analytics.'

Opposition is true friendship.

[Plate 21]

I have always found that angels have the vanity to speak of themselves as the only wise; this they do with a confident insolence sprouting from systematic reasoning.

Thus Swedenborg boasts that what he writes is new, though it is only the contents or index of already published books.

A man carried a monkey about for a show, and, because he was a little wiser than the monkey, grew vain, and conceived himself as much wiser than seven men. It is so with Swedenborg: he shows the folly of churches and exposes hypocrites, till he imagines that all are religious, and himself the single [Plate 22] one on earth that ever broke a net.

Now hear a plain fact: Swedenborg has not written one new truth. Now hear another: he has written all the old falsehoods.

And now hear the reason: he conversed with angels, who are all religious, and conversed not with devils who all hate religion, for he was incapable through his conceited notions.

Thus Swedenborg's writings are a recapitulation of all superficial opinions, and an analysis of the more sublime – but no further.

Have now another plain fact: any man of mechanical talents may, from the writings of Paracelsus or Jacob Behmen,[58] produce ten thousand volumes of equal value with Swedenborg's – and, from those of Dante or Shakespeare, an infinite number.

But when he has done this, let him not say that he knows better than his master, for he only holds a candle in sunshine.

A Memorable Fancy [A Devil, My Friend]

Once I saw a devil in a flame of fire, who arose before an angel that sat on a cloud, and the devil uttered these words:

'The worship of God is honouring his gifts in other men, each according to his genius, and loving the [Plate 23] greatest men best. Those who envy or calumniate great men hate God, for there is no other God.'

The angel hearing this became almost blue; but, mastering himself, he grew yellow, and, at last, white, pink and smiling. And then replied:

---

55   *if space it may be called* the phrasing echoes Milton's description of Death (see p. 5).

56   *seven houses of brick* houses in Swedenborg signify states of mind; possibly also a reference to the seven churches of Asia castigated by John, Revelation 1:4.

57   *Analytics* Aristotle wrote two volumes of *Analytics*, which serve to symbolize an inhuman rationality. The transformation from the monkey skeleton parodies similar transformations in Swedenborg.

58   *Paracelsus or Jacob Behmen* Philippus Aureolus Theophrastus Bombastus von Hohenheim, known as Paracelsus (1493–1541), a Swiss-German physician and alchemist; Jakob Boehme (1575–1624), German cobbler and mystic. Blake placed Paracelsus and Boehme alongside Shakespeare in his personal pantheon.

'Thou idolater! Is not God One? And is not he visible in Jesus Christ? And has not Jesus Christ given his sanction to the law of ten commandments, and are not all other men fools, sinners, and nothings?'

The devil answered, 'Bray a fool in a mortar with wheat, yet shall not his folly be beaten out of him.[59] If Jesus Christ is the greatest man, you ought to love him in the greatest degree; now hear how he has given his sanction to the law of ten commandments. Did he not mock at the Sabbath, and so mock the Sabbath's God? Murder those who were murdered because of him? Turn away the law from the woman taken in adultery? Steal the labour of others to support him? Bear false witness when he omitted making a defence before Pilate? Covet when he prayed for his disciples, and when he bid them shake off the dust of their feet against such as refused to lodge them? I tell you, no virtue can exist without breaking these ten commandments: Jesus was all virtue, and acted from impulse [Plate 24] – not from rules.'

When he had so spoken, I beheld the angel who stretched out his arms embracing the flame of fire, and he was consumed and arose as Elijah.[60]

Note: This angel, who is now become a devil, is my particular friend. We often read the Bible together in its infernal or diabolical sense, which the world shall have if they behave well.

I have also the Bible of Hell,[61] which the world shall have whether they will or no.

One law for the lion and ox is oppression.[62]

[Plate 25]

A Song of Liberty

1. The Eternal Female groaned![63] It was heard over all the earth:
2. Albion's[64] coast is sick, silent; the American meadows faint!
3. Shadows of prophecy shiver along by the lakes and the rivers, and mutter across the ocean! France, rend down thy dungeon![65]
4. Golden Spain, burst the barriers of old Rome![66]
5. Cast thy keys,[67] oh Rome, into the deep, down falling, even to eternity down falling,
6. And weep![68]
7. In her trembling hands, she took the new-born terror howling;
8. On those infinite mountains of light now barred out by the Atlantic sea,[69] the new-born fire stood before the starry king![70]
9. Flagged[71] with grey-browed snows and thunderous visages, the jealous wings[72] waved over the deep.
10. The speary hand burned aloft, unbuckled was the shield, forth went the hand of jealousy among the flaming hair, and [Plate 26] hurled the new-born wonder[73] through the starry night.
11. The fire, the fire, is falling!
12. Look up! Look up! Oh, citizen of London, enlarge thy countenance! Oh Jew, leave counting gold, return to thy oil and wine! Oh African, black African! (Go, winged thought, widen his forehead.)[74]

---

59 *Bray a fool . . . him* cf. Proverbs 27:22: 'Though thou shouldest bray [crush] a fool in a mortar among wheat with a pestle, yet will not his foolishness depart from him'.

60 *I beheld . . . Elijah* Elijah is taken up to heaven in a chariot of fire, II Kings 2:11.

61 *the Bible of Hell* possibly a work projected by Blake, which might have included the Proverbs of Hell and *Urizen*.

62 Above this motto in Blake's plate, a bearded man, looking at the reader with an expression of anguish, crawls along the ground on all fours, naked.

63 *The Eternal Female groaned* This momentous birth (of Revolution) heralds an apocalypse.

64 *Albion* England.

65 *France, rend down thy dungeon* The Bastille prison was stormed by the mob, and demolished, in July 1789.

66 *Rome* the Roman Catholic Church.

67 *keys* keys of St Peter, symbolic of papal power.

68 This line originally read: 'And weep and bow thy reverend locks'.

69 *On those . . . sea* the ancient kingdom of Atlantis.

70 *the starry king* Urizen ('your reason'), the primeval priest, in this case the epitome of all oppressive rulers.

71 *Flagged* covered.

72 *the jealous wings* of Urizen; cf. *Earth's Answer* 7 and n. in *Songs of Experience* p. 71.

73 *the new-born wonder* Orc, spirit of revolution.

74 *Oh, citizen . . . forehead* Blake foresees revolution across the world, from England to the Middle East and Africa.

13. The fiery limbs, the flaming hair, shot like the sinking sun into the western sea.

14. Waked from his eternal sleep, the hoary element[75] roaring fled away;

15. Down rushed, beating his wings in vain, the jealous king;[76] his grey-browed counsellors, thunderous warriors, curled veterans, among helms and shields and chariots, horses, elephants, banners, castles, slings and rocks,

16. Falling, rushing, ruining! – buried in the ruins, on Urthona's[77] dens.

17. All night beneath the ruins; then, their sullen flames faded, emerge round the gloomy king.

18. With thunder and fire, leading his starry hosts through the waste wilderness, [Plate 27] he promulgates his ten commands,[78] glancing his beamy eyelids over the deep in dark dismay,

19. Where the son of fire in his eastern cloud, while the morning plumes her golden breast,

20. Spurning the clouds written with curses, stamps the stony law[79] to dust, loosing the eternal horses from the dens of night, crying,

'Empire is no more! And now the lion and wolf shall cease.'[80]

Chorus

Let the priests of the raven of dawn no longer, in deadly black, with hoarse note, curse the sons of joy; nor his accepted brethren (whom, tyrant, he calls free) lay the bound or build the roof; nor pale religious lechery call that virginity that wishes but acts not.

For everything that lives is holy.[81]

Visions of the Daughters of Albion (1793)

[Plate 1]
The eye sees more than the heart knows.[1]

[Plate 3]

The Argument

I loved Theotormon[2]
And I was not ashamed;
I trembled in my virgin fears
And I hid in Leutha's vale!

I plucked Leutha's flower,[3]   5
And I rose up from the vale;
But the terrible thunders tore
My virgin mantle[4] in twain.

---

[75] *the hoary element* the sea, which prepares the way for the re-emergence of Atlantis. The disappearance of the sea is prophesied by John, Revelation 21:1.

[76] *the jealous king* Urizen, who is falling.

[77] Urthona is the creative, imaginative principle.

[78] *ten commands* cf. God's handing down to Moses of the Ten Commandments, Exodus 20.

[79] *the stony law* the Ten Commandments were inscribed on tablets of stone.

[80] *And now ... cease* cf. Isaiah's prophecy of a new heaven and new earth where 'the wolf and the lamb shall feed together' (Isaiah 65:25).

[81] *For everything ... holy* a parodic reversal of Revelation 15:4: 'For thou [God] only art holy: for all nations shall come and worship before thee'.

VISIONS OF THE DAUGHTERS OF ALBION

[1] The motto appears on the poem's title page.

[2] *Theotormon* Blake's coinage; the speaker in the argument is Oothoon, who represents thwarted love. The name Theotormon probably means 'tormented of god' or 'tormented of law'

[3] *I plucked Leutha's flower* symbolic of an attempt to acquire sexual experience. Leutha has a number of sources, including Lutha, a stream in Ossian's *Berrathon*, and Leucothea, goddess of the dawn in Greek myth. Like that of many other Blake characters, her significance is very difficult to pin down and varies depending on the context in which she appears.

[4] *My virgin mantle* the hymen.

[Plate 4]

Visions

Enslaved,[5] the Daughters of Albion[6] weep: a trembling lamentation
Upon their mountains, in their valleys, sighs toward America.   10
For the soft soul of America,[7] Oothoon wandered in woe
Along the vales of Leutha seeking flowers to comfort her;
And thus she spoke to the bright marigold of Leutha's vale:
  'Art thou a flower? Art thou a nymph? I see thee now a flower,
Now a nymph! I dare not pluck thee from thy dewy bed!'   15
  The golden nymph replied, 'Pluck thou my flower, Oothoon the mild;
Another flower shall spring, because the soul of sweet delight
Can never pass away.' She ceased and closed her golden shrine.
  Then Oothoon plucked the flower, saying, 'I pluck thee from thy bed,
Sweet flower, and put thee here to glow between my breasts;[8]   20
And thus I turn my face to where my whole soul seeks.'
Over the waves she went in winged exulting swift delight,
And over Theotormon's reign[9] took her impetuous course.
  Bromion rent her with his thunders.[10] On his stormy bed
Lay the faint maid, and soon her woes appalled his thunders hoarse.   25
Bromion spoke: 'Behold this harlot here on Bromion's bed,
And let the jealous dolphins[11] sport around the lovely maid.
Thy soft American plains are mine, and mine thy north and south.
Stamped with my signet are the swarthy children of the sun —[12]
They are obedient, they resist not, they obey the scourge;   30
Their daughters worship terrors and obey the violent.
[Plate 5]
Now thou may'st marry Bromion's harlot, and protect the child
Of Bromion's rage that Oothoon shall put forth in nine moons' time.'
  Then storms rent Theotormon's limbs; he rolled his waves around
And folded his black jealous waters round the adulterate pair.   35
Bound back to back in Bromion's caves,[13] terror and meekness dwell.
At entrance Theotormon sits wearing the threshold hard
With secret tears; beneath him sound like waves on a desert shore
The voice of slaves beneath the sun, and children bought with money
That shiver in religious caves beneath the burning fires   40
Of lust, that belch incessant from the summits of the earth.
Oothoon weeps not – she cannot weep! Her tears are locked up
But she can howl incessant writhing her soft snowy limbs,
And calling Theotormon's eagles to prey upon her flesh.[14]
   'I call with holy voice, kings of the sounding air!   45
Rend away this defiled bosom that I may reflect

---

5 *Enslaved* Wollstonecraft had described women as 'the slaves of injustice'.
6 *Albion* England.
7 America has been 'raped' by European exploitation.
8 *between my breasts* In Homer's *Iliad*, Juno places the 'bridle' (girdle) of Venus between her breasts as a sign of sexual awakening.
9 *Theotormon's reign* the sea.
10 *Bromion . . . thunders* On her way to her beloved Theotormon, Oothoon is raped by Bromion. Bromion also embodies the cruelty of slave owners (lines 29–30). His name means 'roarer' or 'thunderer' in Greek.

11 *jealous dolphins* representative of the feelings of Theotormon, who Bromion is addressing.
12 *Stamped . . . sun* newly-bought slaves were branded with their owner's name.
13 *Bound back to back . . . caves* Oothoon and Bromion are bound back to back in Theotormon's cave, while he guards its entrance. This is depicted in one of the most famous and impressive of Blake's illustrations (see Blake, *Early Illuminated Books* 268–9).
14 *And calling . . . flesh* When Zeus chained Prometheus on the mountain top (when he refused to reveal the prophecy of Zeus's fall), an eagle preyed on Prometheus's liver.

The image of Theotormon on my pure transparent breast.'
The eagles at her call descend and rend their bleeding prey:
Theotormon severely smiles – her soul reflects the smile
As the clear spring mudded with feet of beasts grows pure and smiles.   50
The Daughters of Albion hear her woes, and echo back her sighs.
   'Why does my Theotormon sit weeping upon the threshold,
And Oothoon hovers by his side, persuading him in vain?[15]
I cry, "Arise, oh Theotormon, for the village dog
Barks at the breaking day; the nightingale has done lamenting;   55
The lark does rustle in the ripe corn, and the eagle returns
From nightly prey, and lifts his golden beak to the pure east,
Shaking the dust from his immortal pinions to awake
The sun that sleeps too long. Arise, my Theotormon, I am pure
Because the night is gone that closed me in its deadly black."   60
They told me that the night and day were all that I could see;
They told me that I had five senses to enclose me up,
And they enclosed my infinite brain into a narrow circle,
And sunk my heart into the abyss, a red round globe, hot burning,
Till all from life I was obliterated and erased.   65
Instead of morn arises a bright shadow like an eye
In the eastern cloud; instead of night, a sickly charnel house,
That Theotormon hears me not! To him the night and morn
Are both alike: a night of sighs, a morning of fresh tears –
[Plate 6]
And none but Bromion can hear my lamentations.   70
   With what sense is it that the chicken shuns the ravenous hawk?
With what sense does the tame pigeon measure out the expanse?
With what sense does the bee form cells? Have not the mouse and frog
Eyes and ears and sense of touch? Yet are their habitations
And their pursuits as different as their forms and as their joys.   75
Ask the wild ass why he refuses burdens; and the meek camel
Why he loves man – is it because of eye, ear, mouth or skin
Or breathing nostrils? No, for these the wolf and tiger have.
Ask the blind worm the secrets of the grave, and why her spires
Love to curl round the bones of death; and ask the rav'nous snake   80
Where she gets poison; and the winged eagle why he loves the sun –
And then tell me the thoughts of man that have been hid of old.
   Silent I hover all the night, and all day could be silent
If Theotormon once would turn his loved eyes upon me.
How can I be defiled when I reflect thy image pure?   85
Sweetest the fruit that the worm feeds on, and the soul preyed on by woe,
The new-washed lamb tinged with the village smoke, and the bright swan
By the red earth of our immortal river! I bathe my wings
And I am white and pure to hover round Theotormon's breast.'
   Then Theotormon broke his silence, and he answered.   90
'Tell me what is the night or day to one o'erflowed with woe?
Tell me what is a thought, and of what substance is it made?

---

[15] Theotormon's ineffectual response to the rape of Oothoon by Bromion is probably suggested by the behaviour of J. G. Stedman (see headnote, p. 54), who wrote of how he fell in love with Joanna, a slave. After a brief affair, he failed to buy her freedom and returned to England without her. He remem- bered how 'I fancied I saw her tortured, insulted, and bowing under the weight of her chains, calling aloud, but in vain, for my assistance'. Although he disapproved of the treatment of female slaves, Stedman did nothing to prevent the cruelty he witnessed.

Tell me what is a joy, and in what gardens do joys grow?
And in what rivers swim the sorrows, and upon what mountains
[Plate 7]
Wave shadows of discontent? And in what houses dwell the wretched   95
Drunken with woe forgotten, and shut up from cold despair?
Tell me where dwell the thoughts forgotten till thou call them forth?
Tell me where dwell the joys of old, and where the ancient loves?
And when will they renew again, and the night of oblivion past?[16]
That I might traverse times and spaces far remote, and bring   100
Comforts into a present sorrow and a night of pain.
Where goest thou, oh thought? To what remote land is thy flight?
If thou returnest to the present moment of affliction
Wilt thou bring comforts on thy wings, and dews and honey and balm?
Or poison from the desert wilds, from the eyes of the envier?'   105
   Then Bromion said (and shook the cavern with his lamentation),
'Thou knowest that the ancient trees seen by thine eyes have fruit,
But knowest thou that trees and fruits flourish upon the earth
To gratify senses unknown? Trees, beasts and birds unknown?
Unknown, not unperceived, spread in the infinite microscope,   110
In places yet unvisited by the voyager, and in worlds
Over another kind of seas, and in atmospheres unknown.
Ah, are there other wars, beside the wars of sword and fire?
And are there other sorrows, beside the sorrows of poverty?
And are there other joys, beside the joys of riches and ease?   115
And is there not one law for both the lion and the ox?
And is there not eternal fire, and eternal chains
To bind the phantoms of existence from eternal life?'
   Then Oothoon waited silent all the day and all the night,
[Plate 8]
But when the morn arose, her lamentation renewed –   120
The Daughters of Albion hear her woes, and echo back her sighs.
'Oh Urizen,[17] creator of men, mistaken demon of heaven!
Thy joys are tears, thy labour vain – to form men to thine image.
How can one joy absorb another? Are not different joys
Holy, eternal, infinite? And each joy is a love!   125
Does not the great mouth laugh at a gift, and the narrow eyelids mock
At the labour that is above payment? And wilt thou take the ape
For thy counsellor? Or the dog, for a schoolmaster to thy children?
Does he who contemns poverty, and he who turns with abhorrence
From usury, feel the same passion? Or are they moved alike?   130
How can the giver of gifts experience the delights of the merchant?
How the industrious citizen the pains of the husbandman?
How different far the fat-fed hireling with hollow drum
Who buys whole cornfields into wastes,[18] and sings upon the heath –
How different their eye and ear! How different the world to them!   135
With what sense does the parson claim the labour of the farmer?[19]
What are his nets and gins and traps, and how does he surround him

---

[16] *And when . . . past* i.e. when will the thoughts, joys, and loves renew; when will the night of oblivion be past?

[17] *Urizen* ('your reason') the creator of the fallen, fragmented world.

[18] *cornfields into wastes* Expenditure of harvests and men on war is associated with enclosure and agricultural decline. The enlistment of young men in the army left a dearth of farmers to till the land, which in turn led to food shortages.

[19] *With what sense . . . farmer* a reference to tithes, taxes paid by peasants to the church.

With cold floods of abstraction, and with forests of solitude,
To build him castles and high spires where kings and priests may dwell?
Till she who burns with youth, and knows no fixed lot, is bound   140
In spells of law to one she loathes. And must she drag the chain
Of life in weary lust?[20] Must chilling murderous thoughts obscure
The clear heaven of her eternal spring? – to bear the wintry rage
Of a harsh terror, driv'n to madness, bound to hold a rod[21]
Over her shrinking shoulders all the day, and all the night   145
To turn the wheel of false desire? – and longings that wake her womb
To the abhorred birth of cherubs in the human form
That live a pestilence and die a meteor, and are no more?
Till the child dwell with one he hates, and do the deed he loathes,
And the impure scourge force his seed into its unripe birth   150
Ere yet his eyelids can behold the arrows of the day.
   Does the whale worship at thy footsteps as the hungry dog?
Or does he scent the mountain prey because his nostrils wide
Draw in the ocean? Does his eye discern the flying cloud
As the raven's eye? Or does he measure the expanse like the vulture?   155
Does the still spider view the cliffs where eagles hide their young?
Or does the fly rejoice because the harvest is brought in?
Does not the eagle scorn the earth and despise the treasures beneath?
But the mole knoweth what is there, and the worm shall tell it thee.
Does not the worm erect a pillar in the mouldering churchyard,   160
[Plate 9]
And a palace of eternity in the jaws of the hungry grave?
Over his porch these words are written: "Take thy bliss, oh man,
And sweet shall be thy taste, and sweet thy infant joys renew!"
   Infancy – fearless, lustful, happy! – nestling for delight
In laps of pleasure. Innocence! – honest, open, seeking   165
The vigorous joys of morning light, open to virgin bliss –
Who taught thee modesty, subtle modesty, child of night and sleep?
When thou awakest, wilt thou dissemble all thy secret joys
Or wert thou not awake when all this mystery was disclosed?
Then com'st thou forth a modest virgin knowing to dissemble[22]   170
With nets found under thy night pillow, to catch virgin joy,
And brand it with the name of whore, and sell it in the night[23]
In silence, ev'n without a whisper, and in seeming sleep.
Religious dreams and holy vespers light thy smoky fires;
Once were thy fires lighted by the eyes of honest morn.   175
And does my Theotormon seek this hypocrite modesty,
This knowing, artful, secret, fearful, cautious, trembling hypocrite?
Then is Oothoon a whore indeed, and all the virgin joys
Of life are harlots, and Theotormon is a sick man's dream,
And Oothoon is the crafty slave of selfish holiness.   180
   But Oothoon is not so: a virgin filled with virgin fancies,
Open to joy and to delight wherever beauty appears.

---

[20]   *And must ... lust* Wollstonecraft probably inspired the notion of marriage as slavery.
[21]   *rod* yoke for bearing burdens over the shoulders; though perhaps also the rod or whip of her slave-driving husband.
[22]   *a modest virgin ... dissemble* Wollstonecraft lamented the tendency of women to spend so much time in front of mirrors,
'for this exercise of cunning is only an instinct of nature to enable them to obtain indirectly a little of that power of which they are unjustly denied a share'.
[23]   *sell it in the night* prostitution.

If in the morning sun I find it, there my eyes are fixed
[Plate 10]
In happy copulation; if in evening mild, wearied with work,
Sit on a bank and draw the pleasures of this free-born joy.   185
   The moment of desire! The moment of desire! The virgin
That pines for man shall awaken her womb to enormous joys
In the secret shadows of her chamber;[24] the youth shut up from
The lustful joy shall forget to generate, and create an amorous image
In the shadows of his curtains and in the folds of his silent pillow.[25]   190
Are not these the places of religion? The rewards of continence?
The self-enjoyings of self-denial? Why dost thou seek religion?
Is it because acts are not lovely that thou seekest solitude
Where the horrible darkness is impressed with reflections of desire?
   Father of jealousy,[26] be thou accursed from the earth!   195
Why hast thou taught my Theotormon this accursed thing?
Till beauty fades from off my shoulders, darkened and cast out,
A solitary shadow wailing on the margin of nonentity.
   I cry, "Love! Love! Love! Happy, happy Love! Free as the mountain wind!"
Can that be love, that drinks another as a sponge drinks water?   200
That clouds with jealousy his nights, with weepings all the day?
To spin a web of age around him, grey and hoary, dark,
Till his eyes sicken at the fruit that hangs before his sight?[27]
Such is self-love that envies all! – a creeping skeleton
With lamp-like eyes, watching around the frozen marriage bed.   205
   But silken nets and traps of adamant will Oothoon spread,
And catch for thee girls of mild silver, or of furious gold;
I'll lie beside thee on a bank and view their wanton play
In lovely copulation, bliss on bliss, with Theotormon;
Red as the rosy morning, lustful as the first-born beam,   210
Oothoon shall view his dear delight, nor e'er with jealous cloud
Come in the heaven of generous love, nor selfish blightings bring.
   Does the sun walk in glorious raiment on the secret floor
[Plate 11]
Where the cold miser spreads his gold? Or does the bright cloud drop
On his stone threshold? Does his eye behold the beam that brings   215
Expansion to the eye of pity? Or will he bind himself
Beside the ox to thy hard furrow? Does not that mild beam blot
The bat, the owl, the glowing tiger, and the king of night?
The sea-fowl takes the wintry blast for a cov'ring to her limbs
And the wild snake the pestilence to adorn him with gems and gold;   220
And trees and birds and beasts and men behold their eternal joy.
Arise, you little glancing wings, and sing your infant joy!
Arise and drink your bliss, for everything that lives is holy!'
   Thus every morning wails Oothoon, but Theotormon sits
Upon the margined ocean, conversing with shadows dire.   225
   The Daughters of Albion hear her woes, and echo back her sighs.

The End

---

24 *The virgin . . . chamber* female masturbation.
25 *the youth . . . pillow* male masturbation.
26 *Father of jealousy* Urizen.

27 *Till his eyes . . . sight* In Greek myth, Tantalus was tormented in Hades by delicious fruit growing just beyond reach.

The First Book of Urizen[1] (1794)

[Plate 2]

Preludium to the First Book of Urizen

Of the primeval priests' assumed power,[2]
When Eternals spurned back his[3] religion
And gave him a place in the north –
Obscure, shadowy, void, solitary.

Eternals, I hear your call gladly[4] –   5
Dictate swift-winged words, and fear not
To unfold your dark visions of torment!

[Plate 3]

Chapter I

1. Lo, a shadow of horror is risen
In eternity – unknown, unprolific,
Self-closed, all-repelling! What demon   10
Hath formed this abominable void,[5]
This soul-shudd'ring vacuum? Some said,
'It is Urizen'.[6] But unknown, abstracted,
Brooding secret,[7] the dark power hid.

2. Times on times he divided,[8] and measured   15
Space by space in his ninefold darkness,[9]
Unseen, unknown; changes appeared
In his desolate mountains,[10] rifted furious
By the black winds of perturbation.

3. For he strove in battles dire,   20
In unseen conflictions, with shapes
Bred from his forsaken wilderness,
Of beast, bird, fish, serpent and element,
Combustion, blast, vapour and cloud.[11]

THE FIRST BOOK OF URIZEN

1   The title is designed to contrast Blake's poem with the first five books of the Bible, the Pentateuch. Perhaps *Urizen* was intended to be the first part of Blake's 'Bible of Hell' mentioned in *The Marriage of Heaven and Hell* (p. 93). Urizen himself has been aligned in the past with Reason – 'your reason'. Blake was no admirer of reason in its purest state; it is, in the context of this poem, the force of division and separation, and is responsible for the making of unjust laws. There is, to that extent, a demonic aspect to Urizen, though it is worth remembering that Blake's attitude to hell is ambiguous.

2   *Of the . . . power* Blake imitates the usual opening to an epic poem (e.g. 'Of arms and the man I sing . . .'). It echoes the anti-clericalism of *The Marriage of Heaven and Hell*.

3   *his* Urizen's.

4   *I hear your call gladly* Blake, the poet, receives the dictation of the Eternals.

5   *What demon . . . void* cf. Genesis 1:2: 'And the earth was without form, and void'.

6   *Some said . . . Urizen* the first act of naming in the poem.

7   *Brooding secret* an allusion to the moment of creation in *Paradise Lost* i 21–2, where the Holy Spirit 'Dove-like sat'st brooding on the vast abyss / And madest it pregnant'.

8   *divided* the Creation begins with Urizen's splitting away from the Eternals into selfhood.

9   *ninefold darkness* Milton's Satan lay for nine days in the abyss of hell.

10   *mountains* Urizen becomes a landscape: Creation and the Fall are one and the same.

11   *Of beast . . . cloud* the elements (l. 24) are accompanied by emblematic beasts (l. 23).

4. Dark, revolving in silent activity, 25
Unseen in tormenting passions,
An activity unknown and horrible;
A self-contemplating shadow
In enormous labours occupied.

5. But Eternals beheld his vast forests. 30
Age on ages he lay, closed, unknown,
Brooding, shut in the deep; all avoid
The petrific[12] abominable chaos.

6. His cold horrors silent, dark Urizen
Prepared: his ten thousands of thunders 35
Ranged in gloomed array stretch out across
The dread world, and the rolling of wheels,
As of swelling seas, sound in his clouds,
In his hills of stored snows, in his mountains
Of hail and ice; voices of terror 40
Are heard, like thunders of autumn,
When the cloud blazes over the harvests.

Chapter II[13]

1. Earth was not, nor globes of attraction.[14]
The will of the Immortal[15] expanded
Or contracted his all-flexible senses. 45
Death was not, but eternal life sprung.

2. The sound of a trumpet! The heavens
Awoke, and vast clouds of blood rolled
Round the dim rocks of Urizen (so named
That solitary one in immensity). 50

3. Shrill the trumpet, and myriads of eternity
[Plate 4]
Muster around the bleak deserts,
Now filled with clouds, darkness, and waters
That rolled perplexed, lab'ring, and uttered
Words articulate, bursting in thunders 55
That rolled on the tops of his mountains.

4. 'From the depths of dark solitude,[16] from
The eternal abode in my holiness
Hidden, set apart in my stern counsels,
Reserved for the days of futurity, 60
I have sought for a joy without pain,
For a solid without fluctuation.

---

[12] *petrific* a Miltonic coinage meaning stony, static (see *Paradise Lost* x 294). The point is that chaos is static when compared to all-flexible eternity.
[13] In this chapter Blake tells the story of the Creation a second time.

[14] *globes of attraction* solar systems; planets held together by gravity. In Blake's plate, 'attraction' is split into two parts, 'attrac- / -tion', with the second part hovering above the first, mimicking a gravity-less state.
[15] *the Immortal* Urizen.
[16] Lines 57–91 comprise Urizen's account of the Creation.

Why will you die, oh Eternals?[17]
Why live in unquenchable burnings?

5. First I fought with the fire, consumed   65
Inwards, into a deep world within,
A void immense, wild, dark and deep,
Where nothing was: nature's wide womb.
And self-balanced, stretched o'er the void,
I alone (even I!) the winds merciless   70
Bound. But condensing, in torrents
They fall and fall; strong, I repelled
The vast waves, and arose on the waters,
A wide world of solid obstruction.

6. Here alone I, in books formed of metals,   75
Have written the secrets of wisdom,[18]
The secrets of dark contemplation,
By fightings and conflicts dire
With terrible monsters sin-bred,
Which the bosoms of all inhabit,   80
Seven deadly sins of the soul.

7. Lo! I unfold my darkness. And on
This rock place with strong hand the book
Of eternal brass, written in my solitude:

8. Laws of peace, of love, of unity,   85
Of pity,[19] compassion, forgiveness.
Let each choose one habitation,
His ancient infinite mansion.
One command, one joy, one desire,
One curse, one weight, one measure   90
One king, one God, one law.'[20]

Chapter III

1. The voice ended. They saw his pale visage
Emerge from the darkness, his hand
On the rock of eternity unclasping
The book of brass. Rage seized the strong,   95

2. Rage, fury, intense indignation,
In cataracts of fire, blood and gall,
In whirlwinds of sulphurous smoke
And enormous forms of energy;
All the seven deadly sins of the soul   100

---

[17] *Why will you die, oh Eternals?* an echo of Ezekiel 18:31: 'why will ye die, oh house of Israel?'
[18] *Here alone . . . wisdom* parodic of God's handing down to Moses of the Ten Commandments, Exodus 20.
[19] *pity* not, for Blake, a desirable quality, as it consolidates division.
[20] *One king, one God, one law* Blake regarded the imposition of these things as tyranny.

[Plate 5]
In living creations appeared
In the flames of eternal fury.

3. Sund'ring, dark'ning, thund'ring!
Rent away with a terrible crash,
Eternity rolled wide apart,   105
Wide asunder rolling,
Mountainous, all around
Departing, departing, departing,
Leaving ruinous fragments of life,
Hanging frowning cliffs, and all between   110
An ocean of voidness unfathomable.

4. The roaring fires ran o'er the heav'ns
In whirlwinds and cataracts of blood,
And o'er the dark deserts of Urizen
Fires pour through the void on all sides   115
On Urizen's self-begotten armies.

5. But no light from the fires: all was darkness
In the flames of eternal fury.

6. In fierce anguish and quenchless flames
To the deserts and rocks he ran raging   120
To hide, but he could not; combining,
He dug mountains and hills in vast strength,
He piled them in incessant labour,
In howlings and pangs and fierce madness;
Long periods in burning fires labouring   125
Till hoary and age-broke and aged,
In despair and the shadows of death.

7. And a roof, vast, petrific, around,
On all sides he framed, like a womb
Where thousands of rivers in veins   130
Of blood pour down the mountains to cool
The eternal fires beating without
From Eternals; and, like a black globe
Viewed by sons of eternity, standing
On the shore of the infinite ocean,   135
Like a human heart struggling and beating,
The vast world of Urizen appeared.

8. And Los,[21] round the dark globe of Urizen,
Kept watch for Eternals, to confine
The obscure separation alone;   140
For eternity stood wide apart,
[Plate 7]
As the stars are apart from the earth.

---

[21] *Los* the imagination, now separated from Urizen.

9. Los wept, howling around the dark demon
And cursing his lot; for in anguish
Urizen was rent from his side[22] –   145
And a fathomless void for his feet,
And intense fires for his dwelling.

10. But Urizen laid in a stony sleep
Unorganized, rent from eternity.

11. The Eternals said, 'What is this? Death.[23]   150
Urizen is a clod of clay!'
[Plate 9]
12. Los howled in a dismal stupor,
Groaning, gnashing, groaning,
Till the wrenching apart was healed.

13. But the wrenching of Urizen healed not;   155
Cold, featureless, flesh or clay,
Rifted with direful changes,
He lay in a dreamless night

14. Till Los roused his fires, affrighted
At the formless unmeasurable death.   160

[Plate 10]
Chapter IVa

1. Los, smitten with astonishment,
Frightened at the hurtling bones,

2. And at the surging, sulphureous,
Perturbed Immortal, mad-raging

3. In whirlwinds and pitch and nitre   165
Round the furious limbs of Los;

4. And Los formed nets and gins,[24]
And threw the nets round about.

5. He watched in shudd'ring fear
The dark changes, and bound every change   170
With rivets of iron and brass.

6. And these were the changes of Urizen.

[Plate 12]
Chapter IVb

1. Ages on ages rolled over him!
In stony sleep ages rolled over him!
Like a dark waste stretching, changeable,   175

---

[22]   *Urizen was rent from his side* cf. the creation of Eve from   [23]   *What is ... Death* the second act of naming in the poem.
Adam's rib, Genesis 2:21.   [24]   *gins* snares, traps.

By earthquakes riv'n, belching sullen fires,
On ages rolled ages in ghastly
Sick torment; around him in whirlwinds
Of darkness, the Eternal Prophet[25] howled,
Beating still on his rivets of iron,   180
Pouring sodor[26] of iron, dividing
The horrible night into watches.

2. And Urizen (so his eternal name)
His prolific delight obscured more and more
In dark secrecy, hiding in surging   185
Sulphureous fluid his fantasies.
The Eternal Prophet heaved the dark bellows
And turned restless the tongs, and the hammer
Incessant beat, forging chains new and new,
Numb'ring with links, hours, days, and years.[27]   190

3. The Eternal Mind bounded began to roll
Eddies of wrath ceaseless, round and round,
And the sulphureous foam surging thick
Settled – a lake, bright and shining clear,
White as the snow on the mountains cold.   195

4. Forgetfulness, dumbness, necessity!
In chains of the mind locked up
Like fetters of ice shrinking together,
Disorganized, rent from eternity.
Los beat on his fetters of iron,   200
And heated his furnaces, and poured
Iron sodor and sodor of brass.

5. Restless turned the Immortal enchained,
Heaving dolorous, anguished, unbearable,
Till a roof, shaggy, wild, enclosed   205
In an orb[28] his fountain of thought.

6. In a horrible dreamful slumber
Like the linked infernal chain,
A vast spine writhed in torment
Upon the winds, shooting pained   210
Ribs, like a bending cavern,
And bones of solidness froze
Over all his nerves of joy.
And a first age passed over
And a state of dismal woe.   215

[Plate 13]
7. From the caverns of his jointed spine
Down sunk with fright a red

---

[25] *the Eternal Prophet* Los.
[26] *sodor* solder – which, like rivets, is used to join metal components.

[27] *Numb'ring . . . years* Los constructs a calendar.
[28] *an orb* the skull.

Round globe,[29] hot burning, deep
Deep down into the abyss,
Panting, conglobing, trembling,   220
Shooting out ten thousand branches
Around his solid bones.
And a second age passed over
And a state of dismal woe.

8. In harrowing fear rolling round   225
His nervous brain shot branches
Round the branches of his heart
On high into two little orbs;[30]
And fixed in two little caves
Hiding carefully from the wind,   230
His eyes beheld the deep.
And a third age passed over
And a state of dismal woe.

9. The pangs of hope began,
In heavy pain, striving, struggling;   235
Two ears in close volutions[31]
From beneath his orbs of vision
Shot spiring out and petrified
As they grew. And a fourth age passed
And a state of dismal woe.   240

10. In ghastly torment sick,
Hanging upon the wind,
[Plate 15]
Two nostrils bent down to the deep.
And a fifth age passed over
And a state of dismal woe.   245

11. In ghastly torment sick,
Within his ribs bloated round,
A craving hungry cavern;
Thence arose his channelled throat,
And like a red flame a tongue   250
Of thirst and of hunger appeared.
And a sixth age passed over
And a state of dismal woe.

12. Enraged and stifled with torment,
He threw his right arm to the north,   255
His left arm to the south,
Shooting out in anguish deep;
And his feet stamped the nether abyss
In trembling and howling and dismay.
And a seventh age passed over   260
And a state of dismal woe.

---

[29]   *a red / Round globe* the heart.   [31]   *close volutions* inner ear.
[30]   *two little orbs* the eyes.

Chapter V

1. In terrors Los shrunk from his task –
His great hammer fell from his hand;
His fires beheld and, sickening,
Hid their strong limbs in smoke.   265
For with noises, ruinous, loud,
With hurtlings and clashings and groans,
The Immortal endured his chains
Though bound in a deadly sleep.

2. All the myriads of eternity,   270
All the wisdom and joy of life,
Roll like a sea around him,
Except what his little orbs
Of sight by degrees unfold.

3. And now his eternal life,   275
Like a dream, was obliterated.

4. Shudd'ring, the Eternal Prophet smote
With a stroke, from his north to south region.
The bellows and hammer are silent now,
A nerveless silence; his prophetic voice   280
Seized; a cold solitude and dark void
The Eternal Prophet and Urizen closed.

5. Ages on ages rolled over them,
Cut off from life and light, frozen
Into horrible forms of deformity.   285
Los suffered his fires to decay,
Then he looked back with anxious desire.
But the space undivided by existence
Struck horror into his soul.

6. Los wept, obscured with mourning;   290
His bosom earthquaked with sighs;
He saw Urizen, deadly black,
In his chains bound, and pity began,

7. In anguish dividing and dividing
(For pity divides the soul),[32]   295
In pangs, eternity on eternity,
Life in cataracts poured down his cliffs.
The void shrunk the lymph into nerves
Wand'ring wide on the bosom of night,
And left a round globe of blood   300
Trembling upon the void.

---

[32] *For pity divides the soul* Pity is a divisive – and therefore unfavourable – quality for Blake, since it is allied to fear and selfishness. It leads Los to split into two parts, a fallen Los (or Adam) and Enitharmon (or Eve).

[Plate 16]
Thus the Eternal Prophet was divided
Before the death-image of Urizen;
For in changeable clouds and darkness
In a winterly night beneath,   305
The abyss of Los stretched immense.
And now seen, now obscured, to the eyes
Of Eternals the visions remote
Of the dark separation appeared.
As glasses discover worlds   310
In the endless abyss of space,
So the expanding eyes of Immortals
Beheld the dark visions of Los,
And the globe of life-blood trembling.

[Plate 18]
8. The globe of life-blood trembled   315
Branching out into roots,
Fibrous, writhing upon the winds,
Fibres of blood, milk, and tears,[33]
In pangs, eternity on eternity.
At length, in tears and cries embodied,   320
A female form, trembling and pale,
Waves before his deathy face.

9. All eternity shuddered at sight
Of the first female now separate,[34]
Pale as a cloud of snow,   325
Waving before the face of Los.

10. Wonder, awe, fear, astonishment,
Petrify the eternal myriads
At the first female form now separate.
[Plate 19]
They called her Pity, and fled.   330

11. 'Spread a tent,[35] with strong curtains around them;
Let cords and stakes bind in the void,[36]
That Eternals may no more behold them!'

12. They began to weave curtains of darkness;
They erected large pillars round the void   335
With golden hooks fastened in the pillars.
With infinite labour the Eternals
A woof wove, and called it 'science'.

---

[33] *Fibrous ... tears* Blake's description of blood seems strange to us, but was up-to-date at the time of writing. Blood was thought to contain fibres and red globules. Other vessels were believed to carry blood, milk chyle, and tears.
[34] *All eternity ... separate* the Eternals are horrified at the creation of the first female because it implies infinite human division.

[35] *a tent* the sky, the firmament.
[36] *Spread a tent ... void* Blake recalls Isaiah 54:2: 'Enlarge the place of thy tent, and let them stretch forth the curtains of thine habitations: spare not, lengthen thy cords, and strengthen thy stakes.'

Chapter VI

1. But Los saw the female and pitied;
He embraced her, she wept, she refused.
In perverse and cruel delight
She fled from his arms, yet he followed.   340

2. Eternity shuddered when they saw
Man begetting his likeness
On his own divided image.   345

3. A time passed over, the Eternals
Began to erect the tent —
When Enitharmon sick
Felt a worm[37] within her womb.

4. Yet helpless it lay like a worm   350
In the trembling womb,
To be moulded into existence.

5. All day the worm lay on her bosom,
All night within her womb
The worm lay till it grew to a serpent,   355
With dolorous hissings and poisons
Round Enitharmon's loins folding.

6. Coiled within Enitharmon's womb,
The serpent grew, casting its scales;
With sharp pangs the hissings began   360
To change to a grating cry;
Many sorrows and dismal throes,
Many forms of fish, bird and beast,
Brought forth an infant form[38]
Where was a worm before.   365

7. The Eternals their tent finished,
Alarmed with these gloomy visions,
When Enitharmon groaning
Produced a man-child to the light.

8. A shriek ran through eternity,   370
And a paralytic stroke
At the birth of the human shadow.

9. Delving earth in his resistless way,
Howling, the child with fierce flames
Issued from Enitharmon.   375

---

37 *a worm* in 1786 'seminal worms' were believed to be the seed of the human nervous system.

38 *Brought forth an infant form* the apocalyptic tone of all this is heightened by the echo of Revelation 12:5, where the 'woman clothed with the sun' 'brought forth a man child'.

10. The Eternals closed the tent.
They beat down the stakes, the cords
[Plate 20]
Stretched for a work of eternity.
No more Los beheld eternity.

11. In his hands he seized the infant,[39]   380
He bathed him in springs of sorrow,
He gave him to Enitharmon.

Chapter VII

1. They named the child Orc; he grew
Fed with milk of Enitharmon.

2. Los awoke her – oh sorrow and pain!   385
A tight'ning girdle grew
Around his bosom. In sobbings
He burst the girdle in twain,
But still another girdle
Oppressed his bosom. In sobbings   390
Again he burst it. Again
Another girdle succeeds;
The girdle was formed by day,
By night was burst in twain.

3. These, falling down on the rock   395
Into an iron chain,
In each other link by link locked.

4. They took Orc to the top of a mountain –
Oh how Enitharmon wept!
They chained his young limbs to the rock[40]   400
With the chain of jealousy,
Beneath Urizen's deathful shadow.

5. The dead heard the voice of the child
And began to awake from sleep;
All things heard the voice of the child   405
And began to awake to life.

6. And Urizen craving with hunger,
Stung with the odours of nature,
Explored his dens around.

7. He formed a line and a plummet   410
To divide the abyss beneath.
He formed a dividing rule;

---

39 *he seized the infant* cf. the child of the 'woman clothed with the sun' in Revelation, which 'was caught up unto God, and to his throne' (Revelation 12:5).

40 *They chained . . . rock* cf. Abraham's binding of Isaac to the altar (Genesis 22:9); Laius's piercing of Oedipus's ankles when abandoning him to the wolves; and Jupiter's nailing of Prometheus to the rock of the Caucasus.

8. He formed scales to weigh;
He formed massy weights;
He formed a brazen quadrant;   415
He formed golden compasses
And began to explore the abyss,
And he planted a garden of fruits.

9. But Los encircled Enitharmon
With fires of prophecy   420
From the sight of Urizen and Orc.

10. And she bore an enormous race.

Chapter VIII

1. Urizen explored his dens —
Mountain, moor and wilderness,
With a globe of fire lighting his journey,   425
A fearful journey, annoyed
By cruel enormities, forms
[Plate 22]
Of life on his forsaken mountains.

2. And his world teemed vast enormities,
Fright'ning, faithless, fawning.   430
Portions of life, similitudes
Of a foot, or a hand, or a head,
Or a heart, or an eye, they swam, mischievous
Dread terrors, delighting in blood.

3. Most Urizen sickened to see   435
His eternal creations appear —
Sons and daughters of sorrow on mountains
Weeping, wailing! First Thiriel appeared,
Astonished at his own existence
Like a man from a cloud born; and Utha,   440
From the waters emerging, laments;
Grodna rent the deep earth howling
Amazed, his heavens immense cracks
Like the ground parched with heat; then Fuzon
Flamed out! — first begotten, last born.[41]   445
All his eternal sons in like manner,
His daughters from green herbs and cattle,
From monsters and worms of the pit.

4. He, in darkness closed, viewed all his race
And his soul sickened![42] He cursed   450
Both sons and daughters, for he saw
That no flesh nor spirit could keep
His iron laws one moment.

---

[41] Thiriel (air), Utha (water), Grodna (earth), and Fuzon (fire) correspond to the four elements.

[42] *He . . . sickened* there is no way the fall from a state of original innocence can be reversed, as Urizen realizes.

5. For he saw that life lived upon death;
[Plate 25]
The ox in the slaughterhouse moans,   455
The dog at the wintry door.
And he wept, and he called it 'pity',
And his tears flowed down on the winds.

6. Cold he wandered on high, over their cities
In weeping and pain and woe!   460
And wherever he wandered in sorrows
Upon the aged heavens
A cold shadow followed behind him
Like a spider's web – moist, cold, and dim,
Drawing out from his sorrowing soul   465
The dungeon-like heaven dividing,
Wherever the footsteps of Urizen
Walked over the cities in sorrow.

7. Till a web dark and cold, throughout all
The tormented element stretched   470
From the sorrows of Urizen's soul;
And the web is a female in embryo.
None could break the web, no wings of fire,

8. So twisted the cords, and so knotted
The meshes, twisted like to the human brain.   475

9. And all called it 'the net of religion'.

Chapter IX

1. Then the inhabitants of those cities[43]
Felt their nerves change into marrow,
And hardening bones began
In swift diseases and torments,   480
In throbbings and shootings and grindings
Through all the coasts; till, weakened,
The senses inward rushed, shrinking,
Beneath the dark net of infection;

2. Till the shrunken eyes, clouded over,   485
Discerned not the woven hypocrisy.
But the streaky slime in their heavens,
Brought together by narrowing perceptions,
Appeared transparent air; for their eyes
Grew small like the eyes of a man,   490
And in reptile forms, shrinking together,
Of seven feet stature they remained.

---

[43] *the inhabitants of those cities* an allusion to the inhabitants
of Sodom and Gomorrah, Genesis 19:25: 'And he overthrew

those cities, and all the plain, and all the inhabitants of those
cities, and that which grew upon the ground'.

3. Six days they shrunk up from existence,
And on the seventh day they rested;
And they blessed the seventh day, in sick hope,   495
And forgot their eternal life.

4. And their thirty cities divided
In form of a human heart;
No more could they rise at will
In the infinite void, but, bound down   500
To earth by their narrowing perceptions,
[Plate 27]
They lived a period of years,
Then left a noisome[44] body
To the jaws of devouring darkness.

5. And their children wept, and built   505
Tombs in the desolate places,
And formed laws of prudence, and called them
The eternal laws of God.

6. And the thirty cities remained,
Surrounded by salt floods, now called   510
Africa; its name was then Egypt.

7. The remaining sons of Urizen
Beheld their brethren shrink together
Beneath the net of Urizen;
Persuasion was in vain,   515
For the ears of the inhabitants
Were withered and deafened and cold,
And their eyes could not discern
Their brethren of other cities.

8. So Fuzon called all together   520
The remaining children of Urizen,
And they left the pendulous earth;[45]
They called it Egypt, and left it.[46]

9. And the salt ocean rolled englobed.

The End of the first book of Urizen

---

[44] *noisome* noxious, foul, rotten.
[45] *the pendulous earth* cf. *Paradise Lost* iv 1000: 'The pendulous round earth with balanced air'.
[46] *They called it Egypt, and left it* a reworking of the story of how the Israelites were conducted out of Egypt by God, commemorated in the Passover: 'Remember this day, in which ye came out from Egypt, out of the house of bondage; for by strength of hand the Lord brought you out from this place' (Exodus 18:3).

Letter to Revd Dr Trusler,[1] 23 August 1799 (extract)

Reverend Sir,

I really am sorry that you are fall'n out with the spiritual world, especially if I should have to answer for it. I feel very sorry that your ideas and mine on moral painting differ so much as to have made you angry with my method of study. If I am wrong, I am wrong in good company. I had hoped your plan comprehended all species of this art, and especially that you would not regret that species which gives existence to every other – namely, visions of eternity. You say that I want somebody to elucidate my ideas, but you ought to know that what is grand is necessarily obscure to weak men. That which can be made explicit to the idiot is not worth my care. The wisest of the ancients considered what is not too explicit as the fittest for instruction because it rouses the faculties to act – I name Moses, Solomon, Aesop, Homer, Plato. . . .

I have therefore proved your reasonings ill-proportioned, which you can never prove my figures to be. They are those of Michelangelo, Raphael, and the antique, and of the best living models. I perceive that your eye is perverted by caricature prints, which ought not to abound so much as they do. Fun I love, but too much fun is, of all things, the most loathsome. Mirth is better than fun, and happiness is better than mirth. I feel that a man may be happy in this world. And I know that this world is a world of imagination and vision. I see everything I paint in this world, but everybody does not see alike. To the eyes of a miser, a guinea[2] is more beautiful than the sun, and a bag worn with the use of money has more beautiful proportions than a vine filled with grapes. The tree which moves some to tears of joy is, in the eyes of others, only a green thing that stands in the way. Some see nature all ridicule and deformity (and by these I shall not regulate my proportions), and some scarce see nature at all. But to the eyes of the man of imagination, nature is imagination itself. As a man is, so he sees; as the eye is formed, such are its powers.

You certainly mistake when you say that the visions of fancy are not be found in this world. To me, this world is all one continued vision of fancy or imagination, and I feel flattered when I am told so. What is it sets Homer, Virgil, and Milton in so high a rank of art? Why is the Bible more entertaining and instructive than any other book? Is it not because they are addressed to the imagination (which is spiritual sensation), and but mediately to the understanding or reason? Such is true painting, and such was alone valued by the Greeks and the best modern artists. Consider what Lord Bacon says: 'Sense sends over to imagination before reason have judged, and reason sends over to imagination before the decree can be acted' (see *Advancement of Learning* Part 2, p. 47 of first edition).[3]

But I am happy to find a great majority of fellow mortals who can elucidate my visions – and particularly they have been elucidated by children, who have taken a greater delight in contemplating my pictures than I even hoped. Neither youth nor childhood is folly or incapacity; some children are fools and so are some old men. But there is a vast majority on the side of imagination or spiritual sensation . . .

The Mental Traveller

From THE PICKERING MANUSCRIPT (composed 1800–4)

I travelled through a land of men,
A land of men and women too,
And heard and saw such dreadful things
As cold earth-wanderers never knew.

LETTER TO REVD DR TRUSLER
[1] Blake had been introduced to John Trusler with a view to his illustrating some of Trusler's works, but they fell out when Trusler told him that 'Your fancy seems to be in the other world, or the world of spirits, which accords not with my intentions'. Trusler wrote on this letter the comment: 'Blake, dimmed with superstition'.

[2] *guinea* gold coin worth 21 shillings, not minted since 1813.
[3] Francis Bacon, Baron Verulam, Viscount St Albans (1561–1626) published his *Of the Advancement of Learning* in 1605.

For there the babe is born in joy   5
That was begotten in dire woe;
Just as we reap in joy the fruit
Which we in bitter tears did sow.

And, if the babe is born a boy,
He's given to a woman old   10
Who nails him down upon a rock,
Catches his shrieks in cups of gold.

She binds iron thorns around his head,
She pierces both his hands and feet,
She cuts his heart out at his side   15
To make it feel both cold and heat.

Her fingers number every nerve
Just as a miser counts his gold,
She lives upon his shrieks and cries,
And she grows young as he grows old.   20

Till he becomes a bleeding youth
And she becomes a virgin bright;
Then he rends up his manacles
And binds her down for his delight.

He plants himself in all her nerves   25
Just as a husbandman[1] his mould,[2]
And she becomes his dwelling-place,
And garden fruitful seventy-fold.

An aged shadow soon he fades,
Wand'ring round an earthly cot,[3]   30
Full filled all with gems and gold
Which he by industry had got.

And these are the gems of the human soul,
The rubies and pearls of a lovesick eye,
The countless gold of the aching heart,   35
The martyr's groan and the lover's sigh.

They are his meat, they are his drink;
He feeds the beggar and the poor,
And the wayfaring traveller –
Forever open is his door.   40

His grief is their eternal joy;
They make the roofs and walls to ring,
Till from the fire on the hearth
A little female babe does spring.

THE MENTAL TRAVELLER
[1] *husbandman* farmer.

[2] *mould* soil, earth.
[3] *cot* cottage.

And she is all of solid fire,   45
And gems and gold, that none his hand
Dares stretch to touch her baby form
Or wrap her in his swaddling-band.

But she comes to the man she loves,
If young or old, or rich or poor.   50
They soon drive out the aged host –
A beggar at another's door.

He wanders weeping far away
Until some other take him in;
Oft blind and age-bent, sore distressed,
Until he can a maiden win.

And to allay his freezing age
The poor man takes her in his arms;
The cottage fades before his sight,
The garden and its lovely charms;   60

The guests are scattered through the land.
For the eye altering, alters all;
The senses roll themselves in fear
And the flat earth becomes a ball;

The stars, sun, moon – all shrink away,   65
A desert vast without a bound;
And nothing left to eat or drink,
And a dark desert all around.

The honey of her infant lips,
The bread and wine of her sweet smile,   70
The wild game[4] of her roving eye
Does him to infancy beguile.

For as he eats and drinks he grows
Younger and younger every day,
And on the desert wild they both   75
Wander in terror and dismay.

Like the wild stag she flees away,
Her fear plants many a thicket wild;
While he pursues her night and day,
By various arts of love beguiled,   80

By various arts of love and hate;
Till the wide desert planted o'er
With labyrinths of wayward love,
Where roams the lion, wolf, and boar;

---

[4]   *game* sport.

Till he becomes a wayward babe 85
And she a weeping woman old.
Then many a lover wanders here;
The sun and stars are nearer rolled;

The trees bring forth sweet ecstasy
To all who in the desert roam – 90
Till many a city there is built,
And many a pleasant shepherd's home.

But when they find the frowning babe,
Terror strikes through the region wide;
They cry, 'The babe, the babe is born!' 95
And flee away on every side.

For who dare touch the frowning form –
His arm is withered to its root;
Lions, boars, wolves, all howling flee
And every tree does shed its fruit. 100

And none can touch that frowning form
Except it be a woman old;
She nails him down upon the rock
And all is done as I have told.

The Crystal Cabinet

From THE PICKERING MANUSCRIPT (composed 1800–4)

The maiden caught me in the wild
Where I was dancing merrily,
She put me into her cabinet
And locked me up with a golden key.

This cabinet is formed of gold 5
And pearl and crystal, shining bright,
And within it opens into a world
And a little lovely moony night.

Another England there I saw,
Another London with its Tower, 10
Another Thames and other hills
And another pleasant Surrey bower,

Another maiden like herself,
Translucent, lovely, shining clear –
Threefold each in the other closed: 15
Oh, what a pleasant trembling fear!

Oh, what a smile, a threefold smile
Filled me that like a flame I burned;
I bent to kiss the lovely maid
And found a threefold kiss returned. 20

I strove to seize the inmost form
With ardour fierce and hands of flame,
But burst the crystal cabinet
And like a weeping babe became –

A weeping babe upon the wild   25
And weeping woman, pale, reclined.
And in the outward air again
I filled with woes the passing wind.

[*Enion's Lamentation*]

From THE FOUR ZOAS (composed 1803–7) (from *Night the Second*, pp. 35–6)

I am made to sow the thistle for wheat, the nettle for a nourishing dainty.   390
I have planted a false oath in the earth; it has brought forth a poison tree.
I have chosen the serpent for a counsellor, and the dog
For a schoolmaster to my children.[1]
I have blotted out from light and living the dove and nightingale.
And I have caused the earthworm to beg from door to door.   395
I have taught the thief a secret path into the house of the just.
I have taught pale artifice to spread his nets upon the morning.
My heavens are brass, my earth is iron, my moon a clod of clay,
My sun a pestilence burning at noon and a vapour of death in night.
    What is the price of experience? Do men buy it for a song?   400
Or wisdom for a dance in the street? No, it is bought with the price
Of all that a man hath – his house, his wife, his children.
Wisdom is sold in the desolate market where none come to buy,
And in the withered field where the farmer ploughs for bread in vain.
    It is an easy thing to triumph in the summer's sun   405
And in the vintage, and to sing on the wagon loaded with corn.
It is an easy thing to talk of patience to the afflicted,
To speak the laws of prudence to the houseless wanderer,
To listen to the hungry raven's cry in wintry season
When the red blood is filled with wine and with the marrow of lambs.   410
    It is an easy thing to laugh at wrathful elements,
To hear the dog howl at the wintry door, the ox in the slaughterhouse moan;[2]
To see a god on every wind and a blessing on every blast;
To hear sounds of love in the thunderstorm that destroys our enemy's house;
To rejoice in the blight that covers his field, and the sickness that cuts off his children,   415
While our olive and vine sing and laugh round our door, and our children bring
    fruits and flowers.
Then the groan and the dolour are quite forgotten, and the slave grinding at the mill,
And the captive in chains, and the poor in the prison, and the soldier in the field,
When the shattered bone hath laid him groaning among the happier dead.
    It is an easy thing to rejoice in the tents of prosperity;   420
Thus could I sing and thus rejoice – but it is not so with me.

ENION'S LAMENTATION   [2] *To hear . . . moan* cf. *Urizen* 455–6.
[1] *and the dog . . . children* cf. *Visions of the Daughters of Albion*
ll. 127–8.

[Revival of the Eternal Man]

From THE FOUR ZOAS (composed 1803–7) (from *Night the Ninth*, pp. 133–5)

When morning dawned, the Eternals rose to labour at the vintage.
Beneath they saw their sons and daughters wondering inconceivable
At the dark myriads in shadows in the worlds beneath.   640
      The morning dawned, Urizen rose, and in his hand the flail
Sounds, on the floor heard terrible by all beneath the heavens;
Dismal loud redounding, the nether floor shakes with the sound,
And all nations were threshed out, and the stars threshed from their husks.
      Then Tharmas[1] took the winnowing fan, the winnowing wind furious   645
Above, veered round by the violent whirlwind driven west and south,
Tossed the nations like chaff[2] into the seas of Tharmas.
'Oh Mystery[3] fierce!' Tharmas cries, 'Behold thy end is come!
Art thou she that made the nations drunk with the cup of religion?
Go down, ye kings and councillors and giant warriors,   650
Go down into the depths, go down and hide yourselves beneath!
Go down with horse and chariots and trumpets of hoarse war!'
      Lo! how the pomp of Mystery goes down into the caves:
Her great men howl and throw the dust and rend their hoary hair;
Her delicate women and children shriek upon the bitter wind,   655
Spoiled of their beauty, their hair rent, and their skin shrivelled up.
Lo! darkness covers the long pomp of banners on the wind,
And black horses and armed men and miserable bound captives.
Where shall the graves receive them all, and where shall be their place?
And who shall mourn for Mystery, who never loosed her captives?   660
      Let the slave grinding at the mill run out into the field;
Let him look up into the heavens and laugh in the bright air;
Let the enchained soul shut up in darkness and in sighing,
Whose face has never seen a smile in thirty weary years,
Rise and look out! – his chains are loose, his dungeon doors are open.   665
And let his wife and children return from the oppressor's scourge:
They look behind at every step and believe it is a dream.
      Are these the slaves that groaned along the streets of Mystery?
Where are your bonds and task-masters? Are these the prisoners?
Where are your chains? Where are your tears? Why do you look around?   670
If you are thirsty, there is the river; go bathe your parched limbs:
The good of all the land is before you, for Mystery is no more!
      Then all the slaves from every earth in the wide universe
Sing a new song, drowning confusion in its happy notes,
While the flail of Urizen sounded loud and the winnowing wind of Tharmas   675
So loud, so clear in the wide heavens! And the song that they sung was this,
Composed by an African black from the little earth of Sotha:
'Aha! Aha! How came I here, so soon in my sweet native land?
How came I here? Methinks I am as I was in my youth,
When in my father's house I sat, and heard his cheering voice.   680
Methinks I see his flocks and herds, and feel my limbs renewed –
And lo! my brethren in their tents, and their little ones around them!'
      The song arose to the golden feast: the Eternal Man rejoiced.

REVIVAL OF THE ETERNAL MAN
[1]   *Tharmas* In Blake's scheme, Tharmas represents the senses.
Here, he is one of the forces of liberation.

[2]   *chaff* The process of threshing and winnowing here has the
same apocalyptic significance it is given in the Bible.
[3]   *Mystery* the devious goddess of false religion, who has mis-
led humanity.

[*And did those feet in ancient time*]

From MILTON (composed 1803–8)

And did those feet[1] in ancient time
Walk upon England's mountains green?
And was the holy lamb of God
On England's pleasant pastures seen?

And did the countenance divine   5
Shine forth upon our clouded hills?
And was Jerusalem builded here,
Among these dark Satanic mills?

Bring me my bow of burning gold!
Bring me my arrows of desire!   10
Bring me my spear – oh clouds unfold!
Bring me my chariot of fire![2]

I will not cease from mental fight
Nor shall my sword sleep in my hand,
Till we have built Jerusalem   15
In England's green and pleasant land.

Mary Robinson (*née* Darby)   (1758–1800)

She was born and brought up in Bristol, the younger daughter of John Darby, a whaling captain from America, and Mary Seys. Unlike many women of her time, she was fortunate in receiving an education, first at the school run by Hannah More's sisters, and later at Meribah Lorington's academy in Chelsea. She concluded her formal education at a finishing school in Marylebone. Her dancing master introduced her to luminaries in the theatrical world, including David Garrick, who encouraged her interest in acting.

In April 1774 she married Thomas Robinson, an articled clerk at Lincoln's Inn, who was thought to be comfortably off. This was not, alas, the case, and within months he was driven out of the capital to evade his creditors. Mary gave birth to their daughter, Mary Elizabeth, in Wales, November 1774. In 1775 Robinson was imprisoned for debt and, like Charlotte Smith, Mary partook of her husband's punishment, nursing her daughter in the cells. During her incarceration she began to write; her first volume, *Poems* (1775), was funded partly by Georgiana Cavendish, Duchess of Devonshire, one of the few women to respond to her requests for assistance.

Thanks to Garrick and Sheridan, Mary found employment as an actress at Drury Lane Theatre on release from prison; she became famous almost immediately, when acting the part of Juliet in December 1776. In the next few years she enjoyed tremendous success; her starring roles included Ophelia, Viola, Rosalind, Lady Macbeth and Perdita. It was while playing Perdita, in late 1779, that she attracted the attentions of the seventeen-year-old Prince of Wales (see her account of this, p. 124, below). She became his mistress in return for a promised £20,000, which was never paid. He abandoned her the following year, leaving her to much ridicule in the press, which compelled her to retire from the stage. Subsequent lovers included Charles James Fox, who secured an annuity for her of £500, and Colonel Bastre Tarleton, a veteran of the American War, who became the father of the child she was carrying when, at the age of twenty-four, she suffered the miscarriage that left her paralysed from the waist down.

After several years on the continent with Tarleton, she returned to England in 1788. By then she relied increasingly on her writing for income, and in succeed-

---

AND DID THOSE FEET IN ANCIENT TIME
[1]   *those feet* a reference to the feet of Joseph of Arimathea, one of Christ's disciples, believed to have brought Christianity to England, and to be buried in Glastonbury.

[2]   *Bring me my chariot of fire* a reference to the chariot of fire that carried Elijah to heaven, II Kings 2:11.

ing years her productivity was remarkable. Between 1775 and 1800 she produced six volumes of poetry, eight novels, and two plays, with remarkable success. Her gothic chiller *Vancenza, or The Dangers of Credulity* (1792) sold out in a day.

She was best known to the romantics as a contributor to the *Morning Post*, where her poems appeared under the name 'Tabitha Bramble'. Coleridge, Southey and Wordsworth were fellow contributors, and it was Coleridge who engaged in dialogue with her, in both verse and prose. Most famously, he sent her a manuscript copy of *Kubla Khan*, which inspired *Mrs Robinson to the Poet Coleridge*. In addition, her *The Snow-Drop* prompted Coleridge's poem of the same name, and her celebratory ode to the new-born Derwent Coleridge, *Ode Inscribed to the Infant Son of S. T. Coleridge*,[1] sent to Coleridge in manuscript, inspired his address to her, *A Stranger Minstrel*.[2] Her *Lyrical Tales* (1800) were influenced by *Lyrical Ballads*, and almost persuaded Wordsworth to change the title of the second edition of his work. By the time the reviews appeared, she was dead.

'She is a woman of undoubted genius', Coleridge remarked of her in 1800, 'I never knew a human being with so full a mind – bad, good, and indifferent, I grant you – but full and overflowing' (Griggs i 562). On first reading *The Haunted Beach*, he told Southey to include it in his forthcoming *Annual Anthology*: 'it falls off sadly to the last – wants tale and interest; but the images are new and very distinct – that "silvery carpet" is so *just* that it is unfortunate it should *seem* so bad, for it is *really* good – but the metre – aye, that woman has an ear!'[3] It is not hard to see why Coleridge enjoyed the poem so much. Like some of his own, it plays on our susceptibility to the uncanny, the sinister, the spooky. The anonymous author of the biography appended to her *Memoirs* recounted the circumstances of its composition:

> On one of these nights of melancholy inspiration, she discovered from her window a small boat struggling in the spray, which dashed against the wall of her garden. Presently two fishermen brought on shore in their arms a burden which, notwithstanding the distance, Mrs Robinson perceived to be a human body, which the fishermen, after covering it with a sail from their boat, left on the land and disappeared. But a short time elapsed before the men returned, bringing with them fuel, with which they vainly endeavoured to reanimate their unfortunate charge. Struck with a circumstance so affecting, which the stillness of the night ren-

dered yet more impressive, Mrs Robinson remained for some time at her window, motionless with horror. At length, recovering her recollection, she alarmed the family, but before they could gain the beach, the men had again departed. The morning dawned, and day broke in upon the tragical scene. The bathers passed and repassed with little concern, while the corpse continued, extended on the shore, not twenty yards from the Steine. During the course of the day many persons came to look on the body, which still remained unclaimed and unknown. Another day wore away, and the corpse was unburied, the lord of the manor having refused to a fellow-being a grave in which his bones might decently repose, alleging as an excuse *that he did not belong to that parish*. Mrs Robinson, humanely indignant at the scene which passed, exerted herself, but without success, to procure by subscription a small sum for performing the last duties to a wretched outcast. Unwilling, by an ostentatious display of her name, to offend the higher and more fastidious powers, she presented to the fishermen her own contribution, and declined further to interfere. The affair dropped, and the body of the stranger, being dragged to the cliff, was covered by a heap of stones without the ceremony of a prayer.

> These circumstances made on the mind of Mrs Robinson a deep and lasting impression; even at a distant period she could not repeat them without horror and indignation. This incident gave rise to the poem entitled *The Haunted Beach*, written but a few months before her death.[4]

Further reading

Stuart Curran, 'Mary Robinson's *Lyrical Tales* in Context', *RR* 17–35

Jerome J. McGann, *The Poetics of Sensibility: A Revolution in Literary Style* (Oxford, 1996), pp. 94–116

Martin J. Levy, 'Coleridge, Mary Robinson, and *Kubla Khan*', *Charles Lamb Bulletin* NS 77 (1992) 156–67

Susan Luther, 'A Stranger Minstrel: Coleridge's Mrs Robinson', *SIR* 33 (1994) 391–409

Eleanor Ty, 'Engendering a Female Subject: Mary Robinson's (Re)Presentations of the Self', *English Studies in Canada* 21 (1995) 407–31

Lisa Vargo, 'The Claims of "real life and manners": Coleridge and Mary Robinson', *TWC* 26 (1995) 134–7

MARY ROBINSON

[1] A text of *Ode Inscribed to the Infant Son of S. T. Coleridge* is included in my *Romantic Women Poets: An Anthology* (1997), along with a complete text of her sonnet sequence, *Sappho and Phaon* (1796).

[2] See EHC i 356–8, Griggs i 639–42, EHC i 350–2.

[3] Griggs i 576. See also Coleridge's letter to Mary Elizabeth Robinson, Griggs ii 903–6.

[4] *Memoirs of the late Mrs Robinson* (2 vols, 1803), ii 121–4.

The Haunted Beach[1]

From LYRICAL TALES (1800)

Upon a lonely desert beach
   Where the white foam was scattered,
A little shed upreared its head,
   Though lofty barks were shattered.
The seaweeds gath'ring near the door   5
   A sombre path displayed,
And all around, the deaf'ning roar
Re-echoed on the chalky shore,
   By the green billows made.

Above, a jutting cliff was seen   10
   Where seabirds hovered, craving,
And all around the crags were bound
   With weeds, forever waving;
And here and there, a cavern wide
   Its shad'wy jaws displayed,   15
And near the sands, at ebb of tide,
A shivered mast was seen to ride
   Where the green billows strayed.

And often, while the moaning wind
   Stole o'er the summer ocean,   20
The moonlight scene was all serene,
   The waters scarce in motion;
Then while the smoothly slanting sand
   The tall cliff wrapped in shade,
The fisherman beheld a band   25
Of spectres gliding hand in hand,
   Where the green billows played.

And pale their faces were as snow,
   And sullenly they wandered;
And to the skies, with hollow eyes,   30
   They looked, as though they pondered.
And sometimes from their hammock shroud
   They dismal howlings made;
And while the blast blew strong and loud
The clear moon marked the ghastly crowd   35
   Where the green billows played.

And then above the haunted hut,
   The curlews, screaming, hovered;
And the low door, with furious roar,
   The frothy breakers covered.   40
For in the fisherman's lone shed

THE HAUNTED BEACH
[1]   Robinson's biographer relates the story of how this poem
came to be written, headnote, p. 121, above.

A murdered man was laid,
With ten wide gashes on his head;
And deep was made his sandy bed
   Where the green billows played.   45

A shipwrecked mariner was he,
   Doomed from his home to sever,
Who swore to be, through wind and sea,
   Firm and undaunted ever;
And when the wave resistless rolled,   50
   About his arm he made
A packet rich of Spanish gold,
And, like a British sailor bold,
   Plunged where the billows played.

The spectre band, his messmates brave,   55
   Sunk in the yawning ocean,
While to the mast he lashed him fast
   And braved the storm's commotion.
The winter moon upon the sand
   A silv'ry carpet[2] made,   60
And marked the sailor reach the land,
And marked his murd'rer wash his hand,
   Where the green billows played.

And since that hour the fisherman
   Has toiled and toiled in vain;   65
For all the night, the moony light
   Gleams on the spectred main.
And when the skies are veiled in gloom,
   The murd'rer's liquid way
Bounds o'er the deeply yawning tomb,   70
And flashing fires the sands illume
   Where the green billows play.

Full thirty years his task has been,
   Day after day more weary;
For Heaven designed his guilty mind   75
   Should feed on prospects dreary.
Bound by a strong and mystic chain,
   He has not pow'r to stray,
But destined mis'ry to sustain,
He wastes, in solitude and pain,   80
   A loathsome life away.

---

[2] *silv'ry carpet* For Coleridge's comment on this phrase, see
headnote, p. 121, above.

[*My First Encounter with the Prince of Wales*] (vol. ii pp. 36–7, 38–9)

From MEMOIRS OF THE LATE MRS ROBINSON (4 vols, 1801)

The play of 'The Winter's Tale' was this season commanded by their Majesties. I never had performed before the Royal family, and the first character in which I was destined to appear was that of Perdita. I had frequently played the part, both with the Hermione of Mrs Hartley and of Miss Farren, but I felt a strange degree of alarm when I found my name announced to perform it before the Royal family.

In the green room I was rallied on the occasion, and Mr Smith (whose gentlemanly manners and enlightened conversation rendered him an ornament to the profession) who performed the part of Leontes, laughingly exclaimed, 'By Jove, Mrs Robinson, you will make a conquest of the Prince, for tonight you look handsomer than ever.' I smiled at the unmerited compliment, and little foresaw the vast variety of events that would arise from that night's exhibition! ... I hurried through the first scene – not without much embarrassment, owing to the fixed attention with which the Prince of Wales honoured me. Indeed, some flattering remarks which were made by his Royal Highness met my ear as I stood near his box, and I was overwhelmed with confusion.

The Prince's particular attention was observed by everyone, and I was again rallied at the end of the play. On the last curtsey, the Royal Family[1] condescendingly returned a bow to the performers, but, just as the curtain was falling, my eyes met those of the Prince of Wales. And, with a look that I *never shall forget*, he gently inclined his head a second time: I felt the compliment, and blushed my gratitude.

Mrs Robinson to the Poet Coleridge (composed October 1800)

From MEMOIRS OF THE LATE MRS ROBINSON (4 vols, 1801)

Rapt in the visionary theme,
    Spirit divine, with thee I'll wander,
Where the blue, wavy, lucid stream
    Mid forest glooms shall slow meander!
With thee I'll trace the circling bounds   5
    Of thy new paradise, extended,
And listen to the varying sounds
    Of winds and foamy torrents blended!

Now by the source, which lab'ring heaves
    The mystic fountain, bubbling, panting,   10
While gossamer its network weaves[1]
    Adown the blue lawn, slanting –
I'll mark thy 'sunny dome' and view
Thy 'caves of ice',[2] thy fields of dew,
Thy ever-blooming mead, whose flow'r   15
Waves to the cold breath of the moonlight hour!
Or, when the day-star,[3] peering bright
On the grey wing of parting night;
While more than vegetating pow'r

MY FIRST ENCOUNTER WITH THE PRINCE OF WALES
[1] *the Royal Family* consisting probably of George III and his wife, Charlotte of Mecklenburg, and their children, including the Prince of Wales (the future George IV).

MRS ROBINSON TO THE POET COLERIDGE
[1] *While gossamer ... weaves* fine filmy substance, consisting of cobwebs, spun by small spiders, seen spread over the lawn.
[2] *Kubla Khan* 36.
[3] *day-star* morning star.

Throbs, grateful to the burning hour,   20
As summer's whispered sighs unfold
Her million million buds of gold! –
Then will I climb the breezy bounds
    Of thy new paradise, extended,
And listen to the distant sounds   25
    Of winds and foamy torrents blended!

        Spirit divine, with thee I'll trace
        Imagination's boundless space!
With thee, beneath thy 'sunny dome'
    I'll listen to the minstrel's lay   30
    Hymning the gradual close of day;
In 'caves of ice' enchanted roam,
Where on the glitt'ring entrance plays
The moon's beam with its silv'ry rays;
Or when the glassy stream   35
    That through the deep dell flows,
Flashes the noon's hot beam –
    The noon's hot beam that midway shows
Thy flaming temple, studded o'er
With all Peruvia's lustrous store!⁴   40
There will I trace the circling bounds
    Of thy new paradise, extended,
And listen to the awful sounds
    Of winds and foamy torrents blended.

And now I'll pause to catch the moan   45
    Of distant breezes, cavern-pent;
Now, ere the twilight tints are flown,
    Purpling the landscape far and wide,
    On the dark promontory's side
    I'll gather wild-flow'rs, dew-besprent,   50
And weave a crown for thee,
Genius of heav'n-taught poesy!
While, op'ning to my wond'ring eyes,
Thou bid'st a new creation rise,
I'll raptured trace the circling bounds   55
    Of thy rich paradise, extended,
And listen to the varying sounds
    Of winds and foamy torrents blended.

And now, with lofty tones inviting,
Thy nymph, her dulcimer swift-smiting,   60
Shall wake me in ecstatic measures
Far, far removed from mortal pleasures,
In cadence rich, in cadence strong,
Proving the wondrous witcheries of song!
I hear her voice – thy 'sunny dome',   65
    Thy 'caves of ice' aloud repeat –

----

⁴   *With all . . . store* Peru had long been celebrated for its nat-
ural reserves of gold, silver and precious stones.

Vibrations, madd'ning sweet,
Calling the visionary wand'rer home!
She sings of thee, oh favoured child
Of minstrelsy, sublimely wild! –
Of thee whose soul can feel the tone
Which gives to airy dreams a magic all thy own!

70

Robert Burns (1759–1796)

If Scotland's greatest poet died just at the dawn of romanticism, he was nonetheless a powerful influence on it, not least as one of Wordsworth and Coleridge's favourite writers. As Wordsworth once said, 'Who but some impenetrable dunce, or narrow-minded puritan in works of art, ever read without delight the picture which he has drawn of the convivial exaltation of the rustic adventurer, Tam o' Shanter?' (Owen and Smyser iii 124).

Robert Burns was the oldest child of Agnes Broun and William Burnes, a tenant farmer. His father rejected the harsh Calvinism so widespread in Scotland in favour of the humanist virtues of kindness and tolerance. In due course, Robert took over as chief labourer when his father's health went into decline. William Burnes died in 1784, leaving Robert head of a large family. He was twenty-five. During the next two years he composed a vast amount of poetry. He had intended to emigrate to Jamaica as a means of escape from the labouring life, but before he could do so his *Poems, Chiefly in the Scottish Dialect* (1786) was published to enormous acclaim. It sold out in its first month of publication, being read by, among many others, the sixteen-year-old William Wordsworth, who 'admired many of the pieces very much' (*EY* 13).[1]

*Epistle to J. L*****k, an Old Scotch Bard* shows Burns's colloquial, lyric style at its most engaging; his advocacy of 'nature's fire' reveals a poetic creed that would strongly influence *Lyrical Ballads*. *To a Mouse* (one of Dorothy Wordsworth's favourite poems) underlines Burns's sympathy with the natural world. *Man*

was Made to Mourn is a precursor of such Lyrical Ballads as *Simon Lee* and *The Last of the Flock*; the old man at its centre anticipates such characters as Wordsworth's leech-gatherer.

Tam o' Shanter was Burns's most important single work, and his only significant one after 1787. It has endured not just for its power as a Gothic chiller, but for its distinctive energy and brio, a product of Burns's control of the language. 'I have seldom in my life tasted of higher enjoyment from any work of genius than I have received from this composition', wrote the critic, Alexander Fraser Tytler, 'and I am much mistaken if this poem alone, had you never written another syllable, would not have been sufficient to have transmitted your name down to posterity with high reputation.'[2]

Further reading

Franklyn Snyder, *The Life of Robert Burns* (London, 1932)
Maurice Lindsay, *The Burns Encyclopaedia* (London, 1959)
Tom Crawford, *Burns: A Study* (Edinburgh, 1960)
David Daiches, *Robert Burns: The Poet* (London, 1950, rev. 1966)
Robert Burns, *The Kilmarnock Poems* ed. Donald A. Low (London, 1985)
Carol McGuirk, *Robert Burns and the Sentimental Era* (Athens, Georgia, 1985)
James Mackay, *Burns: A Biography* (Edinburgh, 1992)

ROBERT BURNS
[1] See also the note in my *Wordsworth's Reading 1800–1815* (Cambridge, 1995), p. 254.

[2] *Robert Burns: The Critical Heritage* ed. Donald A. Low (London, 1974), p. 95.

*Epistle to J. L*****k,*[1] *An Old Scotch Bard, 1 April 1785*

FROM POEMS, CHIEFLY IN THE SCOTTISH DIALECT (1786)

While briers an' woodbines budding green,
An' paitricks[2] scraichan loud at e'en,
And morning poossie[3] whiddan[4] seen,
    Inspire my muse,
This freedom, in an *unknown* frien',
    I pray excuse.   5

On Fasteneen[5] we had a rockin,[6]
To ca' the crack[7] and weave our stockin;
And there was muckle fun and jokin,
    Ye need na doubt;   10
At length we had a hearty yokin,[8]
    At sang about.[9]

There was ae sang[10] amang the rest,
Aboon them a'[11] it pleased me best,
That some kind husband had addressed   15
    To some sweet wife:
It thirled the heart-strings through the breast,
    A' to the life.

I've scarce heard aught described[12] sae weel
What gen'rous,[13] manly bosoms feel;   20
Thought I, 'Can this be Pope or Steele
    Or Beattie's wark?'[14]
They tald me 'twas an odd kind chiel[15]
    About Muirkirk.[16]

It pat me fidgean-fain[17] to hear't,   25
An' sae about him there I spier't;[18]
Then a' that kent him round declared
    He had ingine,[19]
That nane excelled it, few cam near't,
    It was sae fine.   30

AN OLD SCOTCH BARD

[1] *J. L*****k* John Lapraik (1727–1807) was a tenant-farmer imprisoned for debt in Ayr, 1785. He composed poetry in prison, and published his *Poems on Several Occasions* in Kilmarnock, 1788. Burns had not met him at the time he composed this epistolary poem.

[2] *paitricks* partridges.

[3] *poossie* hare.

[4] *whiddan* scudding.

[5] *Fasteneen* Shrove Tuesday evening.

[6] *rockin* social evening featuring stories and songs.

[7] *ca' the crack* have a chat.

[8] *yokin* set-to.

[9] *sang about* singing in turn.

[10] *ae sang* one song, Lapraik's 'When I upon thy bosom lean', addressed to his wife at a time when she was anxious about their misfortunes. It was published in Lapraik's *Poems on Several Occasions* (1788).

[11] *Aboon them a'* above them all.

[12] *aught described* anything that described.

[13] *gen'rous* kind, sympathetic.

[14] *Can this be . . . wark* all writers skilled at describing tender feelings – Pope in such poems as *Elegy to the Memory of an Unfortunate Lady*, Steele in his essays, James Beattie (1735–1803) in *The Minstrel*, a semi-autobiographical poem in Spenserian stanzas. Burns is almost certainly recalling Beattie's account of Edwin's sensitivity and kindness.

[15] *chiel* man.

[16] *Muirkirk* Lapraik lived at Dalfram, on Ayr Water, near the village of Muirkirk.

[17] *fidgean-fain* fidgeting with eagerness.

[18] *spier't* asked about him.

[19] *ingine* genius, ingenuity.

That set him to a pint of ale,
An' either douse[20] or merry tale,
Or rhymes an' sangs he'd made himsel,
    Or witty catches –
'Tween Inverness and Tiviotdale[21]   35
    He had few matches.

Then up I gat, an swoor an aith,[22]
Though I should pawn my pleugh an' graith,[23]
Or die a cadger pownie's[24] death
    At some dyke-back,[25]   40
A pint an' gill I'd gie them baith
    To hear your crack.

But first an' foremost, I should tell,
Amaist as soon as I could spell,
I to the crambo-jingle[26] fell,   45
    Though rude an' rough,
Yet crooning to a body's sel[27]
    Does weel eneugh.

I am nae poet, in a sense,
But just a rhymer like by chance,   50
An' hae to learning nae pretence –
    Yet what the matter?
Whene'er my muse does on me glance,
    I jingle at her.

Your critic-folk may cock their nose   55
And say, 'How can you e'er propose
You wha ken[28] hardly verse frae prose,
    To mak a sang?'
But by your leaves, my learned foes,
    Ye're maybe wrang.   60

What's a' your jargon o' your schools,
Your Latin names for horns an' stools?
If honest nature made you fools,
    What sairs[29] your Grammars?
Ye'd better taen up spades and shools[30]   65
    Or knappin-hammers.[31]

A set o' dull, conceited hashes[32]
Confuse their brains in College classes!
They gang in stirks[33] and come out asses,[34]
    Plain truth to speak;   70

[20] *douse* sweet.
[21] *'Tween Inverness and Tiviotdale* between the north and south of Scotland.
[22] *swoor an aith* swore an oath.
[23] *pleugh an' graith* plough and harness.
[24] *cadger pownie* pony belonging to a hawker.
[25] *dyke-back* behind a wall.
[26] *crambo-jingle* rhyming songs.

[27] *crooning to a body's sel* singing to oneself.
[28] *ken* know.
[29] *sairs* serves.
[30] *shools* shovels.
[31] *knappin-hammers* hammers for breaking stones or flints.
[32] *hashes* fools.
[33] *stirks* steers.
[34] *asses* young bullocks.

An' syne[35] they think to climb Parnassus
    By dint o' Greek!

    Gie me ae spark o' nature's fire,
That's a' the learning I desire;
Then, though I drudge through dub[36] an' mire   75
    At pleugh or cart,
My muse, though hamely in attire,
    May touch the heart.

    Oh for a spunk[37] o' Allan's glee,
Or Ferguson's,[38] the bauld an' slee,[39]   80
Or bright Lapraik's, my friend to be,
    If I can hit it!
That would be lear[40] eneugh for me,
    If I could get it.

    Now sir, if ye hae friends enow,   85
Though real friends I b'lieve are few,
Yet, if your catalogue be fow,[41]
    I'se no insist;
But gif ye want ae friend that's true,
    I'm on your list.   90

    I winna blaw[42] about mysel,
As ill I like my fauts to tell;
But friends an' folk that wish me well,
    They sometimes roose[43] me –
Though I maun own as monie[44] still   95
    As far abuse me.

    There's ae wee faut they whiles lay to me:
I like the lasses (Gude forgie me!);
For monie a plack[45] they wheedle frae me
    At dance or fair –   100
Maybe some ither thing they gie me
    They weel can spare.

    But Mauchline Race or Mauchline Fair,
I should be proud to meet you there;
We'se gie ae night's discharge to care   105
    If we forgather,
An' hae a swap o' rhymin-ware
    Wi' ane anither.

---

[35] *syne* then.
[36] *dub* puddle.
[37] *spunk* spark.
[38] Allan Ramsay (1686–1758), Scottish poet; Robert Fergusson (1750–74), whose *Poems* (Edinburgh, 1773) strongly influenced Burns.
[39] *bauld an' slee* bold and clever.

[40] *lear* learning.
[41] *fow* full.
[42] *blaw* boast.
[43] *roose* praise.
[44] *I maun as monie* I must admit as many.
[45] *plack* coin.

The four-gill chap,[46] we'se gar him clatter,
An' kirs'n[47] him wi' reekin[48] water;   110
Syne we'll sit down an' tak our whitter[49]
    To cheer our heart;
An' faith, we'se be acquainted better
    Before we part.

Awa ye selfish, warly[50] race,   115
Wha think that havins,[51] sense an' grace,
Ev'n love an' friendship should give place
    To 'catch-the-plack'![52]
I dinna like to see your face,
    Nor hear your crack.   120

But ye whom social pleasure charms,
Whose hearts the tide of kindness warms,
Who hold your being on the terms,
    'Each aid the others' –
Come to my bowl, come to my arms,   125
    My friends, my brothers!

But to conclude my lang epistle,
As my auld pen's worn to the grissle;
Twa lines frae you wad gar me fissle,[53]
    Who am, most fervent,   130
While I can either sing or whistle,
    Your friend and servant.

Man was Made to Mourn, A Dirge (composed August 1785)

From POEMS, CHIEFLY IN THE SCOTTISH DIALECT (1786)

I

When chill November's surly blast
    Made fields and forests bare,
One ev'ning, as I wand'red forth
    Along the banks of Aire,[1]
I spied a man whose aged step   5
    Seemed weary, worn with care;[2]
His face was furrowed o'er with years
    And hoary was his hair.

---

46 *chap* cup. A 'gill' is a measure (of alcohol).
47 *kirs'n* christen.
48 *reekin* steaming.
49 *whitter* draught.
50 *warly* worldly.
51 *havins* good manners.
52 *catch-the-plack* money-making.
53 *gar me fissle* make me fidget (with excitement).

MAN WAS MADE TO MOURN, A DIRGE
1 The River Ayr rises on the western border of Scotland and flows east to the sea.
2 *I spied a man ... care* this solitary was an influence on Wordsworth's leech-gatherer in *Resolution and Independence*.

II

'Young stranger, whither wand'rest thou?'
    Began the rev'rend sage,   10
'Does thirst of wealth thy step constrain,
    Or youthful pleasure's rage?
Or haply, pressed with cares and woes,
    Too soon thou hast began
To wander forth, with me to mourn   15
    The miseries of man.

III

The sun that overhangs yon moors,
    Out-spreading far and wide,
Where hundreds labour to support
    A haughty lordling's pride;   20
I've seen yon weary winter sun
    Twice forty times return,
And ev'ry time has added proofs
    That man was made to mourn.

IV

Oh man, while in thy early years,   25
    How prodigal of time!
Misspending all thy precious hours,
    Thy glorious, youthful prime!
Alternate follies take the sway,
    Licentious passions burn,   30
Which tenfold force gives nature's law
    That man was made to mourn.

V

Look not alone on youthful prime
    Or manhood's active might;
Man then is useful to his kind,   35
    Supported is his right:
But see him on the edge of life,
    With cares and sorrows worn,
Then age and want (oh, ill-matched pair!)
    Show man was made to mourn.   40

VI

A few seem favourites of fate,
    In pleasure's lap caressed;
Yet think not all the rich and great
    Are likewise truly blessed.

But oh! what crowds in ev'ry land,   45
   All wretched and forlorn,
Through weary life this lesson learn –
   That man was made to mourn!

VII

Many and sharp the num'rous ills
   Enwoven with our frame!   50
More pointed still we make ourselves
   Regret, remorse and shame!
And man, whose heav'n-erected face
   The smiles of love adorn,
Man's inhumanity to man[3]   55
   Makes countless thousands mourn!

VIII

See yonder poor, o'erlaboured wight,
   So abject, mean and vile,
Who begs a brother of the earth
   To give him leave to toil;[4]   60
And see his lordly fellow-worm
   The poor petition spurn –
Unmindful, though a weeping wife
   And helpless offspring mourn.

IX

If I'm designed yon lordling's slave,   65
   By nature's law designed,
Why was an independent wish
   E'er planted in my mind?
If not, why am I subject to
   His cruelty or scorn?   70
Or why has man the will and pow'r
   To make his fellow mourn?

X

Yet let not this too much, my son,
   Disturb thy youthful breast;
This partial view of humankind   75
   Is surely not the last!
The poor, oppressed, honest man

---

[3] *Man's inhumanity to man* Donald Low notes an allusion to Edward Young, *Night Thoughts* viii 104–5: 'Man's . . . endless inhumanities to man'.

[4] *To give him leave to toil* As Low notes, De Quincey refers to 'those groans which ascended to heaven from [Burns's] over-burdened heart – those harrowing words, "To give him leave to toil", which record almost a reproach to the ordinances of God' (Masson ii 137).

Had never, sure, been born,
Had there not been some recompense
To comfort those that mourn!   80

XI

Oh death – the poor man's dearest friend,
  The kindest and the best!
Welcome the hour, my aged limbs
  Are laid with thee at rest!
The great, the wealthy, fear thy blow,   85
  From pomp and pleasure torn;
But oh, a blessed relief for those
  That weary-laden mourn!'

To a Mouse, on Turning her up in her Nest, with the Plough, November 1785[1]

From POEMS, CHIEFLY IN THE SCOTTISH DIALECT (1786)

Wee, sleeket,[2] cowran,[3] tim'rous beastie,
Oh what a panic's in thy breastie![4]
Thou need na start awa sae hasty
  Wi' bickering brattle![5]
I wad be laith[6] to rin[7] an' chase thee   5
  Wi' murd'ring pattle![8]

I'm truly sorry man's dominion
Has broken nature's social union,
An' justifies that ill opinion
  Which makes thee startle   10
At me, thy poor earth-born companion
  An' fellow mortal!

I doubt na, whyles,[9] but thou may thieve;
What then? Poor beastie, thou maun live!
A daimen-icker in a thrave[10]   15
  'S a sma' request:
I'll get a blessin wi' the lave,[11]
  An' never miss't!

TO A MOUSE, ON TURNING HER UP IN HER NEST, WITH THE PLOUGH
[1] The title is correct; according to Burns's brother Gilbert, the poem was composed 'while the author was holding the plough'. John Blane, who worked on the plough with Burns, later recalled that he had chased the mouse with the intention of killing it, but was stopped by the poet, who then became 'thoughtful and abstracted'.
[2] *sleeket* smooth, sleek.
[3] *cowran* cowering.
[4] *breastie* little breast.
[5] *bickering brattle* scampering sounds.

[6] *laith* loath.
[7] *rin* run.
[8] *pattle* spade used to clear mud from the plough.
[9] *whyles* sometimes.
[10] *A daimen-icker in a thrave* the occasional ear of corn in a couple of stooks.
[11] *lave* rest, remainder. Donald Low notes the allusion to Deuteronomy 24:19: 'When thou cuttest down thine harvest in thy field, and hast forgot a sheaf in the field, thou shalt not go again to fetch it; it shall be for the stranger, for the fatherless, and for the widow: that the Lord thy God may bless thee in all the work of thine hands'.

Thy wee-bit housie, too, in ruin!
It's silly wa's[12] the win's are strewin!   20
An' naething, now, to big[13] a new ane
    O' foggage[14] green!
An' bleak December's winds ensuin,
    Baith snell[15] an' keen!

Thou saw the fields laid bare an' wast,[16]   25
An' weary winter comin fast,
An' cozie here, beneath the blast,
    Thou thought to dwell;
Till crash! the cruel coulter[17] passed
    Out through thy cell.   30

That wee-bit heap o' leaves an' stibble[18]
Has cost thee monie a weary nibble!
Now thou's turned out, for a' thy trouble,
    But[19] house or hald,
To thole[20] the winter's sleety dribble,   35
    An' cranreuch[21] cauld!

But mousie, thou art no thy-lane[22]
In proving foresight may be vain:
The best-laid schemes o' mice an' men
    Gang aft agley,[23]   40
An' lea'e us nought but grief an' pain
    For promised joy!

Still, thou art blessed compared wi' me![24]
The present only toucheth thee:
But och! I backward cast my e'e   45
    On prospects drear!
An' forward, though I canna see,
    I guess an' fear!

Tam o' Shanter. A Tale (composed late 1790)

From FRANCIS GROSE, THE ANTIQUITIES OF SCOTLAND (1791 vol. ii pp. 199–201)

When chapman billies[1] leave the street,
And drouthy[2] neebors, neebors meet,

---

[12] *silly wa's* helpless walls.
[13] *big* build.
[14] *foggage* rank grass.
[15] *snell* sharp, severe.
[16] *wast* waste.
[17] *coulter* cutting blade of the plough.
[18] *stibble* stubble.
[19] *But* without.
[20] *thole* endure.
[21] *cranreuch* hoar frost.
[22] *no thy-lane* not alone.
[23] *agley* awry.
[24] Donald Low notes the allusion to *Rasselas* chapter 2: 'As he passed through the fields, and saw the animals around him,

"Ye", said he, "are happy, and need not envy me that walk thus among you, burdened with myself; nor do I, ye gentle beings, envy your felicity, for it is not the felicity of man. I have many distresses from which ye are free; I fear pain when I do not feel it; I sometimes shrink at evils recollected, and sometimes start at evils anticipated. Surely the equity of Providence has balanced peculiar sufferings with peculiar enjoyments".'

TAM O' SHANTER. A TALE
[1] *chapman billies* pedlars.
[2] *drouthy* thirsty.

As market-days are wearing late,
And folk begin to tak the gate;[3]
While we sit bowsing at the nappy,[4]   5
And gettin fou, and unco[5] happy,
We think na on the lang Scots miles,[6]
The waters, mosses, slaps[7] and styles
That lie between us and our hame,
Where sits our sulky sullen dame,   10
Gathering her brows like gathering storm,
Nursing her wrath to keep it warm.
    This truth fand honest Tam o' Shanter,
As he frae Ayr ae[8] night did canter
(Auld Ayr, whom ne'er a town surpasses   15
For honest men and bonnie lasses).
    Oh Tam, hadst thou but been sae wise
As taen thy ain wife Kate's advice!
She tauld thee weel, thou was a skellum,[9]
A bletherin, blusterin, drunken blellum;[10]   20
That frae November till October,
Ae market-day thou was na sober;
That ilka melder[11] wi' the miller,
Thou sat as long as thou had siller;[12]
That every naig was ca'd a shoe on,   25
The smith and thee gat roarin fou[13] on;
That at the L——d's house, even on Sunday,
Thou drank wi' Kirkton Jean till Monday.
She prophesied that late or soon,
Thou wad be found deep drowned in Doon;[14]   30
Or catched wi' warlocks in the mirk,
By Alloway's auld haunted kirk.
    Ah, gentle dames, it gars me greet,[15]
To think how mony counsels sweet,
How mony lengthened sage advices,   35
The husband frae the wife despises!
    But to our tale: ae market-night
Tam had got planted[16] unco right,
Fast by an ingle bleezing[17] finely,
Wi' reamin swats[18] that drank divinely;   40
And at his elbow, souter[19] Johnie,
His ancient, trusty, drouthy crony —
Tam lo'ed him like a vera brither,
They had been fou for weeks tegither.
The night drave on wi' sangs and clatter,   45

---

3   *gate* road.
4   *nappy* ale.
5   *fou and unco* full (drunk), and mighty.
6   *the lang Scots miles* Scottish miles were traditionally longer than English ones; they were also variable. One measurement offered is 1,976 yards (as opposed to 1,760). Wordsworth borrows this idea in *Peter Bell*.
7   *slaps* bogs.
8   *ae* one.
9   *skellum* good-for-nothing.
10   *blellum* chatterer.

11   *melder* meal-grinding.
12   *siller* silver.
13   *fou* drunk.
14   *drowned in Doon* The River Doon runs through Ayrshire, to the sea beyond Burns's birthplace at Alloway.
15   *gars me greet* makes me weep.
16   *planted* settled.
17   *an ingle bleezing* a fire blazing.
18   *reamin swats* foaming new ale.
19   *souter* cobbler.

And ay the ale was growing better;
The landlady and Tam grew gracious
With favours secret, sweet and precious;
The souter tauld his queerest stories,
The landlord's laugh was ready chorus;   50
The storm without might rair and rustle,
Tam did na mind the storm a whistle.
    Care, mad to see a man sae happy,
E'en drowned himsel amang the nappy;
As bees flee hame wi' lades o' treasure,   55
The minutes winged their way wi' pleasure –
Kings may be blessed, but Tam was glorious,
O'er a' the ills o' life victorious![20]
    But pleasures are like poppies spread:
You seize the flower, its bloom is shed;   60
Or like the snow-falls in the river,
A moment white, then melts for ever;[21]
Or like the borealis race[22]
That flit ere you can point their place;
Or like the rainbow's lovely form,   65
Evanishing amid the storm.
Nae man can tether time or tide,
The hour approaches Tam maun[23] ride;
That hour, o' night's black arch the keystane,[24]
That dreary hour he mounts his beast in;   70
And sic a night he taks the road in,
As ne'er poor sinner was abroad in.
    The wind blew as 'twad blawn its last,
The rattling showers rose on the blast,
The speedy gleams the darkness swallowed,   75
Loud, deep and lang, the thunder bellowed:
That night, a child might understand,
The Deil had business on his hand.
    Weel mounted on his grey mare, Meg
(A better never lifted leg),   80
Tam skelpit[25] on through dub[26] and mire,
Despising wind and rain and fire,
Whyles[27] holding fast his gude blue bonnet,
Whyles crooning o'er an auld Scots sonnet,
Whyles glowring round wi' prudent cares   85
Lest bogles[28] catch him unawares:
Kirk Alloway[29] was drawing nigh,
Whare ghaists and houlets nightly cry.

---

[20]   *Kings may be blessed . . . victorious* important lines, as they make a political, as much as a moral, point. Wordsworth was especially keen on them, as Henry Crabb Robinson recalled: 'He praised Burns for his introduction to *Tam o' Shanter*. He had given a poetical apology for drunkenness by bringing together all the circumstances which can serve to render excusable what is in itself disgusting, thus interesting our feelings and making us tolerant of what would otherwise be not endurable' (Morley (1938) i 88).
[21]   *Or like . . . ever* In a letter of 1814 Byron described these lines as 'very graceful and pleasing' (Marchand iv 56).

[22]   *borealis race* aurora borealis, the play of (apparently) cosmic light in the night sky.
[23]   *maun* must.
[24]   *keystane* the keystone is to be an important image (see l. 210).
[25]   *skelpit* hurried.
[26]   *dub* mud.
[27]   *Whyles* sometimes.
[28]   *bogles* spectres.
[29]   *Kirk Alloway* Alloway Church.

By this time he was cross the ford
Where in the snaw the chapman smoored,[30]   90
And past the birks and meikle stane[31]
Where drunken Charlie brak's neck-bane;[32]
And through the whins and by the cairn
Where hunters fand the murdered bairn;
And near the tree aboon the well   95
Whare Mungo's mither hanged hersel.
Before him, Doon[33] pours all his floods;
The doubling storm roars through the woods;
The lightnings flash from pole to pole;
Near and more near, the thunders roll: 100
When, glimmering through groaning trees,
Kirk Alloway seemed in a bleeze –
Through ilka bore[34] the beams were glancing,
And loud resounded mirth and dancing.

Inspiring, bold John Barleycorn,[35]   105
What dangers thou canst make us scorn!
Wi' tippeny,[36] we fear nae evil;
Wi' usquabae,[37] we'll face the Devil!
The swats sae reamed in Tammie's noddle,
Fair play, he cared na deils a boddle.[38]   110
But Maggie stood right sair astonished
Till, by the heel and hand admonished,
She ventured forward on the light,
And, wow, Tam saw an unco sight!
Warlocks and witches in a dance,   115
Nae cotillon brent new frae France,
But hornpipes, jigs, strathspeys and reels
Put life and mettle in their heels.
A winnock-bunker in the east,[39]
There sat auld Nick in shape o' beast: 120
A towzie tyke,[40] black, grim and large –
To gie them music was his charge.
He screwed the pipes and gart them skirl[41]
Till roof and rafters a' did dirl!
Coffins stood round like open presses   125
That shawed the dead in their last dresses,
And by some devilish cantraip[42] slight
Each in its cauld hand held a light
By which heroic Tam was able
To note upon the haly table   130
A murderer's banes in gibbet airns;[43]

---

[30] *smoored* was smothered.
[31] *birks and meikle stane* birch trees and large rocks.
[32] *braks neck-bone* broke his neck.
[33] *Doon* the River Doon.
[34] *ilka bore* every gap.
[35] *John Barleycorn* malt whisky.
[36] *tippeny* ale.
[37] *usquabae* whisky.
[38] *he cared na deils a boddle* he didn't care about devils (a boddle is a worthless copper coin).

[39] *A winnock-bunker in the east* a bunker beneath the small east window, at the far end of the church.
[40] *towzie tyke* shaggy dog.
[41] *He screwed the pipes and gart them skirl* He turned ('screwed') the drones on the bagpipes and made them squeal ('skirl').
[42] *cantraip* witchcraft.
[43] *gibbet airns* gibbet irons. Gibbeted bodies were strung up in irons until they had literally rotted away; cf. Wordsworth *The Two-Part Prelude* i 309–10, where 'A man, the murderer of his wife, was hung/In irons'.

Twa span-lang, wee, unchirstened bairns;
A thief new-cutted frae a rape,
Wi' his last gasp his gab did gape;
Five tomahawks, wi' blood red-rusted;   135
Five scymitars, wi' murder crusted;
A garter which a babe had strangled;
A knife a father's throat had mangled,
Whom his ain son of life bereft,
The grey hairs yet stak to the heft;   140
Wi' mair of horrible and awefu',
That even to name wad be unlawfu':
Three lawyers' tongues turned inside out,
Wi' lies seamed like a beggar's clout;
Three priests' hearts, rotten, black as muck,   145
Lay stinking, vile, in every neuk.44

    As Tammie glow'red, amazed and curious,
The mirth and fun grew fast and furious.
The piper loud and louder blew;
The dancers quick and quicker flew –   150
They reeled, they set, they crossed, they cleekit,
Till ilka carlin swat and reekit45
And coost her duddies46 on the wark,
And linket47 at it in her sark.48

    Now Tam, oh Tam! had thae been queans49   155
A' plump and strappin in their teens,
Their sarks, instead o' creeshie flainen,
Been snaw-white seventeen-hunder linen50 –
Thir breeks o' mine, my only pair,
That ance were plush, o' gude blue hair,   160
I wad hae gien them off my hurdies51
For ae blink o' the bonie burdies!
But withered beldams, auld and droll,
Rigwoodie hags wad spean a foal,52
Loupin and flingin on a crumock –   165
I wonder didna turn thy stomach.

    But Tam kend what was what fu' brawlie,
There was ae winsome wench and walie53
That night enlisted in the core
(Lang after kend on Carrick shore,   170
For mony a beast to dead she shot
And perished mony a bonnie boat,
And shook baith meikle corn and bear,
And kept the countryside in fear);
Her cutty sark o' Paisley harn,54   175

---

44   *Three lawyers' tongues . . . neuk* Lines 143–6 were removed
from later versions of the poem; *neuk* corner.
45   *They reeled . . . reekit* They whirled round in the reel, faced
their partners, passed across the circle of the dance, linked
arms, and turned, till every witch sweated and steamed.
46   *duddies* clothes.
47   *linket* tripped.
48   *sark* shirt.
49   *queans* young girls.

50   *Their sarks . . . linen . . .* had their shirts, instead of being
filthy flannels, been quality linen . . .
51   *hurdies* buttocks.
52   *Rigwoodie hags wad spean a foal* ancient hags who would
wean a foal.
53   *ae winsome wench and walie* one choice, handsome wench.
54   *Her cutty sark o' Paisley harn* Her shortened undershirt was
made of 'harn' (coarse linen).

That while a lassie she had worn,
In longitude though sorely scanty,
It was her best, and she was vauntie.[55]
Ah, little thought thy reverend graunie,
That sark she coft[56] for her wee Nannie,   180
Wi' twa pund Scots ('twas a' her riches)
Should ever graced a dance o' witches!

    But here my muse her wing maun cour
(Sic flights are far beyond her power)
To sing how Nannie lap and flang –   185
A souple jad she was, and strang –
And how Tam stood, like ane bewitched,
And thought his very een enriched;
Even Satan glow'red and fidged fu' fain,
And hotched, and blew wi' might and main;   190
Till first ae caper – syne anither –
Tam lost his reason a' thegither
And roars out, 'Weel done, Cutty Sark!'
And in an instant all was dark:
And scarcely had he Maggie rallied,   195
When out the hellish legion sallied.

    As bees bizz out wi' angry fyke
When plundering herds assail their byke;[57]
As open pussie's[58] mortal foes,
When, pop! she starts before their nose;   200
As eager rins the market-croud,
When 'Catch the thief!' resounds aloud;
So Maggie rins, the witches follow,
Wi' mony an eldritch[59] shout and hollo.

    Ah Tam, ah Tam, thou'll get thy fairin!   205
In hell they'll roast thee like a herrin!
In vain thy Kate awaits thy comin,
Kate soon will be a woefu' woman!!!
Now do thy speedy utmost, Meg,
And win the keystane o' the brig;[60]   210
There at them thou thy tail may toss –
A running stream they dare na cross!
    But ere the keystane she could make,
The fient a tail she had to shake;
For Nannie, far before the rest,   215
Hard upon noble Maggie pressed,
And flew at Tam with furious ettle –
But little kend she Maggie's mettle!
Ae spring brought off her master hale,
But left behind her ain grey tail: 220
The carlin claught her by the rump

---

[55] *vauntie* proud.
[56] *coft* bought.
[57] *byke* hive.
[58] *pussie's* hare's.
[59] *eldritch* ghostly.
[60] *the keystane of the brig* the keystone of the bridge. 'It is a well-known fact that witches, or any evil spirits, have no power to follow a poor wight any farther than the middle of the next running stream. It may be proper likewise to mention to the benighted traveller, that when he falls in with "bogles", whatever danger may be in his going forward, there is much more hazard in turning back' (Burns's footnote).

And left poor Maggy scarce a stump.
  Now wha this tale o' truth shall read,
Ilk man and mother's son, take heed:
Whene'er to drink you are inclined,   225
Or cutty sarks rin in your mind –
Think, ye may buy the joys o'er dear,
Remember Tam o' Shanter's mare!

Song (composed by November 1793, published 1796, edited from MS)

Oh my love's like the red, red rose,
  That's newly sprung in June;
My love's like the melody
  That's sweetly played in tune.

As fair art thou, my bonny lass,   5
  So deep in love am I;
And I can love thee still, my dear,
  Till a' the seas gang dry.

Till a' the seas gang dry, my dear,
  And the rocks melt wi' the sun;   10
I will love thee still, my dear,
  While the sands o' life shall run.

And fare thee weel, my only love,
  Oh fare thee weel awhile!
And I will come again, my love,   15
  Though 'twere ten thousand mile.

Mary Wollstonecraft   (1759–1797)

Prolific lady of letters, moral writer and novelist, her most influential single work was *A Vindication of the Rights of Woman* (1792), which used the egalitarian ideals of the French Revolution as the springboard for a demand for women's rights. She is widely regarded as the mother of modern feminism.

She was the second of seven children, the first daughter of Edward John Wollstonecraft and Elizabeth Dickson. Home life was difficult: her father was abusive and prone to drink; her mother doted on the eldest of her sons. Mary left home at nineteen, to support herself as a writer.

In 1784, Mary, her sister Eliza, and Mary's 'soulmate' Fanny Blood opened a school in the London suburb of Islington, later moving it to Newington Green; two years later it was in financial trouble and closed. By this time Mary was becoming known in intellectual circles, a friend of Richard Price and Dr Johnson. She became one of the stable of writers published by the Unitarian, Joseph Johnson (others included Anna Laetitia Barbauld, Blake, Wordsworth, Cowper and Paine); early works include *Thoughts on the Education of Daughters* (1786), *Original Stories from Real Life* (1787) and *Mary: A Fiction* (1788). In 1788 she began contributing to Johnson's periodical, the *Analytical Review*.

A Vindication of the Rights of Men was published anonymously, 29 November 1790, within a month of Burke's *Reflections*, to which it was the first major response. It was a scathing attack on the old order of hereditary property which Burke had been so anxious to defend; as she argued, it served only to confer on the undeserving a false sense of power and worth. Conversely, those who work hard often have little or nothing to show for it. In the extract below Wollstonecraft deplores the poverty and oppression that led to the French Revolution, and criticizes Burke's tendency to resort to pure rhetoric.

Her great work, *A Vindication of the Rights of Woman* (1792), argues that true political freedom implies equality of the sexes. Her principal precursors were the bluestockings (see p. 28) – the likes of Hannah More, Anna Laetitia Barbauld and Catherine Macaulay – but none of them went as far as she did. Indeed, she criticizes Barbauld's *To a Lady, with Some Painted Flowers* for writing, of women, 'Your best and sweetest empire is – to please'.[1] Mary observed that femininity was a socially constructed concept; over-refinement, sensibility, concern with appearances, and seductiveness were parts of a false consciousness fostered by males. To this Mary traced the cultivation in women of a catalogue of unnatural and crippling inversions: reputation favoured over genuine modesty; looks over reason and understanding; sensibility over physical and mental vigour; and deceit and cunning over love. Finally, and perhaps most devastatingly, she argues that the legal disempowerment of women encourages them to become social outlaws. This was to be the theme of her last novel, *Maria or the Wrongs of Woman* (1798).

In her personal life she flouted social convention. Rejected by the painter Fuseli and his wife when she proposed a platonic *ménage*, she went to France in December 1792 to witness the Revolution. There she fell in love with Gilbert Imlay, the traveller and writer, by whom she had a daughter, Fanny, 14 May 1794. The following year she twice attempted suicide when she discovered that Imlay was living with an actress. In 1796 she and William Godwin became lovers, before marrying, 29 March 1797. This kind of behaviour was unacceptable for respectable women in the eighteenth century, and Tory critics attacked her for it. A year after her death, when she no longer posed a threat to them, the reviewers used Godwin's *Memoirs* as an excuse for reiterating their criticisms; not untypical was the *Anti-Jacobin Review*, which observed that, 'Although they married, yet, as the philosopher him-

self bears testimony, they lived for several months in a state of illicit commerce'.[2] The same reviewer attacked the *Vindication of the Rights of Woman*, 'which the superficial fancied to be profound, and the profound knew to be superficial: it indeed had very little title to the character of ingenuity'.[3] And the *European Magazine* commented that Godwin's *Memoirs*

will be read with disgust by every female who has any pretensions to delicacy; with detestation by everyone attached to the interests of religion and morality; and with indignation by anyone who might feel any regard for the unhappy woman whose frailties should have been buried in oblivion. Licentious as the times are, we trust it will obtain no imitators of the heroine in this country.[4]

No one ever found it easy to be a freethinker in England, and Wollstonecraft had the added disadvantage of being a woman at a time when females were either ornaments or slaves. It was over a century before her life and work attained anything like the recognition it deserved.

She was probably happiest during her marriage to Godwin, which did not, alas, last very long. On 30 August 1797 she gave birth to Mary Wollstonecraft Godwin (the future Mary Shelley), and died ten days later of puerperal fever.

Further reading

A Wollstonecraft Anthology ed. Janet Todd (Bloomington, Indiana, 1977)
William Godwin, *Memoirs of the Author of A Vindication of the Rights of Woman* 1798 introduced by Jonathan Wordsworth (Oxford and New York, 1990)
The Works of Mary Wollstonecraft ed. Janet Todd and Marilyn Butler (7 vols, London, 1993)
Anne K. Mellor, 'A Revolution in Female Manners', *Romanticism: A Critical Reader* 408–16
Claire Tomalin, *The Life and Death of Mary Wollstonecraft* (London, 1974)

[On Poverty]

From A VINDICATION OF THE RIGHTS OF MEN (1790) (pp. 141–5)

In this great city[1] that proudly rears its head and boasts of its population and commerce, how much misery lurks in pestilential corners, whilst idle mendicants assail, on every side, the man who hates to

MARY WOLLSTONECRAFT
[1]   See Mary Wollstonecraft, *A Vindication of the Rights of Woman* ed. Carol H. Poston (New York, 1975), p. 53.
[2]   *Anti-Jacobin Review* 1 (1798) 94–102, p. 98.

[3]   Ibid., p. 95.
[4]   *European Magazine* 33 (1798) 246–51, p. 251.

ON POVERTY
[1]   *this great city* London.

encourage impostors, or repress, with angry frown, the plaints of the poor! How many mechanics,[2] by a flux of trade or fashion, lose their employment – whom misfortunes (not to be warded off) lead to the idleness that vitiates their character and renders them afterwards averse to honest labour! Where is the eye that marks these evils, more gigantic than any of the infringements of property which you piously deprecate? Are these remediless evils? And is the human heart satisfied in turning the poor over to another world to receive the blessings this could afford?

If society was regulated on a more enlarged plan; if man was contented to be the friend of man, and did not seek to bury the sympathies of humanity in the servile appellation of master; if, turning his eyes from ideal regions of taste and elegance, he laboured to give the earth he inhabited all the beauty it is capable of receiving, and was ever on the watch to shed abroad all the happiness which human nature can enjoy – he who, respecting the rights of men, wishes to convince or persuade society that this is true happiness and dignity, is not the cruel oppressor of the poor, nor a short-sighted philosopher – *he* fears God and loves his fellow-creatures. Behold the whole duty of man! The citizen who acts differently is a sophisticated being.

Surveying civilized life, and seeing with undazzled eye the polished vices of the rich, their insincerity, want of natural affections, with all the specious train that luxury introduces, I have turned impatiently to the poor to look for man undebauched by riches or power. But alas, what did I see? A being scarcely above the brutes over which it tyrannized – a broken spirit, worn-out body, and all those gross vices which the example of the rich, rudely copied, could produce. Envy built a wall of separation that made the poor hate, whilst they bent to their superiors who, on their part, stepped aside to avoid the loathsome sight of human misery.

What were the outrages of a day[3] to these continual miseries? Let those sorrows hide their diminished head before the tremendous mountain of woe that thus defaces our globe! Man preys on man – and you[4] mourn for the idle tapestry that decorated a gothic pile, and the dronish bell that summoned the fat priest to prayer. You mourn for the empty pageant of a name, when slavery flaps her wing, and the sick heart retires to die in lonely wilds far from the abodes of man. Did the pangs you felt for insulted nobility, the anguish that rent your heart when the gorgeous robes were torn off the idol human weakness had set up, deserve to be compared with the long-drawn sigh of melancholy reflection, when misery and vice thus seem to haunt our steps, and swim on the top of every cheering prospect? Why is our fancy to be appalled by terrific perspectives of a hell beyond the grave? Hell stalks abroad: the lash resounds on the slave's naked sides, and the sick wretch, who can no longer earn the sour bread of unremitting labour, steals to a ditch to bid the world a long goodnight – or, neglected in some ostentatious hospital, breathes its last amidst the laugh of mercenary attendants.

Such misery demands more than tears. I pause to recollect myself, and smother the contempt I feel rising for your rhetorical flourishes and infantine sensibility.

[*On the Lack of Learning*]

From A VINDICATION OF THE RIGHTS OF WOMAN (1792) (pp. 40–2)

Many are the causes that, in the present corrupt state of society, contribute to enslave women by cramping their understandings and sharpening their senses. One, perhaps, that silently does more mischief than all the rest, is their disregard of order.

To do everything in an orderly manner is a most important precept which women who, generally speaking, receive only a disorderly kind of education, seldom attend to with that degree of exactness that men, who from their infancy are broken into method, observe. This negligent kind of guesswork

---

[2]   *mechanics* manual labourers.
[3]   *a day* specifically, 6 October 1789, when the people marched on the Palace of Versailles and 'conducted' the King and Queen back to Paris. Burke had realized that this was a harbinger of the larger threat to the persons of the French Royal family, and he had lamented it at length in his *Reflections* (see pp. 5–6).
[4]   *you* Mary is addressing Edmund Burke.

(for what other epithet can be used to point out the random exertions of a sort of instinctive common sense never brought to the test of reason?) prevents their generalizing matters of fact, so they do today what they did yesterday, merely because they did it yesterday.

This contempt of the understanding in early life has more baneful consequences than is commonly supposed, for the little knowledge which women of strong minds attain is, from various circumstances, of a more desultory kind than the knowledge of men, and it is acquired more by sheer observations on real life than from comparing what has been individually observed with the results of experience generalized by speculation. Led by their dependent situation and domestic employments more into society, what they learn is rather by snatches; and as learning is with them, in general, only a secondary thing, they do not pursue any one branch with that persevering ardour necessary to give vigour to the faculties and clearness to the judgement.

In the present state of society, a little learning is required to support the character of a gentleman, and boys are obliged to submit to a few years of discipline. But in the education of women, the cultivation of the understanding is always subordinate to the acquirement of some corporeal accomplishment. Even while enervated by confinement and false notions of modesty, the body is prevented from attaining that grace and beauty which relaxed half-formed limbs never exhibit. Besides, in youth their faculties are not brought forward by emulation, and having no serious scientific study, if they have natural sagacity it is turned too soon on life and manners. They dwell on effects and modifications without tracing them back to causes, and complicated rules to adjust behaviour are a weak substitute for simple principles.

As a proof that education gives this appearance of weakness to females, we may instance the example of military men, who are, like them, sent into the world before their minds have been stored with knowledge or fortified by principles. The consequences are similar: soldiers acquire a little superficial knowledge snatched from the muddy current of conversation; and, from continually mixing with society, they gain what is termed a knowledge of the world; and this acquaintance with manners and customs has frequently been confounded with a knowledge of the human heart.

But can the crude fruit of casual observation, never brought to the test of judgement, formed by comparing speculation and experience, deserve such a distinction? Soldiers, as well as women, practise the minor virtues with punctilious politeness. Where is then the sexual difference, when the education has been the same? All the difference that I can discern arises from the superior advantage of liberty, which enables the former to see more of life.

[A Revolution in Female Manners]

From A VINDICATION OF THE RIGHTS OF WOMAN (1792) (pp. 92–3)

Let not men then in the pride of power use the same arguments that tyrannic kings and venal ministers have used, and fallaciously assert that woman ought to be subjected because she has always been so. But when man, governed by reasonable laws, enjoys his natural freedom, let him despise woman if she do not share it with him – and, till that glorious period arrives, in descanting on the folly of the sex, let him not overlook his own.

Women, it is true, obtaining power by unjust means by practising or fostering vice, evidently lose the rank which reason would assign them, and they become either abject slaves or capricious tyrants. They lose all simplicity, all dignity of mind, in acquiring power, and act as men are observed to act when they have been exalted by the same means.

It is time to effect a revolution in female manners, time to restore to them their lost dignity, and make them (as a part of the human species) labour, by reforming themselves, to reform the world. It is time to separate unchangeable morals from local manners. If men be demi-gods, why let us serve them! And if the dignity of the female soul be as disputable as that of animals; if their reason does not afford sufficient light to direct their conduct whilst unerring instinct is denied, they are surely of all creatures the most miserable, and, bent beneath the iron hand of destiny, must submit to be a fair defect in creation. But to justify the ways of providence respecting them,[1] by pointing out some irrefragable reason for thus making such a large portion of mankind accountable and not accountable, would puzzle the subtlest casuist.

[On State Education]

From A VINDICATION OF THE RIGHTS OF WOMAN (1792) (pp. 386–90)

When, therefore, I call women slaves, I mean in a political and civil sense, for indirectly they obtain too much power, and are debased by their exertions to obtain illicit sway.

Let an enlightened nation[1] then try what effect reason would have to bring them back to nature and their duty; and allowing them to share the advantages of education and government with man, see whether they will become better, as they grow wiser and become free. They cannot be injured by the experiment, for it is not in the power of man to render them more insignificant than they are at present.

To render this practicable, day schools for particular ages should be established by government in which boys and girls might be educated together. The school for the younger children, from five to nine years of age, ought to be absolutely free and open to all classes.[2] A sufficient number of masters should also be chosen by a select committee in each parish, to whom any complaint of negligence, etc., might be made, if signed by six of the children's parents.

Ushers[3] would then be unnecessary, for I believe experience will ever prove that this kind of subordinate authority is particularly injurious to the morals of youth. What, indeed, can tend to deprave the character more than outward submission and inward contempt? Yet how can boys be expected to treat an usher with respect, when the master seems to consider him in the light of a servant, and almost to countenance the ridicule which becomes the chief amusement of the boys during the play hours?

But nothing of this kind could occur in an elementary day-school, where boys and girls, the rich and poor, should meet together. And to prevent any of the distinctions of vanity, they should be dressed alike, and all obliged to submit to the same discipline, or leave the school. The schoolroom ought to be surrounded by a large piece of ground in which the children might be usefully exercised, for at this age they should not be confined to any sedentary employment for more than an hour at a time. But these relaxations might all be rendered a part of elementary education, for many things improve and amuse the senses when introduced as a kind of show, to the principles of which, drily laid down, children would turn a deaf ear – for instance, botany, mechanics, and astronomy. Reading, writing, arithmetic, natural history and some simple experiments in natural philosophy might fill up the day, but these pursuits should never encroach on gymnastic plays in the open air. The elements of religion, history, the history of man, and politics, might also be taught by conversations in the socratic form.

After the age of nine, girls and boys intended for domestic employments or mechanical trades ought to be removed to other schools, and receive instruction in some measure appropriated to the destination of each individual, the two sexes being still together in the morning. But in the afternoon, the girls should attend a school where plain-work, mantua-making, millinery, etc., would be their employment.

The young people of superior abilities or fortune might now be taught, in another school, the dead

---

A REVOLUTION IN FEMALE MANNERS
[1] *But to justify . . . them* an ironic echo of *Paradise Lost* i 25–6: 'I may assert Eternal Providence, / And justify the ways of God to men'.

ON STATE EDUCATION
[1] *an enlightened nation* 'France' (Wollstonecraft's note).
[2] 'Treating this part of the subject, I have borrowed some hints from a very sensible pamphlet written by the late Bishop of Autun on public education' (Wollstonecraft's note). She refers to Talleyrand's *Rapport sur L'Instruction Publique* (1791).
[3] *Ushers* assistant masters.

and living languages, the elements of science, and continue the study of history and politics on a more extensive scale, which would not exclude polite literature.

'Girls and boys still together?' I hear some readers ask. Yes. And I should not fear any other consequence than that some early attachment might take place – which, whilst it had the best effect on the moral character of the young people, might not perfectly agree with the views of the parents (for it will be a long time, I fear, before the world is so enlightened that parents, only anxious to render their children virtuous, will let them choose companions for life themselves).

Besides, this would be a sure way to promote early marriages, and from early marriages the most salutary physical and moral effects naturally flow. What a different character does a married citizen assume from the selfish coxcomb who lives but for himself, and who is often afraid to marry lest he should not be able to live in a certain style. Great emergencies excepted, which would rarely occur in a society of which equality was the basis, a man can only be prepared to discharge the duties of public life by the habitual practice of those inferior ones which form the man.

In this plan of education the constitution of boys would not be ruined by the early debaucheries which now make men so selfish, nor girls rendered weak and vain by indolence and frivolous pursuits. But I presuppose that such a degree of equality should be established between the sexes as would shut out gallantry and coquetry, yet allow friendship and love to temper the heart for the discharge of higher duties.

[On Capital Punishment]

From Letters Written During a Short Residence in Sweden, Norway, and Denmark (1796) (pp. 207–8)

Business having obliged me to go a few miles out of town this morning, I was surprised at meeting a crowd of people of every description – and enquiring the cause of a servant who spoke French, I was informed that a man had been executed two hours before, and the body afterwards burnt.

I could not help looking with horror around; the fields lost their verdure, and I turned with disgust from the well-dressed women who were returning with their children from this sight. What a spectacle for humanity! The seeing such a flock of idle gazers plunged me into a train of reflections on the pernicious effects produced by false notions of justice. And I am persuaded that till capital punishments be entirely abolished, executions ought to have every appearance of horror given to them, instead of being (as they are now) a scene of amusement for the gaping crowd, where sympathy is quickly effaced by curiosity

I have always been of opinion that the allowing actors to die in the presence of the audience has an immoral tendency – but trifling when compared with the ferocity acquired by viewing the reality as a show. For it seems to me that in all countries the common people go to executions to see how the poor wretch plays his part, rather than to commiserate his fate, much less to think of the breach of morality which has brought him to such a deplorable end. Consequently executions, far from being useful examples to the survivors, have, I am persuaded, a quite contrary effect, by hardening the heart they ought to terrify. Besides, the fear of an ignominious death, I believe, never deterred anyone from the commission of a crime – because, in committing it, the mind is roused to activity about present circumstances. It is a game at hazard, at which all expect the turn of the die in their own favour, never reflecting on the chance of ruin till it comes.

[Norwegian Morals]

From Letters Written During a Short Residence in Sweden, Norway, and Denmark (1796) (pp. 213–14)

Love here seems to corrupt the morals, without polishing the manners, by banishing confidence and truth – the charm as well as cement of domestic life. A gentleman who has resided in this city some time assures me that he could not find language to give me an idea of the gross debaucheries into which the lower order of people fall; and the promiscuous amours of the men of the middling class with their female servants debases both beyond measure, weakening every species of family affection.

I have everywhere been struck by one characteristic difference in the conduct of the two sexes: women, in general, are seduced by their superiors, and men jilted by their inferiors. Rank and manners awe the one, and cunning and wantonness subjugate the other, ambition creeping into the woman's passion, and tyranny giving force to the man's – for most men treat their mistresses as kings do their favourites: *ergo* is not man then the tyrant of the creation?

Still harping on the same subject, you will exclaim. How can I avoid it, when most of the struggles of an eventful life have been occasioned by the oppressed state of my sex? We reason deeply, when we forcibly feel.

Helen Maria Williams   (1761–1827)

Helen was born in London in 1761 to Charles Williams, an army officer, and Helen Hay. When her father died in 1769 she and her mother moved to Berwick-upon-Tweed, where her mother educated her at home. She returned to London in 1781 and, with the help of the dissenting minister Dr Andrew Kippis, published her first poem, *Edwin and Eltruda, A Legendary Tale* (1782). She had begun a successful career as a poet and rapidly became known in literary circles, counting among her friends Fanny Burney, William Hayley, Samuel Johnson, Elizabeth Montagu, Anna Seward, the Wartons, Samuel Rogers, and Charlotte Smith. More than 1,500 people subscribed to her collected *Poems* of 1786. It was read, among others, by the young William Wordsworth, then a schoolboy of sixteen at Hawkshead Grammar School.

Helen's *Julia, A Novel; Interspersed with Some Poetical Pieces* (1790) revised Rousseau's *Nouvelle Héloïse*, making the triangle one of a man, who dies, leaving two women to bring up a child together. *The Bastille, A Vision* (one of those poetical pieces with which it is 'interspersed') offers a heady cocktail of gothicism and radicalism in which her target is the French *ancien régime*, its many injustices symbolized by the Bastille (stormed 14 July 1789). By the time it was published Helen was renowned as one of the keenest supporters of the French Revolution, and it was no surprise that she visited Paris and saw the ruins of the Bastille for herself – an experience described in her *Letters Written in France in the Summer of 1790* (1790). Events were unfolding as she wrote, and it was still possible for radicals to feel optimistic. Her thoughts 'On Revolution' are typical of apologies for its violent effects, and may be compared with James Mackintosh's thoughts on the same subject (pp. 172–4).

When he visited Paris in 1791, Wordsworth obtained a letter of introduction to Helen from Charlotte Smith, though in the event he did not meet her until 1820. She was prominent in British circles, being acquainted with Paine and Wollstonecraft. The months following the execution of Louis XVI in January 1793 were difficult ones for English radicals. Helen's support for the Revolution did not waver, and that fidelity was to cost her dearly; the outbreak of war with Britain in February, and the Reign of Terror, which began in July 1793, made life precarious for English men and women in Paris. Helen, her mother and sister were arrested under the general order of 7 October, placing all British and Hanoverian subjects 'in a state of arrest in houses of security'.

While in confinement she continued to record her impressions of revolutionary France in the *Letters Containing a Sketch of the Politics of France* (1795). Although her account of the Revolution has often been criticized for inaccuracy, it is nonetheless valuable for its firsthand account of the affairs of the day. She emphasizes the part played by women in the Revolution, their efforts to fight tyranny, and their fortitude, regarding these records of the Revolution as among her most important works: 'My narratives make a part of that marvellous story which the eighteenth century has to record to future times, and the testimony of a witness will be heard. Perhaps, indeed, I have written too little of events which I have known so well; but the convulsions of states form accumulations of private calamity that distract the attention by overwhelming the heart, and it is difficult to describe the shipwreck when sinking in the storm.'[1] All of which did her little credit with her compatriots, who were coming to regard her as a traitor to the British cause; the *British Critic* com-

---

HELENA MARIA WILLIAMS
1   *Poems on Various Subjects* (1823), p. x.

mented, not untypically, of the 1795 *Letters*: 'As usual, the French are all wise, generous, good, great, etc. etc. etc. and every other nation, her own in particular, contemptible in the balance'.[2]

Helen and her family owed their release from prison to Jean Debry, a humane deputy to the Convention, who risked much suspicion, and danger to himself, in pleading their cause. They were released in July 1794, when Helen left her family in Paris and joined John Hurford Stone in Switzerland. Stone, a Unitarian and fellow radical, was a married man. Their affair scandalized London, and made it virtually impossible for her to return. As with Mary Wollstonecraft, reviewers now had two sticks with which to beat her: her politics and her morals. Her apparent loyalty to France was particularly controversial as the war with England showed no sign of abating (it would continue until 1815). She continued to express her radical views in her volumes on French history (1815, 1819), became a naturalized French citizen in 1817, and published her collected poems in 1823. Vilified by the English, she died in Paris in 1827. She was buried next to Stone, whom she may secretly have married in 1794.

Fuller treatment is accorded Helen in my *Romantic Women Poets: An Anthology* (1997), which includes complete texts of *A Poem on the Bill Lately Passed for Regulating the Slave-Trade* (1788) and *A Farewell, for Two Years, to England* (1791).

Further reading

Mary A. Favret, *Romantic Correspondence: Women, Politics, and the Fiction of Letters* (Cambridge, 1993), chapter 3

Chris Jones, 'Helen Maria Williams and Radical Sensibility', *Prose Studies* 12 (1989) 3–24

Deborah Kennedy, ' "Storms of Sorrow": The Poetry of Helen Maria Williams', *Lumen* 10 (1991) 77–91

Nicola J. Watson, 'Novel Eloisas: Revolutionary and Counter-Revolutionary Narratives in Helen Maria Williams, Wordsworth and Byron', *TWC* 23 (1992) 18–23

Vivien Jones, 'Femininity, Nationalism, and Romanticism: The Politics of Gender in the Revolution Controversy', *History of European Ideas* 16 (1993) 299–305

The Bastille, A Vision[1]

FROM JULIA, A NOVEL (1790)

I.1
'Drear cell, along whose lonely bounds
Unvisited by light
Chill silence dwells with night,
Save when the clanging fetter sounds!
Abyss where mercy never came,   5
Nor hope the wretch can find,
Where long inaction wastes the frame,
And half annihilates the mind!

I.2
Stretched helpless in this living tomb,
Oh haste, congenial death!   10
Seize, seize this ling'ring breath,
And shroud me in unconscious gloom –
Britain, thy exiled son no more

---

[2] *British Critic* 8 (1796) 321.

THE BASTILLE, A VISION
[1] This poem is preceded in the novel by the following passage: 'Mr F. called at Mr Clifford's one evening, and finding Charlotte and Julia sitting at work, he desired their permission to read to them a poem written by a friend lately arrived from France, and who, for some supposed offence against the state, had been immured several years in the Bastille, but was at length liberated by the interference of a person in power. The horrors of his solitary dungeon were one night cheered by the following prophetic dream.' The prison of the Bastille had for years symbolized the injustice of the *ancien régime*, and its storming on 14 July 1789 (still celebrated today) was welcomed by many on both sides of the English Channel. Williams visited the ruins of the Bastille when she went to Paris in 1790; see pp. 150–1

Thy blissful vales shall see;
Why did I leave thy hallowed shore,   15
Distinguished land, where all are free?'

I.3
Bastille! within thy hideous pile
Which stains of blood defile,
Thus rose the captive's sighs,
Till slumber sealed his weeping eyes –   20
Terrific visions hover near!
He sees an awful form appear
Who drags his step to deeper cells
Where stranger wilder horror dwells.

II.1
'Oh tear me from these haunted walls   25
Or those fierce shapes control,
Lest madness seize my soul;
That pond'rous mask of iron[2] falls,
I see.' 'Rash mortal, ha! Beware,
Nor breathe that hidden name!   30
Should those dire accents wound the air,
Know death shall lock thy stiff'ning frame.

II.2
Hark, that loud bell which sullen tolls!
It wakes a shriek of woe
From yawning depths below;   35
Shrill through this hollow vault it rolls!
A deed was done in this black cell
Unfit for mortal ear;
A deed was done, when tolled that knell,
No human heart could live and hear!   40

II.3
Rouse thee from thy numbing trance,
Near on thick gloom advance,
The solid cloud has shook;
Arm all thy soul with strength to look –
Enough! Thy starting locks have rose,   45
Thy limbs have failed, thy blood has froze;
On scenes so foul, with mad affright,
I fix no more thy fastened sight.'

III.1
'Those troubled phantoms melt away,
I lose the sense of care!   50
I feel the vital air –
I see, I *see* the light of day!

---

[2] 'Alluding to the prisoner who has excited so many conjec-
tures in Europe' (Williams's note). The man in the iron mask
was a state prisoner during the reign of Louis XIV, and was
confined in the Bastille. His identity was concealed and he
wore a mask covered in black velvet; who he was remains a
mystery.

Visions of bliss, eternal powers!
What force has shook those hated walls?
What arm has rent those threat'ning towers?   55
It falls – the guilty fabric falls!'

III.2
'Now favoured mortal, now behold!
To soothe thy captive state
I ope the book of fate –
Mark what its registers unfold!   60
Where this dark pile in chaos lies,
With nature's execrations hurled,
Shall freedom's sacred temple rise
And charm an emulating world!

III.3
'Tis her awak'ning voice commands   65
Those firm, those patriot bands,
Armed to avenge her cause
And guard her violated laws!
Did ever earth a scene display
More glorious to the eye of day   70
Than millions with according mind
Who claim the rights of humankind?

IV.1
Does the famed Roman page sublime
An hour more bright unroll
To animate the soul   75
Than this, loved theme of future time?
Posterity, with rev'rence meet,
The consecrated act shall hear;
Age shall the glowing tale repeat
And youth shall drop the burning tear!   80

IV.2
The peasant, while he fondly sees
His infants round the hearth
Pursue their simple mirth
Or emulously climb his knees,
No more bewails their future lot   85
By tyranny's stern rod oppressed,
While freedom guards his straw-roofed cot
And all his useful toils are blessed.

IV.3
Philosophy,[3] oh share the meed
Of freedom's noblest deed!
'Tis thine each truth to scan,   90
Guardian of bliss and friend of man!

---

[3] The works of numerous philosophers, including Rousseau
and Holbach, were credited with having generated an intellec-
tual climate favourable to the Revolution.

'Tis thine all human wrongs to heal,
'Tis thine to love all nature's weal,
To give each gen'rous purpose birth
And renovate the gladdened earth.'[4]

95

[*A Visit to the Bastille*]

From LETTERS WRITTEN IN FRANCE IN THE SUMMER OF 1790 (1790)
(pp. 22–4, 29–30)

Before I suffered my friends at Paris to conduct me through the usual routine of convents, churches and palaces, I requested to visit the Bastille, feeling a much stronger desire to contemplate the ruins of that building than the most perfect edifices of Paris. When we got into the carriage, our French servant called to the coachman, with an air of triumph, 'A la Bastille – mais nous n'y resterons pas.'[1]

We drove under that porch which so many wretches have entered never to repass,[2] and alighting from the carriage descended with difficulty into the dungeons, which were too low to admit of our standing upright, and so dark that we were obliged at noonday to visit them with the light of a candle. We saw the hooks of those chains by which the prisoners were fastened round the neck to the walls of their cells – many of which, being below the level of the water, are in a constant state of humidity; and a noxious vapour issued from them, which more than once extinguished the candle, and was so insufferable that it required a strong spirit of curiosity to tempt one to enter. Good God! – and to these regions of horror were human creatures dragged at the caprice of despotic power. What a melancholy consideration, that

Man, proud man,
Dressed in a little brief authority,
Plays such fantastic tricks before high heaven
As make the angels weep.[3]

There appears to be a greater number of these dungeons than one could have imagined the hard heart of tyranny itself would contrive, for, since the destruction of the building, many subterraneous cells have been discovered underneath a piece of ground which was enclosed within the walls of the Bastille, but which seemed a bank of solid earth before the horrid secrets of this prison-house were disclosed. Some skeletons were found in these recesses with irons still fastened on their decaying bones.

After having visited the Bastille, we may indeed be surprised that a nation so enlightened as the French submitted so long to the oppressions of their government. But we must cease to wonder that their indignant spirits at length shook off the galling yoke. . . .

When the Bastille was taken, and the old man of whom you have no doubt heard, and who had been confined in a dungeon thirty-five years, was brought into daylight, which had not for so long a space of time visited his eyes, he staggered, shook his white beard, and cried faintly, 'Messieurs, vous m'avez rendu un grand service, rendez m'en un autre, tuez moi! Je ne sais pas où aller'.[4] 'Allons, allons', the crowd answered with one voice, 'la nation te nourrira.'[5]

---

[4] *And renovate the gladdened earth* Williams's language in this line is full of millennial optimism; many believed that the French Revolution was the harbinger of a universal spiritual revolution to come.

A VISIT TO THE BASTILLE
[1] 'To the Bastille – but we shall not remain there' (Williams's translation).

[2] *have entered never to repass* because they were tortured and executed there.
[3] *Measure for Measure* II ii 117–20.
[4] 'Gentlemen, you have rendered me one great service; render me another: kill me, for I know not where to go' (Williams's translation).
[5] 'Come along, come along, the nation will provide for you' (Williams's translation).

As the heroes of the Bastille passed along the streets after its surrender, the citizens stood at the doors of their houses loaded with wine, brandy, and other refreshments which they offered to these deliverers of their country. But they unanimously refused to taste any strong liquors, considering the great work they had undertaken as not yet accomplished, and being determined to watch the whole night, in case of any surprise.

[On Revolution]

From LETTERS WRITTEN IN FRANCE IN THE SUMMER OF 1790 (1790) (pp. 80–2)

As we came out of La Maison de Ville, we were shown, immediately opposite, the far-famed lantern at which, for want of a gallows, the first victims of popular fury were sacrificed. I own that the sight of La Lanterne chilled the blood within my veins. At that moment, for the first time, I lamented the revolution, and, forgetting the imprudence or the guilt of those unfortunate men, could only reflect with horror on the dreadful expiation they had made. I painted in my imagination the agonies of their families and friends, nor could I for a considerable time chase these gloomy images from my thoughts.

It is forever to be regretted that so dark a shade of ferocious revenge was thrown across the glories of the revolution. But alas! Where do the records of history point out a revolution unstained by some actions of barbarity? When do the passions of human nature rise to that pitch which produces great events, without wandering into some irregularities? If the French Revolution should cost no further bloodshed, it must be allowed, notwithstanding a few shocking instances of public vengeance, that the liberty of twenty-four millions of people will have been purchased at a far cheaper rate than could ever have been expected from the former experience of the world.

[Retrospect from England]

From LETTERS WRITTEN IN FRANCE IN THE SUMMER OF 1790 (1790) (pp. 217–21)

Every visitor brings me intelligence from France full of dismay and horror. I hear of nothing but crimes, assassinations, torture and death. I am told that every day witnesses a conspiracy, that every town is the scene of a massacre, that every street is blackened with a gallows, and every highway deluged with blood. I hear these things, and repeat to myself: Is this the picture of France? Are these the images of that universal joy which called tears into my eyes and made my heart throb with sympathy? To me, the land which these mighty magicians have suddenly covered with darkness where, waving their evil wand, they have reared the dismal scaffold, have clotted the knife of the assassin with gore, have called forth the shriek of despair and the agony of torture – to me, this land of desolation appeared dressed in additional beauty beneath the genial smile of liberty. The woods seemed to cast a more refreshing shade, and the lawns to wear a brighter verdure, while the carols of freedom burst from the cottage of the peasant, and the voice of joy resounded on the hill and in the valley.

Must I be told that my mind is perverted, that I am become dead to all sensations of sympathy, because I do not weep with those who have lost a part of their superfluities, rather than rejoice that the oppressed are protected, that the wronged are redressed, that the captive is set at liberty, and that the poor have bread? Did the universal parent of the human race implant the feelings of pity in the heart, that they should be confined to the artificial wants of vanity, the ideal deprivations of greatness; that they should be fixed beneath the dome of the palace, or locked within the gate of the chateau; without extending one commiserating sigh to the wretched hamlet, as if its famished inhabitants, though not ennobled by man, did not bear, at least, the ensigns of nobility stamped on our nature by God?

Must I hear the charming societies in which I found all the elegant graces of the most polished manners, all the amiable urbanity of liberal and cultivated minds, compared with the most rude, ferocious, and barbarous levellers that ever existed? Really, some of my English acquaintance (whatever objections they may have to republican principles) do, in their discussions of French politics, adopt a most free and republican style of censure. Nothing can be more democratical than their mode of expression, or display a more levelling spirit, than their unqualified contempt of *all* the leaders of the revolution.

It is not my intention to shiver[1] lances in every society I enter, in the cause of the National Assembly. Yet I cannot help remarking that, since the Assembly does not presume to set itself up as an example to this country, we seem to have very little right to be furiously angry, because they think proper to try another system of government themselves. Why should they not be suffered to make an experiment in politics? I have always been told that the improvement of every science depends upon experiment. But I now hear that, instead of their new attempt to form the great machine of society upon a simple principle of general amity upon the Federation of its members, they ought to have repaired the feudal wheels and springs by which their ancestors directed its movements.

Yet if mankind had always observed this retrograde motion, it would surely have led them to few acquisitions in virtue or in knowledge, and we might even have been worshipping the idols of paganism at this moment. To forbid, under the pains and penalties of reproach, all attempts of the human mind to advance to greater perfection, seems to be proscribing every art and science. And we cannot much wonder that the French, having received so small a legacy of public happiness from their forefathers, and being sensible of the poverty of their own patrimony, should try new methods of transmitting a richer inheritance to their posterity.

[*Madame Roland*]

From LETTERS CONTAINING A SKETCH OF THE POLITICS OF FRANCE (1795)
(pp. 195–7, 200–1)

At this period one of the most accomplished women that France has produced perished on the scaffold. This lady was Madame Roland, the wife of the late minister. On the 31st of May he had fled from his persecutors, and his wife who remained was carried to prison. The wits observed on this occasion that the body of Roland was missing, but that he had left his soul behind.

Madame Roland was indeed possessed of the most distinguished talents and a mind highly cultivated by the study of literature. I had been acquainted with her since I first came to France, and had always observed in her conversation the most ardent attachment to liberty and the most enlarged sentiments of philanthropy – sentiments which she developed with an eloquence peculiar to herself, with a flow and power of expression which gave new graces and new energy to the French language. With these extraordinary endowments of mind she united all the warmth of a feeling heart and all the charms of the most elegant manners. She was tall and well-shaped, her air was dignified, and although more than thirty-five years of age she was still handsome. Her countenance had an expression of uncommon sweetness, and her full dark eyes beamed with the brightest rays of intelligence.

I visited her in the prison of St Pelagie, where her soul, superior to circumstances, retained its accustomed serenity, and she conversed with the same animated cheerfulness in her little cell as she used to do in the hotel of the minister. She had provided herself with a few books, and I found her reading Plutarch.[1] She told me she expected to die, and the look of placid resignation with which she spoke of it convinced me that she was prepared to meet death with a firmness worthy of her exalted character. . . .

When more than one person is led at the same time to execution, since they can suffer only in succession, those who are reserved to the last are condemned to feel multiplied deaths at the sound of the falling instrument and the sight of the bloody scaffold. To be the first victim was therefore considered as a privilege, and had been allowed to Madame Roland as a woman. But when she observed the dis-

---

RETROSPECT FROM ENGLAND
[1]   *shiver* shatter.

MADAME ROLAND
[1]   Plutarch (*c.* AD 46–*c.*120), Greek biographer and moral philosopher, author of the *Lives*, relating the lives of eminent Greek and Roman statesmen and soldiers.

may of her companion, she said to him, 'Allez le premier: que je vous épargne au moins la douleur de voir couler mon sang.'[2] She then turned to the executioner and begged that this sad indulgence might be granted to her fellow sufferer. The executioner told her that he had received orders that she should perish first.

'But you cannot, I am sure', said she with a smile, 'refuse the last request of a lady.' The executioner complied with her demand. When she mounted the scaffold and was tied to the fatal plank, she lifted up her eyes to the statue of Liberty near which the guillotine was placed, and exclaimed, 'Ah Liberté, comme on t'a jouée!'[3] The next moment she perished. But her name will be recorded in the annals of history as one of those illustrious women whose superior attainments seem fitted to exalt her sex in the scale of being.

Joanna Baillie (1762–1851)

Joanna was the younger daughter of Dorothea Hunter and James Baillie, a presbyterian minister of Bothwell, Lanarkshire, later Professor of Divinity at the University of Glasgow (where a cache of her letters is now retained in the library). Her mother's family was distinguished: her aunt was Anne Hunter (1742–1821), the poet and bluestocking; her uncles were the famous surgeons, William and John Hunter. In 1783 William bequeathed his London house in Great Windmill Street to Matthew, Joanna's brother, a physician and anatomist. In 1784 his mother and sisters joined him there, and on his marriage in 1791 moved to Hampstead. After Mrs Baillie's death in 1806, Joanna lived with her sister for the remainder of her life.

Her first publication was the little-noticed *Poems; wherein it is attempted to describe certain views of nature and of rustic manners* (1790). The volume has much charm, and is in fact quite experimental, as the various poems not merely evoke different scenes, but different psychological states. All the same, they are apprentice pieces, and look forward to her *Series of Plays; in which it is attempted to delineate the stronger passions of the mind* (3 vols, 1798–1812), the work which attracts most critical attention today. The first volume contained two plays on hate, and two on love. It appeared anonymously, leading to widespread speculation about the identity of its author. Her authorship was acknowledged in 1800, the year that saw the first performance of her *De Monfort* with Sarah Siddons in the starring role. She became widely known in literary circles, being acquainted with Wordsworth, Scott, Samuel Rogers and Anna Laetitia Barbauld (who included

some of the 1790 poems in an anthology). Her reputation went into decline after a particularly harsh review from Jeffrey in 1803. In subsequent years she concentrated on poetry.

Her 'Introductory Discourse' of 1798 argues for a drama faithful to 'passion that is permanent in its nature', just as the Preface to *Lyrical Ballads* was to justify the preoccupation with 'low and rustic life' with the claim that 'in that situation the passions of men are incorporated with the beautiful and permanent forms of nature' (p. 357). No doubt this was something she discussed with Wordsworth when they became acquainted in literary circles in London in the 1810s, though critical investigation indicates that Wordsworth borrowed from her as early as 1799.

Some of the best of Joanna's poems are included in my *Romantic Women Poets: An Anthology* (1997) pp. 254–60.

Further reading

Margaret S. Carhart, *The Life and Work of Joanna Baillie* (New Haven, 1923)

Catherine B. Burroughs, 'English Romantic Women Writers and Theatre Theory: Joanna Baillie's Prefaces to the *Plays on the Passions*', RR 274–96

Marjean D. Purinton, *Romantic Ideology Unmasked: The Mentally-Constructed Tyrannies in Dramas of William Wordsworth, Lord Byron, Percy Shelley, and Joanna Baillie* (Newark and London, 1994)

Anne K. Mellor, 'Joanna Baillie and the Counter-Public Sphere', SIR 33 (1994) 559–67

---

[2] 'Go first; let me at least spare you the pain of seeing my blood shed' (Williams's translation).

[3] 'Ah Liberty, how hast thou been sported with!' (Williams's translation); apparently the source of Wordsworth, *Thirteen-Book Prelude* x 352–4.

[On Passion]

From A SERIES OF PLAYS (1798) (from *Introductory Discourse*, PP. 38–9)

But the last part of the task which I have mentioned as peculiarly belonging to tragedy – unveiling the human mind under the dominion of those strong and fixed passions which, seemingly unprovoked by outward circumstances, will from small beginnings brood within the breast till all the better dispositions, all the fair gifts of nature, are borne down before them – her poets in general have entirely neglected, and even her first and greatest have but imperfectly attempted. They have made use of the passions to mark their several characters and animate their scenes, rather than to open to our view the nature and portraitures of those great disturbers of the human breast with whom we are all, more or less, called upon to contend.

With their strong and obvious features, therefore, they have been presented to us stripped almost entirely of those less obtrusive (but not less discriminating) traits which mark them in their actual operation. To trace them in their rise and progress in the heart seems but rarely to have been the object of any dramatist. We commonly find the characters of a tragedy affected by the passions in a transient, loose, unconnected manner. Or, if they are represented as under the permanent influence of the more powerful ones, they are generally introduced to our notice in the very height of their fury, when all that timidity, irresolution, distrust, and a thousand delicate traits which make the infancy of every great passion more interesting perhaps than its full-blown strength, are fled. The impassioned character is generally brought into view under those irresistible attacks of their power which it is impossible to repel, whilst those gradual steps that led him into this state (in some of which a stand might have been made against the foe) are left entirely in the shade.

These passions that may be suddenly excited and are of short duration, as anger, fear, and oftentimes jealousy, may in this manner be fully represented. But those great masters of the soul (ambition, hatred, love – every passion that is permanent in its nature and varied in progress), if represented to us but in one stage of its course, is represented imperfectly.

It is a characteristic of the more powerful passions that they will increase and nourish themselves on very slender aliment: it is from within that they are chiefly supplied with what they feed on, and it is in contending with opposite passions and affections of the mind that we least discover their strength – not with events. But in tragedy it is events more frequently than opposite affections which are opposed to them, and those often of such force and magnitude that the passions themselves are almost obscured by the splendour and importance of the transactions to which they are attached.

William Lisle Bowles   (1762–1851)

Bowles's career demonstrates that it was not necessary to be an adventurer, a revolutionary, an opium addict, to die young, or indeed to have a life of any intrinsic interest at all, to have been a poet in the romantic period. Born into a clergy family at Kings Sutton, Northamptonshire, he was the pupil of Joseph Warton at Winchester, and Thomas Warton at Trinity College, Oxford, where he matriculated in 1781 (graduated 1792). Rejected in love by the niece of Sir Samuel Romilly, he went on a walking tour of northern England, Scotland, and the continent, during which he composed his *Fourteen Sonnets* (1789). The edition of 100 copies sold out immediately, and a second, this time containing 21 sonnets, was published within weeks. They had reached a ninth edition by 1805. He published much else, but nothing as popular and influential as the sonnets. Wordsworth and Coleridge read them in 1789, and in *Biographia Literaria* Coleridge praised 'the genial influence of a style of poetry, so tender, and yet so manly, so natural and real, and yet so dignified, and harmonious, as the sonnets, etc., of Mr Bowles!'[1] True, it was the combination of the same melancholy as that found in the sonnets of his Oxford tutor, Thomas Warton, with a sophisticated sense of

---

WILLIAM LISLE BOWLES
[1]   CC *Biographia* i 17. He also included three of Bowles's sonnets in his *Sonnets from Various Authors* (1796).

the picturesque and sublime, that made his sonnets distinctive and, in their day, fashionable. His sonnet to the Itchin looks back to Warton's *To the River Lodon* (see pp. 3–4), and forward to Coleridge's *To the River Otter* (p. 450).

Further reading

A Wiltshire Parson and his Friends: The Correspondence of William Lisle Bowles ed. Garland Greever (Boston and New York, 1926)

A. Harris Fairbanks, ' "Dear Native Brook": Coleridge, Bowles, and Thomas Warton the Younger', *TWC* 6 (1975) 313–15

Bill Ruddick, ' "Genius of the Sacred Fountain of Tears": A Bicentenary Tribute to the Sonnets of William Lisle Bowles', *Charles Lamb Bulletin* NS 72 (1990) 276–84

Sonnet VIII. To the River Itchin,[1] near Winton

From FOURTEEN SONNETS (1789)

Itchin, when I behold thy banks again,
   Thy crumbling margin, and thy silver breast
   On which the self-same tints still seem to rest,
Why feels my heart the shiv'ring sense of pain?
   Is it that many a summer's day has passed   5
Since in life's morn I carolled on thy side?
Is it that oft since then my heart has sighed
   As youth, and hope's delusive gleams, flew fast?
Is it that those who circled on thy shore,
Companions of my youth, now meet no more?   10
   Whate'er the cause, upon thy banks I bend
Sorrowing, yet feel such solace at my heart,
   As at the meeting of some long-lost friend
From whom, in happier hours, we wept to part.

Ann Radcliffe (*née* Ward)   (1764–1823)

Ann Radcliffe was born in London on 9 July 1764, the only child of William Ward and Ann Oates. Ward may have been a haberdasher by trade, but he was nonetheless well connected. His uncle was William Cheselden, surgeon to George II, and Ann Oates was the cousin of Sir Richard Jebb, a famous physician of the day. Her maternal uncle-in-law was Thomas Bentley, of the pottery firm Wedgwood and Bentley.

On 15 January 1787, at the age of twenty-three, Ann married William Radcliffe at St Michael's Church in Bath. Radcliffe was an Oxford graduate who trained as a lawyer at the Inner Temple, but he gave up his training and they moved to London where he became editor and proprietor of a newspaper, *The English Chronicle*. The couple were to remain childless, but the marriage seems to have been happy. In leisure hours

Ann read, sang, and went to operas, oratorios and plays. She also began to write. Six works appeared, with remarkable speed, between 1789 and 1797. Her first three novels were published, anonymously, within three years.

The Castles of Athlin and Dunbayne, A Highland Story (1789) is comparatively short and experimental, but full of the rugged landscapes that were to become the stock-in-trade of the Radcliffe chiller. It received little critical attention, and no reviews that she would have found encouraging. But she persisted. The following year she published *A Sicilian Romance*, set in Catholic Europe, featuring a heroine who is the focus of debased and perverted lust. All the same, it is still a step away from her best work – the three novels that were to follow: *The Romance of the Forest* (1791), *The Mysteries of*

SONNET VIII. TO THE RIVER ITCHIN
[1] The Itchin runs through Winchester, where Bowles went to school, and a favourite walk of Wykehamists (Winchester College pupils) runs along its banks.

Udolpho (1794) and *The Italian* (1797). *The Romance of the Forest* was greeted with rave reviews, which encouraged its anonymous author to reveal her identity on publication of a second edition in 1792. This established her reputation beyond doubt. *The Mysteries of Udolpho* was, if anything, even more successful. It received a lukewarm reception from the reviewers, who criticized the poetry, anachronisms, improbabilities, and so forth (all the lumber of the gothic, in other words), but this had little effect on sales. *Udolpho* was an enormous success with the reading public, selling in vast numbers.

After its publication, in the summer of 1794, the Radcliffes went on holiday to Holland, Germany and the Lake District. Travel books were all the rage, and as a result of the tour Ann wrote her own, *A Journey Made in the Summer of* 1794 (1795). It contains some memorable landscape descriptions, particularly of the Lakes. The extracts below, particularly that about Borrowdale (p. 157), show how well the scenery suited her gothic sensibilties. Ann never again went abroad, but the Radcliffes went on holiday, within England, at least once a year after this tour.

Ann's father died on 24 July 1798, leaving her interests in the rents of property in Houghton-on-the-Hill, near Leicester; her mother died two years later, leaving most of her property to her. Combined with earnings from her novels, she found herself comfortably off for the first time in her life. She did not need to write for financial motives, and indeed published no more during her life. Of course, by the 1800s her novels were so well established in the literary world that they were attracting the attention of satirists, imitators, and those who, like Jane Austen in *Northanger Abbey*, disapproved of the 'debased' public appetite for the gothic. Ann composed a final novel in 1802, *Gaston de Blondeville*, which appeared after her death, in 1826. In subsequent years she continued to write poetry, but in seclusion, and with no expectation of publication. Her virtual disappearance from the public eye aroused speculation that the author of the gothic chillers of the 1790s had gone mad, or even that she had died. Sir Walter Scott for one was taken in by rumours that, 'in consequence of brooding over the terrors which she depicted, her reason had at length been overturned, and that the author of *The Mysteries of Udolpho* only existed as the melancholy inmate of a private madhouse'.[1] Her last twelve years were dogged by respiratory ailments, mainly asthma.

The best of her poems are included in my *Romantic Women Poets: An Anthology* (1997).

Further reading

Clare Frances McIntyre, *Ann Radcliffe in Relation to her Time* (New Haven, 1920)
The Critical Response to Ann Radcliffe ed. Deborah D. Rogers (Westport, CT, 1994)
Robert Miles, *Ann Radcliffe: The Great Enchantress* (Manchester and New York, 1995)
Deborah D. Rogers, *Ann Radcliffe: A Bio-Bibliography* (Westport, CT, 1996)

Rondeau

From THE MYSTERIES OF UDOLPHO (4 vols, 1794) (II 59–60)

Soft as yon silver ray that sleeps
Upon the ocean's trembling tide;
Soft as the air that lightly sweeps
Yon sail, that swells in stately pride;

Soft as the surge's stealing note   5
That dies along the distant shores,
Or warbled strain that sinks remote –
So soft the sigh my bosom pours!

True as the wave to Cynthia's ray,[1]
True as the vessel to the breeze,   10

ANN RADCLIFFE
[1]   Quoted Deborah D. Rogers, *Ann Radcliffe: A Bio-Bibliography* (1996), p. 13.

RONDEAU
[1]   *Cynthia's ray* moonlight; Cynthia is the Roman name for the moon.

True as the soul to music's sway
Or music to Venetian seas;

Soft as yon silver beams that sleep
Upon the ocean's trembling breast;
So soft, so true, fond love shall weep,   15
So soft, so true, with thee shall rest.

[The Road to Emont]

From A JOURNEY MADE IN THE SUMMER OF 1794 (1795) (pp. 407–8)

Soon after, the road brought us to the brows of Emont, a narrow well-wooded vale,[1] the river from which it takes its name meandering through it from Ullswater[2] among pastures and pleasure-grounds, to meet the Lowther near Brougham Castle.[3] Penrith and its Castle and beacon[4] look up the vale from the north, and the astonishing fells of Ullswater close upon it in the south, while Delemain, the house and beautiful grounds of Mr Hassel; Hutton St John, a venerable old mansion; and the single tower called Dacre Castle adorn the valley.

But who can pause to admire the elegancies of art, when surrounded by the wonders of nature? The approach to this sublime lake along the heights of Emont is exquisitely interesting, for the road (being shrouded by woods) allows the eye only partial glimpses of the gigantic shapes that are assembled in the distance and, awakening high expectation, leaves the imagination thus elevated to paint the 'forms of things unseen'. Thus it was when we caught a first view of the dark broken tops of the fells that rise round Ullswater,[5] of size and shape most huge, bold, and awful, overspread with a blue mysterious tint that seemed almost supernatural, though according in gloom and sublimity with the severe features it involved.

[The Jaws of Borrowdale] (p. 465)

From A JOURNEY MADE IN THE SUMMER OF 1794 (1795) (p. 465)

Dark rocks yawn at its entrance, terrific as the wildness of a maniac, and disclose a narrow pass running up between mountains of granite that are shook into almost every possible form of horror. All above resembles the accumulations of an earthquake – splintered, shivered,[1] piled, amassed. Huge cliffs have rolled down into the glen below, where, however, is still a miniature of the sweetest pastoral beauty on the banks of the river Derwent. But description cannot paint either the wildness of the mountains, or the pastoral and sylvan peace and softness that wind at their base.

THE ROAD TO EMONT
[1]   Radcliffe describes the countryside just south of Penrith, in the north of the Lake District. The River Eamont flows from Penrith to Ullswater.
[2]   Ullswater lake on the borders of what used to be Westmoreland and Cumberland, in the north-east of the Lake District.
[3]   Brougham Castle two miles south-east of Penrith; the castle was in ruins even in Radcliffe's day, and was believed to have been built by the Romans.

[4]   Penrith beacon was built in 1719 to warn of invasion from Scotland and is still to be seen. It features in one of Wordsworth's 'spots of time' (see Two-Part Prelude i 296–327, pp. 307–8).
[5]   The fells around Ullswater play an important part in one of Wordsworth's spots of time; see Two-Part Prelude i 81–122, pp. 302–3.

THE JAWS OF BORROWDALE
[1]   shivered shattered.

[*Grasmere*]

From A JOURNEY MADE IN THE SUMMER OF 1794 (1795) (p. 470)

Beyond Dunmail Raise,[1] one of the grand passes from Cumberland into Westmorland, Helm Crag rears its crest, a strange fantastic summit – round, yet jagged and splintered like the wheel of a water-mill – overlooking Grasmere, which soon after opened below. A green spreading circle of mountains embosoms this small lake and, beyond, a wider range rises in amphitheatre, whose rocky tops are rounded and scalloped, yet are great, wild, irregular, and were then overspread with a tint of faint purple. The softest verdure margins the water and mingles with corn enclosures and woods that wave up the hills, but scarcely a cottage anywhere appears, except at the northern end of the lake, where the village of Grasmere and its very neat white church stand among trees near the shore, with Helm Crag and a multitude of fells rising over it and beyond each other in the perspective.

John Thelwall   (1764–1834)

'Citizen John Thelwall had something good about him', Coleridge recalled in 1830, 'We were once sitting in Somersetshire in a beautiful recess. I said to him, "Citizen John! This is a fine place to talk treason in!" "Nay, Citizen Samuel!", replied he, "it is a place to make a man forget that there is any necessity for treason." '[1] As one of the defendants at the treason trials of 1794, Thelwall had good reason to want to forget.

The son of a silk mercer in London, he had been involved in the theatre, the law, and the family business, before becoming a journalist. His interest in politics was stimulated by involvement in the Society for Free Debate at Coachmakers' Hall in Southwark. In autumn 1793 he joined the London Corresponding Society, and on 21 October became a member of the General Committee. The Society had been founded by Thomas Hardy, a Scottish cobbler, 25 January 1792, as a means of agitating among those wishing for political reform. The low subscription fee of one penny a week was intended to encourage the involvement of tradesmen and artisans. Thelwall came to the fore at a crowded general meeting, 20 January 1794, which was followed by an anniversary dinner at the Globe Tavern in Fleet Street. By this time he had already begun to prove his extraordinary talents as a political orator, poet and publicist. After the dinner he took the chair to propose the toasts, including one to *The Rights of Man*, after which he sang republican songs of his own composition, copies of which were later sold to members of the society and the audiences at his political lectures.

At a time of comparative political freedom it is not easy to imagine how dangerous it was to be a radical in 1794. England had been at war with France for a year (and would remain so until 1815), and Pitt's government was increasingly intolerant of French sympathizers at home. By the spring of 1794 the Terror in Paris was at its height: Robespierre executed Danton and other eminent French politicians in March and April 1794. Undaunted, the London Corresponding Society held a mass meeting on the bowling green at Chalk Farm, 14 April, of which the master of ceremonies was Thelwall. By this time he was under constant surveillance by government spies, who reported that, when quenching his thirst after the five-hour meeting, he had removed the froth from his tankard with a knife, remarking, 'So should all tyrants be served!' That meeting, and another, of the radical Society for Constitutional Information on 2 May, rang alarm bells in Pitt's ministry. Fears of a French invasion made it imperative that the government stifle dissident voices in its midst. On 12 May, Thomas Hardy, secretary of the London Corresponding Society, and Daniel Adams, secretary of the Society for Constitutional Information were arrested at home on the charge of treason. Thelwall and the Revd Jeremiah Joyce were arrested the following day; Horne Tooke, John Lovett, John Richter, and John Augustus Bonney on the 16th. Pitt then suspended habeas corpus, allowing him to detain the prisoners in the Tower of London for up to eight months without trial. This was no vacation; all suffered ill health while in the damp, draughty, uncom-

---

GRASMERE
[1] *Dunmail Raise* pass at the north end of Grasmere vale, on the border of Cumberland and Westmoreland, so called after the Cumbrian King Dunmail who was slaughtered there by the forces of the Saxon King Edmund in 945 AD.

JOHN THELWALL
[1] CC *Table Talk* i 180–1.

fortable prison, aware that the penalty they faced was death, English-style: hanging, drawing, and quartering. Thelwall distracted himself by composing his *Poems Written in Close Confinement* (1795).

A few days before the trials, Godwin published an attack on the government case under the title *Cursory Strictures on the Charge delivered by Lord Chief Justice Eyre to the Grand Jury*. It appeared in the *Morning Chronicle* for 21 October, and was extremely influential. The treason trials began on 25 October; one by one, the accused were either acquitted or had the charges dropped, largely thanks to the devastating effect of Godwin's pamphlet.

A passionately committed freethinker, Thelwall continued to agitate and lecture in spite of the fact that government spies followed him everywhere, often paying stooges to heckle or break up his meetings by force. His lectures, delivered in Beaufort Buildings off the Strand, were published in his periodical, *The Tribune*. They attracted audiences of 400–500, who paid the relatively high entrance fee of one shilling and sixpence, and he claimed they contained a number of 'aristocrats'. The government was constantly seeking ways of suppressing political dissent; their chance came on 29 October 1795, when the King was attacked by a mob on his way to open Parliament. This, and a large meeting of the London Corresponding Society in the fields near Copenhagen House, Islington, in which Thelwall was involved, provided the government with the excuse they needed: on 6 November two bills were introduced into both chambers of the House, forbidding meetings of fifty or more without the consent of a magistrate, and requiring that treason consist of various offences including 'inciting the people to hatred or contempt of His Majesty'. The Two Bills, or 'Gagging Acts', as they were known among the radicals, became law on 18 December. Thelwall warned in *The Tribune* that such measures would give rise to even worse problems for the government, and in the last issue of *The Tribune* he published his moving *Civic Oration*, announcing his decision to retire from politics (see pp. 162–3). Not without cause, his view was that the Acts were aimed at him. There were many protests by societies across the land, but the government finally won.

In summer 1796 he left London for Norwich, where he delivered a course of twenty-two lectures, admitting no more than forty-nine persons, on the subject of 'Classical History, and particularly the Laws and Revolutions of Rome' – a title that provided him with a cover under which to continue his political disquisitions on contemporary events. Later in the year he lectured at Great Yarmouth, where the third meeting was broken up by ninety sailors armed with bludgeons. The three remaining lectures were safely delivered, and Thelwall went on to speak at meetings at King's Lynn and Wisbech. Throughout these times he was the victim of constant harassment by government agents. Lectures at Derby, Stockport, and Norwich were broken up by soldiers, and he was chased 15 miles out of Ashby de la Zouch when passing through on private business.

He was finally driven out of political agitation altogether. When he set off, on 29 June 1797, for a pedestrian tour of the west of England and Wales, he was on the lookout for a suitable retreat. Among those who welcomed him were Coleridge, Wordsworth and Dorothy, who he met at Nether Stowey. Coleridge, whose own political lectures were curtailed by the two bills,[2] had begun a correspondence with Thelwall in late April 1796, with the words: 'Pursuing the same end by the same means we ought not to be strangers to each other'.[3] He had enclosed a copy of his *Poems* (1796), which Thelwall read and analysed in his letter of 10 May 1796 (see pp. 163–4). He criticized Coleridge's ornate manner, reminding him of the importance of writing simply and lucidly; the principles he prescribed were exactly the same as those commended in the Preface to *Lyrical Ballads*, and they are followed in Thelwall's proto-conversation poems, 'Lines written at Bridgwater' and 'To the Infant Hampden'.[4] As 'Lines written at Bridgwater' reveals, Thelwall was at ease among the poets, and for a while entertained the possibility of settling among them. But they were already under surveillance by a government spy,[5] and the landlord of Alfoxden House was sufficiently alarmed to deny the Wordsworths occupation for a further year.

Thelwall moved on, returned to Bristol, Gloucestershire, and finally Wales, where he found a small farm in the hamlet of Llys Wen, on the banks of the Wye, to which he retired with his family. This proved disastrous; the locals harassed him, his efforts at farming failed, and his beloved daughter, Maria, died. In later years he returned to lecturing, but this time on the subject of elocution. Years after his death, Wordsworth recalled: 'He really was a man of extraordinary talent, an affectionate husband and a good father. Though brought up in the city on a tailor's board he was truly sensible of the beauty of natural objects'.[6]

---

2   See Samuel Taylor Coleridge, *Lectures 1795 On Politics and Religion* ed. Lewis Patton and Peter Mann (Princeton, NJ, 1971), Editors' Introduction.
3   Griggs i 204.
4   For further discussion see my 'Coleridge, Thelwall, and the Politics of Poetry', *The Coleridge Bulletin* 4 (1994) 23–44.
5   For more on which, see Nicholas Roe, *Wordsworth and Coleridge: The Radical Years* (Oxford, 1988), pp. 234–62.
6   *FN* 4.

Further reading

C. Cestre, *John Thelwall: A Pioneer of Democracy in England* (London, 1906)

E. P. Thompson, 'Disenchantment or Default? A Lay Sermon', *Power and Consciousness* ed. Conor Cruise O'Brien and William Dean Vanech (London and New York, 1969), pp. 149–81

Nicholas Roe, *Wordsworth and Coleridge: The Radical Years* (Oxford, 1988)

—, 'Coleridge and John Thelwall: The Road to Nether Stowey', *The Coleridge Connection* ed. Richard Gravil and Molly Lefebure (Basingstoke, 1990), pp. 60–80

E. P. Thompson, 'Hunting the Jacobin Fox', *Past and Present* 142 (1994) 94–140

[*The Old Peasant*]

From THE PERIPATETIC (1793) (vol. iii pp. 137–41)

'Detested villains! Proud parochial tyrants! And are these violators of all that endears society the objects who are to monopolize your generosity, while the oppressed mechanic groans in our streets unpitied, and the aged and infirm, whose strength has been exhausted in the labours most important to the community, feel the oppressions of want and sorrow accumulated to the infirmities of years, and apply for relief in vain? How different, my Wentworth – oh, how different were the appearance, the sentiments, and the fate of the honest unfortunate peasant whom (bending with age, and propping his feeble steps upon his hoe) we met upon Ewell[1] common on a late excursion! Do you not see him again in fancy? Does not the tear start again into your eye as he lifts his hat in humble obeisance from his hairless forehead as we approach him? Unmerited complacency! Why was that obeisance paid to us? For aught you knew, poor victim, we might have been in the number of your oppressors, and that distinction of appearance which claimed your reverence might have entitled us to your execration. But the bruised reed turns not upon its destroyer, but bends beneath the foot that tramples it; else what proud gentility! In this insolence of thy oppression, what must be thy instant fate? Poor old man! At such a time of life to be doomed to wander from place to place for employment, and be doomed to wander in vain! To be repulsed from every door on account of those infirmities which former toils and former sorrows had brought upon thee, and to have thy appeals for charity retorted by the unfeeling malevolence of that upstart opulence which, in thy better days, had crouched to thee for obligations!'

'Your lamentation is interesting', said Ambulator, 'but you forget that here are two of us unacquainted with the story it alludes to'.

'It is short and simple, but it is not therefore the less pathetic. My wife', said he, with a mixed expression of anguish and resignation, 'is out of her distresses. Heaven has taken her from her sorrows. I have but one to care for – but that is *one too much*. Times go very hard, particularly with us who are grown old and slow. I have wandered from place to place, and though I am willing to work for less wages, nobody will employ a feeble old man now there are so many young ones out of other works, who are glad to go into the fields. I have applied to the parish here, for I was an inhabitant about five and twenty years ago, and lived in a better way. I had a little farm, and a few cows, and two or three sheep of my own, till my landlord turned me out that he might make three or four joining farms into one. So as I could not afford to take a large farm, I was obliged to sell my stock and go into another country. The churchwarden as is now, who is grown so proud and lives so grand, was a poor man then, and owed me seven pounds. But as it is so long since, I find I can't demand it. And when I asked him for relief, and told him the times were very hard, he told me he had nothing for me, and that if times were hard, I must live hard. And so shut the door in my face. I would have asked him else, what we were to do when times are so hard that we cannot live at all? Everything is very dear,

---

THE OLD PEASANT

[1]   *Ewell* market town in Surrey, about thirteen miles south of London.

there is no work to be had, and I am too old to go a-soldiering. Beside, why should we poor folks go and help the rich to fight against the poor?'

Perhaps, with some, this concluding sentiment may destroy all the compassion excited by his tale. But oh! that I had a voice like thunder, to shout the solemn truth in the ears of all the poor in Europe, that the kings and nobles of the earth might be reduced to the sole option of fighting their own battle, or restoring peace!

Stanzas on Hearing for Certainty that We Were to be Tried for High Treason (composed 28 September 1794)

From Poems Written in Close Confinement in the Tower and Newgate upon a Charge of Treason (1795)

Short is perhaps our date of life,[1]
  But let us while we live be gay –
To those be thought and anxious care
  Who build upon the distant day.

Though in our cup tyrannic power[2]   5
  Would dash the bitter dregs of fear,
We'll gaily quaff the mantling draught,[3]
  While patriot toasts the fancy cheer.

Sings not the seaman, tempest-tossed,
  When surges wash the riven shroud,[4]   10
Scorning the threat'ning voice of fate
  That pipes in rocking winds aloud?

Yes, he can take his cheerful glass,
  And toast his mistress in the storm,
While duty and remembered joys   15
  By turns his honest bosom warm.

And shall not we, in storms of state,
  At base oppression's fury laugh,
And while the vital spirits flow,
  To freedom fill, and fearless quaff?   20

Short is perhaps our date of life,
  But let us while we live be gay –
To those be thought and anxious care
  Who build upon the distant day.

Tower, 28 September 1794

Stanzas on Hearing for Certainty that We Were to be Tried for High Treason

[1] *Short is perhaps ... life* the penalty for treason was death (see headnote).

[2] *tyrannic power* Thelwall had cause to regard Pitt's government as tyrannical. They had arrested him and his radical friends without specific cause, and had confiscated their possessions.

[3] *mantling draught* the draught of beer is 'mantled' by a head of foam.

[4] *riven shroud* severed rigging.

Dangerous Tendency of the Attempt to Suppress Political Discussion (published 21 March 1795)

From THE TRIBUNE (1795, vol. i pp. 25–6)

While prudent and moderate measures leave the door open to peaceful investigation, men of talents and moral character step forward into the field of politics, and never fail to take the lead in popular meetings and associations, for which nature seems to have intended them.

While this continues, all is peaceful and rational enquiry, and the people, though bold, are orderly. Nor even when persecution inflames their passions, are they easily provoked to actual intemperance. But when words are construed into treason, and men can no longer unbosom themselves to their friends at a tavern, or associate together for the diffusion of political information, but at the peril of their lives, the benevolent and moderate part of mankind retire from the scene of action, to brood, with prophetic anxiety, over the melancholy prospect.[1]

Enquiry is thus, it is true, in some degree suppressed, and the counsellors of these overbearing measures are apt to congratulate themselves on their supposed success. But the calm is more dreadful than the hurricane they pretended to apprehend. In the ferment of half-smothered indignation, feelings of a more gloomy complexion are generated, and characters of a very different stamp are called into action.

Men who have neither genius nor benevolence succeed those who had both, and, with no other stimulus than fury, and no other talent than hypocrisy and intrigue, embark in projects which every friend of humanity must abhor – and which, while the free, open, and manly character of the species was yet uncrushed by the detestable system of persecuting opinions, never could have entered the imagination.

Whoever will consult the page of history will find that in every country on the earth where liberty has been alternately indulged and trampled, this has been but too uniformly the progress of the human mind.

Let us ask then this serious question: is it possible for any person to be a more dangerous enemy to the peace and personal safety of the sovereign, than he who advises the persecution of opinion and the suppression of peaceable associations?

Civic Oration on the Anniversary of the Acquittal of the Lecturer {5 December},[1] Being a Vindication of the Principles, and a Review of the Conduct, that Placed Him at the Bar of the Old Bailey. Delivered Wednesday 9 December 1795 (extract)

From THE TRIBUNE (1795) (vol. iii pp. 257–60)

I was born near this place.[2] My residence can be traced with ease during every part of my life, and if there had been any disgraceful particulars in my history, the industrious malice of faction need not have been confined to general abuses. There have been times in which poverty and misfortune frowned upon my youth, and in which I had to struggle with the bitterest disadvantages to which an independent spirit could be subjected; when without a profession (for I could not eat the bread of legal peculation), I had to support an aged mother and a brother robbed of every faculty of reason.

DANGEROUS TENDENCY OF THE ATTEMPT TO SUPPRESS POLITICAL DISCUSSION

1 *melancholy prospect* Thelwall writes in anticipation of the Gagging Acts of December 1795, which banned 'seditious meetings' and aimed to ensure the 'safety of His Majesty's person' (see headnote).

CIVIC ORATION ON THE ANNIVERSARY OF THE ACQUITTAL OF THE LECTURER

1 This is a reference to Thelwall's acquittal at the treason trials in 1794.
2 *this place* Beaufort Buildings, off the Strand; Thelwall was born in Chandos Street, Covent Garden (about 5 minutes' walk away), 27 July 1764.

Yet upon all these embarrassments, when a debating society and a magazine brought me together but about £50 or £60 a year, I look back with the proud consciousness of never having stooped even to a mean action. Search then, probe me to the quick, and if you can find one stain upon my character, think me in reality a plunderer and an assassin. But if you cannot, what will you think of a profligate administration, with more vices upon their heads than I have words to speak them? What will you think of their assassins, and the black epithets and calumnies with which they have so incessantly pursued me? . . .

When our beloved associates – when those men of mind and virtue, whose names I will cherish with veneration so long as 'memory holds her seat'[3] – when Gerrald, Margarot, Muir, Palmer and Skirving[4] were doomed to Botany Bay without having violated one law or principle of our constitution, it was natural (though it was not wise) for men who revered their talents and their virtues to indulge the British vice of intemperance – for it is a British vice, and we are too apt to be proud of it. It was natural that under such circumstances, our blood should boil, and that we should say angry things, and pass vapouring, intemperate resolutions. But the minister knew that the 'very head and jut of our offending went but to this – no further!'[5]

What, then, is that administration, which wishes to hang every man who makes use of an intemperate word against them?

But they have been disappointed – and what do they now attempt? They attempt to pass laws which will make all those things treason which they endeavoured to make treason before without any law whatever.

The minister introduces Two Bills.[6] What are they? Bills that subject a man to all the penalties of High Treason who shall publish, or even write, *without publishing*, any dissertation which approves any form of government but the existing government of the country. . . .

I cannot be ignorant that these acts are made in a very considerable degree with a view to my destruction. I know also that the time will come when – in consequence of the persecutions I have endured, and the temper (permit me to say) with which I have faced those persecutions – I may be an instrument of some service to the liberties and happiness of my country. I shall not therefore give the minister an opportunity to destroy me upon any trifling contest. I have here maintained myself in decency, and cleared away the encumbrances which former persecutions had brought upon me. With something less than £100 in my pocket I shall retire from this place, for the cultivation of my mind, and, carrying the consciousness of my own integrity into retirement, maintain myself by the labours of my pen.

Having been so long seeking for my country, and having endured so much persecution in that search, I think I shall not be accused either of selfishness or pusillanimity, when I say that I shall now wait till my country seeks for me, and that when my country does seek for me, she shall find me ready for my post, whatever may be the difficulty or the danger.

Letter from John Thelwall to Samuel Taylor Coleridge, 10 May 1796 (extract; edited from MS)[1]

Of your favourite poem I fear I shall speak in terms that will disappoint you. There are passages most undoubtedly in the *Religious Musings* of very great merit, and perhaps there is near half of the poem

---

[3]   *Hamlet* I v 96.

[4]   Scottish radicals who fell foul of the oppressive policies of the government: Joseph Gerrald, a delegate to Edinburgh of the London Corresponding Society, was tried for sedition in March 1794 and sentenced to 14 years transportation to Botany Bay, where he died in 1796; Maurice Margarot, the first chairman of the LCS, was tried for sedition in January 1794 and sentenced to transportation (he was returned in 1809, and died in 1815); Thomas Muir (1765–98) was tried in August 1793, sentenced to 14 years transportation, but escaped to France, where he died; the Revd. Thomas Fyshe Palmer (1747–1802), a Unitarian minister, was found guilty of sedition and sentenced to 7 years transportation (after serving his time he died on the journey home); William Skirving was sentenced to 14 years transportation in January 1794, but died in Botany Bay, 1796.

[5]   *Othello* I iii 80–1.

[6]   The Two Bills were introduced in November 1795 and became law on 18 December.

LETTER FROM JOHN THELWALL TO SAMUEL TAYLOR COLERIDGE

[1]   This letter has been published in full by Warren E. Gibbs, 'An Unpublished Letter from John Thelwall to S. T. Coleridge', *MLR* 25 (1930) 85–90.

that no poet in our language need have been ashamed to own. But this praise belongs almost exclusively to those parts that are not at all religious. As for the generality of those passages which are most so, they are certainly anything in the world rather than poetry (unless indeed the mere glowing rapidity of the blank verse may entitle them to that distinction).

They are the very acme of abstruse, metaphysical, mystical rant, and all ranting abstraction, metaphysics and mysticism are wider from true poetry than the equator from the poles. The whole poem also is infected with inflation and turgidity.... 'a vision *shadowy* of truth', '*wormy* grave', and a heap of like instances might be selected worthy of Blackmore[2] himself. ('Ye petrify th' *imbrothelled atheist's* heart' is one of those illiberal and unfounded calumnies with which Christian meekness never yet disdained to supply the want of argument – but this by the way.) '*Lovely* was the *death* of him whose life was love' is certainly enough to make any man sick whose taste has not been corrupted by the licentious (I mean 'pious') nonsense of the conventicle.[3]

You may, if you please, 'lay the flattering unction to your soul'[4] that my irreligious principles dictate the severity of this criticism, and, though it may strengthen you in the suspicion, I must confess that your religious verses approach much nearer to poetry than those of Milton on the same subject. In short, while I was yet a Christian, and a very zealous one (i.e. when I was about your age),[5] I became thoroughly convinced that Christian poetry was very vile stuff – that religion was a subject which none but a rank infidel could handle poetically.

Before I wipe the gall from my pen, I must notice an affectation of the Della Crusca[6] school which blurs almost every one of your poems – I mean the frequent accent upon the adjectives and weak words.... 'For chiefly in the oppressed *good* man's face' etc.

Having dwelt thus largely upon the defects, I shall proceed to prove my qualifications to set up for a critic by running very slightly over the numerous beauties with which it abounds. 'The *thought-benighted sceptic*' is very happy, as is also 'Mists dim-floating of idolatry – misshaped the omnipresent sin'. (The word 'Split' appears to me ill-chosen and unpoetical.) The whole passage 'Thus from the elect'... (ll. 102–118), though not quite free either from mysticism or turgidity, is upon the whole very grand and very poetical. Lines 133–5 and 138–44 are also equally fine in sentiment, conception and expression. And though '*connatural* mind', '*tortuous* folds', '*savagery* of holy zeal', 'at his mouth *im*breathe', and '*fiendish* deeds', offend me not a little as being affected and pedantic (and therefore of course unpoetical), yet the whole passage, lines 181–255, delights me very much. The satire is dignified, the poetry sublime and ardent. Of the ensuing paragraph, 'In the primeval age' etc., the first and third lines are bad; but the ensuing passage consisting of 144 lines beginning with 'soon imagination conjured up a host of new desires', and ending at line 364 breathes a rapture and energy of mind seldom to be met with among modern bards. I must however in sincerity add that, according to my judgement, all that follows hangs like a dead weight upon the poem.

Lines Written at Bridgwater in Somersetshire, on 27 July 1797, During a Long Excursion in Quest of a Peaceful Retreat[1]

From POEMS WRITTEN CHIEFLY IN RETIREMENT (1801)

Day of my double birth! who gave me first
To breathe life's troubled air, and, kindlier far,

---

[2]   Sir Richard Blackmore (1654–1729), author of indifferent epics including *Creation: A Philosophical Poem* (1712).

[3]   *conventicle* religious meeting.

[4]   Hamlet to his mother: 'Lay not that flattering unction to your soul, / That not your trespass but my madness speaks' (*Hamlet* III iv 145–6).

[5]   *your age* Coleridge was twenty-four; Thelwall is looking back to *c.*1788.

[6]   The Della Cruscans of the late eighteenth century advocated an affected, ornamented sentimentality, and are probably in Wordsworth's mind when he mentions the 'gaudiness and inane phraseology of many modern writers' in the Advertisement to *Lyrical Ballads* (1798), p. 191, below.

LINES WRITTEN AT BRIDGEWATER IN SOMERSETSHIRE

[1]   Thelwall was at this point walking to Bristol from Nether Stowey, where he had been Coleridge's guest.

Gave all that makes life welcome – gave me her[2]
Who now, far distant,[3] sheds, perchance, the tear
In pensive solitude, and chides the hours   5
That keep her truant wanderer from her arms –
Hers and our smiling babies; eventful day!
How shall I greet thee[4] now, at thy return,
So often marked with sadness? Art thou, say,
Once more arrived a harbinger of woes,   10
Precursor of a year of miseries,
Of storms and persecutions, of the pangs
Of disappointed hope, and keen regrets,
Wrung from the bosom by a sordid world
That kindness pays with hatred, and returns   15
Evil for good? – a world most scorpion-like
That stings what warms it, and the ardent glow
Of blessed benevolence too oft transmutes
To sullen gloom and sour misanthropy,
Wounding, with venomed tooth, the fostering breast   20
That her milk turns to gall. Or art thou come,
In most unwonted guise, oh fateful day,
With cheering prophecy of kindlier times?
Of hours of sweet retirement, tranquil joys
Of friendship, and of love – of studious ease,   25
Of philosophic thought – poetic dreams
In dell romantic, or by bubbling brook,
High wood, or rocky shore; where fancy's train,
Solemn or gay, shall in the sunbeam sport,
Or murmur in the gloom, peopling earth, air,   30
Ocean, and woodland haunt, mountain and cave
With wildest fantasies – wild, but not vain,
For, but for dreams like these, Meonides[5]
Had never shook the soul with epic song,
Nor Milton, slumbering underneath the shade   35
Of fancy-haunted oak, heard the loud strain
Of heavenly minstrelsy – nor yet had he,
Shakespeare (in praise of whom smooth Avon still
Flows eloquent to every Briton's ear),
Pierced the dark womb of nature with keen glance,   40
Tracing the embryo passions ere their birth,
And every mystic movement of the soul
Baring to public ken. Oh bards, to whom
Youth owes its emulation, age the bliss
Of many a wintry evening, dull and sad   45
But for your cheering aid! Ye from whose strains,
As from a font of inspiration, oft
The quickening mind, else stagnant, learns to flow
In tides of generous ardour, scattering wide
Smiling fertility, fresh fruits and flowers   50

---

[2] *her* Susan Thelwall (*née* Vellum), whom he married on 27
July 1791. He was born 27 July 1764.
[3] *far distant* Thelwall had left his family in Derby while on a
walking tour of the west of England and Wales, in search of a
suitable retreat from politics.

[4] *thee* i.e. Thelwall's birthday.
[5] *Meonides* Homer, author of *The Iliad* and *The Odyssey*.

Of intellectual worth![6] Oh might my soul
Henceforth with yours hold converse, in the scenes
Where nature cherishes poetic thought,
Best cradled in the solitary haunts
Where bustling cares intrude not, nor the throng   55
Of cities or of courts. Yet not for aye
In hermit-like seclusion would I dwell
(My soul estranging from my brother man)
Forgetful and forgotten; rather oft,
With some few minds congenial, let me stray   60
Along the muses' haunts, where converse, meet
For intellectual beings, may arouse
The soul's sublimer energies, or wing
The fleeting time most cheerily – the time
Which, though swift-fleeting, scatters, as he flies,   65
Seeds of delight, that, like the furrowed grain,
Strewed by the farmer as he onward stalks
Over his well-ploughed acres, shall produce,
In happy season, its abundant fruits.

    Day of my double birth,[7] if such the year   70
Thou usherest in, most welcome! For my soul
Is sick of public turmoil[8] – ah, most sick
Of the vain effort to redeem a race
Enslaved, because degenerate; lost to hope
Because to virtue lost – wrapped up in self,   75
In sordid avarice, luxurious pomp,
And profligate intemperance – a race
Fierce without courage, abject and yet proud,
And most licentious, though most far from thee.

    Ah, let me then, far from the strifeful scenes   80
Of public life (where reason's warning voice
Is heard no longer, and the trump of truth
Who blows but wakes The Ruffian Crew of Power
To deeds of maddest anarchy and blood) –
Ah, let me, far in some sequestered dell,   85
Build my low cot! Most happy might it prove,
My Samuel,[9] near to thine, that I might oft
Share thy sweet converse, best-beloved of friends,
Long-loved ere known[10] – for kindred sympathies
Linked (though far distant) our congenial souls!   90
Ah! 'twould be sweet, beneath the neighb'ring thatch,[11]
In philosophic amity to dwell,
Inditing moral verse, or tale, or theme,

---

[6] *Ye from whose strains ... worth* The 'strains' (verses) of Milton and Shakespeare inspire the young poet to compose poetry.

[7] *Day of my double birth* he was born on 27 July 1764; the date of his second birth was his wedding day: 27 July 1791.

[8] *public turmoil* Thelwall had been persecuted by government agents, his lectures broken up by force, he had been chased out of towns, and caballed against even by other radicals.

[9] *My Samuel* Coleridge, who Thelwall described in February 1797 as 'one of the most extraordinary geniuses and finest scholars of the age'.

[10] *Long-loved ere known* Their earliest contact was the letter of April 1796 (see above); they seem not to have met until summer 1797.

[11] *beneath the neighb'ring thatch* it was hoped that Thelwall and his family might move in next door to Coleridge at Nether Stowey, but animosity towards radicalism made that impossible.

Gay or instructive.[12] And it would be sweet,
With kindly interchange of mutual aid,   95
To delve our little garden plots, the while
Sweet converse flowed, suspending oft the arm
And half-driven spade, while, eager, one propounds,
And listens one, weighing each pregnant word,
And pondering fit reply that may untwist   100
The knotty point – perchance of import high –
Of moral truth, of causes infinite
(Creating power, or uncreated worlds
Eternal and uncaused!), or whatsoe'er
Of metaphysic or of ethic lore   105
The mind with curious subtlety[13] pursues,
Agreeing or dissenting – sweet alike,
When wisdom, and not victory, the end.
      And 'twould be sweet, my Samuel (ah, most sweet!),
To see our little infants[14] stretch their limbs   110
In gambols unrestrained, and early learn
Practical love, and – wisdom's noblest lore –
Fraternal[15] kindliness, while rosiest health
Bloomed on their sunburnt cheeks. And 'twould be sweet
(When what to toil was due, to study what,[16]   115
And literary effort, had been paid)[17]
Alternate in each other's bower to sit,
In summer's genial season. Or, when bleak,
The wintry blast had stripped the leafy shade,
Around the blazing hearth, social and gay,   120
To share our frugal viands, and the bowl
Sparkling with home-brewed beverage – by our sides
Thy Sara and my Susan,[18] and, perchance,
Alfoxden's musing tenant, and the maid
Of ardent eye who with fraternal love   125
Sweetens his solitude.[19] With these should join
Arcadian pool, swain of a happier age
When Wisdom and Refinement loved to dwell
With rustic Plainness, and the pastoral vale
Was vocal to the melodies of verse,   130
Echoing sweet minstrelsy.
                        With such, my friend –
With such, how pleasant to unbend awhile,
Winging the idle hour with song or tale,
Pun or quaint joke or converse, such as fits
Minds gay, but innocent. And we would laugh   135
(Unless, perchance, Pity's more kindly tear

---

[12] *Inditing ... instructive* Thelwall worked for years on an epic poem, 'The Hope of Albion' that, he believed, would establish him as one of the finest poets of the age.
[13] *The mind with curious subtlety* perhaps the source of Coleridge's phrase, 'the self-watching subtilizing mind' (*Frost at Midnight* 27).
[14] *our little infants* Hartley Coleridge (b. 1796), Algernon Sydney Thelwall (b. 1795), Maria Thelwall (b. 1794).
[15] *Fraternal* one of the goals of the French Revolution was *fraternité*.

[16] *to study what* what was due to study.
[17] *When what ... paid* when we had fully laboured, studied, and written ...
[18] Sara Fricker married Coleridge, 4 October 1795; Susan Vellum married Thelwall, 27 July 1791.
[19] *Alfoxden's ... solitude* William and Dorothy Wordsworth, who were living at Alfoxden House not far away.

Check the obstreperous mirth) at such who waste
Life's precious hours in the delusive chase
Of wealth and worldly gewgaws, and contend
For honours emptier than the hollow voice   140
That rings in echo's cave, and which, like that,
Exists but in the babbling of a world
Creating its own wonder. Wiselier we
To intellectual joys will thus devote
Our fleeting years, mingling Arcadian sports   145
With healthful industry. Oh, it would be
A golden age revived! Nor would we lack
Woodnymph, or naiad,[20] to complete the group
Of classic fable; for, in happy time,
Sylvanus, Chester,[21] in each hand should bring   150
The sister nymphs, Julia of radiant eye
And stately tread, the dryad[22] of the groves,
And she, of softer mien, the meek-eyed maid,
Pensively sweet, whom Fancy well might deem
The fairy of the brooks that bubble round.   155
    Ah, fateful day! what marvel if my soul
Receive thy visits awfully,[23] and fain[24]
With fancy's glowing characters would trace
Thy yet to me blank legend, painting most
What most my bosom yearns for – friendship's joys,   160
And social happiness, and tranquil hours
Of studious indolence? Or, sweeter far,
The high poetic rapture that becalms
Even while it agitates? Ah, fateful day,
If that the year thou lead'st (as fain my soul   165
Would augur, from some hours of joy late passed,
And friendships unexpected) – if the year
Thou usherest in, has aught, perchance, in store
To realize this vision, welcome most –
Ah most, most welcome! for my soul, at peace,   170
Shall to its native pleasures then return,
And in my Susan's arms, each pang forgot,
Nightly will I repose – yielding my soul
(Unshared, unharassed, by a thankless world)
To the domestic virtues, calm and sweet,   175
Of husband and of father – to the joys
Of relative affiance; its mild cares
And stingless ecstasies; while gentlest sleep,
Unwooed, uncalled, on the soft pillow waits
Of envyless obscurity. Ah, come!   180
Hours of long wished tranquillity, ah come!
Snatch from my couch the thorn of anxious thought,
That I may taste the joys my soul best loves,
And find, once more, 'that Being is a Bliss!'

---

[20] *naiad* water-nymph.
[21] *Sylvanus, Chester* John Chester, a nearby farmer who encouraged Coleridge in his quest for agricultural knowledge, is cast as Sylvanus, Roman god of the country (usually represented as half-man, half-goat). For more on Chester see

Hazlitt, 'My First Acquaintance with Poets', pp. 600–10.
[22] *dryad* wood-nymph.
[23] *awfully* with awe.
[24] *fain* willingly.

To the Infant Hampden. Written during a Sleepless Night. Derby. October 1797[1]

From POEMS WRITTEN CHIEFLY IN RETIREMENT (1801)

Sweet babe, that on thy mother's guardian breast
Slumberest, unheedful of the autumnal blast
That rocks our lowly dwelling,[2] nor dost dream
Of woes, or cares, or persecuting rage,
Or rending passions, or the pangs that wait   5
On ill-requited services[3] – sleep on,
Sleep, and be happy! 'Tis the sole relief
This anxious mind can hope from the dire pangs
Of deep corroding wrong, that thou, my babe,
And the sweet twain (the firstlings of my love!)[4]   10
As yet are blessed; and that my heart's best pride,[5]
Who, with maternal fondness, pillows thee
Beside thy life's warm fountain,[6] is not quite
Hopeless or joyless, but with matron cares
And calm domestic virtues can avert   15
The melancholy fiend, and in your smiles
Read nameless consolations.
                                    Ah, sleep on,
As yet unconscious of the patriot's name
Or of a patriot's sorrows, of the cares
For which thy name-sire bled.[7] And, more unblessed,   20
Thy natural father in his native land
Wanders an exile, and of all that land
Can find no spot his home.[8] Ill-omened babe,
Conceived in tempests, and in tempests born –
What destiny awaits thee? Reekless[9] thou.   25
Oh blessed inapprehension – let it last!
Sleep on, my babe, now while the rocking wind
Pipes mournful, length'ning my nocturnal plaint
With troubled symphony! Ah, sleep secure,
And may thy dream of life be ne'er disturbed   30
With visions such as mar thy father's peace –
Visions (ah, that they were but such indeed!)
That show this world a wilderness of wrongs,
A waste of troubled waters, whelming floods
Of tyrannous injustice canopied   35

TO THE INFANT HAMPDEN

[1] The setting and theme of this poem, about Thelwall's son Hampden, invite comparison with Coleridge's *Frost at Midnight*, which draws inspiration from Coleridge's son Hartley.

[2] *our lowly dwelling* Thelwall composed this poem at a small cottage in Derby, where he and his family were housed, temporarily, shortly before he found what he hoped would be a more permanent residence, at Llys Wen in Wales.

[3] *woes ... services* Thelwall had been the victim of all these things (see headnote).

[4] *the sweet twain (the firstlings of my love!)* Algernon Sydney Thelwall (b. 1795) and Maria Thelwall (b. 1794).

[5] *my heart's best pride* his wife, Susan Thelwall (*née* Vellum).

[6] Hampden Thelwall was breast-fed.

[7] *For which ... bled* Hampden Thelwall was named after John Hampden (1594–1643), leader of the Long Parliament, famous for his historic refusal in 1636 to pay the ship money exacted by Charles I, mortally wounded at Chalgrove Field, near Oxford.

[8] *Thy natural father ... home* Thelwall had been searching for a permanent residence for his family since June 1797. He found a farm in Llys Wen in Wales by 25 October, a matter of days after completing this poem.

[9] *Reekless* unknowing.

With clouds dark-louring, whence the pelting storms
Of cold unkindness the rough torrents swell
On every side resistless. There my ark,
The scanty remnant of my deluged joys,
Floats anchorless, while through the dreary round,   40
Fluttering on anxious pinion, the tired foot
Of persecuted virtue cannot find
One spray on which to rest, or scarce one leaf
To cheer with promise of subsiding woe.

Mary Anne Lamb   (1764–1847)

She was born 3 December 1764, and educated at William Bird's Academy, Bond Stables, off Fetter Lane in London. She went to work as a mantua (gown) maker until 1796. From the start, she was close to her youngest brother Charles, the future Elia (see pp. 577–8).

She will always be associated with the family tragedy that changed her life forever. On 22 September 1796 she stabbed her mother to death in a fit of insanity and embedded a fork in her father's forehead. Charles apparently helped get her admitted to an asylum, where she remained until the following year. She recovered in the spring and lived in Hackney; after a relapse at the end of 1797 she again recovered, and in 1799, after her father's death, returned to live with Charles. Periodic attacks of insanity continued to strike, which became more frequent and of longer duration as she aged. Her elder brother John argued that she be placed in a madhouse permanently, but Charles looked after her at home for as long as he lived.

This proved to be the best strategy. For much of the time they led happy, normal lives together, and she was a particular favourite with Charles' friends, including Landor (see p. 571), Hazlitt (who described her as the only reasonable woman he knew), Leigh Hunt (who praised her fine brain), Hood, Procter and the Wordsworths. She was bridesmaid to William Hazlitt and Sarah Stoddart in 1808, frequently went on holiday with Charles, and travelled as far afield as France in 1822 (although she suffered a seizure there and had to remain until she recovered). She features in her brother's essays as Bridget Elia, specifically in 'Mrs Battle's Opinions on Whist', 'Mackery End in Hertfordshire', and 'Old China', and was the author, with her brother, of *Tales from Shakespear* (1807), *Mrs Leicester's School* (1809), and *Poetry for Children* (1809). Her letters are one of the delights of the period, and that on the death of John Wordsworth reveals her at her most sensitive and shrewd. She died 20 May 1847, and was buried with her brother in Edmonton churchyard.

Further reading

Jane Aaron, ' "On Needle-Work": Protest and Contradiction in Mary Lamb's Essay', *Romanticism and Feminism* ed. Anne K. Mellor (Bloomington, 1988), pp. 167–84
Susan Wolfson, ' "Explaining to Their Sisters": Mary Lamb's *Tales from Shakespear*', *Women's (Re)visions of Shakespeare* ed. Marianne Novy (Urbana, IL, 1990), pp. 16–40
Charles and Mary Lamb, *Mrs Leicester's School* 1809 introduced by Jonathan Wordsworth (Poole, 1995)
Pamela Woof, 'Dorothy Wordsworth and Mary Lamb, Writers', *Charles Lamb Bulletin* NS 66–7 (1989) 41–53, 82–93
Susan Sage Heinzelman, 'Women's Petty Treason: Feminism, Narrative, and the Law', *Journal of Narrative Technique* 20 (1990) 89–106
Mary Blanchard Balle, 'Mary Lamb: Her Mental Health Issues', *Charles Lamb Bulletin* NS 93 (1996) 2–11

Letter from Mary Anne Lamb to Dorothy Wordsworth, 7 May 1805 (extract)

My dear Miss Wordsworth,
I thank you, my kind friend, for your most comfortable letter. Till I saw your own handwriting, I could not persuade myself that I should do well to write to you, though I have often attempted it, but

I always left off dissatisfied with what I had written, and feeling that I was doing an improper thing to intrude upon your sorrow.[1] I wished to tell you that you would one day feel the kind of peaceful state of mind, and sweet memory of the dead, which you so happily describe as now almost begun. But I felt that it was improper, and most grating to the feelings of the afflicted, to say to them that the memory of their affliction would in time become a constant part not only of their 'dream, but of their most wakeful sense of happiness'.[2] That you would see every object with and through your lost brother, and that that would at last become a real and everlasting source of comfort to you, I felt, and well knew, from my own experience in sorrow; but till you yourself began to feel this I did not dare tell you so. But I send you some poor lines which I wrote under this conviction of mind, and before I heard Coleridge was returning home.[3] I will transcribe them now before I finish my letter, lest a false shame prevent me then, for I know they are much worse than they ought to be. Written as they were with strong feeling and on such a subject, every line seems to me to be borrowed, but I had no better way of expressing my thoughts, and I never have the power of altering or amending anything I have once laid aside with dissatisfaction.

Why is he wandering o'er the sea?
Coleridge should now with Wordsworth be.
By slow degrees he'd steal away
Their woe, and gently bring a ray
(So happily he'd time relief)   5
Of comfort from their very grief;
He'd tell them that their brother dead,
When years have passed o'er their head,
Will be remembered with such holy,
True, and perfect melancholy,   10
That ever this lost brother John
Will be their heart's companion.
His voice they'll always hear, his face they'll always see;
There's nought in life so sweet as such a memory.

The Two Boys[1]

From THE LONDON MAGAZINE 6 (1822, p. 36)

I saw a boy with eager eye
Open a book upon a stall,
And read as he'd devour it all,
Which, when the stall-man did espy,
Soon to the boy I heard him call,   5
'You, sir, you never buy a book,
Therefore in one you shall not look!'
The boy passed slowly on, and with a sigh
He wished he never had been taught to read,
Then of the old churl's books he should have had no need.   10

LETTER FROM MARY ANNE LAMB TO DOROTHY WORDSWORTH
[1] *your sorrow* The Wordsworths were devastated by the death of their brother, John Wordsworth, drowned at sea 5 February 1805 – a loss that inspired Wordsworth's *Elegiac Stanzas* (pp. 405–7).
[2] Quoted, apparently, from Dorothy Wordsworth's 'most comfortable' letter to Mary Lamb, which has not survived.

[3] On 2 April 1805, Dorothy told Catherine Clarkson that Coleridge had written to Southey in February that he intended returning to England in March. Dorothy presumably passed this information on to Mary Lamb in her 'most comfortable' letter.

THE TWO BOYS
[1] This poem was published at the end of Charles Lamb's essay, 'Detached Thoughts on Books and Reading', July 1822.

Of sufferings the poor have many,
Which never can the rich annoy.
I soon perceived another boy –
Who looked as if he'd not had any
Food, for that day at least – enjoy   15
The sight of cold meat in a tavern larder.
This boy's case, then thought I, is surely harder;
Thus hungry, longing thus without a penny,
Beholding choice of dainty-dressed meat –
No wonder if he wish he ne'er had learned to eat.   20

What is Love? (signed 'M.L.')

From THE KEEPSAKE FOR 1829 (1828) (p. 237)

Love is the passion which endureth,
Which neither time nor absence cureth;
Which nought of earthly change can sever:
Love is the light which shines for ever.

What cold and selfish breasts deem madness   5
Lives in its depths of joy and sadness;
In hearts, on lips, of flame it burneth –
One is its world, to *one* it turneth.

Its chain of gold – what hand can break it?
Its deathless hold – what force can shake it?   10
Mere passion aught of earth may sever,
But *souls* that love, love on for ever.

James Mackintosh (1765–1832)

The son of an army officer, Mackintosh was educated at King's College, Aberdeen, and trained as a physician in Edinburgh; from 1790 he read for the bar. He moved to London in 1788, already an admirer of Priestley, and quickly became involved in the radical cause. In 1790 he joined the Society for Constitutional Information. The Society had been founded in April 1780 by Major John Cartwright with the intention of reviving in the minds of the citizenry 'a knowledge of their lost rights', and agitating for parliamentary reform.[1] In the 1790 general election Mackintosh campaigned on behalf of Horne Tooke, the leading figure in the Society, who was a candidate in the Westminster ward. Of all the radical societies, the SCI was one

of the more moderate, and so it was that Mackintosh himself leaned more towards moderate Whiggery than outright radicalism.

With *Vindiciae Gallicae* (1791) he produced one of the most effective replies to Burke's *Reflections*. It was one of the more considered, and delayed: Burke published in November 1790; Wollstonecraft within the month; Paine's *Rights of Man* in March 1791; and Mackintosh on 7 May. Hazlitt described him as 'a man of the world and a scholar',[2] and his defence of the French Revolution was thorough and brilliantly argued. Mackintosh provides a scholarly assessment of Burke's argument, showing how distorted his understanding of French politics actually was. By compari-

JAMES MACKINTOSH
[1] For more about the Society see Albert Goodwin, *The Friends of Liberty* (London, 1979), pp. 63–116.

[2] *Spirit of the Age* (London, 1825), p. 209.

son with Mackintosh's mastery of the facts, and clear-sighted analysis, Burke emerges as devious and emotional.

How ironic that, having penned one of the most distinguished of the replies to Burke, he was to become one of his disciples. No doubt the course taken by the French Revolution was instrumental; Mackintosh was one of many who, with the outbreak of war against France in 1793, and the Reign of Terror in 1793–4, renounced their former sympathies. Like that of his mentor, Mackintosh's conversion was public. His opposition to the Revolution was confirmed by three days' conversation with the dying Burke at his house at Beaconsfield in 1796, and in early 1799 he gave a popular and widely-reported series of lectures 'On the Law of Nature and of Nations', in which he vowed to 'abhor, abjure, and forever renounce' his former allegiances; he then proceeded to demolish the logical foundations of Godwinian rationalism. Hazlitt, who attended the lectures, recalled:

> He grew wanton with success. Dazzling others by the brilliancy of his acquirements, dazzled himself by the admiration they excited, he lost fear as well as prudence; dared everything, carried everything before him. . . . The volcano of the French Revolution was seen expiring in its own flames, like a bonfire made of straw: the principles of reform were scattered in all directions, like chaff before the keen northern blast.

He laid about him like one inspired; nothing could withstand his envenomed tooth.[3]

When they heard about the lectures in 1799 Wordsworth and Coleridge had been shocked; Wordsworth alludes to the apostasy at *Two-Part Prelude* ii 478–86. Mackintosh delivered them a second time, January–March 1800, and Coleridge attended; he heartily disliked them. He had been indebted to Mackintosh for recommending him to Daniel Stuart (Mackintosh's brother-in-law) as a contributor to the *Morning Post* in 1797, but was so disappointed by the apostasy of his old acquaintance that, in a letter to Godwin of May 1800, he referred to 'the great dung-fly Mackintosh' (Griggs i 588). See also Lamb's 'On Mackintosh', p. 580, below.

Mackintosh went on to be a lawyer, a Whig MP (from 1813), a student of German philosophy, and a reviewer for the *Edinburgh Review*. He died suddenly from complications after swallowing a chicken bone in 1832.

Further reading

William Hazlitt, 'Sir James Mackintosh', *The Spirit of the Age* (London, 1825), pp. 209–27

James Mackintosh, *Vindiciae Gallicae (Defence of the French Revolution) 1791* introduced by Jonathan Wordsworth (Spelsbury, 1989)

Popular Excesses which Attended the Revolution[1]

From Vindiciae Gallicae (1791) (pp. 162–4)

That no great revolutions can be accomplished without excesses and miseries at which humanity revolts is a truth which cannot be denied.

This unfortunately is true, in a peculiar manner, of those revolutions which, like that of France, are strictly *popular*. Where the people are led by a faction, its leaders find no difficulty in the re-establishment of that order which must be the object of their wishes, because it is the sole security of their power. But when a general movement of the popular mind levels a despotism with the ground, it is far less easy to restrain excess. There is more resentment to satiate, and less authority to control. The passion which produced an effect so tremendous is too violent to subside in a moment into serenity and submission. The spirit of revolt breaks out with fatal violence after its object is destroyed, and turns against the order of freedom those arms by which it had subdued the strength of tyranny. The attempt to punish the spirit that actuates a people, if it were just, would be vain, and, if it were possible, would be cruel. They are too many to be punished in a view of justice, and too strong to be pun-

---

[3] *Spirit of the Age* (London, 1825), pp. 215–16.

POPULAR EXCESSES WHICH ATTENDED THE REVOLUTION
[1] The readiness of radical writers to justify the violence of the Revolution was always a good index of the strength of

their sympathies. Helen Maria Williams felt sufficiently strongly to make the case (see '*On Revolution*', p. 151), as did William Wordsworth in his *Letter to the Bishop of Llandaff* (written 1793, but not published until 1876).

ished in a view of policy. The ostentation of vigour would in such a case prove the display of impotence, and the rigour of justice conduct to the cruelty of extirpation.[2]

No remedy is therefore left but the progress of instruction, the force of persuasion, the mild authority of opinion. These remedies, though infallible, are of slow operation, and in the interval which elapses before a calm succeeds the boisterous moments of a revolution, it is vain to expect that a people inured to barbarism by their oppressors, and which has ages of oppression to avenge, will be punctiliously generous in their triumph, nicely discriminative in their vengeance, or cautiously mild in their mode of retaliation: 'they will break their chains on the heads of their oppressors.'[3]

Robert Bloomfield   (1766–1823)

'What Wordsworth and I have seen of *The Farmer's Boy* (only a few short extracts) pleased us very much', Coleridge wrote, 17 September 1800 (Griggs i 623). They were among the first readers of this Suffolk farm labourer and cobbler turned poet, and were apparently impressed by the close observation of the natural world evident throughout his poem, which described the life of Giles, an orphan peasant, during the agricultural year.

Like Ann Yearsley and Isabella Lickbarrow, Bloomfield was an anomaly: a working-class poet. He made shoes for a living, and, on occasion, Aeolian harps. Self-educated, he composed poetry from an early age, and his first published work, *The Village Girl*, was printed when he was only sixteen. *The Farmer's Boy*, probably the most important of his poems, was complete by 22 April 1798. Unable to find a publisher, he sent the poem to Capel Lofft (1751–1824), the Whig

barrister and magistrate, who wrote a Preface for the work and arranged for its publication on 1 March 1800. It sold out within a fortnight, and went straight to a second edition. A third was out by the end of the year, and a fourth early in 1801. By the seventh, in 1803, it had sold 30,000 copies. Bloomfield became a literary celebrity, made a lot of money in royalties, and bought a house in London's City Road. He made friends with the Prince Regent, Beau Brummel, Samuel Rogers and Anna Laetitia Barbauld, among others. Subsequent works included *Rural Tales, Ballads, and Songs* (1802), *Good Tidings or News From the Farm* (1804), and *Wild Flowers* (1806).

Further reading

William Wickett and Nicholas Duval, *The Farmer's Boy: The Story of a Suffolk Poet* (Lavenham, 1971)

Spring (extract)

From THE FARMER'S BOY (1800)

Neglected now the early daisy lies,
Nor thou, pale primrose, bloom'st the only prize;   270
Advancing spring profusely spreads abroad
Flow'rs of all hues, with sweetest fragrance stored.
Where'er she treads, love gladdens every plain,
Delight on tiptoe bears her lucid train,
Sweet hope with conscious brow before her flies,   275
Anticipating wealth from summer skies.
All nature feels her renovating sway,[1]

---

[2]   *extirpation* extermination.
[3]   'The eloquent expression of Mr Curran in the Parliament of Ireland, respecting the Revolution' (Mackintosh's note). It was in the Irish House of Commons, of which John Philpot Curran (1750–1817) was a member, that this phrase was used. Curran was a tireless advocate of parliamentary reform and the

rights of Catholics. He was implicated in the rising of the United Irishmen in 1798.

SPRING
[1]   *renovating sway* revitalizing power.

The sheep-fed pasture, and the meadow gay,
And trees and shrubs, no longer budding seen,
Display the new-grown branch of lighter green.   280
On airy downs the shepherd idling lies,
And sees tomorrow in the marbled skies;
Here then, my soul, thy darling theme pursue,
For every day was Giles a shepherd too.

    Small was his charge – no wilds had they to roam,   285
But bright enclosures circling round their home.
Nor[2] yellow-blossomed furze, nor stubborn thorn
(The heath's rough produce) had their fleeces torn;
Yet ever roving, ever seeking thee,
Enchanting spirit, dear variety!   290
Oh happy tenants, prisoners of a day,
Released to ease, to pleasure, and to play!
Indulged through every field by turns to range,
And taste them all in one continual change –
For though luxuriant their grassy food,   295
Sheep long confined but loathe the present good;
Instinctively they haunt the homeward gate,
And starve and pine with plenty at their feet.

    Loosed from the winding lane, a joyful throng,
See, o'er yon pasture how they pour along!   300
Giles round their boundaries takes his usual stroll,
Sees every pass secured, and fences whole –
High fences, proud to charm the gazing eye,
Where many a nestling[3] first assays to fly;
Where blows the woodbine,[4] faintly streaked with red,   305
And rests on every bough its tender head;
Round the young ash its twining branches meet,
Or crown the hawthorn with its odours sweet.
Say, ye that know, ye who have felt and seen
Spring's morning smiles, and soul-enliv'ning green,   310
Say, did you give the thrilling transport way?
Did your eye brighten, when young lambs at play
Leaped o'er your path with animated pride,
Or gazed in merry clusters by your side?
Ye who can smile (to wisdom no disgrace)   315
At the arch meaning of a kitten's face,
If spotless innocence and infant mirth
Excites to praise, or gives reflection birth;
In shades like these pursue your fav'rite joy,
Midst nature's revels, sports that never cloy.   320
A few begin a short but vigorous race,
And indolence abashed soon flies the place;
Thus challenged forth, see thither one by one,
From every side assembling playmates run.
A thousand wily antics mark their stay,   325
A starting crowd impatient of delay;

---

[2] *Nor* neither.
[3] *nestling* young bird still in its nest.
[4] *woodbine* honeysuckle.

Like the fond dove from fearful prison freed,
Each seems to say, 'Come, let us try our speed!'
Away they scour, impetuous, ardent, strong,
The green turf trembling as they bound along;   330
Adown the slope, then up the hillock climb,
Where every molehill is a bed of thyme;
There panting stop, yet scarcely can refrain –
A bird, a leaf, will set them off again!
Or if a gale with strength unusual blow,   335
Scatt'ring the wild-brier roses into snow,
Their little limbs increasing efforts try,
Like the torn flower the fair assemblage fly.
    Ah, fallen rose, sad emblem of their doom;
Frail as thyself, they perish while they bloom!   340
Though unoffending innocence may plead,
Though frantic ewes may mourn the savage deed,
Their shepherd comes, a messenger of blood,
And drives them bleating from their sports and food.
Care loads his brow, and pity wrings his heart,   345
For lo, the murd'ring butcher with his cart
Demands the firstlings of his flock to die,
And makes a sport of life and liberty!
His gay companions Giles beholds no more –
Closed are their eyes, their fleeces drenched in gore;   350
Nor can compassion, with her softest notes,
Withhold the knife that plunges through their throats.
    Down, indignation! Hence, ideas foul!
Away the shocking image from my soul!
Let kindlier visitants attend my way   355
Beneath approaching summer's fervid ray;
Nor thankless glooms obtrude, nor cares annoy,
Whilst the sweet theme is universal joy.

Summer (extract)[1]

From THE FARMER'S BOY (1800)

Now ere sweet summer bids its long adieu,
And winds blow keen where late the blossom grew,
The bustling day and jovial night must come,
The long accustomed feast of harvest-home.[2]   290
No blood-stained victory in story bright
Can give the philosophic mind delight;
No triumph please whilst rage and death destroy –
Reflection sickens at the monstrous joy.
And where the joy, if rightly understood,   295
Like cheerful praise for universal good?
The soul nor check nor doubtful anguish knows,
But free and pure the grateful current flows.

SUMMER
[1] This account of the rite of harvest-home should be compared with Clare's account of the celebrations following sheepshearing in *The Shepherd's Calendar* (1827), pp. 972–3.

[2] *harvest-home* party to celebrate the successful gathering of the corn.

Behold the sound oak table's massy frame
Bestride the kitchen floor! The careful dame 300
And gen'rous host invite their friends around,
While all that cleared the crop or tilled the ground
Are guests by right of custom, old and young.
And many a neighbouring yeoman[3] join the throng
With artisans that lent their dextrous aid 305
When o'er each field the flaming sunbeams played.
  Yet Plenty reigns and, from her boundless hoard
(Though not one jelly trembles on the board),
Supplies the feast with all that sense can crave,
With all that made our great forefathers brave 310
Ere the cloyed palate countless flavours tried,
And cooks had nature's judgement set aside.
With thanks to Heaven, and tales of rustic lore,
The mansion echoes when the banquet's o'er.
A wider circle spreads, and smiles abound, 315
As quick the frothing horn[4] performs its round
(Care's mortal foe), that sprightly joys imparts
To cheer the frame and elevate their hearts.
Here, fresh and brown, the hazel's produce lies
In tempting heaps; and peals of laughter rise, 320
And crackling music with the frequent song,
Unheeded bear the midnight hour along.
  Here once a year distinction[5] low'rs its crest –
The master, servant and the merry guest
Are equal all, and round the happy ring 325
The reaper's eyes exulting glances fling
And, warmed with gratitude, he quits his place
With sunburnt hands and ale-enlivened face,
Refills the jug his honoured host to tend,
To serve at once the master and the friend, 330
Proud thus to meet his smiles, to share his tale,
His nuts, his conversation, and his ale.
  Such were the days, of days long past I sing,
When pride gave place to mirth without a sting;
Ere tyrant customs strength sufficient bore 335
To violate the feelings of the poor,
To leave them distanced in the mad'ning race
Where'er refinement shows its hated face –
Nor causeless hated: 'tis the peasant's curse
That hourly makes his wretched station worse, 340
Destroys life's intercourse, the social plan
That rank to rank cements, as man to man.
Wealth flows around him, fashion lordly reigns;
Yet poverty is his, and mental pains.

---

[3] *yeoman* servant in a noble household; Bloomfield celebrates a time when the servants of lords mixed with peasants.

[4] *frothing horn* animal's horn filled with ale and used as a drinking vessel.
[5] *distinction* social status.

Ann Batten Cristall   (born *c.*1769)

Ann was introduced to Robert Southey in March 1797, and in a letter to his Bristol publisher, Joseph Cottle, he wrote enthusiastically: 'But Miss Christal, have you seen her Poems? A fine, artless, sensible girl. Now, Cottle, that word "sensible" must not be construed here in its dictionary acceptation.[1] Ask a Frenchman what it means, and he will understand it, though, perhaps, he can by no circumlocution explain its French meaning. Her heart is alive. She loves poetry. She loves retirement. She loves the country. Her verses are very incorrect,[2] and the literary circle say she has no genius – but she has genius, Joseph Cottle, or there is no truth in physiognomy.'[3] Southey's critical opinion of other writers was not always reliable,[4] but on this occasion, against the prevailing view, he was right. Ann Batten Cristall was one of the most compelling poetic talents of her time. She was to publish only one book of poetry, but it stands as an extraordinary and original achievement of its kind.

She was born at Penzance, Cornwall, to Joseph Alexander Cristall, ship's captain, and his wife Elizabeth Batten, daughter of John Batten, a local merchant. She was the eldest child in a family of four sons and two daughters. Her father, a Scotsman, was often away from home, but eventually set up yards in Fowey and Penzance where he made sails, masts, and blocks. The date of her birth is not known, but she was baptized 7 December 1769 in Penzance.

Ann became a schoolteacher in 1788, and by March of that year had encountered first Everina Wollstonecraft and, through her, her famous sister Mary. Both are listed among the subscribers to her *Poetical Sketches*. By 1790 Joshua, her brother, had moved on from dealing in china to become a painter of china in the potteries in Staffordshire and Shropshire operated by Thomas Turner, from which the Blue Willow and Brosely Blue Dragon patterns originate. He would later become a celebrated watercolourist, engraver, and, in 1804, founder-member of the Society of Painters in Watercolours. He was in correspondence with Mary Wollstonecraft by 1790, when she reproached him for an occasion on which 'you selfishly forgot your sister's peace of mind', and exhorted him

to look after her: 'I know that you earnestly wish to be the friend and protector of your amiable sister and hope no inconsiderate act or thoughtless mode of conduct will add to her cares – for her comfort very much depends on you.'[5] Later that year Wollstonecraft regretted that she herself may have hurt Ann's 'tender affectionate heart'.[6] It is likely, given Wollstonecraft's counsel, that she was already in the habit of giving Joshua financial help (she regretted giving him 'all the money I had' in March 1797),[7] and equally likely that Ann was financially dependent on Joshua. Their father was paralysed by a stroke in the 1790s, and his business began to fail.

Ann's *Poetical Sketches* was published by Joseph Johnson in 1795, with an engraved title page featuring an engraving made from a drawing by her brother, depicting her fictional character Holbain. The poems themselves are, I think, startlingly original, though I cannot be the first to have noted that there are times when her verse sounds like that of Blake. Might she have seen Blake's own *Poetical Sketches*? Some of her characters have names that sound a shade Blakean – Eyzion, Thelmon, Carmel (though Macpherson is another likely influence here). And some of her poems occasionally catch the tone of some of Blake's *Songs* – as, for instance, in the case of *A Fragment: The Blind Man*. Her use of language is original in a way that is sometimes highly redolent of Blake, as when one of her characters is said to have 'unzoned passions'.[8] But when her work is closely examined, the few suggestions as to influence appear rather tenuous, and the case for Ann's originality in her own right becomes stronger. For one thing, the religious world of her poems is more conventional than that of Blake's. She is in no doubt as to the existence of an omnipresent, benevolent deity. What is not so expected is the quasi-pantheistic manner in which her characters deliquesce into the natural world around them. The voice of one of them, Rosamonde, is, at one point, 'pinioned on the wind'[9] – a rather paradoxical way of describing how her song has detached itself from its physical source and assumed its own life. Later we are told that sorrow 'Racked her celestial system with its rage'[10] – an

ANN BATTEN CRISTALL
[1] Southey means 'highly sensitive', as opposed to 'endowed with good sense'.
[2] That is, formally irregular ('incorrect' by the standards of the time).
[3] Joseph Cottle, *Reminiscences of Samuel Taylor Coleridge and Robert Southey* (London, 1847), p. 204.
[4] Particularly female ones – as witness the letter he sent to the young Charlotte Brontë in March 1837, when he told her

that 'literature cannot be the business of a woman's life, and it ought not to be' (BL MS 44,355, f.236).
[5] *Collected Letters of Mary Wollstonecraft* ed. Ralph M. Wardle (Ithaca, NY, 1979), p. 188.
[6] Ibid., p. 196.
[7] Ibid., p. 384.
[8] *Elegy on a Young Lady* 55.
[9] *Morning. Rosamonde* 21.
[10] Ibid., line 113.

astonishing turn of phrase which breaks down the barrier between her physical being and the divinely-ordered cosmos in which she moves. Ann even harnesses Greek myth to her distinctive purpose, as when Iris, messenger of the gods, is invoked in her traditional guise as rainbow,

> Reflecting each celestial ray,
> As if the flowers that decked the May
> Were there exhaled, and through its watery
> pores did glow.[11]

That she should describe the rainbow as having pores is surprising enough – but 'watery pores'? There is a baroque element here, even something of the grotesque, but it works because it is, finally, part of an integrated vision of a universe in which man and nature comprise elements of the same living being – a 'concord', to use Ann's term. The most telling phrases of all are those which describe that most pantheistic of elements – the air. In Ann's poems, the air is 'pregnant'[12] – a distinctive phrasing that manages not just to give it being, but to allude to its seed-bearing function. Elsewhere, we are told that the 'ambient air breathes nature's rich perfumes'[13] – a beautifully compact line that turns the air, decisively, into a physical entity, inhaling the odours of the flowers. It is in the matter of that heightened sensitivity to the numinous in nature that Ann is most romantic, at a moment when Wordsworth, moving in similar company, was still experimenting with an oddly politicized gothic mode, in *Adventures on Salisbury Plain*. The final stanza of one of the last poems in the volume, *An Ode*, tells us a great deal about the essential beliefs that inform her work:

> Stupendous nature – rugged, beauteous, wild!
>   Impressed with awe, thy wondrous book I read;
> Beyond this stormy tract, some realm more mild,
>   My spirit tells me, is for man decreed,
> Where, unallayed, bliss reigns without excess –
> Thus hope eccentric points to happiness![14]

It is not so much that nature is central to her vision of human life, but that it is imperfect in its present state – 'Beasts, birds, fish, insects, war with cruel strife!'[15] What confirms her essential optimism is that within such a postlapsarian vision she comprehends a realm in which 'bliss reigns without excess'. We are very close to the millennial vision of Blake's work, and that of Wordsworth in *The Recluse* – and, indeed, Ann may well have believed, with many of her contemporaries, that the millennium was close at hand. But that does not have to be inferred here. What she is telling us is that the flawed, fallen world before her is a promise of future happiness. Paradoxically enough, that 'hope eccentric' provides the spiritual centre from which so much of her poetry emanates. A complete text of *Poetical Sketches* (1795) is included in my *Romantic Women Poets: An Anthology* (1997).

'Unknown, and nothing in the scale of things', Ann says of herself in one of her poems[16] – and indeed, after her father's death in 1802, she drifts into obscurity. One of the kindest references to her occurs in Dyer's *Poems* (1801), where he comments: 'The names of Smith, More, Williams, Robinson, Carter, Seward, Opie, and Cristall, are well known'.[17] If that was so in 1801, little was heard of her subsequently. She is named in the *Biographical Dictionary of Living Authors* in 1816. Joshua too won praise from Dyer, in *Poetics* (1812), where he was praised for his 'delicate classical hand',[18] so that it is possible that Dyer was still acquainted with both Cristalls at that time. Joshua became President of the Watercolour Society in 1821 and moved to Herefordshire in 1822, where he remained until 1841. In that year he returned to London until his death in 1847. His household is said to have consisted of two young servants and 'two lady wards, between whom and himself there existed a strong attachment'. These were, one presumes, his sisters. Elizabeth is believed to have been alive in 1851; we do not know when Ann died. She seems never to have married.

Further reading

Jerome J. McGann, *The Poetics of Sensibility: A Revolution in Literary Style* (Oxford, 1996), pp. 195–206

---

11 *Evening. Gertrude* 55–7.
12 *Verses Written in the Spring* 23.
13 *The Triumph of Superstition. Raphael and Ianthe* 82.
14 *An Ode* 25–30.
15 Ibid., line 14.

16 Ibid., line 19.
17 *Poems* (1801), p. 301.
18 *Poetics: or, A Series of Poems, and Disquisitions on Poetry* (2 vols, 1812), ii 179.

Morning. Rosamonde

From POETICAL SKETCHES (1795)

Wild midst the teeming buds of opening May,
Breaking large branches from the flow'ry thorn,
  O'er the ferned hills see Rosamonda stray,
Scattering the pearls which the gay leaves adorn;
  Her ringlets o'er her temples play,   5
Flushed with the orient splendour of the morn.
The sun broke forth, and wide its glories threw,
Blushing along the sky, and sparkling in the dew.
    The plains gay-glittered with ethereal light,
      And the field-melody,   10
      Nature's wild harmony,
    Breathed love, and sang delight!

Fresh Rosamonde the glowing scene surveys,
  Her youthful bosom inly stung with pain;
Early amid the shadowy trees she strays,   15
  Her shining eyes the starting tears restrain;
While tyrant Love within her pulses plays,
  O'er the wet grass she flew with wild disdain.
She flew from thought, and far
She sang, and hailed the morning star.   20
    Her voice was pinioned[1] on the wind,
    Which wafts her notes around;
    Encircling zephyrs caught each sound,
    And bore them echoing through the wood,
    Where pleased offended Urban stood   25
    With archest smile, yet musical and kind.
Conquering the sigh, she gaily sung,
And scorn loud-trembled on her wiry tongue.

While Urban stood, and held her in his eyes,
He to his lips applies   30
    The soft-breathed flute
Whose notes, when touched with art,
Steal to the inmost heart,
And throw the tyrannizing spirit down
    While vanity and pride are charmed and mute.   35

Those lays reached Rosamonda's ear –
She fluttering like a bird whom fear
Has drawn within the fascinating serpent's fangs,
Unable to conceal the pangs
Of pride conflicting with returning love,   40
To hide her blushes darts amid the grove.
    Sweet showers fast sprinkle from her lovely eyes

MORNING. ROSAMONDE
[1] *pinioned* bound to.

Which drown her short-lived scorn;
   But as she moves the young musician flies,
Leaves her all wild, sad, weeping, and forlorn!   45

Evening. Gertrude

From POETICAL SKETCHES (1795)

In clouds drew on the evening's close,
Which 'cross the west in ranges stood,
As pensive Gertrude sought the wood,
And there the darkest thicket chose;
While from her eyes amid the wild-briar flows   5
A sad and briny flood.
   Dark o'er her head
Rolled heavy clouds, while showers,
Perfumed by summer's wild and spicy flowers,
   Their ample torrents shed.   10

Why does she mourn?
   Why droop, like flowret nipped in early spring?
Alas, her tenderness meets no return!
Love hovers round her with his airy wing
And warms her youthful heart with vain delight   15
While Urban's graceful form enchants her sight,
   And from his eyes shoots forth the poisonous sting;
Another's charms th' impassioned youth inspired –
The sportive Rosamonde his genius fired.

The drops which glide down Gertrude's cheeks   20
Mid bitter agonies did flow;
And though awhile her pallid lips might glow,
'Twas as a blossom blighted soon with woe.
   Her disregarded tresses, wet with tears,
Hung o'er her panting bosom straight and sleek;   25
   Her faithful heart was all despondency and fears.

The skies disgorged, their last large drops refrain,
   The cloudy hemisphere's no more perturbed;
The leafy boughs that had received the rain,
   With gusts of wind disturbed,   30
Shake wild their scattering drops o'er glade and plain;
They fall on Gertrude's breast, and her white garments stain.
Sighing, she threw her mantle o'er her head,
And through the brakes towards her mansion sped;
Unheedingly her vestments drew along,   35
Sweeping the tears that to the branches hung,
     And as she passed
O'er the soaked road, from off the shining grass,
In clods around her feet the moist earth clung.

The clouds dispersed, again to sight   40
The evening sun glowed lambent bright;

And forcing back the louring shades,
Spread its enlivening beams, and kindled mid the glades.
With high-wrought verdure every object glowed,
And purple hills their glittering mansions showed.   45
    The universal gleam invites to sport,
       For toil and care cease with the ebbing day;
    Th' industrious youths to plains or groves resort,
       Dance on the lawn, or o'er the hillocks stray.

    Gertrude, wandering up a lane   50
From among the winding trees,
Fanned by a refreshing breeze,
    Ascends upon the glistening plain.
Across gay Iris[1] flung her bow
    Reflecting each celestial ray,   55
    As if the flowers that decked the May[2]
Were there exhaled, and through its watery pores did glow.

From a fair covert, Urban's gay resort,
    A whistling pipe in warbling notes respired;
The well-known sound invites each youth to sport,   60
    And every heart its harmony inspired;
      While from each mead
      So thick with daisies spread,
The bounding nymphs with fairy lightness sprung,
And gaily wild their sportive sonnets sung;   65
The air was scented by the odorous flowers,
Bright-sprinkled with the dew of fresh-fall'n show'rs.

Of lively grace, and dimpled smiles,
    Slim Cynthia, the refined,
Came with neat Phillis, full of tricksome wiles,   70
    While Silvius strolled behind,
    Chased by the marble-hearted Rosalind,
The loud and witty large-mouthed Madge
With her obsequious servant Hodge.

Blithe from the mill which, briskly turning round,   75
Made the young zephyrs breathe a rural sound,
Leaped Charles, gay-glowing with industrious heat,
Active to lead in every rustic feat;
Back from his brows he shook his wavy locks,
    And turning quick his lively eyes   80
    His lovely, modest Peggy spies
Returning with her aged father's flocks.
Straight with his hand he gave his heart sincere,
Devoid of order danced, and whistled loud and clear.
Hebe, a blooming, sprightly fair,   85
With shallow Ned (an ill-matched pair);
Simple Daphne, rosy John,

EVENING. GERTRUDE
[1] *Iris* in Greek myth, the goddess who was messenger of the
gods, and appeared as the rainbow.

[2] *the May* despite the article, Ann means the month, rather
than the hawthorn.

And ever-blundering Heleson;
From a large mansion, gloomed by shading trees,
Forth sprung the star-eyed Luisse;   90
Graceful her tresses flowed around,
   Like scattered clouds that catch the moon's pale beams;
Scarcely she seemed to touch the verdant ground,
   But, as inspired,[3] along the plain she streams.
More join the flock - they spring in air,   95
Light as winged doves, and like to doves they pair;
The sun's last ray now lingered o'er their head,
And sweets delectable around were spread.

Poor Gertrude, hid amongst the trees, surveyed
Each ardent youth, each blooming maid,   100
   And as she gazed,
Pleasure by slow degrees within her senses steals;
   Her eyes, with tears impearled, she raised,
Her heart each sweet sensation feels;
   Lightly her feet the grassy meadows tread,   105
While music's power deludes her from her cares;
   Among the nymphs, by its soft influence led,
Her sympathetic breast their raptures shares.

Thus while she felt, and joined the lively throng,
   Lo! quick ascends the plain   110
   The glory of each swain,
Urban, with sportive song,
   Whose cheerful notes in frolic measures fled;
     While Rosamonde –
Fleet-footed, glowing Rosamonde – he led.   115
The rapture of the lark her voice sent forth –
Too well, ah, Gertrude knew its worth;
Dire tremblings soon her spirits seize.
Could she, vain untaught nymph, aspire to please?
Her body owns no grace;   120
No smiles, no dimples deck her eyes or face.
   She feels that she has nought to prize,
Yet totally devoid of art,
   Expression's charm was hers, with beaming eyes,
A voice far-reaching, and a feeling heart.   125

She turned around –
The flying breezes loosened to the air
Her ill-beseeming vests,[4] her scattered hair.
   So sad she looked, so artless was her woe,
As from a thinking mind had drawn a tear;   130
But joy through every vein had stole,
   And mirth shut out the sympathetic glow.
The heart's gay dance admits of no control,
Sweet joys but seldom through our senses steal –
'Tis pity then we should forget to feel.   135

---

[3] *as inspired* i.e. as if inspired.   [4] *vests* loose outer garments.

Gay wicked wit amid the circle spread,
And wanton round the lively sallies[5] sped;
Each neat-trimmed maiden laughed with playful glee,
Whom whispering swains divert with mimicry.
    Fair Rosamonde, whose rival bosom burned,   140
With taunting mirth directs young Urban's eyes;
    He, with mischievous archness, smiles returned,
Amid whose circles wounding satires[6] rise;
Their sportive feet still beat the flowery ground,
While wicked looks, and jests, and jeers went round.   145

Pierced by their insults, stung with bitter smart,
Sad fell poor Gertrude's tears, high-heaved her heart.
Distant she flew and, sitting on a stone
Concealed, gave sorrow vent, and wept alone,
    Till mid her grief, a virtuous just disdain   150
        Came to her aid, and made her bosom glow;
        With shame she burns, she blushes at her woe,
And wonders at her weakness and her pain.

'Unhappy maid!' she cried, 'thou art to blame,
Thus to expose thy virtuous breast to shame;   155
    Poor heart, thy love is laughed at for its truth;
Yet 'tis a holy treasure, though disdained,
And wantonly by thoughtlessness profaned.
    Ah, why then waste the blessings of thy youth?
No more fair reason's sacred light despise;   160
    Thy heart may blessings find
That dwell not in the eyes,
    But in the virtues of the feeling mind.'

Verses Written in the Spring

From POETICAL SKETCHES (1795)

From yon fair hill, whose woody crest
The mantling[1] hand of spring has dressed,
Where gales imbibe the May perfume,
And strew the blushing almond's bloom,
I view the verdant plains below   5
And lucid streams which gently flow;
The opening foliage, drenched with showers,
Weeps o'er the odorous vernal flowers,
And while before my tempered eye
From glancing clouds swift shadows fly,   10
While nature seems serene and blessed,
And inward concord tunes my breast,
I sigh for those by fortune crossed
Whose souls to nature's charms are lost —

---

5 *sallies* witticisms, banter.
6 *wounding satires* against Gertrude.

VERSES WRITTEN IN THE SPRING
1 *mantling* enveloping; cf. the 'mantling vine' at *Comus* 294.

Whether by love of wealth betrayed,   15
Absorbed in all the arts of trade,
Or deep engrossed in mighty schemes,
Tossed in ambition's empty dreams,
Or proud amid the learned schools,
Stiffened by dull pedantic rules,   20
Or those who ne'er from forms depart,
The slaves of fashion[2] and of art.[3]
  Oh lost to bliss – the pregnant[4] air,
The rising sun, the ripening year,
The embryos[5] that on every bush   25
Midst the wild notes of songsters blush;
The violet's scent, the varying hues
Which morn's light ray strikes mid the dews,
To them are lost – involved in care,
They cannot feel, they cannot share.   30
  I grieve when round I cast my eyes
And feel a thousand pleasures rise
That this fair earth, by Heaven bestowed
(Which human fury stains with blood),
Should teem with joys which reach the heart,   35
And man be thus absorbed in art.

An Ode

From POETICAL SKETCHES (1795)

Almighty Power, who rul'st this world of storms,
 Eternal spirit of infinity
Whose wisdom nature's boundless space informs –
 Oh look with mercy on man's misery,
Who, tossed on all the elements by turns,   5
With languor droops, or with fierce passion burns.

Submissive to life's casualties I sing;
 Though short our mortal day, and stored with pains,
And strongly nature's truths conviction bring
 That no firm happiness this world contains,   10
Yet hope, sweet hope, supports the pious breast,
Whose boundless views no earthly griefs arrest.

What dire disorder ravages the world;
 Beasts, birds, fish, insects, war with cruel strife!
Created matter in contention whirled   15
 Spreads desolation as it bursts to life!
And men, who mental light from heaven enjoy,
Pierce the fraternal[1] breast, and impiously destroy.

---

[2] *fashion* outward action or display.
[3] *art* formulated rules, learning.
[4] *pregnant* fertile, fertilising.
[5] *embryos* buds, as at Thomson, *Spring* 99–101: 'while the promised fruit / Lies yet a little embryo, unperceived / Within its crimson folds'.

AN ODE
[1] *fraternal* brotherly; it is possible that this line has an immediate political context, as *fraternité* was one of the ideals of the French Revolution which, by the time Ann was writing, had given way to the violence of the Terror.

Unknown, and nothing in the scale of things,
   Yet would I wisdom's ways aloud rehearse,   20
Touched by humanity, strike loud the strings,
   And pour a strain of more inspired verse;
But reason, truth, and harmony are vain,
No power man's boundless passions can restrain.

Stupendous nature – rugged, beauteous, wild!   25
   Impressed with awe, thy wondrous book I read;
Beyond this stormy tract, some realm more mild,
   My spirit tells me, is for man decreed,
Where, unallayed, bliss reigns without excess –
Thus hope eccentric points to happiness!   30

Amelia Opie (*née* Alderson)   (1769–1853)

Born at Norwich on 12 November 1769, Amelia Alderson was the only child of prosperous Unitarians, Amelia Briggs and the physician James Alderson. Although she had little formal education, she learnt French and was encouraged both as a musician and writer. Her mother was sickly, but gave Amelia, by her own account, a fairly disciplined upbringing.

Her mother died on 31 December 1784, at the age of thirty-nine. Thereafter Amelia took over the running of the household and her father adopted her as his constant companion, introducing her to the fashionable society of Norwich. She was writing poetry by 1790, and published in the Norwich-based dissenting periodical, *The Cabinet* (1795). She had radical political views, and this was no doubt one of the factors that drew her to William Godwin, whom she first met in Norwich in 1793. She met him again when she visited London for the celebrated treason trials of 1794, at which a number of celebrated radicals, including John Thelwall, were threatened with capital punishment (see pp. 158–9, above). The Aldersons had much in common with the accused, and Amelia attended the trials in the anxiety that, if they were found guilty, many in her father's circle would have to leave the country.

She seems to have enjoyed at least a mild flirtation with Godwin, who wrote a love poem to her, probably in February 1796. (Ironically, Amelia would, in succeeding years, write two anti-Godwinian novels.) Another acquaintance at this moment was Anna Laetitia Barbauld, who may have told her about an interesting new volume of poems that was being published by the dissenting bookseller, Joseph Johnson – Ann Batten Cristall's *Poetical Sketches* (1795). She decided to subscribe; another subscriber was Mary Wollstonecraft, whom she met in spring 1796.

On 8 May 1798 she married the divorced painter John Opie and moved to London. After this point she began to distance herself from the radicals. Opie encouraged her writing, and she wrote a good deal of poetry during ensuing years. The first book-length work bearing her name on the title page was *The Father and Daughter, a Tale in Prose* (1801). Others followed, including her *Poems* (1802), in its sixth edition by 1811, and *The Warrior's Return, and Other Poems* (1808). John Opie died on 9 April 1807, after which she returned to Norwich, visiting London for a few weeks each year. She edited his *Lectures on Painting* (1809), contributed to annuals, and wrote novels until 1825, when she became a Quaker and devoted herself to charitable works.

If the *Ode to Borrowdale in Cumberland* is very much of its time in terms of manner, it is revolutionary in content. Inspired by Amelia's visit to the Lake District, it recalls the landscape through the lens of someone well-read in the works of the picturesque theorist William Gilpin. It begins as a neoclassical fantasy, envisaging the 'genius of the storm' sitting on the mountains, recounts the poet's sensation of terror and delight, and concludes with the hope that the memory of the landscape will 'hush my tortured breast's alarms' – presumably a reference to the anxious response of radicals to the repression of Pitt's administration. In reposing its faith in the powers of memory to soothe anxiety, it anticipates Wordsworth in *Tintern Abbey*, who describes the same effect when remembering the Wye valley 'in lonely rooms, and mid the din / Of towns and cities'.

Further reading

Cecilia Lucy Brightwell, *Memorials of the Life of Amelia Opie* (Norwich, 1854)

Ann H. Jones, *Ideas and Innovations: Best Sellers in Jane Austen's Age* (New York, 1986), chapter 2

Gary Kelly, 'Amelia Opie, Lady Caroline Lamb, and Maria Edgeworth: Official and Unofficial Ideology', *Ariel* 12 (1981) 3–24

Ode to Borrowdale in Cumberland (written in 1794)

From THE WARRIOR'S RETURN, AND OTHER POEMS (1808)

Hail, Derwent's beauteous pride!
Whose charms rough rocks in threatening grandeur guard,
Whose entrance seems to mortals barred,
But to the genius of the storm thrown wide.

He on thy rock's dread height,   5
Reclined beneath his canopy of clouds,
His form in darkness shrouds,
And frowns as fixed to keep thy beauties from the sight.
But rocks and storms are vain;
Midst mountains rough and rude   10
Man's daring feet intrude,
Till lo, upon the ravished eye
Burst thy clear stream, thy smiling sky,
Thy wooded valley, and thy matchless plain!

Bright vale, the muse's choicest theme,   15
My morning thought, my midnight dream;
Still memory paints thee, smiling scene,
Still views the robe of purest green,
Refreshed by beauty-shedding rains,
Which wraps thy flower-enamelled plains;   20
Still marks thy mountains' fronts sublime,
Force graces from the hand of time;
Still I thy rugged rocks recall,
Which seem as nodding to their fall,
Whose wonders fixed my aching sight,   25
Till terror yielded to delight,[1]
And my surprises, pleasures, fears,
Were told by slow delicious tears.

But suddenly the smiling day
That cheered the valley, flies away;   30
The wooded rocks, the rapid stream,
No longer boast the noontide beam;
But storms athwart the mountains sail,
And darkly brood o'er Borrowdale.
The frightened swain his cottage seeks,   35
Ere the thick cloud in terror speaks –
And see, pale lightning flashes round!
While as the thunder's awful sound
On Echo's pinion widely flies,
Yon cataract's[2] roar unheeded dies;   40
And thee, sublimity, I hail,
Throned on the gloom of Borrowdale!

ODE TO BORROWDALE IN CUMBERLAND
[1] *Till terror yielded to delight* Amelia uses the concepts and terminology of the Burkean sublime.

[2] The cataract is the Lodore Falls, on the bank of Derwent-water.

But soon the thunder dies away,
The flash withdraws its fearful ray;
Again upon the silver stream   45
Waves in bright wreaths the noontide beam.

Oh scene sequestered, varied, wild,
Scene formed to soothe Affliction's child,
How blessed were I to watch each charm
That decks thy vale in storm or calm!   50

To see Aurora's[3] hand unbind
The mists by night's chill power confined;
Upon the mountain's dusky brow
Then mark their colours as they flow,
Gliding the colder west to seek,   55
As from the east day's splendours break.[4]
Now the green plain enchants the sight,
Adorned with spots of yellow light;
While, by its magic influence, shade
With contrast seems each charm to aid,   60
And clothes the woods in deeper dyes
To suit the azure-vested skies.
While, lo, the lofty rocks above,
Where proudly towers the bird of Jove;[5]
See from the view yon radiant cloud   65
His broad and sable pinions shroud,
Till, as he onward wings his flight,
He vanishes in floods of light;
Where feathered clouds on ether sail
And glittering hang o'er Borrowdale.   70
Or at still midnight's solemn hour,
When the dull bat revolves no more,
In search of nature's awful grace
I'd go, with slow and cautious pace,
Where the loud torrent's foaming tide   75
Lashes the rock's uneven side –
That rock which, o'er the stream below
Bending its moss-clad crumbling brow,
Makes pale with fear the wanderer's cheek,
Nor midnight's silence fails to break   80
By fragments from its aged head,
Which, rushing to the river's bed,
Cause, as they dash the waters round,
A dread variety of sound;
While I the gloomy grandeur hail   85
And awestruck rove through Borrowdale.

---

3   *Aurora* goddess of dawn.
4   In lines 51–6, Amelia follows the picturesque writer
William Gilpin in his approval of contrasting lights and
shades in the mountains: 'It is an agreeable amusement to
attend these vast shadows in their slow, and solemn march
over the mountains – to observe how the morning sun sheds

only a faint catching light upon the summits of the hills,
through one general mass of hazy shade . . .' (*Observations on the
Lakes* i 90).
5   *the bird of Jove* the eagle, now an endangered species in the
Lake District.

Yes, scene sequestered, varied, wild,
So formed to soothe Affliction's child,
Sweet Borrowdale, to thee I'll fly,
To hush my bosom's ceaseless sigh.   90
If yet in nature's store there be
One kind heart-healing balm for me,
Now the long hours are told by sighs,[6]
And sorrow steals health's crimson dyes –
If aught can smiles and bloom restore,   95
Ah, surely thine's the precious power!
   Then take me to thy world of charms,
And hush my tortured breast's alarms;[7]
Thy scenes with unobtrusive art
Shall steal the mourner from her heart;   100
The hands in sorrow clasped unclose,
Bid her sick soul on Heaven repose,
And, soothed by time and nature, hail
Health, peace, and hope in Borrowdale.

William Wordsworth and Samuel Taylor Coleridge, *Lyrical Ballads* (1798)

Lyrical Ballads (1798) is arguably the most important single volume of the romantic period. It signalled a literary revolution, and has generated a vast amount of critical literature in the two hundred years since its first publication. It is presented separately here from the author selections, preserving the distinctive form in which it was first published – a collaborative venture by Wordsworth and Coleridge.

It sprang directly out of the *annus mirabilis* of 1797–8. Its authors spent virtually every day in each other's company, from the moment the Wordsworths moved into Alfoxden House in June 1797, four miles' walk from Coleridge's cottage at Nether Stowey, to the following summer when they moved out. It was an astonishing year, and was to change the lives and careers of both men forever. Wordsworth was twenty-seven, Coleridge twenty-five, and Dorothy twenty-six. Over the next twelve months Coleridge was to concoct the plan for the poem, *The Recluse*, that would help precipitate the millennium (Christ's thousand-year rule on earth) and persuade Wordsworth that he was the only poet fitted to compose it (see p. 271). He himself would compose his three greatest poems, *The*

Ancient Mariner, *Kubla Khan* and *Christabel* (Part I), before handing over the reins to Wordsworth. Together they would plan, write, and publish the *Lyrical Ballads*. Dorothy played a crucial and indispensable part in all this, though it is not easy to say how. Certainly, her Alfoxden journal (the manuscript of which has been lost) is vital to our understanding of what took place. It describes in detail the experiences and observations that fuelled the poetry of the moment, and served as a source for much of Wordsworth's poetry (see, for instance, *A Night-Piece* and *The Discharged Soldier*). Its sensitive, precise accounts of the natural world constitute a remarkable literary achievement in their own right.

The proposal for a joint volume was already in the air when, on 20 November 1797, Dorothy noted that *The Ancient Mariner* was to be published 'with some pieces of William's'.[1] By the following spring Wordsworth was working on *Peter Bell* as a counterpart to Coleridge's 'supernatural' work (it became too long for inclusion and was not published until 1819). Coleridge was composing *Christabel*, but in the event got no further than Part I.[2] Despite his efforts, he had

---

[6] *by sighs* as opposed to bells, which toll the hours.
[7] *alarms* presumably political; Pitt was waging a campaign of repression against radicals like Amelia and her father, of which the treason trials of 1794 were the most obvious manifestation.

WILLIAM WORDSWORTH AND SAMUEL TAYLOR COLERIDGE
[1] *EY* 94.
[2] For Coleridge's account of how *Lyrical Ballads* came to be composed, see pp. 526–7.

trouble composing anything to order for the volume – *The Dungeon* and *The Foster-Mother's Tale* were quarried from *Osorio*, the play he completed in 1797 – and I doubt whether *The Nightingale* was composed with *Lyrical Ballads* in mind. However, Wordsworth seems very confidently and deliberately to have composed thirteen of the nineteen poems that make up his share of the book within a few months. Terms for publication were agreed in late May with the Bristol publisher, Joseph Cottle; *Tintern Abbey* was composed and added at the last moment in July; copies were being distributed by September. It was published anonymously.

As Coleridge suggests in *Biographia Literaria*, his was the shaping genius of the volume. *The Ancient Mariner* has enormous impact as the first of its contents, and although Wordsworth probably penned the *Advertisement*, its preoccupations are those of the younger man. Moreover, Coleridge's influence permeates Wordsworth's poetry of 1798 more strongly than at any other time. His Unitarian pantheism is seen memorably in his own *Ancient Mariner*, at the blessing of the water-snakes (ll. 273–6), and is evident in Wordsworth's *Lines Written at a Small Distance from My House* (ll. 33–6), and the central claim of *Tintern Abbey*:

> And I have felt
> A presence that disturbs me with the joy
> Of elevated thoughts, a sense sublime
> Of something far more deeply interfused,
> Whose dwelling is the light of setting suns,
> And the round ocean, and the living air,
> And the blue sky, and in the mind of man –
> A motion and a spirit that impels
> All thinking things, all objects of all thought,
> And rolls through all things. (ll. 94–103)

Wordsworth would not hold such beliefs for long; he had always been aware of his closeness to the natural world, and would continue so for the rest of his life. The peculiarly Coleridgean element is the way that love of nature has been incorporated into a spiritual vision of all-embracing unity; at the back of his mind he has Coleridge's *Religious Musings* (see p. 455), in which "'tis God / Diffused through all that doth make all one whole' (ll. 144–5).

At the time of its publication, no one recognized its significance. Sales over the next decade were respectable[3] (such that by 1807 Francis Jeffrey could remark that 'The *Lyrical Ballads* were unquestionably popular'),[4] but few copies sold at first, and despite one or two favourable reviews by allies such as Francis Wrangham, the volume caused no immediate ripples in the literary world. There was, on the other hand, one hostile review from an unexpected source – Robert Southey.[5] On the face of it, he had no reason to give *Lyrical Ballads* the thumbs down. As an old friend of Coleridge's (see p. 558), he had seen its contents in manuscript, and even borrowed from *The Idiot Boy* for his own poem, *The Idiot*.[6] His main argument is that the volume pays insufficient attention to the need for narrative interest; thus, having written off *The Idiot Boy* as 'bald in story' he comments that the other ballads 'are not so highly embellished in narration'.[7] He is, in other words, precisely the kind of reader who is invited, in the *Advertisement*, to cast away 'our own pre-established codes of decision', and respond to a new kind of poetry concerned with 'a natural delineation of human passions, human characters, and human incidents'. To make such a demand of even an educated readership was asking a good deal. It meant changing peoples' expectation of poetry, as well as the way in which they read it. That couldn't happen overnight, and if in 1798 Wordsworth and Coleridge expected that it would, they had changed their ideas by 1815, by which time they had both received a good deal of criticism for what many regarded as the strangeness and obscurity of the *Lyrical Ballads*, and Wordsworth observed that 'every author, as far as he is great and at the same time original, has had the task of creating the taste by which he is to be enjoyed: so has it been, so will it continue to be'.[8] For all the criticism, Wordsworth and Coleridge had the last laugh. The *Lyrical Ballads* were sufficiently successful to be enlarged, with the addition of a second volume (consisting of poems by Wordsworth only), in 1800, and to enjoy reprintings in 1802 and 1805. It has had a decisive influence on virtually every poet that has followed, and in doing so has shaped the way in which verse is read and interpreted today.

Further reading

William Hazlitt, 'My First Acquaintance with Poets', pp. 600–10, below

Wordsworth: Lyrical Ballads ed. Alun R. Jones and William M. Tydeman (London, 1972)

Coleridge: The Ancient Mariner and Other Poems ed. Alun R. Jones and William M. Tydeman (London, 1973)

---

3 See W. J. B. Owen, 'Costs, Sales, and Profits of Longman's Editions of Wordsworth', *The Library* 12 (1957) 93–107.

4 In his review of *Poems in Two Volumes* (1807), *Edinburgh Review* 11 (1807).

5 Southey's review is on pp. 564–5.

6 For *The Idiot*, see pp. 562–4. The relationship between the two poems is further discussed in my 'Looking for Johnny: Wordsworth's "The Idiot Boy"', *Charles Lamb Bulletin* NS 88 (1994) 166–76.

7 See p. 564.

8 *Prose Works* iii 80.

Stephen Maxfield Parrish, *The Art of the Lyrical Ballads* (Cambridge, Mass., 1973)

Mary Jacobus, *Tradition and Experiment in Wordsworth's Lyrical Ballads 1798* (Oxford, 1976)

George Whalley, 'The Mariner and the Albatross', *Studies in Literature and the Humanities: Innocence of Intent* (Basingstoke, 1985), pp. 15–34

Jerome J. McGann, 'The Meaning of the Ancient Mariner', *Spirits of Fire: English Romantic Writers and Contemporary Historical Methods* ed. G. A. Rosso and Daniel P. Watkins (London and Toronto, 1990), pp. 208–39

Tom Mayberry, *Coleridge and Wordsworth in the West Country* (Stroud, 1992)

Vincent Newey, 'Indeterminacy of Meaning in "The Ancient Mariner" ', *Centring the Self* (Aldershot, 1995), pp. 87–96

Robert Mayo, 'The Contemporaneity of the *Lyrical Ballads*', *PMLA* 69 (1954) 486–522

Richard Gravil, '*Lyrical Ballads* (1798): Wordsworth as Ironist', *Critical Quarterly* 24 (1982) 39–57

Seamus Perry, 'The Ancient Mariner Controversy', *Charles Lamb Bulletin* NS 92 (1995) 208–23

Advertisement (by Wordsworth,[1] composed June 1798)

From LYRICAL BALLADS (1798)

It is the honourable characteristic of poetry that its materials are to be found in every subject which can interest the human mind. The evidence of this fact is to be sought not in the writings of critics, but in those of poets themselves.

The majority of the following poems are to be considered as experiments. They were written chiefly with a view to ascertain how far the language of conversation in the middle and lower classes of society is adapted to the purposes of poetic pleasure.

Readers accustomed to the gaudiness and inane phraseology of many modern writers,[2] if they persist in reading this book to its conclusion, will perhaps frequently have to struggle with feelings of strangeness and awkwardness: they will look round for poetry, and will be induced to enquire by what species of courtesy these attempts can be permitted to assume that title. It is desirable that such readers, for their own sakes, should not suffer the solitary word 'poetry' (a word of very disputed meaning) to stand in the way of their gratification, but that while they are perusing this book, they should ask themselves if it contains a natural delineation of human passions, human characters, and human incidents; and, if the answer be favourable to the author's wishes, that they should consent to be pleased in spite of that most dreadful enemy to our pleasures: our own pre-established codes of decision.[3]

Readers of superior judgement may disapprove of the style in which many of these pieces are executed. It must be expected that many lines and phrases will not exactly suit their taste. It will perhaps appear to them that, wishing to avoid the prevalent fault of the day,[4] the author has sometimes descended too low, and that many of his expressions are too familiar, and not of sufficient dignity. It is apprehended that the more conversant the reader is with our elder writers, and with those in modern times who have been the most successful in painting manners[5] and passions,[6] the fewer complaints of this kind will he have to make.

ADVERTISEMENT

[1] Throughout this text of *Lyrical Ballads*, I have provided the reader with authorship details for each work. It should be borne in mind that the volume was published anonymously, so that its first readers were unaware not only of who wrote what, but of the fact that it contained the work of more than one person. Though by Wordsworth, the Advertisement and its ideas would have been worked out with Coleridge.

[2] *the gaudiness ... writers* based on Hugh Blair's attack on modern poetry in his *Lectures on Rhetoric and Belles Lettres* (1783): 'In after ages, when poetry became a regular art, studied for reputation and for gain, authors began to affect what they did not feel. Composing coolly in their closets, they endeavoured to imitate passion, rather than to express it ...' (ii 323).

[3] *pre-established codes of decision* prejudices.

[4] *the prevalent fault of the day* gaudy and inane phraseology.

[5] *manners* in a letter of 1799, Wordsworth commends the appearance, in Burns's poetry, of 'manners connected with the permanent objects of nature, and partaking of the simplicity of those objects' (*EY* 255–6).

[6] *elder writers ... passions* Wordsworth probably has in mind Milton and Shakespeare ('elder writers'), and Burns, Cowper, and Joanna Baillie (see pp. 126, 8 and 153) ('those in modern times').

An accurate taste in poetry and in all the other arts, Sir Joshua Reynolds[7] has observed, is an acquired talent which can only be produced by severe thought, and a long continued intercourse with the best models of composition. This is mentioned not with so ridiculous a purpose as to prevent the most inexperienced reader from judging for himself, but merely to temper the rashness of decision, and to suggest that if poetry be a subject on which much time has not been bestowed, the judgement may be erroneous, and that in many cases it necessarily will be so.

The tale of 'Goody Blake and Harry Gill' is founded on a well-authenticated fact which happened in Warwickshire. Of the other poems in the collection, it may be proper to say that they are either absolute inventions of the author, or facts which took place within his personal observation or that of his friends.

The poem of 'The Thorn', as the reader will soon discover, is not supposed to be spoken in the author's own person: the character of the loquacious narrator will sufficiently show itself in the course of the story. 'The Rime of the Ancyent Marinere' was professedly written in imitation of the style, as well as of the spirit, of the elder poets. But with a few exceptions, the author believes that the language adopted in it has been equally intelligible for these three last centuries. The lines entitled 'Expostulation and Reply', and those which follow, arose out of conversation with a friend[8] who was somewhat unreasonably attached to modern books of moral philosophy.

The Rime of the Ancyent Marinere, in Seven Parts (by Coleridge, composed between November 1797 and March 1798)[1]

From LYRICAL BALLADS (1798)

Argument

How a ship, having passed the line,[2] was driven by storms to the cold country towards the South Pole, and how from thence she made her course to the tropical latitude of the great Pacific Ocean; and of the strange things that befell, and in what manner the ancyent marinere came back to his own country.

I

It is an ancyent marinere,
    And he stoppeth one of three:
'By thy long grey beard and thy glittering eye
    Now wherefore stoppest me?

The bridegroom's doors are opened wide,   5
    And I am next of kin;
The guests are met, the feast is set –
    Mayst hear the merry din.'

But still he holds the wedding-guest:
    'There was a ship', quoth he –   10

---

[7] Sir Joshua Reynolds (1723–92), was the most renowned portrait painter of the age. His first discourse was delivered in 1769, and subsequent lectures became yearly fixtures at the Royal Academy. For further details see my *Wordsworth's Reading 1770–1799* (1993), p. 116. Extracts from Reynolds' *Discourses* appear in *British Literature 1640–1789*, (Oxford, 1996) in the same series as the present volume.

[8] *a friend* William Hazlitt.

THE RIME OF THE ANCYENT MARINERE
[1] For circumstances of composition see Fenwick Note to *We are Seven*, pp. 418–19, below. From 1800 to 1817 the poem was subtitled *A Poet's Reverie*.
[2] *line* equator.

'Nay, if thou'st got a laughsome tale,
    Marinere, come with me!'

He holds him with his skinny hand,
    Quoth he, 'There was a ship –'
'Now get thee hence, thou grey-beard loon,   15
    Or my staff shall make thee skip!'

He holds him with his glittering eye –
    The wedding-guest stood still,
And listens like a three years' child:
    The marinere hath his will.[3]   20

The wedding-guest sat on a stone,
    He cannot choose but hear;
And thus spake on that ancyent man,
    The bright-eyed marinere:

'The ship was cheered, the harbour cleared,   25
    Merrily did we drop
Below the kirk, below the hill,
    Below the lighthouse top.

The sun came up upon the left,
    Out of the sea came he;   30
And he shone bright, and on the right
    Went down into the sea.

Higher and higher every day,
    Till over the mast at noon –'
The wedding-guest here beat his breast,   35
    For he heard the loud bassoon.

The bride hath paced into the hall,
    Red as a rose is she;
Nodding their heads before her goes
    The merry minstrelsy.[4]   40

The wedding-guest he beat his breast,
    Yet he cannot choose but hear;
And thus spake on that ancyent man,
    The bright-eyed marinere.

'Listen, stranger! Storm and wind,   45
    A wind and tempest strong!
For days and weeks it played us freaks –
    Like chaff we drove along.

Listen, stranger! Mist and snow,
    And it grew wondrous cauld: 50

---

[3]   Lines 19–20 are by Wordsworth; see p. 419, below.
[4]   *before her ... minstrelsy* cf. Chaucer, *Squire's Tale* 268:
'Toforn hym gooth the loude mynstralcye'.

And ice mast-high came floating by
　　As green as emerauld.

And through the drifts[5] the snowy clifts[6]
　　Did send a dismal sheen;
Ne shapes of men ne beasts we ken —   55
　　The ice was all between.

The ice was here, the ice was there,
　　The ice was all around;
It cracked and growled, and roared and howled
　　Like noises of a swound.[7]   60

At length did cross an albatross,[8]
　　Thorough the fog it came;
And an[9] it were a Christian soul,[10]
　　We hailed it in God's name.

The marineres gave it biscuit-worms,[11]   65
　　And round and round it flew:
The ice did split with a thunder-fit;
　　The helmsman steered us through.

And a good south wind sprung up behind,
　　The albatross did follow;   70
And every day, for food or play,
　　Came to the marineres' hollo!

In mist or cloud, on mast or shroud,
　　It perched for vespers[12] nine,
Whiles all the night, through fogsmoke white,   75
　　Glimmered the white moonshine.'

'God save thee, ancyent marinere,
　　From the fiends that plague thee thus!
Why look'st thou so?' 'With my crossbow
　　I shot the albatross.[13]   80

---

5   *drifts* floating ice.
6   *clifts* clefts.
7   *swound* swoon.
8   *albatross* large sea-bird with a wing span of over ten feet.
9   *an* as if.
10 *a Christian soul* i.e. a human being.
11 This detail was removed from later versions of the poem.
12 *vespers* evening prayers.
13 No explanation for the action is given; it was suggested by Wordsworth after reading Shelvocke's *Voyage Round the World* (1726): '. . . we had continual squalls of sleet, snow and rain, and the heavens were perpetually hid from us by gloomy dismal clouds. In short, one would think it impossible that any thing living could subsist in so rigid a climate; and, indeed, we all observed, that we had not had the sight of one fish of any kind, since we were come to the southward of the streights of le Mair, nor one seabird, except a disconsolate black Albitross, who accompanied us for several days, hovering about us as if he had lost himself, till Hatley (my second Captain), observing, in one of his melancholy fits, that this bird was always hovering near us, imagined, from his colour, that it might be some ill omen. That which, I suppose, induced him the more to encourage his superstition, was the continued series of contrary tempestuous winds, which had oppressed us ever since we had got into this sea. But be that as it would, he, after some fruitless attempts, at length, shot the Albitross, not doubting (perhaps) that we should have a fair wind after it. I must own that this navigation was truly melancholy, and was the more so to us, who were by ourselves without a companion' (pp. 72–3). In 1804 Coleridge saw a hawk shot at during his sea-voyage to Malta, and commented in his notebook: 'Poor hawk! Oh strange lust of murder in man! It is not cruelty; it is mere non-feeling from non-thinking' (*Notebooks* ii 2090).

II

The sun came up upon the right,
    Out of the sea came he;
And broad as a weft[14] upon the left
    Went down into the sea.

And the good south wind still blew behind,   85
    But no sweet bird did follow,
Ne any day for food or play
    Came to the marineres' hollo!

And I had done an hellish thing
    And it would work 'em woe: 90
For all averred[15] I had killed the bird
    That made the breeze to blow.

Ne dim ne red, like God's own head
    The glorious sun uprist:
Then all averred I had killed the bird   95
    That brought the fog and mist.
"'Twas right", said they, "such birds to slay,
    That bring the fog and mist."

The breezes[16] blew, the white foam flew,
    The furrow followed free: 100
We were the first that ever burst
    Into that silent sea.

Down dropt the breeze, the sails dropt down,
    'Twas sad as sad could be,
And we did speak only to break   105
    The silence of the sea.

All in a hot and copper sky
    The bloody sun at noon
Right up above the mast did stand,
    No bigger than the moon.   110

Day after day, day after day,
    We stuck, ne breath ne motion,
As idle as a painted ship
    Upon a painted ocean.

Water, water, everywhere,   115
    And all the boards did shrink;
Water, water, everywhere,
    Ne any drop to drink.

---

[14] *weft* signal-flag.
[15] *averred* maintained that.
[16] *breezes* Trade Winds.

The very deeps did rot: oh Christ,
   That ever this should be!   120
Yea, slimy things did crawl with legs
   Upon the slimy sea.

About, about, in reel and rout
   The death-fires danced at night;
The water, like a witch's oils,   125
   Burnt green and blue and white.

And some in dreams assured were
   Of the spirit that plagued us so;
Nine fathom deep he had followed us
   From the land of mist and snow.   130

And every tongue, through utter drouth,[17]
   Was withered at the root;
We could not speak, no more than if
   We had been choked with soot.

Ah wel-a-day! what evil looks   135
   Had I from old and young!
Instead of the cross the albatross
   About my neck was hung.

III

I saw a something in the sky
   No bigger than my fist;   140
At first it seemed a little speck
   And then it seemed a mist;
It moved and moved, and took at last
   A certain shape, I wist.[18]

A speck, a mist, a shape, I wist!   145
   And still it nered and nered:
And an it dodged a water-sprite,
   It plunged and tacked and veered.

With throat unslaked, with black lips baked,
   Ne could we laugh, ne wail;   150
Then while through drouth all dumb they stood,
I bit my arm, and sucked the blood,
   And cried, "A sail! A sail!"

With throat unslaked, with black lips baked,
   Agape they heard me call: 155
Gramercy![19] they for joy did grin
And all at once their breath drew in
   As they were drinking all.

---

[17] *drouth* dryness.
[18] *wist* was aware of.
[19] *Gramercy!* mercy on us!

She doth not tack from side to side
    Hither to work us weal;[20]   160
Withouten wind, withouten tide
    She steddies with upright keel.

The western wave was all aflame,
    The day was well nigh done!
Almost upon the western wave   165
    Rested the broad bright sun;
When that strange shape[21] drove suddenly
    Betwixt us and the sun.

And strait the sun was flecked with bars
    (Heaven's Mother send us grace!),   170
As if through a dungeon-grate he peered
    With broad and burning face.

Alas! thought I, and my heart beat loud,
    How fast she neres and neres!
Are those *her* sails that glance in the sun   175
    Like restless gossameres?

Are these *her* naked ribs, which flecked
    The sun that did behind them peer?
And are these two all, all the crew,
    That woman and her fleshless pheere?[22]   180

His bones were black with many a crack,
    All black and bare, I ween;
Jet black and bare, save where with rust
Of mouldy damps and charnel crust
    They're patched with purple and green.   185

Her lips are red, *her* looks are free,
    Her locks are yellow as gold;
Her skin is as white as leprosy,
And she is far liker death than he,
    Her flesh makes the still air cold.   190

The naked hulk alongside came,
    And the twain were playing dice;
"The game is done! I've won! I've won!"
    Quoth she, and whistled thrice.

A gust of wind sterte up behind   195
    And whistled through his bones;
Through the holes of his eyes and the hole of his mouth
    Half-whistles and half-groans.

---

[20] *weal* harm.
[21] *strange shape* According to Wordsworth, the ghost-ship was suggested by a dream of Coleridge's friend and neighbour

John Cruikshank, who is said to have seen 'a skeleton ship with figures in it'.
[22] *pheere* companion.

With never a whisper in the sea
    Off darts the spectre-ship;   200
While clombe²³ above the eastern bar
The horned moon, with one bright star
    Almost atween the tips.

One after one by the horned moon
    (Listen, oh stranger, to me!)   205
Each turned his face with a ghastly pang
    And cursed me with his ee.

Four times fifty living men,
    With never a sigh or groan,
With heavy thump, a lifeless lump,   210
    They dropped down one by one.

Their souls did from their bodies fly,
    They fled to bliss or woe;
And every soul, it passed me by
    Like the whiz of my crossbow.'   215

IV

'I fear thee, ancyent marinere,
    I fear thy skinny hand;
And thou art long and lank and brown
    As is the ribbed sea-sand.²⁴

I fear thee and thy glittering eye,   220
    And thy skinny hand so brown –'
'Fear not, fear not, thou wedding-guest,
    This body dropt not down.

Alone, alone, all all alone,
    Alone on the wide wide sea;   225
And Christ would take no pity on
    My soul in agony.

The many men so beautiful,
    And they all dead did lie!
And a million million slimy things   230
    Lived on – and so did I.

I looked upon the rotting sea
    And drew my eyes away;
I looked upon the eldritch²⁵ deck,
    And there the dead men lay.   235

---

²³ *clombe* climbed; still used in everyday speech at the time of writing.

²⁴ *And thou art long . . . sea-sand* these two lines are by Wordsworth (see pp. 418–19).

²⁵ *eldritch* ghostly.

I looked to heaven and tried to pray
    But or ever a prayer had gusht,
A wicked whisper came and made
    My heart as dry as dust.

I closed my lids and kept them close   240
    Till the balls like pulses beat;
For the sky and the sea, and the sea and the sky
Lay like a load on my weary eye,
    And the dead were at my feet.

The cold sweat melted from their limbs,   245
    Ne rot, ne reek did they;
The look with which they looked on me
    Had never passed away.

An orphan's curse would drag to hell
    A spirit from on high;   250
But oh! more horrible than that
    Is the curse in a dead man's eye!
Seven days, seven nights, I saw that curse
    And yet I could not die.

The moving moon went up the sky   255
    And nowhere did abide;
Softly she was going up
    And a star or two beside;

Her beams bemocked the sultry main
    Like morning frosts yspread;   260
But where the ship's huge shadow lay
The charmed[26] water burnt alway
    A still and awful red.

Beyond the shadow of the ship
    I watched the water-snakes;   265
They moved in tracks of shining white,
And when they reared, the elfish light
    Fell off in hoary flakes.

Within the shadow of the ship
    I watched their rich attire: 270
Blue, glossy green, and velvet black,
They coiled and swam, and every track
    Was a flash of golden fire.

Oh happy living things! no tongue
    Their beauty might declare: 275
A spring of love gusht from my heart
    And I blessed them unaware!

---

[26] *charmed* dead calm.

Sure my kind saint took pity on me,
And I blessed them unaware.

The self-same moment I could pray,   280
And from my neck so free
The albatross fell off and sank
Like lead into the sea.

V

Oh sleep, it is a gentle thing
Beloved from pole to pole!   285
To Mary Queen[27] the praise be yeven;[28]
She sent the gentle sleep from heaven
That slid into my soul.

The silly[29] buckets on the deck
That had so long remained,   290
I dreamt that they were filled with dew
And when I awoke it rained.

My lips were wet, my throat was cold,
My garments all were dank;
Sure I had drunken in my dreams   295
And still my body drank.

I moved and could not feel my limbs,
I was so light, almost
I thought that I had died in sleep
And was a blessed ghost.   300

The roaring wind – it roared far off,
It did not come anear;
But with its sound it shook the sails
That were so thin and sere.[30]

The upper air bursts into life   305
And a hundred fire-flags sheen,[31]
To and fro they are hurried about;
And to and fro, and in and out
The stars dance on between.[32]

The coming wind doth roar more loud,   310
The sails do sigh like sedge;
The rain pours down from one black cloud,
And the moon is at its edge.

---

[27] *Mary Queen* the Virgin Mary.
[28] *yeven* given.
[29] *silly* plain, rustic, homely.
[30] *sere* worn.

[31] *sheen* shining.
[32] *The upper air … between* the Aurora Borealis, which also features in Wordsworth's *The Complaint of a Forsaken Indian Woman*.

Hark, hark! The thick black cloud is cleft
    And the moon is at its side;   315
Like waters shot from some high crag,
The lightning falls with never a jag,
    A river steep and wide.

The strong wind reached the ship, it roared
    And dropped down like a stone!   320
Beneath the lightning and the moon
    The dead men gave a groan.

They groaned, they stirred, they all uprose,
    Ne spake, ne moved their eyes;
It had been strange, even in a dream,   325
    To have seen those dead men rise.

The helmsman steered, the ship moved on,
    Yet never a breeze up-blew;
The marineres all 'gan work the ropes
    Where they were wont to do;   330
They raised their limbs like lifeless tools –
    We were a ghastly crew.

The body of my brother's son
    Stood by me, knee to knee;
The body and I pulled at one rope   335
    But he said nought to me –
And I quaked to think of my own voice,
    How frightful it would be!

The daylight dawned, they dropped their arms
    And clustered round the mast;   340
Sweet sounds rose slowly through their mouths
    And from their bodies passed.

Around, around, flew each sweet sound
    Then darted to the sun;
Slowly the sounds came back again,   345
    Now mixed, now one by one.

Sometimes a-dropping from the sky
    I heard the lavrock[33] sing;
Sometimes all little birds that are,
How they seemed to fill the sea and air   350
    With their sweet jargoning![34]

And now 'twas like all instruments,
    Now like a lonely flute,
And now it is an angel's song
    That makes the heavens be mute.   355

---

[33] *lavrock* lark.   [34] *jargoning* birdsong.

It ceased, yet still the sails made on
 A pleasant noise till noon,
A noise like of a hidden brook
 In the leafy month of June,
That to the sleeping woods all night   360
 Singeth a quiet tune –

Listen, oh listen, thou wedding-guest!'
 'Marinere, thou hast thy will!
For that which comes out of thine eye doth make
 My body and soul to be still.'   365

'Never sadder tale was told
 To a man of woman born;
Sadder and wiser thou wedding-guest
 Thou'lt rise tomorrow morn!

Never sadder tale was heard   370
 By a man of woman born;
The marineres all returned to work
 As silent as beforne.

The marineres all 'gan pull the ropes,
 But look at me they n'old;[35]   375
Thought I, I am as thin as air –
 They cannot me behold.

Till noon we silently sailed on,
 Yet never a breeze did breathe;
Slowly and smoothly went the ship,   380
 Moved onward from beneath.

Under the keel nine fathom deep,
 From the land of mist and snow,
The spirit slid, and it was he
 That made the ship to go.   385
The sails at noon left off their tune
 And the ship stood still also.

The sun right up above the mast
 Had fixed her to the ocean;
But in a minute she 'gan stir   390
 With a short uneasy motion –
Backwards and forwards half her length,
 With a short uneasy motion.

Then like a pawing horse let go,
 She made a sudden bound;   395
It flung the blood into my head,
 And I fell into a swound.

---

[35] *n'old* would not.

How long in that same fit I lay,
   I have not to declare;
But ere my living life returned,
I heard and in my soul discerned
   Two voices in the air.

400

"Is it he?" quoth one, "Is this the man?
   By him who died on cross,
With his cruel bow he laid full low
   The harmless albatross.

405

The spirit who bideth by himself
   In the land of mist and snow,
He loved the bird that loved the man
   Who shot him with his bow."

410

The other was a softer voice,
   As soft as honey-dew;
Quoth he, "The man hath penance done
   And penance more will do." '

VI

FIRST VOICE
But tell me, tell me! speak again,
   Thy soft response renewing –
What makes that ship drive on so fast?
   What is the ocean doing?

415

SECOND VOICE
Still as a slave before his lord,
   The ocean hath no blast;
His great bright eye most silently
   Up to the moon is cast –

420

If he may know which way to go,
   For she guides him smooth or grim.
See, brother, see – how graciously
   She looketh down on him!

425

FIRST VOICE
But why drives on that ship so fast
   Withouten wave or wind?
SECOND VOICE
The air is cut away before
   And closes from behind.

430

Fly, brother, fly! more high, more high,
   Or we shall be belated;
For slow and slow that ship will go
   When the marinere's trance is abated.

'I woke, and we were sailing on   435
    As in a gentle weather;
'Twas night, calm night, the moon was high –
    The dead men stood together.

All stood together on the deck,
    For a charnel-dungeon[36] fitter;   440
All fixed on me their stony eyes
    That in the moon did glitter.

The pang, the curse, with which they died
    Had never passed away;
I could not draw my een from theirs   445
    Ne turn them up to pray.

And in its time the spell was snapt
    And I could move my een;
I looked far forth but little saw
    Of what might else be seen –   450

Like one that on a lonely road
    Doth walk in fear and dread,
And having once turned round walks on
    And turns no more his head,
Because he knows a frightful fiend   455
    Doth close behind him tread.

But soon there breathed a wind on me,
    Ne sound ne motion made;
Its path was not upon the sea,
    In ripple or in shade.   460

It raised my hair, it fanned my cheek,
    Like a meadow-gale of spring –
It mingled strangely with my fears,
    Yet it felt like a welcoming.

Swiftly, swiftly flew the ship,   465
    Yet she sailed softly too;
Sweetly, sweetly blew the breeze –
    On me alone it blew.

Oh dream of joy! Is this indeed
    The lighthouse top I see?   470
Is this the hill? Is this the kirk?
    Is this mine own countrée?

We drifted o'er the harbour-bar,[37]
    And I with sobs did pray,
"Oh let me be awake, my God!   475
    Or let me sleep alway!"

---

[36]   *charnel-dungeon* a dungeon containing dead bodies.   [37]   *harbour-bar* bank of silt across the mouth of the harbour.

The harbour-bay was clear as glass,
    So smoothly it was strewn![38]
And on the bay the moonlight lay
    And the shadow of the moon.   480

The moonlight bay was white all o'er
    Till rising from the same,
Full many shapes that shadows were
    Like as of torches came.

A little distance from the prow   485
    Those dark red shadows were;
But soon I saw that my own flesh
    Was red as in a glare.

I turned my head in fear and dread
    And by the holy rood,[39]   490
The bodies had advanced, and now
    Before the mast they stood.

They lifted up their stiff right arms,
    They held them strait and tight;
And each right arm burnt like a torch,   495
    A torch that's borne upright.
Their stony eyeballs glittered on
    In the red and smoky light.

I prayed and turned my head away
    Forth looking as before;   500
There was no breeze upon the bay,
    No wave against the shore.

The rock shone bright, the kirk no less
    That stands above the rock;
The moonlight steeped in silentness   505
    The steady weathercock.

And the bay was white with silent light,
    Till rising from the same
Full many shapes that shadows were
    In crimson colours came.   510

A little distance from the prow
    Those crimson shadows were;
I turned my eyes upon the deck –
    Oh Christ! what saw I there?

Each corse lay flat, lifeless and flat,   515
    And by the holy rood
A man all light, a seraph-man[40]
    On every corse there stood.

---

[38] *strewn* levelled.
[39] *rood* cross.

[40] *seraph-man* the seraphim were the highest order of angels, whose purpose was to glow with the love of God.

This seraph-band, each waved his hand –
   It was a heavenly sight!
They stood as signals to the land,
   Each one a lovely light;   520

This seraph-band, each waved his hand,
   No voice did they impart –
No voice, but oh! the silence sank   525
   Like music on my heart.

Eftsones I heard the dash of oars,
   I heard the pilot's cheer;
My head was turned perforce away
   And I saw a boat appear.   530

Then vanished all the lovely lights,
   The bodies rose anew;
With silent pace each to his place
   Came back the ghastly crew.
The wind that shade nor motion made,   535
   On me alone it blew.

The pilot and the pilot's boy,
   I heard them coming fast –
Dear Lord in heaven! it was a joy
   The dead men could not blast.   540

I saw a third, I heard his voice –
   It is the hermit good!
He singeth loud his godly hymns
   That he makes in the wood.
He'll shrieve my soul, he'll wash away   545
   The albatross's blood.

VII

This hermit good lives in that wood
   Which slopes down to the sea;
How loudly his sweet voice he rears!
He loves to talk with marineres   550
   That come from a far countrée.

He kneels at morn, and noon and eve,
   He hath a cushion plump;
It is the moss that wholly hides
   The rotted old oak-stump.   555

The skiff-boat nered, I heard them talk:
   "Why, this is strange, I trow!
Where are those lights so many and fair,
   That signal made but now?"

"Strange, by my faith!" the hermit said,
　　"And they answered not our cheer! 560
The planks look warped, and see those sails,
　　How thin they are and sere!
I never saw aught like to them
　　Unless perchance it were 565

The skeletons of leaves that lag
　　My forest brook along,
When the ivy-tod[41] is heavy with snow
And the owlet whoops to the wolf below
　　That eats the she-wolf's young." 570

"Dear Lord! it has a fiendish look",
　　The pilot made reply,
"I am a-feared." "Push on, push on!"
　　Said the hermit cheerily.

The boat came closer to the ship 575
　　But I ne spake ne stirred;
The boat came close beneath the ship
　　And strait a sound was heard!

Under the water it rumbled on,
　　Still louder and more dread; 580
It reached the ship, it split the bay –
　　The ship went down like lead.

Stunned by that loud and dreadful sound
　　Which sky and ocean smote,
Like one that hath been seven days drowned, 585
　　My body lay afloat;
But swift as dreams, myself I found
　　Within the pilot's boat.

Upon the whirl where sank the ship
　　The boat spun round and round, 590
And all was still, save that the hill
　　Was telling of the sound.

I moved my lips – the pilot shrieked
　　And fell down in a fit;
The holy hermit raised his eyes 595
　　And prayed where he did sit.

I took the oars; the pilot's boy,
　　Who now doth crazy go,
Laughed loud and long, and all the while
　　His eyes went to and fro: 600
"Ha! ha!" quoth he, "full plain I see
　　The Devil knows how to row."

---

[41]　*ivy-tod* ivy-bush.

And now all in my own countrée
   I stood on the firm land!
The hermit stepped forth from the boat,   605
   And scarcely he could stand.

"Oh shrieve me, shrieve me, holy man!"
   The hermit crossed his brow.
"Say quick", quoth he, "I bid thee say
   What manner man art thou?"   610

Forthwith this frame of mine was wrenched
   With a woeful agony,
Which forced me to begin my tale –
   And then it left me free.

Since then, at an uncertain hour,   615
   Now oft-times and now fewer,
That anguish comes and makes me tell
   My ghastly aventure.

I pass, like night, from land to land,
   I have strange power of speech;   620
The moment that his face I see
I know the man that must hear me –
   To him my tale I teach.

What loud uproar bursts from that door!
   The wedding-guests are there;   625
But in the garden bower the bride
   And bridemaids singing are;
And hark, the little vesper bell[42]
   Which biddeth me to prayer.

Oh wedding-guest! this soul hath been   630
   Alone on a wide wide sea;
So lonely 'twas, that God himself
   Scarce seemed there to be.

Oh sweeter than the marriage-feast,
   'Tis sweeter far to me   635
To walk together to the kirk
   With a goodly company!

To walk together to the kirk
   And all together pray,
While each to his great Father bends,   640
Old men, and babes, and loving friends,
   And youths and maidens gay.

---

[42] *vesper bell* bell used to summon the congregation for ves-
pers, evensong.

Farewell, farewell! but this I tell
  To thee, thou wedding-guest!
He prayeth well who loveth well   645
  Both man and bird and beast.

He prayeth best who loveth best
  All things both great and small,
For the dear God who loveth us,
  He made and loveth all.'[43]   650

[handwritten annotation: moral version]

The marinere, whose eye is bright,
  Whose beard with age is hoar,
Is gone; and now the wedding-guest
  Turned from the bridegroom's door.

He went like one that hath been stunned   655
  And is of sense forlorn:
A sadder and a wiser man
  He rose the morrow morn.

The Foster-Mother's Tale: A Dramatic Fragment (by Coleridge, extracted from *Osorio*, composed 1797)

From LYRICAL BALLADS (1798)

FOSTER-MOTHER I never saw the man whom you describe.
MARIA. 'Tis strange! He spake of you familiarly
As mine and Albert's common foster-mother.
FOSTER-MOTHER Now blessings on the man, whoe'er he be,
That joined your names with mine! Oh my sweet lady,   5
As often as I think of those dear times
When you two little ones would stand at eve
On each side of my chair, and make me learn
All you had learnt in the day; and how to talk
In gentle phrase, then bid me sing to you –   10
'Tis more like heaven to come than what *has* been!
MARIA Oh my dear mother! This strange man has left me
Troubled with wilder fancies than the moon
Breeds in the lovesick maid who gazes at it,
Till, lost in inward vision, with wet eye   15
She gazes idly! But that entrance,[1] Mother!
FOSTER-MOTHER Can no one hear? It is a perilous tale.
MARIA No one.

---

43 *For the dear God . . . all* The failure of the moral satisfactorily to account for the events of the poem, and the mariner's continuing penance, has been noted by many critics, not least Coleridge himself, as Henry Nelson Coleridge recalled: 'Mrs Barbauld, meaning to be complimentary, told our poet, that she thought *The Ancient Mariner* very beautiful, but that it had the fault of containing no moral. "Nay, madam," replied the poet, "if I may be permitted to say so, the only fault in the poem is that there is *too much!* In a work of such pure imagination I ought not to have stopped to give reasons for things, or inculcate humanity to beasts"' (CC *Table Talk* i 273n7; see also ii 272–3).

THE FOSTER-MOTHER'S TALE: A DRAMATIC FRAGMENT
1 *entrance* the entrance to a dungeon, the existence of which has to be explained by the play.

FOSTER-MOTHER My husband's father told it me,
Poor old Leoni! (Angels rest his soul!)
He was a woodman, and could fell and saw   20
With lusty[2] arm. You know that huge round beam
Which props the hanging wall of the old chapel?
Beneath that tree, while yet it was a tree,
He found a baby wrapped in mosses lined
With thistle-beards[3] and such small locks of wool   25
As hang on brambles. Well, he brought him home
And reared him at the then Lord Velez's cost.
And so the babe grew up a pretty boy –
A pretty boy, but most unteachable,
And never learnt a prayer, nor told a bead,[4]   30
But knew the names of birds, and mocked[5] their notes,
And whistled as he were a bird himself.
And all the autumn 'twas his only play
To get the seeds of wild-flowers, and to plant them
With earth and water on the stumps of trees.   35
A friar who gathered simples[6] in the wood,
A grey-haired man, he loved this little boy,
The boy loved him. And when the friar taught him,
He soon could write with the pen, and from that time
Lived chiefly at the convent or the castle.   40
So he became a very learned youth.
     But oh, poor wretch – he read, and read, and read,
Till his brain turned! And ere his twentieth year
He had unlawful thoughts of many things,
And though he prayed, he never loved to pray   45
With holy men, nor in a holy place.
But yet his speech – it was so soft and sweet,
The late Lord Velez ne'er was wearied with him.
And once, as by the north side of the chapel
They stood together, chained in deep discourse,   50
The earth heaved under them with such a groan
That the wall tottered, and had well-nigh fallen
Right on their heads. My Lord was sorely frightened;
A fever seized him, and he made confession
Of all the heretical and lawless talk   55
Which brought this judgement: so the youth was seized
And cast into that hole. My husband's father
Sobbed like a child – it almost broke his heart.
And once as he was working in the cellar,
He heard a voice distinctly: 'twas the youth's,   60
Who sung a doleful song about green fields,
How sweet it were on lake or wild savannah[7]
To hunt for food and be a naked man,[8]
And wander up and down at liberty.
He always doted on the youth and now   65

---

[2] *lusty* strong.
[3] *thistle-beards* the down or pappus which crowns the seeds of
the thistle, and by which they are carried along by the wind.
[4] *told a bead* i.e. counted a bead on a rosary.

[5] *mocked* imitated.
[6] *simples* medicinal herbs.
[7] *savannah* treeless plain in tropical America.
[8] *naked man* i.e. savage.

His love grew desperate; and, defying death,
He made that cunning entrance I described –
And the young man escaped.
MARIA   'Tis a sweet tale,
Such as would lull a listening child to sleep,
His rosy face besoiled with unwiped tears.   70
And what became of him?
FOSTER-MOTHER   He went on shipboard
With those bold voyagers who made discovery
Of golden lands.[9] Leoni's younger brother
Went likewise, and when he returned to Spain,
He told Leoni that the poor mad youth,   75
Soon after they arrived in that new world,
In spite of his dissuasion, seized a boat,
And all alone set sail by silent moonlight
Up a great river, great as any sea,
And ne'er was heard of more. But 'tis supposed   80
He lived and died among the savage men.

Lines Left upon a Seat in a Yew-Tree which Stands near the Lake of Esthwaite, on a Desolate Part of the Shore, yet Commanding a Beautiful Prospect[1] (by Wordsworth, composed April–May 1797)

From Lyrical Ballads (1798)

Nay, traveller, rest! This lonely yew-tree stands
Far from all human dwelling. What if here
No sparkling rivulet spread the verdant herb?[2]
What if these barren boughs the bee not loves?
Yet, if the wind breathe soft, the curling waves   5
That break against the shore shall lull thy mind,
By one soft impulse saved from vacancy.
                              Who he was
That piled these stones, and with the mossy sod
First covered o'er, and taught this aged tree,   10
Now wild, to bend its arms in circling shade,[3]
I well remember. He was one who owned
No common soul. In youth by genius nursed,
And big with[4] lofty views, he to the world
Went forth, pure in his heart, against the taint   15
Of dissolute tongues, 'gainst jealousy and hate
And scorn, against all enemies prepared –
All but neglect. And so his spirit damped
At once, with rash disdain he turned away,
And with the food of pride sustained his soul   20

---

9   *golden lands* South and Central America.

Lines Left upon a Seat in a Yew-Tree
1   Wordsworth had in mind a particular place near Esthwaite Water; the solitary he describes is partly based on the Revd William Braithwaite, who built a yew-tree seat there.
2   *spread the verdant herb* help the grass to grow.

3   *to bend ... shade* in his *Unpublished Tour* Wordsworth recalled how 'the boughs had been trained to bend round the seat and almost embrace the person who might occupy the seat within, allowing only an opening for the beautiful landscape' (*Prose Works* ii 336).
4   *big with* full of.

In solitude. Stranger, these gloomy boughs
Had charms for him[5] – and here he loved to sit,
His only visitants a straggling sheep,
The stonechat or the glancing sandpiper;
And on these barren rocks, with juniper   25
And heath and thistle thinly sprinkled o'er,
Fixing his downward eye, he many an hour
A morbid pleasure nourished, tracing here
An emblem of his own unfruitful life.
And lifting up his head, he then would gaze   30
On the more distant scene – how lovely 'tis
Thou seest – and he would gaze till it became
Far lovelier, and his heart could not sustain
The beauty still more beauteous. Nor, that time,
Would he forget those beings to whose minds,   35
Warm from the labours of benevolence,
The world, and man himself, appeared a scene
Of kindred loveliness: then he would sigh
With mournful joy, to think that others felt
What he must never feel. And so, lost man,   40
On visionary views would fancy feed,
Till his eye streamed with tears. In this deep vale
He died, this seat his only monument.
    If thou be one whose heart the holy forms
Of young imagination have kept pure,   45
Stranger, henceforth be warned – and know that pride,
Howe'er disguised in its own majesty,
Is littleness; that he who feels contempt
For any living thing hath faculties
Which he has never used; that thought with him   50
Is in its infancy. The man whose eye
Is ever on himself doth look on one
The least of nature's works – one who might move
The wise man to that scorn which wisdom holds
Unlawful ever. Oh be wiser thou!   55
Instructed that true knowledge leads to love,
True dignity abides with him alone
Who, in the silent hour of inward thought,
Can still suspect, and still revere himself,
In lowliness of heart.   60

The Nightingale; A Conversational Poem, Written in April 1798
(by Coleridge)

From LYRICAL BALLADS (1798)

No cloud, no relic of the sunken day
Distinguishes the west,[1] no long thin slip

---

5   *Had charms for him* an echo of Charlotte Smith's *Sonnet XII. Written on the Sea Shore* 7: 'But the wild gloomy scene has charms for me'.

THE NIGHTINGALE
1   *the west* the sun sets in the west.

Of sullen[2] light, no obscure trembling hues.
Come, we will rest on this old mossy bridge.
You see the glimmer of the stream beneath   5
But hear no murmuring: it flows silently
O'er its soft bed of verdure. All is still,
A balmy night, and though the stars be dim
Yet let us think upon the vernal showers
That gladden the green earth, and we shall find   10
A pleasure in the dimness of the stars.
And hark, the nightingale begins its song –
'Most musical, most melancholy' bird![3]
A melancholy bird? Oh idle thought!
In nature there is nothing melancholy.   15
     But some night-wandering man whose heart was pierced
With the remembrance of a grievous wrong
Or slow distemper[4] or neglected love
(And so, poor wretch, filled all things with himself
And made all gentle sounds tell back the tale   20
Of his own sorrows) – he, and such as he,
First named these notes a melancholy strain,
And many a poet echoes the conceit[5] –
Poet who hath been building up the rhyme
When he had better far have stretched his limbs   25
Beside a brook in mossy forest-dell[6]
By sun or moonlight, to the influxes[7]
Of shapes and sounds and shifting elements
Surrendering his whole spirit, of his song
And of his fame forgetful! So his fame   30
Should share in nature's immortality
(A venerable thing!), and so his song
Should make all nature lovelier, and itself
Be loved, like nature! But 'twill not be so;
And youths and maidens most poetical[8]   35
Who lose the deep'ning twilights of the spring
In ballrooms and hot theatres, they still,
Full of meek sympathy, must heave their sighs
O'er Philomela's[9] pity-pleading strains.
     My friend, and my friend's sister,[10] we have learnt   40
A different lore; we may not thus profane
Nature's sweet voices always full of love
And joyance! 'Tis the merry nightingale
That crowds and hurries and precipitates

---

[2] *sullen* dim.
[3] *'Most musical, most melancholy' bird* Milton, *Il Penseroso* 62. 'This passage in Milton possesses an excellence far superior to that of mere description: it is spoken in the character of the melancholy man, and has therefore a *dramatic* propriety. The author makes this remark to rescue himself from the charge of having alluded with levity to a line in Milton – a charge than which none could be more painful to him, except perhaps that of having ridiculed his Bible' (Coleridge's note).
[4] *distemper* depression.
[5] *conceit* thought, fancy.

[6] *stretched his limbs … forest-dell* cf. Gray, *Elegy* 103: 'His listless length at noontide would he stretch, / And pore upon the brook that babbles by'.
[7] *influxes* perceptions entering the mind.
[8] *poetical* immersed in poetical conventions.
[9] *Philomela* most poets of the time identified the nightingale with Philomela, raped by her brother-in-law, Tereus, King of Thrace. When she revealed to her sister what had happened, she was saved from his rage by being turned into a nightingale.
[10] *My friend, and my friend's sister* William and Dorothy Wordsworth.

With fast thick warble his[11] delicious notes,   45
As he were fearful that an April night
Would be too short for him to utter forth
His love-chant, and disburden his full soul
Of all its music! And I know a grove
Of large extent, hard by a castle huge[12]   50
Which the great lord inhabits not – and so
This grove is wild with tangling underwood,
And the trim walks are broken up, and grass,
Thin grass and king-cups grow within the paths.
But never elsewhere in one place I knew   55
So many nightingales. And far and near
In wood and thicket over the wide grove,
They answer and provoke each other's songs
With skirmish and capricious passagings,[13]
And murmurs musical and swift jug jug   60
And one low piping sound more sweet than all,
Stirring the air with such an harmony,
That should you close your eyes, you might almost
Forget it was not day. On moonlight bushes
Whose dewy leafits are but half-disclosed,   65
You may perchance behold them on the twigs,
Their bright, bright eyes, their eyes both bright and full,
Glist'ning, while many a glow-worm in the shade
Lights up her love-torch.[14]

A most gentle maid[15]
Who dwelleth in her hospitable home   70
Hard by the castle, and at latest eve
(Even like a lady vowed and dedicate
To something more than nature in the grove)
Glides through the pathways. She knows all their notes,
That gentle maid, and oft, a moment's space,   75
What time the moon was lost behind a cloud,
Hath heard a pause of silence; till the moon
Emerging hath awakened earth and sky
With one sensation, and those wakeful birds
Have all burst forth in choral minstrelsy,   80
As if one quick and sudden gale had swept
An hundred airy harps![16] And she hath watched
Many a nightingale perch giddily
On blos'my twig still swinging from the breeze,
And to that motion tune his wanton song,   85
Like tipsy joy that reels with tossing head.
        Farewell, oh warbler, till tomorrow eve!
And you, my friends – farewell, a short farewell!

---

[11] *his* despite the traditional identification of the nightingale with Philomela, Coleridge is technically correct; male nightingales sing as part of the courtship ritual.
[12] *a castle huge* Coleridge probably has in mind Enmore Castle, home of Lord Egmont. It was demolished in 1834.
[13] *passagings* of music.
[14] *Lights up her love-torch* technically correct; the female glow-worm emits a green light to attract males.

[15] *A most gentle maid* Ellen Cruikshank, sister of John Cruikshank (friend of Coleridge, and source of the idea of the ghost-ship in *The Ancient Mariner*), whose father was agent to the Earl of Egmont.
[16] *airy harps* i.e. Aeolian harps, stringed instruments that were placed by open windows or hung on trees, to be 'played' by the wind.

We have been loitering long and pleasantly,
And now for our dear homes. That strain again!   90
Full fain it would delay me! My dear babe[17]
Who, capable of no articulate sound,
Mars all things with his imitative lisp –
How he would place his hand beside his ear,
His little hand, the small forefinger up,   95
And bid us listen! And I deem it wise
To make him nature's playmate. He knows well
The evening star; and once, when he awoke
In most distressful mood (some inward pain
Had made up that strange thing, an infant's dream)   100
I hurried with him to our orchard-plot
And he beholds the moon, and hushed at once
Suspends his sobs and laughs most silently,
While his fair eyes that swam with undropped tears
Did glitter in the yellow moonbeam! Well,   105
It is a father's tale. But if that Heaven
Should give me life, his childhood shall grow up
Familiar with these songs, that with the night
He may associate joy. Once more farewell,
Sweet nightingale! Once more, my friends, farewell!   110

The Female Vagrant (by Wordsworth, derived from *Salisbury Plain*, probably composed late summer 1793)

From LYRICAL BALLADS (1798)

'By Derwent's side[1] my father's cottage stood',
The woman thus her artless story told,
'One field, a flock, and what the neighbouring flood
Supplied, to him were more than mines of gold.
Light was my sleep, my days in transport[2] rolled;   5
With thoughtless joy I stretched along the shore
My father's nets, or watched (when from the fold
High o'er the cliffs I led my fleecy store[3]),
A dizzy depth below, his boat and twinkling oar.

My father was a good and pious man,   10
An honest man by honest parents bred,
And I believe that, soon as I began
To lisp, he made me kneel beside my bed,
And in his hearing there my prayers I said;
And afterwards, by my good father taught,   15
I read, and loved the books in which I read –

---

[17] *My dear babe* Hartley Coleridge. In a notebook entry for 1797, Coleridge describes how Hartley 'fell down and hurt himself. I caught him up crying and screaming, and ran out of doors with him. The moon caught his eye, he ceased crying immediately, and his eyes and the tears in them – how they glittered in the moonlight!' (*Notebooks* i 219).

THE FEMALE VAGRANT
[1] *By Derwent's side* her father was a fisherman on Derwent-water.
[2] *transport* happiness.
[3] *fleecy store* sheep.

For books in every neighbouring house I sought,
And nothing to my mind a sweeter pleasure brought.

Can I forget what charms did once adorn
My garden, stored with peas and mint and thyme,   20
And rose and lily for the Sabbath morn?
The Sabbath bells, and their delightful chime;
The gambols and wild freaks at shearing time;
My hen's rich nest through long grass scarce espied;
The cowslip-gathering at May's dewy prime;   25
The swans that, when I sought the waterside,
From far to meet me came, spreading their snowy pride.

The staff I yet remember, which upbore
The bending body of my active sire;
His seat beneath the honeyed sycamore   30
When the bees hummed, and chair by winter fire;
When market-morning came, the neat attire
With which, though bent on haste, myself I decked;
My watchful dog, whose starts of furious ire
When stranger passed, so often I have checked;   35
The redbreast known for years, which at my casement⁴ pecked.

The suns of twenty summers danced along –
Ah, little marked, how fast they rolled away!
Then rose a mansion proud our woods among,
And cottage after cottage owned its sway;⁵   40
No joy to see a neighbouring house, or stray
Through pastures not his own, the master took.
My father dared his greedy wish gainsay:
He loved his old hereditary nook,
And ill could I the thought of such sad parting brook.   45

But when he had refused the proffered gold,
To cruel injuries he became a prey –
Sore traversed⁶ in whate'er he bought and sold.
His troubles grew upon him day by day
Till all his substance fell into decay: 50
His little range of water was denied,⁷
All but the bed where his old body lay,
All, all was seized, and weeping side by side
We sought a home where we uninjured might abide.

Can I forget that miserable hour   55
When from the last hilltop my sire surveyed,
Peering above the trees, the steeple tower
That on his marriage-day sweet music made?
Till then he hoped his bones might there be laid
Close by my mother in their native bowers.   60
Bidding me trust in God, he stood and prayed;

---

⁴ *casement* window.
⁵ *owned its sway* yielded to its power, i.e. was abandoned by
its inhabitants.
⁶ *traversed* thwarted.

⁷ 'Several of the lakes in the north of England are let out to
different fishermen, in parcels marked out by imaginary lines
drawn from rock to rock' (Wordsworth's note).

I could not pray – through tears that fell in showers
Glimmered our dear loved home: alas, no longer ours!

There was a youth whom I had loved so long
That when I loved him not I cannot say.   65
Mid the green mountains many and many a song
We two had sung like little birds in May.
When we began to tire of childish play
We seemed still more and more to prize each other:
We talked of marriage and our marriage-day,   70
And I in truth did love him like a brother,
For never could I hope to meet with such another.

His father said that to a distant town
He must repair to ply the artist's[8] trade:
What tears of bitter grief till then unknown!   75
What tender vows our last sad kiss delayed!
To him we turned – we had no other aid.
Like one revived, upon his neck I wept,
And her whom he had loved in joy, he said
He well could love in grief: his faith he kept,   80
And in a quiet home once more my father slept.

Four years each day with daily bread was blessed,
By constant toil and constant prayer supplied.
Three lovely infants lay upon my breast,
And often, viewing their sweet smiles, I sighed   85
And knew not why. My happy father died
When sad distress reduced the children's meal –
Thrice happy, that from him the grave did hide
The empty loom,[9] cold hearth and silent wheel,[10]
And tears that flowed for ills which patience could not heal.   90

'Twas a hard change, an evil time was come.
We had no hope, and no relief could gain.
But soon with proud parade, the noisy drum
Beat round to sweep the streets of want and pain.[11]
My husband's arms now only served to strain[12]   95
Me and his children hungering in his view.
In such dismay my prayers and tears were vain;
To join those miserable men he flew,
And now to the sea-coast, with numbers more we drew.

There foul neglect for months and months we bore,   100
Nor yet the crowded fleet its anchor stirred.
Green fields before us and our native shore,

---

8 *artist* craftsman, artisan.
9 *empty loom* her husband was a weaver, and can no longer find work.
10 *wheel* spinning-wheel, which, in former times, she would have used when work was to be found.
11 *the noisy drum . . . pain* soldiers were enlisted for the American War of Independence in exactly this manner: drummer-boys would parade round provincial towns, followed by conscription officers promising relief from poverty and hunger if men signed up for war. In 1793, when this poem was written, Wordsworth would have seen this process taking place in aid of the war with revolutionary France (declared February 1793).
12 *strain* clasp tightly.

By fever, from polluted air incurred,[13]
Ravage was made for which no knell was heard.[14]
Fondly we wished and wished away, nor knew   105
Mid that long sickness, and those hopes deferred,
That happier days we never more must view.
The parting signal streamed,[15] at last the land withdrew,

But from delay the summer calms were passed.
On as we drove, the equinoctial[16] deep   110
Ran mountains high before the howling blast.
We gazed with terror on the gloomy sleep
Of them that perished in the whirlwind's sweep,
Untaught that soon such anguish must ensue,
Our hopes such harvest of affliction reap,   115
That we the mercy of the waves should rue.
We reached the western world,[17] a poor devoted[18] crew.

Oh dreadful price of being to resign
All that is dear *in* being: better far
In Want's most lonely cave till death to pine,   120
Unseen, unheard, unwatched by any star;
Or, in the streets and walks where proud men are,
Better our dying bodies to obtrude,[19]
Than dog-like, wading at the heels of war,
Protract a cursed existence with the brood   125
That lap (their very nourishment) their brother's blood.

The pains and plagues that on our heads came down –
Disease and famine, agony and fear,
In wood or wilderness, in camp or town –
It would thy brain unsettle even to hear.   130
All perished; all, in one remorseless year,
Husband and children! One by one, by sword
And ravenous plague, all perished. Every tear
Dried up, despairing, desolate, on board
A British ship I waked, as from a trance restored.   135

Peaceful as some immeasurable plain
By the first beams of dawning light impressed,[20]
In the calm sunshine slept the glittering main.
The very ocean has its hour of rest
That comes not to the human mourner's breast.   140
Remote from man and storms of mortal care,
A heavenly silence did the waves invest;[21]

---

[13]   *incurred* caught.
[14]   *Ravage ... heard* those who died from fever were not
given a church funeral.
[15]   *streamed* the signal flag streamed in the wind.
[16]   *equinoctial* equatorial.
[17]   *the western world* America, where the female vagrant's hus-
band was to fight in the War of Independence on the British
side. Wordsworth later recalled that 'All that relates to her suf-
ferings as a soldier's wife in America, and her condition of mind
during her voyage home, were faithfully taken from the report

made to me of her own case by a friend who had been subjected
to the same trials and affected in the same way' (*FN* 62).
[18]   *devoted* doomed.
[19]   *Better ... obtrude* very poor people did starve to death in
the streets of London at this time.
[20]   *impressed* imprinted, as when, in *Paradise Lost*, the sun
'impressed his beams' on Eden (iv 150).
[21]   *the waves invest* cf. Milton's invocation to 'holy light',
which 'as with a mantle didst invest / The rising world of
waters' (*Paradise Lost* iii 10–11).

I looked and looked along the silent air,
Until it seemed to bring a joy to my despair.

Ah, how unlike those late terrific[22] sleeps!   145
And groans, that rage of racking[23] famine spoke,
Where looks inhuman dwelt on festering heaps![24]
The breathing pestilence that rose like smoke![25]
The shriek that from the distant battle broke!
The mine's[26] dire earthquake, and the pallid host[27]   150
Driven by the bomb's incessant thunderstroke
To loathsome vaults[28] where heartsick anguish tossed,
Hope died, and fear itself in agony was lost!

Yet does that burst of woe congeal my frame
When the dark streets appeared to heave and gape,   155
While like a sea the storming army[29] came,
And Fire from hell reared his gigantic shape,
And Murder, by the ghastly gleam, and Rape
Seized their joint prey – the mother and the child!
But from these crazing thoughts, my brain, escape!   160
For weeks the balmy air breathed soft and mild,
And on the gliding vessel heaven and ocean smiled.

Some mighty gulf of separation passed,
I seemed transported to another world:
A thought resigned with pain, when from the mast   165
The impatient mariner the sail unfurled,
And, whistling, called the wind that hardly curled
The silent sea. From the sweet thoughts of home
And from all hope I was forever hurled.
For me, farthest from earthly port to roam   170
Was best, could I but shun the spot where man might come.

And oft, robbed of my perfect mind,[30] I thought
At last my feet a resting-place had found.
Here will I weep in peace (so fancy wrought),
Roaming the illimitable waters[31] round;   175
Here watch, of every human friend disowned,
All day, my ready tomb the ocean flood.
To break my dream the vessel reached its bound,
And homeless near a thousand homes I stood,
And near a thousand tables pined, and wanted[32] food.   180

---

[22] *terrific* terrifying.
[23] *racking* hunger racks the body with pain.
[24] *Where looks . . . heaps* the image is of heaps of decomposing, unburied corpses, dead from hunger.
[25] *The breathing . . . smoke* disease was thought to be airborne; there is a hint that the 'festering heaps' of corpses mentioned in the preceding line were the source of disease.
[26] *mine* tunnel in which explosives, once detonated, would cause the ground to give way.
[27] *the pallid host* the host (of soldiers) are 'pallid' (wan, pale) because they are starving.

[28] *loathsome vaults* soldiers blown up by mines would be buried alive by the 'dire earthquake'.
[29] *the storming army* American troops storm the town occupied by the British.
[30] *robbed of . . . mind* cf. *King Lear* IV vii 62: 'I fear I am not in my perfect mind'.
[31] *the illimitable waters* the sea is like Chaos, 'a dark / Illimitable ocean without bound' (*Paradise Lost* ii 891–2).
[32] *wanted* lacked.

By grief enfeebled was I turned adrift,
Helpless as sailor cast on desert rock;
Nor morsel to my mouth that day did lift,
Nor dared my hand at any door to knock.
I lay where, with his drowsy mates, the cock   185
From the cross timber of an outhouse hung.[33]
How dismal tolled that night the city clock!
At morn my sick heart-hunger scarcely stung,
Nor to the beggar's language could I frame my tongue.

So passed another day, and so the third.   190
Then did I try (in vain) the crowd's resort;
In deep despair by frightful wishes stirred,
Near the seaside I reached a ruined fort.
There pains which nature could no more support,
With blindness linked, did on my vitals fall;   195
Dizzy my brain, with interruption short
Of hideous sense.[34] I sunk, nor step could crawl,
And thence was borne away to neighbouring hospital.

Recovery came with food. But still my brain
Was weak, nor of the past had memory.   200
I heard my neighbours in their beds complain
Of many things which never troubled me:
Of feet still bustling round with busy glee,
Of looks where common kindness had no part,
Of service done with careless cruelty,   205
Fretting the fever round the languid heart,
And groans which, as they said, would make a dead man start.

These things just served to stir the torpid sense,
Nor pain nor pity in my bosom raised;
Memory, though slow, returned with strength; and thence   210
Dismissed, again on open day I gazed
At houses, men and common light, amazed.
The lanes I sought and, as the sun retired,
Came where beneath the trees a faggot blazed.
The wild brood saw me weep, my fate enquired,   215
And gave me food and rest – more welcome, more desired.

My heart is touched to think that men like these,
The rude earth's tenants, were my first relief.
How kindly did they paint their vagrant ease!
And their long holiday[35] that feared not grief –   220
For all belonged to all, and each was chief.
No plough their sinews strained; on grating road
No wain they drove; and yet the yellow sheaf
In every vale for their delight was stowed:
For them in nature's meads the milky udder flowed.[36]   225

---

[33] *outhouse* barn; the cock sleeps with his hens ('mates') in the upper reaches of the barn. This is an early instance of Wordsworth's exploitation of the imaginative power of the word 'hung', explained by him in the *Preface* of 1815 (see pp. 411–12).

[34] *hideous sense* when conscious she was in severe pain.

[35] *their long holiday* life, to them, was a holiday from care.

Semblance, with straw and panniered ass, they made
Of potters wandering on from door to door.
But life of happier sort to me portrayed,
And other joys my fancy to allure:
The bagpipe dinning on the midnight moor   230
In barn uplighted, and companions boon
Well-met from far with revelry secure
In depth of forest glade, when jocund June
Rolled fast along the sky his warm and genial moon.

But ill it suited me, in journey dark   235
O'er moor and mountain, midnight theft to hatch;
To charm the surly housedog's faithful bark,
Or hang on tiptoe at the lifted latch.
The gloomy lantern and the dim blue match,
The black disguise, the warning whistle shrill,   240
And ear still busy on its nightly watch,
Were not for me, brought up in nothing ill.
Besides, on griefs so fresh my thoughts were brooding still.

What could I do, unaided and unblessed?
Poor father, gone was every friend of thine!   245
And kindred of dead husband are at best
Small help, and after marriage such as mine,
With little kindness would to me incline.
Ill was I then for toil or service fit:
With tears whose course no effort could confine,   250
By highway-side forgetful would I sit
Whole hours, my idle arms in moping sorrow knit.[37]

I lived upon the mercy of the fields,
And oft of cruelty the sky accused;
On hazard, or what general bounty yields[38] –   255
Now coldly given, now utterly refused
The fields I for my bed have often used.
But what afflicts my peace with keenest ruth[39]
Is that I have my inner self abused,
Foregone the home[40] delight of constant truth   260
And clear and open soul, so prized in fearless youth.

Three years a wanderer, often have I viewed,
In tears, the sun towards that country tend[41]
Where my poor heart lost all its fortitude.
And now across this moor my steps I bend –   265
Oh tell me whither, for no earthly friend
Have I!' She ceased and, weeping, turned away,

---

[36] *and yet the yellow sheaf . . . flowed* they took milk and corn wherever they found them.
[37] *knit* folded.
[38] *On hazard . . . yields* she lived on charity or what she chanced to find.

[39] *ruth* remorse.
[40] *home* inner.
[41] *the sun . . . tend* the sun sets in the west.

As if because her tale was at an end.
She wept because she had no more to say
Of that perpetual weight which on her spirit lay.   270

Goody Blake and Harry Gill: A True Story (by Wordsworth, composed 7–13 March 1798)[1]

From LYRICAL BALLADS (1798)

Oh what's the matter? What's the matter?
What is't that ails young Harry Gill,
That evermore his teeth they chatter,
Chatter, chatter, chatter still?
Of waistcoats Harry has no lack,   5
Good duffle grey, and flannel fine;
He has a blanket on his back,
And coats enough to smother nine.

In March, December, and in July,[2]
'Tis all the same with Harry Gill;   10
The neighbours tell, and tell you truly,
His teeth they chatter, chatter still.
At night, at morning, and at noon,
'Tis all the same with Harry Gill;
Beneath the sun, beneath the moon,   15
His teeth they chatter, chatter still.

Young Harry was a lusty drover,[3]
And who so stout of limb as he?
His cheeks were red as ruddy clover,
His voice was like the voice of three.   20
Auld Goody[4] Blake was old and poor,
Ill fed she was, and thinly clad;
And any man who passed her door
Might see how poor a hut she had.

All day she spun in her poor dwelling,   25
And then her three hours' work at night –
Alas, 'twas hardly worth the telling,

GOODY BLAKE AND HARRY GILL
[1] This poem has a source in a medical treatise, Erasmus Darwin's *Zoönomia* (1794–6), which Wordsworth read in early March 1798: 'A young farmer in Warwickshire, finding his hedges broke, and the sticks carried away during a frosty season, determined to watch for the thief. He lay many cold hours under a haystack, and at length an old woman, like a witch in a play, approached and began to pull up the hedge. He waited till she had tied up her bottle of sticks and was carrying them off, that he might convict her of the theft; and then, springing from his concealment, he seized his prey with violent threats. After some altercation, in which her load was left upon the ground, she kneeled upon her bottle of sticks, and raising her arms to heaven, beneath the bright moon, then at the full, spoke to the farmer (already shivering with cold): "Heaven grant that thou never mayest know again the blessing to be warm!" He complained of cold all the next day, and wore an upper coat – and in a few days another – and in a fortnight took to his bed, always saying nothing made him warm. He covered himself with very many blankets, and had a sieve over his face as he lay; and from this one insane idea he kept his bed above twenty years for fear of the cold air, till at length he died' (ii 359).
[2] *July* stressed on the first syllable.
[3] *drover* cattle farmer.
[4] *Goody* 'goodwife'; traditional address for a countrywoman, often implying age.

It would not pay for candlelight.
This woman dwelt in Dorsetshire,[5]
Her hut was on a cold hillside,   30
And in that country[6] coals are dear,[7]
For they come far by wind and tide.

By the same fire to boil their pottage,[8]
Two poor old dames (as I have known)
Will often live in one small cottage,   35
But she, poor woman, dwelt alone.
'Twas well enough when summer came,
The long, warm, lightsome summer day;
Then at her door the canty[9] dame
Would sit, as any linnet gay.   40

But when the ice our streams did fetter,[10]
Oh, then how her old bones would shake!
You would have said, if you had met her,
'Twas a hard time for Goody Blake.
Her evenings then were dull and dead –   45
Sad case it was, as you may think,
For very cold to go to bed,
And then for cold not sleep a wink.

Oh joy for her, whene'er in winter
The winds at night had made a rout,[11]   50
And scattered many a lusty splinter,
And many a rotten bough about.
Yet never had she, well or sick
(As every man who knew her says),
A pile beforehand, wood or stick,   55
Enough to warm her for three days.

Now when the frost was past enduring
And made her poor old bones to ache,
Could anything be more alluring
Than an old hedge to Goody Blake?   60
And now and then, it must be said,
When her old bones were cold and chill,
She left her fire or left her bed
To seek the hedge of Harry Gill.

Now Harry he had long suspected   65
This trespass of old Goody Blake,
And vowed that she should be detected,
And he on her would vengeance take.

---

5   *Dorsetshire* although Erasmus Darwin (Wordsworth's
source) had located the story in Warwickshire, Wordsworth
places it in Dorset, where he and Dorothy had lived, 1795–7.
6   *country* region.
7   *coals are dear* coal was shipped from Wales; it was of poor
quality and expensive.

8   *pottage* soup.
9   *canty* cheerful.
10   *fetter* chain, bind. The 1790s was a decade notorious for
the coldness of its winters; it has been described as a mini ice
age.
11   *rout* party.

And oft from his warm fire he'd go,
And to the fields his road would take,
And there at night, in frost and snow,   70
He watched to seize old Goody Blake.

And once, behind a rick[12] of barley,
Thus looking out did Harry stand;
The moon was full and shining clearly,   75
And crisp with frost the stubble-land.
He hears a noise, he's all awake —
Again? On tiptoe down the hill
He softly creeps: 'tis Goody Blake,
She's at the hedge of Harry Gill.   80

Right glad was he when he beheld her:
Stick after stick did Goody pull.
He stood behind a bush of elder
Till she had filled her apron full.
When with her load she turned about,   85
The by-road back again to take,
He started forward with a shout
And sprang upon poor Goody Blake.

And fiercely by the arm he took her,
And by the arm he held her fast,   90
And fiercely by the arm he shook her,
And cried, 'I've caught you then at last!'
Then Goody, who had nothing said,
Her bundle from her lap let fall,
And kneeling on the sticks she prayed   95
To God that is the judge of all.

She prayed, her withered hand uprearing,
While Harry held her by the arm:
'God, who art never out of hearing —
Oh may he never more be warm!'[13]   100
The cold, cold moon above her head,
Thus on her knees did Goody pray,
Young Harry heard what she had said,
And icy cold he turned away.

He went complaining all the morrow   105
That he was cold and very chill;
His face was gloom, his heart was sorrow —
Alas that day for Harry Gill!
That day he wore a riding-coat
But not a whit the warmer he;   110
Another was on Thursday brought,
And ere the Sabbath he had three.

---

[12]   *rick* corn-stack; barley and other grain was cut with a scythe and bound into sheaves, which were stacked and thatched to await threshing.

[13]   *Oh may . . . warm* Joseph Cottle recalled how this line gave particular pleasure to Hannah More when she heard the poem:

'. . . she said, "I must hear *Harry Gill* once more". On coming up to the words, "Oh may he never more be warm", she lifted up her hands in smiling horror' (*Reminiscences of Samuel Taylor Coleridge and Robert Southey* (London, 1847), p. 260).

'Twas all in vain, a useless matter,
And blankets were about him pinned;
Yet still his jaws and teeth they clatter   115
Like a loose casement[14] in the wind.
And Harry's flesh it fell away,
And all who see him say 'tis plain
That, live as long as live he may,
He never will be warm again.   120

No word to any man he utters,
Abed or up, to young or old,
But ever to himself he mutters,
'Poor Harry Gill is very cold.'[15]
Abed or up, by night or day,   125
His teeth they chatter, chatter still;
Now think, ye farmers all, I pray,
Of Goody Blake and Harry Gill.

Lines Written at a Small Distance from My House,[1] and Sent by My Little Boy[2] to the Person to Whom They are Addressed[3]
(by Wordsworth, composed 1–9 March 1798)

From LYRICAL BALLADS (*1798*)

It is the first mild day of March,
Each minute sweeter than before,
The redbreast sings from the tall larch
That stands beside our door.

There is a blessing in the air   5
Which seems a sense of joy to yield
To the bare trees and mountains bare,[4]
And grass in the green field.

My sister, 'tis a wish of mine
Now that our morning meal is done –   10
Make haste, your morning task resign,
Come forth and feel the sun!

Edward[5] will come with you – and pray
Put on with speed your woodland dress,
And bring no book, for this one day   15
We'll give to idleness.

---

14 *casement* window.
15 *Poor . . . cold* cf. *King Lear* III iv 147: 'Poor Tom's a-cold'.

LINES WRITTEN AT A SMALL DISTANCE FROM MY HOUSE
1 *my house* Alfoxden House, where the Wordsworths resided,
June 1797–July 1798.
2 *my little boy* Basil Montagu Jr., whose mother had died,
and whose father, a friend of Wordsworth's, was unable to
look after him.

3 Wordsworth later exchanged the cumbersome original
title for *To my Sister*.
4 *mountains bare* an exaggeration; the Quantock Hills in
which Alfoxden House is located do not compare with the
mountains of the Lake District, where Wordsworth grew up.
5 *Edward* Basil Montagu Jr.

No joyless forms[6] shall regulate
Our living calendar;
We from today, my friend, will date
The opening of the year.[7]   20

Love, now an universal birth,
From heart to heart is stealing,
From earth to man, from man to earth –
It is the hour of feeling.

One moment now may give us more   25
Than fifty years of reason;
Our minds shall drink at every pore
The spirit of the season.

Some silent laws[8] our hearts may make
Which they shall long obey;   30
We for the year to come may take
Our temper[9] from today.

And from the blessed power that rolls
About, below, above,
We'll frame the measure[10] of our souls –   35
They shall be tuned to love.[11]

Then come, my sister, come, I pray,
With speed put on your woodland dress;
And bring no book, for this one day
We'll give to idleness.   40

Simon Lee, the Old Huntsman, with an Incident in Which He Was Concerned (by Wordsworth, composed between March and 16 May 1798)

From LYRICAL BALLADS (1798)

In the sweet shire of Cardigan[1]
Not far from pleasant Ivor Hall,
An old man dwells, a little man,
I've heard he once was tall.
Of years he has upon his back,   5
No doubt, a burden weighty;

---

[6] *forms* rules, conventions.
[7] *We from . . . year* In 1793 the French completely reorganized their calendar to begin from the birth of the republic (22 September 1792) rather than the birth of Christ.
[8] *silent laws* effectively, New Year's resolutions.
[9] *temper* constitution.
[10] *measure* rhythm, harmony.
[11] *And from . . . love* a memorable expression of the pantheistic credo that was imparted to Wordsworth by Coleridge, also to be found in *Tintern Abbey* 94–103.

SIMON LEE, THE OLD HUNTSMAN
[1] *Cardigan* Cardiganshire is on the west coast of Wales; however, Simon Lee's real-life counterpart was Christopher Tricky, the huntsman who lived in a cottage on the common near Alfoxden Park.

He says he is three score and ten,
But others say he's eighty.

A long blue livery-coat[2] has he
That's fair behind and fair before;   10
Yet meet him where you will, you see
At once that he is poor.
Full five and twenty years he lived
A running huntsman[3] merry,
And though he has but one eye left,   15
His cheek is like a cherry.

No man like him the horn could sound,
And no man was so full of glee;
To say the least, four counties round
Had heard of Simon Lee.   20
His master's dead, and no one now
Dwells in the Hall of Ivor,
Men, dogs, and horses – all are dead;
He is the sole survivor.

His hunting feats have him bereft   25
Of his right eye, as you may see;
And then, what limbs those feats have left
To poor old Simon Lee!
He has no son, he has no child;
His wife, an aged woman,   30
Lives with him near the waterfall,
Upon the village[4] common.

And he is lean and he is sick,
His little body's half awry,[5]
His ankles they are swoln and thick,   35
His legs are thin and dry.
When he was young he little knew
Of husbandry or tillage,[6]
And now he's forced to work, though weak –
The weakest in the village.   40

He all the country[7] could outrun,
Could leave both man and horse behind;
And often, ere the race was done,
He reeled and was stone-blind.[8]
And still there's something in the world   45
At which his heart rejoices,
For when the chiming[9] hounds are out
He dearly loves their voices![10]

---

[2] *livery-coat* as worn by the retainer to an aristocratic family.
[3] *running huntsman* Simon would have hunted on foot, running alongside the gentry who rode on horseback.
[4] *village* Holford.
[5] *awry* twisted, bent.
[6] *tillage* cultivation of the land.
[7] *country* region.
[8] *stone-blind* totally blind (with exhaustion).
[9] *chiming* barking together.
[10] *He dearly ... voices* Wordsworth later recalled: 'The expression when the hounds were out, "I dearly love their voice", was word for word from his own lips' (*FN* 37).

Old Ruth works out of doors with him
And does what Simon cannot do;   50
For she, not over-stout of limb,
Is stouter of the two.
And though you with your utmost skill
From labour could not wean them,
Alas, 'tis very little, all   55
Which they can do between them!

Beside their moss-grown hut of clay
Not twenty paces from the door,
A scrap of land they have, but they
Are poorest of the poor.   60
This scrap of land he from the heath
Enclosed when he was stronger,
But what avails the land to them
Which they can till no longer?

Few months of life has he in store   65
As he to you will tell,
For still, the more he works, the more
His poor old ankles swell.
My gentle reader, I perceive
How patiently you've waited,   70
And I'm afraid that you expect
Some tale will be related.

Oh reader, had you in your mind
Such stores as silent thought[11] can bring –
Oh gentle reader, you would find   75
A tale in every thing.[12]
What more I have to say is short,
I hope you'll kindly take it;
It is no tale, but, should you think,
Perhaps a tale you'll make it.   80

One summer day I chanced to see
This old man doing all he could
About the root of an old tree,
A stump of rotten wood.
The mattock[13] tottered in his hand;   85
So vain was his endeavour,
That at the root of the old tree
He might have worked forever.

'You're overtasked, good Simon Lee,
Give me your tool', to him I said;[14]   90
And at the word, right gladly he

---

[11] *silent thought* cf. Shakespeare, *Sonnet* 30: 'When to the sessions of sweet silent thought . . .'
[12] *A tale in every thing* cf. *As You Like It* II i 15–17, where Duke Senior remarks that his life in Arden 'Finds tongues in trees, books in the running brooks, / Sermons in stones, and good in every thing'.
[13] *mattock* tool for tilling the ground.
[14] *You're overtasked . . . said* a response to Burns, *Man was Made to Mourn* 57–60 (see p. 132).

Received my proffered aid.[15]
I struck, and with a single blow
The tangled root I severed,
At which the poor old man so long   95
And vainly had endeavoured.

The tears into his eyes were brought,
And thanks and praises seemed to run
So fast out of his heart, I thought
They never would have done.   100
I've heard of hearts unkind, kind deeds
With coldness still returning;
Alas, the gratitude of men
Has oft'ner left me mourning.[16]

Anecdote for Fathers, Showing How the Art of Lying May be Taught
(by Wordsworth, composed between April and 16 May 1798)

From LYRICAL BALLADS (1798)

I have a boy of five years old,[1]
His face is fair and fresh to see,
His limbs are cast in beauty's mould,
And dearly he loves me.

One morn we strolled on our dry walk,   5
Our quiet house all full in view,
And held such intermitted talk
As we are wont[2] to do.

My thoughts on former pleasures ran;
I thought of Kilve's[3] delightful shore –   10
My pleasant home when spring began
A long long year before.

A day it was when I could bear
To think, and think, and think again;
With so much happiness to spare   15
I could not feel a pain.

My boy was by my side, so slim
And graceful in his rustic dress!

---

[15] *right gladly ... aid* critics have seen this poem as a response to Godwin who, in *Political Justice*, attacked gratitude as an unjust and degrading sentiment, having its origin in the unequal distribution of wealth and influence.
[16] *Alas, the gratitude ... mourning* a highly inventive reworking of the conclusion to Burns' *Man was Made to Mourn*: 'Man's inhumanity to man / Makes countless thousands mourn'.

ANECDOTE FOR FATHERS
[1] *a boy of five years old* Basil Montagu Jr, the son of Wordsworth's friend Basil Montagu, who was a lawyer in London, and whose wife was dead.
[2] *wont* used.
[3] *Kilve* small village on the Somersetshire coast, not far from Alfoxden. It is pronounced as a single syllable. See Berta Lawrence, 'Kilve by the Green Sea', *Charles Lamb Bulletin* NS 91 (1995) 157–8. It is generally agreed that by Kilve Wordsworth means Racedown in Dorset, and that by Liswyn he means Alfoxden.

And oftentimes I talked to him
In very idleness.   20

The young lambs ran a pretty race,
The morning sun shone bright and warm;
'Kilve', said I, 'was a pleasant place,
And so is Liswyn farm.[4]

My little boy, which like you more?'   25
I said and took him by the arm,
'Our home by Kilve's delightful shore,
Or here at Liswyn farm?

And tell me, had you rather be
(I said and held him by the arm)   30
At Kilve's smooth shore by the green sea
Or here at Liswyn farm?'

In careless mood he looked at me
While still I held him by the arm
And said, 'At Kilve I'd rather be   35
Than here at Liswyn farm.'

'Now, little Edward, say why so,
My little Edward, tell me why.'
'I cannot tell, I do not know.'
'Why this is strange!' said I.   40

'For here are woods and green hills warm;
There surely must some reason be
Why you would change sweet Liswyn farm
For Kilve by the green sea.'

At this, my boy, so fair and slim,   45
Hung down his head, nor made reply,
And five times did I say to him,
'Why? Edward, tell me why?'

His head he raised; there was in sight –
It caught his eye, he saw it plain –   50
Upon the house-top, glittering bright,
A broad and gilded vane.[5]

Then did the boy his tongue unlock
And thus to me he made reply;
'At Kilve there was no weathercock,   55
And that's the reason why.'

---

4   *Liswyn farm* John Thelwall, who visited Wordsworth and   5   *vane* weather-cock.
Coleridge in Somerset in July 1797, had retreated to Llys
Wen farm in Wales. Dorothy and William went there for the
first time in early August 1798.

Oh dearest, dearest boy! my heart
For better lore would seldom yearn,
Could I but teach the hundredth part
Of what from thee I learn.   60

We are Seven (by Wordsworth, composed between April and 16 May 1798)

From LYRICAL BALLADS (1798)

A simple child, dear brother Jim,[1]
That lightly draws its breath,
And feels its life in every limb –
What should it know of death?

I met a little cottage girl,[2]   5
She was eight years old, she said;
Her hair was thick with many a curl
That clustered round her head.

She had a rustic woodland air
And she was wildly clad;   10
Her eyes were fair, and very fair –
Her beauty made me glad.

'Sisters and brothers, little maid,
How many may you be?'
'How many? Seven in all', she said,   15
And wondering looked at me.

'And where are they, I pray you tell?'
She answered, 'Seven are we,
And two of us at Conway[3] dwell,
And two are gone to sea.   20

Two of us in the churchyard lie
(My sister and my brother),
And in the churchyard cottage I
Dwell near them with my mother.'

'You say that two at Conway dwell   25
And two are gone to sea,
Yet you are seven – I pray you tell,
Sweet maid, how this may be?'

Then did the little maid reply,
'Seven boys and girls are we;   30

WE ARE SEVEN
[1] *Jim* James Tobin, a friend of Wordsworth and Coleridge's. The first line of the poem was written impromptu by Coleridge.

[2] *I met . . . girl* the poem is based on Wordsworth's meeting with a child near Goodrich Castle on the River Wye in summer 1793.
[3] *Conway* a sea-port in North Wales, about 120 miles north of Goodrich Castle.

Two of us in the churchyard lie
Beneath the churchyard tree.'

'You run about, my little maid,
Your limbs they are alive;
If two are in the churchyard laid,   35
Then ye are only five.'

'Their graves are green, they may be seen',[4]
The little maid replied,
'Twelve steps or more from my mother's door,
And they are side by side.   40

My stockings there I often knit,
My kerchief[5] there I hem,
And there upon the ground I sit,
I sit and sing to them.

And often after sunset, sir,   45
When it is light and fair,
I take my little porringer[6]
And eat my supper there.

The first that died was little Jane,
In bed she moaning lay,   50
Till God released her of her pain
And then she went away.

So in the churchyard she was laid
And all the summer dry,
Together round her grave we played,   55
My brother John and I.

And when the ground was white with snow,
And I could run and slide,
My brother John was forced to go,
And he lies by her side.'   60

'How many are you then', said I,
'If they two are in heaven?'
The little maiden did reply,
'Oh master, we are seven!'

'But they are dead – those two are dead!   65
Their spirits are in heaven!'
'Twas throwing words away, for still
The little maid would have her will
And said, 'Nay, we are seven!'

---

4   *Their graves . . . seen* the child regards the graves as proof   5   *kerchief* headscarf.
that her siblings are alive.   6   *porringer* wooden soup-bowl.

Lines Written in Early Spring (by Wordsworth, composed *c.* 12 April 1798)[1]

From Lyrical Ballads (1798)

I heard a thousand blended notes[2]
While in a grove I sat reclined
In that sweet mood when pleasant thoughts
Bring sad thoughts to the mind.

To her fair works did nature link   5
The human soul that through me ran,
And much it grieved my heart to think
What man has made of man.[3]

Through primrose-tufts, in that sweet bower,
The periwinkle[4] trailed its wreaths;   10
And 'tis my faith that every flower
Enjoys the air it breathes.[5]

The birds around me hopped and played,
Their thoughts I cannot measure,
But the least motion which they made –   15
It seemed a thrill of pleasure.

The budding twigs spread out their fan
To catch the breezy air;
And I must think, do all I can,
That there was pleasure there.   20

If I these thoughts may not prevent,
If such be of my creed[6] the plan,
Have I not reason to lament
What man has made of man?

Lines Written in Early Spring
[1] According to Wordsworth this poem was 'composed while I was sitting by the side of the brook that runs down the coomb (in which stands the village of Holford), through the grounds of Alfoxden. It was a chosen resort of mine. The brook fell down a sloping rock so as to make a waterfall considerable for that country, and, across the pool below, had fallen a tree, an ash if I rightly remember, from which rose perpendicularly boughs in search of the light intercepted by the deep shade above' (FN 36).

[2] *notes* pronounced so as to rhyme with 'thoughts', as Wordsworth, with his Cumbrian accent, would have done.
[3] *And much . . . man* Wordsworth has in mind the conclusion to Burns' *Man was Made to Mourn*: 'Man's inhumanity to man / Makes countless thousands mourn'.
[4] *periwinkle* evergreen trailing plant with light blue flower (US myrtle).
[5] *And 'tis . . . breathes* Wordsworth was up-to-date in his botanical knowledge; in 1791 Erasmus Darwin had written, in *The Economy of Vegetation*, that leaves function as lungs.
[6] *creed* credo, belief.

The Thorn (by Wordsworth, composed between 19 March and 20 April 1798)[1]

From LYRICAL BALLADS (1798)

I

'There is a thorn, it looks so old,
In truth you'd find it hard to say
How it could ever have been young,
It looks so old and grey.
Not higher than a two years' child,   5
It stands erect, this aged thorn;
No leaves it has, no thorny points –
It is a mass of knotted joints,
A wretched thing forlorn.
It stands erect and, like a stone,   10
With lichens[2] it is overgrown.

II

Like rock or stone, it is o'ergrown
With lichens to the very top,
And hung with heavy tufts of moss,
A melancholy crop;   15
Up from the earth these mosses creep,
And this poor thorn they clasp it round
So close, you'd say that they were bent
With plain and manifest intent
To drag it to the ground –   20
And all had joined in one endeavour
To bury this poor thorn for ever.

III

High on a mountain's highest ridge
Where oft the stormy winter gale
Cuts like a scythe, while through the clouds   25
It sweeps from vale to vale;
Not five yards from the mountain path
This thorn you on your left espy,
And to the left, three yards beyond,
You see a little muddy pond   30

THE THORN
[1] Wordsworth recalled that this poem 'arose out of my observing, on the ridge of Quantock Hill, on a stormy day, a thorn which I had often passed in calm and bright weather without noticing it. I said to myself, "Cannot I by some invention do as much to make this thorn permanently an impressive object as the storm has made it to my eyes at this moment?" I began the poem accordingly, and composed it with great rapidity' (*FN* 14). See also the 'Note to *The Thorn*' (1800), pp. 344–5, below. The poem is in the form of a dialogue; an interlocutor enters the poem at ll. 78–88, 100–3, and 210–13. For Southey's hostile comments on it in his review, see pp. 564–5.
[2] *lichens* slow-growing grey-green plants encrusting the surface of old walls, trees, and thorn bushes.

Of water, never dry.
I've measured it from side to side;
'Tis three feet long and two feet wide.

IV

And close beside this aged thorn
There is a fresh and lovely sight,   35
A beauteous heap, a hill of moss,
Just half a foot in height.
All lovely colours there you see,
All colours that were ever seen,
And mossy net-work[3] too is there,   40
As if by hand of lady fair
The work had woven been,
And cups,[4] the darlings of the eye,
So deep is their vermilion dye.

V

Ah me, what lovely tints are there   45
Of olive-green and scarlet bright!
In spikes, in branches, and in stars,
Green, red, and pearly white.
This heap of earth o'ergrown with moss,
Which close beside the thorn you see,   50
So fresh in all its beauteous dyes,
Is like an infant's grave in size,
As like as like can be;
But never, never, anywhere
An infant's grave was half so fair.   55

VI

Now would you see this aged thorn,
This pond and beauteous hill of moss,
You must take care and choose your time
The mountain when to cross.
For oft there sits, between the heap   60
That's like an infant's grave in size
And that same pond of which I spoke,
A woman in a scarlet cloak,[5]
And to herself she cries,
"Oh misery! Oh misery!   65
Oh woe is me! Oh misery!"

---

3   *net-work* embroidery.
4   *cups* blooms

5   *a scarlet cloak* traditionally associated with guilt and sin; cf.
the whore of Babylon 'arrayed in purple, and scarlet colour'
(Revelation 17:4).

VII

At all times of the day and night
This wretched woman thither goes,
And she is known to every star
And every wind that blows;   70
And there beside the thorn she sits
When the blue daylight's in the skies,
And when the whirlwind's on the hill,
Or frosty air is keen and still,
And to herself she cries,   75
"Oh misery! Oh misery!
Oh woe is me! Oh misery!" '

VIII

'Now wherefore thus, by day and night,
In rain, in tempest, and in snow,
Thus to the dreary mountain-top   80
Does this poor woman go?
And why sits she beside the thorn
When the blue daylight's in the sky,
Or when the whirlwind's on the hill,
Or frosty air is keen and still,   85
And wherefore does she cry?
Oh wherefore, wherefore, tell me why
Does she repeat that doleful cry?'

IX

'I cannot tell, I wish I could;
For the true reason no one knows.   90
But if you'd gladly view the spot,
The spot to which she goes –
The heap that's like an infant's grave,
The pond, and thorn so old and grey –
Pass by her door ('tis seldom shut),   95
And if you see her in her hut,[6]
Then to the spot away!
I never heard of such as dare
Approach the spot when she is there.'

X

'But wherefore to the mountain-top   100
Can this unhappy woman go,
Whatever star is in the skies,

---

[6]   *hut* cottage.

Whatever wind may blow?'
'Nay rack your brain, 'tis all in vain –
I'll tell you everything I know;   105
But to the thorn, and to the pond
Which is a little step beyond,
I wish that you would go.
Perhaps when you are at the place
You something of her tale may trace.   110

point of conversation & voice?

XI

I'll give you the best help I can:
Before you up the mountain go,
Up to the dreary mountain-top,
I'll tell you all I know.
'Tis now some two and twenty years   115
Since she (her name is Martha Ray)[7]
Gave with a maiden's true goodwill
Her company to Stephen Hill,
And she was blithe and gay,
And she was happy, happy still   120
Whene'er she thought of Stephen Hill.

XII

And they had fixed the wedding-day,
The morning that must wed them both,
But Stephen to another maid
Had sworn another oath,   125
And with this other maid to church
Unthinking Stephen went –
Poor Martha! On that woeful day
A cruel, cruel fire, they say,
Into her bones was sent: 130
It dried her body like a cinder
And almost turned her brain to tinder.

XIII

They say full six months after this,
While yet the summer leaves were green,
She to the mountain-top would go,   135
And there was often seen;
'Tis said a child was in her womb,
As now to any eye was plain –

---

7   *Martha Ray* the mother of Wordsworth's friend Basil
Montagu, and grandmother of Basil Montagu Jr whom he and
Dorothy were looking after at Alfoxden (featured in *Anecdote
for Fathers*). She had been the mistress of the 4th Earl of Sand-
wich, and on 7 April 1779 had been shot dead on the steps of
Covent Garden Theatre by a jealous lover, the Revd James
Hackman. Why Wordsworth should have used a name with
such painful associations remains unexplained.

She was with child and she was mad,
Yet often she was sober-sad   140
From her exceeding pain.
Oh me! Ten thousand times I'd rather
That he had died, that cruel father!

XIV

Sad case for such a brain to hold
Communion with a stirring child!   145
Sad case (as you may think) for one
Who had a brain so wild!
Last Christmas when we talked of this,
Old Farmer Simpson did maintain
That in her womb the infant wrought   150
About its mother's heart, and brought
Her senses back again;
And when at last her time drew near,
Her looks were calm, her senses clear.

XV

No more I know – I wish I did,   155
And I would tell it all to you.
For what became of this poor child
There's none that ever knew;
And if a child was born or no,
There's no one that could ever tell;   160
And if 'twas born alive or dead,
There's no one knows, as I have said.
But some remember well
That Martha Ray about this time
Would up the mountain often climb.   165

XVI

And all that winter, when at night
The wind blew from the mountain-peak,
'Twas worth your while, though in the dark,
The churchyard path to seek:
For many a time and oft were heard   170
Cries coming from the mountain-head.
Some plainly living voices were,
And others, I've heard many swear,
Were voices of the dead.
I cannot think, whate'er they say,   175
They had to do with Martha Ray.

XVII

But that she goes to this old thorn,
The thorn which I've described to you,
And there sits in a scarlet cloak,
I will be sworn is true.   180
For one day with my telescope,[8]
To view the ocean wide and bright,
When to this country[9] first I came,
Ere I had heard of Martha's name,
I climbed the mountain's height;   185
A storm came on, and I could see
No object higher than my knee.

XVIII

'Twas mist and rain, and storm and rain,
No screen, no fence could I discover;[10]
And then the wind – in faith, it was   190
A wind full ten times over!
I looked around, I thought I saw
A jutting crag, and off I ran
Head-foremost through the driving rain,
The shelter of the crag to gain;   195
And, as I am a man,
Instead of jutting crag, I found
A woman seated on the ground.

XIX

I did not speak – I saw her face,
Her face it was enough for me;   200
I turned about and heard her cry,
"Oh misery! Oh misery!"
And there she sits, until the moon
Through half the clear blue sky will go,
And when the little breezes make   205
The waters of the pond to shake,
As all the country know,
She shudders and you hear her cry,
"Oh misery! Oh misery!" '

XX

'But what's the thorn? And what's the pond?   210
And what's the hill of moss to her?
And what's the creeping breeze that comes

---

[8] *my telescope* the one piece of evidence to corroborate
Wordsworth's later assertion that the speaker of the poem was
the retired 'captain of a small trading vessel' (see p. 344).

[9] *country* area, district.

[10] *discover* see.

The little pond to stir?'
'I cannot tell, but some will say
She hanged her baby on the tree;   215
Some say she drowned it in the pond
Which is a little step beyond;
But all and each agree
The little babe was buried there,
Beneath that hill of moss so fair.   220

XXI

I've heard the scarlet moss is red
With drops of that poor infant's blood –
But kill a new-born infant thus?
I do not think she could.
Some say, if to the pond you go,   225
And fix on it a steady view,
The shadow of a babe you trace,
A baby and a baby's face,
And that it looks at you;
Whene'er you look on it, 'tis plain   230
The baby looks at you again.

XXII

And some had sworn an oath that she
Should be to public justice brought,
And for the little infant's bones
With spades they would have sought.   235
But then the beauteous hill of moss
Before their eyes began to stir,
And for full fifty yards around,
The grass it shook upon the ground.
But all do still aver[11]   240
The little babe is buried there,
Beneath that hill of moss so fair.

XXIII

I cannot tell how this may be,
But plain it is, the thorn is bound
With heavy tufts of moss that strive   245
To drag it to the ground.
And this I know, full many a time
When she was on the mountain high,
By day, and in the silent night,
When all the stars shone clear and bright,   250
That I have heard her cry,
"Oh misery! Oh misery!
Oh woe is me! Oh misery!" '

---

[11] *aver* maintain.

The Last of the Flock (by Wordsworth, composed between March and 16 May 1798)[1]

From LYRICAL BALLADS (1798)

In distant countries I have been,
And yet I have not often seen
A healthy man, a man full grown,
Weep in the public roads alone.
But such a one on English ground   5
And in the broad highway, I met;
Along the broad highway he came,
His cheeks with tears were wet.
Sturdy he seemed, though he was sad,
And in his arms a lamb he had.   10

He saw me and he turned aside
As if he wished himself to hide;
Then with his coat he made essay[2]
To wipe those briny tears away.
I followed him, and said, 'My friend,   15
What ails you? Wherefore weep you so?'
'Shame on me, sir! This lusty lamb,
He makes my tears to flow;
Today I fetched him from the rock –
He is the last of all my flock.   20

When I was young, a single man,
And after youthful follies ran,
Though little given to care and thought,
Yet so it was a ewe I bought;
And other sheep from her I raised,   25
As healthy sheep as you might see.
And then I married, and was rich
As I could wish to be;
Of sheep I numbered a full score,[3]
And every year increased my store.   30

Year after year my stock it grew,
And from this one, this single ewe,
Full fifty comely sheep I raised –
As sweet a flock as ever grazed!

THE LAST OF THE FLOCK
[1] In later years Wordsworth recalled that the encounter described here 'occurred in the village of Holford, close by Alfoxden' (*FN* 9). It was apparently relayed to him by one of those who had taken part: 'I never in my whole life saw a man weep alone in the roads; but a friend of mine did see this poor man weeping alone, with the lamb, the last of the flock, in his arms' (*LY* iii 292). Critics observe that this poem refutes the Godwinian argument that 'property was the cause of every vice, and the source of all the wretchedness, of the poor'. It also illustrates the disastrous effects of the 'Speenhamland sys-tem' for paying from parish rates the difference between what a man earned and what he needed to live. Wages were so low that a man could not live without supplementing his earnings from the parish. But if he possessed anything, even a few pounds saved over the years, he was refused both help and employment. As farmers preferred the parish to subsidize their wage bill they always preferred to take on paupers rather than anyone with resources.
[2] *made essay* tried.
[3] *a full score* twenty.

Upon the mountain did they feed,   35
They throve, and we at home did thrive.
This lusty lamb of all my store
Is all that is alive;
And now I care not if we die
And perish all of poverty.   40

Ten children, sir, had I to feed –
Hard labour in a time of need!
My pride was tamed, and in our grief
I of the parish asked relief.
They said I was a wealthy man;   45
My sheep upon the mountain fed
And it was fit that thence I took
Whereof to buy us bread.
"Do this. How can we give to you"
They cried, "what to the poor is due?"   50

I sold a sheep as they had said,
And bought my little children bread,
And they were healthy with their food;
For me it never did me good.
A woeful time it was for me   55
To see the end of all my gains,
The pretty flock which I had reared
With all my care and pains,
To see it melt like snow away!
For me it was a woeful day.   60

Another still, and still another!
A little lamb and then its mother!
It was a vein that never stopped,
Like blood-drops from my heart they dropped
Till thirty were not left alive;   65
They dwindled, dwindled, one by one,
And I may say that many a time
I wished they all were gone:
They dwindled one by one away –
For me it was a woeful day.   70

To wicked deeds I was inclined,
And wicked fancies crossed my mind,
And every man I chanced to see,
I thought he knew some ill of me.
No peace, no comfort could I find,   75
No ease, within doors or without,
And crazily, and wearily,
I went my work about.
Oft-times I thought to run away;
For me it was a woeful day.   80

Sir, 'twas a precious flock to me,
As dear as my own children be;
For daily with my growing store

I loved my children more and more.
Alas, it was an evil time,   85
God cursed me in my sore distress;
I prayed, yet every day I thought
I loved my children less;
And every week, and every day
My flock, it seemed to melt away.   90

They dwindled, sir, sad sight to see,
From ten to five, from five to three –
A lamb, a wether,[4] and a ewe;
And then at last, from three to two.
And of my fifty, yesterday   95
I had but only one,
And here it lies upon my arm –
Alas, and I have none!
Today I fetched it from the rock;
It is the last of all my flock.'   100

The Dungeon (by Coleridge, extracted from *Osorio*, composed 1797)[1]

From LYRICAL BALLADS (1798)

And this place our forefathers made for man!
This is the process of our love and wisdom
To each poor brother who offends against us;
Most innocent, perhaps – and what if guilty?
Is this the only cure, merciful God?   5
Each pore and natural outlet shrivelled up
By ignorance and parching poverty,
His energies roll back upon his heart
And stagnate and corrupt; till, changed to poison,
They break out on him like a loathsome plague-spot.   10
Then we call in our pampered mountebanks
And this is their best cure: uncomforted
And friendless solitude, groaning and tears
And savage faces at the clanking hour,
Seen through the steams and vapour of his dungeon,   15
By the lamp's dismal twilight. So he lies
Circled with evil, till his very soul
Unmoulds its essence, hopelessly deformed
By sights of ever more deformity!
        With other ministrations, thou, oh nature,   20
Healest thy wandering and distempered child:

---

4 *wether* castrated male sheep.

THE DUNGEON
[1] In Coleridge's play, this was part of a soliloquy by the pro-
tagonist, Albert, when jailed by the Inquisition. Like
Wordsworth's *The Convict* (pp. 263–5), this poem is a plea for
penal reform.

Thou pourest on him thy soft influences,
Thy sunny hues, fair forms, and breathing sweets,
Thy melodies of woods, and winds, and waters,
Till he relent, and can no more endure   25
To be a jarring and a dissonant thing
Amid this general dance and minstrelsy;
But, bursting into tears, wins back his way,
His angry spirit healed and harmonized
By the benignant touch of love and beauty.[2]   30

The Mad Mother (by Wordsworth, composed between March and 16 May 1798)[1]

From LYRICAL BALLADS (1798)

Her eyes are wild, her head is bare,
The sun has burnt her coal-black hair,
Her eyebrows have a rusty stain,
And she came far from over the main.[2]
She has a baby on her arm,   5
Or else she were alone;
And underneath the haystack warm,
And on the greenwood stone,
She talked and sung the woods among –
And it was in the English tongue.   10

'Sweet babe, they say that I am mad,
But nay, my heart is far too glad;
And I am happy when I sing
Full many a sad and doleful thing.
Then, lovely baby, do not fear!   15
I pray thee, have no fear of me,
But safe as in a cradle, here
My lovely baby, thou shalt be;
To thee I know too much I owe,
I cannot work thee any woe.   20

A fire was once within my brain,
And in my head a dull, dull pain;
And fiendish faces – one, two, three,
Hung at my breasts, and pulled at me.
But then there came a sight of joy,   25
It came at once to do me good;
I waked and saw my little boy,

---

[2]   *Till he relent . . . beauty* The experience of being harmonized and healed by nature is celebrated in Coleridge's Alfoxden poems – *This Lime-Tree Bower My Prison*, *Frost at Midnight*; conversely, *The Ancient Mariner* and *Christabel* are concerned with the suffering of those alienated from nature's healing power.

THE MAD MOTHER
[1]   In later years, Wordsworth recalled that 'The subject was reported to me by a lady of Bristol who had seen the poor creature' (*FN* 11). In a letter of 1836 he remarked: 'though she came from far, English was her native tongue – which shows her either to be of these islands, or a North American. On the latter supposition, while the distance removes her from us, the fact of her speaking our language brings us at once into close sympathy with her' (*LY* iii 293).
[2]   *main* sea.

My little boy of flesh and blood –
Oh joy for me that sight to see!
For he was here, and only he.   30

Suck, little babe, oh suck again!
It cools my blood, it cools my brain;
Thy lips I feel them, baby, they
Draw from my heart the pain away.
Oh, press me with thy little hand,   35
It loosens something at my chest;
About that tight and deadly band
I feel thy little fingers pressed.
The breeze I see is in the tree,
It comes to cool my babe and me.[3]   40

Oh love me, love me, little boy!
Thou art thy mother's only joy;
And do not dread the waves below,
When o'er the sea-rock's edge[4] we go.
The high crag cannot work me harm,   45
Nor leaping torrents when they howl;
The babe I carry on my arm,
He saves for me my precious soul.
Then happy lie, for blessed am I –
Without me my sweet babe would die.   50

Then do not fear, my boy, for thee
Bold as a lion I will be;
And I will always be thy guide
Through hollow snows and rivers wide.
I'll build an Indian bower;[5] I know   55
The leaves that make the softest bed;
And if from me thou wilt not go,
But still be true till I am dead –
My pretty thing, then thou shalt sing,
As merry as the birds in spring.   60

Thy father cares not for my breast;
'Tis thine, sweet baby, there to rest,
'Tis all thine own! And if its hue
Be changed, that was so fair to view,
'Tis fair enough for thee, my dove!   65
My beauty, little child, is flown;
But thou wilt live with me in love –
And what if my poor cheek be brown?
'Tis well for me; thou canst not see
How pale and wan it else would be.   70

---

[3] *The breeze ... me* In *Biographia Literaria* Coleridge described these lines as 'so expressive ... of that deranged state, in which from the increased sensibility the sufferer's attention is abruptly drawn off by every trifle, and in the same instant plucked back again by the one despotic thought, and bringing home with it, by the blending, fusing power of imagination and passion, the alien object to which it had been so abruptly diverted, no longer an alien but an ally and an inmate' (CC *Biographia* ii 150–1).

[4] *o'er the sea-rock's edge* along the cliff-top.

[5] *I'll build ... bower* The mad mother was either an American Indian, or lived among them.

Dread not their taunts, my little life!
I am thy father's wedded wife,
And underneath the spreading tree
We two will live in honesty.
If his sweet boy he could forsake, 75
With me he never would have stayed;
From him no harm my babe can take,
But he, poor man, is wretched made;
And every day we two will pray
For him that's gone and far away. 80

I'll teach my boy the sweetest things,
I'll teach him how the owlet sings.
My little babe, thy lips are still,
And thou hast almost sucked thy fill.
Where art thou gone, my own dear child? 85
What wicked looks are those I see?
Alas, alas! that look so wild,
It never, never came from me;
If thou art mad, my pretty lad,
Then I must be forever sad. 90

Oh smile on me, my little lamb,
For I thy own dear mother am.
My love for thee has well been tried;
I've sought thy father far and wide.
I know the poisons of the shade, 95
I know the earth-nuts fit for food;
Then, pretty dear, be not afraid –
We'll find thy father in the wood.
Now laugh and be gay, to the woods away,
And there, my babe, we'll live for aye.' 100

The Idiot Boy (by Wordsworth, composed between March and 16 May 1798)[1]

From LYRICAL BALLADS (1798)

'Tis eight o'clock, a clear March night,
The moon is up, the sky is blue,
The owlet[2] in the moonlight air –
He shouts from nobody knows where,
He lengthens out his lonely shout: 5
Halloo, halloo! A long halloo!

Why bustle thus about your door?
What means this bustle, Betty Foy?

THE IDIOT BOY
[1] According to Wordsworth this poem was 'composed in the groves of Alfoxden almost extempore; not a word, I believe, being corrected, though one stanza was omitted. I mention this in gratitude to those happy moments, for, in truth, I never wrote anything with so much glee' (*FN* 10). For Southey's less than charitable comments on the poem, see p. 564.
[2] *owlet* young owl.

Why are you in this mighty fret?
And why on horseback have you set   10
Him whom you love, your idiot boy?

Beneath the moon that shines so bright,
Till she is tired, let Betty Foy
With girt³ and stirrup fiddle-faddle;
But wherefore set upon a saddle   15
Him whom she loves, her idiot boy?

There's scarce a soul that's out of bed –
Good Betty, put him down again!
His lips with joy they burr at you,
But, Betty, what has he to do   20
With stirrup, saddle, or with rein?

The world will say 'tis very idle –
Bethink you of the time of night?
There's not a mother – no not one,
But when she hears what you have done,   25
Oh Betty, she'll be in a fright!

But Betty's bent on her intent,
For her good neighbour, Susan Gale
(Old Susan, she who dwells alone)
Is sick and makes a piteous moan   30
As if her very life would fail.

There's not a house within a mile,
No hand to help them in distress,
Old Susan lies abed in pain,
And sorely puzzled are the twain,   35
For what she ails⁴ they cannot guess.

And Betty's husband's at the wood
Where by the week he doth abide,
A woodman in the distant vale;
There's none to help poor Susan Gale –   40
What must be done? What will betide?

And Betty from the lane has fetched
Her pony that is mild and good
Whether he be in joy or pain,
Feeding at will along the lane,   45
Or bringing faggots⁵ from the wood.

And he is all in travelling trim,⁶
And by the moonlight, Betty Foy
Has up upon the saddle set
(The like was never heard of yet)   50
Him whom she loves, her idiot boy.

---

³ *girt* saddle-girth.
⁴ *what she ails* what ails her.

⁵ *faggots* bundles of sticks for fuel.
⁶ *in travelling trim* i.e. saddled.

And he must post[7] without delay
Across the bridge that's in the dale,
And by the church and o'er the down
To bring a Doctor from the town,   55
Or she will die, old Susan Gale.

There is no need of boot or spur,
There is no need of whip or wand,[8]
For Johnny has his holly-bough,
And with a hurly-burly now   60
He shakes the green bough in his hand.

And Betty o'er and o'er has told
The boy who is her best delight
Both what to follow, what to shun,
What do, and what to leave undone,   65
How turn to left, and how to right,

And Betty's most especial charge[9]
Was, 'Johnny, Johnny! Mind that you
Come home again, nor stop at all,
Come home again whate'er befall –   70
My Johnny do, I pray you do.'

To this did Johnny answer make
Both with his head and with his hand,
And proudly shook the bridle too,
And then! his words were not a few,   75
Which Betty well could understand.

And now that Johnny is just going,
Though Betty's in a mighty flurry,
She gently pats the pony's side
On which her idiot boy must ride,   80
And seems no longer in a hurry.

But when the pony moved his legs –
Oh then for the poor idiot boy!
For joy he cannot hold the bridle,
For joy his head and heels are idle,   85
He's idle all for very joy.

And while the pony moves his legs,
In Johnny's left hand you may see
The green bough's motionless and dead;
The moon that shines above his head   90
Is not more still and mute than he.

His heart it was so full of glee
That till full fifty yards were gone
He quite forgot his holly whip

---

7 *post* travel quickly.   9 *charge* instruction.
8 *wand* stick, cane.

And all his skill in horsemanship –   95
Oh happy, happy, happy John!

And Betty's standing at the door,
And Betty's face with joy o'erflows,[10]
Proud of herself and proud of him,
She sees him in his travelling trim;   100
How quietly her Johnny goes!

The silence of her idiot boy –
What hopes it sends to Betty's heart!
He's at the guide-post,[11] he turns right,
She watches till he's out of sight,   105
And Betty will not then depart.

Burr, burr, now Johnny's lips they burr[12]
As loud as any mill or near it;
Meek as a lamb the pony moves,
And Johnny makes the noise he loves,   110
And Betty listens, glad to hear it.

Away she hies to Susan Gale,
And Johnny's in a merry tune;[13]
The owlets hoot, the owlets curr,
And Johnny's lips they burr, burr, burr,   115
And on he goes beneath the moon.

His steed and he right well agree,
For of this pony there's a rumour
That should he lose his eyes and ears,
And should he live a thousand years,   120
He never will be out of humour.

But then he is a horse that thinks!
And when he thinks his pace is slack;
Now, though he knows poor Johnny well,
Yet for his life he cannot tell   125
What he has got upon his back.

So through the moonlight lanes they go
And far into the moonlight dale,
And by the church and o'er the down
To bring a Doctor from the town   130
To comfort poor old Susan Gale.

---

[10] *And ... o'erflows* defending this poem in a letter to John Wilson, Wordsworth remarked that 'I have indeed often looked upon the conduct of fathers and mothers of the lower classes of society towards idiots as the great triumph of the human heart. It is there that we see the strength, disinterestedness, and grandeur of love' (*EY* 357).

[11] *guide-post* sign-post.
[12] *Burr ... burr* Coleridge attacked the poem in *Biographia Literaria*, on the grounds of its 'disgusting images of ordinary morbid idiocy'; Wordsworth 'has even, by the "burr, burr, burr" ... assisted in recalling them' (CC *Biographia* ii 48–9).
[13] *tune* mood.

And Betty, now at Susan's side,
Is in the middle of her story,
What comfort Johnny soon will bring,
With many a most diverting thing   135
Of Johnny's wit and Johnny's glory.[14]

And Betty's still at Susan's side –
By this time she's not quite so flurried;
Demure with porringer[15] and plate
She sits, as if in Susan's fate   140
Her life and soul were buried.

But Betty (poor good woman!), she –
You plainly in her face may read it –
Could lend out of that moment's store
Five years of happiness or more   145
To any that might need it.

But yet I guess that now and then
With Betty all was not so well,
And to the road she turns her ears,
And thence full many a sound she hears,   150
Which she to Susan will not tell.

Poor Susan moans, poor Susan groans;
'As sure as there's a moon in heaven',
Cries Betty, 'he'll be back again –
They'll both be here, 'tis almost ten;   155
They'll both be here before eleven.'

Poor Susan moans, poor Susan groans,
The clock gives warning for eleven –
'Tis on the stroke. 'If Johnny's near',
Quoth Betty, 'he will soon be here,   160
As sure as there's a moon in heaven.'

The clock is on the stroke of twelve
And Johnny is not yet in sight;
The moon's in heaven, as Betty sees,
But Betty is not quite at ease –   165
And Susan has a dreadful night.

And Betty, half an hour ago,
On Johnny vile reflections cast;
'A little idle sauntering thing!'
With other names, an endless string,   170
But now that time is gone and past.

---

[14] *Johnny's glory* Defending this poem in a letter to John
Wilson, Wordsworth remarked that, 'I have often applied to
idiots, in my own mind, that sublime expression of scripture
that, "their life is hidden with God" ' (*EY* 357).

[15] *porringer* wooden soup bowl.

And Betty's drooping at the heart,
That happy time all past and gone;
'How can it be he is so late?
The Doctor, he has made him wait –   175
Susan, they'll both be here anon!'

And Susan's growing worse and worse,
And Betty's in a sad quandary,[16]
And then there's nobody to say
If she must go or she must stay –   180
She's in a sad quandary.

The clock is on the stroke of one,
But neither Doctor nor his guide
Appear along the moonlight road;
There's neither horse nor man abroad,   185
And Betty's still at Susan's side.

And Susan, she begins to fear
Of sad mischances not a few;
That Johnny may perhaps be drowned,
Or lost perhaps, and never found –   190
Which they must both forever rue.

She prefaced half a hint of this
With, 'God forbid it should be true!'
At the first word that Susan said,
Cried Betty, rising from the bed,   195
'Susan, I'd gladly stay with you;

I must be gone, I must away.
Consider, Johnny's but half-wise;
Susan, we must take care of him,
If he is hurt in life or limb –'   200
'Oh God forbid!' poor Susan cries.

'What can I do?' says Betty, going,
'What can I do to ease your pain?
Good Susan tell me, and I'll stay;
I fear you're in a dreadful way,   205
But I shall soon be back again.'

'Good Betty go, good Betty go,
There's nothing that can ease my pain.'
Then off she hies, but with a prayer
That God poor Susan's life would spare   210
Till she comes back again.

So through the moonlight lane she goes
And far into the moonlight dale;
And how she ran and how she walked
And all that to herself she talked   215
Would surely be a tedious tale.

---

[16] *quandary* stressed on the second syllable.

In high and low, above, below,
In great and small, in round and square,
In tree and tower was Johnny seen,
In bush and brake, in black and green,   220
'Twas Johnny, Johnny, everywhere.

She's past the bridge that's in the dale,
And now the thought torments her sore –
Johnny perhaps his horse forsook
To hunt the moon that's in the brook,   225
And never will be heard of more.

And now she's high upon the down,
Alone amid a prospect wide;
There's neither Johnny nor his horse
Among the fern or in the gorse;   230
There's neither Doctor nor his guide.

'Oh saints! What is become of him?
Perhaps he's climbed into an oak
Where he will stay till he is dead;
Or sadly he has been misled   235
And joined the wandering gipsy-folk;

Or him that wicked pony's carried
To the dark cave, the goblin's hall;
Or in the castle he's pursuing,
Among the ghosts, his own undoing,   240
Or playing with the waterfall.'

At poor old Susan then she railed,
While to the town she posts away;
'If Susan had not been so ill,
Alas! I should have had him still,   245
My Johnny, till my dying day.'

Poor Betty, in this sad distemper,
The Doctor's self would hardly spare;
Unworthy things she talked, and wild –
Even he, of cattle[17] the most mild,   250
The pony had his share.

And now she's got into the town
And to the Doctor's door she hies;
'Tis silence all on every side –
The town so long, the town so wide   255
Is silent as the skies.

And now she's at the Doctor's door,
She lifts the knocker – rap, rap, rap!
The Doctor at the casement[18] shows

---

[17]   *cattle* animals.   [18]   *casement* window.

His glimmering eyes that peep and doze,   260
And one hand rubs his old nightcap.

'Oh Doctor, Doctor! Where's my Johnny?'
'I'm here, what is't you want with me?'
'Oh sir, you know I'm Betty Foy
And I have lost my poor dear boy –   265
You know him, him you often see;

He's not so wise as some folks be.'
'The devil take his wisdom!' said
The Doctor, looking somewhat grim,
'What, woman, should I know of him?'   270
And grumbling, he went back to bed.

'Oh woe is me! Oh woe is me!
Here will I die, here will I die;
I thought to find my Johnny here,
But he is neither far nor near –   275
Oh what a wretched mother I!'

She stops, she stands, she looks about,
Which way to turn she cannot tell.
Poor Betty, it would ease her pain
If she had heart to knock again;   280
The clock strikes three – a dismal knell!

Then up along the town she hies,
No wonder if her senses fail,
This piteous news so much it shocked her
She quite forgot to send the Doctor   285
To comfort poor old Susan Gale.

And now she's high upon the down
And she can see a mile of road;
'Oh cruel! I'm almost threescore;
Such night as this was ne'er before,   290
There's not a single soul abroad.'

She listens, but she cannot hear
The foot of horse, the voice of man;
The streams with softest sound are flowing,
The grass you almost hear it growing,   295
You hear it now if e'er you can.

The owlets through the long blue night
Are shouting to each other still,
Fond lovers, yet not quite hob-nob,
They lengthen out the tremulous sob   300
That echoes far from hill to hill.

Poor Betty now has lost all hope,
Her thoughts are bent on deadly sin;

A green-grown pond she just has passed
And from the brink she hurries fast
Lest she should drown herself therein.   305

And now she sits her down and weeps,
Such tears she never shed before;
'Oh dear, dear pony! My sweet joy!
Oh carry back my idiot boy   310
And we will ne'er o'erload thee more.'

A thought is come into her head;
'The pony he is mild and good
And we have always used him well;
Perhaps he's gone along the dell   315
And carried Johnny to the wood.'

Then up she springs as if on wings –
She thinks no more of deadly sin;
If Betty fifty ponds should see,
The last of all her thoughts would be   320
To drown herself therein.

Oh reader, now that I might tell[19]
What Johnny and his horse are doing,
What they've been doing all this time –
Oh could I put it into rhyme,   325
A most delightful tale pursuing!

Perhaps (and no unlikely thought)
He with his pony now doth roam
The cliffs and peaks so high that are,
To lay his hands upon a star   330
And in his pocket bring it home.

Perhaps he's turned himself about,
His face unto his horse's tail,
And still and mute, in wonder lost,
All like a silent horseman-ghost   335
He travels on along the vale.

And now, perhaps, he's hunting sheep,
A fierce and dreadful hunter he!
Yon valley that's so trim and green,
In five months' time, should he be seen,   340
A desert wilderness will be.

Perhaps, with head and heels on fire,
And like the very soul of evil,
He's galloping away, away,

---

[19]   Lines 322–51 convey the sense that Johnny enjoyed a
heightened experience of some kind; for further discussion see
'Looking for Johnny: Wordsworth's "The Idiot Boy"', *Charles
Lamb Bulletin* NS 88 (1994) 166–76.

And so he'll gallop on for aye,   345
The bane of all that dread the devil.

I to the muses have been bound
These fourteen years by strong indentures;[20]
Oh gentle muses, let me tell
But half of what to him befell,   350
For sure he met with strange adventures.

Oh gentle muses, is this kind?
Why will ye thus my suit repel?
Why of your further aid bereave[21] me?
And can ye thus unfriended leave me,   355
Ye muses, whom I love so well?

Who's yon, that, near the waterfall
Which thunders down with headlong force,
Beneath the moon, yet shining fair,
As careless as if nothing were,   360
Sits upright on a feeding horse?

Unto his horse that's feeding free
He seems, I think, the rein to give;
Of moon or stars he takes no heed,
Of such we in romances read –   365
'Tis Johnny, Johnny, as I live!

And that's the very pony too!
Where is she, where is Betty Foy?
She hardly can sustain her fears;
The roaring waterfall she hears,   370
And cannot find her idiot boy.

Your pony's worth his weight in gold,
Then calm your terrors, Betty Foy!
She's coming from among the trees,
And now, all full in view, she sees   375
Him whom she loves, her idiot boy,

And Betty sees the pony too.
Why stand you thus, good Betty Foy?
It is no goblin, 'tis no ghost –
'Tis he whom you so long have lost,   380
He whom you love, your idiot boy.

She looks again, her arms are up,
She screams, she cannot move for joy;
She darts as with a torrent's force,
She almost has o'erturned the horse,   385
And fast she holds her idiot boy.

---

[20] *indentures* contract by which apprentice is bound to a master who will teach him a trade. Wordsworth's apprenticeship to the muses of poetry, by his reckoning, began in 1784, when he was fourteen.
[21] *bereave* deprive.

And Johnny burrs and laughs aloud –
Whether in cunning or in joy
I cannot tell; but while he laughs,
Betty a drunken pleasure quaffs   390
To hear again her idiot boy.

And now she's at the pony's tail,
And now she's at the pony's head,
On that side now, and now on this,
And almost stifled with her bliss,   395
A few sad tears does Betty shed.

She kisses o'er and o'er again
Him whom she loves, her idiot boy;
She's happy here, she's happy there,
She is uneasy everywhere;   400
Her limbs are all alive with joy.

She pats the pony, where or when
She knows not, happy Betty Foy!
The little pony glad may be,
But he is milder far than she,   405
You hardly can perceive his joy.

'Oh Johnny, never mind the Doctor;
You've done your best, and that is all.'
She took the reins when this was said,
And gently turned the pony's head   410
From the loud waterfall.

By this the stars were almost gone,
The moon was setting on the hill
So pale you scarcely looked at her;
The little birds began to stir,   415
Though yet their tongues were still.

The pony, Betty, and her boy,
Wind slowly through the woody dale;
And who is she, betimes abroad,
That hobbles up the steep rough road?   420
Who is it but old Susan Gale?

Long Susan lay deep lost in thought
And many dreadful fears beset her,
Both for her messenger and nurse;
And as her mind grew worse and worse,   425
Her body it grew better.

She turned, she tossed herself in bed,
On all sides doubts and terrors met her,
Point after point did she discuss,
And while her mind was fighting thus,   430
Her body still grew better.

'Alas, what is become of them?
These fears can never be endured –
I'll to the wood.' The word scarce said,
Did Susan rise up from her bed,   435
As if by magic cured.

Away she posts up hill and down,
And to the wood at length is come,
She spies her friends, she shouts a greeting –
Oh me, it is a merry meeting   440
As ever was in Christendom!

The owls have hardly sung their last
While our four travellers homeward wend;
The owls have hooted all night long,
And with the owls began my song,   445
And with the owls must end.

For while they all were travelling home,
Cried Betty, 'Tell us Johnny, do,
Where all this long night you have been,
What you have heard, what you have seen –   450
And Johnny, mind you tell us true.'

Now Johnny all night long had heard
The owls in tuneful concert strive;
No doubt too he the moon had seen,
For in the moonlight he had been   455
From eight o'clock till five.

And thus to Betty's question he
Made answer like a traveller bold
(His very words I give to you):
'The cocks did crow to-whoo, to-whoo,   460
And the sun did shine so cold.'[22]
Thus answered Johnny in his glory,
And that was all his travel's story.

Lines Written near Richmond, upon the Thames, at Evening (by Wordsworth, derived from a sonnet written 1789, complete in this form by 29 March 1797)[1]

From Lyrical Ballads (1798)

How rich the wave in front, impressed
With evening twilight's summer hues,
While, facing thus the crimson west,

---

[22] *The cocks . . . cold* According to Wordsworth, these words
were spoken by a local idiot and reported to him at Alfoxden
by his friend Thomas Poole. They provided the starting-point
for the poem (*FN* 10).

Lines Written near Richmond
[1] The title was concocted for the poem's appearance in *Lyri-
cal Ballads*: 'The title is scarcely correct. It was during a soli-
tary walk on the banks of the Cam that I was first struck with
this appearance, and applied it to my own feelings in the man-
ner here expressed, changing the scene to the Thames, near
Windsor' (*FN* 36).

The boat her silent path pursues![2]
And see how dark the backward stream,   5
A little moment past, so smiling!
And still, perhaps, with faithless gleam,
Some other loiterer beguiling.[3]

Such views the youthful bard allure,
But heedless of the following gloom,   10
He deems their colours shall endure
Till peace go with him to the tomb.
And let him nurse his fond deceit;
And what if he must die in sorrow?
Who would not cherish dreams so sweet,   15
Though grief and pain[4] may come tomorrow?

Glide gently, thus forever glide,
Oh Thames! that other bards may see
As lovely visions by thy side
As now, fair river, come to me!   20
Oh glide, fair stream, forever so;
Thy quiet soul on all bestowing,
Till all our minds forever flow,
As thy deep waters now are flowing.

Vain thought! Yet be as now thou art,   25
That in thy waters may be seen
The image of a poet's heart,
How bright, how solemn, how serene!
Such heart did once the poet[5] bless
Who, pouring here a *later* ditty,   30
Could find no refuge from distress
But in the milder grief of pity.

Remembrance! as we glide along,
For him suspend the dashing oar,[6]
And pray that never child of song   35
May know his freezing sorrows[7] more.

---

[2]   *How rich ... beguiling* the poem begins with a picturesque
sunset, described in the manner of the picturesque theorist,
William Gilpin, whose *Observations on the Lakes* (1786)
Wordsworth admired from his schooldays onwards. Gilpin
had described such a scene in exactly this manner: 'its fires,
glowing in the west, light up a new radiance through the
landscape; and spread over it, instead of sober light and shade,
all the colours of nature, in one bright, momentary gleam' (i
91).

[3]   *Some ... beguiling* the brilliant sky at sunset draws the loi-
terer's attention away from the darkness coming up behind.
Wordsworth is imitating Bowles's *Sonnet VIII. On Leaving a
Village in Scotland*:

  Yet still your brightest images shall *smile*,
  To charm the lingering stranger, and *beguile*
  His way ... (ll. 10–12)

[4]   *grief and pain* a comment that anticipates the doleful
judgement of *Resolution and Independence* 48–9: 'We poets in

our youth begin in gladness, / But thereof comes in the end
despondency and madness.'

[5]   'Collins' "Ode on the Death of Thomson" – the last writ-
ten, I believe, of the poems which were published during his
lifetime. This Ode is also alluded to in the next stanza'
(Wordsworth's note). William Collins (1721–59) actually
published the *Ode* in June 1749, a year before *The Passions* in
1750. James Thomson (1700–48), poet and author of *The Sea-
sons*, was buried in Richmond Church. Wordsworth was a life-
long admirer of both.

[6]   *For him ... oar* cf. Collins, *Ode on the Death of Mr. Thomson*
13–16:

  Remembrance oft shall haunt the shore
    When Thames in summer wreaths is dressed,
  And oft suspend the dashing oar
    To bid his gentle spirit rest!

[7]   *his freezing sorrows* Collins suffered spells of insanity and
poverty.

How calm, how still! the only sound
The dripping of the oar suspended!
The evening darkness gathers round
⌈By virtue's holiest powers attended.⌉   40

Expostulation and Reply (by Wordsworth, composed probably 23 May 1798)[1]

From LYRICAL BALLADS (1798)

'Why, William, on that old grey stone,
Thus for the length of half a day,
Why, William, sit you thus alone
And dream your time away?

Where are your books that light bequeathed   5
To beings else forlorn and blind?
Up, up, and drink the spirit breathed
From dead men to their kind!

You look round on your mother earth
As if she for no purpose bore you;   10
As if you were her first-born birth,
And none had lived before you!'

One morning thus, by Esthwaite Lake,[2]
When life was sweet I knew not why,
To me my good friend Matthew spake,   15
And thus I made reply.

'The eye it cannot choose but see,
We cannot bid the ear be still;
Our bodies feel where'er they be,
Against or with our will.   20

Nor less I deem that there are powers[3]
Which of themselves our minds impress,
That we can feed this mind of ours
In a wise passiveness.[4]

Think you, mid all this mighty sum   25
Of things forever speaking,

EXPOSTULATION AND REPLY
[1]   See Advertisement to *Lyrical Ballads* (1798) above, for
Wordsworth's explanation of the poem. It is based on a con-
versation which took place on a walk at Alfoxden with
William Hazlitt. Hazlitt was twenty, and was writing his
Essay on the Principles of Human Action (1805). For Hazlitt's
recollection, see p. 608.
[2]   *Esthwaite Lake* Wordsworth attended school at Hawk-
shead, on Esthwaite Water in the Lake District. Although this
poem was inspired by a discussion with William Hazlitt at

Alfoxden in 1798, Wordsworth locates it in the Lakes, and
characterizes Matthew as his schoolmaster.
[3]   *powers* i.e. external to us; natural forces.
[4]   *wise passiveness* 'Oh how few can transmute activity of mind
into emotion', Coleridge exclaimed in a notebook entry of
1804, 'yet there are [those] who, active as the stirring tempest
and playful as a May blossom in a breeze of May, can yet for
hours together remain with hearts broad awake, and the
understanding asleep in all but its retentiveness and receptiv-
ity' (*Notebooks* i 1834).

That nothing of itself will come,
But we must still[5] be seeking?

Then ask not wherefore, here, alone,
Conversing as I may,[6]   30
I sit upon this old grey stone
And dream my time away.'

The Tables Turned: an Evening Scene, on the Same Subject (by Wordsworth, composed probably 23 May 1798)[1]

From LYRICAL BALLADS (1798)

Up, up, my friend, and clear your looks!
Why all this toil and trouble?[2]
Up, up, my friend, and quit your books,
Or surely you'll grow double!

The sun above the mountain's head   5
A freshening lustre mellow
Through all the long green fields has spread,
His first sweet evening yellow.

Books! 'tis a dull and endless strife;
Come hear the woodland linnet –   10
How sweet his music! On my life,
There's more of wisdom in it.

And hark, how blithe the throstle[3] sings!
And he is no mean preacher;
Come forth into the light of things,   15
Let nature be your teacher.

She has a world of ready wealth,
Our minds and hearts to bless –
Spontaneous wisdom breathed by health,
Truth breathed by cheerfulness.   20

One impulse from a vernal wood
May teach you more of man,
Of moral evil and of good
Than all the sages can.

Sweet is the lore which nature brings;   25
Our meddling intellect
Misshapes the beauteous forms of things –
We murder to dissect.[4]

---

5   *still* always.
6   *Conversing . . . may* i.e. with the natural world.

THE TABLES TURNED
1   The speaker is William from the preceding poem, who simply continues his argument.

2   *toil and trouble* an echo of the witches in *Macbeth*: 'Double, double, toil and trouble' (IV i 10–11).
3   *throstle* thrush.
4   *We murder to dissect* i.e. in analysing what we perceive, we destroy it.

Enough of science[5] and of art,[6]
Close up these barren leaves;[7]   30
Come forth, and bring with you a heart
That watches and receives.

Old Man Travelling; Animal Tranquillity and Decay, A Sketch (by Wordsworth, composed by June 1797)

From LYRICAL BALLADS (1798)

The little hedgerow birds
That peck along the road, regard him not.
He travels on, and in his face, his step,
His gait, is one expression; every limb,
His look and bending figure, all bespeak   5
A man who does not move with pain, but moves
With thought. He is insensibly subdued
To settled quiet; he is one by whom
All effort seems forgotten, one to whom
Long patience has such mild composure given,   10
That patience now doth seem a thing of which
He hath no need. He is by nature led
To peace so perfect that the young behold
With envy what the old man hardly feels.
    I asked him whither he was bound, and what   15
The object of his journey; he replied:
'Sir, I am going many miles to take
A last leave of my son, a mariner,
Who from a sea-fight has been brought to Falmouth,
And there is dying in an hospital.'[1]   20

The Complaint of a Forsaken Indian Woman (by Wordsworth, composed between early March and 16 May 1798)

From LYRICAL BALLADS (1798)

When a Northern Indian, from sickness, is unable to continue his journey with his companions, he is left behind, covered over with deer-skins, and is supplied with water, food, and fuel, if the situation of the place will afford it. He is informed of the track which his companions intend to pursue, and, if he is unable to follow or overtake them, he perishes alone in the desert (unless he should have the good fortune to fall in with some other tribes of Indians). It is unnecessary to add that the females are equally, or still more, exposed to the same fate; see that very interesting work, Hearne's *Journey from Hudson's Bay to the Northern Ocean.*[1] When the Northern Lights[2] (as the same writer informs us) vary

---

[5] *science* knowledge.
[6] *art* skill, artfulness.
[7] *barren leaves* pages of books.

OLD MAN TRAVELLING
[1] Lines 15–20 may have been a late addition to the poem and were removed from texts published after 1815.

THE COMPLAINT OF A FORSAKEN INDIAN WOMAN
[1] A reference to Samuel Hearne's *Journey from Prince of Wales' Fort in Hudson Bay, to the Northern Ocean* (1795), which describes the plight of a sick Indian woman left behind by her tribe: 'The poor woman ... came up with us three several times, after having been left in the manner described. At length, poor creature, she dropped behind, and no one attempted to go back in search of her' (p. 203).
[2] *Northern Lights* the aurora borealis.

their position in the air, they make a rustling and a crackling noise. This circumstance is alluded to in the first stanza of the following poem.

> Before I see another day
> Oh let my body die away!
> In sleep I heard the northern gleams,[3]
> The stars they were among my dreams;
> In sleep did I behold the skies,   5
> I saw the crackling flashes drive,
> And yet[4] they are upon my eyes,
> And yet I am alive.
> Before I see another day
> Oh let my body die away!   10
>
> My fire is dead[5] – it knew no pain,
> Yet is it dead, and I remain.
> All stiff with ice the ashes lie,
> And they are dead, and I will die.
> When I was well, I wished to live,   15
> For[6] clothes, for warmth, for food and fire;
> But they to me no joy can give,
> No pleasure now, and no desire.
> Then here contented will I lie,
> Alone I cannot fear to die.   20
>
> Alas, you might have dragged me on
> Another day, a single one!
> Too soon despair o'er me prevailed,
> Too soon my heartless[7] spirit failed;
> When you were gone my limbs were stronger –   25
> And oh, how grievously I rue
> That afterwards, a little longer,
> My friends, I did not follow you!
> For strong and without pain I lay,
> My friends, when you were gone away.   30
>
> My child, they gave thee to another,
> A woman who was not thy mother;
> When from my arms my babe they took,
> On me how strangely did he look!
> Through his whole body something ran,   35
> A most strange something did I see –
> As if he strove to be a man,

---

[3] *northern gleams* Hearne writes: 'I do not remember to have met with any travellers into high northern latitudes, who remarked their having heard the Northern Lights make any noise in the air as they vary their colours or position – which may probably be owing to the want of perfect silence at the time they made their observations on those meteors. I can positively affirm that in still nights I have frequently heard them make a rustling and crackling noise, like the waving of a large flag in a fresh gale of wind' (*Journey*, p. 224).

[4] *yet* still.

[5] *My fire is dead* According to Hearne, members of the tribe abandoned to die were left with some provisions: 'the friends or relations of the sick generally leave them some victuals and water, and, if the situation of the place will afford it, a little firing. When those articles are provided, the person to be left is acquainted with the road which the others intend to go, and then, after covering them well up with deer-skins, etc., they take their leave, and walk away crying' (*Journey*, p. 202–3).

[6] *For* i.e. I wished for . . .

[7] *heartless* disheartened.

That he might pull the sledge for me.
And then he stretched his arms, how wild!
Oh mercy, like a little child!   40

My little joy! My little pride!
In two days more I must have died.
Then do not weep and grieve for me;
I feel I must have died with thee.
Oh wind, that o'er my head art flying   45
The way my friends their course did bend,
I should not feel the pain of dying
Could I with thee a message send.
Too soon, my friends, you went away,
For I had many things to say.   50

I'll follow you across the snow,
You travel heavily and slow;
In spite of all my weary pain,
I'll look upon your tents again.
My fire is dead, and snowy white   55
The water which beside it stood;
The wolf has come to me tonight
And he has stolen away my food.
Forever left alone am I,
Then wherefore should I fear to die?   60

My journey will be shortly run,[8]
I shall not see another sun,
I cannot lift my limbs to know
If they have any life or no.
My poor forsaken child, if I   65
For once could have thee close to me,
With happy heart I then would die
And my last thoughts would happy be.
I feel my body die away,
I shall not see another day.   70

The Convict (by Wordsworth, composed between 21 March and October 1796)[1]

From LYRICAL BALLADS (1798)

The glory of evening was spread through the west –
On the slope of a mountain I stood;
While the joy that precedes the calm season of rest[2]
Rang loud through the meadow and wood.

---

8   *My journey will be shortly run* cf. *Samson Agonistes* 597–8: 'My race of glory run, and race of shame, / And I shall shortly be with them that rest'.

THE CONVICT
1   Prison reform was a topical issue at the time this poem was first composed, thanks partly to Godwin, who had argued,

in the second edition of *Political Justice* (1796), that it was wrong to punish someone 'for what is past and irrecoverable' (ii 322).
2   *the calm season of rest* i.e. night-time.

'And must we then part from a dwelling so fair?'   5
    In the pain of my spirit I said,
And with a deep sadness I turned to repair
    To the cell where the convict is laid.

The thick-ribbed walls that o'ershadow the gate
    Resound, and the dungeons unfold;   10
I pause,[3] and at length through the glimmering grate[4]
    That outcast of pity behold.

His black matted head on his shoulder is bent,
    And deep is the sigh of his breath,
And with steadfast dejection his eyes are intent   15
    On the fetters that link him to death.

'Tis sorrow enough on that visage to gaze,
    That body dismissed from his care;
Yet my fancy has pierced to his heart, and portrays[5]
    More terrible images there.   20

His bones are consumed and his life-blood is dried,
    With wishes the past to undo;
And his crime, through the pains that o'erwhelm him, descried,
    Still[6] blackens and grows on his view.

When from the dark synod[7] or blood-reeking field,[8]   25
    To his chamber the monarch is led,
All soothers of sense their soft virtue shall yield,
    And quietness pillow his head.

But if grief, self-consumed, in oblivion would doze,
    And conscience her tortures appease,   30
Mid tumult and uproar this man must repose
    In the comfortless vault of disease.

When his fetters at night have so pressed on his limbs
    That the weight can no longer be borne,
If, while a half-slumber his memory bedims,   35
    The wretch on his pallet should turn;

While the jail-mastiff howls at the dull-clanking chain,
    From the roots of his hair there shall start
A thousand sharp punctures of cold-sweating pain,
    And terror shall leap at his heart.   40

But now he half-raises his deep-sunken eye,
    And the motion unsettles a tear;

---

[3] *I pause* i.e. to allow his eyes to adjust to the darkness.
[4] *grate* barred window to the prison cell.
[5] *portrays* visualizes.
[6] *Still* continually.

[7] *dark synod* secret council.
[8] *blood-reeking field* the battlefield that literally stinks of blood. The monarch is, by implication, far more culpable than the convict. Britain had been at war with France since 1793.

The silence of sorrow it seems to supply,
    And asks of me why I am here.

'Poor victim! No idle intruder has stood   45
    With o'erweening complacence our state to compare –
But one whose first wish is the wish to be good
    Is come as a brother thy sorrows to share.[9]

At thy name, though Compassion her nature resign,
    Though in Virtue's proud mouth thy report be a stain,[10]
My care, if the arm of the mighty were mine,
    Would plant thee where yet thou might'st blossom again.'[11]

Lines Written a Few Miles above Tintern Abbey, on Revisiting the Banks of the Wye During a Tour, 13 July 1798 (by Wordsworth, composed 10–13 July 1798)[1]

From LYRICAL BALLADS (1798)

Five years have passed; five summers, with the length
Of five long winters![2] And again I hear
These waters, rolling from their mountain springs
With a sweet inland murmur.[3] Once again
Do I behold these steep and lofty cliffs,   5
Which on a wild secluded scene impress
Thoughts of more deep seclusion, and connect
The landscape with the quiet of the sky.[4]
The day is come when I again repose
Here, under this dark sycamore, and view   10
These plots of cottage-ground, these orchard-tufts,
Which, at this season, with their unripe fruits,
Among the woods and copses lose themselves,
Nor, with their green and simple hue, disturb

[handwritten margin notes: — not just the nature; how the nature effects human perception]

[handwritten margin note: but humans don't disturb the landscape]

---

9 *No idle ... share* the narrator tells the convict that he comes not to gloat over, but to share his grief.

10 *At thy ... stain* Compassionate people feel nothing for convicts, while the virtuous cannot mention them without feeling tainted.

11 *My care ... again* perhaps a plea for the humane transportation of convicts, though it is just as likely that Wordsworth is just suggesting that they be given a second chance.

LINES WRITTEN A FEW MILES ABOVE TINTERN ABBEY
1 'No poem of mine was composed under circumstances more pleasant for me to remember than this: I began it upon leaving Tintern, after crossing the Wye, and concluded it just as I was entering Bristol in the evening, after a ramble of four or five days, with my sister. Not a line of it was altered, and not any part of it written down till I reached Bristol. It was published almost immediately after in the little volume of which so much has been said in these notes' (*FN* 15). In conversation and correspondence Wordsworth and his circle usually referred to the poem as *Tintern Abbey*.

2 *Five years ... winters* Wordsworth's first visit to the Wye was in August 1793.

3 'The river is not affected by the tides a few miles above Tintern' (Wordsworth's note). Wordsworth later commented: 'The Wye is a stately and majestic river from its width and depth, but never slow and sluggish; you can always hear its murmur. It travels through a woody country, now varied with cottages and green meadows, and now with huge and fantastic rocks' (Christopher Wordsworth, *Memoirs of William Wordsworth* (2 vols, London, 1851), i 117).

4 *connect ... sky* the fusing of landscape and sky is a picturesque touch derived from William Gilpin, *Observations on the River Wye* (1782): 'Many of the furnaces on the banks of the river consume charcoal which is manufactured on the spot, and the smoke (which is frequently seen issuing from the sides of the hills, and spreading its thin veil over a part of them) beautifully breaks their lines, and unites them with the sky' (p. 12).

The wild green landscape. Once again I see   15
These hedgerows – hardly hedgerows, little lines
Of sportive wood run wild; these pastoral farms[5]
Green to the very door; and wreaths of smoke
Sent up in silence from among the trees,
With some uncertain notice,[6] as might seem,   20
Of vagrant dwellers in the houseless woods,
Or of some hermit's cave, where by his fire
The hermit sits alone.[7]
                                    Though absent long,
These forms of beauty[8] have not been to me
As is a landscape to a blind man's eye;   25
But oft, in lonely rooms, and mid the din
Of towns and cities, I have owed to them,
In hours of weariness, sensations sweet,
Felt in the blood, and felt along the heart,
And passing even into my purer mind[9]   30
With tranquil restoration;[10] feelings too
Of unremembered pleasure – such, perhaps,
As may have had no trivial influence
On that best portion of a good man's life,
His little, nameless, unremembered acts   35
Of kindness and of love. Nor less, I trust,
To them I may have owed another gift,
Of aspect more sublime; that blessed mood
In which the burden of the mystery,[11]
In which the heavy and the weary weight   40
Of all this unintelligible world
Is lightened – that serene and blessed mood
In which the affections gently lead us on
Until the breath of this corporeal frame[12]
And even the motion of our human blood   45
Almost suspended, we are laid asleep
In body, and become a living soul,[13]
While with an eye made quiet by the power
Of harmony, and the deep power of joy,[14]
We see into the life of things.[15]
                                    If this   50
Be but a vain belief – yet oh, how oft
In darkness, and amid the many shapes

---

[5] *pastoral farms* farms consisting largely of pasture leaving the overall greenness of the landscape undisturbed.

[6] *With some uncertain notice* faintly discernible.

[7] *as might seem ... alone* the 'vagrant dwellers' (gypsies) and hermit are figments of the imagination; the smoke comes from the charcoal-furnaces (see note 4, above).

[8] *forms of beauty* natural objects, impressed on the mind in the manner described at *Pedlar* 27–43.

[9] *my purer mind* i.e. the spiritual element of his being.

[10] *restoration* the memory of the 'forms of beauty' is spiritually restorative, like the 'spots of time', *Two-Part Prelude* i 294, by which the mind is 'nourished and invisibly repaired'.

[11] *the burden of the mystery* life is burdensome because the affairs of the world are so often 'unintelligible' (l. 41).

[12] *corporeal frame* the physical body.

[13] *become a living soul* alluding to the moment at which Adam was created by God: 'And the Lord God formed man of the dust of the ground, and breathed into his nostrils the breath of life; and man became a living soul' (Genesis 2:7).

[14] *the deep power of joy* 'joy', during the Alfoxden period, is the name given by Coleridge and Wordsworth to the pantheist perception of Nature as unified by a universal life-force; see *Pedlar* 217–18: 'in all things / He saw one life, and felt that it was joy'.

[15] *Until the breath ... things* the 'forms of beauty' induce a mystic state in which the poet is released from the confines of the body and instead engages, in a completely spiritual manner, with the life-force of the universe.

Of joyless daylight, when the fretful stir
Unprofitable,[16] and the fever of the world,
Have hung upon the beatings of my heart,   55
How oft, in spirit, have I turned to thee,
Oh sylvan[17] Wye! Thou wanderer through the woods,
How often has my spirit turned to thee!
    And now, with gleams of half-extinguished thought,
With many recognitions dim and faint   60
And somewhat of a sad perplexity,[18]
The picture of the mind revives again;
While here I stand, not only with the sense
Of present pleasure, but with pleasing thoughts
That in this moment there is life and food   65
For future years.[19] And so I dare to hope,
Though changed, no doubt, from what I was when first
I came among these hills, when like a roe[20]
I bounded o'er the mountains[21] by the sides
Of the deep rivers and the lonely streams   70
Wherever nature led, more like a man
Flying from something that he dreads than one
Who sought the thing he loved.[22] For nature then
(The coarser pleasures of my boyish days
And their glad animal movements all gone by)   75
To me was all in all.
          I cannot paint
What then I was. The sounding cataract
Haunted me like a passion;[23] the tall rock,
The mountain, and the deep and gloomy wood,
Their colours and their forms, were then to me   80
An appetite, a feeling and a love
That had no need of a remoter charm
By thought supplied, or any interest
Unborrowed from the eye. That time is past,
And all its aching joys are now no more,   85
And all its dizzy raptures. Not for this
Faint I, nor mourn, nor murmur; other gifts
Have followed – for such loss, I would believe,
Abundant recompense. For I have learned
To look on nature not as in the hour   90
Of thoughtless youth, but hearing oftentimes
The still, sad[24] music of humanity,

[handwritten margin notes: "– not earthy passion now; more subtle, soul" and "def. perception"]

---

[16] *Unprofitable* probably an echo of *Hamlet*: 'How ... unprofitable / Seem to me all the uses of this world' (I ii 133–4).

[17] *sylvan* wooded.

[18] *sad perplexity* due to the fact that the 'recognitions' are only 'dim and faint'; the memorized 'forms of beauty' do not match up to what is before the poet as he looks down at the same scene five years later.

[19] *pleasing thoughts ... future years* in the five years since his first visit he has derived pleasure from recollections of the Wye valley; he hopes that the present visit will provide similar benefits in future. The habit of storing mental pictures is described, months before, in *Pedlar* 30–43.

[20] *roe* small deer.

[21] *like a roe ... mountains* from *Song of Solomon* 2:8–9: 'The voice of my beloved! Behold, he cometh leaping upon the mountains, skipping upon the hills. My beloved is like a roe, or a young hart'.

[22] *more like ... loved* In August 1793 Wordsworth was wandering across the countryside in a state of severe emotional distress, as the newly-declared war on France prevented him from returning to Annette Vallon who, in December 1792, had given birth to their illegitimate daughter, Caroline.

[23] *The sounding ... passion* cf. *Pedlar* 31–4, where images of landscape 'almost seemed / To haunt the bodily sense'.

[24] *still, sad* Wordsworth alludes to the 'still, small' voice of God that speaks to Elijah, I Kings 19:12.

Not harsh nor grating, though of ample power
To chasten and subdue. And I have felt
A presence that disturbs me with the joy   95
Of elevated thoughts, a sense sublime
Of something[25] far more deeply interfused,
Whose dwelling is the light of setting suns,
And the round ocean, and the living air,
And the blue sky, and in the mind of man[26] –   100
A motion and a spirit that impels
All thinking things, all objects of all thought,
And rolls through all things.[27] Therefore am I still
A lover of the meadows and the woods
And mountains, and of all that we behold   105
From this green earth, of all the mighty world
Of eye and ear (both what they half-create[28]
And what perceive) – well-pleased to recognize
In nature and the language of the sense,[29]
The anchor of my purest[30] thoughts, the nurse,   110
The guide, the guardian of my heart, and soul
Of all my moral being.

                           Nor, perchance,
If I were not thus taught, should I the more
Suffer my genial spirits[31] to decay;
For thou[32] art with me,[33] here, upon the banks   115
Of this fair river – thou, my dearest friend,
My dear, dear friend, and in thy voice I catch
The language of my former heart, and read
My former pleasures in the shooting lights
Of thy wild eyes. Oh, yet a little while   120
May I behold in thee what I was once,
My dear, dear sister! And this prayer I make,
Knowing that Nature never did betray
The heart that loved her;[34] 'tis her privilege,
Through all the years of this our life, to lead   125
From joy to joy, for she can so inform[35]
The mind that is within us, so impress
With quietness and beauty, and so feed
With lofty thoughts, that neither evil tongues,[36]
Rash judgements, nor the sneers of selfish men,   130

---

[25]   *something* Wordsworth is deliberately unspecific, but there is little doubt that he is thinking in terms of a universal, pantheistic life-force – the One Life.
[26]   *the light . . . man* probably, as critics argue, a recollection of Virgil, *Aeneid* vi 724–7 (translated): 'an inner spirit sustains the sky and the earth and the sea, the bright globe of the moon, the sun and the stars, and mind activates the whole frame, pervading all its members, and blends with the great body'.
[27]   *And I have felt . . . things* this remarkable affirmation of the pantheist one life should be compared with *Pedlar* 204–22, composed only months before.
[28]   *half-create* Wordsworth notes a borrowing from Young, *Night Thoughts* vi 427: 'And half-create the wondrous world they [the senses] see'.

[29]   *the language of the sense* what the senses perceive.
[30]   *purest* most spiritual.
[31]   *genial spirits* creative energies, vitality. Cf. *Samson Agonistes* 594: 'So much I feel my genial spirits droop'.
[32]   *thou* Dorothy Wordsworth.
[33]   *For thou art with me* an allusion to the most famous of the Psalms: 'Yea, though I walk through the valley of the shadow of death, I will fear no evil: for thou art with me; thy rod and thy staff, they comfort me' (23:4).
[34]   *that Nature . . . her* probably an allusion to Samuel Daniel, *The Civil Wars* ii 225–6: 'Here have you craggy rocks to take your part, / That never will betray their faith to you'.
[35]   *inform* imbue.
[36]   *evil tongues* Milton describes himself as 'On evil times though fallen, and evil tongues' (*Paradise Lost* vii 26).

Nor greetings where no kindness is, nor all
The dreary intercourse of daily life,
Shall e'er prevail against us, or disturb
Our cheerful faith that all which we behold
Is full of blessings. Therefore let the moon 135
Shine on thee in thy solitary walk,
And let the misty mountain-winds be free
To blow against thee. And in after-years,
When these wild ecstasies shall be matured
Into a sober pleasure, when thy mind 140
Shall be a mansion[37] for all lovely forms,
Thy memory be as a dwelling-place
For all sweet sounds and harmonies – oh then
If solitude, or fear, or pain, or grief
Should be thy portion,[38] with what healing thoughts 145
Of tender joy wilt thou remember me,
And these my exhortations! Nor perchance,
If I should be where I no more can hear
Thy voice, nor catch from thy wild eyes these gleams
Of past existence, wilt thou then forget 150
That on the banks of this delightful stream
We stood together; and that I, so long
A worshipper of nature, hither came
Unwearied in that service – rather say
With warmer love, oh with far deeper zeal 155
Of holier love! Nor wilt thou then forget
That, after many wanderings, many years
Of absence, these steep woods and lofty cliffs
And this green pastoral landscape, were to me
More dear, both for themselves, and for thy sake. 160

a like where she isn't drawn down by daily human life – revitalated by nature

---

37 _mansion_ home, abiding-place.
38 _portion_ lot, fate.

William Wordsworth   (1770–1850)

William Wordsworth was born 7 April 1770, second son of John Wordsworth Sr (1741–83), legal agent for Sir James Lowther, later Earl of Lonsdale, the most powerful landowner in the Lake District. The family was relatively well off, and lived in the grandest house in the main street of the small town of Cockermouth. In March 1778 his mother Ann died of pneumonia at the age of thirty. In May 1779 he was sent to Hawkshead Grammar School, at the other side of the Lake District. Here he received an excellent education in the English Grammar School tradition – particularly in Latin, Greek and mathematics. He lodged with the kindly Ann Tyson, and prospered under two teachers in particular, William Taylor and Thomas Bowman. During his time there he and his siblings (Richard, Christopher, John and Dorothy) were orphaned by the death of their father in December 1783 – an event that was devastating, and which caused them financial hardship for years.

At Hawkshead, Wordsworth began to compose poetry – his earliest extant verse dates from 1785. He continued to write poetry and study the classics at St John's College, Cambridge, where he matriculated in 1787. His performance in university examinations was variable, but not because he lacked ability. The university syllabus was concerned chiefly with the work of the Greek mathematician Euclid, which Wordsworth had mastered at Hawkshead;[1] in later years he suggested that the level of proficiency he had reached at school was so high that he felt unchallenged by the Cambridge course. Nonetheless, he always did well in examinations on Latin and Greek literature which he enjoyed translating in his spare time.

At Cambridge he became interested in the French Revolution, and witnessed it at first hand when he toured France on foot in 1790 with a college friend, Robert Jones. He returned in 1791–2, and stayed for a time at Blois near Orleans. Here he met Michel Beaupuy, the soldier who was to serve as a kind of mentor (see *Thirteen-Book Prelude* ix 294ff.), and had an affair with a French girl, Annette Vallon. She gave birth to a child, Caroline Wordsworth, in December 1792. By then Wordsworth was in London; although we cannot be certain of his motives, it seems likely that he intended to publish his two poems, *An Evening Walk* and *Descriptive Sketches*, as a means of raising money, before returning to France to join his family. Although he succeeded in publishing the poems (they

appeared in late January 1793), his return to France was precluded by the execution of Louis XVI in February, which led immediately to war between Britain and France.

His failure to return to Annette and their child caused Wordsworth profound distress – a response that must have strengthened his attachment to the French cause. One symptom of this was the composition in spring 1793 of a pamphlet defending regicide, *A Letter to the Bishop of Llandaff*. Fortunately for him, it remained unpublished; had it gone into print, he would almost certainly have been imprisoned in accordance with the repressive policies of Pitt's Tory administration. In ensuing months he went on a walking tour that took him to Portsmouth, where he saw the British fleet preparing to fight the French; Salisbury Plain, which he crossed in a hallucinatory state (recalled in the *Thirteen-Book Prelude* xii 312ff.); Tintern Abbey, which he saw for the first time (see *Tintern Abbey*, especially ll. 76–84), and finally Wales, where he stayed with Robert Jones.

At this period Godwin's *Political Justice* (see pp. 47–50) had a strong appeal for him in its reaffirmation of revolutionary ideals, but by 1796 he was profoundly disillusioned with it, violently rejecting Godwin's emotionless fantasies of reason (see *Thirteen-Book Prelude* x 805–48). He was rescued from despair by Coleridge and by his sister Dorothy (see *Thirteen-Book Prelude* x 904–15). His closeness to his sister dated back to their childhood, though it may be that they first discovered an affinity in the wake of their father's death in 1783. In any case, they had lived together from 1794 onwards – first at Windy Brow at Keswick, and then, 1795–7, at Racedown Lodge in Dorset. Her healing influence provided the environment in which Wordsworth was able to compose the earliest, no longer extant, version of *The Ruined Cottage*, which Coleridge probably heard when he visited the Wordsworths in June 1797.

The Ruined Cottage is the first indisputably great poem composed by Wordsworth. It has been aptly described by its first editor, Jonathan Wordsworth, as a 'tragedy'; what distinguishes the version presented here (completed in the spring of 1798) is the profound optimism of its conclusion, in which, confronted by the pain and suffering of the ill-fated Margaret, we are directed to feel consolation at the sight of the spear-grass and other plants in her garden:

WILLIAM WORDSWORTH

[1] The Pedlar, too, is a mathematician (*Pedlar* 146–53). Euclid makes an appearance in Book V of *The Thirteen-Book Prelude* (p. 387).

I well remember that those very plumes,
Those weeds, and the high speargrass on that wall,
By mist and silent raindrops silvered o'er,
As once I passed did to my mind convey
So still an image of tranquillity,
So calm and still, and looked so beautiful
Amid the uneasy thoughts which filled my mind,
That what we feel of sorrow and despair
From ruin and from change, and all the grief
The passing shows of being leave behind,
Appeared an idle dream that could not live
Where meditation was. (ll. 513–24)

This is one of the seminal statements in English romantic poetry: life is indeed full of sorrow and despair, but in this hopeful, meditative mood, Wordsworth sees such things as no more than an 'idle dream'. Such unwavering certainty reflects the influence of Coleridge, and their plans for an epic philosophical poem called *The Recluse*, of which *The Ruined Cottage* was to have been part. The first thing to be said about *The Recluse* is that it was never completed, and was probably never likely to be. Seeing around them the continuing hardship and suffering which the French Revolution was intended to counteract, Wordsworth and Coleridge asked themselves how the poet might do his part to bring about the betterment of mankind. The answer incorporated elements of both men's thought. Its central tenet (later to be the subject of the *Thirteen-Book Prelude* Book VIII) was that love of Nature led to love of mankind; that is to say, the intensely perceived, and imaginatively enhanced, engagement with the pantheist life-force running through the natural world could lead, in turn, to a sympathy and compassion for all things, including other members of the human race. The emphasis on the role of Nature was distinctively Wordsworthian, and is attributed to him when it appears for the first time in Coleridge's poetry, in *This Lime-Tree Bower My Prison*, in July 1797 (pp. 457–9); the Unitarian pantheism came from Coleridge, who had espoused his conviction in a unifying, all-embracing divinity since at least 1794, when he wrote the first version of *Religious Musings* (see pp. 455–6). A poem that explained how the love of Nature led to a brotherhood of mankind could, Wordsworth and Coleridge believed, generate substantial political and material improvements in the world. They even looked forward with enthusiasm to the possibility of their poem helping to

bring about the millennium prophesied by St John the Divine – Christ's thousand-year rule on earth. Coleridge had for years wanted to write a poem of this kind (he had wanted to call it *The Brook*), but he so idolized Wordsworth that he persuaded him that he was the only poet fitted to compose it, and it dominated Wordsworth's poetic ambitions for the next forty years of his life.

Wordsworth absorbed Coleridge's enthusiasm for pantheism, and it appears throughout the poetry of 1798, but thereafter it virtually disappears – and, with it, any chance that he could compose *The Recluse*. He returned to the project many times over the years, and numerous associated fragments survive.[2] In due course he came to regard all his poetry as contributing to it. When in 1814 he published *The Excursion*, which he thought of as his greatest work, he said that it, and all his shorter poems, from *Lyrical Ballads* and *Poems, in Two Volumes* (1807), were part of *The Recluse*. Even *The Prelude* took its title from the fact that it was a kind of introduction to *The Recluse*. But the great work itself was not to be. Coleridge's disappointed response to *The Excursion* reveals that he had imposed on Wordsworth the task of writing such a densely complex and challenging work that it is unlikely anyone could have written it (see pp. 519–21, 548). Instead, what survives are poems and fragments that would have been part of *The Recluse* had Wordsworth finished it in 1798: *The Ruined Cottage*, *The Pedlar*, 'There is an active principle', 'Not useless do I deem', and *The Discharged Soldier*, all of which are included here.

The Recluse was distinctively a product of that optimistic year, the *annus mirabilis* of 1797–8, which began in July 1797 when Coleridge brought the Wordsworths to live at Alfoxden House in Somerset, four miles from his cottage at Nether Stowey (see pp. 457–8). That year also saw the composition of the first volume of *Lyrical Ballads* (pp. 189–91), and the beginning of Wordsworth's greatest poem, *The Prelude*. After leaving Alfoxden in summer 1798, the Wordsworths went to Germany, where William was to get on with the task of composing *The Recluse*. But he was unable to do so. Instead, he and his sister found themselves, in the midst of the coldest winter of the century, alienated from the local people (who spoke a language they, for the most part, were struggling to grasp), and missing England. Thrown back on his own resources, Wordsworth found himself scribbling in his notebook the despairing question, 'Was it for this?' It

2 See *Home at Grasmere* ed. Beth Darlington (Ithaca, NY, 1977) and '*The Tuft of Primroses*', with Other Late Poems for '*The Recluse*' ed. Joseph Kishel (Ithaca, NY, 1986).

was not clear to him what he was writing, but he continued, and found himself writing a blank verse account of his life. This was the start of what was to become *The Prelude*. Over the next few months he completed Part I of *The Two-Part Prelude*; Part II was finished in late 1799, just as the Wordsworths, back in England, moved into Dove Cottage in Grasmere. He intended to write a third part, and attempted to do so in 1801. In early 1804 he returned to the poem and completely reorganized it, revising what he had written, and adding such passages as the description of the ascent of Snowdon, the Winander boy, and the infant prodigy, to produce the *Five-Book Prelude*.[3] He continued work on it throughout 1804–5, and completed a much larger work, in early 1806 – *The Thirteen-Book Prelude*. Instead of publishing it, he continued to revise and add to it on and off for the rest of his life, leaving it in manuscript in fourteen books at the time of his death in 1850. It was known only to Coleridge, Dorothy, De Quincey, and the poet's immediate circle; had it been read by Wordsworth's contemporaries, and the second-generation romantics, the course of literary history would have been very different indeed.

The Prelude was published posthumously in 1850, but had little appeal for Victorian readers. Its success has come in the last hundred years – and not surprisingly: Wordsworth's concentration on his psychological development – his education, his response to his father's death, the 'spots of time', his reaction to the French Revolution and its aftermath, his horrified fascination with London, his flirtation and disillusionment with Godwinism, and the supportive influence of his sister – contrive to make it distinctly appealing to the twentieth-century sensibility. Addressed to Coleridge, it describes the intellectual growth of the poet who aims one day to compose the great philosophical epic of *The Recluse*, and in so doing presents him as an exemplar of those redeemed by the intensity of imaginative vision (see especially *Thirteen-Book Prelude*, xiii. 166–84).

Today Wordsworth is regarded as one of the foremost of the romantics; during the early 1800s, however, his poetry was not widely known and often misunderstood – in particular, *The Thorn*, *We Are Seven* and *The Excursion* (see pp. 410–11) came in for vitriolic attack and ridicule. By the 1820s, he had acquired the eminence of a father-figure to second generation writers such as Keats, Byron and Shelley, who nonetheless saw him as having betrayed the radical leanings of earlier work (see *To Wordsworth*, p. 819, and the Dedication to *Don Juan*, pp. 752–5). By 1843, when he was appointed Poet Laureate, Wordsworth's reputation had grown tremendously; he had outlived all the other major romantic writers and was still composing and revising. In his final years he was awarded honorary degrees from Durham and Oxford and supervised the final lifetime edition of his poetry in 1849–50.

Further reading

Herbert Lindenberger, *On Wordsworth's Prelude* (Princeton, NJ, 1963)

Geoffrey Hartman, *Wordsworth's Poetry 1787–1814* (New Haven, 1964)

Mark L. Reed, *Wordsworth: the Chronology of the Early Years, 1770–1799* (Cambridge, Mass., 1967)

W. J. B. Owen, *Wordsworth as Critic* (Oxford, 1969)

Jonathan Wordsworth, *The Music of Humanity* (London and New York, 1969)

Richard Onorato, *The Character of the Poet: Wordsworth in The Prelude* (Princeton, NJ, 1971)

Stephen M. Parrish, *The Art of the Lyrical Ballads* (Cambridge, Mass., 1973)

Mark L. Reed, *Wordsworth: the Chronology of the Middle Years, 1800–1815* (Cambridge, Mass., 1975)

Mary Jacobus, *Tradition and Experiment in Lyrical Ballads, 1798* (Oxford, 1976)

Jonathan Wordsworth, *William Wordsworth: The Borders of Vision* (Oxford, 1982)

Kenneth R. Johnston, *Wordsworth and The Recluse* (New Haven, 1984)

Lucy Newlyn, *Coleridge, Wordsworth, and the Language of Allusion* (Oxford, 1986)

Nicholas Roe, *Wordsworth and Coleridge: The Radical Years* (Oxford, 1988)

Stephen Gill, *William Wordsworth: A Life* (Oxford, 1989)

Alan Liu, *Wordsworth: The Sense of History* (Stanford, 1989)

Wordsworth's complete poetical works are available in the Cornell Wordsworth Series under the general editorship of Stephen M. Parrish. *The Wordsworth Circle*, a quarterly journal edited by Marilyn Gaull, publishes articles on Wordsworth and his contemporaries.

---

[3]   See William Wordsworth, *The Five-Book Prelude* ed. Duncan Wu (Oxford, 1997).

A *Night-Piece* (composed by 25 January 1798; edited from MS)[1]

                        The sky is overspread
        With a close veil of one continuous cloud
        All whitened by the moon, that just appears
        A dim-seen orb, yet chequers not the ground
        With any shadow – plant, or tower, or tree.   5
        At last, a pleasant gleam breaks forth at once,
        An instantaneous light; the musing man
        Who walks along with his eyes bent to earth
        Is startled. He looks about, the clouds are split
        Asunder, and above his head he views   10
        The clear moon, and the glory of the heavens.
        There in a black-blue vault she sails along,
        Followed by multitudes of stars, that small,
        And bright, and sharp, along the gloomy vault
        Drive as she drives. How fast they wheel away,   15
        Yet vanish not! The wind is in the trees,
        But they are silent;[2] still they roll along
        Immeasurably distant, and the vault
        Built round by those white clouds, enormous clouds,
        Still deepens its interminable depth.   20
        At length the vision closes, and the mind,
        Not undisturbed by the deep joy it feels,
        Which slowly settles into peaceful calm,
        Is left to muse upon the solemn scene.

[*The Discharged Soldier*] (edited from MS; composed late January 1798)[1]

                            I love to walk
        Along the public way, when, for the night
        Deserted in its silence, it assumes
        A character of deeper quietness
        Than pathless solitudes. At such a time   5
        I slowly mounted up a steep ascent[2]
        Where the road's watery surface, to the ridge
        Of that sharp rising, glittered in the moon,

A NIGHT-PIECE
[1] This poem was, Wordsworth recalled many years after its composition, 'Composed upon the road between Nether Stowey and Alfoxden, extempore. I distinctly recollect the very moment I was struck, as described, "He looks up at the clouds, etc." ' (*FN* 13). Critics note that it reworks a number of images and expressions from a journal entry by Dorothy of 25 January 1798: 'The sky spread over with one continuous cloud, whitened by the light of the moon, which, though her dim shape was seen, did not throw forth so strong a light as to chequer the earth with shadows. At once the clouds seemed to cleave asunder, and left her in the centre of a black-blue vault. She sailed along, followed by multitudes of stars, small, and

bright, and sharp. Their brightness seemed concentrated (half-moon)' (*DWJ* i 2).
[2] *But they are silent* David Chandler suggests that this is a reply to the question posed by Mrs Barbauld in *A Summer Evening's Meditation*: 'But are they silent all? Or is there not / A tongue in every star that talks with man . . ?' (ll. 48–9)

THE DISCHARGED SOLDIER
[1] This poem was for a time regarded as constituting part of Wordsworth's never-completed epic poem, *The Recluse* (see p. 271), before being incorporated first into *Five-Book Prelude* iv 185–321, and then into *Thirteen-Book Prelude* iv 363–504.
[2] *a steep ascent* Briers Brow, above the ferry on the western shore of Windermere.

And seemed before my eyes another stream[3]
Stealing with silent lapse[4] to join the brook[5]   10
That murmured in the valley.
                                    On I passed
Tranquil, receiving in my own despite
Amusement as I slowly passed along,
From such near objects as from time to time
Perforce disturbed the slumber of the sense   15
Quiescent[6] and disposed to sympathy,
With an exhausted mind worn out by toil
And all unworthy of the deeper joy
Which waits on distant prospect – cliff or sea,
The dark blue vault, and universe of stars.   20
        Thus did I steal along that silent road,
My body from the stillness drinking in
A restoration like the calm of sleep,
But sweeter far. Above, before, behind,
Around me, all was peace and solitude: 25
I looked not round, nor did the solitude
Speak to my eye, but it was heard and felt.
Oh happy state, what beauteous pictures now
Rose in harmonious imagery! They rose
As from some distant region of my soul   30
And came along like dreams; yet such as left
Obscurely mingled with their passing forms
A consciousness of animal delight,
A self-possession felt in every pause
And every gentle movement of my frame.[7]   35
        While thus I wandered, step by step led on,
It chanced a sudden turning of the road
Presented to my view an uncouth shape,[8]
So near that, stepping back into the shade
Of a thick hawthorn, I could mark him well,   40
Myself unseen. He was in stature tall,
A foot above man's common measure tall,
And lank, and upright. There was in his form
A meagre stiffness. You might almost think
That his bones wounded him. His legs were long,   45
So long and shapeless that I looked at them
Forgetful of the body they sustained.
His arms were long and lean, his hands were bare;
His visage, wasted though it seemed, was large
In feature, his cheeks sunken, and his mouth   50
Showed ghastly[9] in the moonlight; from behind

---

[3]   *And seemed . . . stream* a few days before this line was com-
posed, 31 January 1798, Dorothy had written: 'The road to
the village of Holford glittered like another stream' (*DWJ* i
5).
[4]   *lapse* flow; cf. *Paradise Lost* viii 263: 'And liquid lapse of
murmuring streams'.
[5]   *brook* Sawrey Brook.
[6]   *Quiescent* at repose, inert.

[7]   *self-possession . . . frame* awareness of physical well-being dif-
fused through the body and its activity.
[8]   *an uncouth shape* perhaps a reminiscence of *Paradise Lost* ii
666, which describes Death: 'The other shape, / If shape it
might be called that shape had none'. Wordsworth would
have known Burke's comments on the lines (see p. 5, above).
[9]   *ghastly* ghostlike, pale.

A milestone propped him,[10] and his figure seemed
Half-sitting and half-standing. I could mark
That he was clad in military garb,
Though faded yet entire. His face was turned   55
Towards the road, yet not as if he sought
For any living object. He appeared
Forlorn and desolate, a man cut off
From all his kind, and more than half detached
From his own nature.
                 He was alone,   60
Had no attendant, neither dog, nor staff,
Nor knapsack; in his very dress appeared
A desolation, a simplicity
That appertained[11] to solitude. I think
If but a glove had dangled in his hand,   65
It would have made him more akin to man.
Long time I scanned him with a mingled sense
Of fear and sorrow. From his lips meanwhile
There issued murmuring sounds, as if of pain
Or of uneasy thought, yet still his form   70
Kept the same fearful steadiness. His shadow
Lay at his feet and moved not.
                 In a glen
Hard by, a village stood,[12] whose silent doors
Were visible among the scattered trees,
Scarce distant from the spot an arrow's flight.[13]   75
I wished to see him move, but he remained
Fixed to his place, and still from time to time
Sent forth a murmuring voice of dead[14] complaint,
A groan scarce audible. Yet all the while
The chained mastiff in his wooden house   80
Was vexed, and from among the village trees
Howled, never ceasing. Not without reproach
Had I prolonged my watch, and now, confirmed,
And my heart's specious cowardice[15] subdued,
I left the shady nook where I had stood   85
And hailed the stranger. From his resting-place
He rose, and with his lean and wasted arm
In measured gesture lifted to his head
Returned my salutation. A short while
I held discourse on things indifferent   90
And casual matter. He meanwhile had ceased
From all complaint, his station he resumed,
Propped by the milestone as before. And when, erelong,
I asked his history, he in reply
Was neither slow nor eager; but, unmoved,[16]   95
And with a quiet uncomplaining voice,

---

[10] *A milestone propped him* the third milestone from Hawkshead, just beyond Far Sawrey; the milestone has since disappeared from that spot.
[11] *appertained* belonged.
[12] *a village stood* Far Sawrey.

[13] *an arrow's flight* approximately 300 yards.
[14] *dead* muffled, deadened.
[15] *my heart's specious cowardice* he was motivated by fear rather than kindness.
[16] *unmoved* without emotion.

A stately air of mild indifference,
He told a simple fact – that he had been
A soldier, to the tropic isles[17] had gone,
Whence he had landed now some ten days past;   100
That on his landing he had been dismissed,
And with the little strength he yet had left
Was travelling to regain his native home.
At this I turned and through the trees looked down
Into the village. All were gone to rest,   105
Nor smoke nor any taper[18] light appeared,
But every silent window to the moon
Shone with a yellow glitter. 'No one there',
Said I, 'is waking; we must measure back
The way which we have come. Behind yon wood   110
A labourer dwells, an honest man and kind;
He will not murmur should we break his rest,
And he will give you food (if food you need)
And lodging for the night.' At this he stooped
And from the ground took up an oaken staff   115
By me yet unobserved – a traveller's staff
Which I suppose from his slack hand had dropped,
And, such the languor of the weary man,
Had lain till now neglected in the grass,
But not forgotten.
                    Back we turned and shaped   120
Our course toward the cottage. He appeared
To travel without pain, and I beheld
With ill-suppressed astonishment his tall
And ghostly figure moving at my side.
As we advanced I asked him for what cause   125
He tarried there, nor had demanded rest
At any inn or cottage. He replied,
'My weakness made me loath to move; in truth
I felt myself at ease, and much relieved,
But that the village mastiff fretted me,   130
And every second moment rang a peal
Felt at my very heart. I do not know
What ailed him, but it seemed as if the dog
Were howling to the murmur of the stream.'
            While thus we travelled on I did not fail   135
To question him of what he had endured
From war, and battle, and the pestilence.[19]
He all the while was in demeanour calm,
Concise in answer. Solemn and sublime
He might have seemed, but that in all he said   140
There was a strange half-absence, and a tone
Of weakness and indifference, as of one
Remembering the importance of his theme

---

[17]   *tropic isles* West Indies. An anachronism: Wordsworth has
in mind the campaigns against the French that occurred in the
mid 1790s, although the encounter took place during the
long vacation of 1788. Conditions were bad – 40,000 British

troops had died of yellow fever by 1796. Survivors were often
diseased, and had no alternative but to beg in the streets.
[18]   *taper* candle.
[19]   *the pestilence* yellow fever.

But feeling it no longer. We advanced
Slowly, and ere we to the wood were come,   145
Discourse had ceased. Together on we passed
In silence through the shades gloomy and dark;
Then, turning up along an open field,
We gained the cottage. At the door I knocked,
And called aloud, 'My friend, here is a man   150
By sickness overcome. Beneath your roof
This night let him find rest, and give him food –
The service if need be I will requite.'
Assured that now my comrade would repose
In comfort, I entreated that henceforth   155
He would not linger in the public ways
But at the door of cottage or of inn
Demand the succour which his state required,
And told him, feeble as he was, 'twere fit
He asked relief or alms. At this reproof,   160
With the same ghastly mildness in his look,
He said, 'My trust is in the God of Heaven,
And in the eye of him that passes me.'
    By this the labourer had unlocked the door,
And now my comrade touched his hat again   165
With his lean hand, and in a voice that seemed
To speak with a reviving interest
Till then unfelt, he thanked me; I returned
The blessing of the poor unhappy man,
And so we parted.   170

The Ruined Cottage (composed 1797–8; edited from MS)[1]

First Part

'Twas summer and the sun was mounted high;
Along the south the uplands feebly glared
Through a pale steam, and all the northern downs,
In clearer air ascending, showed far off
Their surfaces with shadows dappled o'er   5
Of deep embattled clouds.[2] Far as the sight
Could reach those many shadows lay in spots
Determined and unmoved, with steady beams
Of clear and pleasant sunshine interposed –
Pleasant to him who on the soft cool moss   10
Extends his careless limbs beside the root

THE RUINED COTTAGE

[1] In its brief original form, which does not survive, *The Ruined Cottage* was read to Coleridge on 5 June 1797. The form in which it appears here stems from work of February–March 1798, when it was lengthened, and given a more formal structure, by the addition of the opening section (ll. 1–54), the central transition (ll. 185–237), and the final lines of reconciliation (ll. 493–538). Wordsworth also added, with Coleridge's encouragement, a long philosophical account of the narrator's life, which, though important in its own right, had the effect of unbalancing the poem. Wordsworth therefore removed it, and until 1804 it was regarded as a separate work, *The Pedlar* (see pp. 289–98). *The Ruined Cottage* meanwhile was left as the compact and tightly constructed poem printed here. It was later revised with *The Pedlar* for *The Excursion* (1814), on which see Jeffrey's comments at pp. 556–8.

[2] *deep embattled clouds* an allusion to Charlotte Smith, *Sonnet LIX* 3–4: 'Sudden, from many a deep embattled cloud / Terrific thunders burst'.

Of some huge oak whose aged branches make
A twilight[3] of their own, a dewy shade
Where the wren warbles while the dreaming man,
Half-conscious of that soothing melody,   15
With sidelong eye looks out upon the scene,
By those impending branches made more soft,
More soft and distant.
                              Other lot was mine.
Across a bare wide common I had toiled
With languid feet which by the slippery ground   20
Were baffled still; and when I stretched myself
On the brown earth my limbs from very heat
Could find no rest, nor my weak arm disperse
The insect host which gathered round my face
And joined their murmurs to the tedious noise   25
Of seeds of bursting gorse that crackled round.
I rose and turned towards a group of trees
Which midway in that level stood alone;
And thither come at length, beneath a shade
Of clustering elms[4] that sprang from the same root   30
I found a ruined house, four naked walls[5]
That stared upon each other. I looked round,
And near the door I saw an aged man
Alone and stretched upon the cottage bench;
An iron-pointed staff lay at his side.   35
With instantaneous joy I recognized
That pride of nature and of lowly life,
The venerable Armytage, a friend
As dear to me as is the setting sun.[6]
                                     Two days before   40
We had been fellow-travellers. I knew
That he was in this neighbourhood, and now
Delighted found him here in the cool shade.
He lay, his pack of rustic merchandise
Pillowing his head. I guess he had no thought   45
Of his way-wandering life. His eyes were shut,
The shadows of the breezy elms above
Dappled his face. With thirsty heat oppressed
At length I hailed him, glad to see his hat
Bedewed with water-drops, as if the brim   50
Had newly scooped a running stream. He rose

---

3 *twilight* The 'twilight' in the midst of sunshine is highly
reminiscent of Milton's 'darkness visible', and looks back to
Virgil's 'ingenti ramorum protegat umbra' (*Georgics* ii 489).

4 *clustering elms* Elms tend to grow in clusters as groups of
them spring from a single root; they are now a rare sight in
England thanks to the ravages of Dutch Elm disease in the
1970s.

5 *four naked walls* The nakedness of the walls tends to
humanize them and emphasize their vulnerability; cf. *Two-
Part Prelude* i 343.

6 *a friend ... sun* In the original *Ruined Cottage* of summer
1797 the Pedlar had addressed the poet as 'stranger'. By Feb-
ruary 1798, he had become the mouthpiece for Wordsworth's
new philosophy of redemption, and the two protagonists had
been made old friends as a way of increasing the reader's confi-
dence. It should be noted that it was daring of Wordsworth to
make his narrator a Pedlar; when published in 1814 critics
like Francis Jeffrey disapproved of a lower-class character
being given such an exalted role in the poem: 'Did Mr
Wordsworth really imagine that his favourite doctrines were
likely to gain anything in point of effect or authority by being
put into the mouth of a person accustomed to higgle about
tape, or brass sleeve-buttons?' For Jeffrey's comments, see pp.
556–8.

And pointing to a sunflower, bade me climb
The [   ]⁷ wall where that same gaudy flower
Looked out upon the road.
     It was a plot
Of garden-ground now wild, its matted weeds   55
Marked with the steps of those whom as they passed,
The gooseberry-trees that shot in long lank slips,
Or currants hanging from their leafless stems
In scanty strings, had tempted to o'erleap
The broken wall. Within that cheerless spot,   60
Where two tall hedgerows of thick willow boughs
Joined in a damp cold nook, I found a well
Half covered up with willow-flowers and weeds.
I slaked my thirst and to the shady bench
Returned, and while I stood unbonneted⁸   65
To catch the motion of the cooler air
The old man said, 'I see around me here
Things which you cannot see. We die, my friend,
Nor we alone, but that which each man loved
And prized in his peculiar nook of earth   70
Dies with him, or is changed, and very soon
Even of the good is no memorial left.
The poets, in their elegies and songs
Lamenting the departed, call the groves,
They call upon the hills and streams to mourn,   75
And senseless rocks – nor idly, for they speak
In these their invocations with a voice
Obedient to the strong creative power
Of human passion. Sympathies there are
More tranquil, yet perhaps of kindred birth,   80
That steal upon the meditative mind
And grow with thought. Beside yon spring I stood,
And eyed its waters till we seemed to feel
One sadness, they and I. For them a bond
Of brotherhood is broken: time has been   85
When every day the touch of human hand
Disturbed their stillness, and they ministered
To human comfort. When I stooped to drink
A spider's web hung to the water's edge,
And on the wet and slimy footstone lay   90
The useless fragment of a wooden bowl;⁹
It moved my very heart.
       The day has been
When I could never pass this road but she
Who lived within these walls, when I appeared,
A daughter's welcome gave me, and I loved her   95
As my own child. Oh sir! The good die first,
And they whose hearts are dry as summer dust

---

⁷ There is a gap in the MS at this point.
⁸ *unbonneted* without his hat.
⁹ *The useless . . . bowl* cf. the final chapter of Ecclesiastes, 'Remember now thy Creator in the days of thy youth . . . Or ever the silver cord be loosed, or the golden bowl be broken, or the pitcher be broken at the fountain, or the wheel broken at the cistern. Then shall the dust return to the earth as it was: and the spirit shall return unto God who gave it.'

Burn to the socket.[10] Many a passenger[11]
Has blessed poor Margaret for her gentle looks
When she upheld the cool refreshment drawn   100
From that forsaken spring, and no one came
But he was welcome, no one went away
But that it seemed she loved him. She is dead,
The worm is on her cheek,[12] and this poor hut,
Stripped of its outward garb of household flowers,   105
Of rose and sweetbriar, offers to the wind
A cold bare wall whose earthy top is tricked[13]
With weeds and the rank speargrass. She is dead,
And nettles rot and adders sun themselves
Where we have sat together while she nursed   110
Her infant at her breast. The unshod colt,
The wandering heifer and the potter's ass,
Find shelter now within the chimney-wall
Where I have seen her evening hearthstone blaze
And through the window spread upon the road   115
Its cheerful light. You will forgive me, sir,
But often on this cottage do I muse
As on a picture, till my wiser mind
Sinks, yielding to the foolishness of grief.

     She had a husband, an industrious man,   120
Sober and steady. I have heard her say
That he was up and busy at his loom
In summer ere the mower's scythe had swept
The dewy grass, and in the early spring
Ere the last star had vanished. They who passed   125
At evening, from behind the garden-fence
Might hear his busy spade, which he would ply
After his daily work till the daylight
Was gone, and every leaf and flower were lost
In the dark hedges. So they passed their days   130
In peace and comfort, and two pretty babes
Were their best hope next to the God in heaven.
You may remember, now some ten years gone,
Two blighting seasons when the fields were left
With half a harvest. It pleased heaven to add   135
A worse affliction in the plague of war;[14]
A happy land was stricken to the heart –
'Twas a sad time of sorrow and distress.
A wanderer among the cottages,
I with my pack of winter raiment[15] saw   140
The hardships of that season. Many rich
Sunk down as in a dream among the poor,
And of the poor did many cease to be,

---

[10] *Burn to the socket* The image is of a candle burning down
to its socket in a candlestick-holder; for a possible source see
my *Wordsworth's Reading 1770–1799* (1993), p. 152.
[11] *passenger* passer-by.
[12] *The worm is on her cheek* cf. Viola, in *Twelfth Night* II iv
110–12: 'she never told her love, / But let concealment, like a
worm in the bud, / Feed on her damask cheek'.

[13] *tricked* decked.
[14] *war* England had been at war with France for five years as
Wordsworth was writing in 1798; it should be borne in mind,
however, that the poem itself is set during the aftermath of
the American War, which ended in 1783.
[15] *winter raiment* warm clothes to sell to cottagers.

And their place knew them not. Meanwhile, abridged
Of daily comforts, gladly reconciled   145
To numerous self-denials, Margaret
Went struggling on through those calamitous years
With cheerful hope. But ere the second autumn,
A fever seized her husband. In disease
He lingered long, and when his strength returned   150
He found the little he had stored to meet
The hour of accident, or crippling age,
Was all consumed. As I have said, 'twas now
A time of trouble: shoals of artisans[16]
Were from their daily labour turned away   155
To hang for bread on parish charity,[17]
They and their wives and children – happier far
Could they have lived as do the little birds
That peck along the hedges, or the kite[18]
That makes her dwelling in the mountain rocks.   160
Ill fared it now with Robert, he who dwelt
In this poor cottage. At his door he stood
And whistled many a snatch of merry tunes
That had no mirth in them, or with his knife
Carved uncouth[19] figures on the heads of sticks;   165
Then idly sought about through every nook
Of house or garden any casual task
Of use or ornament, and with a strange,
Amusing but uneasy novelty
He blended where he might the various tasks   170
Of summer, autumn, winter, and of spring.
But this endured not; his good humour soon
Became a weight in which no pleasure was,
And poverty brought on a petted[20] mood
And a sore temper. Day by day he drooped,[21]   175
And he would leave his home, and to the town
Without an errand would he turn his steps,
Or wander here and there among the fields.
One while he would speak lightly of his babes
And with a cruel tongue; at other times   180
He played with them wild freaks of merriment,
And 'twas a piteous thing to see the looks
Of the poor innocent children. "Every smile",
Said Margaret to me here beneath these trees,
"Made my heart bleed." '

                            At this the old man paused,   185
And looking up to those enormous elms
He said, ''Tis now the hour of deepest noon.
At this still season of repose and peace,
This hour when all things which are not at rest
Are cheerful, while this multitude of flies   190

---

[16] *shoals of artisans* crowds of workmen.
[17] *parish charity* Until the early part of the century, the poor were the responsibility of their local parish, which received no government funding to help them.
[18] *kite* large hawk.
[19] *uncouth* grotesque, ugly.
[20] *petted* peevish.
[21] *he drooped* an echo of Milton, *Samson Agonistes* 594: 'So much I feel my genial spirits droop'.

Fills all the air with happy melody,
Why should a tear be in an old man's eye?
Why should we thus with an untoward[22] mind,
And in the weakness of humanity,
From natural wisdom turn our hearts away,   195
To natural comfort shut our eyes and ears,
And feeding on disquiet, thus disturb
The calm of Nature with our restless thoughts?'

Second Part

He spake with somewhat of a solemn tone,
But when he ended there was in his face   200
Such easy cheerfulness, a look so mild,
That for a little time it stole away
All recollection, and that simple tale
Passed from my mind like a forgotten sound.
A while on trivial things we held discourse,   205
To me soon tasteless.[23] In my own despite
I thought of that poor woman as of one
Whom I had known and loved. He had rehearsed
Her homely tale with such familiar power,
With such an active countenance, an eye   210
So busy, that the things of which he spake
Seemed present, and, attention now relaxed,
There was a heartfelt chillness in my veins.
I rose, and turning from that breezy shade
Went out into the open air, and stood   215
To drink the comfort of the warmer sun.
Long time I had not stayed ere, looking round
Upon that tranquil ruin, I returned
And begged of the old man that for my sake
He would resume his story.
                            He replied,   220
'It were a wantonness,[24] and would demand
Severe reproof, if we were men whose hearts
Could hold vain dalliance with[25] the misery
Even of the dead, contented thence to draw
A momentary pleasure, never marked   225
By reason, barren of all future good.
But we have known that there is often found
In mournful thoughts, and always might be found,
A power to virtue friendly; were't not so
I am a dreamer among men, indeed   230
An idle dreamer. 'Tis a common tale
By moving accidents uncharactered,
A tale of silent suffering, hardly clothed
In bodily form, and to the grosser sense
But ill adapted – scarcely palpable   235
To him who does not think. But at your bidding

---

22   *untoward* stubborn, perverse.
23   *tasteless* without taste, insipid.
24   *wantonness* self-indulgence.
25   *hold vain dalliance with* draw entertainment from.

I will proceed.
                    While thus it fared with them
To whom this cottage till that hapless year
Had been a blessed home, it was my chance
To travel in a country far remote;   240
And glad I was when, halting by yon gate
That leads from the green lane, again I saw
These lofty elm-trees. Long I did not rest –
With many pleasant thoughts I cheered my way
O'er the flat common. At the door arrived,   245
I knocked, and when I entered, with the hope
Of usual greeting, Margaret looked at me
A little while, then turned her head away
Speechless, and sitting down upon a chair
Wept bitterly. I wist[26] not what to do,   250
Or how to speak to her. Poor wretch! At last
She rose from off her seat – and then, oh sir!
I cannot tell how she pronounced my name:
With fervent love, and with a face of grief
Unutterably helpless, and a look   255
That seemed to cling upon me, she enquired
If I had seen her husband. As she spake
A strange surprise and fear came to my heart,
Nor had I power to answer ere she told
That he had disappeared – just two months gone.   260
He left his house: two wretched days had passed,
And on the third by the first break of light,
Within her casement[27] full in view she saw
A purse of gold.[28] "I trembled at the sight",
Said Margaret, "for I knew it was his hand   265
That placed it there. And on that very day
By one, a stranger, from my husband sent,
The tidings came that he had joined a troop
Of soldiers going to a distant land.[29]
He left me thus. Poor man, he had not heart   270
To take a farewell of me, and he feared
That I should follow with my babes, and sink
Beneath the misery of a soldier's life."
      This tale did Margaret tell with many tears,
And when she ended I had little power   275
To give her comfort, and was glad to take
Such words of hope from her own mouth as served
To cheer us both. But long we had not talked
Ere we built up a pile of better thoughts,
And with a brighter eye she looked around   280
As if she had been shedding tears of joy.
We parted. It was then the early spring;
I left her busy with her garden tools,
And well remember, o'er that fence she looked,

---

26 *wist* knew.
27 *casement* window.
28 *A purse of gold* a 'bounty' of three guineas was paid to men
when they enlisted – a strong incentive for those with starving families to enlist.
29 *a distant land* America.

And, while I paced along the footway path,   285
Called out and sent a blessing after me,
With tender cheerfulness, and with a voice
That seemed the very sound of happy thoughts.
    I roved o'er many a hill and many a dale
With this my weary load, in heat and cold,   290
Through many a wood and many an open ground,
In sunshine or in shade, in wet or fair,
Now blithe, now drooping, as it might befall;
My best companions now the driving winds
And now the "trotting brooks"[30] and whispering trees,   295
And now the music of my own sad steps,
With many a short-lived thought that passed between
And disappeared. I came this way again
Towards the wane of summer, when the wheat
Was yellow, and the soft and bladed grass   300
Sprang up afresh and o'er the hayfield spread
Its tender green. When I had reached the door
I found that she was absent. In the shade
Where we now sit, I waited her return.
Her cottage in its outward look appeared   305
As cheerful as before, in any show
Of neatness little changed – but that I thought
The honeysuckle crowded round the door
And from the wall hung down in heavier wreaths,
And knots of worthless stonecrop started out   310
Along the window's edge, and grew like weeds
Against the lower panes. I turned aside
And strolled into her garden. It was changed.
The unprofitable bindweed spread his bells
From side to side, and with unwieldy wreaths   315
Had dragged the rose from its sustaining wall
And bent it down to earth.[31] The border tufts,
Daisy, and thrift, and lowly camomile,
And thyme, had straggled out into the paths
Which they were used to deck.
                        Ere this an hour   320
Was wasted. Back I turned my restless steps,
And as I walked before the door it chanced
A stranger passed, and guessing whom I sought,
He said that she was used to ramble far.
The sun was sinking in the west, and now   325
I sat with sad impatience. From within
Her solitary infant cried aloud.
The spot though fair seemed very desolate,
The longer I remained more desolate;
And looking round I saw the corner-stones,   330
Till then unmarked, on either side the door
With dull red stains discoloured, and stuck o'er

---

[30]   *trotting brooks* an allusion to Burns's *To William Simpson*, about the poet and his relationship to nature:
   The Muse, nae poet ever fand her,
   Till by himsel he learned to wander
   Adown some trottin burn's meander . . . (ll. 85–7)

[31]   *the rose . . . earth* a symbol of Margaret herself, without the support of her husband.

With tufts and hairs of wool, as if the sheep
That feed upon the commons thither came
Familiarly, and found a couching-place   335
Even at her threshold.
             The house-clock struck eight:
I turned and saw her distant a few steps.
Her face was pale and thin, her figure too
Was changed. As she unlocked the door she said,
"It grieves me you have waited here so long,   340
But in good truth I've wandered much of late,
And sometimes – to my shame I speak – have need
Of my best prayers to bring me back again."
While on the board[32] she spread our evening meal
She told me she had lost her elder child,   345
That he for months had been a serving-boy,
Apprenticed by the parish.[33] "I perceive
You look at me, and you have cause. Today
I have been travelling far, and many days
About the fields I wander, knowing this   350
Only, that what I seek I cannot find.
And so I waste my time: for I am changed,
And to myself", said she, "have done much wrong,
And to this helpless infant. I have slept
Weeping, and weeping I have waked. My tears   355
Have flowed as if my body were not such
As others are, and I could never die.
But I am now in mind and in my heart
More easy, and I hope", said she, "that Heaven
Will give me patience to endure the things   360
Which I behold at home."
             It would have grieved
Your very soul to see her. Sir, I feel
The story linger in my heart. I fear
'Tis long and tedious, but my spirit clings
To that poor woman. So familiarly   365
Do I perceive her manner and her look
And presence, and so deeply do I feel
Her goodness, that not seldom in my walks
A momentary trance comes over me
And to myself I seem to muse on one   370
By sorrow laid asleep or borne away,
A human being destined to awake
To human life, or something very near
To human life, when he shall come again
For whom she suffered. Sir, it would have grieved   375
Your very soul to see her: evermore
Her eyelids drooped, her eyes were downward cast,
And when she at her table gave me food
She did not look at me. Her voice was low,
Her body was subdued. In every act   380

---

[32] *board* table.
[33] *Apprenticed by the parish* Margaret has allowed her son to
become an apprentice, largely because she would no longer be
responsible for clothing and feeding him.

Pertaining to her house-affairs appeared
The careless stillness which a thinking mind
Gives to an idle matter. Still she sighed,
But yet no motion of the breast was seen,
No heaving of the heart. While by the fire   385
We sat together, sighs came on my ear –
I knew not how, and hardly whence, they came.
I took my staff, and when I kissed her babe
The tears stood in her eyes. I left her then
With the best hope and comfort I could give: 390
She thanked me for my will, but for my hope
It seemed she did not thank me.
                                    I returned
And took my rounds along this road again
Ere on its sunny bank the primrose flower
Had chronicled the earliest day of spring.   395
I found her sad and drooping. She had learned
No tidings of her husband. If he lived,
She knew not that he lived: if he were dead,
She knew not he was dead. She seemed the same
In person or appearance, but her house   400
Bespoke a sleepy hand of negligence.
The floor was neither dry nor neat, the hearth
Was comfortless,[34]
The windows too were dim, and her few books,[35]
Which one upon the other heretofore   405
Had been piled up against the corner-panes
In seemly order, now with straggling leaves
Lay scattered here and there, open or shut,
As they had chanced to fall. Her infant babe
Had from its mother caught the trick[36] of grief,   410
And sighed among its playthings. Once again
I turned towards the garden-gate, and saw
More plainly still that poverty and grief
Were now come nearer to her. The earth was hard,
With weeds defaced and knots of withered grass;   415
No ridges there appeared of clear black mould,[37]
No winter greenness. Of her herbs and flowers
It seemed the better part were gnawed away
Or trampled on the earth. A chain of straw,
Which had been twisted round the tender stem   420
Of a young apple-tree, lay at its root;
The bark was nibbled round by truant sheep.
Margaret stood near, her infant in her arms,
And, seeing that my eye was on the tree,
She said, "I fear it will be dead and gone   425
Ere Robert come again."
                        Towards the house
Together we returned, and she enquired

---

34 Line defective in the MS.
35 *her few books* Margaret, like Michael and his wife (see
Michael l. 445, p. 355), is literate. This was not usual. In 1795
sixty per cent of the female population was unable to read or
write.

36 *trick* habit.
37 *mould* earth.

If I had any hope. But for her babe,
And for her little friendless boy, she said,
She had no wish to live – that she must die   430
Of sorrow. Yet I saw the idle loom
Still in its place. His Sunday garments hung
Upon the self-same nail, his very staff
Stood undisturbed behind the door. And when
I passed this way beaten by autumn winds,   435
She told me that her little babe was dead
And she was left alone. That very time,
I yet remember, through the miry lane
She walked with me a mile, when the bare trees
Trickled with foggy damps, and in such sort   440
That any heart had ached to hear her, begged
That wheresoe'er I went I still would ask
For him whom she had lost. We parted then,
Our final parting; for from that time forth
Did many seasons pass ere I returned   445
Into this tract[38] again.
           Five tedious years[39]
She lingered in unquiet widowhood,
A wife and widow. Needs must it have been
A sore heart-wasting. I have heard, my friend,
That in that broken arbour she would sit   450
The idle length of half a sabbath day –
There, where you see the toadstool's lazy head –
And when a dog passed by she still would quit
The shade and look abroad. On this old bench
For hours she sat, and evermore her eye   455
Was busy in the distance, shaping things
Which made her heart beat quick. Seest thou that path? –
The greensward now has broken its grey line –
There to and fro she paced through many a day
Of the warm summer, from a belt of flax   460
That girt her waist, spinning the long-drawn thread
With backward steps.[40] Yet ever as there passed
A man whose garments showed the soldier's red,[41]
Or crippled mendicant[42] in sailor's garb,
The little child who sat to turn the wheel   465
Ceased from his toil, and she, with faltering voice,
Expecting still[43] to learn her husband's fate,
Made many a fond enquiry; and when they
Whose presence gave no comfort were gone by,
Her heart was still more sad. And by yon gate   470
Which bars the traveller's road, she often stood,
And when a stranger horseman came, the latch
Would lift, and in his face look wistfully,

---

[38] *tract* district.
[39] *Five tedious years* Ll. 446–92 were the first to be written. They were inspired by Southey's account of a war widow in *Joan of Arc* (1797), Book VII, who is described as 'tortured with vain hope' for her absent husband.

[40] *from a belt . . . steps* Robert had been a weaver, and Margaret supports herself in her last years by spinning flax.
[41] *the soldier's red* the British army wore red uniforms, making them easy targets on the battlefield.
[42] *mendicant* beggar.
[43] *still* always.

Most happy if from aught discovered there
Of tender feeling she might dare repeat   475
The same sad question.
                         Meanwhile her poor hut
Sunk to decay; for he was gone, whose hand
At the first nippings of October frost
Closed up each chink, and with fresh bands of straw
Chequered the green-grown thatch. And so she lived   480
Through the long winter, reckless[44] and alone,
Till this reft[45] house, by frost, and thaw, and rain,
Was sapped; and when she slept, the nightly damps
Did chill her breast, and in the stormy day
Her tattered clothes[46] were ruffled by the wind   485
Even at the side of her own fire. Yet still
She loved this wretched spot, nor would for worlds
Have parted hence; and still that length of road,
And this rude bench, one torturing hope endeared,
Fast rooted at her heart. And here, my friend,   490
In sickness she remained; and here she died,
Last human tenant of these ruined walls.'[47]

     The old man ceased; he saw that I was moved.
From that low bench, rising instinctively,
I turned aside in weakness, nor had power   495
To thank him for the tale which he had told.
I stood, and leaning o'er the garden gate
Reviewed that woman's sufferings; and it seemed
To comfort me while with a brother's love
I blessed her in the impotence of grief.   500
At length towards the cottage I returned
Fondly, and traced with milder interest
That secret spirit of humanity
Which, mid the calm oblivious[48] tendencies
Of Nature, mid her plants, her weeds and flowers,   505
And silent overgrowings, still survived.
The old man, seeing this, resumed, and said,
'My friend, enough to sorrow have you given,
The purposes of wisdom ask no more:
Be wise and cheerful, and no longer read   510
The forms of things with an unworthy eye:
She sleeps in the calm earth, and peace is here.
I well remember that those very plumes,
Those weeds, and the high speargrass on that wall,
By mist and silent raindrops silvered o'er,   515
As once I passed did to my mind convey
So still an image of tranquillity,
So calm and still, and looked so beautiful
Amid the uneasy thoughts which filled my mind,
That what we feel of sorrow and despair   520
From ruin and from change, and all the grief

---

[44] *reckless* not caring (i.e. for herself).
[45] *reft* bereft (i.e. without Robert).
[46] *Her tattered clothes* a detail picked up from Cowper's *Crazy Kate* (see p. 9).

[47] The poem originally ended at this point. All that follows was composed in spring 1798.
[48] *oblivious* Nature carries on oblivious to human affairs.

The passing shows of being leave behind,
Appeared an idle dream that could not live
Where meditation was. I turned away,
And walked along my road in happiness.'[49]   525
　　　He ceased. By this the sun declining shot
A slant and mellow radiance, which began
To fall upon us where beneath the trees
We sat on that low bench. And now we felt,
Admonished thus, the sweet hour coming on: 530
A linnet warbled from those lofty elms,
A thrush sang loud, and other melodies
At distance heard peopled the milder air.
The old man rose and hoisted up his load;
Together casting then a farewell look   535
Upon those silent walls, we left the shade,
And ere the stars were visible attained
A rustic inn, our evening resting-place.

The Pedlar (composed February–March 1798, edited from MS)[1]

Him had I seen the day before, alone
And in the middle of the public way,
Standing to rest himself. His eyes were turned
Towards the setting sun, while, with that staff
Behind him fixed, he propped a long white pack   5
Which crossed his shoulders, wares for maids who live
In lonely villages or straggling huts.[2]
I knew him[3] – he was born of lowly race
On Cumbrian hills, and I have seen the tear
Stand in his luminous[4] eye when he described   10
The house in which his early youth was passed,

---

49 *happiness* an astonishing ending, all things considered. The philosophy of consolation and, ultimately, redemption, that underlies this work asks that we regard injustice and suffering as an 'idle dream', mere shadows of a higher, and brighter, reality to come. A principle influence is Bishop Berkeley, whose ideas Wordsworth knew through Coleridge's *Religious Musings*:

　　　　Believe thou, oh my soul,
　　Life is a vision shadowy of truth,
　　And vice, and anguish, and the wormy grave,
　　Shapes of a dream. The veiling clouds retire,
　　And lo! – the throne of the redeeming God . . . (ll. 413–19)

Unlike Coleridge (and many others at this period), Wordsworth did not expect a Christian apocalypse, but the Pedlar's meditation does nevertheless ask us to see Margaret's life, and death, in terms of universal harmony.

THE PEDLAR
1 *The Pedlar* begins abruptly because it was composed originally for insertion into *The Ruined Cottage*, as background on the narrator who tells the story of Margaret. It is Wordsworth's earliest piece of autobiographical and philosophical poetry, and can be regarded as a dry run for both *The*

Recluse and *The Prelude* (though Wordsworth had no idea, as he composed this poem, that he would soon be writing an autobiographical poem; see *Two-Part Prelude* headnote, below). He decided within the year that these verses were too long for incorporation into *The Ruined Cottage* and by October 1800 had turned them into an independent work entitled *The Pedlar*. For a time it was planned to publish the poem with *Christabel*, and it was revised in 1801–2 with this in mind. However, it remained unpublished (as did *Christabel*) when, in spring 1804, Wordsworth planned *The Excursion*, in which the Pedlar, renamed the Wanderer, was a central character. *The Pedlar* and *The Ruined Cottage* were once again brought together and revised as a single entity for *The Excursion*, published in 1814, and given a damning review by Francis Jeffrey (see pp. 556–8). *The Pedlar* remained in manuscript in this early form until 1969.
2 *huts* cottages.
3 *I knew him* 'At Hawkshead also, while I was a schoolboy, there occasionally resided a packman . . . with whom I had frequent conversations upon what had befallen him, and what he had observed during his wandering life, and, as was natural, we took much to each other' (*FN* 79).
4 *luminous* shining.

And found I was no stranger to the spot.
I loved to hear him talk of former days
And tell how when a child, ere[5] yet of age
To be a shepherd, he had learned to read   15
His bible in a school that stood alone,
Sole building on a mountain's dreary edge,
Far from the sight of city spire, or sound
Of minster clock. From that bleak tenement[6]
He many an evening to his distant home   20
In solitude returning saw the hills
Grow larger in the darkness, all alone
Beheld the stars come out above his head,
And travelled through the wood, no comrade near
To whom he might confess the things he saw.   25
    So the foundations of his mind were laid.
In such communion, not from terror free,[7]
While yet a child, and long before his time,
He had perceived the presence and the power
Of greatness, and deep feelings had impressed   30
Great objects on his mind with portraiture
And colour so distinct that on his mind
They lay like substances, and almost seemed
To haunt the bodily sense.[8] He had received
A precious gift, for as he grew in years   35
With these impressions would he still compare
All his ideal stores, his shapes and forms,
And, being still unsatisfied with aught
Of dimmer character, he thence attained
An *active* power to fasten images   40
Upon his brain, and on their pictured lines
Intensely brooded, even[9] till they acquired
The liveliness of dreams.[10] Nor did he fail,
While yet a child, with a child's eagerness
Incessantly to turn his ear and eye   45
On all things which the rolling seasons brought
To feed such appetite. Nor this alone
Appeased his yearning – in the after-day[11]
Of boyhood, many an hour in caves forlorn
And in the hollow depths of naked crags   50
He sate, and even in their fixed lineaments,
Or[12] from the power of a peculiar eye,[13]
Or by creative feeling[14] overborne,

---

5 *ere* before.
6 *tenement* building.
7 *not from terror free* Burke had celebrated the importance
of fear in aesthetic terms in his *Sublime and Beautiful* (1757)
(see p. 5). For Wordsworth, fear is important as it stimulates
and intensifies imaginative thought; cf. *Two-Part Prelude* i
67–80.
8 *deep feelings ... sense* sublime natural forms are literally
stamped ('impressed') on the child's mind as mental 'images',
thanks partly to strong feelings (of fear, pain, pleasure) that he
experienced in their presence.
9 *even* to be scanned as a single syllable, 'e'en'.

10 *he thence ... dreams* recollections of landscape are valued
because they can be compared with the imaginary ('ideal')
scenes that the child creates and stores in his head. The
process by which the mind thinks about remembered land-
scapes ('Intensely brooded'), giving them more and more
vividness, was especially important, and underlies the great
pantheist claims of *Tintern Abbey* 23–50, and much of the
poetry in the *Two-Part Prelude*.
11 *after-day* later time.
12 *Or* either.
13 *the power of a peculiar eye* especially sharp observation.
14 *creative feeling* imaginative sympathy.

Or by predominance of thought[15] oppressed,
Even in their fixed and steady lineaments   55
He traced an ebbing and a flowing mind,
Expression ever varying.[16]
                Thus informed,
He had small need of books; for many a tale
Traditionary round the mountains hung,[17]
And many a legend peopling the dark woods   60
Nourished imagination in her growth,
And gave the mind that apprehensive power
By which she is made quick to recognize
The moral properties[18] and scope of things.
But greedily he read and read again   65
Whate'er the rustic vicar's shelf supplied:
The life and death of martyrs who sustained
Intolerable pangs,[19] and here and there
A straggling volume, torn and incomplete,
Which left half-told the preternatural tale,   70
Romance of giants, chronicle of fiends,
Profuse in garniture of wooden cuts[20]
Strange and uncouth, dire faces, figures dire,
Sharp-kneed, sharp-elbowed, and lean-ankled too,
With long and ghostly shanks, forms which once seen   75
Could never be forgotten[21] – things though low,
Though low and humble, not to be despised
By such as have observed the curious links
With which the perishable hours of life
Are bound together, and the world of thought   80
Exists and is sustained.[22] Within his heart
Love was not yet, nor the pure joy of love,[23]
By sound diffused, or by the breathing air,
Or by the silent looks of happy things,
Or flowing from the universal face –   85
Of earth and sky. But he had felt the power
Of Nature, and already was prepared
By his intense conceptions to receive
Deeply the lesson deep of love, which he
Whom Nature, by whatever means, has taught   90

---

[15] *predominance of thought* dominance of thought over other kinds of response.

[16] *Even in ... varying* even in the solid and unmoveable rocks, the Pedlar perceived the ebb and flow of a pantheistic life-force.

[17] *for many a tale ... hung* legends and folklore nourish the imagination as well as fear. Wordsworth presumably has in mind the kind of story that inspired *The Brothers* (see p. 332 n.1).

[18] *moral properties* it was important to Wordsworth and Coleridge that a natural education be not merely creative, but provide the individual with an understanding ('apprehensive power') of the relationships between people, and enable him to see his relationship to the world around him.

[19] *The life and death ... pangs* Wordsworth read Foxe's *Book of Martyrs* as a schoolboy at Hawkshead.

[20] *Profuse in garniture of wooden cuts* with many woodcut illustrations.

[21] *the preternatural tale ... forgotten* Coleridge and Wordsworth believed that children should read fairy tales, as they did when young; see Coleridge's letter to Poole, p. 460.

[22] *the curious links ... sustained* a reference to the associationist philosophy of David Hartley, which informs much of Wordsworth's thinking at this moment. The 'links' that connect the 'perishable hours of life' are emotions (arising, in this case, out of the romances of giants and chronicles of fiends) that confirm the underlying unity and order of the imaginative mind.

[23] *Within his heart ... love* Although he can see it in the rocks (ll. 56–7) the boy cannot yet feel within himself the pantheist life-force ('love').

To feel intensely, cannot but receive.
    Ere his ninth year he had been sent abroad[24]
To tend his father's sheep; such was his task
Henceforward till the later day of youth.
Oh then, what soul was his, when on the tops   95
Of the high mountains he beheld the sun
Rise up and bathe the world in light! He looked,
The ocean and the earth beneath him lay
In gladness and deep joy. The clouds were touched,
And in their silent faces he did read   100
Unutterable love. Sound needed none,
Nor any voice of joy: his spirit drank
The spectacle. Sensation, soul, and form,
All melted into him; they swallowed up
His animal being. In them did he live,   105
And by them did he live – they were his life.[25]
In such access of mind,[26] in such high hour
Of visitation from the living God,[27]
He did not feel the God, he felt his works.
Thought was not; in enjoyment it expired.   110
Such hour by prayer or praise was unprofaned;
He neither prayed, nor offered thanks or praise;
His mind was a thanksgiving to the power
That made him. It was blessedness and love.
    A shepherd on the lonely mountain-tops,   115
Such intercourse[28] was his, and in this sort
Was his existence oftentimes possessed.
Oh *then* how beautiful, how bright, appeared
The written promise.[29] He had early learned
To reverence the volume which displays   120
The mystery, the life which cannot die,
But in the mountains did he FEEL his faith,
There did he see the writing. All things there
Breathed immortality, revolving life,
And greatness still revolving, infinite.   125
There littleness was not, the least of things
Seemed infinite, and there his spirit shaped
Her prospects – nor did he *believe;* he saw.
What wonder if his being thus became
Sublime and comprehensive?[30] Low desires,   130
Low thoughts, had there no place; yet was his heart
Lowly, for he was meek in gratitude
Oft as he called to mind those ecstacies,
And whence they flowed; and from them he acquired

---

[24] *abroad* out.
[25] *The clouds ... life* Wordsworth draws on Coleridge's *Reflections on Having left a Place of Retirement* 26–42 (see pp. 453–4), in which the poet enjoys a similar pantheistic experience atop a hill.
[26] *access of mind* the boy is incorporated into the larger consciousness of 'the living God'. 'Mind' in this case probably means 'spirit'.
[27] *in such high hour ... God* cf. Charles Lloyd's *London* 82,

which celebrates the visionary who 'holds high converse with the present God' (p. 592).
[28] *intercourse* communion.
[29] *The written promise* this phrase, and the reference to 'the writing' at l. 123, show that Wordsworth is recalling Bishop Berkeley's theory that the natural world is the symbolic language of God's thought. In the same month as *The Pedlar* Coleridge composed *Frost at Midnight* 63–7 (see p. 464).
[30] *Sublime and comprehensive* noble, lofty, or well-balanced.

Wisdom which works through patience – thence he learned 135
In many a calmer hour of sober thought
To look on Nature with an humble heart,
Self-questioned where it did not understand,
And with a superstitious[31] eye of love.
    Thus passed the time, yet to the neighbouring town 140
He often went with what small overplus
His earnings might supply, and brought away
The book which most had tempted his desires
While at the stall he read. Among the hills
He gazed upon that mighty orb[32] of song, 145
The divine Milton.[33] Lore of different kind,
The annual savings of a toilsome life,
The schoolmaster supplied – books that explain
The purer elements of truth involved
In lines and numbers, and by charm severe, 150
Especially perceived where Nature droops
And feeling is suppressed, preserve the mind
Busy in solitude and poverty.[34]
And thus employed he many a time o'erlooked[35]
The listless hours when in the hollow vale, 155
Hollow and green, he lay on the green turf
In lonesome idleness. What could he do?
Nature was at his heart, and he perceived,
Though yet he knew not how, a wasting[36] power
In all things which from her sweet influence 160
Might tend to wean[37] him. Therefore with her hues,
Her forms, and with the spirit of her forms,
He clothed the nakedness of austere truth.[38]
While yet he lingered in the elements
Of science, and among her simplest laws, 165
His triangles they were the stars of heaven,
The silent stars; his altitudes[39] the crag
Which is the eagle's birthplace, or some peak
Familiar with forgotten years which shows
Inscribed, as with the silence of the thought, 170
Upon its bleak and visionary[40] sides
The history of many a winter storm,
Or obscure records of the path of fire.[41]
Yet with these lonesome sciences he still
Continued to amuse the heavier hours 175
Of solitude. Yet not the less he found

---

31   *superstitious* conscientious.
32   *orb* world.
33   *Milton* a favourite poet with young Wordsworth.
34   *books . . . poverty* mathematics is here regarded as inhumane, constricted, and deadly. In later years Wordsworth admitted to being so good at it that he was put in the fast stream: 'When at school, I, with the other boys of the same standing, was put upon reading the first six books of Euclid, with the exception of the fifth; and also in algebra I learnt simple and quadratic equations' (*Prose Works* iii 373).
35   *o'erlooked* didn't notice, whiled away.
36   *wasting* destructive, consuming.

37   *wean* a child is 'weaned' from its mother when she ceases to breastfeed it. The damaging power of schooling will wean the boy away from the sweet influence of Nature.
38   *Therefore . . . truth* the boy clothes the 'austere truth' of geometry with the colours and shapes of the landscape he loves.
39   *altitudes* in geometrical terms, the height of a triangle measured by a perpendicular from the peak to the base.
40   *visionary* embodying truth.
41   *the path of fire* an apocalyptic and tumultuous event in the past, to which the mountains bear witness by their markings.

In cold elation, and the lifelessness
Of truth by oversubtlety dislodged
From grandeur and from love, an idle toy,[42]
The dullest of all toys. He saw in truth   180
A holy spirit and a breathing soul;[43]
He reverenced her and trembled at her look,
When with a moral beauty in her face
She led him through the worlds.

    But now, before his twentieth year was passed,   185
Accumulated feelings pressed his heart
With an increasing weight; he was o'erpowered
By Nature, and his spirit was on fire
With restless thoughts. His eye became disturbed,[44]
And many a time he wished the winds might rage   190
When they were silent. Far more fondly now
Than in his earlier season did he love
Tempestuous nights, the uproar and the sounds
That live in darkness. From his intellect,
And from the stillness of abstracted thought,   195
He sought repose in vain. I have heard him say
That at this time he scanned the laws of light
Amid the roar of torrents, where they send
From hollow clefts up to the clearer air
A cloud of mist, which in the shining sun   200
Varies its rainbow hues.[45] But vainly thus,
And vainly by all other means he strove
To mitigate[46] the fever of his heart.

    From Nature and her overflowing soul
He had received so much that all his thoughts   205
Were steeped in feeling.[47] He was only then
Contented when with bliss ineffable[48]
He felt the sentiment of being spread
O'er all that moves, and all that seemeth still,[49]
O'er all which, lost beyond the reach of thought   210
And human knowledge, to the human eye
Invisible, yet liveth to the heart;
O'er all that leaps, and runs, and shouts, and sings,
Or beats the gladsome air; o'er all that glides
Beneath the wave, yea, in the wave itself,   215
And mighty depth of waters. Wonder not
If such his transports[50] were; for in all things
He saw one life, and felt that it was joy.[51]
One song they sang, and it was audible –
Most audible then when the fleshly ear,   220

---

[42] *toy* hobby.
[43] *A holy spirit and a breathing soul* Nature.
[44] *disturbed* i.e. with intense passion and creative thought.
[45] *I have heard . . . hues* the Pedlar attempts to reconcile Newtonian optics with his perceptions of Nature.
[46] *mitigate* reduce.
[47] *steeped in feeling* filled with emotion. For Wordsworth and Coleridge profound thought was possible only for those capable of deep feeling.
[48] *ineffable* indescribable.

[49] *He felt . . . still* the Pedlar is aware of some divine presence, not unlike the Platonic world soul, infused throughout the natural world.
[50] *transports* raptures.
[51] *He saw one life, and felt that it was joy* primary statement of Wordsworth's pantheistic belief; he came to it only under Coleridge's influence in 1798. It recurs in some of the 1798 lyrical ballads (including *Tintern Abbey*), but virtually disappears from his writing after that year.

O'ercome by grosser prelude of that strain,[52]
Forgot its functions, and slept undisturbed.[53]
   These things he had sustained[54] in solitude
Even till his bodily strength began to yield
Beneath their weight.[55] The mind within him burnt,   225
And he resolved to quit his native hills.
The father strove to make his son perceive
As clearly as the old man did himself
With what advantage he might teach a school
In the adjoining village. But the youth,   230
Who of this service made a short essay,[56]
Found that the wanderings of his thought were then
A misery to him, that he must resign
A task he was unable to perform.
He asked his father's blessing, and assumed   235
This lowly occupation. The old man
Blessed him and prayed for him, yet with a heart
Foreboding[57] evil.
            From his native hills
He wandered far. Much did he see of men,
Their manners,[58] their enjoyments and pursuits,   240
Their passions and their feelings, chiefly those
Essential and eternal in the heart,
Which mid the simpler forms of rural life
Exist more simple in their elements,
And speak a plainer language.[59] Many a year   245
Of lonesome meditation and impelled
By curious thought he was content to toil
In this poor[60] calling, which he now pursued
From habit and necessity. He walked
Among the impure haunts of vulgar men   250
Unstained; the talisman[61] of constant thought
And kind sensations in a gentle heart
Preserved him. Every show of vice to him
Was a remembrancer[62] of what he knew,
Or a fresh seed of wisdom, or produced   255
That tender interest[63] which the virtuous feel
Among the wicked, which when truly felt
May bring the bad man nearer to the good,

[52] *grosser prelude of that strain* the 'music' of ordinary sense experience – so intense that it leads to loss of bodily awareness and a perception of the mystic 'song' of the one life.

[53] *From Nature . . . undisturbed* ll. 204–22 were transferred to the *Two-Part Prelude* in autumn 1799, to describe the poet's own feelings when he was sixteen; see *Two-Part Prelude* ii 446–64.

[54] *sustained* suffered.

[55] *These things . . . weight* the transcendent experiences are so intense that they sap his strength.

[56] *essay* trial.

[57] *Foreboding* anticipating.

[58] *manners* way of life.

[59] *chiefly those . . . language* Partly in reaction to the ornamented and overwrought diction of much late eighteenth-century verse, Wordsworth composed a poetry reflecting the less 'sophisticated' language and experiences of country folk, which he regarded as truer to the emotions. Cf. Preface to *Lyrical Ballads* (1800): 'Low and rustic life was generally chosen because in that situation the essential passions of the heart find a better soil in which they can attain their maturity, are less under restraint, and speak a plainer and more emphatic language' (see p. 357).

[60] *poor* humble. When *The Pedlar* was published as part of *The Excursion* in 1814, Francis Jeffrey attacked the poem for the lowly origins of its protagonist (see pp. 557–8).

[61] *talisman* the Pedlar's thoughts act as a charm that protects him.

[62] *remembrancer* reminder.

[63] *tender interest* compassion.

But, innocent of evil, cannot sink
The good man to the bad.
                Among the woods   260
A lone enthusiast, and among the hills,
Itinerant[64] in this labour he had passed
The better portion of his time, and there
From day to day had his affections[65] breathed
The wholesome air of Nature; there he kept   265
In solitude and solitary thought,
So pleasant were those comprehensive views,
His mind in a just equipoise[66] of love.
Serene it was, unclouded by the cares
Of ordinary life – unvexed, unwarped   270
By partial bondage.[67] In his steady course
No piteous revolutions[68] had he felt,
No wild varieties of joy or grief.
Unoccupied by sorrow of its own,
His heart lay open; and, by Nature tuned   275
And constant disposition of his thoughts
To sympathy with man,[69] he was alive
To all that was enjoyed where'er he went,
And all that was endured; and, in himself
Happy, and quiet in his cheerfulness,   280
He had no painful pressure from within
Which made him turn aside from wretchedness
With coward fears. He could afford to suffer
With those whom he saw suffer. Hence it was
That in our best experience he was rich,   285
And in the wisdom of our daily life.
For hence, minutely, in his various rounds
He had observed the progress and decay
Of many minds, of minds and bodies too –
The history of many families,   290
And how they prospered, how they were o'erthrown
By passion or mischance, or such misrule
Among the unthinking masters of the earth
As makes the nations groan. He was a man,
One whom you could not pass without remark[70] – 295
If you had met him on a rainy day
You would have stopped to look at him. Robust,
Active, and nervous,[71] was his gait; his limbs
And his whole figure breathed intelligence.
His body, tall and shapely, showed in front   300
A faint line of the hollowness of age,
Or rather what appeared the curvature
Of toil; his head looked up steady and fixed.
Age had compressed the rose upon his cheek

---

[64] *Itinerant* travelling.
[65] *affections* feelings.
[66] *equipoise* balance.
[67] *partial bondage* i.e. to the cares of daily life.
[68] *revolutions* reversals, changes.

[69] *by Nature tuned . . . man* Wordsworth's first statement of the belief that love of Nature leads to love of mankind, the central tenet of *The Recluse*.
[70] *without remark* without noticing.
[71] *nervous* vigorous.

Into a narrower circle of deep red,   305
But had not tamed his eye, which, under brows
Of hoary grey, had meanings which it brought
From years of youth, which, like a being made
Of many beings, he had wondrous skill
To blend with meanings of the years to come,   310
Human, or such as lie beyond the grave.
Long had I loved him. Oh, it was most sweet
To hear him teach in unambitious style
Reasoning and thought, by painting as he did
The manners[72] and the passions. Many a time   315
He made a holiday and left his pack
Behind, and we two wandered through the hills
A pair of random travellers. His eye
Flashing poetic fire he would repeat
The songs of Burns,[73] or many a ditty wild   320
Which he had fitted to the moorland harp –
His own sweet verse – and, as we trudged along,
Together did we make the hollow grove
Ring with our transports.
                         Though he was untaught,
In the dead lore of schools[74] undisciplined,   325
Why should he grieve? He was a chosen son.
He yet retained an ear which deeply felt
The voice of Nature in the obscure wind,
The sounding mountain, and the running stream.
From deep analogies by thought supplied,   330
Or consciousnesses not to be subdued,
To every natural form, rock, fruit, and flower,
Even the loose stones that cover the highway,
He gave a moral life;[75] he saw them feel,
Or linked them to some feeling. In all shapes   335
He found a secret and mysterious soul,
A fragrance and a spirit of strange meaning.
Though poor in outward show, he was most rich:
He had a world about him – 'twas his own,
He made it – for it only lived to him,   340
And to the God who looked into his mind.
Such sympathies would often bear him far
In outward gesture, and in visible look,
Beyond the common seeming[76] of mankind.
Some called it madness; such it might have been,   345
But that he had an eye which evermore
Looked deep into the shades of difference[77]
As they lie hid in all exterior forms,
Near or remote, minute or vast – an eye
Which from a stone, a tree, a withered leaf,   350

72 *manners* way of life.
73 *The songs of Burns* Burns was Wordsworth's model of the poet of everyday life.
74 *the dead lore of schools* philosophy.
75 *To every . . . life* he attributed to natural things the ability to act as independent moral agents; effectively, he endowed them with human emotions.
76 *seeming* conduct, behaviour.
77 *shades of difference* small and subtle differences perceptible only to the trained mind.

To the broad ocean and the azure heavens
Spangled with kindred multitudes of stars,
Could find no surface where its power might sleep –
Which spake perpetual logic to his soul,
And by an unrelenting agency   355
Did bind his feelings even as in a chain.[78]

[*There is an active principle*] (extract) (composed February–March 1798; edited from MS)[1]

There is an active principle alive
In all things[2] – in all natures, in the flowers
And in the trees, in every pebbly stone
That paves the brooks, the stationary rocks,
The moving waters, and the invisible air.   5
All beings have their properties which spread[3]
Beyond themselves, a power by which they make
Some other being conscious of their life –
Spirit that knows no insulated spot,
No chasm, no solitude. From link to link   10
It circulates, the soul of all the worlds.[4]
This is the freedom of the universe,
Unfolded still the more, more visible
The more we know[5] – and yet is reverenced least,
And least respected, in the human mind,   15
Its most apparent home.

[*Not useless do I deem*] (extract) (composed early March 1798; edited from MS)[1]

Not useless do I deem
These quiet sympathies with things that hold
An inarticulate language,[2] for the man

---

[78] *such it might . . . chain* not satisfied with 'exterior forms'
(l. 348), or with any single 'surface' or outward appearance
(l. 353), the Pedlar's eye is trained to perceive the essential –
the 'perpetual logic' of existence. Because it sees through to
what is permanent, it is continously active ('unrelenting' in its
'agency'), and has the effect of regulating his feelings, linking
them into a chain of beneficial associations.

THERE IS AN ACTIVE PRINCIPLE
[1] Had Wordsworth been able to complete *The Recluse* in
1798, this fragment would have comprised one of its central
statements, along with '*Not useless do I deem*' (pp. 298–300). Its
overt pantheism looks forward to *Tintern Abbey* and is related
to the central pantheist episode of *The Pedlar* (ll. 204–22). In
later years it was drastically revised to form the opening of
Excursion Book IX (1814).
[2] *In all things* cf. *Pedlar* 217–18: 'in all things / He saw one
life, and felt that it was joy'.

[3] *spread* cf. *Pedlar* 208–9: 'He felt the sentiment of being
spread / O'er all that moves, and all that seemeth still'.
[4] *the soul of all the worlds* Wordsworth has in mind the Pla-
tonic world soul.
[5] *Unfolded . . . know* the divine spirit becomes more evident
to us as we acquire experience.

NOT USELESS DO I DEEM
[1] This fragment articulates the philosophy of Wordsworth's
ambitious, never-completed epic poem, *The Recluse*, focusing
on the means by which love of Nature would lead to love of
mankind. It was composed in early March 1798, just after
composition of *The Ruined Cottage*, and would have formed
part of a new conclusion to that poem, spoken by the Pedlar.
Years later it was revised and incorporated into *The Excursion*
Book IV (ll. 1198–1292).
[2] *Not useless . . . language* in the background is the notion,
derived from Bishop Berkeley, that all natural things are part
of a mental 'language' spoken by God.

Once taught to love such objects as excite
No morbid passions, no disquietude,   5
No vengeance and no hatred, needs must feel[3]
The joy of that pure principle of love
So deeply that, unsatisfied with aught
Less pure and exquisite,[4] he cannot choose
But[5] seek for objects of a kindred love   10
In fellow natures, and a kindred joy.
Accordingly he by degrees perceives
His feelings of aversion softened down,
A holy tenderness pervade his frame.[6]
His sanity of reason not impaired   15
(Say rather all his thoughts now flowing clear,
From a clear fountain flowing), he looks round,
He seeks for good, and finds the good he seeks –
Till execration[7] and contempt are things
He only knows by name, and if he hears   20
From other mouth the language which they speak
He is compassionate, and has no thought,
No feeling, which can overcome his love.
And further, by contemplating these forms
In the relations which they bear to man,   25
We shall discover what a power is theirs
To stimulate our minds, and multiply
The spiritual presences of absent things.[8]
Then weariness[9] will cease: we shall acquire
The [   ] habit by which sense is made   30
Subservient still to moral purposes[10] –
A vital essence and a saving power.
Nor shall we meet an object but may read
Some sweet and tender lesson[11] to our minds
Of human suffering or of human joy.   35
All things shall speak of man, and we shall read
Our duties[12] in all forms; and general laws
And local accidents[13] shall tend alike
To quicken and to rouse,[14] and give the will

---

[3] *needs must feel* Wordsworth's language indicates that the process he is describing is necessitarian. The individual has no choice but to feel 'the joy of that pure principle of love' emanating from natural objects.

[4] *exquisite* refined.

[5] *he cannot choose / But* Once again, the language indicates that Wordsworth is talking about a necessitarian process; having felt the pantheist impulse of pure love passing through him from the natural world, the individual has no choice but to seek out 'objects of a kindred love' – that is, other people.

[6] *Accordingly ... frame* one of the effects of the pure principle of love is to dissolve petty feelings of dislike or hostility, allowing a reciprocal love of other people to 'pervade' his spirit.

[7] *execration* hatred.

[8] *And further ... things* A central belief behind *The Recluse*: as in *Tintern Abbey*, memories of natural forms are impressed on the mind so that the individual can contemplate them at will. Their effect is to 'stimulate' or refresh the mind (cf. the 'tranquil restoration' of *Tintern Abbey* 31), and place the individual

in contact, on a spiritual level, with natural objects that are not physically present. Essentially Wordsworth is claiming that everyone may experience what is described at *Tintern Abbey* 26–50.

[9] *weariness* cf. 'the heavy and the weary weight / Of all this unintelligible world', *Tintern Abbey* 40–1.

[10] *The [   ] habit ... purposes* i.e. the way in which perceived natural forms ('sense') make us 'seek for objects of a kindred love / In fellow natures' (ll. 10–11, above). Nature compels us to love our fellow man.

[11] *lesson* sermon.

[12] *Our duties* i.e. the moral duty to love our fellow human beings.

[13] *and general laws / And local accidents* i.e. the general laws by which love of nature leads to love of man, and unforeseen incidents ('local accidents') which bring us into contact with natural forms.

[14] *To quicken and to rouse* i.e. stimulate the mind, as at l. 27, above.

And power by which a [   ] chain of good[15]   40
Shall link us to our kind. No naked hearts,
No naked minds, shall then be left to mourn
The burden of existence.[16]

[*The Two-Part Prelude*] (Part I composed between October 1798 and February 1799; Part II, autumn 1799; edited from MS)[1]

First Part

Was it for this
That one, the fairest of all rivers, loved
To blend his murmurs with my nurse's song,
And from his alder shades and rocky falls,
And from his fords and shallows, sent a voice   5
That flowed along my dreams?[2] For this didst thou,
Oh Derwent, travelling over the green plains
Near my 'sweet birthplace',[3] didst thou, beauteous stream,
Make ceaseless music through the night and day,
Which with its steady cadence tempering   10
Our human waywardness, composed my thoughts
To more than infant softness, giving me,
Among the fretful dwellings of mankind,
A knowledge, a dim earnest[4] of the calm
Which nature breathes among the fields and groves?   15
    Beloved Derwent, fairest of all streams,
Was it for this that I, a four years' child,
A naked boy, among thy silent pools,
Made one long bathing of a summer's day,
Basked in the sun, or plunged into thy streams   20
Alternate all a summer's day, or coursed[5]
Over the sandy fields, and dashed the flowers
Of yellow grunsel;[6] or, when crag and hill,
The woods, and distant Skiddaw's lofty height[7]
Were bronzed with a deep radiance, stood alone,   25
A naked savage in the thunder shower?
    And afterwards, 'twas in a later day,

---

[15]   *chain of good* a chain of association – that is, the beneficial chain that inspires love of mankind through love of nature.
[16]   *No naked hearts . . . burden of existence* the ills of mankind – disease, war, poverty, and other social ills – would be alleviated.

THE TWO-PART PRELUDE
[1]   This is the earliest complete version of Wordsworth's masterpiece, *The Prelude*. There were to be three further versions: one in Five Books (completed February 1804); one in Thirteen (completed early 1806); and one in Fourteen (published posthumously in 1850). It was known only to Wordsworth's close friends, such as Coleridge and De Quincey. No one expected Wordsworth to write an autobiographical poem; he began it in Germany in the winter of 1798–9, which he believed to be the coldest of the century, in a state of despair at

not managing to get on with *The Recluse*, the great millennial epic poem proposed by Coleridge (see pp. 271, 519–21, 548).
[2]   *Was it for this . . . dreams* This question expresses Wordsworth's disappointment at being unable to compose *The Recluse*. The river is the Derwent which, as present-day visitors can see, flows along the far side of the garden wall of Wordsworth's house in Cockermouth.
[3]   *sweet birthplace* The quotation marks, which appear in the manuscript, refer the reader to Coleridge's *Frost at Midnight* 33; it is particularly appropriate that the *Prelude*, which is addressed to Coleridge, should allude to his work.
[4]   *earnest* foretaste, pledge.
[5]   *coursed* ran.
[6]   *grunsel* ragwort.
[7]   *distant Skiddaw's lofty height* Skiddaw is the fourth highest peak in the Lake District at 3,053 feet.

Though early,[8] when upon the mountain-slope
The frost and breath of frosty wind had snapped
The last autumnal crocus, 'twas my joy   30
To wander half the night among the cliffs
And the smooth hollows where the woodcocks ran
Along the moonlight turf. In thought and wish
That time, my shoulder all with springes[9] hung,
I was a fell destroyer. Gentle powers   35
Who give us happiness and call it peace,
When scudding on from snare to snare I plied
My anxious visitation – hurrying on,
Still hurrying, hurrying onward – how my heart
Panted among the scattered yew-trees and the crags   40
That looked upon me, how my bosom beat
With expectation! Sometimes strong desire,
Resistless, overpowered me, and the bird
Which was the captive of another's toils[10]
Became my prey; and when the deed was done   45
I heard among the solitary hills
Low breathings coming after me, and sounds
Of undistinguishable motion, steps
Almost as silent as the turf they trod.[11]

    Nor less in springtime, when on southern banks   50
The shining sun had from his knot of leaves
Decoyed the primrose flower, and when the vales
And woods were warm, was I a rover then
In the high places, on the lonesome peaks
Among the mountains and the winds. Though mean   55
And though inglorious were my views, the end
Was not ignoble.[12] Oh, when I have hung
Above the raven's nest, by knots of grass
Or half-inch fissures in the slipp'ry rock
But ill sustained, and almost (as it seemed)   60
Suspended by the blast which blew amain,[13]
Shouldering the naked crag[14] – oh, at that time,
While on the perilous ridge I hung alone,[15]
With what strange utterance did the loud dry wind
Blow through my ears! The sky seemed not a sky   65
Of earth, and with what motion moved the clouds!
    The mind of man is fashioned and built up
Even as a strain of music; I believe
That there are spirits which, when they would form

---

8 *And . . . early* Wordsworth jumps forward to his time at Hawkshead Grammar School which he joined in May 1779; he left Hawkshead for Cambridge in the autumn of 1787.

9 *springes* traps; Wordsworth is thinking of *Hamlet* I iii 115: 'Ay, springes to catch woodcocks.'

10 *toils* a pun, meaning both 'trap' and 'labours'.

11 *and when . . . trod* Wordsworth's guilt might be explained partly by the fact that woodcock were a delicacy and fetched a good price for those who could catch them – sixteen or twenty pence a couple on the spot before being sent to London on the Kendal stagecoach. They were trapped by snares set at the end

of narrowing avenues of stones which the birds would not jump over.

12 *the end . . . ignoble* Ravens preyed on lambs and those who destroyed their eggs were rewarded by the parish. The 'end' (result) was not, in Wordsworth's case, monetary.

13 *amain* strongly.

14 *Shouldering the naked crag* the slightly inflated diction suggests that Wordsworth is recalling Atlas, the Titan of myth, who bore the world on his shoulders.

15 *I hung alone* see Wordsworth's comments in the 1815 *Preface*, pp. 411–12.

A favoured being, from his very dawn   70
Of infancy do open out the clouds
As at the touch of lightning, seeking him
With gentle visitation – quiet powers,
Retired and seldom recognized, yet kind
And to the very meanest not unknown.   75
With me, though rarely, in my early days,
They communed; others too there are who use,
Yet haply aiming at the self-same end,
Severer interventions, ministry[16]
More palpable – and of their school was I.   80
    They guided me. One evening, led by them,
I went alone into a shepherd's boat,
A skiff that to a willow-tree was tied
Within a rocky cave, its usual home.
The moon was up, the lake was shining clear   85
Among the hoary mountains; from the shore
I pushed, and struck the oars, and struck again
In cadence, and my little boat moved on
Just like a man who walks with stately step
Though bent on speed.[17] It was an act of stealth   90
And troubled pleasure; not without the voice
Of mountain-echoes did my boat move on,
Leaving behind her still on either side
Small circles glittering idly in the moon
Until they melted all into one track   95
Of sparkling light.[18] A rocky steep uprose
Above the cavern of the willow-tree,
And now, as suited one who proudly rowed
With his best skill, I fixed a steady view
Upon the top of that same craggy ridge,   100
The bound of the horizon, for behind
Was nothing but the stars and the grey sky.
She was an elfin pinnace;[19] twenty times
I dipped my oars into the silent lake,
And, as I rose upon the stroke, my boat   105
Went heaving through the water like a swan –
When, from behind that rocky steep (till then
The bound of the horizon), a huge cliff,[20]
As if with voluntary power instinct,[21]
Upreared its head. I struck and struck again,   110
And, growing still in stature, the huge cliff
Rose up between me and the stars, and still,
With measured motion, like a living thing
Strode after me. With trembling hands I turned,

---

[16] *ministry* guidance.

[17] *Just like ... speed* Wordsworth recalls the description of Michael from *Paradise Lost* xii 1–2: 'As one who in his journey bates at noon, / Though bent on speed.'

[18] *sparkling light* probably a recollection of the 'tracks of shining white' made by the water-snakes in Coleridge's *Ancient Mariner* (1798) 266.

[19] *elfin pinnace* the language embodies the child's imaginative absorption; the boat seems to be enchanted.

[20] *a huge cliff* Glenridding Dodd, the stepped-back summit of which causes its peak to make a sudden, delayed appearance above the 'craggy steep' of Stybarrow Crag as one rows out from the shores of Patterdale (see Grevel Lindop, *A Literary Guide to the Lake District* (1993), pp. 317–18).

[21] *instinct* imbued, filled.

And through the silent water stole my way   115
Back to the cavern of the willow-tree.
There in her mooring-place I left my bark,
And through the meadows homeward went with grave
And serious thoughts; and after I had seen
That spectacle, for many days my brain   120
Worked with a dim and undetermined sense
Of unknown modes of being.[22] In my thoughts
There was a darkness – call it solitude
Or blank desertion; no familiar shapes
Of hourly objects,[23] images of trees,   125
Of sea or sky, no colours of green fields,
But huge and mighty forms that do not live
Like living men moved slowly through my mind
By day, and were the trouble of my dreams.[24]

    Ah, not in vain, ye beings of the hills,   130
And ye that walk the woods and open heaths
By moon or starlight, thus from my first dawn
Of childhood did ye love to intertwine
The passions that build up our human soul,
Not with the mean and vulgar works of man,   135
But with high objects, with eternal things,
With life and nature, purifying thus
The elements of feeling and of thought,
And sanctifying by such discipline
Both pain and fear, until we recognize   140
A grandeur in the beatings of the heart.[25]

    Nor was this fellowship vouchsafed to me
With stinted kindness.[26] In November days,
When vapours rolling down the valleys made
A lonely scene more lonesome, among woods   145
At noon, and mid the calm of summer nights
When by the margin of the trembling lake
Beneath the gloomy hills I homeward went
In solitude, such intercourse[27] was mine.

    And in the frosty season, when the sun   150
Was set, and visible for many a mile,
The cottage windows through the twilight blazed,
I heeded not the summons;[28] clear and loud
The village clock tolled six; I wheeled about,
Proud and exulting like an untired horse   155
That cares not for its home. All shod with steel

---

[22] *unknown modes of being* forms of life beyond human experience. The vagueness and imprecision is meant to evoke the child's fear.
[23] *hourly objects* objects that can be depended on to be the same from one hour to the next.
[24] *But huge . . . dreams* as the alien mountain-forms take hold of his imagination, the boy is 'deserted' by the reassuring memories of ordinary things.
[25] *Ah, not in vain . . . heart* The feelings and thoughts of Wordsworth's childhood were purer for having been associated not with man-made things (as in a town), but with the enduring forms of Nature. This natural education has sanctified – that is to say, has given value to – the otherwise unpleasant sensations of pain and fear; thus, when his heart beat with terror, he recognized the 'grandeur' of the experience.
[26] *Nor was . . . kindness* This special relationship with Nature ('fellowship') was not given grudgingly.
[27] *intercourse* companionship (with Nature).
[28] *The cottage . . . summons* candle- and fire-light through the cottage windows tell the boy that it is time to go home.

We hissed along the polished ice[29] in games
Confederate,[30] imitative of the chase
And woodland pleasures – the resounding horn,
The pack loud bellowing, and the hunted hare.   160
So through the darkness and the cold we flew,
And not a voice was idle. With the din,
Meanwhile, the precipices rang aloud,
The leafless trees and every icy crag
Tinkled like iron, while the distant hills   165
Into the tumult sent an alien sound
Of melancholy not unnoticed – while the stars
Eastward were sparkling clear, and in the west
The orange sky of evening died away.

    Not seldom from the uproar I retired   170
Into a silent bay, or sportively
Glanced sideway, leaving the tumultuous throng,
To cut across the shadow[31] of a star
That gleamed upon the ice. And oftentimes,
When we had given our bodies to the wind,   175
And all the shadowy banks on either side
Came sweeping through the darkness, spinning still
The rapid line of motion – then at once
Have I, reclining back upon my heels,
Stopped short: yet still the solitary cliffs   180
Wheeled by me, even as if the earth had rolled
With visible motion her diurnal[32] round;
Behind me did they stretch in solemn train[33]
Feebler and feebler, and I stood and watched
Till all was tranquil as a summer sea.   185

    Ye powers of earth, ye genii of the springs!
And ye that have your voices in the clouds
And ye that are familiars of the lakes
And of the standing pools,[34] I may not think
A vulgar hope was yours when ye employed   190
Such ministry[35] – when ye through many a year
Thus by the agency of boyish sports
On caves and trees, upon the woods and hills,
Impressed[36] upon all forms the characters[37]
Of danger or desire, and thus did make   195
The surface of the universal earth
With meanings of delight, of hope and fear,
Work like a sea.[38]

---

[29]   *We hissed . . . ice* Wordsworth's phrasing recalls Erasmus Darwin's *Botanic Garden*, 'Hang o'er the sliding steel, and hiss along the ice' (*Economy of Vegetation* iii 570).

[30]   *Confederate* collective; games played in groups.

[31]   *shadow* reflection; altered to 'image' in the *Thirteen-Book Prelude*, and 'reflex' for *Fourteen-Book Prelude*.

[32]   *diurnal* daily, as in '*A slumber did my spirit seal*', in which Lucy is 'Rolled round in earth's diurnal course / With rocks and stones and trees' (ll. 7–8).

[33]   *train* sequence, succession.

[34]   *Ye powers . . . pools* the tutelary spirits have their source in Shakespeare, *Tempest* V i 33: 'Ye elves of hills, brooks, standing lakes and groves'.

[35]   *ministry* guidance

[36]   *Impressed* stamped, printed.

[37]   *characters* signs, marks.

[38]   *Work like a sea* See Cowper, *Task* vi 737–8: 'this tempestuous state of human things, / Is merely as the working of a sea'. Their association with 'boyish sports' has given the impression of movement to the poet's recollection of the landscape in which he grew up.

Not uselessly employed,
I might pursue this theme through every change
Of exercise and sport to which the year   200
Did summon us in its delightful round.
We were a noisy crew; the sun in heaven
Beheld not vales more beautiful than ours,
Nor saw a race in happiness and joy
More worthy of the fields where they were sown.   205
I would record with no reluctant voice
Our home amusements by the warm peat-fire
At evening, when with pencil and with slate,
In square divisions parcelled out, and all
With crosses and with cyphers scribbled o'er,[39]   210
We schemed and puzzled, head opposed to head,
In strife too humble to be named in verse;
Or round the naked table, snow-white deal,
Cherry or maple, sat in close array,
And to the combat, loo or whist,[40] led on   215
A thick-ribbed army[41] – not (as in the world)
Discarded and ungratefully thrown by
Even for the very service they had wrought,[42]
But husbanded[43] through many a long campaign.
Oh with what echoes on the board they fell!   220
Ironic diamonds, hearts of sable hue,
Queens gleaming through their splendour's last decay,
Knaves wrapped in one assimilating gloom,
And kings indignant at the shame incurred
By royal visages. Meanwhile abroad   225
The heavy rain was falling, or the frost
Raged bitterly with keen and silent tooth,[44]
Or, interrupting the impassioned game,[45]
Oft from the neighbouring lake the splitting ice,
While it sank down towards the water, sent   230
Among the meadows and the hills its long
And frequent yellings,[46] imitative some
Of wolves that howl along the Bothnic main.[47]
        Nor with less willing heart would I rehearse
The woods of autumn and their hidden bowers   235
With milk-white clusters[48] hung, the rod and line

---

[39] *With crosses ... o'er* noughts and crosses (tick-tack-toe); the line echoes *Paradise Lost*, where man is ridiculed for attempting to map the heavens, 'With centric and eccentric scribbled o'er' (viii 83).

[40] *loo or whist* The description of these eighteenth-century card-games recalls the game of ombre in Pope's *Rape of the Lock* iii. See J. R. Watson, 'Wordsworth's Card Games', *TWC* 6 (1975) 299–302.

[41] *A thick-ribbed army* The cards' edges have thickened through use.

[42] *not ... wrought* cf. for example, the discharged soldier (see preceding poem).

[43] *husbanded* saved up; they were survivors.

[44] *keen and silent tooth* 'Thy tooth is not so keen', Amiens

tells the winter wind in *As You Like It* II vii 177. But as Owen *TWC* 107 points out, ll. 225–7 are based on Cowper's *Winter Evening*: 'how the frost / Raging abroad, and the rough wind, endear / The silence and the warmth enjoyed within' (*Task* iv 308–10; see pp. 11–12).

[45] *the impassioned game* a particularly persuasive detail; the game fully engages the players' emotions ('passions').

[46] *its long ... yellings* the ice makes a yelling noise as it breaks up; Coleridge had used this detail in *The Ancient Mariner* (1798) 57–60.

[47] *Bothnic main* the northern Baltic.

[48] *milk-white clusters* hazel nuts. *Nutting*, composed for the *Two-Part Prelude*, was discarded immediately and published in *Lyrical Ballads* (1800) as an independent work; see pp. 325–6.

(True symbol of the foolishness of hope)
Which with its strong enchantment led me on
By rocks and pools where never summer star
Impressed its shadow,[49] to forlorn cascades   240
Among the windings of the mountain-brooks;
The kite, in sultry calms from some high hill
Sent up, ascending thence till it was lost
Among the fleecy clouds, in gusty days
Launched from the lower grounds, and suddenly   245
Dashed headlong – and rejected by the storm.
All these and more with rival claims demand
Grateful acknowledgement. It were a song
Venial, and such as if I rightly judge
I might protract unblamed, but I perceive   250
That much is overlooked, and we should ill
Attain our object if from delicate fears
Of breaking in upon the unity
Of this my argument[50] I should omit
To speak of such effects as cannot here   255
Be regularly classed, yet tend no less
To the same point, the growth of mental power
And love of nature's works.
                              Ere I had seen
Eight summers[51] – and 'twas in the very week
When I was first entrusted to thy vale,   260
Beloved Hawkshead! – when thy paths, thy shores
And brooks, were like a dream of novelty
To my half-infant mind, I chanced to cross
One of those open fields which, shaped like ears,[52]
Make green peninsulas on Esthwaite's Lake.   265
Twilight was coming on, yet through the gloom
I saw distinctly on the opposite shore,
Beneath a tree and close by the lakeside,
A heap of garments, as if left by one
Who there was bathing. Half an hour I watched   270
And no one owned them; meanwhile the calm lake
Grew dark with all the shadows on its breast,
And now and then a leaping fish disturbed
The breathless stillness. The succeeding day
There came a company, and in their boat   275
Sounded with iron hooks and with long poles.
At length the dead man,[53] mid that beauteous scene
Of trees and hills and water, bolt upright
Rose with his ghastly face. I might advert[54]
To numerous accidents in flood or field,[55]   280
Quarry or moor, or mid the winter snows,

---

49   *shadow* reflection.
50   *argument* theme; cf. *Paradise Lost* i 24: 'the hight of this great argument'.
51   *Ere I had . . . summers* despite Wordsworth's claims, he went to Hawkshead Grammar School in May 1779 at the age of nine.
52   *shaped like ears* There are three such peninsulas on the map; the one Wordsworth has in mind is Strickland Ees.

53   *the dead man* John Jackson, village schoolmaster from Sawrey, was drowned while bathing in Esthwaite Water, 18 June 1779.
54   *advert* refer.
55   *To numerous . . . field* an echo of *Othello* I iii 134–5: 'Wherein I spake of most disastrous chances, / Of moving accidents by flood and field'.

Distresses and disasters, tragic facts
Of rural history that impressed my mind
With images to which, in following years,
Far other feelings were attached, with forms   285
That yet exist with independent life,
And, like their archetypes, know no decay.[56]
There are in our existence spots of time
Which with distinct pre-eminence retain
A fructifying[57] virtue, whence, depressed   290
By trivial occupations and the round
Of ordinary intercourse, our minds
(Especially the imaginative power)
Are nourished, and invisibly repaired.[58]
Such moments chiefly seem to have their date   295
In our first childhood.

            I remember well
('Tis of an early season that I speak,
The twilight of rememberable life)
While I was yet an urchin,[59] one who scarce
Could hold a bridle, with ambitious hopes   300
I mounted, and we rode towards the hills.
We were a pair of horsemen: honest James[60]
Was with me, my encourager and guide.
We had not travelled long ere some mischance
Disjoined me from my comrade and, through fear   305
Dismounting, down the rough and stony moor
I led my horse, and, stumbling on, at length
Came to a bottom where in former times
A man, the murderer of his wife, was hung
In irons; mouldered was the gibbet-mast,   310
The bones were gone, the iron and the wood,
Only a long green ridge of turf remained
Whose shape was like a grave.[61] I left the spot
And, reascending the bare slope, I saw
A naked pool that lay beneath the hills,   315
The beacon on the summit,[62] and, more near,
A girl who bore a pitcher on her head
And seemed with difficult steps to force her way
Against the blowing wind. It was in truth
An ordinary sight, but I should need   320

---

[56] *tragic facts ... decay* A change has taken place in Wordsworth's thought since *The Pedlar* and *Tintern Abbey* (composed only months before). As in those works, he is concerned with the storing-up of visual memories in the mind as a result of deep emotional response. However, the images are now treasured not for their permanence but because of quite distinct new feelings that have become attached to them over the years.

[57] *fructifying* the power to make fruitful.

[58] *repaired* as in *Tintern Abbey* 40–2, the essential characteristic of these remembered 'spots of time' is to restore the mind.

[59] *an urchin* Wordsworth was five at the time this incident took place. He was staying with his grandparents at Penrith.

[60] *honest James* identified in the *Fourteen-Book Prelude* as being 'An ancient Servant of my Father's house' (xii 229).

[61] *Mouldered was the gibbet-mast ... like a grave* the valley-bottom was Cowdrake Quarry, east of Penrith, where Thomas Nicholson was hanged in 1767 for having murdered a butcher. However, *The Prelude* is not a record of fact, and it is worth noting that Nicholson's gibbet had not 'mouldered down' in 1775, and a five-year-old would not have ridden that far. Wordsworth may also have in mind a rotted gibbet in the water-meadows near Ann Tyson's cottage, the last remains of Thomas Lancaster, hanged in 1672 for poisoning his wife.

[62] *The beacon on the summit* built in 1719 to warn of invasion from Scotland; it is still to be seen, a short building with a pointed roof on the hill above Penrith.

Colours and words that are unknown to man
To paint the visionary dreariness[63]
Which, while I looked all round for my lost guide,
Did at that time invest the naked pool,
The beacon on the lonely eminence,   325
The woman and her garments vexed and tossed
By the strong wind.
                                      Nor less I recollect,
Long after, though my childhood had not ceased,
Another scene which left a kindred power
Implanted in my mind. One Christmas-time,   330
The day before the holidays began,[64]
Feverish and tired and restless, I went forth
Into the fields, impatient for the sight
Of those three horses which should bear us home,
My brothers and myself.[65] There was a crag,[66]   335
An eminence which from the meeting-point
Of two highways ascending, overlooked
At least a long half-mile of those two roads,
By each of which the expected steeds might come,
The choice uncertain. Thither I repaired   340
Up to the highest summit. 'Twas a day
Stormy, and rough, and wild, and on the grass
I sat, half-sheltered by a naked wall;
Upon my right hand was a single sheep,
A whistling hawthorn on my left, and there,   345
Those two companions at my side, I watched,
With eyes intensely straining, as the mist
Gave intermitting prospects of the wood
And plain beneath. Ere I to school returned
That dreary time, ere I had been ten days   350
A dweller in my father's house, he died,[67]
And I and my two brothers, orphans then,
Followed his body to the grave. The event,
With all the sorrow which it brought, appeared
A chastisement,[68] and when I called to mind   355
That day so lately past, when from the crag
I looked in such anxiety of hope,
With trite reflections of morality,
Yet with the deepest passion, I bowed low

---

[63]   *visionary dreariness* a phrase that has generated much critical commentary. Wordsworth's point is that the ordinariness and bleakness of the scene was so intense as to be impressed on his mind with the potency of a vision. At the back of his mind is Milton's hell, a 'dismal situation waste and wild', where there was no light, 'but rather darkness visible' (*Paradise Lost* i 60, 63).

[64]   *One Christmas-time ... began* probably 19 December 1783, when Wordsworth was thirteen.

[65]   *My brothers and myself* Wordsworth's brothers, Richard (1768–1816) and John (1772–1805), also attended Hawkshead Grammar School. The horses were to take them home to Cockermouth; it was a fairly lengthy journey as Hawkshead and Cockermouth were at opposite ends of the Lake District.

Whether they chose to go round the coastal route, or towards the east, to Keswick, through Ambleside and thence to Hawkshead, it was necessary to travel around the central mountains. The horses were in fact delayed; for the circumstances surrounding this see my article, 'Wordsworth's Poetry of Grief', *TWC* 21 (1990) 114–17.

[66]   *a crag* probably the ridge north of Borwick Lodge, a mile and a half from Hawkshead Grammar School.

[67]   *he died* John Wordsworth Sr died on 30 December 1783 after spending a shelterless night lost during his return from the Seignory of Millom two weeks before. His wife, Ann, had died five years previously, just before Wordsworth's eighth birthday.

[68]   *chastisement* punishment (stressed on the first syllable).

To God, who thus corrected my desires.[69]   360
And afterwards the wind and sleety rain
And all the business of the elements,
The single sheep, and the one blasted tree,
And the bleak music of that old stone wall,
The noise of wood and water, and the mist   365
Which on the line of each of those two roads
Advanced in such indisputable shapes[70] –
All these were spectacles and sounds to which
I often would repair, and thence would drink
As at a fountain.[71] And I do not doubt   370
That in this later time, when storm and rain
Beat on my roof at midnight, or by day
When I am in the woods, unknown to me
The workings of my spirit thence are brought.[72]

  Nor, sedulous[73] as I have been to trace   375
How nature by collateral[74] interest
And by extrinsic passion[75] peopled first
My mind with forms or beautiful or grand[76]
And made me love them, may I well forget
How other pleasures have been mine, and joys   380
Of subtler origin – how I have felt,
Not seldom, even in that tempestuous time,
Those hallowed and pure motions of the sense
Which seem in their simplicity to own
An intellectual[77] charm, that calm delight   385
Which, if I err not, surely must belong
To those first-born affinities[78] that fit
Our new existence to existing things,
And in our dawn of being constitute
The bond of union betwixt life and joy.   390

  Yes, I remember when the changeful earth
And twice five seasons on my mind had stamped
The faces of the moving year; even then,
A child, I held unconscious intercourse
With the eternal beauty, drinking in   395
A pure organic[79] pleasure from the lines
Of curling mist, or from the level plain
Of waters coloured by the steady clouds.

  The sands of Westmorland, the creeks and bays
Of Cumbria's rocky limits, they can tell   400
How when the sea threw off his evening shade
And to the shepherd's hut beneath the crags

---

69 *I bowed low to God ... desires* The child believes he has been punished for looking forward too eagerly to the Christmas holidays – in effect, he has killed his father.

70 *indisputable shapes* De Selincourt notes an interesting echo of Hamlet addressing his father's ghost: 'Thou com'st in such a questionable shape / That I will speak to thee' (I iv 43–4).

71 *fountain* stream or well.

72 *unknown to me ... brought* Spots of time mould the adult mind by the power of association, though it remains unaware of their workings.

73 *sedulous* careful, anxious.

74 *collateral* indirect, sideways.

75 *extrinsic passion* emotions not directly related to the natural scenes that were to 'educate' the poet. Nature operated on the boy without his being aware of it.

76 *or ... or* either ... or.

77 *intellectual* spiritual – the sense in which Wordsworth often uses the word.

78 *first-born affinities* affinities with which the child is born.

79 *organic* sensuous, bodily.

Did send sweet notice of the rising moon,
How I have stood, to images like these
A stranger, linking with the spectacle   405
No body of associated forms[80]
And bringing with me no peculiar sense
Of quietness or peace – yet I have stood,
Even while my eye has moved o'er three long leagues[81]
Of shining water, gathering, as it seemed,   410
Through the wide surface of that field of light
New pleasure like a bee among the flowers.

    Thus often in those fits of vulgar[82] joy
Which through all seasons on a child's pursuits
Are prompt attendants, mid that giddy bliss   415
Which like a tempest works along the blood
And is forgotten – even then I felt
Gleams like the flashing of a shield. The earth
And common face of nature spake to me
Rememberable things – sometimes, 'tis true,   420
By quaint associations, yet not vain
Nor profitless if haply they impressed
Collateral objects and appearances,[83]
Albeit lifeless then, and doomed to sleep
Until maturer seasons called them forth   425
To impregnate and to elevate the mind.
And if the vulgar joy by its own weight
Wearied itself out of the memory,
The scenes which were a witness of that joy
Remained in their substantial lineaments   430
Depicted on the brain,[84] and to the eye
Were visible, a daily sight. And thus,
By the impressive agency of fear,[85]
By pleasure, and repeated happiness,
So frequently repeated, and by force   435
Of obscure feelings representative
Of joys that were forgotten, these same scenes
So beauteous and majestic in themselves,
Though yet the day was distant, did at length
Become habitually dear, and all   440
Their hues and forms were by invisible links[86]
Allied to the affections.[87]

---

[80] *linking ... forms* Wordsworth emphasizes that he has enjoyed these things in and for themselves, rather than for any association they may have with other things. He has been a 'stranger' to them insofar as he has not seen them before and sees them freshly.

[81] *three long leagues* at least nine miles (a league is a varying measure of about three miles).

[82] *vulgar* ordinary, unremarkable.

[83] *sometimes ... appearances* the 'associations' (or juxtapositions) are quaint, but not vain or without benefit if indirectly ('collaterally') they impress natural objects and appearances on the mind.

[84] *in their substantial lineaments ... brain* The storing up of visual images is described in similar terms at *Pedlar* 32–4: 'on

his mind / They lay like substances, and almost seemed / To haunt the bodily sense'.

[85] *the impressive agency of fear* fear's ability to stamp 'impressions' on the memory.

[86] *invisible links* associative links in the mind. Wordsworth draws on the theory of the mind's association of ideas derived from sense-experience, as expounded by David Hartley (1705–57) in his *Observations of Man* (1749) – a strong influence on Coleridge.

[87] *And thus ... affections* Fear, pleasure, and repeated happiness all work to make the natural world constantly precious ('habitually dear'), and to connect its colours and shapes to the poet's emotions ('affections').

I began
My story early, feeling, as I fear,
The weakness of a human love for days
Disowned by memory, ere the birth of spring   445
Planting my snowdrops among winter snows.[88]
Nor will it seem to thee, my friend,[89] so prompt
In sympathy, that I have lengthened out
With fond and feeble tongue a tedious tale.
Meanwhile my hope has been that I might fetch   450
Reproaches from my former years, whose power
May spur me on, in manhood now mature,
To honourable toil.[90] Yet should it be
That this is but an impotent desire,
That I by such enquiry am not taught   455
To understand myself, nor thou to know
With better knowledge how the heart was framed
Of him thou lovest, need I dread from thee
Harsh judgements if I am so loath to quit
Those recollected hours that have the charm   460
Of visionary things,[91] and lovely forms
And sweet sensations that throw back our life
And make our infancy a visible scene
On which the sun is shining?

Second Part

Thus far, my friend, have we retraced the way
Through which I travelled when I first began
To love the woods and fields. The passion yet
Was in its birth, sustained (as might befall)
By nourishment that came unsought;[1] for still   5
From week to week, from month to month, we lived
A round of tumult. Duly were our games
Prolonged in summer till the daylight failed;
No chair remained before the doors; the bench
And threshold steps were empty; fast asleep   10
The labourer, and the old man who had sat
A later lingerer – yet the revelry
Continued, and the loud uproar! At last,
When all the ground was dark, and the huge clouds
Were edged with twinkling stars, to bed we went,   15
With weary joints and with a beating mind.[2]
    Ah, is there one who ever has been young
And needs a monitory voice to tame
The pride of virtue and of intellect?[3]

---

88   *ere the birth ... snows* In Wordsworth's metaphor, he has
attributed (or 'planted') his memories (snowdrops) to a time
from which, in actual fact, no memories survive ('winter
snows').
89   *my friend* Coleridge, to whom the poem is addressed.
90   *honourable toil* When he composed these lines in February
1799, Wordsworth expected to go on with *The Recluse*.
91   *visionary things* things seen imaginatively.

SECOND PART
1   *nourishment that came unsought* Where in Part I Wordsworth
discussed his unconscious reponse to the influence of nature,
he aims to show in Part II how nature in adolescence was
'sought / For her own sake'.
2   *a beating mind* cf. *The Tempest* IV i 162–3: 'A turn or two
I'll walk, / To still my beating mind'.
3   *Ah, is ... intellect* How can anyone who remembers what it
was like to be young need a warning ('monitory voice') not to
overrate the achievements of maturity?

And is there one, the wisest and the best   20
Of all mankind, who does not sometimes wish
For things which cannot be, who would not give,
If so he might, to duty and to truth
The eagerness of infantine desire?
A tranquillizing spirit presses now   25
On my corporeal frame,[4] so wide appears
The vacancy between me and those days
Which yet have such self-presence[5] in my heart
That sometimes, when I think of them, I seem
Two consciousnesses – conscious of myself   30
And of some other being. A grey stone
Of native rock, left midway in the square
Of our small market-village, was the home
And centre of these joys; and when, returned
After long absence, thither I repaired,   35
I found that it was split, and gone to build
A smart assembly-room[6] that perked and flared
With wash and rough-cast, elbowing the ground
Which had been ours. But let the fiddle scream
And be ye happy! Yet I know, my friends,[7]   40
That more than one of you will think with me
Of those soft starry nights, and that old dame
From whom the stone was named, who there had sat
And watched her table with its huckster's wares,
Assiduous for the length of sixty years.[8]   45
We ran a boisterous race, the year span round
With giddy motion. But the time approached
That brought with it a regular desire
For calmer pleasures, when the beauteous scenes
Of nature were collater..ly attached   50
To every scheme of holiday delight
And every boyish sport – less grateful[9] else,
And languidly pursued.[10]
               When summer came
It was the pastime of our afternoons
To beat along the plain[11] of Windermere   55
With rival oars, and the selected bourn[12]
Was now an island musical with birds
That sang for ever; now a sister isle
Beneath the oak's umbrageous[13] covert, sown
With lilies-of-the-valley like a field;   60
And now a third small island[14] where remained

---

4   *corporeal frame* body; the effect is similar to that described
in *Tintern Abbey* 44–6.

5   *self-presence* presence to himself – actuality, immediacy.

6   *A smart assembly-room* Hawkshead Town Hall, built 1790,
covered with gravel stucco ('rough-cast') and white-wash.
Wordsworth didn't like white buildings because of the way
they stuck out in the landscape.

7   *my friends* An address to Coleridge and John Wordsworth
(the poet's brother), with whom the poet visited Hawkshead
on 2 November 1799.

8   *that old dame . . . years* Ann Holme, who set out her wares –
cakes, pies, and sweets – on the large stone at the end of the
market square in Hawkshead

9   *grateful* pleasing.

10   *languidly pursued* Natural beauty is still only an additional
('collateral') pleasure, though it is beginning to be valued.

11   *plain* flat surface of the lake.

12   *bourn* aim, destination.

13   *umbrageous* shady.

14   *a third small island* Lady Holm, where there was once a
chapel to the Virgin Mary.

An old stone table and one mouldered cave –
A hermit's history. In such a race,
So ended, disappointment could be none,
Uneasiness, or pain, or jealousy;   65
We rested in the shade, all pleased alike,
Conquered and conqueror. Thus our selfishness
Was mellowed down, and thus the pride of strength
And the vainglory of superior skill
Were interfused[15] with objects which subdued   70
And tempered them, and gradually produced
A quiet independence of the heart.
And to my friend who knows me, I may add,
Unapprehensive of reproof, that hence
Ensued a diffidence and modesty,   75
And I was taught to feel, perhaps too much,
The self-sufficing power of solitude.
       No delicate viands[16] sapped our bodily strength;
More than we wished we knew the blessing then
Of vigorous hunger, for our daily meals   80
Were frugal, Sabine fare;[17] and then, exclude
A little weekly stipend,[18] and we lived
Through three divisions of the quartered year
In penniless poverty. But now, to school
Returned from the half-yearly holidays,   85
We came with purses more profusely filled,[19]
Allowance which abundantly sufficed
To gratify the palate with repasts
More costly than the dame of whom I spake,
That ancient woman,[20] and her board, supplied.   90
Hence inroads into distant vales, and long
Excursions far away among the hills;
Hence rustic dinners on the cool green ground,
Or in the woods, or by a riverside
Or fountain[21] – festive banquets that provoked   95
The languid action of a natural scene
By pleasure of corporeal appetite.
       Nor is my aim neglected if I tell
How twice in the long length of those half-years
We from our funds perhaps with bolder hand   100
Drew largely – anxious for one day, at least,
To feel the motion of the galloping steed.
And with the good old innkeeeper,[22] in truth,
I needs must say that sometimes we have used
Sly subterfuge, for the intended bound   105
Of the day's journey was too distant far

---

[15] *interfused* mingled; cf. *Tintern Abbey* 97.
[16] *delicate viands* decorative delicacies of no nutritional value.
[17] *Sabine fare* The Roman poet Horace had a Sabine farm
and recommended a frugal diet, although Ann Tyson,
Wordsworth's landlady, fed the poet pasties, cakes,
dumplings, eggs, and porridge for breakfast.
[18] *A little weekly stipend* In 1787, the year he left Hawks-
head, Wordsworth received sixpence a week.

[19] *But now ... filled* When Wordsworth returned to school
in January 1787, after the half-yearly holiday, he had an extra
guinea (worth 42 'weekly stipends').
[20] *That ancient woman* Ann Tyson was seventy-three in Janu-
ary 1787.
[21] *fountain* spring or stream.
[22] *innkeeper* who hired out the horses.

For any cautious man – a structure famed
Beyond its neighbourhood, the antique walls
Of that large abbey with its fractured arch,[23]
Belfry, and images, and living trees,   110
A holy scene! Along the smooth green turf
Our horses grazed. In more than inland peace
Left by the winds that overpass the vale
In that sequestered ruin trees and towers,
Both silent and both motionless alike,   115
Hear all day long the murmuring sea that beats
Incessantly upon a craggy shore.
    Our steeds remounted, and the summons given,
With whip and spur we by the chantry[24] flew
In uncouth[25] race, and left the cross-legged knight,   120
And the stone abbot,[26] and that single wren
Which one day sang so sweetly in the nave
Of the old church that, though from recent showers
The earth was comfortless, and, touched by faint
Internal breezes from the roofless walls,   125
The shuddering ivy dripped large drops, yet still
So sweetly mid the gloom the invisible bird
Sang to itself that there I could have made
My dwelling-place, and lived for ever there
To hear such music.[27] Through the walls we flew   130
And down the valley, and, a circuit made
In wantonness of heart, through rough and smooth
We scampered homeward. Oh, ye rocks and streams,
And that still spirit of the evening air,
Even in this joyous time I sometimes felt   135
Your presence, when with slackened step we breathed[28]
Along the sides of the steep hills, or when,
Lightened by gleams of moonlight from the sea,
We beat with thundering hoofs the level sand.[29]
    There was a row of ancient trees, since fallen,   140
That on the margin of a jutting land
Stood near the lake of Coniston, and made
With its long boughs above the water stretched
A gloom through which a boat might sail along
As in a cloister. An old hall[30] was near,   145
Grotesque and beautiful, its gavel-end[31]
And huge round chimneys to the top o'ergrown
With fields of ivy. Thither we repaired,
'Twas even a custom with us, to the shore

---

[23]   *that large abbey with its fractured arch* Furness Abbey is
about 20 miles south of Hawkshead, near Barrow-in-Furness.
It was founded by Cistercian monks in 1127 and dissolved by
Henry VIII in 1539. The fractured arch is still to be seen. Its
roof-timbers, stripped of their valuable lead, had long since
fallen by Wordsworth's day.
[24]   *chantry* chapel where masses were once said for the dead.
[25]   *uncouth* unseemly, indecorous (because of their surround-
ings).

[26]   *the cross-legged knight ... abbot* The stone figures of several
cross-legged knights and an abbot may still be seen in the
museum at Furness Abbey.
[27]   *So sweetly ... music* cf. Shakespeare, *Sonnet 73*: 'Bare ruined
choirs, where late the sweet birds sang'.
[28]   *breathed* i.e. let the horses get their breath back.
[29]   *the level sand* The return journey took them along Levens
Sands from Rampside to Greenodd.
[30]   *An old hall* Coniston Hall, dating from 1580, was the seat
of the wealthy Le Fleming family.
[31]   *gavel-end* gable.

And to that cool piazza.[32] They who dwelt 150
In the neglected mansion-house supplied
Fresh butter, tea-kettle, and earthenware,
And chafing-dish with smoking coals,[33] and so
Beneath the trees we sat in our small boat
And in the covert[34] ate our delicate meal 155
Upon the calm smooth lake. It was a joy
Worthy the heart of one who is full-grown
To rest beneath those horizontal boughs
And mark the radiance of the setting sun,
Himself unseen, reposing on the top 160
Of the high eastern hills. And there I said,
That beauteous sight before me, there I said
(Then first beginning in my thoughts to mark
That sense of dim similitude which links
Our moral feelings with external forms) 165
That in whatever region I should close
My mortal life I would remember you,
Fair scenes, that dying I would think on you,
My soul would send a longing look to you,
Even as that setting sun while all the vale 170
Could nowhere catch one faint memorial gleam
Yet with the last remains of his last light
Still lingered, and a farewell lustre threw
On the dear mountain-tops where first he rose.[35]
'Twas then my fourteenth summer, and these words 175
Were uttered in a casual access
Of sentiment, a momentary trance
That far outran the habit of my mind.
    Upon the eastern shore of Windermere
Above the crescent of a pleasant bay, 180
There was an inn[36] – no homely-featured shed,
Brother of the surrounding cottages,
But 'twas a splendid place, the door beset
With chaises,[37] grooms, and liveries,[38] and within
Decanters, glasses, and the blood-red wine.[39] 185
In ancient times, or ere the hall was built
On the large island,[40] had this dwelling been

---

[32] *cool piazza* the shady colonnade formed by the branches of the sycamore trees.

[33] *chafing-dish with smoking coals* portable charcoal stove used to cook trout, or char, from the lake.

[34] *covert* shade.

[35] *Even as ... rose* in later years Wordsworth recalled this this image 'suggested itself to me while I was resting in a boat along with my companions under the shade of a magnificent row of sycamores, which then extended their branches from the shore of the promontory upon which stands the ancient, and at that time the more picturesque, Hall of Coniston, the seat of the Le Flemings, from very early times' (*FN* 6).

[36] *an inn* the White Lion at Bowness, now the Royal Hotel.

[37] *chaises* light carriages.

[38] *liveries* uniforms.

[39] *the blood-red wine* an echo of the anonymous ballad, *Sir Patrick Spence*: 'The king sits in Dunfermling toune, / Drink-ing the blude-reid wine' (ll. 1–2). Wordsworth knew it from Percy's *Reliques of Ancient English Poetry* (1765), a copy of which he purchased in Hamburg shortly before starting work on the *Two-Part Prelude*.

[40] *the hall ... island* The first and finest of the neo-classical villas in the Lakes was the circular mansion on Belle Isle in Windermere, designed by John Plaw in 1774 for Thomas English, but not completed until the early 1780s when John Christian Curwen had become its owner. Wordsworth follows the guide-book writers of the day – Hutchinson, West, and Gilpin – in deploring the changes that had taken place, including the felling of many trees and the demolition of the old buildings (including, perhaps, the 'hut' mentioned here). Dorothy had harsh words for the circular mansion in June 1802: '... & that great house! Mercy upon us! If it *could* be concealed it would be well for all who are pained to see the pleasantest of earthly spots deformed by man' (Grasmere Journals 107; her italics).

More worthy of a poet's love, a hut[41]
Proud of its one bright fire and sycamore shade.
But though the rhymes were gone which once inscribed 190
The threshold, and large golden characters[42]
On the blue-frosted signboard had usurped
The place of the old lion, in contempt
And mockery of the rustic painter's hand,
Yet to this hour the spot to me is dear 195
With all its foolish pomp. The garden lay
Upon a slope surmounted by the plain
Of a small bowling-green; beneath us stood
A grove, with gleams of water through the trees
And over the tree-tops — nor did we want 200
Refreshment, strawberries and mellow cream.
And there, through half an afternoon, we played
On the smooth platform, and the shouts we sent
Made all the mountains ring. But ere the fall
Of night, when in our pinnace we returned 205
Over the dusky lake, and to the beach
Of some small island steered our course, with one,[43]
The minstrel of our troop, and left him there,
And rowed off gently while he blew his flute
Alone upon the rock — oh then the calm 210
And dead still water lay upon my mind
Even with a weight of pleasure, and the sky,
Never before so beautiful, sank down
Into my heart, and held me like a dream.

    Thus day by day my sympathies increased, 215
And thus the common range of visible things
Grew dear to me. Already I began
To love the sun — a boy I loved the sun
Not as I since have loved him (as a pledge
And surety[44] of our earthly life, a light 220
Which while I view I feel I am alive),
But for this cause: that I had seen him lay
His beauty on the morning hills, had seen
The western mountain touch his setting orb
In many a thoughtless hour, when from excess 225
Of happiness my blood appeared to flow
With its own pleasure, and I breathed with joy.
And from like feelings, humble though intense
(To patriotic and domestic love
Analogous),[45] the moon to me was dear, 230
For I would dream away my purposes,
Standing to look upon her while she hung
Midway between the hills, as if she knew
No other region, but belonged to thee —

---

41 *hut* cottage.
42 *characters* letters.
43 *one* Robert Greenwood, another of Ann Tyson's boarders, who was elected Fellow of Trinity College, Cambridge in 1792. Wordsworth remained in touch with him for many years.

44 *surety* guarantee.
45 *To patriotic ... analogous* His love for the moon was like love of country and family ('domestic love') because it gave him pleasure in the region where he lived.

Yea, appertained by a peculiar right   235
To thee and thy grey huts,[46] my native vale.
    Those incidental charms which first attached
My heart to rural objects day by day
Grew weaker, and I hasten on to tell
How Nature – intervenient till this time,   240
And secondary[47] – now at length was sought
For her own sake. But who shall parcel out[48]
His intellect by geometric rules,
Split like a province into round and square?
Who knows the individual hour in which   245
His habits were first sown, even as a seed?
Who that shall point as with a wand, and say,
'This portion of the river of my mind
Came from yon fountain'? Thou, my friend,[49] art one
More deeply read in thy own thoughts, no slave   250
Of that false secondary power[50] by which
In weakness we create distinctions, then
Believe our puny boundaries are things
Which we perceive, and not which we have made.
To thee, unblinded by these outward shows,   255
The unity of all has been revealed;[51]
And thou wilt doubt with me, less aptly skilled
Than many are to class the cabinet
Of their sensations,[52] and in voluble[53] phrase
Run through the history and birth of each   260
As of a single independent thing.
Hard task[54] to analyse a soul, in which
Not only general habits and desires,
But each most obvious and particular thought –
Not in a mystical[55] and idle sense,   265
But in the words of reason deeply weighed –
Hath no beginning.
           Blessed the infant babe[56]
(For with my best conjectures I would trace
The progress of our being)[57] – blessed the babe
Nursed in his mother's arms, the babe who sleeps   270
Upon his mother's breast, who when his soul
Claims manifest kindred with an earthly soul,

---

[46] *grey huts* cottages built of grey stone.

[47] *intervenient ... secondary* Nature had been experienced in the midst of other distractions.

[48] *parcel out* divide up, categorize, analyse.

[49] *my friend* Wordsworth turns once more to Coleridge, to whom this poem is dedicated.

[50] *that false secondary power* the power of rational analysis, as opposed to the imaginative perception of unity.

[51] *To thee ... revealed* Coleridge was a Unitarian, and capable of writing: ''tis God / Diffused through all that doth make all one whole' (*Religious Musings* 144–5).

[52] *to class ... sensations* classify sensations as if they were exhibits in a cabinet. The metaphor is borrowed from Locke's *Essay on Human Understanding*: 'The senses at first let in particular ideas, and furnish the yet empty cabinet'.

[53] *voluble* glib, fluent.

[54] *Hard task* a deliberate echo of Milton, who speaks of having to describe the war in heaven as 'Sad task and hard' (*Paradise Lost* v 564); describing the growth of the mind is just as worthy of epic treatment for Wordsworth.

[55] *mystical* mysterious, occult.

[56] *Blessed the infant babe* The Infant Babe passage was probably inspired partly by the death of Coleridge's baby son Berkeley, news of which reached Coleridge in Germany in April 1799, several months after it had taken place; for Coleridge's reaction see his letter to Poole of 6 April 1799, pp. 473–4.

[57] *The progress of our being* Just as Milton charted progress from the Garden of Eden, Wordsworth will trace that of the growing mind.

Doth gather passion from his mother's eye![58]
Such feelings pass into his torpid[59] life
Like an awakening breeze, and hence his mind,   275
Even in the first trial of its powers,
Is prompt and watchful, eager to combine
In one appearance all the elements
And parts of the same object, else detached
And loath to coalesce.[60] Thus day by day   280
Subjected to the discipline of love,
His organs and recipient faculties[61]
Are quickened,[62] are more vigorous; his mind spreads,
Tenacious of the forms which it receives.[63]
In one beloved presence – nay and more,   285
In that most apprehensive habitude[64]
And those sensations which have been derived
From this beloved presence, there exists
A virtue which irradiates and exalts
All objects through all intercourse of sense.[65]   290
No outcast he, bewildered and depressed:
Along his infant veins are interfused
The gravitation and the filial bond
Of nature that connect him with the world.[66]
Emphatically such a being lives   295
An inmate of this *active* universe.
From nature largely he receives, nor so
Is satisfied, but largely[67] gives again –
For feeling has to him imparted strength;
And, powerful in all sentiments of grief,   300
Of exultation, fear and joy, his mind,
Even as an agent of the one great mind
Creates, creator and receiver both,[68]
Working but in alliance with the works
Which it beholds. Such, verily, is the first   305
Poetic spirit of our human life,
By uniform control of after-years
In most abated and suppressed, in some
Through every change of growth or of decay
Pre-eminent till death.
　　　　　　　　　From early days,   310
Beginning not long after that first time
In which, a babe, by intercourse of touch,

---

[58] *who when ... eye* When his soul first forms a relationship with another, the baby learns to love by seeing its mother's love in her eyes.
[59] *torpid* dormant.
[60] *loath to coalesce* reluctant to come together, making wholes. Inspired by its mother's love, the baby becomes able to form parts into wholes, ordering what he perceives; in other words, his mind is working imaginatively.
[61] *recipient faculties* senses.
[62] *quickened* enlivened.
[63] *Tenacious ... receives* The mind retains visual images; cf. *Tintern Abbey* 23–50.

[64] *most apprehensive habitude* a relationship ('habitude') best suited to learning ('most apprehensive').
[65] *this beloved presence ... sense* The mother's love is a power ('virtue') that infuses all objects which the child perceives, exalting them; cf. *Tintern Abbey* 101–2: 'A motion and a spirit that impels / All thinking things, all objects of all thought'.
[66] *Along his infant veins ... world* The child's loving relationship with his mother is what connects him to natural objects.
[67] *largely* abundantly.
[68] *Creates ... both* The child's mind becomes creative as well as receptive; it is imaginative – working in harmony with Nature. In doing so it acts as an agent of God.

I held mute dialogues with my mother's heart,
I have endeavoured to display the means
Whereby the infant sensibility, 315
Great birthright of our being, was in me
Augmented and sustained. Yet is a path
More difficult before me, and I fear
That in its broken windings we shall need
The chamois'[69] sinews and the eagle's wing. 320
For now a trouble came into my mind
From unknown causes: I was left alone,
Seeking this visible world, nor knowing why.
The props of my affections were removed,
And yet the building stood, as if sustained 325
By its own spirit.[70] All that I beheld
Was dear to me, and from this cause it came:
That now to nature's finer influxes[71]
My mind lay open to that more exact
And intimate communion which our hearts 330
Maintain with the minuter properties[72]
Of objects which already are beloved,
And of those only.
          Many are the joys
Of youth, but oh what happiness to live
When every hour brings palpable access[73] 335
Of knowledge, when all knowledge is delight,
And sorrow is not there! The seasons came,
And every season brought a countless store
Of modes and temporary qualities[74]
Which, but for this most watchful power of love, 340
Had been neglected – left a register
Of permanent relations,[75] else unknown.
Hence life, and change, and beauty, solitude
More active even than 'best society',[76]
Society made sweet as solitude 345
By silent inobtrusive sympathies
And gentle agitations of the mind
From manifold distinctions (difference
Perceived in things where to the common eye
No difference is) – and hence, from the same source, 350
Sublimer joy.[77] For I would walk alone[78]

---

69 *chamois* mountain antelope which Wordsworth may have seen on his 1790 walking tour which took him through the Alps.

70 *The props . . . spirit* The 'props' of the boy's feelings are the 'incidental charms which first attached / My heart to rural objects day by day' (ll. 237–8); they are no longer required for his love of nature to exist in its own right.

71 *influxes* influences.

72 *minuter properties* qualities known only to those who possess a well-established love of nature.

73 *palpable access* perceptible increase.

74 *modes and temporary qualities* short-lived weather or seasonal conditions.

75 *register . . . relations* permanent recollection in the mind of changing scenes in nature.

76 *best society* Wordsworth alludes to *Paradise Lost*, where Adam in Eden says: 'For solitude sometimes is best society' (ix 249).

77 *sublimer joy* A series of things follows from the permanently impressed features of Nature on the poet's mind: change, beauty, solitude more active than society, society as sweet as solitude, and the 'gentle agitations' produced by noticing many distinctions not observable to the untrained eye. From this last feature is produced 'sublimer joy'.

78 ll. 351–71 were composed in January–February 1798, as part of a passage describing the narrator of *The Ruined Cottage*. While boarding with the Tysons at Colthouse, Wordsworth was prone to going for walks at 1a.m.

In storm and tempest, or in starlight nights
Beneath the quiet heavens, and at that time
Would feel whate'er there is of power in sound
To breathe[79] an elevated mood, by form   355
Or image unprofaned. And I would stand
Beneath some rock, listening to sounds that are
The ghostly language of the ancient earth
Or make their dim abode in distant winds:
Thence did I drink the visionary power.   360
I deem not profitless these fleeting moods
Of shadowy exultation – not for this,
That they are kindred to our purer mind[80]
And intellectual life, but that the soul,
Remembering how she felt, but what she felt   365
Remembering not, retains an obscure sense
Of possible sublimity, to which
With growing faculties she doth aspire,
With faculties still growing, feeling still
That whatsoever point they gain they still   370
Have something to pursue.
                                        And not alone
In grandeur and in tumult, but no less
In tranquil scenes, that universal power
And fitness[81] in the latent qualities
And essences of things, by which the mind   375
Is moved with feelings of delight, to me
Came strengthened with a superadded soul,[82]
A virtue not its own. My morning walks
Were early; oft before the hours of school[83]
I travelled round our little lake, five miles   380
Of pleasant wandering – happy time more dear
For this, that one was by my side, a friend
Then passionately loved. With heart how full
Will he peruse these lines, this page (perhaps
A blank to other men), for many years   385
Have since flowed in between us, and, our minds
Both silent to each other, at this time
We live as if those hours had never been.
Nor seldom did I lift our cottage latch
Far earlier, and before the vernal[84] thrush   390
Was audible, among the hills I sat
Alone upon some jutting eminence
At the first hour of morning, when the vale
Lay quiet in an utter solitude.
How shall I trace the history, where seek   395

---

[79] *breathe* inspire.
[80] *kindred to our purer mind* of a spiritual nature.
[81] *fitness* harmony.
[82] *superadded soul* The 'superadded soul' is presumably an element of the 'visionary power' of l. 360. It is additional to natural objects, and is not conferred on them by the perceiving mind: it comes from beyond.

[83] *oft before the hours of school* School began at 6 or 6.30 a.m. during the summer; the five mile walk would have taken Wordsworth round Esthwaite Water – although that seems a generous estimate for a lake which is little more than a mile long. The friend was John Fleming, who went up to Cambridge in 1785.
[84] *vernal* springtime.

The origin of what I then have felt?
Oft in those moments such a holy calm
Did overspread my soul, that I forgot
The agency of sight, and what I saw
Appeared like something in myself – a dream, 400
A prospect[85] in my mind.
     'Twere long to tell
What spring and autumn, what the winter snows,
And what the summer shade, what day and night,
The evening and the morning, what my dreams
And what my waking thoughts supplied, to nurse 405
That spirit of religious love in which
I walked with nature. But let this at least
Be not forgotten – that I still retained
My first creative sensibility,
That by the regular action of the world 410
My soul was unsubdued. A plastic[86] power
Abode with me, a forming hand,[87] at times
Rebellious, acting in a devious mood,
A local spirit of its own, at war
With general tendency, but for the most 415
Subservient strictly to the external things
With which it communed.[88] An auxiliar[89] light
Came from my mind, which on the setting sun
Bestowed new splendour; the melodious birds,
The gentle breezes, fountains that ran on 420
Murmuring so sweetly in themselves, obeyed
A like dominion, and the midnight storm
Grew darker in the presence of my eye.
Hence my obeisance, my devotion hence,
And *hence* my transport.[90]
     Nor should this perchance 425
Pass unrecorded, that I still had loved
The exercise and produce of a toil
Than analytic industry to me
More pleasing, and whose character I deem
Is more poetic, as resembling more 430
Creative agency – I mean to speak
Of that interminable building[91] reared
By observation of affinities
In objects where no brotherhood exists
To common minds. My seventeenth year was come, 435
And, whether from this habit[92] rooted now
So deeply in my mind, or from excess
Of the great social principle of life[93]

---

85 *prospect* landscape, view.
86 *plastic* shaping, forming.
87 *forming hand* an allusion to the creation of Eve at *Paradise Lost* viii 470: 'Under his forming hands a creature grew'.
88 *at times . . . communed* The imagination sometimes behaves with a will of its own, but is usually subordinate to the natural world (i.e. prepared to enhance it).
89 *auxiliar* enhancing; the 'auxiliar light' is the imagination.

90 *transport* ecstasy. It is because the mind is believed to be 'lord and master' over what it perceives that the poet devotes himself to Nature.
91 *interminable building* mental structure.
92 *this habit* the 'observation of affinities' (l. 433).
93 *the great social principle of life* love, which might have led Wordsworth to see his feelings reflected in inanimate objects ('unorganic natures').

Coercing all things into sympathy,
To unorganic natures I transferred   440
My own enjoyments,[94] or, the power of truth
Coming in revelation, I conversed
With things that really are; I at this time
Saw blessings spread around me like a sea.
Thus did my days pass on, and now at length   445
From Nature and her overflowing soul[95]
I had received so much that all my thoughts
Were steeped in feeling.
                            I was only then
Contented when with bliss ineffable[96]
I felt the sentiment of being spread   450
O'er all that moves, and all that seemeth still,
O'er all that, lost beyond the reach of thought
And human knowledge, to the human eye
Invisible, yet liveth to the heart;
O'er all that leaps and runs, and shouts and sings,   455
Or beats the gladsome air; o'er all that glides
Beneath the wave, yea in the wave itself
And mighty depth of waters. Wonder not
If such my transports[97] were, for in all things
I saw one life, and felt that it was joy.   460
One song they sang, and it was audible –
Most audible then when the fleshly ear,
O'ercome by grosser prelude of that strain,[98]
Forgot its functions and slept undisturbed.
        If this be error,[99] and another faith   465
Find easier access to the pious mind,
Yet were I grossly destitute of all
Those human sentiments which make this earth
So dear, if I should fail with grateful voice
To speak of you, ye mountains and ye lakes   470
And sounding cataracts, ye mists and winds
That dwell among the hills where I was born.
If in my youth I have been pure in heart,
If, mingling with the world, I am content
With my own modest pleasures, and have lived   475
With God and nature communing, removed
From little enmities and low desires,
The gift is yours; if in these times of fear,
This melancholy waste[100] of hopes o'erthrown,
If, mid indifference and apathy   480
And wicked exultation, when good men

---

94   *or, from excess . . . own enjoyments* Wordsworth has in mind
Coleridge's lines in the 1798 text of *Frost at Midnight*:
    But still the living spirit in our frame
    That loves not to behold a lifeless thing,
    Transfuses into all its own delights
    Its own volition . . . (ll. 21–4)
95   ll. 446–64 comprise *Pedlar* 204–22, incorporated here in
autumn 1799, with the necessary change of pronoun from 'he'
to 'I'.

96   *ineffable* indescribable.
97   *transports* raptures.
98   *grosser prelude of that strain* sensual joy preceding the more
refined pleasures of the pantheist's perception of the 'one life'.
99   *If this be error* Wordsworth sometimes sounds certain, but
it is characteristic of him sometimes to express doubt; cf. *Tin-
tern Abbey* 50ff.: 'If this / Be but a vain belief . . .' The phrasing
is in fact borrowed from Shakespeare, Sonnet 116, l. 13.
100   *waste* desert.

On every side fall off we know not how,
To selfishness, disguised in gentle names
Of peace and quiet and domestic love,
Yet mingled not unwillingly with sneers   485
On visionary minds[101] – if in this time
Of dereliction and dismay I yet
Despair not of our nature, but retain
A more than Roman confidence,[102] a faith
That fails not, in all sorrow my support,   490
The blessing of my life, the gift is yours,
Ye mountains! – thine, oh nature! Thou hast fed
My lofty speculations, and in thee,
For this uneasy heart of ours, I find
A never-failing principle[103] of joy   495
And purest passion.
        Thou, my friend, wast reared
In the great city, mid far other scenes,[104]
But we by different roads at length have gained
The self-same bourn. And from this cause to thee
I speak unapprehensive of contempt,   500
The insinuated scoff of coward tongues,
And all that silent language which so oft
In conversation betwixt man and man
Blots from the human countenance all trace
Of beauty and of love. For thou hast sought   505
The truth in solitude, and thou art one,
The most intense of nature's worshippers,
In many things my brother, chiefly here
In this my deep devotion.
               Fare thee well![105]
Health and the quiet of a healthful mind   510
Attend thee, seeking oft the haunts of men,
And yet more often living with thyself,
And for thyself. So haply shall thy days
Be many, and a blessing to mankind.

End of the Second Part[106]

---

[101] *when good men ... minds* Wordsworth is reacting to Coleridge's exhortation to incorporate into *The Recluse* an address to 'those, who, in consequence of the complete failure of the French Revolution, have thrown up all hopes of the amelioration of mankind, and are sinking into an almost epicurean selfishness, disguising the same under the soft titles of domestic attachment and contempt for visionary *philosophes*' (Griggs i 527). The most obvious example is that of Sir James Mackintosh, former apologist for the French Revolution, who, in a series of notorious lectures of February–June 1799, attacked the progressive causes he had once advocated (see pp. 172–4). His apostasy drew comments in Hazlitt's essay on Mackintosh in *The Spirit of the Age* (1825), an uncharacteristically harsh epigram by Lamb (p. 580), and a notebook entry by Coleridge: 'Did Mackintosh change his opinions, with a cold clear predetermination, formed at one moment, to make £5000 a year by that change?' (*Notebooks* i 947).

[102] *more than Roman confidence* Although Maxwell adduced the example of the Roman general, Varro, commended after his defeat by Hannibal at Cannae (216 BC) for not despairing of the republic, Wordsworth may simply be recommending Stoicism. His admiration for Roman history and thought is analysed by Jane Worthington, *Wordsworth's Reading of Roman Prose* (1946).

[103] *principle* source.

[104] *Thou, my friend ... other scenes* In *Frost at Midnight*, Coleridge had written: 'For I was reared / In the great city, pent mid cloisters dim' (ll. 56–7).

[105] *Fare thee well!* Coleridge in November 1799 was about to go south to become a journalist in London; the Wordsworths were about to move into Dove Cottage.

[106] *End of the Second Part* entered by Dorothy when she copied the poem. She thought it would be continued, and Wordsworth indeed attempted to write a third part at the end of 1801. However, when he next made a serious start on the poem, in January 1804, he decided to completely reorganize the work, and ended up creating the *Five-Book Prelude*.

[*There was a boy*] (composed between 6 October and early December 1798)[1]

From LYRICAL BALLADS (2nd edn, 2 vols, 1800)

There was a boy – ye knew him well, ye cliffs
And islands of Winander![2] Many a time
At evening, when the stars had just begun
To move along the edges of the hills,
Rising or setting, would he stand alone   5
Beneath the trees or by the glimmering lake,
And there, with fingers interwoven, both hands
Pressed closely palm to palm and to his mouth
Uplifted, he, as through an instrument,
Blew mimic hootings to the silent owls   10
That they might answer him. And they would shout
Across the watery vale, and shout again
Responsive to his call, with quivering peals
And long halloos, and screams, and echoes loud
Redoubled and redoubled – a wild scene   15
Of mirth and jocund din! And when it chanced
That pauses of deep silence mocked his skill,
Then sometimes in that silence while he hung
Listening, a gentle shock of mild surprise
Has carried far[3] into his heart the voice   20
Of mountain torrents; or the visible scene
Would enter unawares[4] into his mind
With all its solemn imagery, its rocks,
Its woods, and that uncertain heaven, received
Into the bosom of the steady lake.[5]   25
Fair are the woods, and beauteous is the spot,
The vale where he was born. The churchyard hangs
Upon a slope above the village school,
And there, along that bank, when I have passed
At evening, I believe that near his grave   30
A full half-hour together I have stood
Mute – for he died when he was ten years old.[6]

THERE WAS A BOY
[1] In early 1804 this poem was incorporated into *Five-Book Prelude* iv 471–504, and then into *Thirteen-Book Prelude* v 389–422. It was originally composed in the first person, with all the experiences attributed to the poet.
[2] *Winander* Windermere.
[3] 'The very expression, "far", by which space and its infinities are attributed to the human heart, and to its capacities of re-echoing the sublimities of nature, has always struck me as with a flash of sublime revelation', wrote De Quincey of this passage in 1839; see pp. 640–2.
[4] *unawares* unbidden, unpremeditated; it is important to Wordsworth and Coleridge that moments of vision occur spontaneously – cf. *The Ancient Mariner* (1798): 'A spring of love gusht from my heart / And I blessed them unaware!' (ll. 276–7).

[5] After reading '*There was a boy*' in December 1798, Coleridge wrote of ll. 24–5: 'I should have recognised [them] any where; and had I met these lines running wild in the deserts of Arabia, I should have instantly screamed out "Wordsworth!"' (Griggs i 453). Wordsworth offered a gloss on ll. 21–5 in his 1815 Preface: 'The Boy, there introduced, is listening, with something of a feverish and restless anxiety, for the recurrence of the riotous sounds which he had previously excited; and, at the moment when the intenseness of his mind is beginning to remit, he is surprised into a perception of the solemn and tranquillizing images which the Poem describes' (*Prose Works* iii 35n).
[6] Although, as Wordsworth later recalled, the boy who hooted at the owls was a conflation of himself and a schoolfriend called William Raincock, the dead boy was in fact John Tyson, who died in 1782 at the age of twelve.

Nutting (composed between 6 October and 28 December 1798)[1]

From LYRICAL BALLADS (2nd edn, 2 vols, 1800)

It seems a day,
One of those heavenly days which cannot die,
When forth I sallied from our cottage-door,
And with a wallet o'er my shoulder slung,
A nutting-crook in hand, I turned my steps   5
Towards the distant woods, a figure quaint,
Tricked out in proud disguise of beggar's weeds[2]
Put on for the occasion, by advice
And exhortation of my frugal dame.[3]
Motley accoutrement! of power to smile   10
At thorns, and brakes, and brambles, and, in truth,
More ragged than need was. Among the woods,
And o'er the pathless rocks, I forced my way
Until, at length, I came to one dear nook
Unvisited, where not a broken bough   15
Drooped with its withered leaves (ungracious sign
Of devastation), but the hazels rose
Tall and erect, with milk-white clusters hung,
A virgin scene! A little while I stood,
Breathing with such suppression of the heart   20
As joy delights in; and, with wise restraint
Voluptuous, fearless of a rival, eyed
The banquet, or beneath the trees I sate
Among the flowers, and with the flowers I played;
A temper known to those who, after long   25
And weary expectation, have been blessed
With sudden happiness beyond all hope.
   Perhaps it was a bower beneath whose leaves
The violets of five seasons reappear
And fade, unseen by any human eye,   30
Where fairy water-breaks[4] do murmur on
For ever; and I saw the sparkling foam,
And, with my cheek on one of those green stones
That, fleeced with moss, beneath the shady trees,
Lay round me scattered like a flock of sheep,   35
I heard the murmur and the murmuring sound,
In that sweet mood when pleasure loves to pay
Tribute to ease; and, of its joy secure,
The heart luxuriates with indifferent[5] things,
Wasting its kindliness on stocks and stones,   40
And on the vacant air. Then up I rose,

NUTTING
[1] 'Written in Germany, intended as part of a poem on my own life [*The Two-Part Prelude*], but struck out as not being wanted there. Like most of my schoolfellows I was an impassioned nutter.... These verses arose out of the remembrance of feelings I had often had when a boy, and particularly in the extensive woods that still stretch from the side of Esthwaite Lake towards Graythwaite, the seat of the ancient family of Sandys' (*FN* 13).
[2] *weeds* clothes.
[3] *my frugal dame* Ann Tyson, Wordsworth's landlady at Hawkshead. Cf. *Two-Part Prelude* ii 88–90.
[4] *water-breaks* stretches of rapid water.
[5] *indifferent* not insensible but neutral, impartial, disinterested.

And dragged to earth both branch and bough, with crash
And merciless ravage, and the shady nook
Of hazels, and the green and mossy bower,
Deformed and sullied, patiently gave up   45
Their quiet being; and, unless I now
Confound my present feelings with the past,
Even then, when from the bower I turned away,
Exulting, rich beyond the wealth of kings,
I felt a sense of pain when I beheld   50
The silent trees, and the intruding sky.
    Then, dearest maiden, move along these shades
In gentleness of heart; with gentle hand
Touch – for there is a spirit in the woods.

[*Strange fits of passion I have known*] (composed between 6 October and 28 December 1798)[1]

From LYRICAL BALLADS (2nd edn, 2 vols, 1800)

Strange fits of passion I have known,
And I will dare to tell,
But in the lover's ear alone,
What once to me befell.

When she I loved was strong and gay   5
And like a rose in June,
I to her cottage bent my way
Beneath the evening moon.

Upon the moon I fixed my eye,
All over the wide lea;[2]   10
My horse trudged on, and we drew nigh
Those paths so dear to me.

And now we reached the orchard-plot,
And as we climbed the hill,
Towards the roof of Lucy's cot   15
The moon descended still.

In one of those sweet dreams I slept,
Kind nature's gentlest boon!
And all the while my eyes I kept
On the descending moon.   20

My horse moved on; hoof after hoof
He raised and never stopped:
When down behind the cottage roof
At once the planet dropped.

STRANGE FITS OF PASSION I HAVE KNOWN
[1] This poem, the three that follow it, and '*I travelled among unknown men*' (pp. 356–7), comprise what have come to be known as the Lucy poems. '*She was a phantom of delight*' is often classed among them. Much ink has been expended on the question of Lucy's identity; for Coleridge's suggestion that the poems were inspired by the fear of Dorothy's death, see his letter to Poole, 6 April 1799, p. 474.
[2] *lea* meadow.

What fond[3] and wayward thoughts will slide   25
Into a lover's head;
'Oh mercy!' to myself I cried,
'If Lucy should be dead!'

Song (composed between 6 October and 28 December 1798)

From LYRICAL BALLADS (2nd edn, 2 vols, 1800)

She dwelt among th' untrodden ways
    Beside the springs of Dove,[1]
A maid whom there were none to praise
    And very few to love.

A violet by a mossy stone   5
    Half-hidden from the eye,
Fair as a star when only one
    Is shining in the sky!

She *lived* unknown, and few could know
    When Lucy ceased to be;
But she is in her grave, and oh!   10
    The difference to me.

[*A slumber did my spirit seal*] (composed between 6 October and 28 December 1798)

From LYRICAL BALLADS (2nd edn, 2 vols, 1800)

A slumber did my spirit seal,[1]
    I had no human fears;
She seemed a thing that could not feel
    The touch of earthly years.

No motion has she now, no force;   5
    She neither hears nor sees;
Rolled round in earth's diurnal[2] course
    With rocks and stones and trees!

---

[3] *fond* meaning either 'foolish' or 'loving, affectionate'.

SONG
[1] *Dove* there are three English rivers with this name. Wordsworth probably meant the one in Derbyshire, rather than those in Yorkshire or Cumbria.

A SLUMBER DID MY SPIRIT SEAL
[1] *seal* contain, lock up.
[2] *diurnal* daily; cf. *Two-Part Prelude* i 182.

[*Three years she grew in sun and shower*] (composed between 6 October and 28 December 1798)

From LYRICAL BALLADS (2nd edn, 2 vols, 1800)

Three years she grew in sun and shower,
Then Nature said, 'A lovelier flower
On earth was never sown;
This child I to myself will take,
She shall be mine, and I will make   5
A lady of my own.

Myself will to my darling be
Both law and impulse, and with me
The girl in rock and plain,
In earth and heaven, in glade and bower,   10
Shall feel an overseeing power
To kindle or restrain.

She shall be sportive as the fawn
That wild with glee across the lawn
Or up the mountain springs,   15
And hers shall be the breathing balm
And hers the silence and the calm
Of mute insensate[1] things.

The floating clouds their state shall lend
To her, for her the willow bend,   20
Nor shall she fail to see
Even in the motions of the storm
A beauty that shall mould her form
By silent sympathy.

The stars of midnight shall be dear   25
To her, and she shall lean her ear
In many a secret place
Where rivulets dance their wayward round,
And beauty born of murmuring sound
Shall pass into her face.   30

And vital feelings of delight
Shall rear her form to stately height,
Her virgin bosom swell,
Such thoughts to Lucy I will give
While she and I together live   35
Here in this happy dell.'

Thus Nature spake – the work was done –
How soon my Lucy's race was run!

THREE YEARS SHE GREW IN SUN AND SHOWER
[1] *insensate* inanimate.

She died and left to me
This heath, this calm and quiet scene,   40
The memory of what has been,
And never more will be.

[*The Prelude: Glad Preamble*] (composed late November 1799; edited from MS)[1]

Oh there is blessing in this gentle breeze
That blows from the green fields, and from the clouds,
And from the sky: it beats against my cheek,
And seems half-conscious of the joy it gives.
Oh welcome messenger, oh welcome friend!   5
A captive greets thee, coming from a house
Of bondage, from yon city's walls set free,
A prison where he hath been long immured.[2]
Now I am free, enfranchised and at large,
May fix my habitation where I will.   10
What dwelling shall receive me? In what vale
Shall be my harbour? Underneath what grove
Shall I take up my home, and what sweet stream
Shall with its murmur lull me to my rest?
The earth is all before me:[3] with a heart   15
Joyous, nor scared at its own liberty,
I look about, and should the guide I choose
Be nothing better than a wandering cloud,[4]
I cannot miss my way. I breathe again;
Trances of thought and mountings of the mind   20
Come fast upon me. It is shaken off,
As by miraculous gift 'tis shaken off,
The heavy weight of many a weary day
Not mine, and such as were not made for me.
Long months of peace (if such bold word accord   25
With any promises of human life),
Long months of ease and undisturbed delight
Are mine in prospect — whither shall I turn?
By road or pathway, or through open field,
Or shall a twig or any floating thing   30
Upon the river, point me out my course?

THE PRELUDE: GLAD PREAMBLE
[1] Wordsworth began work on this passage while walking
from Ullswater to Grasmere, 18 November 1799, and com-
pleted it soon after moving into Dove Cottage two days later.
It was used as the opening to *Prelude* Book I in all versions of
the poem after January 1804.
[2] *immured* confined, walled up. The city from which
Wordsworth has been released is probably a mixture of Goslar
in Germany (where he spent the cold winter of 1798–9) and
London.
[3] *The earth is all before me* an allusion to the conclusion of
Paradise Lost, as Adam and Eve are driven out of Eden:

Some natural tears they dropped, but wiped them
    soon;
The world was all before them, where to choose
Their place of rest, and Providence their guide.
They hand in hand, with wandering steps and
    slow,
Through Eden took their solitary way.

Wordsworth's poem begins where Milton leaves off. He too is
making a new start, but does so in a spirit of profound opti-
mism.
[4] Providence guided Adam and Eve out of Eden (see preced-
ing note).

Enough that I am free, embrace today
An uncontrolled enfranchisement; for months
To come may live a life of chosen tasks,
May quit the tiresome sea and dwell on shore –   35
If not a settler on the soil, at least
To drink wild waters, and to pluck green herbs,
And gather fruits fresh from their native tree.
Nay more: if I may trust myself, this hour
Hath brought a gift that consecrates my joy,   40
For I, methought, while the sweet breath of heaven
Was blowing on my body, felt within
A corresponding mild creative breeze,[5]
A vital breeze which travelled gently on
O'er things which it had made, and is become   45
A tempest, a redundant[6] energy
Vexing its own creation. 'Tis a power
That does not come unrecognized, a storm
Which, breaking up a long-continued frost,
Brings with it vernal promises, the hope   50
Of active days, of dignity and thought,
Of prowess in an honourable field,[7]
Pure passion, virtue, knowledge, and delight,
The holy life of music and of verse.

[*Prospectus to 'The Recluse'*] (composed probably November or December 1799; edited from MS)[1]

On man, on nature, and on human life,
Thinking in solitude, from time to time
I find sweet passions traversing my soul
Like music;[2] unto these, where'er I may,
I would give utterance in numerous verse.[3]   5
Of truth, of grandeur, beauty, love, and hope,
Of joy in various commonalty[4] spread,
Of the individual mind that keeps its own
Inviolate retirement, and consists[5]
With being limitless – the one great life[6] –   10
I sing: fit audience let me find, though few!
    'Fit audience find, though few!'[7] Thus prayed the bard,
Holiest of men. Urania,[8] I shall need
Thy guidance, or a greater muse (if such
Descend to earth, or dwell in highest heaven),   15

---

[5]   *A corresponding mild creative breeze* the subject of much comment among recent critics; see, most notably, M. H. Abrams' title essay in *The Correspondent Breeze: Essays on English Romanticism* (New York and London, 1984).
[6]   *redundant* overflowing, exuberant.
[7]   *prowess in an honourable field* a reference to the composition of *The Recluse*; see p. 271.

PROSPECTUS TO 'THE RECLUSE'
[1]   Composed soon after arrival in Grasmere, 19 November 1799, published in much revised form in *The Excursion* (1814), as an announcement of the plan of *The Recluse*.

[2]   *I find . . . music* passions (emotions) play across the poet's soul just as the winds cross the strings on an Aeolian harp.
[3]   *numerous verse* poetic metre.
[4]   *commonalty* community.
[5]   *consists* co-exists.
[6]   *the one great life* the pantheist perception of *Pedlar* 204–22 and *Tintern Abbey* 94–103.
[7]   *Paradise Lost* vii 31.
[8]   Urania, muse of astronomy, is invoked by Milton, *Paradise Lost* Book VII.

For I must tread on shadowy ground, must sink
Deep, and ascend aloft, and breathe in worlds
To which the heaven of heavens[9] is but a veil.
All strength, all terror, single or in bands,
That ever was put forth by personal forms[10] –   20
Jehovah with his thunder, and the choir
Of shouting angels, and th' empyreal thrones[11] –
I pass them unalarmed. The darkest pit
Of the profoundest hell,[12] night, chaos, death,
Nor aught of blinder vacancy scooped out   25
By help of dreams, can breed such fear and awe
As fall upon me often when I look
Into my soul, into the soul of man –
My haunt, and the main region of my song.

    Beauty, whose living home is the green earth,   30
Surpassing far what hath by special craft[13]
Of delicate[14] poets been culled forth and shaped
From earth's materials, waits upon my steps,
Pitches her tents before me as I move,
My hourly neighbour. Paradise and groves   35
Elysian,[15] blessed islands in the deep
Of choice seclusion – wherefore need they be
A history, or but a dream, when minds
Once wedded to this outward frame of things
In love, find these the growth of common day?[16]   40

    Such pleasant haunts foregoing, if my song
Must turn elsewhere, and travel near the tribes
And fellowships of man, and see ill sights
Of passions ravenous from each other's rage,[17]
Insult and injury, and wrong and strife;   45
Must hear humanity in fields and groves
Pipe solitary anguish; or must hang
Brooding above the fierce confederate[18] storm
Of sorrow, barricadoed[19] evermore
Within the walls of cities,[20] to these sounds   50
Let me find meaning more akin to that
Which to God's ear they carry, that even these
Hearing, I be not heartless[21] or forlorn.

    Come thou, prophetic spirit, soul of man,
Thou human soul of the wide earth, that hast   55
Thy metropolitan temple[22] in the hearts
Of mighty poets, unto me vouchsafe[23]

---

9   *the heaven of heavens is but a veil* cf. *Paradise Lost* vii 553.
10 *personal forms* celestial beings to whom individual forms are usually attributed.
11 *empyreal thrones* high-ranking angels, as at *Paradise Lost* ii 430.
12 *profoundest hell* an echo of *Paradise Lost* i 251.
13 *craft* skill.
14 *delicate* fastidious.
15 *groves Elysian* the Elysian fields, where the souls of the blessed were believed to live in an eternal spring.
16 *Paradise . . . day* paradise materializes in different forms before the poet in everyday sights.

17 *passions ravenous from each other's rage* emotions stirred up by the sight of passion in other people.
18 *confederate* aggregated, accumulated. Wordsworth is recalling how in *Paradise Lost* the Holy Spirit 'Dove-like sat'st brooding' over chaos, 'And madest it pregnant' (i 21–2).
19 *barricadoed* cf. *Paradise Lost* viii 241.
20 *the fierce . . . cities* those confined within the hell of city life are united in misery.
21 *heartless* unhappy.
22 *metropolitan temple* throne.
23 *vouchsafe* grant.

Thy foresight, teach me to discern, and part
Inherent things from casual, what is fixed
From fleeting,[24] that my soul may live, and be   60
Even as a light hung up in heaven to cheer
The world in times to come. And if with this
I mingle humbler matter – with the thing
Contemplated describe the mind and man
Contemplating, and who he was, and what   65
The transitory being that beheld
This vision, when and where and how he lived
With all his little realities of life
(In part a fellow-citizen, in part
An outlaw and a borderer of his age) –   70
Be not this labour useless.
                        Oh great God!
To less than thee I cannot make this prayer;
Innocent mighty spirit, let my life
Express the image of a better time,
Desires more wise and simpler manners, nurse   75
My heart in genuine freedom, all pure thoughts
Be with me and uphold me to the end.

The Brothers: A Pastoral Poem (composed between December 1799 and early March 1800)[1]

From LYRICAL BALLADS (2nd edn, 2 vols, 1800)

'These tourists,[2] Heaven preserve us, needs must live
A profitable life! Some glance along,
Rapid and gay, as if the earth were air,
And they were butterflies to wheel about
Long as their summer lasted; some, as wise,   5
Upon the forehead of a jutting crag
Sit perched with book and pencil on their knee,
And look and scribble, scribble on and look,
Until a man might travel twelve stout miles[3]
Or reap an acre of his neighbour's corn.   10
    But, for that moping[4] son of idleness –
Why can he tarry *yonder*? In our churchyard
Is neither epitaph nor monument,

---

[24] *part . . . fleeting* innate qualities will be separated from the random; the permanent from the ephemeral.

THE BROTHERS: A PASTORAL POEM
[1] *The Brothers* is based on a story told to Wordsworth and Coleridge while on a walking tour of the Lakes in 1799. They heard about Jerome Bowman (who broke his leg near Scale Force, crawled three miles at night on hands and knees, and then died from his injuries) and his son who 'broke his neck before this, by falling off a crag', as Coleridge puts it. The son was believed 'to have laid down and slept, but walked in his sleep, and so came to this crag and fell off. This was at Proud

Knot on the mountain called Pillar up Ennerdale. His pike-staff stuck midway and stayed there till it rotted away' (*Note-books* i 540). In 1800 Wordsworth appended the following note to the title: 'This poem was intended to be the concluding poem of a series of pastorals the scene of which was laid among the mountains of Cumberland and Westmorland. I mention this to apologise for the abruptness with which the poem begins'.
[2] *tourists* even in 1800, the Lake District was a popular tourist resort.
[3] *stout miles* the old English 'long mile' of 2,428 yards.
[4] *moping* aimless, purposeless.

Tombstone nor name,[5] only the turf we tread
And a few natural graves.' To Jane, his wife,   15
Thus spake the homely priest of Ennerdale.
It was a July evening, and he sat
Upon the long stone-seat beneath the eaves
Of his old cottage – as it chanced that day,
Employed in winter's work. Upon the stone   20
His wife sat near him, teasing matted wool,
While from the twin cards[6] toothed with glittering wire,
He fed the spindle of his youngest child,
Who turned her large round wheel in the open air
With back and forward steps.[7] Towards the field   25
In which the parish chapel stood alone
Girt round with a bare ring of mossy wall,
While half an hour went by, the priest had sent
Many a long look of wonder; and at last,
Risen from his seat, beside the snowy ridge   30
Of carded wool which the old man had piled
He laid his implements with gentle care,
Each in the other locked, and down the path
Which from his cottage to the churchyard led
He took his way, impatient to accost   35
The stranger whom he saw still lingering there.
   'Twas one well known to him in former days:
A shepherd-lad, who ere his thirteenth year[8]
Had changed his calling – with the mariners   40
A fellow-mariner – and so had fared
Through twenty seasons; but he had been reared
Among the mountains, and he in his heart
Was half a shepherd on the stormy seas.
Oft in the piping shrouds[9] had Leonard heard
The tones of waterfalls, and inland sounds   45
Of caves and trees. And when the regular wind
Between the tropics[10] filled the steady sail
And blew with the same breath through days and weeks,
Lengthening invisibly its weary line
Along the cloudless main, he, in those hours   50
Of tiresome indolence, would often hang
Over the vessel's side, and gaze and gaze;
And while the broad green wave and sparkling foam
Flashed round him images and hues that wrought

---

5 *neither epitaph ... name* several Lake District churchyards
had no tombstones.
6 *twin cards* a pair of combs used for teasing out the hairs of
wool before they are spun into thread.
7 *Upon the stone ... steps* In the Fenwick Notes of 1843,
Wordsworth recalled: 'I could write a treatise of lamentation
upon the changes brought about among the cottages of West-
morland by the silence of the spinning wheel. During long
winter nights and wet days, the wheel upon which wool was
spun gave employment to a great part of a family. The old
man, however infirm, was able to card the wool, as he sate in
the corner by the fireside; and often, when a boy, have I

admired the cylinders of carded wool which were softly laid
upon each other by his side. Two wheels were often at work
on the same floor, and others of the family, chiefly the little
children, were occupied in teasing and cleaning the wool to fit
it for the hand of the carder. So that all except the smallest
infants were contributing to mutual support' (*FN* 20).
8 *ere his thirteenth year* John Wordsworth, the poet's younger
brother, also decided early on that he would be a sailor.
9 *shrouds* ropes supporting the mast of a ship, climbed when
changing sails. The wind plays ('pipes') through them.
10 *the regular wind ... tropics* trade winds blowing towards
the equator from the tropics of cancer and capricorn.

In union with the employment of his heart,   55
He – thus by feverish passion overcome –
Even with the organs of his bodily eye,
Below him in the bosom of the deep
Saw mountains, saw the forms of sheep that grazed
On verdant hills, with dwellings among trees,   60
And shepherds clad in the same country grey
Which he himself had worn.[11]
                        And now at length,
From perils manifold, with some small wealth
Acquired by traffic in the Indian Isles,[12]
To his paternal home he is returned   65
With a determined purpose to resume
The life which he lived there – both for the sake
Of many darling[13] pleasures, and the love
Which to an only brother he has borne
In all his hardships, since that happy time   70
When, whether it blew foul or fair, they two
Were brother shepherds on their native hills.
They were the last of all their race;[14] and now,
When Leonard had approached his home, his heart
Failed in him, and not venturing to enquire   75
Tidings of one whom he so dearly loved,
Towards the churchyard he had turned aside[15]
That (as he knew in what particular spot
His family were laid) he thence might learn
If still his brother lived, or to the file[16]   80
Another grave was added. He had found
Another grave, near which a full half-hour
He had remained; but as he gazed there grew
Such a confusion in his memory
That he began to doubt, and he had hopes   85
That he had seen this heap of turf before –
That it was not another grave, but one
He had forgotten. He had lost his path
As up the vale he came that afternoon
Through fields which once had been well known to him,   90

---

[11] 'This description of the calenture is sketched from an imperfect recollection of an admirable one in prose, by Mr Gilbert, author of *The Hurricane*' (Wordsworth's note). The calenture was defined by Johnson as 'a distemper peculiar to sailors in hot climates, wherein they imagine the sea to be green fields, and will throw themselves into it'. Gilbert's *Hurricane* (1796) may have been read by Wordsworth in the year of its publication; in later years at Rydal Mount he owned a copy.

[12] *traffic in the Indian Isles* trade in the East Indies.

[13] *darling* dearly loved.

[14] *They were the last of all their race* As in *Michael*, Wordsworth is concerned in this poem with the dying-out of small landowners – 'statesmen', whose small plots of land had descended through the same families for generations. Wordsworth made this point when he sent the Whig leader, Charles James Fox, a copy of *Lyrical Ballads* (1800): 'The domestic affections will always be strong amongst men who live in a country not crowded with population, if these men are placed above poverty. But if they are proprietors of small estates, which have descended to them from their ancestors, the power which these affections will acquire amongst such men is inconceivable by those who have only had an opportunity of observing hired labourers, farmers, and the manufacturing poor. Their little tract of land serves as a kind of permanent rallying point for their domestic feelings, as a tablet upon which they are written which makes them objects of memory in a thousand instances when they would otherwise be forgotten' (*EY* 314–15).

[15] *When Leonard … aside* probably based on John Wordsworth's arrival in Grasmere at the end of January 1800; according to Dorothy, 'twice did he approach the door and lay his hand upon the latch, and stop, and turn away without the courage to enter (we had not met for several years). He then went to the inn and sent us word that he was come' (*EY* 649).

[16] *file* row, line.

And oh, what joy the recollection now
Sent to his heart! He lifted up his eyes,
And looking round he thought that he perceived
Strange alteration wrought on every side
Among the woods and fields, and that the rocks,   95
And the eternal hills themselves, were changed.
    By this the priest, who down the field had come
Unseen by Leonard, at the churchyard gate
Stopped short; and thence, at leisure, limb by limb
He scanned him with a gay complacency.[17]   100
'Aye', thought the vicar, smiling to himself,
''Tis one of those who needs must leave the path
Of the world's business, to go wild alone –
His arms have a perpetual holiday.
The happy man will creep about the fields   105
Following his fancies by the hour, to bring
Tears down his cheek, or solitary smiles
Into his face, until the setting sun
Write Fool upon his forehead.' Planted thus
Beneath a shed[18] that overarched the gate   110
Of this rude churchyard, till the stars appeared
The good man might have communed with himself,
But that the stranger, who had left the grave,
Approached. He recognized the priest at once,
And after greetings interchanged (and given   115
By Leonard to the vicar as to one
Unknown to him), this dialogue ensued.

LEONARD
You live, sir, in these dales, a quiet life.
Your years make up one peaceful family,
And who would grieve and fret, if – welcome come   120
And welcome gone – they are so like each other
They cannot be remembered? Scarce a funeral
Comes to this churchyard once in eighteen months;
And yet, some changes must take place among you.
And you who dwell here, even among these rocks   125
Can trace the finger of mortality,[19]
And see that with our threescore years and ten[20]
We are not all that perish. I remember
(For many years ago I passed this road)
There was a footway all along the fields   130
By the brook-side; 'tis gone. And that dark cleft –
To me it does not seem to wear the face
Which then it had.

PRIEST
              Why, sir, for aught I know,
That chasm is much the same.

---

[17] *complacency* self-satisfaction.
[18] *shed* porchway, roof.
[19] *the finger of mortality* signs of death or change.

[20] *threescore years and ten* seventy years, man's allotted life-span: 'the days of our years are threescore years and ten' (Psalm 90:10).

LEONARD

              But surely, yonder –

PRIEST

Aye, there indeed your memory is a friend	135
That does not play you false. On that tall pike	
(It is the loneliest place of all these hills)	
There were two springs which bubbled side by side	
As if they had been made that they might be	
Companions for each other! Ten years back,	140
Close to those brother fountains, the huge crag	
Was rent with lightning – one is dead and gone,	
The other, left behind, is flowing still.[21]	
For accidents and changes such as these,	
Why, we have store[22] of them! A water-spout	145
Will bring down half a mountain – what a feast	
For folks that wander up and down like you,	
To see an acre's breadth of that wide cliff	
One roaring cataract! A sharp May storm	
Will come with loads of January snow	150
And in one night send twenty score of sheep	
To feed the ravens; or a shepherd dies	
By some untoward death among the rocks;	
The ice breaks up, and sweeps away a bridge;	
A wood is felled. And then, for our own homes –	155
A child is born or christened, a field ploughed,	
A daughter sent to service,[23] a web spun,[24]	
The old house-clock is decked with a new face[25] –	
And hence, so far from wanting facts or dates	
To chronicle the time, we all have here	160
A pair of diaries: one serving, sir,	
For the whole dale, and one for each fireside.[26]	
Yours was a stranger's judgment[27] – for historians	
Commend me to these vallies!	

LEONARD

Yet your churchyard	
Seems (if such freedom may be used with you)	165
To say that you are heedless of the past:	
An orphan could not find his mother's grave.	
Here's neither head nor foot-stone, plate of brass,	
Cross-bones or skull, type of our earthly state	
Or emblem of our hopes. The dead man's home	170
Is but a fellow to that pasture field.[28]	

---

[21] 'The impressive circumstance here described actually took place some years ago in this country, upon an eminence called Kidstow Pike, one of the highest of the mountains that surround Hawes Water. The summit of the Pike was stricken by lightning, and every trace of one of the fountains disappeared, while the other continued to flow as before' (Wordsworth's note).

[22] *store* a good store, plenty.

[23] *sent to service* put to work as a servant.

[24] *a web spun* a piece of cloth woven.

[25] *decked with a new face* re-painted.

[26] *we all . . . fireside* time is measured by the public events, shared by the community, and private ones, known to each family.

[27] *Yours was a stranger's judgment* painfully ironic; the priest is still unaware of Leonard's identity.

[28] *The dead . . . field* the graveyard looks the same as the meadow.

PRIEST

Why there, sir, is a thought that's new to me.
The stonecutters, 'tis true, might beg their bread
If every English churchyard were like ours;
Yet your conclusion wanders from the truth.   175
We have no need of names and epitaphs,
We talk about the dead by our firesides.
And then for our immortal part[29] – *we* want
No symbols, sir, to tell us that plain tale.
The thought of death sits easy on the man   180
Who has been born and dies among the mountains.[30]

LEONARD

Your dalesmen, then, do in each other's thoughts
Possess a kind of second life. No doubt
You, sir, could help me to the history
Of half these graves?

PRIEST

                        For eight-score winters past[31] –   185
With what I've witnessed, and with what I've heard –
Perhaps I might; and on a winter's evening,
If you were seated at my chimney's nook,
By turning o'er these hillocks one by one
We two could travel, sir, through a strange round,   190
Yet all in the broad highway of the world.[32]
Now there's a grave – your foot is half upon it –
It looks just like the rest, and yet that man
Died broken-hearted.

LEONARD

                    'Tis a common case –
We'll take another. Who is he that lies   195
Beneath yon ridge, the last of those three graves? –
It touches on that piece of native[33] rock
Left in the churchyard wall.

PRIEST

                        That's Walter Ewbank.
He had as white a head and fresh a cheek
As ever were produced by youth and age   200
Engendering in the blood of hale fourscore.[34]
For five long generations had the heart
Of Walter's forefathers o'erflowed the bounds

---

[29] *our immortal part* i.e. the soul.

[30] 'There is not anything more worthy of remark in the manners of the inhabitants of these mountains, than the tranquillity – I might say indifference – with which they think and talk upon the subject of death. Some of the country churchyards, as here described, do not contain a single tombstone, and most of them have a very small number' (Wordsworth's note).

[31] *eight-score winters past* i.e. the last 160 years (a score is 20).

[32] *By turning ... world* the life stories of those buried before them comprise a wide range ('strange round') of experience, which, taken as a whole, would be revealed as entirely normal ('in the broad highway of the world').

[33] *native* a piece of rock embedded in the ground even before the graveyard was put there.

[34] *He had ... fourscore* Walter was eighty, but he was healthy and vigorous ('hale') thanks to his combination of youth and age.

Of their inheritance[35] – that single cottage
(You see it yonder), and those few green fields.   205
They toiled and wrought, and still, from sire[36] to son,
Each struggled, and each yielded as before
A little – yet a little. And old Walter –
They left to him the family heart, and land
With other burdens than the crop it bore.   210
Year after year the old man still preserved
A cheerful mind, and buffeted with bond,
Interest and mortgages, at last he sank,[37]
And went into his grave before his time.
Poor Walter – whether it was care that spurred him   215
God only knows, but to the very last
He had the lightest foot in Ennerdale.
His pace was never that of an old man –
I almost see him tripping down the path
With his two grandsons after him. But you,   220
Unless our landlord be your host tonight,[38]
Have far to travel, and in these rough paths
Even in the longest day of midsummer –

LEONARD
But these two orphans . . .

PRIEST
             Orphans – such they were,
Yet not while Walter lived. For though their parents   225
Lay buried side by side as now they lie,
The old man was a father to the boys –
Two fathers in one father – and if tears
Shed when he talked of them where they were not,
And hauntings from the infirmity of love,   230
Are aught of what makes up a mother's heart,
This old man in the day of his old age
Was half a mother to them. If you weep, sir,
To hear a stranger talking about strangers,[39]
Heaven bless you when you are among your kindred!   235
Aye, you may turn that way – it is a grave
Which will bear looking at.

LEONARD
             These boys, I hope
They loved this good old man?

PRIEST
               They did, and truly –

---

[35] *the heart . . . inheritance* the Ewbanks were more generous than they could afford.
[36] *sire* father.
[37] *buffeted . . . time* The cost of Walter's independence was that the land he inherited was burdened by mortgages and debt.

[38] *Unless our landlord be your host tonight* unless you plan to stay at the inn.
[39] *If you weep . . . strangers* again, painfully ironic. The Priest is still unaware that the story he has been telling is that of Leonard's family.

But that was what we almost overlooked,
They were such darlings of each other. For   240
Though from their cradles they had lived with Walter,
The only kinsman near them in the house,
Yet he being old they had much love to spare,
And it all went into each other's hearts.
Leonard, the elder by just eighteen months,   245
Was two years taller – 'twas a joy to see,
To hear, to meet them! From their house the school
Was distant three short miles; and in the time
Of storm, and thaw, when every water-course
And unbridged stream (such as you may have noticed,   250
Crossing our roads at every hundred steps)
Was swoln into a noisy rivulet,
Would Leonard then, when elder boys perhaps
Remained at home, go staggering through the fords[40]
Bearing his brother on his back. I've seen him   255
On windy days, in one of those stray brooks –
Aye, more than once I've seen him mid-leg deep,
Their two books lying both on a dry stone
Upon the hither side. And once I said,
As I remember, looking round these rocks   260
And hills on which we all of us were born,
That God who made the great book of the world[41]
Would bless such piety.[42]

LEONARD
                        It may be then –

PRIEST
Never did worthier lads break English bread:
The finest Sunday that the autumn saw,   265
With all its mealy[43] clusters of ripe nuts,
Could never keep these boys away from church
Or tempt them to an hour of sabbath breach.[44]
Leonard and James! I warrant, every corner
Among these rocks, and every hollow place   270
Where foot could come, to one or both of them
Was known as well as to the flowers that grow there.
Like roebucks they went bounding o'er the hills;[45]
They played like two young ravens on the crags.
Then they could write, aye, and speak too, as well   275
As many of their betters.[46] And for Leonard –
The very night before he went away,
In my own house I put into his hand
A bible, and I'd wager twenty pounds
That if he is alive he has it yet.   280

---

[40] *fords* a ford is a shallow place in a river where people and animals can wade across.
[41] *the great book of the world* i.e. the natural world.
[42] *piety* virtue.
[43] *mealy* meal-coloured.

[44] *sabbath breach* violating the command not to work on the Sabbath (Sunday).
[45] *Like roebucks ... hills* cf. *Tintern Abbey* 68–9.
[46] *betters* social superiors.

LEONARD
It seems these brothers have not lived to be
A comfort to each other?

PRIEST
             That they might
Live to that end, is what both old and young
In this our valley all of us have wished –
And what for my part I have often prayed.   285
But Leonard –

LEONARD
         Then James still is left among you?

PRIEST
'Tis of the elder brother I am speaking –
They had an uncle (he was at that time
A thriving man and trafficked[47] on the seas[48]),
And but for this same uncle, to this hour   290
Leonard had never handled rope or shroud.
For the boy loved the life which we lead here;
And, though a very stripling, twelve years old,
His soul was knit[49] to this his native soil.
But, as I said, old Walter was too weak   295
To strive with such a torrent. When he died,
The estate and house were sold, and all their sheep –
A pretty flock, and which, for aught I know,
Had clothed the Ewbanks for a thousand years.
Well – all was gone, and they were destitute;   300
And Leonard, chiefly for his brother's sake,
Resolved to try his fortune on the seas.
'Tis now twelve years since we had tidings from him.
If there was one among us who had heard
That Leonard Ewbank was come home again,   305
From the Great Gavel, down by Leeza's Banks,
And down the Enna, far as Egremont,[50]
The day would be a very festival,
And those two bells of ours, which there you see
Hanging in the open air – but oh, good sir,   310
This is sad talk; they'll never sound for him,
Living or dead. When last we heard of him
He was in slavery among the Moors
Upon the Barbary Coast.[51] 'Twas not a little
That would bring down his spirit, and no doubt   315
Before it ended in his death, the lad

---

[47] *trafficked* traded.
[48] *he was ... seas* the poet's cousin, another John Wordsworth, was a successful captain working for the East India Company. Wordsworth's brother John succeeded him as captain of the *Earl of Abergavenny.*
[49] *knit* joined, attached.
[50] 'The Great Gavel, so called, I imagine, from its resemblance to the gable end of a house, is one of the highest of the Cumberland mountains. It stands at the head of the several vales of Ennerdale, Wastdale, and Borrowdale. The Leeza is a river which flows into the Lake of Ennerdale; on issuing from the Lake, it changes its name and is called the End, or Eyne, or Enna. It falls into the sea a little below Egremont' (Wordsworth's note).
[51] *Barbary Coast* north coast of Africa.

Was sadly crossed.[52] Poor Leonard, when we parted
He took me by the hand and said to me
If ever the day came when he was rich
He would return, and on his father's land   320
He would grow old among us.

LEONARD

               If that day
Should come, 'twould needs be a glad day for him;
He would himself, no doubt, be then as happy
As any that should meet him.

PRIEST

                  Happy, sir –

LEONARD

You said his kindred were all in their graves,   325
And that he had one brother . . .

PRIEST

                That is but
A fellow[53] tale of sorrow. From his youth
James, though not sickly, yet was delicate;
And Leonard being always by his side
Had done so many offices about him[54]   330
That, though he was not of a timid nature,
Yet still the spirit of a mountain boy
In him was somewhat checked. And when his brother
Was gone to sea and he was left alone,
The little colour that he had was soon   335
Stolen from his cheek; he drooped, and pined and pined . . .

LEONARD

But these are all the graves of full grown men . . .

PRIEST

Aye, sir, that passed away. We took him to us –
He was the child of all the dale. He lived
Three months with one, and six months with another,   340
And wanted neither food, nor clothes, nor love;
And many, many happy days were his.
But, whether blithe or sad, 'tis my belief
His absent brother still was at his heart.
And when he lived beneath our roof, we found   345
(A practice till this time unknown to him)
That often, rising from his bed at night,
He in his sleep would walk about, and sleeping
He sought his brother Leonard. You are moved;
Forgive me, sir – before I spoke to you   350
I judged you most unkindly.

---

⁵² *crossed* grieved.
⁵³ *fellow* similar.

⁵⁴ *Had done so many offices about him* had looked after him so
much.

LEONARD
                                    But this youth,
How did he die at last?

PRIEST
                              One sweet May morning
(It will be twelve years since, when spring returns)
He had gone forth among the new-dropped lambs
With two or three companions, whom it chanced   355
Some further business summoned to a house
Which stands at the dale-head.[55] James, tired perhaps,
Or from some other cause, remained behind.
You see yon precipice? It almost looks
Like some vast building made of many crags,   360
And in the midst is one particular rock
That rises like a column from the vale,
Whence by our shepherds it is called the Pillar.[56]
James pointed to its summit, over which
They all had purposed to return together,   365
Informed them that he there would wait for them.
They parted, and his comrades passed that way
Some two hours after, but they did not find him
At the appointed place – a circumstance
Of which they took no heed. But one of them,   370
Going by chance, at night, into the house
Which at this time was James' home, there learned
That nobody had seen him all that day.
The morning came, and still he was unheard of;
The neighbours were alarmed, and to the brook   375
Some went, and some towards the lake. Ere noon
They found him at the foot of that same rock,
Dead, and with mangled limbs. The third day after,
I buried him, poor lad, and there he lies.

LEONARD
And that then *is* his grave. Before his death   380
You said that he saw many happy years?

PRIEST
Aye, that he did.

LEONARD
                        And all went well with him?

PRIEST
If he had one, the lad had twenty homes.

LEONARD
And you believe then, that his mind was easy?

---

[55]   *dale-head* head of the valley.   [56]   *the Pillar* a mountain in Ennerdale.

PRIEST

Yes, long before he died he found that time 385
Is a true friend to sorrow; and unless
His thoughts were turned on Leonard's luckless fortune,
He talked about him with a cheerful love.

LEONARD

He could not come to an unhallowed end![57]

PRIEST

Nay, God forbid! You recollect I mentioned 390
A habit which disquietude and grief
Had brought upon him; and we all conjectured
That as the day was warm he had lain down
Upon the grass, and waiting for his comrades
He there had fallen asleep – that in his sleep 395
He to the margin of the precipice
Had walked, and from the summit had fallen headlong.
And so no doubt he perished. At the time
We guess that in his hands he must have had
His shepherd's staff; for midway in the cliff 400
It had been caught, and there for many years
It hung – and mouldered there.

The priest here ended.
The stranger would have thanked him, but he felt
Tears rushing in. Both left the spot in silence,
And Leonard, when they reached the churchyard gate, 405
As the priest lifted up the latch, turned round,
And looking at the grave he said, 'My brother'.
The vicar did not hear the words; and now,
Pointing towards the cottage, he entreated
That Leonard would partake his homely fare. 410
The other thanked him with a fervent voice,
But added that, the evening being calm,
He would pursue his journey. So they parted.
It was not long ere Leonard reached a grove
That overhung the road. He there stopped short, 415
And sitting down beneath the trees, reviewed
All that the priest had said.

His early years
Were with him in his heart – his cherished hopes,
And thoughts which had been his an hour before,
All pressed on him with such a weight that now 420
This vale where he had been so happy seemed
A place in which he could not bear to live.
So he relinquished all his purposes.
He travelled on to Egremont; and thence
That night addressed a letter to the priest 425
Reminding him of what had passed between them,
And adding – with a hope to be forgiven –

---

[57] *an unhallowed end* In 1800 suicide was still regarded as a sin.

That it was from the weakness of his heart
He had not dared to tell him who he was.
This done, he went on shipboard, and is now   430
A seaman, a grey-headed mariner.

Note to 'The Thorn' (composed late September 1800)[1]

From LYRICAL BALLADS (2nd edn, 2 vols, 1800) (I 211–14)

This poem ought to have been preceded by an introductory poem which I have been prevented from writing by never having felt myself in a mood when it was probable that I should write it well.

The character which I have here introduced speaking is sufficiently common. The reader will perhaps have a general notion of it if he has ever known a man (a captain of a small trading vessel, for example)[2] who, being past the middle age of life, had retired upon an annuity or small independent income to some village or country town of which he was not a native, or in which he had not been accustomed to live. Such men, having little to do, become credulous and talkative from indolence. And from the same cause (and other predisposing causes by which it is probable that such men may have been affected) they are prone to superstition. On which account it appeared to me proper to select a character like this to exhibit some of the general laws by which superstition acts upon the mind. Superstitious men are almost always men of slow faculties and deep feelings. Their minds are not loose but adhesive.[3] They have a reasonable share of imagination, by which word I mean the faculty which produces impressive effects out of simple elements. But they are utterly destitute of fancy – the power by which pleasure and surprise are excited by sudden varieties of situation and by accumulated imagery.

It was my wish in this poem to show the manner in which such men cleave[4] to the same ideas, and to follow the turns of passion (always different, yet not palpably different) by which their conversation is swayed. I had two objects to attain: first, to represent a picture which should not be unimpressive, yet consistent with the character that should describe it; secondly (while I adhered to the style in which such persons describe), to take care that words – which in their minds are impregnated with passion[5] – should likewise convey passion to readers who are not accustomed to sympathize with men feeling in that manner, or using such language. It seemed to me that this might be done by calling in the assistance of lyrical and rapid metre. It was necessary that the poem, to be natural, should in reality move slowly. Yet I hoped that by the aid of the metre, to those who should at all enter into the spirit of the poem, it would appear to move quickly. (The reader will have the kindness to excuse this note, as I am sensible that an introductory poem is necessary to give this poem its full effect.)

Upon this occasion I will request permission to add a few words closely connected with 'The Thorn', and many other poems in these volumes. There is a numerous class of readers who imagine that the same words cannot be repeated without tautology. This is a great error. Virtual tautology is much oftener produced by using different words when the meaning is exactly the same. Words – a poet's words more particularly – ought to be weighed in the balance of feeling, and not measured by the space which they occupy upon paper. For the reader cannot be too often reminded that poetry is passion: it is the history or science of feelings. Now every man must know that an attempt is rarely made to communicate impassioned feelings without something of an accompanying consciousness of the inadequateness of our own powers, or the deficiencies of language. During such efforts there will be a craving[6] in the mind, and as long as it is unsatisfied the speaker will cling to the same words, or words of the same character.

NOTE TO 'THE THORN'
[1] *The Thorn* (see pp. 234–40) was originally published in *Lyrical Ballads* (1798) without any explanation. This essay, which is significant both for what it says about its subject and for what it says about Wordsworth's use of tautology, was published first in the second edition of *Lyrical Ballads* (1800), in anticipation of the widespread misunderstanding of the poem that was to follow.

[2] *a captain . . . example* The telescope at line 181 of the poem is the only piece of evidence that supports this suggestion.
[3] *adhesive* persevering, tending to worry at certain ideas. Wordsworth is talking about the psychology of obsession.
[4] *cleave* cling, stick.
[5] *passion* emotion.
[6] *craving* i.e. an emotional craving, or frustration.

There are also various other reasons why repetition and apparent tautology are frequently beauties of the highest kind. Among the chief of these reasons is the interest which the mind attaches to words not only as symbols of the passion, but as *things*, active and efficient, which are of themselves part of the passion. And further, from a spirit of fondness, exultation, and gratitude, the mind luxuriates in the repetition of words which appear successfully to communicate its feelings.

The truth of these remarks might be shown by innumerable passages from the Bible, and from the impassioned poetry of every nation.

Awake, awake, Deborah! Awake, awake, utter a song! Arise, Barak, and lead thy
  captivity captive, thou son of Abinoam!
At her feet he bowed, he fell, he lay down. At her feet he bowed, he fell. Where he
  bowed, there he fell down dead.
Why is his chariot so long in coming? Why tarry the wheels of his chariot?
(Judges 5:12, 27, and part of 28; see also the whole of that tumultuous and wonderful poem)

Note to 'Ancient Mariner' (composed early October 1800)[1]

From LYRICAL BALLADS (2nd edn, 2 vols, 1800)

I cannot refuse myself the gratification of informing such readers as may have been pleased with this poem, or with any part of it, that they owe their pleasure in some sort to me, as the author[2] was himself very desirous that it should be suppressed. This wish had arisen from a consciousness of the defects of the poem, and from a knowledge that many persons had been much displeased with it.[3] The poem of my friend has indeed great defects: first, that the principal person has no distinct character, either in his profession of mariner, or as a human being who having been long under the control of supernatural impressions might be supposed himself to partake of something supernatural; secondly, that he does not act, but is continually acted upon; thirdly, that the events having no necessary connection do not produce each other; and lastly, that the imagery is somewhat too laboriously accumulated. Yet the poem contains many delicate touches of passion, and indeed the passion is everywhere true to nature; a great number of the stanzas present beautiful images and are expressed with unusual felicity of language; and the versification, though the metre is itself unfit for long poems, is harmonious and artfully varied, exhibiting the utmost powers of that metre, and every variety of which it is capable. It therefore appeared to me that these several merits (the first of which, namely that of the passion, is of the highest kind)[4] gave to the poem a value which is not often possessed by better poems. On this account I requested of my friend to permit me to republish it.

NOTE TO 'ANCIENT MARINER'
[1] Wordsworth appended this brief note to the text of Coleridge's poem when published in the second edition of *Lyrical Ballads* (1800), sending it to the printer a few days before the decision to exclude *Christabel* (see p. 475 n. 1). His doubts about the *Ancient Mariner* may have been reinforced by Southey's comment in his review in the *Critical Review* (see pp. 564–5). The note must have contributed to the 'change' in the relationship between the two men, lamented in Wordsworth's *A Complaint* (pp. 407–8). And in 1818 Coleridge recalled the Wordsworths' 'cold praise and effective discouragement of every attempt of mine to roll onward in a distinct current of

my own – who admitted that the Ancient Mariner and the Christabel ... were not without merit, but were abundantly anxious to acquit their judgements of any blindness to the very numerous defects' (Griggs i 631n2).
[2] *the author* Coleridge.
[3] *many persons ... with it* probably a reference to Southey's damning comment that it was 'a poem of little merit' (see p. 565).
[4] *the first of which ... kind* a comment consistent with Wordsworth's *Note to 'The Thorn'*, which states that 'poetry is passion; it is the history or science of feelings' (p. 344).

Michael: A Pastoral Poem (composed October–December 1800)

From LYRICAL BALLADS (2nd edn, 2 vols, 1800)

If from the public way you turn your steps
Up the tumultuous brook of Greenhead Gill[1]
You will suppose that with an upright path
Your feet must struggle, in such bold ascent
The pastoral mountains front you, face to face.   5
But courage! for beside that boisterous brook
The mountains have all opened out themselves,
And made a hidden valley of their own.
No habitation there is seen; but such
As journey thither find themselves alone   10
With a few sheep, with rocks and stones, and kites[2]
That overhead are sailing in the sky.[3]
    It is in truth an utter solitude,
Nor should I have made mention of this dell
But for one object which you might pass by –   15
Might see and notice not. Beside the brook
There is a straggling heap of unhewn stones;
And to that place a story appertains,
Which, though it be ungarnished with events,
Is not unfit, I deem, for the fireside   20
Or for the summer shade. It was the first,
The earliest of those tales that spake to me
Of shepherds, dwellers in the vallies, men
Whom I already loved – not verily
For their own sakes, but for the fields and hills   25
Where was their occupation and abode.
And hence this tale, while I was yet a boy –
Careless of books, yet having felt the power
Of nature – by the gentle agency
Of natural objects led me on to feel   30
For passions that were not my own, and think
(At random and imperfectly indeed)
On man, the heart of man, and human life.[4]
Therefore, although it be a history[5]
Homely and rude,[6] I will relate the same   35
For the delight of a few natural hearts[7] –
And with yet fonder feeling, for the sake
Of youthful poets who among these hills

MICHAEL: A PASTORAL POEM
[1] *Greenhead Gill* Greenhead Gill (a gill is a Lake District term for a mountain stream) is in the Vale of Grasmere, Cumbria. Wordsworth later recalled that this poem was based on memories of a family who once owned Dove Cottage.
[2] *kite* bird of prey.
[3] *but such . . . sky* lines indebted to Dorothy's account of her walk with her brother to the sheepfold on 11 October 1800: 'Kites sailing in the sky above our heads – sheep bleating and in lines and chains and patterns scattered over the mountains' (*Grasmere Journals* 44–5).

[4] *man, the heart of man, and human life* the subject of Wordsworth's never-completed epic, *The Recluse*; see 'Prospectus to *The Recluse*', pp. 330–2.
[5] *history* story.
[6] *rude* unsophisticated, simple.
[7] *a few natural hearts* Wordsworth is painfully aware that in relating a story about poor country folk he is working against public taste. The 'few' for whom he saw himself writing would have included, primarily, Dorothy and Coleridge. ' "Fit audience find, though few!" Thus prayed the bard, / Holiest of men' ('Prospectus to *The Recluse*' 12–13).

Will be my second self when I am gone.

    Upon the forest-side in Grasmere vale   40
There dwelt a shepherd, Michael was his name,
An old man, stout of heart and strong of limb.
His bodily frame had been from youth to age
Of an unusual strength; his mind was keen,
Intense, and frugal, apt for all affairs;[8]   45
And in his shepherd's calling he was prompt
And watchful more than ordinary men.
Hence he had learned the meaning of all winds,
Of blasts of every tone; and oftentimes
When others heeded not, he heard the south   50
Make subterraneous music, like the noise
Of bagpipers on distant Highland hills.
The shepherd, at such warning, of his flock
Bethought him, and he to himself would say,
'The winds are now devising work for me!'   55
And truly at all times the storm that drives
The traveller to a shelter, summoned him
Up to the mountains: he had been alone
Amid the heart of many thousand mists
That came to him and left him on the heights.   60
So lived he till his eightieth year was passed;
And grossly that man errs who should suppose
That the green valleys, and the streams and rocks,
Were things indifferent to the shepherd's thoughts.[9]
Fields, where with cheerful spirits he had breathed   65
The common air, the hills which he so oft
Had climbed with vigorous steps – which had impressed
So many incidents upon his mind
Of hardship, skill or courage, joy or fear;
Which like a book preserved the memory   70
Of the dumb animals whom he had saved,
Had fed or sheltered, linking to such acts,
So grateful in themselves, the certainty
Of honourable gains – these fields, these hills,
Which were his living being even more   75
Than his own blood (what could they less?), had laid
Strong hold on his affections, were to him
A pleasurable feeling of blind love,
The pleasure which there is in life itself.

    He had not passed his days in singleness: 80
He had a wife, a comely matron – old,
Though younger than himself full twenty years.
She was a woman of a stirring life,
Whose heart was in her house. Two wheels she had
Of antique form – this, large for spinning wool,   85
That, small for flax – and if one wheel had rest
It was because the other was at work.[10]

---

[8] *apt for all affairs* suitable for all kinds of work.

[9] *And grossly ... thoughts* Wordsworth told the Whig leader, Charles James Fox, that this poem and *The Brothers* 'were written with a view to show that men who do not wear fine clothes can feel deeply'.

[10] *Two wheels ... work* see Wordsworth's comment on the cottage industry of spinning, p. 333 n. 7.

The pair had but one inmate[11] in their house,
An only child, who had been born to them
When Michael telling[12] o'er his years began   90
To deem that he was old – in shepherd's phrase,
With one foot in the grave. This only son,
With two brave sheep dogs tried in many a storm
(The one of an inestimable worth),
Made all their household. I may truly say   95
That they were as a proverb in the vale
For endless industry. When day was gone,
And from their occupations out of doors
The son and father were come home, even then
Their labour did not cease, unless when all   100
Turned to their cleanly supper-board, and there
Each with a mess of pottage[13] and skimmed milk,
Sat round their basket piled with oaten cake,[14]
And their plain home-made cheese. Yet when their meal
Was ended, Luke (for so the son was named)   105
And his old father both betook themselves
To such convenient work as might employ
Their hands by the fireside – perhaps to card[15]
Wool for the housewife's spindle, or repair
Some injury done to sickle, flail, or scythe,[16]   110
Or other implement of house or field.
    Down from the ceiling by the chimney's edge
(Which in our ancient uncouth country style
Did with a huge projection overbrow[17]
Large space beneath) as duly as the light   115
Of day grew dim, the housewife hung a lamp,
An aged utensil which had performed
Service beyond all others of its kind.
Early at evening did it burn, and late,
Surviving comrade of uncounted[18] hours   120
Which going by from year to year had found
And left the couple neither gay perhaps
Nor cheerful, yet with objects[19] and with hopes
Living a life of eager industry.
And now, when Luke was in his eighteenth year,   125
There by the light of this old lamp they sat,
Father and son, while late into the night
The housewife plied her own peculiar[20] work,
Making the cottage through the silent hours
Murmur as with the sound of summer flies.   130
Not with a waste of words, but for the sake
Of pleasure which I know that I shall give
To many living now, I of this lamp

---

11 *inmate* dependent.
12 *telling* counting.
13 *pottage* porridge.
14 *oaten cake* a kind of bread eaten by local statesmen (small landowners).
15 *card* comb out.

16 *sickle, flail, or scythe* implements that reveal Michael's other labours: growing hay (cut with the scythe) and corn (cut with the scythe and threshed with the flail).
17 *overbrow* overhang.
18 *uncounted* countless.
19 *objects* objectives, aims.
20 *peculiar* particular.

Speak thus minutely; for there are no few
Whose memories will bear witness to my tale.   135
The light was famous in its neighbourhood,
And was a public symbol of the life
The thrifty pair had lived. For as it chanced
Their cottage on a plot of rising ground
Stood single, with large prospect north and south,   140
High into Easedale, up to Dunmail Raise,
And westward to the village near the lake.
And from this constant light so regular
And so far-seen, the house itself by all
Who dwelt within the limits of the vale,   145
Both old and young, was named The Evening Star.

    Thus living on through such a length of years
The shepherd, if he loved himself, must needs
Have loved his helpmate;[21] but to Michael's heart
This son of his old age was yet more dear –   150
Effect which might perhaps have been produced
By that instinctive tenderness, the same
Blind[22] spirit which is in the blood of all,
Or that a child more than all other gifts,
Brings hope with it, and forward-looking thoughts,   155
And stirrings of inquietude,[23] when they
By tendency of nature[24] needs must fail.
From such, and other causes, to the thoughts
Of the old man his only son was now
The dearest object that he knew on earth.   160
Exceeding was the love he bare to him,
His heart and his heart's joy! For oftentimes
Old Michael, while he was a babe in arms,
Had done him female service,[25] not alone
For dalliance[26] and delight, as is the use   165
Of fathers, but with patient mind enforced
To acts of tenderness; and he had rocked
His cradle with a woman's gentle hand.

    And in a later time, ere yet the boy
Had put on boy's attire,[27] did Michael love   170
(Albeit of a stern unbending mind)
To have the young one in his sight when he
Had work by his own door, or when he sat
With sheep before him on his shepherd's stool
Beneath that large old oak, which near their door   175
Stood, and from its enormous breadth of shade
Chosen for the shearer's covert[28] from the sun,
Thence in our rustic dialect was called
The Clipping[29] Tree – a name which yet it bears.

---

[21] *helpmate* wife.
[22] *Blind* unquestioning.
[23] *inquietude* anxiety about Luke.
[24] *tendency of nature* age.
[25] *Old Michael . . . female service* Michael tended his baby son as if he had been his mother.
[26] *For dalliance* for playfulness.

[27] *ere yet . . . attire* Until well into the nineteenth century, boys and girls were dressed in frocks until, between the ages of three and seven, boys were 'breeched'.
[28] *covert* shade.
[29] 'Clipping is the word used in the north of England for shearing' (Wordsworth's note).

There, while they two were sitting in the shade   180
With others round them, earnest all and blithe,
Would Michael exercise his heart with looks
Of fond correction and reproof, bestowed
Upon the child if he disturbed the sheep
By catching at their legs, or with his shouts   185
Scared them while they lay still beneath the shears.
And when by Heaven's good grace the boy grew up
A healthy lad, and carried in his cheek
Two steady roses that were five years old,
Then Michael from a winter coppice[30] cut   190
With his own hand a sapling, which he hooped
With iron, making it throughout in all
Due requisites a perfect shepherd's staff,
And gave it to the boy; wherewith equipped,
He as a watchman oftentimes was placed   195
At gate or gap, to stem[31] or turn the flock;
And, to his office[32] prematurely called,
There stood the urchin, as you will divine,
Something between a hindrance and a help –
And for this cause not always, I believe,   200
Receiving from his father hire[33] of praise,
Though nought was left undone which staff, or voice,
Or looks, or threatening gestures, could perform.
But soon as Luke, now ten years old, could stand
Against the mountain blasts, and to the heights,   205
Not fearing toil, nor length of weary ways,
He with his father daily went, and they
Were as companions – why should I relate
That objects which the shepherd loved before
Were dearer now? – that from the boy there came   210
Feelings and emanations, things which were
Light to the sun and music to the wind,
And that the old man's heart seemed born again?
Thus in his father's sight the boy grew up
And now when he had reached his eighteenth year,   215
He was his comfort and his daily hope.
        While this good household thus were living on
From day to day, to Michael's ear there came
Distressful tidings. Long before the time
Of which I speak, the shepherd had been bound   220
In surety for his brother's son,[34] a man
Of an industrious life and ample means,
But unforeseen misfortunes suddenly
Had pressed upon him, and old Michael now
Was summoned to discharge the forfeiture –   225
A grievous penalty, but little less
Than half his substance.[35] This unlooked-for claim,

---

30 *coppice* a small wood.
31 *stem* stop.
32 *office* job, work.
33 *hire* reward.
34 *In surety for his brother's son* Michael made himself liable
for his nephew's debt.

35 *Long before ... substance* The failure of his nephew to pay
off the loan Michael had guaranteed, using his land as secu-
rity, means that he is now forced to pay the penalty – a sum
amounting to only slightly less than half his entire capital.

At the first hearing, for a moment took
More hope out of his life than he supposed
That any old man ever could have lost. 230
As soon as he had gathered so much strength
That he could look his trouble in the face,
It seemed that his sole refuge was to sell
A portion of his patrimonial fields.[36]
Such was his first resolve; he thought again, 235
And his heart failed him. 'Isabel', said he,
Two evenings after he had heard the news,
'I have been toiling more than seventy years,
And in the open sunshine of God's love
Have we all lived, yet if these fields of ours 240
Should pass into a stranger's hand, I think
That I could not lie quiet in my grave.
Our lot is a hard lot;[37] the sun itself
Has scarcely been more diligent than I,
And I have lived to be a fool at last 245
To my own family. An evil man
That was, and made an evil choice, if he
Were false to us; and if he were not false,
There are ten thousand to whom loss like this
Had been no sorrow. I forgive him – but 250
'Twere better to be dumb than to talk thus.
When I began, my purpose was to speak
Of remedies and of a cheerful hope.
Our Luke shall leave us, Isabel; the land
Shall not go from us, and it shall be free – 255
He shall possess it, free as is the wind
That passes over it. We have, thou knowest,
Another kinsman; he will be our friend
In this distress. He is a prosperous man,
Thriving in trade, and Luke to him shall go 260
And with his kinsman's help and his own thrift
He quickly will repair this loss, and then
May come again to us. If here he stay
What can be done? Where everyone is poor
What can be gained?'[38]
            At this the old man paused 265
And Isabel sat silent, for her mind
Was busy looking back into past times.
'There's Richard Bateman', thought she to herself,

---

[36] *patrimonial fields* the land he had inherited from his forefathers. This poem is preoccupied with the plight of small landowners – families who passed the same small plot of land from one generation to the next over many centuries. When Wordsworth sent Charles James Fox, the Whig leader, a copy of *Lyrical Ballads* in 1801, he drew his attention to *Michael*: 'The domestic affections will always be strong amongst men who live in a country not crowded with population, if these men are placed above poverty. But if they are proprietors of small estates, which have descended to them from their ancestors, the power which these affections will acquire amongst such men is inconceivable by those who have only had an opportunity of observing hired labourers, farmers, and the manufacturing poor. Their little tract of land serves as a kind of permanent rallying point for their domestic feelings, as a tablet upon which they are written, which makes them objects of memory in a thousand instances when they would otherwise be forgotten. It is a fountain fitted to the nature of social man from which supplies of affection, as pure as his heart was intended for, are daily drawn. This class of men is rapidly disappearing' (*EY* 314–15).

[37] *lot* way of life.

[38] *Where everyone . . . gained* no one in the village has enough money to employ Luke.

'He was a parish-boy[39] – at the church door
They made a gathering for him, shillings, pence,[40]   270
And halfpennies, wherewith the neighbours bought
A basket which they filled with pedlar's wares,
And with this basket on his arm the lad
Went up to London, found a master[41] there,
Who out of many chose the trusty boy   275
To go and overlook his merchandise
Beyond the seas, where he grew wondrous rich
And left estates and monies to the poor,
And at his birthplace built a chapel, floored
With marble which he sent from foreign lands.'[42]   280
These thoughts, and many others of like sort,
Passed quickly through the mind of Isabel,
And her face brightened. The old man was glad,
And thus resumed: 'Well, Isabel, this scheme
These two days has been meat and drink to me: 285
Far more than we have lost is left us yet.
We have enough – I wish indeed that I
Were younger, but this hope is a good hope.
Make ready Luke's best garments; of the best
Buy for him more, and let us send him forth   290
Tomorrow, or the next day, or tonight –
If he could go, the boy should go tonight.'
    Here Michael ceased, and to the fields went forth
With a light heart. The housewife for five days
Was restless morn and night, and all day long   295
Wrought on with her best fingers[43] to prepare
Things needful for the journey of her son.
But Isabel was glad when Sunday came
To stop her in her work; for when she lay
By Michael's side, she for the last two nights   300
Heard him, how he was troubled in his sleep;
And when they rose at morning she could see
That all his hopes were gone. That day at noon
She said to Luke, while they two by themselves
Were sitting at the door: 'Thou must not go,   305
We have no other child but thee to lose,
None to remember – do not go away,
For if thou leave thy father he will die.'
The lad made answer with a jocund[44] voice,
And Isabel, when she had told her fears,   310
Recovered heart. That evening her best fare
Did she bring forth, and all together sat
Like happy people round a Christmas fire.
    Next morning Isabel resumed her work,
And all the ensuing week the house appeared   315

---

[39] *parish-boy* supported by the parish.
[40] *shillings, pence* before decimalization in 1971, there were
12 pence to the shilling, and 20 shillings to the pound.
[41] *master* employer.
[42] 'The story alluded to here is well known in the country.
The chapel is called Ings Chapel, and is on the right hand side

of the road leading from Kendal to Ambleside' (Wordsworth's
note). Bateman's marble floor is still to be seen.
[43] *Wrought on with her best fingers* idiomatic; she worked as
hard as she possibly could.
[44] *jocund* happy.

As cheerful as a grove in spring. At length
The expected letter from their kinsman came,
With kind assurances that he would do
His utmost for the welfare of the boy –
To which requests were added that forthwith   320
He might be sent to him. Ten times or more
The letter was read over; Isabel
Went forth to show it to the neighbours round;
Nor was there at that time on English land
A prouder heart than Luke's. When Isabel   325
Had to her house returned the old man said,
'He shall depart tomorrow.' To this word
The housewife answered, talking much of things
Which, if at such short notice he should go,
Would surely be forgotten – but at length   330
She gave consent, and Michael was at ease.
    Near the tumultuous brook of Greenhead Gill
In that deep valley, Michael had designed
To build a sheepfold,[45] and before he heard
The tidings of his melancholy loss   335
For this same purpose he had gathered up
A heap of stones, which close to the brook-side
Lay thrown together, ready for the work.
With Luke that evening thitherward[46] he walked,
And soon as they had reached the place he stopped,   340
And thus the old man spake to him: 'My son,
Tomorrow thou wilt leave me. With full heart
I look upon thee, for thou art the same
That wert a promise to me ere thy birth,
And all thy life hast been my daily joy.   345
I will relate to thee some little part
Of our two histories; 'twill do thee good
When thou art from me, even if I should speak
Of things thou canst not know of. After thou
First cam'st into the world, as it befalls   350
To new-born infants, thou didst sleep away
Two days, and blessings from thy father's tongue
Then fell upon thee. Day by day passed on,
And still I loved thee with increasing love.
Never to living ear came sweeter sounds   355
Than when I heard thee by our own fireside
First uttering without words a natural tune –
When thou, a feeding babe, didst in thy joy
Sing at thy mother's breast. Month followed month,
And in the open fields my life was passed,   360
And in the mountains, else I think that thou
Hadst been brought up upon thy father's knees.
But we were playmates, Luke; among these hills,

---

[45] 'It may be proper to inform some readers that a sheepfold in these mountains is an unroofed building of stone walls, with different divisions. It is generally placed by the side of a brook for the convenience of washing the sheep; but it is also useful as a shelter for them, and as a place to drive them into, to enable the shepherds conveniently to single out one or more for any particular purpose' (Wordsworth's note).
[46] *thitherward* in that direction, to that place.

As well thou know'st, in us the old and young
Have played together – nor with me didst thou   365
Lack any pleasure which a boy can know.'
    Luke had a manly heart, but at these words
He sobbed aloud. The old man grasped his hand,
And said, 'Nay do not take it so – I see
That these are things of which I need not speak.   370
Even to the utmost I have been to thee
A kind and a good father; and herein
I but repay a gift which I myself
Received at others' hands, for, though now old
Beyond the common life of man,[47] I still   375
Remember them who loved me in my youth.
Both of them sleep together – here they lived
As all their forefathers had done; and when
At length their time was come, they were not loath
To give their bodies to the family mould.[48]   380
I wished that thou should'st live the life they lived;
But 'tis a long time to look back, my son,
And see so little gain from sixty years.
These fields were burdened when they came to me;[49]
Till I was forty years of age, not more   385
Than half of my inheritance was mine.
I toiled and toiled; God blessed me in my work,
And till these three weeks past the land was free –
It looks as if it never could endure
Another master. Heaven forgive me, Luke,   390
If I judge ill for thee, but it seems good
That thou should'st go.'
                    At this the old man paused,
Then pointing to the stones near which they stood,
Thus after a short silence he resumed:
'This was a work for us, and now, my son,   395
It is a work for me. But lay one stone –
Here, lay it for me, Luke, with thine own hands –
I for the purpose brought thee to this place.
Nay, boy, be of good hope: we both may live
To see a better day. At eighty-four   400
I still am strong and stout; do thou thy part,
I will do mine. I will begin again
With many tasks that were resigned to thee;
Up to the heights, and in among the storms,
Will I without thee go again, and do   405
All works which I was wont to do alone
Before I knew thy face. Heaven bless thee, boy;
Thy heart these two weeks has been beating fast
With many hopes. It should be so – yes, yes,
I knew that thou could'st never have a wish   410
To leave me, Luke – thou hast been bound to me

---

[47] *the common life of man* the usual lifespan of a man (three-score years and ten); he is eighty-four.
[48] *mould* the earth from which man was formed, and to which he returns in the grave.

[49] *These fields were burdened when they came to me* Michael inherited his land with the burden of a mortgage.

Only by links of love. When thou art gone
What will be left to us? But I forget
My purposes. Lay now the corner-stone
As I requested, and hereafter, Luke,   415
When thou art gone away, should evil men
Be thy companions, let this sheepfold be
Thy anchor and thy shield. Amid all fear
And all temptation, let it be to thee
An emblem of the life thy fathers lived,   420
Who, being innocent,[50] did for that cause
Bestir them in good deeds. Now fare thee well.
When thou return'st, thou in this place wilt see
A work which is not here. A covenant[51]
'Twill be between us – but whatever fate   425
Befall thee, I shall love thee to the last,
And bear thy memory with me to the grave.'
      The shepherd ended here, and Luke stooped down
And as his father had requested, laid
The first stone of the sheepfold. At the sight   430
The old man's grief broke from him; to his heart
He pressed his son, he kissed him and wept –
And to the house together they returned.
Next morning, as had been resolved, the boy
Began his journey; and when he had reached   435
The public way he put on a bold face,
And all the neighbours as he passed their doors
Came forth with wishes and with farewell prayers
That followed him till he was out of sight.
      A good report did from their kinsman come   440
Of Luke and his well-doing; and the boy
Wrote loving letters, full of wondrous news,
Which, as the housewife phrased it, were throughout
The prettiest letters that were ever seen.
Both parents read them with rejoicing hearts.   445
So many months passed on, and once again
The shepherd went about his daily work
With confident and cheerful thoughts; and now
Sometimes when he could find a leisure hour
He to that valley took his way, and there   450
Wrought at the sheepfold. Meantime Luke began
To slacken in his duty, and at length
He in the dissolute city gave himself
To evil courses; ignominy and shame
Fell on him, so that he was driven at last   455
To seek a hiding-place beyond the seas.
      There is a comfort in the strength of love,
'Twill make a thing endurable which else
Would break the heart – old Michael found it so.
I have conversed with more than one who well   460
Remember the old man, and what he was

---

[50]   *innocent* uncorrupted.

[51]   *covenant* cf. the covenant of Jacob and his father-in-law Laban, Genesis 31:43–55.

Years after he had heard this heavy news.
His bodily frame had been from youth to age
Of an unusual strength. Among the rocks
He went, and still looked up upon the sun,   465
And listened to the wind, and, as before,
Performed all kinds of labour for his sheep
And for the land, his small inheritance.
And to that hollow dell from time to time
Did he repair, to build the fold of which   470
His flock had need. 'Tis not forgotten yet
The pity which was then in every heart
For the old man; and 'tis believed by all
That many and many a day he thither went,
And never lifted up a single stone.   475
        There by the sheepfold sometimes was he seen
Sitting alone, with that his faithful dog –
Then old – beside him, lying at his feet.
The length of full seven years from time to time
He at the building of this sheepfold wrought,   480
And left the work unfinished when he died.[52]
        Three years, or little more, did Isabel
Survive her husband; at her death the estate
Was sold, and went into a stranger's hand.
The cottage which was named The Evening Star   485
Is gone; the ploughshare has been through the ground
On which it stood. Great changes have been wrought
In all the neighbourhood; yet the oak is left
That grew beside their door, and the remains
Of the unfinished sheepfold may be seen   490
Beside the boisterous brook of Greenhead Gill.

[*I travelled among unknown men*] (composed *c.* 29 April 1801)

From POEMS IN TWO VOLUMES (1807)

I travelled among unknown men
    In lands beyond the sea;[1]
Nor, England, did I know till then
    What love I bore to thee.

'Tis passed, that melancholy dream!   5
    Nor will I quit thy shore
A second time, for still I seem
    To love thee more and more.

Among thy mountains did I feel
    The joy of my desire;   10
And she I cherished turned her wheel
    Beside an English fire.

---

[52] *when he died* on Wordsworth's evidence, Michael would have been ninety-one or ninety-two.

I TRAVELLED AMONG UNKNOWN MEN
[1] *I travelled . . . sea* Wordsworth is probably recalling his visit to Germany, 1798–9.

Thy mornings showed, thy nights concealed
The bowers where Lucy played;
And thine is, too, the last green field   15
Which Lucy's eyes surveyed!

Preface (extracts) (composed September 1800; this version revised January–April 1802)[1]

From LYRICAL BALLADS (2 vols, 1802)

The principal object, then, which I proposed to myself in these poems, was to choose incidents and situations from common life, and to relate or describe them throughout, as far as was possible, in a selection of language really used by men, and at the same time to throw over them a certain colouring of imagination, whereby ordinary things should be presented to the mind in an unusual way. And further, and above all, to make these incidents and situations interesting by tracing in them (truly,[2] though not ostentatiously) the primary laws of our nature,[3] chiefly as far as regards the manner in which we associate ideas[4] in a state of excitement.[5]

Low and rustic life was generally chosen because in that condition the essential passions of the heart find a better soil in which they can attain their maturity, are less under restraint, and speak a plainer and more emphatic language;[6] because in that condition of life our elementary feelings coexist in a state of greater simplicity, and consequently may be more accurately contemplated and more forcibly communicated; because the manners of rural life germinate from those elementary feelings,[7] and (from the necessary character of rural occupations) are more easily comprehended and are more durable; and, lastly, because in that condition the passions of men are incorporated[8] with the beautiful and permanent forms of nature.[9]

The language, too, of these men is adopted (purified indeed from what appear to be its real defects – from all lasting and rational causes of dislike or disgust) because such men hourly communicate with the best objects[10] from which the best part of language is originally derived, and because, from their rank in society and the sameness and narrow circle of their intercourse being less under the influence of social vanity, they convey their feelings and notions in simple and unelaborated expressions. Accordingly, such a language, arising out of repeated experience and regular feelings, is a more permanent and a far more philosophical language[11] than that which is frequently substituted for it by poets who think that they are conferring honour upon themselves and their art, in proportion as they separate themselves from the sympathies of men and indulge in arbitrary and capricious habits of expression, in order to furnish food for fickle tastes and fickle appetites[12] of their own creation.[13]

PREFACE

[1] The first edition of *Lyrical Ballads*, published 1798, carried a brief 'Advertisement' to prepare readers for the unusual fare within (see pp. 191–2). The second edition in two volumes, 1800, contained a much longer *Preface* that was revised and expanded for the 1802 edition. Extracts from that second version are presented here. The *Preface* was written at Coleridge's insistence, and drew on ideas conceived or gathered by him; as he told Southey, 29 July 1802, 'Wordsworth's Preface is half a child of my own brain' (Griggs ii 830).

[2] *truly* truthfully.

[3] *the primary laws of our nature* i.e. (in this context) the workings of the mind.

[4] *we associate ideas* the association of ideas – that is to say, the way in which emotions are connected with, for instance, memories, is an important element in Wordsworth's thinking. See *Pedlar* 78–81, *Two-Part Prelude* i 418–24, 432–42.

[5] *a state of excitement* i.e. when we feel intensely.

[6] *Low and rustic . . . language* a belief first expressed in February 1798, *Pedlar* 239–45.

[7] *the manners of rural life . . . feelings* there is an implied comparison with the social life ('manners') of the city, which has become detached from 'elementary' human emotion.

[8] *incorporated* interfused, united, blended.

[9] *the passions . . . nature* as, for instance, in the way that Michael's unfinished sheepfold becomes a symbol of his tragedy, or that Margaret's ruined cottage embodies hers. The search for permanence – of language and symbol – is fundamental to Wordsworth's aesthetic.

[10] *the best objects* for example, natural objects.

[11] *philosophical language* i.e. fit for philosophical discourse.

[12] *fickle tastes and fickle appetites* tastes and appetites governed by literary fashion.

[13] 'It is worthwhile here to observe that the affecting parts of Chaucer are almost always expressed in language pure and universally intelligible even to this day' (Wordsworth's note). Wordsworth believed that 'every great and original writer, in proportion as he is great or original, must himself create the taste by which he is to be relished' (*MY* i 150).

I cannot, however, be insensible to the present outcry against the triviality and meanness both of thought and language which some of my contemporaries have occasionally introduced into their metrical compositions. And I acknowledge that this defect, where it exists, is more dishonourable to the writer's own character than false refinement or arbitrary innovation (though I should contend at the same time that it is far less pernicious in the sum of its consequences).

From such verses the poems in these volumes will be found distinguished at least by one mark of difference – that each of them has a worthy purpose. Not that I mean to say that I always began to write with a distinct purpose formally conceived, but I believe that my habits of meditation have so formed my feelings, as that my descriptions of such objects as strongly excite those feelings will be found to carry along with them a purpose. If in this opinion I am mistaken, I can have little right to the name of a poet; for all good poetry is the spontaneous overflow of powerful feelings. But though this be true, poems to which any value can be attached were never produced on any variety of subjects but by a man who, being possessed of more than usual organic[14] sensibility, had also thought long and deeply.[15] For our continued influxes of feeling[16] are modified and directed by our thoughts, which are indeed the representatives of all our past feelings.[17] And, as by contemplating the relation of these general representatives[18] to each other we discover what is really important to men, so, by the repetition and continuance of this act, our feelings will be connected with important subjects. Till at length (if we be originally possessed of much sensibility) such habits of mind will be produced that, by obeying blindly and mechanically[19] the impulses of those habits, we shall describe objects and utter sentiments of such a nature, and in such connection with each other, that the understanding of the being to whom we address ourselves – if he be in a healthful state of association[20] – must necessarily be in some degree enlightened, and his affections ameliorated.[21]

I have said that each of these poems has a purpose. I have also informed my reader what this purpose will be found principally to be; namely, to illustrate the manner in which our feelings and ideas are associated in a state of excitement.[22] But (speaking in language somewhat more appropriate) it is to follow the fluxes and refluxes[23] of the mind when agitated by the great and simple affections of our nature. This object I have endeavoured in these short essays[24] to attain by various means: by tracing the maternal passion through many of its more subtle windings (as in the poems of 'The Idiot Boy' and 'The Mad Mother'); by accompanying the last struggles of a human being at the approach of death, cleaving in solitude to life and society (as in the poem of the forsaken Indian); by showing, as in the stanzas entitled 'We are Seven', the perplexity and obscurity which in childhood attend our notion of death – or rather our utter inability to admit that notion; or by displaying the strength of fraternal or (to speak more philosophically) of moral attachment when early associated with the great and beautiful objects of nature (as in 'The Brothers'); or, as in the incident of 'Simon Lee', by placing my reader in the way of receiving from ordinary moral sensations another and more salutary impression than we are accustomed to receive from them.[25]

It has also been part of my general purpose to attempt to sketch characters under the influence of less impassioned feelings (as in 'The Two April Mornings', 'The Fountain', the 'Old Man Travelling', 'The Two Thieves', etc.); characters of which the elements are simple, belonging rather to nature than to manners,[26] such as exist now and will probably always exist, and which from their constitution may be distinctly and profitably contemplated.

---

[14] *organic* innate, inherent.

[15] *If in this opinion ... deeply* Wordsworth's championing of 'powerful feelings' is strongly modified by the insistence on long and profound thought.

[16] *influxes of feeling* i.e. 'flowing-in' of emotion; cf. the Pedlar's 'access of mind' (*Pedlar* 107).

[17] *For our ... feelings* our emotions are modified by our thoughts, which are themselves the products of our past feelings.

[18] *these general representatives* thoughts deriving from feelings in the past.

[19] *by obeying blindly and mechanically* it is crucial to the creative act that the poet completely surrender to associations, and habits of thought and feeling.

[20] *a healthful state of association* i.e. a state of mind in which the reader is receptive, and does not impose on the poetry irrelevant prejudices or assumptions.

[21] *ameliorated* improved. Poetry should be emotionally uplifting.

[22] *the manner ... excitement* the way in which emotions and ideas interact associatively when the mind is stimulated.

[23] *fluxes and refluxes* ebb and flow.

[24] *essays* attempts.

[25] *by placing ... them* the initial pity, which leads the narrator to offer to help Simon Lee, gives way to the more complex sentiment expressed in the final lines of the poem.

[26] *manners* customs.

I will not abuse the indulgence of my reader by dwelling longer upon this subject, but it is proper that I should mention one other circumstance which distinguishes these poems from the popular poetry of the day. It is this – that the feeling therein developed gives importance to the action and situation, and not the action and situation to the feeling.[27] My meaning will be rendered perfectly intelligible by referring my reader to the poems entitled 'Poor Susan' and 'The Childless Father'[28] (particularly to the last stanza of the latter poem).

I will not suffer a sense of false modesty to prevent me from asserting that I point my reader's attention to this mark of distinction far less for the sake of these particular poems than from the general importance of the subject. The subject is indeed important! For the human mind is capable of being excited without the application of gross and violent stimulants,[29] and he must have a very faint perception of its beauty and dignity who does not know this, and who does not further know that one being is elevated above another in proportion as he possesses this capability.[30]

It has therefore appeared to me that to endeavour to produce or enlarge this capability is one of the best services in which (at any period) a writer can be engaged – but this service, excellent at all times, is especially so at the present day. [For a multitude of causes, unknown to former times, are now acting with a combined force to blunt the discriminating powers of the mind and, unfitting it for all voluntary exertion, to reduce it to a state of almost savage torpor.[31] The most effective of these causes are the great national events[32] which are daily taking place, and the increasing accumulation of men in cities, where the uniformity of their occupations produces a craving for extraordinary incident, which the rapid communication[33] of intelligence hourly gratifies.] To this tendency of life and manners the literature and theatrical exhibitions[34] of the country have conformed themselves. The invaluable works of our elder writers (I had almost said the works of Shakespeare and Milton) are driven into neglect by frantic novels, sickly and stupid German tragedies, and deluges of idle and extravagant stories in verse.[35]

When I think upon this degrading thirst after outrageous[36] stimulation, I am almost ashamed to have spoken of the feeble effort with which I have endeavoured to counteract it. And, reflecting upon the magnitude of the general evil, I should be oppressed with no dishonourable melancholy had I not a deep impression of certain inherent and indestructible qualities of the human mind (and likewise of certain powers in the great and permanent objects[37] that act upon it which are equally inherent and indestructible), and did I not further add to this impression a belief that the time is approaching when the evil will be systematically opposed by men of greater powers and with far more distinguished success.

Having dwelt thus long on the subjects and aim of these poems, I shall request the reader's permission to apprise him of a few circumstances relating to their style, in order (among other reasons) that I may not be censured for not having performed what I never attempted. The reader will find that personifications of abstract ideas rarely occur in these volumes, and I hope are utterly rejected as an ordinary device to elevate the style and raise it above prose. I have proposed to myself to imitate – and as far as is possible, to adopt – the very language of men, and assuredly such personifications do not make any natural or regular part of that language. They are, indeed, a figure of speech occasionally prompted by passion (and I have made use of them as such), but I have endeavoured utterly to reject them as a mechanical device of style or as a family[38] language which writers in metre seem to lay

---

[27] *the feeling … feeling* a crucial distinction between Wordsworth's poetry and that of many of his more fashionable contemporaries: his poetry is inspired primarily by the emotion behind it rather than by the incidents or the social class of those it describes.

[28] These poems, first published in *Lyrical Ballads* (1800), are not included in this anthology, but Wordsworth's point is borne out just as well by *Simon Lee, The Last of the Flock, Complaint of a Forsaken Indian Woman, The Thorn*, and *The Idiot Boy*.

[29] *gross and violent stimulants* a reference to the sort of violent or salacious detail often found in gothic chillers of the day.

[30] *this capability* imaginative sympathy.

[31] *savage torpor* barbaric laziness.

[32] *national events* Britain had been at war with France since 1793.

[33] *rapid communication* the telegraph (invented 1792) and the stagecoach.

[34] *exhibitions* performances.

[35] *frantic novels … verse* Gothic novels, and plays by sentimental writers like Kotzebue, were popular at this time.

[36] *outrageous* excessive.

[37] *the great and permanent objects* i.e. primarily the internalized images of objects in the natural world, such as mountains, lakes, trees.

[38] *family* generic; widely used by all poets.

claim to by prescription. I have wished to keep my reader in the company of flesh and blood, persuaded that by so doing I shall interest him. I am, however, well aware that others who pursue a different track may interest him likewise. I do not interfere with their claim; I only wish to prefer a different claim of my own.

There will also be found in these volumes little of what is usually called poetic diction: I have taken as much pains to avoid it as others ordinarily take to produce it. This I have done for the reason already alleged – to bring my language near to the language of men, and, further, because the pleasure which I have proposed to myself to impart is of a kind very different from that which is supposed by many persons to be the proper object of poetry. I do not know how, without being culpably particular,[39] I can give my reader a more exact notion of the style in which I wished these poems to be written than by informing him that I have at all times endeavoured to look steadily at my subject. Consequently, I hope that there is in these poems little falsehood of description, and that my ideas are expressed in language fitted to their respective importance.[40]

Something I must have gained by this practice, as it is friendly to one property of all good poetry – namely, good sense. But it has necessarily cut me off from a large portion of phrases and figures of speech which, from father to son, have long been regarded as the common inheritance of poets. I have also thought it expedient to restrict myself still further, having abstained from the use of many expressions in themselves proper and beautiful, but which have been foolishly repeated by bad poets till such feelings of disgust are connected with them as it is scarcely possible by any art of association to overpower. . . .

Taking up the subject, then, upon general grounds, I ask what is meant by the word poet? What is a poet? To whom does he address himself? And what language is to be expected from him? He is a man speaking to men – a man (it is true) endued[41] with more lively sensibility, more enthusiasm and tenderness, who has a greater knowledge of human nature, and a more comprehensive[42] soul, than are supposed to be common among mankind; a man pleased with his own passions and volitions,[43] and who rejoices more than other men in the spirit of life that is in him, delighting to contemplate similar volitions and passions as manifested in the goings-on of the universe,[44] and habitually impelled to create them where he does not find them.

To these qualities he has added a disposition to be affected more than other men by absent things as if they were present,[45] an ability of conjuring up in himself passions which are indeed far from being the same as those produced by real events, yet (especially in those parts of the general sympathy which are pleasing and delightful) do more nearly resemble the passions produced by real events than anything which, from the motions of their own minds merely, other men are accustomed to feel in themselves – whence, and from practice, he has acquired a greater readiness and power in expressing what he thinks and feels, and especially those thoughts and feelings which, by his own choice, or from the structure of his own mind, arise in him without immediate external excitement.

But whatever portion of this faculty we may suppose even the greatest poet to possess, there cannot be a doubt but that the language which it will suggest to him must in liveliness and truth fall far short of that which is uttered by men in real life under the actual pressure of those passions – certain shadows of which the poet thus produces, or feels to be produced, in himself.

However exalted a notion we would wish to cherish of the character of a poet, it is obvious that, while he describes and imitates passions, his situation is altogether slavish and mechanical compared with the freedom and power of real and substantial action and suffering. So that it will be the wish of

---

39 *culpably particular* too meticulously detailed.
40 *fitted to their respective importance* i.e. by the weight of emotion behind them.
41 *endued* endowed.
42 *more comprehensive* more intense, profound, and all-embracing.
43 *volitions* impulses, good deeds.
44 *the universe* the created world.
45 *To these qualities . . . present* so vividly does the poet recall

natural objects, which have 'impressed' themselves on his mind, that they seem to be present; the process is described in *Tintern Abbey* 23–50, and elucidated for the first time in *Not Useless do I Deem* 24–8:

    And further, by contemplating these forms
    In the relations which they bear to man,
    We shall discover what a power is theirs
    To stimulate our minds, and multiply
    The spiritual presences of absent things . . .

the poet to bring his feelings near to those of the persons whose feelings he describes – nay, for short spaces of time, perhaps, to let himself slip into an entire delusion, and even confound[46] and identify his own feelings with theirs, modifying only the language which is thus suggested to him by a consideration that he describes for a particular purpose: that of giving pleasure. Here, then, he will apply the principle on which I have so much insisted – namely, that of selection. On this he will depend for removing what would otherwise be painful or disgusting in the passion; he will feel that there is no necessity to trick out[47] or elevate nature.[48] And the more industriously he applies this principle, the deeper will be his faith that no words which his fancy or imagination can suggest will be compared with those which are the emanations of reality and truth. . . .

Aristotle, I have been told,[49] hath said that poetry is the most philosophic of all writing.[50] It is so. Its object is truth,[51] not individual and local, but general and operative;[52] not standing upon external testimony, but carried alive into the heart by passion – truth which is its own testimony, which gives strength and divinity to the tribunal to which it appeals, and receives them from the same tribunal.

Poetry is the image of man and nature. The obstacles which stand in the way of the fidelity of the biographer and historian (and of their consequent utility) are incalculably greater than those which are to be encountered by the poet who has an adequate notion of the dignity[53] of his art. The poet writes under one restriction only – namely, that of the necessity of giving immediate pleasure to a human being possessed of that information which may be expected from him, not as a lawyer, a physician, a mariner, an astronomer, or a natural philosopher, but as a man.[54] Except this one restriction, there is no object standing between the poet and the image of things; between this, and the biographer and historian, there are a thousand.

Nor let this necessity of producing immediate pleasure be considered as a degradation of the poet's art; it is far otherwise. It is an acknowledgement of the beauty of the universe, an acknowledgement the more sincere because it is not formal, but indirect; it is a task light and easy to him who looks at the world in the spirit of love. Further, it is a homage paid to the native and naked dignity of man, to the grand elementary principle of pleasure[55] by which he knows, and feels, and lives, and moves. . . .

I have said that poetry is the spontaneous overflow of powerful feelings; it takes its origin from emotion recollected in tranquillity.[56] The emotion is contemplated till, by a species of reaction, the tranquillity gradually disappears, and an emotion kindred to that which was before the subject of contemplation is gradually produced, and does itself actually exist in the mind.[57] In this mood successful composition generally begins, and in a mood similar to this it is carried on. But the emotion (of whatever kind and in whatever degree) from various causes is qualified by various pleasures, so that in describing any passions whatsoever which are voluntarily described, the mind will upon the whole be in a state of enjoyment.[58] Now, if nature be thus cautious in preserving in a state of enjoyment a being thus employed, the poet ought to profit by the lesson thus held forth to him, and ought especially to take care that, whatever passions he communicates to his reader, those passions (if his reader's mind be sound and vigorous) should always be accompanied with an overbalance of pleasure.

Now, the music of harmonious metrical language,[59] the sense of difficulty overcome, and the blind association of pleasure which has been previously received from works of rhyme or metre of the same or similar construction, an indistinct perception perpetually renewed of language closely resembling that of real life (and yet, in the circumstance of metre, differing from it so widely) – all these imper-

---

[46] *confound* confuse; effectively, the poet cannot tell the difference between his own feelings and those of his subject.

[47] *trick out* dress up.

[48] *nature* natural utterance.

[49] *I have been told* probably by Coleridge, who had been a Grecian (boy in the highest class) at Christ's Hospital.

[50] *Aristotle . . . writing* Wordsworth aimed, of course, to compose the great philosophical epic of his day – *The Recluse* (see p. 271).

[51] *truth* effectively, the real world – real people and real things, as opposed to abstract personifications.

[52] *operative* practical.

[53] *dignity* high status.

[54] *not as . . . man* i.e. the poet is concerned with fidelity to psychological truth, rather than with facts.

[55] *pleasure* positive sensations (spiritual and physical) deriving from our involvement with the external world.

[56] *emotion recollected in tranquillity* in August–September 1800 Coleridge recorded in his notebook that poetry was a 'recalling of passion in tranquillity' (*Notebooks* i 787).

[57] *The emotion . . . in the mind* what the poet experiences is related to the original emotion, rather than the original emotion itself.

[58] *so that . . . enjoyment* Wordsworth emphasizes that we gain aesthetic pleasure even from reading poetry that is tragic in theme.

[59] *harmonious metrical language* poetry.

ceptibly make up a complex feeling of delight, which is of the most important use in tempering[60] the painful feeling which will always be found intermingled with powerful descriptions of the deeper passions.[61] This effect is always produced in pathetic[62] and impassioned poetry, while, in lighter compositions, the ease and gracefulness with which the poet manages his numbers[63] are themselves confessedly a principal source of the gratification of the reader.

I might perhaps include all which it is necessary to say upon this subject by affirming what few persons will deny – that, of two descriptions, either of passions, manners, or characters, each of them equally well-executed, the one in prose and the other in verse, the verse will be read a hundred times where the prose is read once. We see that Pope, by the power of verse alone, has contrived to render the plainest common sense interesting, and even frequently to invest it with the appearance of passion. In consequence of these convictions I related in metre the tale of 'Goody Blake and Harry Gill', which is one of the rudest of this collection. I wished to draw attention to the truth that the power of the human imagination is sufficient to produce such changes even in our physical nature as might almost appear miraculous. The truth is an important one; the fact (for it is a fact[64]) is a valuable illustration of it. And I have the satisfaction of knowing that it has been communicated to many hundreds of people[65] who would never have heard of it had it not been narrated as a ballad, and in a more impressive metre than is usual in ballads.

Having thus explained a few of my reasons why I have written in verse and why I have chosen subjects from common life, and endeavoured to bring my language near to the real language of men – if I have been too minute[66] in pleading my own cause, I have at the same time been treating a subject of general interest. And it is for this reason that I request the reader's permission to add a few words with reference solely to these particular poems, and to some defects which will probably be found in them. I am sensible that my associations must have sometimes been particular instead of general, and that, consequently – giving to things a false importance, sometimes from diseased impulses – I may have written upon unworthy subjects. But I am less apprehensive on this account, than that my language may frequently have suffered from those arbitrary connections of feelings and ideas with particular words and phrases from which no man can altogether protect himself. Hence I have no doubt that in some instances, feelings even of the ludicrous may be given to my readers by expressions which appeared to me tender and pathetic.

Such faulty expressions, were I convinced they were faulty at present, and that they must necessarily continue to be so, I would willingly take all reasonable pains to correct. But it is dangerous to make these alterations on the simple authority of a few individuals, or even of certain classes of men. For where the understanding of an author is not convinced, or his feelings altered, this cannot be done without great injury to himself, for his own feelings are his stay and support[67] – and if he sets them aside in one instance, he may be induced to repeat this act till his mind loses all confidence in itself, and becomes utterly debilitated.

To this it may be added that the reader ought never to forget that he is himself exposed to the same errors as the poet – and perhaps in a much greater degree. For there can be no presumption in saying that it is not probable he will be so well acquainted with the various stages of meaning through which words have passed, or with the fickleness or stability of the relations of particular ideas to each other – and above all, since he is so much less interested in the subject, he may decide lightly and carelessly. . . .

I have one request to make of my reader, which is, that in judging these poems he would decide by his own feelings genuinely, and not by reflection upon what will probably be the judgement of others. How common is it to hear a person say, 'I myself do not object to this style of composition, or this or that expression, but to such and such classes of people it will appear mean or ludicrous.' This mode of

---

60 *tempering* modifying.
61 *deeper passions* serious, darker emotions, such as grief.
62 *pathetic* passionate, deeply felt.
63 *numbers* i.e. verse, metre.
64 *for it is a fact* it is based on a true story; see p. 222 n. 1.
65 *it has been . . . people* Goody Blake and Harry Gill was in

1800 the most reprinted of the 1798 *Lyrical Ballads*, having appeared in the *Edinburgh Magazine* 14 (1799) 387–9, the *Ipswich Magazine* (1799) 118–19, *New Annual Register* 19 (1799) 200–3, and the *Universal Magazine* 105 (1799) 270–1.
66 *minute* detailed.
67 *stay and support* cf. *Resolution and Independence* 146–7.

criticism, so destructive of all sound unadulterated judgement, is almost universal. I have therefore to request that the reader would abide independently by his own feelings, and that if he finds himself affected he would not suffer such conjectures to interfere with his pleasure.

If an author by any single composition has impressed us with respect for his talents, it is useful to consider this as affording a presumption that, on other occasions where we have been displeased, he nevertheless may not have written ill or absurdly. And further, to give him so much credit for this one composition as may induce us to review what has displeased us with more care than we should otherwise have bestowed upon it. This is not only an act of justice but, in our decisions upon poetry especially, may conduce in a high degree to the improvement of our own taste. For an *accurate* taste in poetry, and in all the other arts (as Sir Joshua Reynolds[68] has observed) is an *acquired* talent which can only be produced by thought and a long continued intercourse with the best models of composition. This is mentioned not with so ridiculous a purpose as to prevent the most inexperienced reader from judging for himself (I have already said that I wish him to judge for himself), but merely to temper the rashness of decision, and to suggest that if poetry be a subject on which much time has not been bestowed, the judgement may be erroneous, and that in many cases it necessarily will be so.

I know that nothing would have so effectually contributed to further the end which I have in view, as to have shown of what kind the pleasure is, and how that pleasure is produced which is confessedly produced by metrical composition essentially different from that which I have here endeavoured to recommend. For the reader will say that he has been pleased by such composition, and what can I do more for him?

The power of any art is limited, and he will suspect that, if I propose to furnish him with new friends, it is only upon condition of his abandoning his old friends. Besides, as I have said, the reader is himself conscious of the pleasure which he has received from such composition – composition to which he has peculiarly attached the endearing name of poetry – and all men feel an habitual gratitude and something of an honourable bigotry for the objects which have long continued to please them. We not only wish to be pleased, but to be pleased in that particular way in which we have been accustomed to be pleased.

There is a host of arguments in these feelings, and I should be the less able to combat them successfully, as I am willing to allow that, in order entirely to enjoy the poetry which I am recommending, it would be necessary to give up much of what is ordinarily enjoyed. But would my limits have permitted me to point out how this pleasure is produced, I might have removed many obstacles and assisted my reader in perceiving that the powers of language are not so limited as he may suppose, and that it is possible that poetry may give other enjoyments, of a purer, more lasting, and more exquisite nature. This part of my subject I have not altogether neglected, but it has been less my present aim to prove that the interest excited by some other kinds of poetry is less vivid and less worthy of the nobler powers of the mind, than to offer reasons for presuming that, if the object which I have proposed to myself were adequately attained, a species of poetry would be produced which is genuine poetry, in its nature well adapted to interest mankind permanently, and likewise important in the multiplicity and quality of its moral relations.

From what has been said, and from a perusal of the poems, the reader will be able clearly to perceive the object which I have proposed to myself. He will determine how far I have attained this object and (what is a much more important question) whether it be worth attaining. And upon the decision of these two questions will rest my claim to the approbation of the public.

Appendix (extracts) (composed early 1802)

From LYRICAL BALLADS (2 vols, 1802)

As perhaps I have no right to expect from a reader of an introduction to a volume of poems that attentive perusal without which it is impossible, imperfectly as I have been compelled to express my mean-

---

[68] Sir Joshua Reynolds (1723–92), was the most renowned portrait painter of the age. His first discourse was delivered in 1769, and subsequent lectures became yearly fixtures at the Royal Academy.

ing, that what I have said in the preface should throughout be fully understood, I am the more anxious to give an exact notion of the sense in which I use the phrase 'poetic diction'. And for this purpose I will here add a few words concerning the origin of the phraseology which I have condemned under that name.

The earliest poets of all nations generally wrote from passion excited by real events.[1] They wrote naturally, and as men. Feeling powerfully as they did, their language was daring and figurative. In succeeding times, poets and men ambitious of the fame of poets, perceiving the influence of such language and desirous of producing the same effect without having the same animating passion, set themselves to a mechanical adoption of those figures of speech, and made use of them, sometimes with propriety, but much more frequently applied them to feelings and ideas with which they had no natural connection whatsoever. A language was thus insensibly produced, differing materially from the real language of men *in any situation*.

The reader or hearer of this distorted language found himself in a perturbed and unusual state of mind; when affected by the genuine language of passion he had been in a perturbed and unusual state of mind also. In both cases he was willing that his common judgement and understanding should be laid asleep, and he had no instinctive and infallible perception of the true[2] to make him reject the false; the one served as a passport for the other.[3] The agitation and confusion of mind were in both cases delightful, and no wonder if he confounded the one with the other, and believed them both to be produced by the same, or similar, causes. Besides, the poet spake to him in the character of a man to be looked up to, a man of genius and authority.

Thus, and from a variety of other causes, this distorted language was received with admiration, and poets (it is probable) who had before contented themselves for the most part with misapplying only expressions which at first had been dictated by real passion, carried the abuse still further, and introduced phrases composed apparently in the spirit of the original figurative language of passion, yet altogether of their own invention, and distinguished by various degrees of wanton deviation from good sense and nature.

It is indeed true that the language of the earliest poets was felt to differ materially from ordinary language because it was the language of extraordinary occasions – but it was really spoken by men, language which the poet himself had uttered when he had been affected by the events which he described, or which he had heard uttered by those around him. To this language it is probable that metre of some sort or other was early superadded. This separated the genuine language of poetry still further from common life, so that whoever read or heard the poems of these earliest poets felt himself moved in a way in which he had not been accustomed to be moved in real life, and by causes manifestly different from those which acted upon him in real life. This was the great temptation to all the corruptions which have followed. Under the protection of this feeling, succeeding poets constructed a phraseology which had one thing, it is true, in common with the genuine language of poetry – namely, that it was not heard in ordinary conversation, that it was unusual. But the first poets, as I have said, spake a language which, though unusual, was still the language of men. This circumstance, however, was disregarded by their successors. They found that they could please by easier means. They became proud of a language which they themselves had invented, and which was uttered only by themselves. And, with the spirit of a fraternity, they arrogated[4] it to themselves as their own. In process of time metre became a symbol or promise of this unusual language, and whoever took upon him to write in metre, according as he possessed more or less of true poetic genius, introduced less or more of this adulterated phraseology into his compositions, and the true and the false became so inseparably interwoven that the taste of men was gradually perverted, and this language was received as a natural language – and at length, by the influence of books upon men, did to a certain degree really become so.[5] Abuses of this kind were imported from one nation to another, and with the

---

APPENDIX

[1] *passion excited by real events* cf. Wordsworth's insistence that the proper object of poetry is truth, p. 361, above.

[2] *the true* i.e. the real – real emotions, real objects.

[3] *the one . . . other* in other words, language became detached from reality.

[4] *arrogated* claimed.

[5] *by the influence . . . so* the artificial, distorted language of poets was picked up in colloquial speech and thus, to some extent, became the 'natural language'.

progress of refinement this diction became daily more and more corrupt, thrusting out of sight the plain humanities of nature by a motley masquerade of tricks, quaintnesses, hieroglyphics,[6] and enigmas. . . .

Perhaps I can in no way, by positive example, more easily give my reader a notion of what I mean by the phrase 'poetic diction' than by referring him to a comparison between the metrical paraphrases which we have of passages in the Old and New Testament, and those passages as they exist in our common translation; see Pope's 'Messiah' throughout; Prior's 'Did sweeter sounds adorn my flowing tongue', etc., etc.; 'Though I speak with the tongues of men and of angels', etc., etc; see I Corinthians 13.

By way of immediate example, take the following of Dr Johnson:

> Turn on the prudent ant thy heedless eyes,
> Observe her labours, sluggard, and be wise!
> No stern command, no monitory voice[7]
> Prescribes her duties, or directs her choice;
> Yet, timely provident, she hastes away
> To snatch the blessings of a plenteous day.
> When fruitful summer loads the teeming plain,
> She crops the harvest and she stores the grain.
> How long shall sloth usurp thy useless hours,
> Unnerve thy vigour, and enchain thy powers?
> While artful shades thy downy couch enclose,
> And soft solicitation courts repose,
> Amidst the drowsy charms of dull delight
> Year chases year with unremitted flight;
> Till want now following, fraudulent and slow,
> Shall spring to seize thee, like an ambushed foe. (*The Ant*)

From this hubbub of words pass to the original: 'Go to the ant, thou sluggard, consider her ways and be wise – which having no guide, overseer, or ruler, provideth her meat in the summer, and gathereth her food in the harvest. How long wilt thou sleep, oh sluggard? When wilt thou arise out of thy sleep? Yet a little sleep, a little slumber, a little folding of the hands to sleep. So shall thy poverty come as one that travaileth, and thy want as an armed man' (Proverbs 6).

One more quotation and I have done. It is from Cowper's 'Verses Supposed to be Written by Alexander Selkirk'.

> Religion – what treasure untold
> Resides in that heavenly word!
> More precious than silver and gold
> Or all that this earth can afford.
> But the sound of the church-going bell
> These valleys and rocks never heard,
> Ne'er sighed at the sound of a knell,
> Or smiled when a sabbath appeared.
>
> Ye winds that have made me your sport,
> Convey to this desolate shore
> Some cordial endearing report
> Of a land I must visit no more.

---

6 *hieroglyphics* words of unknown or mysterious meaning.
7 *monitory voice* warning. Wordsworth was evidently recalling Johnson when he used this phrase at *Two-Part Prelude* ii 18.

> My friends, do they now and then send
> A wish or a thought after me?
> Oh tell me I yet have a friend,
> Though a friend I am never to see.

I have quoted this passage as an instance of three different styles of composition. The first four lines are poorly expressed. Some critics would call the language prosaic; the fact is it would be bad prose – so bad that it is scarcely worse in metre. The epithet 'church-going' applied to a bell (and that by so chaste a writer as Cowper) is an instance of the strange abuses which poets have introduced into their language till they and their readers take them as matters of course, if they do not single them out expressly as objects of admiration. The two lines 'Ne'er sighed at the sound', etc., are in my opinion an instance of the language of passion wrested from its proper use, and, from the mere circumstance of the composition being in metre, applied upon an occasion that does not justify such violent expressions – and I should condemn the passage (though perhaps few readers will agree with me) as vicious poetic diction.

The last stanza is throughout admirably expressed. It would be equally good whether in prose or verse, except that the reader has an exquisite pleasure in seeing such natural language so naturally connected with metre. The beauty of this stanza tempts me here to add a sentiment which ought to be the pervading spirit of a system, detached parts of which have been imperfectly explained in the preface – namely, that in proportion as ideas and feelings are valuable, whether the composition be in prose or in verse, they require and exact one and the same language.

To H.C., Six Years Old (composed probably between 4 March and 4 April 1802)[1]

From POEMS IN TWO VOLUMES (1807)

> Oh thou, whose fancies from afar are brought,
> Who of thy words dost make a mock apparel,
> And fittest to unutterable thought
> The breeze-like motion and the self-born carol;
> Thou fairy voyager, that dost float   5
> In such clear water, that thy boat
> May rather seem
> To brood on air than on an earthly stream,[2]
> Suspended in a stream as clear as sky,
> Where earth and heaven do make one imagery;   10
> Oh blessed vision, happy child,
> That art so exquisitely wild,
> I think of thee with many fears
> For what may be thy lot in future years.

TO H.C., SIX YEARS OLD
[1] Hartley Coleridge (b. 1796) had already featured in Coleridge's *Frost at Midnight*, *Christabel*, *The Nightingale*, and would appear again in Wordsworth's *Ode* (pp. 375–80). Lucy Newlyn has observed that this poem is 'close to the rhythms and language' of Marvell's *On a Drop of Dew* ('The Little Actor and his Mock Apparel', *TWC* 14 (1983) 30–9). The dating of the poem is debated; see my *Wordsworth's Reading 1800–1815* (1995), p. 142.
[2] 'See Carver's description of his situation upon one of the lakes of America' (Wordsworth's note). Wordsworth has in mind Carver's account of Lake Superior: 'The water in general

appeared to lie on a bed of rocks. When it was calm, and the sun shone bright, I could sit in my canoe, where the depth was upwards of six fathoms, and plainly see huge piles of stones at the bottom, of different shapes, some of which appeared as if they were hewn. The water at this time was as pure and transparent as air; and my canoe seemed as if it hung suspended in that element. It was impossible to look attentively through this limpid medium at the rocks below, without finding, before many minutes were elapsed, your head swim, and your eyes no longer able to behold the dazzling scene' (Jonathan Carver, *Travels through the interior parts of North America* (1778), pp. 132–3).

I thought of times when Pain might be thy guest,   15
Lord of thy house and hospitality;
And Grief, uneasy lover, never rest
But when she sate within the touch of thee.
Oh too industrious folly!
Oh vain and causeless melancholy!   20
Nature will either end thee quite,
Or, lengthening out thy season of delight,
Preserve for thee, by individual right,
A young lamb's heart among the full-grown flocks.
What hast thou to do with sorrow   25
Or the injuries of tomorrow?
Thou art a dew-drop, which the morn brings forth,
Not doomed to jostle with unkindly shocks,
Or to be trailed along the soiling earth;
A gem that glitters while it lives,   30
And no forewarning gives;
But, at the touch of wrong, without a strife,
Slips in a moment out of life.

The Rainbow (composed probably 26 March 1802)

From POEMS IN TWO VOLUMES (1807)

My heart leaps up when I behold
    A rainbow in the sky;
So was it when my life began,
So is it now I am a man,
So be it when I shall grow old   5
    Or let me die!
The child is father of the man,
And I could wish my days to be
Bound each to each by natural piety.

[*These chairs they have no words to utter*] (composed *c.* 22 April 1802; edited from MS)[1]

These chairs they have no words to utter,
No fire is in the grate to stir or flutter,
The ceiling and floor are mute as a stone,
My chamber is hushed and still,
        And I am alone,
        Happy and alone.   5

Oh, who would be afraid of life,
    The passion, the sorrow, and the strife,
        When he may lie

THESE CHAIRS THEY HAVE NO WORDS TO UTTER
[1]   These two poems should be read in the light of Dorothy
Wordsworth's journal entry of 29 April 1802, p. 434, below.

Sheltered so easily –   10
May lie in peace on his bed,
Happy as they who are dead?

  Half an hour afterwards
I have thoughts that are fed by the sun;[2]
    The things which I see
    Are welcome to me,   15
    Welcome every one;
    I do not wish to lie
      Dead, dead,
Dead, without any company.[3]
    Here alone on my bed,   20
With thoughts that are fed by the sun
And hopes that are welcome every one,
    Happy am I.

Oh life, there is about thee
A deep delicious peace;   25
I would not be without thee –
  Stay, oh stay!
Yet be thou ever as now,
Sweetness and breath with the quiet of death,
  Peace, peace, peace.   30

Resolution and Independence (composed probably between 3 May and 4 July 1802)[1]

From POEMS IN TWO VOLUMES (1807)

There was a roaring in the wind all night,
The rain came heavily and fell in floods;
But now the sun is rising calm and bright,
The birds are singing in the distant woods;
Over his own sweet voice the stockdove broods,[2]   5
The jay makes answer as the magpie chatters,
And all the air is filled with pleasant noise of waters.

All things that love the sun are out of doors,
The sky rejoices in the morning's birth,
The grass is bright with raindrops, on the moors   10
The hare is running races in her mirth
And with her feet she from the plashy earth
Raises a mist which, glittering in the sun,
Runs with her all the way, wherever she doth run.

---

[2]   *I have thoughts that are fed by the sun* an echo of Anna Laetitia Barbauld's *A Summer Evening's Meditation*, in which Contemplation 'fed on thoughts unripened by the sun' (l. 22).
[3]   *without any company* Wordsworth echoes Arcite's dying speech in Chaucer's *Knight's Tale*:
  What is this world? What askest men to have?
  Now with his love, now in his colde grave
  Allone, withouten any compaignye? (ll. 2777–9)

RESOLUTION AND INDEPENDENCE
[1]   The incident which inspired this poem is recounted by Dorothy Wordsworth, p. 433.
[2]   *Over . . . broods* see Wordsworth's comments on this line in the 1815 Preface, pp. 412–13.

I was a traveller then upon the moor;[3]   15
I saw the hare that raced about with joy;
I heard the woods and distant waters roar,
Or heard them not, as happy as a boy –
The pleasant season did my heart employ.
My old remembrances went from me wholly,   20
And all the ways of men, so vain and melancholy.

But as it sometimes chanceth, from the might
Of joy in minds that can no farther go,
As high as we have mounted in delight
In our dejection do we sink as low –   25
To me that morning did it happen so,
And fears and fancies thick upon me came,
Dim sadness, and blind thoughts I knew not nor could name.

I heard the skylark singing in the sky,[4]
And I bethought me of the playful hare;   30
Even such a happy child of earth am I,
Even as these blissful creatures do I fare;
Far from the world I walk, and from all care.
But there may come another day to me –
Solitude, pain of heart, distress, and poverty.   35

My whole life I have lived in pleasant thought
As if life's business were a summer mood,
As if all needful things would come unsought
To genial faith, still rich in genial good;
But how can he expect that others should   40
Build for him, sow for him, and at his call
Love him, who for himself will take no heed at all?

I thought of Chatterton,[5] the marvellous boy,
The sleepless soul that perished in its pride;
Of him[6] who walked in glory and in joy   45
Behind his plough[7] upon the mountainside.
By our own spirits are we deified;[8]
We poets in our youth begin in gladness,
But thereof comes in the end despondency and madness.

Now whether it were by peculiar grace,[9]   50
A leading from above, a something given,

---

3 *I was then ... moor* In the Fenwick Notes, Wordsworth recalls: 'This old man I met a few hundred yards from my cottage at Town End, Grasmere, and the account of him is taken from his own mouth' (*FN* 14). As in *The Prelude*, he is not concerned with factual truth, but with truth to the emotions.
4 *I heard ... sky* cf. *The Ancient Mariner* (1798) 347–8: 'Sometimes a-dropping from the sky / I heard the lavrock sing'.
5 During his short life, Thomas Chatterton (1752–70) composed a number of forged medieval poems supposedly by the fifteenth-century poet, Thomas Rowley. Wordsworth and Coleridge both admired these works as schoolboys. It is often noted that this poem imitates the metre of Chatterton's *Excellent Ballade of Charitie*.
6 Robert Burns.
7 *Behind his plough* Burns was a farmer, and in some of his poems, such as 'To a Mouse' (pp. 133–4), described himself at the plough.
8 *deified* made godlike, divine.
9 *grace* divine influence.

Yet it befell that, in this lonely place,
When up and down my fancy thus was driven,
And I with these untoward thoughts had striven,
I saw a man before me unawares –   55
The oldest man he seemed that ever wore grey hairs.

My course I stopped as soon as I espied
The old man in that naked wilderness;
Close by a pond, upon the further side,
He stood alone. A minute's space I guess   60
I watched him, he continuing motionless.
To the pool's further margin then I drew,
He being all the while before me full in view.

As a huge stone is sometimes seen to lie[10]
Couched on the bald top of an eminence,   65
Wonder to all who do the same espy
By what means it could thither come, and whence;
So that it seems a thing endued with sense,
Like a sea-beast crawled forth, which on a shelf
Of rock or sand reposeth, there to sun itself –   70

Such seemed this man, not all alive nor dead,
Nor all asleep, in his extreme old age.
His body was bent double, feet and head
Coming together in their pilgrimage,
As if some dire constraint of pain, or rage   75
Of sickness felt by him in times long past,
A more than human weight upon his frame had cast.

Himself he propped, his body, limbs, and face,
Upon a long grey staff of shaven wood;
And still as I drew near with gentle pace,   80
Beside the little pond or moorish flood,
Motionless as a cloud the old man stood
That heareth not the loud winds when they call,
And moveth altogether, if it move at all.

At length, himself unsettling, he the pond   85
Stirred with his staff, and fixedly did look
Upon the muddy water, which he conned[11]
As if he had been reading in a book.
And now such freedom as I could I took,
And drawing to his side, to him did say,   90
'This morning gives us promise of a glorious day.'

A gentle answer did the old man make
In courteous speech which forth he slowly drew,
And him with further words I thus bespake,
'What kind of work is that which you pursue?   95
This is a lonesome place for one like you.'

---

[10] For Wordsworth's important comments on ll. 64–84 see   [11] *conned* studied.
pp. 413–14.

He answered me with pleasure and surprise,
And there was, while he spake, a fire about his eyes.

His words came feebly, from a feeble chest,
Yet each in solemn order followed each, 100
With something of a lofty utterance dressed,
Choice word and measured phrase, above the reach
Of ordinary men – a stately speech
Such as grave livers[12] do in Scotland use,
Religious men, who give to God and man their dues. 105

He told me that he to this pond had come
To gather leeches, being old and poor –
Employment hazardous and wearisome![13]
And he had many hardships to endure;
From pond to pond he roamed, from moor to moor, 110
Housing, with God's good help, by choice or chance;
And in this way he gained an honest maintenance.[14]

The old man still stood talking by my side,
But now his voice to me was like a stream
Scarce heard, nor word from word could I divide; 115
And the whole body of the man did seem
Like one whom I had met with in a dream,
Or like a man from some far region sent
To give me human strength, and strong admonishment.

My former thoughts returned: the fear that kills, 120
The hope that is unwilling to be fed,
Cold, pain, and labour, and all fleshly ills,
And mighty poets in their misery dead.
And now, not knowing what the old man had said,
My question eagerly did I renew, 125
'How is it that you live, and what is it you do?'

He with a smile did then his words repeat,
And said that gathering leeches far and wide
He travelled, stirring thus about his feet
The waters of the ponds where they abide. 130
'Once I could meet with them on every side
But they have dwindled long by slow decay;
Yet still I persevere, and find them where I may.'

While he was talking thus, the lonely place,
The old man's shape and speech, all troubled me; 135
In my mind's eye I seemed to see him pace
About the weary moors continually,
Wandering about alone and silently.

---

[12] *livers* folk.
[13] *He told me . . . wearisome* leeches were widely used in med-
ical treatment. Many illnesses, including fevers, were thought
to be caused by an excess of blood; leeches were applied to
bleed the patient.

[14] *maintenance* living.

While I these thoughts within myself pursued,
He, having made a pause, the same discourse renewed.   140

And soon with this he other matter blended,
Cheerfully uttered, with demeanour kind,
But stately in the main; and when he ended,
I could have laughed myself to scorn to find
In that decrepit man so firm a mind.   145
'God', said I, 'be my help and stay[15] secure;
I'll think of the leech-gatherer on the lonely moor.'

[*The world is too much with us*] (composed May/June 1802)

From POEMS IN TWO VOLUMES (1807)

The world is too much with us; late and soon,
Getting and spending, we lay waste our powers:
Little we see in nature that is ours;
We have given our hearts away – a sordid boon!
This sea that bares her bosom to the moon,   5
The winds that will be howling at all hours
And are up-gathered now like sleeping flowers –
For this, for everything, we are out of tune,
It moves us not. Great God! I'd rather be
A pagan suckled in a creed outworn;   10
So might I, standing on this pleasant lea,[1]
Have glimpses that would make me less forlorn;
Have sight of Proteus coming from the sea;[2]
Or hear old Triton blow his wreathed horn.[3]

To Toussaint L'Ouverture[1] (composed August 1802)

From POEMS IN TWO VOLUMES (1807)

Toussaint, the most unhappy man of men!
Whether the rural milkmaid by her cow
Sing in thy hearing, or thou liest now
Alone in some deep dungeon's earless den –
Oh miserable chieftain, where and when   5
Wilt thou find patience? Yet die not! Do thou
Wear rather in thy bonds a cheerful brow;

---

[15] *stay* support.

THE WORLD IS TOO MUCH WITH US
[1] *lea* meadow.
[2] *Have sight ... sea* cf. *Paradise Lost* iii 603–4: 'call up unbound / In various shapes old Proteus from the sea'.
[3] *Have sight ... horn* cf. Spenser, *Colin Clouts Come Home Againe* 245–8: 'Triton blowing loud his wreathed horne ... And Proteus eke with him does drive his heard'.

TO TOUSSAINT L'OUVERTURE
[1] François Dominique Toussaint L'Ouverture (born 1743), son of a Negro slave, became governor of San Domingo (Haiti), then a French colony, in 1801. He resisted Napoleon's attempts to reintroduce slavery, leading a popular uprising. French forces eventually suppressed the revolt, and Toussaint was taken to France, and imprisoned and tortured at the Castle of Joux, where he died, April 1803. His heroic life and death aroused tremendous sympathy in England, where the movement for the Abolition of the Slave Trade was gathering pace.

Though fallen thyself, never to rise again,
Live, and take comfort. Thou hast left behind
Powers that will work for thee – air, earth, and skies;   10
There's not a breathing of the common wind
That will forget thee; thou hast great allies;
Thy friends are exultations, agonies,
And love, and man's unconquerable mind.

[*It is a beauteous evening, calm and free*] (composed 1–29 August 1802)[1]

From POEMS IN TWO VOLUMES (1807)

It is a beauteous evening, calm and free;
The holy time is quiet as a nun
Breathless with adoration; the broad sun
Is sinking down in its tranquillity;
The gentleness of heaven is on the sea;   5
Listen! The mighty Being is awake
And doth with his eternal motion make
A sound like thunder – everlastingly.
Dear child![2] Dear girl! that walkest with me here,
If thou appear'st untouched by solemn thought,   10
Thy nature is not therefore less divine;
Thou liest in Abraham's bosom[3] all the year,
And worshipp'st at the Temple's inner shrine,
God being with thee when we know it not.

1 September 1802 (composed between 29 August and 1 September 1802)[1]

From POEMS IN TWO VOLUMES (1807)

We had a fellow-passenger who came
From Calais with us, gaudy in array –
A Negro woman, like a lady gay,
Yet silent as a woman fearing blame;
Dejected, meek – yea, pitiably tame   5
She sat, from notice turning not away,
But on our proffered kindness still did lay

IT IS A BEAUTEOUS EVENING, CALM AND FREE
[1]   This poem was composed on the beach at Calais. The poet and Dorothy took advantage of the Peace of Amiens in the summer of 1802 to visit France to see his former French girlfriend, Annette Vallon, and their daughter, Caroline Wordsworth, whom he had not seen.
[2]   *Dear child* Wordsworth's daughter, Caroline.
[3]   *Abraham's bosom* see Luke 16:22: 'And it came to pass that the beggar died, and was carried by the angels into Abraham's bosom'.

1 SEPTEMBER 1802
[1]   Composed during Wordsworth's brief visit to France during the Treaty of Amiens, 1802. In 1827, he added a headnote: 'Among the capricious acts of tyranny that disgraced these times was the chasing of all Negroes from France by decree of the government. We had a fellow-passenger who was one of the expelled.'

A weight of languid speech, or at the same
Was silent, motionless in eyes and face.
She was a Negro woman driv'n from France,   10
Rejected like all others of that race,
Not one of whom may now find footing there;
This the poor outcast did to us declare,
Nor murmured at the unfeeling ordinance.

Composed upon Westminster Bridge, 3 September 1802 (composed between 31 July and 3 September 1802)

From POEMS IN TWO VOLUMES (1807)

Earth has not any thing to show more fair:
Dull would he be of soul who could pass by
A sight so touching in its majesty.
This city now doth like a garment wear
The beauty of the morning – silent, bare,   5
Ships, towers, domes, theatres, and temples lie
Open unto the fields, and to the sky,
All bright and glittering in the smokeless air.
Never did sun more beautifully steep
In his first splendour valley, rock, or hill;   10
Ne'er saw I, never felt, a calm so deep.
The river glideth at his own sweet will[1] –
Dear God! the very houses seem asleep;
And all that mighty heart is lying still.

London 1802 (composed September 1802)

From POEMS IN TWO VOLUMES (1807)

Milton, thou shouldst be living at this hour,
England hath need of thee! She is a fen
Of stagnant waters. Altar, sword, and pen,
Fireside, the heroic wealth of hall and bower,
Have forfeited their ancient English dower   5
Of inward happiness. We are selfish men;
Oh raise us up, return to us again,
And give us manners, virtue, freedom, power!
Thy soul was like a star and dwelt apart;
Thou hadst a voice whose sound was like the sea,   10
Pure as the naked heavens, majestic, free –
So didst thou travel on life's common way,
In cheerful godliness, and yet thy heart
The lowliest duties on itself did lay.

COMPOSED UPON WESTMINSTER BRIDGE
[1] *own sweet will* Shakespeare, *Sonnet 16*, l. 14: 'And you must
live, drawn by your own sweet will'.

[*Great men have been among us*] (composed summer 1802)

From POEMS IN TWO VOLUMES (1807)

Great men have been among us; hands that penned
And tongues that uttered wisdom, better none:
The later Sidney, Marvell, Harrington,
Young Vane,[1] and others who called Milton friend.
These moralists could act and comprehend: 5
They knew how genuine glory was put on;
Taught us how rightfully a nation shone
In splendour; what strength was, that would not bend
But in magnanimous meekness. France, 'tis strange,
Hath brought forth no such souls as we had then.   10
Perpetual emptiness! Unceasing change!
No single volume paramount, no code,
No master spirit, no determined road;
But equally a want of books and men!

Ode (from 1815 entitled, *Ode. Intimations of Immortality from Recollections of Early Childhood*) (composed between March 1802 and March 1804)[1]

From POEMS IN TWO VOLUMES (1807)

Paulò majora canamus.[2]

There was a time when meadow, grove, and stream,
The earth, and every common sight,
    To me did seem
    Apparelled in celestial light,
The glory and the freshness of a dream.   5
It is not now as it has been of yore;
    Turn wheresoe'er I may
      By night or day
The things which I have seen I now can see no more.

    The rainbow comes and goes   10
    And lovely is the rose,
    The moon doth with delight

GREAT MEN HAVE BEEN AMONG US
[1] *Great men . . . Vane* all English republicans of the civil war period. Algernon Sidney was a distinguished republican and was beheaded for complicity in the Rye House plot, 1683; he was the author of a republican tract, *Discourse concerning Civil Government* (1698), which Wordsworth probably read while an undergraduate. He had read the work of Andrew Marvell (1621–78), poet, friend, and secretary to Milton, by 1795. James Harrington (1611–77) was the author of the republican classic, *Commonwealth of Oceana* (1656); Wordsworth is likely to have read it during his time in France, 1791–2. As Wordsworth would have known, Milton had written a sonnet

To Henry Vane the Younger, beginning: 'Vane, young in years, but in sage counsel old'. Vane was executed 14 January 1662.

ODE
[1] Probably some or all of stanzas 1–4 composed 27 March 1802. Further composition – possibly including some or, less probably, all of stanzas 5–8 – on 17 June 1802. Most of the last seven stanzas probably composed, and the poem completed, early 1804, by 6 March. See also the Fenwick Note to this poem, pp. 417–18.
[2] 'Let us sing of somewhat more exalted things' (Virgil, *Eclogue* iv 1).

Look round her when the heavens are bare;
    Waters on a starry night
    Are beautiful and fair;
The sunshine is a glorious birth;
But yet I know, where'er I go,
That there hath passed away a glory from the earth.   15

Now while the birds thus sing a joyous song,
    And while the young lambs bound   20
    As to the tabor's³ sound,
To me alone there came a thought of grief;
A timely utterance gave that thought relief
    And I again am strong.
The cataracts blow their trumpets from the steep –   25
No more shall grief of mine the season wrong;
I hear the echoes through the mountains throng,
The winds come to me from the fields of sleep
    And all the earth is gay;
        Land and sea   30
Give themselves up to jollity,
    And with the heart of May
Doth every beast keep holiday.
    Thou child of joy
Shout round me, let me hear thy shouts, thou happy shepherd-boy!   35

    Ye blessed creatures, I have heard the call
Ye to each other make; I see
The heavens laugh with you in your jubilee;
    My heart is at your festival,
    My head hath its coronal⁴ –   40
The fullness of your bliss, I feel, I feel it all.
    Oh evil day! if I were sullen
    While the earth herself is adorning
      This sweet May morning,
    And the children are pulling
      On every side   45
In a thousand valleys far and wide
Fresh flowers, while the sun shines warm
And the babe leaps up on his mother's arm –
    I hear, I hear, with joy I hear!
    But there's a tree, of many one,   50
A single field which I have looked upon,
Both of them speak of something that is gone;
      The pansy at my feet
      Doth the same tale repeat:
Whither is fled the visionary gleam?   55
Where is it now, the glory and the dream?

Our birth is but a sleep and a forgetting.
The soul that rises with us, our life's star,
    Hath had elsewhere its setting   60

---

³ *tabor* a small drum.   ⁴ *coronal* small garland of flowers worn on the head.

And cometh from afar.[5]
Not in entire forgetfulness,
And not in utter nakedness,
But trailing clouds of glory do we come
    From God, who is our home.   65
Heaven lies about us in our infancy!
Shades of the prison-house begin to close
    Upon the growing boy,[6]
But he beholds the light and whence it flows,
    He sees it in his joy;   70
The youth who daily farther from the east
    Must travel, still is nature's priest,
      And by the vision splendid
      Is on his way attended:
At length the man perceives it die away   75
And fade into the light of common day.

Earth fills her lap with pleasures of her own;
Yearnings she hath in her own natural kind,
And even with something of a mother's mind
      And no unworthy aim,   80
    The homely nurse doth all she can
To make her foster-child, her inmate man,
    Forget the glories he hath known
And that imperial palace whence he came.

Behold the child[7] among his new-born blisses,   85
A four years' darling of a pygmy size!
See where mid work of his own hand he lies,
Fretted by sallies of his mother's kisses
With light upon him from his father's eyes!
See at his feet some little plan or chart,   90
Some fragment from his dream of human life
Shaped by himself with newly-learned art –
      A wedding or a festival,
      A mourning or a funeral;
      And this hath now his heart,   95
      And unto this he frames his song.
      Then will he fit his tongue
To dialogues of business, love, or strife;
      But it will not be long
      Ere this be thrown aside,   100
      And with new joy and pride
The little actor cons[8] another part,
Filling from time to time his 'humorous stage'[9]

---

[5] *The soul ... afar* Wordsworth suggests that we exist, before birth, in spiritual form. For his later comments on pre-existence, see pp. 417–18.

[6] *Shades ... boy* Wordsworth probably has in mind Coleridge's recollection of his schooldays at Christ's Hospital: 'For I was reared / In the great city, pent mid cloisters dim' (*Frost at Midnight* 56–7).

[7] *the child* Hartley Coleridge, who had already been celebrated as a gifted being by Wordsworth in *To H.C., Six Years Old* (pp. 366–7), and by Coleridge in *Frost at Midnight*, *Christabel* 644–65, and *The Nightingale* 91–105.

[8] *cons* learns.

[9] *humorous stage* the theatre is full of characters with difference moods ('humours'). The quotation is from Samuel Daniel's dedicatory sonnet to *Musophilus, To the Right Worthy and Judicious Favourer of Virtue, Mr Fulke Grevill* 1–2: 'I do not here upon this hum'rous stage / Bring my transformed verse'. Wordsworth is also recalling the seven ages of man speech, *As You Like It* II vii 139–66.

With all the persons down to palsied Age
That Life brings with her in her equipage[10] –   105
    As if his whole vocation
    Were endless imitation.

Thou[11] whose exterior semblance doth belie
    Thy soul's immensity;
Thou best philosopher who yet dost keep   110
Thy heritage; thou eye among the blind
That, deaf and silent, read'st the eternal deep,
Haunted forever by the eternal mind;
    Mighty prophet! Seer blessed!
    On whom those truths do rest   115
Which we are toiling all our lives to find;
Thou, over whom thy immortality
Broods like the day, a master o'er a slave,
A presence which is not to be put by,
    To whom the grave   120
Is but a lonely bed without the sense or sight
    Of day or the warm light,
A place of thought where we in waiting lie;[12]
Thou little child, yet glorious in the might
Of untamed pleasures, on thy being's height –   125
Why with such earnest pains dost thou provoke
The years to bring the inevitable yoke,
Thus blindly with thy blessedness at strife?
Full soon thy soul shall have her earthly freight,
And custom lie upon thee with a weight   130
Heavy as frost, and deep almost as life.

    Oh joy! that in our embers
    Is something that doth live,
    That nature yet remembers
    What was so fugitive!   135
The thought of our past years in me doth breed
Perpetual benedictions, not indeed
For that which is most worthy to be blessed –
Delight and liberty, the simple creed
Of childhood, whether fluttering or at rest,   140
With new-born hope forever in his breast –
    Not for these I raise
    The song of thanks and praise;
    But for those obstinate questionings
    Of sense and outward things,[13]   145
    Fallings from us, vanishings,[14]
    Blank misgivings of a creature

---

[10] *equipage* retinue, attendant following.

[11] *Thou* Hartley Coleridge.

[12] *To whom ... lie* See Dorothy Wordsworth's journal, p. 434, below, and 'These chairs, they have no words to utter' 11–12. Lines 120–3 were cut in versions of the poem after 1815.

[13] *obstinate ... things* the soul constantly challenges the notion that the outward, material reality of the physical world might be all there is.

[14] *vanishings* Years later, Wordsworth is reported to have said, 'There was a time in my life when I had to push against something that resisted, to be sure that there was anything outside me. I was sure of my own mind; everything else fell away and vanished into thought' (*WPW* iv 467); see also Fenwick Note to this poem, pp. 417–18, below.

Moving about in worlds not realized,
High instincts before which our mortal nature
Did tremble like a guilty thing surprised;[15]   150
    But for those first affections,
    Those shadowy recollections
       Which, be they what they may,
Are yet the fountain-light of all our day,
Are yet a master-light of all our seeing;   155
       Uphold us, cherish us, and make
Our noisy years seem moments in the being
Of the eternal silence – truths that wake
        To perish never,
Which neither listlessness nor mad endeavour,   160
       Nor man nor boy,
Nor all that is at enmity with joy
Can utterly abolish or destroy!
    Hence, in a season of calm weather,
       Though inland far we be,   165
Our souls have sight of that immortal sea
       Which brought us hither,
       Can in a moment travel thither
And see the children sport upon the shore,
And hear the mighty waters rolling evermore.   170

Then sing, ye birds; sing, sing a joyous song!
    And let the young lambs bound
    As to the tabor's sound!
    We in thought will join your throng,
      Ye that pipe and ye that play,   175
      Ye that through your hearts today
      Feel the gladness of the May!
What though the radiance which was once so bright
Be now for ever taken from my sight?
    Though nothing can bring back the hour   180
Of splendour in the grass, of glory in the flower,
      We will grieve not, rather find
      Strength in what remains behind,
      In the primal sympathy
      Which having been must ever be,   185
      In the soothing thoughts that spring
      Out of human suffering,
      In the faith that looks through death,
In years that bring the philosophic mind.

And oh, ye fountains, meadows, hills and groves,   190
Think not of any severing of our loves!
Yet in my heart of hearts I feel your might;
I only have relinquished one delight
To live beneath your more habitual sway.
I love the brooks which down their channels fret[16]   195

---

[15] *like a guilty thing surprised* cf. Horatio talking about the
ghost at *Hamlet* I i 148–9: 'And then it started like a guilty
thing / Upon a fearful summons'.

[16] *fret* move in an agitated manner.

Even more than when I tripped lightly as they;
The innocent brightness of a new-born day
   Is lovely yet;
The clouds that gather round the setting sun
Do take a sober colouring from an eye   200
That hath kept watch o'er man's mortality;
Another race hath been, and other palms are won.
Thanks to the human heart by which we live,
Thanks to its tenderness, its joys and fears,
To me the meanest flower[17] that blows can give   205
Thoughts that do often lie too deep for tears.

From [*The Five-Book Prelude*] (composed February–March 1804; edited from MS)[1]

[*The Infant Prodigy*] (from Book IV)

Rarely, and with reluctance, would I stoop
To transitory themes,[2] yet I rejoice –
And, by these thoughts admonished, must speak out
Thanksgivings from my heart – that I was reared
Safe from an evil which these days have laid   375
Upon the children of the land, a pest[3]
That might have dried me up, body and soul.
Let few words paint it: 'tis a child – no child,
But a dwarf man – in knowledge, virtue, skill,
In what he is not and in what he is,   380
The noontide shadow of a man complete;
A worshipper of worldly seemliness,
Not quarrelsome (for that were far beneath
His dignity), with gifts he bubbles o'er
As generous as a fountain. Selfishness   385
May not come near him, gluttony or pride;
The wandering beggars propagate his name,
Dumb creatures find him tender as a nun.[4]
Yet deem him not for this a naked dish

---

[17] *the meanest flower* borrowed from Gray, *Ode on the Pleasure Arising from Vicissitude* 49: 'The meanest flowret of the vale'.

THE FIVE-BOOK PRELUDE
[1] In February–March 1804, Wordsworth returned to *The Prelude* with the aim of turning it into a poem consisting of five Books. He reorganized the *Two-Part Prelude*, placing the spots of time at the end of the poem, and used the 'glad preamble', composed in 1799 (pp. 329–30), as an introduction to the poem. Among the various passages he composed towards the five-Book version was this satirical attack on educational theorists of the day. It was followed immediately by 'There was a boy', which had been published as an independent poem in *Lyrical Ballads* (1800) (p. 324). In early March Wordsworth abandoned the five-Book poem, dismembered it, and began working towards a new version in thirteen Books. The description of the infant prodigy was later revised to form *Thirteen-Book Prelude* v 223–9, 294–388.
[2] *transitory themes* Wordsworth rightly recognized the controversy over different ways of educating children to be of its time.

[3] *pest* plague. Wordsworth's target is the tradition of educationalists who followed in the wake of Locke's *Some Thoughts Concerning Education* (1693). These include Rousseau's *Emile* (1762) – which Wordsworth had read by 1796; Richard and Maria Edgeworth's *Practical Education* (1798) (read by Coleridge shortly after publication) and Thomas Day's *Sandford and Merton* (1783–6). See also James Chandler, 'Wordsworth, Rousseau and the Politics of Education', *Romanticism: A Critical Reader* 57–83, and Alan Richardson, *Literature, Education and Romanticism* (Cambridge, 1994), pp. 51–8.
[4] *Selfishness . . . nun* Thomas Day's protagonist, Harry Sandford, is 'brave, generous to beggars, kind to animals, even cockchafers, calm in the presence of an angry bull. Even the cattle were glad when he came back after an absence'. The literary model is Chaucer's portrait of the prioress (*General Prologue* 118–62).

Of goodness merely, he is garnished out: 390
Arch are his notices,[5] and nice his sense
Of the ridiculous; deceit and guile
He can look through and through in pleasant spleen,[6]
At the broad follies of the licensed world;[7]
Though shrewd, yet innocent himself withal,   395
And can read lectures upon innocence.[8]
    He is fenced round – nay armed, for aught we know,
In panoply complete;[9] and fear itself,
Unless it leap upon him in a dream,
Touches him not.[10] In brief, the moral part   400
Is perfect; in learning and in books
He is a prodigy. His discourse moves slow,
Massy and ponderous as a prison door,
Tremendously embossed with terms of art;[11]
With propositions are the younker's[12] brains   405
Filled to the brim; the path in which he treads
Is choked with grammars; cushion of divine
Was never such a type of thought profound
As is the pillow where he rests his head.[13]
The ensigns of the empire which he holds,   410
The globe and sceptre of his royalties,
Are telescopes and crucibles and maps.[14]
Ships he can guide across the pathless sea,
And tell you all their cunning;[15] he can read
The inside of the earth, and spell the stars;   415
He knows the policies of foreign lands,
Can string you names of districts, cities, towns
The whole world over,[16] tight as beads of dew
Upon a gossamer thread! His teachers stare,
The country people pray for God's good grace   420
And shudder at his deep experiments.[17]
He sifts, he weighs, takes nothing upon trust –
All things are put to question.[18] He must live

---

5 *Arch are his notices* his observations are clever, crafty, even mischievous.

6 *pleasant spleen* amusement, as at *Twelfth Night* III ii 68–9: 'If you desire the spleen, and will laugh yourselves into stitches, follow me.'

7 *the licensed world* The world is 'licensed' in that it has the liberty to do as it pleases; it is also, of course, licentious.

8 *And can read . . . innocence* Richly ironic. The child's sophistication belies his 'goodness'. He is in no position to speak learnedly on the subject of innocence.

9 *panoply complete* full armour; cf. Cowper's satirical portrait of the clergyman, 'armed himself in panoply complete' (*Task* ii 345).

10 *fear itself . . . touches him not* without fear, the infant prodigy is deprived of a principal formative influence; cf. *Two-Part Prelude* i 139–41.

11 *terms of art* technical jargon.

12 *younker's* youngster's.

13 *cushion of divine . . . head* The prodigy's pillow is a better symbol ('type') of profound thought than the cushion on which the parson rests his bible in front of a pulpit. The image is suggested by the Cowper's 'plump convivial parson' who 'lays'

His rev'rence and his worship both to rest
On the same cushion of habitual sloth. (*Task* iv 595–8)

14 *maps* The scientific instruments and maps indicate the prodigy's intellectual authority, just as flags ('ensigns'), orb and sceptre symbolize a king's sovereignty.

15 *cunning* secrets (of their operation).

16 *He knows . . . over* cf. John Locke, *Some Thoughts Concerning Education*: 'I now live in the house with a child . . . [who] knew the limits of the four parts of the world, could readily point, being asked, to any country upon the globe . . . and could find the longitude and latitude of any place, before he was six years old.'

17 Country people, being closer to Nature and God, perceive the danger of the prodigy's course.

18 *he sifts . . . trust* cf. Coleridge's outrage at this tendency, in a letter to Poole, 16 October 1797: 'I have known some who have been *rationally* educated, as it is styled. They were marked by a microscopic acuteness; but when they looked at great things, all became a blank and they saw nothing – and denied (very illogically) that any thing could be seen . . . [they] called the want of imagination Judgment, and the never being moved to rapture Philosophy!' (Griggs i 354–5).

Knowing that he grows wiser every day
Or else not live at all[19] – and seeing too   425
Each little drop of wisdom as it falls
Into the dimpling cistern[20] of his heart.[21]
Meanwhile old Grandam Earth is grieved to find
The playthings which her love designed for him
Unthought of: in their woodland beds the flowers   430
Weep, and the riversides are all forlorn.
      Now this is hollow, 'tis a life of lies
From the beginning, and in lies must end.
Forth bring him to the air of common sense,
And, fresh and showy as it is, the corpse   435
Slips from us into powder. Vanity,
That is his soul, there lives he, and there moves –
It is the soul of everything he seeks;
That gone, nothing is left which he can love.
Nay, if a thought of purer birth should rise   440
To carry him towards a better clime,
Some busy helper still is on the watch
To drive him back, and pound[22] him like a stray
Within the pinfold[23] of his own conceit,
Which is his home, his natural dwelling-place.   445
Oh, give us once again the wishing-cap
Of Fortunatus, and the invisible coat
Of Jack the giant-killer, Robin Hood,
And Sabra in the forest with St George![24]
The child whose love is here at least does reap   450
One precious gain – that he forgets himself.[25]
      These mighty workmen of our latter age[26]
Who with a broad highway have overbridged
The froward[27] chaos of futurity,[28]
Tamed to their bidding; they who have the art   455
To manage books, and things, and make them work

---

[19] *He must live ... at all* Wordsworth regarded knowledge, as opposed to understanding, as redundant: 'Lastly comes that class of objects which are interesting almost solely because they are known, and the knowledge may be displayed; and this unfortunately comprehends three fourths of what, according to the plan of modern education, children's heads are stuffed with, that is, minute remote or trifling facts in geography, topography natural history chronology etc., or acquisitions in art, or accomplishments which the child makes by rote and which are quite beyond its age' (*MY* i 287).
[20] *dimpling cistern* The surface of the water in the barrel ('cistern') dimples with each drop that falls into it.
[21] cf. the manner in which the Wordsworths reared Basil Montagu at Alfoxden: 'You ask to be informed of our system respecting Basil; it is a very simple one, so simple that in this age of systems you will hardly be likely to follow it. We teach him nothing at present but what he learns from the evidence of his senses. He has an insatiable curiosity which we are always careful to satisfy to the best of our ability. It is directed to everything he sees, the sky, the fields, trees, shrubs, corn, the making of tools, carts, etc., etc., etc. He knows his letters, but we have not attempted any further step in the path of *book learn-*

ing. Our grand study has been to make him *happy* ...' (*EY* 180).
[22] *pound* impound.
[23] *pinfold* enclosure for stray animals.
[24] Fortunatus's hat took him wherever he wanted; Jack's coat made him invisible while killing giants; St George married Sabra, daughter of the King of Egypt, after rescuing her from a dragon.
[25] Wordsworth recommended that children be allowed to read 'fairy tales, romances, the best biographies and histories, and such parts of natural history relating to the powers and appearances of the earth and elements, and the habits and structures of animals, as belong to it not as an art or science, but as a magazine of form and feeling' (*MY* i 287). See also Coleridge on fairy tales, p. 460.
[26] ll. 452–70 derive from a fragment probably composed in Goslar during the winter of 1798–9, intended as an introduction to 'There was a boy'.
[27] *froward* wayward, uncontrollable.
[28] *Who with a broad highway ... futurity* educationalists are compared to Milton's Sin and Death who in *Paradise Lost* build a bridge over Chaos to their new empire on earth (x 282–305).

Gently on infant minds as does the sun
Upon a flower – the tutors of our youth,
The guides, the wardens of our faculties
And stewards of our labour, watchful men   460
And skilful in the usury of time,
Sages who in their prescience would control
All accidents, and to the very road which they
Have fashioned would confine us down
Like engines[29] – when will they be taught   465
That in the unreasoning progress of the world
A wiser spirit is at work for us,
A better eye than theirs, most prodigal
Of blessings and most studious of our good,
Even in what seem our most unfruitful hours?   470

Daffodils (composed between March 1804 and April 1807)[1]

From POEMS IN TWO VOLUMES (1807)

I wandered lonely as a cloud
That floats on high o'er vales and hills,
When all at once I saw a crowd,
A host of dancing daffodils;[2]
Along the lake, beneath the trees,   5
Ten thousand dancing in the breeze.[3]

The waves beside them danced, but they
Outdid the sparkling waves in glee;
A poet could not but be gay
In such a laughing company.   10
I gazed, and gazed, but little thought
What wealth the show to me had brought –

For oft when on my couch I lie
In vacant or in pensive mood,
They flash upon that inward eye   15
Which is the bliss of solitude,[4]
And then my heart with pleasure fills,
And dances with the daffodils.

---

[29] *engines* educational theories are as imprisoning as manu-
facturing machines – machine-looms, for instance – which
were just coming into use.

DAFFODILS
[1] For the incident that inspired this poem see Dorothy
Wordsworth's journal, p. 434, below. In 1815 Wordsworth
attached a note: 'The subject of these stanzas is rather an ele-
mentary feeling and simple impression (approaching to the
nature of an ocular spectrum) upon the imaginative faculty,
than an *exertion* of it'.
[2] *daffodils* not the garden daffodils of today but the small,
pale, and wild *pseudo-narcissi*.

[3] At this point in 1815 Wordsworth added an extra stanza:
Continuous as the stars that shine
And twinkle on the milky way,
They stretched in never-ending line
Along the margin of a bay –
Ten thousand saw I at a glance,
Tossing their heads in sprightly dance.
[4] *They flash ... solitude* these two lines were written by
Wordsworth's wife, Mary. Coleridge commented in his note-
book, 1808–11: '"To flash upon that inward eye / Which is
the bliss of solitude" – and to make every thing present by a
series of images – this an absolute essential of poetry, and of
itself would form a poet, though not of the highest class'
(*Notebooks* iii 3247).

Stepping Westward (composed 3 June 1805)

From POEMS IN TWO VOLUMES (1807)

While my fellow-traveller and I were walking by the side of Loch Ketterine one fine evening after sunset,[1] in our road to a hut[2] where, in the course of our tour, we had been hospitably entertained some weeks before, we met in one of the loneliest parts of that solitary region two well-dressed women, one of whom said to us by way of greeting, 'What you are stepping westward?'

'What you are stepping westward?' 'Yea.'
'Twould be a wildish destiny
If we, who thus together roam
In a strange land, and far from home,
Were in this place the guests of Chance –   5
Yet who would stop, or fear to advance,
Though home or shelter he had none,
With such a sky to lead him on?

The dewy ground was dark and cold;
Behind, all gloomy to behold;   10
And stepping westward seemed to be
A kind of *heavenly* destiny.
I liked the greeting – 'twas a sound
Of something without place or bound,
And seemed to give me spiritual right   15
To travel through that region bright.

The voice was soft, and she who spake
Was walking by her native lake;
The salutation had to me
The very sound of courtesy: 20
Its power was felt, and while my eye
Was fixed upon the glowing sky,
The echo of the voice enwrought[3]
A human sweetness with the thought
Of travelling through the world that lay   25
Before me in my endless way.

The Solitary Reaper (composed 5 November 1805)[1]

FROM POEMS IN TWO VOLUMES (1807)

Behold her, single in the field,
Yon solitary highland lass!
Reaping and singing by herself –

STEPPING WESTWARD
[1]   *While ... sunset* Wordsworth and Dorothy toured Scotland in 1803.
[2]   *hut* cottage.
[3]   *enwrought* interwove, combined.

THE SOLITARY REAPER
[1]   'This poem was suggested by a beautiful sentence in a MS tour in Scotland written by a friend, the last line being taken

from it verbatim' (Wordsworth's note). Thomas Wilkinson, the Lake District poet, was a friend of Wordsworth, and his *Tours to the British Mountains* was published in 1824. The sentence that inspired Wordsworth runs as follows: 'Passed a female who was reaping alone: she sung in Erse as she bended over her sickle; the sweetest human voice I ever heard: her strains were tenderly melancholy, and felt delicious, long after they were heard no more' (p. 12).

Stop here, or gently pass!
Alone she cuts, and binds the grain,   5
And sings a melancholy strain;
Oh listen! for the vale profound
Is overflowing with the sound.

No nightingale did ever chaunt
So sweetly to reposing bands   10
Of travellers in some shady haunt
Among Arabian sands;
No sweeter voice was ever heard
In springtime from the cuckoo-bird,
Breaking the silence of the seas   15
Among the farthest Hebrides.

Will no one tell me what she sings?
Perhaps the plaintive numbers flow
For old, unhappy, far-off things
And battles long ago;   20
Or is it some more humble lay,
Familiar matter of today?
Some natural sorrow, loss, or pain
That has been, and may be again?

Whate'er the theme, the maiden sang   25
As if her song could have no ending;
I saw her singing at her work
And o'er the sickle bending;
I listened till I had my fill,
And as I mounted up the hill,   30
The music in my heart I bore
Long after it was heard no more.

From [*The Thirteen-Book Prelude*] (composed 1804–6; edited from MS)[1]

[*The Arab Dream*] (from Book V)[2]

Hitherto
In progress through this verse, my mind hath looked
Upon the speaking face of earth and heaven[3]
As her prime teacher, intercourse with man
Established by the sovereign intellect
Who through that bodily image hath diffused   15
A soul divine which we participate,[4]

THE ARAB DREAM
[1] Wordsworth began work on the *Thirteen-Book Prelude* as soon as he abandoned and dismembered the five-Book version of the poem in early March 1804. He continued working on it, with occasional breaks, until the spring of 1805.
[2] The title of Book V is 'Books', though in fact Wordsworth is preoccupied less with the literary works that have most influenced him than with explaining the purpose of artistic

endeavour, and its place within the larger scheme of things.
[3] *the speaking face of earth and heaven* Wordsworth has in mind Coleridge's account of nature as 'The lovely shapes and sounds intelligible / Of that eternal language which thy God / Utters' (*Frost at Midnight* 64–6).
[4] *intercourse . . . participate* God has diffused his divine soul through the medium of the natural world (his 'bodily image'), so that mankind literally partakes of his being.

A deathless spirit. Thou also, man, hast wrought,
For commerce of thy nature with itself,
Things worthy of unconquerable life;[5]
And yet we feel, we cannot choose but feel   20
That these must perish. Tremblings of the heart
It gives to think that the immortal being
No more shall need such garments; and yet man,
As long as he shall be the child of earth,
Might almost 'weep to have'[6] what he may lose,   25
Nor be himself extinguished, but survive
Abject, depressed, forlorn, disconsolate.[7]
A thought is with me sometimes, and I say:
'Should earth by inward throes be wrenched throughout,
Or fire[8] be sent from far to wither all   30
Her pleasant habitations, and dry up
Old ocean in his bed, left singed and bare,
Yet would the living presence still subsist
Victorious, and composure would ensue,
And kindlings like the morning – presage sure   35
(Though slow perhaps) of a returning day.
But all the meditations of mankind,
Yea, all the adamantine holds[9] of truth
By reason built, or passion[10] (which itself
Is highest reason in a soul sublime),   40
The consecrated works of bard and sage,[11]
Sensuous or intellectual, wrought by men,
Twin labourers and heirs of the same hopes –
Where would they be? Oh, why hath not the mind
Some element to stamp her image on   45
In nature somewhat nearer to her own?[12]
Why, gifted with such powers to send abroad
Her spirit, must it lodge in shrines so frail?'[13]
     One day, when in the hearing of a friend[14]
I had given utterance to thoughts like these,   50
He answered with a smile that in plain truth
'Twas going far to seek disquietude;[15]
But on the front[16] of his reproof confessed
That he at sundry seasons had himself
Yielded to kindred hauntings[17] – and forthwith   55
Added that once upon a summer's noon
While he was sitting in a rocky cave

---

[5] *Things worthy of unconquerable life* i.e. works of art, that
deserve to be immortal.

[6] *weep to have* Shakespeare, *Sonnet* 64: 'This thought is as a
death, which cannot choose / But weep to have that which it
fears to lose' (ll. 13–14).

[7] *yet man ... disconsolate* man, while still living ('unextin-
guished'), must regret possession of earthly achievements that
he fears losing, and live on, abject, and disconsolate.

[8] *fire* Some of Wordsworth's ideas here may derive from
Thomas Burnet's *Sacred Theory of the Earth*, Book III of which
is entitled 'Concerning the Conflagration'; Wordsworth
owned a copy of Burnet at Rydal Mount.

[9] *adamantine holds* indestructible fortresses.

[10] *passion* emotion; 'Poetry is passion: it is the history or sci-
ence of feeling' (Note to *The Thorn*, p. 344).

[11] *The consecrated ... sage* works of the imagination and the
intellect.

[12] *Oh why ... own* Wordsworth laments the fact that there is
no substance as durable as the mind itself (which he regards as
immortal), on which its thoughts might be recorded.

[13] *shrines so frail* i.e. books.

[14] *a friend* Coleridge.

[15] *disquietude* anxiety.

[16] *on the front* immediately after.

[17] *kindred hauntings* similar worries.

By the sea-side (perusing, as it chanced,
The famous history of the errant knight
Recorded by Cervantes[18]), these same thoughts   60
Came to him, and to height unusual rose
While listlessly he sat, and, having closed
The book, had turned his eyes towards the sea.
On poetry and geometric truth
(The knowledge that endures), upon these two   65
And their high privilege of lasting life
Exempt from all internal injury,[19]
He mused; upon these chiefly – and at length,
His senses yielding to the sultry air,
Sleep seized him and he passed into a dream.   70
   He saw before him an Arabian waste,
A desert, and he fancied that himself
Was sitting there in the wide wilderness
Alone upon the sands. Distress of mind
Was growing in him when, behold, at once   75
To his great joy a man was at his side,
Upon a dromedary mounted high!
He seemed an Arab of the bedouin tribes;
A lance he bore,[20] and underneath one arm
A stone, and in the opposite hand a shell   80
Of a surpassing brightness. Much rejoiced
The dreaming man that he should have a guide
To lead him through the desert, and he thought –
While questioning himself what this strange freight
Which the newcomer carried through the waste   85
Could mean – the Arab told him that the stone
(To give it in the language of the dream)
Was Euclid's *Elements*.[21] ' "And this", said he,
"This other", pointing to the shell, "this book,
Is something of more worth." And at the word   90
The stranger', said my friend continuing,
'Stretched forth the shell towards me, with command
That I should hold it to my ear. I did so,
And heard that instant in an unknown tongue,
Which yet I understood, articulate sounds,   95
A loud prophetic blast of harmony,
An ode in passion uttered, which foretold
Destruction to the children of the earth
By deluge now at hand.'
       No sooner ceased
The song, but with calm look the Arab said   100
That all was true, that it was even so
As had been spoken, and that he himself
Was going then to bury those two books –

---

[18] *The famous history ... Cervantes* Miguel de Cervantes Saavedra, *Don Quixote*; Wordsworth and Coleridge would have known it from early childhood.

[19] *Exempt ... injury* poetry and geometry may be subject to external injury (that is to say, books can be damaged), but are perfect in themselves.

[20] *A lance he bore* shades of the Don, who famously used his lance to tilt at windmills.

[21] *Euclid's Elements* Euclid was a Greek mathematician of the third century BC, whose *Elements* was the basic textbook of geometry used by Wordsworth at Hawkshead and Cambridge.

The one that held acquaintance with the stars
And wedded man to man by purest bond   105
Of nature, undisturbed by space or time;
The other that was a god – yea, many gods,
Had voices more than all the winds, and was
A joy, a consolation, and a hope.
My friend continued, 'Strange as it may seem,   110
I wondered not, although I plainly saw
The one to be a stone, the other a shell,
Nor doubted once but that they both were books,
Having a perfect faith in all that passed.
A wish was now engendered[22] in my fear   115
To cleave unto[23] this man, and I begged leave
To share his errand with him. On he passed
Not heeding me; I followed, and took note
That he looked often backward with wild look,
Grasping his twofold treasure to his side.   120
Upon a dromedary, lance in rest
He rode, I keeping pace with him; and now
I fancied that he was the very knight
Whose tale Cervantes tells, yet not the knight,
But was an Arab of the desert too –   125
Of these was neither, and was both at once.
His countenance meanwhile grew more disturbed,
And, looking backwards when he looked, I saw
A glittering light, and asked him whence it came.
"It is", said he, "the waters of the deep   130
Gathering upon us." Quickening then his pace,
He left me. I called after him aloud;
He heeded not, but with his twofold charge[24]
Beneath his arm, before me, full in view,
I saw him riding o'er the desert sands   135
With the fleet waters of the drowning world
In chase of him. Whereat I waked in terror,
And saw the sea before me, and the book
In which I had been reading at my side.'
Full often, taking from the world of sleep   140
This Arab phantom which my friend beheld,
This semi-Quixote, I to him have given
A substance, fancied him a living man,
A gentle dweller in the desert, crazed
By love and feeling and internal thought   145
Protracted among endless solitudes –
Have shaped him, in the oppression of his brain,[25]
Wandering upon this quest, and thus equipped.
And I have scarcely pitied him, have felt
A reverence for a being thus employed,   150
And thought that in the blind and awful lair
Of such a madness, reason did lie couched.

---

[22] *engendered* created.
[23] *cleave unto* stick to.

[24] *charge* burden.
[25] *oppression of his brain* derangement, anxiety.

Enow[26] there are on earth to take in charge
Their wives, their children, and their virgin loves,
Or whatsoever else the heart holds dear –   155
Enow to think of these; yea, will I say,
In sober contemplation of the approach
Of such great overthrow, made manifest
By certain evidence, that I methinks
Could share that maniac's anxiousness, could go   160
Upon like errand. Oftentimes, at least,
Me hath such deep entrancement half possessed
When I have held a volume in my hand
(Poor earthly casket of immortal verse)[27] –
Shakespeare or Milton, labourers divine!   165

[*Crossing the Alps*] (from *Thirteen-Book Prelude* Book VI)[1]

That day we first
Beheld the summit of Mont Blanc, and grieved
To have a soulless image on the eye
Which had usurped upon a living thought   455
That never more could be.[2] The wondrous Vale
Of Chamouny did on the following dawn,
With its dumb cataracts and streams of ice,
A motionless array of mighty waves,
Five rivers broad and vast, make rich amends,   460
And reconciled us to realities.
There small birds warble from the leafy trees,
The eagle soareth in the element;
There doth the reaper bind the yellow sheaf,
The maiden spread the haycock in the sun,   465
While winter like a tamed lion walks,
Descending from the mountain to make sport
Among the cottages by beds of flowers.
    Whate'er in this wide circuit we beheld
Or heard was fitted to our unripe state   470
Of intellect and heart. By simple strains
Of feeling, the pure breath of real life,
We were not left untouched. With such a book[3]
Before our eyes we could not choose but read
A frequent lesson of sound tenderness,   475
The universal reason of mankind,
The truth of young and old. Nor, side by side
Pacing, two brother pilgrims, or alone
Each with his humour, could we fail to abound
(Craft this which hath been hinted at before)   480
In dreams and fictions pensively composed,

---

[26] *Enow* enough.
[27] *Poor earthly casket of immortal verse* a brilliant paradox; verse, which is immortal, is contained within the casket, or coffin, of the book.

CROSSING THE ALPS
[1] Wordsworth is recounting his tour of the continent in summer 1790, which he undertook with his college friend, Robert Jones. Wordsworth was twenty.
[2] *That day ... be* the actual image of the mountain displaced, in the mind, the image of the unseen mountain, which was more 'alive' because it was imaginatively generated.
[3] *book* the book of nature.

Dejection taken up for pleasure's sake,
And gilded sympathies. The willow wreath,
Even among those solitudes sublime,
And sober posies of funereal flowers   485
Culled from the gardens of the Lady Sorrow,
Did sweeten many a meditative hour.[4]
  Yet still in me, mingling with these delights,
Was something of stern mood, an under-thirst[5]
Of vigour never utterly asleep.   490
Far different dejection once was mine,
A deep and genuine sadness then I felt,
The circumstances I will here relate
Even as they were. Upturning with a band
Of travellers, from the Valais we had clomb[6]   495
Along the road that leads to Italy;
A length of hours, making of these our guides
Did we advance, and having reached an inn
Among the mountains, we together ate
Our noon's repast, from which the travellers rose   500
Leaving us at the board. Erelong we followed,
Descending by the beaten road that led
Right to a rivulet's edge, and there broke off.
The only track now visible was one
Upon the further side, right opposite,   505
And up a lofty mountain. This we took
After a little scruple[7] and short pause,
And climbed with eagerness – though not, at length
Without surprise and some anxiety
On finding that we did not overtake   510
Our comrades gone before. By fortunate chance,
While every moment now increased our doubts,
A peasant met us, and from him we learned
That to the place which had perplexed[8] us first
We must descend, and there should find the road   515
Which in the stony channel of the stream
Lay a few steps, and then along its banks –
And further, that thenceforward all our course
Was downwards with the current of that stream.
Hard of belief, we questioned him again,   520
And all the answers which the man returned
To our enquiries, in their sense and substance,
Translated by the feelings which we had,
Ended in this – that we had crossed the Alps.
  Imagination! lifting up itself   525
Before the eye and progress of my song
Like an unfathered vapour; here that power,
In all the might of its endowments, came
Athwart me. I was lost as in a cloud,

---

4 *The willow wreath … hour* the somewhat artificial manner
of all this indicates that Wordsworth is affectionately mock-
ing his youthful self, preoccupied with poetic sorrows.
5 *under-thirst* a typically original way of talking about his
inner world.

6 *clomb* climbed.
7 *scruple* hesitation, uncertainty.
8 *perplexed* confused.

Halted without a struggle to break through,   530
And now, recovering, to my soul I say,
'I recognize thy glory'.[9] In such strength
Of usurpation,[10] in such visitings
Of awful promise, when the light of sense
Goes out in flashes that have shown to us   535
The invisible world, doth greatness make abode,
There harbours whether we be young or old.
Our destiny, our nature, and our home,
Is with infinitude, and only there –
With hope it is, hope that can never die,   540
Effort, and expectation, and desire,
And something evermore about to be.[11]
The mind beneath such banners militant[12]
Thinks not of spoils or trophies, nor of aught
That may attest its prowess, blessed in thoughts   545
That are their own perfection and reward –
Strong in itself, and in the access of joy
Which hides it like the overflowing Nile.
    The dull and heavy slackening which ensued
Upon those tidings by the peasant given   550
Was soon dislodged. Downwards we hurried fast,
And entered with the road which we had missed
Into a narrow chasm. The brook and road
Were fellow-travellers in this gloomy pass,
And with them did we journey several hours   555
At a slow step. The immeasurable height
Of woods decaying, never to be decayed,
The stationary blasts of waterfalls,
And everywhere along the hollow rent[13]
Winds thwarting winds, bewildered and forlorn,   560
The torrents shooting from the clear blue sky,
The rocks that muttered close upon our ears,
Black drizzling crags that spake by the wayside
As if a voice were in them, the sick[14] sight
And giddy prospect of the raving stream,   565
The unfettered clouds and region of the heavens,
Tumult and peace, the darkness and the light,
Were all like workings of one mind, the features
Of the same face, blossoms upon one tree,
Characters[15] of the great Apocalypse,[16]   570

---

[9] *Imagination ... glory* against the moment in August 1790 when his imagination had been disappointed, Wordsworth places the 'glory' of the present (i.e. the moment of composition, spring 1804).

[10] *usurpation* another usurpation (cf. l. 455, above). This time, however, the usurpation proves the strength, rather than the weakness, of the imagination; it may sound forced, but Wordsworth needs to believe that the imagination can overcome the deadening influences of reality.

[11] *something evermore about to be* few phrases more succinctly characterize Wordsworth's literary personality; in his poetry sublimity is always beyond reach.

[12] *such banners militant* i.e. effort, expectation, and desire, and something evermore about to be.

[13] *rent* ravine.

[14] *sick* probably means 'sickening', given the 'giddy prospect' in the next line.

[15] *Characters* letters.

[16] *Characters ... Apocalypse* contemporary geological theory held that all but the highest Alpine peaks were created by the retreating waters of the Flood. Thus the features of the landscape would indeed have been engraved ('charactered') by the first apocalyptic event in the history of mankind. They also function as a reminder of the apocalypse to come.

The types[17] and symbols of eternity,
Of first, and last, and midst, and without end.[18]

[*The London Beggar*] (from *Thirteen-Book Prelude* Book VII)[1]

Oh friend,[2] one feeling was there which belonged
To this great city by exclusive right:
How often in the overflowing streets
Have I gone forwards with the crowd, and said   595
Unto myself, 'The face of everyone
That passes by me is a mystery!'
Thus have I looked, nor ceased to look, oppressed
By thoughts of what and whither, when and how,
Until the shapes before my eyes became   600
A second-sight[3] procession, such as glides
Over still mountains, or appears in dreams,
And all the ballast of familiar life –
The present and the past, hope, fear, all stays,[4]
All laws, of acting, thinking, speaking man –   605
Went from me, neither knowing me, nor known.
And once, far travelled in such mood, beyond
The reach of common indications, lost
Amid the moving pageant, 'twas my chance
Abruptly to be smitten with the view   610
Of a blind beggar who, with upright face,
Stood propped against a wall, upon his chest
Wearing a written paper to explain
The story of the man and who he was.
My mind did at this spectacle turn round   615
As with the might of waters, and it seemed
To me that in this label was a type
Or emblem of the utmost that we know
Both of ourselves and of the universe;
And, on the shape of this unmoving man,   620
His fixed face and sightless eyes, I looked
As if admonished[5] from another world.

[*London and the Den of Yordas*][1] (from *Thirteen-Book Prelude* Book VIII)

Preceptress[2] stern, that didst instruct me next –
London, to thee I willingly return!

---

[17] *types* letters, as in typeface.
[18] *The unfettered clouds … without end* Wordsworth's source is
Pope, *Essay on Man* ii 266–72:
   All are but parts of one stupendous whole,
   Whose body nature is, and God the soul,
   That (changed through all, and yet in all the same) …
   Warms in the sun, refreshes in the breeze,
   Glows in the sun, and blossoms in the trees …
l. 572 echoes Milton's description of God, *Paradise Lost* v 165:
'Him first, Him last, Him midst, and without end'.

THE LONDON BEGGAR
[1] Book VII is about Wordsworth's residence in London dur-
ing the 1790s.
[2] *Oh friend* Coleridge.
[3] *second-sight* mystic; second sight is the power by which
occurrences in the future are perceived as though they were
present.
[4] *stays* emotional and psychological support.
[5] *admonished* cf. the 'strong admonishment' administered by
the leech-gatherer (*Resolution and Independence* 119).

LONDON AND THE DEN OF YORDAS
[1] *Yordas* See note 11 below.
[2] *Preceptress* teacher.

Erewhile[3] my verse played only with the flowers   680
Enwrought upon thy mantle,[4] satisfied
With this amusement, and a simple look
Of childlike inquisition[5] now and then
Cast upwards on thine eye to puzzle out
Some inner meanings which might harbour there.   685
Yet did I not give way to this light mood
Wholly beguiled, as one incapable
Of higher things, and ignorant that high things
Were round me. Never shall I forget the hour,[6]
The moment rather say, when, having thridded   690
The labyrinth of suburban villages,
At length I did unto myself first seem
To enter the great city. On the roof
Of an itinerant vehicle[7] I sat,
With vulgar[8] men about me, vulgar forms   695
Of houses, pavement, streets, of men and things,
Mean shapes on every side, but at the time
When to myself it fairly might be said
(The very moment that I seemed to know)
'The threshold now is overpassed' – great God!   700
That aught external to the living mind
Should have such mighty sway, yet so it was.
A weight of ages[9] did at once descend
Upon my heart – no thought embodied, no
Distinct remembrances, but weight and power,   705
Power growing with the weight. Alas, I feel
That I am trifling; 'twas a moment's pause,
All that took place within me came and went
As in a moment, and I only now
Remember that it was a thing divine.   710
    As when a traveller hath from open day
With torches passed into some vault of earth,
The grotto of Antiparos[10] or the den
Of Yordas among Craven's mountain tracts;[11]
He looks and sees the cavern spread and grow,   715
Widening itself on all sides, sees, or thinks
He sees,[12] erelong the roof above his head,
Which instantly unsettles and recedes –
Substance and shadow, light and darkness, all
Commingled, making up a canopy   720

---

[3] *Erewhile* up to now, hitherto.
[4] *Enwrought upon thy mantle* in Milton's *Lycidas*, the River Cam has a 'mantle hairy . . . Inwrought with figures dim' (ll. 104–5).
[5] *inquisition* enquiry.
[6] *the hour* i.e. of Wordsworth's first sight of London.
[7] *an itinerant vehicle* i.e. a vehicle that travels around, a stage-coach, probably from Cambridge to London (Wordsworth was probably an undergraduate when he first visited London).
[8] *vulgar* ordinary.
[9] *A weight of ages* effectively, Wordsworth was conscious of the history of the city.

[10] *The grotto of Antiparos* famous cave on the island of Antiparos in the Aegean.
[11] *the den . . . tracts* limestone cave near Ingleton in West Yorkshire, visited by Wordsworth and his brother John in May 1800. In the *Fourteen-Book Prelude* Wordsworth referred to 'the den / In old time haunted by that Danish witch, / Yordas' (vii 562–4), though as Jonathan Wordsworth points out, he was perhaps 'being fanciful'. Wu and Trott identify 'Three Sources for Wordsworth's Prelude Cave', *N&Q* 38 (1991) 298–9.
[12] *sees, or thinks / He sees* from Virgil, *Aeneid* vi 454: 'aut videt, aut vidisse putat', borrowed also by Milton, *Paradise Lost* i 783–4.

Of shapes and forms and tendencies to shape
That shift and vanish, change and interchange
Like spectres, ferment quiet and sublime
Which after a short space works[13] less and less,
Till, every effort, every motion gone,   725
The scene before him lies in perfect view,
Exposed and lifeless as a written book.
But let him pause awhile and look again
And a new quickening[14] shall succeed, at first
Beginning timidly, then creeping fast   730
Through all which he beholds. The senseless mass,
In its projections, wrinkles, cavities,
Through all its surface, with all colours streaming
Like a magician's airy pageant,[15] parts,
Unites, embodying everywhere some pressure[16]   735
Or image, recognized or new, some type
Or picture of the world; forests and lakes,
Ships, rivers, towers, the warrior clad in mail,
The prancing steed, the pilgrim with his staff,
The mitred bishop and the throned king –   740
A spectacle to which there is no end.

[*Paris, December* 1791] (from *Thirteen-Book Prelude* Book IX)[1]

Where silent zephyrs[2] sported with the dust
Of the Bastille[3] I sat in the open sun,
And from the rubbish gathered up a stone   65
And pocketed the relic in the guise
Of an enthusiast; yet, in honest truth,
Though not without some strong incumbences[4]
And glad[5] (could living man be otherwise?),
I looked for something which I could not find,   70
Affecting more emotion than I felt.
For 'tis most certain that the utmost force
Of all these various objects which may show
The temper of my mind as then it was
Seemed less to recompense the traveller's pains –   75
Less moved me, gave me less delight – than did
A single picture merely, hunted out
Among other sights: the 'Magdalene' of Le Brun,[6]
A beauty exquisitely wrought, fair face
And rueful, with its ever-flowing tears.   80

---

[13] *works* seethes.
[14] *quickening* invigoration.
[15] *magician's airy pageant* cf. Prospero's 'insubstantial pageant faded', *Tempest* IV i 155.
[16] *pressure* imprint.

PARIS, DECEMBER 1791
[1] Wordsworth is remembering his visit to Paris in December 1791. It was on this residence in France that he met Annette Vallon, with whom he had a child, Caroline, born December 1792. His immediate excuse for visiting revolutionary France was to perfect his command of the language so as to qualify as a gentleman's travelling companion or tutor.

[2] *zephyrs* small breezes.
[3] *the dust / Of the Bastille* the dust was all that was left of it. The Bastille, a large prison in the centre of Paris, symbol of the tyranny of the *ancien régime*, had been stormed by the Paris mob on 14 July 1789, and then demolished.
[4] *incumbences* feelings of obligation – presumably to the revolutionary cause (in spite of his posturing as an 'enthusiast').
[5] *glad* i.e. about the Revolution.
[6] *the 'Magdalene' of Le Brun* Charles le Brun (1616–90) painted a picture of St Mary Magdalene (the repentant prostitute who washed Christ's feet with her tears). Wordsworth would have seen it at the Carmelite convent at Rue d'Enfer. It is now in the Louvre.

[*Blois, Spring* 1792] (from *Thirteen-Book Prelude* Book IX)[1]

    A knot of military officers
That to a regiment appertained which then
Was stationed in the city[2] were the chief
Of my associates; some of these wore swords   130
Which had been seasoned in the wars, and all
Were men well-born[3] – at least laid claim to such
Distinction, as the chivalry of France.
In age and temper differing, they had yet
One spirit ruling in them all, alike   135
(Save only one, hereafter to be named)[4]
Were bent upon undoing what was done.
This was their rest, and only hope; therewith
No fear had they of bad becoming worse,
For worst to them was come – nor would have stirred,   140
Or deemed it worth a moment's while to stir,
In anything, save only as the act
Looked thitherward. One, reckoning by years,
Was in the prime of manhood, and erewhile
He had sat lord in many tender hearts,   145
Though heedless of such honours now, and changed:
His temper[5] was quite mastered by the times,
And they had blighted him, had eat away
The beauty of his person, doing wrong
Alike to body and to mind. His port,[6]   150
Which once had been erect and open, now
Was stooping and contracted, and a face,
By nature lovely in itself, expressed
As much as any that was ever seen
A ravage out of season, made by thoughts   155
Unhealthy and vexatious. At the hour,
The most important of each day, in which
The public news was read, the fever came,
A punctual visitant, to shake this man,
Disarmed his voice and fanned his yellow cheek   160
Into a thousand colours. While he read,
Or mused, his sword was haunted by his touch
Continually, like an uneasy place
In his own body.
           'Twas in truth an hour
Of universal ferment. Mildest men   165
Were agitated, and commotions, strife
Of passion and opinion, filled the walls
Of peaceful houses with unquiet sounds.
The soil of common life was at that time
Too hot to tread upon! Oft said I then,   170

BLOIS, SPRING 1792
[1] Wordsworth moved to Blois, near Orleans, early in 1792.
[2] *city* Blois.
[3] *men well-born* in spring 1792 the French army was staffed largely by royalist officers, sympathetic to the Austrians, who were waging war with France on the borders.

[4] *Save . . . named* Wordsworth's friend, Michel Beaupuy, who converted Wordsworth to the revolutionary cause.
[5] *temper* character.
[6] *port* bearing.

And not then only, 'What a mockery this
Of history, the past and that to come!
Now do I feel how I have been deceived,
Reading of nations and their works in faith –
Faith given to vanity and emptiness;   175
Oh, laughter for the page that would reflect
To future times the face of what now is!'[7]
The land all swarmed with passion, like a plain
Devoured by locusts – Carra, Gorsas[8] – add
A hundred other names forgotten now,   180
Nor to be heard of more. Yet were they powers
Like earthquakes, shocks repeated day by day,
And felt through every nook of town and field.

[*Beaupuy*] (from *Thirteen-Book Prelude* Book IX)

Among that band of officers was one,[1]
Already hinted at, of other mould[2] –
A patriot, thence rejected by the rest,   295
And with an oriental loathing spurned
As of a different caste.[3] A meeker man
Than this lived never, or a more benign,
Meek though enthusiastic to the height   300
Of highest expectation. Injuries
Made him more gracious, and his nature then
Did breathe its sweetness out most sensibly,[4]
As aromatic flowers on Alpine turf
When foot hath crushed them. He through the events   305
Of that great change[5] wandered in perfect faith
As through a book, an old romance or tale
Of fairy,[6] or some dream of actions wrought
Behind the summer clouds. By birth he ranked
With the most noble,[7] but unto the poor   310
Among mankind he was in service bound
As by some tie invisible, oaths professed
To a religious order. Man he loved
As man, and to the mean and the obscure,
And all the homely in their homely works,   315
Transferred a courtesy which had no air
Of condescension, but did rather seem
A passion and a gallantry, like that
Which he, a soldier, in his idler day
Had paid to woman. Somewhat vain he was,   320

---

7 *Oh laughter ... is* he who would attempt to record the events of the Revolution for posterity would only bring mockery upon himself, so complex have things become.
8 *Carra, Gorsas* journalist deputies in the French National Assembly, and members of the Girondin faction with which Beaupuy and Wordsworth consorted. They were probably known to Wordsworth. Carra was guillotined on 31 October 1793, Gorsas on the 7th.

BEAUPUY
1 *one* Michel Beaupuy (1755–96).
2 *mould* clay, substance.

3 *And with ... caste* he was spurned by the others with the same kind of loathing shown by Indians towards those of a lower caste.
4 *sensibly* perceptibly.
5 *that great change* the Revolution.
6 *fairy* magic.
7 *By birth ... noble* Beaupuy was an aristocrat, descended on his mother's side from Montaigne. Many French aristocrats were in favour of the Revolution, though his rank separated him from his fellow soldiers in Blois. He was thirty-six when he befriended the 22-year-old Wordsworth.

Or seemed so; yet it was not vanity
But fondness, and a kind of radiant joy
That covered him about when he was bent
On works of love or freedom, or revolved
Complacently[8] the progress of a cause   325
Whereof he was a part – yet this was meek
And placid, and took nothing from the man
That was delightful. Oft in solitude
With him did I discourse about the end[9]
Of civil government, and its wisest forms,   330
Of ancient prejudice and chartered[10] rights,
Allegiance, faith, and laws by time matured,
Custom and habit, novelty and change –
Of self-respect and virtue in the few
For patrimonial honour set apart,   335
And ignorance in the labouring multitude.
For he, an upright man and tolerant,
Balanced these contemplations in his mind;
And I, who at that time was scarcely dipped
Into the turmoil, had a sounder judgement   340
Than afterwards,[11] carried about me yet
With less alloy to its integrity
The experience of past ages, as (through help
Of books and common life) it finds its way
To youthful minds, by objects over-near   345
Not pressed upon, nor dazzled or misled
By struggling with the crowd for present ends. . . .
                    And when my friend
Pointed upon occasion to the site
Of Romorantin,[12] home of ancient kings;
To the imperial edifice of Blois;
Or to that rural castle, name now slipped   485
From my remembrance (where a lady lodged,
By the first Francis[13] wooed, and, bound to him
In chains of mutual passion, from the tower,
As a tradition of the country tells,
Practised to commune with her royal knight   490
By cressets[14] and love-beacons, intercourse
'Twixt her high-seated residence and his
Far off at Chambord[15] on the plain beneath) –
Even here, though less than with the peaceful house
Religious, mid these frequent monuments   495
Of kings, their vices or their better deeds,
Imagination, potent to inflame
At times with virtuous wrath and noble scorn,
Did also often mitigate the force
Of civic prejudice, the bigotry   500

---

8   *Complacently* with pleasure.
9   *end* aim, objective.
10   *chartered* legislated.
11   *a sounder ... afterwards* i.e. in 1793–5, during his disillusioning flirtation with Godwinian thought (see next extract).

12   *Romorantin* small town in the Loire, once a provincial capital.
13   *the first Francis* Francis I (1514–57); attempts to identify the chateau and the mistress have been unsuccessful.
14   *cressets* torches.
15   *Chambord* chateau in the Loire valley, built by Francis I.

(So call it) of a youthful patriot's mind;
And on these spots with many gleams I looked
Of chivalrous delight. Yet not the less,
Hatred of absolute rule, where will of one
Is law for all, and of that barren pride   505
In those who, by immunities unjust,
Betwixt the sovereign and the people stand
(His helpers and not theirs), laid stronger hold
Daily upon me – mixed with pity too
And love, for where hope is, there love will be   510
For the abject multitude. And when we chanced
One day to meet a hunger-bitten girl,
Who crept along, fitting her languid self
Unto a heifer's motion, by a cord
Tied to her arm, and picking thus from the lane   515
Its sustenance, while the girl with her two hands
Was busy knitting in a heartless[16] mood
Of solitude – and at the sight my friend
In agitation said "Tis against that
Which we are fighting', I with him believed   520
Devoutly that a spirit was abroad
Which could not be withstood; that poverty,
At least like this, would in a little time
Be found no more; that we should see the earth
Unthwarted in her wish to recompense   525
The industrious and the lowly child of toil,
All institutes[17] for ever blotted out
That legalized exclusion, empty pomp
Abolished, sensual state and cruel power,
Whether by edict of the one or few;   530
And finally, as sum and crown of all,
Should see the people having a strong hand
In making their own laws, whence better days
To all mankind.[18]

[*Godwinism*] (from *Thirteen-Book Prelude* Book X)[1]

This was the time when all things tended fast   805
To depravation; the philosophy
That promised to abstract the hopes of man
Out of his feelings,[2] to be fixed thenceforth
For ever in a purer element[3]
Found ready welcome. Tempting region that   810

---

[16]   *heartless* despondent, without heart.
[17]   *institutes* laws, edicts, judgements.
[18]   *To all mankind* like many supporters of the Revolution, Wordsworth believed that the rest of the world would follow France's example.

GODWINISM
[1]   For an outline of Godwin's life and ideas, see pp. 47–8. Wordsworth's attachment to Godwinian rationalism occurred in 1794–5, and coincided with a period during which he and Godwin met several times in London.

[2]   *Out of his feelings* Godwin put forward a philosophy by which, true to his origins as a Sandemanian (by which religious belief was completely intellectual), political aspiration was divorced from the emotions.
[3]   *a purer element* ironic. At the time of writing, ten years after the event, he certainly does not believe in anything purer than the emotions; it seemed at the time, however, to him and many other believers in Godwin's system, that radical aspirations could be justified through a completely anti-emotional philosophy.

For Zeal to enter and refresh herself,
Where passions had the privilege to work,
And never hear the sound of their own names![4]
But (speaking more in charity) the dream
Was flattering to the young ingenuous mind   815
Pleased with extremes, and not the least with that
Which makes the human reason's naked self
The object of its fervour. What delight!
How glorious, in self-knowledge and self-rule,
To look through all the frailties of the world!   820
And, with a resolute mastery shaking off
The accidents of nature, time and place,
That make up the weak being of the past,
Build social freedom on its only basis,
The freedom of the individual mind,   825
Which (to the blind restraint of general laws
Superior) magisterially adopts
One guide, the light of circumstances, flashed
Upon an independent intellect.[5]

[*Confusion and Recovery; Racedown, spring* 1796] (from *Thirteen-Book Prelude* Book X)[1]

                              Time may come
When some dramatic story may afford
Shapes livelier to convey to thee, my friend,   880
What then[2] I learned, or think I learned, of truth,
And the errors into which I was betrayed
By present objects, and by reasonings false
From the beginning, inasmuch as drawn
Out of a heart which had been turned aside   885
From nature by external accidents,
And which was thus confounded[3] more and more,
Misguiding and misguided. Thus I fared,
Dragging all passions, notions, shapes of faith,
Like culprits to the bar;[4] suspiciously   890
Calling the mind to establish in plain day
Her titles and her honours;[5] now believing,
Now disbelieving; endlessly perplexed
With impulse, motive, right and wrong, the ground
Of moral obligation, what the rule   895

---

4 *Where passions . . . names* Wordsworth points out that God-win was essentially repressive; emotion was involved in one's commitment to his philosophy, but it was not recognized as such.
5 *What delight . . . intellect* these lines are all heavily ironic, and satirize Wordsworth's younger self.

CONFUSION AND RECOVERY; RACEDOWN, SPRING 1796
1 From London, where his attachment to Godwinism peaked in 1795, Wordsworth retreated to Racedown Lodge in Dorset, where he lived with Dorothy and made his first serious attempts to write poetry. It was here that, according to *The Prelude*, he had an emotional crisis precipitated jointly by a disillusionment with Godwin and disappointment at the failure of the Revolution. On 21 March 1796 he described the second edition of *Political Justice* in terms that indicate his distaste: 'Such a piece of barbarous writing I have not often seen. It contains scarce one sentence decently written' (*EY* 170–1).
2 *then* i.e. during his experience of the Revolution, and in the years following it.
3 *confounded* confused.
4 *bar* The barrier or wooden rail marking off the immediate precinct of the judge's seat, at which prisoners are stationed for arraignment, trial or sentence. In Wordsworth's simile, he analysed his former beliefs and emotions as rigorously as a lawyer cross-examining a witness in a courtroom.
5 *Calling the mind . . . honours* Wordsworth's crisis involved a doubt over the value of imaginative thought.

And what the sanction – till, demanding proof,
And seeking it in everything, I lost
All feeling of conviction, and (in fine)[6]
Sick, wearied out with contrarieties,[7]
Yielded up moral questions in despair,   900
And for my future studies, as the sole
Employment of the enquiring faculty,
Turned towards mathematics, and their clear
And solid evidence.[8]
                Ah, then it was
That thou, most precious friend,[9] about this time   905
First known to me,[10] didst lend a living help
To regulate my soul. And then it was
That the beloved woman[11] in whose sight
Those days were passed (now speaking in a voice
Of sudden admonition, like a brook   910
That does but cross a lonely road; and now
Seen, heard and felt, and caught at every turn,
Companion never lost through many a league)[12]
Maintained for me a saving intercourse
With my true self. For, though impaired and changed   915
Much, as it seemed, I was no further changed
Than as a clouded, not a waning moon.
She, in the midst of all, preserved me still
A poet, made me seek beneath that name
My office[13] upon earth, and nowhere else.   920
And lastly Nature's self, by human love
Assisted, through the weary labyrinth
Conducted me again to open day,
Revived the feelings of my earlier life,
Gave me that strength and knowledge full of peace,   925
Enlarged and never more to be disturbed,
Which through the steps of our degeneracy,
All degradation of this age, hath still
Upheld me, and upholds me at this day[14]
In the catastrophe (for so they dream,   930
And nothing less) when finally to close
And rivet up[15] the gains of France, a Pope
Is summoned in to crown an Emperor[16] –
This last opprobrium,[17] when we see the dog

---

[6] *in fine* in the end.

[7] *contrarieties* unresolved, opposing arguments.

[8] *Turned . . . evidence* against the continual doubt that seemed to surround the morality of, for instance, regicide, or the suppression of emotion by false prophets like Godwin, Wordsworth turns to mathematics which provides the solace of 'clear / And solid evidence', with no moral ambiguity.

[9] *most precious friend* Coleridge.

[10] *about this time . . . me* not true; Wordsworth met Coleridge in September 1795, and no doubt kept in touch in ensuing months, but close contact did not occur until June 1797.

[11] *the beloved woman* Dorothy, with whom Wordsworth resided at Racedown Lodge from September 1795 to June 1797.

[12] *league* about three miles; by 'many a league', Wordsworth just means over a long time.

[13] *office* role, vocation.

[14] *this day* Wordsworth moves forward from 1796 to the time of writing, December 1804.

[15] *to close . . . up* Wordsworth's language underlines his dismay; all the gains of the Revolution have now been imprisoned – effectively thrown away.

[16] *a Pope . . . Emperor* Napoleon had been emperor since May 1804, but summoned Pope Pius VII to crown him on 2 December.

[17] *opprobrium* disgrace.

Returning to his vomit;[18] when the sun 935
That rose in splendour, was alive, and moved
In exultation among living clouds,
Hath put his function and his glory off,[19]
And, turned into a gewgaw,[20] a machine,
Sets like an opera phantom.[21] 940

[The Climbing of Snowdon] (from *Thirteen-Book Prelude* Book XIII)[1]

In one of these excursions, travelling then
Through Wales on foot and with a youthful friend,
I left Bethgelert's huts[2] at couching-time[3]
And westward took my way to see the sun
Rise from the top of Snowdon. Having reached 5
The cottage at the mountain's foot, we there
Roused up the shepherd who by ancient right
Of office is the stranger's usual guide,
And after short refreshment sallied forth.
    It was a summer's night, a close warm night, 10
Wan, dull and glaring,[4] with a dripping mist
Low-hung and thick that covered all the sky,
Half threatening storm and rain; but on we went
Unchecked, being full of heart and having faith
In our tried pilot.[5] Little could we see, 15
Hemmed round on every side with fog and damp,
And, after ordinary travellers' chat
With our conductor, silently we sunk
Each into commerce with his private thoughts.
Thus did we breast the ascent, and by myself 20
Was nothing either seen or heard the while
Which took me from my musings, save that once
The shepherd's cur did to his own great joy
Unearth a hedgehog in the mountain crags
Round which he made a barking turbulent. 25
This small adventure (for even such it seemed
In that wild place and at the dead of night)
Being over and forgotten, on we wound
In silence as before.
                With forehead bent
Earthward, as if in opposition set 30
Against an enemy, I panted up
With eager pace, and no less eager thoughts.

---

[18] *the dog . . . vomit* the French have returned to a monarchy.
The image is taken from Proverbs 26:11: 'As a dog returneth
to his vomit, so a fool returneth to his folly'.
[19] *put . . . off* cast . . . away.
[20] *gewgaw* worthless toy.
[21] *the sun . . . phantom* the sun of the French Republic, that
once rose in glory, now sets, looking more like a clumsy the-
atrical effect ('opera phantom').

THE CLIMBING OF SNOWDON
[1] For the final episode of *The Prelude*, Wordsworth goes back
in time to June–August 1791, when he made a walking tour
of north Wales with his Welsh college friend, Robert Jones.
The account of the climb itself was composed for the final
Book of the *Five-Book Prelude* in February 1804.
[2] *Bethgelert's huts* the cottages of Beddgelert, a village at the
foot of Snowdon.
[3] *couching-time* bed time.
[4] *glaring* Maxwell suggests that this word is used in the
dialect sense of dull, rainy, sticky, clammy.
[5] *tried pilot* experienced guide.

Thus might we wear perhaps an hour away,
Ascending at loose distance each from each,
And I, as chanced, the foremost of the band –   35
When at my feet the ground appeared to brighten,
And with a step or two seemed brighter still;
Nor had I time to ask the cause of this,
For instantly a light upon the turf
Fell like a flash.[6] I looked about, and lo!   40
The moon stood naked in the heavens at height
Immense above my head, and on the shore
I found myself of a huge sea of mist,
Which meek and silent rested at my feet.
A hundred hills their dusky backs upheaved   45
All over this still ocean;[7] and beyond,
Far, far beyond, the vapours shot themselves
In headlands, tongues, and promontory shapes,
Into the sea – the real sea, that seemed
To dwindle and give up its majesty,   50
Usurped[8] upon as far as sight could reach.
Meanwhile, the moon looked down upon this show
In single glory, and we stood, the mist
Touching our very feet. And from the shore
At distance not the third part of a mile   55
Was a blue chasm, a fracture in the vapour,
A deep and gloomy breathing-place through which
Mounted the roar of waters, torrents, streams
Innumerable, roaring with one voice.
The universal spectacle throughout   60
Was shaped for admiration and delight,
Grand in itself alone, but in that breach
Through which the homeless voice of waters rose,
That dark deep thoroughfare, had nature lodged
The soul, the imagination of the whole.[9]   65
    A meditation rose in me that night[10]
Upon the lonely mountain when the scene
Had passed away, and it appeared to me
The perfect image of a mighty mind,
Of one that feeds upon infinity,   70
That is exalted by an under-presence,
The sense of God, or whatsoe'er is dim
Or vast in its own being.[11] Above all,
One function of such mind had nature there
Exhibited by putting forth,[12] in midst   75
Of circumstance most awful and sublime:

---

[6]   *a light . . . flash* cf. the central event described in *A Night-Piece* (p. 273).
[7]   *A hundred hills their dusky backs upheaved . . . ocean* borrowed from Milton's account of Creation, *Paradise Lost* vii 285–7:
         the mountains huge appear
     Emergent, and their broad backs upheave
     Into the clouds . . .
[8]   *Usurped* cf. other imaginative usurpations at Book VI, ll. 455 and 533 (pp. 389, 391).
[9]   *The soul, the imagination of the whole* the revelation offered on Snowdon is of the identity of soul and imagination.

[10]   *that night* the 'meditation' took place in May 1805, as he composed these lines, fourteen months after describing the climbing of Snowdon itself.
[11]   *it appeared . . . being* the experience has been internalized: what is remembered becomes a symbol of the imaginative mind itself, which contains an 'under-presence' of power, whether divine or otherwise. Infinity and vastness exist within the poet's mind.
[12]   *Exhibited by putting forth* demonstrated by analogy.

That domination which she[13] oftentimes
Exerts upon the outward face of things,
So moulds them, and endues, abstracts, combines,[14]
Or by abrupt and unhabitual influence   80
Doth make one object so impress itself
Upon all others, and pervade them so,
That even the grossest minds must see and hear
And cannot choose but feel.[15]
                              The power which these
Acknowledge when thus moved, which Nature thus   85
Thrusts forth upon the senses, is the express
Resemblance, in the fullness of its strength
Made visible, a genuine counterpart
And brother, of the glorious faculty
Which higher minds[16] bear with them as their own.   90
This is the very spirit in which they deal
With all the objects of the universe;
They from their native selves can send abroad
Like transformation, for themselves create
A like existence, and, whene'er it is   95
Created for them, catch it by an instinct.[17]
Them the enduring and the transient both
Serve to exalt. They build up greatest things
From least suggestions,[18] ever on the watch,
Willing to work and to be wrought upon.   100
They need not extraordinary calls
To rouse them: in a world of life they live,
By sensible impressions not enthralled,
But quickened, roused, and made thereby more fit
To hold communion with the invisible world.[19]   105
Such minds are truly from the Deity
For they are Powers,[20] and hence the highest bliss
That can be known is theirs – the consciousness
Of whom they are,[21] habitually infused
Through every image and through every thought,   110
And all impressions. Hence religion, faith,
And endless occupation for the soul,
Whether discursive or intuitive;[22]

---

[13] *she* the mind (from l.74).
[14] *So moulds them, and endues, abstracts, combines* the mist transforms the slopes of the mountain into a sea; in the same way, the imagination is capable of transforming any object it recalls. Cf. Wordsworth's comments on the imagination in the 1815 Preface (pp. 411–14).
[15] *That even . . . feel* it is crucial to the millennial scheme of *The Recluse* that all people, however insensitive to the lure of the metaphysical, should be susceptible to the improving effects of imaginative thought.
[16] *higher minds* Wordsworth believes that some people are particularly prone to imaginative vision.
[17] *whene'er it is . . . instinct* the imagination is both creative and receptive; on occasion, the transformation occurs outside the individual, and is 'caught' by the perceiving mind.
[18] *They build . . . suggestions* a crucial element in Wordsworth's thinking. Reviewers of the day criticized him for writ-

ing about subjects they considered trivial, but for him the imagination was 'the faculty that produces impressive effects out of simple elements' (p. 344).
[19] *By sensible . . . world* Wordsworth's elect are not imprisoned by their senses (the view of some enlightenment thinkers), but are enlivened imaginatively and enabled to perceive the higher world that lies beyond them.
[20] *Powers* divinely empowered beings.
[21] *the consciousness . . . are* because the imaginative mind creates and perceives, the very act of perception confirms its individual identity.
[22] *Whether discursive or intuitive* Wordsworth is thinking of the distinction made by Milton between discursive reason (belonging to man), and a higher, 'intuitive' reason, to which man may aspire, which is possessed by angels (*Paradise Lost* v 487–90).

Hence sovereignty within[23] and peace at will,
Emotion which best foresight need not fear,   115
Most worthy then of trust when most intense;
Hence cheerfulness in every act of life;
Hence truth in moral judgements, and delight
That fails not in the external universe.[24]

    Oh, who is he that hath his whole life long   120
Preserved, enlarged, this freedom in himself? –
For this alone is genuine liberty.[25]
Witness, ye solitudes where I received
My earliest visitations,[26] careless then
Of what was given me, and where now I roam   125
A meditative, oft a suffering, man,
And yet I trust with undiminished powers –
Witness – whatever falls[27] my better mind,
Revolving with the accidents of life,
May have sustained – that, howsoe'er misled,   130
I never, in the quest of right and wrong,
Did tamper with myself from private aims;[28]
Nor was in any of my hopes the dupe
Of selfish passions; nor did wilfully
Yield ever to mean cares and low pursuits,   135
But rather did with jealousy[29] shrink back
From every combination that might aid
The tendency, too potent in itself,
Of habit to enslave the mind – I mean
Oppress it by the laws of vulgar sense   140
And substitute a universe of death,[30]
The falsest of all worlds, in place of that
Which is divine and true.

               To fear and love
(To love as first and chief, for there fear ends)[31]
Be this ascribed, to early intercourse   145
In presence of sublime and lovely forms
With the adverse principles of pain and joy –
Evil as one is rashly named by those
Who know not what they say.[32] From love (for here
Do we begin and end) all grandeur comes,   150
All truth and beauty – from pervading love;
That gone, we are as dust. Behold the fields

---

[23] *sovereignty within* complete spiritual mastery.
[24] *delight . . . universe* unfailing pleasure at beholding natural objects.
[25] *liberty* one of the primary objectives of the (now failed) French Revolution. Wordsworth is implicitly revising this political term, turning it into a spiritual one. The 'liberty' of the Wordsworthian visionary is interior, a freedom of the soul.
[26] *ye solitudes . . . visitations* the landscape of the Lakes. The 'visitations' are from the life-force within the natural world – effectively, God (cf. *Pedlar* 108).
[27] *falls* befalls.
[28] *never . . . from private aims* clearer in the *Fourteen-Book Prelude*:

Never did I, in quest of right and wrong,
Tamper with conscience from a private aim . . . (xiv 150–1)
[29] *with jealousy* scrupulously.
[30] *a universe of death* in which the individual is enslaved by unimaginative reliance on the senses; the phrase is from *Paradise Lost* ii 622.
[31] *To love . . . ends* fear leads to love of nature, and thence to love of mankind. Cf. *Thirteen-Book Prelude* i 305–6: 'Fair seed-time had my soul, and I grew up / Fostered alike by beauty and by fear'.
[32] *Evil . . . say* Neither fear nor pain are evil, because they play their part in shaping the imaginative mind.

In balmy[33] springtime full of rising flowers
And happy creatures! See that pair, the lamb
And the lamb's mother, and their tender ways   155
Shall touch thee to the heart. In some green bower
Rest, and be not alone, but have thou there
The one who is thy choice of all the world –
There linger, lulled and lost, and rapt away –
Be happy to thy fill! Thou call'st this love,   160
And so it is, but there is higher love
Than this, a love that comes into the heart
With awe and a diffusive sentiment;[34]
Thy love is human merely – this proceeds
More from the brooding soul,[35] and is divine.   165

    This love more intellectual[36] cannot be
Without imagination, which in truth
Is but another name for absolute strength
And clearest insight, amplitude of mind[37]
And reason[38] in her most exalted mood.   170
This faculty hath been the moving soul
Of our long labour: we have traced the stream
From darkness and the very place of birth
In its blind cavern, whence is faintly heard
The sound of waters; followed it to light   175
And open day, accompanied its course
Among the ways of nature; afterwards
Lost sight of it bewildered and engulfed,
Then given it greeting as it rose once more
With strength, reflecting in its solemn breast   180
The works of man and face of human life;
And lastly, from its progress have we drawn
The feeling of life endless,[39] the great thought
By which we live, infinity and God.

Elegiac Stanzas, Suggested by a Picture of Peele Castle[1] in a Storm, Painted by Sir George Beaumont[2] (composed between 20 May and 27 June 1806)

From POEMS IN TWO VOLUMES (1807)

I was thy neighbour once, thou rugged pile![3]
Four summer weeks I dwelt in sight of thee;
I saw thee every day, and all the while
Thy form was sleeping on a glassy sea.

---

33 *balmy* mild, fragrant.
34 *diffusive sentiment* a love that comes from outside the individual, and spreads from soul to soul ('diffusive').
35 *the brooding soul* i.e. that of God, as suggested by the allusion to the moment of creation in *Paradise Lost* i 21–2, where the Holy Spirit 'Dove-like sat'st brooding on the vast abyss / And madest it pregnant'.
36 *intellectual* spiritual.
37 *amplitude of mind* effectively, greatness of soul.
38 *reason* i.e. intuitive reason, the theme of Book XIII.
39 *life endless* the afterlife.

ELEGIAC STANZAS
1 Piel Castle is in northern Lancashire, on a promontory opposite Rampside, where Wordsworth spent the summer of 1794. Beaumont's painting is now at the Wordsworth Museum, Grasmere.
2 Sir George Howland Beaumont, 7th Baronet (1753–1827), of Coleorton Hall, near Ashby de la Zouch, Leicestershire. He had sketched in the Lakes in 1798, and given Wordsworth a farmstead at Applethwaite, less than two miles north of Greta Hall at the foot of Skiddaw, in 1803.
3 *thou rugged pile* Piel Castle.

So pure the sky, so quiet was the air!   5
So like, so very like, was day to day!
Whene'er I looked, thy image still was there –
It trembled, but it never passed away.

How perfect was the calm; it seemed no sleep,
No mood which season takes away, or brings;   10
I could have fancied that the mighty deep
Was even the gentlest of all gentle things.

Ah *then*, if mine had been the painter's hand
To express what then I saw, and add the gleam,
The light that never was, on sea or land,   15
The consecration, and the poet's dream,

I would have planted thee, thou hoary pile,
Amid a world how different from this! –
Beside a sea that could not cease to smile,
On tranquil land, beneath a sky of bliss;   20

Thou shouldst have seemed a treasure-house, a mine
Of peaceful years, a chronicle of heaven –
Of all the sunbeams that did ever shine
The very sweetest had to thee been given.

A picture had it been of lasting ease,   25
Elysian quiet,[4] without toil or strife;
No motion but the moving tide, a breeze,
Or merely silent nature's breathing life.

Such, in the fond delusion of my heart,
Such picture would I at that time have made;   30
And seen the soul of truth in every part –
A faith, a trust that could not be betrayed.

So once it would have been – 'tis so no more;
I have submitted to a new control:
A power is gone, which nothing can restore –   35
A deep distress hath humanized my soul.[5]

Not for a moment could I now behold
A smiling sea[6] and be what I have been;
The feeling of my loss will ne'er be old –
This, which I know, I speak with mind serene.   40

---

4 *Elysian quiet* i.e. as peaceful as the Elysian fields, where in
Greek myth the souls of dead heroes enjoyed eternal life.
5 *A deep distress . . . soul* the drowning of Wordsworth's
brother John (b.1773) in the wreck of the Earl of Aber-
gavenny, of which he was Captain, 25 February 1805. The
news inspired Mary Lamb to write her own poem, pp. 170–1,
and a reading of Wordsworth's lines led Mary Shelley to com-
pose an elegy for her drowned husband, pp. 1096–7.

6 *Not for a moment . . . sea* cf. Wordsworth's comment in a
letter: 'since the loss of my dear brother, we have all had such
painful and melancholy thoughts connected with the ocean
that nothing but a paramount necessity could make us live
near it' (*MY* i 212).

Then, Beaumont, friend! who would have been the friend,
If he had lived, of him[7] whom I deplore,[8]
This work of thine[9] I blame not, but commend;
This sea in anger, and that dismal shore.

Oh 'tis a passionate work! – yet wise and well,   45
Well-chosen is the spirit that is here;
That hulk which labours in the deadly swell,
This rueful sky, this pageantry of fear!

And this huge castle, standing here sublime,
I love to see the look with which it braves,   50
Cased in the unfeeling armour of old time,
The lightning, the fierce wind, and trampling waves.

Farewell, farewell the heart that lives alone,
Housed in a dream, at distance from the kind![10]
Such happiness, wherever it be known,   55
Is to be pitied, for 'tis surely blind.

But welcome fortitude, and patient cheer,
And frequent sights of what is to be borne!
Such sights, or worse, as are before me here –
Not without hope we suffer and we mourn.[11]   60

A *Complaint* (composed between 30 October 1806 and April 1807)[1]

From POEMS IN TWO VOLUMES (1807)

There is a change – and I am poor;
Your love hath been, nor long ago,
A fountain at my fond heart's door
Whose only business was to flow –
And flow it did, not taking heed   5
Of its own bounty,[2] or my need.

What happy moments did I count!
Blessed was I then all bliss above!
Now, for this consecrated fount
Of murmuring, sparkling, living love,   10
What have I? Shall I dare to tell?
A comfortless and hidden well.

---

7   *him* John Wordsworth.
8   *deplore* lament.
9   *This work of thine* Sir George Beaumont's *A Storm: Peele Castle* was exhibited at the Royal Academy, 2 May 1806, where Wordsworth probably saw it.
10   *kind* humankind.
11   *Not without hope . . . mourn* Edward Wilson notes that this line echoes the Book of Common Prayer's 'Order for the Burial of the Dead': '. . . who also hath taught us, by his holy Apostle St. Paul, not to be sorry, as men without hope, for them that sleep in him' ('An Echo of St. Paul and Words of Consolation in Wordsworth's "Elegiac Stanzas"', *RES* 43 [1992] 75–80).

A COMPLAINT
1   'Suggested by a change in the manners of a friend' (*FN* 9). The friend was Coleridge. Strains had been developing between the Wordsworths and Coleridge since around 1802, the period of *Dejection*.
2   *bounty* its gift of love.

A well of love – it may be deep –
I trust it is, and never dry;
What matter if the waters sleep   15
In silence and obscurity?
Such change, and at the very door
Of my fond heart, hath made me poor.

Star Gazers (composed November 1806)[1]

From POEMS IN TWO VOLUMES (1807)

What crowd is this? What have we here? We must not pass it by;
A telescope upon its frame and pointed to the sky,
Long is it as a barber's pole, or mast of little boat,
Some little pleasure-skiff that doth on Thames' waters float.

The showman chooses well his place – 'tis Leicester's busy Square;   5
And he's as happy in his night, for the heavens are blue and fair;
Calm, though impatient, are the crowd, each is ready with the fee,
And envies him that's looking – what an insight it must be!

Now, showman, where can lie the cause? Shall thy implement have blame –
A boaster that, when he is tried, fails and is put to shame?   10
Or is it good as others are, and be their eyes at fault?
Their eyes or minds? Or finally, is this resplendent vault?[2]

Is nothing of that radiant pomp so good as we have here?
Or gives a thing but small delight that never can be dear?
The silver moon with all her vales, and hills of mightiest fame,   15
Do they betray us when they're seen? And are they but a name?

Or is it rather that conceit[3] rapacious[4] is and strong?
And bounty[5] never yields so much but it seems to do her wrong?
Or is it that when human souls a journey long have had
And are returned into themselves they cannot but be sad?   20

Or does some deep and earnest thought the blissful mind employ[6]
Of him who gazes, or has gazed – a grave and steady joy
That doth reject all show of pride, admits no outward sign,
Because not of this noisy world, but silent and divine?

Or is it (last unwelcome thought!) that these spectators rude,   25
Poor in estate, of manners base, men of the multitude,
Have souls which never yet have risen, and therefore prostrate[7] lie,
Not to be lifted up at once to power and majesty?

STAR GAZERS
[1] 'Observed by me in Leicester Square as here described,
1806' (*FN* 14). Wordsworth probably saw the showman
charging customers to look through his telescope when walk-
ing through Leicester Square with Charles Lamb during a visit
to London, April-May 1806.
[2] *resplendent vault* the sky; cf. the vault in *A Night-Piece*
(p. 273).

[3] *conceit* conception, expectation of what we will see down
the telescope.
[4] *rapacious* greedy; i.e. people expect too much.
[5] *bounty* i.e. the reward of seeing the moon down the tele-
scope.
[6] *employ* preoccupy.
[7] *prostrate* overcome, defeated.

Whate'er the cause, 'tis sure that they who pry and pore
Seem to meet with little gain, seem less happy than before;   30
One after one they take their turns, nor have I one espied
That does not slackly go away as if dissatisfied.

[*St Paul's*] (composed 1808; edited from MS)[1]

From POEMS IN TWO VOLUMES (1807)

Pressed[2] with conflicting thoughts of love and fear,
I parted from thee, friend,[3] and took my way
Through the great city, pacing with an eye
Downcast, ear sleeping, and feet masterless,
That were sufficient guide unto themselves,   5
And step by step went pensively. Now, mark
Not how my trouble was entirely hushed
(That might not be), but how by sudden gift,[4]
Gift of imagination's holy power,
My soul in her uneasiness received   10
An anchor of stability. It chanced
That, while I thus was pacing, I raised up
My heavy eyes and instantly beheld,
Saw at a glance in that familiar spot
A visionary scene: a length of street   15
Laid open[5] in its morning quietness,
Deep, hollow, unobstructed, vacant, smooth,
And white with winter's purest white, as fair,
As fresh and spotless as he ever sheds
On field or mountain. Moving form was none,   20
Save here and there a shadowy passenger,
Slow, shadowy, silent, dusky, and beyond
And high above this winding length of street,
This noiseless and unpeopled avenue,
Pure, silent, solemn, beautiful, was seen   25
The huge majestic temple of St Paul
In awful sequestration,[6] through a veil,
Through its own sacred veil of falling snow.

ST PAUL'S
[1] This poem was never published by Wordsworth. It was inspired by his departure early on the morning of 3 April 1808 from Coleridge's lodgings above the *Courier* offices in the Strand to start his journey back to Grasmere. On 8 April he described it to Sir George Beaumont: 'I left Coleridge at 7 o'clock on Sunday morning; and walked towards the city in a very thoughtful and melancholy state of mind. I had passed through Temple Bar and by St Dunstan's, noticing nothing, and entirely occupied by my own thoughts, when, looking up, I saw before me the avenue of Fleet Street, silent, empty, and pure white, with a sprinkling of new-fallen snow, not a cart or carriage to obstruct the view, no noise, only a few soundless and dusky foot-passengers here and there; you remember the elegant curve of Ludgate Hill in which this avenue would terminate, and beyond and towering above it was the huge and majestic form of St Paul's, solemnized by a thin veil of falling snow. I cannot say how much I was affected at this unthought-of sight in such a place, and what a blessing I felt there is in habits of exalted imagination. My sorrow was controlled, and my uneasiness of mind, not quieted and relieved altogether, seemed at once to receive the gift of an anchor of security' (*MY* i 209).
[2] *Pressed* oppressed.
[3] *friend* Coleridge.
[4] *by sudden gift* cf. *Resolution and Independence* 50–1: 'Now whether it were by peculiar grace, / A leading from above, a something given . . .'
[5] *Laid open* cf. *Composed upon Westminster Bridge, 3 September 1802*, in which 'Ships, towers, domes, theatres, and temples lie / Open unto the fields, and to the sky'.
[6] *awful sequestration* awe-inspiring seclusion.

[*Cloudscape New Jerusalem*] (composed between 1809 and 1812)[2]

From THE EXCURSION (1814)[1] (from BOOK II)

The shepherds homeward moved
Through the dull mist, I following – when a step,
A single step, that freed me from the skirts   860
Of the blind vapour, opened to my view
Glory beyond all glory ever seen
By waking sense or by the dreaming soul.
Though I am conscious that no power of words
Can body forth, no hues of speech can paint   865
That gorgeous spectacle too bright and fair
Even for remembrance, yet the attempt may give
Collateral[3] interest to this homely tale.
   The appearance, instantaneously disclosed,
Was of a mighty city – boldly say   870
A wilderness of building, sinking far
And self-withdrawn into a wondrous depth,
Far sinking into splendour, without end!
Fabric[4] it seemed of diamond and of gold,
With alabaster domes, and silver spires,   875
And blazing terrace upon terrace high
Uplifted: here, serene pavilions bright
In avenues disposed; there, towers begirt[5]
With battlements that on their restless fronts
Bore stars – illumination of all gems!   880
By earthly nature had the effect been wrought
Upon the dark materials of the storm
And pacified; on them, and on the coves
And mountain-steeps and summits, whereunto
The vapours had receded, taking there   885
Their station under a cerulean[6] sky.
      Oh 'twas an unimaginable sight!
Clouds, mists, streams, watery rocks and emerald turf,
Clouds of all tincture, rocks and sapphire sky,
Confused,[7] commingled,[8] mutually inflamed,[9]   890
Molten together, and composing thus,
Each lost in each, that marvellous array
Of temple, palace, citadel, and huge
Fantastic pomp of structure without name,
In fleecy folds voluminous, enwrapped.   895
Right in the midst, where interspace[10] appeared

---

[1] Despite their reservations about *The Excursion* as a whole, this important set-piece vision in the clouds was a big influence on Shelley and Keats (pp. 834 n. 77, 848 n. 28, 1026 n. 30).

[2] *The Excursion* was the published work of which Wordsworth was most proud. (*The Prelude* was posthumously published, and therefore not known to most of his contemporaries.) It contained drastically revised versions of *The Ruined Cottage*, *The Pedlar*, and '*Not useless do I deem*' (all composed 1798), as well as passages such as this one, composed especially for the volume.

[3] *Collateral* additional.

[4] *Fabric* the substance from which it was made.

[5] *begirt* surrounded.

[6] *cerulean* azure.

[7] *Confused* mixed together.

[8] *commingled* blended.

[9] *mutually inflamed* glowing together.

[10] *interspace* a gap, opening.

Of open court, an object like a throne
Beneath a shining canopy of state
Stood fixed, and fixed resemblances were seen
To implements of ordinary use,   900
But vast in size, in substance glorified,
Such as by Hebrew prophets were beheld
In vision – forms uncouth of mightiest power,
For admiration and mysterious awe.
Below me was the earth – this little vale   905
Lay low beneath my feet; 'twas visible,
I saw not, but I felt that it was there.
That which I *saw* was the revealed abode
Of spirits in beatitude:[11] my heart
Swelled in my breast. 'I have been dead', I cried,   910
'And now I live. Oh, wherefore do I live?'
And with that pang I prayed to be no more!

[*Surprised by joy – impatient as the wind*] (composed between 1812 and 1814)[1]

From POEMS (1815)

Surprised by joy – impatient as the wind
I wished to share the transport[2] – oh, with whom
But thee,[3] long buried in the silent tomb,
That spot which no vicissitude[4] can find?
Love, faithful love recalled thee to my mind –   5
But how could I forget thee? Through what power,
Even for the least division of an hour,
Have I been so beguiled[5] as to be blind
To my most grievous loss? That thought's return
Was the worst pang that sorrow ever bore,   10
Save one, one only, when I stood forlorn,
Knowing my heart's best treasure was no more;
That neither present time, nor years unborn
Could to my sight that heavenly face restore.

Preface (extract)

From POEMS (1815) (pp. xx–xxviii)[1]

Imagination (in the sense of the word as giving title to a class[2] of the following poems) has no reference to images that are merely a faithful copy existing in the mind of certain external objects, but is a

---

[11] *beatitude* supreme happiness.

SURPRISED BY JOY – IMPATIENT AS THE WIND
[1] 'This was in fact suggested by my daughter Catherine long after her death' (*FN* 21). Catherine Wordsworth died 4 June 1812.
[2] *transport* ecstasy.
[3] *thee* his dead daughter Catherine.
[4] *vicissitude* change, development in human affairs.

[5] *beguiled* deceived.

PREFACE
[1] *Poems* (1815) was Wordsworth's first attempt to collect his shorter works. For the occasion he composed an important Preface that outlines his ideas about the imagination.
[2] *a class* In *Poems* (1815) Wordsworth divided his collected works into 'classes' or categories, one of which was 'Imagination'.

word of higher import, denoting operations of the mind upon those objects, and processes of creation or of composition governed by certain fixed laws. I proceed to illustrate my meaning by instances.

A parrot *hangs* from the wires of his cage by his beak or by his claws, or a monkey from the bough of a tree by his paws or his tail: each creature does so literally and actually. In the first *Eclogue* of Virgil, the shepherd, thinking of the time when he is to take leave of his farm, thus addresses his goats:

> Non ego vos posthac viridi projectus in antro
> Dumosa *pendere* procul de rupe videbo . . .[3]

> . . . half way up
> *Hangs* one who gathers samphire[4]

is the well-known expression of Shakespeare, delineating an ordinary image upon the cliffs of Dover. In these two instances is a slight exertion of the faculty which I denominate[5] imagination, in the use of one word. Neither the goats nor the samphire-gatherer[6] do literally hang (as does the parrot or the monkey), but, presenting to the senses something of such an appearance, the mind in its activity, for its own gratification, contemplates them as hanging.

> As when far off at sea a fleet descried
> *Hangs* in the clouds, by equinoxial winds
> Close sailing from Bengala or the Isles
> Of Ternate or Tydore, whence merchants bring
> Their spicy drugs; they on the trading flood
> Through the wide Ethiopian to the Cape
> Ply, stemming nightly toward the pole – so seemed
> Far off the flying fiend.[7]

Here is the full strength of the imagination involved in the word *hangs* and exerted upon the whole image. First the fleet (an aggregate of many ships) is represented as one mighty person whose track, we know and feel, is upon the waters; but, taking advantage of its appearance to the senses, the poet dares to represent it as *hanging in the clouds*, both for the gratification of the mind in contemplating the image itself, and in reference to the motion and appearance of the sublime object to which it is compared.[8]

From images of sight we will pass to those of sound: 'Over his own sweet voice the stock-dove broods . . .'.[9] Of the same bird:

> His voice was *buried* among trees,
> Yet to be come at by the breeze . . .[10]

> Oh cuckoo! shall I call thee *bird*
> Or but a wandering *voice?*[11]

---

3 Virgil, *Eclogue* i 76–7: 'No more, stretched in some mossy grot, shall I watch you [i.e. my flock of goats] in the distance hanging from a bushy crag'.
4 *King Lear* IV vi 15–16.
5 *denominate* call.
6 *samphire-gatherer* one who gathers samphire, a plant that grows on rocks by the sea, the leaves of which were used in pickles.
7 *Paradise Lost* ii 636–43.
8 Wordsworth first discussed his ideas relating to Milton's image in a letter to Sir George Beaumont, 28 August 1811:

> We had another fine sight one evening, walking along a rising ground about two miles distant from the shore. It was about the hour of sunset, and the sea was perfectly calm, and in a quarter where its surface was indistinguish-

able from the western sky, hazy and luminous with the setting sun, appeared a tall sloop-rigged vessel, magnified by the atmosphere through which it was viewed, and seeming rather to hang in the air than to float upon the waters. Milton compares the appearance of Satan to a fleet descried far off at sea; the visionary grandeur and beautiful form of this single vessel, could words have conveyed to the mind the picture which Nature presented to the eye, would have suited his purpose as well as the largest company of vessels that ever associated together with the help of a trade wind. (MY i 508)

9 *Resolution and Independence* 5.
10 'Oh nightingale' 13–14.
11 *To the Cuckoo* 3–4.

The stock-dove is said to *coo*, a sound well imitating the note of the bird. But by the intervention of the metaphor *broods*, the affections[12] are called in by the imagination to assist in marking the manner in which the bird reiterates and prolongs her soft note, as if herself delighting to listen to it, and participating of a still and quiet satisfaction like that which may be supposed inseparable from the continuous process of incubation.

'His voice was buried among trees': a metaphor expressing the love of seclusion by which this bird is marked, and characterizing its note as not partaking of the shrill and the piercing, and therefore more easily deadened by the intervening shade – yet a note so peculiar, and withal so pleasing, that the breeze, gifted with that love of the sound which the poet feels, penetrates the shade in which it is entombed, and conveys it to the ear of the listener.

> . . . shall I call thee bird
> Or but a wandering voice?

This concise interrogation[13] characterizes the seeming ubiquity of the voice of the cuckoo, and dispossesses the creature almost of a corporeal existence – the imagination being tempted to this exertion of her power by a consciousness in the memory that the cuckoo is almost perpetually heard throughout the season of spring, but seldom becomes an object of sight.

Thus far of images independent of each other, and immediately endowed by the mind with properties that do not inhere in them,[14] upon an incitement[15] from properties and qualities the existence of which is inherent and obvious. These processes of imagination are carried on either by conferring additional properties upon an object, or abstracting[16] from it some of those which it actually possesses, and thus enabling it to react upon the mind which hath performed the process, like a new existence.

I pass from the imagination acting upon an individual image to a consideration of the same faculty employed upon images in a conjunction[17] by which they modify each other. The reader has already had a fine instance before him in the passage quoted from Virgil, where the apparently perilous situation of the goat hanging upon the shaggy precipice is contrasted with that of the shepherd contemplating it from the seclusion of the cavern in which he lies stretched at ease and in security. Take these images separately, and how unaffecting the picture compared with that produced by their being thus connected with, and opposed to, each other!

> As a huge stone is sometimes seen to lie
> Couched on the bald top of an eminence,
> Wonder to all who do the same espy
> By what means it could thither come, and whence;
> So that it seems a thing endued with sense,
> Like a sea-beast crawled forth, which on a shelf
> Of rock or sand reposeth, there to sun himself –
>
> Such seemed this man, not all alive nor dead,
> Nor all asleep, in his extreme old age. . . .
> Motionless as a cloud the old man stood
> That heareth not the loud winds when they call
> And moveth altogether, if it move at all.[18]

In these images, the conferring, the abstracting, and the modifying powers of the imagination, immediately and mediately acting, are all brought into conjunction.[19] The stone is endowed with some-

---

12 *affections* feelings.
13 *interrogation* question.
14 *do not inhere in them* i.e. qualities and properties not actually possessed by the objects themselves.
15 *incitement* stimulus.

16 *abstracting* removing.
17 *conjunction* combination.
18 *Resolution and Independence* 64–72, 82–4.
19 *brought into conjunction* i.e. act together.

thing of the power of life to approximate it to the sea-beast, and the sea-beast stripped of some of its vital qualities to assimilate it to the stone – which intermediate image is thus treated for the purpose of bringing the original image (that of the stone) to a nearer resemblance to the figure and condition of the aged man, who is divested of so much of the indications of life and motion as to bring him to the point where the two objects unite and coalesce in just comparison. After what has been said, the image of the cloud need not be commented upon.

Thus far of an endowing or modifying power. But the imagination also shapes and *creates* – and how? By innumerable processes, and in none does it more delight than in that of consolidating numbers into unity, and dissolving and separating unity into number – alternations proceeding from, and governed by, a sublime consciousness of the soul in her own mighty and almost divine powers. Recur to the passage already cited from Milton.[20] When the compact fleet, as one person, has been introduced 'sailing from Bengala', 'they' (i.e. the 'merchants' representing the fleet resolved into a multitude of ships) 'Ply' their voyage towards the extremities of the earth; 'so' (referring to the word 'As' in the commencement) 'seemed the flying fiend' – the image of his person acting to recombine the multitude of ships into one body, the point from which the comparison set out.

'So seemed': and to whom 'seemed'? To the heavenly muse who dictates the poem, to the eye of the poet's mind, and to that of the reader, present at one moment in the wide Ethiopian, and the next in the solitudes, then first broken in upon, of the infernal regions!

Conclusion (composed 1818–20)

From THE RIVER DUDDON (1820)[1]

I thought of thee,[2] my partner and my guide,
As being passed away. Vain sympathies!
For *backward*, Duddon, as I cast my eyes,
I see what was, and is, and will abide;
Still glides the stream, and shall for ever glide;   5
The form remains, the function never dies,
While *we*, the brave, the mighty, and the wise,[3]
We men who, in our morn of youth, defied
The elements, must vanish; be it so!
Enough, if something from our hands have power   10
To live, and act, and serve the future hour;
And if, as tow'rd the silent tomb we go,
Through love, through hope, and faith's transcendent dower,[4]
We feel that we are greater than we know.

---

[20] *the passage ... Milton* i.e. *Paradise Lost* ii 636–43, quoted p. 412.

CONCLUSION

[1] Wordsworth composed a sequence of sonnets describing the Duddon valley, which he published in 1820. This concluding sonnet is probably the most famous, and the best. The River Duddon springs from the top of the Wrynose Pass and then descends through one of the most picturesque valleys in the Lake District.

[2] *thee* the River Duddon.

[3] *While we ... wise* borrowed from Wordsworth's early translation of Moschus's *Lament for Bion* (1789) 5: 'But we, the great, the mighty and the wise'. Shelley, who frequently alludes to Moschus's *Lament*, also echoes the line at *Mont Blanc* 82.

[4] *dower* gift.

From [*The Fourteen-Book Prelude*] (1850)

[*Genius of Burke!*] (composed by 1832; edited from MS)[1]

Genius of Burke! forgive the pen seduced
By specious wonders,[2] and too slow to tell
Of what the ingenuous, what bewildered men
Beginning to mistrust their boastful guides,[3]   515
And wise men, willing to grow wiser, caught
(Rapt auditors!) from thy most eloquent tongue –
Now mute, for ever mute, in the cold grave.[4]
I see him, old but vigorous in age,
Stand, like an oak whose stag-horn branches start   520
Out of its leafy brow, the more to awe
The younger brethren of the grove. But some –
While he forewarns, denounces, launches forth,
Against all systems built on abstract rights,[5]
Keen ridicule; the majesty[6] proclaims   525
Of institutes and laws hallowed by time;[7]
Declares the vital power of social ties
Endeared by custom, and with high disdain
Exploding upstart theory, insists
Upon the allegiance to which men are born –   530
Some (say at once a froward[8] multitude)
Murmur (for truth is hated where not loved)
As the winds fret within the Eolian cave,
Galled by their monarch's chain.[9] The times[10] were big
With ominous change which, night by night, provoked   535
Keen struggles, and black clouds of passion raised;
But memorable moments intervened
When Wisdom, like the goddess from Jove's brain,[11]
Broke forth in armour of resplendent words,
Startling the synod.[12] Could a youth, and one   540
In ancient story versed, whose breast had heaved
Under the weight of classic eloquence,
Sit, see, and hear, unthankful, uninspired?[13]

GENIUS OF BURKE!
[1] This is one of the best-known instances of how Wordsworth's political views had altered since his republican youth. Edmund Burke's *Reflections on the Revolution in France* (1790) had argued eloquently against the Revolution (pp. 5–8), and Wordsworth certainly did not approve of it at the time of its publication. By 1832, however, he had become a fervent admirer of its author.
[2] *specious wonders* i.e. the work of radical writers like Paine, Wollstonecraft and Godwin.
[3] *the ingenuous . . . guides* young men taken in by radical ideologues like Thomas Paine – of which Wordsworth had been one.
[4] Burke died in 1797.
[5] *abstract rights* an allusion to Paine's *Rights of Man* (1791–2), written in response to Burke (pp. 14–17).
[6] *the majesty* 'he' (i.e. Burke) of line 523.
[7] *Of institutes . . . time* one of Burke's central arguments in the *Reflections* was that society and its laws constituted 'a part-

nership not only between those who are living, but between those who are living, those who are dead, and those who are to be born' (p. 7).
[8] *froward* wayward, undisciplined.
[9] *As the winds . . . chain* Aeolus, god of the winds, was given command of the winds by Zeus, and kept them in a cave, releasing them at will.
[10] *The times* Wordsworth is looking back to the French Revolution, 1789–95.
[11] *the goddess . . . brain* Athene, daughter of Zeus (Roman 'Jove'), was born without a mother, springing fully armed from her father's head when it was split open by the axe of Prometheus.
[12] *synod* House of Commons, where Burke was known for his passionate oratory.
[13] *Could a youth . . . uninspired* the question is not as rhetorical as it looks. Wordsworth in youth was no admirer of Burke, and would not, presumably, have confessed to feeling inspired by his words.

Airey-Force Valley (composed September 1835)[1]

From YARROW REVISITED, AND OTHER POEMS (1835)

> Not a breath of air
> Ruffles the bosom of this leafy glen.
> From the brook's margin, wide around, the trees
> Are steadfast as the rocks; the brook itself,
> Old as the hills that feed it from afar,
> Doth rather deepen than disturb the calm
> Where all things else are still and motionless.
> And yet, even now, a little breeze, perchance
> Escaped from boisterous winds that rage without,
> Has entered, by the sturdy oaks unfelt,
> But to its gentle touch how sensitive
> Is the light ash that, pendent from the brow
> Of yon dim cave, in seeming silence makes
> A soft eye-music of slow-waving boughs,
> Powerful almost as vocal harmony
> To stay the wanderer's steps and soothe his thoughts.

Extempore Effusion, Upon Reading, in the Newcastle Journal, the Notice of the Death of the Poet, James Hogg[1] (composed *c*. 30 November 1835)

From THE NEWCASTLE JOURNAL 4 (5 December 1835) No. 188

> When first,[2] descending from the moorlands,
> I saw the stream of Yarrow glide
> Along a bare and open valley,
> The Ettrick Shepherd[3] was my guide;
>
> When last[4] along its banks I wandered   5
> Through groves that had begun to shed
> Their golden leaves upon the pathways,
> My steps the Border Minstrel[5] led.
>
> The mighty Minstrel breathes no longer,
> Mid mouldering ruins[6] low he lies;   10
> And death upon the braes of Yarrow
> Has closed the Shepherd-poet's eyes.

AIREY-FORCE VALLEY
[1] Aira Force is a waterfall on the north shore of Ullswater. This poem celebrates the gorge that rises above it.

EXTEMPORE EFFUSION
[1] James Hogg, died 21 November 1835. For more on Hogg, see pp. 419–20. Wordsworth later commented: 'These verses were written extempore immediately after reading a notice of the Ettrick Shepherd's death in the Newcastle paper, to the editor of which I sent a copy for publication. The persons lamented in these verses were all either of my friends or acquaintance' (*FN* 58). A cogent line by line analysis of the poem is available in William Ruddick's 'Subdued Passion and Controlled Emotion: Wordsworth's "Extempore Effusion upon the Death of James Hogg"', *Charles Lamb Bulletin* NS 87 (1994) 98–110.

[2] *When first* Wordsworth first walked along the banks of the River Yarrow in September 1814.
[3] *The Ettrick Shepherd* the name under which Hogg published and appeared in *Noctes Ambrosianae* (see pp. 627–8). After his father went bankrupt when he was six, he was removed from school and spent most of his life as a shepherd.
[4] *When last* Wordsworth returned to the Yarrow in September–October 1831, when his guide was Sir Walter Scott, a friend since the early 1800s.
[5] *the Border Minstrel* Sir Walter Scott, died 21 September 1832. His earliest literary success had come with *The Minstrelsy of the Scottish Border* (1802–3).
[6] *Mid mouldering ruins* Scott was buried at Dryburgh Abbey, 26 September 1832.

Nor has the rolling year twice measured,
From sign to sign, his steadfast course,
Since every mortal power of Coleridge[7]   15
Was frozen at its marvellous source;

The rapt one of the godlike forehead,
The heaven-eyed creature sleeps in earth;[8]
And Lamb,[9] the frolic and the gentle,
Has vanished from his lonely hearth.   20

Like clouds that rake the mountain-summits,
Or waves that own no curbing hand,
How fast has brother followed brother
From sunshine to the sunless land!

Yet I, whose lids from infant slumbers   25
Were earlier raised, remain to hear
A timid voice that asks in whispers,
'Who next will drop and disappear?'

Our haughty life is crowned with darkness,
Like London with its own black wreath,[10]   30
On which with thee, oh Crabbe,[11] forth-looking
I gazed from Hampstead's breezy heath;

As if but yesterday departed,
Thou too art gone before – yet why
For ripe fruit seasonably gathered   35
Should frail survivors[12] heave a sigh?[13]

No more of old romantic[14] sorrows
For slaughtered youth and love-lorn maid;
With sharper grief is Yarrow smitten,
And Ettrick[15] mourns with her their Shepherd dead!   40

[On the 'Ode'] (extract)

From THE FENWICK NOTES (dictated 1843)

Nothing was more difficult for me in childhood than to admit the notion of death as a state applicable to my own being. I have said elsewhere: 'A simple child ... that lightly draws its breath, / And feels

---

7 Samuel Taylor Coleridge, died 25 July 1834.
8 *The rapt one ... earth* all these qualities are attributed to Coleridge.
9 Charles Lamb, died 27 December 1834. Lamb remained a good friend of Wordsworth from the time of their first meeting at Nether Stowey in June 1797 (see p. 458). It is appropriate that he follows Coleridge in this list, as they had been friends since their time together at Christ's Hospital.
10 *Like London ... wreath* a reference to the pall of black smoke hanging over central London.
11 George Crabbe, died 3 February 1832; see p. 36.
12 *frail survivors* Wordsworth was sixty-five.

13 When Wordsworth published this poem in a new edition of his collected works, 1837, he added a stanza at this point lamenting Felicia Hemans (d. 16 May 1835):
    Mourn rather for that holy spirit,
    Sweet as the spring, as ocean deep;
    For her who, ere her summer faded,
    Has sunk into a breathless sleep.
14 *romantic* i.e. from old medieval romances, which provided much of Scott's subject-matter.
15 *Ettrick* the village of Ettrick, where Hogg lived, worked, and is buried, is in the Scottish lowlands.

its life in every limb – / What should it know of death?'[1] But it was not so much from [excess][2] of animal vivacity that *my* difficulty came, as from a sense of the indomitableness[3] of the spirit within me. I used to brood over the stories of Enoch and Elijah, and almost to persuade myself that, whatever might become of others, I should be translated in something of the same way to heaven.

With a feeling congenial to this, I was often unable to think of external things as having external existence, and I communed with all that I saw as something not apart from, but inherent in, my own immaterial nature.[4] Many times while going to school have I grasped at a wall or tree to recall myself from this abyss of idealism to the reality. At that time I was afraid of such processes. In later periods of life I have deplored (as we have all reason to do) a subjugation of an opposite character, and have rejoiced over the remembrances, as is expressed in the lines, 'obstinate questionings',[5] etc. To that dreamlike vividness and splendour which invest objects of sight in childhood, everyone (I believe, if he would look back) could bear testimony, and I need not dwell upon it here.

But having in the poem regarded it as presumptive evidence of a prior state of existence, I think it right to protest against a conclusion which has given pain to some good and pious persons that I meant to inculcate such a belief. It is far too shadowy a notion to be recommended to faith as more than an element in our instincts of immortality. But let us bear in mind that, though the idea is not advanced in revelation, there is nothing there to contradict it, and the fall of man presents an analogy in its favour. Accordingly, a pre-existent state has entered into the popular creeds of many nations, and among all persons acquainted with classic literature is known as an ingredient in Platonic philosophy.

Archimedes said that he could move the world if he had a point whereon to rest his machine. Who has not felt the same aspirations as regards the world of his own mind? Having to wield some of its elements when I was impelled to write this poem on the immortality of the soul, I took hold of the notion of pre-existence as having sufficient foundation in humanity for authorizing me to make for my purpose the best use of it I could as a poet.

[On 'We are Seven'] (extract)

From THE FENWICK NOTES (dictated 1843)

In reference to this poem, I will here mention one of the most remarkable facts in my own poetic history and that of Mr Coleridge.

In the spring of the year 1798,[1] he, my sister and myself started from Alfoxden, pretty late in the afternoon, with a view to visit Lynton and the Valley of Stones near it. And as our united funds were very small, we agreed to defray the expense of the tour by writing a poem to be sent to the new *Monthly Magazine* set up by Phillips the bookseller, and edited by Dr Aikin.[2] Accordingly we set off and proceeded along the Quantock Hills towards Watchet, and in the course of this walk was planned the poem of 'The Ancient Mariner', founded on a dream (as Mr Coleridge said) of his friend Mr Cruikshank.[3] Much the greatest part of the story was Mr Coleridge's invention, but certain parts I myself suggested; for example, some crime was to be committed which should bring upon the Old Navigator (as Coleridge afterwards delighted to call him) the spectral persecution, as a consequence of that crime and his own wanderings.

ON THE 'ODE'

[1] *We are Seven* 1–4.

[2] *excess* editorial conjecture, necessary to fill a gap left in the MS.

[3] *indomitableness* effectively, strength, power.

[4] *my own immaterial nature* spirit.

[5] *obstinate questionings* see *Ode* 144ff.

ON 'WE ARE SEVEN'

[1] *In the year . . . 1798* The walking tour took place not in spring 1798 but in mid-November 1797.

[2] *The Monthly Magazine*, influential radical periodical founded 1796 by Richard Phillips and edited by Dr John Aikin (1747–1822), brother of Mrs Barbauld.

[3] John Cruikshank, land agent to Lord Egmont at Nether Stowey, and Coleridge's neighbour there. He was the brother of Ellen Cruikshank, the 'most gentle maid' of Coleridge's *The Nightingale* 69.

I had been reading in Shelvocke's *Voyages*[4] a day or two before, that while doubling Cape Horn they frequently saw albatrosses – in that latitude the largest sort of seafowl, some extending their wings 12 or 13 feet. 'Suppose', I said, 'you represent him as having killed one of these birds on entering the South Sea, and that the tutelary spirits of these regions take upon them to avenge the crime?' The incident was thought fit for the purpose, and adopted accordingly. I also suggested the navigation of the ship by the dead men, but do not recollect that I had anything more to do with the scheme of the poem.

The gloss with which it was subsequently accompanied was not thought of by either of us at the time – at least, not a hint of it was given to me – and I have no doubt it was a gratuitous afterthought.[5] We began the composition together on that (to me) memorable evening; I furnished two or three lines at the beginning of the poem, in particular:

> And listened like a three years' child:
> The mariner had his will.[6]

These trifling contributions all but one (which Mr Coleridge has with unnecessary scrupulosity recorded)[7] slipped out of his mind – as they well might. As we endeavoured to proceed conjointly[8] (I speak of the same evening), our respective manners[9] proved so widely different that it would have been quite presumptuous in me to do anything but separate from an undertaking upon which I could only have been a clog.

James Hogg   (1770–1835)

Hogg was born in 1770 in the parish of Ettrick, an isolated village on the Scottish borders, where he spent his entire childhood. He was six years old when his father, a tenant farmer, became bankrupt. Hogg was removed from school (where he had been only a few months), and spent the rest of his childhood as a shepherd and farmhand. He later testified that between the ages of six and fifteen 'I neither read nor wrote; nor had I access to any book save the Bible'. At fifteen, he bought himself a fiddle and taught himself to play; within five years he was playing it at local fairs and weddings. In his twenties he joined a library; for the first time he read Shakespeare, Spenser, Milton, Fielding, Smollett, Dryden and Pope. He also began to write under the name of the Ettrick Shepherd.

He was forty-two when his poem *The Queen's Wake* was published in 1813. It was a major success, and established him as a major literary force. *The Witch of Fife*, presented below, was one of its most celebrated poems; Wordsworth thought that it was the best in the volume, and commended it for having 'much spirit'.[1] Shortly after its publication Byron described Hogg as 'a man of great powers and deserving of encouragement'.[2]

When *Blackwood's Edinburgh Magazine* was founded in 1817, Hogg became one if its main contributors. However, *Blackwood's* took advantage of him by publishing under his name a number of articles he did not write, and ridiculing his Scots language and lowly origins in the *Noctes Ambrosianae* (see pp. 627–8), some episodes of which he nonetheless composed.

His greatest work was to come. In 1824 he published his novel, *The Private Memoirs and Confessions of a Justified Sinner*. It is an astonishing literary achievement and received no serious critical attention until an appreciative essay by André Gide in 1947. Only in recent years has it been recognized for the great work that it really is. He died in poverty, and was celebrated in fine style by Wordsworth in his *Extempore Effusion Upon the Death of James Hogg*.

Finally, after years of comparative neglect, the Stirling/South Carolina edition of Hogg's collected works

---

4   George Shelvocke, *Voyage round the World, by the way of the Great South Sea* (1726); for the passage to which Wordsworth refers, see p. 194 n. 13.
5   *The gloss ... afterthought* The 1817 text of *The Ancient Mariner* carries a series of marginal glosses; see pp. 528–44.
6   *The Ancient Mariner* (1798) 19–20.
7   *which Mr Coleridge ... recorded* See note to the 1817 text of *The Ancient Mariner* 227, p. 534 n. 21.

8   *conjointly* together.
9   *manners* literary styles.

JAMES HOGG
1   MY ii 170.
2   Marchand iv 151.

began to appear in 1995 with *The Three Perils of Woman* ed. David Groves, Antony Hasler and Douglas S. Mack, *A Queer Book* ed. P. D. Garside, and *The Shepherd's Calendar* ed. Douglas S. Mack. The edition is expected to run to 31 volumes when complete.

Further reading

James Hogg, *The Private Memoirs and Confessions of a Justified Sinner* ed. John Carey (Oxford, 1969)

—, *Selected Poems* ed. Douglas S. Mack (Oxford, 1970)

—, *Memoirs of the Author's Life and Familiar Anecdotes of Sir Walter Scott* ed. Douglas S. Mack (Edinburgh and London, 1972)

—, *Selected Sketches and Stories* ed. Douglas S. Mack (Edinburgh, 1982)

—, *A Shepherd's Delight: A James Hogg Anthology* ed. Judy Steel (Edinburgh, 1985)

—, *Tales of Love and Mystery* ed. David Groves (Edinburgh, 1985)

—, *Selected Poems and Songs* ed. David Groves (Edinburgh, 1987)

David Groves, *James Hogg: The Growth of a Writer* (Edinburgh, 1988)

A journal dedicated to Hogg, *Studies in Hogg and his World*, is published annually by the James Hogg Society (1990 onwards).

The Witch of Fife

From THE QUEEN'S WAKE (1813)

'Quhare haif ye been, ye ill womyne,[1]
    These three lang nightis fra hame?
Quhat garris[2] the sweit drap fra yer brow,
    Like clotis of the saut sea faem?[3]

It fearis[4] me muckil[5] ye haif seen   5
    Quhat[6] good man never knew;
It fearis me muckil ye haif been
    Quhare the grey cock never crew.[7]

But the spell may crack and the brydel breck,
    Then sherpe yer werde will be;   10
Ye had better sleipe in yer bed at hame
    Wi yer deire littil bairnis and me.'

'Sit dune, sit dune, my leile[8] auld man,
    Sit dune and listin to me;
I'll gar the hayre stand on yer crown   15
    And the cauld sweit blind yer e'e.[9]

But tell nae wordis, my gude auld man,
    Tell never word again;
Or deire shall be yer courtisye,[10]
    And driche[11] and sair yer pain.[12]   20

The first leet-night,[13] quhan the new moon set,
    Quhan all was douffe[14] and mirk,

THE WITCH OF FIFE
[1] *ill womyne* bad woman.
[2] *garris* makes.
[3] *clotis of the saut sea faem* masses of the salt sea foam.
[4] *fearis* worries.
[5] *muckil* much.
[6] *Quhat* what.
[7] *Quhare the grey cock never crew* i.e. in hell.

[8] *leile* honest.
[9] *e'e* eye.
[10] *courtisye* apology.
[11] *driche* dreary.
[12] *pain* punishment.
[13] *leet-night* chosen night.
[14] *douffe* dull.

We saddled ouir naigis[15] wi the moon-fern[16] leif
  And rode fra Kilmerrin kirk.

Some horses ware[17] of the brume-cow[18] framit[19]   25
  And some of the greine bay-tree,
But mine was made of ane humloke schaw,[20]
  And a stout stallion was he.

We raide[21] the tod[22] doune on the hill,
  The martin on the law,[23]   30
And we huntyd the hoolet[24] out of brethe,
  And forcit him doune to fa.'

'Quhat guid was that, ye ill womyne?
  Quhat guid was that to thee?
Ye wald better haif bein in yer bed at hame   35
  Wi yer deire littil bairnis and me.'

'And ay we raide and se merrily we raide
  Throw the merkist gloffis[25] of the night,
And we swam the floode and we darnit[26] the woode
  Till we cam to the Lommond height.[27]   40

And quhen we cam to the Lommond height,
  Se lythlye[28] we lychtid doune;
And we drank fra the hornis[29] that never grew,
  The beer that was never browin.

Than up there rase ane wee wee man,   45
  Franethe[30] the moss-grey stane;
His fece was wan like the collifloure,
  For he nouthir had blude nor bane.[31]

He set ane reid-pipe till his muthe
  And he playit se bonnilye,   50
Till the grey curlew and the black-cock flew
  To listen his melodye.

It rang se sweet through the green Lommond
  That the nycht-winde lowner[32] blew,
And it soupit[33] alang the Loch Leven   55
  And wakinit the white seamew.

---

[15] *naigis* horses.
[16] *moon-fern* moonwort (a fern).
[17] *ware* were.
[18] *brume-cow* broom.
[19] *framit* made.
[20] *ane humloke schaw* a small piece of hemlock wood.
[21] *raide* raced.
[22] *tod* fox.
[23] *law* hill.
[24] *hoolet* owl.

[25] *merkist gloffis* darkest fears.
[26] *darnit* zigzagged through.
[27] *the Lommond height* the Lomond Hills overlook Loch Leven.
[28] *lythlye* with agility.
[29] *hornis* drinking-horns.
[30] *Franethe* from beneath.
[31] *For he nouthir had blude nor bane* i.e. he was a ghost.
[32] *lowner* more gently.
[33] *soupit* swept.

It rang se sweet through the grein Lommond,
　　Se sweitly butt[34] and se shill,[35]
That the wezilis laup out of their mouldy holis
　　And dancit on the mydnycht hill.　　　　　　　　　60

The corby-craw[36] cam gledgin[37] near,
　　The ern[38] gede veeryng bye,
And the troutis laup[39] out of the Leven Louch,[40]
　　Charmit with the melodye.

And ay we dancit on the green Lommond　　　　　　65
　　Till the dawn on the ocean grew —
Ne wonder I was a weary wycht
　　Quhan I cam hame to you!'

'Quhat guid, quhat guid, my weird weird wyfe,
　　Quhat guid was that to thee?　　　　　　　　　70
Ye wald better haif bein in yer bed at hame
　　Wi yer deire littil bairnis and me.'

'The second nychte quhan the new moon set,
　　O'er the roaryng sea we flew;
The cockle-shell our trusty bark,　　　　　　　　75
　　Our sailis of the grein sea-rue.[41]

And the bauls windis blew, and the fire flauchtis[42] flew,
　　And the sea ran to the skie;
And the thunner it growlit and the sea-dogs[43] howlit
　　As we gaed scouryng bye.　　　　　　　　　　80

And ay we mountit the sea-green hillis,
　　Quhill we brushit thro' the cludis of the hevin;
Than sousit[44] dounright like the stern-shot light
　　Fra the liftis[45] blue casement driven.

But our taickil stood and our bark was good,　　　85
　　And se pang[46] was our pearily[47] prowe;
Quhan we culdna speil[48] the brow of the wavis,
　　We needilit them throu belowe.

As fast as the hail, as fast as the gale,
　　As fast as the midnycht leme,[49]　　　　　　90
We borit the breiste of the burstyng swale,[50]
　　Or fluffit i' the flotyng faem.

---

[34]　*butt* verily (used for emphasis).
[35]　*shill* shrill.
[36]　*corby-craw* carrion crow.
[37]　*gledgin* looking slyly at.
[38]　*ern* eagle.
[39]　*laup* jumped.
[40]　*Leven Louch* Loch Leven.
[41]　*sea-rue* shrub that grows on sea shores.
[42]　*flauchtis* flies.

[43]　*sea-dogs* seals.
[44]　*sousit* fell.
[45]　*liftis* sky's.
[46]　*pang* strong.
[47]　*pearily* tiny.
[48]　*speil* climb.
[49]　*leme* gleam.
[50]　*swale* swelling wave.

And quhan to the Norraway shore we wan,
    We muntyd our steedis of the wynd,
And we splashit the floode, and we darnit the woode,
    And we left the shouir behynde.   95

Fleet is the roe on the green Lommond
    And swift is the couryng grew;[51]
The reindeir dun[52] can eithly[53] run
    Quhan the houndis and the hornis pursue.   100

But nowther the roe nor the reindeir dun,
    The hinde nor the couryng grew,
Culde fly owr muntaine, muir[54] and dale,
    As owr braw[55] steedis they flew.

The dales war deep, and the Doffrinis steep,[56]   105
    And we rase to the skyis ee-bree;[57]
Quhite, quhite was ouir rode, that was never trode,
    Owr the snawis of eternity!

And quhan we cam to the Lapland lone[58]
    The fairies war all in array,   110
For all the genii of the north
    War keepyng their holeday.

The warlock men and the weerd wemyng
    And the fays of the wood and the steep,
And the phantom hunteris all war there,   115
    And the mermaidis of the deep.

And they washit us all with the witch-water
    Distillit fra the moorland dew,
Quhill our beauty blumit like the Lapland rose,
    That wylde in the foreste grew.'   120

'Ye lee,[59] ye lee, ye ill womyne,
    Se loud as I heir ye lee!
For the warst-faurd[60] wyfe on the shoris of Fife
    Is cumlye[61] comparet wi thee.'

'Then the mermaidis sang and the woodlandis rang,   125
    Se sweetly swellit the quire;
On every cliff a herpe they hang,
    On every tree a lyre.

And ay they sang and the woodlandis rang,
    And we drank and we drank se deep;   130

---

51 *the couryng grew* the cowering greyhound.
52 *dun* brown.
53 *eithly* easily.
54 *muir* moor.
55 *braw* handsome.
56 *the Doffrinis steep* the Dovre Fjeld mountain range, Norway.

57 *ee-bree* eyebrows.
58 *lone* common.
59 *Ye lee* you lie.
60 *warst-faurd* most ugly.
61 *cumlye* comely, good-looking.

Then soft in the armis of the warlock men,
    We laid us dune to sleep.'

'Away, away, ye ill womyne,
    An ill deide met ye dee![62]
Quhan ye hae pruvit se false to yer God   135
    Ye can never pruve trew to me.'

'And there we lernit fra the fairy foke
    And fra our master true,
The wordis that can beire us throu the air,
    And lokkis and baris[63] undo.   140

Last nycht we met at Maisry's cot,[64]
    Richt weil the wordis we knew;
And we set a foot on the black cruik-shell,[65]
    And out at the lum[66] we flew.

And we flew owr hill and we flew owr dale   145
    And we flew owr firth and sea,
Until we cam to merry Carlisle[67]
    Quhar we lightit on the lea.[68]

We gaed[69] to the vault beyound the towir[70]
    Quhar we enterit free as ayr;   150
And we drank and we drank of the bishopis wine
    Quhill we culde drynk ne mair.'

'Gin[71] that be trew, my gude auld wyfe,
    Whilk[72] thou hast tauld to me,
Betide my death, betide my lyfe,   155
    I'll beire thee companye.

Neist tyme ye gaung[73] to merry Carlisle
    To drynk of the blude-reid wine –
Beshrew my heart, I'll fly with thee,
    If the diel[74] shulde fly behynde.'   160

'Ah, littil do ye ken, my silly auld man,
    The daingeris we maun dree;[75]
Last nichte we drank of the bishopis wyne
    Quhill near near taen[76] war we.

Afore we wan to the sandy ford   165
    The gorcockis[77] nichering[78] flew;

---

[62] *An ill deide met ye dee* may you die a terrible death.
[63] *lokkis and baris* locks and bars (on doors).
[64] *cot* cottage. Maisry is another of the witches.
[65] *cruik-shell* hook for hanging a pot over a fire.
[66] *lum* chimney-top.
[67] *Carlisle* just over the border in England.
[68] *lightit on the lea* landed on the meadow.
[69] *gaed* went.
[70] *towir* in Carlisle castle.

[71] *Gin* If.
[72] *Whilk* which.
[73] *Neist tyme ye gaung* next time you go.
[74] *diel* devil.
[75] *dree* endure.
[76] *taen* captured.
[77] *gorcockis* moorcocks.
[78] *nichering* squawking, screeching.

The lofty crest of Ettrick Pen[79]
    Was wavit about with blew,
And flichtering throu the air we fand
    The chill chill mornyng dew.   170

As we flew owr the hillis of Braid,[80]
    The sun rase fair and clear;
There gurly James[81] and his baronis braw[82]
    War out to hunt the deere.

Their bowis they drew, their arrowis flew,   175
    And peircit the ayr with speede,
Quhill purpil fell the mornyng dew
    With witch-blude rank and reide.

Littil do ye ken, my silly auld man,
    The dangeris we maun dree;   180
Ne wonder I am a weary wycht
    Quhan I come hame to thee.'

'But tell me the *word*, my gude auld wyfe,
    Come tell it me speedilye;
For I lang to drink of the gude reide wyne,   185
    And to wyng the ayr with thee.

Yer hellish horse I wilna ryde,
    Nor sail the seas in the wynd;
But I can flee as well as thee
    And I'll drynk quhill ye be blynd.'   190

'O fy! O fy! my leil auld man,
    That word I darena tell;
It wald turn this warld all upside down,
    And make it warse than hell,

For all the lasses in the land   195
    Wald munt the wynd and fly;
And the men wald doff their doublets syde[83]
    And after them wald ply.'

But the auld gudeman was ane cunnyng auld man,
    And ane cunnyng auld man was he;   200
And he watchit and he watchit for mony a night
    The witches' flychte to see.

Ane nychte he darnit[84] in Maisry's cot,
    The fearless haggs came in;
And he heard the word of awsome weird,   205
    And he saw their deedis of synn.

---

79   *Ettrick Pen* a mountain in the Scottish Borders near Moffat.
80   *the hillis of Braid* The Braid Hills south of Edinburgh.
81   *gurly James* deceitful James IV, King of Scotland (1488–1513).
82   *braw* strong.
83   *doff their doublets syde* remove their long doublets.
84   *darnit* hid.

Then ane by ane they said that word
   As fast to the fire they drew,
Then set a foot on the black cruik-shell
   And out at the lum they flew.   210

The auld gude-man cam fra his hole
   With feire and muckil dreide,
But yet he culdna think to rue,
   For the wyne came in his head.

He set his foot in the black cruik-shell   215
   With ane fixit and ane wawlyng[85] ee,
And he said the word that I darena say
   And out at the lum flew he.

The witches skalit the moonbeam pale,
   Deep groanit the trembling wynde;
But they never wist till our auld gudeman   220
   Was hoveryng them behynde.

They flew to the vaultis of merry Carlisle
   Quhair they enterit free as ayr,
And they drank and they drank of the byshopis wyne   225
   Quhill they culde drynk ne mair.

The auld gudeman he grew se crouse,[86]
   He dancit on the mouldy ground,
And he sang the bonniest sangis of Fife,
   And he tuzzlit the kerlyngs[87] round.   230

And ay he percit the tither butt,
   And he suckit and he suckit se lang,
Quhill his een they closit, and his voice grew low,
   And his tongue wold hardly gang.

The kerlyngs drank of the bishopis wyne   235
   Quhill they scentit the mornyng wynde,
Then clove again the yeilding ayr
   And left the auld man behynde.

And ay he slepit on the damp damp floor,
   He slepit and he snorit amain;   240
He never dremit he was far fra hame,
   Or that the auld wyvis war gane.

And ay he slepit on the damp damp floor
   Quhill past the midday highte,
Quhan wakenit by five rough Englishmen   245
   That trailit him to the lychte.

---

[85] *wawlyng* wildly-gazing.
[86] *crouse* cheerful.

[87] *he tuzzlit the kerlyngs* he boisterously hugged the old women.

'Now quha are ye, ye silly auld man,
　That sleepis se sound and se weil?
Or how gat ye into the bishopis vault
　Throu lokkis and barris of steel?'　　　　　　　250

The auld gudeman he tryit to speak
　But ane word he culdna fynde;
He tryit to think but his head whirlit round,
　And ane thing he culdna mynde;
'I cam fra Fife', the auld man cryit,　　　　　　255
　'And I cam on the midnycht wynde.'

They nickit the auld man and they prickit[88] the auld man,
　And they yerkit[89] his limbis with twine,
Quhill the reid blude ran in his hose and shoon,
　But some cryit it was wyne.　　　　　　　260

They lickit[90] the auld man and they prickit the auld man,
　And they tyit him till ane stone;
And they set ane bele-fire[91] him about,
　And they burnit him skin and bone.

Now wae be to the puir auld man　　　　　　　265
　That ever he saw the day!
And wae be to all the ill wemyng
　That lead puir men astray!

Let never ane auld man after this
　To lawless greide inclyne;　　　　　　　270
Let never an auld man after this
　Rin post to the diel[92] for wyne.[93]

88　*nickit ... prickit* hit ... cut.
89　*yerkit* tightly bound.
90　*lickit* beat, struck.
91　*bele-fire* large fire.
92　*Rin post to the diel* run straight to the devil.

93　This is how the earliest version of the poem ended. However, Sir Walter Scott persuaded Hogg to change the ending, which he felt jarred with its comic tone. In the revised version of the poem the man is saved when his wife flies down, whispers the magic word, which he then utters, and flies off after her.

Sir Walter Scott   (1771–1832)

'My birth was neither distinguished nor sordid', Scott wrote in his autobiography.[1] His father was a Writer to the Signet – a legal position in Scotland which allowed the holder to conduct cases in the Court of Session in Edinburgh. Of Scott's twelve brothers and sisters only five survived infancy. Scott himself was born on 15 August 1771, and being of poor health spent much time in the countryside as he grew up, particularly in the Border country. He matriculated at the University of Edinburgh, was called to the bar in 1792, and became an advocate.

He began his literary career as the translator of popular German poems of the day: Bürger's *Lenore* and *Der wilde Jäger* (1796) and Goethe's *Götz von Berlichingen* (1799). He became Sheriff Depute for Selkirkshire in 1799 and obtained the post of Principal Clerk of the Quarter Session in 1805. Neither position was particularly distinguished, but both allowed him a steady income and time to pursue his literary interests.

His first major work was *Minstrelsy of the Scottish Border* (1802–3), an immediate success which established his reputation. It was essentially a collection of folk ballads and songs which he had edited and annotated. He followed this up with poems of his own composition: *The Lay of the Last Minstrel* (1805), *Marmion: A Tale of Flodden Field* (1808), *The Lady of the Lake* (1810) – his greatest success as a poet, *The Lord of the Isles* (1815), and *Harold the Dauntless* (1817). These works made Scott one of the best-selling poets of day. His distinctive brand of Scottish hokum was based on a cocktail of medievalism,

supernaturalism (inherited from the gothic ballads of Bürger), picturesque description of landscape, and Highland epic. It was a winner, and much the same ingredients contributed to a stream of wildly successful novels: *Waverley* (1814), *Old Mortality* (1816), *Rob Roy* (1817), *The Heart of Midlothian* (1818), *Ivanhoe* (1820) and *Redgauntlet* (1824), to name but a few. Bad investments ruined Scott financially in 1826, and forced him to continue writing fiction in order to reimburse his creditors. When he died his health was broken by overwork; he was lamented, along with other writers of the time, in Wordsworth's *Extempore Effusion Upon the Death of James Hogg* (see pp. 416–17).

His masterpiece was the 'Waverley' novels. Byron liked them so much that he claimed, in 1821, to have read each one fifty times,[2] and in 1812 he told Scott that even the Prince Regent 'preferred you to every bard past and present'.[3] The poems presented here offer a taste of Scott's verse – some of which was contained in the novels – and the extract from his diary provides valuable insight into his technique.

Further reading

J. G. Lockhart, *The Life of Sir Walter Scott, Bart.* (Edinburgh, 1879)

Jane Millgate, *Walter Scott: The Making of the Novelist* (Buffalo, NY, 1984)

Judith Wilt, *Secret Leaves: The Novels of Sir Walter Scott* (Chicago, 1985)

Caledonia

From THE LAY OF THE LAST MINSTREL (1805) (from Canto Six)

I

Breathes there the man, with soul so dead,
Who never to himself hath said,
    'This is my own, my native land!' –
Whose heart hath ne'er within him burned
As home his footsteps he hath turned
    From wandering on a foreign strand?[1]
If such there breathe, go mark him well;

5

SIR WALTER SCOTT
[1]   J. G. Lockhart, *The Life of Sir Walter Scott, Bart.* (Edinburgh, 1879), p. 3.
[2]   Marchand viii 13.

[3]   Marchand ii 182.

CALEDONIA
[1]   *strand* shore.

For him no minstrel raptures swell;
High though his titles, proud his name,
Boundless his wealth as wish can claim;   10
Despite those titles, power and pelf,[2]
The wretch, concentred all in self,
Living, shall forfeit fair renown,
And, doubly dying, shall go down
To the vile dust from whence he sprung –   15
Unwept, unhonoured, and unsung.

II

Oh Caledonia, stern and wild,
Meet nurse for a poetic child!
Land of brown heath and shaggy wood,
Land of the mountain and the flood,   20
Land of my sires! What mortal hand
Can e'er untie the filial band
That knits me to thy rugged strand?
Still as I view each well-known scene,
Think what is now, and what hath been,   25
Seems as, to me, of all bereft,
Sole friends, thy woods and streams were left;
And thus I love them better still,
Even in extremity of ill.
By Yarrow's stream[3] still let me stray,   30
Though none should guide my feeble way;
Still feel the breeze down Ettrick[4] break
Although it chill my withered cheek;
Though there, forgotten and alone,
The bard may draw his parting groan.   35

Lochinvar

From MARMION (1808) (from Canto Five)

Oh, young Lochinvar is come out of the west,
Through all the wide Border[1] his steed was the best;
And save[2] his good broadsword he weapons had none,
He rode all unarmed, and he rode all alone.
So faithful in love, so dauntless in war,   5
There never was knight like the young Lochinvar.

He stayed not for brake[3] and he stopped not for stone,
He swam the Esk river where ford there was none;

---

2   *pelf* booty, plunder.
3   *Yarrow's stream* the River Yarrow runs through the Scottish lowlands, where Scott spent much of his boyhood.
4   Ettrick is a small village in the Scottish lowlands.

LOCHINVAR
1   *Border* the region on either side of the English and Scottish border.
2   *save* except.
3   *brake* briers.

But ere he alighted at Netherby gate,
The bride had consented, the gallant came late: 10
For a laggard[4] in love and a dastard[5] in war
Was to wed the fair Ellen of brave Lochinvar.

So boldly he entered the Netherby Hall
Among bridesmen and kinsmen and brothers and all;
Then spoke the bride's father, his hand on his sword   15
(For the poor craven[6] bridegroom said never a word),
'Oh come ye in peace here, or come ye in war,
Or to dance at our bridal, young Lord Lochinvar?'

'I long wooed your daughter, my suit you denied;
Love swells like the Solway[7] but ebbs like its tide.   20
And now am I come, with this lost love of mine
To lead but one measure, drink one cup of wine.
There are maidens in Scotland more lovely by far
That would gladly be bride to the young Lochinvar.'

The bride kissed the goblet; the knight took it up,   25
He quaffed off the wine and he threw down the cup.
She looked down to blush and she looked up to sigh
With a smile on her lips and a tear in her eye.
He took her soft hand ere her mother could bar,
'Now tread we a measure!'[8] said young Lochinvar.   30

So stately his form and so lovely her face
That never a hall such a galliard[9] did grace;
While her mother did fret and her father did fume
And the bridegroom stood dangling his bonnet and plume,
And the bride-maidens whispered, ''Twere better by far   35
To have matched our fair cousin with young Lochinvar.'

One touch to her hand and one word in her ear;
When they reached the hall-door, and the charger[10] stood near –
So light to the croupe[11] the fair lady he swung,
So light to the saddle before her he sprung!   40
'She is won! We are gone over bank, bush, and scaur![12]
They'll have fleet steeds that follow', quoth young Lochinvar.

There was mounting 'mong Graemes of the Netherby clan;
Forsters, Fenwicks, and Musgraves, they rode and they ran;
There was racing and chasing on Cannobie Lee   45
But the lost bride of Netherby ne'er did they see.
So daring in love and so dauntless in war,
Have ye e'er heard of gallant like young Lochinvar?

---

4   *laggard* a ditherer.
5   *dastard* base coward.
6   *craven* cowardly, weak-hearted.
7   *Solway* The Solway Firth is an arm of the sea extending
between Cumbria and Dumfriesshire.

8   *measure* dance.
9   *galliard* quick and lively dance in triple time.
10   *charger* horse.
11   *croupe* hind end of the saddle.
12   *scaur* ridge of a hill.

[*Lucy Ashton's Song*]

From TALES OF MY LANDLORD (4 vols, 1819); *The Bride of Lammermoor*
(vol. i p. 68)

Look not thou on beauty's charming,
Sit thou still when kings are arming,
Taste not when the wine-cup glistens,
Speak not when the people listens,
Stop thine ear against the singer,
From the red gold keep thy finger;
Vacant heart, and hand, and eye,
Easy live and quiet die.

Scott's Diary. 12 February 1826

From J. G. LOCKHART, MEMOIRS OF THE LIFE OF SCOTT (1837–8)

Having ended the second volume of *Woodstock* last night, I had to begin the third this morning.[1] Now I have not the slightest idea how the story is to be wound up to a catastrophe.[2] I am just in the same case as I used to be when I lost myself in former days in some country to which I was a stranger. I always pushed for the pleasantest route, and either found or made it the nearest. It is the same in writing. I never could lay down a plan – or, having laid it down, I never could adhere to it. The action of composition always extended some passages, and abridged or omitted others; and personages were rendered important or insignificant, not according to their agency in the original conception of the piece, but according to the success (or otherwise) with which I was able to bring them out. I only tried to make that which I was actually writing diverting and interesting, leaving the rest to fate.

I have been often amused with the critics distinguishing some passages as particularly laboured, when the pen passed over the whole as fast as it could move, and the eye never again saw them, except in proof. Verse I write twice, and sometimes three times over. This hab nab[3] at a venture is a perilous[4] style, I grant, but I cannot help it. When I strain my mind to ideas which are purely imaginative (for argument is a different thing), it seems to me that the sun leaves the landscape – that I think away the whole vivacity of my original conception, and that the results are cold, tame and spiritless. It is the difference between a written oration and one bursting from the unpremeditated exertions of the speaker which have always something of the air of enthusiasm and inspiration. I would not have young authors imitate my carelessness, however.

Dorothy Wordsworth   (1771–1855)

She was born in Cockermouth in 1771. When she was six her mother died, at which point she was brought up by her mother's cousin, Elizabeth Threlkeld, in Halifax. The ensuing years were not all unhappy, but they were marred by her separation from her brothers. In 1783 her father died, and the Wordsworth children were orphaned; she was unable to attend his funeral. Between the ages of fifteen and seventeen she was brought up by her grandmother in Penrith, and from 1788 to 1794 by her kindly uncle, William Cookson, at Forncett Rectory in Norfolk. By then a young woman, she spent time with a variety of people in various places: with Elizabeth Threlkeld in Halifax, in Newcastle with the Miss Griffiths (other cousins of her mother), with the Hutchinson

---

SCOTT'S DIARY
[1] Scott's novel, *Woodstock*, was published in three volumes, 1826.

[2] *catastrophe* climax.
[3] *hab nab* hit or miss.
[4] *perilous* risky.

family at Sockburn, at Rampside with more cousins (this time on her father's side), and so on.

Her life changed forever in the summer of 1795 when, for the first time since childhood, she was able to live with her brother William at Racedown Lodge in Dorset. Here they lived a settled, domestic existence which neither had known in adulthood. This continued at Alfoxden House in Somerset, where they moved to be close to Coleridge, four miles away in Nether Stowey. She had already written many letters which reveal a precocious and developing literary talent, but it was at Alfoxden that her abilities blossomed with the writing of a journal. The manuscripts of the Alfoxden journal are now lost, but the transcripts that survive reveal that already at this stage her close, detailed observations of the natural world were the inspiration for much of her brother's poetry, and constituted a remarkable literary achievement in themselves.

She went to Germany with her brother in 1798 and settled with him at Dove Cottage in Grasmere on 20 December 1799. It was probably the most important event in her life. Here she was to write the Grasmere journals which, besides continuing to provide the source for much of Wordsworth's poetry, documented the goings-on of life over the first three years of their lives at Dove Cottage. It was her masterpiece. As Pamela Woof has written:

> There is simply nothing like it anywhere else. This Journal calls out to us directly across almost two hundred years, and its writer and her world come alive. It sometimes moves in little rushes when days can be noted with a staccato speed; it sometimes slows down to linger on a single figure: a beggar woman, a leech-gatherer, a child catching hailstones at a cottage door, a bow-bent postman with his little wooden box at his back, an old seaman with a beard like grey plush; it sometimes slows to linger on a whole scene: a funeral, or children with their mother by a fire, or a lakeshore on a windy day with daffodils, or a man with carts going up a hill and a little girl putting stones behind the wheels.... The Journal conveys directly the unpremeditated

rhythms; they seem comfortable with Dorothy's nature; they reflect her wholehearted acceptance of the experience of living.[1]

The most important thing about the journals is, of course, their naturalness and unliterariness – Dorothy never intended them to be published; they were private documents, intended only for her eyes and those of her brother. And yet it is the same perspective as that of the great poet of *The Prelude*, for here are the same characters, the same village folk, the same sharp observation of the natural world. They are guileless, undeceived, full of compassion and wisdom about the ways of the world. I am indebted in my work on the journals to Pamela Woof's exemplary edition, which contains the most accurate text and most helpful notes of any thus far published.

Some of her poetry was published during her lifetime, mainly alongside her brother's poetry in his collected works. She began writing in about 1805, and seems to have continued writing, very occasionally, until after the onset of dementia in 1829. Her last years were marked by a sad and slow decline; she survived her brother by five years, and was nursed until her death by Mary Wordsworth. A broad range of her verse is presented here, edited from Dorothy's Commonplace Book at Dove Cottage.

Further reading

Beth Darlington, 'Reclaiming Dorothy Wordsworth's Legacy', *The Age of William Wordsworth* ed. Kenneth R. Johnston and Gene W. Ruoff (New Brunswick and London, 1987), pp. 160–72

Susan M. Levin, *Dorothy Wordsworth and Romanticism* (New Brunswick, 1987)

Pamela Woof, *Dorothy Wordsworth, Writer* (Grasmere, 1988)

Dorothy Wordsworth, *Journal of my Second Tour in Scotland, 1822* ed. Jiro Nagasawa (Tokyo, 1989)

—, *The Grasmere Journals* ed. Pamela Woof (Oxford, 1991)

Pamela Woof, 'Dorothy Wordsworth and Mary Lamb, Writers', *Charles Lamb Bulletin* NS 66–7 (1989) 41–53, 82–93

DOROTHY WORDSWORTH
[1]   *Grasmere Journals* ix–x.

From The Grasmere Journals, Wednesday 3 September 1800

Coleridge, William and John[1] went from home to go upon Helvellyn[2] with Mr Simpson. They set out after breakfast. I accompanied them up near the blacksmith's – a fine, coolish morning. I ironed till half past three, now very hot. I then went to a funeral at John Dawson's[3] – about ten men and four women. Bread, cheese and ale; they talked sensibly and cheerfully about common things. The dead person, 56 years of age, buried by the parish; the coffin was neatly lettered and painted black and covered with a decent cloth. They set the corpse down at the door and, while we stood within the threshold, the men with their hats off sang with decent and solemn countenances a verse of a funeral psalm. The corpse was then borne down the hill and they sang till they had got past the Town End.[4]

I was affected to tears while we stood in the house, the coffin lying before me. There were no near kindred, no children. When we got out of the dark house, the sun was shining and the prospect looked so divinely beautiful as I never saw it. It seemed more sacred than I had ever seen it, and yet more allied to human life. The green fields, neighbours of the churchyard, were green as possible and, with the brightness of the sunshine, looked quite gay. I thought she was going to a quiet spot and I could not help weeping very much.

When we came to the bridge, they began to sing again and stopped during four lines before they entered the churchyard. The priest[5] met us – he did not look as a man ought to do on such an occasion (I had seen him half-drunk the day before in a pothouse).[6] Before we came with the corpse one of the company observed he wondered what sort of cue[7] 'our parson would be in'? N.B. It was the day after the fair.[8] I had not finished ironing till 7 o'clock. The wind was now high and I did not walk. Writing my journal now at 8 o'clock. William and John came home at 10 o'clock.

From The Grasmere Journals, Friday 3 October 1800 (extract)[1]

When William and I returned from accompanying Jones, we met an old man almost double. He had on a coat thrown over his shoulders above his waistcoat and coat. Under this he carried a bundle and had an apron on and a nightcap. His face was interesting. He had dark eyes and a long nose (John, who afterwards met him at Wythburn, took him for a Jew). He was of Scotch parents but had been born in the army. He had had a wife, 'and a good woman, and it pleased God to bless us with ten children'; all these were dead but one of whom he had not heard for many years, a sailor. His trade was to gather leeches,[2] but now leeches are scarce and he had not strength for it. He lived by begging and was making his way to Carlisle where he should buy a few godly books to sell. He said leeches were very scarce partly owing to this dry season, but many years they have been scarce. He supposed it owing to their being much sought-after, that they did not breed fast, and were of slow growth. Leeches were formerly 2s. 6d. per 100; they are now 30s. He had been hurt in driving a cart: his leg broke, his body driven over, his skull fractured. He felt no pain till he recovered from his first insensibility;[3] it was then 'late in the evening, when the light was just going away.'

THE GRASMERE JOURNALS, WEDNESDAY 3 SEPTEMBER 1800
[1] John Wordsworth (1773–1805), brother of William and Dorothy, a sea-captain, visited Dove Cottage, January–September 1800.
[2] Helvellyn is a large mountain (3116 ft) that towers above Grasmere.
[3] John Dawson's farm was on the Rydal road at the top of the hill behind Dove Cottage. The funeral was that of a pauper, Susan Shacklock.
[4] *Town End* the small cluster of cottages (including Dove Cottage) just off the main road to Keswick, half a mile from the village of Grasmere.
[5] *The priest* Edward Rowlandson, curate of Grasmere for more than forty years. He was notorious for getting drunk.

[6] *pothouse* ale-house, tavern.
[7] *cue* condition.
[8] *the fair* Grasmere fair is held yearly in the meadows between Town End and the village of Grasmere.

THE GRASMERE JOURNALS, FRIDAY 3 OCTOBER 1800
[1] This entry was written a week after the encounter had taken place; it is a source for Wordsworth's *Resolution and Independence*, composed eighteen months later.
[2] *leeches* blood-letting was the usual method of treating physical ailments such as fevers, and a favoured means of performing this operation was to apply leeches to the patient's skin.
[3] *insensibility* unconsciousness.

From The Grasmere Journals, Thursday 15 April 1802[1]

It was a threatening misty morning, but mild. We set off after dinner from Eusemere; Mrs Clarkson[2] went a short way with us but turned back. The wind was furious and we thought we must have returned. We first rested in the large boathouse, then under a furze-bush opposite Mr Clarkson's; saw the plough going in the field. The wind seized our breath, the lake was rough. There was a boat by itself floating in the middle of the bay below Water Millock; we rested again in the Water Millock lane. The hawthorns are black and green, the birches here and there greenish but there is yet more of purple to be seen on the twigs. We got over into a field to avoid some cows – people working, a few primroses by the roadside, woodsorrel flowers, the anemone, scentless violets, strawberries, and that starry yellow flower which Mrs Clarkson calls pilewort.[3]

When we were in the woods beyond Gowbarrow Park[4] we saw a few daffodils[5] close to the waterside. We fancied that the lake had floated the seeds ashore and that the little colony had so sprung up. But as we went along there were more and yet more, and at last, under the boughs of the trees, we saw that there was a long belt of them along the shore, about the breadth of a country turnpike road. I never saw daffodils so beautiful. They grew among the mossy stones, about and about them; some rested their heads upon these stones as on a pillow for weariness, and the rest tossed and reeled and danced, and seemed as if they verily laughed with the wind that blew upon them over the lake. They looked so gay – ever-glancing, ever-changing. This wind blew directly over the lake to them. There was, here and there, a little knot, and a few stragglers a few yards higher up – but they were so few as not to disturb the simplicity and unity and life of that one busy highway. We rested again and again.

The bays were stormy, and we heard the waves at different distances and in the middle of the water like the sea. Rain came on; we were wet when we reached Luff's but we called in. Luckily all was cheerless and gloomy, so we faced the storm – we *must* have been wet if we had waited; put on dry clothes at Dobson's. I was very kindly treated by a young woman, the landlady looked sour but it is her way. She gave us a goodish supper, excellent ham and potatoes. We paid 7s. when we came away. William was sitting by a bright fire when I came downstairs; he soon made his way to the library piled up in a corner of the window. He brought out a volume of Enfield's *Speaker*,[6] another miscellany, and an odd volume of Congreve's plays. We had a glass of warm rum and water; we enjoyed ourselves and wished for Mary.[7] It rained and blew when we went to bed. N.B. Deer in Gowbarrow Park like to skeletons.

From The Grasmere Journals, Thursday 29 April 1802

A beautiful morning. The sun shone and all was pleasant. We sent off our parcel to Coleridge by the wagon. Mr Simpson heard the cuckoo today. Before we went out, after I had written down 'The Tinker', which William finished this morning, Luff called.[1] He was very lame, limped into the kitchen (he came on a little pony).

We then went to John's Grove,[2] sat a while at first. Afterwards William lay and I lay in the trench under the fence – he with his eyes shut and listening to the waterfalls and the birds. There was no one

THE GRASMERE JOURNALS, THURSDAY 15 APRIL 1802

[1] This entry is a source for Wordsworth's *Daffodils* (p. 383), composed probably two years later when he re-read Dorothy's journal entry.

[2] *Mrs Clarkson* Catherine Clarkson (1772–1856), wife of Thomas Clarkson (1760–1846), agitator for abolition of the slave trade, from about 1785 onwards. After his health collapsed in 1794 he built a house, Eusemere, on Ullswater. Dorothy had been friendly with the Clarksons since meeting them in September 1800.

[3] *pilewort* the lesser celandine.

[4] *beyond Gowbarrow Park* on the western shore of Ullswater, the Park belonged to the Duke of Norfolk.

[5] *daffodils* not the garden daffodils of today but the small, pale, and wild *pseudo-narcissi*.

[6] *Enfield's Speaker* William Enfield, *The Speaker; or Miscellaneous Pieces Selected from the Best English Writers* (1774), popular anthology, frequently reprinted. Dorothy had met Enfield in 1788.

[7] *Mary* i.e. Mary Hutchinson, who would marry William in October (see next page).

THE GRASMERE JOURNALS, THURSDAY 29 APRIL 1802

[1] Capt. Charles Luff (or Lough) (d. 1815). He and his wife Letitia, friends of the Wordsworths, resided in Patterdale but occasionally (as here) lodged in Ambleside.

[2] *John's Grove* formerly a small grove of fir trees almost opposite the Wishing Gate beyond How Top on the old Rydal Road beyond Dove Cottage. The firs had been cut down in 1801.

waterfall above another – it was a sound of waters in the air, the voice of the air. William heard me breathing and rustling now and then, but we both lay still and unseen by one another. He thought that it would be as sweet thus to lie so in the grave, to hear the *peaceful* sounds of the earth and just to know that one's dear friends were near.[3] The lake was still; there was a boat out. Silver How[4] reflected with delicate purple and yellowish hues as I have seen [in] spar.[5] Lambs on the island[6] and running races together by the half-dozen in the round field near us. The copses green*ish*, hawthorn green.

Came home to dinner, then went to Mr Simpson.[7] We rested a long time under a wall. Sheep and lambs were in the field – cottages smoking. As I lay down on the grass, I observed the glittering silver line on the ridges of the backs of the sheep, owing to their situation respecting the sun, which made them look beautiful but with something of strangeness, like animals of another kind – as if belonging to a more splendid world. Met old Mr Simpson at the door; Mrs Simpson poorly. I got mullens[8] and pansies. I was sick and ill and obliged to come home soon. We went to bed immediately – I slept upstairs. The air coldish where it was felt somewhat frosty.

From The Grasmere Journals, 4 October 1802

On Monday 4 October 1802, my brother William was married to Mary Hutchinson.[1] I slept a good deal of the night and rose fresh and well in the morning. At a little after 8 o'clock I saw them go down the avenue towards the church.[2] William had parted from me upstairs. I gave him the wedding ring – with how deep a blessing! I took it from my forefinger where I had worn it the whole of the night before; he slipped it again onto my finger and blessed me fervently.[3]

When they were absent, my dear little Sara[4] prepared the breakfast. I kept myself as quiet as I could, but when I saw the two men[5] running up the walk, coming to tell us it was over, I could stand it no longer and threw myself on the bed where I lay in stillness, neither hearing or seeing anything till Sara came upstairs to me and said, 'They are coming'. This forced me from the bed where I lay, and I moved I knew not how straightforward, faster than my strength could carry me, till I met my beloved William and fell upon his bosom. He and John Hutchinson led me to the house and there I stayed to welcome my dear Mary. As soon as we had breakfasted we departed.[6] It rained when we set off. Poor Mary was much agitated when she parted from her brothers and sisters and her home.

A Cottage in Grasmere Vale (composed *c*.1805, edited from MS)

> Peaceful our valley, fair and green,
> And beautiful her cottages,
> Each in its nook, its sheltered hold,
> Or guarded by its tuft of trees –

[3] These remarks provide a context for '*These chairs they have no thoughts to utter*', composed a week before, pp. 367–8, above. See also 'Ode' 120–3.
[4] *Silver How* mountain on the western side of Grasmere lake, opposite Town End.
[5] *spar* crystalline mineral.
[6] *the island* in the middle of Grasmere lake.
[7] *Mr Simpson* Revd Joseph Simpson of High Broadraine, Grasmere, vicar of the small church at Wythburn. He died on 27 June 1807 at the age of ninety-two.
[8] *mullens* the mullein is a plant with yellow flowers.

THE GRASMERE JOURNALS, 4 OCTOBER 1802
[1] Wordsworth had known Mary Hutchinson since early childhood, when they attended Ann Birkett's dame school together.

[2] Wordsworth was married at All Saints Church, Brompton-by-Sawdon, Yorkshire, a mile or so down the road from Gallow Hill (today called Gallows Hill), where the Hutchinson family resided. Only five people were present at the service: besides the couple, Mary's siblings, Thomas, John, and Joanna.
[3] Pamela Woof comments: 'That Dorothy wore the ring the night before denotes her full acceptance of Mary Hutchinson and the marriage, and that Wordsworth slipped it for a moment back on to her finger was surely a pledge that the marriage would not exclude her' (*Grasmere Journals* 249). The ring may be seen in the Wordsworth Museum, Grasmere.
[4] Sara Hutchinson, Mary's sister.
[5] *the two men* John and Thomas Hutchinson, Mary's brothers, were witnesses.
[6] *we departed* for Dove Cottage.

Many and beautiful they are,   5
But there is *one* that I love best,
A lowly shed in truth it is,
A brother of the rest.

Yet when I sit on rock or hill,
Down looking on the valley fair,   10
That cottage with its clustering trees
Summons my heart – it settles there.

Others there are whose small domain
Of fertile fields and hedgerows green
Might more entice a wanderer's mind   15
To wish that *there* his home had been.

Such wish be his! I blame him not,
My fancy is unfettered, wild!
I love that house because it is
The very mountains' child.   20

Fields hath it of its own, green fields,
But they are craggy, steep and bare;
Their fence is of the mountain stone
And moss and lichen flourish there.

And when the storm comes from the north   25
It lingers near that pastoral spot,
And piping through the mossy walls,
It seems delighted with its lot.

And let it take its own delight,
And let it range the pastures bare;   30
Until it reach that group of trees
It may not enter there.

A green unfading grove it is,
Skirted with many a lesser tree –
Hazel and holly, beech and oak –   35
A bright and flourishing company!

Precious the shelter of those trees,
They screen the cottage that I love;
The sunshine pierces to the roof
And the tall pine-trees tower above.   40

After-recollection at Sight of the Same Cottage (edited from MS)

When first I saw that dear abode
It was a lovely winter's day;[1]
After a night of perilous storm
The west wind ruled with gentle sway –

A day so mild it might have been   5
The first day of the gladsome spring;
The robins warbled, and I heard
One solitary throstle[2] sing.

AFTER-RECOLLECTION AT SIGHT OF THE SAME COTTAGE   [2] *throstle* thrush.
[1] *When first ... day* 20 November 1799, when the
Wordsworths moved into Dove Cottage.

A Winter's Ramble in Grasmere Vale (edited from MS)

A stranger, Grasmere, in thy vale,
All faces then to me unknown,
I left my sole companion-friend[1]
To wander out alone.

Lured by a little winding path,   5
Quickly I left the public road,
A smooth and tempting path it was,
By sheep and shepherds trod.

Eastward, towards the lofty hills
That pathway led me on   10
Until I reached a stately rock
With velvet moss o'ergrown.

With russet oak and tufts of fern
Its top was richly garlanded,
Its sides adorned with eglantine   15
Bedropped with hips of glossy red.

There, too, in many a sheltered chink
The foxglove's broad leaves flourished fair,
And silver birch whose purple twigs
Bend to the softest breathing air.   20

Beneath that rock my course I stayed,
And, looking to its summit high,
'Thou wear'st', said I, 'a splendid garb –
Here winter keeps his revelry.

Full long a dweller on the plains,[2]   25
I grieved when summer days were gone;
No more I'll grieve, for winter here
Hath pleasure-gardens of his own.

What need of flowers? The splendid moss
Is gayer than an April mead –   30
More rich its hues of varied green,
Orange, and gold, and glowing red.'

Beside that gay and lovely rock
There came with merry voice
A foaming streamlet glancing by –   35
It seemed to say, 'Rejoice!'

My youthful wishes all fulfilled,
Wishes matured by thoughtful choice,
I stood an inmate of this vale –
How *could* I but rejoice?   40

A WINTER'S RAMBLE IN GRASMERE VALE
[1] *my sole companion-friend* almost certainly her brother.
[2] *the plains* after their parents' deaths Dorothy was brought up by her uncle William Cookson at Forncett Rectory in Norfolk, 1788–94. Norfolk, a low-lying county, must indeed have seemed flat to someone used to the Lake District.

A Sketch (composed by 1826; edited from MS)

There is one cottage in our dale,
In naught distinguished from the rest,
Save by a tuft of flourishing trees,
The shelter of that little nest.

The public road through Grasmere vale   5
Winds close beside that cottage small,
And there 'tis hidden by the trees
That overhang the orchard wall.

You lose it there – its serpent line
Is lost in that close household grove;   10
A moment lost – and then it mounts
The craggy hills above.

Floating Island at Hawkshead: An Incident in the Schemes of Nature (composed during the 1820s; edited from MS)[1]

Harmonious powers with nature work
On sky, earth, river, lake and sea;
Sunshine and storm, whirlwind and breeze,
All in one duteous task agree.

Once did I see a slip of earth   5
By throbbing waves long undermined,
Loosed from its hold – *how* no one knew,
But all might see it float, obedient to the wind;

Might see it from the verdant shore
Dissevered float upon the lake,   10
Float with its crest of trees adorned
On which the warbling birds their pastime take.

Food, shelter, safety, there they find;
There berries ripen, flowerets bloom;
There insects live their lives and die –   15
A peopled *world* it is, in size a tiny room.

And thus through many seasons' space
This little island may survive,
But nature (though we mark her not)
Will take away, may cease to give.   20

FLOATING ISLAND AT HAWKSHEAD: AN INCIDENT IN THE
SCHEMES OF NATURE
[1]   As Wordsworth mentions in his *Guide through the District
of the Lakes* (1835), 'on one of the pools near the lake of Esth-
waite may sometimes be seen a mossy islet, with trees upon it,
shifting about before the wind' (*Prose Works* ii 184).

Perchance when you are wandering forth
Upon some vacant sunny day
Without an object, hope, or fear,
Thither your eyes may turn – the isle is passed away.

Buried beneath the glittering lake,   25
Its place no longer to be found,
Yet the lost fragments shall remain
To fertilize some other ground.

Thoughts on my Sickbed (composed *c*.1831; edited from MS)[1]

And has the remnant of my life
Been pilfered of this sunny spring?
And have its own prelusive sounds[2]
Touched in my heart no echoing string?

Ah, say not so! The hidden life,   5
Couchant[3] within this feeble frame,
Hath been enriched by kindred gifts
That undesired, unsought-for, came

With joyful heart in youthful days,
When fresh each season in its round   10
I welcomed the earliest celandine
Glittering upon the mossy ground.

With busy eyes I pierced the lane
In quest of known and unknown things;
The primrose a lamp on its fortress rock,   15
The silent butterfly spreading its wings,

The violet betrayed by its noiseless breath,
The daffodil dancing in the breeze,
The carolling thrush on his naked perch,
Towering above the budding trees.   20

Our cottage-hearth no longer our home,
Companions of nature were we;
The stirring, the still, the loquacious, the mute –
To all we gave our sympathy.

Yet never in those careless days   25
When springtime in rock, field, or bower
Was but a fountain of earthly hope
A promise of fruits and the *splendid* flower –

THOUGHTS ON MY SICKBED
[1] In 1829 Dorothy developed a serious illness, apparently pre-
senile dementia, from which she never fully recovered. From
1830 to 1835 she experienced shorter and shorter remissions
until being permanently debilitated.

[2] *its own prelusive sounds* i.e. sounds that herald the spring,
such as birdsong, etc.
[3] *Couchant* lying.

No! – then I never felt a bliss
That might with *that* compare,   30
Which, piercing to my couch of rest,
Came on the vernal air.

When loving friends an offering brought,
The first flowers of the year,
Culled from the precincts of our home,   35
From nooks to memory dear,

With some sad thoughts the work was done,
Unprompted and unbidden,
But joy it brought to my *hidden* life,
To consciousness no longer hidden.   40

I felt a power unfelt before,
Controlling weakness, languor, pain;
It bore me to the terrace-walk,[4]
I trod the hills again.

No prisoner in this lonely room,   45
I *saw* the green banks of the Wye,[5]
Recalling thy prophetic words –
Bard, brother, friend from infancy!

No need of motion or of strength
Or even the breathing air,   50
I thought of nature's loveliest scenes,
And with memory I was there.

[*When shall I tread your garden path*] (composed 11 November 1835; edited from MS)

When shall I tread your garden path
Or climb your sheltering hill?
When shall I wander, free as air,
And track the foaming rill?

A prisoner on my pillowed couch,   5
Five years in feebleness I've lain –
Oh shall I e'er with vigorous step
Travel the hills again?

---

[4]   *the terrace-walk* at Rydal Mount, where the Wordsworths lived at this time, there was a terrace leading from the house along the side of the mountain overlooking Rydal Water and Windermere. It can still be seen today.

[5]   *I saw ... Wye* Dorothy visited the Wye valley with her brother in July 1798; she is addressed in *Tintern Abbey* (pp. 265–9).

'Charlotte Dacre' (Charlotte Byrne, *née* King) (?1771/2–1825)

'Rosa Matilda' was 'one of the most licentious writers of romance of the time',[1] her books devoured eagerly in their thousands by the reading and borrowing public in the first two decades of the nineteenth century; as 'Charlotte Dacre' she was the author of some of the most forthright, impressive love lyrics of the day – but she began life as Charlotte King. She and her sister Sophia were daughters of the money-lender,[2] blackmailer, and radical writer Jonathan King (aka Jacob Rey), and his wife Deborah Lara. King was notorious as a wife-beater and adulterer, his amours including Mary Robinson. The divorce of their parents in 1785, by Jewish law, was no doubt a traumatic experience for Charlotte and Sophia; all the same, their father was the dedicatee of the first volume the two girls published together, *Trifles of Helicon* (1798), a collection of sentimental and gothic poems.

Charlotte's most important volume of poems was *Hours of Solitude* (1805). It was dedicated to John Penn, the politician and poet (1760–1834) ('the patron of literature, and the friend of mankind', as the Preface puts it), and begins with an engraved portrait of Charlotte, entitled 'Rosa Matilda' (the name of the demon lover in M. G. Lewis's successful gothic novel, *The Monk*). This was the name by which she was best known, although the title-page offers another pseudonym: *Hours of Solitude. A Collection of Original Poems, now First Published. By Charlotte Dacre, Better Known by the Name of Rosa Matilda*. It was as Charlotte Dacre that she would publish most of her novels and become best known in the literary world; for many years it was believed to be her real name. The volume itself is varied. Some of the poems are early work, reprinted from *Trifles of Helicon*; others are exercises in skin-crawling gothicry, not unlike some of those in her sister's volume the year before[3] – *The Skeleton Priest; or, the Marriage of Death* and *Julia's Murder; or, the Song of Woe*, for instance. But it would be a mistake to dismiss all of the gothic verses. *The Mistress to the Spirit of her Lover* appears once as a piece of Ossianic prose, and then as a curiously haunting poem, which Adriana Craciun has

discussed, usefully, 'in the demon lover tradition in which a woman is haunted by her lover'.[4] The best poems in the volume are, in fact, love poems. Charlotte wrote persuasively, and forthrightly, about the psychology of love. It was evidently something she understood, and perhaps only Lady Caroline Lamb could rival her for conviction and persuasiveness.

In 1805 Charlotte embarked on a career as one of the most popular gothic novelists of the day, first with *The Confessions of the Nun of St Omer* (1805), dedicated to M. G. Lewis, and then the popular *Zofloya; or The Moor* (1806), an outrageous fifteenth-century tale about illicit love in the Apennines. It was in this context that she was best-known to her contemporaries: Shelley read the novel at Eton, and it was a strong influence on his *Zastrozzi* (1811), and Byron alludes to her in *English Bards and Scotch Reviewers* (1808):

> Far be't from me unkindly to upbraid
> The lovely Rosa's prose in masquerade,
> Whose strains, the faithful echoes of her mind,
> Leave wondering comprehension far behind.[5]

He added a note to these lines, which reveals that he had seen *Hours of Solitude*: 'This lovely little Jessica, the daughter of the noted Jew K[ing],[6] seems to be a follower of the Della Cruscan School, and has published two volumes of very respectable absurdities in rhyme, as times go; besides many novels in the style of the first edition of *The Monk*'.[7]

There were more novels to come. *The Libertine* went through three editions in the year of its publication, 1807, and she published another fiction, *The Passions*, in 1811. There was a final volume of poetry, *George the Fourth, a Poem . . . To Which are Added Lyrics Designed for Various Melodies* in 1822.

Charlotte's private life was, apparently, eventful. She had three children, William, Charles and Mary, in 1806, 1807 and 1809, who were baptized in June 1811 at St Paul's, Covent Garden. Her partner at this time was Nicholas Byrne, editor of the *Morning Post*

CHARLOTTE DACRE

[1] Cited Ann H. Jones, *Ideas and Innovations: Best Sellers of Jane Austen's Age* (New York, 1986), p. 224.

[2] King lent money to Percy Bysshe Shelley, among others (Jones i 478).

[3] Sophia published a volume of poems about mad people, distressed lovers and the like in 1804, *Poems, Legendary, Pathetic and Descriptive*. By this time she was well known as the author of such gothic novels as *The Fatal Secret* (1801).

[4] '"I hasten to be disembodied": Charlotte Dacre, the Demon Lover, and Representations of the Body', *ERR* 6 (1995) 75–97, p. 76.

[5] Lines 755–8.

[6] The 'Jew King' was one of Jonathan King's soubriquets; Shelley referred to him in this way in a letter of 24 June 1816 (Jones i 478).

[7] *The Complete Poetical Works* ed. Jerome J. McGann and Barry Weller (7 vols, Oxford, 1980–93), i 413.

from 1803–33, who was still married. After the death of his wife Louisa they married at St James, Westminster, 1 July 1815. Charlotte died on 7 November 1825, 'after a long and painful illness', according to *The Times* (9 November 1825). A fuller selection of her poetry is included in my *Romantic Women Poets: An Anthology* (1997).

Further reading

Ann H. Jones, *Ideas and Innovations: Best Sellers of Jane Austen's Age* (New York, 1986)

Adriana Craciun, ' "I hasten to be disembodied": Charlotte Dacre, the Demon Lover, and Representations of the Body', *ERR* 6 (1995) 75–97

Charlotte Dacre, *Zofloya* ed. Adriana Craciun (Peterborough, Ontario, 1997)

Il Trionfo del Amor

From HOURS OF SOLITUDE (1805)

So full my thoughts are of thee, that I swear
   All else is hateful to my troubled soul;
   How thou hast o'er me gained such vast control,
   How charmed my stubborn spirit, is most rare!
Sure thou hast mingled philtres[1] in my bowl,   5
   Or what thine high enchanted arts declare
   Fearless of blame – for truth I will not care
   (So charms the witchery), whether fair or foul.
Yet well my lovesick mind thine arts can tell;
   No magic potions gav'st thou, save what I   10
   Drank from those lustrous eyes when they did dwell
   With dying fondness on me – or thy sigh
Which sent its perfumed poison to my brain.
   Thus known thy spells, thou bland seducer, see –
   Come practise them again, and oh! again;   15
Spellbound I *am*, and spellbound *wish* to be.

To Him Who Says He Loves

From HOURS OF SOLITUDE (1805)

You tell me that you truly love;
   Ah! know you well what love does mean?
Does neither whim nor fancy move
   The rapture of your transient dream?

Tell me, when absent do you think   5
   O'er ev'ry look and ev'ry sigh?
Do you in melancholy sink,
   And hope and doubt you know not why?

When present, do you die to say
   How much you love, yet fear to tell?   10
Does her breath melt your soul away?
   A touch, your nerves with transport swell?

IL TRIONFO DEL AMOR
[1] *philtres* magic potions.

Or do you faint with sweet excess
  Of pleasure rising into pain,
When hoping you may e'er possess   15
  The object you aspire to gain?

The charms of every other fair
  With coldness could you learn to view?
Fondly unchanged to her repair,
  With transports ever young and new?   20

Could you for her, fame, wealth despise?
  In poverty and toil feel blessed?
Drink sweet delusion from her eyes
  Or smile at ruin on her breast?

And tell me, at her loss or hate,   25
  Would death your only refuge prove?
Ah! if in aught you hesitate –
  Coward! you dare not say you love.

Mary Tighe (*née* Blachford)   (1772–1810)

Mary Tighe (pronounced 'Tie') was born in Dublin on 9 October 1772, the daughter of the Methodist leader Theodosia Tighe and the Revd William Blachford, a clergyman and landowner who was librarian of Marsh's Library and St Patrick's Library in Dublin. Theodosia was self-educated, as governesses were out of fashion during her childhood. Her husband died early, in May 1773, and, as a keen believer in a liberal education for women, she devoted herself to educating both her daughter and Mary's brother, John. Theodosia herself took responsibility for Mary's strict religious education (she herself was a Wesleyan, and founded the House of Refuge for Unprotected Female Servants in Dublin).

In 1793 Mary married her first cousin Henry Tighe, of Woodstock, County Wicklow, who represented the borough of Inistioge, Kilkenny, in the Irish Parliament. She did not love him, and never would. The marriage was unhappy, and they had no children.

Henry had a yearly allowance of £1,000. As this was thought inadequate, the newly-married couple went to London, where he was to read for the bar. But he lacked the application and settled into an unproductive life, mingling with other uncommitted trainee lawyers, most of whom flocked to the Tighes' house so as to dally with his beautiful wife. Mary spent her mornings studying Latin, sometimes with her hus-

band, which was to prove highly useful in her poetry.

In 1801 the Tighes returned to Ireland, and it was here that Mary composed *Psyche*. Contrary to her *DNB* entry, there was no 1795 edition of the poem; it was completed only in 1803. At the same time that she composed *Psyche*, Mary also wrote a novel, *Selena*, which was never published, the manuscript of which is now at the National Library of Ireland. Partly autobiographical, it concerns a heroine, Selena, tricked by parental manoeuvring into marrying her first cousin with whom she is not in love. From 1802 onwards *Psyche* – or parts of it – were circulating in manuscript. One of its earliest readers was Thomas Moore, who was inspired by it to compose his 1802 lyric, *To Mrs Henry Tighe on Reading her 'Psyche'*. Mary's poem was privately published in a limited edition of fifty copies in 1805, by which time she had contracted the consumption that was to kill her. Her health took a serious turn for the worse in 1804. Her final years were spent at Dublin and Rosanna, County Wicklow. Her final poem, *On Receiving a branch of Mezereon which flowered at Woodstock, December 1809*, was written months before her death at Woodstock, 24 March 1810. Countess de Charleville told Sydney Owenson that Mary had been 'the first genius of her day'.[1] In future years her grave

MARY TIGHE
[1] Sydney Owenson, Lady Morgan's Memoirs: Autobiography, Diaries, and Correspondence (2 vols, London, 1862), i 384.

would be visited by many admirers of her poetry; before going there, Felicia Hemans composed a poem about Mary, *The Grave of a Poetess* (see pp. 997–8).

Psyche was given wider circulation after her death, when it was published with other poems in 1811, edited by her cousin and brother-in-law, William Tighe. Profits went to Theodosia's House of Refuge. In the same year William published *Mary, a Series of Reflections During Twenty Years*, a privately printed series of facsimiles of poems by Mary copied out in his hand.

The 1811 edition of *Psyche* was an immediate success, and had entered a fourth edition within the year. One of its readers was Keats, who enjoyed its subdued eroticism,[2] and it seems to have influenced Shelley as well. But *Psyche* is an extraordinary poem in its own right, irrespective of its influence on other writers. Its primary source is the story of Psyche as told by Apuleius. According to him, Psyche's beauty was so great that she distracted from the worship of Venus. Venus arranged for Cupid to make Psyche fall in love with 'some base wretch to foul disgrace allied'.[3] Her lover (Cupid himself) promised that she would give birth to 'an immortal boy'[4] so long as she did not look at him or seek to discover his identity. Out of jealousy, her sisters persuade her that she is in fact sleeping with a monster, and urge her to kill him. With a lamp and a knife close by, she discovers her lover to be Cupid. He is scared away when she drops the lamp and deserts her. At this point in Apuleius Psyche is scolded by Venus and given a series of hard and worthless labours, such as sorting grain, that ultimately cause her death.

But Mary sends her heroine off on an allegorical journey in which she is tested by encounters with such personages as Vanity, Flattery (Canto III), Credulity, Jealousy (Canto IV), and Indifference (Canto VI), before being reunited with Love. It is a kind of latter-day odyssey (making, incidentally, a number of references to that of Ulysses), which aims to value love as a romantic ideal. Despite the allegorical framework, there is nothing abstract about this; it is a genuinely moving work. Furthermore, Mary's handling of the Spenserian stanza is expert: the poetry is carried effortlessly by strong, fluent rhythms, and a language and a style that is plainer, and in some ways more engaging, than Spenser's. *Psyche* is one of the great love poems in the language; a complete text is included in my *Romantic Women Poets: An Anthology* (Oxford, 1997).

Further reading

Keats and Mary Tighe: The Poems of Mary Tighe, with Parallel Passages from the Work of John Keats ed. Earle Vonard Weller (New York, 1928)

Marlon B. Ross, *The Contours of Masculine Desire: Romanticism and the Rise of Women's Poetry* (New York, 1989), pp. 153–67

Mary Tighe, *Psyche 1811* introduced by Jonathan Wordsworth (Spelsbury, 1992)

Greg Kucich, 'Gender Crossings: Keats and Tighe', *Keats-Shelley Journal* 44 (1995) 29–39

Harriet Kramer Linkin, 'Romanticism and Mary Tighe's *Psyche*: Peering at the Hem of Her Blue Stockings', *SIR* 35 (1996) 55–72

Psyche; or The Legend of Love

From PSYCHE, WITH OTHER POEMS (3RD EDN, 1811) (FROM CANTO ONE)[1]

> Here Cupid tempers his unerring darts
> And in the fount of bliss delights to play;   200
> Here mingles balmy sighs and pleasing smarts,
> And here the honeyed draught will oft allay[2]
> With that black poison's all-polluting sway,
> For wretched man. Hither, as Venus willed,
> For Psyche's punishment he bent his way;   205
> From either stream his amber vase he filled,
> For her were meant the drops which grief alone distilled.

---

[2] Numerous echoes of Tighe are noted by Earle Vonard Weller in *Keats and Mary Tighe: The Poems of Mary Tighe with Parallel Passages from the work of John Keats* (New York, 1928). The more persuasive of these are included in my footnotes, below.

[3] *Psyche* i 124.

[4] Ibid., i 560.

PSYCHE; OR THE LEGEND OF LOVE

[1] The extract comes from the beginning of *Psyche*. Jealous of Psyche's superior beauty, Cytherea has sent Cupid to make her fall in love with 'some base wretch to foul disgrace allied'. Cupid finds Psyche sleeping in Pleasure's garden, where two fountains are playing – one the fountain of jealousy and shame, the other of desire and pleasure.

[2] *allay* mix.

His quiver, sparkling bright with gems and gold,
From his fair-plumed shoulder graceful hung,
And from its top in brilliant chords enrolled   210
Each little vase resplendently was slung.
Still as he flew, around him sportive clung
His frolic train of winged zephyrs light,
Wafting the fragrance which his tresses flung,
While odours dropped from every ringlet bright,   215
And from his blue eyes beamed ineffable delight.

Wrapped in a cloud unseen by mortal eye[3]
He sought the chamber of the royal maid;
There, lulled by careless soft security,
Of the impending mischief nought afraid,   220
Upon her purple couch was Psyche laid,
Her radiant eyes a downy slumber sealed;
In light transparent veil alone arrayed,
Her bosom's opening charms were half-revealed,
And scarce the lucid folds her polished limbs concealed.   225

A placid smile plays o'er each roseate lip:
Sweet severed lips, why thus your pearls disclose
That, slumbering thus, unconscious she may sip
The cruel presage of her future woes?
Lightly, as fall the dews upon the rose,   230
Upon the coral gates of that sweet cell[4]
The fatal drops he pours – nor yet he knows,
Nor, though a god, can he presaging tell
How he himself shall mourn the ills of that sad spell!

Nor yet content, he from his quiver drew,   235
Sharpened with skill divine, a shining dart;
No need had he for bow, since thus too true
His hand might wound her all exposed heart;
Yet her fair side he touched with gentlest art,
And half relenting on her beauties gazed: 240
Just then awaking with a sudden start
Her opening eye in humid lustre blazed –
Unseen he still remained, enchanted and amazed.

The dart which in his hand now trembling stood
As o'er the couch he bent with ravished eye,   245
Drew with its daring point celestial blood
From his smooth neck's unblemished ivory.
Heedless of this, but with a pitying sigh
The evil done now anxious to repair,
He shed in haste the balmy drops of joy   250
O'er all the silky ringlets of her hair,
Then stretched his plumes divine, and breathed celestial air.

---

[3] *unseen by mortal eye* Cf. the sylphs in Pope's *The Rape of the Lock* ii 61, 'too fine for mortal sight'.

[4] *the coral gates ... cell* i.e. her lips, the 'cell' being her mouth.

Unhappy Psyche! Soon the latent wound
The fading roses of her cheek confess;
Her eyes' bright beams, in swimming sorrows drowned,   255
Sparkle no more with life and happiness,
Her parents' fond exulting heart to bless;
She shuns adoring crowds, and seeks to hide
The pining sorrows which her soul oppress,
Till to her mother's tears no more denied,   260
The secret grief she owns, for which she lingering sighed.

A dream of mingled terror and delight
Still heavy hangs upon her troubled soul;
An angry form still swims before her sight,
And still the vengeful thunders seem to roll;   265
Still crushed to earth she feels the stern control
Of Venus unrelenting, unappeased.
The dream returns, she feels the fancied dole;[5]
Once more the furies on her heart have seized,
But still she views the youth who all her sufferings eased.   270

Of wondrous beauty did the vision seem,
And in the freshest prime of youthful years;
Such at the close of her distressful dream
A graceful champion to her eyes appears;
Her loved deliverer from her foes and fears   275
She seems in grateful transport still to press;
Still his soft voice sounds in her ravished ears;
Dissolved in fondest tears of tenderness
His form she oft invokes her waking eyes to bless.

Nor was it quite a dream,[6] for as she woke   280
Ere heavenly mists concealed him from her eye,
One sudden transitory view she took
Of Love's most radiant bright divinity;
From the fair image never can she fly,
As still consumed with vain desire she pines,   285
While her fond parents heave the anxious sigh,
And to avert her fate seek holy shrines,
The threatened ills to learn by auguries and signs.

---

5   *dole* grief, distress.
6   *Nor was it quite a dream* this episode would have had an obvious importance for Keats, who reworks the episode of 'dreaming' a lover into reality in *The Eve of St Agnes*, and who describes the imagination as being like Adam's dream: 'He awoke and found it truth' (p. 1018).

Samuel Taylor Coleridge (1772–1834)

Coleridge was the tenth and last child of John Coleridge, the vicar of the village of Ottery St Mary and headmaster of the local grammar school. Although he died when his son was only eight, John Coleridge had by then filled him with an unquenchable love of ideas and books (see Coleridge's letter to Poole, p. 462). Shortly after his death, Coleridge was sent to Christ's Hospital in the City of London, where he was to meet his lifelong friend, Charles Lamb (see *This Lime-Tree Bower My Prison* and headnote to Lamb, pp. 577–8). A more precocious classicist than Wordsworth, Coleridge benefited enormously from an excellent education in Latin and Greek, although the techniques used to impart such skills were, by modern standards, brutal.[1]

Coleridge had a turbulent time at Jesus College, Cambridge, where he matriculated in 1791 at the age of nineteen. It was here that he began to espouse republicanism and became interested in the brand of Unitarianism promoted by the theologian and scientist, Joseph Priestley (the discoverer of oxygen, among other things). He was a fervent supporter of William Frend, whose *Peace and Union* (1793), a pamphlet advocating parliamentary reform and increased suffrage, led to its author's expulsion from the University of Cambridge. In the midst of this, Coleridge ran away and joined the King's Light Dragoons under the name of Silas Tomkyn Comberbache (S.T.C.). Thanks to the efforts of his brother George, he was discharged from the army and returned to the university in April 1794. It was at around this time Coleridge met Robert Southey, at that time an undergraduate at Oxford. Together they planned a 'pantisocracy' – a sort of commune on the banks of the Susquehanna in America. The first step was marriage, and they found their prospective wives in two sisters – Edith and Sara Fricker. Although the pantisocratic scheme fell through, and Coleridge quarrelled with Southey, he nonetheless married Sara on 4 October 1795, something he would later regret. She features in a number of poems – notably *The Eolian Harp, Reflections on Having Left a Place of Retirement*, and *This Lime-Tree Bower My Prison* (see pp. 451–3, 453–5, 457–9).

The mid-1790s were a period of frenetic activity. Coleridge delivered lectures espousing his distinctive philosophical and religious notions in Bristol in 1795, and founded and largely wrote his own periodical, *The Watchman*, in 1796. A cornerstone of his beliefs at this period was that the millennium – Christ's thousand-year rule on earth – was nigh, and that it was presaged by the French Revolution; as he puts it in the final line of *Reflections on Having Left a Place of Retirement*: 'Speed it, oh Father! Let thy Kingdom come!' Humanity would not be able to resist these redemptive forces, and all would be united in a common apprehension of good – notions he expounded in *Religious Musings* (see pp. 455–6).

The intense period of association with Wordsworth began in July 1797 when Coleridge brought him and his sister, Dorothy, from Dorset, and settled them in Alfoxden House in Somerset, a few miles down the road from his cottage in Nether Stowey (see pp. 457–8). Wordsworth's influence may be seen immediately in *This Lime-Tree Bower My Prison*, which contains an element new to Coleridge's writing: a Wordsworthian belief in the morally-improving powers of love of nature. This is developed in *Frost at Midnight*, which confers the Wordsworthian childhood Coleridge did not have on his infant son Hartley; it also reworks Cowper's more effacing and tentative vision of nature from *The Task* (see pp. 11–12). Although it was an exhilarating period in his life, the *annus mirabilis* of 1797–8 was also somewhat uncertain. He lived on very little, and had a growing family to support. In December 1797 the Wedgwood brothers, famous for their pottery, sent him a gift of £100, but Coleridge returned it in January saying that he needed a secure income. Instead, he took up the post of a Unitarian minister and travelled to Shrewsbury, where he delivered a sermon on 14 January. Here he met the young William Hazlitt, who describes their first meeting in his important essay, 'On my First Acquaintance with Poets' (pp. 600–10). This would have brought the *annus mirabilis* and the close working relationship with Wordsworth to a premature end had it not been for the Wedgwoods; Coleridge had spent the night with the Hazlitts at Wem, and the next morning, on 15 January, he received a letter from the Wedgwoods offering him £150 a year for life so as to devote himself to poetry and philosophy. Two days later Coleridge wrote to accept the offer, and returned to Stowey, via the Wedgwoods, in early February.

The *annus mirabilis* saw the composition of (or the beginning of work on) Coleridge's most important poems: *The Ancient Mariner, Kubla Khan* and *Christabel*. *The Ancient Mariner* is presented here in both the 1798 version (published in *Lyrical Ballads* (1798), see pp. 192–209), and that of 1817 – the first to introduce the

---

SAMUEL TAYLOR COLERIDGE
[1] His teacher, the Revd James Boyer (or Bowyer) was an enthusiastic flogger; see Rosemary Ashton, *The Life of Samuel Taylor Coleridge* (1996), pp. 20–1.

marginal glosses which serve as both a commentary and counterpoint to the narrative (see pp. 528–44). The Mariner's tale is essentially one of continuing damnation, apparently unrelieved even by the blessing of the water-snakes. *Kubla Khan* appears here in both the manuscript text and that published in 1816, with Coleridge's Preface (pp. 461–2, 523–4). Like Eden, Kubla's idyll is not without its flaws: the ancestral voices prophesying war presumably speak from deep within the human psyche. *Christabel* was complete by 1801, and was to have been published in the second edition of *Lyrical Ballads*, but Wordsworth and Coleridge seemed to have decided not to include it and for years it circulated in manuscript. It was published with *Kubla Khan* and *The Pains of Sleep* in 1816 thanks largely to Byron, who encouraged his own publisher, John Murray, to put it into print. Christabel is an ambiguous figure, and critics have argued both that she is an innocent and that she is complicit in what happens to her. It can be no accident that the poem's protagonist has a name which brings together those of two suffering innocents from the Bible (Christ/Abel). What is clear is that Geraldine passes onto Christabel some of her serpentine qualities, and that the power of the poem depends in some measure on our understanding that Geraldine was once the comparative innocent that Christabel is at the beginning, and that the passing on of her 'shame' and 'sorrow' is part of a necessary process.

Curiously, the most important product of the *annus mirabilis* of 1797–8 was a poem that neither Coleridge nor Wordsworth actually wrote: *The Recluse*. For some time Coleridge had wanted to write an epic poem about man, nature, and society, entitled *The Brook*. Its central themes had been outlined in *Religious Musings* (1794–6), but Coleridge was interested in writing a much more ambitious work that would play its part in precipitating the millennium. When he met Wordsworth he realized he had met the only person capable of writing such a work. Many of its ideas – such as its reworking of the idealist philosophy of Berkeley and the associationist thought of Hartley – went straight into Wordsworth's poems; but the main result of all this is that Wordsworth resolved to write the great millennial epic of the day. He composed a number of passages intended for it immediately: *The Pedlar*, 'Not useless do I deem', and *The Discharged Soldier* (*The Ruined Cottage* was revised with it in mind). But the tragedy of Wordsworth's career was that he would never be able to complete it. He hoped, when he published *The Excursion* (1814), that it would stand as part of *The Recluse*, but Coleridge was disappointed with it, and his letter to Wordsworth of 1815 explicates the mind-boggling ambitions of *The Recluse* – which suggest that no human being could have written a poem so grandiose in its scale and content (pp. 519–21).

Dejection: An Ode is the last of Coleridge's great so-called 'conversation' poems, and is presented here in three versions: (i) the manuscript *Letter to Sara Hutchinson* (pp. 495–504); (ii) the *Morning Post* text of 1802 (pp. 507–11); and (iii) the *Sibylline Leaves* text of 1817 (pp. 544–8). By the time he composed the first of these, Coleridge was at odds with his wife, and hopelessly in love with Sara Hutchinson (the sister of Wordsworth's wife, Mary). He had begun to despair of his ability to write poetry or even to achieve a fraction of the tasks he had set himself – a state not helped by increasingly fragile health aggravated by opium addiction. Its composition was probably a response to the first four stanzas of Wordsworth's *Ode*, composed between late March and early April 1802 (pp. 375–6). Coleridge distressed both Wordsworths with a reading of the 'Letter to Sara Hutchinson' on 21 April, and, apparently in response, Wordsworth went on to compose *Resolution and Independence* (pp. 368–72). The formal publication of *Dejection: An Ode* in the *Morning Post* was a sort of gift from Coleridge to Wordsworth, as it was published on the latter's wedding-day. This was apparently a period of strain between them, as is suggested by Coleridge's *Spots in the Sun* (p. 511) and Wordsworth's *A Complaint* (pp. 407–8).

To William Wordsworth, edited here from the earliest complete manuscript, is Coleridge's immediate response to the *Thirteen-Book Prelude* which he heard its author recite in January 1807. Like Wordsworth, Coleridge was an inveterate reviser of his poetry, and new texts of most of his major poems continued to appear until his death in 1834. But it seems likely that his faith in Wordsworth's ability to compose *The Recluse* (the philosophical epic poem that would herald the millennium), as well as Wordsworth's underrating of his work (exemplified by the last-minute exclusion of *Christabel* from the second edition of *Lyrical Ballads*) led to a drastic loss of confidence in his poetic abilities.

Coleridge fell out with Wordsworth in 1810; there had been strains between them for years, but they would no doubt have remained friends had it not been for the unnecessary indiscretion of a mutual friend, Basil Montagu. While having an argument with Coleridge in London, Montagu falsely claimed that Wordsworth had asked him to say that Coleridge had been a complete nuisance to his family because he was a 'rotten drunkard'. True or not, the remark stung, and Wordsworth's high-minded refusal to write to Coleridge, even when Montagu himself had reported events to him, did not improve matters. Wordsworth visited London in 1812 to effect a reconciliation with his old friend, but despite the intercession of several mutual acquaintances, frequent meetings in London, and a tour of the continent together in 1822, their old comradeship was forever lost.

In his later years Coleridge was famous as a conversationalist – or rather, as a talker (see Hazlitt's comments on him, pp. 611–17), and this, combined with the effects of his addiction to opium, led to him being regarded as someone whose promise far outweighed his achievements; in fact, only in the late twentieth century, with the continuing publication of his notebooks, letters and marginalia, and of the multi-volume Collected Coleridge series, has the true extent of his accomplishment become recognized. Only now do we have reliable texts of such works as the 'Lectures on the Drama' (May and June 1812); lectures on Milton and Cervantes (April 1814); *The Statesman's Manual* (1816); *Biographia Literaria* (1817); lectures on Shakespeare, Milton, Dante, Spenser, Ariosto, and Cervantes (1819); lectures on philosophy (1818–19); *Aids to Reflection* (1825); and *On the Constitution of Church and State* (1829). Coleridge's great prose work, the *Opus Maximum*, is still, at the time of writing, unpublished.

It should be noted that Coleridge's poems appear both here and under *Lyrical Ballads*, pp. 189–269, above. I have taken the view that early and late versions of the poems effectively constitute separate works, and for that reason have presented different texts in their appropriate chronological position; hence the appearance here of two versions of *The Eolian Harp* (pp. 451–3, 549–50), *This Lime-Tree Bower My Prison* (pp. 458–9, 551–3), *Kubla Khan* (pp. 461–2, 523–4), *Frost at Midnight* (pp. 462–5, 553–5), *The Ancient Mariner* (pp. 192–209, 528–44), *The Pains of Sleep* (pp. 512–13, 524–5), and, as already noted above, the *Letter to Sara Hutchinson* and two versions of *Dejection: An Ode*.

Further reading

The Collected Works of Samuel Taylor Coleridge is Bollingen Series LXXV, published by Princeton University Press and Routledge.

Joseph Cottle, *Reminiscences of Samuel Taylor Coleridge and Robert Southey* (London, 1847)

Stephen Potter, *Coleridge and S.T.C.* (London, 1935)

George Whalley, *Coleridge and Sara Hutchinson and the Asra Poems* (London, 1955)

John Beer, *Coleridge the Visionary* (London, 1959)

J. A. Appleyard, S.J., *Coleridge's Philosophy of Literature: The Development of a Concept of Poetry 1791–1819* (Cambridge, Mass., 1965)

Walter Jackson Bate, *Coleridge* (London, 1968)

J. R. de J. Jackson, *Method and Imagination in Coleridge's Criticism* (London, 1969)

Thomas McFarland, *Coleridge and the Pantheist Tradition* (Oxford, 1969)

Basil Willey, *Samuel Taylor Coleridge* (London, 1972)

Coleridge: The Ancient Mariner and Other Poems ed. Alun R. Jones and William Tydeman (London, 1973)

Coleridge's Variety: Bicentenary Studies ed. John Beer (London, 1974)

Kathleen Coburn, *The Self Conscious Imagination* (London, 1974)

Molly Lefebure, *Samuel Taylor Coleridge: A Bondage of Opium* (London, 1974)

John Beer, *Coleridge's Poetic Intelligence* (London, 1977)

John Livingston Lowes, *The Road to Xanadu: A Study in the ways of the Imagination* (London, 1978)

Richard Holmes, *Coleridge: Early Visions* (London, 1982)

George Whalley, 'The Mariner and the Albatross', *Studies in Literature and the Humanities: Innocence of Intent* (Basingstoke, 1985), pp. 15–34

Jonathan Wordsworth, ' "The Infinite I AM": Coleridge and the Ascent of Being', *Coleridge's Imagination* ed. Richard Gravil, Lucy Newlyn, and Nicholas Roe (Cambridge, 1985), pp. 22–52

Nicholas Roe, *Wordsworth and Coleridge: The Radical Years* (Oxford, 1988)

Ian Wylie, *Young Coleridge and the Philosophers of Nature* (Oxford, 1989)

Jerome J. McGann, 'The Meaning of the Ancient Mariner', *Spirits of Fire: English Romantic Writers and Contemporary Historical Methods* ed. G. A. Rosso and Daniel P. Watkins (London and Toronto, 1990), pp. 208–39

Samuel Taylor Coleridge: Poems ed. John Beer (2nd edn, London, 1993)

Critical Essays on Samuel Taylor Coleridge ed. Leonard Orr (New York, 1994)

Vincent Newey, 'Indeterminacy of Meaning in "The Ancient Mariner" ', *Centring the Self* (Aldershot, 1995), pp. 87–96

Rosemary Ashton, *The Life of Samuel Taylor Coleridge: A Critical Biography* (Oxford, 1996)

Seamus Perry, 'The Ancient Mariner Controversy', *Charles Lamb Bulletin* NS 92 (1995) 208–23

A journal dedicated to Coleridge, *The Coleridge Bulletin*, is published twice-yearly by the Friends of Coleridge.

Sonnet V. To the River Otter[1] (composed *c.*1793)

From SONNETS FROM VARIOUS AUTHORS (1796)[2]

Dear native brook, wild streamlet of the west![3]
   How many various-fated years have passed,
   What blissful and what anguished hours, since last
I skimmed the smooth thin stone along thy breast,
   Numbering its light leaps! Yet so deep impressed   5
   Sink the sweet scenes of childhood, that mine eyes
I never shut amid the sunny blaze,
   But straight with all their tints thy waters rise,
Thy crossing plank, thy margin's willowy maze,
   And bedded sand that, veined with various dyes,   10
Gleamed through thy bright transparence to the gaze!
   Visions of childhood, oft have ye beguiled
Lone manhood's cares, yet waking fondest sighs –
Ah, that once more I were a careless child!

Letter from S. T. Coleridge to George Dyer,[1] 10 March 1795 (extract)

There is one sentence in your last letter which affected me greatly: 'I feel a degree of languor, etc. etc., and, by seeing and frequently feeling much illiberality, acquire something of misanthropy'! It is melancholy to think that the best of us are liable to be shaped and coloured by surrounding objects – and a demonstrative proof that man was not made to live in great cities![2] Almost all the physical evil in the world depends on the existence of moral evil, and the long-continued contemplation of the latter does not tend to meliorate[3] the human heart. The pleasures which we receive from rural beauties are of little consequence compared with the moral effect of these pleasures;[4] beholding constantly the best possible, we at last become ourselves the best possible. In the country, all around us smile good and beauty, and the images of this divine καλοκἀγαθοῦ[5] are miniatured on the mind of the beholder as a landscape on a convex mirror.[6] Thomson,[7] in that most lovely poem, *The Castle of Indolence*, says,

    I care not, Fortune, what you me deny –
    You cannot rob me of free nature's grace!

SONNET V. TO THE RIVER OTTER
[1] Coleridge was born at Ottery St Mary in Devon on the River Otter.
[2] In 1796 Coleridge published a short pamphlet of sonnets by himself, Charlotte Smith, Bowles and Warton, among others. This sonnet is indebted to nativity sonnets by two eighteenth-century poets: Warton's *To the River Lodon* and Bowles's *To the Itchin* (see pp. 3–4, 155).
[3] *the west* i.e. the west of England.

LETTER FROM S. T. COLERIDGE TO GEORGE DYER
[1] For Dyer, see pp. 44–5. Coleridge met Dyer in London in August 1794, when he persuaded him of the merits of pantisocracy ('he was enraptured – pronounced it impregnable', Griggs i 98).

[2] *man was not made . . . cities* Dyer lived in London.
[3] *meliorate* improve.
[4] *The pleasures . . . pleasures* it was always important to Coleridge that love of nature had an improving moral effect on the individual. It would be amplified and reworked by Wordsworth into the central principle of *The Recluse*: that love of nature leads to love of mankind (see Wordsworth, *Not Useless do I Deem*, pp. 298–300).
[5] καλοκἀγαθοῦ nobility and beauty.
[6] *as a landscape on a convex mirror* The Claude Lorraine Glass was a dark or coloured hand-mirror, used by picturesque tourists to reflect the features of the landscape in subdued tones.
[7] James Thomson (1700–48), author of *The Seasons*, a popular nature poem of the mid eighteenth century.

Through which the morning shows her dewy face;
You cannot bar my constant feet to rove
Through wood and vale by living stream at eve . . .[8]

Alas, alas! She *can* deny us all this, and can force us, fettered and handcuffed by our dependencies and wants, to *wish* and *wish* away the bitter little of life in the felon-crowded dungeon of a great city!

God love you, my very dear sir! I would that we could form a pantisocracy[9] in England and that you could be one of us! The finely-fibred heart that, like the statue of Memnon,[10] trembles into melody on the sunbeam touch of benevolence, is most easily jarred into the dissonance of misanthropy. But you will never suffer your feelings to be benumbed by the torpedo touch of that fiend – I know you, and know that you will drink of every mourner's sorrows even while your own cup is trembling over its brink!

Effusion XXXV. Composed 20 August 1795, at Clevedon, Somersetshire[1]

From Poems on Various Subjects (1796)

My pensive Sara,[2] thy soft cheek reclined
Thus on mine arm, most soothing sweet it is
To sit beside our cot, our cot o'ergrown
With white-flowered jasmine and the broad-leaved myrtle
(Meet emblems they of innocence and love),   5
And watch the clouds that late were rich with light
Slow-sad'ning round, and mark the star of eve
Serenely brilliant (such should wisdom be)
Shine opposite! How exquisite the scents
Snatched from yon bean-field! And the world *so* hushed!   10
The stilly murmur of the distant sea
Tells us of silence. And that simplest lute
Placed lengthways in the clasping casement – hark
How by the desultory breeze caressed![3]
Like some coy maid half-yielding to her lover,   15
It pours such sweet upbraidings as must needs
Tempt to repeat the wrong. And now its strings
Boldlier swept, the long sequacious[4] notes
Over delicious surges sink and rise,
Such a soft floating witchery of sound   20
As twilight elfins make when they at eve
Voyage on gentle gales from fairyland,
Where melodies round honey-dropping flowers
Footless and wild, like birds of paradise,
Nor pause nor perch, hov'ring on untamed wing.   25

---

[8] *The Castle of Indolence* ii 19–24.

[9] *pantisocracy* Coleridge and Southey wished to go to America and set up an ideal society in which everyone was equal, and all possessions were shared.

[10] *like the statue of Memnon* The statue of Memnon at Thebes in Egypt was believed to give forth a musical sound when touched by the dawn or the setting sun. See Robin C. Dix, 'The Harps of Memnon and Aeolus: A Study in the Propagation of an Error', *Modern Philology* 85 (1988) 288–93.

Effusion XXXV

[1] This is the first of the so-called conversation poems, and the earliest version of the poem revised and retitled *The Eolian*

Harp; for the later, better-known version, see pp. 549–50.

[2] *Sara* Sara Fricker, with whom Coleridge was in love. He was to marry her less than two months after this poem was composed, 4 October 1795. In early August he told Southey that 'Domestic happiness is the greatest of things sublunary – and of things celestial it is perhaps impossible for unassisted man to believe anything greater' (Griggs i 158).

[3] The Aeolian harp is a stringed instrument placed in front of an open window so as to catch the breeze; it is not unlike modern wind-chimes.

[4] *sequacious* following one another.

And thus, my love, as on the midway slope
Of yonder hill I stretch my limbs at noon,
Whilst through my half-closed eyelids I behold
The sunbeams dance, like diamonds, on the main,
And tranquil muse upon tranquillity,   30
Full many a thought uncalled and undetained,
And many idle flitting fantasies
Traverse my indolent and passive brain –
As wild and various as the random gales
That swell or flutter on this subject lute!   35
And what if all of animated nature
Be but organic harps diversely framed,
That tremble into thought, as o'er them sweeps,
Plastic[5] and vast, one intellectual[6] breeze,
At once the soul of each, and God of all?[7]   40
    But thy more serious eye a mild reproof
Darts, oh beloved woman![8] – nor such thoughts
Dim and unhallowed dost thou not reject,
And biddest me walk humbly with my God.
Meek daughter in the family of Christ,[9]   45
Well hast thou said and holily dispraised[10]
These shapings of the unregenerate mind,
Bubbles that glitter as they rise and break
On vain philosophy's aye-babbling spring.[11]
For never guiltless may I speak of Him,   50
Th' Incomprehensible! save when with awe
I praise him, and with faith that inly[12] *feels* –

---

[5] *Plastic* shaping, formative, creative. It is important to Coleridge that God's spiritual influence shape the sensibility of the beings it enters.

[6] *intellectual* spiritual.

[7] *And what if all . . . all* A major pantheist declaration: 'And what if all natural things are like Aeolian harps, each unique and individual in itself ("diversely framed"), receiving, just as the harps receive the breeze, the spiritual ("intellectual") apprehension of the one God?' An early MS of the poem contains a more detailed and explicit version of ll. 36–40:

And what if all of animated life
Be but as instruments diversely framed,
That tremble into thought, while through them breathes
One infinite and intellectual breeze,
And all in different heights so aptly hung
That murmurs indistinct and bursts sublime,
Shrill discords and most soothing melodies,
Harmonious form Creation's vast consent?
Thus God would be the universal soul,
Mechanized matter as th' organic harps,
And each one's tunes be that which each calls 'I'.

[8] *But thy . . . woman* Referring to these lines, Lamb told Coleridge that he and his sister enjoyed the 'pleasing picture of Mrs C. checking your wild wanderings, which we were so fond of hearing you indulge when among us. It has endeared us more than anything to your good lady, and your own self-reproof that follows delighted us' (Marrs i 12).

[9] *Meek daughter . . . Christ* Coleridge's language is, of course, figurative. Sara's father was a Bristol manufacturer who died bankrupt in 1786, leaving his wife and six children penniless. Sara's mother ran a dress shop.

[10] *holily dispraised* piously attacked. Coleridge's unease about the pantheist experience of ll. 36–40 is transferred completely to Sara.

[11] *Bubbles . . . spring* Can Sara really have thought all this so early in her relationship with Coleridge? He attributes to her the criticisms that he is 'vain' (impractical) and 'aye-babbling'.

[12] ' "L'athée n'est point à mes yeux un faux esprit; je puis vivre avec lui aussi bien et mieux qu'avec le dévot, car il raisonne davantage, mais il lui manque un sens, et mon ame ne se fond point entièrement avec la sienne: il est froid au spectacle le plus ravissant, et il cherche un syllogisme lorsque je rends une action de grace." *Appel a l'impartiale postérité, par la Citoyenne Roland*, troisieme partie, p. 67.' (Coleridge's note to the 1796 text, dropped from versions of the poem after 1803.) 'The atheist is not, to my eyes, deceived; I can live with him as well as – if not better than with – the zealot, because he reasons more. But he is lacking in a certain sense, and my soul does not entirely combine with his: he is untouched by the most ravishing spectacle, and searches for a syllogism when I thank God.' French copies of Madame Roland's memoirs were available in England by late July 1795; their popularity led to an English translation later that year, published by Joseph Johnson (who had published Wordsworth's *An Evening Walk* in 1793, and who would publish *Frost at Midnight* in 1798). See my *Wordsworth's Reading 1770–1799* (1993), p. 118.

I praise him, and with faith that inly[12] *feels* –
Who with his saving mercies healed me,
A sinful and most miserable man
Wildered and dark, and gave me to possess   55
Peace, and this cot,[13] and thee, heart-honoured maid!

Reflections on Having Left a Place of Retirement (first published as *Reflections on Entering into Active Life. A Poem which Affects Not To Be Poetry*; composed November 1795[1])

From POEMS (1797)
Sermoni propriora.[2]

Low was our pretty cot;[3] our tallest rose
Peeped at the chamber-window. We could hear
At silent noon, and eve, and early morn,
The sea's faint murmur. In the open air
Our myrtles blossomed, and across the porch   5
Thick jasmines twined;[4] the little landscape round
Was green and woody and refreshed the eye.[5]
It was a spot which you might aptly call
The Valley of Seclusion. Once I saw
(Hallowing his sabbath-day by quietness)   10
A wealthy son of commerce saunter by,
Bristowa's[6] citizen; methought it calmed
His thirst of idle gold, and made him muse
With wiser feelings – for he paused and looked
With a pleased sadness, and gazed all around,   15
Then eyed our cottage, and gazed round again,
And sighed, and said it was a blessed place.
And we *were* blessed. Oft with patient ear,
Long-listening to the viewless skylark's note
(Viewless, or haply for a moment seen   20
Gleaming on sunny wing), in whispered tones
I've said to my beloved, 'Such,[7] sweet girl,
The inobtrusive song of happiness,
Unearthly minstrelsy – then only heard
When the soul seeks to hear, when all is hushed   25
And the heart listens!'
                              But the time when first
From that low dell, steep up the stony mount

---

[13]   *cot* cottage.

REFLECTIONS OF HAVING LEFT A PLACE OF RETIREMENT
[1]   Coleridge married Sara Fricker on 4 October 1795 in Bristol. They honeymooned at a cottage in Clevedon, Somerset, on the Bristol Channel, and in November left Sara in the cottage with her mother, while he returned to Bristol. It was at this stage that the present work was composed.
[2]   Horace, *Satires* I iv 42. In a note to *Fears in Solitude* (1798), he was to write: 'The above is perhaps not poetry but rather a sort of middle thing between poetry and oratory – *sermoni propriora* [more appropriate for a sermon]. Some parts are, I am conscious, too tame even for animated prose'.
[3]   *cot* cottage.
[4]   *myrtles ... jasmines* 'Meet emblems they of innocence and love', *Eolian Harp* 5.
[5]   *the little landscape ... eye* cf. Coleridge's letter to Poole, 7 October 1795: 'The prospect around us is perhaps more various than any in the kingdom – Mine Eye gluttonizes. – The Sea – the distant Islands! – the opposite Coasts! – I shall assuredly write Rhymes' (Griggs i 160).
[6]   *Bristowa's* Bristol's.
[7]   *Such* i.e. similar to this (the skylark's song).

I climbed with perilous toil and reached the top –
Oh, what a goodly scene! *Here* the bleak mount,
The bare bleak mountain speckled thin with sheep;   30
Grey clouds, that shadowing spot the sunny fields;
And river, now with bushy rocks o'erbrowed,
Now winding bright and full with naked banks;
And seats, and lawns, the abbey and the wood,
And cots, and hamlets, and faint city-spire;   35
The channel *there*, the islands and white sails,
Dim coasts, and cloudlike hills, and shoreless ocean –
It seemed like Omnipresence![8] God, methought,
Had built him there a temple: the whole world
Seemed *imaged* in its vast circumference.   40
No wish profaned my overwhelmed heart[9] –
Blessed hour! It was a luxury – to be!
    Ah, quiet dell, dear cot, and mount sublime!
I was constrained to quit you. Was it right,
While my unnumbered brethren toiled and bled,[10]   45
That I should dream away the trusted hours
On rose-leaf beds, pamp'ring the coward heart
With feelings all too delicate for use?
Sweet is the tear that from some Howard's[11] eye
Drops on the cheek of one he lifts from earth;   50
And he that works me good with unmoved face
Does it but half – he chills me while he aids –
My benefactor, not my brother man.[12]
Yet even this, this cold beneficence
Seizes my praise, when I reflect on those   55
(The sluggard pity's vision-weaving tribe!)
Who sigh for wretchedness, yet shun the wretched,
Nursing in some delicious solitude
Their slothful loves and dainty sympathies!
I therefore go and join head, heart and hand,   60
Active and firm, to fight the bloodless fight
Of Science,[13] Freedom, and the Truth in Christ.[14]
    Yet oft when after honourable toil
Rests the tired mind, and waking loves to dream,
My spirit shall revisit thee, dear cot!   65
Thy jasmine and thy window-peeping rose,
And myrtles fearless of the mild sea-air;

---

[8] *Omnipresence* the godlike perspective granted Coleridge from the top of the 'stony mount' is comparable with that of the visionary of *Religious Musings*, who 'Views all creation, and he loves it all / And blesses it' (ll. 126–7). This is the first poem by either Coleridge or Wordsworth to present the ascent of a mountain as a meeting with divine forces; compare the ascent of Snowdon, *Prelude* Book XIII (pp. 401–5).
[9] *No wish ... heart* any materialistic ambitions at such a moment of divine apprehension would be a kind of profanity.
[10] *While my ... bled* Britain had been at war with France since 1793.

[11] John Howard (1726–90), prison reformer and philanthropist.
[12] *My benefactor ... man* a spiritual affirmation of brotherhood is more desirable on its own than a good deed without it.
[13] *Science* knowledge, which would have included such things as chemistry.
[14] *I therefore ... Christ* Coleridge was not actually going to sign up as a soldier; the 'bloodless fight' will consist of his editing of a new journal dedicated to the causes of Unitarianism and radical politics: *The Watchman*.

It might be so, but the time is not yet: 70
Speed it, oh Father! Let thy Kingdom come!¹⁵

Religious Musings (extract) (composed 1794–6)¹

From POEMS (1797)

There is one Mind,² one omnipresent Mind
Omnific.³ His most holy name is LOVE –   120
Truth of subliming⁴ import! with the which
Who feeds and saturates his constant soul,
He from his small particular orbit flies
With blessed outstarting!⁵ From himself he flies,
Stands in the sun, and with no partial gaze⁶   125
Views all creation, and he loves it all
And blesses it,⁷ and calls it very good!⁸
This is indeed to dwell with the most high –
Cherubs and rapture-trembling seraphim
Can press no nearer to th' Almighty's throne.   130
But that we roam unconscious, or with hearts
Unfeeling of our universal Sire,
And that in his vast family no Cain⁹
Injures uninjured (in her best-aimed blow
Victorious murder a blind suicide),¹⁰   135
Haply for this some younger angel now
Looks down on human nature – and behold!
A sea of blood¹¹ bestrewed with wrecks where mad
Embattling interests on each other rush
With unhelmed rage!¹²
                            'Tis the sublime of man,   140
Our noontide majesty,¹³ to know ourselves
Parts and proportions of one wondrous whole;

---

¹⁵ *Speed it . . . come* Coleridge looks forward to the millennium (Christ's thousand-year rule on earth), when all people will share his love of nature, and 'fond wishes'.

RELIGIOUS MUSINGS
¹ In this important poem the young Coleridge set out, though in very dense and frequently obscure terms, his central religious and political beliefs. He presents the French Revolution in terms of his expectation of the millennium (Christ's thousand-year rule on earth, thought to be nigh), and in this important extract explicates his Unitarian principles. For a detailed analysis of the entire poem see Ian Wylie, *Young Coleridge and the Philosophers of Nature* (Oxford, 1989), chapter 6.
² *There is one Mind* Coleridge was a fervent Unitarian, and this opening remark expresses the central Unitarian belief in the absolute unity of the godhead.
³ *Omnific* all-creating, as at *Paradise Lost* vii 217: ' "Silence, ye troubled waves, and thou Deep, peace", / Said then th' Omnific Word.'
⁴ *subliming* exalting.
⁵ *Who feeds . . . outstarting* He who feeds and saturates his

soul in the truth that God is Love may transcend (outstart) his earthly state ('particular orbit').
⁶ *with no partial gaze* i.e. with a vision as universal, and all-embracing, as that of God.
⁷ *And blesses it* other Coleridgean blessings can be found in *The Ancient Mariner* (1798) 277 and *Frost at Midnight* (1798) 49ff.
⁸ *Views all . . . good* from Genesis 1:31: 'And God saw every thing that he had made, and behold, it was very good'.
⁹ *Cain* the son of Adam and Eve, who killed his brother Abel and brought murder into the world; see Genesis 4:8.
¹⁰ *Victorious murder a blind suicide* Because we are united in a common humanity, murder is as destructive of the aggressor as it is of the victim.
¹¹ *A sea of blood* the image is from Revelation 16:3.
¹² *A sea of blood . . . rage* during the period in which this poem was written, the Reign of Terror had come to an end with Robespierre's execution, and had given way to full-scale war as France had taken on the European allies (1793 onwards). As a committed republican, Coleridge was horrified by what he saw.
¹³ *Our noontide majesty* the height of our spiritual existence.

Our noontide majesty,[13] to know ourselves
Parts and proportions of one wondrous whole;
This fraternizes[14] man, this constitutes
Our charities and bearings – but 'tis God
Diffused through all that doth make all one whole.[15]   145
This the worst superstition: Him except,
Aught to desire,[16] supreme reality,
The plenitude and permanence of bliss!
Oh fiends of superstition![17] – not that oft
Your pitiless rites have floated with man's blood   150
The skull-piled temple, not for this shall wrath
Thunder against you from the Holy One!
But (whether ye, th' unclimbing bigot, mock
With secondary gods, or if more pleased
Ye petrify th' imbrothelled atheist's heart[18] –   155
The atheist your worst slave) I o'er some plain
Peopled with death, and to the silent sun
Steaming with tyrant-murdered multitudes,
Or where mid groans and shrieks loud-laughing trade[19]
More hideous packs his bales of living anguish –   160
I will raise up a mourning, oh ye fiends,
And curse your spells that film the eye of faith,[20]
Hiding the present God, whose presence lost,
The moral world's cohesion, we become
An anarchy of spirits! Toy-bewitched,[21]   165
Made blind by lusts, disherited of soul,
No common centre man, no common sire
Knoweth![22] A sordid solitary thing,
Mid countless brethren with a lonely heart,
Through courts and cities the smooth savage roams   170
Feeling himself, his own low self the whole,
When he by sacred sympathy might make
The whole one self![23] Self, that no alien knows!
Self, far diffused as fancy's wing can travel!
Self, spreading still, oblivious of its own,   175
Yet all of all possessing! This is faith![24]
This the Messiah's destined victory!

---

[14] *fraternizes* 'fraternité' was one of the ideals of the French Revolution. Coleridge believes our brotherhood to be affirmed by a collective perception of ourselves as part of the godhead.

[15] *'tis God ... whole* a reiteration of the pantheist belief in a single divinity diffused through the universe; cf. *Eolian Harp* 36–40.

[16] *This the ... desire* i.e the worst superstition is to desire anything except Him.

[17] *fiends of superstition* an attack on European Christians, who are responsible for using superstition as a means of perpetuating the slave trade.

[18] *th' imbrothelled atheist's heart* the atheist is, effectively, in the brothel of hell; for Thelwall's view of this phrase, see p. 164, above.

[19] *trade* the slave trade.

[20] *I o'er some plain ... faith* it is not clear whether Coleridge has some specific event in mind, but in general terms he is saying that the present war between France and the allies is leading people to lose faith in God. The image of a film over the eyes echoes the conversion of Saul, the persecutor of the Christians, when 'there fell from his eyes as it had been scales' (Acts 9:18).

[21] *Toy-bewitched* seduced by idle pastimes.

[22] *An anarchy ... Knoweth* Coleridge is attacking Godwinian thought, which he despised for its atheism and disapproval of marriage. In April 1796, he wrote: 'I do consider Mr Godwin's principles as vicious, and his book as a pander to sensuality' (Griggs i 199). See Nicola Trott, 'The Coleridge Circle and the "Answer to Godwin"', *RES* 41 (1990) 212–29.

[23] *A sordid ... self* instead of enjoying the Unitarian perception of himself as part of the godhead, the Godwinian is a selfish moral degenerate.

[24] *Self, far diffused ... faith* faith consists of self diffused through the world, integrated with the Unitarian God.

Letter from S. T. Coleridge to John Thelwall,[1] 19 November 1796
(extract)

Your portrait of yourself interested me. As to me, my face, unless when animated by immediate eloquence, expresses great sloth and great (indeed almost idiotic) good nature. 'Tis a mere carcass of a face – fat, flabby, and expressive chiefly of inexpression. Yet I am told that my eyes, eyebrows, and forehead are physiognomically good,[2] but of this the deponent[3] knoweth not. As to my shape, 'tis a good shape enough if measured – but my gait is awkward, and the walk and the whole man indicates *indolence capable of energies*. I am, and ever have been, a great reader, and have read almost everything – a library-cormorant. I am deep in all out of the way books, whether of the monkish times or of the puritanical era.[4] I have read and digested most of the historical writers but I do not *like* history. Metaphysics and poetry and 'facts of mind' (i.e. accounts of all the strange phantasms that ever possessed your philosophy-dreamers[5] from Thoth the Egyptian[6] to Taylor the English pagan[7]) are my darling studies.

In short, I seldom read except to amuse myself, and I am almost always reading. Of useful knowledge, I am a so-so chemist, and I love chemistry.[8] All else is blank, but I *will* be (please God) an horticulturist and a farmer.[9] I compose very little and I absolutely hate composition. Such is my dislike that even a sense of duty is sometimes too weak to overpower it.

I cannot breathe through my nose, so my mouth, with sensual thick lips, is almost always open. In conversation I am impassioned, and oppose what I deem error with an eagerness which is often mistaken for personal asperity[10] – but I am ever so swallowed up in the *thing*, that I perfectly forget my opponent. Such am I.

Letter from S. T. Coleridge to Robert Southey, 17 July 1797 (including
early version of *This Lime-Tree Bower My Prison*)[1] (extract)

... I am as much a Pangloss as ever – only less *contemptuous*, than I used to be, when I argue how unwise it is to feel contempt for any thing.[2]

LETTER FROM S. T. COLERIDGE TO JOHN THELWALL
[1] For Thelwall, see pp. 158–60. Coleridge first wrote to Thelwall in late April 1796, with the words: 'Pursuing the same end by the same means we ought not to be strangers to each other' (Griggs i 204). Coleridge probably meant their shared antipathy to private property, and their republicanism.
[2] *physiognomically good* i.e. that they indicate good character traits.
[3] *deponent* witness.
[4] *monkish times ... era* i.e. from the middle ages to the seventeenth century.
[5] *philosophy-dreamers* visionaries.
[6] *Thoth the Egyptian* Thoth is the Egyptian name for Hermes Trismegistus, who wrote in Greek and Latin on philosophical, theological and occult subjects.
[7] *Taylor the English pagan* Thomas Taylor (1758–1835), classical scholar and Neoplatonist. Coleridge's copy of Taylor's translation of Plato's *Cratylus* (1793) was retained at Rydal Mount in later years; see my *Wordsworth's Reading 1800–1815* (1995), pp. 167–8.
[8] *chemistry* one of Coleridge's greatest mentors, Joseph Priestley, the founder of modern Unitarianism, was an accomplished chemist, and discovered oxygen.
[9] *an horticulturalist and a farmer* Coleridge enjoyed the theory, rather than the practice, of farming. He was a regular

reader of the *Letters and Papers on Agriculture, Planting, etc., Selected from the Correspondence of the Bath and West of English Society* (see my *Wordsworth's Reading 1770–1799* (1993), pp. 183–4).
[10] *asperity* roughness, boisterousness.

LETTER FROM S. T. COLERIDGE TO ROBERT SOUTHEY
[1] The earliest extant text of *This Lime-Tree Bower My Prison* survives in this revealing letter to Coleridge's former mentor, Robert Southey. The poem was first published in Southey's *Annual Anthology* (1800), as *This Lime-Tree Bower My Prison, A Poem Addressed to Charles Lamb of the India House, London*, but probably the best-known and most polished version is that in Coleridge's collected poetical works of 1834, presented pp. 551–3. By this time some bitterness existed between Coleridge and Southey, thanks largely to the collapse of the pantisocracy scheme.
[2] *I am as much ... thing* Pangloss was the eternal optimist of Voltaire's *Candide*. Coleridge's emphatic respect for natural things represents a distinctively Wordsworthian way of thinking; he even echoes Wordsworth's *Lines Left Upon a Seat in A Yew-Tree* (composed by July 1797): 'he who feels contempt / For any living thing, hath faculties / Which he has never used' (ll. 48–50).

I had been on a visit to Wordsworth's at Racedown near Crewkerne[3] – and I brought him and his sister back with me and here[4] I have settled them. By a combination of curious circumstances a gentleman's seat,[5] with a park and woods, elegantly and completely furnished, with nine lodging rooms, three parlours and a hall, in a most beautiful and romantic situation by the sea-side, four miles from Stowey – this we have got for Wordsworth at the rent of £23 *a year, taxes included*!! The park and woods are *his* for all purposes he wants them – i.e. he may walk, ride, and keep a horse in them, and the large gardens are altogether and entirely his. Wordsworth is a very great man – the only man to whom *at all times* and in *all modes of excellence* I feel myself inferior – the only one, I mean, whom I have yet met with[6] (for the London literati appear to me to be very much like little potatoes – i.e. no great things, a compost of nullity and dullity!).

Charles Lamb[7] has been with me for a week; he left me Friday morning. The second day after Wordsworth came to me, dear Sara accidentally emptied a skillet of boiling milk on my foot, which confined me during the whole time of C. Lamb's stay and still prevents me from all walks longer than a furlong. While Wordsworth, his sister, and C. Lamb were out one evening, sitting in the arbour of T. Poole's garden,[8] which communicates with mine, I wrote these lines, with which I am pleased.

> Well, they are gone; and here must I remain,
> Lamed by the scathe of fire,[9] lonely and faint,
> This lime-tree bower my prison. They, meantime,
> My friends, whom I may never meet again,[10]
> On springy[11] heath, along the hilltop edge,[12]   5
> Wander delighted, and look down, perchance,
> On that same rifted dell, where many an ash
> Twists its wild limbs beside the ferny rock,
> Whose plumy ferns[13] forever nod and drip
> Sprayed by the waterfall. But chiefly thou,   10
> My gentle-hearted Charles![14] – thou who hast pined
> And hungered after nature many a year
> In the great city pent, winning thy way,
> With sad yet bowed soul, through evil and pain
> And strange calamity.[15] Ah, slowly sink   15

---

[3] *I had been ... Crewkerne* Wordsworth and his sister had been resident at Racedown Lodge in Dorset since July 1795. Coleridge visited them there in June 1797.

[4] *here* i.e. at Alfoxden House, four miles away from where Coleridge lived at Nether Stowey, Somerset. It was here that Wordsworth's close association with Coleridge began to bear fruit: *The Ruined Cottage* (completed February 1798); *Lyrical Ballads* (composed spring–summer 1798); and blank verse fragments which later contributed to *The Prelude* and *The Excursion*. The house is now a hotel.

[5] *seat* residence.

[6] *Wordsworth ... met with* A loaded comment, as Coleridge had, only a few years before, idolized Southey in much the same way (see p. 447).

[7] *Charles Lamb* Coleridge's friend since their shared schooldays at Christ's Hospital; for more on Lamb, see pp. 577–8.

[8] The incompatibility that was to ruin his marriage with Sara Fricker is evident even at this early moment: the overemphatic claim that his injury had been accidental begs the question. The garden attached to Tom Poole's house adjoins that of Coleridge Cottage, as visitors may still observe today.

[9] *Lamed ... fire* an interesting phrase, eliminated from subsequent versions of the poem, which recasts Coleridge as Vulcan, whose leg was broken when he was flung out of Olympus.

[10] *whom I may never meet again* an exaggeration; as he has just told Southey, Wordsworth and his sister had moved into Alfoxden House only days before. They would certainly remain for at least a year.

[11] 'Elastic, I mean' (Coleridge's note) – meaning, simply, that the furze and heather reassumes its original shape after having been trodden on. In the course of the poem the poet will reassume his original mood, having been depressed by the 'accident' and its consequences.

[12] *the hilltop edge* the Wordsworths and Lamb would have climbed up the Quantock Hills behind Coleridge's cottage.

[13] 'The ferns that grow in moist places, grow five or six together and form a complete "Prince of Wales' feather" – i.e. plumy' (Coleridge's note).

[14] *My gentle-hearted Charles!* 'For God's sake', Lamb wrote to Coleridge, when the poem was published in 1800, 'don't make me ridiculous any more by terming me gentle-hearted in print, or do it in better verses. . . . the meaning of "gentle" is equivocal at best, and almost always means "poor-spirited"' (Marrs i 217–18).

[15] *strange calamity* In September 1796 Lamb's sister Mary stabbed their mother to death in a fit of insanity; see p. 578. Lamb had been working in East India House in the City of London since 1792.

Behind the western ridge, thou glorious sun!
Shine in the slant beams of the sinking orb,
Ye purple heath-flowers! Richlier burn, ye clouds!
Live in the yellow light, ye distant groves!
And kindle, thou blue ocean! So my friend,   20
Struck with joy's deepest calm, and gazing round
On the wide view, may gaze till all doth seem
Less gross than bodily,[16] a living thing
That acts upon the mind, and with such hues
As clothe the Almighty Spirit, when he makes   25
Spirits perceive His presence![17]
                              A delight
Comes sudden on my heart, and I am glad
As I myself were there! Nor in this bower
Want I sweet sounds or pleasing shapes. I watched
The sunshine of each broad transparent leaf   30
Broke by the shadows of the leaf or stem
Which hung above it; and that walnut tree
Was richly tinged; and a deep radiance lay
Full on the ancient ivy which usurps
Those fronting elms, and now with blackest mass   35
Makes their dark foliage gleam a lighter hue
Through the last twilight. And though the rapid bat
Wheels silent by, and not a swallow twitters,
Yet still the solitary humble-bee[18]
Sings in the bean-flower. Henceforth I shall know   40
That nature ne'er deserts the wise and pure;
No scene so narrow but may well employ
Each faculty of sense, and keep the heart
Awake to love and beauty.[19] And sometimes
'Tis well to be bereaved of promised good,   45
That we may lift the soul and contemplate
With lively joy the joys we cannot share.
My sister and my friends! when the last rook
Beat its straight path along the dusky air
Homewards, I blessed it, deeming its black wing   50
Crossed, like a speck, the blaze of setting day,
While ye stood gazing; or when all was still,
Flew creaking o'er your heads, and had a charm
For you, my sister and my friends, to whom
No sound is dissonant which tells of Life!   55

---

[16] *Less gross than bodily* a difficult phrase, meaning, presumably, that the world becomes more spiritualized as Lamb gazes upon it, granting him the Unitarian experience described in *Reflections on Having Left a Place of Retirement* 26–42.

[17] 'You remember, I am a Berkeleian' (Coleridge's note). George Berkeley, Bishop of Cloyne (1685–1753), denied the existence of the material world in favour of an invisible world created by God, perceptible by human beings in moments of heightened vision.

[18] *humble-bee* against a copy of the 1817 printed text, Coleridge entered the following note: 'Cows without horns are called Hummel cows, in the country as the Hummel bee, as stingless (unless it be a corruption of *humming*, from the sound observable).'

[19] *Awake to love and beauty* at around this time Coleridge would describe how the 'wandering and distempered child' would be 'healed and harmonized / By the benignant touch of love and beauty' (*The Dungeon* 29–30).

Letter from S. T. Coleridge to John Thelwall, 14 October 1797 (extract)

I can at times feel strongly the beauties you describe – in themselves and for themselves. But more frequently all things appear little – all the knowledge that can be acquired, child's play; the universe itself, what but an immense heap of *little* things? I can contemplate nothing but parts, and parts are all little! My mind feels as if it ached to behold and know something *great*, something *one* and *indivisible*[1] – and it is only in the faith of this that rocks or waterfalls, mountains or caverns, give me the sense of sublimity or majesty! But in this faith *all things* counterfeit infinity! 'Struck with the deepest calm of joy', I stand

> Silent, with swimming sense, and gazing round
> On the wide landscape, gaze till all doth seem
> Less gross than bodily, a living thing
> Which acts upon the mind, and with such hues
> As clothe th' Almighty Spirit, when he makes
> Spirits perceive his presence![2]

Letter from S. T. Coleridge to Thomas Poole,[1] 16 October 1797 (extract)

I read every book that came in my way without distinction. And my father was fond of me, and used to take me on his knee, and hold long conversations with me.[2] I remember that at eight years old I walked with him one winter evening from a farmer's house a mile from Ottery, and he told me the names of the stars, and how Jupiter was a thousand times larger than our world, and that the other twinkling stars were suns that had worlds rolling round them. And when I came home, he showed me how they rolled round. I heard him with a profound delight and admiration, but without the least mixture of wonder or incredulity. For, from my early reading of fairy tales and genii etc. etc., my mind had been habituated *to the Vast* – and I never regarded my senses in any way as the criteria of my belief. I regulated all my creeds by my conceptions – not by my sight, even at that age.

Should children be permitted to read romances, and relations of giants and magicians and genii? I know all that has been said against it, but I have formed my faith in the affirmative. I know no other way of giving the mind a love of 'the Great' and 'the Whole'.[3] Those who have been led to the same truths step by step through the constant testimony of their senses, seem to me to want a sense which I possess: they contemplate nothing but *parts*, and all parts are necessarily little. And the universe to them is but a mass of *little things*. It is true that the mind *may* become credulous and prone to superstition by the former method – but are not the experimentalists[4] credulous even to madness in believing any absurdity rather than believe the grandest truths, if they have not the testimony of their own senses in their favour? I have known some who have been *rationally* educated, as it is styled. They were marked by a microscopic acuteness, but when they looked at great things, all became a blank and they saw nothing – and denied (very illogically) that anything could be seen, and uniformly put the negation of a power for the possession of a power, and called the want of imagination 'judgement', and the never being moved to rapture 'philosophy'!

LETTER FROM S. T. COLERIDGE TO JOHN THELWALL
[1]   *My mind feels ... indivisible* Coleridge yearns for the transcendental experience described in *Religious Musings* 140–2.
[2]   See the preceding text of *This Lime-Tree Bower My Prison* 21–6.

LETTER FROM S. T. COLERIDGE TO THOMAS POOLE
[1]   Thomas Poole (1765–1837) was a well-to-do tanner of Nether Stowey. He encouraged and materially helped Coleridge from about 1794 onwards. He found Coleridge a cottage in Nether Stowey which adjoined his own back garden, funded Coleridge's magazine, *The Watchman*, and looked after Sara Coleridge and the children during Coleridge's many absences.
[2]   *And my father ... me* Coleridge was the youngest of John Coleridge's many children, and probably the favourite. John was headmaster of the King Henry VII Grammar School at Ottery St Mary and vicar of St Mary's, until his death in 1781.
[3]   *Should children ... Whole* cf. Wordsworth's views on education as expressed in the passage on the infant prodigy in the *Five-Book Prelude* (pp. 380–3).
[4]   *experimentalists* those who base their religious faith and beliefs only on what is perceived by the five senses, and on the reason.

Kubla Khan (composed early November 1797;[1] edited from MS)[2]

In Xannadù did Cubla Khan[3]
A stately pleasure-dome decree,
Where Alph, the sacred river, ran
Through caverns measureless to man
Down to a sunless sea.   5
So twice six[4] miles of fertile ground
With walls and towers were compassed[5] round;
And here were gardens bright with sinuous rills
Where blossomed many an incense-bearing tree;
And here were forests ancient as the hills,   10
Enfolding sunny spots of greenery.
But oh, that deep romantic chasm that slanted
Down a green hill athwart a cedarn cover!
A savage place, as holy and enchanted
As e'er beneath a waning moon was haunted   15
By woman wailing for her demon-lover!
And from this chasm, with hideous[6] turmoil seething,
As if this earth in fast thick pants were breathing,
A mighty fountain momently was forced
Amid whose swift half-intermitted burst   20
Huge fragments vaulted like rebounding hail,
Or chaffy grain beneath the thresher's flail!
And mid these dancing rocks at once and ever,
It flung up momently the sacred river.
Five miles meandering with a mazy motion   25
Through wood and dale the sacred river ran,
Then reached the caverns measureless to man
And sank in tumult to a lifeless ocean.
And mid this tumult Cubla heard from far
Ancestral voices prophesying war![7]   30

KUBLA KHAN

[1] The exact date of composition is unknown; for Coleridge's accounts see note at the end of this poem, and Preface to the published version, pp. 522–3. If, as seems likely, Coleridge's retirement to a farmhouse occurred during the walking tour to the Valley of the Rocks with the Wordsworths, the probable date is early November 1797.

[2] This text is edited from the earliest surviving MS in Coleridge's hand, the precise date of which remains in question, though it may be assumed to date from the period of composition; the MS is widely reproduced, for instance in Rosemary Ashton, *The Life of Samuel Taylor Coleridge* (1996), plate 8. The poem was not published until 1816, and only then through the intervention of Byron, who, having heard its author recite it, urged his publisher, John Murray, to put it into print (Marchand iv 285–6, Griggs iv 636n4). Some of the more interesting variants are indicated in the footnotes. For comment on the two versions of the poem see John Beer, 'The Languages of *Kubla Khan*', *Coleridge's Imagination* ed. Richard Gravil, Lucy Newlyn, and Nicholas Roe (1985), pp. 218–62. The 1816 version and its intriguing introduction are at pp. 522–4.

[3] As Coleridge recalled in his 1816 introduction to the poem, his source for its opening was a passage in Samuel Purchas, *Purchas his Pilgrimage* (1613), p. 350: 'In Xaindu did Cublai Can build a stately pallace, encompassing sixteene miles of plaine ground with a wall, wherein are fertile meddowes, pleasant springs, delightfull streames, and all sorts of beasts of chase and game, and in the middest thereof a sumptuous house of pleasure, which may be removed from place to place'.

[4] *six* five (1816).

[5] *compassed* girdled (1816).

[6] *hideous* ceaseless (1816).

[7] *Ancestral voices prophesying war* presumably the voices of ancestors looking forward to war in the present; though another way of reading it would be to regard the ancestral voices as speaking to the individual psyche. In March 1798 Coleridge told his brother George: 'I believe most steadfastly in original sin; that from our mothers' wombs our understandings are darkened; and even where our understandings are in the light, that our organization is depraved, and our volitions imperfect' (Griggs i 396).

> The shadow of the dome of pleasure
> Floated midway on the wave,
> Where was heard the mingled measure
> From the fountain and the cave;
> It was a miracle of rare device,   35
> A sunny pleasure-dome with caves of ice!
>
> A damsel with a dulcimer
> In a vision once I saw:
> It was an Abyssinian maid
> And on her dulcimer she played,   40
> Singing of Mount Amara.[8]
> Could I revive within me
> Her symphony[9] and song,
> To such a deep delight 'twould win me
> That with music loud and long,   45
> I would build that dome in air,
> That sunny dome, those caves of ice!
> And all who heard should see them there,
> And all should cry, 'Beware, beware!
> His flashing eyes, his floating hair!   50
> Weave a circle round him thrice,
> And close your eyes in holy dread –
> For he on honey-dew hath fed
> And drank the milk of paradise.'

This fragment with a good deal more, not recoverable, composed in a sort of reverie brought on by two grains of opium taken to check a dysentery,[10] at a farm-house between Porlock and Lynton, a quarter of a mile from Culbone Church, in the fall of the year 1797. S. T. Coleridge

Frost at Midnight (composed February 1798)[1]

From FEARS IN SOLITUDE, WRITTEN IN 1798 DURING THE ALARM OF AN INVASION; TO WHICH ARE ADDED FRANCE: AN ODE; AND FROST AT MIDNIGHT (1798)

> The frost performs its secret ministry
> Unhelped by any wind. The owlet's cry
> Came loud – and hark, again! loud as before.
> The inmates of my cottage, all at rest,
> Have left me to that solitude which suits   5

---

[8] *Mount Amara* Coleridge originally wrote 'Amora' in the MS – a reading that alludes to Latin 'amor' (love). Mount Amara alludes to *Purchas his Pilgrimage*, in which it is said to be 'situate as the navel of the Ethopian body, and centre of their empire, under the equinoctial line where the sun may take his best view thereof, as not encountering in all his long journey with the like theatre ... the sun himself so in love with the sight, that the first and last thing he vieweth in all those parts is this hill.' See also *Paradise Lost* iv 281. The allusion was suppressed in 1816 with the revision to 'Mount Abora'.

[9] *symphony* possibly means 'dulcimer'; see Joseph Sgammato, 'A Note on Coleridge's "symphony and song"', *TWC* 6 (1975) 303–6.

[10] *two grains ... dysentery* it is worth bearing in mind that the only available treatment for stomach disorders and pains of various kinds (including toothache) was opium or its derivatives. Many people consumed it for entirely legitimate medicinal purposes, and became addicted as a result.

FROST AT MIDNIGHT
[1] This is the earliest version; the better-known text of 1834 is on pp. 553–5. The main difference is the conclusion to this text, ll. 80–5, eliminated in 1834. Coleridge's literary source is Cowper's description of a winter evening in *The Task*, pp. 11–12.

Abstruser musings, save that at my side
My cradled infant[2] slumbers peacefully.
'Tis calm indeed! – so calm that it disturbs
And vexes meditation with its strange
And extreme silentness. Sea, hill, and wood,   10
This populous village! Sea, and hill, and wood,
With all the numberless goings-on of life,
Inaudible as dreams! The thin blue flame
Lies on my low-burnt fire, and quivers not;
Only that film[3] which fluttered on the grate   15
Still flutters there, the sole unquiet thing.
Methinks its motion in this hush of nature
Gives it dim sympathies with me who live,
Making it a companionable form
With which I can hold commune. Idle thought!   20
But still the living spirit in our frame
That loves not to behold a lifeless thing,
Transfuses into all its own delights
Its own volition – sometimes with deep faith
And sometimes with fantastic playfulness.[4]   25
　　　Ah me! amused by no such curious toys
Of the self-watching subtilizing[5] mind,
How often in my early schoolboy days,[6]
With most believing superstitious wish
Presageful have I gazed upon the bars,   30
To watch the *stranger* there! – and oft belike,
With unclosed lids, already had I dreamt
Of my sweet birthplace, and the old church-tower
Whose bells, the poor man's only music, rang
From morn to evening all the hot fair-day,   35
So sweetly that they stirred and haunted me
With a wild pleasure, falling on mine ear
Most like articulate sounds of things to come!

---

[2] *My cradled infant* Hartley Coleridge, born 19 September 1796. He was one-and-a-half years old. This is the first of numerous appearances in the poetry of Wordsworth and Coleridge, including *The Nightingale* 91–105, *Christabel* 644–65, *To H.C., Six Years Old*, and *Ode* 85–131.

[3] 'In all parts of the kingdom these films are called "strangers", and supposed to portend the arrival of some absent friend' (Coleridge's note). The same detail turns up in Cowper's description of a winter evening, p. 11.

[4] *But still ... playfulness* Coleridge's language indicates that the mind, when it infers the existence of an inner life in external objects, is engaging in an essentially fanciful act – it is making patterns (in the terms of Coleridge's much later definition of fancy, pp. 525–6) out of fixities and definites. This is emphasized in ll. 20–5 which, in versions of the poem from 1812 to 1817, were expanded:

With which I can hold commune. Haply hence,
That still the living spirit in our frame
Which loves not to behold a lifeless thing,
Transfuses into all things its own Will
And its own pleasures; sometimes with deep faith,
And sometimes with a wilful playfulness,
That stealing pardon from our common sense

Smiles, as self-scornful, to disarm the scorn
For these wild relics of our childish thought,
That flit about, oft go, and oft return
Not uninvited. Ah, there was a time,
When oft, amused by no such subtle toys
Of the self-watching mind, a child at school,
With most believing superstitious wish ...

The 1817 text was briefer:

Making it a companionable form,
To which the living spirit in our frame,
That loves not to behold a lifeless thing,
Transfuses its own pleasures, its own will.
How oft, at school, with most believing mind,
Presageful, have I gazed upon the bars
To watch that fluttering stranger! And as oft ...

In 1834 this passage was replaced by a formulation even more sceptical of the charms of fancy; see pp. 553–4, below.

[5] *subtilizing* given to subtle reasoning.

[6] *my early schoolboy days* a reference to Coleridge's time at Christ's Hospital in the City of London, 1782–91. His lack of enthusiasm for those years in this poem may owe something to the use of violence by many of the masters at the school.

So gazed I till the soothing things I dreamt
Lulled me to sleep, and sleep prolonged my dreams!   40
And so I brooded all the following morn,
Awed by the stern preceptor's[7] face, mine eye
Fixed with mock study on my swimming book;
Save if the door half-opened, and I snatched
A hasty glance, and still my heart leaped up,   45
For still I hoped to see the *stranger's* face –
Townsman, or aunt, or sister more beloved,
My playmate when we both were clothed alike![8]

 Dear babe,[9] that sleepest cradled by my side,
Whose gentle breathings heard in this dead calm   50
Fill up the interspersed vacancies
And momentary pauses of the thought;
My babe so beautiful, it fills my heart
With tender gladness thus to look at thee,
And think that thou shalt learn far other lore   55
And in far other scenes! For I was reared
In the great city, pent mid cloisters dim,
And saw nought lovely but the sky and stars.
But *thou*, my babe, shalt wander like a breeze
By lakes and sandy shores, beneath the crags   60
Of ancient mountain, and beneath the clouds
Which image in their bulk both lakes and shores
And mountain crags;[10] so shalt thou see and hear
The lovely shapes and sounds intelligible
Of that eternal language which thy God   65
Utters,[11] who from eternity doth teach
Himself in all, and all things in himself.
Great universal teacher! He shall mould[12]
Thy spirit, and by giving make it ask.

 Therefore all seasons shall be sweet to thee,   70
Whether the summer clothe the general earth
With greenness, or the redbreasts sit and sing
Betwixt the tufts of snow on the bare branch
Of mossy apple-tree, while all the thatch
Smokes in the sun-thaw; whether the eave-drops fall   75
Heard only in the trances[13] of the blast,
Or whether the secret ministry of cold
Shall hang them up in silent icicles,
Quietly shining to the quiet moon;

---

[7] *preceptor* teacher.

[8] *sister ... alike* Until well into the nineteenth century, small boys and girls were dressed in frocks until boys were breeched. Coleridge was deeply attached to his sister Anne (1767–91), whose early death from consumption distressed him greatly. In September 1794 he told Edith Fricker that Anne had been 'beautiful and accomplished – like you, she was lowly of heart. Her eye beamed with meekest sensibility' (Griggs i 102).

[9] *Dear babe* Coleridge turns again to his son Hartley.

[10] *But thou ... crags* Coleridge had not actually seen the Lake District in February 1798, when these lines were written; Cumbrian lakes do not have 'sandy shores'. He is no doubt thinking of the account of the mountains and lakes in Wordsworth's *The Pedlar*, which was being written at the same time as this poem.

[11] *so shalt ... utters* a reference to Bishop Berkeley's theory that the natural world is the symbolic language of God's thought. At more or less the same time that this was written, Wordsworth was describing the Pedlar's perception of the 'written promise' (*Pedlar* 119).

[12] *mould* the pantheist perception Coleridge confers on Hartley is formative of the individual; cf. the intellectual breeze of *The Eolian Harp* (1795), which is 'Plastic' (l. 39).

[13] *trances* moments of suspension, when the blast stills.

Like those, my babe, which ere tomorrow's warmth   80
Have capped their sharp keen points with pendulous drops,
Will catch thine eye, and with their novelty
Suspend thy little soul; then make thee shout
And stretch and flutter from thy mother's arms,
As thou would'st fly for very eagerness.[14]   85

France: An Ode (composed February 1798)[1]

From FEARS IN SOLITUDE, WRITTEN IN 1798, DURING THE ALARM OF AN INVASION; TO
WHICH ARE ADDED FRANCE: AN ODE; AND FROST AT MIDNIGHT (1798)

I

Ye clouds, that far above me float and pause,
Whose pathless march no mortal may control!
Ye ocean waves, that, wheresoe'er ye roll,
Yield homage only to eternal laws!
Ye woods, that listen to the night-bird's singing,   5
Midway the smooth and perilous steep reclined;
Save when your own imperious branches swinging
Have made a solemn music of the wind!
Where, like a man beloved of God,
Through glooms which never woodman trod,   10
How oft, pursuing fancies holy,
My moonlight way o'er flow'ring weeds I wound,
Inspired beyond the guess of folly
By each rude[2] shape, and wild unconquerable sound!
Oh ye loud waves, and oh ye forests high,   15

---

[14] ll.80–5 were removed from subsequent versions of the poem, as Coleridge explained in a marginal note made in a copy of the 1798 volume: 'The six last lines I omit because they destroy the rondo, and return upon itself of the poem. Poems of this kind of length ought to lie coiled with its tail round its head. S.T.C.' For Hartley's sensitivity to natural things, see Coleridge's notebook entry, p. 215 n. 17 above.

FRANCE: AN ODE
[1] This poem is Coleridge's response to the suppression of the Swiss cantons by the French government. It was an important moment for radicals in Britain, because it was the first time that the French had acted contrary to the principles of the Revolution. When first published in the *Morning Post*, 16 April 1798 (under the title *The Recantation: An Ode*), this poem was prefaced by a brief note by the paper's editor, Daniel Stuart: 'The following excellent Ode will be in unison with the feelings of every friend to liberty and foe to oppression; of all who, admiring the French Revolution, detest and deplore the conduct of France towards Switzerland. It is very satisfactory to find so zealous and steady an advocate for freedom as Mr Coleridge concur with us in condemning the conduct of France towards the Swiss Cantons.' When reprinted with corrections by the same paper in 1802, it was accompanied by an Argument:

First stanza: An invocation to those objects in nature the contemplation of which had inspired the poet with a devotional love of liberty. *Second stanza*. The exultation of the poet at the commencement of the French Revolution, and his unqualified abhorrence of the Alliance against the Republic. *Third stanza*: The blasphemies and horrors during the domination of the Terrorists regarded by the poet as a transient storm, and as the natural consequence of the former despotism and of the foul superstition of Popery. Reason, indeed, began to suggest many apprehensions; yet still the poet struggled to retain the hope that France would make conquests by no other means than by presenting to the observation of Europe a people more happy and better instructed than under other forms of government. *Fourth stanza*: Switzerland, and the poet's recantation. *Fifth stanza*: An address to Liberty, in which the poet expresses his conviction that those feelings and that grand ideal of freedom which the mind attains by its contemplation of its individual nature, and of the sublime surrounding objects (see stanza the first) do not belong to men, as a society, nor can possibly be either gratified or realized, under any form of human government; but belong to the individual man, so far as he is pure, and inflamed with the love and adoration of God in nature.
[2] *rude* rough.

And oh ye clouds, that far above me soared!
Thou rising sun! Thou blue rejoicing sky!
Yea, every thing that is and will be free,
Bear witness for me wheresoe'er ye be,
With what deep worship I have still adored   20
The spirit of divinest liberty.

II

When France in wrath her giant limbs upreared,[3]
And with that oath which smote earth, air, and sea,
Stamped her strong foot and said she would be free,
Bear witness for me, how I hoped and feared!   25
With what a joy, my lofty gratulation[4]
Unawed, I sung amid a slavish band;
And when to whelm the disenchanted nation,
Like fiends embattled by a wizard's wand,
The monarchs marched in evil day,   30
And Britain joined the dire array[5] –
Though dear her shores, and circling ocean,
Though many friendships, many youthful loves
Had swoln the patriot emotion,
And flung a magic light o'er all her hills and groves;   35
Yet still my voice unaltered sang defeat
To all that braved the tyrant-quelling lance,[6]
And shame too long delayed, and vain retreat!
For ne'er, oh Liberty! with partial[7] aim
I dimmed thy light, or damped thy holy flame;   40
But blessed the paeans of delivered France,
And hung my head, and wept at Britain's name!

III

'And what', I said, 'though blasphemy's loud scream
With that sweet music of deliv'rance strove;
Though all the fierce and drunken passions wove
A dance more wild than ever maniac's dream;[8]   45
Ye storms, that round the dawning east assembled,
The sun was rising, though ye hid his light!'
And when to soothe my soul, that hoped and trembled,
The dissonance ceased, and all seemed calm and bright;   50
When France, her front deep-scarred and gory,
Concealed with clust'ring wreaths of glory;
When insupportably advancing,
Her arm made mock'ry of the warrior's ramp,

---

3 *When France ... upreared* i.e. when the Revolution began.
4 *gratulation* pleasure, exultation.
5 *And Britain ... array* England joined the alliance of Austria and Prussia against France shortly after the execution of Louis XVI, February 1793.
6 *the tyrant-quelling lance* i.e. of revolutionary France, with whose interests the young Coleridge identified.

7 *partial* selfish.
8 *And what ... dream* during Robespierre's Reign of Terror (October 1793 to July 1794) the clergy was persecuted and executed, along with the aristocrats, politicians of all colours, foreigners, and anyone identifiable as alien to the interests of the state.

While, timid looks of fury glancing,   55
Domestic treason, crushed beneath her fatal stamp,
Writhed like a wounded dragon in his gore –
Then I reproached my fears that would not flee,
'And soon', I said, 'shall wisdom teach her lore
In the low huts of them that toil and groan!   60
And conqu'ring by her happiness alone,
Shall France compel the nations to be free,[9]
Till love and joy look round, and call the earth their own!'

The sun will rise to it's zenith [handwritten marginalia]

IV

Forgive me, Freedom! Oh forgive these dreams!
I hear thy voice, I hear thy loud lament   65
From bleak Helvetia's[10] icy caverns sent –
I hear thy groans upon her bloodstained streams!
Heroes, that for your peaceful country perished,
And ye, that fleeing spot the mountain snows
With bleeding wounds – forgive me, that I cherished   70
One thought that ever blessed your cruel foes![11]
To scatter rage and trait'rous guilt
Where Peace her jealous home had built;
Swiss [marginalia] A patriot race to disinherit
Of all that made their stormy wilds so dear,   75
And with inexpiable[12] spirit
To taint the bloodless freedom of the mountaineer.
Oh France! that mockest heav'n, adult'rous,[13] blind,
And patriot only in pernicious toils! –
Are these thy boasts, champion of humankind?   80
To mix with kings in the low lust of sway,[14]
Yell in the hunt, and share the murd'rous prey;
T' insult the shrine of liberty with spoils
From freemen torn; to tempt and to betray!

V

The sensual and the dark rebel in vain,   85
Slaves by their own compulsion! In mad game
They burst their manacles, and wear the name
Of freedom graven on a heavier chain!
Oh Liberty! with profitless endeavour
Have I pursued thee many a weary hour: 90
But thou nor swell'st the victor's strain, nor ever
Didst breathe thy soul in forms of human pow'r.[15]

---

9   *Shall France ... free* it was believed that revolution would spread to other countries.
10   *Helvetia* Switzerland.
11   *your cruel foes* i.e. France.
12   *inexpiable* unpardonable, unforgiveable.
13   *adult'rous* France has adulterated the principle of liberty.
14   *sway* power – in this case, over Switzerland.

15   *But thou ... pow'r* Coleridge felt a general disillusionment with those in power at this moment; in March 1798 he told his brother George: 'As to the rulers of France, I see in their views, speeches, and actions, nothing that distinguishes them to their advantage from other animals of the same species. History has taught me that rulers are much the same in all ages and under all forms of government: they are as bad as they dare to be' (Griggs i 395).

Alike from all, howe'er they praise thee
(Nor pray'r, nor boastful name delays thee),
Alike from priesthood's harpy minions   95
And factious blasphemy's obscener slaves,
Thou speedest on thy subtle pinions,
To live amid the winds, and move upon the waves![16]
And then I felt thee on the sea-cliff's verge,
Whose pines, scarce travelled by the breeze above,   100
Had made one murmur with the distant surge!
Yes, while I stood and gazed, my temples bare,
And shot my being through earth, sea, and air,
Possessing all things with intensest love,
Oh Liberty, my spirit felt thee there![17]   105

Fears in Solitude. Written April 1798, During the Alarms of an Invasion[1] (composed 20 April 1798)[2]

From Fears in Solitude, Written in 1798, During the Alarm of an Invasion; to Which are Added France: An Ode; and Frost at Midnight (1798)

A green and silent spot amid the hills![3]
A small and silent dell! O'er stiller place
No singing skylark ever poised himself!
The hills are heathy, save that swelling slope
Which hath a gay and gorgeous covering on,   5
All golden with the never-bloomless furze,
Which now blooms most profusely; but the dell,
Bathed by the mist, is fresh and delicate
As vernal cornfield, or the unripe flax,
When through its half-transparent stalks, at eve,   10
The level sunshine glimmers with green light.
Oh 'tis a quiet, spirit-healing nook,
Which all, methinks, would love – but chiefly he,
The humble man, who in his youthful years
Knew just so much of folly as had made   15
His early manhood more securely wise;

---

[16]   *Alike from all ... waves* the point of the poem is that true liberty is found neither with institutionalized religion ('priesthood's harpy minions') nor with atheistic revolutionaries ('factious blasphemy's obscener slaves'); it is found in nature.

[17]   *And shot ... love* the poem culminates in another moment of godlike apprehension (cf. *Reflections on Having Left a Place of Retirement* 26–42). In this case, Coleridge claims that his investment of love in the landscape enabled him to perceive the pantheist life-force in nature – which he regards as representing true liberty.

FEARS IN SOLITUDE

[1]   In February 1797 the French had landed no less than 1,200 men at Fishguard in preparation for an invasion of England; it was widely feared that they would try again in spring 1798, and that the west country would be their landing-point. For useful discussion of this poem see Peter Larkin,

'"Fears in Solitude": Reading (from) the Dell', *TWC* 22 (1991) 11–14.

[2]   The central argument of the poem is the fear that, in declaring war on himself, man has, like the ancient mariner, declared war on God. In an undated but initialled MS of the poem, Coleridge comments: 'The above is perhaps not poetry, but rather a sort of middle thing between poetry and oratory – *sermoni propriora*. Some parts are, I am conscious, too tame even for animated prose.' The phrase 'sermoni propriora' means 'more appropriate for a sermon' – that is, Coleridge explicitly acknowledges his didacticism. As an anti-war poem, *Fears in Solitude* should be compared with Wordsworth's *The Female Vagrant*, which was being prepared at this moment for publication in *Lyrical Ballads* (1798); see pp. 215–22.

[3]   *the hills* the Quantock hills in Somerset, close to Nether Stowey.

Here he might lie on fern or withered heath,
While from the singing lark (that sings unseen –
The minstrelsy which solitude loves best),
And from the sun, and from the breezy air,   20
Sweet influences trembled o'er his frame;[4]
And he with many feelings, many thoughts,
Made up a meditative joy, and found
Religious meanings in the forms of nature!
And so, his senses gradually wrapped   25
In a half-sleep, he dreams of better worlds,
And dreaming hears thee still, oh singing lark,
That singest like an angel in the clouds!
    My God! it is a melancholy thing
For such a man, who would full fain preserve   30
His soul in calmness, yet perforce must feel
For all his human brethren; oh my God,
It is indeed a melancholy thing,
And weighs upon the heart, that he must think
What uproar and what strife may now be stirring   35
This way or that way o'er these silent hills –
Invasion, and the thunder and the shout,
And all the crash of onset; fear and rage
And undetermined conflict – even now,
Ev'n now, perchance, and in his native isle,   40
Carnage and screams beneath this blessed sun!
We have offended, oh my countrymen!
We have offended very grievously,
And have been tyrannous. From east to west
A groan of accusation pierces heaven!   45
The wretched plead against us, multitudes
Countless and vehement, the sons of God,
Our brethren! Like a cloud that travels on,
Steamed up from Cairo's swamps of pestilence,
Ev'n so, my countrymen, have we gone forth   50
And borne to distant tribes slavery and pangs –
And, deadlier far, our vices, whose deep taint
With slow perdition murders the whole man,
His body and his soul! Meanwhile, at home,
We have been drinking with a riotous thirst   55
Pollutions from the brimming cup of wealth –
A selfish, lewd, effeminated race,
Contemptuous of all honourable rule,
Yet bartering freedom, and the poor man's life,
For gold, as at a market! The sweet words   60
Of Christian promise (words that even yet
Might stem destruction, were they wisely preached)
Are muttered o'er by men, whose tones proclaim
How flat and wearisome they feel their trade.
Rank scoffers some, but most too indolent   65
To deem them falsehoods, or to *know* their truth.

---

[4] *Sweet influences ... frame* the humble man is responsive to
the influence of nature, as recommended in *The Eolian Harp*
36–40.

Oh blasphemous! the book of life is made
A superstitious instrument on which
We gabble o'er the oaths we mean to break,[5]
For all must swear – all, and in every place,　　　　　　　70
College and wharf, council and justice-court,
All, all must swear, the briber and the bribed,
Merchant and lawyer, senator and priest,
The rich, the poor, the old man, and the young,
All, all make up one scheme of perjury,　　　　　　　75
That faith doth reel; the very name of God
Sounds like a juggler's charm; and bold with joy,
Forth from his dark and lonely hiding-place
(Portentous sight!), the owlet Atheism,
Sailing on obscene wings athwart the noon,　　　　　　　80
Drops his blue-fringed lids, and holds them close,
And, hooting at the glorious sun in heaven,
Cries out, 'Where is it?'
　　　　　　　Thankless too for peace
(Peace long preserved by fleets and perilous seas),
Secure from actual warfare, we have loved　　　　　　　85
To swell the war-whoop, passionate for war![6]
Alas! for ages ignorant of all
Its ghastlier workings (famine or blue plague,
Battle, or siege, or flight through wintry snows),
We, this whole people, have been clamorous　　　　　　　90
For war and bloodshed, animating sports,
The which we pay for,[7] as a thing to talk of –
Spectators and not combatants! No guess
Anticipative of a wrong unfelt,
No speculation on contingency,[8]　　　　　　　95
However dim and vague, too vague and dim
To yield a justifying cause – and forth
(Stuffed out with big preamble, holy names,
And adjurations of [9] the God in heaven)
We send our mandates[10] for the certain death　　　　　　　100
Of thousands and ten thousands! Boys and girls,
And women that would groan to see a child
Pull off an insect's leg – all read of war,
The best amusement for our morning meal!
The poor wretch, who has learnt his only prayers　　　　　　　105
From curses, who knows scarcely words enough
To ask a blessing of his heavenly Father,
Becomes a fluent phraseman, absolute
And technical in victories and defeats,
And all our dainty terms for fratricide,　　　　　　　110
Terms which we trundle smoothly o'er our tongues

---

[5] *We gabble . . . break* Coleridge's target is subscription to the Thirty-nine Articles, the practice whereby dissenters from the established church were compelled to swear allegiance to its founding principles.
[6] *passionate for war* Coleridge's target is popular support for the war with France.

[7] *animating sports . . . pay for* this is a pious attack on such sports as boxing, cockfighting, and the like. The obvious comparison is with gladiatorial combat in ancient Rome.
[8] *No guess . . . contingency* i.e. there is no attempt to anticipate the harm that will come to those fighting on our behalf.
[9] *adjurations of* appeals to.
[10] *mandates* orders.

Like mere abstractions, empty sounds to which
We join no feeling and attach no form,
As if the soldier died without a wound,
As if the fibres of this godlike frame   115
Were gored without a pang, as if the wretch,
Who fell in battle doing bloody deeds,
Passed off to heaven, *translated* and not killed,
As though he had no wife to pine for him,
No God to judge him! Therefore evil days   120
Are coming on us, oh my countrymen!
And what if all-avenging Providence,
Strong and retributive, should make us know
The meaning of our words, force us to feel
The desolation and the agony   125
Of our fierce doings?[11]
                Spare us yet awhile,
Father and God! Oh spare us yet awhile!
Oh let not English women drag their flight
Fainting beneath the burden of their babes,
Of the sweet infants, that but yesterday   130
Laughed at the breast! Sons, brothers, husbands, all
Who ever gazed with fondness on the forms
Which grew up with you round the same fireside,
And all who ever heard the sabbath bells
Without the infidel's scorn, make yourselves pure!   135
Stand forth! Be men! Repel an impious foe,
Impious and false, a light yet cruel race
That laugh away all virtue, mingling mirth
With deeds of murder; and still promising
Freedom, themselves too sensual to be free,   140
Poison life's amities,[12] and cheat the heart
Of faith and quiet hope, and all that soothes
And all that lifts the spirit! Stand we forth;
Render them back upon th' insulted ocean,
And let them toss as idly on its waves   145
As the vile seaweeds which some mountain blast
Swept from our shores! And oh! may we return
Not with a drunken triumph, but with fear,
Repenting of the wrongs with which we stung
So fierce a foe to frenzy!
               I have told,   150
Oh Britons! Oh my brethren! I have told
Most bitter truth, but without bitterness.
Nor deem my zeal or factious or mistimed;[13]
For never can true courage dwell with them
Who, playing tricks with conscience, dare not look   155
At their own vices. We have been too long

---

[11] *And what if . . . doings* Coleridge's point is that God will punish English people for the way in which they have become hardened to the reality of war.
[12] *amities* friendships.

[13] *or . . . or* either . . . or; *factious* Coleridge was disillusioned with politics; as he told his brother George in March 1798, 'I am of no party. It is true, I think the present ministry weak and perhaps unprincipled men, but I could not with a safe conscience vote for their removal' (Griggs i 396).

Dupes of a deep delusion![14] Some, belike,
Groaning with restless enmity, expect
All change from change of constituted power –
As if a government had been a robe   160
On which our vice and wretchedness were tagged
Like fancy-points and fringes,[15] with the robe
Pulled off at pleasure.[16] Fondly these attach
A radical causation to a few
Poor drudges of chastising Providence,   165
Who borrow all their hues and qualities
From our own folly and rank wickedness,
Which gave them birth, and nurse them.[17] Others, meanwhile,
Dote with a mad idolatry; and all
Who will not fall before their images   170
And yield them worship, they are enemies
Ev'n of their country! Such have I been deemed.[18]
But oh dear Britain! Oh my mother isle!
Needs must thou prove a name most dear and holy
To me, a son, a brother, and a friend,   175
A husband and a father, who revere
All bonds of natural love, and find them all
Within the limits of thy rocky shores.
Oh native Britain! Oh my mother isle!
How shouldst thou prove aught else but dear and holy   180
To me, who from thy lakes and mountain-hills,
Thy clouds, thy quiet dales, thy rocks, and seas,
Have drunk in all my intellectual[19] life,
All sweet sensations, all ennobling thoughts,
All adoration of the God in nature,   185
All lovely and all honourable things,
Whatever makes this mortal spirit feel
The joy and greatness of its future being?[20]
There lives nor form nor feeling in my soul
Unborrowed from my country! Oh divine   190
And beauteous island, thou hast been my sole
And most magnificent temple, in the which
I walk with awe, and sing my stately songs,
Loving the God that made me!
                         May my fears,
My filial fears, be vain! and may the vaunts   195

---

[14] *a deep delusion* namely, the radical hope that the French Revolution would lead to a new era of justice and enlightenment in human affairs.

[15] *fancy-points and fringes* buttons and bows. As his mother-in-law ran a dress shop, Coleridge would have known that fancy-points were ornate laces used for fastening clothes; their undoing would allow a robe to be 'pulled off'. The fringes would have consisted of lace edgings.

[16] *As if ... pleasure* the vice and wretchedness of the *ancien régime* is compared with a robe that has been removed; Coleridge is saying that vice and wretchedness are not so easily done away with – they are endemic in humanity.

[17] *Fondly ... nurse them* it is a foolish (fond) delusion to ascribe radicalism to those responsible for destroying the

ancien régime; they are really the servants (drudges) of God, empowered by the inherent evil of those who gave them power – the people.

[18] *Such have I been deemed* during his support of France in the war against England, Coleridge was considered an enemy of the state. He has now, of course, changed his mind (see preceding poem), though it is worth noting that Pitt's spies were watching both Wordsworth and Coleridge at this moment.

[19] *intellectual* spiritual.

[20] *How shouldst thou prove ... being* the point is that Coleridge's moral and spiritual being has been shaped by the English countryside – by nature, in fact.

And menace of the vengeful enemy
Pass like the gust that roared and died away
In the distant tree, which heard, and only heard;
In this low dell bowed not the delicate grass.
But now the gentle dew-fall sends abroad   200
The fruitlike perfume of the golden furze;
The light has left the summit of the hill,
Though still a sunny gleam lies beautiful
On the long-ivied beacon.[21] Now farewell,
Farewell awhile, oh soft and silent spot!   205
On the green sheep-track, up the heathy hill,
Homeward I wind my way; and lo! recalled
From bodings, that have well-nigh wearied me,
I find myself upon the brow, and pause
Startled! And after lonely sojourning   210
In such a quiet and surrounded scene,
This burst of prospect (here the shadowy main,
Dim-tinted, there the mighty majesty
Of that huge amphitheatre of rich
And elmy fields) seems like society   215
Conversing with the mind, and giving it
A livelier impulse, and a dance of thought;
And now, beloved Stowey, I behold
Thy church-tower, and (methinks) the four huge elms
Clust'ring, which mark the mansion of my friend;[22]   220
And close behind them, hidden from my view,
Is my own lowly cottage, where my babe
And my babe's mother[23] dwell in peace! With light
And quickened footsteps thitherward I tend,
Rememb'ring thee, oh green and silent dell!   225
And grateful that by nature's quietness
And solitary musings all my heart
Is softened, and made worthy to indulge
Love, and the thoughts that yearn for humankind.

Letter from S. T. Coleridge to Thomas Poole, 6 April 1799[1] (extract)

My baby has not lived in vain! This life has been to him what it is to all of us – education and development! Fling yourself forward into your immortality only a few thousand years, and how small will not the difference between one year old and sixty years appear! Consciousness! It is no otherwise necessary to our conceptions of future continuance than as connecting the *present link* of our being with the one *immediately* preceding it – and *that* degree of consciousness, *that* small portion of *memory*, it would not only be arrogant, but in the highest degree absurd, to deny even to a much younger infant.

---

[21] *the long-ivied beacon* a chain of beacons were built across the countryside to warn of threats of invasion from France. That this one is covered in ivy testifies to its prolonged redundancy; Coleridge's implicit hope is that it will remain so.

[22] *the mansion of my friend* Alfoxden House, four miles from Nether Stowey, where Coleridge had lodged the Wordsworths (see p. 458).

[23] *my babe ... mother* Hartley Coleridge and Sara, who was pregnant with Berkeley Coleridge (see next letter).

LETTER FROM S. T. COLERIDGE TO THOMAS POOLE
[1] Coleridge's son, Berkeley (born 14 May 1798), died 10 February 1799 during his father's stay in Germany. At first the news was kept from Coleridge, but later Poole thought it better to let him know. This letter is Coleridge's first written response to the news, from Göttingen. Berkeley's death seems to have been a catalyst for the 'Infant Babe' passage in *Two-Part Prelude* ii 267–310.

'Tis a strange assertion that the essence of identity lies in *recollective* consciousness; 'twere scarcely less ridiculous to affirm that the 8 miles from Stowey to Bridgwater consist in the 8 milestones. Death in a doting old age falls upon my feelings ever as a more hopeless phenomenon than death in infancy – but *nothing* is hopeless.

What if the vital force which I sent from my arm into the stone, as I flung it in the air and skimmed it upon the water – what if even that did not perish? It was *Life*! It was a particle of *Being*! It was *Power*! – and *how could* it perish? *Life, Power, Being*! – organization may be and probably *is* their *effect*; their *cause* it *cannot* be! I have indulged very curious fancies concerning that force, that *swarm* of motive powers which I sent out of my body into that stone – and which, one by one, left the untractable or already possessed mass, and – but the German ocean lies between us. It is all too far to send you such fancies as these! Grief indeed,

> Doth love to dally with fantastic thoughts,
> And smiling, like a sickly moralist,
> Finds some resemblance to her own concerns
> In the straws of chance, and things inanimate![2]

But I cannot truly say that I grieve. I am perplexed, I am sad – and a little thing, a very trifle, would make me weep. But for the death of the baby I have *not* wept! Oh, this strange, strange, strange scene-shifter, death! – that giddies one with insecurity, and so unsubstantiates the living things that one has grasped and handled! Some months ago Wordsworth transmitted to me a most sublime epitaph;[3] whether it had any reality, I cannot say. Most probably, in some gloomier moment he had fancied the moment in which his sister might die.

Lines Written in the Album at Elbingerode, in the Hartz Forest (composed by 17 May 1799)[1]

From THE ANNUAL ANTHOLOGY (1800)

I stood on Brocken's sovran height,[2] and saw
Woods crowding upon woods, hills over hills,
A *surging* scene, and only limited
By the blue distance. Heavily my way
Homeward I dragged through fir-groves evermore,   5
Where bright green moss heaves in sepulchral forms,
Speckled with sunshine; and, but seldom heard,
The sweet bird's song became an hollow sound;
And the breeze murmuring indivisibly
Preserved its solemn murmur most distinct   10
From many a note of many a waterfall,
And the brook's chatter, mid whose islet stones
The dingy kidling with its tinkling bell
Leapt frolicsome, or old romantic goat

---

[2]   Coleridge quotes himself: *Osorio* V i 11–14.
[3]   *a most sublime epitaph* 'A slumber did my spirit seal', p. 327.

LINES WRITTEN IN THE ALBUM AT ELBINGERODE, IN THE HARTZ FOREST
[1]   Coleridge sent this poem in a letter to his wife, 17 May 1799, with the introduction: 'At the inn they brought us an Album, or Stammbuch, requesting that we would write our

names and something or other as a remembrance that we had been there. I wrote the following lines, which I send to you not that they possess a grain of merit as poetry, but because they contain a true account of my journey from the Brocken to Elbinrode' (Griggs i 504).
[2]   *Brocken's sovran height* Coleridge notes that the Great Brocken is 'the highest mountain in the Hartz, and indeed in north Germany.'

Sat, his white beard slow-waving. I moved on   15
In low and languid mood,[3] for I had found
That grandest scenes have but imperfect charms,
Where the sight vainly wanders, nor beholds
One spot with which the heart associates
Holy remembrances of friend or child,   20
Or gentle maid, our first and early love,
Or father, or the venerable name
Of our adored country!
                Oh thou Queen,
Thou delegated deity of earth,
Oh dear, dear, England! How my longing eye   25
Turned westward, shaping in the steady clouds
Thy sand and high white cliffs! Oh native land,
Filled with the thought of thee, this heart was proud,
Yea, mine eye swam with tears, that all the view
From sovran Brocken, woods and woody hills,   30
Floated away like a departing dream,
Feeble and dim! Stranger, these impulses
Blame thou not lightly, nor will I profane
With hasty judgement or injurious doubt
That man's sublimer spirit, who can feel   35
That God is everywhere! – the God who framed
Mankind to be one mighty family,
Himself our Father, and the world our home.

Christabel[1]

From CHRISTABEL; KUBLA KHAN: A VISION; THE PAINS OF SLEEP (1816)

Part I (composed *c*. February 1798)

'Tis the middle of night by the castle clock,
And the owls have awakened the crowing cock;
Tu-whit! Tu-whoo!
And hark, again! the crowing cock,
How drowsily it crew.   5

---

[3] *In low and languid mood* Coleridge glosses this with a quotation from Southey:

    When I have gazed
From some high eminence on goodly vales,
And cots and villages embowered below,
The thought would rise that all to me was strange
Amid the scenes so fair, nor one small spot
Where my tired mind might rest, and call it 'home'.

              Southey's *Hymn to the Penates*

CHRISTABEL
[1] *Christabel* was not published until 1816. It had come close to appearing in the second edition of *Lyrical Ballads* (1800). Coleridge even sent Part I to the publishers in early September 1800, and was working towards its completion when, on 6 October 1800, Wordsworth decided to omit it. A few days later, in a demoralized state, Coleridge told Humphry Davy

that the poem 'was in direct opposition to the very purpose for which the *Lyrical Ballads* were published, viz. an experiment to see how far those passions, which alone give any value to extraordinary incidents, were capable of interesting, in and for themselves, in the incidents of common life' (Griggs i 631). A few months later Wordsworth remarked, less delicately, that 'the style of this poem was so discordant from my own that it could not be printed along with my poems with any propriety' (*EY* 309). Wordsworth's sceptical opinion of Coleridge's verse led him to append a stinging criticism of *The Ancient Mariner* to the poem as it appeared in *Lyrical Ballads* (1800) (see p. 345), and was recalled by Coleridge when, in 1818, he noted the 'cold praise and effective discouragement of every attempt of mine to roll onward in a distinct current of my own' (Griggs i 631n2). See also my 'Wordsworth's Fisher King', *Charles Lamb Bulletin* NS 98 (1997) 54–63.

Sir Leoline, the Baron rich,
Hath a toothless mastiff bitch;
From her kennel beneath the rock
She makes answer to the clock –
Four for the quarters and twelve for the hour,   10
Ever and aye, moonshine or shower,
Sixteen short howls not over loud;
Some say she sees my lady's shroud.

Is the night chilly and dark?
The night is chilly, but not dark –   15
The thin grey cloud is spread on high,
It covers but not hides the sky.
The moon is behind, and at the full,
And yet she looks both small and dull;
The night is chill, the cloud is grey –   20
'Tis a month before the month of May
And the spring comes slowly up this way.

The lovely lady, Christabel,
Whom her father loves so well,
What makes her in the wood so late,   25
A furlong² from the castle gate?
She had dreams all yesternight
Of her own betrothed knight –
Dreams that made her moan and leap
As on her bed she lay in sleep;   30
And she in the midnight wood will pray
For the weal³ of her lover that's far away.

She stole along, she nothing spoke,
The breezes they were still also;
And nought was green upon the oak   35
But moss and rarest mistletoe;
She kneels beneath the huge oak tree
And in silence prayeth she.

The lady leaps up suddenly,
The lovely lady, Christabel!   40
It moaned as near as near can be,
But what it is, she cannot tell:
On the other side it seems to be
Of the huge, broad-breasted, old oak tree.

The night is chill, the forest bare –   45
Is it the wind that moaneth bleak?
There is not wind enough in the air
To move away the ringlet curl

---

²   *A furlong* an eighth of a mile (220 yards).   ³   *weal* welfare.

From the lovely lady's cheek;
There is not wind enough to twirl   50
The one red leaf, the last of its clan,
That dances as often as dance it can,
Hanging so light and hanging so high
On the topmost twig that looks up at the sky.

Hush, beating heart of Christabel!   55
Jesu Maria, shield her well!
She folded her arms beneath her cloak
And stole to the other side of the oak:
    What sees she there?

There she sees a damsel bright   60
Dressed in a silken robe of white;
Her neck, her feet, her arms were bare,
And the jewels disordered in her hair.
I guess 'twas frightful there to see
A lady so richly clad as she –   65
Beautiful exceedingly!

'Mary Mother, save me now!'
Said Christabel, 'And who art thou?'

The lady strange made answer meet
And her voice was faint and sweet.   70
'Have pity on my sore distress,
I scarce can speak for weariness!'
'Stretch forth thy hand, and have no fear',
Said Christabel, 'How cam'st thou here?'
And the lady whose voice was faint and sweet   75
Did thus pursue her answer meet:
'My sire is of a noble line,
And my name is Geraldine.
Five warriors seized me yestermorn –
Me, even me, a maid forlorn;   80
They choked my cries with force and fright
And tied me on a palfrey[4] white.
The palfrey was as fleet as wind,
And they rode furiously behind.
They spurred amain,[5] their steeds were white,   85
And once we crossed the shade of night.
As sure as Heaven shall rescue me,
I have no thought what men they be;
Nor do I know how long it is
(For I have lain in fits, I wis)   90
Since one, the tallest of the five,
Took me from the palfrey's back,
A weary woman scarce alive.
Some muttered words his comrades spoke,

---

[4] *palfrey* saddle-horse for ordinary riding, as opposed to a   [5] *amain* violently.
war-horse.

He placed me underneath this oak,   95
He swore they would return with haste;
Whither they went I cannot tell –
I thought I heard, some minutes past,
Sounds as of a castle-bell.
Stretch forth thy hand (thus ended she)   100
And help a wretched maid to flee.'

Then Christabel stretched forth her hand
And comforted fair Geraldine,
Saying that she should command
The service of Sir Leoline,   105
And straight be convoyed,[6] free from thrall,[7]
Back to her noble father's hall.

So up she rose and forth they passed
With hurrying steps, yet nothing fast;
Her lucky stars the lady blessed,   110
And Christabel, she sweetly said,
'All our household are at rest,
Each one sleeping in his bed.
Sir Leoline is weak in health
And may not well awakened be,   115
So to my room we'll creep in stealth
And you tonight must sleep with me.

They crossed the moat, and Christabel
Took the key that fitted well –
A little door she opened straight   120
All in the middle of the gate,
The gate that was ironed[8] within and without
Where an army in battle array had marched out.

The lady sank, belike through pain,
And Christabel with might and main   125
Lifted her up, a weary weight,
Over the threshold of the gate;
Then the lady rose again
And moved as she were not in pain.

So free from danger, free from fear,   130
They crossed the court – right glad they were.
And Christabel devoutly cried
To the lady by her side,
'Praise we the Virgin all divine
Who hath rescued thee from thy distress!'   135
'Alas, alas,' said Geraldine,
'I cannot speak for weariness.'
So free from danger, free from fear,
They crossed the court – right glad they were.

---

6   *convoyed* escorted.
7   *thrall* captivity.

8   *ironed* reinforced with iron.

Outside her kennel, the mastiff old   140
Lay fast asleep in moonshine cold.
The mastiff old did not awake,
Yet she an angry moan did make.
And what can ail the mastiff bitch?
Never till now she uttered yell   145
Beneath the eye of Christabel.
Perhaps it is the owlet's scritch,
For what can ail the mastiff bitch?

They passed the hall that echoes still,
Pass as lightly as you will.   150
The brands[9] were flat, the brands were dying,
Amid their own white ashes lying;
But when the lady passed, there came
A tongue of light, a fit of flame,
And Christabel saw the lady's eye,   155
And nothing else saw she thereby
Save the boss of the shield of Sir Leoline tall
Which hung in a murky old nitch[10] in the wall.
'Oh softly tread', said Christabel,
'My father seldom sleepeth well.'   160

Sweet Christabel, her feet she bares
And they are creeping up the stairs,
Now in glimmer and now in gloom,
And now they pass the Baron's room,
As still as death with stifled breath;   165
And now have reached her chamber door,
And now with eager feet press down
The rushes of her chamber floor.

The moon shines dim in the open air
And not a moonbeam enters here.   170
But they without its light can see
The chamber carved so curiously,
Carved with figures strange and sweet
All made out of the carver's brain
For a lady's chamber meet;   175
The lamp with twofold silver chain
Is fastened to an angel's feet.

The silver lamp burns dead and dim,
But Christabel the lamp will trim.[11]
She trimmed the lamp and made it bright   180
And left it swinging to and fro,
While Geraldine in wretched plight
Sank down upon the floor below.

---

9   *brands* wood burnt in the hearth.
10   *nitch* niche.

11   *trim* to clean the wick of a lamp for fresh burning.

'Oh weary lady Geraldine,
I pray you, drink this cordial[12] wine.   185
It is a wine of virtuous powers –
My mother made it of wild-flowers.'

'And will your mother pity me,
Who am a maiden most forlorn?'
Christabel answered, 'Woe is me!   190
She died the hour that I was born.
I have heard the grey-haired friar tell
How on her deathbed she did say
That she should hear the castle bell
Strike twelve upon my wedding day.   195
Oh mother dear, that thou wert here!'
'I would', said Geraldine, 'she were.'

But soon with altered voice said she,
'Off, wandering mother! Peak and pine!
I have power to bid thee flee.'[13]   200
Alas, what ails poor Geraldine?
Why stares she with unsettled eye?
Can she the bodiless dead espy?
And why with hollow voice cries she,
'Off, woman, off! this hour is mine –   205
Though thou her guardian spirit be,
Off, woman, off! – 'tis given to me'?

Then Christabel knelt by the lady's side,
And raised to heaven her eyes so blue;
'Alas!' said she, 'this ghastly ride –   210
Dear lady, it hath wildered[14] you!'
The lady wiped her moist cold brow,
And faintly said, ''Tis over now!'

Again the wild-flower wine she drank;
Her fair large eyes 'gan[15] glitter bright,   215
And from the floor whereon she sank,
The lofty lady stood upright:
She was most beautiful to see,
Like a lady of a far countrée.

And thus the lofty lady spake: 220
'All they who live in the upper sky
Do love you, holy Christabel!
And you love them, and for their sake,
And for the good which me befell,
Even I, in my degree will try,   225
Fair maiden, to requite you well.
But now unrobe yourself, for I
Must pray, ere yet in bed I lie.'

---

[12] *cordial* reviving, restorative.
[13] *Off . . . flee* in a marginal note entered in a copy of the 1816 printed text, Coleridge explained: 'The mother of Christabel, who is now her guardian spirit, appears to Geral-
dine, as in answer to her wish. Geraldine fears the spirit, but yet has power over it for a time'.
[14] *wildered* perplexed, bewildered.
[15] *'gan* began to.

Quoth Christabel, 'So let it be!'
And as the lady bade, did she.   230
Her gentle limbs did she undress,
And lay down in her loveliness.

But through her brain, of weal and woe
So many thoughts moved to and fro
That vain it were her lids to close;   235
So halfway from the bed she rose,
And on her elbow did recline
To look at the lady Geraldine.

Beneath the lamp the lady bowed
And slowly rolled her eyes around;   240
Then drawing in her breath aloud
Like one that shuddered, she unbound
The cincture[16] from beneath her breast:
Her silken robe and inner vest
Dropped to her feet, and full in view,   245
Behold! her bosom and half her side –
A sight to dream of, not to tell!
And she is to sleep by Christabel.[17]

She took two paces and a stride,
And lay down by the maiden's side;   250
And in her arms the maid she took,
        Ah wel-a-day!
And with low voice and doleful look
        These words did say:
'In the touch of this bosom there worketh a spell   255
Which is lord of thy utterance, Christabel![18]
Thou knowest tonight, and wilt know tomorrow,
This mark of my shame, this seal of my sorrow;
        But vainly thou warrest,
            For this is alone in   260
        Thy power to declare,
            That in the dim forest
            Thou heard'st a low moaning,
And found'st a bright lady surpassingly fair,
And didst bring her home with thee in love and in charity,   265
To shield her and shelter her from the damp air.'

The Conclusion to Part I (composed *c.* February 1798)

It was a lovely sight to see
The lady Christabel, when she

---

[16] *cincture* belt.
[17] *Behold . . . Christabel* The MS text of 1800, in the Christa-
bel notebook at the Wordsworth Library, Grasmere, makes
Geraldine less human:
    Behold! her bosom and half her side
    Are lean and old and foul of hue –
    A sight to dream of, not to tell,
    And she is to sleep with Christabel.

In a MS version of 1816, Geraldine's side is 'dark and rough as
the sea-wolf's hide'.
[18] *In the touch . . . Christabel* a marginal note to a copy of the
1816 printed text by Coleridge reads: 'As soon as the wicked
bosom, with the mysterious sign of evil stamped thereby,
touches Christabel, she is deprived of the power of disclosing
what had occurred'.

Was praying at the old oak tree.
>Amid the jagged shadows 270
>Of mossy leafless boughs,
>Kneeling in the moonlight
>To make her gentle vows;
Her slender palms together pressed,
Heaving sometimes on her breast; 275
Her face resigned to bliss or bale,
Her face – oh call it fair, not pale!
And both blue eyes more bright than clear,
Each about to have a tear.

With open eyes (ah woe is me!) 280
Asleep, and dreaming fearfully,
Fearfully dreaming, yet I wis,
Dreaming that alone, which is –
Oh sorrow and shame! Can this be she,
The lady who knelt at the old oak tree? 285
And lo! the worker of these harms
That holds the maiden in her arms,
Seems to slumber still and mild,
As a mother with her child.

A star hath set, a star hath risen, 290
Oh Geraldine, since arms of thine
Have been the lovely lady's prison!
Oh Geraldine, one hour was thine –
Thou'st had thy will! By tairn[19] and rill
The night-birds all that hour were still; 295
But now they are jubilant anew,
From cliff and tower, tu-whoo! tu-whoo!
Tu-whoo! tu-whoo! from wood and fell!

And see! the lady Christabel
Gathers herself from out her trance; 300
Her limbs relax, her countenance
Grows sad and soft; the smooth thin lids
Close o'er her eyes, and tears she sheds –
Large tears that leave the lashes bright;
And oft the while she seems to smile 305
As infants at a sudden light!

Yea she doth smile and she doth weep
Like a youthful hermitess
Beauteous in a wilderness,
Who praying always, prays in sleep. 310
And if she move unquietly,

---

[19] *tairn* the earliest MS version of the poem has a note: 'Tairn or tarn (derived by Lye from the Icelandic *tiorn*, stagnum, palus) is rendered in our dictionaries as synonymous with mere or lake; but it is properly a large pool or reservoir in the mountains, commonly the feeder of some mere in the valleys. Tarn Watling and Blellum Tarn, though on lower ground than other tarns, are yet not exceptions – for both are on elevations, and Blellum Tarn feeds the Winander mere'. This is the first clear indication that the poem is set in the Lake District.

Perchance 'tis but the blood so free
Comes back and tingles in her feet.
No doubt she hath a vision sweet:
What if her guardian spirit 'twere?   315
What if she knew her mother near?
But this she knows – in joys and woes,
That saints will aid if men will call,
For the blue sky bends over all.

Part II (composed by 18 August 1800)

'Each matin bell',[20] the Baron saith,   320
'Knells us back to a world of death.'
These words Sir Leoline first said
When he rose and found his lady dead;
These words Sir Leoline will say
Many a morn to his dying day.   325
And hence the custom and law began
That still at dawn the sacristan[21]
Who duly pulls the heavy bell
Five and forty beads must tell[22]
Between each stroke – a warning knell   330
Which not a soul can choose but hear
From Bratha Head[23] to Windermere.[24]

Saith Bracy the bard, 'So let it knell!
And let the drowsy sacristan[25]
Still count as slowly as he can!   335
There is no lack of such, I ween,
As well fill up the space between.
In Langdale Pike[26] and Witch's Lair[27]
And Dungeon Ghyll[28] (so foully rent),
With ropes of rock and bells of air   340
Three sinful sextons' ghosts are pent,
Who all give back, one after t'other,
The death-note to their living brother;
And oft too, by the knell offended,
Just as their one! – two! – three! is ended,   345
The Devil mocks the doleful tale
With a merry peal from Borrowdale.[29]

The air is still – through mist and cloud
That merry peal comes ringing loud;
And Geraldine shakes off her dread   350
And rises lightly from the bed,

---

[20] *matin bell* sounded at midnight or 2 a.m.
[21] *sacristan* sexton of a parish church.
[22] *tell* count.
[23] *Bratha Head* i.e. the length of Langdale, through which
the River Brathay runs until it reaches Windermere.
[24] *Windermere* Windermere lake.
[25] *sacristan* (or sexton) officer responsible for the fabric of the
church; his main duties were ringing bells and digging graves.

[26] *Langdale Pike* consists of two mountains of over 2,300 ft.
each, called Harrison Stickle and Pike of Stickle.
[27] *Witch's Lair* probably the cave on Pike of Stickle.
[28] *Dungeon Ghyll* stream going up between the two Lang-
dale Pikes to a height of 2,400 ft.
[29] *Borrowdale* the valley of Borrowdale is due north of the
Langdale Pikes.

Puts on her silken vestments white
And tricks her hair in lovely plight,[30]
And nothing doubting of her spell
Awakens the lady Christabel.   355
'Sleep you, sweet lady Christabel?
I trust that you have rested well.'

And Christabel awoke and spied
The same who lay down by her side —
Oh rather say, the same whom she   360
Raised up beneath the old oak tree!
Nay, fairer yet, and yet more fair,
For she belike hath drunken deep
Of all the blessedness of sleep!
And while she spake, her looks, her air   365
Such gentle thankfulness declare,
That (so it seemed) her girded vests
Grew tight beneath her heaving breasts.
'Sure I have sinned!' said Christabel,
'Now heaven be praised if all be well!'   370
And in low faltering tones, yet sweet,
Did she the lofty lady greet
With such perplexity of mind
As dreams too lively leave behind.[31]

So quickly she rose, and quickly arrayed   375
Her maiden limbs, and having prayed
That He who on the cross did groan
Might wash away her sins unknown,
She forthwith led fair Geraldine
To meet her sire, Sir Leoline.   380

The lovely maid and the lady tall
Are pacing both into the hall,
And pacing on through page and groom,
Enter the Baron's presence-room.[32]

The Baron rose, and while he pressed   385
His gentle daughter to his breast,
With cheerful wonder in his eyes
The lady Geraldine espies,
And gave such welcome to the same,
As might beseem so bright a dame!   390

But when he heard the lady's tale,
And when she told her father's name,
Why waxed[33] Sir Leoline so pale,
Murmuring o'er the name again —
Lord Roland de Vaux of Tryermaine?   395

---

³⁰ *plight* fashion.
³¹ *With such ... behind* in a MS marginal note to a copy of
the 1816 printed text, Coleridge wrote: 'Christabel is made to
believe that the fearful sight had taken place only in a dream'.

³² *presence-room* room where Sir Leoline receives guests;
reception room.
³³ *waxed* became.

Alas, they had been friends in youth,
But whispering tongues can poison truth,
And constancy lives in realms above;
And life is thorny, and youth is vain,
And to be wroth[34] with one we love   400
Doth work like madness in the brain.
And thus it chanced, as I divine,
With Roland and Sir Leoline;
Each spake words of high disdain
And insult to his heart's best brother –   405
They parted, ne'er to meet again!
But never either found another
To free the hollow heart from paining;
They stood aloof, the scars remaining
Like cliffs which had been rent asunder.   410
A dreary sea now flows between,
But neither heat, nor frost, nor thunder
Shall wholly do away, I ween,
The marks of that which once hath been.

Sir Leoline a moment's space   415
Stood gazing on the damsel's face,
And the youthful Lord of Tryermaine
Came back upon his heart again.

Oh then the Baron forgot his age,
His noble heart swelled high with rage;   420
He swore by the wounds in Jesu's side
He would proclaim it far and wide
With trump and solemn heraldry,
That they who thus had wronged the dame
Were base as spotted infamy!   425
'And if they dare deny the same,
My herald shall appoint a week,
And let the recreant traitors seek
My tournay court[35] – that there and then
I may dislodge their reptile souls   430
From the bodies and forms of men!'
He spake – his eye in lightning rolls,
For the lady was ruthlessly seized, and he kenned[36]
In the beautiful lady the child of his friend.

And now the tears were on his face,   435
And fondly in his arms he took
Fair Geraldine, who met th' embrace,
Prolonging it with joyous look,
Which when she viewed, a vision fell
Upon the soul of Christabel –   440
The vision of fear, the touch and pain!

---

34   *wroth* angry.
35   *My tournay court* The sheriff's county court usually met
twice a year.

36   *kenned* recognized.

She shrunk and shuddered, and saw again
(Ah woe is me! Was it for thee,
Thou gentle maid, such sights to see?)[37] —
Again she saw that bosom old,   445
Again she felt that bosom cold,
And drew in her breath with a hissing sound.
Whereat the knight turned wildly round,
And nothing saw but his own sweet maid
With eyes upraised, as one that prayed.   450

The touch, the sight, had passed away,
And in its stead that vision blessed,
Which comforted her after rest,[38]
While in the lady's arms she lay,
Had put a rapture in her breast,   455
And on her lips and o'er her eyes
Spread smiles like light!
                With new surprise,
'What ails then my beloved child?'
The Baron said. His daughter mild
Made answer, 'All will yet be well!'   460
I ween she had no power to tell
Aught else, so mighty was the spell.
Yet he who saw this Geraldine
Had deemed her sure a thing divine,
Such sorrow with such grace she blended,   465
As if she feared she had offended
Sweet Christabel, that gentle maid!
And with such lowly tones she prayed
She might be sent without delay
Home to her father's mansion.
                      'Nay,   470
Nay, by my soul!' said Leoline.
'Ho! Bracy the bard, the charge be thine!
Go thou with music sweet and loud,
And take two steeds with trappings proud,
And take the youth whom thou lov'st best   475
To bear thy harp and learn thy song,
And clothe you both in solemn vest,
And over the mountains haste along,
Lest wand'ring folk that are abroad
Detain you on the valley road.   480
And when he has crossed the Irthing flood,
My merry bard, he hastes, he hastes
Up Knorren Moor, through Halegarth Wood,[39]
And reaches soon that castle good
Which stands and threatens Scotland's wastes.   485

---

[37] *Which when she viewed . . . to see* Coleridge's MS note in a copy of the 1816 volume reads: 'Christabel then recollects the whole, and knows that it was not a dream, but yet cannot disclose the fact that the strange lady is a supernatural being with the stamp of the Evil Ones on her'.

[38] *The touch . . . after rest* in a MS marginal note to a copy of the 1816 printed text, Coleridge wrote: 'Christabel for a moment sees her mother's spirit'.

[39] *Irthing flood . . . Halegarth Wood* in a MS marginal note to a copy of the 1816 printed text, Coleridge wrote: 'How gladly Sir Leoline repeats the names and shows how familarly he had once been acquainted with all the spots and paths in the neighbourhood of his former friend's castle and residence'.

Bard Bracy! Bard Bracy! Your horses are fleet,
Ye must ride up the hall, your music so sweet,
More loud than your horses' echoing feet!
And loud and loud to Lord Roland call,
"Thy daughter is safe in Langdale hall!   490
Thy beautiful daughter is safe and free —
Sir Leoline greets thee thus through me.
He bids thee come without delay
With all thy numerous array,
And take thy lovely daughter home;   495
And he will meet thee on the way
With all his numerous array,
White with their panting palfreys' foam!"
And, by mine honour, I will say
That I repent me of the day   500
When I spake words of fierce disdain
To Roland de Vaux of Tryermaine!
For since that evil hour hath flown,
Many a summer's sun have shone;
Yet ne'er found I a friend again   505
Like Roland de Vaux of Tryermaine.'

The lady fell and clasped his knees,
Her face upraised, her eyes o'erflowing;
And Bracy replied, with faltering voice,
His gracious hail⁴⁰ on all bestowing: 510
'Thy words, thou sire of Christabel,
Are sweeter than my harp can tell;
Yet might I gain a boon⁴¹ of thee,
This day my journey should not be,
So strange a dream hath come to me,   515
That I had vowed with music loud
To clear yon wood from thing unblessed,
Warned by a vision in my rest!
For in my sleep I saw that dove,
That gentle bird whom thou dost love,   520
And call'st by thy own daughter's name —
Sir Leoline! I saw the same
Fluttering and uttering fearful moan
Among the green herbs⁴² in the forest alone;
Which when I saw, and when I heard,   525
I wondered what might ail the bird,
For nothing near it could I see
Save the grass and green herbs underneath the old tree.

And in my dream methought I went
To search out what might there be found,   530
And what the sweet bird's trouble meant

---

⁴⁰ *hail* greeting.   ⁴² *herbs* plants.
⁴¹ *boon* favour.

That thus lay fluttering on the ground.
I went, and peered, and could descry
No cause for her distressful cry;
But yet for her dear lady's sake   535
I stooped, methought the dove to take,
When lo! I saw a bright green snake
Coiled around its wings and neck.
Green as the herbs on which it couched,
Close by the dove's its head it crouched,   540
And with the dove it heaves and stirs,
Swelling its neck as she swelled hers!
I woke – it was the midnight hour,
The clock was echoing in the tower;
But though my slumber was gone by,   545
This dream it would not pass away –
It seems to live upon my eye!
And thence I vowed this self-same day,
With music strong and saintly song,
To wander through the forest bare   550
Lest aught unholy loiter there.'

Thus Bracy said. The Baron the while,
Half-listening, heard him with a smile,
Then turned to Lady Geraldine,
His eyes made up of wonder and love;   555
And said, in courtly accents fine,
'Sweet maid, Lord Roland's beauteous dove,
With arms more strong than harp or song,
Thy sire and I will crush the snake!'
He kissed her forehead as he spake,   560
And Geraldine, in maiden wise,
Casting down her large bright eyes,
With blushing cheek and courtesy fine
She turned her from Sir Leoline,
Softly gathering up her train   565
That o'er her right arm fell again,
And folded her arms across her chest,
And couched her head upon her breast,
And looked askance at Christabel –
Jesu Maria, shield her well!   570

A snake's small eye blinks dull and shy,
And the lady's eyes they shrunk in her head,
Each shrunk up to a serpent's eye;
And with somewhat of malice and more of dread
At Christabel she looked askance!   575
One moment and the sight was fled;
But Christabel, in dizzy trance,
Stumbling on the unsteady ground,
Shuddered aloud with a hissing sound;
And Geraldine again turned round   580
And like a thing that sought relief,
Full of wonder and full of grief,

She rolled her large bright eyes divine
Wildly on Sir Leoline.

The maid, alas, her thoughts are gone,   585
She nothing sees, no sight but one!
The maid, devoid of guile and sin,
I know not how, in fearful wise
So deeply had she drunken in
That look, those shrunken serpent eyes,   590
That all her features were resigned
To this sole image in her mind,
And passively did imitate
That look of dull and treacherous hate.
And thus she stood in dizzy trance,   595
Still picturing that look askance
With forced unconscious sympathy
Full before her father's view –
As far as such a look could be,
In eyes so innocent and blue!   600

But when the trance was o'er, the maid
Paused awhile and inly prayed,
Then falling at her father's feet,
'By my mother's soul do I entreat
That thou this woman send away!'   605
She said – and more she could not say,
For what she knew she could not tell,
O'er-mastered by the mighty spell.

Why is thy cheek so wan and wild,
Sir Leoline? Thy only child   610
Lies at thy feet, thy joy, thy pride,
So fair, so innocent, so mild –
The same for whom thy lady died!
Oh by the pangs of her dear mother,
Think thou no evil of thy child!   615
For her and thee, and for no other
She prayed the moment ere she died,
Prayed that the babe for whom she died
Might prove her dear lord's joy and pride!
   That prayer her deadly pangs beguiled,   620
     Sir Leoline!
   And would'st thou wrong thy only child,
     Her child and thine?
Within the Baron's heart and brain,
If thoughts like these had any share,   625
They only swelled his rage and pain
And did but work confusion there;
His heart was cleft with pain and rage,
His cheeks they quivered, his eyes were wild –
Dishonoured thus in his old age,   630
Dishonoured by his only child,
And all his hospitality
To th' insulted daughter of his friend

By more than woman's jealousy
Brought thus to a disgraceful end.   635
He rolled his eye with stern regard
Upon the gentle minstrel bard,
And said in tones abrupt, austere,
'Why, Bracy, dost thou loiter here?
I bade thee hence!' The bard obeyed;   640
And, turning from his own sweet maid,
The aged knight, Sir Leoline,
Led forth the lady Geraldine.[43]

The Conclusion to Part II (composed *c.* 6 May 1801)[44]

A little child,[45] a limber elf,
Singing, dancing to itself,   645
A fairy thing with red round cheeks
That always finds and never seeks,
Makes such a vision to the sight
As fills a father's eyes with light,
And pleasures flow in so thick and fast   650
Upon his heart, that he[46] at last
Must needs express his love's excess
With words of unmeant bitterness.
Perhaps 'tis pretty to force together
Thoughts so all unlike each other,   655
To mutter and mock a broken charm,
To dally with wrong that does no harm.
Perhaps 'tis tender too and pretty
At each wild word to feel within
A sweet recoil of love and pity.   660
And what if, in a world of sin
(Oh sorrow and shame should this be true!),
Such giddiness of heart and brain
Comes seldom save from rage and pain,
So talks as it's most used to do.   665

---

[43]   The poem was never concluded, and partly for this reason did not appear in *Lyrical Ballads* (1800). In later years Coleridge gave varying accounts of how it might have ended, including this, the most lengthy, recorded by James Gillman: 'Over the mountains, the Bard, as directed by Sir Leoline, "hastes" with his disciple; but in consequence of one of those inundations supposed to be common to this country, the spot only where the castle once stood is discovered, the edifice itself being washed away. He determines to return. Geraldine being acquainted with all that is passing, like the Weird Sisters in *Macbeth*, vanishes. Reappearing, however, she waits the return of the Bard, exciting in the meantime, by her wily arts, all the anger she could rouse in the Baron's breast, as well as that jealousy of which he is described to have been susceptible. The old Bard and the youth at length arrive, and therefore she can no longer personate the character of Geraldine, the daughter of Lord Roland de Vaux, but changes her appearance to that of the accepted though absent lover of Christabel. Next ensues a courtship most distressing to Christabel, who feels (she knows not why) great disgust for her once favoured knight. This coldness is very painful to the Baron, who has no more conception than herself of the supernatural transformation. She at last yields to her father's entreaties, and consents to approach the altar with this hated suitor. The real lover returning, enters at this moment, and produces the ring which she had once given him in sign of her betrothment. Thus defeated, the supernatural being Geraldine disappears. As predicted, the castle bell tolls, the mother's voice is heard, and to the exceeding great joy of the parties, the rightful marriage takes place, after which follows a reconciliation and explanation between the father and daughter' (James Gillman, *The Life of Samuel Taylor Coleridge,* (1838), pp. 301–2).

[44]   These lines were sent as a fragment to Southey in a letter of 6 May 1801 (Griggs ii 728); it is not clear as to whether they were at that time considered to form part of *Christabel* (quite possibly not). They appeared as the conclusion to Part II in the printed text of 1816.

[45]   *A little child* Hartley Coleridge.

[46]   *he* i.e. the father of l. 649.

The Day-Dream (composed probably March 1802, published *The Morning Post* 19 October 1802; edited from MS)[1]

1

If thou wert here, these tears were tears of light!
But from as sweet a day-dream did I start
As ever made these eyes grow idly bright;
And though I weep, yet still about the heart
A dear and playful tenderness doth linger,   5
Touching my heart as with a baby's finger.

2

My mouth half-open like a witless man,
I saw the couch, I saw the quiet room,
The heaving shadows and the firelight gloom;
And on my lips I know not what there ran –   10
On my unmoving lips a subtile[2] feeling;
I know not what, but had the same been stealing

3

Upon a sleeping mother's lips, I guess
It would have made the loving mother dream
That she was softly stooping down to kiss   15
Her babe, that something more than babe did seem –
An obscure presence of its darling father,
Yet still its own sweet baby self far rather!

4

Across my chest there lived a weight so warm
As if some bird had taken shelter there;   20
And lo, upon the couch, a woman's form! –
Thine, Sara,[3] thine! Oh joy, if thine it were!
I gazed with anxious hope, and feared to stir it –
A deeper trance ne'er rapt a yearning spirit!

THE DAY-DREAM
[1] The date of composition must remain conjectural, though I have accepted George Whalley's argument that this poem was written prior to *A Letter to Sara Hutchinson*, probably at Greta Hall. When published in the *Morning Post*, in somewhat revised form, it appeared under the title, *The Day-Dream, from an Emigrant to his Absent Wife*.

[2] *subtle* delicate, fine.
[3] Sara Hutchinson (1775–1835), Coleridge's 'Asra', was Wordsworth's sister-in-law. Coleridge's love for her was hopeless, tormenting (for them both), and unconsummated.

5

And now, when I seemed *sure* my love to see,   25
Her very self in her own quiet home,
There came an elfish laugh, and wakened me!
'Twas Hartley,[4] who behind my chair had clomb,[5]
And with his bright eyes at my face was peeping;
I blessed him, tried to laugh – and fell a-weeping.   30

The Picture; or, The Lover's Resolution (composed March 1802)[1]

From THE MORNING POST NO. 10,584 (6 September 1802)

Through weeds and thorns, and matted underwood
I force my way; now climb, and now descend
O'er rocks, or bare or mossy, with blind foot
Crushing the purple whorts;[2] while oft unseen,
Hurrying along the drifted forest leaves,   5
The scared snake rustles. Onward still I toil,
I know not, ask not whither. A new joy
Lovely as light, sudden as summer gust
And gladsome as the first-born of the spring,
Beckons me on, or follows from behind,   10
Playmate or guide.[3] The master-passion quelled,
I feel that I am free. With dun-red bark
The fir-trees and th' unfrequent slender oak
Forth from this tangle wild of bush and brake
Soar up, and form a melancholy vault   15
High o'er me, murm'ring like a distant sea.
No myrtle-walks are here![4] These are no groves
For Love[5] to dwell in; the low stumps would gore
His dainty feet; the briar and the thorn
Make his plumes haggard; till, like wounded bird,   20
Easily caught, the dusky dryads,[6]
With prickles sharper than his darts, would mock
His little godship, making him perforce
Creep through a thorn-bush on yon hedgehog's back.
This is my hour of triumph! I can now   25
With my own fancies play the merry fool,
And laugh away worse folly, being free.
Here will I seat myself beside this old,
Hollow, and woody oak, which ivy-twine
Clothes, as with network;[7] here will couch my limbs   30
Close by this river, in this silent shade,

---

4   Hartley Coleridge (b. 1796).
5   *clomb* climbed.

THE PICTURE; OR, THE LOVER'S RESOLUTION
1   In March 1802 Coleridge made the following entry in a notebook: 'A poem on the endeavour to emancipate the soul from day-dreams and note the different attempts and the vain ones' (*Notebooks* i 1153). The poem was *The Picture*.
2   *whorts* whortleberries.

3   ll. 7–11 recall Wordsworth's search for a guide in the '*Glad Preamble*' (composed early 1800) (see pp. 329–30).
4   *No myrtle-walks are here* Coleridge may be recalling the myrtle at Clevedon, mentioned at *Eolian Harp* (1795) 4–5 and *Reflections on Having Left a Place of Retirement* l. 5.
5   *Love* cupid.
6   *dryads* wood-nymphs.
7   *network* light fabric made of netted threads.

As safe and sacred from the step of man
As an invisible world – unheard, unseen,[8]
And list'ning only to the pebbly stream
That murmurs with a dead yet bell-like sound   35
Tinkling, or bees, that in the neighb'ring trunk
Make honey-hoards. This breeze that visits me
Was never Love's accomplice, never raised
The tendril ringlets from the maiden's brow,
And the blue, delicate veins above her cheek;   40
Ne'er played the wanton, never half-disclosed
The maiden's snowy bosom, scatt'ring thence
Eye-poisons for some love-distempered youth,
Who ne'er, henceforth, may see an aspen-grove
Shiver in sunshine, but his feeble heart   45
Shall flow away like a dissolving thing.
Sweet breeze! thou only, if I guess aright,
Liftest the feathers of the robin's breast,
Who swells his little breast, so full of song,
Singing above me on the mountain ash.   50
And thou too, desert stream! No pool of thine,
Though clear as lake in latest summer eve,
Did e'er reflect the stately virgin's robe,
The face, the form divine, her downcast look
Contemplative, her cheek upon her palm   55
Supported; the white arm and elbow rest
On the bare branch of half-uprooted tree,
That leans towards its mirror! He, meanwhile,
Who from her count'nance turned, or looked by stealth
(For fear is true love's cruel nurse), he now,   60
With steadfast gaze and unoffending eye,
Worships the wat'ry idol, dreaming hopes
Delicious to the soul – but fleeting, vain
Ev'n as that phantom-world on which he gazed!
She (sportive tyrant) with her left hand plucks   65
The heads of tall flow'rs that behind her grow –
Lychnis, and willow-herb, and foxglove-bells;
And suddenly, as one that toys with time,
Scatters them on the pool! Then all the charm
Is broken – all that phantom world so fair   70
Vanishes, and a thousand circlets spread,
And each misshape the other. Stay awhile,
Poor youth, who scarcely dar'st lift up thine eyes –
The stream will soon renew its smoothness, soon
The visions will return! And lo, he stays,   75
And soon the fragments dim of lovely forms
Come trembling back, unite, and now once more
The pool becomes a mirror;[9] and behold
Each wild-flow'r on the marge inverted there,
And there the half-uprooted tree – but where,   80

---

[8] *Close by ... unseen* cf. Coleridge's notebook entry, March
1802: 'A river, so translucent as not to be seen – and yet mur-
muring – shadowy world – and these a dream / Enchanted
river' (*Notebooks* i 1124).

[9] Lines 69–78 are quoted by Coleridge in the introduction to
the printed text of *Kubla Khan* (1816), p. 522.

Oh where the virgin's snowy arm, that leaned
On its bare branch? He turns, and she is gone!
Homeward she steals through many a woodland maze
Which he shall seek in vain. Ill-fated youth,
Go, day by day, and waste thy manly prime   85
In mad love-gazing on the vacant brook,
Till sickly thoughts bewitch thine eyes, and thou
Behold'st her shadow still abiding there,
The naiad of the mirror![10]
                              Not to thee,
Oh wild and desert stream, belongs this tale.   90
Gloomy and dark art thou; the crowded firs
Tow'r from thy shores, and stretch across thy bed,
Making thee doleful as a cavern well!
Save when the shy kingfishers build their nest
On thy steep banks, no loves hast thou, wild stream!   95
This be my chosen haunt – emancipate[11]
From passion's dreams, a freeman, and alone,
I rise and trace its devious course. Oh lead,
Lead me to deeper shades, to lonelier glooms.
Lo! stealing through the canopy of firs,   100
How fair the sunshine spots that mossy rock,
Isle of the river, whose disparted[12] waters
Dart off asunder with an angry sound,
How soon to reunite! They meet, they join
In deep embrace, and open to the sun   105
Lie calm and smooth. Such the delicious hour
Of deep enjoyment, foll'wing love's brief quarrels!
And hark, the noise of a near waterfall!
I come out into light – I find myself
Beneath a weeping birch (most beautiful   110
Of forest trees, the lady of the woods)
Hard by the brink of a tall weedy rock
That overbrows the cataract. How bursts
The landscape on my sight! Two crescent hills
Fold in behind each other, and so make   115
A circular vale, and landlocked, as might seem,
With brook and bridge, and grey-stone cottages,
Half hid by rocks and fruit-trees. Beneath my feet
The whortleberries are bedewed with spray,
Dashed upwards by the furious waterfall.   120
How solemnly the pendent ivy mass
Swings in its winnow![13] All the air is calm,
The smoke from cottage chimneys, tinged with light,
Rises in columns; from this house alone
Close by the waterfall, the column slants   125
And feels its ceaseless breeze. But what is this?
That cottage, with its slanting chimney smoke,
And close beside its porch a sleeping child,
His dear head pillowed on a sleeping dog,

---

[10] *naiad of the mirror* nymph of the pond.
[11] *emancipate* free (i.e. from romantic entanglement).
[12] *disparted* divided (by the rock).
[13] *winnow* swinging motion caused by the spray of the waterfall.

One arm between its forelegs, and the hand   130
Holds loosely its small handful of wild-flow'rs,
Unfilleted,[14] and of unequal lengths –
A curious picture, with a master's haste
Sketched on a strip of pinky-silver skin
Peeled from the birchen bark! Divinest maid –   135
Yon bark her canvas, and these purple berries
Her pencil! See, the juice is scarcely dried
On the fine skin! She has been newly here,
And lo! Yon patch of heath has been her couch –
The pressure still remains! Oh blessed couch,   140
For this may'st thou flow'r early, and the sun
Slanting, at eve rest bright, and linger long
Upon thy purple bells! Oh Isabel,
Daughter of genius, stateliest of our maids,
More beautiful than whom Alcaeus wooed,   145
The Lesbian woman of immortal song,[15]
Oh child of genius, stately, beautiful,
And full of love to all, save only one,
And not ungentle ev'n to me! My heart,
Why beats it thus? Through yonder coppice-wood   150
Needs must the pathway turn, that leads away
On to her father's house. She is alone!
The night draws on – such ways are hard to hit –
And fit it is I should restore this sketch
Dropped unawares, no doubt. Why should I yearn   155
To keep the relic? 'Twill but idly feed
The passion that consumes me. Let me haste!
This picture in my hand, which she has left;
She cannot blame me, that I followed her,
And I may be her guide the long wood through!   160

Letter to Sara Hutchinson,[1] *4 April 1802. Sunday Evening* (earliest version of *Dejection: An Ode*; edited from MS)[2]

I

Well! if the bard was weather-wise who made
The dear old ballad of Sir Patrick Spence,[3]
This night, so tranquil now, will not go hence

---

[14] *Unfilleted* i.e. the stems of the bunch of flowers are not tied up together.
[15] *whom Alcaeus . . . song* Sappho, as in Wordsworth's *Alcaeus to Sappho*, published *Morning Post* 2 October 1800 (see Griggs i 629).

LETTER TO SARA HUTCHINSON
[1] In the MS the title actually reads 'A Letter to ------------', but there is no doubt that the addressee was Sara Hutchinson.
[2] This, the earliest version of the shorter *Dejection: An Ode*, is also published here in texts of 1802 and 1817 (pp. 507–11, 544–8). The MS from which the present text is edited is the so-called 'Cornell Manuscript', now retained at the

Wordsworth Library, Grasmere. Coleridge was, at least at the moment he composed this poem, in a state of considerable turmoil. He had decisively passed on the torch of poet to Wordsworth, in whom he vested all his hopes of *The Recluse* coming to fruition, and was hopelessly in love with Sara Hutchinson (Wordsworth's sister-in-law), who preferred Wordsworth's company to his. This poem initiated a dialogue with Wordsworth, who 'replied' with the first version of *Resolution and Independence* (3–9 May).
[3] *the bard . . . Spence* unknown; Coleridge knew *The Ballad of Sir Patrick Spens* from Thomas Percy's *Reliques of Ancient English Poetry* (1765).

Unroused by winds that ply a busier trade
Than that which moulds yon clouds in lazy flakes,   5
Or the dull sobbing draught that drones and rakes
Upon the strings of this Eolian lute,[4]
Which better far were mute.
For lo! the new moon, winter-bright,
And all suffused[5] with phantom light   10
(With swimming phantom light o'erspread,
But rimmed and circled with a silver thread);
I see the old moon in her lap, foretelling
The coming-on of rain and squally blast.
Ah Sara![6] that the gust ev'n now were swelling,   15
And the slant night-shower driving loud and fast.

2

A grief without a pang – void, dark, and drear;
A stifling, drowsy, unimpassioned grief
That finds no natural outlet, no relief
In word, or sigh, or tear –   20
This, Sara, well thou know'st,
Is that sore evil which I dread the most
And oft'nest suffer in this heartless mood,
To other thoughts by yonder throstle wooed,
That pipes within the larch-tree not unseen   25
(The larch which pushes out in tassels green
Its bundled leafits), wooed to mild delights
By all the tender sounds and gentle sights
Of this sweet primrose-month – and *vainly* wooed,
Oh dearest Sara, in this heartless[7] mood.   30

3

All this long eve so balmy and serene
Have I been gazing on the western sky
And its peculiar tint of yellow-green;
And still I gaze, and with how blank an eye!
And those thin clouds above, in flakes and bars,   35
That give away their motion to the stars,
Those stars that glide behind them and between,
Now sparkling, now bedimmed, but always seen;
Yon crescent moon, as fixed as if it grew
In its own cloudless, starless lake of blue –   40
A boat becalmed! Dear William's sky canoe![8]
I see them all, so excellently fair;
I *see*, not *feel*, how beautiful they are!

---

[4] *Eolian lute* Aeolian harps were placed lengthways in front
of open windows, where their strings were 'played' by the
wind; see Coleridge's *The Eolian Harp*, pp. 451–3.

[5] *suffused* overspread.

[6] Sara Hutchinson (1775–1835), Coleridge's 'Asra', was
Wordsworth's sister-in-law. Coleridge's love for her was hope-
less, tormenting (for them both), and unconsummated.

[7] *heartless* depressed, discouraged.

[8] *Dear William's sky canoe* as featured in the prologue to
Wordsworth's *Peter Bell* (1798, published 1819).

4

My genial spirits fail,[9]
And what can these avail   45
To lift the smoth'ring weight from off my breast?
It were a vain endeavour,
Though I should gaze forever
On that green light that lingers in the west:
I may not hope from outward forms to win   50
The passion and the life, whose fountains are within;
These lifeless shapes, around, below, above –
Oh dearest Sara, what can they impart?
Even when the gentle thought that thou, my love,
Art gazing now like me   55
And see'st the heaven I see –
Sweet thought it is, yet feebly stirs my heart! –

5

Feebly, oh feebly! Yet
(I well remember it)
In my first dawn of youth, that fancy stole   60
With many gentle yearnings on my soul.
At eve, sky-gazing in 'ecstatic fit'[10]
(Alas, far-cloistered in a city school,[11]
The sky was all I knew of beautiful),
At the barred window often did I sit,   65
And often on the leaded school-roof lay,
    And to myself would say,
'There does not live the man so stripped of good affections
As not to love to see a maiden's quiet eyes
Upraised and linking on sweet dreams by dim connections   70
To moon, or evening star, or glorious western skies!'
While yet a boy, this thought would so pursue me,
That often it became a kind of vision to me.

6

Sweet thought, and dear of old
To hearts of finer mould[12] –   75
Ten thousand times by friends and lovers blessed!
    I spake with rash despair,
    And ere I was aware,
The weight was somewhat lifted from my breast!
Dear Sara! in the weather-fended wood,[13]   80
Thy loved haunt where the stock-doves coo at noon,
    I guess that thou hast stood

---

9   *My genial spirits fail* an echo of Milton, *Samson Agonistes*
594: 'my genial spirits droop'.
10   Milton, *The Passion* 42.
11   *a city school* Christ's Hospital in the City of London; cf.
Frost at Midnight (1798) 26–48.

12   *mould* substance.
13   *the weather-fended wood* the wood provides cover from wind
and rain, and is therefore weather (de)fended.

And watched yon crescent and that ghost-like moon;
    And yet far rather, in my present mood,
I would that thou'dst been sitting all this while   85
Upon the sod-built seat of camomile,[14]
And though thy robin may have ceased to sing,
Yet needs for *my* sake must thou love to hear
The beehive murmuring near —
That ever-busy and most quiet thing   90
Which I have heard at midnight murmuring.

7

    I feel my spirit moved:
    And wheresoe'er thou be,
    Oh sister, oh beloved!
Thy dear mild eyes that see   95
The very heaven *I* see —
There is a prayer in them, it is for *me*!
And I, dear Sara, *I* am blessing *thee*![15]

8

It was as calm as this, the happy night[16]
When Mary, thou and I together were,   100
The low decaying fire our only light,
And listened to the stillness of the air!
Oh, that affectionate and blameless maid,
Dear Mary, on her lap my head she laid —
    Her hand was on my brow   105
    Even as my own is now,
And on my cheek I felt thy eyelash play.[17]
Such joy I had that I may truly say
My spirit was awe-stricken with the excess
And trance-like depth of its brief happiness.   110

9

Ah fair remembrances, that so revive
My heart, and fill it with a living power —
Where were they, Sara? Or did I not strive
To win them to me on the fretting hour
Then when I wrote thee that complaining scroll,[18]   115
Which even to bodily sickness bruised thy soul?

---

[14]   *the sod-built seat of camomile* 'Sara's seat' was built by Coleridge and the Wordsworths on White Moss Common, Rydal, 10 October 1801 (*Grasmere Journals* 35, 182).

[15]   *I am blessing thee* one in a long line of benedictions; cf. those of Hartley in *Frost at Midnight* and Charles Lamb in *This Lime-Tree Bower My Prison*.

[16]   *the happy night* the exact date is not known, although Whalley suggested that it was some time during Coleridge's visit to Gallow Hill, 2–13 March 1802, and Parrish suggests a date during the summer of 1801. Cf. *A Day-Dream* and *The Day-Dream* (pp. 491–2, 504–5).

[17]   *And on my cheek . . . play* cf. *A Day-Dream* 31–2: 'Thine eyelash on my cheek doth play – / 'Tis Mary's hand upon my brow!'

[18]   *that complaining scroll* a letter to Sara. The 'bodily sickness' of l.116 may be the sickness into which she had fallen by 29 February 1802, which drew Coleridge back to Gallow Hill from London. He remained at Gallow Hill from 2 to 13 March, weeping aloud when he left for Keswick.

And yet thou blam'st thyself alone, and yet
    Forbidd'st me all regret.[19]

10

And must I not *regret* that I distressed   120
Thee, best beloved, who lovest me the best?
My better mind had fled I know not whither –
For oh! was this an absent friend's employ,
To send from far both pain and sorrow thither,
Where still his blessings should have called down joy?   125
I read thy guileless letter o'er again,
I hear thee of thy blameless self complain,
And only this I learn – and this, alas, I know –
That thou art weak and pale with sickness, grief, and pain,
And *I – I* made thee so!

11

Oh, *for my own sake*, I regret *perforce*   130
Whatever turns *thee*, Sara, from the course
Of calm well-being and a heart at rest.
When thou and, with thee, those whom thou lov'st best
Shall dwell together in one quiet home,
One home the sure *abiding* home of all,   135
I too will crown me with a coronal;[20]
Nor shall this heart in idle wishes roam
    Morbidly soft!
No, let me trust that I shall wear away
In no inglorious toils the manly day;   140
And only now and then, and not too oft,
Some dear and memorable eve shall bless,
Dreaming of all your love and happiness.

12

Be happy, and I need thee not in sight!
Peace in thy heart, and quiet in thy dwelling,   145
Health in thy limbs, and in thy eyes the light
Of love, and hope, and honourable feeling;
Where'er I am, I needs must be content –
Not near thee, haply shall be more content!
To all things I prefer the permanent.[21]   150
And better seems it for a heart like mine
Always to *know*, than sometimes to *behold*

---

[19] Coleridge's letters not infrequently caused Sara distress. On 13 December 1801 Dorothy recorded: 'The boy brought letters from Coleridge and from Sara. Sara in bad spirits about Coleridge' (*Grasmere Journals* 48).
[20] *I too . . . coronal* an allusion to Wordsworth's *Ode*: 'My heart is at your festival, / My head hath its coronal' (ll. 39–40).

[21] *To all things . . . permanent* cf. Wordsworth's reference to the 'beautiful and permanent forms of nature', *Preface to Lyrical Ballads*, p. 357.

Their happiness and thine:
For change doth trouble me with pangs untold!
To see thee, hear thee, feel thee, then to part –   155
    Oh, it weighs down the heart!
To visit those I love, as I love *thee*,
Mary, William, and dear Dorothy,
It is but a temptation to repine!
The transientness is poison in the wine,   160
Eats out the pith of joy, makes all joy hollow,
All pleasure a dim dream of pain to follow!
My own peculiar lot, my household life,
It is (and will remain) indifference or strife;
While ye are well and happy, 'twould but wrong you   165
If I should fondly yearn to be among you –
Wherefore, oh wherefore, should I wish to be
A withered branch upon a blossoming tree?

                                 13

But (let me say it, for I vainly strive
To beat away the thought) – but if thou pined,   170
Whate'er the cause, in body or in mind,
I were the miserablest man alive
To know it and be absent! Thy delights
Far off or near, alike shall I partake –
But oh! to mourn for thee, and to forsake   175
All power, all hope of giving comfort to thee;
To know that thou art weak and worn with pain
And not to hear thee, Sara, not to view thee,
    Not sit beside thy bed,
    Not press thy aching head,   180
    Not bring thee health again,
    At least to hope, to try
By this voice which thou lov'st, and by this earnest eye –

                                 14

Nay, wherefore did I let it haunt my mind,
    This dark distressful dream?   185
I turn from it and listen to the wind
Which long has howled unnoticed; what a scream
Of agony, by torture lengthened out,
That lute sent forth! Oh, thou wild storm without!
Or crag, or tairn,[22] or lightning-blasted tree,   190
Or pine-grove whither woodman never clomb,[23]
Or lonely house long held the witches' home,
Methinks were fitter instruments for thee,
Mad lutanist, that in this month of showers,
Of dark-brown gardens and of peeping flowers,   195

---

[22] *tairn* expanse of water high among the mountains; see   [23] *clomb* climbed.
Coleridge's note to *Dejection: An Ode*, p. 510 n. 15.

Mak'st devil's yule,[24] with worse than wintry song,
The blooms and buds and timorous leaves among!
Thou actor, perfect in all tragic sounds,
Thou mighty poet,[25] even to frenzy bold,
    What tell'st thou now about?   200
'Tis of a rushing of an host[26] in rout,
And many groans from men with smarting wounds,[27]
That groan at once from smart, and shudder with the cold!
But hush, there is a break of deepest silence –
Again! But that dread sound, as of a rushing crowd,   205
And groans and tremulous shuddering – all are over.
And it has other sounds, and all less deep, less loud;
    A tale of less affright,
    And tempered with delight,
As William's self had made the tender lay!   210
    'Tis of a little child
    Upon a heathy wild[28]
Not far from home, but it has lost its way,
And now moans low in utter grief and fear,
And now screams loud, and hopes to make its mother hear!   215

15

'Tis midnight, and small thought have I of sleep;
Full seldom may my friend[29] such vigils keep –
Oh breathe she softly in her gentle sleep!
Cover her, gentle sleep, with wings of healing,
And be this tempest but a mountain birth;   220
May all the stars hang bright above her dwelling,
Silent, as though they watched the sleeping earth,
Like elder sisters with love-twinkling eyes!
Healthful and light, my darling, may'st thou rise,
And of the same good tidings to me send –   225
For oh, beloved friend,
I am not the buoyant thing I was of yore,
When like an own child,[30] I to joy belonged;
For others mourning oft, myself oft sorely wronged,
Yet bearing all things then as if I nothing bore.   230

16

Ere I was wedded,[31] though my path was rough,
The joy within me dallied with distress,

---

[24] *yule* festival; yule was the pagan festival that became Christmas. This is the devil's yule because it is April rather than December.
[25] *Thou actor . . . Thou mighty poet* i.e. the 'wild storm' of l. 189.
[26] *host* army.
[27] *an host . . . wounds* Coleridge was very conscious of the war against France, which had been going on since 1793; see also *Reflections on Having Left a Place of Retirement* 43–8, *Fears in Solitude*.

[28] *a little child . . . wild* Coleridge has in mind Wordsworth's *Lucy Gray*, published in *Lyrical Ballads* (1800).
[29] *my friend* Sara Hutchinson.
[30] *an own child* a beloved child. Coleridge was the youngest of ten children and was spoilt, especially by his father, who died when Coleridge was only eight.
[31] *Ere I was wedded* Coleridge married Sara Fricker on 4 October 1795 at St Mary Redcliffe, Bristol. He had in the preceding year enjoyed a celebrated career as a political lecturer and pamphleteer.

And all misfortunes were but as the stuff
Whence fancy made me dreams of happiness;
For hope grew round me like the climbing vine,   235
And leaves and fruitage not my own, seemed mine!
But now ill tidings bow me down to earth,
Nor care I that they rob me of my mirth;
    But oh! each visitation
Suspends what nature gave me at my birth –   240
My shaping spirit of imagination!
I speak not now of those habitual ills
That wear out life, when two unequal minds
Meet in one house, and two discordant wills –
    This leaves me where it finds,   245
Past cure and past complaint, a fate austere
Too fixed and hopeless to partake of fear!

17

But thou, *dear* Sara – dear indeed thou art,
My comforter, a heart within my heart! –
Thou and the few we love (though few ye be)   250
Make up a world of hopes and fears for me;
And when affliction or distempering pain
Or wayward chance befall you, I complain.
Not that I mourn – oh friends most dear, most true,
    Methinks to weep with you   255
Were better far than to rejoice alone –
But that my coarse domestic life[32] has known
No griefs but such as dull and deaden me,
No habits of heart-nursing sympathy,
No mutual mild enjoyments of its own,   260
No hopes of its own vintage – none, oh none! –
Whence, when I mourn for you, my heart must borrow
Fair forms and living motions for its sorrow.
For not to think of what I needs must feel,
But to be still and patient all I can,   265
And haply by abstruse research to steal
From my own nature all the natural man –
This was my sole resource, my wisest plan;
And that which suits a part infects the whole,
And now is almost grown the temper of my soul.[33]   270

18

My little children[34] are a joy, a love,
    A good gift from above!
But what is bliss that ever calls up woe,

---

32   *my coarse domestic life* Coleridge's marriage was disintegrat-
ing. On 20 October 1802 he told Thomas Wedgwood of what
he had endured at Greta Hall: 'Ill-tempered speeches sent
after me when I went out of the house; ill-tempered speeches
on my return; my friends received with freezing looks' (Griggs
ii 876).

33   *For not . . . soul* these lines were not included in *Dejection:
An Ode* in 1802, but were readmitted to the 1817 text.
34   *My little children* Hartley (b.1796) and Derwent (b.1800).
Sara would be born 23 December 1802.

And makes it doubly keen,
Compelling me to feel what well I know –   275
What a most blessed lot mine *might* have been?
Those little angel children (woe is me!),
There have been hours when, feeling how they bind
And pluck out the wing-feathers of my mind,
Turning my error to necessity,   280
I have half-wished they never had been born.[35]
That, seldom; but sad thought they always bring,
And, like the poet's nightingale, I sing
My love-song with my breast against a thorn.

19

With no unthankful spirit I confess   285
This clinging grief, too, in its turn awakes
That love and father's joy – but oh! it makes
The love the greater, and the joy far less.
These mountains too, these vales, these woods, these lakes,
Scenes full of beauty and of loftiness   290
Where all my life I fondly hope to live –
I were sunk low indeed, did they *no* solace give.
But oft I seem to feel, and evermore to fear,
They are not to me now the things which once they were.[36]

20

Oh Sara, we receive but what we give,   295
And in *our* life alone does nature live;
Ours is her wedding-garment, ours her shroud!
And would we aught behold of higher worth
Than that inanimate cold world allowed
To the poor, loveless, ever-anxious crowd –   300
Ah! from the soul itself must issue forth
A light, a glory,[37] and a luminous cloud
    Enveloping the earth!
And from the soul itself must there be sent
A sweet and potent voice, of its own birth,   305
Of all sweet sounds the life and element.
Oh pure of heart![38] thou need'st not ask of me
What this strange music in the soul may be,
What and wherein it doth exist,
This light, this glory, this fair luminous mist,   310
This beautiful and beauty-making power!
Joy, innocent Sara! Joy that ne'er was given
Save to the pure and in their purest hour,

---

35   *I have . . . born* the unsatisfactoriness of his marriage was largely the cause of these guilty feelings about his children, with whom he was spending less and less time. Cf. *The Day-Dream* 25–30, and his comment to his wife in a letter of Christmas Day 1801: 'Oh my dear Hartley, my Derwent! My children! The night before last I dreamt I saw them so vividly, that I was quite ill in the morning and wept my eyes red' (Griggs ii 776).

36   *They are not . . . were* a reworking of Wordsworth, *Ode* 9: 'The things which I have seen I now can see no more'.

37   *glory* divine effulgence of light, as at Wordsworth, *Ode* 18.

38   *Oh pure of heart* Sara Hutchinson.

Joy, Sara, is the spirit and the power
That, wedding nature to us, gives in dower[39]   315
    A new earth and new heaven
Undreamt of by the sensual and the proud!
Joy is that sweet voice, joy that luminous cloud –
    We, we ourselves rejoice!
And thence flows all that charms or ear or sight,   320
All melodies the echoes of that voice,
All colours a suffusion from that light.
Sister and friend[40] of my devoutest choice;
Thou being innocent and full of love,
And nested with the darlings of thy love;   325
And feeling in thy soul, heart, lips, and arms
Even what the conjugal and mother dove
That borrows genial warmth from these she warms
Feels in her thrilled wings, blessedly outspread;[41]
Thou, freed awhile from cares and human dread   330
By the immenseness of the good and fair
    Which thou seest everywhere –
Thus, thus would'st thou rejoice!
To thee would all things *live* from pole to pole,[42]
Their life the eddying of thy living soul.   335
Oh dear! Oh innocent! Oh full of love!
Sara, thou friend of my devoutest[43] choice,
As dear as light and impulse from above –
So may'st thou ever, evermore rejoice!

A *Day-Dream* (composed June 1802; published 1828)[1]

From THE BIJOU (1828)

My eyes make pictures, when they are shut:
    I see a fountain, large and fair,
A willow and a ruined hut,[2]
    And thee,[3] and me, and Mary[4] there.
Oh Mary, make thy gentle lap our pillow!   5
Bend o'er us, like a bower, my beautiful green willow!

A wild rose roofs the ruined shed,
    And that and summer well agree;
And lo! where Mary leans her head –
    Two dear names carved upon the tree!   10

---

[39] *dower* a wedding-gift.
[40] *Sister and friend* Dorothy and William Wordsworth.
[41] *Even what . . . outspread* Coleridge has in mind the moment of creation, *Paradise Lost* i 21–2, where the Holy Spirit 'Dove-like sat'st brooding on the vast abyss / And madest it pregnant'.
[42] *To thee . . . pole* Coleridge blesses Sara with the pantheist perception of the one life in the natural world, as he had done Charles Lamb in *This Lime-Tree Bower My Prison*.
[43] *devoutest* most devoted, most attached.

A DAY-DREAM
[1] The date of composition remains conjectural, but Coleridge himself says that it was written in June (l. 16); the likely year is 1802. Coleridge spent most of June 1802 at Dove Cottage.
[2] *hut* cottage.
[3] *thee* Sara Hutchinson (1775–1835), Coleridge's 'Asra', was Wordsworth's sister-in-law. Coleridge's love for her was hopeless and unconsummated.
[4] Mary Hutchinson (1770–1859), who married Wordsworth on 4 October 1802.

And Mary's tears, they are not tears of sorrow:
Our sister and our friend[5] will both be here tomorrow.

'Twas day, but now few, large, and bright,
　　The stars are round the crescent moon!
And now it is a dark warm night,
　　The balmiest of the month of June!
A glow-worm fall'n, and on the marge remounting
Shines, and its shadow[6] shines – fit stars for our sweet fountain.

Oh ever, ever be thou blessed!
　　For dearly, Asra, love I thee!
This brooding warmth across my breast,[7]
　　This depth of tranquil bliss – ah me!
Fount, tree and shed are gone, I know not whither,
But in one quiet room we three are still together.

The shadows dance upon the wall
　　By the still dancing fire-flames made,
And now they slumber, moveless all,
　　And now they melt to one deep shade!
But not from me shall this mild darkness steal thee;
I dream thee with mine eyes, and at my heart I feel thee.

Thine eyelash on my cheek doth play –
　　'Tis Mary's hand upon my brow![8]
But let me check this tender lay,
　　Which none may hear but she and thou!
Like the still hive at quiet midnight humming;
Murmur it to yourselves, ye two beloved women!

Chamouny; the Hour Before Sunrise. A Hymn. (composed not before 26 August 1802)[1]

From THE MORNING POST No. 10,589 (11 September 1802)

Chamouny is one of the highest mountain valleys of the Barony of Faucigny in the Savoy Alps, and exhibits a kind of fairy world in which the wildest appearances (I had almost said horrors) of nature alternate with the softest and most beautiful. The chain of Mont Blanc is its boundary, and, besides the Arve, it is filled with sounds from the Arveiron, which rushes from the melted glaciers like a giant mad with joy from a dungeon, and forms other torrents of snow-water, having their rise in the

---

5　*Our sister and our friend* Dorothy and William Wordsworth.
6　*shadow* reflection (in the fountain).
7　*This brooding warmth . . . breast* Sara has become the 'the conjugal and mother dove' of *A Letter to Sara Hutchinson* 327–9.
8　*Thine eyelash . . . brow* Cf. *A Letter to Sara Hutchinson* 104–7.

CHAMOUNY; THE HOUR BEFORE SUNRISE. A HYMN
1　On 10 September 1802 Coleridge told William Sotheby that he composed this poem 'when I was on Scafell. I involuntarily poured forth a hymn in the manner of the Psalms, though afterwards I thought the ideas etc. disproportionate to

our humble mountains, and, accidentally lighting on a short note in some Swiss poems concerning the Vale of Chamouni and its mountains, I transferred myself thither, in the spirit, and adapted my former feelings to these grander external objects' (Griggs ii 864–5). However, Griggs notes that the poem could not have been composed until after 26 August 1802 – three weeks after Coleridge's ascent of Scafell. Coleridge had certainly not seen Chamouni when this poem was written; the main literary inspiration was Frederika Brun's 'Chamouny beym Sonnenaufgange', reprinted EHC ii 1131; see Griggs ii 865n. Coleridge's poem is often contrasted with the religious scepticism of Shelley's poem about the same locale, *Mont Blanc* (pp. 845–9).

glaciers which slope down into the valley. The beautiful *gentiana major*, or greater gentian, with blossoms of the brightest blue, grows in large companies a few steps from the never-melted ice of the glaciers. I thought it an affecting emblem of the boldness of human hope, venturing near, and, as it were, leaning over, the brink of the grave. Indeed, the whole vale, its every light, its every sound, must needs impress every mind not utterly callous with the thought, Who *would* be, who *could* be an atheist in this valley of wonders? If any readers of *The Morning Post* have visited this vale in their journeys among the Alps, I am confident that they will not find the sentiments and feelings expressed, or attempted to be expressed, in the following poem, extravagant.

Hast thou a charm to stay[2] the morning star
In his steep course? So long he seems to pause
On thy bald awful head, oh Chamouny!
The Arvè and Arveiron at thy base
Rave ceaselessly; but thou, dread mountain form,   5
Risest from forth thy silent sea of pines
How silently! Around thee and above,
Deep is the sky, and black – transpicuous,[3] deep,
An ebon mass. Methinks thou piercest it
As with a wedge! But when I look again,   10
It seems thy own calm home, thy crystal shrine,
Thy habitation from eternity.
Oh dread and silent form! I gazed upon thee
Till thou, still present to my bodily eye,
Didst vanish from my thought. Entranced in pray'r,   15
I worshipped the Invisible alone.
Yet thou, meantime, wast working on my soul,
E'en like some deep enchanting melody,
So sweet, we know not we are list'ning to it.
But I awake, and with a busier mind   20
And active will self-conscious, offer now,
Not, as before, involuntary pray'r
And passive adoration.
                        Hand and voice,
Awake, awake! And thou, my heart, awake!
Awake, ye rocks! Ye forest pines, awake!   25
Green fields and icy cliffs, all join my hymn!
And thou, oh silent mountain, sole and bare,
Oh blacker than the darkness, all the night,
And visited all night by troops of stars,
Or when they climb the sky, or when they sink;   30
Companion of the morning star at dawn,
Thyself earth's rosy star, and of the dawn
Co-herald! Wake, oh wake, and utter praise!
Who sank thy sunless pillars deep in earth?
Who filled thy countenance with rosy light?   35
Who made thee father of perpetual streams?
And you, ye five wild torrents, fiercely glad,
Who called you forth from night and utter death,
From darkness let you loose, and icy dens,
Down those precipitous, black, jagged rocks   40

---

[2]   *stay* stop.

[3]   *transpicuous* transparent, as at *Paradise Lost* viii 141.

For ever shattered, and the same for ever?
Who gave you your invulnerable life,
Your strength, your speed, your fury, and your joy,
Unceasing thunder, and eternal foam?
And who commanded (and the silence came), 45
'Here shall the billows stiffen, and have rest'?
   Ye ice-falls! Ye that from yon dizzy heights
Adown enormous ravines steeply slope –
Torrents, methinks, that heard a mighty voice,
And stopped at once amid their maddest plunge! 50
Motionless torrents! Silent cataracts!
Who made you glorious as the gates of heav'n
Beneath the keen full moon? Who bade the sun
Clothe you with rainbows? Who with lovely flow'rs
Of living blue spread garlands at your feet? 55
'God, God!' the torrents, like a shout of nations,
Utter. The ice-plain bursts, and answers 'God!'
'God!' sing the meadow-streams with gladsome voice,
And pine-groves, with their soft and soul-like sound!
The silent snow-mass, loos'ning, thunders 'God!' 60
Ye dreadless flow'rs that fringe th' eternal frost!
Ye wild goats bounding by the eagle's nest!
Ye eagles, playmates of the mountain blast!
Ye lightnings, the dread arrows of the clouds!
Ye signs and wonders of the element 65
Utter forth 'God!' and fill the hills with praise!
   And thou, oh silent form, alone and bare,
Whom, as I lift again my head bowed low
In adoration, I again behold,
And to thy summit upward from thy base 70
Sweep slowly with dim eyes suffused[4] by tears,
Awake, thou mountain form! Rise like a cloud!
Rise like a cloud of incense from the earth!
Thou kingly spirit throned among the hills,
Thou dread ambassador from earth to heav'n – 75
Great hierarch,[5] tell thou the silent sky,
And tell the stars, and tell the rising sun,
Earth with her thousand voices calls on God!

Dejection: An Ode, written 4 April 1802

From THE MORNING POST NO. 10,608 (4 OCTOBER 1802)[1]

> *Late, late yestreen I saw the new moon*
> *With the old moon in her arms;*
> *And I fear, I fear, my master dear,*
> *We shall have a deadly storm*
>
>   *Ballad of Sir Patrick Spence*[2]

---

4   *suffused* filled.
5   *hierarch* priest.

DEJECTION: AN ODE
1   Coleridge composed *A Letter to Sara Hutchinson* on 4 April 1802 (see pp. 495–504); in the months that followed he revised it drastically, and published it in the text presented here, in *The Morning Post*, 4 October 1802, as a sort of gift to Wordsworth, whose wedding-day it was. It next appeared in Sibylline Leaves (1817), further revised; see pp. 544–8.
2   Coleridge knew *The Ballad of Sir Patrick Spens* from Thomas Percy's *Reliques of Ancient English Poetry* (1765).

I

Well! if the bard was weather-wise who made
   The grand old ballad of Sir Patrick Spence,[3]
   This night, so tranquil now, will not go hence
Unroused by winds that ply a busier trade
Than those which mould yon clouds in lazy flakes,   5
Or this dull sobbing draught that drones and rakes
Upon the strings of this Eolian lute,[4]
Which better far were mute.
For lo! the new moon, winter-bright,
And overspread with phantom light   10
(With swimming phantom light o'erspread,
But rimmed and circled by a silver thread);
I see the old moon in her lap, foretelling
   The coming-on of rain and squally blast.
And oh, that even now the gust were swelling,   15
   And the slant night-show'r driving loud and fast.
Those sounds which oft have raised me while they awed
And sent my soul abroad,
Might now perhaps their wonted[5] impulse give,
Might startle this dull pain, and make it move and live!   20

II

A grief without a pang – void, dark, and drear;
   A stifled, drowsy, unimpassioned grief
   Which finds no nat'ral outlet, no relief
In word, or sigh, or tear –
Oh Edmund![6] in this wan and heartless mood,   25
To other thoughts by yonder throstle wooed
All this long eve so balmy and serene,
   Have I been gazing on the western sky
And its peculiar tint of yellow-green;
   And still I gaze, and with how blank an eye!   30
And those thin clouds above, in flakes and bars,
That give away their motion to the stars,
Those stars that glide behind them or between,
Now sparkling, now bedimmed, but always seen;
Yon crescent moon, as fixed as if it grew   35
In its own cloudless, starless lake of blue –
A boat becalmed! A lovely sky-canoe![7]
I see them all, so excellently fair;
I *see*, not *feel*, how beautiful they are!

---

[3] *the bard . . . Spence* unknown; the ballad is anonymous.

[4] *Eolian lute* Aeolian harps were placed lengthways in front of open windows, where their strings were 'played' by the wind; see Coleridge's *The Eolian Harp*, pp. 451–3.

[5] *wonted* expected, usual.

[6] *Edmund* poetic name for Wordsworth. In each of the four successive versions of this poem, Coleridge changed the person to whom it was addressed: (i) Sara Hutchinson in *Letter to Sara Hutchinson*, presented pp. 495–504, above; (ii) Wordsworth (letters to William Sotheby, July 1802, and Sir George Beaumont, August 1803, Griggs ii 815–19, 970–2); (iii) 'Edmund' (in the version presented here); (iv) 'Lady' (Sara Hutchinson) (*Sibylline Leaves* (1817), pp. 544–8).

[7] *A sky-canoe* This reference to the Prologue of Wordsworth's *Peter Bell* (composed 1798) would not have been understood by most of the readers of *The Morning Post* since the poem was unpublished, and would remain so until 1819.

III

My genial spirits fail,[8]   40
　And what can these avail
To lift the smoth'ring weight from off my breast?
　　It were a vain endeavour,
　　Though I should gaze forever
On that green light that lingers in the west: 45
I may not hope from outward forms to win
The passion and the life, whose fountains are within!

IV

Oh Edmund, we receive but what we give,
And in *our* life alone does nature live;
Ours is her wedding-garment, ours her shroud!   50
And would we aught behold of higher worth
Than that inanimate cold world allowed
To the poor, loveless, ever-anxious crowd –
Ah! from the soul itself must issue forth
A light, a glory,[9] a fair luminous cloud   55
Enveloping the earth!
And from the soul itself must there be sent
A sweet and potent voice, of its own birth,
Of all sweet sounds the life and element.
Oh pure of heart![10] thou need'st not ask of me   60
What this strong music in the soul may be,
What and wherein it doth exist,
This light, this glory, this fair luminous mist,
This beautiful and beauty-making pow'r!
Joy, virtuous Edmund! Joy that ne'er was given   65
Save to the pure and in their purest hour,
Joy, Edmund, is the spirit and the pow'r
Which, wedding nature to us, gives in dow'r[11]
　　A new earth and new heaven
Undreamed of by the sensual and the proud!   70
Joy is the sweet voice, Joy the luminous cloud –
　　We, we ourselves rejoice!
And thence flows all that charms or ear or sight,[12]
All melodies the echoes of that voice,
All colours a suffusion from that light.   75

V

Yes, dearest Edmund, yes!
　There was a time[13] when, though my path was rough,
　　This joy within me dallied with distress,

---

[8] *My genial spirits fail* an echo of Milton, *Samson Agonistes* 594: 'my genial spirits droop'.

[9] *glory* divine effulgence of light, as at Wordsworth, *Ode* 18.

[10] *Oh pure of heart* i.e. Edmund.

[11] *dow'r* a wedding-gift.

[12] *sight* other versions of the poem give 'sight', suggesting that 'light', the reading of the *Morning Post* text at this point, is an error.

[13] *There was a time* echoes Wordsworth, *Ode* l. 1. In the *Letter to Sara Hutchinson*, this was the time 'Ere I was wedded' (l. 231).

And all misfortunes were but as the stuff
    Whence fancy made me dreams of happiness;   80
For hope grew round me like the twining vine,
And fruits and foliage not my own, seemed mine!
But now afflictions bow me down to earth,
Nor care I that they rob me of my mirth;
    But oh! each visitation   85
Suspends what nature gave me at my birth –
    My shaping spirit of imagination!

[The sixth and seventh stanzas omitted.][14]

VIII

Oh, wherefore did I let it haunt my mind,
    This dark distressful dream?
I turn from it and listen to the wind   90
    Which long has raved unnoticed; what a scream
Of agony, by torture lengthened out,
That lute sent forth! Oh wind, that rav'st without!
    Bare crag, or mountain tairn,[15] or blasted tree,
Or pine-grove whither woodman never clomb,[16]   95
Or lonely house long held the witches' home,
    Methinks were fitter instruments for thee,
Mad lutanist, who in this month of show'rs,
Of dark-brown gardens and of peeping flow'rs,
Mak'st devil's yule,[17] with worse than wintry song,   100
The blossoms, buds, and tim'rous leaves among!
    Thou actor, perfect in all tragic sounds,
        Thou mighty poet,[18] ev'n to frenzy bold,
What tell'st thou now about?
'Tis of the rushing of an host[19] in rout,   105
    With many groans of men with smarting wounds[20] –
        At once they groan with pain, and shudder with the cold!
But hush, there is a pause of deepest silence!
    And all that noise, as of a rushing crowd,
        With groans and tremulous shudderings – all is over.   110
It tells another tale, with sounds less deep and loud,
        A tale of less affright
        And tempered with delight,
As Edmund's self had framed the tender lay –
        'Tis of a little child   115
        Upon a lonesome wild[21]

---

[14] *{The sixth and seventh stanzas omitted.}* There is no textual evidence to support this claim.

[15] ' "Tairn": a small lake, generally (if not always) applied to the lakes up in the mountains, and which are the feeders of those in the valleys. This address to the wind will not appear extravagant to those who have heard it at night in a mountainous country' (Coleridge's note).

[16] *clomb* climbed.

[17] *yule* festival; yule was the pagan festival that became Christmas. This is the devil's yule because it is April rather than December.

[18] *Thou actor . . . Thou mighty poet* i.e. the 'wind' of l. 93.

[19] *host* army.

[20] *an host . . . wounds* Coleridge was very conscious of the war against France, which had been going on since 1793; see also *Reflections on Having Left a Place of Retirement* 43–8, *Fears in Solitude*.

[21] *'Tis of . . . wild* Coleridge has in mind Wordsworth's *Lucy Gray*.

Not far from home, but she has lost her way,
And now moans low in utter grief and fear,
And now screams loud, and hopes to make her mother *hear!*

IX

'Tis midnight, and small thoughts have I of sleep;   120
Full seldom may my friend such vigils keep!
Visit him, gentle sleep, with wings of healing,
   And may this storm be but a mountain birth;
May all the stars hang bright above his dwelling,
     Silent, as though they *watched* the sleeping earth!   125
       With light heart may he rise,
        Gay fancy, cheerful eyes,
And sing his lofty song, and teach me to rejoice!
Oh Edmund, friend of my devoutest choice,
Oh, raised from anxious dread and busy care,   130
By the immenseness of the good and fair
Which thou see'st ev'rywhere[22] –
Joy lifts thy spirit, joy attunes thy voice,
To thee do all things live from pole to pole,
Their life the eddying of thy living soul!   135
Oh simple spirit, guided from above;
Oh lofty poet, full of light and love;
Brother and friend of my devoutest[23] choice,
Thus may'st thou ever, evermore rejoice!

Spots in the Sun[1]

From The Morning Post No. 10,614 (11 October 1802)

    My father confessor is strict and holy,
    'Mi fili', still he cries, 'peccare noli.'[2]
    And yet how oft I find the pious man
    At Annette's door, the lovely courtesan![3]
    Her soul's deformity the good man wins,   5
    And not her charms – he comes to hear her sins!
    Good father, I would fain not do thee wrong,
    But ah! I fear that they who oft and long
    Stand gazing at the sun, to count each spot,
    Must sometimes find the sun itself too hot.   10

---

[22] Lines 128–32 were removed from subsequent texts.
[23] *devoutest* most devoted, most attached. This had been Sara Hutchinson in *Letter to Sara Hutchinson* 337.

Spots in the Sun
[1] Like Wordsworth's *A Complaint*, this poem arose out of the strains that had crept into Coleridge's relationship with Wordsworth.

[2] *Mi . . . noli* 'Sin not, my son.'
[3] *At Annette's door, the lovely courtesan* hardly diplomatic in view of Wordsworth's marriage just days before. Coleridge was aware of Wordsworth's abandonment of Annette Vallon and their child, Caroline, in 1792, and of his visit to Calais to see them in August 1802 (see '*It is a beauteous evening, calm and free*', p. 373).

Letter from S. T. Coleridge to Robert Southey, 11 September 1803
(extract) (including early version of *The Pains of Sleep*)[1]

I have been on a wild journey – taken up for a spy and clapped into Fort Augustus – and I am afraid they may have frightened poor Sara by sending her off a scrap of a letter I was writing to her.[2] I have walked 263 miles in eight days, so I must have strength somewhere, but my spirits are dreadful, owing entirely to the horrors of every night. I truly dread to sleep; it is no shadow with me, but substantial misery foot-thick that makes me sit by my bedside of a morning and *cry*. I have abandoned all opiates except ether be one, and that only in *fits* – and that is a blessed medicine! and when you see me drink a glass of spirit and water, except by prescription of a physician, you shall despise me – but I still cannot get quiet rest –

> When on my bed my limbs I lay,
> It hath not been my use to pray
> With moving lips or bended knees;
> But silently, by slow degrees,
> My spirit I to love compose,   5
> In humble trust my eyelids close
> With reverential resignation;
> No wish conceived, no thought expressed!
> Only a *sense* of supplication,
> A *sense* o'er all my soul impressed   10
> That I am weak, yet not unblessed –
> Since *round* me, *in* me, everywhere,
> Eternal strength and goodness are!
>
> But yesternight I prayed aloud
> In anguish and in agony,   15
> Awaking from the fiendish crowd
> Of shapes and thoughts that tortured me!
> Desire with loathing strangely mixed,
> On wild or hateful objects fixed:
> Pangs of revenge, the powerless will,   20
> Still baffled, and consuming still,
> Sense of intolerable wrong,
> And men whom I despised made strong
> Vainglorious threats, unmanly vaunting,
> Bad men my boasts and fury taunting –   25
> Rage, sensual passion, mad'ning brawl,
> And shame and terror over all!
> Deeds to be hid that were not hid,
> Which all confused I might not know,

LETTER FROM S. T. COLERIDGE TO ROBERT SOUTHEY
[1]   The letter in which Coleridge enshrined this early version of *The Pains of Sleep*, and the early readings themselves, make the poem more powerful than the version published in 1816 with *Christabel* and *Kubla Khan* (see pp. 524–5, below). Coleridge had embarked on 15 August 1803 on a tour of Scotland with the Wordsworths. Badly depressed, partly thanks to his unfulfilled love for Sara Hutchinson, partly to his opium addiction, he accompanied them as far as Loch Lomond, but departed from them at Arrochar. Attempting to withdraw from opium, he embarked on a marathon walk, covering 263 miles in eight days before reaching Perth on 11 September.
[2]   Probably Sara Hutchinson, with whom Coleridge was hopelessly in love. In August 1803, shortly after setting off on the Scottish tour, he had confided to his notebook: 'Oh Asra, wherever I am, and am impressed, my heart aches for you' (*Notebooks* i 1451).

Whether I suffered or I did –   30
For all was horror, guilt and woe,
My own or others, still the same
Life-stifling fear, soul-stifling shame!

Thus two nights passed: the night's dismay
Saddened and stunned the boding day.   35
I feared to sleep – sleep seemed to be
Disease's worst malignity.
The third night when my own loud scream
Had freed me from the fiendish dream,
O'ercome with sufferings dark and wild,   40
I wept as I had been a child –
And having thus by tears subdued
My trouble to a milder mood,
Such punishments, I thought, were due
To natures deepliest stained with sin: 45
Still to be stirring up anew
The self-created hell within,
The horror of their crimes to view,
To know and loathe, yet wish and do!
With such let fiends make mockery –   50
But I – oh wherefore this on *me*?
Frail is my soul, yea, strengthless wholly,
Unequal, restless, melancholy,
But free from hate and sensual folly!
To live beloved is all I need,   55
And whom I love, I love indeed.

Letter from S. T. Coleridge to Thomas Poole, 14 October 1803 (extract)[1]

Wordsworth is in good health, and all his family. He has one LARGE boy, christened John. He has made a beginning to his *Recluse*.[2] He was here on Sunday last. His wife's sister, who is on a visit at Grasmere, was in a bad hysterical way, and he rode in to consult our excellent medical men.[3] I now see very little of Wordsworth. My own health makes it inconvenient and unfit for me to go thither one third as often, as I used to do – and Wordsworth's indolence, etc., keeps him at home. Indeed, were I an irritable man (and an unthinking one), I should probably have considered myself as having been very unkindly used by him in this respect, for I was at one time confined for two months, and he never came in to see me – me, who had ever paid such unremitting attentions to him!

But we must take the good and the ill together – and by seriously and habitually reflecting on our own faults and endeavouring to amend them, we shall then find little difficulty in confining our attention (as far as it acts on our friends' characters) to their good qualities. Indeed, I owe it to truth

LETTER FROM S. T. COLERIDGE TO THOMAS POOLE

[1] This important letter, written from Greta Hall, Keswick, where Coleridge's family were now living with Southey, indicates something of the strain that had crept into the relationship with Wordsworth. Compare Wordsworth's *A Complaint*, pp. 407–8, above.

[2] *The Recluse* was the epic poem planned in 1798 which, Coleridge and Wordsworth believed, would help precipitate the millennium (Christ's 1000-year rule on earth predicted in the Bible). Coleridge was becoming increasingly impatient at Wordsworth's failure to get on with it.

[3] Joanna Hutchinson suffered a 'hysteric and fainting fit' at Dove Cottage on the evening of 7 October 1803. Wordsworth rode to Keswick to consult Mr Edmondson about it the next day, meeting Southey and Coleridge on 9 October before returning to Grasmere that evening.

and justice, as well as to myself, to say that the concern which I have felt in this instance (and one or two other more *crying* instances) of self-involution in Wordsworth, has been almost wholly a feeling of friendly regret and disinterested apprehension. I saw him more and more benetted in hypochondriacal fancies, living wholly among *devotees*, having every the minutest thing, almost his very eating and drinking, done for him by his sister or wife – and I trembled lest a film should rise and thicken on his moral eye.

The habit too of writing such a multitude of small poems was in this instance hurtful to him – such things as that sonnet of his in Monday's *Morning Post* about Simonides and the ghost.[4] I rejoice, therefore, with a deep and true joy, that he has at length yielded to my urgent and repeated (almost unremitting) requests and remonstrances, and will go on with *The Recluse* exclusively – a great work in which he will sail on an open ocean and a steady wind, unfretted by short tacks, reefing and hauling and disentangling the ropes; great work necessarily comprehending his attention and feelings within the circle of great objects and elevated conceptions. This is his natural element. The having been out of it has been his disease; to return into it is the specific remedy – both remedy and health. It is what food is to famine.

I have seen enough positively to give me feelings of hostility towards the plan of several of the poems in the *Lyrical Ballads*, and I really consider it as a misfortune that Wordsworth ever deserted his former mountain-track to wander in lanes and alleys – though in the event it may prove to have been a great benefit to him. He will steer, I trust, the middle course.

Letter from S. T. Coleridge to Richard Sharp, 15 January 1804 (extract)

Wordsworth is a poet, a most original poet. He no more resembles Milton than Milton resembles Shakespeare – no more resembles Shakespeare than Shakespeare resembles Milton: he is himself. And I dare affirm that he will hereafter be admitted as the first and greatest philosophical poet – the only man who has effected a complete and constant synthesis of thought and feeling, and combined them with poetic forms, with the music of pleasurable passion and with imagination, or the *modifying* power in that highest sense of the word in which I have ventured to oppose it to fancy, or the *aggregating* power (in that sense in which it is a dim analogue of creation – not all that we can *believe* but all that we can *conceive* of creation). Wordsworth is a poet, and I feel myself a better poet, in knowing how to honour *him*, than in all my own poetic compositions – all I have done or hope to do. And I prophesy immortality to his *Recluse*, as the first and finest philosophical poem, if only it be (as it undoubtedly will be) a faithful transcript of his own most august and innocent life, of his own habitual feelings and modes of seeing and hearing.

To William Wordsworth. Lines composed, for the greater part, on the night on which he finished the recitation of his poem in Thirteen Books, concerning the growth and history of his own mind, January 1807, Coleorton, near Ashby-de-la-Zouch (composed January 1807; first published 1817; edited from MS)[1]

> Oh friend! Oh teacher! God's great gift to me!
> Into my heart have I received that lay
> More than historic, that prophetic lay

---

4 *I find it written of Simonides*, composed by 7 October 1803, published *Morning Post* 10 October 1803. Coleridge may also have in mind some of the poems which were to appear in *Poems in Two Volumes* (1807).

To William Wordsworth
1 This poem is important as one of the earliest literary responses to Wordsworth's greatest poem. Wordsworth,

Dorothy, Mary, Coleridge, Hartley and Sara Hutchinson, all spent the Christmas of 1806 at Coleorton, the country seat of Sir George Beaumont, and in the New Year, January 1807, Wordsworth read them the *Thirteen-Book Prelude* in its entirety. During its author's lifetime, the poem would be read or heard by members of the Wordsworth circle, but it remained unpublished until 1850.

Wherein (high theme by thee first sung aright)
Of the foundations and the building-up   5
Of thy own spirit, thou hast loved to tell
What may be told, to th' understanding mind
Revealable; and what within the mind
May rise enkindled. Theme as hard as high!
Of smiles spontaneous, and mysterious fear   10
(The first-born they of reason, and twin-birth);
Of tides obedient to external force,
And currents self-determined, as might seem,
Or by interior power; of moments awful,[2]
Now in thy hidden life, and now abroad,   15
Mid festive crowds, *thy* brows too garlanded,
A brother of the feast; of fancies fair,
Hyblaean[3] murmurs of poetic thought,
Industrious in its joy, by lilied streams
Native or outland, lakes and famous hills!   20
Of more than fancy – of the hope of man
Amid the tremor of a realm aglow,[4]
Where France in all her towns lay vibrating,
Ev'n as a bark becalmed on sultry seas
Beneath the voice from heaven, the bursting crash   25
Of heaven's immediate thunder, when no cloud
Is visible, or shadow on the main!
Ah, soon night rolled on night, and every cloud
Opened its eye of fire; and hope aloft
Now fluttered, and now tossed upon the storm   30
Floating![5] Of hope afflicted, and struck down,
Thence summoned homeward – homeward to thy heart,
Oft from the watchtower of man's absolute self,
With light unwaning on her eyes, to look
Far on – herself a glory to behold,   35
The angel of the vision! Then (last strain!)
Of duty, chosen laws controlling[6] choice,
Virtue and love! An Orphic[7] tale indeed,
A tale divine of high and passionate thoughts
To their own music chaunted!
                    Ah great bard!   40
Ere yet that last swell dying awed the air,
With steadfast ken[8] I viewed thee in the choir
Of ever-enduring men. The truly great
Have all one age, and from one visible space
Shed influence;[9] for they, both power and act,   45
Are permanent, and time is now with them,
Save as it worketh for them, they in it.

---

[2] *awful* i.e. full of awe.

[3] *Hyblaean* honeyed; Hybla was a Sicilian mountain near Syracuse known for honey and herbs.

[4] *of the hope . . . aglow* a reference to Books IX and X of *The Prelude*, in which Wordsworth describes his residence in France, 1791–2.

[5] *and hope aloft . . . Floating* a reference to the Reign of Terror, which led radicals in England to lose hope in the French Revolution.

[6] In the MS Coleridge writes: 'Impelling? Directing?'

[7] *Orphic* oracular; communicated by God.

[8] *ken* gaze.

[9] *Shed influence* Coleridge is thinking of Milton's description of the Pleiades 'Shedding sweet influence' (*Paradise Lost* vii 375).

Nor less a sacred roll, than those of old,
And to be placed, as they, with gradual fame
Among the archives of mankind, thy work   50
Makes audible a linked song of truth,
Of truth profound a sweet continuous song
Not learnt but native, her own natural notes!
Dear shall it be to every human heart,
To me how more than dearest! Me, on whom   55
Comfort from thee and utterance of thy love
Came with such heights and depths of harmony,
Such sense of wings uplifting, that the storm
Scattered and whirled me, till my thoughts became
A bodily tumult! And thy faithful hopes,   60
Thy hopes of me, dear friend, by me unfelt
Were troublous[10] to me, almost as a voice
Familiar once and more than musical
To one cast forth, whose hope had seemed to die,
A wanderer with a worn-out heart,   65
Mid strangers pining with untended wounds![11]
      Oh friend, too well thou know'st, of what sad years
The long suppression had benumbed my soul,[12]
That even as life returns upon the drowned,
Th' unusual joy awoke a throng of pains —   70
Keen pangs of *love*, awakening, as a babe,
Turbulent, with an outcry in the heart;
And fears self-willed, that shunned the eye of hope,
And hope, that would not know itself from fear;
Sense of passed youth, and manhood come in vain;   75
And genius given, and knowledge won in vain;
And all which I had culled in wood-walks wild,
And all which patient toil had reared, and all
Commune with thee had opened out, but[13] flowers
Strewed on my corse, and borne upon my bier,   80
In the same coffin, for the self-same grave!
      That way no more! And ill beseems it me,
Who came a welcomer in herald's guise,
Singing of glory and futurity,
To wander back on such unhealthful road   85
Plucking the poisons of self-harm! And ill
Such intertwine beseems triumphal wreaths
Strewed before thy advancing! Thou too, friend!
Oh injure not the memory of that hour
Of thy communion with my nobler mind[14]   90
By pity or grief,[15] already felt too long!
Nor let my words import more blame than needs.
The tumult rose and ceased; for peace is nigh

---

[10] *troublous* confusing (because Coleridge had lost hope in himself).

[11] *Mid strangers . . . wounds* cf. the *Letter to Sara Hutchinson*, where Coleridge compares the sound of the wind with 'many groans from men with smarting wounds' (l. 202).

[12] *benumbed my soul* as at *Letter to Sara Hutchinson* 43: 'I see, not *feel*, how beautiful they are!'

[13] *but* i.e. [nothing] but.

[14] *that hour . . . mind* a reference to the *annus mirabilis* of 1797–8.

[15] *pity or grief* i.e. felt for Coleridge in his present, miserable state.

Where Wisdom's voice has found a list'ning heart.
Amid the howl of more than wintry storms   95
The halcyon[16] hears the voice of vernal hours,
Already on the wing!
                    Eve following eve,[17]
Dear tranquil time, when the sweet sense of home
Becomes most sweet! Hours for their own sake hailed,
And more desired, more precious, for thy song!   100
In silence list'ning, like a devout child,
My soul lay passive, by thy various strain[18]
Driven as in surges now, beneath the stars,
With momentary stars of my own birth,
Fair constellated foam still darting off   105
Into the darkness! – now a tranquil sea
Outspread and bright, yet swelling to the moon!
        And when, oh friend, my comforter, my guide,
Strong in thyself and powerful to give strength,
Thy long-sustained lay finally closed,   110
And thy deep voice had ceased (yet thou thyself
Wert still before mine eyes, and round us both
That happy vision of beloved faces,
All whom I deepliest love, in one room all!),
Scarce conscious and yet conscious of its close,   115
I sat, my being blended in one thought
(Thought was it? Or aspiration? Or resolve?)
Absorbed, yet hanging still upon the sound:
And when I rose, I found myself in prayer!

On Donne's First Poem (composed *c.* 2 May 1811; edited from MS)[1]

Be proud as Spaniards! Leap for pride, ye fleas!
Henceforth in nature's minim[2] world grandees,[3]
In Phoebus' archives registered are ye –
And this[4] your patent of nobility.
No skipjacks[5] now, nor civiller skip-johns,   5
Dread Anthropophagi![6] Specks of living bronze,
I hail you one and all, sans pros or cons,
Descendants from a noble race of Dons.[7]

---

[16] *halcyon* kingfisher which, according to classical legend, brought the seas and winds to a calm when it bred in a nest which floated on the ocean.
[17] *Eve following eve* the evenings when Wordsworth recited *The Thirteen-Book Prelude* to Coleridge.
[18] *thy various strain* i.e. *The Prelude*.

On Donne's First Poem
[1] Parts of this poem have previously appeared in print as *Limbo* and *Ne Plus Ultra*. In fact, both derive from this larger work; for a detailed account, see *Notebooks* iii 4073n, and Frederick Burwick, 'Coleridge's "Limbo" and "Ne Plus Ultra": The Multeity of Intertextuality', *Romanticism Past and Present* 9 (1985) 35–45. The poem was inspired by a reading of Donne's

Poems (1669), which Coleridge annotated 2 May 1811. *The Flea* is the first poem in the volume.
[2] *minim* smallest.
[3] *grandees* people of high rank; nobles. The point is that the fleas jump higher than other insects, and are therefore 'higher' than others of their species.
[4] *this* i.e. the ability to jump.
[5] *skipjacks* hoppers, jumpers.
[6] *Dread Anthropophagi* man-eaters (fleas suck human blood); first mentioned by Pliny, who described them drinking out of skulls and using scalps as napkins. Their most famous literary appearance is in *Othello* I iii 143–4: 'the cannibals that each other eat, / The Anthropophagi'.
[7] *Dons* Spanish noblemen (presumably a reference back to the 'grandees' of l. 2), although 'don' can also mean 'teacher'.

What though that great ancestral flea be gone,
Immortal with immortalizing Donne –   10
His earthly spots bleached off as Papists gloze
In purgatory fire on Bardolph's nose?[8]
For skimming in the wake, it mocked the care
Of the old boat-god for his farthing fare,[9]
Though Irus' ghost[10] he ne'er frowned blacker on,   15
The skin and skin-pent druggist crossed the Acheron,[11]
Styx and with Puriphlegethon Cocytus[12]
(The very names, methinks, might thither fright us);
Unchanged it crossed, and shall keep in ghost-light
Of lank half-nothings his, the thinnest sprite,   20
The sole true something[13] – this in limbo den:
It frightens ghosts as ghosts here frighten men.
Thence crossed unseized, and shall, some fated hour,
Be pulverized by Demogorgon's[14] power,
And given as poison to annihilate souls –   25
Even now it shrinks them! They shrink in, as moles
(Nature's mute monks, live mandrakes of the ground)
Creep back from light, then listen for its sound –
See but to dread, and dread they know not why –
The natural alien of their negative eye.[15]   30

'Tis a strange place, this limbo![16] Not a place,
Yet name it so – where Time and weary Space
Fettered from flight, with nightmare sense of fleeing,
Strive for their last crepuscular[17] half-being;
Lank Space, and scytheless Time with branny[18] hands,   35
Barren and soundless as the measuring sands,[19]
Marked but by flit of shades – unmeaning[20] they
As moonlight on the dial of the day.
But that is lovely – looks like human time,
An old man with a steady look sublime,   40
That stops his earthly task to watch the skies;
But he is blind – a statue hath such eyes –
Yet having moonward turned his face by chance,
Gazes[21] the orb with moonlike countenance,
With scant white hairs, with foretop bald and high,   45
He gazes still, his eyeless face all eye,
As 'twere an organ full of silent sight;
His whole face seemeth to rejoice in light.

---

[8]   *In purgatory fire . . . nose* Coleridge alludes to the flea mentioned by the Boy in *Henry V*: 'Do you not remember, 'a saw a flea stick upon Bardolph's nose, and 'a said it was a black soul burning in hell?' (II iii 40–2).

[9]   *Of the old . . . fare* Charon was the ferryman who took the souls of the properly buried dead across the Styx (river surrounding Hades) for a fee of one obol. The flea got across without paying.

[10]   *Irus' ghost* the voracious beggar of Ithaca, in the *Odyssey*.

[11]   *Acheron* another river of Hades.

[12]   *Puriphlegethon Cocytus* Phlegethon and Cocytus are rivers of hell.

[13]   *The sole true something* in Hades the flea is the only real being, with both spirit and body.

[14]   *Demogorgon* terrifying deity.

[15]   *The natural alien of their negative eye* light is alien to the eye used only in pitch darkness (a 'negative eye' because used to see nothing).

[16]   *limbo* Hades, hell.

[17]   *crepuscular* twilight, dim.

[18]   *branny* coarse-textured (like bran).

[19]   *the measuring sands* sands running through an hourglass.

[20]   *unmeaning* meaningless. In Hell, Time and Space have no meaning.

[21]   *Gazes* i.e. gazes at.

Lip touching lip – all moveless, bust and limb,
He seems to gaze at that which seems to gaze on him!   50

No such sweet sights doth limbo den immure,²²
Walled round and made a spirit-jail²³ secure,
By the mere horror of blank nought-at-all,
Whose circumambience²⁴ doth these ghosts enthrall.²⁵
A lurid thought is growthless dull privation,   55
Yet that is but a purgatory²⁶ curse;
Hell knows a fear far worse –
A fear, a future fate: 'tis positive negation!

    Sole Positive of Night!
      Antipathist of light!   60
Fate's only essence! Primal scorpion rod!
    The one permitted opposite of God!
      Condensed blackness, and abysmal storm
        Compacted to one sceptre
        Arms the grasp enorm²⁷ –   65
        The Intercepter!
The substance, that still casts the shadow, death!
    The dragon foul and fell!
    The unrevealable
And hidden one, whose breath   70
Gives wind and fuel to the fires of hell!
    Ah sole despair
Of both th' eternities in heaven!
Sole interdict²⁸ of all-bedewing²⁹ prayer,
    The All-compassionate!   75
Save to the lampads seven³⁰
Revealed to none of all th' angelic state,
    Save to the lampads seven
    That watch the throne of heaven!

Letter from S. T. Coleridge to William Wordsworth, 30 May 1815 (extract)¹

What did my criticism amount to, reduced to its full and naked sense? This: that, *comparatively* with the former poem, *The Excursion*, as far as it was new to me, had disappointed my expectations; that the excellences were so many and of so high a class, that it was impossible to attribute the inferiority (if any such really existed) to any flagging of the writer's own genius; and that I conjectured that it

---

²² *immure* contain.
²³ *spirit-jail* prison of the soul.
²⁴ *circumambience* surrounding presence.
²⁵ *enthrall* enslave.
²⁶ *purgatory* a place of suffering, where spirits are ultimately cleansed of venial sins.
²⁷ *enorm* enormous.
²⁸ *interdict* (pronounced 'interdite') prohibition.
²⁹ *all-bedewing* dew is a symbol of purification.
³⁰ *the lampads seven* the seven lamps of fire burning before the throne of God (Revelation 4:5).

LETTER FROM S. T COLERIDGE TO WILLIAM WORDSWORTH
¹ Coleridge writes to Wordsworth to explain his disappointment with *The Excursion* (1814). This important letter outlines what he had hoped Wordsworth would achieve in *The Recluse* (of which *The Excursion* was part), though the reader should bear in mind that it was written seventeen years after *The Recluse* was originally formulated, and that Coleridge's response may be coloured by his quarrel with Wordsworth in 1810. Another account of *The Recluse* may be found at p. 548, below.

might have been occasioned by the influence of self-established convictions having given to certain thoughts and expressions a depth and force which they had not for readers in general. In order, therefore, to explain the disappointment, I must recall to your mind what my expectations were; and as these again were founded on the supposition that (in whatever order it might be published) the poem on the growth of your own mind[2] was as the ground-plat[3] and the roots out of which *The Recluse* was to have sprung up as the tree. As far as the same sap in both, I expected them doubtless to have formed one complete whole, but in matter, form, and product to be different, each not only a distinct but a different work. In the first I had found 'themes by thee first sung aright'[4]:

> Of smiles spontaneous, and mysterious fears
> (The first-born they of reason, and twin-birth);
> Of tides obedient to external force,
> And currents self-determined, as might seem,
> Or by some central breath; of moments awful,
> Now in thy inner life, and now abroad,
> When power streamed from thee, and thy soul received
> The light reflected as a light bestowed!
> Of fancies fair, and milder hours of youth,
> Hyblaean[5] murmurs of poetic thought,
> Industrious in its joy, in vales and glens
> Native or outland, lakes and famous hills!
> Or on the lonely high-road, when the stars
> Were rising, or by secret mountain streams,
> The guides and the companions of thy way;
> Of more than fancy – of the social sense
> Distending wide, and man beloved as man,
> Where France in all her towns lay vibrating,
> Ev'n as a bark becalmed beneath the burst
> Of heaven's immediate thunder, when no cloud
> Is visible, or shadow on the main!
> For thou wert there,[6] thy own brows garlanded
> Amid the tremor of a realm aglow,
> Amid a mighty nation jubilant,
> When from the general heart of humankind
> Hope sprang forth, like a full-born deity!
> Of that dear hope afflicted, and amazed,
> So homeward summoned! Thenceforth calm and sure
> From the dread watchtower of man's absolute self,
> With light unwaning on her eyes, to look
> Far on – herself a glory[7] to behold,
> The angel of the vision! Then (last strain!)
> Of duty, chosen laws controlling choice,
> Action and joy! An Orphic[8] song indeed,
> *A song divine of high and passionate truths*
> *To their own music chaunted!*

---

2   *the poem . . . mind* i.e. *The Prelude.*
3   *ground-plat* ground-plot, plot of ground on which the edifice of *The Recluse* would be built.
4   *themes by thee . . . aright* Coleridge's *To William Wordsworth* 4; he goes on to quote ll. 10–40.

5   *Hyblaean* honeyed; Hybla was a Sicilian mountain near Syracuse known for honey and herbs.
6   *For thou wert there* i.e. in Revolutionary France, 1791–2.
7   *a glory* an effulgent light.
8   *Orphic* oracular; communicated by God.

Indeed through the whole of that poem με Αύρα τις είσέπνευσε μυστικωτάτη.[9] *This* I considered as *The Excursion*, and the second as *The Recluse* I had (from what I had at different times gathered from your conversation on the plan) anticipated as commencing with you set down and settled in an abiding home, and that with the description of that home you were to begin a *Philosophical Poem*, the result and fruits of a spirit so framed and so disciplined, as had been told in the former.

Whatever in Lucretius[10] is poetry is not philosophical; whatever is philosophical is not poetry – and in the very pride of confident hope I looked forward to *The Recluse* as the *first* and *only* true philosophical poem in existence. Of course, I expected the colours, music, imaginative life, and passion of *poetry*, but the matter and arrangement of *philosophy* – not doubting from the advantages of the subject that the totality of a system was not only capable of being harmonized with, but even calculated to aid, the unity (beginning, middle, and end) of a *poem*. Thus, whatever the length of the work might be, still it was a *determinate* length.

Of the subjects announced each would have its own appointed place and, excluding repetitions, each would relieve and rise in interest above the other. I supposed you first to have meditated the faculties of man in the abstract; in their correspondence with his sphere of action – and first, in the feeling, touch, and taste, then in the eye, and last in the ear; to have laid a solid and immovable foundation for the edifice by removing the sandy sophisms[11] of Locke and the mechanic dogmatists;[12] and demonstrating that the senses were living growths and developments of the mind and spirit in a much juster as well as higher sense than the mind can be said to be formed by the senses. Next I understood that you would take the human race in the concrete, have exploded the absurd notion of Pope's *Essay on Man*,[13] Darwin,[14] and all the countless believers (even, strange to say, among Christians) of man's having progressed from an orang-utan state – so contrary to all history, to all religion, nay, to all possibility; to have affirmed a fall, in some sense, as a fact the possibility of which cannot be understood from the nature of the will, but the reality of which is attested by experience and conscience; fallen men contemplated in the different ages of the world, and in the different states – savage – barbarous – civilized – the lonely cot or borderer's wigwam – the village – the manufacturing town – sea-port – city – universities – and, not disguising the sore evils under which the whole creation groans, to point out, however, a manifest scheme of redemption from this slavery, of reconciliation from this enmity with nature (What are the obstacles? The Antichrist that must be and already is); and to conclude by a grand didactic swell on the necessary identity of a true philosophy with true religion, agreeing in the results and differing only as the analytic and synthetic process, as discursive from intuitive,[15] the former chiefly useful as perfecting the latter.

In short, the necessity of a general revolution in the modes of developing and disciplining the human mind by the substitution of life and intelligence (considered in its different powers, from the plant up to that state in which the difference of degree becomes a new kind – man, self-consciousness – but yet not by essential opposition), for the philosophy of mechanism which in everything that is needworthy of the human intellect strikes *death*, and cheats itself by mistaking clear images for distinct conceptions, and which idly demands conceptions where intuitions alone are possible or adequate to the majesty of the truth. In short, facts elevated into theory, theory into laws, and laws into living and intelligent powers – true idealism necessarily perfecting itself in realism, and realism refining itself into idealism.

9   'a certain most mystical breeze blew into me' (Aristophanes, *The Frogs* 313–14).

10   Lucretius, *De Rerum Natura*, philosophical poem in six Books.

11   *Sandy sophisms* dry and specious arguments.

12   *Locke . . . mechanic dogmatists* John Locke (1632–1704), author of the *Essay concerning Human Understanding* (1690); other 'dogmatists' probably include Isaac Newton (1642–1727) and Francis Bacon (1561–1626).

13   *Essay on Man* (1732–4), a philosophical poem, part of a larger work never completed by Pope, in which he seeks to vindicate the ways of God to man and prove that the universe is the best of all possible schemes.

14   Erasmus Darwin (1731–1802), grandfather of Charles Darwin, author of *The Botanic Garden* (1789–91) and *Zoönomia* (1794–6).

15   *discursive or intuitive* the same distinction is mentioned by Wordsworth in *Thirteen-Book Prelude* xiii 113 (p. 403). Milton had differentiated discursive reason (belonging to man), from a higher, 'intuitive' reason, to which man may aspire, and which is possessed by angels (*Paradise Lost* v 487–90).

Kubla Khan: or A Vision in a Dream

From CHRISTABEL; KUBLA KHAN: A VISION; THE PAINS OF SLEEP (1816)

Of the Fragment of 'Kubla Khan'[1]

The following fragment is here published at the request of a poet of great and deserved celebrity,[2] and as far as the author's own opinions are concerned, rather as a psychological curiosity than on the ground of any supposed *poetic* merits.

In the summer of the year 1797,[3] the author, then in ill health, had retired to a lonely farmhouse between Porlock and Lynton on the Exmoor confines of Somerset and Devonshire. In consequence of a slight indisposition, an anodyne had been prescribed,[4] from the effects of which he fell asleep in his chair at the moment that he was reading the following sentence, or words of the same substance, in *Purchas's Pilgrimage*: 'Here the Khan Kubla commanded a palace to be built, and a stately garden thereunto. And thus ten miles of fertile ground were enclosed with a wall.'[5]

The author continued for about three hours in a profound sleep (at least of the external senses) during which time he has the most vivid confidence that he could not have composed less than from two to three hundred lines – if that indeed can be called composition in which all the images rose up before him as *things*, with a parallel production of the correspondent expressions, without any sensation or consciousness of effort. On awaking he appeared to himself to have a distinct recollection of the whole, and taking his pen, ink, and paper, instantly and eagerly wrote down the lines that are here preserved. At this moment he was unfortunately called out by a person on business from Porlock and detained by him above an hour, and on his return to his room, found to his no small surprise and mortification that though he still retained some vague and dim recollection of the general purpose of the vision, yet, with the exception of some eight or ten scattered lines and images, all the rest had passed away like the images on the surface of a stream into which a stone has been cast – but, alas! without the after-restoration of the latter:

> Then all the charm
> Is broken – all that phantom-world so fair
> Vanishes, and a thousand circlets spread,
> And each misshapes the other. Stay awhile,
> Poor youth, who scarcely dar'st lift up thine eyes –
> The stream will soon renew its smoothness, soon
> The visions will return! And lo, he stays,
> And soon the fragments dim of lovely forms
> Come trembling back, unite, and now once more
> The pool becomes a mirror.[6]

Yet from the still-surviving recollections in his mind, the author has frequently purposed to finish for himself what had been originally, as it were, given to him. Σάμερον ἄδιον ἄσω,[7] but the tomorrow is yet to come.

KUBLA KHAN: OR A VISION IN A DREAM

[1]   This short essay was prefaced to *Kubla Khan* on its first publication in 1816. The narrative given here should be compared with the briefer account of the poem's composition appended to the MS version of the poem (p. 462).

[2]   *a poet of great and deserved celebrity* Lord Byron, who described it as 'a fine wild poem' (Marchand v 108). *Kubla Khan* and *Christabel* circulated in MS in literary circles for years before they were formally published. Other early readers included Charles Lamb, Sir Walter Scott, and Mrs Robinson (see pp. 124–6, above).

[3]   *In the summer . . .* 1797 The correct date is early November 1797.

[4]   *an anodyne . . . prescribed* Opium was generally used for the treatment of dysentery at this time.

[5]   'In Xaindu did Cublai Can build a stately pallace, encompassing sixteene miles of plaine ground with a wall, wherein are fertile meddowes, pleasant springs, delightfull streames, and all sorts of beasts of chase and game, and in the middest thereof a sumptuous house of pleasure, which may be removed from place to place' (Samuel Purchas, *Purchas his Pilgrimage* [1613], p. 350).

[6]   Coleridge quotes his own *The Picture* 69–78.

[7]   'Today I shall sing more sweetly', adapted by Coleridge from Theocritus, *Idyll* i 145.

As a contrast to this vision, I have annexed a fragment of a very different character, describing with equal fidelity the dream of pain and disease.[8]

Kubla Khan (composed early November 1797)[1]

From CHRISTABEL; KUBLA KHAN: A VISION; THE PAINS OF SLEEP (1816)

In Xanadu did Kubla Khan
A stately pleasure-dome decree,
Where Alph, the sacred river, ran
Through caverns measureless to man
    Down to a sunless sea.   5
So twice five miles of fertile ground
With walls and towers were girdled round;
And here were gardens bright with sinuous rills
Where blossomed many an incense-bearing tree;
And here were forests ancient as the hills,   10
And folding sunny spots of greenery.

But oh, that deep romantic chasm which slanted
Down the green hill athwart a cedarn cover!
A savage place, as holy and enchanted
As e'er beneath a waning moon was haunted   15
By woman wailing for her demon-lover!
And from this chasm, with ceaseless turmoil seething,
As if this earth in fast thick pants were breathing,
A mighty fountain momently was forced
Amid whose swift half-intermitted burst   20
Huge fragments vaulted like rebounding hail,
Or chaffy grain beneath the thresher's flail!
And mid these dancing rocks at once and ever,
It flung up momently the sacred river.
Five miles meandering with a mazy motion   25
Through wood and dale the sacred river ran,
Then reached the caverns measureless to man
And sank in tumult to a lifeless ocean.
And mid this tumult Kubla heard from far
Ancestral voices prophesying war![2]   30

The shadow of the dome of pleasure
Floated midway on the waves,
Where was heard the mingled measure
From the fountain and the caves;
It was a miracle of rare device,   35
A sunny pleasure-dome with caves of ice!

---

[8] *a fragment . . . disease The Pains of Sleep*; see pp. 524–5.

KUBLA KHAN
[1] The earlier, MS text of this poem is at pp. 461–2.
[2] *Ancestral voices prophesying war* presumably the voices of ancestors looking forward to war in the present; though another way of reading it would be to regard the ancestral voices as speaking to the individual psyche. In March 1798 Coleridge told his brother George: 'I believe most steadfastly in original sin; that from our mothers' wombs our understandings are darkened; and even where our understandings are in the light, that our organization is depraved, and our volitions imperfect' (Griggs i 396).

A damsel with a dulcimer
In a vision once I saw:
It was an Abyssinian maid
And on her dulcimer she played,   40
Singing of Mount Abora.[3]
Could I revive within me
Her symphony[4] and song,
To such a deep delight 'twould win me
That with music loud and long,   45
I would build that dome in air,
That sunny dome, those caves of ice!
And all who heard should see them there,
And all should cry, 'Beware, beware!
His flashing eyes, his floating hair!   50
Weave a circle round him thrice,
And close your eyes with holy dread –
For he on honey-dew hath fed
And drank the milk of paradise.'

The Pains of Sleep (composed by 10 September 1803)[1]

From Christabel; Kubla Khan: A Vision; The Pains of Sleep (1816)

Ere on my bed my limbs I lay,
It hath not been my use to pray
With moving lips or bended knees;
But silently, by slow degrees,
My spirit I to love compose,   5
In humble trust mine eyelids close
With reverential resignation;
No wish conceived, no thought expressed!
Only a *sense* of supplication,
A sense o'er all my soul impressed   10
That I am weak, yet not unblessed –
Since in me, round me, everywhere,
Eternal strength and wisdom are.

But yesternight I prayed aloud
In anguish and in agony,   15
Upstarting from the fiendish crowd
Of shapes and thoughts that tortured me;
A lurid light, a trampling throng,
Sense of intolerable wrong,
And whom I scorned, those only strong!   20
Thirst of revenge, the powerless will
Still baffled, and yet burning still!

---

3   *Mount Abora* changed from 'Mount Amara' in the MS (see p. 462).
4   *symphony* possibly means 'dulcimer'; see Joseph Sgammato, 'A Note on Coleridge's "symphony and song"', *TWC* 6 (1975) 303–6.

The Pains of Sleep
1   For the context in which this poem was composed, see the MS version and notes, pp. 512–13.

Desire with loathing strangely mixed,
On wild or hateful objects fixed.
Fantastic passions! Mad'ning brawl!   25
And shame and terror over all!
Deeds to be hid which were not hid,
Which all confused I could not know,
Whether I suffered or I did –
For all seemed guilt, remorse or woe,   30
My own or others, still the same
Life-stifling fear, soul-stifling shame!

So two nights passed: the night's dismay
Saddened and stunned the coming day.
Sleep, the wide blessing, seemed to me   35
Distemper's worst calamity.
The third night when my own loud scream
Had waked me from the fiendish dream,
O'ercome with sufferings strange and wild,
I wept as I had been a child –   40
And having thus by tears subdued
My anguish to a milder mood,
Such punishments, I said, were due
To natures deepliest stained with sin:
For aye entempesting anew   45
Th' unfathomable hell within,
The horror of their deeds to view,
To know and loathe, yet wish and do!
Such griefs with such men well agree,
But wherefore, wherefore fall on me?   50
To be beloved is all I need,
And whom I love, I love indeed.

Biographia Literaria (1847)[1] (extracts)

Chapter 13 (extract)[2] (vol. i pp. 297–8)

The imagination then I consider either as primary or secondary. The primary imagination I hold to be the living power and prime agent of all human perception, and as a repetition in the finite mind of the eternal act of creation in the infinite I AM. The secondary imagination I consider as an echo of the former, coexisting with the conscious will, yet still as identical with the primary in the *kind* of its agency, and differing only in *degree*, and in the *mode* of its operation. It dissolves, diffuses, dissipates, in order to recreate; or, where this process is rendered impossible, yet still at all events it struggles to idealize and to unify. It is essentially *vital*, even as all objects (*as* objects) are essentially fixed and dead.

Fancy, on the contrary, has no other counters to play with but fixities and definites. The fancy is

---

BIOGRAPHIA LITERARIA

[1] Although I have used the 1847 text of *Biographia* (ed. Henry Nelson and Sara Coleridge, 2 vols), it should be noted that it was first published in 1817. Coleridge began dictating it in July 1815, and it was intended to be a combination of autobiography, a defence of Wordsworth against reviewers such as Jeffrey (see pp. 555–8), and a treatise on philosophy and religion.

[2] The first of the extracts from *Biographia* consists of the famous definition of the primary and secondary imagination; for detailed discussion, see Jonathan Wordsworth, 'The Romantic Imagination', in *A Companion to Romanticism* ed. Duncan Wu (1997), pp. 490–2.

indeed no other than a mode of memory emancipated from the order of time and space – while it is blended with, and modified by, that empirical phenomenon of the will which we express by the word 'choice'. But equally with the ordinary memory the fancy must receive all its materials ready-made from the law of association.

Chapter 14 (extracts)[1] (vol. ii pp. 1–9, 13–14)

During the first year that Mr Wordsworth and I were neighbours,[2] our conversations turned frequently on the two cardinal points of poetry: the power of exciting the sympathy of the reader by a faithful adherence to the truth of nature, and the power of giving the interest of novelty by the modifying colours of imagination. The sudden charm which accidents of light and shade, which moonlight or sunset diffused over a known and familiar landscape, appeared to represent the practicability of combining both. These are the poetry of nature.

The thought suggested itself (to which of us I do not recollect) that a series of poems might be composed of two sorts. In the one, the incidents and agents were to be (in part at least) supernatural – and the excellence aimed at was to consist in the interesting of the affections by the dramatic truth of such emotions as would naturally accompany such situations, supposing them real. And real in this sense they have been to every human being who, from whatever source of delusion, has at any time believed himself under supernatural agency. For the second class, subjects were to be chosen from ordinary life. The characters and incidents were to be such as will be found in every village and its vicinity, where there is a meditative and feeling mind to seek after them or to notice them when they present themselves.

In this idea originated the plan of the *Lyrical Ballads*, in which it was agreed that my endeavours should be directed to persons and characters supernatural, or at least romantic – yet so as to transfer, from our inward nature, a human interest and a semblance of truth sufficient to procure for these shadows of imagination that willing suspension of disbelief for the moment, which constitutes poetic faith. Mr Wordsworth, on the other hand, was to propose to himself as his object, to give the charm of novelty to things of every day, and to excite a feeling analogous to the supernatural, by awakening the mind's attention to the lethargy of custom, and directing it to the loveliness and the wonders of the world before us – an inexhaustible treasure but for which, in consequence of the film of familiarity and selfish solicitude, we have eyes yet see not, ears that hear not, and hearts that neither feel nor understand.

With this view I wrote 'The Ancient Mariner', and was preparing (among other poems) 'The Dark Ladie' and the 'Christabel', in which I should have more nearly realised my ideal than I had done in my first attempt. But Mr Wordsworth's industry had proved so much more successful, and the number of his poems so much greater, that my compositions, instead of forming a balance, appeared rather an interpolation of heterogeneous matter. Mr Wordsworth added two or three poems written in his own character, in the impassioned, lofty, and sustained diction which is characteristic of his genius. In this form the *Lyrical Ballads* were published, and were presented by him, as an 'experiment'[3] whether subjects, which from their nature rejected the usual ornaments and extra-colloquial style of poems in general, might not be so managed in the language of ordinary life as to produce the pleasurable interest which it is the peculiar business of poetry to impart.

To the second edition he added a Preface of considerable length in which (notwithstanding some passages of apparently a contrary import) he was understood to contend for the extension of this style to poetry of all kinds, and to reject as vicious and indefensible all phrases and forms of speech that were not included in what he – unfortunately, I think, adopting an equivocal expression – called the

---

CHAPTER 14
[1] The account given by Coleridge of the evolution of *Lyrical Ballads* is important, but fictionalizes in retrospect; it differs markedly from that later given by Wordsworth (see pp. 418–19, above). The facts may be found in the Introduction to *Lyrical Ballads, and Other Poems, 1797–1800* ed. James Butler and Karen Green (Ithaca, NY, 1992), pp. 3–12.

[2] *the first year . . . neighbours* July 1797 to July 1798, when Wordsworth was at Alfoxden and Coleridge four miles away at Nether Stowey (see pp. 457–8, above).
[3] *experiment* see the Advertisement to *Lyrical Ballads* (1798), p. 191, above. See also his remarks to Hazlitt, p. 609, below.

language of *real* life.[4] From this Preface, prefixed to poems in which it was impossible to deny the presence of original genius (however mistaken its direction might be deemed), arose the whole long-continued controversy.[5] For, from the conjunction of perceived power with supposed heresy, I explain the inveteracy and (in some instances, I grieve to say) the acrimonious passions with which the controversy has been conducted by the assailants.

Had Mr Wordsworth's poems been the silly, the childish things which they were for a long time described as being; had they been really distinguished from the compositions of other poets merely by meanness of language and inanity of thought; had they indeed contained nothing more than what is found in the parodies and pretended imitations of them – they must have sunk at once, a dead weight, into the slough of oblivion, and have dragged the Preface along with them. But year after year increased the number of Mr Wordsworth's admirers. They were found, too, not in the lower classes of the reading public, but chiefly among young men of strong sensibility and meditative minds,[6] and their admiration (inflamed perhaps in some degree by opposition) was distinguished by its intensity – I might almost say, by its religious fervour.

These facts, and the intellectual energy of the author (which was more or less consciously felt, where it was outwardly and even boisterously denied), meeting with sentiments of aversion to his opinions, and of alarm at their consequences, produced an eddy of criticism which would of itself have borne up the poems by the violence with which it whirled them round and round.

With many parts of this Preface in the sense attributed to them and which the words undoubtedly seem to authorize, I never concurred – but on the contrary objected to them as erroneous in principle, and as contradictory (in appearance at least) both to other parts of the same Preface, and to the author's own practice in the greater part of the poems themselves.[7] Mr Wordsworth in his recent collection[8] has, I find, degraded this prefatory disquisition to the end of his second volume, to be read or not at the reader's choice. But he has not (as far as I can discover) announced any change in his poetic creed. At all events, considering it as the source of a controversy in which I have been honoured more than I deserve by the frequent conjunction of my name with his, I think it expedient to declare once for all, in what points I coincide with the opinions supported in that Preface, and in what points I altogether differ. . . .

'What is poetry?' is so nearly the same question with 'what is a poet?' that the answer to the one is involved in the solution of the other. For it is a distinction resulting from the poetic genius itself, which sustains and modifies the images, thoughts, and emotions of the poet's own mind. The poet, described in ideal perfection, brings the whole soul of man into activity, with the subordination of its faculties to each other, according to their relative worth and dignity. He diffuses a tone and spirit of unity that blends and (as it were) *fuses* each into each by that synthetic and magical power to which I would exclusively appropriate the name of imagination. This power, first put in action by the will and understanding, and retained under their irremissive, though gentle and unnoticed, control (*laxis effertur habenis*[9]), reveals itself in the balance or reconcilement of opposite or discordant qualities; of sameness with difference; of the general with the concrete; the idea with the image; the individual with the representative; the sense of novelty and freshness, with old and familiar objects; a more than usual state of emotion, with more than usual order; judgement ever awake and steady self-possession, with enthusiasm and feeling profound or vehement – and, while it blends and harmonizes the natural and the artificial, still subordinates art to nature; the manner to the matter; and our admiration of the poet to our sympathy with the poetry.

---

[4]   *To the second edition . . . life* Coleridge's account of the Preface is not strictly accurate; here he distances himself from it, though it was, as he said at the time, 'half the child of my own brain'. Wordsworth referred to the 'real language of men', see p. 364, above.

[5]   *controversy* Coleridge refers to the criticism Wordsworth received particularly from the *Edinburgh Review*, culminating with Jeffrey's review of *The Excursion*, see pp. 556–8, below.

[6]   *young men . . . minds* such as John Wilson and Thomas De Quincey, both of whom, as young men, wrote admiringly to Wordsworth of the *Lyrical Ballads*.

[7]   *With many parts . . . themselves* not true; Coleridge was the mastermind behind the Preface, and its fundamental principles were drawn largely from his reading.

[8]   *his recent collection* Wordsworth published his first collected *Poems* in 1815.

[9]   'carried on with slackened reins' (Petrarch, *Epistola Barbato Sulmonensi* 39); see *Notebooks* iii 4178 and n.

The Rime of the Ancient Mariner. In Seven Parts.[1]

From SIBYLLINE LEAVES (1817)

Facile credo, plures esse Naturas invisibiles quam visibiles in rerum universitate. Sed horum omnium familiam quis nobis enarrabit? et gradus et cognationes et discrimina et singulorum munera? Quid agunt? quae loca habitant? Harum rerum notitiam semper ambivit ingenium humanum, nunquam attigit. Juvat, interea, non diffiteor, quandoque in animo, tanquam in Tabulâ, majoris et melioris mundi imaginem contemplari: ne mens assuefacta hodierniae vitae minutiis se contrahat nimis, et tota subsidat in pusillas cogitationes. Sed veritati interea invigilandum est, modusque servandus, ut certa ab incertis, diem a nocte, distinguamus.[2]

Thomas Burnet, Archaeologiae Philosophicae *{London, 1692}, p. 68–9*

Part the First

An ancient mariner
meeteth three gallants
bidden to a wedding-
feast, and detaineth one.

It is an ancient mariner,
And he stoppeth one of three:
'By thy long grey beard and glittering eye
Now wherefore stopp'st thou me?

The bridegroom's doors are opened wide,   5
And I am next of kin;
The guests are met, the feast is set –
Mayst hear the merry din.'

He holds him with his skinny hand,
'There was a ship', quoth he;   10
'Hold off! Unhand me, grey-beard loon!'
Eftsoons his hand dropped he.

The wedding-guest is
spellbound by the eye of
the old seafaring man,
and constrained to hear
his tale.

He holds him with his glittering eye –
The wedding-guest stood still,
And listens like a three years' child: 15
The mariner hath his will.

The wedding-guest sat on a stone,
He cannot choose but hear;
And thus spake on that ancient man,
The bright-eyed mariner: 20

'The ship was cheered, the harbour cleared,
Merrily did we drop
Below the kirk, below the hill,
Below the lighthouse top.

THE RIME OF THE ANCIENT MARINER. IN SEVEN PARTS
[1]   This was the fifth published text of *The Ancient Mariner*, and the first where Coleridge was identified as the author. It is radically different from previous texts in containing the Latin epigraph, marginal glosses, and numerous revisions to the poem itself. The earliest, 1798 version of the poem appears in the present volume with the other *Lyrical Ballads* of 1798, pp. 192–209.
[2]   This adaptation from Burnet may be translated: 'I can easily believe that there are more invisible than visible beings in the universe. But who will describe to us their families, ranks, affinities, differences, and functions? What do they do? Where do they live? The human mind has always sought knowledge of these things, but has never attained it. I admit that it is good sometimes to contemplate in thought, as in a picture, the image of a greater and better world; otherwise the mind, used to the minor concerns of daily life, may contract itself too much, and concentrate entirely on trivia. But meanwhile we must be vigilant for truth and moderation, that we may distinguish certainty from doubt, day from night.' Coleridge entered Burnet's remarks in his notebook, 1801 or 1802; see *Notebooks* i 1000H and n.

The mariner tells how
the ship sailed
southward with a good
wind and fair weather
till it reached the
line.[3]

The sun came up upon the left,　　　　　　　　25
Out of the sea came he;
And he shone bright, and on the right
Went down into the sea.

Higher and higher every day,
Till over the mast at noon –'　　　　　　　　30
The wedding-guest here beat his breast,
For he heard the loud bassoon.

The wedding-guest
heareth the bridal
music, but the mariner
continueth his tale.

The bride hath paced into the hall,
Red as a rose is she;
Nodding their heads before her goes　　　　　35
The merry minstrelsy.[4]

The wedding-guest he beat his breast,
Yet he cannot choose but hear;
And thus spake on that ancient man,
The bright-eyed mariner.　　　　　　　　　　40

The ship drawn by a
storm toward the South
Pole.

'And now the storm-blast came, and he
Was tyrannous and strong;
He struck with his o'ertaking wings,
And chased us south along.

With sloping masts and dipping prow,　　　　45
As who pursued with yell and blow
Still treads the shadow of his foe
And forward bends his head,
The ship drove fast, loud roared the blast,
And southward aye we fled.　　　　　　　　　50

And now there came both mist and snow,
And it grew wondrous cold:
And ice mast-high came floating by
As green as emerald.

The land of ice, and of
fearful sounds where no
living thing was to be
seen.

And through the drifts[5] the snowy clift[6]　　55
Did send a dismal sheen;
Nor shapes of men nor beasts we ken –
The ice was all between.

The ice was here, the ice was there,
The ice was all around;　　　　　　　　　　60
It cracked and growled, and roared and howled
Like noises in a swound.[7]

3　*line* equator.
4　*before her . . . minstrelsy* cf. Chaucer, *Squire's Tale* 268:
'Toforn hym gooth the louds mynstralcye'.

5　*drifts* floating ice.
6　*clift* cleft.
7　*swound* swoon.

Till a great sea-bird, called the albatross, came through the snow-fog, and was received with great hospitality.	At length did cross an albatross, Thorough the fog it came; As if it had been a Christian soul,[8] 65 We hailed it in God's name.
	It ate the food it ne'er had eat, And round and round it flew: The ice did split with a thunder-fit; The helmsman steered us through. 70
And lo! the albatross proveth a bird of good omen, and followeth the ship as it returned northward through fog and floating ice.	And a good south wind sprung up behind, The albatross did follow; And every day, for food or play, Came to the mariners' hollo!
	In mist or cloud, on mast or shroud, 75 It perched for vespers[9] nine, Whiles all the night, through fogsmoke white, Glimmered the white moonshine.'
The ancient mariner inhospitably killeth the pious bird of good omen.	'God save thee, ancient mariner, From the fiends that plague thee thus! 80 Why look'st thou so?' 'With my crossbow I shot the albatross.[10]

Part the Second

The sun now rose upon the right,
Out of the sea came he;
Still hid in mist, and on the left   85
Went down into the sea.

And the good south wind still blew behind,
But no sweet bird did follow,
Nor any day for food or play
Came to the mariners' hollo!   90

His shipmates cry out against the ancient mariner, for killing the bird of good luck.

And I had done an hellish thing
And it would work 'em woe:
For all averred[11] I had killed the bird
That made the breeze to blow.
"Ah wretch!" said they, "the bird to slay   95
That made the breeze to blow!"

But when the fog cleared off, they justify the same – and thus make themselves accomplices in the crime.

Nor dim nor red, like God's own head
The glorious sun uprist:
Then all averred I had killed the bird
That brought the fog and mist.   100

---

8   *a Christian soul* i.e. a human being.
9   *vespers* evenings.
10   The central event of the poem was suggested by a travel book which Wordsworth read, Shelvocke's *Voyage Round the World* (1726); see p.194 n. 13.

11   *averred* maintained that.

"'Twas right", said they, "such birds to slay,
That bring the fog and mist."

The fair breeze continues; the ship enters the Pacific Ocean and sails northward, even till it reaches the line.

The fair breeze blew, the white foam flew,
The furrow[12] streamed off free:
We were the first that ever burst   105
Into that silent sea.

The ship hath been suddenly becalmed.

Down dropped the breeze, the sails dropped down,
'Twas sad as sad could be,
And we did speak only to break
The silence of the sea.   110

All in a hot and copper sky
The bloody sun at noon
Right up above the mast did stand,
No bigger than the moon.

Day after day, day after day,   115
We stuck, nor breath nor motion,
As idle as a painted ship
Upon a painted ocean.

And the albatross begins to be avenged.

Water, water, everywhere,
And all the boards did shrink;   120
Water, water, everywhere,
Nor any drop to drink.

The very deeps did rot: oh Christ,
That ever this should be!
Yea, slimy things did crawl with legs   125
Upon the slimy sea.

About, about, in reel and rout
The death-fires danced at night;
The water, like a witch's oils,
Burnt green and blue and white.   130

A spirit had followed them; one of the invisible inhabitants of this planet, neither departed souls nor angels; concerning whom the learned Jew, Josephus,[13] and the Platonic Constantinopolitan,[14] Michael Psellus,[15] may be consulted. They are very numerous, and there is no climate or element without one or more.

And some in dreams assured were
Of the spirit that plagued us so;
Nine fathom deep he had followed us
From the land of mist and snow.

---

[12] 'In the former edition the line was "The furrow followed free". But I had not been long on board a ship before I perceived that this was the image as seen by a spectator from the shore, or from another vessel. From the ship itself the wake appears like a brook flowing off from the stern' (Coleridge's note).
[13] Flavius Josephus (*c*.37–*c*.100), author of *Antiquitates Judaicae* and, more famously, *De Bello Judaico*, which Coleridge read in November 1800 (*Notebooks* i 851).
[14] *Platonic Constantinopolitan* neo-Platonic philosopher who comes from Constantinople.
[15] Michael Constantine Psellus (*c*.1018–*c*.1105), whose commentary to the *Chaldaean Oracles*, as John Livingston Lowes has pointed out, informed both this poem and *Kubla Khan*; see Lowes, *The Road to Xanadu* (1978), pp. 216–17.

And every tongue, through utter drought,   135
Was withered at the root;
We could not speak, no more than if
We had been choked with soot.

The shipmates in their
sore distress would fain
throw the whole guilt
on the ancient mariner:
in sign whereof they
hang the dead sea- bird
round his neck.

Ah wel-a-day! what evil looks
Had I from old and young!   140
Instead of the cross the albatross
About my neck was hung.

Part the Third

There passed a weary time. Each throat
Was parched, and glazed each eye.
A weary time! a weary time!   145
How glazed each weary eye!
When looking westward, I beheld
A something in the sky.

The ancient mariner
beholdeth a sign in the
element afar off.

At first it seemed a little speck
And then it seemed a mist;   150
It moved and moved, and took at last
A certain shape, I wist.[16]

A speck, a mist, a shape, I wist!
And still it neared and neared:
And as if it dodged a water-sprite,   155
It plunged and tacked and veered.

At its nearer approach, it
seemeth to him to be a
ship; and at a dear
ransom he freeth his
speech from the bonds of
thirst.

With throat unslaked, with black lips baked,
We could nor laugh nor wail;
Through utter drought all dumb we stood!
I bit my arm, I sucked the blood,   160
And cried, "A sail! A sail!"

With throat unslaked, with black lips baked,
Agape they heard me call:

A flash of joy.

Gramercy![17] they for joy did grin
And all at once their breath drew in   165
As they were drinking all.

And horror follows. For
can it be a *ship* that
comes onward without
wind or tide?

"See, see!" I cried, "She tacks no more,
Hither to work us weal;[18]
Without a breeze, without a tide,
She steadies with upright keel."   170

The western wave was all a-flame,
The day was well nigh done!
Almost upon the western wave
Rested the broad bright sun;

---

[16]   *wist* was aware of.   [18]   *weal* harm.
[17]   *Gramercy!* mercy on us!

When that strange shape drove suddenly   175
Betwixt us and the sun.

It seemeth him but the
skeleton of a ship.

And straight the sun was flecked with bars
(Heaven's Mother send us grace!),
As if through a dungeon-grate he peered
With broad and burning face.   180

Alas! thought I, and my heart beat loud,
How fast she nears and nears!
Are those *her* sails that glance in the sun
Like restless gossameres?

And its ribs are seen as
bars on the face of the
setting sun.

Are those *her* ribs through which the sun   185
Did peer, as through a grate?
And is that woman all her crew?

The spectre-woman and
her death- mate, and no
other on board the
skeleton-ship.

Is that a Death? And are there two?
Is Death that woman's mate?

Her lips were red, *her* looks were free,   190
Her locks were yellow as gold;

Like vessel, like crew!

Her skin was as white as leprosy,
The nightmare Life-in-Death was she
Who thicks man's blood with cold.

Death and Life-in-Death
have diced for the ship's
crew, and she (the latter)
winneth the ancient
mariner.

The naked hulk alongside came,   195
And the twain were casting dice;
"The game is done! I've won! I've won!"
Quoth she, and whistles thrice.

The sun's rim dips, the stars rush out,
At one stride comes the dark;[19]   200
With far-heard whisper, o'er the sea,
Off shot the spectre bark.

We listened and looked sideways up!
Fear at my heart, as at a cup,
My life-blood seemed to sip!   205
The stars were dim, and thick the night,
The steersman's face by his lamp gleamed white;
From the sails the dews did drip –

At the rising of the
moon,

Till clomb[20] above the eastern bar
The horned moon, with one bright star   210
Within the nether tip.

One after another,

One after one, by the star-dogged moon
Too quick for groan or sigh,
Each turned his face with a ghastly pang
And cursed me with his eye.   215

---

[19]   *The sun's rim . . . dark* Coleridge added a marginal gloss in MS in copies of *Sibylline Leaves* to explain: 'Between the tropics there is no twilight. As the sun's last segment dips down, and the evening gun is fired, the constellations appear arrayed'. Subsequent printed texts included the terser gloss: 'No twilight within the courts of the sun'.
[20]   *clomb* climbed.

His shipmates drop
down dead.

Four times fifty living men
(And I heard nor sigh nor groan)
With heavy thump, a lifeless lump,
They dropped down one by one.

But Life-in-Death
begins her work on the
ancient mariner.

The souls did from their bodies fly,   220
They fled to bliss or woe!
And every soul, it passed me by
Like the whiz of my crossbow.'

Part the Fourth

The wedding-guest
feareth that a spirit is
talking to him;

'I fear thee, ancient mariner,
I fear thy skinny hand;   225
And thou art long and lank and brown
As is the ribbed sea-sand.[21]

I fear thee and thy glittering eye,
And thy skinny hand so brown –'

But the ancient mariner
assureth him of his
bodily life, and
proceedeth to relate his
horrible penance.

'Fear not, fear not, thou wedding-guest,   230
This body dropped not down.

Alone, alone, all all alone,
Alone on a wide wide sea;
And never a saint took pity on
My soul in agony.   235

He despiseth the
creatures of the calm,

The many men so beautiful,
And they all dead did lie!
And a thousand thousand slimy things
Lived on – and so did I.

And envieth that *they*
should live, and so many
lie dead.

I looked upon the rotting sea   240
And drew my eyes away;
I looked upon the rotting deck,
And there the dead men lay.

I looked to heaven and tried to pray
But or ever a prayer had gushed,   245
A wicked whisper came and made
My heart as dry as dust.

I closed my lids and kept them close
And the balls like pulses beat;
For the sky and the sea, and the sea and the sky   250
Lay like a load on my weary eye,
And the dead were at my feet.

---

[21]   'For the last two lines of this stanza I am indebted to Mr Wordsworth. It was on a delightful walk from Nether Stowey to Dulverton, with him and his sister, in the autumn of 1797, that this poem was planned and in part composed' (Coleridge's note). For Wordsworth's comment on this note, see p. 419.

But the curse liveth for
him in the eye of the
dead men.

The cold sweat melted from their limbs,
Nor rot nor reek did they;
The look with which they looked on me   255
Had never passed away.

An orphan's curse would drag to hell
A spirit from on high;
But oh! more horrible than that
Is the curse in a dead man's eye!   260
Seven days, seven nights, I saw that curse
And yet I could not die.

In his loneliness and
fixedness, he yearneth
towards the journeying
moon, and the stars that
still sojourn, yet still
move onward; and
everywhere the blue sky
belongs to them, and is
their appointed rest, and
their native country, and
their own natural
homes, which they enter
unannounced, as lords
that are certainly
expected, and yet there
is a silent joy at their
arrival.

By the light of the moon
he beholdeth God's
creatures of the great
calm.

The moving moon went up the sky
And nowhere did abide;
Softly she was going up   265
And a star or two beside;

Her beams bemocked the sultry main
Like April hoar-frost spread;
But where the ship's huge shadow lay
The charmed[22] water burnt alway   270
A still and awful red.

Beyond the shadow of the ship
I watched the water-snakes;
They moved in tracks of shining white,
And when they reared, the elfish light   275
Fell off in hoary flakes.

Within the shadow of the ship
I watched their rich attire:
Blue, glossy green, and velvet black,
They coiled and swam, and every track   280
Was a flash of golden fire.

Their beauty and their
happiness.

Oh happy living things! no tongue
Their beauty might declare:
A spring of love gushed from my heart

He blesseth them in his
heart.

And I blessed them unaware!   285
Sure my kind saint took pity on me,
And I blessed them unaware.

The spell begins to
break.

The self-same moment I could pray,
And from my neck so free
The albatross fell off and sank   290
Like lead into the sea.

---

[22] *charmed* dead calm.

Part the Fifth

Oh sleep, it is a gentle thing
Beloved from pole to pole!
To Mary Queen[23] the praise be given;
She sent the gentle sleep from heaven   295
That slid into my soul.

By grace of the holy
Mother, the ancient
mariner is refreshed with
rain.

The silly[24] buckets on the deck
That had so long remained,
I dreamt that they were filled with dew
And when I awoke it rained.   300

My lips were wet, my throat was cold,
My garments all were dank;
Sure I had drunken in my dreams
And still my body drank.

I moved and could not feel my limbs,   305
I was so light, almost
I thought that I had died in sleep
And was a blessed ghost.

He heareth sounds, and
seeth strange sights and
commotions in the sky
and the element.

And soon I heard a roaring wind,
It did not come anear;   310
But with its sound it shook the sails
That were so thin and sere.[25]

The upper air bursts into life
And a hundred fire-flags sheen,[26]
To and fro they were hurried about;   315
And to and fro, and in and out
The wan stars danced between.[27]

And the coming wind did roar more loud,
And the sails did sigh like sedge;
And the rain poured down from one black cloud,   320
The moon was at its edge.

The thick black cloud was cleft, and still
The moon was at its side;
Like waters shot from some high crag,
The lightning fell with never a jag,   325
A river steep and wide.

The bodies of the ship's
crew are inspirited,[28]
and the ship moves on;

The loud wind never reached the ship,
Yet now the ship moved on!
Beneath the lightning and the moon
The dead men gave a groan.   330

---

23 *Mary Queen* the Virgin Mary.
24 *silly* plain, rustic, homely.
25 *sere* worn.

26 *sheen* shining.
27 *The upper air . . . between* the Aurora Borealis.
28 *inspirited* quickened, animated.

They groaned, they stirred, they all uprose,
Nor spake, nor moved their eyes;
It had been strange, even in a dream,
To have seen those dead men rise.

The helmsman steered, the ship moved on,   335
Yet never a breeze up-blew;
The mariners all 'gan work the ropes
Where they were wont to do;
They raised their limbs like lifeless tools –
We were a ghastly crew.   340

The body of my brother's son
Stood by me, knee to knee;
The body and I pulled at one rope
But he said nought to me.'

But not by the souls of the men, nor by demons of earth or the middle air, but by a blessed troop of angelic spirits, sent down by the invocation of the guardian saint.

'I fear thee, ancient mariner!'   345
'Be calm, thou wedding-guest!
'Twas not those souls that fled in pain,
Which to their corses came again,
But a troop of spirits blessed;

For when it dawned, they dropped their arms   350
And clustered round the mast;
Sweet sounds rose slowly through their mouths
And from their bodies passed.

Around, around, flew each sweet sound
Then darted to the sun;   355
Slowly the sounds came back again,
Now mixed, now one by one.

Sometimes a-dropping from the sky
I heard the skylark sing;
Sometimes all little birds that are,   360
How they seemed to fill the sea and air
With their sweet jargoning![29]

And now 'twas like all instruments,
Now like a lonely flute,
And now it is an angel's song   365
That makes the heavens be mute.

It ceased, yet still the sails made on
A pleasant noise till noon,
A noise like of a hidden brook
In the leafy month of June,   370
That to the sleeping woods all night
Singeth a quiet tune.

---

[29] *jargoning* birdsong.

Till noon we quietly sailed on,
Yet never a breeze did breathe;
Slowly and smoothly went the ship,   375
Moved onward from beneath.

The lonesome spirit
from the South Pole
carries on the ship as far
as the line, in obedience
to the angelic troop, but
still requireth vengeance.

Under the keel nine fathom deep,
From the land of mist and snow,
The spirit slid, and it was he
That made the ship to go.   380
The sails at noon left off their tune
And the ship stood still also.

The sun right up above the mast
Had fixed her to the ocean;
But in a minute she 'gan stir   385
With a short uneasy motion –
Backwards and forwards half her length,
With a short uneasy motion.

Then like a pawing horse let go,
She made a sudden bound;   390
It flung the blood into my head,
And I fell down in a swound.

The Polar Spirit's fellow
demons, the invisible
inhabitants of the
element, take part in his
wrong; and two of them
relate, one to the other,
that penance long and
heavy for the ancient
mariner hath been
accorded to the Polar
Spirit, who returneth
southward.

How long in that same fit I lay,
I have not to declare;
But ere my living life returned,   395
I heard and in my soul discerned
Two voices in the air.

"Is it he?" quoth one, "Is this the man?
By him who died on cross,
With his cruel bow he laid full low   400
The harmless albatross.

The spirit who bideth by himself
In the land of mist and snow,
He loved the bird that loved the man
Who shot him with his bow."   405

The other was a softer voice,
As soft as honey-dew;
Quoth he, "The man hath penance done
And penance more will do." '

Part the Sixth

FIRST VOICE
But tell me, tell me! speak again,   410
Thy soft response renewing –
What makes that ship drive on so fast?
What is the ocean doing?

SECOND VOICE
Still as a slave before his lord,
The ocean hath no blast;   415
His great bright eye most silently
Up to the moon is cast –

If he may know which way to go,
For she guides him smooth or grim.
See, brother, see – how graciously   420
She looketh down on him!

FIRST VOICE
But why drives on that ship so fast
Without or wave or wind?
SECOND VOICE
The air is cut away before
And closes from behind.   425

Fly, brother, fly! more high, more high,
Or we shall be belated;
For slow and slow that ship will go
When the mariner's trance is abated.

'I woke, and we were sailing on   430
As in a gentle weather;
'Twas night, calm night, the moon was high –
The dead men stood together.

All stood together on the deck,
For a charnel-dungeon[30] fitter;   435
All fixed on me their stony eyes
That in the moon did glitter.

The pang, the curse, with which they died
Had never passed away;
I could not draw my eyes from theirs   440
Nor turn them up to pray.

And now this spell was snapped; once more
I viewed the ocean green,
And looked far forth, yet little saw
Of what had else been seen –   445

Like one that on a lonesome road
Doth walk in fear and dread,
And having once turned round walks on
And turns no more his head,
Because he knows a frightful fiend   450
Doth close behind him tread.

The mariner hath been cast into a trance; for the angelic power causeth the vessel to drive northward, faster than human life could endure.

The supernatural motion is retarded; the mariner awakes, and his penance begins anew.

The curse is finally expiated.

---

[30] *charnel-dungeon* dungeon containing dead prisoners' bodies.

But soon there breathed a wind on me,
Nor sound nor motion made;
Its path was not upon the sea,
In ripple or in shade.   455

It raised my hair, it fanned my cheek,
Like a meadow-gale of spring –
It mingled strangely with my fears,
Yet it felt like a welcoming.

Swiftly, swiftly flew the ship,   460
Yet she sailed softly too;
Sweetly, sweetly blew the breeze –
On me alone it blew.

And the ancient mariner
beholdeth his native
country.

Oh dream of joy! Is this indeed
The lighthouse top I see?   465
Is this the hill? Is this the kirk?
Is this mine own countree?

We drifted o'er the harbour-bar,[31]
And I with sobs did pray,
"Oh let me be awake, my God!   470
Or let me sleep alway!"

The harbour-bay was clear as glass,
So smoothly it was strewn![32]
And on the bay the moonlight lay
And the shadow of the moon.   475

The rock shone bright, the kirk no less
That stands above the rock;
The moonlight steeped in silentness
The steady weathercock.

And the bay was white with silent light,   480
Till rising from the same,

The angelic spirits leave
the dead bodies,

Full many shapes that shadows were
In crimson colours came.

And appear in their own
forms of light.

A little distance from the prow
Those crimson shadows were;   485
I turned my eyes upon the deck –
Oh Christ! What saw I there!

Each corse lay flat, lifeless and flat,
And by the holy rood,[33]
A man all light, a seraph-man[34]   490
On every corse there stood.

---

[31] *bar* bank of silt across the mouth of the harbour.
[32] *strewn* levelled.
[33] *rood* cross.

[34] *seraph-man* the seraphim were the highest order of angels,
whose purpose was to glow with the love of God.

This seraph-band, each waved his hand –
It was a heavenly sight!
They stood as signals to the land,
Each one a lovely light;   495

This seraph-band, each waved his hand,
No voice did they impart –
No voice, but oh! the silence sank
Like music on my heart.

But soon I heard the dash of oars,   500
I heard the pilot's cheer;
My head was turned perforce away
And I saw a boat appear.

The pilot and the pilot's boy,
I heard them coming fast –   505
Dear Lord in heaven! it was a joy
The dead men could not blast.

I saw a third, I heard his voice –
It is the hermit good!
He singeth loud his godly hymns   510
That he makes in the wood.
He'll shrieve my soul, he'll wash away
The albatross's blood.

Part the Seventh

The hermit of the wood,

This hermit good lives in that wood
Which slopes down to the sea;   515
How loudly his sweet voice he rears!
He loves to talk with mariners
That come from a far countree.

He kneels at morn, and noon and eve,
He hath a cushion plump;   520
It is the moss that wholly hides
The rotted old oak-stump.

The skiff-boat neared, I heard them talk:
"Why, this is strange, I trow!
Where are those lights so many and fair,   525
That signal made but now?"

Approacheth the ship
with wonder.

"Strange, by my faith!" the hermit said,
"And they answered not our cheer!
The planks look warped, and see those sails,
How thin they are and sere!   530
I never saw aught like to them
Unless perchance it were

The skeletons of leaves that lag
My forest brook along,
When the ivy-tod[35] is heavy with snow   535
And the owlet whoops to the wolf below
That eats the she-wolf's young."

"Dear Lord! it hath a fiendish look",
The pilot made reply,
"I am a-feared." "Push on, push on!"   540
Said the hermit cheerily.

The boat came closer to the ship
But I nor spake nor stirred;
The boat came close beneath the ship
And straight a sound was heard!   545

The ship suddenly sinketh.

Under the water it rumbled on,
Still louder and more dread;
It reached the ship, it split the bay –
The ship went down like lead.

The ancient mariner is saved in the pilot's boat.

Stunned by that loud and dreadful sound   550
Which sky and ocean smote,
Like one that hath been seven days drowned,
My body lay afloat;
But swift as dreams, myself I found
Within the pilot's boat.   555

Upon the whirl where sank the ship
The boat spun round and round,
And all was still, save that the hill
Was telling of the sound.

I moved my lips – the pilot shrieked   560
And fell down in a fit;
The holy hermit raised his eyes
And prayed where he did sit.

I took the oars; the pilot's boy,
Who now doth crazy go,   565
Laughed loud and long, and all the while
His eyes went to and fro:
"Ha! ha!" quoth he, "full plain I see
The Devil knows how to row."

And now all in my own countrée   570
I stood on the firm land!
The hermit stepped forth from the boat,
And scarcely he could stand.

---

[35] *ivy-tod* ivy-bush.

The ancient mariner
earnestly entreateth the
hermit to shrieve him;
and the penance of life
falls on him.

"Oh shrieve me, shrieve me, holy man!"
The hermit crossed his brow.   575
"Say quick", quoth he, "I bid thee say
What manner of man art thou?"

Forthwith this frame of mine was wrenched
With a woeful agony,
Which forced me to begin my tale –   580
And then it left me free.

And ever and anon
throughout his future
life an agony
constraineth him to
travel from land to land,

Since then, at an uncertain hour,
That agony returns,
And till my ghastly tale is told,
This heart within me burns.   585

I pass, like night, from land to land,
I have strange power of speech;
The moment that his face I see,
I know the man that must hear me –
To him my tale I teach.   590

What loud uproar bursts from that door!
The wedding-guests are there;
But in the garden bower the bride
And bridemaids singing are;
And hark, the little vesper-bell[36]   595
Which biddeth me to prayer.

Oh wedding-guest! this soul hath been
Alone on a wide wide sea;
So lonely 'twas, that God himself
Scarce seemed there to be.   600

Oh sweeter than the marriage-feast,
'Tis sweeter far to me
To walk together to the kirk
With a goodly company!

To walk together to the kirk   605
And all together pray,
While each to his great Father bends,
Old men, and babes, and loving friends,
And youths and maidens gay.

And to teach by his own
example love and
reverence to all things
that God made and
loveth.

Farewell, farewell! but this I tell   610
To thee, thou wedding-guest!
He prayeth well who loveth well
Both man and bird and beast.

He prayeth best who loveth best
All things both great and small,   615
For the dear God who loveth us,
He made and loveth all.'

---

[36] *vesper-bell* bell used to summon the congregation for ves-
pers, evensong.

The mariner, whose eye is bright,
Whose beard with age is hoar,
Is gone; and now the wedding-guest   620
Turned from the bridegroom's door.

He went like one that hath been stunned
And is of sense forlorn:
A sadder and a wiser man
He rose the morrow morn.   625

Dejection: An Ode[1]

From SIBYLLINE LEAVES (1817)

Late, late yestreen I saw the new moon
With the old moon in her arms;
And I fear, I fear, my master dear,
We shall have a deadly storm.

Ballad of Sir Patrick Spence[2]

I

Well! if the bard was weather-wise who made
        The grand old ballad of Sir Patrick Spence,[3]
        This night, so tranquil now, will not go hence
Unroused by winds that ply a busier trade
Than those which mould yon clouds in lazy flakes,   5
Or the dull sobbing draught that moans and rakes
        Upon the strings of this Eolian lute,[4]
        Which better far were mute.
For lo! the new moon, winter-bright,
And overspread with phantom light   10
(With swimming phantom light o'erspread,
But rimmed and circled by a silver thread);
I see the old moon in her lap, foretelling
        The coming-on of rain and squally blast.
And oh, that even now the gust were swelling,   15
        And the slant night-shower driving loud and fast.
Those sounds which oft have raised me whilst they awed
        And sent my soul abroad,
Might now perhaps their wonted[5] impulse give,
Might startle this dull pain, and make it move and live!   20

DEJECTION: AN ODE
[1]   This is the best-known version of the poem, as published
in 1817. There are three important versions in this volume: it
was composed originally as a verse-letter to Sara Hutchinson
(pp. 495–504); published in *The Morning Post* in 1802,
addressed to 'Edmund' (pp. 507–11), and substantially revised
and published in this form in 1817.

[2]   Coleridge knew *The Ballad of Sir Patrick Spens* from
Thomas Percy's *Reliques of Ancient English Poetry* (1765).
[3]   *the bard . . . Spence* unknown; the ballad is anonymous.
[4]   *Eolian lute* Aeolian harps were placed lengthways in front
of open windows, where their strings were 'played' by the
wind; see Coleridge's *The Eolian Harp*, pp. 451–3.
[5]   *wonted* expected, usual.

II[6]

A grief without a pang – void, dark, and drear;
   A stifled, drowsy, unimpassioned grief
   Which finds no natural outlet, no relief
      In word, or sigh, or tear –
Oh Lady![7] in this wan and heartless mood,   25
To other thoughts by yonder throstle wooed
   All this long eve so balmy and serene,
Have I been gazing on the western sky
   And its peculiar tint of yellow-green;
And still I gaze, and with how blank an eye!   30
And those thin clouds above, in flakes and bars,
That give away their motion to the stars,
Those stars that glide behind them or between,
Now sparkling, now bedimmed, but always seen;
Yon crescent moon, as fixed as if it grew   35
In its own cloudless, starless lake of blue –
I see them all, so excellently fair;
I see, not feel, how beautiful they are!

III

   My genial spirits fail,[8]
    And what can these avail   40
To lift the smoth'ring weight from off my breast?
    It were a vain endeavour,
    Though I should gaze for ever
On that green light that lingers in the west:
I may not hope from outward forms to win   45
The passion and the life, whose fountains are within!

IV

Oh Lady, we receive but what we give,
And in our life alone does nature live;
Ours is her wedding-garment, ours her shroud!
   And would we aught behold of higher worth   50
Than that inanimate cold world allowed
To the poor loveless ever-anxious crowd –
   Ah! from the soul itself must issue forth
A light, a glory,[9] a fair luminous cloud
      Enveloping the earth!   55
And from the soul itself must there be sent
   A sweet and potent voice, of its own birth,
Of all sweet sounds the life and element.

---

6 This stanza had been reprinted in Coleridge's essay, 'The Principles of Genial Criticism' (1814), prefaced by a short discourse on the distinction between the beautiful and the agreeable; see Coleridge, *Shorter Works and Fragments* ed. H. J. Jackson and J. R. de J. Jackson (2 vols, 1995), i 380.

7 *Lady* Coleridge once again has in mind the original addressee of this work, Sara Hutchinson.
8 *My genial spirits fail* An echo of Milton, *Samson Agonistes* 594: 'my genial spirits droop'.
9 *glory* divine effulgence of light, as at Wordsworth, *Ode* 18.

V

Oh pure of heart![10] thou need'st not ask of me
What this strong music in the soul may be,   60
What and wherein it doth exist,
This light, this glory, this fair luminous mist,
This beautiful and beauty-making power!
        Joy, virtuous Lady! Joy that ne'er was given
Save to the pure and in their purest hour,   65
Life, and life's effluence,[11] cloud at once and shower,[12]
Joy, Lady, is the spirit and the power
Which, wedding nature to us, gives in dower[13]
        A new earth and new heaven
Undreamt of by the sensual and the proud!   70
Joy is the sweet voice, joy the luminous cloud –
        We in ourselves rejoice!
And thence flows all that charms or ear or sight,
        All melodies the echoes of that voice,
All colours a suffusion from that light.   75

VI

There was a time[14] when, though my path was rough,
        This joy within me dallied with distress,
And all misfortunes were but as the stuff
        Whence fancy made me dreams of happiness;
For hope grew round me like the twining vine,   80
And fruits and foliage not my own, seemed mine!
But now afflictions bow me down to earth,
Nor care I that they rob me of my mirth;
        But oh! each visitation
Suspends what nature gave me at my birth –   85
        My shaping spirit of imagination!
For not to think of what I needs must feel,
        But to be still and patient all I can,
And haply by abstruse research to steal
        From my own nature all the natural man –   90
        This was my sole resource, my only plan;
Till that which suits a part infects the whole,
And now is almost grown the habit of my soul.[15]

VII

Hence, viper thoughts, that coil around my mind,
        Reality's dark dream!   95

---

[10] *Oh pure of heart* the addressee of the poem, in this case, 'Lady'.
[11] *effluence* emanation, radiating energies.
[12] This line appears for the first time in this version of the poem. It is corrected in the errata list to *Sibylline Leaves* from 'Life, and life's effulgence, cloud at once and shower'. Jack Stillinger, *Coleridge and Textual Instability* (1994), p. 95, regards 'effulgence' as a misreading of 'effluence'.

[13] *dower* wedding-gift.
[14] *There was a time* echoes Wordsworth, *Ode* 1. In the *Letter to Sara Hutchinson*, this was the time 'Ere I was wedded' (l.231).
[15] Although not included in any earlier version of *Dejection*, lines 87–93 derive from the 1802 *Letter to Sara Hutchinson* 264–70 (see p. 502).

I turn from you, and listen to the wind,
   Which long has raved unnoticed. What a scream
Of agony, by torture lengthened out,
That lute sent forth! Thou wind, that rav'st without!
   Bare crag, or mountain tairn,[16] or blasted tree,   100
Or pine-grove whither woodman never clomb,[17]
Or lonely house long held the witches' home,
   Methinks were fitter instruments for thee,
Mad lutanist, who in this month of show'rs,
Of dark-brown gardens and of peeping flow'rs,   105
Mak'st devil's yule,[18] with worse than wintry song,
The blossoms, buds, and tim'rous leaves among!
   Thou actor, perfect in all tragic sounds,
Thou mighty poet,[19] e'en to frenzy bold,
      What tell'st thou now about?   110
      'Tis of the rushing of an host[20] in rout,
With groans of trampled men with smarting wounds[21] –
At once they groan with pain, and shudder with the cold!
But hush, there is a pause of deepest silence!
   And all that noise, as of a rushing crowd,   115
With groans and tremulous shudderings – all is over.
   It tells another tale, with sounds less deep and loud,
      A tale of less affright
      And tempered with delight,
As Otway's[22] self had framed the tender lay –   120
      'Tis of a little child
      Upon a lonesome wild
Not far from home, but she hath lost her way,
And now moans low in bitter grief and fear,
And now screams loud, and hopes to make her mother hear.   125

VIII

'Tis midnight, but small thoughts have I of sleep;
Full seldom may my friend such vigils keep!
Visit her, gentle sleep, with wings of healing,
   And may this storm be but a mountain birth;
May all the stars hang bright above her dwelling,   130
   Silent, as though they watched the sleeping earth!
      With light heart may she rise,

---

[16] 'Tairn is a small lake, generally if not always applied to the lakes up in the mountains, and which are the feeders of those in the valleys. This address to the storm-wind will not appear extravagant to those who have heard it at night, and in a mountainous country' (Coleridge's note).

[17] *clomb* climbed.

[18] *yule* festival; yule was the pagan festival that became Christmas. This is the devil's yule because it is April rather than December.

[19] *Thou actor . . . Thou mighty poet* i.e. the 'wind' of l. 99.

[20] *host* army.

[21] *an host . . . wounds* only two years before, in 1815,

Britain's long war with France (which had begun in 1793) had come to an end; see also *Reflections on Having Left a Place of Retirement* 43–8, *Fears in Solitude*.

[22] This reference to Thomas Otway (1652–85), who, according to Johnson, died in penury after wandering across a heath in a state of near-nakedness, further veils the reference to Wordsworth ('Edmund' in the 1802 *Morning Post* version), whose *Lucy Gray* tells the story of a lost child. For speculation on the allusion see David V. Erdman, 'The Otway Connection', *Coleridge's Imagination* ed. Richard Gravil, Lucy Newlyn, and Nicholas Roe (1985), pp. 143–60.

Gay fancy, cheerful eyes,
Joy lift her spirit, joy attune her voice:
To her may all things live, from pole to pole,
Their life the eddying of her living soul!
Oh simple spirit, guided from above;
Dear Lady, friend devoutest of my choice,
Thus may'st thou ever, evermore rejoice.

135

[On 'The Ancient Mariner'] (dictated 30 May 1830)

From TABLE TALK (edited from MS)

The fault of 'The Ancient Mariner' consists in making the moral sentiment too apparent and bringing it in too much as a principle or cause in a work of such pure imagination.

[The True Way for a Poet] (dictated 19 September 1830)

Southey picked nature's pockets as a poet, instead of borrowing from her. He went out and took some particular image, for example a water-insect – and then exactly copied its make, colours and motions. This he put in a poem. The true way for a poet is to examine nature, but write from your recollection, and trust more to your imagination than your memory.

[On 'The Recluse'] (dictated 21 July 1832)

Wordsworth should have first published his Thirteen Books on the growth of an individual mind,[1] far superior to any part of *The Excursion*. Then the plan suggested and laid out by me was that he should assume the station of a man in repose, whose mind was made up, and so prepared to deliver upon authority a system of philosophy. He was to treat man as man – a subject of eye, ear, touch, taste, in contact with external nature, informing the senses from the mind and not compounding a mind out of the senses; then the pastoral and other states, assuming a satiric or Juvenalian spirit as he approached the high civilization of cities and towns; and then opening a melancholy picture of the present state of degeneracy and vice; thence revealing the necessity for and proof of the whole state of man and society being subject to and illustrative of a redemptive process in operation, showing how this idea reconciled all the anomalies, and how it promised future glory and restoration. Something of this sort I suggested, and it was agreed on. It is what in substance I have been all my life doing in my system of philosophy.

Wordsworth spoilt many of his best poems by abandoning the contemplative position, which is alone fitted for him, and introducing the object in a dramatic way. This is seen in 'The Leech-Gatherer'[2] and 'Ruth'. Wordsworth had more materials for the great philosophic poet than any man I ever knew or (as I think) has existed in this country for a long time – but he was utterly unfitted for the epic or narrative style. His mental-internal action is always so excessively disproportionate to the actual business that the latter either goes to sleep or becomes ridiculous.[3] In his reasoning you will find no progression: it eddies, it comes round and round again, perhaps with a wider circle, but it is repetition still.

ON 'THE RECLUSE'
[1]   *The Thirteen-Book Prelude*; for Coleridge's immediate reaction to it, see *To William Wordsworth*, pp. 514–17.
[2]   i.e. *Resolution and Independence*.

[3]   Coleridge here echoes the point made by Jeffrey in his review of *The Excursion*, when he notes that its incidents are 'few and trifling', p. 557, below.

[*Keats*]¹ (dictated 11 August 1832)

A loose, not well-dressed youth, met Mr. Green and me in Mansfield Lane. Green knew him and spoke. It was Keats. He was introduced to me, and stayed a minute or so. After he had gone a little, he came back and said, 'Let me carry away the memory, Coleridge, of having pressed your hand.' There is death in *his* hand, said I to Green when he was gone. Yet this was before the consumption showed itself.

The Eolian Harp. Composed at Clevedon, Somersetshire.¹

From THE POETICAL WORKS OF S. T. COLERIDGE (1834)

My pensive Sara,² thy soft cheek reclined
Thus on mine arm, most soothing sweet it is
To sit beside our cot, our cot o'ergrown
With white-flowered jasmine and the broad-leaved myrtle
(Meet emblems they of innocence and love),⁣   5
And watch the clouds that late were rich with light
Slow-sad'ning round, and mark the star of eve
Serenely brilliant (such should wisdom be)
Shine opposite! How exquisite the scents
Snatched from yon bean-field! And the world so hushed!   10
The stilly murmur of the distant sea
Tells us of silence.
⁣   And that simplest lute
Placed lengthways in the clasping casement – hark
How by the desultory breeze caressed!³
Like some coy maid half-yielding to her lover,   15
It pours such sweet upbraidings as must needs
Tempt to repeat the wrong. And now its strings
Boldlier swept, the long sequacious⁴ notes
Over delicious surges sink and rise,
Such a soft floating witchery of sound   20
As twilight elfins make when they at eve
Voyage on gentle gales from fairyland,
Where melodies round honey-dropping flowers
Footless and wild, like birds of paradise,
Nor pause nor perch, hovering on untamed wing.   25
Oh the one life within us and abroad,⁵

KEATS
¹ Keats's account of this meeting may be found on pp. 1053–4; it took place probably on 11 April 1819. Joseph Henry Green (1791–1863) was Coleridge's literary executor, and had been Keats's demonstrator at Guy's Hospital.

THE EOLIAN HARP
¹ This poem was composed in 1795, and published in Coleridge's *Poems* (1796) as *Effusion XXXV*; for the early version see pp. 451–3.
² Sara Fricker, with whom Coleridge was in love at the time

this poem was first written. He was to marry her less than two months later, 4 October 1795.
³ The Aeolian harp is a stringed instrument placed in front of an open window so as to catch the breeze; it is not unlike modern wind-chimes.
⁴ *sequacious* following one another.
⁵ *Oh the one life . . . abroad* it is at first surprising to find that this was written not in 1795 but in 1817 (see next note). Coleridge's celebration of the pantheist one life echoes Wordsworth, *The Pedlar* 217–18: 'for in all things / He saw one life, and felt that it was joy'.

Which meets all motion and becomes its soul,
A light in sound, a sound-like power in light,
Rhythm in all thought, and joyance everywhere –
Methinks it should have been impossible   30
Not to love all things in a world so filled,
Where the breeze warbles, and the mute still air
Is Music slumbering on its instrument!⁶

    And thus, my love, as on the midway slope
Of yonder hill I stretch my limbs at noon,   35
Whilst through my half-closed eyelids I behold
The sunbeams dance, like diamonds, on the main,
And tranquil muse upon tranquillity,
Full many a thought uncalled and undetained,
And many idle flitting fantasies   40
Traverse my indolent and passive brain –
As wild and various as the random gales
That swell and flutter on this subject lute!

    And what if all of animated nature
Be but organic harps diversely framed,   45
That tremble into thought, as o'er them sweeps,
Plastic⁷ and vast, one intellectual⁸ breeze,
At once the soul of each, and God of all?⁹

    But thy more serious eye a mild reproof
Darts, oh beloved woman! – nor such thoughts   50
Dim and unhallowed dost thou not reject,
And biddest me walk humbly with my God.
Meek daughter in the family of Christ,¹⁰
Well hast thou said and holily dispraised¹¹
These shapings of the unregenerate mind,   55
Bubbles that glitter as they rise and break
On vain philosophy's aye-babbling spring.¹²
For never guiltless may I speak of Him,
Th' Incomprehensible! save when with awe
I praise him, and with faith that inly feels –   60
Who with his saving mercies healed me,
A sinful and most miserable man
Wildered and dark, and gave me to possess
Peace, and this cot,¹³ and thee, heart-honoured maid!

---

⁶ Lines 26–33 comprise the most substantial addition to this version of the poem; they were were first published in the errata to *Sibylline Leaves* (1817). Lines 32–3 as published in 1817, uncorrected by the errata, read: 'Where even the breezes, and the common air, / Contain the power and spirit of Harmony.'

⁷ *Plastic* shaping, formative, creative.

⁸ *intellectual* spiritual.

⁹ For the early MS version of ll. 44–8 see p. 452 n. 7.

¹⁰ *Meek daughter . . . Christ* Coleridge's language is figurative. Sara's father was a Bristol manufacturer who died bankrupt in 1786, leaving his wife and six children penniless. Sara's mother ran a dress shop.

¹¹ *holily dispraised* piously attacked. Coleridge's unease about the pantheist experience of ll. 44–8 is transferred to Sara.

¹² *On vain . . . spring* Coleridge is the philosopher accused, presumably by Sara, of endless babbling.

¹³ *cot* cottage.

This Lime-Tree Bower My Prison[1]

From THE POETICAL WORKS OF S. T. COLERIDGE (1834)

In the June of 1797, some long-expected friends paid a visit to the author's cottage, and on the morning of their arrival he met with an accident which disabled him from walking during the whole time of their stay. One evening, when they had left him for a few hours, he composed the following lines in the garden bower.

Well, they are gone, and here must I remain,
This lime-tree bower my prison! I have lost
Beauties and feelings, such as would have been
Most sweet to my remembrance even when age
Had dimmed mine eyes to blindness! They, meanwhile,   5
Friends whom I never more may meet again,[2]
On springy heath, along the hilltop edge,[3]
Wander in gladness, and wind down, perchance,
To that still roaring dell of which I told;
The roaring dell, o'erwooded, narrow, deep,   10
And only speckled by the midday sun;
Where its slim trunk the ash from rock to rock
Flings arching like a bridge – that branchless ash,
Unsunned and damp, whose few poor yellow leaves
Ne'er tremble in the gale, yet tremble still,   15
Fanned by the waterfall! And there my friends
Behold the dark green file of long lank weeds,[4]
That all at once (a most fantastic sight!)
Still nod and drip beneath the dripping edge
Of the blue clay-stone.
              Now, my friends emerge   20
Beneath the wide wide heaven – and view again
The many-steepled tract magnificent
Of hilly fields and meadows, and the sea,
With some fair bark, perhaps, whose sails light up
The slip of smooth clear blue betwixt two isles   25
Of purple shadow! Yes, they wander on
In gladness all – but thou, methinks, most glad,
My gentle-hearted Charles![5] For thou hast pined
And hungered after nature many a year

THIS LIME-TREE BOWER MY PRISON

[1] When first published in *The Annual Anthology* ed. Robert Southey (1800) it was entitled *This Lime-Tree Bower My Prison, A Poem Addressed to Charles Lamb, of the India-House, London*; for the exact circumstances and the earliest version of the poem see Coleridge's letter to Southey, 17 July 1797, pp. 457–9, above.

[2] *Friends . . . meet again* an exaggeration even by Coleridge's standards; they were Charles Lamb (who Coleridge had known since their shared boyhood at Christ's Hospital), and the Wordsworths, who had just arrived in Somerset for a minimum residence of a year.

[3] *the hilltop edge* the Quantock hills, behind Coleridge's cottage at Nether Stowey.

[4] 'The asplenium scolopendrium, called in some countries the Adder's tongue, in others the Hart's tongue; but Withering gives the Adder's tongue as the trivial name of the Ophioglossum only' (Coleridge's note). Coleridge and Wordsworth acquired copies of William Withering's *Arrangement of British Plants* (4 vols, 1796) in August 1800; see my *Wordsworth's Reading 1800–1815* (1996), pp. 245–6.

[5] *My gentle-hearted Charles* Coleridge apparently disregarded his friend's request, made shortly after the poem's first publication in 1800: 'For God's sake, don't make me ridiculous any more by terming me gentle-hearted in print, or do it in better verses. . . . the meaning of "gentle" is equivocal at best, and almost always means "poor-spirited" ' (Marrs i 217–18).

In the great city pent, winning thy way,   30
With sad yet patient soul, through evil and pain
And strange calamity![6] Ah, slowly sink
Behind the western ridge, thou glorious sun!
Shine in the slant beams of the sinking orb,
Ye purple heath-flowers! Richlier burn, ye clouds!   35
Live in the yellow light, ye distant groves!
And kindle, thou blue ocean! So my friend,
Struck with deep joy, may stand, as I have stood,
Silent with swimming sense; yea, gazing round
On the wide landscape, gaze till all doth seem   40
Less gross than bodily,[7] and of such hues
As veil the Almighty Spirit, when yet he makes
Spirits perceive His presence.
                                        A delight
Comes sudden on my heart, and I am glad   45
As I myself were there! Nor in this bower,
This little lime-tree bower, have I not marked
Much that has soothed me. Pale beneath the blaze
Hung the transparent foliage; and I watched
Some broad and sunny leaf, and loved to see   50
The shadow of the leaf and stem above
Dappling its sunshine! And that walnut tree
Was richly tinged, and a deep radiance lay
Full on the ancient ivy which *usurps*
Those fronting elms, and now with blackest mass   55
Makes their dark branches gleam a lighter hue
Through the late twilight; and though now the bat
Wheels silent by, and not a swallow twitters,
Yet still the solitary humble-bee[8]
Sings in the bean-flower! Henceforth I shall know   60
That nature ne'er deserts the wise and pure –
No scene so narrow but may well employ
Each faculty of sense, and keep the heart
Awake to love and beauty![9] And sometimes
'Tis well to be bereaved of promised good,   65
That we may lift the soul, and contemplate
With lively joy the joys we cannot share.
My gentle-hearted Charles! when the last rook
Beat its straight path along the dusky air
Homewards, I blessed it, deeming its black wing   70
(Now a dim speck, now vanishing in the light)
Had crossed the mighty orb's dilated glory
While thou stoodst gazing; or, when all was still,

[6]   *strange calamity* In September 1796 Lamb's sister Mary murdered her mother in a fit of insanity; see p. 578, below. Lamb had been working in East India House in the City of London since 1792.

[7]   *Less gross than bodily* a difficult phrase, meaning, presumably, that the world becomes more spiritualized as Lamb gazes upon it, granting him the Unitarian experience described in *Reflections on Having Left a Place of Retirement* 26–42.

[8]   *humble-bee* against a copy of the 1817 printed text, Coleridge entered the following note: 'Cows without horns are called Hummel cows, in the country as the Hummel bee, as stingless (unless it be a corruption of *humming*, from the sound observable).'

[9]   *Awake to love and beauty* In summer 1797, when this poem was first composed, Coleridge described how the 'wandering and distempered child' would be 'healed and harmonized / By the benignant touch of love and beauty' (*The Dungeon* 29–30).

Flew creaking[10] o'er thy head, and had a charm
For thee, my gentle-hearted Charles! to whom   75
No sound is dissonant which tells of Life.

Frost at Midnight[1]

From THE POETICAL WORKS OF S. T. COLERIDGE (1834)

The frost performs its secret ministry
Unhelped by any wind. The owlet's cry
Came loud — and hark, again! loud as before.
The inmates of my cottage, all at rest,
Have left me to that solitude which suits   5
Abstruser musings, save that at my side
My cradled infant[2] slumbers peacefully.
'Tis calm indeed! — so calm that it disturbs
And vexes meditation with its strange
And extreme silentness. Sea, hill, and wood,   10
This populous village! Sea, and hill, and wood,
With all the numberless goings-on of life,
Inaudible as dreams! The thin blue flame
Lies on my low-burnt fire, and quivers not;
Only that film[3] which fluttered on the grate   15
Still flutters there, the sole unquiet thing.
Methinks its motion in this hush of nature
Gives it dim sympathies with me who live,
Making it a companionable form
Whose puny flaps and freaks the idling spirit   20
By its own moods interprets, everywhere
Echo or mirror seeking of itself,
And makes a toy of thought.[4]
                                    But oh, how oft,
How oft at school,[5] with most believing mind,

---

[10] 'Some months after I had written this line, it gave me pleasure to find that Bartram had observed the same circumstance of the Savanna crane. "When these birds move their wings in flight, their strokes are slow, moderate and regular; and even when at a considerable distance or high above us, we plainly hear the quill-feathers; their shafts and webs upon one another creak as the joints or working of a vessel in a tempestuous sea" ' (Coleridge's note). Coleridge was reading William Bartram's *Travels through North and South Carolina* (1794) by summer 1797, and quickly communicated his enthusiasm for the work to Wordsworth.

FROST AT MIDNIGHT
[1] This poem was composed in February 1798, at around the same time Wordsworth was working on *The Ruined Cottage* and writing *The Pedlar*. An early text was published in the summer of 1798 and can be found on pp. 462–5. This later text, first published in 1834, is different in numerous respects,
most importantly in its omission of the final lines of the 1798 version, which describe baby Hartley's response to the icicles.
[2] *My cradled infant* Hartley Coleridge, born 19 September 1796. He was one-and-a-half years old when the poem was first written. By 1834 he was thoroughly mythologised in such poems as *The Nightingale* 91–105, *Christabel* 644–65, *To H.C., Six Years Old*, and *Ode* 83–131.
[3] *that film* Not footnoted in this version of the poem; in texts from 1798 to 1812 Coleridge had explained to his readers: 'In all parts of the kingdom these films are called "strangers", and supposed to portend the arrival of some absent friend.'
[4] In this late version of the poem Coleridge's debt to Cowper is clearer than ever; cf. Cowper's description of the winter evening, *Task* iv 284–307 (pp. 11–12, above), particularly his reference to the 'brittle toys' of fancy (l. 307). Earlier versions of these lines read very differently; see pp. 463 n. 4.
[5] *at school* Christ's Hospital in the City of London, where Coleridge was a pupil, 1782–91.

Presageful, have I gazed upon the bars,   25
To watch that fluttering stranger! And as oft
With unclosed lids, already had I dreamt
Of my sweet birthplace, and the old church-tower
Whose bells, the poor man's only music, rang
From morn to evening all the hot fair-day,   30
So sweetly that they stirred and haunted me
With a wild pleasure, falling on mine ear
Most like articulate sounds of things to come!
So gazed I till the soothing things I dreamt
Lulled me to sleep, and sleep prolonged my dreams!   35
And so I brooded all the following morn,
Awed by the stern preceptor's face, mine eye
Fixed with mock study on my swimming book;
Save if the door half opened, and I snatched
A hasty glance, and still my heart leaped up,   40
For still I hoped to see the stranger's face –
Townsman, or aunt, or sister more beloved,
My playmate when we both were clothed alike![6]
    Dear babe,[7] that sleepest cradled by my side,
Whose gentle breathings heard in this deep calm   45
Fill up the interspersed vacancies
And momentary pauses of the thought;
My babe so beautiful, it fills my heart
With tender gladness thus to look at thee,
And think that thou shalt learn far other lore   50
And in far other scenes! For I was reared
In the great city, pent mid cloisters dim,
And saw nought lovely but the sky and stars.
But thou, my babe, shalt wander like a breeze
By lakes and sandy shores, beneath the crags   55
Of ancient mountain, and beneath the clouds
Which image in their bulk both lakes and shores
And mountain crags; so shalt thou see and hear
The lovely shapes and sounds intelligible
Of that eternal language which thy God   60
Utters,[8] who from eternity doth teach
Himself in all, and all things in himself.
Great universal teacher! He shall mould[9]
Thy spirit, and by giving make it ask.
    Therefore all seasons shall be sweet to thee,   65
Whether the summer clothe the general earth
With greenness, or the redbreast sit and sing
Betwixt the tufts of snow on the bare branch
Of mossy apple-tree, while the nigh thatch
Smokes in the sun-thaw; whether the eave-drops fall   70

---

[6] *sister . . . alike* until well into the nineteenth century, small boys and girls were dressed in frocks until boys were breeched. Coleridge was deeply attached to his sister Anne (1767–91), whose early death from consumption distressed him greatly.

[7] *Dear babe* Coleridge turns again to his son Hartley.

[8] *so shalt . . . Utters* a reference to Bishop Berkeley's theory that the natural world is the symbolic language of God's thought. At more or less the same time that this was written, Wordsworth was describing the Pedlar's perception of the 'written promise' (*Pedlar* 119).

[9] *mould* the pantheist perception Coleridge wishes on Hartley is formative of the individual; cf. the intellectual breeze of *The Eolian Harp* (1795), which is 'Plastic' (l. 39).

Heard only in the trances[10] of the blast,
Or if the secret ministry of frost
Shall hang them up in silent icicles,
Quietly shining to the quiet moon.

Francis, Lord Jeffrey   (1773–1850)

The son of a deputy clerk in the Edinburgh law courts, Jeffrey was a graduate of the University of Glasgow, and despite a determination to write, trained as a lawyer and in 1794 was admitted to the Scottish bar. He was by then, against the wishes of his high Tory father, a Whig; because the Scottish legal system was dominated by Tories, he gained preferment very slowly.

Jeffrey found solace among other intellectuals such as Henry Brougham and Sydney Smith, who regularly met at his flat in Buccleugh Place. Smith quickly recognized the talents of his friends, and proposed that they establish a critical journal, the *Edinburgh Review*, the first number of which appeared in October 1802. Jeffrey, who had assumed the role of editor, was at first doubtful of success – but he was mistaken. The initial printing was for 750 copies, and a second printing was called for within the month. By the end of 1803, 2150 copies of the first issue had been sold in Edinburgh alone, with many being passed around. Its success was such that, by 1809, 9000 copies were being printed every quarter. Wordsworth had good reason to be irked by the bad reviews of his work that regularly appeared there: they were read by everyone.

Despite his reputation for severity, Jeffrey wrote appreciatively of Crabbe, Scott, Byron and, surprisingly, Keats. But it is true that he bore a particular grudge against Wordsworth, Coleridge and Southey, whom he lumped together as the 'Lake School'. He held them collectively responsible for the Preface to *Lyrical Ballads*, which he saw as a scurrilous attack on Pope and his imitators. For him, Wordsworth's *White Doe of Rylstone* (1815) was 'the very worst poem we ever saw imprinted in a quarto volume'.[1] The main problem with Wordsworth, as Jeffrey saw it, was that he was a poetic genius enslaved to a misguided philosophical system. That system had led him astray, and it was Jeffrey's duty to reveal the errors of his ways lest others be tempted to follow him. His most notorious attack,

parts of which are presented here, was that on *The Excursion*, which focuses his opposition on the grounds of: (i) plainness of diction; (ii) lowly subject-matter; (iii) bogus metaphysics. Wordsworth was no longer the Jacobin he had once been, so he was no longer a target for political reasons, and the review is conducted largely on aesthetic grounds. Its portrayal of Wordsworth as a self-obsessed mystic stuck, and helped depress his popularity for years. In private, Wordsworth remarked that he held the review 'in entire contempt, and therefore shall not pollute my fingers with the touch of it' (*MY* ii 190).[2] In later years, Henry Crabb Robinson reported that Jeffrey told him, ' "I was always among Wordsworth's admirers." I answered him rudely enough (but I did not wish to be civil), "You had an odd way of showing it" ' (Morley ii 838). He emerges with more credit from his friendship with Felicia Hemans, whose *Records of Woman*, he wrote in 1829, 'embraces a great deal of that which gives the very best poetry its chief power of pleasing.'[3]

Unlike Scott (also a lawyer by training), Jeffrey was always more dependent on his legal career than on his literary life for a living. After the Whigs came to power in 1830, he gained the advancement for which he had waited so long. In 1832, he was elected to Parliament, and two years later was made a judge and became Lord Jeffrey. He was a friend of the young Carlyle, and of Dickens. When he died in 1850 (the same year as Wordsworth), he was universally liked and admired.

Further reading

James A. Greig, *Francis Jeffrey of the Edinburgh Review* (Edinburgh, 1948)
Philip Flynn, *Francis Jeffrey* (Canbury, NJ, 1978)
Peter Morgan, *Jeffrey's Criticism* (Edinburgh, 1983)
Francis Jeffrey, *On the Lake Poets* introduced by Jonathan Wordsworth (Poole, 1998)

---

[10]   *trances* moments of suspension, when the blast stills.

FRANCIS, LORD JEFFREY
[1]   *Edinburgh Review* 25 (1815) 355.

[2]   Did Wordsworth ever read it? See my *Wordsworth's Reading 1800–1815* (1995), pp. 118–19.
[3]   For more on Jeffrey and Hemans see my *Romantic Women Poets: An Anthology* (1998), pp. xxii, 490.

Review of William Wordsworth, 'The Excursion' (extracts)

From EDINBURGH REVIEW 24 (1814. pp. 1–30)

This will never do. It bears, no doubt, the stamp of the author's heart and fancy – but unfortunately not half so visibly as that of his peculiar system. His former poems were intended to recommend that system, and to bespeak favour for it by their individual merit, but this, we suspect, must be recommended by the system, and can only expect to succeed where it has been previously established. It is longer, weaker, and tamer, than any of Mr Wordsworth's other productions, with less boldness of originality, and less even of that extreme simplicity and lowliness of tone which wavered so prettily, in the *Lyrical Ballads*, between silliness and pathos. We have imitations of Cowper and even of Milton here, engrafted on the natural drawl of the Lakers – and all diluted into harmony by that profuse and irrepressible wordiness which deluges all the blank verse of this school of poetry, and lubricates and weakens the whole structure of their style.

Though it fairly fills four hundred and twenty good quarto pages, without note, vignette, or any sort of extraneous assistance, it is stated in the title (with something of an imprudent candour) to be but 'a portion' of a larger work,[1] and in the preface – where an attempt is rather unsuccessfully made to explain the whole design – it is still more rashly disclosed that it is but 'a part of the second part of a *long* and laborious work' which is to consist of three parts!

What Mr Wordsworth's ideas of length are, we have no means of accurately judging, but we cannot help suspecting that they are liberal to a degree that will alarm the weakness of most modern readers. As far as we can gather from the preface, the entire poem – or one of them (for we really are not sure whether there is to be one or two) – is of a biographical nature, and is to contain the history of the author's mind and of the origin and progress of his poetical powers up to the period when they were sufficiently matured to qualify him for the great work on which he has been so long employed. Now the quarto before us contains an account of one of his youthful rambles in the vales of Cumberland, and occupies precisely the period of three days; so that, by the use of a very powerful calculus,[2] some estimate may be formed of the probable extent of the entire biography.

This small specimen, however, and the statements with which it is prefaced, have been sufficient to set our minds at rest in one particular. The case of Mr Wordsworth, we perceive, is now manifestly hopeless, and we give him up as altogether incurable, and beyond the power of criticism. We cannot indeed altogether omit taking precautions now and then against the spreading of the malady – but for himself, though we shall watch the progress of his symptoms as a matter of professional curiosity and instruction, we really think it right not to harass him any longer with nauseous remedies, but rather to throw in cordials and lenitives, and wait in patience for the natural termination of the disorder. In order to justify this desertion of our patient, however, it is proper to state why we despair of the success of a more active practice. . . .

The volume before us, if we were to describe it very shortly, we should characterize as a tissue of moral and devotional ravings in which innumerable changes are rung upon a few very simple and familiar ideas – but with such an accompaniment of long words, long sentences, and unwieldy phrases, and such a hubbub of strained raptures and fantastical sublimities, that it is often extremely difficult for the most skilful and attentive student to obtain a glimpse of the author's meaning, and altogether impossible for an ordinary reader to conjecture what he is about.

Moral and religious enthusiasm, though undoubtedly poetical emotions, are at the same time but dangerous inspirers of poetry, nothing being so apt to run into interminable dullness or mellifluous extravagance, without giving the unfortunate author the slightest intimation of his danger. His laudable zeal for the efficacy of his preachments, he very naturally mistakes for the ardour of poetical inspiration – and, while dealing out the high words and glowing phrases which are so readily supplied by themes of this description, can scarcely avoid believing that he is eminently original and

---

REVIEW OF WILLIAM WORDSWORTH, 'THE EXCURSION'   [2]   *calculus* calculation.
[1]   *a larger work* i.e. *The Recluse* (see pp. 271, 519–21).

impressive. All sorts of commonplace notions and expressions are sanctified in his eyes by the sublime ends for which they are employed, and the mystical verbiage of the Methodist pulpit is repeated till the speaker entertains no doubt that he is the elected organ of divine truth and persuasion. But if such be the common hazards of seeking inspiration from those potent fountains, it may easily be conceived what chance Mr Wordsworth had of escaping their enchantment, with his natural propensities to wordiness, and his unlucky habit of debasing pathos with vulgarity. The fact accordingly is that in this production he is more obscure than a Pindaric poet of the seventeenth century, and more verbose 'than even himself of yore', while the wilfulness with which he persists in choosing his examples of intellectual dignity and tenderness exclusively from the lowest ranks of society will be sufficiently apparent from the circumstance of his having thought fit to make his chief prolocutor[3] in this poetical dialogue, and chief advocate of providence and virtue, *an old Scotch Pedlar*, retired indeed from business, but still rambling about in his former haunts, and gossiping among his old customers without his pack on his shoulders. The other persons of the drama are a retired military chaplain, who has grown half an atheist and half a misanthrope; the wife of an unprosperous weaver; a servant girl with her infant; a parish pauper, and one or two other personages of equal rank and dignity.

The character of the work is decidedly didactic, and more than nine-tenths of it are occupied with a species of dialogue, or rather a series of long sermons or harangues which pass between the Pedlar, the author, the old chaplain, and a worthy vicar who entertains the whole party at dinner on the last day of their excursion. The incidents which occur in the course of it are as few and trifling as can be imagined – and those which the different speakers narrate in the course of their discourses, are introduced rather to illustrate their arguments or opinions than for any interest they are supposed to possess of their own. The doctrine which the work is intended to enforce, we are by no means certain that we have discovered. In so far as we can collect, however, it seems to be neither more nor less than the old familiar one that a firm belief in the providence of a wise and beneficent Being must be our great stay and support[4] under all afflictions and perplexities upon earth, and that there are indications of his power and goodness in all the aspects of the visible universe, whether living or inanimate – every part of which should therefore be regarded with love and reverence, as exponents of those great attributes. We can testify, at least, that these salutary and important truths are inculcated at far greater length, and with more repetitions, than in any ten volumes of sermons that we ever perused. It is also maintained, with equal conciseness and originality, that there is frequently much good sense, as well as much enjoyment, in the humbler conditions of life; and that, in spite of great vices and abuses, there is a reasonable allowance both of happiness and goodness in society at large. If there be any deeper or more recondite[5] doctrines in Mr Wordsworth's book, we must confess that they have escaped us – and, convinced as we are of the truth and soundness of those to which we have alluded, we cannot help thinking that they might have been better enforced with less parade and prolixity. His effusions on what may be called the physiognomy[6] of external nature, or its moral and theological expression, are eminently fantastic, obscure, and affected. . . .

Nobody can be more disposed to do justice to the great powers of Mr Wordsworth than we are, and, from the first time that he came before us, down to the present moment, we have uniformly testified in their favour, and assigned indeed our high sense of their value as the chief ground of the bitterness with which we resented their perversion.[7] That perversion, however, is now far more visible than their original dignity; and while we collect the fragments, it is impossible not to mourn over the ruins from which we are condemned to pick them. If anyone should doubt of the existence of such a perversion, or be disposed to dispute about the instances we have hastily brought forward, we would just beg leave to refer him to the general plan and character of the poem now before us. Why should Mr Wordsworth have made his hero a superannuated Pedlar? What but the most wretched affectation, or provoking perversity of taste, could induce anyone to place his chosen advocate of wisdom and

---

3   *prolocutor* spokesman.
4   *stay and support* cheekily, Jeffrey echoes Wordsworth's *Resolution and Independence* 146.
5   *recondite* abstruse, profound.
6   *physiognomy* outward form.

7   *Nobody can . . . perversion* ever so slightly disingenuous; Jeffrey's first direct review of Wordsworth was of *Poems in Two Volumes* (1807), which described the contents as 'trash', and suggested that their author appeared 'like a bad imitator of the worst of his former productions'.

virtue in so absurd and fantastic[8] a condition? Did Mr Wordsworth really imagine that his favourite doctrines were likely to gain anything in point of effect or authority by being put into the mouth of a person accustomed to higgle about tape, or brass sleeve-buttons? Or is it not plain that, independent of the ridicule and disgust which such a personification[9] must excite in many of his readers, its adoption exposes his work throughout to the charge of revolting incongruity, and utter disregard of probability or nature? For, after he has thus wilfully debased his moral teacher by a low occupation, is there one word that he puts into his mouth, or one sentiment of which he makes him the organ, that has the most remote reference to that occupation? Is there anything in his learned, abstract, and logical harangues, that savours of the calling that is ascribed to him? Are any of their materials, the diction, the sentiments, in any, the very smallest degree, accommodated to a person in that condition? Or are they not eminently and conspicuously such as could not by possibility belong to it? A man who went about selling flannel and pocket-handkerchiefs in this lofty diction, would soon frighten away all his customers; and would infallibly pass either for a madman, or for some learned and affected gentleman, who, in a frolic,[10] had taken up a character which he was peculiarly ill qualified for supporting.[11]

The absurdity in this case, we think, is palpable and glaring: but it is exactly of the same nature with that which infects the whole substance of the work – a puerile ambition of singularity[12] engrafted on an unlucky predilection for truisms;[13] and an affected passion for simplicity and humble life, most awkwardly combined with a taste for mystical refinements, and all the gorgeousness of obscure phraseology. His taste for simplicity is evinced by sprinkling up and down his interminable declamations a few descriptions of baby-houses,[14] and of old hats with wet brims;[15] and his amiable partiality for humble life, by assuring us that a wordy rhetorician, who talks about Thebes,[16] and allegorizes all the heathen mythology, was once a pedlar – and making him break in upon his magnificent orations with two or three awkward notices of something that he had seen when selling winter raiment about the country – or of the changes in the state of society, which had almost annihilated his former calling.

Robert Southey   (1774–1843)

Southey was born in Bristol on 12 August 1774. He entered Westminster School in April 1788 but was expelled in April 1792 for writing a pamphlet called *The Flagellant*, an attack on corporal punishment. By the time he went up to Balliol College, Oxford, in November 1792, he was a fervent supporter of the French Revolution. He read Godwin's *Political Justice* as soon as it was published in February 1793, and exclaimed enthusiastically to his friend, Grosvenor Bedford, 'I am studying such a book!'[1] Soon after, he

began writing an epic poem, *Joan of Arc*, which aimed to denounce church and state – the apparatus of the establishment. On 17 June 1794 he met Coleridge, whose hero-worship of him seems to have begun immediately. Together they planned a 'pantisocracy', a sort of commune on the banks of the Susquehanna river in America, and recruited fellow pantisocrats, including George Burnett and Robert Lovell (Oxford friends of Southey's). In August Coleridge met the Fricker family, who instantly became involved in the

---

8   *fantastic* fanciful; perhaps also quaint, eccentric.
9   *personification* dramatic representation of a character; Jeffrey's language emphasizes Wordsworth's artifice.
10   *frolic* fit of amusement; prank.
11   Perhaps with these comments in mind, Wordsworth appended a note to the 1827 edition of the *Excursion*, which quoted Robert Heron's *Observations Made in a Journey through the Western Counties of Scotland* (1793) as follows: 'It is not more than twenty or thirty years, since a young man going from any part of Scotland to England, of purpose to carry the pack, was considered as going to lead the life, and acquire the fortune, of a gentleman'.
12   *singularity* originality.
13   *truisms* commonplace thoughts; Jeffrey's point is that Wordsworth is no philosopher.

14   *baby-houses* see *Excursion* ii 425.
15   *old hats with wet brims* see *Excursion* i 445, or *Ruined Cottage* 50–1 (p. 278).
16   *Thebes* the Pedlar (or the Wanderer, as he is called in *The Excursion*) mentions 'Egyptian Thebes' at Book VIII, l. 216.

ROBERT SOUTHEY
1   Quoted Nicholas Roe, 'Robert Southey and the Origins of Pantisocracy', *The Politics of Nature: Wordsworth and Some Contemporaries* (Houndmills, 1992), pp. 36–55, 45; to which readers should refer for detailed discussion of Southey's radical youth.

project: Lovell had just married the second daughter, Mary; Southey was courting the third, Edith; and, by the middle of the month, Coleridge was engaged to the eldest, Sara. The plan was that Coleridge, Southey and Lovell, would marry the three Fricker sisters and emigrate to America in March 1795.[2] The scheme failed, partly through lack of money, and as soon as he had married Edith on 14 November 1795, Southey left for Portugal alone.

For the next five months he travelled through Spain and Portugal with his uncle, the Revd Herbert Hill, chaplain to the British factory at Lisbon, who wanted him to become a clergyman. There was little chance of that: for one thing, Southey was too contemptuous of the Church of England and its political power to want to become part of it; for another, his vocation as a writer was close to being realized. In 1796 *Joan of Arc* (containing numerous passages partly or wholly written by Coleridge) was published, followed by two volumes of *Poems* (1797–9), and *Letters Written during a Short Residence in Spain and Portugal* (1797). On the basis of *Joan of Arc*, Lamb declared, 'I expect Southey one day to rival Milton. I already deem him equal to Cowper, and superior to all living poets besides' (Marrs i 16). Lamb must have recognized the influence of Coleridge, evident in *Natural Religion*, in which Joan, questioned by doctors of divinity about her faith, gives an account of her upbringing which culminates in a pantheist declaration. In September 1797, Coleridge told Southey that *Hannah* 'is to me the most affecting of all your little pieces' (Griggs i 345); while reflecting the influence of Cowper's *Crazy Kate* (p. 9, above), it is also one of his most Wordsworthian. In fact, it is likely to have been an influence on *The Ruined Cottage*.[3] But it was not typical of the quality of Southey's poetry; several months before, Coleridge had expressed his fear that Southey depended 'too much on story and event in his poems, to the neglect of those lofty imaginings that are peculiar to, and definitive of, the poet' (Griggs i 320) – and a comparison of *The Idiot* with *The Idiot Boy* shows that his fears were well-grounded.[4]

By that time, Coleridge and Southey had fallen out, with much vestigial bitterness over the failure of pantisocracy. When Coleridge brought the Wordsworths from Racedown to Alfoxden in June 1797, he went out of his way to tell Southey that Wordsworth was 'a very great man – the only man to whom *at all times* and in *all modes of excellence* I feel myself inferior' (see p. 458).

This could hardly have improved relations, and it may have been partly responsible for the exceptionally harsh review Southey gave *Lyrical Ballads* (1798) a year later. It provides a foretaste of the kind of criticism Wordsworth was later to receive from Jeffrey, drawing attention to the lowliness of his subject-matter and to the claims of the Advertisement.

In September 1803, grieved by the death of his daughter Margaret, Southey settled with the Coleridges at Greta Hall, Keswick. He spent the rest of his life there, engaged in unremitting literary activity. One cause for this was Coleridge's abandonment of his family, which meant that Southey had two families to provide for. He has had a bad press in our day, and had a terrible press in his own, partly because he had by 1810 renounced his former radical sympathies. His appointment as Poet Laureate in 1813 pretty much sealed his fate, making him a prime target for the likes of Byron. Byron's motives for savaging Southey were complicated. The main thrust of the Dedication to *Don Juan* (which Southey, mercifully, never saw, as it was not published with Cantos I and II), is that Southey had betrayed his earlier radicalism (see pp. 752–5). At the same time, Byron had for years resented the fact that, as he believed, Southey had spread rumours in London that he and Shelley had been involved in a 'league of incest' with Mary Shelley and Claire Clairmont.[5] For this he described Southey, in his letters, as 'a dirty, lying rascal',[6] among other things. When Southey published *A Vision of Judgment*, a tribute to the late George III, in 1821, he made the mistake of referring to Byron, without naming him, as the leader of the Satanic school of writers whose works 'breathe the spirit of Belial in their lascivious parts'. This was the cue for a brilliant *tour de force* by Byron in his own poem, *The Vision of Judgment* (1822), which satirized Southey's verses, depicting the Laureate reading his work and sending the devils howling back to hell.

By this time, Southey was regarded by Byron and Shelley as no more than a Tory lapdog, and he certainly supported the government in such works as *Carmen Triumphale* (1814) and *The Poet's Pilgrimage to Waterloo* (1816). He was an advocate of social order, and a firm opponent of revolution, Catholic emancipation, and parliamentary reform. He never really recovered from the death of his favourite child, Herbert, in 1816, at the age of nine. On his wife's death in 1837, he married the poetess Caroline Bowles. By this time he was exhausted after a lifetime of unremitting liter-

---

2   This was, at least, the date given in Coleridge's letter to Charles Heath of 29 August 1794 (Griggs i 97).
3   See my *Wordsworth's Reading 1770–1799* (1993), p. 130.
4   For a comparison of the two poems, see my 'Looking for Johnny: Wordsworth's "The Idiot Boy" ', *Charles Lamb Bulletin* NS 88 (1994) 166–76.

5   See Peter Cochran, 'Robert Southey, the "Atheist" Inscription, and the "League of Incest" ', *N&Q* 37 (1990) 415–18.
6   Marchand vi 83.

ary toil, and his mind and memory failed. His remaining years were lamentable; increasingly debilitated, unable to read or write, he finally died on 21 March 1843, and was buried in Crosthwaite Church in Keswick, where the Brazilian government paid for his monument out of gratitude for Southey's *History of Brazil* (1810).

Largely unread today, Southey's poetry enjoyed considerable popularity in its time: *Thalaba the Destroyer* (1801), *Madoc* (1805), *The Curse of Kehama* (1810), and *Roderick, the Last of the Goths* (1814) are probably the most distinguished. But it is his prose works that do him most credit. A biography, his *Life of Nelson* (1813), remained compulsory reading for all schoolchildren until well into the present century. And his *Letters from England by Don Manuel Espriella* (1807) remains a compelling read today.

Further Reading

Geoffrey Carnall, *Robert Southey and His Age: The Development of a Conservative Mind* (Oxford, 1960)

Kenneth Curry, *The Contributions of Robert Southey to the Morning Post* (Alabama, 1984)

Robert Southey, *Poems 1797* introduced by Jonathan Wordsworth (Spelsbury, 1989)

—, *Thalaba the Destroyer* introduced by Jonathan Wordsworth (Spelsbury, 1991)

Nicholas Roe, 'Robert Southey and the Origins of Pantisocracy', *The Politics of Nature: Wordsworth and Some Contemporaries* (Houndmills, 1992), pp. 36–55

Robert Southey, *Joan of Arc* introduced by Jonathan Wordsworth (Spelsbury, 1993)

—, *Poems 1799* introduced by Jonathan Wordsworth (Poole, 1997)

Mark Storey, *Robert Southey: A Life* (Oxford, 1997)

Michael Bauman, 'Contributions Toward a Southey Bibliography', *Charles Lamb Bulletin* NS 88 (1994) 177–81

[Natural Religion]

From JOAN OF ARC (1796) (from Book III)

In forest shade my infant years trained up   355
Knew not devotion's forms.[1] The chaunted mass,
The silver altar and religious robe,
The mystic wafer and the hallowed cup,
Gods priest-created, are to me unknown.
Beneath no high-arched roof I bowed in prayer,   360
No solemn light by storied pane disguised,
No trophied pillars and no imaged cross
Waked my young mind to artificial awe
To fear the God I only learnt[2] to love.
I saw th' eternal energy pervade   365
The boundless range of nature, with the sun
Pour life and radiance from his flamy path,
And on the lowliest flowret in the field
The kindly dew-drops shed; all nature's voice
Proclaimed the all-good Parent – nor myself   370
Deemed I by him neglected. This good Power[3]
My more than father taught my youth to know,
Knowing to love, and loving to adore.
At earliest morn to him my grateful heart
Poured forth th' unstudied prayer that spake my thanks   375
For mercies oft vouchsafed, and humbly asked

NATURAL RELIGION
[1] *forms* i.e. ceremonies, rituals.
[2] *I only learnt* i.e. I learnt only . . .
[3] *Power* Joan is trained outside the bounds of formalized religion, as was necessary for Southey's critique of the established church. His use of the word 'Power' provides one hint as to why Shelley so admired his poetry; cf. Shelley's *Hymn to Intellectual Beauty* and *Mont Blanc*.

Protection yet to come. Each flower that bloomed
Expanding in the new-born spring called forth
The soul of full devotion. Every morn
My soaring spirit glorified the god   380
Of light, and every evening thanked the Power
Preserving through the day. For sins confessed
To holy priest and absolution given,
I knew them not – for, ignorant of sin,
Why should I seek forgiveness? Of the points   385
Abstruse of nice[4] religion, and the bounds
Subtle and narrow which confine the path
Of orthodox belief, my artless creed
Knew nought. 'Twas nature taught my early youth
Religion; nature bade me see the God   390
Confessed in all that lives, and moves, and is.

Hannah, A Plaintive Tale (composed by 15 September 1797)[1]

From THE MONTHLY MAGAZINE 4 (1797, p. 287)

The coffin, as I crossed the common lane,
Came sudden on my view; it was not here
A sight of every day, as in the streets
Of the great city – and we paused and asked
Who to the grave was going. It was one,   5
A village girl; they told us she had borne
An eighteen months' strange illness, pined away
With such slow wasting as had made the hour
Of death most welcome. To the house of mirth
We held our way and, with that idle talk   10
That passes o'er the mind and is forgot,
We wore away the hour. But it was eve
When homewardly I went, and in the air
Was that cool freshness, that discolouring shade
That makes the eye turn inward. Then I heard,   15
Over the vale, the heavy toll of death[2]
Sound slow, and questioned of the dead again.
    It was a very plain and simple tale.
She bore, unhusbanded, a mother's name,
And he who should have cherished her, far off   20
Sailed on the seas, self-exiled from his home,
For he was poor. Left thus, a wretched one,
Scorn[3] made a mock of her, and evil tongues
Were busy with her name. She had one ill

---

[4] *nice* strict.

HANNAH, A PLAINTIVE TALE
[1] When *Hannah* was published, revised, in Southey's *Poems* (1799), Southey noted: 'It is proper to remark that the story related in this Eclogue is strictly true. I met the funeral, and learnt the circumstances, in a village in Hampshire. The indifference of the child was mentioned to me; indeed, no addition whatever has been made to the story. I should have thought it wrong to have weakened the effect of a faithful narrative by adding anything' (p. 202). The poem was probably seen by Wordsworth in MS, and may have influenced *The Ruined Cottage*.
[2] *the heavy toll of death* i.e. the death-bell.
[3] *Scorn* i.e. scornful people.

Heavier: neglect, forgetfulness from him   25
Whom she had loved so dearly. Once he wrote,
But only once that drop of comfort came,
To mingle with her cup of wretchedness;
And when his parents had some tidings from him
There was no mention of poor Hannah there;   30
Or 'twas the cold enquiry, bitterer
Than silence. So she pined and pined away,
And for herself and baby toiled and toiled,
Till she sunk with very weakness;[4] her old mother
Omitted no kind office, and she worked   35
Most hard, and with hard working barely earned
Enough to make life struggle. Thus she lay
On the sickbed of poverty, so worn
That she could make no effort to express
Affection for her infant – and the child   40
Whose lisping love perhaps had solaced her,
With strangest infantine ingratitude,
Shunned her as one indifferent. She was past
That anguish, for she felt her hour draw on,
And 'twas her only comfort now to think   45
Upon the grave. 'Poor girl!' her mother said,
'Thou hast suffered much.' 'Aye mother; there is none
Can tell what I have suffered', she replied,
'But I shall soon be where the weary rest.'
And she did rest her soon, for it pleased God   50
To take her to his mercy.

The Idiot[1]

From THE MORNING POST No. 9198 (30 June 1798)

The circumstance related in the following ballad happened some years since in Herefordshire.

It had pleased God to form poor Ned
    A thing of idiot mind,
Yet to the poor unreas'ning man
    God had not been unkind.

Old Sarah loved her helpless child   5
    Whom helplessness made dear,
And life was happiness to him
    Who had no hope nor fear.

---

4   *So she pined . . . weakness* cf. Wordsworth's *The Ruined Cottage* 428–31.

THE IDIOT
1   This poem was first attributed to Southey by B. R. McElderry Jr, 'Southey, and Wordsworth's "The Idiot Boy" ', *N&Q* 200 (1955) 490–1; it is further discussed by Elizabeth Duthie, 'A Fresh Comparison of "The Idiot Boy" and "The Idiot" ', *N&Q* 223 (1978) 219–20.

She knew his wants, she understood
 Each half-artic'late call,
And he was ev'rything to her
 And she to him was all.   10

And so for many a year they dwelt
 Nor knew a wish beside,
But age at length on Sarah came,   15
 And she fell sick and died.

He tried in vain to waken her,
 And called her o'er and o'er;
They told him she was dead – the sound
 To him no import bore.   20

They closed her eyes and shrouded her,
 And he stood wond'ring by;
And when they bore her to the grave
 He followed silently.

They laid her in the narrow house,[2]   25
 They sung the fun'ral stave,[3]
But when the fun'ral train dispersed
 He loitered by the grave.

The rabble boys who used to jeer
 Whene'er they saw poor Ned   30
Now stood and watched him at the grave,
 And not a word they said.

They came and went and came again
 Till night at last came on,
And still he loitered by the grave   35
 Till all to rest were gone.

And when he found himself alone
 He swift removed the clay,
And raised the coffin up in haste
 And bore it swift away.   40

And when he reached his hut he laid
 The coffin on the floor,
And with the eagerness of joy
 He barred the cottage door.

And out he took his mother's corpse   45
 And placed it in her chair,
And then he heaped the hearth and blew
 The kindling fire with care.

---

[2] *narrow house* grave.
[3] *stave* i.e. hymn.

> He placed his mother in her chair
>   And in her wonted place,   50
> And blew the kindling fire that shone
>   Reflected on her face.
>
> And pausing now, her hand would feel,
>   And now her face behold –
> 'Why, mother, do you look so pale   55
>   And why are you so cold?'
>
> It had pleased God from the poor wretch
>   His only friend to call,
> But God was kind to him and soon
>   In death restored him all.[4]   60

Review of William Wordsworth and S. T. Coleridge, 'Lyrical Ballads' (1798)

From CRITICAL REVIEW 24 (1798, pp. 197–204)

The majority of these poems, we are informed in the Advertisement,[1] are to be considered as 'experiments': 'They were written chiefly with a view to ascertain how far the language of conversation in the middle and lower classes of society is adapted to the purposes of poetic pleasure'.

Of these 'experimental' poems, the most important is 'The Idiot Boy', the story of which is simply this: Betty Foy's neighbour Susan Gale is indisposed, and no one can be conveniently sent for the doctor but Betty's idiot boy. She therefore puts him upon her pony at eight o'clock in the evening, gives him proper directions, and returns to take care of her sick neighbour. Johnny is expected with the doctor by eleven, but the clock strikes eleven, and twelve, and one, without the appearance either of Johnny or the doctor. Betty's restless fears become insupportable and she now leaves her friend to look for her idiot son. She goes to the doctor's house but hears nothing of Johnny. About five o'clock, however, she finds him sitting quietly upon his feeding pony. As they go home they meet old Susan, whose apprehensions have cured her, and brought her out to seek them. And they all return merrily together. Upon this subject the author has written nearly five hundred lines. With what spirit the story is told, our extract will evince. [Southey quotes *Idiot Boy* 322–401.]

No tale less deserved the labour that appears to have been bestowed upon this. It resembles a Flemish picture in the worthlessness of its design and the excellence of its execution. From Flemish artists we are satisfied with such pieces; who would not have lamented if Correggio or Raphael[2] had wasted their talents in painting Dutch boors or the humours of a Flemish wake?

The other ballads of this kind are as bald in story, and are not so highly embellished in narration. With that which is entitled 'The Thorn' we were altogether displeased. The Advertisement says it is not told in the person of the author, but in that of some 'loquacious narrator'. The author should have recollected that he who personates tiresome loquacity becomes tiresome himself. The story of a man who suffers the perpetual pain of cold because an old woman prayed that he never might be warm is

---

4   When *The Idiot* was published in *Sarah Farley's Bristol Journal* (21 July 1798), two new stanzas were substituted for the last stanza of this text:

> But, hapless boy, he now found out
>   His efforts were in vain,
> Sarah would warmth again ne'er feel,
>   Her eyes ne'er ope again.
>
> Heaven pitying, saw the wretch had lost
>   The only friend it gave;

> Then shortly had his lifeless limbs
>   Conveyed to Sarah's grave.

REVIEW OF WILLIAM WORDSWORTH AND S. T. COLERIDGE, 'LYRICAL BALLADS'
1   *the Advertisement* i.e. the Advertisement to *Lyrical Ballads*, pp. 191–2, above.
2   *Correggio or Raphael* Italian Renaissance artists who specialized in biblical subjects.

perhaps a good story for a ballad because it is a well-known tale – but is the author certain that it is 'well-authenticated'?[3] And does not such an assertion promote the popular superstition of witchcraft?

In a very different style of poetry is 'The Rime of the Ancyent Marinere' – a ballad (says the Advertisement) 'professedly written in imitation of the *style*, as well as of the spirit, of the elder poets.' We are tolerably conversant with the early English poets and can discover no resemblance whatever, except in antiquated spelling and a few obsolete words. This piece appears to us perfectly original in style as well as in story. Many of the stanzas are laboriously beautiful, but in connection they are absurd or unintelligible. Our readers may exercise their ingenuity in attempting to unriddle what follows. [Southey quotes *Ancient Mariner* 301–22.] We do not sufficiently understand the story to analyse it. It is a Dutch attempt at German sublimity. Genius has here been employed in producing a poem of little merit.

With pleasure we turn to the serious pieces, the better part of the volume. 'The Foster-Mother's Tale' is in the best style of dramatic narrative; 'The Dungeon' and the 'Lines upon the Yew-Tree Seat' are beautiful. The tale of 'The Female Vagrant' is written in the stanza, not the style, of Spenser. We extract a part of this poem. [Southey quotes *Female Vagrant* 91–180.] Admirable as this poem is, the author[4] seems to discover still superior powers in the 'Lines written near Tintern Abbey'. On reading this production it is impossible not to lament that he should ever have condescended to write such pieces as 'The Last of the Flock', 'The Convict', and most of the ballads. In the whole range of English poetry, we scarcely recollect anything superior to a part of the following passage. [Southey quotes *Tintern Abbey* 65–111.]

The 'experiment', we think, has failed, not because the language of conversation is little adapted to 'the purposes of poetic pleasure', but because it has been tried upon uninteresting subjects. Yet every piece discovers genius, and, ill as the author has frequently employed his talents, they certainly rank him with the best of living poets.

The Sailor Who Had Served in the Slave-Trade[1]

From POEMS (1799)

He stopped: it surely was a groan
    That from the hovel came!
He stopped and listened anxiously –
    Again it sounds the same.

It surely from the hovel comes!   5
    And now he hastens there,
And thence he hears the name of Christ
    Amidst a broken prayer.

He entered in the hovel now,
    A sailor there he sees,   10
His hands were lifted up to heaven
    And he was on his knees.

---

[3] Southey was apparently unaware of the poem's source in Erasmus Darwin's *Zoönomia* (see p. 222 n. 1).

[4] *the author* Southey was aware of the joint authorship of Wordsworth and Coleridge despite the fact that *Lyrical Ballads* was published anonymously.

THE SAILOR WHO HAD SERVED IN THE SLAVE-TRADE
[1] During the 1790s and early 1800s Southey was strongly opposed to the slave trade and, like many of his contemporaries, even advised friends not to put sugar in their tea, as it was the product of slave labour. His early poems include many anti-slavery poems, including a series of sonnets and a poem entitled *To the Genius of Africa*, all in his *Poems* (1797). Many efforts were made to abolish the trade during the 1790s, but complete abolition did not come until 1807.

Nor did the sailor so intent
    His entering footsteps heed,
But now the Lord's prayer said, and now   15
    His half-forgotten creed.[2]

And often on his Saviour called
    With many a bitter groan,
In such heart-anguish as could spring
    From deepest guilt alone.   20

He asked the miserable man
    Why he was kneeling there,
And what the crime had been that caused
    The anguish of his prayer.

'Oh I have done a wicked thing!   25
    It haunts me night and day,
And I have sought this lonely place,
    Here undisturbed to pray.

I have no place to pray on board
    So I came here alone,   30
That I might freely kneel and pray
    And call on Christ and groan.

If to the mainmast-head[3] I go,
    The wicked one[4] is there –
From place to place, from rope to rope,   35
    He follows everywhere.

I shut my eyes, it matters not,
    Still still the same I see;
And when I lie me down at night
    'Tis always day with me.   40

He follows, follows everywhere
    And every place is hell!
Oh God! – and I must go with him
    In endless fire to dwell.

He follows, follows everywhere,   45
    He's still above, below –
Oh tell me where to fly from him!
    Oh tell me where to go!'

'But tell me', quoth the stranger then,
    'What this thy crime hath been?   50
So haply I may comfort give
    To one that grieves for sin.'

---

[2] *creed* beliefs of the Christian Church, repeated as a form of devotion.

[3] *mainmast-head* the top of the principal mast in the ship.

[4] *The wicked one* the Devil.

'Oh I have done a cursed deed'
   The wretched man replies,   55
'And night and day and everywhere
    'Tis still before my eyes.

I sailed on board a Guinea-man[5]
   And to the slave-coast went –
Would that the sea had swallowed me   60
   When I was innocent!

And we took in our cargo there,
   Three hundred Negro slaves,
And we sailed homeward merrily
   Over the ocean waves.   65

But some were sulky of the slaves
   And would not touch their meat,
So therefore we were forced by threats
   And blows to make them eat.

One woman sulkier than the rest   70
   Would still refuse her food –
Oh Jesus God! I hear her cries,
   I see her in her blood!

The Captain made me tie her up
   And flog while he stood by,   75
And then he cursed me if I stayed
   My hand to hear her cry.

She groaned, she shrieked – I could not spare,
   For the Captain he stood by –
Dear God! that I might rest one night   80
   From that poor woman's cry!

She twisted from the blows – her blood,
   Her mangled flesh I see;
And still the Captain would not spare –
   Oh, he was worse than me!   85

She could not be more glad than I
   When she was taken down,
A blessed minute – 'twas the last
   That I have ever known!

I did not close my eyes all night,   90
   Thinking what I had done;
I heard her groans and they grew faint
   About the rising sun.

---

5   *Guinea-man* ship trading slaves from Guinea.

She groaned and groaned, but her groans grew
  Fainter at morning tide,
Fainter and fainter still they came
  Till at the noon she died.

95

They flung her overboard – poor wretch,
  She rested from her pain;
But when, oh Christ! oh blessed God!
  Shall I have rest again?

100

I saw the sea close over her,
  Yet she was still in sight;
I see her twisting everywhere,
  I see her day and night.

105

Go where I will, do what I can,
  The wicked one I see –
Dear Christ, have mercy on my soul,
  Oh God deliver me!

Tomorrow I set sail again
  Not to the Negro shore;
Wretch that I am, I will at least
  Commit that sin no more.

110

Oh give me comfort if you can,
  Oh tell me where to fly –
And bid me hope, if there be hope
  For one so lost as I.'

115

'Poor wretch', the stranger he replied,
  'Put thou thy trust in Heaven,
And call on Him for whose dear sake
  All sins shall be forgiven.

120

This night at least is thine – go thou
  And seek the house of prayer,
There shalt thou hear the word of God
  And he will help thee there!'

125

The Battle of Blenheim[1]

From THE ANNUAL ANTHOLOGY (1800)

I

It was a summer evening,
  Old Kaspar's work was done,
And he before his cottage door

THE BATTLE OF BLENHEIM
[1] The Battle of Blenheim, 13 August 1704, the most famous victory in the Wars of the Spanish Succession, was credited to John Churchill, 1st Duke of Marlborough, and Prince Eugene of Savoy; the French and Bavarians were defeated.

Was sitting in the sun,
And by him sported on the green   5
His little grandchild Wilhelmine.

II

She saw her brother Peterkin
　　Roll something large and round
That he beside the rivulet
　　In playing there had found;   10
He came to ask what he had found
That was so large, and smooth, and round.

III

Old Kaspar took it from the boy
　　Who stood expectant by,
And then the old man shook his head   15
　　And with a natural sigh,
''Tis some poor fellow's skull', said he,
'Who fell in the great victory.

IV

I find them in the garden for
　　There's many here about,   20
And often when I go to plough
　　The ploughshare turns them out –
For many thousand men', said he,
'Were slain in the great victory.'

V

'Now tell us what 'twas all about',   25
　　Young Peterkin he cries,
And little Wilhelmine looks up
　　With wonder-waiting eyes,
'Now tell us all about the war
And what they killed each other for.'   30

VI

'It was the English', Kaspar cried,
　　'That put the French to rout,
But what they killed each other for
　　I could not well make out.
But everybody said', quoth he,   35
'That 'twas a famous victory.

VII

My father lived at Blenheim then,
   Yon little stream hard by –
They burnt his dwelling to the ground
   And he was forced to fly;   40
So with his wife and child he fled,
Nor had he where to rest his head.

VIII

With fire and sword the country round
   Was wasted far and wide,
And many a childing mother then   45
   And new-born infant died.
But things like that, you know, must be
At every famous victory.

IX

They say it was a shocking sight
   After the field was won,   50
For many thousand bodies here
   Lay rotting in the sun –
But things like that you know must be
After a famous victory.

X

Great praise the Duke of Marlbro' won,   55
   And our good Prince Eugene.'
'Why 'twas a very wicked thing!'
   Said little Wilhelmine.
'Nay, nay, my little girl', quoth he,
'It was a famous victory,   60

XI

And everybody praised the Duke
   Who such a fight did win.'
'But what good came of it at last?'
   Quoth little Peterkin.
'Why that I cannot tell', said he,   65
'But 'twas a famous victory.'

Walter Savage Landor (1775–1864)

Landor was born at Warwick, the eldest son of a physician who retired early after inheriting the family fortune. Landor in turn was to benefit from that wealth, and should have been financially independent for most of his days, had it not been for his mismanagement of the family estate in Monmouthshire, which bankrupted him. As a result he emigrated to Italy in 1814.

In his schooldays at Rugby, he distinguished himself as a classicist, and learnt to compose poetry in Latin. His passionate temper was expressing itself even then, and after an argument with the headmaster, he was expelled. He was rusticated from Oxford for another fracas in 1793 and left the groves of academe for ever. Most of his life was spent travelling and writing. He published his first volume, the romantic 'oriental' tale, *Gebir*, in 1798, which affirmed his radical and humanitarian convictions.[1] Southey reviewed it generously in the *Critical Review*, and in a letter to his Bristol publisher, Joseph Cottle, of 22 September 1799, remarked that it contained 'some of the most exquisite poetry in the language'.[2] In later years it won the admiration of Shelley and De Quincey.

In 1808 Landor travelled to Corunna to support the Spanish revolt against Napoleon in the Peninsular War; he saw no action, but made a generous financial donation to the cause. Back in England three years later, he married Julia Thullier, a much younger woman of Swiss descent. They had three sons and a daughter, but were not well matched, and spent most of their lives apart. By this time Landor had established himself as one of the most quarrelsome and difficult characters of the day. Having alienated many former friends, and lost the family fortune, it was probably a good idea that in 1814 he left for the continent. He resided in France and Italy until 1832, settling in Florence in 1821. He returned to England, went back to Italy, and finally, in 1838,

removed himself to Bath, where he spent the next twenty-one years. During the last two decades of his life he became friendly with all the new young writers of the moment, including Dickens, who caricatured him as Boythorn in *Bleak House*, Tennyson and the Brownings. In 1858 he emigrated for the last time to Italy, settling in Florence once more the following year. He died there, aged eighty-nine, on 17 September 1864, and was buried in the Protestant Cemetery.

His most important literary achievement is probably the *Imaginary Conversations* (5 vols, 1824–9), free-flowing debates between distinguished thinkers, alive and dead, on historical, political, moral and cultural matters. Even the shortest is too long to include here, and I have instead presented the cream of his poems. His elegiac love-poem, *Rose Aylmer*, concerns a friend who died in 1800 at the age of twenty. In *Regeneration* Landor writes on behalf of the Risorgimento, the movement for Italian reunification, while the delicate sensuousness of *Faesulan Idyl* is a triumph of classical simplicity recalling Coleridge's conversation poems. *Rose Aylmer* was a favourite of Lamb's, and he got on well with its author when they met on 28 September 1832; Landor's *To the Sister of Charles Lamb* was inspired by affection for his old friend.

Further reading

R. H. Super, *Walter Savage Landor: A Biography* (New York and London, 1954)

Landor: An Autobiographical Anthology ed. Herbert Van Thal (London, 1973)

Landor as Critic ed. Charles Proudfit (London, 1979)

Walter Savage Landor, *Selected Poetry and Prose* ed. Keith Hanley (Manchester, 1981)

—, *Gebir 1798* introduced by Jonathan Wordsworth (Spelsbury, 1993)

Rose Aylmer[1]

From SIMONIDEA (1806)

Ah, what avails the sceptred race,
Ah, what the form divine?
What every virtue, every grace?
For, Aylmer, all were thine.

WALTER SAVAGE LANDOR
[1] Lamb was later a good friend of Landor, but in late 1799, when he first read *Gebir*, he had some fun at its expense: 'I have seen Gebor! Gebor aptly so denominated from Geborish, *quasi* Gibberish. But Gebor hath some lucid intervals' (Marrs i 172).
[2] Joseph Cottle, *Reminiscences of Samuel Taylor Coleridge and Robert Southey* (London, 1847), p. 219.

ROSE AYLMER
[1] Although I have given the poem its later, better-known title, it was in fact first published as *II*.

Sweet Aylmer, whom these wakeful eyes 5
May weep, but never see,
A night of sorrows and of sighs
I consecrate to thee.

Regeneration

From IMAGINARY CONVERSATIONS (1824)

We are what suns and winds and waters make us –
The mountains are our sponsors, and the rills
Fashion and win their nursling with their smiles.
But where the land is dim from tyranny,[1]
There tiny pleasures occupy the place 5
Of glories and of duties, as the feet
Of fabled fairies when the sun goes down
Trip o'er the grass where wrestlers strove by day.
Then Justice (called the Eternal One above)
Is more inconstant than the buoyant form 10
That bursts into existence from the froth
Of ever-varying ocean. What is best
Then becomes worst; what loveliest, most deformed.
The heart is hardest in the softest climes,
The passions flourish, the affections die. 15
      Oh, thou vast tablet of these awful truths
That fillest all the space between the seas,
Spreading from Venice's deserted courts
To the Tarentine and Hydruntine mole,[2]
What lifts thee up? What shakes thee? 'Tis the breath 20
Of God – awake, ye nations, spring to life!
Let the last work of his right hand appear
Fresh with his image – man.[3] Thou recreant slave
That sittest afar off and helpest not,
Oh thou degenerate Albion![4] With what shame 25
Do I survey thee, pushing forth the sponge
At thy spear's length, in mockery at the thirst
Of holy Freedom in his agony,
And prompt and keen to pierce the wounded side![5]
      Must Italy then wholly rot away 30
Amid her slime before she germinate
Into fresh vigour, into form again?
What thunder bursts upon mine ear! Some isle
Hath surely risen from the gulfs profound,

REGENERATION
[1] *tyranny* as a classicist, Landor honoured Italy for its republican past. But Napoleon had brought the Venetian republic to an end in 1797, and ruled it as a kingdom of France until it fell to the Austrians in April 1814. In 1815 the Congress of Vienna made Francis I of Austria king of Lombardy-Venetia, dividing the rest of Italy between other dignitaries and heads of state. Real power remained vested in Austrian hands, a fact resented also by Shelley and Byron (see pp. 755 n. 46, 853–4).

[2] Since 1797, from Venice in the north to Taranto and Hydruntum (Otranto) in the south, the country had been carved up first under Napoleon and more recently by his enemies.
[3] *man* created Genesis 1:26–8.
[4] *Albion* England. Since 1812 the British had either failed to intervene to save Italy, or had compromised with its enemies.
[5] Landor recalls the centurion at the crucifixion of Christ; John 19:29–30.

Eager to suck the sunshine from the breast   35
Of beauteous nature, and to catch the gale
From golden Hermus and Melaena's brow.[6]
A greater thing than isle, than continent,
Than earth itself, than ocean circling earth
Hath risen there: regenerate man hath risen.   40
Generous old bard of Chios![7] Not that Jove
Deprived thee in thy latter days of sight
Would I complain, but that no higher theme
Than a disdainful youth,[8] a lawless king,[9]
A pestilence, a pyre,[10] awoke thy song,   45
When on the Chian coast, one javelin's throw
From where thy tombstone, where thy cradle stood,
Twice twenty self-devoted Greeks assailed
The naval host of Asia, at one blow
Scattered it into air – and Greece was free![11]   50
And ere these glories beamed, thy day had closed.
Let all that Elis[12] ever saw, give way,
All that Olympian Jove e'er smiled upon;
The Marathonian[13] columns never told
A tale more glorious, never Salamis,[14]   55
Nor (faithful in the centre of the false)
Plataea,[15] nor Anthela,[16] from whose mount
Benignant Ceres wards the blessed laws
And sees the Amphictyon dip his weary foot
In the warm streamlet of the strait below.   60
    Goddess, although thy brow was never reared
Among the powers that guarded or assailed
Perfidious Ilion,[17] parricidal Thebes,[18]
Or other walls whose war-belt e'er enclosed
Man's congregated crimes and vengeful pain,   65
Yet hast thou touched the extremes of grief and joy –
Grief upon Enna's mead and hell's ascent,
A solitary mother;[19] joy beyond,

---

[6] The River Hermus flows into the Aegean behind the promontory of Melaena, which faces the island of Chios.

[7] *Generous old bard of Chios* Homer, the blind bard, was reputed to have been born at Chios, an island off the Ionian coast between Lesbos and Samos.

[8] *a disdainful youth* Achilles, who sulked in his tent after Agamemnon stole his mistress, Briseis, refusing to come out.

[9] *a lawless king* In order to avert a pestilence that had broken out in the Greek camp, Agamemnon was forced to surrender the maiden who was his prize, and instead abducted Achilles' mistress, Briseis.

[10] *a pyre* Achilles came out to fight in the Trojan wars only when his lover, Patroclus, was slain by Hector. At Patroclus's funeral, Achilles killed twelve Trojans and his friend's corpse was cremated on a huge pyre.

[11] Landor may be alluding to the Greek revenge for the Turks' Massacre of Chios in 1822, when the Turks were driven back into the open sea by a daring raid on their fleet.

[12] *Elis* valley in which the small plain of Olympia is situated, site of the Olympic games, held every four years, founded by Hercules in honour of Jupiter.

[13] *Marathonian* Marathon is thirteen miles north-east of Athens, where the Persians were defeated by Miltiades in 490 BC.

[14] *Salamis* Ionian isle, site of a major naval battle in which the Greeks, heavily outnumbered, defeated the Persians under Xerxes I in 480 BC.

[15] *Plataea* city in Boeotia, protected by Athens; site of a major battle in 479 BC, in which the Greeks defeated the Persians under Xerxes I.

[16] *Anthela* town at the foot of Mount Callidromos, site of the temple of the Greek corn goddess, Demeter (Roman Ceres), where the Amphictyony (group of Greek worshippers) met each year.

[17] *Perfidious Ilion* Paris, son of the King of Troy (Ilion), abducted Helen, wife of Menelaus, causing the Trojan War.

[18] *parricidal Thebes* Oedipus killed his father before being made King of Thebes.

[19] *Grief . . . mother* Persephone, daughter of Jove and Ceres, was carried off to Hades by Pluto who found her gathering flowers in the plain of Enna.

Far beyond, that thy woe, in this thy fane:
The tears were human, but the bliss divine.   70
    I, in the land of strangers,[20] and depressed
With sad and certain presage for my own,
Exult at hope's fresh dayspring, though afar –
There where my youth was not unexercised
By chiefs in willing war and faithful song;[21]   75
Shades as they were, they were not empty shades
Whose bodies haunt our world and blear our sun –
Obstruction worse than swamp and shapeless sands.
Peace, praise, eternal gladness, to the souls
That, rising from the seas into the heavens,   80
Have ransomed first their country with their blood!
    Oh thou immortal Spartan, at whose name
The marble table sounds beneath my palms –
Leonidas![22] Even thou wilt not disdain
To mingle names august as these with thine;   85
Nor thou, twin-star of glory,[23] thou whose rays
Streamed over Corinth on the double sea,
Achaian and Saronic, whom the sons
Of Syracuse, when death removed thy light,
Wept more than slavery ever made them weep   90
But shed (if gratitude is sweet) sweet tears;
For the hand that then poured ashes o'er their heads
Was loosened from its desperate chain by thee.
    What now can press mankind into one mass,
For Tyranny to tread the more secure?   95
From gold alone is drawn the guilty wire
That adulation trills – she mocks the tone
Of duty, courage, virtue, piety,
And under her sits hope! Oh, how unlike
That graceful form in azure vest arrayed,   100
With brow serene and eyes on heaven alone
In patience fixed, in fondness unobscured!
What monsters coil beneath the spreading tree
Of despotism! What wastes extend around!
What poison floats upon the distant breeze!   105
But who are those that cull and deal its fruit?
Creatures that shun the light and fear the shade,
Bloated and fierce – sleep's mien and famine's cry.
Rise up again, rise in thy dignity,
Dejected man, and scare this brood away!   110

---

[20] *the land of strangers* Italy, presumably, as Landor was resident in Florence at that moment.
[21] *my youth . . . song* Landor was eighteen when Britain declared war on France; the war continued until 1815.
[22] Leonidas, King of Sparta, defended the pass of Thermopylae against the Persians, 480 BC. Initially successful, the Spartans were annihilated by a Persian contingent attacking from the rear. Leonidas was beheaded on Xerxes' orders, and celebrated as a martyr. The Greeks set up temples and festivals in his honour.
[23] *twin-star of glory* Gelon, ruler of Syracuse in Sicily (founded by Corinth), suppressed a revolt against the aristocracy, and made the city a great Hellenic power.

Faesulan Idyl (composed *c.*1830)

From GEBIR, COUNT JULIAN, AND OTHER POEMS (1831)

Here, where precipitate[1] spring with one light bound
Into hot summer's lusty arms expires,
And where go forth at morn, at eve, at night,
Soft airs[2] that want the lute to play with them,
And softer sighs that know not what they want,   5
Under a wall, beneath an orange-tree
Whose tallest flowers could tell the lowlier ones
Of sights in Fiesole[3] right up above –
While I was gazing a few paces off
At what they seemed to show me with their nods,   10
Their frequent whispers and their pointing shoots,
A gentle maid came down the garden steps
And gathered the pure treasure in her lap.
I heard the branches rustle and stepped forth
To drive the ox away, or mule, or goat   15
(Such I believed it must be).
       For sweet scents
Are the swift vehicles of still sweeter thoughts,
And nurse and pillow the dull memory
That would let drop without them her best stores.
They bring me tales of youth and tones of love,   20
And 'tis and ever was my wish and way
To let all flowers live freely, and all die,
Whene'er their genius bids their souls depart,
Among their kindred in their native place.
I never pluck the rose; the violet's head   25
Hath shaken with my breath upon its bank
And not reproached me; the ever-sacred cup
Of the pure lily hath between my hands
Felt safe, unsoiled, nor lost one grain of gold.
 I saw the light that made the glossy leaves   30
More glossy; the fair arm, the fairer cheek
Warmed by the eye intent on its pursuit;
I saw the foot that, although half-erect
From its grey slipper, could not lift her up
To what she wanted. I held down a branch   35
And gathered her some blossoms, since their hour
Was come, and bees had wounded them, and flies
Of harder wing were working their way through,
And scattering them in fragments underfoot.
So crisp were some, they rattled unevolved;[4]   40
Others, ere broken off, fell into shells –

FAESULAN IDYL
[1] *precipitate* rushing, hurrying (to become summer).
[2] *Soft airs* perhaps a recollection of *Tempest* III ii 135–6, where Caliban says that 'the isle is full of noises, / Sounds, and sweet airs, that give delight and hurt not'. The soft airs of Faesulae (modern Fiesole) would presumably 'play' the idle strings of a lute, just as the wind blows across the strings of the Aeolian harp in Coleridge's poem.
[3] From autumn 1829 Landor lived in the Villa Gheradescha at Fiesole, on a hillside above Florence.
[4] *unevolved* undeveloped.

For such appear the petals when detached,
Unbending, brittle, lucid, white like snow,
And, like snow, not seen through by eye or sun.
Yet every one her gown received from me   45
Was fairer than the first. I thought not so,
But so she praised them to reward my care.
I said, 'You find the largest.'
                                    'This indeed',
Cried she, 'is large and sweet'. She held one forth,
Whether for me to look at or to take   50
She knew not, nor did I. But taking it
Would best have solved (and this she felt) her doubts.
I dared not touch it, for it seemed a part
Of her own self – fresh, full, the most mature
Of blossoms, yet a blossom; with a touch   55
To fall, and yet unfallen. She drew back
The boon[5] she tendered, and then, finding not
The ribbon at her waist to fix it in,
Dropped it, as loath to drop it, on the rest.

To the Sister of Charles Lamb[1]

From LEIGH HUNT'S LONDON JOURNAL No. 63 (13 JUNE 1835, P. 181)

Comfort thee, oh thou mourner, yet awhile!
    Again shall Elia's smile
Refresh thy heart, when heart can ache no more.
    What is it we deplore?[2]
He leaves behind him, freed from griefs and years,   5
    Far worthier things than tears:
The love of friends without a single foe,
    Unequalled lot below!
His gentle soul, his genius, these are thine;
    Shalt thou for those repine?   10
He may have left the lowly walks of men;
    Left them he has – what then?
Are not his footsteps followed by the eyes
    Of all the good and wise?
Though the warm day is over, yet they seek,   15
    Upon the lofty peak
Of his pure mind, the roseate light that glows
    O'er death's perennial snows.
Behold him! From the spirits of the blessed
    He speaks, he bids thee rest.   20

---

5   *boon* gift.

TO THE SISTER OF CHARLES LAMB
[1]   Mary Anne Lamb (see p. 170); her brother Charles died 27
December 1834, and was buried 3 January 1835.
[2]   *deplore* lament.

Charles Lamb   (1775–1834)

The youngest son of John Lamb and Elizabeth Field, Charles Lamb was born in 1775 at Crown Office Row, London, where his father was clerk to Samuel Salt, a Bencher of the Inner Temple. He had an older brother, John (1763–1821), and a sister, Mary (1764–1847). He was educated at Christ's Hospital in Newgate Street, where he was a contemporary of Coleridge – a period he later recalled in his essay, 'Christ's Hospital Five and Thirty Years Ago'. Lamb spent vacations at Blakesware, Hertfordshire, where his grandmother was housekeeper of a country house. These visits are recalled in the essays, 'Mackery End, in Hertfordshire', and 'Blakesmoor in H————shire'. It was here that he met his first passionate love, Ann Simmons, but the realization that she did not want to marry him destabilized him so much that he suffered a fit of insanity in 1795. By this time he had begun a long career with the East India Company (1792–1825), which kept him in his office for nine hours a day, six days a week. He was always to regret not having gone to university, but suffered from a bad stutter that made it impossible for him to pursue a career in the church (the usual destiny for men of his class and background). Instead, his 'university' was his beloved London, where he was surrounded by his favourite things: old books, theatre, drink, and good conversation (see his letter to Wordsworth, pp. 579–80).

On 22 September 1796 he came home from work to find that his elder sister, Mary had stabbed their mother to death in a fit of insanity.[1] Having suffered bouts of mental instability himself, he knew how best to deal with episodes of this kind: he took her straight to the Islington Asylum, Fisher House, and saved her from permanent incarceration by agreeing in future to look after her at home, which he did for the rest of his life. This was the 'strange calamity' which cast its shadow over him when he was given an offstage role in Coleridge's *This Lime-Tree Bower My Prison* (pp. 551–3).

Lamb's early literary career was promising. He became known in the 1790s for his poetry, much of it inspired by the same Unitarian theology behind Coleridge's *Religious Musings*.[2] Not surprisingly, some of his work appeared in Coleridge's *Poems* (1797) (along with verses by Charles Lloyd); in 1798 he published *Blank Verse* with Coleridge's pupil and acolyte

Charles Lloyd (see pp. 589–90), which contained his best-known poem, 'The Old Familiar Faces' (pp. 578–9). In 1798 Lamb published *Rosamund Gray*, a novella whose eponymous heroine was a thinly-disguised portrait of Ann Simmons, and, in 1802, a play, *John Woodvil, a Tragedy*. Although *Blank Verse* had made him sufficiently famous to be portrayed in Gillray's 1798 caricature of radical intellects, 'New Morality',[3] Lamb's talents did not lie in poetry. In subsequent years he turned to prose, often in collaboration with his sister. Together they produced *Tales from Shakespear* (1807) – so popular it has not been out of print since; *Mrs Leicester's School* and *Poetry for Children* (both 1809). These exercises helped turn him into one of the finest prose stylists of the day. He began to write for journals including Leigh Hunt's *Reflector*, *Examiner* and *Indicator*. He was also cultivating his craft in his enormously entertaining letters, which contain much valuable critical disquisition.[4] Then, in 1820, came the turning-point in his career; he was asked to contribute to John Scott's *London Magazine*. Under the pseudonym of Elia, Lamb began to publish some of the greatest essays in the history of English letters. In due course these were collected as *Elia* (1823) and *Last Essays of Elia* (1833). It was the glory of those essays to seek to retrieve, in fine romantic fashion, that instinct from which the adult has long been cut adrift – a sense of the numinous and magical. They are a distinctive and inimitable combination of romantic yearning for the intensity of childhood vision, combined with an underlying fear that the world may turn out to be no more than the materialist nightmare – matter in motion. Elia's art lay to a large extent in his manner; as Lamb told his publisher, John Taylor, 'The Essays want no Preface: they are *all* Preface. A Preface is nothing but a talk with the reader; and they do nothing else' (Lucas ii 350). Doubtless it was the mask of Elia that enabled Lamb to indulge his prejudices and whims with a freedom he had never enjoyed before. The result was a literary personality that took the world by storm. Such was his success that he was soon the highest paid contributor to the *London Magazine*, and, still pursuing his clerical career at East India House, he became a literary celebrity, being invited to dine with the Lord Mayor at the Guildhall. Two essays are presented here in full: the first, 'Imperfect Sympa-

CHARLES LAMB
[1]   Usefully analysed in detail, Mary Blanchard Balle, 'Mary Lamb: Her Mental Health Issues', *Charles Lamb Bulletin* NS 93 (1996) 2–11.
[2]   See Jonathan Wordsworth, 'Lamb and Coleridge as One-Goddites', *Charles Lamb Bulletin* NS 58 (1987) 37–47.

[3]   See Nicholas Roe, 'The Politics of "New Morality": Lamb, Coleridge, Wordsworth', *The Politics of Nature: Wordsworth and Some Contemporaries* (Houndmills, 1992), pp. 56–72.
[4]   The ideal compendium of Lamb's criticism is *Lamb as Critic* ed. Roy Park (1980).

thies', may be read as the manifesto for a philosophy applied in the second, 'Witches, and Other Night-Fears'.

In 1819 he fell in love again, with an actress, Fanny Kelly; she refused his proposal of marriage, but remained a friend. His eventual retirement from the East India Company was something of a disappointment, as he moved to the London suburbs of Enfield and Edmonton. There he felt exiled from the excitements of the town, and Mary's increasing bouts of insanity left him feeling isolated and lonely. He died of erysipelas after a bad fall on 27 December 1834 and was buried in Edmonton; Mary died in 1847 and was interred with him.

Further reading

Lamb as Critic ed. Roy Park (London, 1980)

Winifred F. Courtney, *Young Charles Lamb 1775–1802* (London, 1982)

Claude A. Prance, *Companion to Charles Lamb: A Guide to People and Places 1760–1847* (London, 1983)

Charles Lamb, *Elia and The Last Essays of Elia* ed. Jonathan Bate (Oxford, 1987)

—, *Elia 1823* introduced by Jonathan Wordsworth (Spelsbury, 1991)

—, *Rosamund Gray 1798* introduced by Jonathan Wordsworth (Spelsbury, 1991)

—, *Charles Lamb and Elia* ed. J. E. Morpurgo (Manchester, 1993)

Charles and Mary Lamb, *Mrs Leicester's School 1809* introduced by Jonathan Wordsworth (Poole, 1995)

Samuel Taylor Coleridge, Charles Lamb, Charles Lloyd, *Poems 1797* introduced by Jonathan Wordsworth (Poole, 1997)

Nicola Trott, ' "The Old Margate Hoy" and Other Depths of Elian Credulity', *Charles Lamb Bulletin* NS 82 (1993) 47–59

A journal dedicated to Lamb and his circle, *The Charles Lamb Bulletin*, is published quarterly by the Charles Lamb Society.

Letter from Charles Lamb to S. T. Coleridge, 27 September 1796 (extract)

My dearest friend –

White or some of my friends or the public papers by this time may have informed you of the terrible calamities that have fallen on our family.[1] I will only give you the outlines. My poor, dear, dearest sister, in a fit of insanity, has been the death of her own mother. I was at hand only time enough to snatch the knife out of her grasp. She is at present in a madhouse from whence I fear she must be moved to an hospital.

God has preserved to me my senses.[2] I eat and drink and sleep, and have my judgement, I believe, very sound. My poor father was slightly wounded, and I am left to take care of him and my aunt. Mr Norris of the Bluecoat school[3] has been very kind to us, and we have no other friend – but, thank God, I am very calm and composed, and able to do the best that remains to do.

The Old Familiar Faces (composed January 1798)

From BLANK VERSE BY CHARLES LLOYD AND CHARLES LAMB (1798)

> Where are they gone, the old familiar faces?
> I had a mother, but she died and left me,
> Died prematurely in a day of horrors –
> All, all are gone, the old familiar faces.

LETTER FROM CHARLES LAMB TO S. T. COLERIDGE
[1] On Thursday 22 September 1796 Mary Lamb stabbed her mother to death (see headnote).
[2] Lamb was a patient at the Hoxton madhouse, December 1795 to January 1796.

[3] Christ's Hospital, where Lamb and Coleridge went to school.

I have had playmates, I have had companions   5
In my days of childhood, in my joyful schooldays –
All, all are gone, the old familiar faces.

I have been laughing, I have been carousing,
Drinking late, sitting late, with my bosom cronies –
All, all are gone, the old familiar faces.   10

I loved a love once, fairest among women;[1]
Closed are her doors on me, I must not see her –
All, all are gone, the old familiar faces.

I have a friend,[2] a kinder friend has no man;
Like an ingrate, I left my friend abruptly,   15
Left him, to muse on the old familiar faces.

Ghostlike, I paced round the haunts of my childhood;
Earth seemed a desert I was bound to traverse,
Seeking to find the old familiar faces.

Friend of my bosom, thou more than a brother![3]   20
Why wert not thou born in my father's dwelling,
So might we talk of the old familiar faces?

For some they have died, and some they have left me,
And some are taken from me[4] – all are departed,
All, all are gone, the old familiar faces.   25

Letter from Charles Lamb to William Wordsworth, 30 January 1801
(extract)

Separate from the pleasure of your company, I don't much care if I never see a mountain in my life.[1] I have passed all my days in London until I have formed as many and intense local attachments as any of you mountaineers can have done with dead nature.

The lighted shops of the Strand and Fleet Street, the innumerable trades, tradesmen and customers, coaches, wagons, playhouses, all the bustle and wickedness round about Covent Garden,[2] the very women of the town, the watchmen, drunken scenes, rattles; life awake, if you awake, at all hours of the night, the impossibility of being dull in Fleet Street, the crowds, the very dirt and mud, the sun shining upon houses and pavements, the print shops, the old book stalls,[3] parsons cheapening[4] books, coffee-houses, steams of soups from kitchens, the pantomimes[5] – London itself a pantomime and a masquerade:[6] all these things work themselves into my mind and feed me without a power of satiating me.

THE OLD FAMILIAR FACES
[1] *a love . . . women* Ann Simmons, Lamb's sweetheart of 1792 (see headnote).
[2] *a friend* Charles Lloyd.
[3] *Friend . . . brother* Coleridge.
[4] *And some are taken from me* Shortly before this poem was written, Mary Lamb suffered a relapse and was returned to hospital.

LETTER FROM CHARLES LAMB TO WILLIAM WORDSWORTH
[1] In fact, Lamb was to visit the Lake District in August 1802, when he was to climb Skiddaw and Helvellyn.
[2] *all the bustle . . . Covent Garden* Covent Garden was in the heart of a red-light district.
[3] *old book stalls* stalls selling old books.
[4] *cheapening* bargaining for.
[5] *pantomimes* dramatic entertainments in which the performers express themselves by gestures to the accompaniment of music.
[6] *a masquerade* i.e. London is as diverse, varied and fantastic as a masked ball.

The wonder of these sights impels me into night-walks about her crowded streets, and I often shed tears in the motley[7] Strand from fullness of joy at so much life. All these emotions must be strange to you; so are your rural emotions to me. But consider, what must I have been doing all my life not to have lent great portions of my heart with usury[8] to such scenes?

My attachments are all local, purely local. I have no passion (or have had none since I was in love – and then it was the spurious engendering of poetry and books) to groves and valleys. The rooms where I was born,[9] the furniture which has been before my eyes all my life, a bookcase which has followed me about like a faithful dog (only exceeding him in knowledge) wherever I have moved, old chairs, old tables, streets, squares where I have sunned myself, my old school[10] – these are my mistresses. Have I not enough, without your mountains? I do not envy you. I should pity you, did I not know that the mind will make friends of anything. Your sun and moon and skies and hills and lakes affect me no more, or scarcely come to me in more venerable characters, than as a gilded room with tapestry and tapers where I might live with handsome visible objects. I consider the clouds above me but as a roof beautifully painted, but unable to satisfy the mind, and at last, like the pictures of the apartment of a connoisseur, unable to afford him any longer a pleasure.

Letter from Charles Lamb to Thomas Manning, 22 August 1801 (extract)

[*On Mackintosh*][1]

Though thou'rt like Judas – an apostate black,
In the resemblance one thing thou dost lack:
When he had gotten his ill-purchased pelf,[2]
He went away and wisely hanged himself.[3]
This thou may do at last – yet much I doubt,
If thou hast any bowels to gush out![4]

Letter from Charles Lamb to John Taylor,[1] 30 June 1821 (extract)

Poor Elia the real (for I am but a counterfeit) is dead. The fact is a person of that name, an Italian, was a fellow-clerk of mine at the South Sea House thirty (not forty) years ago,[2] when the characters I described there existed, but had left it like myself many years – and I having a brother[3] now there, and doubting how he might relish certain descriptions in it, I clapped down the name of Elia to it, which passed off pretty well, for Elia himself added the function of an author to that of a scrivener, like myself.

---

7   *motley* varied, diverse, unpredictable.
8   *usury* interest, advantage.
9   *The rooms . . . born* No. 2 Crown Office Row, Inner Temple (see headnote).
10 *my old school* Christ's Hospital, in the city of London.

LETTER FROM CHARLES LAMB TO THOMAS MANNING
1   Having defended the French Revolution in *Vindiciae Gallicae* (see pp. 172–4, above), James Mackintosh was persuaded by Burke to repudiate it in *A Discourse on the Study of the Law of Nature and Nations* (1799). This was a tremendous blow to radicals like Lamb, and of all the comments on Mackintosh's renunciation this is by far the most bitter; for more on Mackintosh, see pp. 323 n. 101.
2   *pelf* booty, spoil.

3   *hanged himself* Lamb's source is Matthew 27:5, where Judas is said to have repented his betrayal of Christ, 'departed, and went and hanged himself'.
4   *any bowels to gush out* an echo of Acts 1:18, which tells the story of Judas after his betrayal of Christ: 'Now this man purchased a field with the reward of iniquity; and falling headlong, he burst asunder in the midst, and all his bowels gushed out.'

LETTER FROM CHARLES LAMB TO JOHN TAYLOR
1   Taylor was the proprietor of the *London Magazine*, and, with his business partner, James Augustus Hessey (1785–1870), published volumes by Keats, Clare, Hazlitt, De Quincey, Coleridge and Carlyle.
2   *thirty . . . years ago* Lamb was a clerk in the Pacific trade office of the South Sea House, 1791–2.
3   John Lamb the younger (1763–1821).

I went the other day (not having seen him for a year) to laugh over with him at my usurpation of his name, and found him, alas, no more than a name, for he died of consumption eleven months ago, and I knew not of it.

So the name has fairly devolved to me, I think, and 'tis all he has left me.

Imperfect Sympathies[1]

From ELIA (1823)

I am of a constitution so general, that it consorts and sympathizeth with all things; I have no antipathy, or rather idiosyncrasy, in anything. Those national repugnancies do not touch me, nor do I behold with prejudice the French, Italian, Spaniard, or Dutch.

Sir Thomas Browne, Religio Medici[2]

That the author of the *Religio Medici*, mounted upon the airy stilts of abstraction, conversant about notional and conjectural essences, in whose categories of being the possible took the upper hand of the actual, should have overlooked the impertinent individualities[3] of such poor concretions[4] as mankind, is not much to be admired. It is rather to be wondered at, that in the genus of animals he should have condescended to distinguish that species at all.

For myself, earthbound and fettered to the scene of my activities, 'Standing on earth, not rapt above the sky',[5] I confess that I do feel the differences of mankind, national or individual, to an unhealthy excess. I can look with no indifferent eye upon things or persons. Whatever is, is to me a matter of taste or distaste, or, when once it becomes indifferent, it begins to be disrelishing.[6] I am, in plainer words, a bundle of prejudices made up of likings and dislikings, the veriest thrall[7] to sympathies, apathies,[8] antipathies.

In a certain sense, I hope it may be said of me that I am a lover of my species. I can feel for all indifferently,[9] but I cannot feel towards all equally. The more purely English word that expresses sympathy will better explain my meaning. I can be a friend to a worthy man who, upon another account, cannot be my mate or *fellow*. I cannot *like* all people alike.[10]

I have been trying all my life to like Scotchmen and am obliged to desist from the experiment in despair. They cannot like me and, in truth, I never knew one of that nation who attempted to do it. There is something more plain and ingenuous[11] in their mode of proceeding. We know one another at first sight. There is an order of imperfect intellects (under which mine must be content to rank) which in its constitution is essentially anti-Caledonian. The owners of the sort of faculties I allude to have minds rather suggestive[12] than comprehensive.[13] They have no pretences to much clearness or precision in their ideas, or in their manner of expressing them. Their intellectual wardrobe (to confess fairly) has few whole pieces in it. They are content with fragments and scattered pieces of Truth; she presents no full front to them – a feature or side-face at the most. Hints and glimpses, germs and crude essays at a system, is the utmost they pretend to. They beat up a little game peradventure,[14]

IMPERFECT SYMPATHIES
[1] First published, *London Magazine* August 1821, as 'Jews, Quakers, Scotchmen, and other Imperfect Sympathies'.
[2] Sir Thomas Browne (1605–82) was a favourite author of Lamb, Coleridge and Wordsworth.
[3] *impertinent individualities* trivial distinctions.
[4] *concretions* masses.
[5] *Paradise Lost* vii 23.
[6] *disrelishing* disgusting.
[7] *thrall* prisoner.
[8] *apathies* feelings of indifference.
[9] *indifferently* equally, disinterestedly.
[10] 'I would be understood as confining myself to the subject of *imperfect sympathies*. To nations or classes of men there can be

no direct *antipathy*. There may be individuals born and constellated so opposite to another individual nature, that the same sphere cannot hold them. I have met with my moral antipodes, and can believe the story of two men meeting (who never saw one another before in their lives) and instantly fighting' (Lamb's note).
[11] *ingenuous* frank, candid.
[12] *suggestive* fitted to conceive, or comprehend suggestions, rather than to reach final conclusions.
[13] *comprehensive* interested only in understanding conclusively.
[14] *They beat up . . . peradventure* i.e. they put forward an argument as it chances to occur.

and leave it to knottier heads, more robust constitutions, to run it down.[15] The light that lights them is not steady and polar,[16] but mutable and shifting – waxing, and again waning. Their conversation is accordingly.[17] They will throw out a random word in or out of season, and be content to let it pass for what it is worth. They cannot speak always as if they were upon their oath, but must be understood, speaking or writing, with some abatement.[18] They seldom wait to mature a proposition, but e'en bring it to market in the green ear.[19] They delight to impart their defective discoveries as they arise, without waiting for their full development. They are no systematizers, and would but err more by attempting it. Their minds, as I said before, are suggestive merely.

The brain of a true Caledonian (if I am not mistaken) is constituted upon quite a different plan. His Minerva is born in panoply.[20] You are never admitted to see his ideas in their growth – if indeed they do grow, and are not rather put together upon principles of clockwork. You never catch his mind in an undress. He never hints or suggests anything, but unlades[21] his stock of ideas in perfect order and completeness. He brings his total wealth into company, and gravely unpacks it. His riches are always about him. He never stoops to catch a glittering something in your presence to share it with you, before he quite[22] knows whether it be true touch[23] or not. You cannot cry *halves*[24] to anything that he finds – he does not find, but bring. You never witness his first apprehension of a thing. His understanding is always at its meridian;[25] you never see the first dawn, the early streaks. He has no falterings of self-suspicion. Surmises, guesses, misgivings, half-intuitions, semi-consciousnesses, partial illuminations, dim instincts, embryo conceptions, have no place in his brain or vocabulary. The twilight of dubiety[26] never falls upon him. Is he orthodox? He has no doubts. Is he an infidel? He has none either. Between the affirmative and the negative there is no borderland with him. You cannot hover with him upon the confines of truth, or wander in the maze of a probable argument. He always keeps the path. You cannot make excursions with him, for he sets you right. His taste never fluctuates. His morality never abates.[27] He cannot compromise, or understand middle actions. There can be but a right and a wrong. His conversation is as a book. His affirmations have the sanctity of an oath. You must speak upon the square[28] with him. He stops a metaphor like a suspected person in an enemy's country. 'A healthy[29] book!' said one of his countrymen to me, who had ventured to give that appellation to *John Buncle*,[30] 'Did I catch rightly what you said? I have heard of a man in health, and of a healthy state of body, but I do not see how that epithet can be properly applied to a book.'

Above all, you must beware of indirect expressions before a Caledonian. Clap an extinguisher upon your irony if you are unhappily blessed with a vein of it: remember you are upon your oath. I have a print of a graceful female after Leonardo da Vinci,[31] which I was showing off to Mr ****. After he had examined it minutely, I ventured to ask him how he liked 'my beauty' (a foolish name it goes by among my friends), when he very gravely assured me that he had considerable respect for my character and talents (so he was pleased to say) but had not given himself much thought about the degree of my personal pretensions. The misconception staggered me, but did not seem much to disconcert him.

Persons of this nation[32] are particularly fond of affirming a truth which nobody doubts. They do not so properly affirm, as annunciate[33] it. They do indeed appear to have such a love of truth (as if, like virtue, it were valuable for itself) that all truth becomes equally valuable whether the proposition that contains it be new or old, disputed, or such as is impossible to become a subject of disputation. I was present not long since at a party of north Britons[34] where a son of Burns was expected, and hap-

---

[15]   *run it down* i.e. dispute it.

[16]   *polar* fixed; 'as fixed as the poles'.

[17]   *accordingly* i.e. consistent with these tendencies.

[18]   *abatement* i.e. indulgence; it is the expectation of seriousness that must be abated in the listener.

[19]   *in the green ear* prematurely.

[20]   *in panoply* in armour. Minerva sprang fully-armed from the head of her father, Zeus.

[21]   *unlades* discharges.

[22]   *quite* completely.

[23]   *true touch* indisputably correct.

[24]   *cry halves* to claim a half share in anything found or caught by someone else.

[25]   *meridian* fullest height.

[26]   *dubiety* doubt.

[27]   *abates* weakens.

[28]   *upon the square* with extreme exactness and precision. Lamb goes on to criticize extreme literal-mindedness.

[29]   *healthy* in the sense of wholesome.

[30]   Thomas Amory's novel, *The Life and Opinions of John Buncle, Esq.* (1756–66), was one of Lamb's favourite books.

[31]   *The Virgin of the Rocks.*

[32]   *this nation* Scotland, though Lamb means all those of Caledonian tendencies, wherever they may come from.

[33]   *annunciate* proclaim, declare.

[34]   *north Britons* i.e. Scots.

pened to drop a silly expression (in my south British way), that I wished it were the father instead of the son – when four of them started up at once to inform me, that 'that was impossible, because he was dead'. An impracticable wish, it seems, was more than they could conceive. Swift has hit off this part of their character (namely their love of truth) in his biting way, but with an illiberality[35] that necessarily confines the passage to the margin.[36]

The tediousness of these people is certainly provoking. I wonder if they ever tire one another? In my early life I had a passionate fondness for the poetry of Burns. I have sometimes foolishly hoped to ingratiate myself with his countrymen by expressing it. But I have always found that a true Scot resents your admiration of his compatriot even more than he would your contempt of him. The latter he imputes to your 'imperfect acquaintance with many of the words which he uses', and the same objection makes it a presumption in you to suppose that you can admire him. Thomson[37] they seem to have forgotten. Smollett they have neither forgotten nor forgiven for his delineation of Rory and his companion upon their first introduction to our metropolis.[38] Speak of Smollett as a great genius and they will retort upon you Hume's *History* compared with *his* continuation of it.[39] What if the historian had continued *Humphrey Clinker*?[40]

I have, in the abstract, no disrespect for Jews. They are a piece of stubborn antiquity compared with which Stonehenge is in its nonage.[41] They date beyond the pyramids. But I should not care to be in habits of familiar intercourse with any of that nation. I confess that I have not the nerves to enter their synagogues; old prejudices cling about me – I cannot shake off the story of Hugh of Lincoln.[42] Centuries of injury, contempt, and hate, on the one side, of cloaked revenge, dissimulation, and hate, on the other, between our and their fathers, must and ought to affect the blood of the children. I cannot believe it can run clear and kindly yet, or that a few fine words, such as candour, liberality, the light of a nineteenth century, can close up the breaches of so deadly a disunion.

A Hebrew is nowhere congenial to me. He is least distasteful on 'Change,[43] for the mercantile spirit levels all distinctions, as all are beauties in the dark. I boldly confess that I do not relish the approximation[44] of Jew and Christian which has become so fashionable. The reciprocal endearments have, to me, something hypocritical and unnatural in them. I do not like to see the Church and Synagogue kissing and congeeing[45] in awkward postures of an affected civility. If *they* are converted, why do they not come over to us altogether? Why keep up a form of separation when the life of it is fled? If they can sit with us at table, why do they keck[46] at our cookery? I do not understand these half-convertites. Jews christianizing, Christians judaizing, puzzle me. I like fish or flesh. A moderate Jew is a more confounding piece of anomaly than a wet Quaker.[47] The spirit of the Synagogue is essentially *separative*.

B——[48] would have been more in keeping if he had abided by the faith of his forefathers;[49] there is a fine scorn in his face, which nature meant to be of[50] – Christians. The Hebrew spirit is strong in him, in spite of his proselytism.[51] He cannot conquer the shibboleth.[52] How it breaks out

---

[35]   *illiberality* rudeness, ungenerousness.
[36]   *the margin* i.e. of the page. Lamb notes a passage from Swift's 'Hints towards an Essay on Conversation':

There are some people who think they sufficiently acquit themselves, and entertain their company, with relating facts of no consequence, not at all out of the road of such common incidents as happen every day. And this I have observed more frequently among the Scots than any other nation, who are very careful not to omit the minutest circumstances of time or place – which kind of discourse, if it were not a little relieved by the uncouth terms and phrases, as well as accent and gesture peculiar to that country, would be hardly tolerable.

[37]   James Thomson (1700–48), author of *The Seasons*.
[38]   Rory, the eponymous hero of *Roderick Random* (1748) by Tobias Smollett, arrives in London at chapter 13.
[39]   Smollett's *A Complete History of England* (1757–8) was frequently published as a continuation of David Hume's *History of Great Britain* (1754–62).
[40]   *The Expedition of Humphry Clinker* (1771), the most

accomplished of Smollett's novels. Lamb's point is that it is so thoroughly imaginative (and, in effect, anti-Caledonian), that no historian could have written a sequel.
[41]   *nonage* infancy.
[42]   *Hugh of Lincoln* ten-year-old boy supposedly crucified and killed by Jews.
[43]   *'Change* place where merchants meet for the transaction of business, an exchange.
[44]   *approximation* closeness, proximity.
[45]   *congeeing* bowing in courtesy.
[46]   *keck* retch.
[47]   *a wet Quaker* a Quaker lax in the observances of his or her sect.
[48]   *B——* John Braham (1774–1856), renowned tenor of Jewish parentage who converted to Christianity.
[49]   *the faith of his forefathers* Judaism (see preceding note).
[50]   *of* i.e. directed towards.
[51]   *proselytism* conversion.
[52]   *shibboleth* accent or intonation revealing a person's racial origins.

when he sings, 'The Children of Israel passed through the Red Sea!'[53] The auditors, for the moment, are as Egyptians to him, and he rides over our necks in triumph. There is no mistaking him. B—— has a strong expression of sense[54] in his countenance, and it is confirmed by his singing. The foundation of his vocal excellence is sense. He sings with understanding, as Kemble[55] delivered dialogue. He would sing the Commandments and give an appropriate character to each prohibition.

His nation, in general, have not over-sensible countenances. How should they? But you seldom see a silly expression among them. Gain, and the pursuit of gain, sharpen a man's visage. I never heard of an idiot being born among them. Some admire the Jewish female physiognomy.[56] I admire it, but with trembling. Jael[57] had those full dark inscrutable eyes.

In the Negro countenance you will often meet with strong traits of benignity. I have felt yearnings of tenderness towards some of these faces, or rather masks, that have looked out kindly upon one in casual encounters in the streets and highways. I love what Fuller[58] beautifully calls these 'images of God cut in ebony.' But I should not like to associate with them, to share my meals and my goodnights with them — because they are black.

I love Quaker ways and Quaker worship. I venerate the Quaker principles. It does me good for the rest of the day when I meet any of their people in my path. When I am ruffled or disturbed by any occurrence, the sight, or quiet voice of a Quaker, acts upon me as a ventilator, lightening the air and taking off a load from the bosom. But I cannot like the Quakers (as Desdemona would say) 'to live with them.'[59] I am all over-sophisticated[60] – with humours,[61] fancies,[62] craving hourly sympathy. I must have books, pictures, theatres, chit-chat,[63] scandal, jokes, ambiguities, and a thousand whim-whams which their simpler taste can do without. I should starve at their primitive banquet. My appetites are too high for the salads which (according to Evelyn)[64] Eve dressed for the angel, my gusto[65] too excited 'To sit a guest with Daniel at his pulse.'[66]

The indirect answers which Quakers are often found to return to a question put to them may be explained, I think, without the vulgar[67] assumption that they are more given to evasion and equivocating than other people. They naturally look to their words more carefully, and are more cautious of committing themselves. They have a peculiar character to keep up on this head. They stand in a manner upon their veracity.[68] A Quaker is by law exempted from taking an oath. The custom of resorting to an oath in extreme cases, sanctified as it is by all religious antiquity, is apt[69] (it must be confessed) to introduce into the laxer sort of minds the notion of two kinds of truth – the one applicable to the solemn affairs of justice, and the other to the common proceedings of daily intercourse. As truth bound upon the conscience by an oath can be but truth, so in the common affirmations of the shop and the marketplace a latitude is expected and conceded upon questions wanting this solemn covenant. Something less than truth satisfies. It is common to hear a person say, 'You do not expect me to speak as if I were upon my oath.' Hence a great deal of incorrectness and inadvertency (short of falsehood) creeps into ordinary conversation, and a kind of secondary or laic-truth[70] is tolerated, where clergy-truth – oath-truth, by the nature of the circumstances – is not required. A Quaker knows none of this distinction. His simple affirmation being received upon the most sacred occasions,

---

53 Presumably a version of Hebrews 11:29 set to music.
54 *sense* i.e. understanding of what he sings.
55 John Philip Kemble (1757–1823), manager of Drury Lane theatre (1788–1802) and Covent Garden theatre (1803–17), the leading Shakespearian actor–director of his time.
56 *physiognomy* facial cast.
57 Jael was a murderess, Judges 4:21: 'Then Jael Heber's wife took a nail of the tent, and took an hammer in her hand, and went softly unto him, and smote the nail into his temples, and fastened it into the ground: for he was fast asleep and weary. So he died.'
58 Thomas Fuller (1608–61), author of *History of the Worthies of England* (1662), one of Lamb's favourite books.
59 *Othello* I iii 248.
60 *over-sophisticated* completely and utterly lacking in the natural and simple tastes demanded of the Quaker.

61 *humours* inclinations, likings, enthusiasms.
62 *fancies* whims.
63 *chit-chat* gossip.
64 *according to Evelyn* Lamb refers to John Evelyn, *Acetaria* (1699), a learned discourse on salad dressings.
65 *gusto* appetite for good food.
66 *Paradise Regained* ii 278. Daniel refused to eat the food provided for the children of Jewish nobles, preferring the simple diet of 'pulse' (lentils, beans, etc.); see Daniel 1:3–21.
67 *vulgar* usual.
68 *veracity* honesty.
69 *is apt* tends.
70 *laic-truth* the sort of honesty expected of those not under oath.

without any further test, stamps a value upon the words which he is to use upon the most indifferent topics of life. He looks to them, naturally, with more severity.

You can have of him no more than his word. He knows, if he is caught tripping in a casual expression,[71] he forfeits, for himself at least, his claim to the invidious exemption.[72] He knows that his syllables are weighed – and how far a consciousness of this particular watchfulness, exerted against a person, has a tendency to produce indirect answers and a diverting of the question by honest means, might be illustrated (and the practice justified) by a more sacred example than is proper to be adduced upon this occasion. The admirable presence of mind, which is notorious in Quakers upon all contingencies, might be traced to this imposed self-watchfulness, if it did not seem rather an humble and secular scion of that old stock of religious constancy which never bent or faltered in the Primitive Friends,[73] or gave way to the winds of persecution, to the violence of judge or accuser, under trials and racking examinations. 'You will never be the wiser, if I sit here answering your questions till midnight', said one of those upright Justicers[74] to Penn,[75] who had been putting law-cases with a puzzling subtlety. 'Thereafter as the answers may be', retorted the Quaker.

The astonishing composure of this people is sometimes ludicrously displayed in lighter instances. I was travelling in a stagecoach with three male Quakers, buttoned up in the straitest non-conformity of their sect. We stopped to bait[76] at Andover, where a meal (partly tea apparatus, partly supper) was set before us. My friends confined themselves to the tea-table. I in my way took supper. When the landlady brought in the bill, the eldest of my companions discovered that she had charged for both meals. This was resisted. Mine hostess was very clamorous and positive. Some mild arguments were used on the part of the Quakers, for which the heated mind of the good lady seemed by no means a fit recipient. The guard[77] came in with his usual peremptory notice. The Quakers pulled out their money and formally tendered it (so much for tea), I, in humble imitation, tendering mine for the supper which I had taken. She would not relax in her demand. So they all three quietly put up[78] their silver, as did myself, and marched out of the room, the eldest and gravest going first, with myself closing up the rear, who thought I could not do better than follow the example of such grave and warrantable personages. We got in. The steps went up. The coach drove off. The murmurs of mine hostess (not very indistinctly or ambiguously pronounced) became after a time inaudible – and now, my conscience (which the whimsical scene had for a while suspended) beginning to give some twitches, I waited in the hope that some justification would be offered by these serious persons for the seeming injustice of their conduct. To my great surprise not a syllable was dropped on the subject. They sat as mute as at a meeting. At length the eldest of them broke silence, by enquiring of his next neighbour, 'Hast thee heard how indigos[79] go at the India House?' And the question operated as a soporific[80] on my moral feeling as far as Exeter.

Witches, and Other Night-Fears[1]

From ELIA (1823)

We are too hasty when we set down our ancestors in the gross for fools, for the monstrous inconsistencies (as they seem to us) involved in their creed of witchcraft. In the relations of this visible world we find them to have been as rational, and shrewd to detect an historic anomaly, as ourselves. But when once the invisible world was supposed to be opened, and the lawless agency of bad spirits assumed,

---

71   *tripping in . . . expression* committing an error by using a casual expression.
72   *exemption* i.e. as a Quaker.
73   *the Primitive Friends* the Quakers, or Religious Society of Friends, was founded by George Fox in 1648–50, distinguished by its stress on the 'Inner Light' and rejection of sacraments, ordained ministry and set forms of worship.
74   *Justicers* judges.
75   William Penn (1644–1718), English Quaker.

76   *bait* stop at an inn to refresh the horses.
77   *guard* i.e. of the stagecoach, to warn them of its departure.
78   *put up* i.e. put their money back in their pockets.
79   *indigos* plants yielding blue dye, imported from India.
80   *soporific* anaesthetic.

WITCHES, AND OTHER NIGHT-FEARS
1   First published in the *London Magazine*, October 1821.

what measures of probability, of decency, of fitness, or proportion of that which distinguishes the likely from the palpable absurd, could they have to guide them in the rejection or admission of any particular testimony? That maidens pined away, wasting inwardly as their waxen images consumed before a fire; that corn was lodged[2] and cattle lamed;[3] that whirlwinds uptore in diabolic revelry the oaks of the forest; or that spits and kettles only danced a fearful-innocent vagary about some rustic's kitchen when no wind was stirring – were all equally probable where no law of agency was understood. That the Prince of the powers of darkness, passing by the flower and pomp of the earth, should lay preposterous siege to the weak fantasy of indigent eld,[4] has neither likelihood nor unlikelihood *a priori*[5] to us who have no measure to guess at his policy, or standard to estimate what rate those anile[6] souls may fetch in the devil's market. Nor, when the wicked are expressly symbolised by a goat, was it to be wondered at so much, that *he* should come sometimes in that body and assert his metaphor. That the intercourse was opened at all between both worlds was perhaps the mistake – but that once assumed, I see no reason for disbelieving one attested story of this nature more than another on the score of absurdity. There is no law to judge of the lawless, or canon by which a dream may be criticised.

I have sometimes thought that I could not have existed in the days of received witchcraft, that I could not have slept in a village where one of those reputed hags dwelt. Our ancestors were bolder (or more obtuse). Amidst the universal belief that these wretches were in league with the author of all evil, holding hell tributary[7] to their muttering, no simple Justice of the Peace seems to have scrupled issuing, or silly headborough[8] serving, a warrant upon them – as if they should subpoena Satan! Prospero in his boat, with his books and wand about him, suffers himself to be conveyed away at the mercy of his enemies to an unknown island.[9] He might have raised a storm or two, we think, on the passage.[10] His acquiescence is in exact analogy to the non-resistance of witches to the constituted powers. What stops the fiend in Spenser from tearing Guyon to pieces?[11] Or who had made it a condition of his prey that Guyon must take assay of the glorious bait?[12] We have no guess; we do not know the laws of that country.

From my childhood I was extremely inquisitive about witches and witch-stories. My maid, and more legendary aunt, supplied me with good store. But I shall mention the accident which directed my curiosity originally into this channel. In my father's book-closet, the *History of the Bible* by Stackhouse[13] occupied a distinguished station. The pictures with which it abounds – one of the ark, in particular, and another of Solomon's temple, delineated with all the fidelity of ocular admeasurement,[14] as if the artist had been upon the spot – attracted my childish attention. There was a picture, too, of the witch raising up Samuel, which I wish that I had never seen. (We shall come to that hereafter.)

Stackhouse is in two huge tomes, and there was a pleasure in removing folios[15] of that magnitude, which, with infinite straining, was as much as I could manage, from the situation which they occupied upon an upper shelf. I have not met with the work from that time to this, but I remember it consisted of Old Testament stories, orderly set down, with the 'objection' appended to each story, and the 'solution' of the objection regularly tacked to that. The objection was a summary of whatever difficulties had been opposed to the credibility of the history, by the shrewdness of ancient or modern infidelity,[16] drawn up with an almost complimentary[17] excess of candour; the solution was brief, modest, and satisfactory. The bane and antidote were both before you. To doubts so put (and so

---

[2] *lodged* prematurely beaten down as if by supernatural means.

[3] *lamed* crippled.

[4] *indigent eld* people in olden times.

[5] *a priori* prior to investigation.

[6] *anile* imbecilic.

[7] *tributary* contributary.

[8] *silly headborough* rustic constable.

[9] *Prospero . . . island* see *Tempest* I ii 159–68.

[10] *He might . . . passage The Tempest* begins in the midst of a storm raised by Prospero.

[11] *What stops . . . pieces* a reference to *Faerie Queene* II vii st. 64, where Guyon is said not to have been 'rent in thousand

peeces' by the 'dreadfull feend'. Bob Cummings points out to me that Lamb refers again to this episode in his essay, 'Sanity of True Genius'.

[12] *Or who had . . . bait* see *Faerie Queene* II vii st.34, where Guyon is tempted by the 'glorious bayte'. The short answer to Lamb's question is, of course, Mammon.

[13] Thomas Stackhouse, *New History of the Holy Bible* (1737).

[14] *ocular admeasurement* proportions and size as if seen.

[15] *folios* a folio is a book of the largest magnitude, made of sheets of paper folded only once.

[16] *infidelity* lack of religious faith.

[17] *complimentary* respectful.

quashed), there seemed to be an end for ever. The dragon lay dead, for the foot of the veriest babe to trample on.

But (like as was rather feared than realized from that slain monster in Spenser) from the womb of those crushed errors young dragonets[18] would creep, exceeding the prowess of so tender a St George as myself to vanquish. The habit of expecting objections to every passage set me upon starting more objections, for the glory of finding a solution of my own for them. I became staggered[19] and perplexed, a sceptic in long coats. The pretty Bible stories which I had read, or heard read in church, lost their purity and sincerity of impression, and were turned into so many historic or chronologic theses to be defended against whatever impugners. I was not to disbelieve them, but (the next thing to that) I was to be quite sure that someone or other would or had disbelieved them. Next to making a child an infidel is the letting him know that there are infidels at all. Credulity is the man's weakness, but the child's strength. Oh, how ugly sound scriptural doubts from the mouth of a babe and a suckling!

I should have lost myself in these mazes and have pined away, I think, with such unfit sustenance as these husks afforded, but for a fortunate piece of ill-fortune, which about this time befell me. Turning over the picture of the ark with too much haste, I unhappily made a breach in its ingenious fabric – driving my inconsiderate fingers right through the two larger quadrupeds (the elephant and the camel) that stare, as well they might, out of the two last windows next the steerage in that unique piece of naval architecture. Stackhouse was henceforth locked up, and became an interdicted[20] treasure. With the book, the objections and solutions gradually cleared out of my head, and have seldom returned since in any force to trouble me. But there was one impression which I had imbibed from Stackhouse which no lock or bar could shut out, and which was destined to try my childish nerves rather more seriously – that detestable picture!

I was dreadfully alive to nervous terrors. The night-time solitude and the dark were my hell. The sufferings I endured in this nature would justify the expression. I never laid my head on my pillow, I suppose, from the fourth to the seventh or eighth year of my life (so far as memory serves in things so long ago), without an assurance, which realised its own prophecy, of seeing some frightful spectre. Be old Stackhouse then acquitted in part, if I say that to his picture of the witch raising up Samuel[21] (oh, that old man covered with a mantle!)[22] I owe not my midnight terrors, the hell of my infancy, but the shape and manner of their visitation. It was he who dressed up for me a hag that nightly sat upon my pillow – a sure bedfellow when my aunt or my maid was far from me. All day long, while the book was permitted me, I dreamed waking over his delineation,[23] and at night (if I may use so bold an expression) awoke into sleep, and found the vision true. I durst not, even in the daylight, once enter the chamber where I slept, without my face turned to the window, aversely from the bed where my witch-ridden pillow was. Parents do not know what they do when they leave tender babes alone to go to sleep in the dark. The feeling about for a friendly arm, the hoping for a familiar voice when they wake screaming and find none to soothe them – what a terrible shaking it is to their poor nerves! The keeping them up till midnight, through candlelight and the unwholesome hours (as they are called), would, I am satisfied, in a medical point of view, prove the better caution. That detestable picture, as I have said, gave the fashion[24] to my dreams – if dreams they were, for the scene of them was invariably the room in which I lay. Had I never met with the picture, the fears would have come self-pictured in some shape or other – 'Headless bear, black man, or ape'[25] – but, as it was, my imaginations took that form.

It is not book, or picture, or the stories of foolish servants which create these terrors in children; they can at most but give them a direction. Dear little T.H.[26] who, of all children, has been brought up with the most scrupulous exclusion of every taint of superstition, who was never allowed to hear of

18   *dragonets* baby dragons; Lamb has in mind *Faerie Queene* I xii st.10 5–6: 'some hidden nest / Of many dragonets, his fruitfull seed'.

19   *staggered* doubtful.

20   *interdicted* forbidden.

21   *the witch raising up Samuel* the witch of Endor brought Samuel back to life from death; see I Samuel 28:7–14.

22   *that old man . . . mantle* when the witch brought him back to life, Samuel was covered in a cloak (mantle); I Samuel 28:14.

23   *delineation* pictorial representation.

24   *fashion* shape and substance.

25   From 'The Author's Abstract of Melancholy' prefixed to Robert Burton, *The Anatomy of Melancholy* (1621).

26   Thornton Leigh Hunt (1810–73), eldest son of Leigh Hunt, who was to become editor of the *Daily Telegraph*.

goblin or apparition, or scarcely to be told of bad men, or to read or hear of any distressing story, finds all this world of fear, from which he has been so rigidly excluded *ab extra* in his own 'thick-coming fancies'[27] – and from his little midnight pillow, this nurse-child of optimism will start at shapes unborrowed of tradition, in sweats to which the reveries of the cell-damned murderer are tranquillity.

Gorgons and hydras and chimeras,[28] dire stories of Celaeno and the harpies,[29] may reproduce themselves in the brain of superstition – but they were there before. They are transcripts, types; the archetypes are in us, and eternal.[30] How else should the recital of that which we know in a waking sense to be false come to affect us at all? Or 'Names whose sense we see not, / Fray us with things that be not?'[31] Is it that we naturally conceive terror from such objects, considered in their capacity of being able to inflict upon us bodily injury? Oh, least of all! These terrors are of older standing. They date beyond body – or, without the body, they would have been the same. All the cruel, tormenting, defined devils in Dante[32] – tearing, mangling, choking, stifling, scorching demons – are they one half so fearful to the spirit of a man as the simple idea of a spirit unembodied following him?

> Like one that on a lonesome road
> Doth walk in fear and dread,
> And having once turned round walks on
> And turns no more his head
> Because he knows a frightful fiend
> Doth close behind him tread.[33]

That the kind of fear here treated of is purely spiritual, that it is strong in proportion as it is object-less upon earth, that it predominates in the period of sinless infancy – are difficulties, the solution of which might afford some probable insight into our ante-mundane[34] condition, and a peep at least into the shadowland of pre-existence.

My night-fancies have long ceased to be afflictive. I confess an occasional nightmare, but I do not, as in early youth, keep a stud[35] of them. Fiendish faces, with the extinguished taper, will come and look at me – but I know them for mockeries, even while I cannot elude their presence, and I fight and grapple with them. For the credit of my imagination, I am almost ashamed to say how tame and pro-saic my dreams are grown. They are never romantic, seldom even rural. They are of architecture and of buildings – cities abroad, which I have never seen, and hardly have hope to see. I have traversed, for the seeming length of a natural day, Rome, Amsterdam, Paris, Lisbon – their churches, palaces, squares, market-places, shops, suburbs, ruins, with an inexpressible sense of delight, a map-like dis-tinctness of trace, and a daylight vividness of vision, that was all but being awake.

I have formerly travelled among the Westmorland fells (my highest Alps),[36] but they are objects too mighty for the grasp of my dreaming recognition, and I have again and again awoke with ineffec-tual struggles of the inner eye, to make out a shape, in any way whatever, of Helvellyn.[37] Methought I was in that country, but the mountains were gone. The poverty of my dreams mortifies me. There is Coleridge, at his will can conjure up icy domes and pleasure-houses for Kubla Khan, and Abyssinian maids, and songs of Abara, and caverns 'Where Alph, the sacred river, runs', to solace his night soli-

---

27   *Macbeth* V iii 38; *ab extra* from outside.

28   *Gorgons . . . chimeras* an echo of *Paradise Lost* ii 628: 'Gor-gons and hydras and chimeras dire.'

29   *Celaeno . . . harpies* Celaeno was the leader of the harpies in Virgil's *Aeneid* Book III.

30   *They are transcripts . . . eternal* Lamb's claim is that we are born with the archetypal forces, that, in childhood, produce the fear of such things as gorgons and hydras and chimaeras; his phrasing and ideas derive from Wordsworth, *Thirteen-Book Prelude* vi 571: 'the types and symbols of eternity'. See also Wordsworth's disquisition on pre-existence in his *Ode* (pp. 375–80).

31   Spenser, *Epithalamion* 343–4.

32   Dante was a relatively new discovery for those who did not know the language of the original; the first full English translation, by Lamb's friend, Henry Francis Cary (1772–1844), was published in 1814.

33   *The Ancient Mariner* 451–6.

34   *ante-mundane* i.e. before our life on earth.

35   *stud* as in stud-farm; presumably the nightmares were like horses on a stud, in that they multiplied.

36   *I have . . . Alps* Lamb and his sister visited the Lake Dis-trict in August 1802. They stayed with Coleridge at Greta Hall in Keswick, and with Charles Lloyd at Brathay Hall, near Ambleside.

37   Helvellyn is a large mountain (3116 ft) in the centre of the Lake District.

tudes, when I cannot muster a fiddle. Barry Cornwall has his tritons and his nereids gambolling before him in nocturnal visions, and proclaiming sons born to Neptune,[38] when my stretch of imaginative activity can hardly, in the night season, raise up the ghost of a fishwife. To set my failures in somewhat a mortifying light, it was after reading the noble 'Dream' of this poet that my fancy ran strong upon these marine spectra[39] – and the poor plastic[40] power (such as it is) within me set to work, to humour my folly in a sort of dream that very night. Methought I was upon the ocean billows at some sea nuptials, riding and mounted high, with the customary train[41] sounding their conchs before me (I myself, you may be sure, the leading god), and jollily we went careering over the main, till, just where Ino Leucothea[42] should have greeted me (I think it was Ino) with a white embrace, the billows, gradually subsiding, fell from a sea-roughness to a sea-calm, and thence to a river-motion, and that river (as happens in the familiarization of dreams) was no other than the gentle Thames – which landed me, in the wafture of a placid wave or two, alone, safe and inglorious, somewhere at the foot of Lambeth Palace.[43]

The degree of the soul's creativeness in sleep might furnish no whimsical criterion of the quantum[44] of poetical faculty resident in the same soul waking. An old gentleman, a friend of mine, and a humorist, used to carry this notion so far that when he saw any stripling of his acquaintance ambitious of becoming a poet, his first question would be, 'Young man, what sort of dreams have you?' I have so much faith in my old friend's theory that when I feel that idle vein returning upon me, I presently subside into my proper element of prose, remembering those eluding nereids, and that inauspicious inland landing.

Charles Lloyd   (1775–1839)

Lloyd was the eldest of probably fifteen children born to Charles Lloyd Sr (1748–1828), Quaker banker, philanthropist, translator of Horace and Homer, Birmingham worthy, and husband of Mary Farmer (1750–1821). At first it was hoped that Charles would go into the family banking business, but he was clearly not fitted for it and left in 1794 to study medicine in Edinburgh. This failed to work out and he left the same year to live for a while with Wordsworth's friend, Thomas Wilkinson (1751–1836), the Quaker of Yanwath in Cumberland; there he composed his *Poems on Various Subjects* (1795).

Back in Birmingham in 1796 he continued to write poetry, composing *Poems on the Death of Priscilla Farmer by her Grandson* (1796), which was published by the year's end. Lloyd already had something of a reputation in literary circles, therefore, when he met Coleridge in Birmingham, 19 August 1796. He took a strong liking to him and within weeks he had arranged with his father that he would reside with him in Bristol, paying Coleridge £80 per annum for board,

lodging and private tuition. Coleridge described Lloyd enthusiastically to Thomas Poole on 24 September 1796: 'his heart is uncommonly pure, his affections delicate, and his benevolence enlivened, but not sicklied, by sensibility. He is assuredly a man of great genius. . . . His joy, and gratitude to Heaven for the circumstance of his domestication with me, I can scarcely describe to you – and I believe that his fixed plans are of being always with me'.[1] Coleridge modified his views rapidly. On 4 December he wrote to Lloyd's father saying that he could not continue as his son's tutor, although he could lodge with him, adding that the only profession for which Charles was fitted was that of a farmer. One reason for Coleridge's brisk change of heart was the discovery that Lloyd was an epileptic. Coleridge was far from healthy himself, having recently increased his dosage of laudanum from 25 to 70 drops in order to combat the neuralgia that was plaguing him, and he soon exhausted himself in his attempts to nurse Lloyd. He described Lloyd's 'agonizing delirium' to several correspondents in March 1797,

---

[38] *Barry Cornwall . . . Neptune* Bryan Waller Procter (1787–1874) wrote under the name of Barry Cornwall. Lamb refers to his poem, *A Dream*, published in *Dramatic Scenes and Other Poems* (1819).

[39] *spectra* ghosts, apparitions.

[40] *plastic* shaping, imaginative.

[41] *train* wedding procession.

[42] *Ino Leucothea* girl transformed into a sea-goddess in

Homer's *Odyssey*.

[43] *Lambeth Palace* official residence in London of the Archbishop of Canterbury, on Lambeth Palace Road, on the south bank of the Thames.

[44] *quantum* amount.

CHARLES LLOYD

[1] Griggs i 236–7.

adding: 'what with bodily struggles and mental anguish and loss of sleep from sitting up with him, my temples ache, and my frame is feeble'.[2] The arrangement finally came to an end when Lloyd returned home to Birmingham in April 1797, to be treated by Erasmus Darwin. By this time Coleridge had enough of Lloyd's poems to include some by him, alongside others by Lamb, in the second edition of his *Poems*, published 28 October.

In the meantime, Lloyd had begun work on a novel, *Edmund Oliver*, which was published in April 1798. It was dedicated to Charles Lamb, whom Lloyd had met while on a visit to London in January 1797. Its eponymous hero was a thinly-disguised portrayal of his former tutor, his story consisting of loosely reworked episodes from Coleridge's life, including his 'love-fit, debaucheries, leaving college and going into the army'.[3] In later years Coleridge claimed that the distress caused by this episode, which began a breach with Lamb, prevented him from completing *Christabel*. Also in 1798, Lloyd collaborated with Lamb on a volume of poetry, *Blank Verse*. It is from that volume that *London* is taken. It is strongly influenced by Coleridge, but also reflects Lamb's enjoyment of London life. The book was sufficiently successful to cause its authors to be caricatured by Gillray in his famous burlesque of contemporary radicals, *The New Morality*.

Lloyd married Sophia Pemberton in 1799 and settled at Brathay Hall near Ambleside in June 1802. There he entertained the Wordsworths, De Quincey and the Southeys. He continued to write but his health declined. He was taken to an asylum in York in 1816, but escaped to De Quincey, then resident at Dove Cottage. After another spell at the asylum, he was released, continued writing, and published further in London. He continued to suffer fits of insanity and finally entered a sanitarium at Chaillot, in Paris, where he died.

Further reading

Lucy Newlyn, 'Lamb, Lloyd, London: A Perspective on Book Seven of *The Prelude*', *Charles Lamb Bulletin* NS 47–8 (1984) 169–87

David Fairer, 'Baby Language and Revolution: The Early Poetry of Charles Lloyd and Charles Lamb', *Charles Lamb Bulletin* NS 74 (1991) 33–52

London

From BLANK VERSE BY CHARLES LLOYD AND CHARLES LAMB (1798)

> *In solitude*
> *What happiness? Who can enjoy alone?*
> *Or, all enjoying, what contentment find?*[1]

Thou first of human feelings, social love!
I must obey thy powerful sympathies,
E'en though I've often found that those my heart
Most prized were creatures of its warm desires,
Rather than aught which other men (less prone   5
To affections swift, transforming quality)
Might worthy deem or excellent!
                                        Thy scenes,
Thy tainted scenes, proud city, now detain
My restless feet. 'Twill soothe a vacant hour
To trace what dim inexplicable links   10
Of hidden nature have inclined my soul
To love what heretofore it most abhorred.
When first, a little one, I marked far off
The wreathed smoke that capped thy palaces,
Oh, what a joyous fluttering of the heart,   15
Oh, what exulting hopes were mine! Methought

---

[2] Griggs i 316.
[3] Griggs i 404.

LONDON
[1] *Paradise Lost* viii 364–6.

Within thy walls there must be somewhat strange,
Surpassing greatly any wondrous dream
Of fairy grandeur which my childhood loved.
And when I heard the busy hum of men   20
And saw the passing crowd in endless ranks,
The many-coloured equipage,[2] and steeds
Gaily caparisoned,[3] it seemed to me
As though all living things were centred here.
But other feelings soon transformed these shows   25
To merest emptiness, e'en till my soul
Would sicken at their presence; for I've sought
To cherish quiet musings, and disdained
The idle forms which play upon the sense,
Yet give the heart no comfortable thoughts.   30
Yes, I have sought the solitary walk
Where I might number every absent friend
And give a tear to each; I've nursed my soul
With strangest contemplation, till it wore
A sad and lonely character, untouched   35
By th' operation of external shapes.
      Yet, London, now thou'rt pleasant – 'tis e'en so!
For I am sick of hopes that stand aloof
From common sympathy; for I am sick
Of pampering delicate exclusive loves,   40
And silly dreams of rapture that would pull
The shrinking hand from every honest grasp,
The shrinking heart from every honest pledge,
Not tricked in gracefulness poetical!
Sometimes, 'tis true, when I have paced the haunts   45
Of crowded occupation, I have felt
A sad repression looking all around,
Nor catching one known face amid the throng
That answered mine with cordial pleasantness.
I've often thought upon some absent friend,   50
E'en till an assured hope that he was nigh
Has made me lift my head and stretch my arm
To gaze upon the form, and grasp the hand
Of him who lived in my wayward dream.[4]
And I have looked, and all has been to me   55
A crowded desolation! Not one being
Mid that incessant and perturbed throng
Dreamt of *my* hopes or fears!
                        Then have I paced
With breathless eagerness, and if an eye
Has met my gaze, wherein some trace remote   60
Lived of one on whom my heart has leaned,
A gentle thrilling of awakened love
Has warmed my breast, and haply kindled there
A dream of parted days, that so my feet,
It seemed to me, moved on in solitude.   65

---

[2] *equipage* stagecoach.
[3] *caparisoned* fitted out.

[4] *I've often thought . . . dream* cf. Coleridge's *Frost at Midnight*
44–8.

Thus can the heart, by its strange agency,
Extract divine emotion from the scene
Most barren and uncouth, which images
To *him who cannot love*, who never felt
That ever-active warmth commingling still　　　　　70
Its own existence with all present things,
Nought beside forms and bodily substances.
　　　Methinks he acts the purposes of life,
And fills the measure of his destiny
With best-approved wisdom, who retires　　　　　75
To some majestic solitude – his mind
Raised by those visions of eternal love,
The rock, the vale, the forest and the lake,
The sky, the sea, and everlasting hills.
He best performs the purposes of life　　　　　80
And fills the measure of his destiny
Who holds high converse with the present God[5]
(Not mystically meant), and feels him ever
Made manifest to his transfigured soul.
But few there are who know to prize such bliss,　　　　　85
And he who thus would raise his mortal being
Must shake weak nature off, and be content
To live a lonely uncompanioned thing,[6]
Exiled from human loves and sympathies.
Therefore the city must detain *my* feet,　　　　　90
For I would sometimes gaze upon a face
That smiles on me, and speaks intelligibly
Of one that answers all my hopes and fears.
　　　Nor is to me the sentiment of life
Less acceptable, when I contemplate　　　　　95
Numberless living and progressive beings
Acting the infinite varieties
Of this miraculous scene. For though the dim
And inharmonious ministrations here
Of heavenly wisdom may confound the sense,　　　　　100
The partial sense of man, *my soul* is glad –
Trusting that all, yea, every living thing
Shall understand, in the appointed time,
And praise the inwoven mystery of sin,
Losing each hope and each propellant fear　　　　　105
In perfect bliss – and 'God be all in all!'

---

[5] 'The doctrine of Berkeley, of which the author is a believer, is here alluded to' (Lloyd's note).
[6] *To live . . . thing* there is an echo of Coleridge's *The Dungeon*: 'Till he relent, and can no more endure / To be a jarring and a dissonant thing' (ll. 25–6).

Sydney Owenson, Lady Morgan   (1777–1859)

Sydney Owenson was one of the most prolific and successful writers of her time, producing over seventy volumes of fiction, poetry, non-fictional prose, and even an opera. Her total profits from her writing are estimated to have been £25,000 – an enormous amount for the time. And she was the first woman to be granted a pension for her services to literature – £300 per annum, granted by Lord Melbourne (widowed husband of Lady Caroline Lamb) in 1837.

She was apparently born on Christmas Day[1] aboard the Dublin packet in the Irish Sea, the eldest child of the actor and singer Robert MacOwen by his wife Jane Hill, the daughter of a prosperous Shrewsbury tradesman and staunch Methodist (MacOwen later anglicized his name at the behest of a patron). After her mother died in 1789, she was sent first to the school of Madame Terson at Clontarf (one of the best schools in Ireland), and later to a finishing school in Dublin. She grew up feeling pride for her country's traditions and heritage.

Her *Poems* first appeared in 1801, published in both Dublin and London. She also collected a number of Irish tunes, composed lyrics, and published them. They enjoyed much popularity and her example was copied by Thomas Moore.[2] In 1803 she embarked on a wildly successful career as a novelist with *St Clair, or the Heiress of Desmond*; the following year she published *The Novice of St Dominick*, which met with tremendous success. She was offered £300 for her third fiction, *The Wild Irish Girl* (1806). Though not her best, it did even better than its predecessors, and Charles Maturin attempted to cash in on its success by calling his next fiction *The Wild Irish Boy* (1808).

In 1807 she published *The Lay of an Irish Harp; or Metrical Fragments*, her most important volume of poems. She made no claims as a poet, and the two epigraphs to the volume indicate her own valuation: 'trifles light as air' (Shakespeare) and 'vrai papillon de Parnasse' (La Fontaine).

Sydney went on to write many more successful novels and non-fiction works, including *The Missionary* (1811), an Indian novel, with which Shelley was delighted. She married Sir Charles Morgan in 1812, reluctantly, but the two seem to have enjoyed a happy marriage, despite having no children. She died on 14 April 1859, her age a mystery even to her closest friends, leaving a fortune of between £15,000 and £16,000 to be divided between her nieces. She was buried in the Old Brompton cemetery.

Further reading

Ann H. Jones, *Ideas and Innovations: Best Sellers of Jane Austen's Age* (New York, 1986), chapter 7

James Newcomer, *Lady Morgan the Novelist* (Lewisburg, PA, 1990)

Jeanne Moskal, 'Gender, Nationality, and Textual Authority in Lady Morgan's Travel Books', *RWW* 171–93

Richard C. Sha, 'Expanding the Limits of Feminine Writing: The Prose Sketches of Sydney Owenson (Lady Morgan) and Helen Maria Williams', *RWW* 194–206

Joseph W. Lew, 'Sydney Owenson and the Fate of Empire', *Keats-Shelley Journal* 39 (1990) 39–65

The Irish Harp: Fragment I

From THE LAY OF AN IRISH HARP, OR METRICAL FRAGMENTS (1807)

'Voice of the days of old, let me hear you. Awake the soul of song.'
Ossian

I

Why sleeps the harp of Erin's[1] pride?
Why with'ring droops its shamrock wreath?
Why has that song of sweetness died
Which Erin's harp alone can breathe?

SYDNEY OWENSON, LADY MORGAN
[1]   The year of her birth is disputed. Lionel Stevenson argues for 1776, while S. C. Hall who as a personal friend had reason to know, says it was 1777. This is the date favoured by John Andrew Hamilton in the *DNB*, and in the absence of more reliable evidence it is the date I have accepted. It should be noted, however, that Ann Jones favours 1780–?82, while Gayla S. McGlamery chooses ?1778.
[2]   Most notably in his *Irish Melodies*; see pp. 617–19.

THE IRISH HARP: FRAGMENT I
[1]   *Erin* Ireland.

II

Oh 'twas the simplest, wildest thing!   5
The sighs of eve that faintest flow
O'er airy lyres,[2] did never fling
So sweet, so sad, a song of woe.

III

And yet its sadness seemed to borrow
From love, or joy, a mystic spell;   10
'Twas doubtful still if bliss or sorrow
From its melting lapses fell.

IV

For if amidst its tone's soft languish
A note of love or joy e'er streamed,
'Twas the plaint of lovesick anguish,   15
And still the 'joy of grief' it seemed.

V

'Tis said oppression taught the lay
To him (of all the 'sons of song'
That basked in Erin's brighter day)
The *last* of the inspired throng;   20

VI

That not in sumptuous hall or bow'r,
To victor chiefs on tented plain,
To festive souls, in festal hour,
Did he (sad bard) pour forth the strain.

VII

Oh no! For he, oppressed, pursued,[3]   25
Wild, wand'ring, doubtful of his course,
With tears his silent harp bedewed,
That drew from Erin's woes their source.

VIII

It was beneath th' impervious gloom
Of some dark forest's deepest dell,   30
'Twas at some patriot hero's tomb,
Or on the drear heath where *he* fell.

---

[2]   *airy lyres* i.e. Aeolian harps.
[3]   'The persecution begun by the Danes against the Irish
bards finished in almost the total extirpation of that sacred
order in the reign of Elizabeth' (Owenson's note).

IX

It was beneath the loneliest cave
That roofs the brow of misery,
Or stems the ocean's wildest wave,   35
Or mocks the sea-blast's keenest sigh.

X

It was through night's most spectral hours,
When reigns the spirit of dismay,
And terror views demoniac pow'rs
Flit ghastly round in dread array.   40

XI

Such was the time, and such the place,
The bard respired *his* song of woe,
To those who had of Erin's race
Survived their freedom's vital blow.

XII

Oh, what a lay the minstrel breathed!   45
How many bleeding hearts around,
In suff'ring sympathy enwreathed,
Hung desponding o'er the sound!

XIII

For still his harp's wild plaintive tones
Gave back their sorrows keener still,   50
Breathed sadder sighs, heaved deeper moans,
And wilder waked despair's wild thrill.

XIV

For still he sung the ills that flow
From dire oppression's ruthless fang,
And deepened every patriot woe,   55
And sharpened every patriot pang.

XV

Yet, ere he ceased, a prophet's fire
Sublimed his lay, and louder rung
The deep-toned music of his lyre,
And 'Erin go brach'4 he boldly sung.   60

---

4 'Ireland for ever! A national exclamation, and, in less felic-
itous times, the rallying point to which many an Irish heart
revolted from the influence of despair' (Owenson's note).

William Hazlitt   (1778–1830)

Hazlitt was born in Maidstone in Kent, where his father, William Hazlitt Sr (1737–1820), was a Unitarian minister.[1] Hazlitt Sr was the correspondent of two distinguished fellow Unitarians, Richard Price (see pp. 1–3) and Benjamin Franklin, and it was no doubt at their urging that, in 1783, the family moved to America, where he preached at Philadelphia and Boston. Returning in 1784, they settled in Wem, Shropshire, and Hazlitt's education was supervised by his father. At fifteen he went to the Unitarian College in Hackney to prepare for the ministry. He read widely in philosophy, from Locke to Godwin, and came under the influence of radical thinkers like Helvétius and Holbach. This led him to renounce all expectation of a life in the ministry for a career as a philosopher, for which he returned to Wem in 1797.

On 14 January 1798 Coleridge preached a sermon at the Unitarian chapel in Shrewsbury (where he was preparing to take up the post of minister); Hazlitt (aged nineteen) was there to hear him, and fell under his spell immediately. Coleridge spent the following night with the Hazlitts, and the next morning received a letter from the Wedgwoods offering him an annuity of £150 a year for life, thus relieving him from the need to become a Unitarian minister.[2] Coleridge returned to Nether Stowey, urging Hazlitt to visit him there. Hazlitt did so, and through Coleridge met Wordsworth and Charles Lamb – friendships which were to change his life for ever. To Alfoxden he brought the manuscript of his *Essay on the Principles of Human Action* (published 1805), a lengthy disquisition on some of the ideas in Hartley[3] that underlay *The Recluse*. He seems to have discussed it at some length with Wordsworth, appearing 'somewhat unreasonably attached to modern books of moral philosophy' (p. 192); their exchanges provided the inspiration for Wordsworth's *Expostulation and Reply* and *The Tables Turned* (pp. 259–61).

Hazlitt was an enthusiastic painter, and studied with his elder brother John, who was a pupil of Reynolds. During the Peace of Amiens, 1802–3, he went to Paris and copied a number of paintings in the Louvre. In 1808 he married Sarah Stoddart, a friend of the Lambs, and at her cottage in Winterslow, near Salisbury, he began to write. In 1812 he moved his wife and son to London, where he delivered lectures, first on philosophy and then on literature, all of which he published subsequently. He made his name writing parliamentary reports and theatrical criticism for the *Morning Chronicle*; his drama reviews were collected in 1818 as *A View of the English Stage*. Further commissions poured in, and he became one of the most sought-after journalists in the field, being recruited by Leigh Hunt and his brother John for *The Examiner* and by John Scott for the *London Magazine*. It was not just that he had developed one of the most delicious prose styles in literature, but that his judgements on whatever topic – philosophical, political, cultural, literary – were sharp, shrewd, and brilliantly expressed. He possessed, above all, a precision of manner and thought with which he was able to trace the exact profile of the various intellects of the age. No other non-fiction prose writer had the same flawless combination of wit and technique. A series of unmatched collections of essays and lectures poured from him in the first decades of the nineteenth century – notably, *Characters of Shakespeare's Plays* (1817), *The Round Table* (1817, with Leigh Hunt), *Lectures on the English Poets* (1818), *Lectures on the English Comic Writers* (1819), *Political Essays* (1819), *Lectures on the Dramatic Literature of the Age of Elizabeth* (1821), *Table-Talk* (1821–2), *Spirit of the Age* (1825), and his forgotten masterpiece, *The Plain Speaker* (1826). Hazlitt was tremendously prolific, dependent as he was on his writing for his income, and he was responsible for many other works besides these. In recent years he has been criticized for *Liber Amoris, or the New Pygmalion* (1823), a confessional work about his unrequited love for a much younger woman, Sarah Walker. Whatever the rights and wrongs of the case (and they are far from settled), it is only through intellectual intolerance that an anthology dedicated to romanticism could exclude him from the canon.[4]

WILLIAM HAZLITT
1   The Unitarian chapel where Hazlitt Sr preached still stands, and the local museum contains a number of his son's paintings.
2   All this is related, more effectively, by Hazlitt, in 'My First Acquaintance with Poets', pp. 600–10.
3   David Hartley's associationist philosophy, expounded in *Observations on Man* (1749), edited in 1791 by Joseph Priestley), had a profound influence on the work of Wordsworth and Coleridge, providing the philosophical basis for *The Recluse* and much of Wordsworth's greatest poetry (see pp. 519–21).

4   Recent criticism of Hazlitt has tended to focus on this controversial work; see, for instance, Sonia Hofkosh, 'Sexual Politics and Literary History: William Hazlitt's Keswick Escapade and Sarah Hazlitt's *Journal*', *At the Limits of Romanticism* ed. Mary A. Favret and Nicola J. Watson (Bloomington, 1994), pp. 125–42. In *British Literature 1780–1830* ed. Anne K. Mellor and Richard E. Matlak, Hazlitt is represented only by brief extracts from two essays, with the observation that Hazlitt was so 'obsessively' in love with Sarah Walker that 'his sanity was seriously in question'.

He is represented here by the very best of his essays, three of which are included in full: 'On Gusto', 'My First Acquaintance with Poets', and 'Mr Coleridge'. The first of these is a document central to any discussion of the romantic imagination. Hazlitt defines gusto as 'power or passion defining any object', using precisely the same parameters that Wordsworth uses in his note to *The Thorn* (pp. 344–5). Passion, for the romantics, was more than just emotion, it was the index of imaginative truth, the measure of the artist's conviction in the creative act. Thus, Titian's paintings are remarkable to Hazlitt for their flesh tones, which appear 'nor merely to have the look and texture of flesh, but the feeling in itself'. 'My First Acquaintance with Poets' is probably the most important first-hand testimony we have as to the nature of the remarkable *annus mirabilis* of 1797–8, and the aspirations of those involved. It is composed, of course, in the light of what was widely regarded as Coleridge's failure to live up to his early promise, and this matter is fully explored in 'Mr Coleridge', one of the most important chapters from *The Spirit of the Age*. One of the main arguments of *The Spirit of the Age* is that intellectuals of the time could be categorized as rationalists (Godwin, Malthus) and non-rationalists (Lamb, Southey, Leigh Hunt). Coleridge cuts across such distinctions: like the rationalists, he has a towering intellect, and an unquenchable appetite for philosophy, but as the arch non-rationalist, he has been seduced into the interminable vortex of metaphysics. Besides being one of the most poignant of Hazlitt's essays, combining affection for his old mentor with a profound regret at his failure to fulfil his potential, this is also one of his funniest. It is not possible to do justice to Hazlitt in such a brief selection; those with a serious interest will wish to turn, as a first step, to *The Spirit of the Age* and *The Plain Speaker*.

Hazlitt placed enormous hope in his final work, the huge four-volume *Life of Napoleon* (1826–30). It was largely quarried from the work of others, but those passages by Hazlitt are written with his distinctive genius. He died having just completed it, in 1830, destitute, but with his old friend, Charles Lamb, at his side. He was fifty-two.

Further reading

P. P. Howe, *The Life of William Hazlitt* (3rd ed., London, 1947)

Roy Park, *Hazlitt and the Spirit of the Age* (Oxford, 1971)

David Bromwich, *Hazlitt: The Mind of a Critic* (New York and Oxford, 1983)

William Hazlitt ed. Harold Bloom (New York, 1986)

William Hazlitt, *The Spirit of the Age 1825* introduced by Jonathan Wordsworth (Spelsbury, 1989)

—, *Political Essays 1819* introduced by Jonathan Wordsworth (Spelsbury, 1990)

William Hazlitt and Leigh Hunt, *The Round Table 1817* introduced by Jonathan Wordsworth (Spelsbury, 1991)

Stanley Jones, *Hazlitt: A Life* (Oxford, 1991)

William Hazlitt, *Liber Amoris 1823* introduced by Jonathan Wordsworth (Spelsbury, 1992)

A new selected edition of the works, published by Pickering and Chatto in their Modern Masters series, in 9 volumes, is in preparation, edited by Duncan Wu, scheduled for publication in 1998.

On Gusto[1]

From THE ROUND TABLE (1817)

Gusto in art is power or passion defining any object. It is not so difficult to explain this term in what relates to expression (of which it may be said to be the highest degree), as in what relates to things without expression, to the natural appearances of objects, as mere colour or form. In one sense, however, there is hardly any object entirely devoid of expression, without some character of power belonging to it, some precise association with pleasure or pain. And it is in giving this truth of character from the truth of feeling, whether in the highest or the lowest degree (but always in the highest degree of which the subject is capable), that gusto consists.

There is a gusto in the colouring of Titian.[2] Not only do his heads seem to think, his bodies seem to feel. This is what the Italians mean by the *morbidezza*[3] of his flesh colour. It seems sensitive and alive all over – not merely to have the look and texture of flesh, but the feeling in itself. For example,

---

ON GUSTO
[1] First published in *The Examiner*, 26 May 1816.
[2] Tiziano Vecellio (1490–1576), Venetian painter whose work Hazlitt saw at the Louvre in 1802.

[3] *morbidezza* softness, delicacy.

the limbs of his female figures have a luxurious softness and delicacy, which appears conscious of the pleasure of the beholder. As the objects themselves in nature would produce an impression on the sense – distinct from every other object, and having something divine in it which the heart owns and the imagination consecrates – the objects in the picture preserve the same impression, absolute, unimpaired, stamped with all the truth of passion, the pride of the eye, and the charm of beauty. Rubens[4] makes his flesh colour like flowers; Albani's[5] is like ivory – Titian's is like flesh, and like nothing else. It is as different from that of other painters, as the skin is from a piece of white or red drapery thrown over it. The blood circulates here and there, the blue veins just appear, the rest is distinguished throughout only by that sort of tingling sensation to the eye, which the body feels within itself. This is gusto.

Van Dyck's[6] flesh colour, though it has great truth and purity, wants gusto. It has not the internal character, the living principle in it. It is a smooth surface, not a warm, moving mass. It is painted without passion, with indifference. The hand only has been concerned. The impression slides off from the eye, and does not, like the tones of Titian's pencil, leave a sting behind it in the mind of the spectator. The eye does not acquire a taste or appetite for what it sees. In a word, gusto in painting is where the impression made on one sense excites by affinity those of another.

Michelangelo's[7] forms are full of gusto. They everywhere obtrude[8] the sense of power upon the eye. His limbs convey an idea of muscular strength, of moral grandeur, and even of intellectual dignity; they are firm, commanding, broad and massy, capable of executing with ease the determined purposes of the will. His faces have no other expression than his figures, conscious power and capacity. They appear only to think what they shall do, and to know that they can do it. This is what is meant by saying that his style is hard and masculine; it is the reverse of Correggio's,[9] which is effeminate. That is, the gusto of Michelangelo consists in expressing energy of will without proportionable sensibility; Correggio's in expressing exquisite sensibility without energy of will. In Correggio's faces as well as figures we see neither bones nor muscles, but then what a soul is there, full of sweetness and of grace – pure, playful, soft, angelical! There is sentiment enough in a hand painted by Correggio to set up a school of history painters. Whenever we look at the hands of Correggio's women, or of Raphael's,[10] we always wish to touch them.

Again, Titian's landscapes have a prodigious gusto, both in the colouring and forms. We shall never forget one that we saw many years ago in the Orleans Gallery[11] of Actaeon hunting.[12] It had a brown, mellow, autumnal look. The sky was of the colour of stone. The winds seemed to sing through the rustling branches of the trees, and already you might hear the twanging of bows resound through the tangled mazes of the wood. (Mr West,[13] we understand, has this landscape; he will know if this description of it is just.)

The landscape background of the St Peter Martyr[14] is another well-known instance of the power of this great painter to give a romantic interest and an appropriate character to the objects of his pencil, where every circumstance adds to the effect of the scene: the bold trunks of the tall forest trees, the trailing ground plants, with that cold convent spire rising in the distance amidst the blue sapphire mountains and the golden sky.

Rubens has a great deal of gusto in his fauns and satyrs and in all that expresses motion, but in nothing else. Rembrandt[15] has it in everything; everything in his pictures has a tangible character. If

---

4 Peter Paul Rubens (1577–1640), Flemish painter whose work Hazlitt also saw in Paris in 1802.
5 Francesco Albani (1578–1660), painter of the school of Bologna.
6 Sir Anthony Van Dyck (1599–1641), Flemish portraitist.
7 Michelangelo Buonarroti (1475–1564), Italian painter, sculptor, architect.
8 *obtrude* impose, thrust forth.
9 Antonio Allegri da Correggio (1494–1534), eminent Italian painter.
10 Raffaello Santi (1483–1520), Renaissance artist.
11 *Orleans Gallery* exhibition of Italian old masters, so called because most of them came from the collection of the Duke of

Orleans in Paris, and were placed on sale in Pall Mall, December 1798, remaining there until July 1799.
12 *Actaeon hunting* Titian's *Diana and Actaeon*. Actaeon was a hunter who came upon the naked Diana bathing with her train of nymphs on Mount Citheron; she turned him into a stag and he was devoured by his own hounds.
13 Benjamin West (1738–1820), historical painter born in America, who succeeded Reynolds as President of the Royal Academy in 1792.
14 *the St Peter Martyr* Hazlitt saw this painting at the Louvre, 1802, and again in Venice in 1825. It was destroyed by fire in 1867.
15 Rembrandt van Rijn (1606–69), Dutch painter.

he puts a diamond in the ear of a burgomaster's[16] wife, it is of the first water[17] – and his furs and stuffs are proof against a Russian winter. Raphael's gusto was only in expression; he had no idea of the character of anything but the human form. The dryness and poverty of his style in other respects is a phenomenon in the art. His trees are like sprigs of grass stuck in a book of botanical specimens. Was it that Raphael never had time to go beyond the walls of Rome, that he was always in the streets, at church, or in the bath? He was not one of the Society of Arcadians.[18]

Claude's[19] landscapes, perfect as they are, want gusto. This is not easy to explain. They are perfect abstractions of the visible images of things; they speak the visible language of nature truly. They resemble a mirror or a microscope. To the eye only they are more perfect than any other landscapes that ever were or will be painted. They give more of nature as cognizable by one sense alone, but they lay an equal stress on all visible impressions; they do not interpret one sense by another; they do not distinguish the character of different objects as we are taught (and can only be taught) to distinguish them by their effect on the different senses. That is, his eye wanted imagination; it did not strongly sympathize with his other faculties. He saw the atmosphere but he did not feel it. He painted the trunk of a tree or a rock in the foreground as smooth, with as complete an abstraction of the gross, tangible impression, as any other part of the picture; his trees are perfectly beautiful, but quite immovable – they have a look of enchantment. In short, his landscapes are unequalled imitations of nature, released from its subjection to the elements – as if all objects were become a delightful fairy vision, and the eye had rarefied and refined away the other senses.

The gusto in the Greek statues is of a very singular kind. The sense of perfect form nearly occupies the whole mind, and hardly suffers it to dwell on any other feeling. It seems enough for them *to be*, without acting or suffering. Their forms are ideal, spiritual. Their beauty is power. By their beauty they are raised above the frailties of pain or passion; by their beauty they are deified.[20]

The infinite quantity of dramatic invention in Shakespeare takes from his gusto. The power he delights to show is not intense, but discursive. He never insists on anything as much as he might, except a quibble. Milton has great gusto. He repeats his blow twice, grapples with and exhausts his subject. His imagination has a double relish of its objects, an inveterate attachment to the things he describes, and to the words describing them:

> Or where Chinese drive
> With sails and wind their *cany* waggons *light* . . . .
> Wild above rule or art, *enormous* bliss.[21]

There is a gusto in Pope's compliments, in Dryden's satires, and Prior's tales. And among prose writers, Boccacio and Rabelais had the most of it. We will only mention one other work which appears to us to be full of gusto, and that is *The Beggar's Opera*.[22] If it is not, we are altogether mistaken in our notions on this delicate subject.

---

[16] *burgomaster* chief magistrate of a Dutch town, equivalent to a Mayor in England.

[17] *it is of the first water* i.e. it is so well painted that you can tell the quality of the stone. 'Water' is the measure of the quality of a diamond.

[18] *He was not . . . Arcadians* i.e. he didn't like the countryside. 'Raphael not only could not paint a landscape; he could not paint people in a landscape. He could not have painted the heads or the figures, or even the dresses of the St Peter Martyr. His figures have always an *indoor* look – that is, a set, deter-

mined, voluntary, dramatic character, arising from their own passions, or a watchfulness of those of others, and want that wild uncertainty of expression which is connected with the accidents of nature and the changes of the elements. He has nothing *romantic* about him' (Hazlitt's note).

[19] Claude Lorraine (1600–82), French landscape painter.

[20] *by their beauty . . . deified* Hazlitt echoes Wordsworth, *Resolution and Independence* 47: 'By our own spirits are we deified'.

[21] *Paradise Lost* iii 438–9, v 297.

[22] Popular play by John Gay (produced 1728).

My First Acquaintance with Poets[1]

From THE LIBERAL 2 (1823, PP. 23–46)

My father was a Dissenting minister[2] at Wem in Shropshire, and in the year 1798 (the figures that compose that date are to me like the 'dreaded name of Demogorgon'), Mr Coleridge came to Shrewsbury to succeed Mr Rowe in the spiritual charge of a Unitarian congregation there.

He did not come till late on the Saturday afternoon before he was to preach, and Mr Rowe, who himself went down to the coach in a state of anxiety and expectation to look for the arrival of his successor, could find no one at all answering the description but a round-faced man in a short black coat, like a shooting jacket, which hardly seemed to have been made for him, but who seemed to be talking at a great rate to his fellow-passengers. Mr Rowe had scarce returned to give an account of his disappointment, when the round-faced man in black entered, and dissipated all doubts on the subject by beginning to talk. He did not cease while he stayed – nor has he since, that I know of. He held the good town of Shrewsbury in delightful suspense for three weeks that he remained there, 'fluttering the *proud Salopians* like an eagle in a dovecot',[3] and the Welsh mountains that skirt the horizon with their tempestuous confusion agree to have heard no such mystic sounds since the days of 'High-born Hoel's harp or soft Llewellyn's lay!'[4]

As we passed along between Wem and Shrewsbury, and I eyed their blue tops seen through the wintry branches, or the red rustling leaves of the sturdy oak-trees by the roadside, a sound was in my ears as of a siren's song. I was stunned, startled with it, as from deep sleep, but I had no notion then that I should ever be able to express my admiration to others in motley imagery or quaint allusion, till the light of his genius shone into my soul, like the sun's rays glittering in the puddles of the road. I was at that time dumb, inarticulate, helpless, like a worm by the wayside,[5] crushed, bleeding, lifeless – but now, bursting from the deadly bands that 'bound them, / With Styx nine times round them',[6] my ideas float on winged words, and as they expand their plumes, catch the golden light of other years. My soul has indeed remained in its original bondage, dark, obscure, with longings infinite[7] and unsatisfied; my heart, shut up in the prison-house of this rude clay, has never found (nor will it ever find) a heart to speak to – but that my understanding also did not remain dumb and brutish, or at length found a language to express itself, I owe to Coleridge. But this is not to my purpose.

My father lived ten miles from Shrewsbury and was in the habit of exchanging visits with Mr Rowe and with Mr Jenkins of Whitchurch (nine miles farther on), according to the custom of Dissenting ministers in each other's neighborhood. A line of communication is thus established, by which the flame of civil and religious liberty is kept alive, and nourishes its smouldering fire unquenchable, like the fires in the *Agamemnon* of Aeschylus, placed at different stations, that waited for ten long years to announce with their blazing pyramids the destruction of Troy.

Coleridge had agreed to come over to see my father, according to the courtesy of the country, as Mr Rowe's probable successor, but in the meantime I had gone to hear him preach the Sunday after his arrival. A poet and a philosopher getting up into a Unitarian pulpit to preach the gospel was a romance in these degenerate days, a sort of revival of the primitive spirit of Christianity, which was not to be resisted.

It was in January 1798 that I rose one morning before daylight, to walk ten miles in the mud, to hear this celebrated person preach. Never, the longest day I have to live, shall I have such another walk as this cold, raw, comfortless one in the winter of the year 1798. *Il y a des impressions que ni le tems*

MY FIRST ACQUAINTANCE WITH POETS
[1]   The present text is emended on the advice of Stanley Jones in 'A Hazlitt Anomaly', *The Library* 7 (1985) 60–2, and 'A Hazlitt Corruption', *The Library* 33 (1978) 235–8.
[2]   *My father . . . minister* William Hazlitt Sr was a Unitarian minister (see headnote).
[3]   An allusion to *Coriolanus* V vi 114–15.

[4]   Gray, *The Bard* 28.
[5]   *like a worm by the wayside* cf. Chaucer, *The Clerk's Tale* 879–80: 'wherfore I yow preye, / Lat me nat lyk a worm go by the weye'.
[6]   Pope, *Ode on St Cecilia's Day* 90–1.
[7]   *with longings infinite* cf. Wordsworth, *The Affliction of Margaret* 63: 'With love and longings infinite'.

ni les circonstances peuvent effacer. Dusse-je vivre des siècles entiers, le doux tems de ma jeunesse ne peut renaitre pour moi, ni s'effacer jamais dans ma mémoire.[8]

When I got there the organ was playing the 100th Psalm, and, when it was done, Mr Coleridge rose and gave out his text: 'And he went up into the mountain to pray, HIMSELF, ALONE.'[9] As he gave out this text, his voice 'rose like a steam of rich distilled perfumes',[10] and when he came to the two last words, which he pronounced loud, deep, and distinct, it seemed to me, who was then young, as if the sounds had echoed from the bottom of the human heart, and as if that prayer might have floated in solemn silence through the universe. The idea of St John came into mind, 'of one crying in the wilderness, who had his loins girt about, and whose food was locusts and wild honey'.[11]

The preacher then launched into his subject like an eagle dallying with the wind. The sermon was upon peace and war,[12] upon church and state (not their alliance, but their separation), on the spirit of the world and the spirit of Christianity – not as the same, but as opposed to one another. He talked of those who had 'inscribed the cross of Christ on banners dripping with human gore'. He made a poetical and pastoral excursion, and, to show the fatal effects of war, drew a striking contrast between the simple shepherd boy driving his team afield, or sitting under the hawthorn piping to his flock 'as though he should never be old', and the same poor country lad, crimped,[13] kidnapped, brought into town, made drunk at an alehouse, turned into a wretched drummer-boy, with his hair sticking on end with powder and pomatum,[14] a long cue[15] at his back, and tricked out in the loathsome finery of the profession of blood – 'Such were the notes our once-loved poet sung.'[16]

And for myself I could not have been more delighted if I had heard the music of the spheres. Poetry and philosophy had met together, truth and genius had embraced under the eye and with the sanction of religion. This was even beyond my hopes. I returned home well-satisfied. The sun that was still labouring pale and wan through the sky, obscured by thick mists, seemed an emblem of the *good cause*, and the cold dank drops of dew that hung half-melted on the beard of the thistle had something genial and refreshing in them – for there was a spirit of hope and youth in all nature, that turned everything into good. The face of nature had not then the brand of *jus divinum*[17] on it, 'Like to that sanguine flower inscribed with woe.'[18]

On the Tuesday following the half-inspired speaker came. I was called down into the room where he was, and went half-hoping, half-afraid. He received me very graciously, and I listened for a long time without uttering a word. I did not suffer in his opinion by my silence. 'For those two hours', he afterwards was pleased to say, 'he was conversing with W.H.'s forehead'. His appearance was different from what I had anticipated from seeing him before. At a distance, and in the dim light of the chapel, there was to me a strange wildness in his aspect, a dusky obscurity, and I thought him pitted with the smallpox. His complexion was at that time clear, and even bright, 'As are the children of yon azure sheen'.[19] His forehead was broad and high; light, as if built of ivory, with large projecting eyebrows, and his eyes rolling beneath them like a sea with darkened lustre. 'A certain tender bloom his face o'erspread',[20] a purple tinge as we see it in the pale thoughtful complexions of the Spanish portrait-painters, Murillo and Velasquez. His mouth was gross, voluptuous, open, eloquent; his chin good-humoured and round; but his nose, the rudder of the face, the index of the will, was small, feeble, nothing – like what he has done.[21] It might seem that the genius of his face, as from a height, sur-

---

[8] 'There are impressions which neither time nor circumstance is able to efface. Were I to live entire centuries, the sweet time of my youth could never be reborn for me – nor could it ever be erased from my memory'. Hazlitt has adapted Rousseau, *Julie, ou la Nouvelle Héloïse* (6 vols., Amsterdam, 1761), vi 55–6.

[9] Matthew 14:23 and John 6:15.

[10] Milton, *Comus* 556.

[11] Matthew 3:3–4 and Mark 1:3.

[12] *peace and war* Coleridge was at this time much preoccupied with the war with France, which had been in progress since 1793, and which would give rise within months to *Fears in Solitude* and *France: An Ode* (pp. 465–73). Given Hazlitt's remarks here, it is evident that Coleridge's reservations about

the war, fully expressed in *France: An Ode*, were brewing in January 1798.

[13] *crimped* forced into the army.

[14] *pomatum* pomade, a scented ointment.

[15] *cue* pigtail.

[16] Pope, *Epistle to Robert, Earl of Oxford* 1.

[17] 'The divine right' – i.e. of kings.

[18] *that flower . . . woe* the hyacinth; see *Lycidas* 106.

[19] Thomson, *The Castle of Indolence* ii 295.

[20] Thomson, *The Castle of Indolence* i 507: 'A certain tender gloom o'erspread his face'.

[21] Cf. Coleridge's description of himself two years earlier, p. 457.

veyed and projected him (with sufficient capacity and huge aspiration) into the world unknown of thought and imagination, with nothing to support or guide his veering purpose, as if Columbus had launched his adventurous course for the New World in a scallop, without oars or compass. So at least I comment on it after the event.

Coleridge in his person was rather above the common size, inclining to the corpulent, or like Lord Hamlet, 'somewhat fat and pursy'.[22] His hair (now, alas, grey) was then black and glossy as the raven's, and fell in smooth masses over his forehead. This long pendulous hair is peculiar to enthusiasts,[23] to those whose minds tend heavenward, and is traditionally inseparable (though of a different colour) from the pictures of Christ. It ought to belong, as a character, to all who preach Christ crucified, and Coleridge was at that time one of those.

It was curious to observe the contrast between him and my father, who was a veteran in the cause,[24] and then declining into the vale of years.[25] He had been a poor Irish lad, carefully brought up by his parents, and sent to the University of Glasgow, where he studied under Adam Smith,[26] to prepare him for his future destination. It was his mother's proudest wish to see her son a Dissenting minister. So if we look back to past generations as far as eye can reach, we see the same hopes, fears, wishes, followed by the same disappointments, throbbing in the human heart – and so we may see them, if we look forward, rising up forever, and disappearing, like vapourish bubbles, in the human breast. After being tossed about from congregation to congregation in the heats of the Unitarian controversy and squabbles about the American War, he had been relegated to an obscure village where he was to spend the last thirty years of his life far from the only converse that he loved – the talk about disputed texts of scripture, and the cause of civil and religious liberty. Here he passed his days, repining but resigned, in the study of the Bible and the perusal of the commentators[27] – huge folios not easily got through, one of which would outlast a winter. Why did he pore on these from morn to night (with the exception of a walk in the fields or a turn in the garden to gather broccoli plants or kidney beans of his own rearing, with no small degree of pride and pleasure)? Here were 'no figures nor no fantasies',[28] neither poetry nor philosophy, nothing to dazzle, nothing to excite modern curiosity – but to his lacklustre eyes there appeared, within the pages of the ponderous, unwieldy, neglected tomes, the sacred name of JEHOVAH in Hebrew capitals: pressed down by the weight of the style, worn to the last fading thinness of the understanding, there were glimpses, glimmering notions of the patriarchal wanderings, with palm-trees hovering in the horizon, and processions of camels at the distance of three thousand years; there was Moses with the burning bush, the number of the Twelve Tribes, types, shadows, glosses on the law and the prophets; there were discussions (dull enough) on the age of Methuselah[29] (a mighty speculation!); there were outlines, rude guesses at the shape of Noah's Ark and of the riches of Solomon's Temple; questions as to the date of the creation, predictions of the end of all things; the great lapses of time, the strange mutations of the globe were unfolded with the voluminous leaf, as it turned over; and though the soul might slumber with an hieroglyphic veil of inscrutable mysteries drawn over it, yet it was in a slumber ill-exchanged for all the sharpened realities of sense, wit, fancy, or reason. My father's life was comparatively a dream, but it was a dream of infinity and eternity, of death, the resurrection, and a judgement to come.

No two individuals were ever more unlike than were the host and his guest. A poet was to my father a sort of nondescript, yet whatever added grace to the Unitarian cause was to him welcome. He could hardly have been more surprised or pleased if our visitor had worn wings. Indeed, his thoughts had wings, and as the silken sounds rustled round our little wainscoted parlour, my father threw back his spectacles over his forehead, his white hairs mixing with its sanguine hue, and a smile of delight beamed across his rugged cordial face, to think that Truth had found a new ally in Fancy! Besides,

[22] *Hamlet* III iv 153.
[23] *enthusiasts* fanatics.
[24] *the cause* i.e. of Unitarianism.
[25] *declining into the vale of years* as Stanley Jones points out, an allusion to Cowper, *Task* ii 725–6: 'But Discipline, a faithful servant long, / Declined at length into the vale of years'. William Hazlitt Sr was sixty in January 1798.

[26] Adam Smith (1723–90), distinguished Scottish economist and man of letters, author, most notably, of *The Wealth of Nations* (1776).
[27] *the commentators* i.e. biblical interpreters.
[28] *Julius Caesar* II i 231.
[29] *Methuselah* one of the pre-Noachian patriarchs, stated to have lived 969 years (Genesis 5:27), hence used as a type of extreme longevity.

Coleridge seemed to take considerable notice of me, and that of itself was enough. He talked very familiarly, but agreeably, and glanced over a variety of subjects.

At dinnertime he grew more animated, and dilated in a very edifying manner on Mary Wollstonecraft and Mackintosh.[30] The last he said he considered (on my father's speaking of his *Vindiciae Gallicae* as a capital performance) as a clever scholastic man, a master of the topics – or as the ready warehouseman of letters, who knew exactly where to lay his hand on what he wanted, though the goods were not his own. He thought him no match for Burke,[31] either in style or matter. Burke was a metaphysician, Mackintosh a mere logician. Burke was an orator (almost a poet) who reasoned in figures[32] because he had an eye for nature; Mackintosh, on the other hand, was a rhetorician who had only an eye to commonplaces. On this I ventured to say that I had always entertained a great opinion of Burke, and that (as far as I could find) the speaking of him with contempt might be made the test of a vulgar democratical mind. This was the first observation I ever made to Coleridge, and he said it was a very just and striking one. I remember the leg of Welsh mutton and the turnips on the table that day had the finest flavour imaginable. Coleridge added that Mackintosh and Tom Wedgwood[33] (of whom, however, he spoke highly) had expressed a very indifferent opinion of his friend Mr Wordsworth, on which he remarked to them: 'He strides on so far before you that he dwindles in the distance!'

Godwin[34] had once boasted to him of having carried on an argument with Mackintosh for three hours with dubious success; Coleridge told him, 'If there had been a man of genius in the room, he would have settled the question in five minutes.' He asked me if I had ever seen Mary Wollstonecraft, and I said I had once for a few moments,[35] and that she seemed to me to turn off[36] Godwin's objections to something she advanced with quite a playful, easy air. He replied that 'This was only one instance of the ascendancy which people of imagination exercised over those of mere intellect'. He did not rate Godwin very high[37] (this was caprice or prejudice, real or affected), but he had a great idea of Mrs Wollstonecraft's powers of conversation, none at all of her talent for book-making.[38] We talked a little about Holcroft.[39] He had been asked if he was not much struck *with* him, and he said he thought himself in more danger of being struck *by* him. 'I complained that he would not let me get on at all, for he required a definition of every the commonest word, exclaiming, "What do you mean by a *sensation*, sir? What do you mean by an *idea*?"' This, Coleridge said, was barricadoing the road to truth; it was setting up a turnpike-gate at every step we took.[40]

I forget a great number of things (many more than I remember), but the day passed off pleasantly, and the next morning Mr Coleridge was to return to Shrewsbury. When I came down to breakfast I found that he had just received a letter from his friend, T. Wedgwood, making him an offer of £150 a year if he chose to waive his present pursuit and devote himself entirely to the study of poetry and philosophy. Coleridge seemed to make up his mind to close with this proposal in the act of tying on one of his shoes. It threw an additional damp on his departure. It took the wayward enthusiast quite from us to cast him into Deva's winding vales[41] or by the shores of old romance. Instead of living at ten miles' distance, of being the pastor of a Dissenting congregation at Shrewsbury, he was henceforth

---

[30] *Mary Wollstonecraft and Mackintosh* see pp. 140–6, 172–4. Coleridge met Mackintosh only weeks before meeting Hazlitt, in December 1797; it is not known when he met Wollstonecraft, though from Hazlitt's comments it is clear that he had.

[31] *Burke* see pp. 4–8.

[32] *figures* rhetorical devices intended to give force to the composition; perhaps also 'images'.

[33] Thomas Wedgwood (1771–1805), third surviving son of Josiah Wedgwood, the famous potter, was a good friend of Coleridge.

[34] *Godwin* see pp. 47–50.

[35] If Hazlitt met Wollstonecraft, it must have been in September or October 1796 in London; the following year he was in Wem.

[36] *turn off* dismiss.

[37] *He did not . . . high* cf. Coleridge's comment to Southey, 19 December 1799: 'Godwin is no great thing in intellect, but in heart and manner he is all the better for having been the husband of Mary Wollstonecraft' (Griggs i 549).

[38] *book-making* i.e. book-writing.

[39] Thomas Holcroft (1745–1809), dramatist, novelist, man of letters, noted radical. Coleridge met him in London in December 1794, just after the Treason Trials at which he had been a defendant (see pp. 158–9); the most notable work of Hazlitt's early years was his *Memoir of Thomas Holcroft* (1816). Hazlitt probably met Holcroft for the first time in the autumn of 1796.

[40] Coleridge evidently had a trying time with Holcroft, whose atheism he found difficult to take; see Griggs i 138–9.

[41] *Deva's winding vales* Hazlitt has in mind Milton's *Lycidas* 55.

to inhabit the hill of Parnassus,[42] to be a shepherd on the Delectable Mountains.[43] Alas, I knew not the way thither, and felt very little gratitude for Mr Wedgwood's bounty! I was presently relieved from this dilemma, for Mr Coleridge, asking for a pen and ink, and going to a table to write something on a bit of card, advanced towards me with undulating step and, giving me the precious document, said that that was his address – 'Mr Coleridge, Nether Stowey, Somersetshire' – and that he should be glad to see me there in a few weeks' time, and, if I chose, would come halfway to meet me. I was not less surprised than the shepherd boy (this simile is to be found in *Cassandra*)[44] when he sees a thunderbolt fall close at his feet. I stammered out my acknowledgements and acceptance of this offer (I thought Mr Wedgwood's annuity a trifle to it) as well as I could, and, this mighty business being settled, the poet-preacher took leave, and I accompanied him six miles on the road.

It was a fine morning in the middle of winter, and he talked the whole way. The scholar in Chaucer is described as going 'Sounding on his way';[45] so Coleridge went on his. In digressing, in dilating, in passing from subject to subject, he appeared to me to float in air, to slide on ice. He told me in confidence (going along) that he should have preached two sermons before he accepted the situation at Shrewsbury, one on infant baptism, the other on the Lord's Supper, showing that he could not administer either, which would have effectually disqualified him for the object in view. I observed that he continually crossed me on the way by shifting from one side of the footpath to the other. This struck me as an odd movement, but I did not at that time connect it with any instability of purpose or involuntary change of principle, as I have done since. He seemed unable to keep on in a straight line.

He spoke slightingly of Hume,[46] whose 'Essay on Miracles' he said was stolen from an objection started in one of South's[47] sermons – *Credat Judaeus Apella!*[48] I was not very much pleased at this account of Hume, for I had just been reading, with infinite relish, that completest of all metaphysical *choke-pears*,[49] his *Treatise on Human Nature*, to which the *Essays*, in point of scholastic subtlety and close reasoning, are mere elegant trifling, light summer reading. Coleridge even denied the excellence of Hume's general style, which I think betrayed a want of taste or candour.

He however made me amends by the manner in which he spoke of Berkeley. He dwelt particularly on his *Essay on Vision* as a masterpiece of analytical reasoning – so it undoubtedly is.[50] He was exceedingly angry with Dr Johnson for striking the stone with his foot, in allusion to this author's theory of matter and spirit, and saying, 'Thus I confute him, sir!'[51] Coleridge drew a parallel (I don't know how he brought about the connection) between Bishop Berkeley and Tom Paine.[52] He said the one was an instance of a subtle, the other of an acute mind, than which no two things could be more distinct. The one was a shopboy's quality, the other the characteristic of a philosopher. He considered Bishop Butler[53] as a true philosopher, a profound and conscientious thinker, a genuine reader of nature and of his own mind. He did not speak of his *Analogy* but of his *Sermons at the Rolls Chapel*, of which I had never heard. Coleridge somehow always contrived to prefer the *unknown* to the *known*; in this instance he was right. The *Analogy* is a tissue of sophistry, of wire-drawn,[54] theological special pleading; the

---

42 *Parnassus* mountain sacred to the muses in classical literature.
43 In Bunyan's *Pilgrim's Progress* Christian and Hopeful reach the Delectable Mountains after escaping from Doubting Castle and the Giant Despair.
44 Ten-volume romance by Gauthier de Costes de la Calprenède.
45 *Sounding on his way* probably, as P. P. Howe has suggested, a confused recollection of several lines from Chaucer and Wordsworth. In the General Prologue to *The Canterbury Tales*, the Merchant is described as 'Sownynge alwey th' encrees of his wynnyng' (l. 275), and of the Clerk Chaucer writes: 'Sownynge in moral vertu was his speche' (l. 307). Hazlitt may also be recalling Wordsworth, *Excursion* iii 701 ('Went sounding on a dim and perilous way'), to which Coleridge alludes at the end of *Biographia Literaria* chapter 5.

46 David Hume (1711–76), Scottish sceptic and philosopher, whose publications included *Treatise of Human Nature* (1739) and *Essays Moral and Political* (1741–2); Hartley and Berkeley were more to Coleridge's taste.
47 Robert South (1634–1716), noted divine and sermonist.
48 'Apella the Jew may believe it' [but I don't] (Horace, *Satires* I v 100).
49 *choke-pear* something difficult to swallow.
50 George Berkeley (1685–1753), Bishop of Cloyne, *An Essay Towards a New Theory of Vision* (1709, 1710, 1732).
51 Related in Boswell's *Life of Johnson* (1791).
52 *Tom Paine* see pp. 14–17.
53 Joseph Butler, Bishop of Bristol (1692–1752), whose *Fifteen Sermons* (1726) preached at the Rolls Chapel defines his moral philosophy.
54 *wire-drawn* drawn out at great length and with subtle ingenuity.

Sermons (with the Preface to them) are in a fine vein of deep, matured reflection, a candid appeal to our observation of human nature, without pedantry and without bias.

I told Coleridge I had written a few remarks, and was sometimes foolish enough to believe that I had made a discovery on the same subject ('The Natural Disinterestedness of the Human Mind'),[55] and I tried to explain my view of it to Coleridge, who listened with great willingness, but I did not succeed in making myself understood. I sat down to the task shortly afterwards for the twentieth time, got new pens and paper, determined to make clear work of it, wrote a few meagre sentences in the skeleton style of a mathematical demonstration, stopped halfway down the second page, and, after trying in vain to pump up any words, images, notions, apprehensions, facts or observations from that gulf of abstraction in which I had plunged myself for four or five years preceding, gave up the attempt as labour in vain, and shed tears of helpless despondency on the blank unfinished paper. I can write fast enough now. Am I better than I was then? Oh no! One truth discovered, one pang of regret at not being able to express it, is better than all the fluency and flippancy in the world. Would that I could go back to what I then was! Why can we not revive past times as we can revisit old places? If I had the quaint[56] muse of Sir Philip Sidney to assist me, I would write a 'Sonnet to the Road between Wem and Shrewsbury', and immortalize every step of it by some fond enigmatical conceit. I would swear that the very milestones had ears, and that Harmer Hill stooped with all its pines to listen to a poet as he passed!

I remember but one other topic of discourse in this walk. He mentioned Paley,[57] praised the naturalness and clearness of his style, but condemned his sentiments, thought him a mere time-serving casuist, and said that 'the fact of his work on *Moral and Political Philosophy* being made a textbook in our universities was a disgrace to the national character'.

We parted at the six-milestone and I returned homeward, pensive but much pleased. I had met with unexpected notice from a person whom I believed to have been prejudiced against me: 'Kind and affable to me had been his condescension, and should be honoured ever with suitable regard'.[58] He was the first poet I had known, and he certainly answered to that inspired name. I had heard a great deal of his powers of conversation and was not disappointed. In fact, I never met with anything at all like them, either before or since. I could easily credit the accounts which were circulated of his holding forth to a large party of ladies and gentlemen, an evening or two before, on the Berkeleian theory, when he made the whole material universe look like a transparency of fine words;[59] and another story (which I believe he has somewhere told himself) of his being asked to a party at Birmingham, of his smoking tobacco and going to sleep after dinner on a sofa, where the company found him to their no small suprise, which was increased to wonder when he started up of a sudden and, rubbing his eyes, looked about him, and launched into a three hours' description of the third heaven, of which he had had a dream, very different from Mr Southey's *Vision of Judgement*, and also from that other *Vision of Judgement* which Mr. Murray, the Secretary of the Bridge Street junto,[60] has taken into his especial keeping.[61]

On my way back I had a sound in my ears; it was the voice of fancy – I had a light before me: it was the face of Poetry. The one still lingers there, the other has not quitted my side! Coleridge in truth met me halfway on the ground of philosophy, or I should not have been won over to his imaginative creed. I had an uneasy, pleasurable sensation all the time till I was to visit him. During those months the chill breath of winter gave me a welcoming; the vernal air was balm and inspiration to me. The golden sunsets, the silver star of evening, lighted me on my way to new hopes and prospects. *I was to visit Coleridge in the spring.* This circumstance was never absent from my thoughts, and min-

---

55   Published as *An Essay on the Principles of Human Action* (1805).

56   *quaint* clever, ingenious.

57   William Paley (1743–1805), theologian and philosopher, whose *Moral and Political Philosophy* (1785) was a university textbook by the time Wordsworth went up to Cambridge in 1787.

58   *Paradise Lost* viii 648–50.

59   *he made . . . fine words* George Berkeley (1685–1753), Bishop of Cloyne, argued that the material world was no more than an idea in the mind of God.

60   *junto* political clique, cabal.

61   Southey's *A Vision of Judgement* (1821) describes the reception in heaven of George III; Byron's *The Vision of Judgement* (1822) was a satirical response aimed largely at Southey, though Charles Murray of Bridge Street, an officer of the Constitutional Association, prosecuted the publishers of Byron's poem on the grounds of its libellous attack on George III.

gled with all my feelings. I wrote to him at the time proposed and received an answer postponing my intended visit for a week or two, but very cordially urging me to complete my promise then. This delay did not damp, but rather increased my ardour. In the meantime I went to Llangollen Vale by way of initiating myself in the mysteries of natural scenery, and I must say I was enchanted with it. I had been reading Coleridge's description of England in his fine *Ode on the Departing Year*,[62] and I applied it *con amore*[63] to the objects before me. That valley was to me, in a manner, the cradle of a new existence: in the river that winds through it, my spirit was baptized in the waters of Helicon![64]

I returned home and soon after set out on my journey with unworn heart and untired feet. My way lay through Worcester and Gloucester and by Upton – where I thought of Tom Jones and the adventure of the muff.[65] I remember getting completely wet through one day and stopping at an inn (I think it was at Tewkesbury) where I sat up all night to read *Paul and Virginia*.[66] Sweet were the showers in early youth that drenched my body, and sweet the drops of pity that fell upon the books I read! I recollect a remark of Coleridge's upon this very book, that nothing could show the gross indelicacy of French manners and the entire corruption of their imagination more strongly than the behaviour of the heroine in the last fatal scene, who turns away from a person on board the sinking vessel that offers to save her life, because he has thrown off his clothes to assist him in swimming. Was this a time to think of such a circumstance? I once hinted to Wordsworth,[67] as we were sailing in his boat on Grasmere lake, that I thought he had borrowed the idea of his 'Poems on the Naming of Places' from the local inscriptions of the same kind in *Paul and Virginia*. He did not own the obligation, and stated some distinction without a difference in defence of his claim to originality. Any the slightest variation would be sufficient for this purpose in his mind, for whatever *he* added or omitted would inevitably be worth all that anyone else had done, and contain the marrow of the sentiment.

I was still two days before the time fixed for my arrival, for I had taken care to set out early enough. I stopped these two days at Bridgwater, and when I was tired of sauntering on the banks of its muddy river, returned to the inn and read *Camilla*.[68] So have I loitered my life away, reading books, looking at pictures, going to plays, hearing, thinking, writing on what pleased me best. I have wanted only one thing to make me happy – but wanting that, have wanted everything.

I arrived, and was well-received. The country about Nether Stowey is beautiful, green and hilly, and near the seashore. I saw it but the other day[69] after an interval of twenty years from a hill near Taunton. How was the map of my life spread out before me, as the map of the country lay at my feet! In the afternoon, Coleridge took me over to Alfoxden, a romantic old family mansion of the St Aubins, where Wordsworth lived. It was then in the possession of a friend of the poet's who gave him the free use of it.[70] Somehow that period (the time just after the French Revolution) was not a time when nothing was given for nothing. The mind opened, and a softness might be perceived coming over the heart of individuals beneath 'the scales that fence' our self-interest.

Wordsworth himself was from home, but his sister kept house, and set before us a frugal repast – and we had free access to her brother's poems, the *Lyrical Ballads*, which were still in manuscript, or in the form of sibylline leaves.[71] I dipped into a few of these with great satisfaction, and with the faith of a novice. I slept that night in an old room with blue hangings and covered with the round-faced family portraits of the age of George I and II, and from the wooded declivity of the adjoining park that overlooked my window, at the dawn of day, could 'hear the loud stag speak'.[72]

In the outset of life (and particularly at this time I felt it so) our imagination has a body to it. We are in a state between sleeping and waking, and have indistinct but glorious glimpses of strange shapes, and there is always something to come better than what we see. As in our dreams the fullness

---

[62]   Published in pamphlet form, 1796.

[63]   with love.

[64]   The River Dee flows through the Vale of Llangollen; the fountains of Aganippe and Hippocrene rose out of Mount Helicon, sacred to the muses.

[65]   Henry Fielding, *Tom Jones* (1749), Book X, chapters 5–7.

[66]   Popular novel by Jacques-Henri Bernardin de Saint-Pierre (1737–1814), disciple of Rousseau, published 1788.

[67]   *I once hinted to Wordsworth* probably on his visit to the Lakes, August–September 1803.

[68]   Popular novel (1796) by Fanny Burney (1752–1840).

[69]   *I saw it but the other day* Hazlitt visited John Hunt, the radical publisher, near Taunton, in March 1820.

[70]   Wordsworth paid £23 a year; see p. 458, above.

[71]   *sibylline leaves* the title of Coleridge's 1817 collected poems; the allusion is to the oracles and mystic utterances of the sibyl (or prophetess); see Virgil, *Aeneid* vi 74–6.

[72]   Ben Jonson, *To Sir Robert Wroth* 22.

of the blood gives warmth and reality to the coinage of the brain, so in youth our ideas are clothed and fed and pampered with our good spirits; we breathe thick with thoughtless happiness, the weight of future years presses on the strong pulses of the heart, and we repose with undisturbed faith in truth and good. As we advance, we exhaust our fund of enjoyment and of hope. We are no longer wrapped in lamb's wool, lulled in Elysium.[73] As we taste the pleasures of life, their spirit evaporates, the sense palls, and nothing is left but the phantoms, the lifeless shadows of what *has been*.

That morning, as soon as breakfast was over, we strolled out into the park and, seating ourselves on the trunk of an old ash-tree that stretched along the ground, Coleridge read aloud with a sonorous and musical voice the ballad of Betty Foy.[74] I was not critically or sceptically inclined. I saw touches of truth and nature, and took the rest for granted. But in 'The Thorn', 'The Mad Mother', and 'The Complaint of a Poor Indian Woman', I felt that deeper power and pathos which have been since acknowledged, 'In spite of pride, in erring reason's spite',[75] as the characteristics of this author; and the sense of a new style and a new spirit in poetry came over me. It had to me something of the effect that arises from the turning up of the fresh soil, or of the first welcome breath of spring 'While yet the trembling year is unconfirmed'.[76]

Coleridge and myself walked back to Stowey that evening, and his voice sounded high

> Of Providence, foreknowledge, will and fate,
> Fixed fate, free will, foreknowledge absolute,[77]

as we passed through echoing grove, by fairy stream or waterfall gleaming in the summer moonlight. He lamented that Wordsworth was not prone enough to belief in the traditional superstitions of the place, and that there was a something corporeal, a matter-of-factness, a clinging to the palpable, or often to the petty, in his poetry, in consequence. His genius was not a spirit that descended to him through the air; it sprung out of the ground like a flower, or unfolded itself from a green spray on which the goldfinch sang. He said, however (if I remember right), that this objection must be confined to his descriptive pieces, that his philosophic poetry had a grand and comprehensive spirit in it, so that his soul seemed to inhabit the universe like a palace, and to discover truth by intuition rather than by deduction.

The next day Wordsworth arrived from Bristol at Coleridge's cottage. I think I see him now. He answered in some degree to his friend's description of him, but was more gaunt and Don Quixote-like. He was quaintly dressed, according to the costume of that unconstrained period, in a brown fustian jacket and striped pantaloons.[78] There was something of a roll, a lounge in his gait, not unlike his own Peter Bell.[79] There was a severe, worn pressure of thought about his temples; a fire in his eye, as if he saw something in objects more than the outward appearance; an intense, high, narrow forehead; a Roman nose; cheeks furrowed by strong purpose and feeling, and a convulsive inclination to laughter about the mouth, a good deal at variance with the solemn, stately expression of the rest of his face. Chantrey's bust[80] wants[81] the marking[82] traits, but he was teased into making it regular and heavy; Haydon's head of him, introduced into the 'Entrance of Christ into Jerusalem',[83] is the most like his drooping weight of thought and expression.

He sat down and talked very naturally and freely, with a mixture of clear gushing accents in his voice, a deep guttural intonation, and a strong tincture of the northern *burr*, like the crust on wine. He instantly began to make havoc of the half of a Cheshire cheese on the table, and said triumphantly

---

73 *Elysium* state of ideal happiness.

74 *the ballad of Betty Foy The Idiot Boy*, pp. 246–57.

75 Pope, *An Essay on Man* i 293. Hazlitt is presumably thinking of Jeffrey's review of *The Excursion*, pp. 556–8, above.

76 Thomson, *Spring* 18.

77 *Paradise Lost* ii 559–60.

78 *pantaloons* breeches.

79 Wordsworth had completed a version of *Peter Bell* by this time, although the poem was published only in 1819.

80 Sir Francis Leggatt Chantrey (1781–1841) exhibited his bust of Wordsworth at the Royal Academy in 1821.

81 *wants* lacks.

82 *marking* defining.

83 Benjamin Robert Haydon (1786–1846), whose *Christ's Triumphant Entry into Jerusalem* (now at Mount St Mary's Seminary, Norwood, Ohio) contains portraits of Wordsworth, Lamb, Keats and Hazlitt (among others). The pencil sketch of Wordsworth, made for the painting, which Hazlitt refers to here, is now at the Wordsworth Museum, Grasmere.

that 'his marriage with experience had not been so unproductive as Mr Southey's in teaching him a knowledge of the good things of this life'. He had been to see *The Castle Spectre* by Monk Lewis,[84] while at Bristol, and described it very well. He said 'it fitted the taste of the audience like a glove'. This *ad captandum*[85] merit was however by no means a recommendation of it according to the severe principles of the new school, which reject rather than court popular effect.

Wordsworth, looking out of the low, latticed window, said, 'How beautifully the sun sets on that yellow bank!' I thought within myself, 'With what eyes these poets see nature!' And ever after, when I saw the sunset stream upon the objects facing it, conceived I had made a discovery, or thanked Mr Wordsworth for having made one for me.

We went over to Alfoxden again the day following and Wordsworth read us the story of Peter Bell in the open air, and the comment made upon it by his face and voice was very different from that of some later critics. Whatever might be thought of the poem, 'his face was as a book where men might read strange matters',[86] and he announced the fate of his hero in prophetic tones. There is a *chaunt* in the recitation both of Coleridge and Wordsworth which acts as a spell upon the hearer, and disarms the judgement. Perhaps they have deceived themselves by making habitual use of this ambiguous accompaniment. Coleridge's manner is more full, animated, and varied; Wordsworth's more equable, sustained, and internal. The one might be termed more dramatic, the other more lyrical. Coleridge has told me that he himself liked to compose in walking over uneven ground, or breaking through the straggling branches of a copsewood, whereas Wordsworth always wrote (if he could) walking up and down a straight gravel-walk, or in some spot where the continuity of his verse met with no collateral[87] interruption.

Returning that same evening, I got into a metaphysical argument with Wordsworth while Coleridge was explaining the different notes of the nightingale to his sister, in which we neither of us succeeded in making ourselves perfectly clear and intelligible.[88] Thus I passed three weeks at Nether Stowey and in the neighbourhood generally devoting the afternoons to a delightful chat in an arbour made of bark by the poet's friend Tom Poole, sitting under two fine elm-trees, and listening to the bees humming round us while we quaffed our flip.[89] It was agreed, among other things, that we should make a jaunt down the Bristol Channel as far as Lynton.[90] We set off together on foot, Coleridge, John Chester[91] and I. This Chester was a native of Nether Stowey, one of those who were attracted to Coleridge's discourse as flies are to honey, or bees in swarming-time to the sound of a brass pan. He 'followed in the chase like a dog who hunts, not like one that made up the cry'.[92] He had on a brown cloth coat, boots, and corduroy breeches, was low in stature, bow-legged, had a drag in his walk like a drover, which he assisted by a hazel switch,[93] and kept on a sort of trot by the side of Coleridge, like a running footman by a state coach, that he might not lose a syllable or sound that fell from Coleridge's lips. He told me his private opinion that Coleridge was a wonderful man. He scarcely opened his lips, much less offered an opinion the whole way – yet, of the three, had I to choose during that journey, I would be John Chester. He afterwards followed Coleridge into Germany, where the Kantean philosophers were puzzled how to bring him under any of their categories. When he sat down at table with his idol, John's felicity was complete; Sir Walter Scott's, or Mr Blackwood's, when they sat down at the same table with the King, was not more so.[94]

We passed Dunster on our right, a small town between the brow of a hill and the sea. I remember eyeing it wistfully as it lay below us; contrasted with the woody scene around, it looked as clear, as

---

[84]   Matthew Gregory Lewis (1775–1818), author of a popular Gothic novel, *The Monk* (1795), and play, *The Castle Spectre* (1798). Wordsworth attended a performance of the play at the Theatre Royal, Bristol, Monday 21 May 1798; he returned to Alfoxden the following day. Coleridge read and reviewed it for the *Critical Review* in February 1797.

[85]   *ad captandum {vulgus}* [designed] to take the fancy of [the crowd].

[86]   *Macbeth* I v 62–3.

[87]   *collateral* accompanying.

[88]   This argument seems to have inspired *Expostulation and Reply* and *The Tables Turned*.

[89]   *flip* mixture of hot beer and spirits sweetened with sugar.

[90]   *Lynton* village on the north coast of Devon.

[91]   John Chester was a farmer who encouraged Coleridge in his quest for agricultural knowledge. They went to Germany together in 1798 so as to study agricultural techniques.

[92]   *Othello* II iii 363–4.

[93]   *switch* walking stick made of hazel wood.

[94]   William Blackwood (1776–1834), publisher, and Sir Walter Scott (see pp. 428–31), were Tories; they banqueted with George IV in Edinburgh, 24 August 1822.

pure, as embrowned and ideal as any landscape I have seen since, of Gaspar Poussin's or Domenichino's.[95] We had a long day's march (our feet kept time to the echoes of Coleridge's tongue) through Minehead and by the Blue Anchor and on to Lynton, which we did not reach till near midnight, and where we had some difficulty in making a lodgement.[96] We however knocked the people of the house up at last, and we were repaid for our apprehensions and fatigue by some excellent rashers of fried bacon and eggs. The view in coming along had been splendid. We walked for miles and miles on dark brown heaths overlooking the Channel,[97] with the Welsh hills beyond, and at times descended into little sheltered valleys close by the seaside, with a smuggler's face scowling by us, and then had to ascend conical hills with a path winding up through a coppice to a barren top, like a monk's shaven crown, from one of which I pointed out to Coleridge's notice the bare masts of a vessel on the very edge of the horizon and within the red-orbed disk of the setting sun, like his own spectreship in 'The Ancient Mariner'.

At Lynton the character of the sea-coast becomes more marked and rugged. There is a place called the Valley of Rocks[98] (I suspect this was only the poetical name for it) bedded among precipices overhanging the sea, with rocky caverns beneath, into which the waves dash, and where the seagull forever wheels its screaming flight. On the tops of these are huge stones thrown transverse, as if an earthquake had tossed them there, and behind these is a fretwork of perpendicular rocks, something like the Giant's Causeway.[99]

A thunderstorm came on while we were at the inn, and Coleridge was running out bareheaded to enjoy the commotion of the elements in the Valley of Rocks, but, as if in spite, the clouds only muttered a few angry sounds, and let fall a few refreshing drops. Coleridge told me that he and Wordsworth were to have made this place the scene of a prose tale which was to have been in the manner of, but far superior to, *The Death of Abel*,[100] but they had relinquished the design.

In the morning of the second day, we breakfasted luxuriously in an old-fashioned parlour on tea, toast, eggs, and honey, in the very sight of the beehives from which it had been taken, and a garden full of thyme and wild-flowers that had produced it. On this occasion Coleridge spoke of Virgil's *Georgics*, but not well. I do not think he had much feeling for the classical or elegant. It was in this room that we found a little worn-out copy of *The Seasons* lying in a window-seat, on which Coleridge exclaimed, '*That* is true fame!' He said Thomson was a great poet rather than a good one; his style was as meretricious as his thoughts were natural. He spoke of Cowper as the best modern poet. He said the *Lyrical Ballads* were an experiment about to be tried by him and Wordsworth, to see how far the public taste would endure poetry written in a more natural and simple style than had hitherto been attempted – totally discarding the artifices of poetical diction, and making use only of such words as had probably been common in the most ordinary language since the days of Henry II.[101]

Some comparison was introduced between Shakespeare and Milton. He said he hardly knew which to prefer. Shakespeare seemed to him a mere stripling in the art; he was as tall and as strong, with infinitely more activity, than Milton, but he never appeared to have come to man's estate – or if he had, he would not have been a man, but a monster. He spoke with contempt of Gray and with intolerance of Pope. He did not like the versification of the latter. He observed that 'the ears of these couplet-writers might be charged with having short memories, that could not retain the harmony of whole passages'. He thought little of Junius[102] as a writer, he had a dislike of Dr Johnson, and a much higher opinion of Burke as an orator and politician, than of Fox or Pitt.[103] He however thought him very inferior in richness of style and imagery to some of our elder prose writers, particularly

---

95   Gaspar Poussin (1613–75), landscape artist; Domenico Zampieri (1581–1641), Italian artist.
96   *making a lodgement* i.e. finding an inn that could accommodate us.
97   *the Channel* i.e. the Bristol Channel.
98   The Valley of Rocks may have provided the landscape for Coleridge's *Kubla Khan* – see Eugene E. Stelzig, 'The Landscape of *Kubla Khan* and the Valley of Rocks', *TWC* 6 (1975) 316–18. This number of *TWC* contains a photograph of the Valley on its inside back cover.

99   *the Giant's Causeway* beauty-spot on the west coast of Ireland.
100   Salomon Gessner, *The Death of Abel* (1758).
101   Henry II reigned 1154–89.
102   'Junius', Sir Philip Francis (1740–1818), pseudonymous author of a series of letters published in the *Public Advertiser*, January 1769 to January 1772, attacking Tory worthies.
103   Charles James Fox (1749–1806), Whig statesman and orator; William Pitt (1759–1806), Prime Minister 1783–1801.

Jeremy Taylor.[104] He liked Richardson but not Fielding, nor could I get him to enter into the merits of *Caleb Williams*.[105] In short, he was profound and discriminating with respect to those authors whom he liked, and where he gave his judgement fair play; capricious, perverse, and prejudiced in his antipathies and distastes.

We loitered on the 'ribbed sea-sands'[106] in such talk as this a whole morning, and I recollect met with a curious seaweed of which John Chester told us the country name. A fisherman gave Coleridge an account of a boy that had been drowned the day before, and that they had tried to save him at the risk of their own lives. He said he 'did not know how it was that they ventured, but, sir, we have a *nature* towards one another.' This expression, Coleridge remarked to me, was a fine illustration of that theory of disinterestedness which I (in common with Butler)[107] had adopted. I broached to him an argument of mine to prove that *likeness* was not mere association of ideas. I said that the mark in the sand put one in mind of a man's foot not because it was part of a former impression of a man's foot (for it was quite new), but because it was like the shape of a man's foot. He assented to the justness of this distinction (which I have explained at length elsewhere[108] for the benefit of the curious), and John Chester listened not from any interest in the subject, but because he was astonished that I should be able to suggest anything to Coleridge that he did not already know. We returned on the third morning, and Coleridge remarked the silent cottage-smoke curling up the valleys where, a few evenings before, we had seen the lights gleaming through the dark.

In a day or two after we arrived at Stowey, we set out, I on my return home and he for Germany. It was a Sunday morning and he was to preach that day for Dr Toulmin of Taunton. I asked him if he had prepared anything for the occasion. He said he had not even thought of the text, but should as soon as we parted. I did not go to hear him (this was a fault) but we met in the evening at Bridg-water. The next day we had a long day's walk to Bristol, and sat down, I recollect, by a well-side on the road, to cool ourselves and satisfy our thirst, when Coleridge repeated to me some descriptive lines from his tragedy of *Remorse*, which I must say became his mouth and that occasion better than they, some years after, did Mr Elliston's[109] and the Drury Lane boards:

> Oh memory, shield me from the world's poor strife
> And give those scenes thine everlasting life.[110]

I saw no more of him for a year or two, during which period he had been wandering in the Hartz Forest in Germany,[111] and his return was cometary, meteorous (unlike his setting-out). It was not till some time after that I knew his friends Lamb[112] and Southey. The last always appears to me as I first saw him, with a commonplace book under his arm;[113] and the first with a *bon mot* in his mouth. It was at Godwin's that I met him with Holcroft and Coleridge, where they were disputing fiercely which was the best – man as he was, or man as he is to be. 'Give me', says Lamb, 'man as he is *not* to be.' This saying was the beginning of a friendship between us which I believe still continues. Enough of this for the present.

> But there is matter for another rhyme,
> And I to this may add a second tale.[114]

---

[104]   Jeremy Taylor (1613–67), prose stylist famous for *Holy Living* (1650) and *Holy Dying* (1651).
[105]   novel by Godwin (1794).
[106]   *The Ancient Mariner* (1798) 219.
[107]   *Butler* see p. 604 n. 53.
[108]   *elsewhere* in his essay 'Remarks on the Systems of Hartley and Helvetius'.
[109]   Robert William Elliston (1774–1831), famous actor who appeared in *Remorse* when first produced at Drury Lane theatre, 1813.
[110]   The quotation is not to be found in *Remorse* or any other work by Coleridge.

[111]   *during which . . . Germany* Coleridge was in Germany from September 1798 to July 1799.
[112]   Hazlitt was introduced to Lamb by Coleridge in 1804; in that year Hazlitt painted Lamb's portrait, now in the National Portrait Gallery.
[113]   Hazlitt's first serious acquaintance with Southey was in the Lakes, September–November 1803.
[114]   Wordsworth, *Hart-Leap Well* 95–6. Hazlitt wrote no sequel to this essay.

Mr Coleridge

From THE SPIRIT OF THE AGE (1825)

The present is an age of talkers, and not of doers – and the reason is that the world is growing old. We are so far advanced in the arts and sciences, that we live in retrospect and dote on past achievements. The accumulation of knowledge has been so great that we are lost in wonder at the height it has reached, instead of attempting to climb or add to it; while the variety of objects distracts and dazzles the looker-on.

What niche remains unoccupied? What path untried? What is the use of doing anything unless we could do better than all those who have gone before us? What hope is there of this? We are like those who have been to see some noble monument of art, who are content to admire without thinking of rivalling it – or, like guests after a feast, who praise the hospitality of the donor 'and thank the bounteous Pan',[1] perhaps carrying away some trifling fragments – or, like the spectators of a mighty battle, who still hear its sound afar off, and the clashing of armour and the neighing of the warhorse and the shout of victory is in their ears, like the rushing of innumerable waters!

Mr. Coleridge has 'a mind reflecting ages past'.[2] His voice is like the echo of the congregated roar of the 'dark rearward and abyss'[3] of thought. He who has seen a mouldering tower by the side of a crystal lake, hid by the mist but glittering in the wave below, may conceive the dim, gleaming, uncertain intelligence of his eye; he who has marked the evening clouds uprolled (a world of vapours) has seen the picture of his mind – unearthly, unsubstantial, with gorgeous tints and ever-varying forms:

> That which was now a horse, even with a thought
> The rack dislimns, and makes it indistinct
> As water is in water.[4]

Our author's mind is (as he himself might express it) *tangential*. There is no subject on which he has not touched, none on which he has rested. With an understanding fertile, subtle, expansive, 'quick, forgetive,[5] apprehensive'[6] beyond all living precedent, few traces of it will perhaps remain. He lends himself to all impressions alike; he gives up his mind and liberty of thought to none. He is a general lover of art and science, and wedded to no one in particular. He pursues knowledge as a mistress, with outstretched hands and winged speed, but as he is about to embrace her, his Daphne turns – alas, not to a laurel![7] Hardly a speculation has been left on record from the earliest time, but it is loosely folded up in Mr Coleridge's memory, like a rich but somewhat tattered piece of tapestry. We might add (with more seeming than real extravagance) that scarce a thought can pass through the mind of man, but its sound has at some time or other passed over his head with rustling pinions.

On whatever question or author you speak, he is prepared to take up the theme with advantage – from Peter Abelard[8] down to Thomas Moore,[9] from the subtlest metaphysics to the politics of *The Courier*.[10] There is no man of genius in whose praise he descants,[11] but the critic seems to stand above the author, and 'what in him is weak, to strengthen; what is low, to raise and support'.[12] Nor is there any work of genius that does not come out of his hands like an illuminated missal,[13] sparkling even in its defects.

MR COLERIDGE

[1] Milton, *Comus* 175. Pan, god of woods and shepherds, was the subject of festivals in ancient Rome.

[2] I.M.S., 'On Worthy Master Shakespeare and his Poems' 1, prefixed to the second Folio (1632).

[3] *The Tempest* I ii 50.

[4] *Antony and Cleopatra* IV xiv 9–11.

[5] *forgetive* inventive.

[6] *2 Henry IV* IV iii 99.

[7] In Greek myth, Daphne was pursued by Apollo; on the point of capture, she was turned by the gods into a laurel tree.

[8] Pierre Abailard (1079–1142), medieval French theologian.

[9] *Thomas Moore* poet, see pp. 617–19.

[10] *The Courier* was an evening paper to which Coleridge contributed; Hazlitt resented Coleridge's involvement with it because of its Tory sympathies.

[11] *descants* discourses.

[12] *Paradise Lost* i 22–3.

[13] *illuminated missal* book containing Roman Catholic liturgy, with hand-painted illustrations and decorations.

If Mr Coleridge had not been the most impressive talker of his age, he would probably have been the finest writer – but he lays down his pen to make sure of an auditor, and mortgages the admiration of posterity for the stare of an idler. If he had not been a poet, he would have been a powerful logician; if he had not dipped his wing in the Unitarian controversy, he might have soared to the very summit of fancy. But in writing verse, he is trying to subject the muse to *transcendental* theories; in his abstract reasoning, he misses his way by strewing it with flowers. All that he has done of moment, he had done twenty years ago; since then he may be said to have lived on the sounds of his own voice. Mr Coleridge is too rich in intellectual wealth to need to task himself to any drudgery – he has only to draw the sliders[14] of his imagination, and a thousand subjects expand before him, startling him with their brilliancy, or losing themselves in endless obscurity,

> And by the force of blear illusion,[15]
> They draw him on to his confusion.[16]

What is the little he could add to the stock, compared with the countless stores that lie about him, that he should stoop to pick up a name, or to polish an idle fancy? He walks abroad in the majesty of an universal understanding, eyeing the 'rich strond',[17] or golden sky above him, and 'goes sounding on his way',[18] in eloquent accents, uncompelled and free!

Persons of the greatest capacity are often those who, for this reason, do the least – for, surveying themselves from the highest point of view amidst the infinite variety of the universe, their own share in it seems trifling and scarce worth a thought, and they prefer the contemplation of all that is, or has been, or can be, to the making a coil[19] about doing what (when done) is no better than vanity. It is hard to concentrate all our attention and efforts on one pursuit, except from ignorance of others, and, without this concentration of our faculties, no great progress can be made in any one thing. It is not merely that the mind is not capable of the effort; it does not think the effort worth making. Action is one, but thought is manifold. He whose restless eye glances through the wide compass of nature and art will not consent to have 'his own nothings monstered',[20] but he must do this before he can give his whole soul to them. The mind, after 'letting contemplation have its fill',[21] or

> Sailing with supreme dominion
> Through the azure deep of air,[22]

sinks down on the ground, breathless, exhausted, powerless, inactive, or, if it must have some vent to its feelings, seeks the most easy and obvious – is soothed by friendly flattery, lulled by the murmur of immediate applause, thinks as it were aloud, and babbles in its dreams! A scholar (so to speak) is a more disinterested and abstracted character than a mere author: the first looks at the numberless volumes of a library, and says, 'All these are mine'; the other points to a single volume (perhaps it may be an immortal one) and says, 'My name is written on the back of it'. This is a puny and grovelling ambition beneath the lofty amplitude of Mr Coleridge's mind. No, he revolves in his wayward soul, or utters to the passing wind, or discourses to his own shadow things mightier and more various! Let us draw the curtain and unlock the shrine.

Learning rocked him in his cradle, and, while yet a child, 'He lisped in numbers, for the numbers came'.[23] At sixteen he wrote his 'Ode on Chatterton',[24] and he still reverts to that period with

---

[14]   *draw the sliders* open the shutters.
[15]   *blear illusion* Milton, *Comus* 155.
[16]   *Macbeth* III v 28–9.
[17]   *rich strond* Spenser, *Faerie Queene* III iv stanza 34 2
[18]   *goes sounding on his way* probably, as P. P. Howe has suggested, a confused recollection of several lines from Chaucer and Wordsworth. In the General Prologue to *The Canterbury Tales*, the Merchant is described as 'Sownynge alwey th' encrees of his wynnyng' (l.275), and of the Clerk Chaucer writes: 'Sownynge in moral vertu was his speche' (l.307). Hazlitt may also be recalling Wordsworth, *Excursion* iii 701

('Went sounding on a dim and perilous way'), to which Coleridge alludes at the end of *Biographia Literaria* chapter 5.
[19]   *coil* fuss.
[20]   *Coriolanus* II ii 77; *monstered* put on show.
[21]   John Dyer, *Grongar Hill* (1761) 26.
[22]   Gray, *The Progress of Poesy* 116–17.
[23]   Pope, *Epistle to Dr Arbuthnot* 128: 'I lisp'd in numbers, for the numbers came'.
[24]   Coleridge's *Monody on the Death of Chatterton* seems to date from 1790, when he was still at Christ's Hospital.

delight, not so much as it relates to himself (for that string of his own early promise of fame rather jars than otherwise), but as exemplifying the youth of a poet. Mr Coleridge talks of himself without being an egotist, for in him the individual is always merged in the abstract and general. He distinguished himself at school and at the University[25] by his knowledge of the classics, and gained several prizes for Greek epigrams.[26] (How many men are there – great scholars, celebrated names in literature – who, having done the same thing in their youth, have no other idea all the rest of their lives . but of this achievement, of a fellowship and dinner, and who, installed in academic honours, would look down on our author as a mere strolling bard!) At Christ's Hospital where he was brought up, he was the idol of those among his schoolfellows who mingled with their bookish studies the music of thought and of humanity, and he was usually attended round the cloisters by a group of these (inspiring and inspired) whose hearts, even then, burnt within them as he talked, and where the sounds yet linger to mock Elia[27] on his way, still turning pensive to the past![28]

One of the finest and rarest parts of Mr Coleridge's conversation is when he expatiates[29] on the Greek tragedians (not that he is not well-acquainted, when he pleases, with the epic poets, or the philosophers, or orators, or historians of antiquity) – on the subtle reasonings and melting pathos of Euripides; on the harmonious gracefulness of Sophocles, tuning his love-laboured song like sweetest warblings from a sacred grove; on the high-wrought trumpet-tongued eloquence of Aeschylus, whose Prometheus, above all, is like an Ode to Fate and a pleading with Providence, his thoughts being let loose as his body is chained on his solitary rock,[30] and his afflicted will (the emblem of mortality) 'Struggling in vain with ruthless destiny'.[31] As the impassioned critic speaks and rises in his theme, you would think you heard the voice of the man hated by the gods contending with the wild winds as they roar, and his eye glitters with the spirit of antiquity!

Next he was engaged with Hartley's tribes of mind, 'ethereal braid, thought-woven',[32] and he busied himself for a year or two with vibrations and vibratiuncles and the great law of association that binds all things in its mystic chain, and the doctrine of necessity (the mild teacher of charity) and the millennium, anticipative of a life to come;[33] and he plunged deep into the controversy on matter and spirit, and, as an escape from Dr Priestley's materialism[34] (where he felt himself imprisoned by the logician's spell like Ariel in the cloven pine-tree),[35] he became suddenly enamoured of Bishop Berkeley's fairy-world,[36] and used in all companies to build the universe (like a brave poetical fiction) of fine words; and he was deep-read in Malebranche,[37] and in Cudworth's *Intellectual System*[38] (a huge pile of learning – unwieldy, enormous), and in Lord Brook's hieroglyphic theories,[39] and in Bishop Butler's *Sermons*,[40] and in the Duchess of Newcastle's fantastic folios,[41] and in Clarke and South and Tillotson,[42] and all the fine thinkers and masculine reasoners of that age – and Leibniz's *Pre-established Harmony*[43] reared its arch above his head, like the rainbow in the cloud, covenanting with the hopes

[25] Coleridge attended Jesus College, Cambridge, 1791–4.

[26] In June 1792 Coleridge was awarded the Browne Medal for Greek verse at Cambridge.

[27] *Elia* Charles Lamb's pen-name (see pp. 580–1).

[28] Hazlitt refers to Lamb's essay, 'Christ's Hospital Five and Thirty Years Ago'.

[29] *expatiates* discourses at length.

[30] *chained on his solitary rock* Jupiter nailed Prometheus to a rock (the Caucasus) for 30,000 years, with an eagle incessantly devouring his liver.

[31] Wordsworth, *The Excursion* vi 557.

[32] Collins, *Ode to Evening* 7. In *Ode on the Poetical Character* 47, Collins refers to 'the shad'wy tribes of mind'.

[33] *vibrations . . . life to come* features of Hartleian philosophy, also a strong influence on Wordsworth; see p. 291 n. 22.

[34] Joseph Priestley, *Disquisitions Relating to Matter and Spirit* (1777). Coleridge was for a long time a disciple of Priestleyan Unitarianism.

[35] *The Tempest* I ii 277–9.

[36] *Bishop Berkeley's fairy-world* George Berkeley (1685–1753), Bishop of Cloyne, argued that the material world was no more than an idea in the mind of God.

[37] Nicolas Malebranche (1638–1715), *De La Recherche de la Vérité* (1674).

[38] Ralph Cudworth (1617–88), *True Intellectual System of the Universe* (1678).

[39] Robert Greville, second Baron Brooke (1608–43), *The Nature of Truth, its Union and Unity with the Soul* (1640).

[40] Joseph Butler, Bishop of Bristol (1692–1752), whose *Fifteen Sermons* (1726) preached at the Rolls Chapel defines his moral philosophy.

[41] Margaret Cavendish, Duchess of Newcastle (1624–74) published plays, essays and poetry in large folio volumes.

[42] Samuel Clarke (1657–1729), metaphysician; Robert South (1634–1716), divine and sermonist; John Tillotson (1630–94), Archbishop of Canterbury and renowned Anglican sermonist.

[43] Gottfried Wilhelm Leibniz (1646–1716) assumed a 'pre-established harmony' to exist between matter and spirit; see his *Monadology* (1714).

of man; and then he fell plump ten thousand fathoms down (but his wings saved him harmless) into the *hortus siccus* of Dissent,[44] where he pared religion down to the standard of reason and stripped faith of mystery, and preached Christ crucified and the Unity of the Godhead, and so dwelt for a while in the spirit with John Huss and Jerome of Prague and Socinus and old John Zisca,[45] and ran through Neal's *History of the Puritans*, and Calamy's *Non-Conformists' Memorial*[46] (having like thoughts and passions with them); but then Spinoza[47] became his god and he took up the vast chain of being in his hand, and the round world became the centre and the soul of all things in some shadowy sense forlorn of meaning, and around him he beheld the living traces and the sky-pointing proportions of the mighty Pan; but poetry redeemed him from this spectral philosophy,[48] and he bathed his heart in beauty, and gazed at the golden light of heaven, and drank of the spirit of the universe, and wandered at eve by fairy-stream or fountain,

> When he saw nought but beauty,
> When he heard the voice of that Almighty One
> In every breeze that blew, or wave that murmured,[49]

and wedded with truth in Plato's shade, and in the writings of Proclus and Plotinus[50] saw the ideas of things in the eternal mind, and unfolded all mysteries with the schoolmen,[51] and fathomed the depths of Duns Scotus and Thomas Aquinas, and entered the third heaven with Jacob Behmen, and walked hand in hand with Swedenborg[52] through the pavilions of the New Jerusalem, and sung his faith in the promise and in the word in his *Religious Musings*[53] – and lowering himself from that dizzy height, poised himself on Milton's wings, and spread out his thoughts in charity with the glad prose of Jeremy Taylor,[54] and wept over Bowles' sonnets,[55] and studied Cowper's blank verse,[56] and betook himself to Thomson's *Castle of Indolence*,[57] and sported with the wits of Charles the Second's days[58] and of Queen Anne,[59] and relished Swift's style and that of the *John Bull* (Arbuthnot's we mean – not Mr Croker's[60]), and dallied with the *British Essayists* and *Novelists*,[61] and knew all qualities of more modern writers with a learned spirit, Johnson and Goldsmith and Junius[62] and Burke and Godwin, and the *Sorrows of Werter*,[63] and Jean Jacques Rousseau and Voltaire and Marivaux and Crebillon,[64] and thousands more; now 'laughed with Rabelais in his easy chair'[65] or pointed to Hogarth, or afterwards dwelt on Claude's classic scenes or spoke with rapture of Raphael,[66] and compared the women

---

44   *the hortus siccus of Dissent* a *hortus siccus* is a collection of dried flowers. The phrase comes from Burke, *Reflections on the Revolution in France* (1790), p. 15.

45   John Huss (1369–1415), Bohemian theologian; Jerome of Prague (died 1416), colleague of Huss; Socinus was the Latinized name of two Italian theologians, Fausto Paolo Sozzini (1539–1604) and Lelio Sozzini (1525–62); John Zisca (died 1424), Czech soldier and religious leader.

46   Daniel Neal, *History of the Puritans* (1732–8); Edmund Calamy, *Non-Conformists' Memorial* (abridged 1775).

47   Benedict Spinoza (1632–77), Dutch philosopher.

48   *spectral philosophy* philosophy concerned with spectres, ghosts.

49   Coleridge, *Remorse* IV ii 100–2.

50   Proclus (410–85) and Plotinus (204–70), Platonist philosophers.

51   *schoolmen* medieval scholars and theologians.

52   Duns Scotus (1265–1308), Scottish medieval philosopher; Thomas Aquinas (1227–74), medieval philosopher; Jacob Behmen (1575–1624), German mystic; Emanuel Swedenborg (1688–1772), Swedish mystic (for whom see p. 54).

53   Poem by Coleridge, 1794–6, see pp. 455–6.

54   Jeremy Taylor (1613–67), prose stylist famous for *Holy Living* (1650) and *Holy Dying* (1651).

55   *Bowles' sonnets* see pp. 154–5.

56   *Cowper's blank verse* probably *The Task*; see pp. 8–12.

57   James Thomson, *The Castle of Indolence* (1748), popular poem in Spenserian stanzas.

58   Charles II reigned 1660–85.

59   Queen Anne reigned 1702–14.

60   *The History of John Bull*, collection of pamphlets by John Arbuthnot (1667–1735), issued 1712. *John Bull* was also the name of a Tory newspaper which began publishing on 17 December 1820, but there is no evidence that John Wilson Croker (1780–1857), Tory politician and man of letters, was involved in its production.

61   *British Essayists* (1817), issued in 45 volumes; *British Novelists* ed. Mrs. Barbauld (1810).

62   'Junius' was the pseudonym of Sir Philip Francis (1740–1818), author of a series of letters published in the *Public Advertiser*, January 1769 to January 1772, attacking Tory worthies.

63   novel by Goethe (1774).

64   Jean Jacques Rousseau (1712–78), French novelist and philosopher; François-Marie Arouet (1694–1778) wrote under the pseudonym of Voltaire; Pierre Carlet de Chamblain de Marivaux (1688–1763), French novelist; Crébillon the elder (1674–1762), dramatist.

65   Pope, *Dunciad* i 20.

66   Coleridge saw priceless sketches by Raphael at Helmstedt, 3 July 1799.

at Rome[67] to figures that had walked out of his pictures, or visited the Oratory of Pisa,[68] and described the works of Giotto and Ghirlandaio and Massaccio, and gave the moral of the picture of the Triumph of Death[69] (where the beggars and the wretched invoke his dreadful dart but the rich and mighty of the earth quail and shrink before it); and in that land of siren sights and sounds saw a dance of peasant girls, and was charmed with lutes and gondolas; or wandered into Germany and lost himself in the labyrinths of the Hartz Forest[70] and of the Kantean philosophy, and amongst the cabalistic[71] names of Fichte and Schelling and Lessing[72] and God knows who – this was long after, but all the former while he had nerved his heart and filled his eyes with tears, as he hailed the rising orb of liberty (since quenched in darkness and in blood), and had kindled his affections at the blaze of the French Revolution, and sang for joy[73] when the towers of the Bastille and the proud places of the insolent and the oppressor fell,[74] and would have floated his bark, freighted with fondest fancies, across the Atlantic wave with Southey and others[75] to seek for peace and freedom, 'In Philarmonia's[76] undivided dale!'[77]

Alas! 'Frailty, thy name is *Genius*!'[78] What is become of all this mighty heap of hope, of thought, of learning, and humanity? It has ended in swallowing doses of oblivion[79] and in writing paragraphs in the *Courier*. Such, and so little, is the mind of man!

It was not to be supposed that Mr Coleridge could keep on at the rate he set off; he could not realize all he knew or thought, and less could not fix his desultory ambition. Other stimulants supplied the place, and kept up the intoxicating dream, the fever and the madness of his early impressions. Liberty (the philosopher's and the poet's bride) had fallen a victim, meanwhile, to the murderous practices of the hag Legitimacy. Proscribed by court-hirelings, too romantic for the herd of vulgar politicians, our enthusiast stood at bay, and at last turned on the pivot of a subtle casuistry to the *unclean side* – but his discursive reason would not let him trammel himself into a Poet Laureate or stamp-distributor,[80] and he stopped, ere he had quite passed that well-known 'bourne from whence no traveller returns',[81] and so has sunk into torpid, uneasy repose, tantalized by useless resources, haunted by vain imaginings, his lips idly moving but his heart forever still, or, as the shattered chords vibrate of themselves, making melancholy music to the ear of memory!

Such is the fate of genius in an age when, in the unequal contest with sovereign wrong, every man is ground to powder who is not either a born slave, or who does not willingly and at once offer up the yearnings of humanity and the dictates of reason as a welcome sacrifice to besotted prejudice and loathsome power.

Of all Mr Coleridge's productions, *The Ancient Mariner* is the only one that we could with confidence put into any person's hands, on whom we wished to impress a favourable idea of his extraordinary powers. Let whatever other objections be made to it, it is unquestionably a work of genius – of wild, irregular, overwhelming imagination, and has that rich, varied movement in the verse which gives a distant idea of the lofty or changeful tones of Mr Coleridge's voice. In the *Christabel*, there is one splendid passage on divided friendship. The translation of Schiller's *Wallenstein*[82] is also a masterly production in its kind, faithful and spirited. Among his smaller pieces there are occasional

---

[67] Coleridge was at Rome, January–May 1806.

[68] Coleridge travelled to Pisa from Rome, June 1806.

[69] *the picture . . . Death* anonymous painting, sometimes attributed to the fourteenth-century artist, Francesco Traini.

[70] *wandered into Germany . . . Forest* Coleridge visited Germany, 1798–9.

[71] *cabalistic* esoteric, abstruse.

[72] Johann Gottlieb Fichte (1762–1814), Friedrich Wilhelm von Schelling (1775–1854), and Gotthold Ephraim Lessing (1729–81), German philosophers.

[73] *sang for joy* a reference to Coleridge's 1789 poem, *Destruction of the Bastille*, first published 1834.

[74] *when the towers . . . fell* the Bastille prison, symbol of the tyranny of the *ancien régime*, was stormed by the Paris mob on 14 July 1789, and later demolished.

[75] *across the Atlantic . . . others* a reference to pantisocracy; see p. 447.

[76] *Philarmonia* love of order.

[77] Coleridge's *Monody on the Death of Chatterton* (1796) 129.

[78] Compare *Hamlet* I ii 146.

[79] *swallowing . . . oblivion* a reference to Coleridge's opium addiction.

[80] Hazlitt swipes at Southey, who became Poet Laureate in 1813, and Wordsworth, Distributor of Stamps for Westmorland, 1813–42.

[81] *Hamlet* III i 78–9.

[82] Coleridge translated Johann Christoph Friedrich von Schiller (1759–1805), *The Piccolomini, or the first part of Wallenstein* and *The Death of Wallenstein*, and published them both in 1800.

bursts of pathos and fancy equal to what we might expect from him, but these form the exception and not the rule; such, for instance, is his affecting sonnet to the author of *The Robbers*:[83]

> Schiller! that hour I would have wished to die,
>   If through the shudd'ring midnight I had sent
>   From the dark dungeon of the tower time-rent
> That fearful voice, a famished father's cry,
> That in no after-moment aught less vast
>   Might stamp me mortal! A triumphant shout
>   Black horror screamed, and all her goblin rout
> From the more with'ring scene diminished passed.
> Ah, bard tremendous in sublimity!
>   Could I behold thee in thy loftier mood,
> Wand'ring at eve, with finely frenzied eye,
>   Beneath some vast old tempest-swinging wood –
> Awhile, with mute awe gazing, I would brood,
> Then weep aloud in a wild ecstasy.

His tragedy entitled *Remorse*[84] is full of beautiful and striking passages, but it does not place the author in the first rank of dramatic writers. But if Mr Coleridge's works do not place him in that rank, they injure instead of conveying a just idea of the man, for he himself is certainly in the first class of general intellect.

If our author's poetry is inferior to his conversation, his prose is utterly abortive. Hardly a gleam is to be found in it of the brilliancy and richness of those stores of thought and language that he pours out incessantly, when they are lost like drops of water in the ground. The principal work in which he has attempted to embody his general views of things is *The Friend*,[85] of which, though it contains some noble passages and fine trains of thought, prolixity and obscurity are the most frequent characteristics.

No two persons can be conceived more opposite in character or genius than the subject of the present and of the preceding sketch. Mr Godwin, with less natural capacity and with fewer acquired advantages, by concentrating his mind on some given object and doing what he had to do with all his might, has accomplished much and will leave more than one monument of a powerful intellect behind him; Mr Coleridge, by dissipating his and dallying with every subject by turns, has done little or nothing to justify to the world or to posterity the high opinion which all who have ever heard him converse, or known him intimately, with one accord entertain of him. Mr Godwin's faculties have kept house and plied their task in the workshop of the brain, diligently and effectually; Mr Coleridge's have gossipped away their time and gadded about from house to house, as if life's business were[86] to melt the hours in listless talk. Mr Godwin is intent on a subject only as it concerns himself and his reputation; he works it out as a matter of duty, and discards from his mind whatever does not forward his main object as impertinent and vain. Mr Coleridge, on the other hand, delights in nothing but episodes and digressions, neglects whatever he undertakes to perform, and can act only on spontaneous impulses, without object or method: 'He cannot be constrained by mastery.'[87] While he should be occupied with a given pursuit, he is thinking of a thousand other things; a thousand tastes, a thousand objects tempt him and distract his mind, which keeps open house and entertains all comers and, after being fatigued and amused with morning calls from idle visitors, finds the day consumed and its business unconcluded. Mr Godwin, on the contrary, is somewhat exclusive and unsocial in his habits of mind, entertains no company but what he gives his whole time and attention to, and wisely writes over the doors of his understanding, his fancy, and his senses, 'No admittance except on

---

83   *The Robbers* another play by Schiller.
84   Produced at Drury Lane Theatre, 23 January 1813.
85   Weekly periodical edited by Coleridge, 1808–10.
86   *as if life's business were* an echo of Wordsworth *Resolution and Independence* 37: 'As if life's business were a summer mood'.

87   Chaucer, *The Franklin's Tale* 764: 'Love wol nat been constreyned by maistrye'.

business'. He has none of that fastidious refinement and false delicacy which might lead him to balance between the endless variety of modern attainments. He does not throw away his life (nor a single half-hour of it) in adjusting the claims of different accomplishments, and in choosing between them or making himself master of them all. He sets about his task, whatever it may be, and goes through it with spirit and fortitude. He has the happiness to think an author the greatest character in the world, and himself the greatest author in it. Mr Coleridge, in writing an harmonious stanza, would stop to consider whether there was not more grace and beauty in a *pas de trois*,[88] and would not proceed till he had resolved this question by a chain of metaphysical reasoning without end. Not so Mr Godwin. That is best to him which he can do best. He does not waste himself in vain aspirations and effeminate sympathies. He is blind, deaf, insensible to all but the trump of fame. Plays, operas, painting, music, ballrooms, wealth, fashion, titles, lords, ladies, touch him not: all these are no more to him than to the anchorite in his cell, and he writes on to the end of the chapter through good report and evil report. *Pingo in eternitatem*[89] is his motto. He neither envies nor admires what others are, but is contented to be what he is, and strives to do the utmost he can. Mr Coleridge has flirted with the muses as with a set of mistresses; Mr Godwin has been married twice – to Reason and to Fancy – and has to boast no short-lived progeny by each. So to speak, he has *valves* belonging to his mind to regulate the quantity of gas admitted into it, so that, like the bare, unsightly, but well-compacted steam-vessel, it cuts its liquid way, and arrives at its promised end; while Mr Coleridge's bark, 'taught with the little nautilus to sail',[90] the sport of every breath, dancing to every wave, 'Youth at its prow, and Pleasure at its helm',[91] flutters its gaudy pennons in the air, glitters in the sun, but we wait in vain to hear of its arrival in the destined harbour. Mr Godwin, with less variety and vividness, with less subtlety and susceptibility both of thought and feeling, has had firmer nerves, a more determined purpose, a more comprehensive grasp of his subject, and the results are as we find them. Each has met with his reward – for justice has, after all, been done to the pretensions of each, and we must in all cases use means to ends!

Thomas Moore (1779–1852)

Moore was the son of a Dublin grocer, John Moore, and Anastasia Codd, a Catholic convert. He had two younger sisters. At school he was an early success, attending a private school at the age of six, where he won a medal for history, before enrolment at the English Grammar School a year later. He became a distinguished classicist, and enjoyed poetry, music, and acting. His first published poem appeared when he was fourteen.

He entered Trinity College, where he became embroiled in radical politics, and was a friend of Robert Emmet and Edward Hudson, who were involved in the uprising of the United Irishmen under Wolfe Tone in 1798. Tone died in prison, Hudson went into exile, and Emmet was hanged five years later. Moore's suspected involvement was investigated by the university authorities, but he conducted himself with such diplomacy that they allowed him to graduate in 1799.

He published a highly popular translation of the Greek love poet Anacreon in 1800 that won him the soubriquet of 'Anacreon Moore', and followed that up with an equally love-obsessed (some thought lubricious) volume, *Poetical Works of Thomas Little, Esq.* (1801).[1] His new patron, the Earl of Moira, wangled him the sinecure of registrar in the admiralty prize-

---

88 *pas de trois* dance for three people.
89 'I delineate for all time'.
90 Pope, *Essay on Man* iii 177.
91 Gray, *The Bard* 74.

THOMAS MOORE
1 It was shrewd of Moore to publish under the name of Thomas Little; the poems were regarded as virtually pornographic for years after their first appearance. As late as 1853 his editor, Lord John Russell (Bertrand Russell's grandfather) remarked: 'Some of Little's poems should never have been written, far less published, but they must now be classed with those of other amatory poets who have allowed their fancy to roam beyond the limits which morality and decorum would prescribe' (*Memoirs, Journal, and Correspondence of Thomas Moore* ed. Lord John Russell (8 vols, London, 1853), i xxvi).

court in Bermuda, which he took up in January 1804. It took him only three months to discover the true boredom of a desk-job, and he abandoned it to a minion in favour of a tour of America and Canada. Not finding North America to his taste, he returned to literary London and published his *Epistles, Odes, and Other Poems* in 1806. When Jeffrey greeted it with condemnation in the *Edinburgh Review*, he challenged him to a duel, stopped only at the last moment by the intervention of the authorities. As a result, Moore and Jeffrey became good friends, and Moore began reviewing for the *Edinburgh*.

His most important poetic achievement was probably the enterprise launched by James and William Power, brothers who published in London and Dublin. They asked him to set words to a number of traditional Irish tunes recently transcribed at a convocation of harpists. Moore's *Irish Melodies* turned into a lifelong pursuit, extending over ten volumes, from 1808 to 1834. These nationalistic songs portrayed his native country as it suffered under the oppression of the English; they have proved enduringly popular throughout the English-speaking world. They led to friendship with Byron, who was to give him his treasured memoirs at La Mira, near Venice, in 1822. Among friends, Moore often sang his melodies, accompanying himself on the guitar.

Further works included *Lalla Rookh* (1817) and *The Fudge Family in Paris* (1818), both of which sold widely. Moore's luck ran out in 1819, when his deputy in Bermuda absconded with £6,000 for which Moore was liable. He went abroad, travelling through Italy with Lord John Russell, and settling in Paris for nearly two years. In 1822 he returned to England, his debts having been cleared. After Byron's death at Missolonghi in 1824, an argument ensued over the memoirs which had been entrusted to Moore; in the end, Byron's publisher John Murray burnt them, unread, in his fireplace. Moore set about the writing of a biography of his old friend, and published his *Letters, Journals of Lord Byron* in 1830. He continued to write throughout the 1830s and 40s, and set about a mammoth four-volume *History of Ireland* in 1835 (completed 1846). In that year he was awarded a pension of £300 a year, and the esteem in which he was held as a literary figure no doubt encouraged him to embark on his edition of *The Poetical Works of Thomas Moore*, published in ten volumes in 1841. He became senile in 1849, and died in 1852.

Further reading

Thomas Moore, *The Poetical Works of Thomas Little 1801* introduced by Jonathan Wordsworth (Spelsbury, 1990)

Love in a Storm

From THE POETICAL WORKS OF THE LATE THOMAS LITTLE ESQ. (1801)

Loud sung the wind in the ruins above
 Which murmured the warnings of time o'er our head,
While fearless we offered devotions to love,
 The rude rock our pillow, the rushes our bed!

Damp was the chill of the wintery air,   5
 But it made us cling closer, and warmly unite;
Dread was the lightning, and horrid its glare,
 But it showed me my Julia in languid delight.

To my bosom she nestled and felt not a fear
 Though the shower did beat and the tempest did frown; 10
Her sighs were as sweet and her murmurs as dear
 As if she lay lulled on a pillow of down!

[Believe me, if all those endearing young charms]

From IRISH MELODIES (2nd edn, 1822)

Believe me, if all those endearing young charms,
    Which I gaze on so fondly today,
Were to change by tomorrow, and fleet in my arms,
    Like fairy gifts fading away,
Thou wouldst still be adored, as this moment thou art,   5
    Let thy loveliness fade as it will,
And, around the dear ruin, each wish of my heart
    Would entwine itself verdantly still.

It is not – while beauty and youth are thine own,
    And thy cheeks unprofaned by a tear –   10
That the fervour and faith of a soul can be known,
    To which time will but make thee more dear!
Oh, the heart that has truly loved never forgets,
    But as truly loves on to the close,
As the sunflower turns on her god, when he sets,   15
    The same look which she turned when he rose!

[In the morning of life]

From IRISH MELODIES (2nd edn, 1822)

In the morning of life, when its cares are unknown,
    And its pleasures in all their new lustre begin,
When we live in a bright-beaming world of our own,
    And the light that surrounds us is all from within –
Oh it is not, believe me, in that happy time   5
    We can love, as in hours of less transport we may;
Of our smiles, of our hopes, 'tis the gay sunny prime,
    But affection is warmest when these fade away.

When we see the first glory of youth pass us by,
    Like a leaf on the stream that will never return;   10
When our cup, which had sparkled with pleasure so high,
    First tastes of the *other*, the dark flowing urn –
Then, then is the moment affection can sway
    With a depth and a tenderness joy never knew;
Love, nursed among pleasures, is faithless as they,   15
    But the love born of sorrow, like sorrow is true!

In climes full of sunshine, though splendid their dyes,
    Yet faint is the odour the flow'rs shed about;
'Tis the clouds and the mists of our own weeping skies,
    That call the full spirit of fragrancy out.   20
So the wild glow of passion may kindle from mirth,
    But 'tis only in grief true affection appears;
And, ev'n though to smiles it may first owe its birth,
    All the soul of its sweetness is drawn out by tears!

James Henry Leigh Hunt   (1784–1859)

Leigh Hunt was born on 19 October 1784 to Isaac and Mary Hunt, American Loyalists whose allegiance to George III led them to move to England shortly before their son's birth. Hunt was educated at Christ's Hospital (1791–9) in the wake of Dyer, Coleridge and Lamb, and published his youthful verse in *Juvenilia* in 1801. In 1808, with his brother John, he set up *The Examiner*, a radical, reforming newspaper that gained immediate popularity. Also, from 1810 to 1811 he edited *The Reflector*, which contained some of Lamb's best early writings.

He and his brother were imprisoned in 1813 for libelling the Prince Regent in their leading article in *The Examiner* for 22 March 1812 – entitled 'The Prince on St Patrick's Day'. The Hunts had been sailing close to the wind for a while, criticizing the future George IV for his debaucheries and, in the immediate context, expressing their 'indignation at the Regent's breaking his promises to the Irish'.[1] They were convicted, and spent the next two years in prison, widely regarded as martyrs to the radical cause. This made him even more of a literary celebrity than he would otherwise have been, and the authorities of the Surrey Jail had little choice but to make his residence as pleasant as they could. The walls of his cell were covered with rose-trellised wallpaper, he was allowed to have food sent in, as many books as he wanted, continued to edit *The Examiner* from his cell, and received guests at will. Visitors included the Lambs, Byron, Hazlitt, Haydon and Thomas Moore.

After his release in February 1815 he moved to the Vale of Health, Hampstead, where in 1816 he completed *The Story of Rimini*, dedicated to Byron, which he regarded as the most important of his poems. *Foliage* was published in 1818 (by far the most interesting of his volumes), followed by *Hero and Leander* and *Bacchus and Ariadne* (1819). During these years Keats found him an enormous encouragement and help at a time when he needed a mentor, but it has to be said that Hunt was responsible for many of the excesses of Keats's literary style – stemming from an over-indulgence in sensuous language (see p. 1010). For this Keats was pilloried by hostile critics like Lockhart (see pp. 1006–9).[2] Nonetheless, at its best, Hunt's highly mannered poetry could result in such works as *To Hampstead*, and the sonnets to Shelley and

Keats, presented below. For the full context of the Shelley sonnets, the reader should consult the latter's assessment of Hunt's deism (p. 621 n. 1). 'A Now, Descriptive of a Hot Day', written partly in collaboration with Keats, illustrates Hunt's belief that the essay form was primarily a vehicle of 'pleasure'. His *Autobiography* recalls that 'the paper that was most liked by Keats, if I remember, was the one on a hot summer's day, entitled "A Now". He was with me while I was writing and reading it to him, and contributed one or two of the passages' (p. 281). It was published in another of his own journals, *The Indicator*, which ran from 1819 to 1821. Throughout this period Hunt, Keats and Hazlitt came in for fierce criticism, mainly from Tory reviewers hostile to their liberal opinions. One of the most virulent attacks was made by William Gifford in the *Quarterly Review*, to which Shelley mistakenly attributed Keats's early demise.[3]

In 1821, Shelley invited Hunt to live with him in Italy, with the idea that they and Byron might become joint editors of a new journal. Hunt and his family (which by then included seven children) arrived early in July 1822; on 8 July Shelley was drowned. Byron and Hunt went on to produce *The Liberal*, which contained work by Byron, Shelley, Hazlitt, Hunt and Hogg, among others. But the arrangement was unsatisfactory and the Hunts returned home in 1825.

In future years Hunt was very hard-working, publishing, besides others works, *Leigh Hunt's London Journal* (1834–5), *Imagination and Fancy* (1844), *Men, Women, and Books* (1847), his *Autobiography* (1850), *Table Talk* (1851), and many other titles. He was always hard up, but was helped by the award of a civil-list pension in 1847. His reputation was dented by an appearance as Skimpole in Dickens's *Bleak House* (1852–3), but he had the solace of continuing work to the last. He died in Putney and was buried at Kensal Green cemetery. He had been one of the most energetic and adventurous editors and publishers of the age, and the author of some enduringly entertaining poems and essays.

Further reading

Edmund Blunden, *Leigh Hunt: A Biography* (London, 1930)

JAMES HENRY LEIGH HUNT
[1]   Hunt's words, quoted Edmund Blunden, *Leigh Hunt: A Biography* (London, 1930), p. 69n.
[2]   A more detailed account of Hunt's aesthetic influence is given in my 'Leigh Hunt's "Cockney" Aesthetics', *Keats-Shelley Review* 10 (1996) 77–97.

[3]   See the Preface to *Adonais*, pp. 956–7, and James A. W. Heffernan, '*Adonais*: Shelley's Consumption of Keats', *Romanticism: A Critical Reader* 173–91.

The Autobiography of Leigh Hunt ed. J. E. Morpurgo (London, 1949)

Ann Blainey, Immortal Boy: A Portrait of Leigh Hunt (London, 1985)

Leigh Hunt: Selected Writings ed. David Jesson Dibley (Manchester, 1990)

Rodney Stenning Edgecombe, Leigh Hunt and the Poetry of Fancy (London and Toronto, 1994)

The Examiner, 1808–22, is currently being reprinted, in facsimile, by Pickering and Chatto, in 15 volumes.

To Hampstead (composed 7 May 1815)

From THE EXAMINER No. 385 (14 May 1815, p. 316)

As one who after long and far-spent years
   Comes on his mistress in an hour of sleep,
   And half-surprised that he can silence keep
Stands smiling o'er her through a flash of tears,
To see how sweet and self-same she appears;   5
   Till at his touch, with little moving creep
   Of joy, she wakes from out her calmness deep,
And then his heart finds voice, and dances round her ears –
So I, first coming on my haunts again,[1]
   In pause and stillness of the early prime,[2]   10
   Stood thinking of the past and present time
With earnest eyesight, scarcely crossed with pain;
   Till the fresh moving leaves, and startling birds,
   Loosened my long-suspended breath in words.

To Percy Shelley, on the Degrading Notions of Deity[1]

From FOLIAGE (1818)

What wonder, Percy, that with jealous rage
Men should defame the kindly and the wise,[2]
When in the midst of the all-beauteous skies,
And all this lovely world, that should engage
Their mutual search for the old golden age,   5
They seat a phantom,[3] swelled into grim size
Out of their own passions and bigotries,
And then, for fear, proclaim it meek and sage!
And this they call a light and a revealing!
Wise as the clown[4] who, plodding home at night   10

TO HAMPSTEAD

[1] *first coming on my haunts again* this was Hunt's first visit to Hampstead Heath since his incarceration in the Surrey Jail, 1813–15.

[2] *prime* about 6 a.m.

TO PERCY SHELLEY, ON THE DEGRADING NOTIONS OF DEITY

[1] This poem and the one that follows should be read in the light of Shelley's comments on Hunt's atheism, 8 May 1811: 'he is a Deist despising Jesus Christ, etc., etc., yet having a high veneration for the Deity. . . . with him God is neither omnipo-

tent, omnipresent, nor identical . . . he says that God *is* comprehensible, not doubting but an adequate exertion of reason . . . would lead us from a contemplation of his works to a definite knowledge of his attributes, which are by no means limited' (Jones i 77).

[2] *the kindly and the wise* presumably themselves (i.e. Hunt and Shelley). Shelley had been expelled from Oxford for publishing a pamphlet on 'The Necessity of Atheism'.

[3] *a phantom* i.e. conventional notions of God.

[4] *clown* untutored peasant.

In autumn, turns at call of fancied elf,
And sees upon the fog, with ghastly feeling,
A giant shadow in its imminent might,
Which his own lanthorn[5] throws up from himself.

To the Same

From FOLIAGE (1818)

Yet, Percy, not for this, should he whose eye
Sees loveliness, and the unselfish joy
Of justice, turn him, like a peevish boy,
At hindrances and thwartings, and deny
Wisdom's divinest privilege, constancy –   5
That which most proves him free from the alloy
Of useless earth, least prone to the decoy[1]
That clamours down weak pinions from the sky.
The Spirit of Beauty,[2] though by solemn choirs
Hourly blasphemed, stoops not from its calm end,   10
And forward breathing love, but ever on
Rolls the round day, and calls the starry fires
To their glad watch. Therefore, high-hearted friend,
Be still with thine own task in unison.

To John Keats (composed 1 December 1816)[1]

From FOLIAGE (1818)

'Tis well you think me truly one of those
Whose sense discerns the loveliness of things;
For surely as I feel the bird that sings
Behind the leaves, or dawn as it up grows,
Or the rich bee rejoicing as he goes,   5
Or the glad issue of emerging springs,
Or overhead the glide of a dove's wings,
Or turf, or trees, or, midst of all, repose;
And surely as I feel things lovelier still,
The human look, and the harmonious form   10
Containing woman, and the smile in ill,[2]
And such a heart as Charles',[3] wise and warm –
As surely as all this, I see, ev'n now,
Young Keats, a flowering laurel on your brow.

---

[5] *lanthorn* lantern.

TO THE SAME
[1] *decoy* bird trained to lure others into the hunter's trap.
[2] *The Spirit of Beauty* an allusion to Shelley's *Hymn to Intellectual Beauty*, published by Hunt in *The Examiner* for 19 January 1817 (see pp. 841–3), which features an address to the 'Spirit of Beauty' in stanzas 2–4.

TO JOHN KEATS
[1] Keats had first met Hunt in early October 1816. Hunt would have known Keats's sonnet *On First Looking into Chapman's Homer* and *Addressed to Haydon* (pp. 1012–13).
[2] *smile in ill* the eventual good that may result from bad tidings.
[3] Charles Cowden Clarke (1787–1877), mutual friend of Keats and Hunt.

A Now, Descriptive of a Hot Day[1]

From The Indicator 1 (1820, pp. 300–2)

Now the rosy- (and lazy-) fingered Aurora, issuing from her saffron house,[2] calls up the moist vapours to surround her, and goes veiled with them as long as she can; till Phoebus,[3] coming forth in his power, looks everything out of the sky, and holds sharp uninterrupted empire from his throne of beams. Now the mower begins to make his sweeping cuts more slowly, and resorts oftener to the beer. Now the carter sleeps atop of his load of hay, or plods with double slouch of shoulder, looking out with eyes winking under his shading hat, and with a hitch upward of one side of his mouth. Now the little girl at her grandmother's cottage-door watches the coaches that go by, with her hand held up over her sunny forehead. Now labourers look well, resting in their white shirts at the doors of rural alehouses. Now an elm is fine there, with a seat under it; and horses drink out of the trough, stretching their yearning necks with loosened collars; and the traveller calls for his glass of ale, having been without one for more than ten minutes; and his horse stands wincing at the flies, giving sharp shivers of his skin, and moving to and fro his ineffectual docked tail; and now Miss Betty Wilson, the host's daughter, comes streaming forth in a flowered gown and earrings, carrying with four of her beautiful fingers the foaming glass, for which, after the traveller has drank it, she receives with an indifferent eye, looking another way, the lawful two pence: that is to say, unless the traveller, nodding his ruddy face, pays some gallant compliment to her before he drinks – such as, 'I'd rather kiss you, my dear, than the tumbler', or, 'I'll wait for you, my love, if you'll marry me' – upon which, if the man is good-looking, and the lady in good humour, she smiles and bites her lips, and says, 'Ah, men can talk fast enough', upon which the old stagecoachman, who is buckling something near her before he sets off, says in a hoarse voice, 'So can women too for that matter', and John Boots grins through his ragged red locks, and dotes on the repartee all the day after. Now grasshoppers 'fry', as Dryden says.[4] Now cattle stand in water and ducks are envied. Now boots and shoes and trees by the roadside are thick with dust; and dogs, rolling in it, after issuing out of the water into which they have been thrown to fetch sticks, come scattering horror among the legs of the spectators. Now a fellow who finds he has three miles further to go in a pair of tight shoes is in a pretty situation.[5] Now rooms with the sun upon them become intolerable; and the apothecary's apprentice, with a bitterness beyond aloes,[6] thinks of the pond he used to bathe in at school. Now men with powdered heads (especially if thick) envy those that are unpowdered, and stop to wipe them uphill, with countenances that seem to expostulate with destiny. Now boys assemble round the village pump with a ladle to it, and delight to make a forbidden splash and get wet through the shoes. Now also they make suckers of leather,[7] and bathe all day long in rivers and ponds, and follow the fish into their cool corners, and say millions of 'My eyes!' at tittle-bats.[8] Now the bee, as he hums along, seems to be talking heavily of the heat. Now doors and brick walls are burning to the hand; and a walled lane, with dust and broken bottles in it, near a brick-field,[9] is a thing not to be thought of. Now a green lane, on the contrary, thick-set with hedgerow elms, and having the noise of a brook 'rumbling in pebble-stone',[10] is one of the pleasantest things in the world. Now youths and damsels walk through hayfields by chance; and if the

---

A Now, Descriptive of a Hot Day

[1] Hunt does not acknowledge the debt, but this essay was clearly inspired by Mary Robinson's *A London Summer Morning*; see my *Romantic Women Poets* (1997) pp. 183–4.

[2] *Now the . . . house* a deliberately elaborate way of saying that the dawn goddess (Aurora) casts an orange-yellow (saffron) light over the world. The 'rosy-fingered dawn' is a Homeric tag.

[3] *Phoebus* i.e. the sun.

[4] Hunt recalls Dryden, *Virgil's Georgics* iii 510–11, although the word 'fry' is not used.

[5] *pretty situation* ironic; he's in a terrible situation.

[6] *aloes* drug of nauseous odour, bitter taste, and purgative qualities, procured from the juice of the aloe plant.

[7] *suckers of leather* a toy, consisting of a round piece of leather with a string attached at the centre, which, laid wet upon a solid surface and drawn up by the string, adheres by reason of the vacuum created.

[8] *tittlebats* sticklebacks (small, spiny-finned fish).

[9] *brick-field* yard where bricks are made.

[10] Spenser, *Virgil's Gnat* 163: 'caerule streame, rombling in pible stone'.

latter say, 'Ha' done then, William', the overseer[11] in the next field calls out to 'Let thic thear hay thear bide', and the girls persist, merely to plague 'such a frumpish[12] old fellow'.

Now, in town, gossips talk more than ever to one another, in rooms, in doorways, and out of window, always beginning the conversation with saying that the heat is overpowering. Now blinds are let down and doors thrown open and flannel waistcoats left off, and cold meat preferred to hot, and wonder expressed why tea continues so refreshing, and people delight to sliver lettuces into bowls, and apprentices water doorways with tin canisters that lay several atoms of dust. Now the water-cart, jumbling along the middle of the street, and jolting the showers out of its box of water, really does something. Now boys delight to have a water-pipe let out, and see it bubbling away in a tall and frothy volume. Now fruiterers' shops and dairies look pleasant, and ices are the only things to those who can get them. Now ladies loiter in baths; and people make presents of flowers; and wine is put into ice; and the after-dinner lounger recreates[13] his head with applications of perfumed water out of long-necked bottles. Now the lounger, who cannot resist riding his new horse, feels his boots burn him. Now buckskins[14] are not the lawn[15] of Cos. Now jockeys, walking in greatcoats to lose flesh, curse inwardly. Now five fat people in a stagecoach hate the sixth fat one who is coming in, and think he has no right to be so large. Now clerks in offices do nothing but drink soda-water and spruce beer,[16] and read the newspaper. Now the old-clothes-man[17] drops his solitary cry more deeply into the areas on the hot and forsaken side of the street; and bakers look vicious; and cooks are aggravated; and the steam of a tavern-kitchen catches hold of one like the breath of Tartarus.[18] Now delicate skins are beset with gnats; and boys make their sleeping companion start up with playing a burning-glass[19] on his hand; and blacksmiths are super-carbonated;[20] and cobblers in their stalls almost feel a wish to be transplanted; and butter is too easy to spread; and the dragoons wonder whether the Romans liked their helmets; and old ladies, with their lappets[21] unpinned, walk along in a state of dilapidation; and the servant-maids are afraid they look vulgarly hot; and the author, who has a plate of strawberries brought him, finds that he has come to the end of his writing.

Rondeau (composed 1838)

From THE MORNING CHRONICLE 2 (1838, p. 436)

> Nelly kissed me when we met,
> Jumping from the chair she sat in;
> Time, you thief, who love to get
> Sweets into your list, put *that* in.
> Say I'm jaundiced, say I'm sad,   5
> Say that health and wealth have missed me,
> Say I'm growing old, but add,
> Nelly kissed me.

---

[11]   *overseer* supervisor.
[12]   *frumpish* ill-tempered.
[13]   *recreates* revives, refreshes.
[14]   *buckskins* breeches made of buckskin (too warm in the summer).
[15]   *lawn* fine linen, such as that made of the Island of Cos in the Aegean.
[16]   *spruce beer* beer made from leaves and branches of the spruce fir.
[17]   *old-clothes-man* dealer in old or second-hand clothes.

[18]   *Tartarus* in classical literature, the walled and dark underground prison reserved for the punishment of the wicked, surrounded by Phlegethon, the river of fire.
[19]   *burning-glass* lens through which the rays of the sun are concentrated so as to burn.
[20]   *super-carbonated* so hot that they are completely reduced to carbon.
[21]   *lappets* flaps of their dress which would normally be fastened down.

John Wilson ('Christopher North')
(1785–1854)

Wilson was born, 18 May 1785, at Paisley in Scotland, the first son and fourth child of John Wilson Sr, a gauze manufacturer who had recently made his fortune (assets amounting to £50,000), and his wife, Margaret. John Jr went up to the University of Glasgow in 1797, where he remained happily until 1803. While an undergraduate he read *Lyrical Ballads* and wrote a fan letter to Wordsworth: 'In your poems I discovered such marks of delicate feeling, such benevolence of disposition, and such knowledge of human nature, as made an impression on my mind that nothing will ever efface; and while I felt my soul refined by the sentiments contained in them, and filled with those delightful emotions which it would be almost impossible to describe, I entertained for you an attachment made up of love and admiration'.[1] The letter is worth examining for its intelligent early analysis of the volume, and for Wilson's reservations about *The Idiot Boy*, which Wordsworth defended in an eloquent reply shortly after.[2]

In June 1803 he entered Magdalen College, Oxford, as a gentleman-commoner. He took a full part in Oxford life, attending the local cockpit, participating in boxing matches, going on lengthy walking-tours of England and Wales, and even writing poetry. As one of his friends recalled: 'He was considered the strongest, most athletic, and most active man of those days at Oxford; and certainly created more interest amongst the gownsmen than any of his contemporaries, having already greatly distinguished himself in the schools, and as a poet'.[3] He graduated in 1807, having won the coveted Newdigate Prize for Poetry, and moved to Elleray on Windermere in the Lakes, where he built himself a handsome mansion that still stands. He met Wordsworth in 1807, quickly became friendly with him, and through Wordsworth met another acolyte of the poet, who had been up at Oxford at the same time as him – Thomas De Quincey.

He married in 1811, and the following year published *The Isle of Palms and Other Poems*. The two sonnets presented here give some idea of his verse at its best, with its intermittently successful attempts to capture a Wordsworthian sublimity. He was among the few 'lake poets' praised by Jeffrey, who commended the poems in *The Isle of Palms* (1812) on the grounds that Wilson 'is scarcely ever guilty of the offence of building them upon a foundation that is ludicrous or purely fantastic'.[4] Sales were not high, but it was praised in the right journals, and Wilson told a correspondent that it had been 'tolerably successful'.[5] His gentlemanly life in the Lakes came to an abrupt end in 1815 when an improvident uncle cheated him of his fortune, and he was compelled to go to Edinburgh where he was called to the bar.

Blackwood's Edinburgh Magazine was founded in 1817 by the publisher William Blackwood (1776–1834), a Tory who was in competition with the major Whig publisher of the day, Archibald Constable. His first choices as joint editors were James Pringle and Thomas Cleghorn, but he quickly became dissatisfied with their work and appointed in their stead Wilson and John Gibson Lockhart (see pp. 1004–5). Blackwood's choice was vindicated by the dynamism and energy of the revamped journal. Wilson and Lockhart engaged the most talented of their cronies, including the likes of James Hogg, De Quincey and Coleridge, and it became one of the foremost intellectual periodicals of the day. One of its most popular features was the *Noctes Ambrosianae* (nights at Ambrose's Inn), a series of loose, meandering dialogues between fictionalized versions of themselves. It turned the Ettrick Shepherd (Hogg) into a star, and featured Wilson himself as Christopher North. The *Noctes* ran from 1822 to 1835 and were written, often collaboratively, by Wilson, Lockhart, James Hogg and William Maginn (1793–1842). Typically for the *Noctes*, the extract below mingles literary satire with discussion of contemporary politics – in this case, slavery. Abolition of the trade had come with the Bill passed in Parliament on 1 May 1807, but slavery itself continued. By the 1820s, many people wanted to ban slavery, for which a further bill would be necessary. Thomas F. Buxton unsuccessfully introduced such a bill on 15 May 1823, and contemporary milestones in the struggle included Wilberforce's speech of 16 March 1824, and Brougham's of 10 June. The Emancipation Act was passed in Parliament on 25 March 1833.

Wilson and *Blackwood's* were a success. *Blackwood's* continued to publish until 1967, and in later years car-

JOHN WILSON
[1]   The letter is published in Mary Gordon, *Christopher North: A Memoir of John Wilson* (2 vols, Edinburgh, 1862), i 39.
[2]   See *EY* 352–8.

[3]   Ibid., i 77.
[4]   *Edinburgh Review* 19 (1811–12) 374.
[5]   Ibid., i 173.

ried the work of Landor (see pp. 571–6), George Eliot, Anthony Trollope and Joseph Conrad (*Lord Jim* appeared first in its pages). Wilson discovered that his talents lay not so much in verse as in literary journalism; his collected *Noctes*, published in book form, enjoyed tremendous popularity into the present century.

Further reading

Mary Gordon, *'Christopher North': A Memoir of John Wilson* (2 vols., Edinburgh, 1862)

Sonnet III. Written at Midnight, on Helm Crag[1]

From THE ISLE OF PALMS AND OTHER POEMS (1812)

Go up among the mountains when the storm
Of midnight howls, but go in that wild mood
When the soul loves tumultuous solitude,
And through the haunted air each giant form
Of swinging pine, black rock, or ghostly cloud   5
That veils some fearful cataract tumbling loud,
Seems to thy breathless heart with life imbued.
Mid those gaunt, shapeless things thou art alone!
The mind exists, thinks, trembles through the ear,
The memory of the human world is gone,   10
And time and space seem living only *here*.
Oh! worship thou the visions then made known,
While sable glooms round Nature's temple roll,
And her dread anthem peals into thy soul.

Sonnet VII. Written on Skiddaw,[1] during a Tempest

From THE ISLE OF PALMS AND OTHER POEMS (1812)

It was a dreadful day when late I passed
O'er thy dim vastness, Skiddaw! Mist and cloud
Each subject fell[2] obscured, and rushing blast
To thee made darling music, wild and loud,
Thou mountain-monarch! Rain in torrents played   5
As when at sea a wave is borne to heaven –
A watery spire, then on the crew dismayed
Of reeling ship with downward wrath is driven.
I could have thought that every living form
Had fled, or perished in that savage storm,   10
So desolate the day. To me were given
Peace, calmness, joy; then, to myself I said,
Can grief, time, chance, or elements control
Man's chartered pride – the liberty of soul?

SONNET III
[1] Helm Crag is a large, pyramidical mountain that dominates Grasmere Vale.

SONNET VII
[1] Skiddaw is the fourth highest peak in the Lake District (3,053ft).
[2] *fell* mountain.

Noctes Ambrosianae No. XIV

From BLACKWOOD'S EDINBURGH MAGAZINE 15 (1824, pp. 371–3)

Scene: Sky-Blue Parlour[1]

CHRISTOPHER NORTH How did the Border games go off this spring meeting, Shepherd?[2]

THE ETTRICK SHEPHERD The loupin'[3] was gude, and the rinnin'[4] was better, and the ba'[5] was best. Oh man, that ye had been but there!

NORTH What were the prizes?

THE SHEPHERD Bunnets.[6] Blue bunnets – I hae ane o' them in my pouch, that wasna gien awa'. There – try it on.

(The Shepherd puts the blue bonnet on Mr North's head)

NORTH I have seen the day, James, when I could have leaped any man in Ettrick.[7]

THE SHEPHERD A' but ane.[8] The Flying Tailor wad hae been your match ony day. But there's nae deny-ing you used to take awfu' spangs.[9] Gude safe us, on springy meadow grun, rather on the decline, you were a verra grasshopper. But, wae's me – thae crutches! Eheu! fugaces, Posthume, Posthume, labun-tur anni![10]

NORTH Why, even yet, James, if it were not for this infernal gout here, I could leap any man living at hop, step, and jump –

THE SHEPHERD Hech, sirs! Hech, sirs! But the human mind's a strange thing, after a'! Here's you, Mr North, the cleverest man, I'll say't to your face, noo extant, a scholar and a feelosopher, vauntin' o' your loupin'! That's a great wakeness. You should be thinkin' o' ither things, Mr North. But a' you grit men are perfet fules either in ae thing or anither.

NORTH Come James, my dear Hogg, draw your chair a little closer. We are a set of strange devils, I acknowledge, we human beings.

THE SHEPHERD Only luk at the maist celebrated o' us. There's Byron, braggin' o' his soomin',[11] just like yourself o' your loupin'. He informs us that he swom through the streets of Venice, that are a' canals, you ken – nae very decent proceeding – and keepit ploutering on the drumly waves[12] for four hours and a half, like a wild guse, diving too I'se warrant, wi' his tail, and treading water, and lying on the back o' him – wha the deevil cares?

NORTH His Lordship was, after all, but a sorry Leander?[13]

THE SHEPHERD You may say that. To have been like Leander, he should hae swom the Strechts in a storm, and in black midnight, and a' by himself – without boats and gondolas to pick him up gin he tuk the cramp, and had a bonnie lass to dicht him dry – and been drowned at last: but that he'll never be.

NORTH You are too satirical, Hogg.

THE SHEPHERD And there's Tammas Mure[14] braggin' after anither fashion o' his exploits amang the lasses. Oh man, dinna you think it rather contemptible, to sit in a cotch[15] wi' a bonnie thochtless[16]

NOCTES AMBROSIANAE No. XIV

[1]   At Ambrose's Inn.

[2]   Since they last met, Hogg has attended the athletic games in the lowlands of Scotland ('Border').

[3]   *loupin'* leaping, jumping.

[4]   *rinnin'* running.

[5]   *ba'* football.

[6]   *Bunnets* hats, caps.

[7]   *I have seen . . . Ettrick* Wilson was a champion leaper at Oxford, his record being a length of 23ft.

[8]   *A' but ane* all but one.

[9]   *spangs* springs, jumps.

[10]   'Ah Posthumus, the years run on apace!' (Horace, *Odes* II xiv 1–2).

[11]   *soomin'* swimming. Byron swam the Hellespont on 3 May

1810. Everyone knew about it, partly because it had been mentioned in *Don Juan* ii stanza 105 (see p. 798), and partly because it was described in detail in 'Extract from Lord Byron's Journal', published in the *London Magazine* 1 (1820) 295–6.

[12]   *ploutering on the drumly waves* playing idly on the muddy waves.

[13]   Leander of Abydos disobeyed his family's wishes and swam the Hellespont to be with his lover, Hero of Sestos. After numerous excursions of this kind, Leander was drowned while crossing in a storm, and Hero flung herself into the sea.

[14]   *Tammas Mure* Thomas Moore (see pp. 617–19).

[15]   *cotch* stagecoach.

[16]   *thochtless* careless.

lassie, for twa three lang stages,[17] and then publish a sang about it? I ance heard a gran' leddie frae London lauching till I thocht she would hae split her sides, at Thomas Little,[18] as she ca'd him. I could scarcely fadom her – but ye ken't by her face what she was thinking – and it was a' quite right – a severe reproof.

NORTH Mr Coleridge – is he in the habit, Hogg, of making the public the confidants of his personal accomplishments?

THE SHEPHERD I canna weel tell, for deevil the like o' sic books as his did I never see wi' my een beneath the blessed licht. I'm no speakin' o' his poems. I'll aye roose[19] them – but The Freen and the Lay Sermons[20] are aneuch to drive ane to destraction. What's logic?

NORTH Upon my honour as a gentleman, I do not know; if I did, I would tell you with the greatest pleasure.

THE SHEPHERD Weel, weel, Coleridge is aye accusing folk o' haeing nae logic. The want o' a' things is owing to the want o' logic, it seems. Noo, Mr North, gin logic be soun reasoning, and I jalouse[21] as much, he has less o't himsel than onybody I ken, for he never sticks to the point twa pages; and to tell you the truth, I aye feel as I were fuddled after perusing Coleridge. Then he's aye speaking o' himsel – but what he says I never can mak out. Let him stick to his poetry, for – oh man! – he's an unyerthly writer, and gies Superstition sae beautifu' a countenance, that she wiles folk on wi' her, like so many bairns, into the flowery but fearfu' wildernesses, where sleeping and wauking seem a' ae thing, and the very soul within us wonders what has become o' the everyday warld, and asks hersel what creation is this that wavers and glimmers, and keeps up a bonnie wild musical sough,[22] like that o' swarming bees, spring-startled birds, and the voice of a hundred streams, some wimpling awa' ower the Elysian meadows, and ithers roaring at a distance frae the clefts o' Mount Abora.[23] But is't true that they hae made him the Bishop of Barbados?

NORTH No, he is only Dean of Highgate. I long for his 'Wanderings of Cain', about to be published by Taylor and Hessey.[24] That house has given us some excellent things of late. They are spirited publishers. But why did not Coleridge speak to Blackwood? I suppose he could not tell, if he were questioned.

THE SHEPHERD In my opinion, sir, the bishops o' the Wast Indies should be blacks.

NORTH Prudence, James, prudence; we are alone to be sure, but the affairs of the West Indies –

THE SHEPHERD The bishops o' the Wast Indies should be blacks. Naebody'll ever mak me think itherwise. Mr Wilberforce and Mr M'Auley, and Mr Brougham,[25] and a' the ither saints,[26] have tell't us that blacks are equal to whites; and gin that be true, make bishops o' them. What for no?[27]

NORTH James, you are a consistent poet, philosopher, and philanthropist. Pray, how would you like to marry a black woman? How would Mr Wilberforce like it?

THE SHEPHERD I canna answer for Mr Wilberforce, but as for myself, I scunner[28] at the bare idea.

NORTH Why, a black skin, thick lips, grizzly hair, long heels, and convex shins – what can be more delightful? But to be serious, James, do you think there is no difference between black and white?

THE SHEPHERD You're drawing me into an argument about the Wast Indies, and the neegars. I ken naething about it. I hate slavery as an abstract idea, but it's a necessary evil, and I canna believe a' thae stories about cruelty. There's nae fun or amusement in whipping women to death – and as for a skelp[29] or twa, what's the harm? Hand me ower the rum and sugar,[30] sir.

---

[17] *twa three lang stages* two or three long stages; a stage is a regular stopping place on a stage-coach route where horses are changed and travellers taken up and set down.

[18] Thomas Moore published under the name of Thomas Little (see pp. 617–18).

[19] *roose* peruse.

[20] Coleridge's *The Friend* was published in a three-volume edition in 1818; his *Lay Sermons* in 1817.

[21] *jalouse* suspect.

[22] *sough* rushing, murmuring sound.

[23] *Kubla Khan* (1816) 41.

[24] *The Wanderings of Cain* was first published in Coleridge's *Poetical Works* (1828) by William Pickering. John Taylor and James Augustus Hessey had published the work of Keats, Clare, Lamb and De Quincey.

[25] Abolitionists: William Wilberforce (1759–1833) became parliamentary leader of the abolitionist cause in 1787, and published his *Appeal on behalf of Negro Slaves in the West Indies* in 1823; Zachary Macaulay (1768–1838) formed the Anti-Slavery Society in 1823; Henry Peter Brougham, Baron Brougham and Vaux (1778–1868), parliamentary supporter of the abolitionist cause.

[26] *saints* nickname given to the 'Clapham sect', which was instrumental in the abolitionist movement.

[27] *What for no?* Why not?

[28] *scunner* shudder.

[29] *skelp* slap.

[30] *rum and sugar* both produced by slave labour.

Thomas De Quincey   (1785–1859)

He was born Thomas Penson Quincey in Manchester, one of seven children born to Thomas Quincey, a linen merchant, and Elizabeth Penson Quincey. In 1791 the family moved to Greenhay, a newly-built house in the country on the outskirts of Manchester. A year later Thomas' beloved sister Elizabeth died, aged nine (see pp. 642–6); his father died in 1793.

The family moved to Bath in 1796, where he attended Bath Grammar School. At this time the family changed its name to De Quincey from a tradition that an ancestor came over with William the Conqueror. He moved to Winkfield School in Wiltshire in 1799, and it was here that he discovered Wordsworth's poetry, with which he immediately fell in love. After a highly eventful summer holiday in 1800, during which he met George III, he enrolled at Manchester Grammar School. For his first two years he was miserable and in July 1802 ran away to North Wales and London. In London he met the sixteen-year-old prostitute Ann, who saved him from starvation; he went to Bristol to borrow some money from his mother, and when he returned Ann had disappeared (see pp. 630–2).

In March 1803 he was reconciled with his family, and in May sent a fan letter to Wordsworth. Wordsworth wrote a generous reply, and he resolved, at some point, to meet his idol.[1] In December he went up to Worcester College, Oxford. During a visit to London the following spring he was introduced to opium (widely used as a pain-killer), as a treatment for rheumatism. After an abortive attempt to meet Wordsworth in the Lakes in 1805–6, he went to Nether Stowey where he met Coleridge. From there he escorted the Coleridge family to Grasmere, and in the process finally met Wordsworth. In his heart he knew he had discovered his true home, and after attending the first day of finals in Oxford in 1808, he suddenly left for the Lakes.

He gradually gained the trust of both William and Dorothy Wordsworth, always finding Dorothy more approachable than her brother. By 1809 he was sufficiently well regarded by the poet to supervise, on his behalf, the printing of The Convention of Cintra (Wordsworth's pamphlet in support of the Spanish rebellion against Napoleon) in London. In October he moved into Dove Cottage, the Wordsworths having moved to Allan Bank. In 1810–11 he became one of the few people of his day to read The Prelude – in man-

uscript, necessarily, as it was not published until 1850. As might be expected, the poem had a profoundly important influence on him; in particular, his theory of 'involutes', expounded p. 643 below, depends on Wordsworth's spots of time (pp. 306–9); the idea is taken to an extreme in Savannah-la-Mar and The Palimpsest of the Human Brain. During succeeding years strains developed in his relationship with his idol. Wordsworth was unhappy about the chopping down of certain trees at Dove Cottage, disliked De Quincey's addiction to opium (complete by 1813), and then disapproved of his affair with the Wordsworths' serving-girl, Margaret Simpson, which resulted in the birth of a son, William Penson, in 1816. De Quincey married her in 1817.

He had outgrown his mentor, but that knowledge was to some extent a liberation, and in 1818 his journalistic career took off when he became editor of the Westmorland Gazette. He was sacked for inefficiency within the year, but was almost immediately invited by John Wilson (see pp. 625–6) to write for Blackwood's Edinburgh Magazine. In the event he failed to produce, but by 1821 he was in London, writing his most important work – Confessions of an English Opium-Eater, serialized in the London Magazine, and published in book form a year later. The claims it made for opium were shocking even to the likes of Coleridge, who, in 1833, called it 'a wicked book, a monstrous exaggeration' (CC Table Talk i 581). The series of false starts and failures that characterized his early life were due to the influence of the drug, and it set a trend against which he would battle for the remainder of his life. He was expected to produce a third instalment of the Confessions for the London Magazine, but never did so; he returned to Grasmere with an advance for a novel, but never wrote it. All the same, despite his addiction, he wrote a vast quantity of material for a wide variety of newspapers and periodicals, including the London Magazine, John Stoddart's paper The New Times, Blackwood's, the Edinburgh Saturday Post, Edinburgh Literary Gazette, and Tait's Edinburgh Magazine. He suffered throughout his life from financial troubles; in 1829 he was forced to raise a second mortgage on Nab cottage in Rydal, where he then lived; he was imprisoned for debt in 1831, was twice prosecuted two years later (upon which he took refuge in the debtors' sanctuary at Holyrood), and thrice prosecuted in 1837. During these years he continued to write, when he was

---

THOMAS DE QUINCEY
[1]   For the full story of this relationship see John E. Jordan, De Quincey to Wordsworth: A Biography of a Relationship (Berkeley, 1962).

able, on a variety of subjects, including German metaphysics, 'Recollections of the Lake Poets' (which ran intermittently in *Tait's*, 1834–9), and the opium wars (including some anti-Chinese articles). Financial pressure on him was eased in 1840 when his eldest daughter Margaret (aged twenty-two) took control of his affairs.

In 1845 he began work on the second of his great works, *Suspiria De Profundis*, which was serialized in *Blackwood's*, April–July. In spite of his health problems, he came from a long-lived family (his mother died in 1846 at the age of ninety), and survived to see himself become sufficiently venerated to merit publication of a collected works. Interestingly, this was initiated by an American publisher, Ticknor, Reed, and Fields, of Boston, which began publication of *De Quincey's Writings* in 1850; it ran to twenty volumes, and was completed six years later. And in 1853 the Edinburgh publisher James Hogg (not the Ettrick Shepherd) began publication of *Selections Grave and Gay from Writings Published and Unpublished*, which ran to fourteen volumes, completed in 1860. He revised and substantially enlarged the *Confessions* for Hogg's edition, which appeared as volume 5 of *Selections Grave and Gay* (1856). He died at 42 Lothian Street, Edinburgh, 7 December 1859.

With Hazlitt and Lamb, De Quincey ranks as one of the most important writers of non-fiction prose of the romantic period. His great achievement is *The Confessions of an English Opium-Eater* (1822); it is impossible to offer more than mere extracts here, and the serious student of De Quincey is urged to read the complete text of 1822, preferably in Grevel Lindop's fine World's Classics edition, which also contains what survives of *Suspiria De Profundis*. It was as the inheritor of observations first made by Wordsworth and Coleridge that he set himself up as one of the foremost

exponents of 'psychological criticism', seen at its most persuasive and effective in 'On the Knocking at the Gate in *Macbeth*' and 'On Wordsworth's *There was a boy*' (pp. 638–42).

Further reading

Thomas De Quincey, *Reminiscences of the English Lake Poets* ed. John E. Jordan (London and New York, 1961)

—, *Confessions of an English Opium Eater and Other Writings* ed. Aileen Ward (New York and London, 1966)

De Quincey as Critic ed. John E. Jordan (London and Boston, 1973)

Thomas De Quincey, *Confessions of an English Opium-Eater and Other Writings* ed. Grevel Lindop (Oxford, 1985)

Robert M. Maniquis, 'The Dark Interpreter and the Palimpsest of Violence: De Quincey and the Unconscious', *Thomas De Quincey: Bicentenary Studies* ed. Robert Lance Snyder (Norman and London, 1985)

Robert Woof, *Thomas De Quincey: An English Opium-Eater* (Grasmere, 1985)

Jonathan Wordsworth, 'Two Dark Interpreters: Wordsworth and De Quincey', *The Age of William Wordsworth: Critical Essays on the Romantic Tradition* ed. Kenneth R. Johnston and Gene W. Ruoff (New Brunswick and London, 1987), pp. 214–38

John O. Hayden, 'De Quincey's *Confessions* and the Reviewers', *TWC* 6 (1975) 273–9

Charles Rzepka, 'De Quincey and the Malay: Dove Cottage Idolatry', *TWC* 24 (1993) 180–5

A new edition of *The Works of Thomas De Quincey*, General Editor Grevel Lindop, is currently in preparation in 15 volumes. It is scheduled for publication, by Pickering and Chatto, in October 1999.

[Ann of Oxford Street][1]

From CONFESSIONS OF AN ENGLISH OPIUM-EATER (1822) (pp. 47–53)

Being myself at that time of necessity a peripatetic (or a walker of the streets), I naturally fell in more frequently with those female peripatetics who are technically called street-walkers.[2] Many of these women had occasionally taken my part against watchmen who wished to drive me off the steps of houses where I was sitting. But one amongst them, the one on whose account I have at all introduced this subject – yet no, let me not class thee, oh noble-minded Ann, with that order of women! Let me find, if it be possible, some gentler name to designate the condition of her to whose bounty and compassion, ministering to my necessities when all the world had forsaken me, I owe it that I am at this time alive.

ANN OF OXFORD STREET
[1]   De Quincey recalls the period, 1802–3, when he ran away from school, aged seventeen, and lived rough in London.

[2]   *street-walkers* i.e. prostitutes.

For many weeks I had walked at nights with this poor friendless girl up and down Oxford Street,[3] or had rested with her on steps and under the shelter of porticos.[4] She could not be so old as myself; she told me, indeed, that she had not completed her sixteenth year. By such questions as my interest about her prompted, I had gradually drawn forth her simple history. Hers was a case of ordinary occurrence (as I have since had reason to think), and one in which, if London beneficence had better adapted its arrangements to meet it, the power of the law might oftener be interposed to protect and to avenge. But the stream of London charity flows in a channel which, though deep and mighty, is yet noiseless and underground, not obvious or readily accessible to poor houseless wanderers[5] – and it cannot be denied that the outside air and framework of London society is harsh, cruel, and repulsive. In any case, however, I saw that part of her injuries might easily have been redressed, and I urged her often and earnestly to lay her complaint before a magistrate; friendless as she was, I assured her that she would meet with immediate attention, and that English justice, which was no respecter of persons, would speedily and amply avenge her on the brutal ruffian who had plundered her little property. She promised me often that she would, but she delayed taking the steps I pointed out from time to time, for she was timid and dejected to a degree which showed how deeply sorrow had taken hold of her young heart, and perhaps she thought justly that the most upright judge and the most righteous tribunals could do nothing to repair her heaviest wrongs. Something, however, would perhaps have been done, for it had been settled between us at length (but unhappily on the very last time but one that I was ever to see her) that in a day or two we should go together before a magistrate, and that I should speak on her behalf. This little service it was destined, however, that I should never realize.

Meantime, that which she rendered to me, and which was greater than I could ever had repaid her, was this. One night, when we were pacing slowly along Oxford Street, and after a day when I had felt more than usually ill and faint, I requested her to turn off with me into Soho Square.[6] Thither we went, and we sat down on the steps of a house which to this hour I never pass without a pang of grief and an inner act of homage to the spirit of that unhappy girl, in memory of the noble action which she there performed. Suddenly, as we sat, I grew much worse: I had been leaning my head against her bosom, and all at once I sank from her arms and fell backwards on the steps. From the sensations I then had, I felt an inner conviction of the liveliest kind that without some powerful and reviving stimulus I should either have died on the spot or should at least have sunk to a point of exhaustion from which all re-ascent under my friendless circumstances would soon have become hopeless.

Then it was, at this crisis of my fate, that my poor orphan companion – who had herself met with little but injuries in this world – stretched out a saving hand to me. Uttering a cry of terror, but without a moment's delay, she ran off into Oxford Street and in less time than could be imagined returned to me with a glass of port wine and spices, that acted upon my empty stomach (which at that time would have rejected all solid food) with an instantaneous power of restoration – and for this glass the generous girl without a murmur paid out of her own humble purse at a time (be it remembered) when she had scarcely wherewithal to purchase the bare necessaries of life, and when she could have no reason to expect that I should ever be able to reimburse her.

Oh youthful benefactress! How often, in succeeding years, standing in solitary places and thinking of thee with grief of heart and perfect love – how often have I wished that, as in ancient times the curse of a father was believed to have a supernatural power, and to pursue its object with a fatal necessity of self-fulfilment, even so, the benediction of a heart oppressed with gratitude might have a like prerogative,[7] might have power given to it from above to chase, to haunt, to waylay, to overtake, to pursue thee into the central darkness of a London brothel, or (if it were possible) into the darkness of the grave, there to awaken thee with an authentic message of peace and forgiveness, and of final reconciliation!

---

3 *Oxford Street* central thoroughfare in the west end of London. In 1802 its properties were mainly residential.
4 *porticos* porchways, some of which in Oxford Street would at that time have been grand.
5 *wanderers* vagrants.

6 *Soho Square* square of buildings just off the south side of the eastern end of Oxford Street. In 1802 its properties were the residences of professional men – doctors, lawyers, dentists, and architects.
7 *prerogative* privilege.

I do not often weep, for not only do my thoughts on subjects connected with the chief interests of man daily, nay hourly, descend a thousand fathoms 'too deep for tears';[8] not only does the sternness of my habits of thought present an antagonism[9] to the feelings which prompt tears (wanting of necessity to those who, being protected usually by their levity from any tendency to meditative sorrow, would by that same levity be made incapable of resisting it on any casual access of such feelings) – but also I believe that all minds which have contemplated such objects as deeply as I have done, must for their own protection from utter despondency have early encouraged and cherished some tranquillizing belief as to the future balances[10] and the hieroglyphic[11] meanings of human sufferings. On these accounts, I am cheerful to this hour, and, as I have said, I do not often weep. Yet some feelings, though not deeper or more passionate, are more tender than others, and often, when I walk at this time in Oxford Street by dreamy lamplight, and hear those airs played on a barrel-organ which years ago solaced me and my dear companion (as I must always call her), I shed tears, and muse with myself at the mysterious dispensation[12] which so suddenly and so critically separated us for ever.

[The Malay]

From CONFESSIONS OF AN ENGLISH OPIUM-EATER (1822) (pp. 129–34)

One day a Malay knocked at my door.[1] What business a Malay could have to transact amongst English mountains I cannot conjecture, but possibly he was on his road to a seaport about forty miles distant.[2]

The servant who opened the door to him was a young girl born and bred amongst the mountains, who had never seen an Asiatic dress of any sort – his turban, therefore, confounded her not a little – and as it turned out that his attainments in English were exactly of the same extent as hers in the Malay, there seemed to be an impassable gulf fixed between all communication of ideas (if either party had happened to possess any). In this dilemma, the girl, recollecting the reputed learning of her master (and doubtless giving me credit for a knowledge of all the languages of the earth, besides, perhaps, a few of the lunar ones), came and gave me to understand that there was a sort of demon below, whom she clearly imagined that my art could exorcise from the house.

I did not immediately go down, but when I did, the group which presented itself – arranged as it was by accident, though not very elaborate, took hold of my fancy and my eye in a way that none of the statuesque attitudes exhibited in the ballets at the Opera House, though so ostentatiously complex, had ever done. In a cottage kitchen, but panelled on the wall with dark wood that from age and rubbing resembled oak, and looking more like a rustic hall of entrance than a kitchen, stood the Malay, his turban and loose trousers of dingy white relieved upon[3] the dark panelling. He had placed himself nearer to the girl than she seemed to relish, though her native spirit of mountain intrepidity contended with the feeling of simple awe which her countenance expressed as she gazed upon the tiger-cat before her. And a more striking picture there could not be imagined, than the beautiful English face of the girl, and its exquisite fairness, together with her erect and independent attitude, contrasted with the sallow and bilious[4] skin of the Malay, enamelled or veneered with mahogany, by marine air, his small fierce restless eyes, thin lips, slavish gestures and adorations.[5] Half-hidden by the ferocious-looking Malay was a little child from a neighbouring cottage who had crept in after him

---

8   Wordsworth, *Ode* 206: 'Thoughts that do often lie too deep for tears'.
9   *antagonism* opposition.
10   *balances* i.e. the belief that all suffering is balanced with an equal amount of happiness.
11   *hieroglyphic* symbolic, emblematic. De Quincey is comforted by the thought that suffering is not meaningless – that it has some kind of higher significance in the making of the soul.
12   *dispensation* ordering agency (implicitly, of God).

THE MALAY
1   *my door* i.e. that of Dove Cottage, Grasmere, where De Quincey lived from 1809 to 1819. The Malay's visit took place in 1816.
2   *a seaport . . . distant* probably Whitehaven, a trading port in the north of the Lakes.
3   *relieved upon* i.e. standing out against.
4   *bilious* brownish-yellow (like bile, the fluid secreted from the liver).
5   *adorations* gestures of respect.

and was now in the act of reverting its head, and gazing upwards at the turban and the fiery eyes beneath it, whilst with one hand he caught at the dress of the young woman for protection.

My knowledge of the oriental tongues is not remarkably extensive, being indeed confined to two words: the Arabic word for barley, and the Turkish for opium (madjoon), which I have learnt from *Anastasius*.[6] And as I had neither a Malay dictionary, nor even Adelung's *Mithridates*,[7] which might have helped me to a few words, I addressed him in some lines from the *Iliad*, considering that, of such languages as I possessed, Greek, in point of longitude, came geographically nearest to an oriental one. He worshipped me in a most devout manner, and replied in what I suppose was Malay. In this way I saved my reputation with my neighbours, for the Malay had no means of betraying the secret. He lay down upon the floor for about an hour, and then pursued his journey.

On his departure, I presented him with a piece of opium. To him, as an orientalist, I concluded that opium must be familiar, and the expression of his face convinced me that it was. Nevertheless, I was struck with some little consternation when I saw him suddenly raise his hand to his mouth and (in the schoolboy phrase) bolt[8] the whole, divided into three pieces, at one mouthful. The quantity was enough to kill three dragoons and their horses, and I felt some alarm for the poor creature – but what could be done? I had given him the opium in compassion for his solitary life, on recollecting that, if he had travelled on foot from London, it must be nearly three weeks since he could have exchanged a thought with any human being. I could not think of violating the laws of hospitality by having him seized and drenched with[9] an emetic, and thus frightening him into a notion that we were going to sacrifice him to some English idol. No – there was clearly no help for it. He took his leave, and for some days I felt anxious; but as I never heard of any Malay being found dead, I became convinced that he was used to opium, and that I must have done him the service I designed, by giving him one night of respite from the pains of wandering.

This incident I have digressed to mention because this Malay (partly from the picturesque exhibition he assisted to frame, partly from the anxiety I connected with his image for some days) fastened afterwards upon my dreams, and brought other Malays with him worse than himself, that ran amuck at me, and led me into a world of troubles.

[*The Pains of Opium*]

From CONFESSIONS OF AN ENGLISH OPIUM-EATER (1822) (pp. 155–60)

I now pass to what is the main subject of these latter confessions – to the history and journal of what took place in my dreams, for these were the immediate and proximate cause of my acutest suffering.

The first notice I had of any important change going on in this part of my physical economy, was from the reawakening of a state of eye generally incident[1] to childhood or exalted states of irritability.[2] I know not whether my reader is aware that many children – perhaps most – have a power of painting, as it were, upon the darkness, all sorts of phantoms. In some, that power is simply a mechanic affection[3] of the eye; others have a voluntary or a semi-voluntary power to dismiss or to summon them – or, as a child once said to me when I questioned him on this matter, 'I can tell them to go and they go, but sometimes they come when I don't tell them to come.' Whereupon I told him that he had almost as unlimited a command over apparitions as a Roman centurion over his soldiers.[4]

---

6 *Anastasius, or, Memoirs of a Greek* (1819), popular novel by Thomas Hope (1770–1831), attributed to Byron. At one point an old man warns its hero that opium leads to madness.
7 Johann Christoph Adelung (1732–1806), *Grammatisch-kritisches Wörterbuch der hochdeutschen Mundart* (1793), polyglot grammar and dictionary.
8 *bolt* swallow.
9 *drenched with* i.e. forced to drink.

THE PAINS OF OPIUM
1 *incident* relating.
2 *irritability* excitement, rather than annoyance.
3 *mechanic affection* involuntary property.
4 *as a Roman centurion . . . soldiers* a recollection of Matthew 8:8–9.

In the middle of 1817, I think it was, that this faculty became positively distressing to me. At night, when I lay awake in bed, vast processions passed along in mournful pomp,[5] friezes of never-ending stories that to my feelings were as sad and solemn as if they were stories drawn from times before Oedipus or Priam[6] – before Tyre, before Memphis.[7] And at the same time a corresponding change took place in my dreams; a theatre seemed suddenly opened and lighted up within my brain, which presented nightly spectacles of more than earthly splendour. And the four following facts may be mentioned as noticeable at this time:

1. That, as the creative state of the eye increased, a sympathy seemed to arise between the waking and the dreaming states of the brain in one point – that whatsoever I happened to call up and to trace by a voluntary act upon the darkness was very apt to transfer itself to my dreams, so that I feared to exercise this faculty, for, as Midas turned all things to gold[8] that yet baffled his hopes and defrauded his human desires, so whatsoever things capable of being visually represented I did but think of in the darkness, immediately shaped themselves into phantoms of the eye, and, by a process apparently no less inevitable, when thus once traced in faint and visionary colours, like writings in sympathetic ink, they were drawn out by the fierce chemistry of my dreams into insufferable splendour that fretted[9] my heart.

2. For this and all other changes in my dreams were accompanied by deep-seated anxiety and gloomy melancholy, such as are wholly incommunicable by words. I seemed every night to descend – not metaphorically, but literally to descend, into chasms and sunless abysses, depths below depths, from which it seemed hopeless that I could ever reascend. Nor did I, by waking, feel that I *had* reascended. This I do not dwell upon, because the state of gloom which attended these gorgeous spectacles, amounting at least to utter darkness, as of some suicidal despondency, cannot be approached by words.

3. The sense of space and, in the end, the sense of time, were both powerfully affected. Buildings, landscapes, etc., were exhibited in proportions so vast as the bodily eye is not fitted to receive. Space swelled and was amplified to an extent of unutterable infinity. This however did not disturb me so much as the vast expansion of time: I sometimes seemed to have lived for 70 or 100 years in one night – nay, sometimes had feelings representative of a millennium[10] passed in that time, or, however, of a duration far beyond the limits of any human experience.

4. The minutest incidents of childhood, or forgotten scenes of later years, were often revived. I could not be said to recollect them, for if I had been told of them when waking, I should not have been able to acknowledge them as parts of my past experience. But placed as they were before me, in dreams like intuitions, and clothed in all their evanescent circumstances and accompanying feelings, I *recognized* them instantaneously. I was once told by a near relative of mine[11] that, having in her childhood fallen into a river, and being on the very verge of death but for the critical assistance which reached her, she saw in a moment her whole life, in its minutest incidents, arrayed before her simultaneously as in a mirror, and she had a faculty developed as suddenly for comprehending the whole and every part. This, from some opium experiences of mine, I can believe; I have indeed seen the same thing asserted twice in modern books,[12] and accompanied by a remark which I am convinced is true –

---

5   *At night . . . pomp* De Quincey is recalling a fragment composed by Wordsworth at the same time as the *Two-Part Prelude*, 'When in my bed I lay':

      When in my bed I lay
Alone in darkness, I have seen the gloom
Peopled with shapes arrayed in hues more bright
Than flowers or gems or than the evening sky:
Processions . . . (ll. 1–5)

See Cornell *Lyrical Ballads* 316 and W. J. B. Owen, ' "A Second-Sight Procession" in Wordsworth's London', *N&Q* 16 (1969) 49–50.
6   *Oedipus or Priam* Oedipus was the King of Thebes, whose remarkable story is told in classic works by Sophocles; Priam, King of Troy, during the Trojan Wars, which were started when his son, Paris, abducted Helen.

7   Tyre was a Phoenician seaport founded 1,400 BC; the Egyptian city of Memphis dates from 3,000 BC.
8   *as Midas . . . gold* King of Phrygia, known for his generosity, who asked that whatever he touched be turned to gold. He realized he had made an error when his food turned into gold, and he was cured by bathing in the River Pactolus.
9   *fretted* tormented.
10   *a millennium* 1,000 years.
11   *a near relative of mine* a coy reference to his mother, Elizabeth Penson Quincey, who at this time was sixty-five. Her story is told in detail on pp. 646–7.
12   *modern books* probably Swedenborg's *Arcana Coelestia* and Coleridge's *Biographia Literaria*.

viz. that the dread book of account[13] which the scriptures speak of is, in fact, the mind itself of each individual. Of this at least I feel assured: that there is no such thing as *forgetting* possible to the mind; a thousand accidents may and will interpose a veil between our present consciousness and the secret inscriptions on the mind[14] – accidents of the same sort will also rend away this veil. But alike, whether veiled or unveiled, the inscription remains for ever, just as the stars seem to withdraw before the common light of day, whereas in fact we all know that it is the light which is drawn over them as a veil, and that they are waiting to be revealed when the obscuring daylight shall have withdrawn.

[*Oriental Dreams*]

From CONFESSIONS OF AN ENGLISH OPIUM-EATER (1822) (PP. 167–72)

May 1818

The Malay has been a fearful enemy for months. I have been every night, through his means, transported into Asiatic scenes. I know not whether others share in my feelings on this point, but I have often thought that if I were compelled to forego England and to live in China and among Chinese manners and modes of life and scenery, I should go mad.

The causes of my horror lie deep, and some of them must be common to others. Southern Asia, in general, is the seat of awful images and associations. As the cradle of the human race, it would alone have a dim and reverential feeling connected with it. But there are other reasons. No man can pretend that the wild, barbarous, and capricious superstitions of Africa, or of savage tribes elsewhere, affect him in the way that he is affected by the ancient, monumental, cruel, and elaborate religions of Indostan,[1] etc. The mere antiquity of Asiatic things, of their institutions, histories, modes of faith, etc., is so impressive, that to me the vast age of the race and name overpowers the sense of youth in the individual. A young Chinese seems to me an antediluvian man[2] renewed. Even Englishmen, though not bred in any knowledge of such institutions, cannot but shudder at the mystic sublimity of castes that have flowed apart and refused to mix, through such immemorial tracts of time – nor can any man fail to be awed by the names of the Ganges or the Euphrates.

It contributes much to these feelings that southern Asia is, and has been for thousands of years, the part of the earth most swarming with human life – the great *officina gentium*.[3] Man is a weed in those regions. The vast empires also, into which the enormous population of Asia has always been cast, give a further sublimity to the feelings associated with all oriental names or images. In China, over and above what it has in common with the rest of southern Asia, I am terrified by the modes of life, by the manners, and the barrier of utter abhorrence and want of sympathy placed between us by feelings deeper than I can analyse. I could sooner live with lunatics or brute animals.[4] All this, and much more than I can say or have time to say, the reader must enter into before he can comprehend the unimaginable horror which these dreams of oriental imagery and mythological tortures impressed upon me.

Under the connecting feeling of tropical heat and vertical sunlights, I brought together all creatures, birds, beasts, reptiles, all trees and plants, usages[5] and appearances that are found in all tropical regions, and assembled them together in China or Indostan. From kindred feelings I soon brought

---

[13] *the dread book of account* mentioned Revelation 8:8: 'And all that dwell upon the earth shall worship him, whose names are not written in the book of life of the Lamb slain from the foundation of the world'.

[14] *secret inscriptions on the mind* i.e. memories impressed indelibly on the mind. De Quincey is thinking in Wordsworthian terms; cf. *Pedlar* 30–4.

ORIENTAL DREAMS

[1] *Indostan* India.

[2] *antediluvian man* man before the great flood.

[3] *officina gentium* workshop of peoples.

[4] *I am terrified . . . animals* De Quincey wrote a number of anti-Chinese articles inspired by the opium wars in 1839. It should be remembered that racist opinions were so common in his day as to be unremarkable; so common were they that the very concept of racism was unknown (the OED's first usage is dated 1907).

[5] *usages* customs.

Egypt and all her gods under the same law. I was stared at, hooted at, grinned at, chattered at, by monkeys, by parakeets, by cockatoos. I ran into pagodas and was fixed for centuries at the summit, or in secret rooms. I was the idol, I was the priest, I was worshipped, I was sacrificed. I fled from the wrath of Brahma[6] through all the forests of Asia. Vishnu hated me. Siva laid wait for me.[7] I came suddenly upon Isis and Osiris.[8] I had done a deed, they said, which the ibis[9] and the crocodile trembled at. I was buried for a thousand years in stone coffins, with mummies and sphinxes, in narrow chambers at the heart of eternal pyramids. I was kissed with cancerous kisses by crocodiles, and laid confounded with all unutterable slimy things amongst reeds and Nilotic mud.

I thus give the reader some slight abstraction of[10] my oriental dreams, which always filled me with such amazement at the monstrous[11] scenery, that horror seemed absorbed for a while in sheer astonishment. Sooner or later came a reflux[12] of feeling that swallowed up the astonishment, and left me not so much in terror as in hatred and abomination of what I saw. Over every form, and threat, and punishment, and dim sightless incarceration, brooded a sense of eternity and infinity that drove me into an oppression as of madness. Into these dreams only it was (with one or two slight exceptions) that any circumstances of physical horror entered. All before had been moral and spiritual terrors, but here the main agents were ugly birds, or snakes, or crocodiles – especially the last. The cursed crocodile became to me the object of more horror than almost all the rest. I was compelled to live with him, and (as was always the case almost in my dreams) for centuries. I escaped sometimes, and found myself in Chinese houses with cane tables, etc. All the feet of the tables, sofas, etc., soon became instinct[13] with life. The abominable head of the crocodile, and his leering eyes, looked out at me, multiplied into a thousand repetitions – and I stood loathing and fascinated. And so often did this hideous reptile haunt my dreams, that many times the very same dream was broken up in the very same way: I heard gentle voices speaking to me (I hear everything when I am sleeping), and instantly I awoke.

It was broad noon, and my children were standing, hand in hand, at my bedside, come to show me their coloured shoes or new frocks, or to let me see them dressed for going out. I protest that so awful was the transition from the damned crocodile and the other unutterable monsters and abortions of my dreams to the sight of innocent *human* natures and of infancy, that, in the mighty and sudden revulsion of mind, I wept, and could not forbear it, as I kissed their faces.[14]

[*Easter Sunday*]

From CONFESSIONS OF AN ENGLISH OPIUM-EATER (1822) (pp. 173–7)

June 1819

I have had occasion to remark, at various periods of my life, that the deaths of those whom we love – and indeed the contemplation of death generally – is, *caeteris paribus*,[1] more affecting in summer than in any other season of the year. And the reasons are these three, I think:

first, that the visible heavens in summer appear far higher, more distant, and (if such a solecism may be excused) more infinite; the clouds, by which chiefly the eye expounds[2] the distance of the blue pavilion stretched over our heads, are in summer more voluminous, massed, and accumulated in far grander and more towering piles;

---

6   *Brahma* supreme God of Hindu myth.
7   Vishnu and Siva are Hindu deities.
8   *Isis and Osiris* Egyptian deities.
9   *ibis* the Sacred Ibis of Egypt (*Ibis religiosa*), with white and black plumage, was an object of veneration among the ancient Egyptians.
10   *slight abstraction of* brief extract from.
11   *monstrous* unnatural.

12   *reflux* return.
13   *instinct* animated.
14   De Quincey has in mind Coleridge's poem, *The Day-Dream* (see pp. 491–2).

EASTER SUNDAY
1   *caeteris paribus* all other things being equal.
2   *expounds* infers.

secondly, the light and the appearances of the declining and the setting sun are much more fitted to be types and characters of the Infinite;[3]

and thirdly (which is the main reason), the exuberant and riotous prodigality[4] of life naturally forces the mind more powerfully upon the antagonist[5] thought of death and the wintry sterility of the grave – for it may be observed generally that wherever two thoughts stand related to each other by a law of antagonism, and exist, as it were, by mutual repulsion, they are apt to suggest each other.

On these accounts it is that I find it impossible to banish the thought of death when I am walking alone in the endless days of summer, and any particular death, if not more affecting, at least haunts my mind more obstinately and besiegingly in that season. Perhaps this cause, and a slight incident which I omit, might have been the immediate occasions of the following dream – to which, however, a predisposition must always have existed in my mind. But having been once roused, it never left me, and split into a thousand fantastic varieties, which often suddenly reunited and composed again the original dream.

I thought that it was a Sunday morning in May, that it was Easter Sunday, and as yet very early in the morning. I was standing, as it seemed to me, at the door of my own cottage.[6] Right before me lay the very scene which could really be commanded from that situation, but exalted (as was usual) and solemnized by the power of dreams. There were the same mountains and the same lovely valley at their feet, but the mountains were raised to more than Alpine height, and there was interspace[7] far larger between them of meadows and forest lawns. The hedges were rich with white roses, and no living creature was to be seen, excepting that in the green churchyard there were cattle tranquilly reposing upon the verdant graves, and particularly round about the grave of a child[8] whom I had tenderly loved, just as I had really beheld them, a little before sunrise in the same summer, when that child died. I gazed upon the well-known scene, and I said aloud (as I thought) to myself, 'It yet wants much of sunrise; and it is Easter Sunday, and that is the day on which they celebrate the first fruits of resurrection. I will walk abroad. Old griefs shall be forgotten today, for the air is cool and still, and the hills are high, and stretch away to heaven, and the forest-glades are as quiet as the churchyard; and, with the dew, I can wash the fever from my forehead, and then I shall be unhappy no longer.'

And I turned as if to open my garden gate – and immediately I saw upon the left a scene far different, but which yet the power of dreams had reconciled into harmony with the other. The scene was an oriental one, and there also it was Easter Sunday and very early in the morning. And at a vast distance were visible, as a stain upon the horizon, the domes and cupolas of a great city – an image or faint abstraction caught perhaps in childhood from some picture of Jerusalem.[9] And not a bowshot[10] from me, upon a stone and shaded by Judean palms, there sat a woman – and I looked – and it was – Ann! She fixed her eyes upon me earnestly, and I said to her at length, 'So then I have found you at last.' I waited, but she answered me not a word. Her face was the same as when I saw it last, and yet again how different! Seventeen years ago, when the lamplight fell upon her face, as for the last time I kissed her lips (lips, Ann, that to me were not polluted), her eyes were streaming with tears; the tears were now wiped away. She seemed more beautiful than she was at that time, but in all other points the same, and not older. Her looks were tranquil, but with unusual solemnity of expression, and I now gazed upon her with some awe.

But suddenly her countenance grew dim, and, turning to the mountains, I perceived vapours rolling between us. In a moment all had vanished; thick darkness came on, and, in the twinkling of

---

3   *types . . . Infinite* a phrase that reveals De Quincey's understanding of Berkeley's philosophy (imbibed, presumably, from Coleridge), though in fact he echoes Wordsworth, *Thirteen-Book Prelude* vi 571: 'types and symbols of eternity'. Berkeley's central idea was that the material world was merely an idea in the mind of God, and that nature was God's 'writing' (hence 'types', as in the sense of a typeface).

4   *prodigality* rich profusion.

5   *antagonist* opposite.

6   *my own cottage* Dove Cottage in Grasmere. In fact, De Quincey wrote this in London, and had moved out of Dove Cottage after a fire in 1819.

7   *interspace* intervening space.

8   *a child* Catherine Wordsworth (1808–12), the poet's daughter; De Quincey was close to Kate, and devastated by her death. For more than two months after he slept on her grave.

9   De Quincey may have in mind the cloudscape New Jerusalem passage from *The Excursion* (see pp. 410–11).

10   *a bowshot* an arrow's flight; about 300 yards.

an eye, I was far away from mountains, and by lamplight in Oxford Street, walking again with Ann – just as we walked seventeen years before when we were both children.[11]

On the Knocking at the Gate in Macbeth (first published under the pseudonym, 'X.Y.Z.')

From LONDON MAGAZINE 8 (1823, pp. 353–6)

From my boyish days I had always felt a great perplexity on one point in *Macbeth*. It was this: the knocking at the gate[1] which succeeds to the murder of Duncan[2] produced to my feelings an effect for which I never could account. The effect was that it reflected back upon the murder a peculiar awful-ness[3] and a depth of solemnity. Yet however obstinately I endeavoured with my understanding to comprehend this, for many years I never could see *why* it should produce such an effect.[4]

Here I pause for one moment to exhort the reader never to pay any attention to his understanding when it stands in opposition to any other faculty of his mind. The mere understanding, however use-ful and indispensable, is the meanest faculty in the human mind and the most to be distrusted – and yet the great majority of people trust to nothing else, which may do for ordinary life, but not for philosophic purposes. Of this, out of ten thousand instances that I might produce, I will cite one. Ask of any person whatsoever, who is not previously prepared for the demand by a knowledge of perspec-tive, to draw in the rudest way the commonest appearance which depends upon the laws of that sci-ence[5] – as for instance, to represent the effect of two walls standing at right angles to each other, or the appearance of the houses on each side of a street, as seen by a person looking down the street from one extremity. Now in all cases, unless the person has happened to observe in pictures how it is that artists produce these effects, he will be utterly unable to make the smallest approximation to it. Yet why? For he has actually seen the effect every day of his life. The reason is that he allows his under-standing to overrule his eyes. His understanding, which includes no intuitive[6] knowledge of the laws of vision, can furnish him with no reason why a line which is known and can be proved to be a hori-zontal line, should not *appear* a horizontal line; a line that made any angle with the perpendicular less than a right angle would seem to him to indicate that his houses were all tumbling down together. Accordingly he makes the line of his houses a horizontal line and fails of course to produce the effect demanded.

Here then is one instance out of many in which not only the understanding is allowed to overrule the eyes, but where the understanding is positively allowed to obliterate the eyes as it were. For not only does the man believe the evidence of his understanding in opposition to that of his eyes, but (which is monstrous!) the idiot is not aware that his eyes ever gave such evidence. He does not know that he has seen (and therefore *quoad*[7] his consciousness has *not* seen) that which he *has* seen every day of his life.

But to return from this digression. My understanding could furnish no reason why the knocking at the gate in *Macbeth* should produce any effect direct or reflected;[8] in fact, my understanding said posi-tively that it could *not* produce any effect. But I knew better.[9] I felt that it did, and I waited and

---

[11] *both children* De Quincey had been seventeen, Ann six-teen.

ON THE KNOCKING AT THE GATE IN MACBETH
[1] *Macbeth* II ii 54.
[2] *the murder of Duncan* Macbeth, a general in the army, kills King Duncan as a first step to taking the throne.
[3] *awfulness* awesomeness.
[4] De Quincey is pointing out the disparity between a trivial, apparently insignificant stage direction, 'Knock within', and his response (feelings of awe and solemnity).

[5] *that science* i.e. the laws of perspective.
[6] *intuitive* behind this lies the distinction, followed by Coleridge and Wordsworth, between discursive (belonging to man) and intuitive understanding (belonging to angels), as stated in *Paradise Lost* v 486–90. See *Thirteen-Book Prelude* xiii 113.
[7] *quoad* with respect to.
[8] *reflected* i.e. indirect.
[9] *But I knew better* discursive reason tells him that his response is nonsensical; intuitive reason tells him that it is justified.

clung to the problem until further knowledge should enable me to solve it. At length, in 1812, Mr Williams made his début on the stage of Ratcliffe Highway,[10] and executed those unparalleled murders which have procured for him such a brilliant and undying reputation.

On which murders, by the way, I must observe that in one respect they have had an ill effect, by making the connoisseur in murder very fastidious in his taste and dissatisfied with anything that has been since done in that line. All other murders look pale by the deep crimson of his – and, as an amateur once said to me in a querulous tone, 'There has been absolutely nothing *doing* since his time, or nothing that's worth speaking of.' But this is wrong, for it is unreasonable to expect all men to be great artists, and born with the genius of Mr Williams.

Now it will be remembered that in the first of these murders (that of the Marrs) the same incident (of a knocking at the door soon after the work of extermination was complete) did actually occur which the genius of Shakespeare had invented – and all good judges and the most eminent dilettanti acknowledged the felicity of Shakespeare's suggestion as soon as it was actually realized. Here then was a fresh proof that I had been right in relying on my own feeling in opposition to my understanding, and again I set myself to study the problem. At length I solved it to my own satisfaction, and my solution is this. Murder in ordinary cases, where the sympathy is wholly directed to the case of the murdered person, is an incident of coarse and vulgar horror, and for this reason – that it flings the interest exclusively upon the natural but ignoble instinct by which we cleave to life (an instinct which, as being indispensable to the primal law of self-preservation, is the same in kind, though different in degree, amongst all living creatures) – this instinct therefore, because it annihilates all distinctions and degrades the greatest of men to the level of 'the poor beetle that we tread on',[11] exhibits human nature in its most abject and humiliating attitude.

Such an attitude would little suit the purposes of the poet. What then must he do? He must throw the interest on the murderer: our sympathy must be with *him* (of course I mean a sympathy of comprehension, a sympathy by which we enter into his feelings and are made to understand them – not a sympathy of pity or approbation). In the murdered person all strife of thought, all flux and reflux of passion and of purpose, are crushed by one overwhelming panic: the fear of instant death smites him 'with its petrific mace'.[12] But in the murderer, such a murderer as a poet will condescend to, there must be raging some great storm of passion – jealousy, ambition, vengeance, hatred – which will create a hell within him, and into this hell we are to look. In *Macbeth*, for the sake of gratifying his own enormous and teeming faculty of creation, Shakespeare has introduced two murderers,[13] and, as usual in his hands, they are remarkably discriminated. But though in Macbeth the strife of mind is greater than in his wife, the tiger-spirit not so awake, and his feelings caught chiefly by contagion from her – yet, as both were finally involved in the guilt of murder, the murderous mind of necessity is finally to be presumed in both. This was to be expressed; and on its own account, as well as to make it a more proportionable antagonist to the unoffending nature of their victim, 'the gracious Duncan',[14] and adequately to expound 'the deep damnation of his taking off',[15] this was to be expressed with peculiar energy. We were to be made to feel that the human nature (i.e. the divine nature of love and mercy, spread through the hearts of all creatures, and seldom utterly withdrawn from man) was gone, vanished, extinct – and that the fiendish nature had taken its place. And as this effect is marvellously accomplished in the dialogues and soliloquies themselves, so it is finally consummated[16] by the expedient under consideration[17] – and it is to this that I now solicit the reader's attention.

If the reader has ever witnessed a wife, daughter or sister in a fainting fit, he may chance to have observed that the most affecting moment in such a spectacle is that in which a sigh and a stirring announce the recommencement of suspended life. Or if the reader has ever been present in a vast metropolis on the day when some great national idol was carried in funeral pomp to his grave, and chancing to

---

[10]   *Mr Williams . . . Highway* A servant-girl sent out on an errand returned and knocked at the door while Williams, who had murdered the entire family, was still inside the house.

[11]   *Measure for Measure* III i 78.

[12]   *Paradise Lost* x 294.

[13]   *two murderers* i.e. Macbeth and Lady Macbeth.

[14]   *Macbeth* III i 65.

[15]   *Macbeth* I vii 20.

[16]   *consummated* completed.

[17]   *the expedient under consideration* i.e. the knocking at the gate.

walk near to the course through which it passed, has felt powerfully, in the silence and desertion of the streets, and in the stagnation of ordinary business, the deep interest which at that moment was possessing the heart of man; if all at once he should hear the deathlike stillness broken up by the sound of wheels rattling away from the scene, and making known that the transitory vision was dissolved, he will be aware that at no moment was his sense of the complete suspension and pause in ordinary human concerns so full and affecting as at that moment when the suspension ceases, and the goings-on of human life are suddenly resumed. All action in any direction is best expounded, measured, and made apprehensible, by reaction.

Now apply this to the case in *Macbeth*. Here, as I have said, the retiring of the human heart and the entrance of the fiendish heart was to be expressed and made sensible.[18] Another world has stepped in, and the murderers are taken out of the region of human things, human purposes, human desires. They are transfigured: Lady Macbeth is 'unsexed',[19] Macbeth has forgot that he was born of woman,[20] both are conformed to the image of devils, and the world of devils is suddenly revealed. But how shall this be conveyed and made palpable? In order that a new world may step in, this world must for a time disappear. The murderers and the murder must be insulated, cut off by an immeasurable gulf from the ordinary tide and succession of human affairs, locked up and sequestered in some deep recess; we must be made sensible that the world of ordinary life is suddenly arrested, laid asleep,[21] tranced, racked into a dread armistice;[22] time must be annihilated, relation to things without[23] abolished, and all must pass self-withdrawn into a deep syncope[24] and suspension of earthly passion.

Hence it is that, when the deed is done, when the work of darkness is perfect, then the world of darkness passes away like a pageantry in the clouds. The knocking at the gate is heard, and it makes known audibly that the reaction has commenced – the human has made its reflux upon the fiendish, the pulses of life are beginning to beat again, and the re-establishment of the goings-on of the world in which we live first makes us profoundly sensible of the awful parenthesis[25] that had suspended them.

Oh mighty poet![26] Thy works are not as those of other men, simply and merely great works of art, but are also like the phenomena of nature, like the sun and the sea, the stars and the flowers, like frost and snow, rain and dew, hailstorm and thunder – which are to be studied with entire submission of our own faculties, and in the perfect faith that in them there can be no too much or too little, nothing useless or inert, but that the further we press in our discoveries, the more we shall see proofs of design and self-supporting arrangement where the careless eye had seen nothing but accident.

N.B. In the above specimen of psychological criticism, I have purposely omitted to notice another use of the knocking at the gate (viz. the opposition and contrast which it produces in the porter's comments[27] to the scenes immediately preceding) because this use is tolerably obvious to all who are accustomed to reflect on what they read. A third use also, subservient to the scenical illusion, has been lately noticed by a critic in the *London Magazine*.[28] I fully agree with him, but it did not fall in my way to insist on this.

[On Wordsworth's 'There was a boy']¹

From TAIT'S EDINBURGH MAGAZINE 6 (1839, p. 94)

There is amongst the poems of Wordsworth one most ludicrously misconstrued by his critics, which offers a philosophical hint upon this subject, of great instruction. I will preface it with the little incident which first led Wordsworth into a commentary upon his own meaning.

---

18   *sensible* perceptible.
19   *Macbeth* I v 40–1: 'Come, you spirits / That tend on mortal thoughts, unsex me here'.
20   *born of woman* cf. *Macbeth* IV i 80–1: 'for none of woman born / Shall harm Macbeth'.
21   *laid asleep* cf. *Tintern Abbey* 46–7: 'we are laid asleep / In body, and become a living soul'.
22   *racked into a dread armistice* time is stretched into a fearful suspension.
23   *things without* i.e. external reality.
24   *syncope* cessation.

25   *awful parenthesis* awesome interlude.
26   *Oh mighty poet!* Shakespeare.
27   *the porter's comments* see *Macbeth* II iii 1–21.
28   George Darley (as John Lacy) in his 'Third Letter to the Dramatists of the Day', *London Magazine* 8 (1823) 275–83, p. 276.

ON WORDSWORTH'S 'THERE WAS A BOY'
1   This is an extract from a much longer essay about De Quincey's recollections of Wordsworth during his early acquaintance with him.

One night, as often enough happened, during the Peninsular war,[2] he and I walked up Dunmail Raise from Grasmere,[3] about midnight, in order to meet the carrier who brought the London newspapers by a circuitous course from Keswick. The case was this. Coleridge, for many years, received a copy of *The Courier*[4] as a mark of esteem, and in acknowledgement of his many contributions to it, from one of the proprietors, Mr Daniel Stuart. This went up in any case, let Coleridge be where he might,[5] to Mrs Coleridge.[6] For a single day it stayed at Keswick for the use of Southey, and on the next it came on to Wordsworth by the slow conveyance of a carrier, plying with a long train of carts between Whitehaven and Kendal.[7] Many a time the force of storms or floods would compel the carrier to stop on his route, five miles short of Grasmere at Wythburn, or even eight miles short at Legberthwaite. But as there was always hope until one or two o'clock in the morning, often and often it would happen that, in the deadly[8] impatience for earlier intelligence, Wordsworth and I would walk off to meet him about midnight, to a distance of three or four miles.

Upon one of these occasions, when some great crisis in Spain was daily apprehended, we had waited for an hour or more, sitting upon one of the many huge blocks of stone which lie scattered over that narrow field of battle on the desolate frontier of Cumberland and Westmorland, where King Dunmail with all his peerage fell more than a thousand years ago.[9] The time had arrived, at length, that all hope for that night had left us. No sound came up through the winding valleys that stretched to the north, and the few cottage lights, gleaming at wide distances from recesses amidst the rocky hills, had long been extinct. At intervals, Wordsworth had stretched himself at length on the high road, applying his ear to the ground so as to catch any sound of wheels that might be groaning along at a distance.

Once, when he was slowly rising from this effort, his eye caught a bright star that was glittering between the brow of Seat Sandal and of the mighty Helvellyn. He gazed upon it for a minute or so, and then, upon turning away to descend into Grasmere, he made the following explanation. 'I have remarked from my earliest days that if, under any circumstances, the attention is energetically braced up to an act of steady observation or of steady expectation, then, if this intense condition of vigilance should suddenly relax, at that moment any beautiful, any impressive visual object, or collection of objects, falling upon the eye, is carried to the heart with a power not known under other circumstances. Just now, my ear was placed upon the stretch in order to catch any sound of wheels that might come down upon the lake of Wythburn from the Keswick road; at the very instant when I raised my head from the ground in final abandonment of hope for this night, at the very instant when the organs of attention were all at once relaxing from their tension, the bright star hanging in the air above those outlines of massy blackness fell suddenly upon my eye, and penetrated my capacity of apprehension with a pathos and a sense of the infinite that would not have arrested me under other circumstances.'

He then went on to illustrate the same psychological principle from another instance. It was an instance derived from that exquisite poem[10] in which he describes a mountain boy planting himself at twilight on the margin of some solitary bay of Windermere, and provoking the owls to a contest

[2] *the Peninsular war* war in the Spanish and Portuguese peninsula, 1808–14, between the French under Napoleon, and the English, Spanish and Portuguese, under Wellington. Wordsworth's fascination with the campaign, and sympathy with the Spanish freedom fighters, led him to write *The Convention of Cintra*, which De Quincey saw through the press in 1809.

[3] *from Grasmere* the Wordsworths were then living at Allan Bank, De Quincey at Dove Cottage. Dunmail Raise is on the main road leading northwards out of Grasmere to Keswick.

[4] *The Courier* quality evening newspaper of early nineteenth century, to which Coleridge, Wordsworth, Lamb and Southey contributed. Its proprietor was Daniel Stuart (1766–1846), who also published *The Morning Post*.

[5] *let Coleridge be where he might* generally speaking, Coleridge spent little of the first decade of the nineteenth century with

his family, leaving it to Southey to provide for them and bring up his children. He had separated from his wife by 1807.

[6] *Mrs Coleridge* Sara (*née* Fricker), resident, with Southey and his family, at Greta Hall in Keswick.

[7] Whitehaven is a sea-port on the far north-western coast of Cumbria, Kendal a market town in the south.

[8] *deadly* excessive.

[9] Dunmail, King of Cumberland, was defeated by the Saxon King Edmund in the decisive battle at Dunmail Raise, 945 AD. Dunmail was buried under a pile of stones which may still be seen on the Raise today.

[10] *that exquisite poem* 'There was a boy', published *Lyrical Ballads* (1800); see p. 324. De Quincey would have known (though his readers would not) that it was incorporated into *Thirteen-Book Prelude* v 389–422.

with himself by 'mimic hootings' blown through his hands – which of itself becomes an impressive scene to anyone able to realize to his fancy the various elements of the solitary woods and waters, the solemn vesper hour,[11] the solitary bird, the solitary boy. Afterwards, the poem goes on to describe the boy as waiting amidst 'the pauses of his skill' for the answers of the birds, waiting with intensity of expectation. And then at length when, after waiting to no purpose, his attention began to relax – that is, in other words, under the giving way of one exclusive direction of his senses, began suddenly to allow an admission to other objects – then, in that instant, the scene actually before him, the visible scene, would enter unawares, 'With all its solemn imagery'. This complex scenery was – what?

> Was carried *far* into his heart
> With all its pomp, and that uncertain heav'n received
> Into the bosom of the steady lake.[12]

This very expression, 'far', by which space and its infinities are attributed to the human heart, and to its capacities of re-echoing the sublimities of nature, has always struck me as with a flash of sublime revelation.

Suspiria De Profundis: The Affliction of Childhood (extract)

FROM BLACKWOOD'S EDINBURGH MAGAZINE 57 (1845, PP. 278–81)

It was upon a Sunday evening (or so people fancied) that the spark of fatal fire fell upon that train of predispositions to a brain complaint[1] which had hitherto slumbered within her. She had been permitted to drink tea at the house of a labouring man, the father of an old female servant. The sun had set when she returned in the company of this servant through meadows reeking with exhalations after a fervent day. From that time she sickened. Happily a child in such circumstances feels no anxieties. Looking upon medical men as people whose natural commission it is to heal diseases, since it is their natural function to profess it, knowing them only as *ex officio*[2] privileged to make war upon pain and sickness, I never had a misgiving about the result. I grieved indeed that my sister should lie in bed; I grieved still more sometimes to hear her moan. But all this appeared to me no more than a night of trouble on which the dawn would soon arise.

Oh moment of darkness and delirium when a nurse awakened me from that delusion, and launched God's thunderbolt at my heart in the assurance that my sister *must* die! Rightly it is said of utter, utter misery, that it 'cannot be *remembered*';[3] itself, as a rememberable thing, is swallowed up in its own chaos. Mere anarchy and confusion of mind fell upon me. Deaf and blind I was as I reeled under the revelation. I wish not to recall the circumstances of that time, when *my* agony was at its height, and hers in another sense was approaching. Enough to say that all was soon over, and the morning of that day had at last arrived which looked down upon her innocent face, sleeping the sleep from which there is no awaking, and upon me sorrowing the sorrow for which there is no consolation.

On the day after my sister's death, whilst the sweet temple of her brain was yet unviolated by human scrutiny,[4] I formed my own scheme for seeing her once more. Not for the world would I have made this known, nor have suffered a witness to accompany me. I had never heard of feelings that take the name of 'sentimental', nor dreamed of such a possibility. But grief even in a child hates the light, and shrinks from human eyes. The house was large; there were two staircases, and by one of these I knew that about noon, when all would be quiet, I could steal up into her chamber. I imagine

---

[11] *vesper hour* time at which Venus (Vesper), the evening star, and the brightest, emerges in the evening sky.

[12] An inaccurate recollection of 'There was a boy' 20–5.

SUSPIRIA DE PROFUNDIS: THE AFFLICTION OF CHILDHOOD

[1] *a brain complaint* Elizabeth Quincey died in 1792, at the age of nine. De Quincey was six.

[2] *ex officio* by virtue of their office.

[3] Coleridge, *Osorio* iv 411.

[4] *whilst the sweet temple . . . scrutiny* the usual procedure would have been to perform an autopsy as soon as possible to confirm the cause of death.

that it was exactly high noon when I reached the chamber door. It was locked, but the key was not taken away. Entering, I closed the door so softly that, although it opened upon a hall which ascended through all the stories, no echo ran along the silent walls. Then turning round, I sought my sister's face. But the bed had been moved, and the back was now turned. Nothing met my eyes but one large window wide open, through which the sun of midsummer at noonday was showering down torrents of splendour. The weather was dry, the sky was cloudless, the blue depths seemed the express types of infinity,[5] and it was not possible for eye to behold or for heart to conceive any symbols more pathetic[6] of life and the glory of life.

Let me pause for one instant in approaching a remembrance so affecting and revolutionary for my own mind, and one which (if any earthly remembrance) will survive for me in the hour of death, to remind some readers and to inform others that in the original *Opium Confessions*[7] I endeavoured to explain the reason why death, *caeteris paribus*,[8] is more profoundly affecting in summer than in other parts of the year – so far at least as it is liable to any modification at all from accidents of scenery or season. The reason, as I there suggested, lies in the antagonism between the tropical redundancy of life in summer and the dark sterilities of the grave. The summer we see, the grave we haunt with our thoughts; the glory is around us, the darkness is within us. And, the two coming into collision, each exalts the other into stronger relief. But in my case there was even a subtler reason why the summer had this intense power of vivifying[9] the spectacle or the thoughts of death. And, recollecting it, often I have been struck with the important truth that far more of our deepest thoughts and feelings pass to us through perplexed combinations of concrete objects, pass to us as *involutes* (if I may coin that word) in compound[10] experiences incapable of being disentangled, than ever reach us directly, and in their own abstract shapes.

It had happened that amongst our nursery collection of books was the Bible illustrated with many pictures. And in long dark evenings, as my three sisters with myself sat by the firelight round the guard[11] of our nursery, no book was so much in request amongst us. It ruled us and swayed us as mysteriously as music. One young nurse whom we all loved, before any candle was lighted, would often strain her eyes to read it for us – and sometimes, according to her simple powers, would endeavour to explain what we found obscure. We, the children, were all constitutionally touched with pensiveness. The fitful gloom and sudden lambencies[12] of the room by firelight suited our evening state of feelings, and they suited also the divine revelations of power and mysterious beauty which awed us. Above all, the story of a just man[13] – man and yet *not* man, real above all things and yet shadowy above all things, who had suffered the passion of death in Palestine, slept upon our minds like early dawn upon the waters. The nurse knew and explained to us the chief differences in oriental climates, and all these differences (as it happens) express themselves in the great varieties of summer. The cloudless sunlights of Syria – those seemed to argue everlasting summer; the disciples plucking the ears of corn[14] – that *must* be summer; but above all the very name of Palm Sunday[15] (a festival in the English church) troubled me like an anthem. 'Sunday?' What was *that*? That was the day of peace which masked another peace deeper than the heart of man can comprehend. 'Palms?' What were they? *That* was an equivocal word: 'palms' in the sense of 'trophies' expressed the pomps of life; 'palms' as a product of nature expressed the pomps of summer. Yet still even this explanation does not suffice: it was not merely by the peace and by the summer, by the deep sound of rest below all rest and of ascending glory, that I had been haunted. It was also because Jerusalem stood near to those deep images both in time and in place. The great event of Jerusalem was at hand when Palm Sunday

---

[5]   *the express types of infinity* cf. *Thirteen-Book Prelude* vi 571: 'types and symbols of eternity'.

[6]   *pathetic* evocative, emotionally stirring.

[7]   *in the original . . .Confessions* see 'Easter Sunday', pp. 636–8, above.

[8]   *caeteris paribus* all other things being equal.

[9]   *vivifying* reviving. As De Quincey was aware, Wordsworth had used this word to describe the spots of time in early versions of *The Prelude*.

[10]   *compound* i.e. compounded, mixed up.

[11]   *guard* fireguard.

[12]   *lambencies* lightings-up, illuminations.

[13]   *a just man* Christ.

[14]   *the disciples . . . corn* the disciples plucked ears of corn from the fields when they were hungry; see, for instance, Matthew 12:1.

[15]   *Palm Sunday* Christ's followers greeted him with palm branches, when he entered Jerusalem; John 12:13.

came, and the scene of that Sunday was near in place to Jerusalem. Yet what then was Jerusalem? Did I fancy it to be the *omphalos* (navel) of the earth? That pretension had once been made for Jerusalem, and once for Delphi[16] – and both pretensions had become ridiculous, as the figure[17] of the planet became known. Yes – but if not of the earth, for earth's tenant: Jerusalem was the *omphalos* of mortality. Yet how? There on the contrary it was, as we infants understood, that mortality had been trampled underfoot.[18] True, but for that very reason there it was that mortality had opened its very gloomiest crater. There it was indeed that the human had risen on wings from the grave. But for that reason there also it was that the divine had been swallowed up by the abyss; the lesser star could not rise before the greater would submit to eclipse. Summer, therefore, had connected itself with death not merely as a mode of antagonism, but also through intricate relations to scriptural scenery and events.

Out of this digression, which was almost necessary for the purpose of showing how inextricably my feelings and images of death were entangled with those of summer, I return to the bedchamber of my sister. From the gorgeous sunlight I turned round to the corpse. There lay the sweet childish figure, there the angel face – and, as people usually fancy, it was said in the house that no features had suffered any change. Had they not? The forehead indeed, the serene and noble forehead – *that* might be the same. But the frozen eyelids, the darkness that seemed to steal from beneath them, the marble lips, the stiffening hands laid palm to palm as if repeating the supplications of closing anguish – could these be mistaken for life? Had it been so, wherefore did I not spring to those heavenly lips with tears and never-ending kisses? But so it was *not*.

I stood checked for a moment – awe, not fear, fell upon me – and whilst I stood, a solemn wind began to blow, the most mournful that ear ever heard. Mournful! That is saying nothing. It was a wind that had swept the fields of mortality for a hundred centuries. Many times since, upon a summer day, when the sun is about the hottest, I have remarked the same wind arising and uttering the same hollow, solemn, Memnonian,[19] but saintly swell; it is in this world the one sole *audible* symbol of eternity. And three times in my life I have happened to hear the same sound in the same circumstances, viz. when standing between an open window and a dead body on a summer day.

Instantly, when my ear caught this vast Aeolian intonation,[20] when my eye filled with the golden fullness of life, the pomps and glory of the heavens outside, and turning when it settled upon the frost[21] which overspread my sister's face, instantly a trance fell upon me. A vault seemed to open in the zenith of the far blue sky, a shaft which ran up for ever. I in spirit rose as if on billows that also ran up the shaft for ever, and the billows seemed to pursue the throne of God – but that also ran before us and fled away continually. The flight and the pursuit seemed to go on for ever and ever. Frost, gathering frost, some sarsar[22] wind of death, seemed to repel me. I slept, for how long I cannot say; slowly I recovered my self-possession, and found myself standing as before, close to my sister's bed.

Oh flight of the solitary child to the solitary God[23] – flight from the ruined corpse to the throne that could not be ruined! How rich wert thou in truth for after-years! Rapture of grief that, being too mighty for a child to sustain, foundest a happy oblivion in a heaven-born sleep, and within that sleep didst conceal a dream whose meanings in after-years, when slowly I deciphered, suddenly there flashed upon me new light – and even by the grief of a child, as I will show you reader hereafter, were confounded the falsehoods of philosophers.

---

[16] *Delphi* believed in ancient times to be the centre or navel of the earth, because it was close to a ravine.
[17] *figure* i.e. shape; once the earth was known to be spherical, it was no longer possible to think of it having a centre (or navel).
[18] *mortality . . . underfoot* i.e. by Christ's resurrection.
[19] *Memnonian* i.e. sensitive to sunlight. Thanks to a misreading of Juvenal, the romantics believed that the statue of Memnon, King of Ethiopia, which was believed to have been holding a lute, produced music when struck by the rising or setting sun. See Robin C. Dix, 'The Harps of Memnon and Aeolus: A Study in the Propagation of an Error', *Modern Philology* 85 (1988) 288–93.

[20] *Aeolian intonation* De Quincey probably has in mind the other-worldly sound of an Aeolian harp.
[21] *frost* coldness, though De Quincey may also be referring to the frost-like pallor of death.
[22] *sarsar* cold.
[23] 'φυγὴ μόνου πρὸζ μόνου. Plotinus' (De Quincey's note). De Quincey quotes the final words of *Ennead* VI 9 11, line 51, in which Plotinus writes of 'deliverance from the things of this world, a life which takes no delight in the things of this world, *escape in solitude to the solitary*.'

In the *Opium Confessions* I touched a little upon the extraordinary power connected with opium (after long use) of amplifying the dimensions of time.[24] Space also it amplifies by degrees that are sometimes terrific.[25] But time it is upon which the exalting and multiplying power of opium chiefly spends its operation. Time becomes infinitely elastic, stretching out to such immeasurable and vanishing *termini* that it seems ridiculous to compute the sense of it on waking by expressions commensurate to human life. As in starry fields one computes by diameters of the earth's orbit, or of Jupiter's, so in valuing the *virtual* time lived during some dreams, the measurement by generations is ridiculous, by millennia is ridiculous – by aeons, I should say (if aeons were more determinate), would be also ridiculous. On this single occasion, however, in my life, the very inverse phenomenon occurred. But why speak of it in connection with opium? Could a child of six years old have been under that influence? No, but simply because it so exactly reversed the operation of opium. Instead of a short interval expanding into a vast one, upon this occasion a long one had contracted into a minute. I have reason to believe that a *very* long one had elapsed during this wandering or suspension of my perfect mind. When I returned to myself, there was a foot (or I fancied so) on the stairs. I was alarmed. For I believed that, if anybody should detect me, means would be taken to prevent my coming again. Hastily, therefore, I kissed the lips that I should kiss no more, and slunk like a guilty thing[26] with stealthy steps from the room. Thus perished the vision, loveliest amongst all the shows which earth has revealed to me; thus mutilated was the parting which should have lasted for ever; thus tainted with fear was the farewell sacred to love and grief, to perfect love and perfect grief.

Oh Ahasuerus,[27] everlasting Jew! Fable or not a fable,[28] thou when first starting on thy endless pilgrimage of woe, thou when first flying through the gates of Jerusalem and vainly yearning to leave the pursuing curse behind thee, couldst not more certainly have read thy doom of sorrow in the misgivings of thy troubled brain than I when passing for ever from my sister's room. The worm was at my heart – and, confining myself to that stage of life, I may say, the worm that could not die. For if, when standing upon the threshold of manhood, I had ceased to feel its perpetual gnawings, that was because a vast expansion of intellect, it was because new hopes, new necessities, and the frenzy of youthful blood, had translated me into a new creature. Man is doubtless *one* by some subtle nexus[29] that we cannot perceive, extending from the new-born infant to the superannuated dotard; but as regards many affections and passions incident to his nature at different stages, he is *not* one – the unity of man in this respect is coextensive[30] only with the particular stage to which the passion belongs. Some passions, as that of sexual love, are celestial by one half of their origin, animal and earthy by the other half. These will not survive their own appropriate stage. But love which is *altogether* holy, like that between two children, will revisit undoubtedly by glimpses the silence and the darkness of old age – and I repeat my belief that, unless bodily torment should forbid it, that final experience in my sister's bedroom, or some other in which her innocence was concerned, will rise again for me to illuminate the hour of death.

On the day following this which I have recorded, came a body of medical men to examine the brain, and the particular nature of the complaint, for in some of its symptoms it had shown perplexing anomalies. Such is the sanctity of death (and especially of death alighting on an innocent child), that even gossiping people do not gossip on such a subject. Consequently I knew nothing of the purpose which drew together these surgeons, nor suspected anything of the cruel changes which might have been wrought in my sister's head. Long after this I saw a similar case; I surveyed the corpse (it was that of a beautiful boy eighteen years old,[31] who had died of the same complaint) one hour *after* the surgeons had laid the skull in ruins – but the dishonours of this scrutiny were hidden by bandages, and had not disturbed the repose of the countenance. So it might have been here, but if it were *not* so, then I was happy in being spared the shock, from having that marble image of peace, icy and

---

24 *In the Opium Confessions . . . time* see p. 634.
25 *terrific* terrifying.
26 *like a guilty thing* compare *Hamlet* I i 148–9 and Wordsworth, *Ode* 150.
27 *Ahasuerus* Because he denied rest to Christ on the way to the crucifixion, Ahasuerus was doomed to wander the earth until the Day of Judgement.

28 *Fable or not . . . fable* Ahasuerus's story is not in the Bible, and is presumably the stuff of folklore.
29 *nexus* connection.
30 *coextensive* extends over the same space and time.
31 William, De Quincey's son, died 1834.

rigid as it was, unsettled by disfiguring images. Some hours after the strangers had withdrawn, I crept again to the room, but the door was now locked, the key was taken away, and I was shut out for ever.

Suspiria De Profundis: The Palimpsest (extract)

From BLACKWOOD'S EDINBURGH MAGAZINE 57 (1845, pp. 742–3)

What else than a natural and mighty palimpsest[1] is the human brain? Such a palimpsest is my brain; such a palimpsest, oh reader, is yours. Everlasting layers of ideas, images, feelings, have fallen upon your brain softly as light. Each succession has seemed to bury all that went before, and yet in reality not one has been extinguished. And if, in the vellum palimpsest, lying amongst the other *diplomata*[2] of human archives or libraries, there is anything fantastic or which moves to laughter – as oftentimes there is in the grotesque collisions of those successive themes, having no natural connection, which by pure accident have consecutively occupied the roll – yet in our own heaven-created palimpsest, the deep memorial palimpsest of the brain, there are not and cannot be such incoherencies. The fleeting accidents of a man's life and its external shows may indeed be irrelate and incongruous, but the organizing principles which fuse into harmony and gather about fixed predetermined centres, whatever heterogeneous elements life may have accumulated from without, will not permit the grandeur of human unity greatly to be violated, or its ultimate repose to be troubled in the retrospect from dying moments or from other great convulsions.

Such a convulsion is the struggle of gradual suffocation, as in drowning – and in the original *Opium Confessions* I mentioned a case of that nature communicated to me by a lady from her own childish experience.[3] The lady is still living, though now of unusually great age.[4] And I may mention that amongst her faults never was numbered any levity[5] of principle, or carelessness of the most scrupulous veracity[6] – but, on the contrary, such faults as arise from austerity, too harsh perhaps, and gloomy, indulgent neither to others nor herself. And at the time of relating this incident, when already very old, she had become religious to asceticism.

According to my present belief, she had completed her ninth year when, playing by the side of a solitary brook, she fell into one of its deepest pools. Eventually (but after what lapse of time nobody ever knew) she was saved from death by a farmer who, riding in some distant lane, had seen her rise to the surface – but not until she had descended within the abyss of death, and looked into its secrets as far, perhaps, as ever human eye *can* have looked that had permission to return. At a certain stage of this descent, a blow seemed to strike her, phosphoric radiance sprang forth from her eyeballs, and immediately a mighty theatre expanded within her brain. In a moment, in the twinkling of an eye, every act, every design of her past life lived again – arraying themselves not as a succession but as parts of a coexistence. Such a light fell upon the whole path of her life backwards into the shades of infancy, as the light perhaps which wrapped the destined apostle on his road to Damascus.[7] Yet that light blinded for a season, but hers poured celestial vision upon the brain, so that her consciousness became omnipresent at one moment to every feature in the infinite review.

This anecdote was treated sceptically at the time by some critics. But besides that it has since been confirmed by other experiences essentially the same, reported by other parties in the same circumstances who had never heard of each other. The true point for astonishment is not the *simultaneity* of arrangement under which the past events of life – though in fact successive – had formed their dread line of revelation; this was but a secondary phenomenon. The deeper lay in the resurrection itself, and

---

SUSPIRIA DE PROFUNDIS: THE PALIMPSEST

[1]   *palimpsest* parchment, in this case of vellum (sheepskin), written upon twice, the original writing having been erased or rubbed out to make place for the second.

[2]   *diplomata* historical documents.

[3]   *in the original Opium Confessions . . . experience* see p. 634.

[4]   De Quincey's mother, who was ninety.

[5]   *levity* inconstancy, fickleness.

[6]   *And I may mention . . . veracity* i.e. she was always principled and honest.

[7]   *as the light perhaps . . . Damascus* St Paul, who was struck by 'a great light' on the road to Damascus; see Acts 22:6.

the possibility of resurrection for what had so long slept in the dust. A pall deep as oblivion had been thrown by life over every trace of these experiences, and yet suddenly, at a silent command, at the signal of a blazing rocket sent up from the brain, the pall draws up and the whole depths of the theatre are exposed. Here was the greater mystery: now this mystery is liable to no doubt, for it is repeated, and ten thousand times repeated by opium, for those who are its martyrs.

Yes, reader, countless are the mysterious handwritings of grief or joy which have inscribed themselves successively upon the palimpsest of your brain – and like the annual leaves of aboriginal forests,[8] or the undissolving snows on the Himalaya, or light falling upon light, the endless strata have covered up each other in forgetfulness. But by the hour of death, but by fever, but by the searchings of opium, all these can revive in strength. They are not dead, but sleeping. In the illustration imagined by myself, from the case of some individual palimpsest, the Grecian tragedy had seemed to be displaced, but was *not* displaced, by the monkish legend – and the monkish legend had seemed to be displaced, but was *not* displaced, by the knightly romance. In some potent convulsion of the system, all wheels back into its earliest elementary stage. The bewildering romance, light tarnished with darkness, the semi-fabulous legend, truth celestial mixed with human falsehoods, these fade even of themselves as life advances. The romance has perished that the young man adored. The legend has gone that deluded the boy. But the deep, deep tragedies of infancy, as when the child's hands were unlinked for ever from his mother's neck, or his lips for ever from his sister's kisses, these remain lurking below all, and these lurk to the last.

Suspiria De Profundis: Finale to Part I. Savannah-la-Mar

From BLACKWOOD'S EDINBURGH MAGAZINE 57 (1845, pp. 750–1)

God smote Savannah-la-Mar,[1] and in one night, by earthquake, removed her, with all her towers standing and population sleeping, from the steadfast foundations of the shore to the coral floors of ocean. And God said, 'Pompeii did I bury and conceal from men through seventeen centuries: this city I will bury, but not conceal. She shall be a monument to men of my mysterious anger, set in azure light through generations to come – for I will enshrine her in a crystal dome of my tropic seas.'

This city, therefore, like a mighty galleon with all her apparel[2] mounted, streamers flying and tackling perfect, seems floating along the noiseless depths of ocean. And oftentimes in glassy calms, through the translucid[3] atmosphere of water that now stretches like an air-woven awning above the silent encampment, mariners from every clime look down into her courts and terraces, count her gates, and number the spires of her churches. She is one ample cemetery and has been for many a year, but in the mighty calms that brood for weeks over tropic latitudes, she fascinates the eye with a *fata Morgana*[4] revelation, as of human life still subsisting in submarine asylums sacred from the storms that torment our upper air.[5]

Thither lured by the loveliness of cerulean depths, by the peace of human dwellings privileged from molestation, by the gleam of marble altars sleeping in everlasting sanctity, oftentimes in dreams did I and the Dark Interpreter[6] cleave the watery veil that divided us from her streets. We looked into the belfries where the pendulous bells were waiting in vain for the summons which should awaken their marriage peals; together we touched the mighty organ keys that sang no *jubilates*[7] for the ear of Heaven, that sang no requiems for the ear of human sorrow; together we searched the silent nurseries where the children were all asleep – and *had* been asleep through five generations.

---

8   *aboriginal forests* i.e. unexplored jungles.

SUSPIRIA DE PROFUNDIS: FINALE TO PART I. SAVANNAH-LA-MAR
1   Jamaican port destroyed by a tidal wave in 1780.
2   *apparel* outfit and rigging of a ship.
3   *translucid* translucent.

4   *fata Morgana* mirage of a city, seen floating in the Straits of Messina.
5   *upper air* i.e. above water level.
6   *the Dark Interpreter* De Quincey's own personal interpreting angel.
7   *jubilates* songs of rejoicing.

'They are waiting for the heavenly dawn', whispered the Interpreter to himself, 'and when *that* comes, the bells and the organs will u ter a *jubilate* repeated by the echoes of paradise.' Then, turning to me, he said, 'This is sad, this is piteous, but less would not have sufficed for the purposes of God. Look here – put into a Roman clepsydra[8] one hundred drops of water. Let these run out as the sands in an hourglass, every drop measuring the hundredth part of a second, so that each shall represent but the three-hundred-and-sixty-thousandth part of an hour. Now count the drops as they race along, and, when the fiftieth of the hundred is passing, behold! Forty-nine are not because already they have perished, and fifty are not because they are yet to come. You see, therefore, how narrow, how incalculably narrow, is the true and actual present.

Of that time which we call the present, hardly a hundredth part but belongs either to a past which has fled, or to a future which is still on the wing. It has perished, or it is not born. It was, or it is not. Yet even this approximation to the truth is *infinitely* false. For again subdivide that solitary drop which only was found to represent the present into a lower series of similar fractions, and the actual present which you arrest measures now but the thirty-sixth millionth of an hour. And so by infinite declensions the true and very present in which only we live and enjoy, will vanish into a mote of a mote, distinguishable only by a heavenly vision. Therefore the present, which only man possesses, offers less capacity for his footing than the slenderest film that ever spider twisted from her womb. Therefore, also, even this incalculable shadow from the narrowest pencil of moonlight is more transitory than geometry can measure or thought of angel can overtake. The time which *is* contracts into a mathematic point, and even that point perishes a thousand times before we can utter its birth. All is finite in the present, and even that finite is infinite in its velocity of flight towards death. But in God there is nothing finite; but in God there is nothing transitory; but in God there *can* be nothing that tends to death. Therefore it follows that for God there can be no present. The future is the present of God, and to the future it is that he sacrifices the human present. Therefore it is that he works by earthquake. Therefore it is that he works by grief. Oh deep is the ploughing of earthquake! Oh deep' – and his voice swelled like a *sanctus*[9] rising from the choir of a cathedral – 'Oh deep is the ploughing of grief! But oftentimes less would not suffice for the agriculture of God. Upon a night of earthquake he builds a thousand years of pleasant habitations for man. Upon the sorrow of an infant, he raises oftentimes from human intellects glorious vintages that could not else have been. Less than these fierce ploughshares would not have stirred the stubborn soil. The one is needed for earth, our planet – for earth itself as the dwelling-place of man. But the other is needed yet oftener for God's mightiest intrument; yes', and he looked solemnly at myself, 'is needed for the mysterious children of the earth!'

Lady Caroline Lamb (*née* Ponsonby)   (1785–1828)

Caroline was the fourth child and only daughter of Frederick Ponsonby, 3rd Earl of Bessborough, and of his wife Lady Henrietta Frances Spencer (sister of Georgiana Cavendish, Duchess of Devonshire). At the age of four she was sent to Italy for six years and brought up by a servant. On her return she was sent to Devonshire House where she was brought up by her aunt, who treated her kindly, and who she always remembered affectionately; she later told Lady Morgan: 'I was a trouble, not a pleasure, all my childhood, for which reason, after my return from Italy, where I was from the age of four until nine, I was ordered by the late Dr Warre neither to learn anything nor see

anyone, for fear the violent passions and strange whims they found in me should lead to madness; of which, however, he assured everyone there were no symptoms. I differ, but the end was, that until fifteen I learned nothing.'[1]

She married the Hon. William Lamb (later Lord Melbourne) in 1805, with whom she had three children, of whom two died. Her surviving son, George Augustus Frederick, was born 11 August 1807, and had mental problems throughout his life.

One hesitates to make too much of her affair with Byron, but she was obsessed with him from the time she first read Samuel Rogers's advance copy of *Childe*

---

[8]   *clepsydra* water-clock.
[9]   *sanctus* Isaiah 6:3, 'Holy, holy, holy . . .'

LADY CAROLINE LAMB
[1]   *Sydney Owenson, Lady Morgan's Memoirs: Autobiography, Diaries and Correspondence* (2 vols, London, 1862), ii 211.

Harold's Pilgrimage (1812). Their affair began in March 1812 and ended in November – short-lived, but intensely passionate. 'Then your heart, my poor Caro – what a little volcano that pours lava through your veins!', Byron told her.[2] But he soon tired of her and concluded matters in a particularly brutal manner, sending her a letter bearing the seal of his new conquest, Lady Oxford. She told Lady Morgan that 'It destroyed me: I lost my brain. I was bled, leeched; kept for a week in the filthy Dolphin Inn, at Rock. On my return, I was in great prostration of mind and spirit.'[3] For a long time she was effectively what we would today describe as a 'stalker', following Byron wherever he went, even waiting in the street when she knew he was attending a party inside. 'You talked to me about keeping her out', Byron told Lady Melbourne in June 1814, 'it is impossible – she comes at all times – at any time – and the moment the door is open in she walks – I can't throw her out of the window'.[4] He struck back in rhyme, making her the subject of one of the most memorable hate-poems in the language, *Remember me*.

Her revenge was also literary. She claimed that her first novel, *Glenarvon* (1816), was written in secret, at night, in the space of a month. It portrayed Byron as the evil and depraved Earl of Glenarvon, and even reprinted, word for word, the letter he had sent her when he ended their affair. Though published anonymously, it was known to have come from her, and to portray a number of real people. That, and Byron's popularity, then at its height, guaranteed a brisk sale.

The best of her literary works is *A New Canto* (1819), a remarkable act of literary appropriation in which, borrowing the *ottava rima* which Byron had used in the recently-published *Don Juan* Cantos I and II, she ridiculed both him and the society from which she felt increasingly alienated. It is presented here in its entirety; its energy, inventiveness and exuberance make it the most impressive by far of her various literary productions. She continued to write novels, notably *Graham Hamilton* (1822) and *Ada Reis* (1823), published anonymously. They received mixed reviews, but sold well.

Her letters are frequently charming, and always readable.[5] Besides her wit, they reveal her to have been, from time to time, a manic-depressive. Typical is a remark to Lady Morgan that 'The only thoughts that ever can make me lose my senses are these: a want of knowledge as to what is really true; a certainty that I am useless; a fear that I am worthless; a belief that all is vanity and vexation of spirit, and that there is nothing new under the sun.'[6] Nonetheless, she evidently possessed an energy and a brilliance that could, on occasion, produce powerful and inventive poetry, a further selection of which may be found in my *Romantic Women Poets: An Anthology* (1997) pp. 479–88.

Further reading

Elizabeth Jenkins, *Lady Caroline Lamb* (London, 1932)

Henry Blyth, *Caro: The Fatal Passion* (London, 1972)

Malcolm Kelsall, 'The Byronic Hero and Revolution in Ireland: The Politics of *Glenarvon*', *The Byron Journal* 9 (1981) 4–19

Peter W. Graham, 'Fictive Biography in 1816: The Case of *Glenarvon*', *The Byron Journal* 19 (1991) 53–68

James Soderholm, 'Lady Caroline Lamb: Byron's Miniature Writ Large', *Keats-Shelley Journal* 40 (1991) 24–46

Duncan Wu, 'Appropriating Byron: Lady Caroline Lamb's *A New Canto*', *TWC* 26 (1995) 140–6

---

[2] Marchand ii 170.

[3] *Sydney Owenson, Lady Morgan's Memoirs: Autobiography, Diaries and Correspondence*, ii 201.

[4] Marchand iv 132.

[5] Her letters may be found in the following: C. Kegan Paul, *William Godwin: His Friends and Contemporaries* (2 vols, London, 1876), ii 266–8, 285–6, 302–4 (letters to Godwin); *Fugitive Pieces and Reminiscences of Lord Byron* ed. Isaac Nathan (London, 1829), pp. 150, 153, 155–6 (letters to Nathan); *Sydney Owenson, Lady Morgan's Memoirs: Autobiography, Diaries and Correspondence* (2 vols, London, 1862), i 442–3; ii 174–9, 203–4, 206–13, 240 (letters to Morgan); Sydney Owenson, Lady Morgan, *Passages from my Autobiography* (London, 1859), pp. 49–50, 66–71; W. M. Torrens, *Memoirs of the Right Honourable William Second Viscount Melbourne* (2 vols, London, 1878), i 297, 171–2, 173–4, ii 130–1; James O. Hoge, Jr, 'Lady Caroline Lamb on Byron and her own wasted life: two new letters', *N&Q* 21 (1974) 331–3 (letters to Bulwer Lytton); and my 'Appropriating Byron: Lady Caroline Lamb's *A New Canto*', *TWC* 26 (1995) 140–6.

[6] *Sydney Owenson, Lady Morgan's Memoirs: Autobiography, Diaries and Correspondence*, ii 303.

[*My heart's fit to break*]

From GLENARVON (1816)

My heart's fit to break, yet no tear fills my eye,
As I gaze on the moon, and the clouds that flit by;
The moon shines so fair, it reminds me of thee,
But the clouds that obscure it are emblems of me.

They will pass like the dreams of our pleasures and youth,   5
They will pass like the promise of honour and truth,
And bright thou shalt shine when these shadows are gone,
All radiant, serene, unobscured – but alone.

A New Canto (1819)

I

I'm sick of fame[1] – I'm gorged with it, so full
    I almost could regret[2] the happier hour
When northern oracles proclaimed me dull,
    Grieving my Lord should so mistake his power[3] –
E'en they who now my consequence would lull,   5
    And vaunt they hailed and nursed the opening flower.
Vile cheats! He knew not, impudent reviewer,
Clear spring of Helicon[4] from common sewer.

II

'Tis said they killed the gentle-souled Montgomery;[5]
    I'll swear they did not shed for him a tear!   10
He had not spirit to revenge their mummery,
    Nor lordly purse to print and persevere.[6]
I measured stings with 'em[7] – a method summary
    (Not that I doubt their penitence sincere);
And I've a fancy running in my head   15
They'll like – or so by some it will be said.

A NEW CANTO
[1] *I'm sick of fame* the poem is written in the persona of
Byron, the 'Lord' of l. 4.
[2] *regret* long for.
[3] *I almost . . . power* Byron's first volume of poems, *Hours of
Idleness* (1807), was greeted with facetious contempt by the
Edinburgh Review ('northern oracles').
[4] *clear spring of Helicon* Aganippe, the fountain of inspiration,
flowed from the foot of Mt Helicon, seat of the Muses in
ancient Greece.
[5] The poet James Montgomery (1771–1854) was both alive
and popular in 1819. Caroline alludes to Byron's *English Bards
and Scotch Reviewers* 419–25, which laments Montgomery's
supposed death on the grounds of his harsh treatment from
the *Edinburgh Review*.

[6] *Nor lordly purse . . . persevere* a dig at Byron: the implication
is that his poetry has been so unsuccessful that he has had to
fund its publication out of his own purse. Byron's first two
volumes, *Fugitive Pieces* (1806) and *Poems on Various Occasions*
(1807) were, as Caroline must have known, funded out of his
own pocket.
[7] *I measured stings with 'em* a reference to *English Bards and
Scotch Reviewers* (1809), in which Byron attacked most of his
contemporary poets and reviewers, with the exception of
Thomas Campbell (1777–1844), author of *The Pleasures of
Hope* (1799); Samuel Rogers (1763–1855), author of *The Plea-
sures of Memory* (1792), and William Gifford (1756–1826),
satirist (as author of the *Baviad* (1794) and *Maeviad* (1795)),
and editor of the *Quarterly Review*, 1809–24.

III

When doomsday comes, St Paul's[8] will be on fire
    (I should not wonder if we live to see it);
Of us, proof pickles,[9] Heaven must rather tire
    And want a reckoning – if so, so be it: 20
Only about the cupola,[10] or higher,
    If there's a place unoccupied, give me it –
To catch, before I touch my sinner's salary,[11]
The first grand crackle in the whispering gallery.[12]

IV

The ball comes tumbling with a lively crash,   25
    And splits the pavement up, and shakes the shops,
Teeth chatter, china dances, spreads the flash,[13]
    The omnium[14] falls, the Bank of England[15] stops;
Loyal and radical, discreet and rash,
    Each on his knees in tribulation flops;   30
The Regent[16] raves (Moore[17] chuckling at his pain)
And sends about for ministers in vain.

V

The roaring streamers[18] flap, red flakes[19] are shot
    This way and that, the town is a volcano –
And yells are heard, like those provoked by Lot,[20]   35
    Some of the Smithfield[21] sort, and some *soprano*;
Some holy water seek – the font is hot,
    And fizzing in a tea-kettle *piano*.
'Now bring your magistrates, with yeomen[22] backed',
Bawls Belial,[23] 'and read the Riot Act!'[24]   40

---

[8]   St Paul's Cathedral in the City of London, redesigned and rebuilt by Sir Christopher Wren, 1663–98.

[9]   *proof pickles* proven delinquents.

[10]   *the cupola* i.e. of St Paul's.

[11]   *my sinner's salary* i.e. everlasting damnation. Byron was renowned as an atheist and a libertine.

[12]   *the whispering gallery* immediately beneath the 24 windows in the dome of St Paul's Cathedral. It is 100ft from the floor and, if you whisper against the wall, you can be heard clearly on the opposite side of the Gallery 107ft away.

[13]   *the flash* i.e. fire in the sky as the apocalypse begins.

[14]   *omnium* at the Stock Exchange, the aggregate amount of the parcels of different stocks, formerly offered by the government, in raising a loan, for each unit of capital subscribed.

[15]   *the Bank of England* in Threadneedle Street, City of London, from 1734 onwards.

[16]   *The Regent* by 1819 George III was blind and mad; his son (the future George IV) was governing the country as Prince Regent, and would ascend to the throne in 1820 on his father's death.

[17]   Thomas Moore (see pp. 617–19) met Lamb during her affair with Byron, March 1812. He was widely known to be the author of a popular lampoon on court life, *The Twopenny Post Bag* (1813).

[18]   *roaring streamers* flaming debris that roars through the air.

[19]   *flakes* ignited bits of rubble.

[20]   *like those provoked by Lot* Caroline refers to the aggressive behaviour of the Sodomites towards Lot and his family, Genesis 19:9–11.

[21]   *Smithfield* London's largest meat market covering a plain of over ten acres; it was usually a scene of mayhem – drovers often stampeded cattle on the way to market, tormented beasts took refuge in shops and houses (the origin of the phrase 'a bull in a china shop'), live animals were slaughtered in the open, blood flowed through the streets, and entrails were dumped in drainage channels.

[22]   *yeomen* charged with upholding the magistrate's decisions; a sort of civil guard.

[23]   *Belial* one of the fallen angels.

[24]   *read the Riot Act* declare that (unruly) action or conduct must cease. The Riot Act was repealed in 1973.

VI

The Peak of Derbyshire[25] goes to and fro;
   Like drunken sot the Monument[26] is reeling;
Now fierce and fiercer comes the furious glow –
   The planets, like a juggler's ball, are wheeling!
I am a graceless poet, as you know,   45
   Yet would not wish to wound a proper feeling,
Nor hint you'd hear, from saints in agitation,
The *lapsus linguae*[27] of an execration.

VII

Mark yon bright beauty in her tragic airs,[28]
   How her clear white the mighty smother[29] tinges –   50
Delicious chaos, that such beauty bares!
   And now those eyes outstretch their silken fringes,[30]
Staring bewildered – and anon she tears
   Her raven tresses ere the wide flame singes –
Oh would she feel as I could do, and cherish   55
One wild forgetful rapture, ere all perish!

VIII

Who would be vain? Fair maids and ugly men
   Together rush, the dainty and the shabby
(No gallantry will soothe ye, ladies, then),
   High dames, the wandering beggar and her *babby*,   60
In motley agony, a desperate train,
   Flocking to holy places like the Abbey,[31]
Till the black volumes,[32] closing o'er them, scowl,
Muffling forever curse, and shriek, and howl.

IX

A woman then may rail, nor would I stint her;   65
   Her griefs, poor soul, are past redress in law –
And if this matter happen in the winter,
   There'll be at Petersburg a sudden thaw,
And Alexander's palace, every splinter
   Burn Christmas-like and merry, though the jaw   70
Of its imperial master[33] take to trembling,
As when the French were quartered in the Kremlin.[34]

---

[25] *The Peak of Derbyshire* the Peak District in Derbyshire.
[26] *the Monument* Doric column 202ft high, built of Portland stone in 1671–7, to mark the place from which the Great Fire of London began in 1666.
[27] *lapsus linguae* slip of the tongue.
[28] *airs* demeanour, pose.
[29] *smother* dense, stifling smoke.
[30] *silken fringes* eyelashes.

[31] *the Abbey* Westminster Abbey, restored and very largely redesigned by Sir Christopher Wren, 1698–1723. People mistakenly believe it will provide them with sanctuary from the unfolding apocalypse.
[32] *black volumes* masses of black cloud or smoke.
[33] *its imperial master* Tsar Alexander I.
[34] *As when . . . Kremlin* Napoleon took control of Moscow in September 1812, but retreated a month later.

X

Rare doings in the north! as trickle down
    Primeval snows, and white bears swash[35] and caper,
And Bernadotte,[36] that swaggerer[37] of renown,
    To Bonaparte again might hold a taper,[38]   75
Aye, truckle[39] to him, cap in hand or crown,
    To save his distance from the sturdy vapour.
Napoleon, too, will he look blank and paly?
He hung the citizens of Moscow gaily;   80

XI

He made a gallant youth[40] his darkling prey,
    Nor e'er would massacre or murder mince;[41]
And yet I fear, on this important day,
    To see the hero[42] pitifully wince!
Go yield him up to Beelzebub,[43] and say,   85
    'Pray treat him like a gentleman and prince.'
I doubt him thoroughbred, he's not a true one,
A bloodhound spaniel-crossed, and no Don Juan.

XII

Death-watches[44] now, in every baking wall, tick
    Faster and faster, till they tick no more,   90
And Norway's copper-mines about the Baltic
    Swell, heave, and rumble with their boiling ore,
Like some griped giant's motion peristaltic,[45]
    Then burst, and to the sea vast gutters pour;
And as the waters with the fire-stream curl,   95
Zooks! what a whizzing, roaring, sweltering whirl!

XIII

Lo! the great deep laid bare,[46] tremendous yawning,
    Its scalding waves retiring from the shore,
Affrighted whales on dry land sudden spawning,
    And small fish fry where fish ne'er fried before.   100

---

[35] *swash* dash.
[36] The Frenchman Jean Bernadotte was elected Crown Prince of Sweden in 1810, joined the allies against Napoleon in 1813, and became King in 1818.
[37] *swaggerer* quarreller.
[38] *hold a taper* i.e. assist him. At the time of writing, Napoleon was still alive, in exile on the tiny South Atlantic isle of St Helena.
[39] *truckle* kow-tow.
[40] *a gallant youth* Horatio, Lord Nelson (1758–1805), killed at the Battle of Trafalgar, by Napoleon's forces, 21 October 1805.

[41] *mince* restrain, mitigate.
[42] *the hero* i.e. Napoleon (ironic).
[43] *Beelzebub* prince of devils.
[44] *Death-watches* death-watch beetles, which make a ticking sound, supposed to portend death.
[45] *motion peristaltic* action of the intestine as it digests food.
[46] *the great deep laid bare* it is so hot that the sea has evaporated.

No Christian eye shall see another dawning –
  The Turkish infidel may now restore
His wives[47] to liberty, and, ere to hell he go,
  Roll to the bottom of the Archipelago![48]

XIV

And now, ye coward sinners (I'm a bold one,   105
  Scorning all here, nor caring for hereafter –
A radical, a stubborn, and an old one),
  Behold! each riding on a burning rafter,[49]
The devils (in my arms I long to fold one)
  Splitting their blue and brazen sides with laughter,   110
Play at snapdragon[50] in their merry fits,
O'er some conventicle[51] for hypocrites.[52]

XV

Aye, serve the skulkers, with their looks so meek,
  As they've, no doubt, served lobsters[53] in their time
(Poor *blacks*! No Wilberforce[54] for them can speak,   115
  Pleading their colour is their only crime);
Trundle them all to bubble and to squeak[55] –
  No doubt they shut their ears against my rhyme,
Yet sneak, rank elders, fearful of denials,
To pick Susannas up[56] in Seven Dials.[57]   120

XVI

Brave fiends! for usurers and misers melt
  And make a hell-broth of their cursed gold!
On all who mock at want[58] they never felt,
  On all whose consciences are bought and sold,
E'en as on me, be stern damnation dealt –   125
  And lawyers, damn them all! The blood runs cold,
That man should deal with misery to mock it,
And filch an only shilling[59] from its pocket.

---

47 *wives* Caroline imagines the Turk as having a harem.
48 *the Archipelago* the Aegean Sea, between Greece and Turkey.
49 *rafter* raft, sailing on the boiling sea.
50 *snapdragon* game in which the players snatch raisins out of a bowl of burning brandy; the devils amuse themselves by plucking hypocrites out of the boiling sea.
51 *conventicle* meeting.
52 *hypocrites* i.e. religious hypocrites.
53 *lobsters* cooked by being immersed, alive, in boiling water – the same fate as the 'skulkers'.
54 William Wilberforce (1759–1833), leader of the movement for the abolition of the slave trade in Parliament.
55 *to bubble and to squeak* bubble-and-squeak is a dish of meat and cabbage fried up together.

56 *Yet sneak . . . up* Lamb is referring to godfearing people who break their faith by picking up prostitutes. The story of Susanna and the elders is to be found in the apocryphal 'History of Susanna'; two elders watched her bathing, and asked her to 'lie with them' or else they would denounce her as a whore.
57 *Seven Dials* area near Covent Garden, where seven roads converge on a Doric pillar in the middle of a circular area. Although intended at first to be fashionable, it was, by 1819, the haunt of prostitutes, petty thieves and disreputable street vendors.
58 *want* need, e.g. poverty, hunger, homelessness.
59 *an only shilling* i.e. the last shilling (a shilling was equal to 12 old pence).

XVII

Aye, damn them all, a deep damnation wait
 On all such callous, crooked, hopeless souls!   130
Ne'er mince the matter to discriminate,
 But let the devil strike them from the rolls:[60]
'Twill cheer their clients to behold their fate,
 And round their bonfires dance in merry shoals!
Some poor men's tales I've heard upon my journeys   135
Would make a bishop long to roast attorneys!

XVIII

Perhaps the thing may take another turn,
 And one smart shock may split the world in two,
And I in Italy,[61] you soon may learn,
 On t'other half[62] am reeling far from you.   140
No doubt 'twould split where first it ought to burn –
 Across some city that its sins should rue,
Some wicked capital, for instance, Paris,
And stop the melodrames[63] from Mr Harris.[64]

XIX

Save London, none is wickeder or bigger,[65]   145
 An odious place too, in these modern times;
Small incomes, runaways, and swindlers eager
 To fleece[66] and dash; and then their quacks and mimes,
Their morals lax, and literary rigour,
 Their prim caesuras, and their gendered rhymes –   150
Mine never could abide their statutes critical,
They'd call them neutral or hermaphroditical.

XX

True, their poor playwrights (truth, I speak with pain)
 Yield ours a picking, and I beg their pardon;
'Tis needless – down must come poor Drury Lane,   155
 And scarcely less poor, down come Covent Garden![67]

---

[60] *the rolls* official list of those qualified to practise as solicitors.
[61] *And I in Italy* Byron had been in Italy since October 1816.
[62] *t'other half* i.e. of the world, which has split in two.
[63] *melodrames* melodramas – sensational and romantic dramas, often with music. Melodramas flourished in London during the first decades of the nineteenth century, thanks partly to the enormous success of Thomas Holcroft's *A Tale of Mystery* (1802).
[64] Thomas Harris (died 1820), proprietor and manager of Covent Garden theatre.

[65] *none is wickeder or bigger* i.e. than Paris.
[66] *fleece* steal.
[67] Fiercely competitive, Drury Lane and Covent Garden were the only theatres in London licensed to perform 'spoken drama'. Both had 'come down' in recent years: Drury Lane burned down in 1809, and was rebuilt in 1812; Covent Garden burned down in 1808 and reopened the following year. Byron had been on the committee of management of Drury Lane.

If we must blaze, no squabbles will remain
    That actor's hearts against each other harden –
Committees, creditors, all wrapped in flames,
That leave no joke for Horace Smith or James.[68]   160

XXI

In rebus modus est:[69] whene'er I write
    I mean to rhapsodize, and nothing more;
If some poor nervous souls my muse affright,
    I might a strain of consolation pour,
Talk of the spotless spirits, snowy white,   165
    Which, newly clad, refreshing graves restore,
And, silvery wreaths of glory round them curled,
Serenely rise above the blazing world.

XXII

Free, bursting from his mound of lively green,[70]
    Winged light as zephyr of the rosy morn,   170
The poor man smiling on the proud is seen,
    With something of a mild, forgiving scorn –
The marbled proud one, haply with the mean,
    Sole on his prayer of intercession borne:[71]
Upward in peal harmonious they move,   175
Soft as the midnight tide of hallowed love.

XXIII

The rich humane, who with their common clay
    Divided graciously (distinguished few);
Good Christians who had slept their wrongs away,
    In peace with this life, and the next in view;   180
Strugglers with tyrant passion and its prey,
    Love's single-hearted victims, sacred, true,
Who, when dishonour's path alone could save,[72]
Bore a pure pang to an untimely grave –

---

[68] The brothers Horace Smith (1779–1849) and James Smith (1775–1839) were well known for their *Rejected Addresses* (1812). When Drury Lane theatre was reopened in 1812, the management announced a contest for dedicatory verses for the new building. In the end, none of the entrants were accepted and Byron was commissioned to write the address delivered on the opening night. However, the Smiths decided to write parodies of all the rejected addresses by the best-known writers of the day, including Coleridge, Wordsworth, Southey and Scott.

[69] 'There is a measure in things.'

[70] *bursting . . . green* the poor man rises up from the grave, in fulfilment of the prophecy of St John the Divine, Revelation 20:12: 'And I saw the dead, small and great, stand before God'.

[71] The proud man is saved only by a prayer of intercession (i.e. on his behalf) by the humble ('mean') man.

[72] *when dishonour's path alone could save* Caroline again has in mind the story of Susanna, who could have saved herself by surrendering to the impure desires of the elders, but preferred to remain pure in the sight of God.

XXIV

Blessed they, who wear the vital spirit out   185
    Even thus, degrading not the holy fire,[73]
Nor bear a prostituted sense about –
    The misery of never-quenched desire
(Still quenched, still kindling, every thought devout
    Lost in the changeful torment – portion dire!).   190
Return we to our heaven, our fire and smoke,
Though now you may begin to take the joke!

XXV

What joke? My verses – mine, and all beside,
    Wild, foolish tales of Italy and Spain,[74]
The gushing shrieks, the bubbling squeaks, the bride   195
    Of nature, blue-eyed, black-eyed, and her swain,
Kissing in grottos near the moonlit tide,[75]
    Though to all men of commonsense 'tis plain –
Except for rampant and amphibious brute,
Such damp and drizzly places would not suit.   200

XXVI

Mad world! For fame we rant, call names, and fight –
    I scorn it heartily, yet love to dazzle it,
Dark intellects by day, as shops by night,
    All with a bright, new, speculative gas lit,[76]
Wars the blue vapour with the oil-fed light,   205
    Hot sputter Blackwood, Jeffrey, Gifford, Hazlitt[77] –
The muse runs madder, and, as mine may tell,
Like a loose comet, mingles heaven and hell.

XXVII

You shall have more of her another time,
    Since gulled you will be with our flights poetic,   210
Our eight, and ten, and twenty feet[78] sublime,
    Our maudlin, hey-down-derrified[79] pathetic;
For my part, though I'm doomed to write in rhyme,
    To read it would be worse than an emetic –
But something must be done to cure the spleen,[80]   215
And keep my name in capitals, like Kean.[81]

---

73 *the holy fire* i.e. their souls.

74 *Italy and Spain* Don Juan in Byron's poem is born in Seville. *Beppo* (1818) is set in Venice.

75 *Kissing . . . tide* an allusion to Haidee and Juan; see *Don Juan* ii 1465–88 (p. 808).

76 *gas lit* gas lighting was introduced in London, 1792–1808.

77 William Blackwood (1776–1834), publisher of *Blackwood's Edinburgh Magazine*; William Gifford (1756–1826), editor of the *Quarterly Review*; Jeffrey edited the *Edinburgh Review* (see p. 555); and Hazlitt was a journalist (see pp. 596–7).

78 *feet* Caroline means metrical feet; her point is that Byron thinks he is sublime, when he is just long-winded.

79 *hey-down-derrified* 'Hey down derry' is a meaningless refrain in popular ballads. Caroline means that Byron's verse operates at a similarly uninspired level.

80 *the spleen* extreme depression, of which both Caroline and Byron were sufferers.

81 Caroline's point is that Byron writes only for fame, in spite of his protestations to the contrary. Edmund Kean (?1787–1833) was one of the most distinguished actors of the day; he was just about the biggest draw in London from 1814 onwards, when he became famous overnight for his portrayal of Shylock. Byron was a great admirer.

[*Would I had seen thee dead and cold*]

From FUGITIVE PIECES AND REMINISCENCES OF LORD BYRON WITH SOME ORIGINAL POETRY,
LETTERS AND RECOLLECTIONS OF LADY CAROLINE LAMB ed. Isaac Nathan (1829)

Would I had seen thee dead and cold
  In thy lone grave asleep,
Than live, thy falsehood to behold,
  And, penitent, to weep;
For better I thy grave could see   5
Than know that thou art false to me!

Or rather, would that I had died
  When happy on thy breast;
My love had then been satisfied,
  And life's last moments blessed –   10
For they taste bliss without alloy
Who die in the sweet dream of joy.

But no, I feel the fault was mine,
  To think affection's chain
Could thy proud wayward heart confine   15
  When honour's claim was vain:
Who robs the shrine where virtue lies
Will not the stolen relic prize!

Benjamin Robert Haydon   (1786–1846)

Haydon was born at Plymouth on 25 January 1786, to a bookseller and his wife. His artistic talent emerged quickly: at school he taught other pupils. But his father wanted him to take over the family business, and Haydon was formally apprenticed to him for seven years. Frustrated by this prospect, he broke his indentures to his father in 1804, and left for London to study at the Royal Academy. He was never successful as an artist, and suffered frequent bouts of poverty. But the patronage of the likes of Lord Mulgrave and Sir George and Lady Beaumont led to occasional commissions. In 1811 he began to keep a diary, which he called the 'secret history of my mind' and eventually ran to over a million words. Though in many ways a difficult, prickly man, he enjoyed meeting his contemporaries and by the end of 1812 his circle included Hazlitt (pp. 596–617), Lamb (pp. 577–89), and John and Leigh Hunt (pp. 620–4).

One of his most important paintings, *Christ's Entry into Jerusalem* (now at St Mary's Seminary, Ohio), was begun in 1814. It was to occupy him for the next six years, and included portraits of Keats, Wordsworth, Hazlitt and Newton. On 28 December 1817 he gave the 'immortal dinner', described by him in his diary in the extract below; in few other places are the romantics brought so vividly to life.

Important paintings in succeeding years included *Marcus Curtius Leaping into the Gulf* (1836–42) and *Wordsworth on Helvellyn* (1842) – the subject of a sonnet by Elizabeth Barrett (p. 1112). In an age that can boast of two of the greatest English artists of all time – Constable and Turner – Haydon remains a minor attraction, in many ways of more interest for his literary associations than for his painting. He felt his career to have been a failure even as he hung the final exhibition of his works at the Egyptian Hall, Piccadilly, in April 1846. It closed after six weeks, losing him more than £111. Pressurised by debt, persuaded of the uselessness of his life, he cut his own throat on 22 June.

Further reading

Alethea Hayter, *A Sultry Month: Scenes of London Literary Life in 1846* (London, 1965)
Eric George, *The Life and Death of Benjamin Robert Haydon: Historical Painter 1786–1846* (2nd edn, Oxford, 1967)
David Blayney Brown, Robert Woof, and Stephen Hebron, *Benjamin Robert Haydon 1786–1846* (Grasmere, 1996)

[*The Immortal Dinner*]

28 December 1817. Wordsworth dined with me; Keats and Lamb with a friend made up the dinner party, and a very pleasant party we had. Wordsworth was in fine and powerful cue.[1] We had a glorious set-to on Homer, Shakespeare, Milton and Virgil. Lamb got excessively merry and witty, and his fun in the intervals of Wordsworth's deep and solemn intonations of oratory was the fun and wit of the fool in the intervals of Lear's passion.[2] Lamb soon gets tipsy, and tipsy he got very shortly, to our infinite amusement.

'Now, you rascally Lake Poet', said Lamb, 'you call Voltaire[3] a dull fellow.'[4] We all agreed there was a state of mind when he would appear so – and 'Well let us drink his health', said Lamb. 'Here's Voltaire, the Messiah of the French nation, and a very fit one!'

He then attacked me for putting in Newton,[5] 'a fellow who believed nothing unless it was as clear as the three sides of a triangle!' And then he and Keats agreed he had destroyed all the poetry of the rainbow by reducing it to a prism. It was impossible to resist them, and we drank 'Newton's health, and confusion to mathematics!' It was delightful to see the good humour of Wordsworth in giving in to all our frolics without affectation[6] and laughing as heartily as the best of us.

By this time other visitors began to drop in, and a Mr Ritchie,[7] who is going to penetrate into the interior of Africa. I introduced him to Wordsworth as such, and the conversation got into a new train. After some time, Lamb, who had seemingly paid no attention to anyone, suddenly opened his eyes and said, alluding to the dangers of penetrating into the interior of Africa, 'And pray, who is the gentleman we are going *to lose?*' Here was a roar of laughter, the victim Ritchie joining with us.

We now retired to tea, and, among other friends, a gentleman[8] who was Comptroller of the Stamp Office came. He had been peculiarly anxious to know and see Wordsworth. The moment he was introduced he let Wordsworth know *who* he officially was.[9] This was an exquisite touch of human nature. Though Wordsworth of course would not have suffered him to speak indecently or impiously without reproof, yet he had a visible effect on Wordsworth. I felt pain at the slavery of office. In command men are despotic, and those who are dependent on others who have despotic control must and do feel affected by their presence. The Comptroller was a very mild and nice fellow, but rather weak and very fond of talking. He got into conversation with Wordsworth on poetry, and just after he had been putting forth some of his silly stuff, Lamb, who had been dozing as usual, suddenly opened his mouth and said, 'What did you say, sir?'

'Why, sir', said the Comptroller, in his milk and water insipidity, 'I was saying. . .', etc., etc., etc.

'Do you say so, sir?' 'Yes sir', was the reply. 'Why then, sir, I say (hiccup) you are – you are a silly fellow!' This operated like thunder. The Comptroller knew nothing of his previous tipsiness and looked at him like a man bewildered. The venerable anxiety of Wordsworth to prevent the Comptroller being angry, and his expostulations with Lamb, who had sunk back again into his doze, as insensible to the confusion he had produced as a being above it; the astonishment of Landseer the engraver,[10] who was totally deaf, and with his hand to his ear and his eye was trying to catch the meaning of the gestures he saw; and the agonizing attempts of Keats, Ritchie, and I to suppress our laughter; and the smiling struggle of the Comptroller to take all in good part without losing his dignity, made up a story of comic expressions totally unrivalled in nature. I felt pain that such a poet as Wordsworth

---

THE IMMORTAL DINNER

1   *cue* form, condition.
2   *the fool . . . Lear's passion* see *King Lear* III vi.
3   François Marie Arouet de Voltaire (1694–1778), French philosopher and novelist.
4   *you call . . . fellow* a reference to Wordsworth's criticism of *Candide* as the 'dull product of a scoffer's pen' (*Excursion* ii 484). The comment had come in for criticism from Hazlitt in his review of the *Excursion* in the *Examiner*, and Lamb had corresponded with Wordsworth about it on 19 September 1814 (Marrs iii 112).

5   Haydon inserted the face of Sir Isaac Newton into the background of his painting, *Christ's Entry into Jerusalem.*
6   *affectation* pretence.
7   Joseph Ritchie (1788–1819), surgeon and African traveller, who died at Murzuk, Libya.
8   John Kingston, Deputy Comptroller of Stamps.
9   Wordsworth was Distributor of Stamps for Westmorland, 1813–42, and was therefore junior to Kingston.
10   John Landseer (1769–1852), painter and engraver, father of Edwin Landseer.

should be under the supervisorship of such a being as this Comptroller. The people of England have a horror of office, an instinct against it. They are right. A man's liberty is gone the moment he becomes official; he is the slave of superiors, and makes others slaves to him. The Comptroller went on making his profound remarks, and when anything very *deep* came forth,[11] Lamb roared out,

> Diddle iddle don
> My son John
> Went to bed with his breeches on,
> One stocking off and one stocking on,
> My son John.

The Comptroller laughed as if he marked it, and went on; every remark Lamb chorused with

> Went to bed with his breeches on
> Diddle iddle on.

There is no describing this scene adequately. There was not the restraint of refined company, nor the vulgar freedom of low, but a frank natural license such as one sees in an act of Shakespeare, every man expressing his natural emotions without fear. Into this company, a little heated with wine, a Comptroller of the Stamp Office walked, frilled, dressed, and official, with a due awe of the powers above him and a due contempt for those beneath him. His astonishment at finding where he was come cannot be conceived, and in the midst of his mild namby-pamby[12] opinions, Lamb's address deadened his views. When they separated, Wordsworth softened his feelings, but Lamb kept saying in the Painting Room, 'Who is that fellow? Let me go and hold the candle once more to his face –

> My son John
> Went to bed with his breeches on!'

And these were the last words of C. Lamb. The door was closed upon him. There was something interesting in seeing Wordsworth sitting, and Keats and Lamb, and my picture of Christ's entry towering up behind them, occasionally brightened by the gleams of flame that sparkled from the fire, and hearing the voice of Wordsworth repeating Milton with an intonation like the funeral bell of St Paul's[13] and the music of Handel mingled, and then Lamb's wit came sparkling in between, and Keats' rich fancy of satyrs and fauns and doves and white clouds wound up the stream of conversation. I never passed a more delightful day, and I am convinced that nothing in Boswell[14] is equal to what came out from these poets. Indeed there were no such poets in his time.[15] It was an evening worthy of the Elizabethan age, and will long flash upon 'that inward eye which is the bliss of solitude.'[16] Hail and farewell!

---

[11] 'Such as "Pray sir, don't you think Milton a very *great genius?*" This I really recollect. 1823' (Haydon's note).

[12] *namby-pamby* childishly simple.

[13] St Paul's Cathedral in the City of London.

[14] James Boswell, *Life of Johnson* (1791).

[15] *there were no such . . . time* a comment that reveals that by 1817 the likes of Haydon were aware that they lived at a time of tremendous artistic achievement.

[16] Wordsworth, *Daffodils* 15–16.

George Gordon Byron, 6th Baron Byron
(1788–1824)

George Gordon, 6th Lord Byron, that most seductively attractive of major poets, and by far one of the biggest-selling of his day, was born 22 January 1788, to Catherine Gordon and Captain John ('Mad Jack') Byron, in poor lodgings in London. He had a deformed right foot from birth and was lame throughout his life. Abandoned by her husband (he died in France in 1791), and brought to verge of ruin by his extravagant way with money, Catherine took her son to Aberdeen in her native Scotland where she struggled to bring him up as best she could. Here he came to love the Scottish countryside and, in about 1795, fell in love with his cousin, Mary Duff.

He was only ten years old when, with the death of his grand-uncle, he succeeded to the title of the Barony, becoming the 6th Lord Byron. He and his mother moved down to Newstead Abbey, and he received private tuition in Nottingham, in preparation for entrance to a public school. During this time (around 1799), when he was eleven, he was the subject of sexual advances from his nurse, May Gray, who was dismissed when her misdemeanours were discovered.

He became a pupil at Harrow in 1801, where Robert Peel (future Prime Minister) was a contemporary. Having fallen in love with another cousin, Margaret Parker, in 1800, he was in love again with yet another, Mary Chaworth, two years later. In spite of his obvious brilliance, he was never a diligent student, and later said that he had hated Harrow until his last eighteen months there, which he had enjoyed. But those months were turbulent: he fell out with a good friend, Lord Grey (apparently because of Grey's sexual advances towards him); was shocked by Mary Chaworth's decision to marry a rival; and got himself into trouble in May 1805 for leading a rebellion against the new headmaster. His last weeks as a Harrovian were distinguished, however, by a fine performance in the Eton–Harrow cricket match, in which he scored eighteen runs (Harrow lost) – no mean feat for someone with a club foot.

He left Harrow having incurred numerous debts and took every opportunity, after going up to Trinity College, Cambridge, in October 1805, to live even more extravagantly than before. (By January 1808 his debts amounted to over £5,000.) Cambridge brought out his lordliness: the keeping of dogs being prohibited, he kept a tame bear in a turret at the top of a staircase. At Cambridge he had a passionate friendship with the choirboy John Edleston, 'the only *being* I

esteem', who provided the inspiration for the 'Thyrza' poems some years later (see pp. 666–7). In 1806 he gathered his juvenile poetry together under the title of *Fugitive Pieces*, but suppressed it at the last moment; in January 1807 he privately printed a second collection of juvenilia as *Poems on Various Occasions*; and in the summer of 1807 he published a third volume, *Hours of Idleness*. This volume drew damning criticism from Henry Brougham (anonymously) in the *Edinburgh Review* (January 1808); his opening remarks set the tone for what was to come: 'His effusions are spread over a dead flat, and can no more get above or below the level, than if they were so much stagnant water.'

Byron took his revenge in print with a vigorous and uncompromising satire on literary life, *English Bards and Scotch Reviewers* (1809). It branded most of his contemporaries as 'dunces', including his own guardian, the Earl of Carlisle, who had ambitions to be a verse-dramatist. The only writers for whom he had anything good to say were Thomas Campbell, Samuel Rogers and William Gifford. This view, however strange it may seem to us, was crucial to Byron's aesthetic: as far as he was concerned, poets like Rogers were true to the neo-classical tradition of Pope; Wordsworth, Coleridge and Southey, by contrast, had rejected it for a completely bogus system which they used to promote their own intellects. From time to time he could even regard himself and Thomas Moore as seduced by the current trends; he put it like this in a letter to his publisher, John Murray, 15 September 1817:

> With regard to poetry in general I am convinced, the more I think of it, that he [Thomas Moore] and *all* of us – Scott, Southey, Wordsworth, Moore, Campbell, I – are all in the wrong, one as much as another – that we are upon a wrong revolutionary poetical system (or systems) not worth a damn in itself – and from which none but Rogers and Crabbe are free – and that the present and next generations will finally be of this opinion. I am the more confirmed in this by having lately gone over some of our classics, particularly Pope, whom I tried[1] in this way: I took Moore's poems and my own and some others, and went over them side by side with Pope's, and I was really astonished (I ought not to have been so) and mortified at the ineffable distance in point of sense, harmony, effect, and even *Imagination*, passion,

GEORGE GORDON BYRON
[1] *tried* i.e. tested.

and invention, between the little Queen Anne's man [Pope] and us of the lower Empire.[2]

This was the aesthetic position from which Byron attacked contemporary writers in *English Bards*, and which was later to inform his criticism of the Lake poets in *Don Juan*. At any rate, *English Bards and Scotch Reviewers* was popular with the public, and attracted favourable reviews.

By July 1808, when he took his MA from Cambridge, he had established himself as a man about town in London (with no less than four mistresses). Feeling pressurized, no doubt thanks partly to his enormous debts, he left England in July 1809 with his friend Hobhouse, on a tour of Portugal, Spain, Gibraltar, Malta, Albania and Greece. In the course of his travels he met the Ali Pasha (Turkish despot of Albania and western Greece), swam the Hellespont, saved the life of a Turkish girl condemned to death for sexual impropriety, and met the young woman he would celebrate in verse as the 'Maid of Athens'.

After an absence of two years and twelve days, he landed at Sheerness in Kent on 14 July 1811, proceeding straight to London. There he took his seat in the House of Lords and made his maiden speech on 27 February 1812 on behalf of the stocking weavers of Nottingham (the Luddites). He spoke against a vicious piece of legislation by the government, which proposed the death penalty as punishment for frame-breaking. It was a creditable performance, and some of his Whig colleagues regarded it highly; 'I was born for opposition', he later wrote.[3]

Perhaps he might have gone on to be a distinguished politician but for the fact that, a few days later on 3 March, John Murray published *Childe Harold's Pilgrimage* Cantos I and II. It was an instant success: London had seen nothing like it. All 500 copies of the first edition were sold out within three days of publication, and its author became one of the major literary stars of the day. As Samuel Rogers recalled: 'The genius which the poem exhibited, the youth, the rank of the author, his romantic wanderings in Greece, – these combined to make the world stark mad about *Childe Harold* and Byron'. In a favourable notice in the *Edinburgh Review*, Francis Jeffrey described the poem as follows:

> Childe Harold is a sated epicure – sickened with the very fullness of prosperity – oppressed with ennui, and stung by occasional remorse; –

his heart hardened by a long course of sensual indulgence, and his opinion of mankind degraded by his acquaintance with the baser part of them. In this state he wanders over the fairest and most interesting parts of Europe, in the vain hope of stimulating his palsied sensibility by novelty, or at least of occasionally forgetting his mental anguish in the toils and perils of his journey.

It was the identification of Byron with his protagonist that fuelled interest in the poem and its author. At any rate, the formula captured the imagination of his readers (many of whom were women), and aroused an unquenchable thirst for information about his exploits and for more poetry. From this point onwards virtually everything he published would sell in thousands, making him one of the biggest-selling writers of the day.

It was the publication of *Childe Harold* that attracted Lady Caroline Lamb to Byron.[4] Their affair lasted only months, but Caroline became obsessed with him, and followed him around for months afterwards (see pp. 648–9). He consolidated his literary success with some oriental romances that successfully reworked the formula established by *Childe Harold*, in which the dark, brooding hero found himself in exotic locations: *The Giaour* (1813), *The Bride of Abydos* (1813), *The Corsair* (1814) and *Lara* (1814). They were, effectively, literary fantasies for a public eager for escape; as Wordsworth might have said, they fitted the taste of their readership like a glove. Byron gained much credit through his work, and it was only through his urging that John Murray published Coleridge's *Christabel; Kubla Khan: A Vision; The Pains of Sleep* in 1816 (none of which had been published previously).

It was during these years that Byron had one of the most important love affairs of his life. Augusta Byron (1784–1851) was the daughter of Byron's father by his first wife, and hence Byron's half-sister. Her mother had died only two days after her birth, and she had been brought up by a grandmother and then by various relatives. She did not meet Byron as a child; they apparently met while he was at Harrow, and had corresponded from about 1804. In 1807 she had married a cousin, Colonel George Leigh, and over the next six years gave birth to three daughters. Since then Byron had seen little of her, but in the summer of 1813 he visited the Leighs near Newmarket, fell in love with her, and took her back to London with him, showing

---

[2]   Marchand v 265.

[3]   *Don Juan* xv 176. A full text of Byron's maiden speech in the Lords may be found in *Lord Byron: The Complete Miscellaneous Prose* ed. Andrew Rutherford (Oxford, 1991).

[4]   For a detailed account see my 'Appropriating Byron: Lady Caroline Lamb's *A New Canto*', *TWC* 26 (1995) 140–6.

her off at the theatre, balls, and assemblies. An intimate relationship seems to have developed,[5] and it was only by the alarmed counsel of his friend, Lady Melbourne, that he desisted from the plan of taking her abroad with him. No doubt the relationship with Augusta always seemed somehow 'purer' than those with other women because her love for him was, by definition, distinct from theirs; certainly, this was the light in which he wrote of it in his *Stanzas* and *Epistle* to her, and in *Childe Harold's Pilgrimage* III (stanza 55). She would always be genuinely concerned for his well-being in a way no one else was. In the end, she realized how dangerous the liaison had become, and encouraged him to marry.

With Augusta's approval, he married Annabella Milbanke on 2 January 1815. The decision was hastily made, and they turned out to be disastrously ill-matched (though it is hard to conceive what sort of woman might have lived happily with Byron). Their daughter, Augusta Ada, was born on 10 December, by which time the marriage was seriously on the rocks and debt-collectors were once again knocking at the door. They separated in February 1816 amidst veiled (and some not-so-veiled) accusations of infidelity and outright insanity. London was alive with rumours of Byron's private life and, thanks partly to an effective whispering campaign run by Annabella, he soon found himself ostracized from society. He decided to leave England, and on 25 April set out on a tour that took in Bruges, Antwerp, Brussels and Waterloo (already a tourist destination thanks to the decisive Battle fought the previous year).

Travelling through Europe with Hobhouse and another friend, John Polidori, he arrived at the Hotel Angleterre near Geneva on 25 May, where he amused himself by putting his age down in the Hotel register as 100. Two days later he met Shelley, who had arrived over a week before with Mary Godwin and her half-sister Claire Clairmont (with whom Byron had already had an affair in London). Geneva remained his base until the end of September, and during the summer of 1816 he saw a great deal of Shelley, with whom he got on. It was a remarkable moment in literary history, not unlike the *annus mirabilis* of 1797–8 when Wordsworth and Coleridge inspired each other; their regular conversations at the Villa Diodati (where Milton had stayed in 1639), into which Byron moved in June, provided the inspiration for Mary's novel *Frankenstein*, Byron's *Manfred*, *Prometheus*, *Darkness* and *Childe Harold* Canto III (see pp. 672–709, 716–51),

and two of Shelley's most important poems, *Hymn to Intellectual Beauty* and *Mont Blanc* (see pp. 841–3, 845–9).

Complete texts of *Childe Harold* Canto III and *Manfred* are presented below. Each, in their different ways, is extraordinary. Though for most of his life heartily contemptuous of Wordsworth (largely for having rejected Pope), for a brief period, during the summer of 1816, Byron listened to Shelley's recitals of Wordsworth's *Poems* (1815) and *The Excursion* (1814) – as he later told Thomas Medwin, Shelley 'used to dose me with Wordsworth physic even to nausea'.[6] That Wordsworthian influence went straight into *Childe Harold* Canto III, and was noted by Wordsworth himself, when he told Henry Taylor, 26 December 1823, that Byron's 'poetical obligations to me' consisted 'not so much in particular expressions, though there is no want of these, as in the tone (*assumed* rather than natural) of enthusiastic admiration of nature, and a sensibility to her influences'.[7] Wordsworth was right; the weakest, though most intriguing, parts of the Canto are those stanzas which strain to express a love of nature that Byron did not really feel (as, for instance, at stanzas 86–9). It was a false step, and no doubt, as Auden observed, Byron's choice of the Spenserian stanza, with its long, slow-moving cadences, was also a mistake; his comic muse required a more sprightly poetic form.[8]

The odd thing is that, if Canto III presents Byron at his least convincing, it presents Childe Harold at his best. As Jeffrey observed in the *Edinburgh Review*, the reader has no ground for distinguishing Byron's views from those of his hero: 'Not only do the author and his hero travel and reflect together – but, in truth, we scarcely ever have any notice to which of them the sentiments so energetically expressed are to be ascribed'. The poem ranges across Europe following exactly the same trail taken by Byron himself in April–May 1816, visiting Waterloo (for melancholy reflections on the nature of war), travelling up the Rhine (for further reflections of a similar kind), travelling into Switzerland, and finally arriving at Geneva, where Harold celebrates the work of such freethinkers as Rousseau and Voltaire. It is of particular interest for Byron's view of Napoleon, for whom he felt considerable admiration:

> There sunk the greatest, nor the worst of men,
> Whose spirit antithetically mixed
> One moment of the mightiest, and again
> On little objects with like firmness fixed,
> Extreme in all things! (ll. 316–20)

5   This, at any rate, is the view of Leslie A. Marchand, *Byron: A Portrait* (London, 1971), p. 148n.
6   Medwin 237.
7   *LY* i 237.

8   For further discussion of *Childe Harold* Canto III, and its preoccupations, see Michael O'Neill, *Romanticism and the Self-Conscious Poem* (Oxford, 1997), pp. 93–118.

Napoleon is, for Byron, a type of the overreacher, the man who seeks to transcend the frailty of the human condition in his search for a kind of divinity, mixing with his own spirit 'One moment of the mightiest'.[9] With views like this it was impossible that Byron should subscribe to the religious conventions of the day. Neither he nor Shelley believed in God in anything like the conventional sense. Throughout Byron's poetry God is given short shrift; in *Childe Harold* III, he is capable of writing: 'I have not loved the world . . . Nor coined my cheek to smiles, nor cried aloud / In worship of an echo' (stanza 113, p. 706). If he believes in anything, it is in the godlike potential of mankind. Even in 1816, at his most credulous, Byron is willing to admit only the bare possibility of 'the Power which gave' (l.156) – and even then, that divine power is one that has permitted the appalling carnage of the Battle of Waterloo.

If in *Childe Harold* III the plight of the Byronic overreacher is that of Harold, so too is it that of Manfred. *Manfred* was written immediately after and was inspired partly by M. G. Lewis's readings to Byron of his translations of Goethe's *Faust*. But Manfred is distinguished from other versions of the Faust character by his defiance of the spirits he invokes, and passion for his dead sister, Astarte (a passion that echoes that of Byron for Augusta Leigh). It is one of Byron's most serious works, in which the eponymous hero embodies his creator's own frustration at the human condition, and contempt for institutionalized religion. Although a drama, Byron claimed to have 'rendered it *quite impossible* for the stage – for which my intercourse with Drury Lane had given me the greatest contempt'.[10]

He left Switzerland in the autumn and travelled south to Venice. Here, in 1818, he composed the fourth and final Canto of *Childe Harold*, and discovered the *ottava rima*. It was a turning-point in his poetic development, as he realized immediately that it was much better suited to his purposes than the Spenserian stanzas he had used for *Childe Harold*. Why? Because the Italian form was geared to feminine rhymes and a rapid metre – ideal for comedy. He experimented with it in *Beppo* and the *Epistle to Augusta* (pp. 711–15), and then, in 1819, began his masterpiece: *Don Juan*. The first parts to be published were the Dedication and Cantos I and II, presented here in their entirety (pp. 752–812). Byron declared, 'I *have* no plan – I *had* no plan – but I had or have materials',[11] and indeed the manner in which it is written is just as important as

the story – as he observed, 'I mean it for a poetical *Tristram Shandy*'.[12] This was a fairly accurate account; no one in their right mind would read the poem just for its story, as so much is taken up with digressions and disquisitions by the narrator on all kinds of well-chosen irrelevancies. But that was precisely the point: it is sufficiently relaxed to contain all the waywardness, unpredictability and accummulated detritus of life as lived. 'Almost all *Don Juan* is real life', Byron declared, 'either my own, or from people I know'.[13] He worked on it for the remainder of his life, leaving it unfinished at the time of his death. Though published anonymously, everyone knew its author's identity, and they were completely horrified by it. The shipwreck scene in Canto II provided a focus for these anxieties; as the reviewer in the *British Critic* put it:

> In the scenes of confusion and agony attending a shipwreck, in the struggles for self-preservation, in the loss of so many souls, perhaps but too unprepared for their great account, in tracing the protracted sufferings of those whose lot is still to linger on in desperation drearier than death, in viewing a company of fellow-creatures on the wide ocean, devouring their last morsel, in witnessing hunger and thirst increasing upon them, the cannibal passions beginning to rise, the casting of lots for destruction, the self-immolation, the feast upon human blood, the frantic feeling of satiety – surely in bringing all these things home to our hearts, we can ill endure a full-born jest. Much less can we tolerate the mixing up of these fearful events with low doggerel and vapid absurdity.

In one sense, the reviewer was right. *Don Juan* was a calculated and gleeful affront to the tastes of its first readers. You could hardly argue that the shipwreck was not intended to be realistic – it was, and Byron took care to base it on first-hand accounts.[14] But what really upset the reviewer (though he was too shocked to put it in quite this way) was the pleasure Byron takes in undermining human virtue and religious faith, exposing the animalistic urges that underlie almost all social behaviour. Another poet might have had the inhabitants of the lifeboat pray for salvation and receive sustenance, but Byron takes undisguised pleasure in ensuring that it is Pedrillo, Juan's tutor, licensed to carry out religious rites, who is the first to

---

9 Napoleon is, in this sense, a version of Byron himself – and there's little doubt that Byron felt some affinity with him; as he commented at Waterloo, 'Bonaparte and I are the only public persons whose initials are the same' (Marchand ix 171). (Byron's middle name, Noel, enabled him to make this claim.)
10 Marchand v 170.

11 Marchand vi 207.
12 Marchand x 150.
13 Marchand viii 186.
14 He found numerous examples in Sir John Graham Dalyell's *Shipwrecks and Disasters at Sea* (3 vols, 1812).

be eaten. As if this was not enough, he then has those who have dined on Pedrillo go insane, implying that religious belief is a kind of madness. In *Don Juan*, nothing is sacred; everything is reduced to the same materialistic level, everything is profane. Take for instance the moment in the cave when, frying some eggs for the emaciated Juan, Zoe notes that 'the best feelings must have victual'[15] – love is dependent on the state of one's stomach. Not very surprisingly, perhaps, Wordsworth did not see the joke; in late January 1820, he told Henry Crabb Robinson: 'I am persuaded that *Don Juan* will do more harm to the English character than anything of our time'.[16] That copious absence of respect for things sacred and respectable, besides the fact that it is funny, has been the secret of the poem's popularity – which it has achieved only in the twentieth century.

In the year of *Juan*'s appearance, Byron became *cavalier servente* (lover of a married woman) to Countess Teresa Guiccioli, who he pursued to Ravenna in 1820. He would remain persuaded of his love for her until his death, and made her the subject of a moving, and triumphantly undeceived love poem, *To the Po* (pp. 813–14). In 1821 he moved to Pisa to be near Shelley, who, with him and Leigh Hunt, wished to set up a new literary periodical entitled *The Liberal*. In the event Shelley died before it could be done, and Byron and Leigh Hunt found that they could not work together. Only four numbers were published before it was discontinued and Hunt returned with his family to England. Where Wordsworth, Coleridge and Southey had abandoned the radical attachments of their youth (see Dedication to *Don Juan*), Byron prided himself on fidelity to his, and it was characteristic of him to join the fight for Greek Independence. He donated money to the Greek forces, and joined them at Missolonghi. Caught in a heavy rain while riding on 9 April 1824, he developed a fever, and, weakened by repeated bleeding (the usual treatment for fever was to apply leeches to the forehead and arms), died ten days later.

I am grateful to Peter Cochran for advice in resolving some of the textual conundrums in Byron's texts for this second edition of *Romanticism*.

Further reading

Andrew Rutherford, *Byron: A Critical Study* (Stanford, Calif., 1961)

W. H. Auden, 'Don Juan', *The Dyer's Hand and Other Essays* (London, 1963)

M. K. Joseph, *Byron the Poet* (London, 1964)

Jerome J. McGann, *Fiery Dust: Byron's Poetic Development* (London, 1968)

M. G. Cooke, *The Blind Man Traces a Circle* (Princeton, 1969)

Leslie Marchand, *Byron: A Portrait* (London, 1971)

A. B. England, *Byron's Don Juan and Eighteenth-Century Literature: A Study of Some Rhetorical Continuities and Discontinuities* (Lewisburg, 1975)

Jerome J. McGann, *Don Juan in Context* (London, 1976)

Peter Manning, *Byron and His Fictions* (Detroit, 1978)

Bernard Beatty, *Byron's Don Juan* (Basingstoke, 1985)

Frederick L. Beaty, *Byron the Satirist* (Dekalb, Ill., 1985)

Jerome J. McGann, 'The Book of Byron and the Book of a World', *The Beauty of Inflections: Literary Investigations in Historical Method and Theory* (Oxford, 1985), pp. 255–93

The Oxford Authors Byron ed. Jerome J. McGann (Oxford, 1986)

Malcolm Kelsall, *Byron's Politics* (Brighton, 1987)

Michael Foot, *The Politics of Paradise: A Vindication of Byron* (London, 1988)

Anne Barton, *Byron: Don Juan* (Cambridge, 1992)

Byron: Augustan and Romantic ed. Andrew Rutherford (Basingstoke, 1990)

Susan Wolfson, ' "Their She Condition": Cross-Dressing and the Politics of Gender in *Don Juan*', in *Romantic Poetry: Recent Revisionary Criticism* ed. Karl Kroeber and Gene Ruoff (New Brunswick, 1993) 267–89

Jerome J. McGann, 'Byron and the Anonymous Lyric', *Romanticism: A Critical Reader* 243–60

Peter Manning, '*Don Juan* and Byron's Imperceptiveness to the English Word', *Romanticism: A Critical Reader* 217–42

Philip W. Martin, 'Authorial Identity and the Critical Act: John Clare and Lord Byron', in *Questioning Romanticism* ed. John Beer (Baltimore, Maryland, 1995) 71–91

Byron ed. Jane Stabler (Harlow, 1998)

Anne Barton, '*Don Juan* Reconsidered: The Haidée Episode', *The Byron Journal* 15 (1987) 11–20

The Byron Journal is published annually by the Byron Society in London.

---

[15] *Don Juan* ii 1153. It is a reworking of Terence, *Eunuchus* iv 5,6: 'sine Cerere et Libero friget Venus' (without Ceres (i.e. bread) and Bacchus (wine), Venus is frigid), alluded to more explicitly at *Don Juan* ii 1351–2.

[16] *MY* ii 579.

Written Beneath a Picture (composed *c*. January 1812)[1]

From CHILDE HAROLD'S PILGRIMAGE: A ROMAUNT (1812)[2]

1

Dear object of defeated care!
  Though now of love and thee bereft,
To reconcile me with despair
  Thine image and my tears are left.

2

'Tis said with sorrow time can cope,   5
  But this I feel can ne'er be true;
For by the death-blow of my hope
  My memory immortal grew.

Stanzas (composed *c*. February 1812)

From CHILDE HAROLD'S PILGRIMAGE: A ROMAUNT (2nd edn, 1812)

Heu quanto minus est cum reliquis versari quam tui meminisse![1]

1

And thou art dead, as young and fair
  As aught of mortal birth;
And form so soft, and charms so rare,
  Too soon returned to earth!
Though earth received them in her bed,   5
And o'er the spot the crowd may tread
  In carelessness or mirth,
There is an eye which could not brook
A moment on that grave to look.

2

I will not ask where thou liest low,   10
  Nor gaze upon the spot;
There flowers or weeds at will may grow,
  So I behold them not;
It is enough for me to prove
That what I loved and long must love   15
  Like common earth can rot —

WRITTEN BENEATH A PICTURE
[1] This poem was probably written to John Edleston, the boy chorister to whom Byron was passionately attached while at Cambridge, 1805–7. Edleston died in May 1811; Byron heard about this in October, and immediately found relief for his feelings in a series of poems about 'Thyrza'. By using a woman's name he could write freely about the relationship.

[2] Childe Harold's Pilgrimage (1812) contained a number of Byron's shorter works.

STANZAS
[1] 'Alas, how much less it is to deal with things left behind than to remember thee.'

To me there needs no stone to tell
'Tis nothing that I loved so well.

3

Yet did I love thee to the last
   As fervently as thou,   20
Who didst not change through all the past,
   And canst not alter now.
The love where death has set his seal
Nor age can chill, nor rival steal,
   Nor falsehood disavow;   25
And, what were worse, thou canst not see
Or wrong, or change, or fault in me.

4

The better days of life were ours,
   The worst can be but mine;
The sun that cheers, the storm that lours,   30
   Shall never more be thine.
The silence of that dreamless sleep
I envy now too much to weep;
   Nor need I to repine
That all those charms have passed away   35
I might have watched through long decay.

5

The flower in ripened bloom unmatched
   Must fall the earliest prey,
Though by no hand untimely snatched,
   The leaves must drop away;   40
And yet it were a greater grief
To watch it withering leaf by leaf
   Than see it plucked today –
Since earthly eye but ill can bear
To trace the change to foul from fair.   45

6

I know not if I could have borne
   To see thy beauties fade;
The night that followed such a morn
   Had worn a deeper shade;
Thy day without a cloud hath passed,   50
And thou wert lovely to the last,
   Extinguished, not decayed –
As stars that shoot along the sky
Shine brightest as they fall from high.

7

As once I wept, if I could weep,   55
   My tears might well be shed,

To think I was not near to keep
  One vigil o'er thy bed,
To gaze, how fondly, on thy face,
To fold thee in a faint embrace,   60
  Uphold thy drooping head;
And show that love, however vain,
Nor thou nor I can feel again.

8

Yet how much less it were to gain
  (Though thou hast left me free)   65
The loveliest things that still remain,
  Than thus remember thee!
The all of thine that cannot die
Through dark and dread eternity
  Returns again to me,   70
And more thy buried love endears
Than aught, except its living years.

She Walks in Beauty (composed *c.* 12 June 1814)[1]

From HEBREW MELODIES (1815)

I

She walks in beauty like the night
  Of cloudless climes and starry skies,
And all that's best of dark and bright
  Meet in her aspect and her eyes,
Thus mellowed to that tender light   5
  Which heaven to gaudy day denies.

II

One shade the more, one ray the less
  Had half-impaired the nameless grace
Which waves in every raven tress
  Or softly lightens o'er her face –   10
Where thoughts serenely sweet express
  How pure, how dear their dwelling place.

III

And on that cheek and o'er that brow,
  So soft, so calm, yet eloquent,

SHE WALKS IN BEAUTY
[1]   A MS version of the poem is entitled, 'Lines written by
Lord Byron after seeing Mrs Wilmot at Lansdowne House'.
Byron met Anne Wilmot (1784–1871) on 11 June 1814; she
was the wife of his first cousin Robert John Wilmot.

The smiles that win, the tints that glow,   15
    But tell of days in goodness spent,
A mind at peace with all below,
    A heart whose love is innocent.

[*When we two parted*] (composed August or September 1815)[1]

From POEMS (1816)

1

When we two parted
    In silence and tears,
Half broken-hearted,
    To sever for years,
Pale grew thy cheek and cold,   5
    Colder thy kiss –
Truly that hour foretold
    Sorrow to this.

2

The dew of the morning
    Sunk chill on my brow –   10
It felt like the warning
    Of what I feel now.
Thy vows are all broken,
    And light is thy fame;
I hear thy name spoken,   15
    And share in its shame.

3

They name thee before me –
    A knell to mine ear;
A shudder comes o'er me –
    Why wert thou so dear?   20
They know not I knew thee,
    Who knew thee too well;
Long, long shall I rue thee,
    Too deeply to tell.[2]

WHEN WE TWO PARTED
[1] The subject of the poem is Lady Frances Wedderburn
Webster, with whom Byron had a brief, 'platonic' affair late in
1813; its immediate occasion was gossip about her affair with
the Duke of Wellington in Paris in 1815.
[2] Byron's original draft contains an extra stanza at this
point, which refers explicitly to Lady Webster:

Then fare thee well, Fanny,
    Now doubly undone,
To prove false unto many
    As faithless to one.
Thou art past all recalling
    Even would I recall,
For the woman once falling
    Forever must fall.

4

In secret we met, 25
In silence I grieve
That thy heart could forget,
Thy spirit deceive.
If I should meet thee
After long years, 30
How should I greet thee?
With silence and tears.

Fare Thee Well! (composed 18 March 1816)[1]

From POEMS (1816)

Alas! they had been friends in youth;
But whispering tongues can poison truth;
And constancy lives in realms above:
And life is thorny; and youth is vain:
And to be wroth with one we love,
Doth work like madness in the brain . . . .
But never either found another
To free the hollow heart from paining –
They stood aloof, the scars remaining,
Like cliffs which had been rent asunder;
A dreary sea now flows between,
But neither heat, nor frost, nor thunder
Shall wholly do away, I ween,
The marks of that which once hath been.[2]

Fare thee well! and if for ever –
Still for ever, fare *thee well*! –
Even though unforgiving, never
'Gainst thee shall my heart rebel.
Would that breast were bared before thee 5
Where thy head so oft hath lain,
While that placid sleep came o'er thee
Which thou ne'er canst know again;
Would that breast by thee glanced over,
Every inmost thought could show! 10
Then thou wouldst at last discover
'Twas not well to spurn it so.
Though the world for this commend thee
Though it smile upon the blow,
Even its praises must offend thee, 15
Founded on another's woe;

FARE THEE WELL!
[1] This valedictory poem was addressed to Lady Byron the day after ratification of her preliminary Separation Agreement with the poet; the final agreement was signed on 21 April. The poem was sent to her in early April with a view to moving her to a reconciliation. In the event a version appeared in *The Champion* as part of an attack on Byron engineered by his wife's allies.
[2] The epigraph is from Coleridge's *Christabel* 396–414. Byron had been responsible for the first publication of *Christabel* in 1816, eighteen years after the composition of Part I.

Though my many faults defaced me,
    Could no other arm be found
Than the one which once embraced me
    To inflict a cureless wound?   20
Yet, oh yet, thyself deceive not:
    Love may sink by slow decay;
But by sudden wrench, believe not,
    Hearts can thus be torn away.
Still thine own its life retaineth –   25
    Still must mine, though bleeding, beat,
And the undying thought which paineth
    Is – that we no more may meet.
These are words of deeper sorrow
    Than the wail above the dead;   30
Both shall live, but every morrow
    Wake us from a widowed bed.
And when thou wouldst solace gather
    When our child's[3] first accents flow
Wilt thou teach her to say 'Father!'   35
    Though his care she must forgo?
When her little hands shall press thee,
    When her lip to thine is pressed,
Think of him whose prayer shall bless thee,
    Think of him thy love had blessed.   40
Should her lineaments resemble
    Those thou never more may'st see[4]
Then thy heart will softly tremble
    With a pulse yet true to me.
All my faults (perchance thou knowest),   45
    All my madness[5] – none can know;
All my hopes, where'er thou goest,
    Wither – yet with *thee* they go.
Every feeling hath been shaken,
    Pride (which not a world could bow)   50
Bows to thee – by thee forsaken
    Even my soul forsakes me now.
But 'tis done, all words are idle –
    Words from me are vainer still;
But the thoughts we cannot bridle   55
    Force their way without the will.
Fare thee well! – thus disunited,
    Torn from every nearer tie,
Seared in my heart – and lone – and blighted –
    More than this, I scarce can die.   60

---

3   Ada Augusta Byron, born 10 December 1815. After his departure from England in 1816, Byron never saw her again. Knowledge of her father was kept from her as she grew up, but her husband, Lord King, eventually weaned her from her mother's influence, and she came to revere her father's poetry and his memory. She died at the age of thirty-five.

4   *Those thou . . . see* i.e. Byron's.
5   *madness* Annabella accused Byron of madness prior to their separation.

Childe Harold's Pilgrimage

Canto the Third (composed between 25 April and 4 July 1816; published 18 November 1816)[1]

Afin que cette application vous forçât à penser à autre chose. Il n'y a en vérité de remède que celui-là et le temps.

Lettre du Roi de Prusse à D'Alembert, Sept. 7, 1776[2]

1

Is thy face like thy mother's, my fair child,[3]
Ada, sole daughter of my house and heart?
When last I saw thy young blue eyes, they smiled;
And then we parted – not as now we part,
But with a hope. Awaking with a start,   5
The waters heave around me, and on high
The winds lift up their voices. I depart
Whither I know not, but the hour's gone by
When Albion's lessening shores could grieve or glad mine eye.[4]

2

Once more upon the waters, yet once more![5]   10
And the waves bound beneath me as a steed
That knows his rider – welcome to their roar!
Swift be their guidance, wheresoe'er it lead!
Though the strained mast should quiver as a reed
And the rent canvas fluttering strew the gale,   15
Still must I on – for I am as a weed
Flung from the rock on ocean's foam, to sail
Where'er the surge may sweep, the tempest's breath prevail.

3

In my youth's summer I did sing of one,[6]
The wandering outlaw of his own dark mind;   20
Again I seize the theme then but begun,
And bear it with me as the rushing wind
Bears the cloud onwards. In that tale I find
The furrows of long thought, and dried-up tears
Which, ebbing, leave a sterile track behind,   25
O'er which all heavily the journeying years
Plod the last sands of life, where not a flower appears.

CHILDE HAROLD'S PILGRIMAGE

[1] For a general introduction to this poem see headnote, pp. 663–4.

[2] 'So that this work will force you to think of something else. Truly, that and time are the only remedies.'

[3] *my fair child* Byron's only legitimate daughter Ada Augusta, born 10 December 1815. After Lady Byron left him five weeks later, he never saw Ada again.

[4] Byron began writing this Canto while at sea, 25 April 1816. He felt that he had been hounded out of England by the bad publicity whipped up by his wife.

[5] Compare *Henry V* III i 1.

[6] *In my youth's summer . . . one* i.e. Childe Harold. Byron began Canto I on 31 October 1809, when he was twenty-one.

4

Since my young days of passion[7] (joy or pain),
Perchance my heart and harp have lost a string
And both may jar; it may be that in vain   30
I would essay,[8] as I have sung, to sing.
Yet, though a dreary[9] strain, to this I cling,
So that it wean me from the weary dream
Of selfish grief or gladness; so it fling
  Forgetfulness around me. It shall seem   35
To me (though to none else) a not ungrateful theme.

5

He, who grown aged in this world of woe
(In deeds not years), piercing the depths of life
So that no wonder waits him; nor below
Can love or sorrow, fame, ambition, strife,   40
Cut to his heart again with the keen knife
Of silent sharp endurance – he can tell
Why thought seeks refuge in lone caves yet[10] rife
With airy images,[11] and shapes which dwell
Still unimpaired, though old, in the soul's haunted cell.   45

6

'Tis to create, and in creating live
A being more intense, that we endow
With form our fancy, gaining as we give
The life we image – even as I do now.
What am I? Nothing. But not so art thou,   50
Soul of my thought,[12] with whom I traverse earth,
Invisible but gazing, as I glow
Mixed with thy spirit, blended with thy birth,
And feeling still with thee in my crushed feelings' dearth.

7

Yet must I think less wildly. I *have* thought   55
Too long and darkly till my brain became,
In its own eddy, boiling and o'erwrought,
A whirling gulf of fantasy and flame;
And thus, untaught in youth my heart to tame,
My springs of life were poisoned. 'Tis too late!   60

---

7   *Since my young days of passion* Byron was twenty-eight at the time of writing.
8   *essay* attempt.
9   *dreary* melancholy.
10   *yet* still.
11   *airy images* Byron is probably recalling *A Midsummer Night's Dream* V i 14–17:

And as imagination bodies forth
The forms of things unknown, the poet's pen
Turns them to shapes, and gives to aery nothing
A local habitation and a name.

12   *Soul of my thought* Byron is still thinking of his daughter.

Yet am I changed, though still enough the same
In strength to bear what time cannot abate,
And feed on bitter fruits without accusing fate.

8

Something too much of this:[13] but now 'tis past,
And the spell closes with its silent seal.   65
Long absent Harold reappears at last;[14]
He of the breast which fain no more would feel,
Wrung with the wounds which kill not, but ne'er heal;
Yet Time, who changes all, had altered him
In soul and aspect as in age: years steal   70
Fire from the mind as vigour from the limb;
And Life's enchanted cup but sparkles near the brim.

9

His had been quaffed too quickly, and he found
The dregs were wormwood;[15] but he filled again,
And from a purer fount,[16] on holier ground,   75
And deemed its spring perpetual – but in vain!
Still round him clung invisibly a chain
Which galled for ever, fettering though unseen,
And heavy though it clanked not; worn with pain,
Which pined although it spoke not, and grew keen,   80
Entering with every step he took, through many a scene.

10

Secure in guarded coldness, he had mixed
Again in fancied safety with his kind,
And deemed his spirit now so firmly fixed
And sheathed with an invulnerable mind,   85
That, if no joy, no sorrow lurked behind;
And he, as one, might midst the many stand
Unheeded, searching through the crowd to find
Fit speculation – such as in strange land
He found in wonder-works of God and Nature's hand.   90

11

But who can view the ripened rose, nor seek
To wear it? Who can curiously behold
The smoothness and the sheen of Beauty's cheek,
Nor feel the heart can never all grow old?

---

[13]   *Something too much of this Hamlet* III ii 72.
[14]   Although Byron seems to direct attention away from
himself at this point, his readers knew by now that the charac-
ter of Harold was a kind of alter ego, who embodied his cre-
ator's deepest anxieties and preoccupations.

[15]   *wormwood* plant known for its bitter taste.
[16]   *a purer fount* Greece, where Harold had gone in Canto II.

Who can contemplate fame through clouds unfold   95
The star which rises o'er her steep, nor climb?
Harold, once more within the vortex, rolled
On with the giddy circle, chasing Time,
Yet with a nobler aim than in his Youth's fond prime.

12

But soon he knew himself the most unfit   100
Of men to herd with man,[17] with whom he held
Little in common; untaught to submit
His thoughts to others, though his soul was quelled
In youth by his own thoughts; still uncompelled,
He would not yield dominion of his mind   105
To spirits against whom his own rebelled,
Proud though in desolation – which could find
A life within itself, to breathe without mankind.

13

Where rose the mountains, there to him were friends;
Where rolled the ocean, thereon was his home;   110
Where a blue sky, and glowing clime, extends,
He had the passion and the power to roam;
The desert, forest, cavern, breaker's foam,
Were unto him companionship; they spake
A mutual language, clearer than the tome   115
Of his land's tongue, which he would oft forsake
For nature's pages glassed by sunbeams on the lake.

14

Like the Chaldean,[18] he could watch the stars
Till he had peopled them with beings bright
As their own beams; and earth, and earth-born jars,[19]   120
And human frailties, were forgotten quite:
Could he have kept his spirit to that flight
He had been happy; but this clay will sink
Its spark immortal, envying it the light
To which it mounts, as if to break the link   125
That keeps us from yon heaven which woos us to its brink.

15

But in Man's dwellings he became a thing
Restless and worn, and stern and wearisome,
Drooped as a wild-born falcon with clipped wing,
To whom the boundless air alone were home: 130

---

[17] *man* i.e. mankind.   [19] *jars* quarrels.
[18] *Chaldean* the Chaldees were renowned astronomers.

Then came his fit again, which to o'ercome,
As eagerly the barred-up bird will beat
His breast and beak against his wiry dome
Till the blood tinge his plumage – so the heat
Of his impeded soul would through his bosom eat.   135

16

Self-exiled Harold wanders forth again,
With nought of hope left, but with less of gloom;
The very knowledge that he lived in vain,
That all was over on this side the tomb,[20]
Had made Despair a smilingness[21] assume,   140
Which, though 'twere wild (as on the plundered wreck
When mariners would madly meet their doom
With draughts intemperate on the sinking deck),
Did yet inspire a cheer, which he forbore to check.

17

Stop! For thy tread is on an Empire's dust!   145
An earthquake's spoil is sepulchred below![22]
Is the spot marked with no colossal bust?
Nor column trophied for triumphal show?
None; but the moral's truth tells simpler so.
As the ground was before, thus let it be;   150
How that red rain[23] hath made the harvest grow!
And is this all the world has gained by thee,
Thou first and last of fields, king-making Victory?[24]

18

And Harold stands upon this place of skulls,
The grave of France, the deadly Waterloo!   155
How in an hour the Power which gave[25] annuls
Its gifts, transferring fame as fleeting too!
In 'pride of place' here last the eagle flew,[26]
Then tore with bloody talon the rent plain,
Pierced by the shaft[27] of banded nations through;   160
Ambition's life and labours all were vain;
He wears the shattered links of the world's broken chain.

---

[20] *That all was over . . . tomb* i.e. that there was no afterlife.
[21] *a smilingness* a smiling expression.
[22] *Stop! . . . below* Byron visited the battlefield at Waterloo on Saturday 4 May 1816. The 'earthquake's spoil' consists of the corpses of thousands of people – killed, in this case, in the battle.
[23] *red rain* blood shed on the fields in the battle.
[24] *king-making Victory* In fact, Louis XVIII had assumed power, thanks to the allies, shortly after Napoleon's abdication, 6 April 1814. He had gone into exile by the time Napoleon returned to Paris, in March 1815, and was rein-

stated by the allies in July, after Napoleon's defeat at Waterloo. In a letter written soon after his visit to Waterloo, Byron commented on the Battle: 'I detest the cause and the victors – and the victory – including Blucher and the Bourbons' (Marchand v 76).
[25] *the Power which gave* rather than use the word 'God', Byron uses the same term as that used by Shelley in *Hymn to Intellectual Beauty* and *Mont Blanc*.
[26] ' "Pride of place" is a term of falconry, and means the highest pitch of flight. See *Macbeth* [II iv 12], etc.' (Byron's note).
[27] *shaft* arrow.

19

Fit retribution! Gaul[28] may champ the bit
And foam in fetters – but is earth more free?
Did nations combat to make *one*[29] submit?   165
Or league[30] to teach all kings true sovereignty?
What? Shall reviving thraldom[31] again be
The patched-up idol of enlightened days?
Shall we, who struck the lion down, shall we
Pay the wolf homage? Proffering lowly gaze   170
And servile knees to thrones? No! Prove[32] before ye praise!

20

If not, o'er one fallen despot boast no more!
In vain fair cheeks were furrowed with hot tears
For Europe's flowers long rooted up before
The trampler of her vineyards; in vain, years   175
Of death, depopulation, bondage, fears,
Have all been borne, and broken by the accord
Of roused-up millions: all that most endears
Glory, is when the myrtle wreathes a sword,
Such as Harmodius drew on Athens' tyrant lord.[33]   180

21

There was a sound of revelry by night,[34]
And Belgium's capital had gathered then
Her beauty and her chivalry – and bright
The lamps shone o'er fair women and brave men;
A thousand hearts beat happily; and when   185
Music arose with its voluptuous swell,
Soft eyes looked love to eyes which spake again,
And all went merry as a marriage bell;
But hush! hark! a deep sound strikes like a rising knell!

22

Did ye not hear it? No, 'twas but the wind,   190
Or the car rattling o'er the stony street;
On with the dance! Let joy be unconfined;
No sleep till morn, when Youth and Pleasure meet
To chase the glowing Hours with flying feet –
But hark! that heavy sound breaks in once more,   195
As if the clouds its echo would repeat;

---

28 *Gaul* France.
29 *one* i.e. Napoleon.
30 *league* i.e. band together. The Battle of Waterloo was fought by an alliance of the British, Dutch, Belgians, Germans, and the Prussians.
31 *thraldom* slavery. Byron was no friend to monarchy.
32 *Prove* i.e. establish the true value of the victory.

33 Byron alludes to Harmodius and Aristogeiton, their daggers wreathed in myrtle branches, who in 514 BC attempted to kill Hippias and Hipparchus, tyrannical rulers of Athens. The sword wreathed in myrtle leaves is an emblem of the freedom fighter.
34 *There was a sound . . . night* the stanza recalls the famous ball given by the Duchess of Richmond in Brussels on 15 June 1815, the night prior to the inconclusive Battle of Quatre-Bras; Waterloo was fought three days later.

And nearer – clearer – deadlier than before!
Arm! Arm! It is – it is – the cannon's opening roar![35]

23

Within a windowed niche of that high hall
Sate Brunswick's fated chieftain;[36] he did hear   200
That sound the first amidst the festival,
And caught its tone with Death's prophetic ear;
And when they smiled because he deemed it near,
His heart more truly knew that peal too well
Which stretched his father on a bloody bier,   205
And roused the vengeance blood alone could quell;
He rushed into the field, and, foremost fighting, fell.

24

Ah! then and there was hurrying to and fro,
And gathering tears, and tremblings of distress,
And cheeks all pale, which but an hour ago   210
Blushed at the praise of their own loveliness –
And there were sudden partings, such as press
The life from out young hearts, and choking sighs
Which ne'er might be repeated; who could guess
If ever more should meet those mutual eyes,   215
Since upon nights so sweet such awful morn could rise?

25

And there was mounting in hot haste: the steed,
The mustering squadron, and the clattering car,
Went pouring forward with impetuous speed,
And swiftly forming in the ranks of war;   220
And the deep thunder peal on peal afar;
And near, the beat of the alarming drum[37]
Roused up the soldier ere the morning star;
While thronged the citizens with terror dumb,
Or whispering, with white lips, 'The foe! They come! they come!'   225

26

And wild and high the 'Cameron's gathering'[38] rose!
The war-note of Lochiel,[39] which Albyn's[40] hills

---

[35] Wellington discovered the approach of Napoleon not from the sound of cannon but from dispatches sent by the Prussian commander, Blücher.

[36] *Brunswick's fated chieftain* Frederick, Duke of Brunswick (1771–1815), nephew of George III, killed at Quatre-Bras. His father, Charles William Ferdinand, was killed in 1806 at Auerstädt.

[37] *the alarming drum* the drum sounds an alarm to the soldiers.

[38] *Cameron's gathering* rallying-cry of the Cameron clan.

[39] *Lochiel* title of the chief of the Camerons.

[40] *Albyn* Gaelic name for Scotland.

Have heard, and, heard, too, have her Saxon foes:
How in the noon of night that pibroch[41] thrills,
Savage and shrill! But with the breath which fills   230
Their mountain-pipe, so fill the mountaineers
With the fierce native daring which instils
The stirring memory of a thousand years,
And Evan's, Donald's[42] fame rings in each clansman's ears!

27

And Ardennes[43] waves above them her green leaves,   235
Dewy with nature's tear-drops, as they pass,
Grieving, if aught inanimate e'er grieves,
Over the unreturning brave – alas!
Ere evening to be trodden like the grass
Which now beneath them, but above shall grow   240
In its next verdure, when this fiery mass
Of living valour, rolling on the foe
And burning with high hope, shall moulder cold and low.

28

Last noon beheld them full of lusty life,
Last eve in Beauty's circle proudly gay,   245
The midnight brought the signal-sound of strife,
The morn the marshalling in arms, the day
Battle's magnificently-stern array!
The thunder-clouds close o'er it, which when rent
The earth is covered thick with other clay,[44]   250
Which her own clay shall cover, heaped and pent,
Rider and horse, friend, foe, in one red burial blent![45]

29

Their praise is hymned by loftier harps than mine;[46]
Yet one I would select from that proud throng,
Partly because they blend me with his line,[47]   255
And partly that I did his sire some wrong,

---

[41] *pibroch* series of martial variations for the bagpipe, on a theme called the 'urlar'.

[42] Sir Ewan Cameron (1629–1719) resisted Cromwell 1652–8 and fought at Killiecrankie for James II in 1689. His grandson Donald Cameron (1695–1748) fought to restore the Stuarts in 1745 and was wounded at Culloden the following year. Byron spent his formative years in Scotland.

[43] 'The woods of Soignies is supposed to be a remnant of the "forest of Ardennes", famous is Boiardo's *Orlando*, and immortal in Shakespeare's *As You Like It*. It is also celebrated in Tacitus as being the spot of successful defence by the Germans against the Roman encroachments. I have ventured to adopt the name connected with nobler associations than those of mere slaughter' (Byron's note). A note full of errors: Soignies is between Waterloo and Brussels, Ardennes is in Luxembourg, and Arden is English.

[44] *other clay* i.e. dead bodies.

[45] *blent* blended.

[46] *loftier harps than mine* Scott's, in *The Field of Waterloo* (Edinburgh, 1815).

[47] *line* i.e. of descent.

And partly that bright names will hallow song;
And his was of the bravest, and when showered
The death-bolts deadliest the thinned files along,
Even where the thickest of war's tempest loured,　　　　　260
They reached no nobler breast than thine – young, gallant Howard![48]

30

There have been tears and breaking hearts for thee,
And mine were nothing, had I such to give;
But when I stood beneath the fresh green tree,
Which living waves where thou didst cease to live,[49]　　　265
And saw around me the wide field revive
With fruits and fertile promise, and the spring
Come forth her work of gladness to contrive,
With all her reckless[50] birds upon the wing,
I turned from all she brought to those she could not bring.[51]　　　270

31

I turned to thee, to thousands, of whom each
And one as all a ghastly gap did make
In his own kind and kindred, whom to teach
Forgetfulness were mercy for their sake;
The Archangel's trump, not Glory's, must awake　　　275
Those whom they thirst for; though the sound of Fame
May for a moment soothe, it cannot slake
The fever of vain longing, and the name
So honoured but assumes a stronger, bitterer claim.

32

They mourn, but smile at length – and, smiling, mourn:　　　280
The tree will wither long before it fall;
The hull drives on, though mast and sail be torn;

---

[48] The Hon. Frederick Howard (1785–1815), Byron's cousin, son of his guardian, the Earl of Carlisle, whom he had criticized in *English Bards and Scotch Reviewers* (1809) for his ambitions as a verse-dramatist: 'So dull in youth, so drivelling in his age, / His scenes alone had damned our sinking stage' (ll. 733–4).

[49] *didst cease to live* i.e. died.

[50] *reckless* carefree.

[51] 'My guide from Mont St Jean over the field seemed intelligent and accurate. The place where Major Howard fell was not far from two tall and solitary trees (there was a third cut down, or shivered in the battle) which stand a few yards from each other at a pathway's side. Beneath these he died and was buried. The body has since been removed to England. A small hollow for the present marks where it lay, but will probably soon be effaced; the plough has been upon it, and the grain is.

After pointing our the different spots where Picton and other gallant men had perished, the guide said, "Here Major Howard lay; I was near him when wounded." I told him my relationship, and he seemed then still more anxious to point out the particular spot and circumstances. The place is one of the most marked in the field from the peculiarity of the two trees above mentioned.

I went on horseback twice over the field, comparing it with my recollection of similar scenes. As a plain, Waterloo seems marked out for the scene of some great action, though this may be mere imagination: I have viewed with attention those of Platea, Troy, Mantinea, Leuctra, Chaeronea, and Marathon; and the field around Mont St Jean and Hougoumont appears to want little but a better cause, and that undefinable but impressive halo which the lapse of ages throws around a celebrated spot, to vie in interest with any or all of these, except perhaps the last mentioned' (Byron's note).

The roof-tree sinks, but moulders on the hall
In massy hoariness; the ruined wall
Stands when its wind-worn battlements are gone;   285
The bars survive the captive they enthral;[52]
The day drags through though storms keep out the sun;
And thus the heart will break, yet brokenly live on:

33

Even as a broken mirror, which the glass
In every fragment multiplies; and makes   290
A thousand images of one that was,
The same, and still the more, the more it breaks;
And thus the heart will do which not forsakes,
Living in shattered guise; and still, and cold,
And bloodless, with its sleepless sorrow aches,   295
Yet withers on till all without is old,
Showing no visible sign, for such things are untold.

34

There is a very life in our despair,
Vitality of poison – a quick[53] root
Which feeds these deadly branches; for it were   300
As nothing did we die; but Life will suit
Itself to Sorrow's most detested fruit,
Like to the apples on the Dead Sea's shore,
All ashes to the taste.[54] Did man compute
Existence by enjoyment, and count o'er   305
Such hours 'gainst years of life, say, would he name threescore?

35

The Psalmist numbered out the years of man:[55]
They are enough; and if thy tale[56] be *true*,
Thou, who didst grudge him even that fleeting span,
More than enough, thou fatal Waterloo!   310
Millions of tongues record thee, and anew
Their children's lips shall echo them, and say,
'Here, where the sword united nations drew,
Our countrymen were warring on that day!'
And this is much, and all which will not pass away.   315

---

52   *enthral* imprison.
53   *quick* living.
54   'The (fabled) apples on the brink of the Lake Asphaltes were said to be fair without, and within ashes. – Vide Tacitus, *Historia* [Book 5, sec.7]' (Byron's note).

55   Psalm 90:10: 'The days of our years are threescore years and ten; and if by reason of strength they be fourscore years, yet is their strength labour and sorrow; for it is soon cut off, and we fly away.'
56   *tale* a pun, meaning both 'story' and 'counting'.

36

There sunk the greatest, nor the worst of men,[57]
Whose spirit antithetically mixed
One moment of the mightiest, and again
On little objects with like firmness fixed,
Extreme in all things! Hadst thou been betwixt,[58]   320
Thy throne[59] had still been thine, or never been;
For daring made thy rise as fall: thou seek'st
Even now to reassume the imperial mien,[60]
And shake again the world, the Thunderer of the scene!

37

Conqueror and captive of the earth art thou!   325
She trembles at thee still, and thy wild name
Was ne'er more bruited[61] in men's minds than now
That thou art nothing, save the jest of Fame,
Who wooed thee once, thy vassal, and became
The flatterer of thy fierceness – till thou wert   330
A god unto thyself; nor less the same
To the astounded kingdoms all inert,
Who deemed thee for a time whate'er thou didst assert.

38

Oh, more or less than man – in high or low,
Battling with nations, flying from the field;   335
Now making monarchs' necks thy footstool, now
More than thy meanest soldier taught to yield;[62]
An empire thou couldst crush, command, rebuild,
But govern not thy pettiest passion, nor,
However deeply in men's spirits skilled,   340
Look through thine own,[63] nor curb the lust of war,
Nor learn that tempted Fate will leave the loftiest star.

39

Yet well thy soul hath brooked[64] the turning tide
With that untaught innate philosophy,
Which, be it wisdom, coldness, or deep pride,   345
Is gall and wormwood[65] to an enemy.

---

[57] *There sunk . . . men* i.e. Napoleon. Byron's view was that Napoleon had been no worse than the despots who had taken his place.

[58] *betwixt* i.e. between the mightiest and the meanest.

[59] *Thy throne* Napoleon crowned himself Emperor in December 1804.

[60] *thou seek'st . . . mien* Napoleon was at this time in exile on St Helena.

[61] *bruited* celebrated.

[62] *now / More than thy meanest soldier . . . yield* Napoleon has been taught to humble himself even more than the lowest of his soldiers.

[63] *thine own* i.e. spirit.

[64] *brooked* endured.

[65] *gall and wormwood* i.e. very bitter.

When the whole host of hatred stood hard by
To watch and mock thee shrinking, thou hast smiled
With a sedate and all-enduring eye;
When Fortune fled her spoiled and favourite child,   350
He stood unbowed beneath the ills upon him piled.

40

Sager than in thy fortunes; for in them
Ambition steeled thee on too far to show
That just habitual scorn, which could contemn
Men and their thoughts; 'twas wise to feel, not so   355
To wear it ever on thy lip and brow,
And spurn the instruments[66] thou wert to use
Till they were turned unto thine overthrow:
'Tis but a worthless world to win or lose;
So hath it proved to thee, and all such lot who choose.   360

41

If, like a tower upon a headlong rock,
Thou[67] hadst been made to stand or fall alone,
Such scorn of man had helped to brave the shock;
But men's thoughts were the steps which paved thy throne,
Their admiration thy best weapon shone;   365
The part of Philip's son[68] was thine, not then
(Unless aside thy purple[69] had been thrown)
Like stern Diogenes[70] to mock at men:
For sceptred cynics earth were far too wide a den.[71]

42

But quiet to quick[72] bosoms is a hell,   370
And *there* hath been thy bane: there is a fire
And motion of the soul which will not dwell
In its own narrow being, but aspire
Beyond the fitting medium of desire,
And, but once kindled, quenchless evermore,   375
Preys upon high adventure, nor can tire

---

[66] *the instruments* i.e. other men.
[67] *Thou* Napoleon.
[68] *Philip's son* Alexander the Great, son of Philip of Macedonia, who also conquered an empire.
[69] *thy purple* the colour worn by emperors.
[70] *stern Diogenes* Greek, Cynic, philosopher of the fourth century BC, known for austere habits, and choosing to live in the open.
[71] 'The great error of Napoleon, "if we have writ our annals true", was a continued obtrusion on mankind of his want of all community of feeling for or with them; perhaps more offensive to human vanity than the active cruelty of more trembling and suspicious tyranny.

Such were his speeches to public assemblies as well as individuals: and the single expression which he is said to have used on returning to Paris after the Russian winter had destroyed his army, rubbing his hands over a fire, "This is pleasanter than Moscow", would probably alienate more favour from his cause than the destruction and reverses which led to the remark' (Byron's note).
[72] *quick* vital, living.

Of aught but rest – a fever at the core,
Fatal to him who bears, to all who ever bore.[73]

43

This makes the madmen who have made men mad
By their contagion: conquerors and kings,   380
Founders of sects and systems, to whom add
Sophists, bards, statesmen, all unquiet things
Which stir too strongly the soul's secret springs,
And are themselves the fools to those they fool –
Envied, yet how unenviable! What stings   385
Are theirs! One breast laid open were a school
Which would unteach mankind the lust to shine or rule:

44

Their breath is agitation, and their life
A storm whereon they ride, to sink at last;
And yet so nursed and bigoted to strife,   390
That, should their days (surviving perils passed)
Melt to calm twilight, they feel overcast
With sorrow and supineness, and so die;
Even as a flame unfed, which runs to waste
With its own flickering, or a sword laid by   395
Which eats into itself, and rusts ingloriously.

45

He who ascends to mountain-tops shall find
The loftiest peaks most wrapped in clouds and snow;
He who surpasses or subdues mankind
Must look down on the hate of those below.   400
Though high *above* the sun of glory glow
And far *beneath* the earth and ocean spread,
Round him are icy rocks, and loudly blow
Contending tempests on his naked head,
And thus reward the toils which to those summits led.   405

46

Away with these! True wisdom's world will be
Within its own creation, or in thine,
Maternal Nature![74] For who teems like thee,

---

[73] Napoleon is styled here as a type of the Byronic over-reacher, not unlike Manfred.
[74] Byron's celebration of nature was uncharacteristic, and appears largely thanks to the influence of Wordsworth, which Shelley was reading to him in Geneva in the summer of 1816, when this poem was composed.

Thus on the banks of thy majestic Rhine?[75]
There Harold gazes on a work divine,   410
A blending of all beauties; streams and dells,
Fruit, foliage, crag, wood, cornfield, mountain, vine,
And chiefless castles breathing stern farewells
From gray but leafy walls, where Ruin greenly dwells.

47

And there they[76] stand, as stands a lofty mind,   415
Worn, but unstooping to the baser crowd,
All tenantless, save to the crannying[77] wind,
Or holding dark communion with the cloud.
There was a day when they were young and proud;
Banners on high, and battles[78] passed below;   420
But they who fought are in a bloody shroud,
And those which waved[79] are shredless dust ere now,
And the bleak battlements shall bear no future blow.

48

Beneath these battlements, within those walls,
Power dwelt amidst her passions; in proud state   425
Each robber-chief upheld his armed halls,
Doing his evil will, nor less elate[80]
Than mightier heroes of a longer date.
What want these outlaws conquerors should have[81]
But history's purchased page to call them great?[82]   430
A wider space? An ornamented grave?
Their hopes were not less warm, their souls were full as brave.

49

In their baronial feuds and single fields,
What deeds of prowess unrecorded died!
And Love, which lent a blazon[83] to their shields,   435
With emblems well devised by amorous pride,
Through all the mail of iron hearts would glide;
But still their flame was fierceness, and drew on
Keen contest and destruction near allied,

---

[75] Byron travelled up the Rhine via Bonn, Koblenz, and Mannheim, 10–16 May 1816.
[76] *they* i.e. ruined castles.
[77] *crannying* the wind is so strong it penetrates into nooks and crannies of the ruin.
[78] *battles* a pun, meaning both battalions and military engagements.
[79] *those which waved* flags.
[80] *elate* proud.
[81] ' "What wants that knave / That a king should have?" was King James' question on meeting Johnny Armstrong and

his followers in full accoutrements. See the ballad' (Byron's note). Johnnie Armstrong, Laird of Gilnockie, surrendered to James V in such fine attire that the king hanged him for his insolence. Byron knew the ballad of *Johnie Armstrang* from Scott's *Minstrelsy of the Scottish Border* (1802–3).
[82] *What want . . . great* i.e. if they have conquerors, what else do these outlaws need, except for a historian to write up their story and call them great?
[83] *a blazon* the device of a bleeding heart.

And many a tower for some fair mischief won,
Saw the discoloured[84] Rhine beneath its ruin run. 440

50

But thou, exulting and abounding river!
Making thy waves a blessing as they flow
Through banks whose beauty would endure for ever
Could man but leave thy bright creation so, 445
Nor its fair promise from the surface mow
With the sharp scythe of conflict – then to see
Thy valley of sweet waters, were to know
Earth paved like heaven, and to seem such to me,
Even now what wants thy stream? – that it should Lethe[85] be. 450

51

A thousand battles have assailed thy banks,
But these and half their fame have passed away,
And Slaughter heaped on high his weltering ranks:
Their very graves are gone, and what are they?
Thy tide washed down the blood of yesterday, 455
And all was stainless, and on thy clear stream
Glassed, with its dancing light, the sunny ray;
But o'er the blackened memory's blighting dream
Thy waves would vainly roll, all sweeping as they seem.

52

Thus Harold inly said,[86] and passed along, 460
Yet not insensible[87] to all which here
Awoke the jocund birds to early song
In glens which might have made even exile[88] dear:
Though on his brow were graven lines austere,
And tranquil sternness, which had ta'en the place 465
Of feelings fierier far but less severe,
Joy was not always absent from his face,
But o'er it in such scenes would steal with transient trace.

53

Nor was all love shut from him, though his days
Of passion had consumed themselves to dust. 470
It is in vain that we would coldly gaze

---

[84] *discoloured* i.e. with blood.
[85] *Lethe* river of forgetfulness in Hades, from which souls drank in order to forget their previous lives.
[86] *Thus Harold inly said* stanzas 47–51 comprise Harold's inner thoughts.
[87] *insensible* unaware.
[88] *exile* Byron exiled himself from England after separating from his wife in spring 1816 (see headnote).

On such as smile upon us; the heart must
Leap kindly back to kindness, though disgust
Hath weaned it from all worldlings: thus he felt,
For there was soft remembrance, and sweet trust   475
In one fond breast,[89] to which his own would melt,
And in its tenderer hour on that his bosom dwelt.

54

And he had learned to love – I know not why,
For this in such as him seems strange of mood,
The helpless looks of blooming infancy,   480
Even in its earliest nurture; what subdued,
To change like this, a mind so far imbued
With scorn of man, it little boots to know –
But thus it was; and though in solitude
Small power the nipped affections have to grow,   485
In him this glowed when all beside had ceased to glow.

55

And there was one soft breast, as hath been said,
Which unto his was bound by stronger ties
Than the church links withal; and, though unwed,
That love was pure, and, far above disguise,   490
Had stood the test of mortal enmities
Still undivided, and cemented more
By peril, dreaded most in female eyes;
But this was firm, and from a foreign shore
Well to that heart might his these absent greetings pour! 495

1

The castled crag of Drachenfels[90]
Frowns o'er the wide and winding Rhine,
Whose breast of waters broadly swells
Between the banks which bear the vine,
And hills all rich with blossomed trees,   500
And fields which promise corn and wine,
And scattered cities crowning these,
Whose far white walls along them shine,
Have strewed a scene, which I should see
With double joy wert *thou* with me.   505

2

And peasant girls, with deep blue eyes,
And hands which offer early flowers,

---

89   *one fond breast* Augusta Leigh, Byron's half-sister, to
whom he was passionately attached, the subject of his *Stanzas*
and an *Epistle* (pp. 710–15).
90   'The castle of Drachenfels stands on the highest summit
of "the Seven Mountains", over the Rhine banks; it is in ruins,
and connected with some singular traditions. It is the first in
view on the road from Bonn, but on the opposite side of the
river; on this bank, nearly facing it, are the remains of another
called the Jew's castle, and a large cross commemorative of the
murder of a chief by his brother. The number of castles and
cities along the course of the Rhine on both sides is very great,
and their situations remarkably beautiful' (Byron's note).

Walk smiling o'er this Paradise;
Above, the frequent feudal towers
Through green leaves lift their walls of gray;   510
And many a rock which steeply lours,
And noble arch in proud decay,
Look o'er this vale of vintage-bowers;
But one thing want these banks of Rhine –
Thy gentle hand to clasp in mine!   515

3
I send the lilies given to me;
Though long before thy hand they touch,
I know that they must withered be,
But yet reject them not as such;
For I have cherished them as dear,   520
Because they yet may meet thine eye,
And guide thy soul to mine even here,
When thou behold'st them drooping nigh,
And know'st them gathered by the Rhine,
And offered from my heart to thine!   525

4
The river nobly foams and flows,
The charm of this enchanted ground,
And all its thousand turns disclose
Some fresher beauty varying round;
The haughtiest breast its wish might bound   530
Through life to dwell delighted here;
Nor could on earth a spot be found
To nature and to me so dear,
Could thy dear eyes in following mine
Still sweeten more these banks of Rhine!   535

56

By Coblentz, on a rise of gentle ground,
There is a small and simple pyramid,[91]
Crowning the summit of the verdant mound;
Beneath its base are heroes' ashes hid –
Our enemy's[92] – but let not that forbid   540
Honour to Marceau![93] o'er whose early tomb
Tears, big tears, gushed from the rough soldier's lid,[94]
Lamenting and yet envying such a doom,[95]
Falling for France, whose rights he battled to resume.[96]

---

[91] *pyramid* i.e. a memorial.
[92] *Our enemy's* i.e. those of French heroes.
[93] *Marceau* François Sévérin Desgravins Marceau (1769–96)
died in a battle with the forces of the Archduke Charles of
Austria.

[94] *lid* eyelid.
[95] *doom* fate.
[96] *resume* take back.

57

Brief, brave, and glorious was his young career,   545
His mourners were two hosts,[97] his friends and foes;
And fitly may the stranger lingering here
Pray for his gallant spirit's bright repose;
For he was Freedom's champion, one of those,
The few in number, who had not o'erstepped   550
The charter to chastise[98] which she bestows
On such as wield her weapons; he had kept
The whiteness of his soul – and thus men o'er him wept.[99]

58

Here Ehrenbreitstein,[100] with her shattered wall
Black with the miner's blast,[101] upon her height   555
Yet shows of what she was, when shell and ball
Rebounding idly on her strength did light;
A tower of victory! from whence the flight
Of baffled foes was watched along the plain:
But peace destroyed what war could never blight,   560
And laid those proud roofs bare to Summer's rain –
On which the iron shower[102] for years had poured in vain.

59

Adieu to thee, fair Rhine! How long delighted
The stranger fain would linger on his way!
Thine is a scene alike where souls united   565

---

97 *hosts* armies. Marceau was mourned by both forces: the French, retreating from Altenkirchen, had to leave him behind, and the Austrians buried him.

98 *chastise* i.e. teach tyrants (enemies of Freedom) a lesson.

99 'The monument of the young and lamented General Marceau (killed by a rifle-ball at Altenkirchen on the last day of the fourth year of the French Republic) still remains as described.

The inscriptions on his monument are rather too long, and not required; his name was enough. France adored, and her enemies admired; both wept over him. His funeral was attended by the generals and detachments from both armies. In the same grave General Hoche is interred, a gallant man also in every sense of the word, but though he distinguished himself greatly in battle, *he* had not the good fortune to die there; his death was attended by suspicions of poison.

A separate monument (not over his body, which is buried by Marceau's) is raised for him near Andernach, opposite to which one of his most memorable exploits was performed, in throwing a bridge to an island on the Rhine. The shape and style are different from that of Marceau's, and the inscription more simple and pleasing.

The Army of the Sambre and Meuse
to its Commander in Chief
Hoche

This is all, and as it should be. Hoche was esteemed among the first of France's earlier generals before Bonaparte monopolized her triumphs. He was the destined commander of the invading army of Ireland' (Byron's note). Lazare Hoche (1768–97) died of consumption, but the rapid deterioration of his health led to speculation that he had been poisoned.

100 'Ehrenbreitstein (i.e. "the broad stone of honour"), one of the strongest fortresses in Europe, was dismantled and blown up by the French at the Truce of Leoben. It had been and could only be reduced by famine or treachery. It yielded to the former, aided by surprise. After having seen the fortifications of Gibraltar and Malta, it did not much strike by comparison, but the situation is commanding. General Marceau besieged it in vain for some time, and I slept in a room where I was shown a window at which he is said to have been standing observing the progress of the siege by moonlight, when a ball struck immediately below it' (Byron's note). Marceau unsuccessfully besieged Ehrenbreitstein in 1795–6. It was finally taken, after a long siege, in 1799. It was blown up not after the Treaty of Loeben (1797), but after the Treaty of Lunéville (1801). Byron visited the ruins in mid-May 1816.

101 *the miner's blast* the miner would dig tunnels under the walls of the fortresses, for the detonation of explosives – to 'undermine' the building.

102 *the iron shower* i.e. artillery fire directed against the fortress.

Or lonely Contemplation thus might stray;
And could the ceaseless vultures cease to prey
On self-condemning bosoms,[103] it were here,
Where nature, nor too sombre nor too gay,
Wild but not rude, awful yet not austere,   570
Is to the mellow earth as autumn to the year.

60

Adieu to thee again! A vain adieu!
There can be no farewell to scene like thine;
The mind is coloured by thy every hue;
And if reluctantly the eyes resign   575
Their cherished gaze upon thee, lovely Rhine,
'Tis with the thankful glance of parting praise;
More mighty spots may rise – more glaring shine,
But none unite in one attaching maze
The brilliant, fair, and soft – the glories of old days,   580

61

The negligently grand, the fruitful bloom
Of coming ripeness, the white city's sheen,
The rolling stream, the precipice's gloom,
The forest's growth, and gothic walls between,
The wild rocks shaped, as they had turrets been[104]   585
In mockery of man's art; and these withal
A race of faces happy as the scene,
Whose fertile bounties here extend to all,
Still springing o'er thy banks, though empires near them fall.

62

But these recede. Above me are the Alps,   590
The palaces of nature, whose vast walls
Have pinnacled in clouds their snowy scalps,
And throned Eternity in icy halls
Of cold sublimity, where forms and falls
The avalanche – the thunderbolt of snow!   595
All that expands the spirit, yet appals,
Gather around these summits, as to show
How earth may pierce to heaven, yet leave vain man below.

63

But ere these matchless heights I dare to scan,
There is a spot should not be passed in vain –   600

---

[103]   *ceaseless vultures . . . bosoms* Jupiter had Prometheus nailed   [104]   *as they had turrets been* as if they had been turrets.
to a rock for 30,000 years, with an eagle devouring his liver.

Morat,[105] the proud, the patriot field! where man
May gaze on ghastly trophies of the slain,
Nor blush for those who conquered on that plain;
Here Burgundy bequeathed his tombless host,
A bony heap, through ages to remain, 605
Themselves their monument; the Stygian coast
Unsepulchred they roamed, and shrieked each wandering ghost.[106]

64

While Waterloo with Cannae's carnage vies,
Morat and Marathon twin names shall stand;[107]
They were true Glory's stainless victories 610
Won by the unambitious heart and hand
Of a proud, brotherly, and civic band,
All unbought champions in no princely cause
Of vice-entailed[108] Corruption; they no land
Doomed to bewail the blasphemy of laws 615
Making kings' rights divine, by some Draconic[109] clause.[110]

65

By a lone wall a lonelier column rears
A gray and grief-worn aspect of old days;
'Tis the last remnant of the wreck of years,
And looks as with the wild-bewildered gaze 620
Of one to stone converted by amaze,
Yet still with consciousness; and there it stands
Making a marvel that it not decays,
When the coeval pride of human hands,
Levelled Aventicum,[111] hath strewed her subject lands. 625

---

[105] The Battle of Morat was the bloodiest of three battles fought by the Swiss against the French (under Charles the Bold, Duke of Burgundy) in 1476.

[106] 'The chapel is destroyed, and the pyramid of bones diminished to a small number by the Burgundian legion in the service of France, who anxiously effaced this record of their ancestors' less successful invasions. A few still remain notwithstanding the pains taken by the Burgundians for ages (all who passed that way removing a bone to their own country) and the less justifiable larcenies of the Swiss postillions, who carried them off to sell for knife-handles, a purpose for which the whiteness imbibed by the bleaching of years had rendered them in great request. Of these relics I ventured to bring away as much as may have made the quarter of a hero, for which the sole excuse is, that if I had not, the next passer-by might have perverted them to worse uses than the careful preservation which I intend for them' (Byron's note).

[107] Morat and Marathon (490 BC) were victories of men fighting for their freedom; Waterloo and Cannae (216 BC) were battles between countries seeking power over each other.

[108] *vice-entailed* Corruption is inseparable from vice.

[109] *Draconic* harsh, cruel; after Draco, author of the notoriously severe penal code for Athens (624 BC).

[110] Like many radicals of the day, Byron disagreed heartily with the divine right of kings. 'Draco, the author of the first red book on record, was an Athenian special pleader in great business. Hippias, the Athenian Bourbon, was in the Battle of Marathon, and did not keep at the respectful distance from danger of the Ghent refugees – but the English and Prussians resembled the Medes and Persians as little as Blucher and the British General did Datis and Artaphernes and Bonaparte was still more remote in cause and character from Miltiades – and a parallel "after the manner of Plutarch" might have still existed in the fortunes of the sons of Pisistratus and the reigning doctors of right-divinity' (Byron's note). Byron offers an ironic comparison between the principals at Waterloo and those at Marathon. The sons of Pisistratus, Hippias and Hipparchus died inglorious.

[111] 'Aventicum (near Morat) was the Roman capital of Helvetia, where Avenches now stands' (Byron's note).

66

And there – oh, sweet and sacred be the name! –
Julia – the daughter, the devoted – gave
Her youth to heaven; her heart, beneath a claim
Nearest to heaven's, broke o'er a father's grave.
Justice is sworn 'gainst tears, and hers would crave   630
The life she lived in; but the judge was just,
And then she died on him she could not save.
Their tomb was simple, and without a bust,
And held within their urn one mind, one heart, one dust.[112]

67

But these are deeds which should not pass away,   635
And names that must not wither, though the earth
Forgets her empires with a just decay,
The enslavers and the enslaved, their death and birth;
The high, the mountain-majesty of worth
Should be, and shall, survivor of its woe,   640
And from its immortality look forth
In the sun's face, like yonder Alpine snow,
Imperishably pure beyond all things below.

68

Lake Leman[113] woos me with its crystal face,
The mirror where the stars and mountains view   645
The stillness of their aspect in each trace
Its clear depth yields of their far height and hue:
There is too much of man here to look through,
With a fit mind, the might which I behold;
But soon in me shall loneliness renew   650
Thoughts hid, but not less cherished than of old,
Ere mingling with the herd had penned me in their fold.

69

To fly from, need not be to hate, mankind;
All are not fit with them to stir and toil,

---

[112] 'Julia Alpinula, a young Aventian priestess, died soon after a vain endeavour to save her father, condemned to death as a traitor by Aulus Caecina. Her epitaph was discovered many years ago; it is thus –

Julia Alpinula
Hic jaceo
Infelicis patris, infelix proles
Deae Aventiae Sacerdos;
Exorare patris necem non potui
Male mori in fatis illi erat.
Vixi annos XXIII.

I know of no human composition so affecting as this, nor a history of deeper interest. These are the names and actions which ought not to perish, and to which we turn with a true and healthy tenderness, from the wretched and glittering detail of a confused mass of conquests and battles, with which the mind is roused for a time to a false and feverish sympathy, from whence it recurs at length with all the nausea consequent on such intoxication' (Byron's note).

[113] *Lake Leman* Lake Geneva.

Nor is it discontent to keep the mind   655
Deep in its fountain, lest it overboil
In the hot throng, where we become the spoil[114]
Of our infection, till too late and long
We may deplore and struggle with the coil[115]
In wretched interchange of wrong for wrong   660
Midst a contentious world, striving where none are strong.

70

There in a moment we may plunge our years
In fatal penitence, and in the blight
Of our own soul turn all our blood to tears,
And colour things to come with hues of night;   665
The race of life becomes a hopeless flight
To those that walk in darkness: on the sea
The boldest steer but where their ports invite,
But there are wanderers o'er eternity
Whose bark drives on and on, and anchored ne'er shall be.   670

71

Is it not better, then, to be alone,
And love earth only for its earthly sake?
By the blue rushing of the arrowy Rhone[116]
Or the pure bosom of its nursing lake,
Which feeds it as a mother who doth make   675
A fair but froward[117] infant her own care,
Kissing its cries away as these awake?
Is it not better thus our lives to wear
Than join the crushing crowd, doomed to inflict or bear?

72

I live not in myself, but I become   680
Portion of that around me; and to me
High mountains are a feeling, but the hum
Of human cities torture.[118] I can see
Nothing to loathe in nature, save to be
A link reluctant in a fleshly chain,   685
Classed among creatures, when the soul can flee,
And with the sky, the peak, the heaving plain
Of ocean, or the stars, mingle, and not in vain.

---

[114]   *spoil* prey.
[115]   *coil* mortal coil; bustle of life.
[116]   'The colour of the Rhone at Geneva is blue, to a depth of tint which I have never seen equalled in water, salt or fresh, except in the Mediterranean and Archipelago' (Byron's note).

The 'Archipelago' is the Aegean, which he swam in May 1810.
[117]   *froward* refractory.
[118]   Here and in succeeding lines Byron repeats attitudes he had encountered in Wordsworth's *Tintern Abbey*.

73

And thus I am absorbed, and this is life.
I look upon the peopled desert past   690
As on a place of agony and strife
Where for some sin to sorrow I was cast
To act and suffer, but remount at last
With a fresh pinion, which I feel to spring
(Though young, yet waxing vigorous as the blast   695
Which it would cope with) on delighted wing,
Spurning the clay-cold bonds which round our being cling.[119]

74

And when at length the mind shall be all free
From what it hates in this degraded form,[120]
Reft of its carnal life, save what shall be   700
Existent happier in the fly and worm;
When elements to elements conform
And dust is as it should be, shall I not
Feel all I see – less dazzling, but more warm?
The bodiless thought? The spirit of each spot –   705
Of which, even now, I share at times the immortal lot?

75

Are not the mountains, waves and skies a part
Of me and of my soul, as I of them?
Is not the love of these deep in my heart
With a pure passion? Should I not contemn   710
All objects if compared with these, and stem
A tide of suffering, rather than forego
Such feelings for the hard and worldly phlegm[121]
Of those whose eyes are only turned below,
Gazing upon the ground, with thoughts which dare not glow?   715

76

But this is not my theme, and I return
To that which is immediate – and require
Those who find contemplation in the urn
To look on one[122] whose dust was once all fire,
A native of the land where I respire[123]   720
The clear air for a while, a passing guest

---

[119] *Spurning . . . cling* the attitude of the Byronic over-reacher; cf. *Manfred* I ii 39–41: 'we / Half-dust, half-deity, alike unfit / To sink or soar'.
[120] *this degraded form* the human body is inherently degraded as far as Byron is concerned.
[121] *phlegm* coldness, lack of passion.

[122] *one* Jean-Jacques Rousseau, born in Geneva 1712 (d. 1778) whose political, fictional and philosophical writings strongly influenced the outbreak of revolution at the end of the eighteenth century.
[123] *respire* inhale.

Where he became a being whose desire
Was to be glorious ('twas a foolish quest,
The which to gain and keep, he sacrificed all rest).

77

Here the self-torturing sophist,[124] wild Rousseau,   725
The apostle of affliction, he who threw
Enchantment over passion, and from woe
Wrung overwhelming eloquence – first drew
The breath which made him wretched; yet he knew
How to make madness beautiful, and cast   730
O'er erring deeds and thoughts a heavenly hue
Of words like sunbeams, dazzling as they passed
The eyes, which o'er them shed tears feelingly and fast.

78

His love was passion's essence, as a tree
On fire by lightning;[125] with ethereal flame[126]   735
Kindled he was, and blasted – for to be
Thus, and enamoured, were in him the same.
But his was not the love of living dame,
Nor of the dead who rise upon our dreams,[127]
But of ideal beauty,[128] which became   740
In him existence, and o'erflowing teems
Along his burning page, distempered though it seems.

79

This breathed itself to life in Julie,[129] this
Invested her with all that's wild and sweet;
This hallowed, too, the memorable kiss   745
Which every morn his fevered lip would greet
From hers[130] who, but with friendship, his would meet:
But to that gentle touch, through brain and breast
Flashed the thrilled spirit's love-devouring heat –
In that absorbing sigh, perchance more blessed   750
Than vulgar minds may be with all they seek possessed.[131]

---

[124] *sophist* learned man.
[125] *a tree / On fire by lightning* an image used also by Shelley and Mary Shelley.
[126] *ethereal flame* fire from heaven.
[127] *But his . . . dreams* the comparison is with Dante's Beatrice and Petrarch's Laura.
[128] *ideal beauty* cf. Shelley's *Hymn to Intellectual Beauty*.
[129] *Julie* heroine of Rousseau's *Julie, ou la Nouvelle Héloïse* (1761), which Shelley and Byron read in 1816, and deals with the illicit love of Julie and her tutor Saint-Preux.
[130] *hers* Rousseau describes his unrequited love of the Comtesse d'Houdetot in his *Confessions*.

[131] 'This refers to the account in his *Confessions* of his passion for the Comtesse d'Houdetot (the mistress of St Lambert) and his long walk every morning for the sake of the single kiss which was the common salutation of French acquaintance. Rousseau's description of his feelings on this occasion may be considered as the most passionate, yet not impure description and expression of love that ever kindled into words; which after all must be felt, from their very force, to be inadequate to the delineation: a painting can give no sufficient idea of the ocean' (Byron's note).

80

His life was one long war with self-sought foes
Or friends by him self-banished,[132] for his mind
Had grown suspicion's sanctuary, and chose,
For its own cruel sacrifice, the kind,   755
'Gainst whom he raged with fury strange and blind.
But he was frenzied – wherefore, who may know,
Since cause might be which skill could never find?
But he was frenzied by disease or woe
To that worst pitch of all, which wears a reasoning show.   760

81

For then he was inspired, and from him came,
As from the Pythian's[133] mystic cave of yore,
Those oracles[134] which set the world in flame,
Nor ceased to burn till kingdoms were no more.
Did he not this for France, which lay before   765
Bowed to the inborn tyranny of years?
Broken and trembling to the yoke she bore,
Till by the voice of him and his compeers
Roused up to too much wrath, which follows o'ergrown fears?

82

They made themselves a fearful monument!   770
The wreck of old opinions, things which grew
Breathed from the birth of time: the veil they rent,[135]
And what behind it lay, all earth shall view.
But good with ill they also overthrew,
Leaving but ruins, wherewith to rebuild   775
Upon the same foundation, and renew
Dungeons[136] and thrones,[137] which the same hour refilled
As heretofore, because ambition was self-willed.

83

But this will not endure, nor be endured!
Mankind have felt their strength and made it felt.[138]   780

---

[132]   *self-sought foes . . . self-banished* including Madame de
Warens, Madame d'Epinay, Diderot, Grimm, Voltaire, Hume
and St Lambert.

[133]   The Pythian was the priestess of the oracle at Delphi;
she gave utterance in a state of frenzy and sat on a three-
legged stool.

[134]   *oracles* The *Discours* of 1750 and 1753 and *Le Contrat
Social* (1762) helped inspire the French Revolution.

[135]   *the veil they rent* cf. the moment of Christ's death: 'And,
behold, the veil of the temple was rent in twain from the top
to the bottom' (Matthew 27:51).

[136]   *Dungeons* the Bastille prison in Paris, symbol of the
ancien régime, was stormed on 14 July 1789 during the Revo-
lution; it was demolished shortly after.

[137]   *thrones* Ferdinand VII of Spain and Louis XVIII of France
were restored to their respective thrones in 1814.

[138]   *Mankind have felt their strength and made it felt* this stanza
picks up a subject that preoccupied all the revolutionary writ-
ers: the necessity for violence even in the cause of good. Cf.
Helen Maria Williams (p. 151) and James Mackintosh (pp.
173–4).

They might have used it better, but, allured
By their new vigour, sternly have they dealt
On one another; pity ceased to melt
With her once-natural charities. But they
Who in oppression's darkness caved had dwelt,   785
They were not eagles, nourished with the day;
What marvel then, at times, if they mistook their prey?

84

What deep wounds ever closed without a scar?
The heart's[139] bleed longest, and but heal to wear
That which disfigures it; and they who war   790
With their own hopes, and have been vanquished, bear
Silence but not submission. In his lair
Fixed Passion holds his breath until the hour
Which shall atone for years – none need despair:
It came, it cometh, and will come, the power   795
To punish or forgive; in *one* we shall be slower.

85

Clear placid Leman! thy contrasted lake,
With the wild world I dwelt in, is a thing
Which warns me, with its stillness, to forsake
Earth's troubled waters for a purer spring.   800
This quiet sail is as a noiseless wing
To waft me from distraction; once I loved
Torn ocean's roar, but thy soft murmuring
Sounds sweet as if a sister's voice reproved
That I with stern[140] delights should e'er have been so moved. 805

86

It is the hush of night, and all between
Thy margin and the mountains, dusk – yet clear,
Mellowed and mingling, yet distinctly seen
(Save darkened Jura, whose capped heights appear
Precipitously steep); and, drawing near,   810
There breathes a living fragrance from the shore
Of flowers yet fresh with childhood; on the ear
Drops the light drip of the suspended oar,[141]
Or chirps the grasshopper one goodnight carol more

---

139 *The heart's* i.e. the heart's wounds.
140 *stern* uncompromising.
141 *Drops the light . . . oar* an echo of Wordsworth's *Lines
Written near Richmond*: 'Remembrance! as we glide along, / For
him suspend the dashing oar' (ll. 33–4).

87

(He is an evening reveller who makes   815
His life an infancy, and sings his fill);
At intervals, some bird from out the brakes[142]
Starts into voice a moment, then is still.
There seems a floating whisper on the hill,
But that is fancy, for the starlight dews   820
All silently their tears of love instil,
Weeping themselves away, till they infuse
Deep into nature's breast the spirit of her hues.

88

Ye stars which are the poetry of heaven!
If in your bright leaves we would read the fate   825
Of men and empires, 'tis to be forgiven
That in our aspirations to be great,
Our destinies o'erleap their mortal state,
And claim a kindred with you – for ye are
A beauty and a mystery, and create   830
In us such love and reverence from afar
That fortune, fame, power, life, have named themselves a star.[143]

89

All heaven and earth are still – though not in sleep,
But breathless (as we grow when feeling most)
And silent (as we stand in thoughts too deep);[144]   835
All heaven and earth are still: from the high host
Of stars to the lulled lake and mountain-coast,
All is concentred in a life intense
Where not a beam, nor air, nor leaf is lost,
But hath a part of being,[145] and a sense   840
Of that which is of all creator and defence.

90

Then stirs the feeling infinite, so felt
In solitude, where we are least alone –
A truth which through our being then doth melt
And purifies from self; it is a tone,   845
The soul and source of music, which makes known
Eternal harmony, and sheds a charm

---

[142] *brakes* thicket.
[143] Cf. Manfred's affinity with the stars, *Manfred* III iv 1–7.
[144] *thoughts too deep* compare 'Thoughts that do often lie too deep for tears' (Wordsworth, *Ode* 206).

[145] *Where not a beam . . . part of being* the sentiment is virtually identical to the pantheism of Wordsworth's *Tintern Abbey* 96–103.

Like to the fabled Cytherea's zone,[146]
Binding all things with beauty – 'twould disarm
The spectre death, had he substantial power to harm.   850

91

Not vainly did the early Persian make
His altar the high places and the peak
Of earth-o'ergazing mountains,[147] and thus take
A fit and unwalled temple, there to seek
The spirit in whose honour shrines are weak,   855
Upreared of human hands. Come and compare
Columns and idol-dwellings, Goth[148] or Greek,
With nature's realms of worship, earth and air,[149]
Nor fix on fond[150] abodes to circumscribe thy prayer!

92

The sky is changed, and such a change![151] Oh night   860
And storm and darkness, ye are wondrous strong,
Yet lovely in your strength, as is the light
Of a dark eye in woman! Far along
From peak to peak, the rattling crags among,
Leaps the live thunder – not from one lone cloud   865
But every mountain now hath found a tongue,

---

[146] *Cytherea's zone* Aphrodite's girdle ('zone') brought love to those wearing it.

[147] 'It is to be recollected that the most beautiful and impressive doctrines of the founder of Christianity were delivered not in the Temple, but on the mount.

To waive the question of devotion, and turn to human eloquence – the most effectual and splendid specimens were not pronounced within walls. Demosthenes addressed the public and popular assemblies. Cicero spoke in the forum. That this added to their effect on the mind of both orator and hearers, may be conceived from the difference between what we read of the emotions then and there produced, and those we ourselves experience in the perusal in the closet. It is one thing to read the *Iliad* at Sigaeum and on the tumuli, or by the springs with Mount Ida above, and the plain and rivers and Archipelago around you, and another to trim your taper over it in a snug library – *this* I know.

Were the early and rapid progress of what is called Methodism to be attributed to any cause beyond the enthusiasm excited by its vehement faith and doctrines (the truth or error of which I presume neither to canvas nor to question) I should venture to ascribe it to the practice of preaching in the *fields*, and the unstudied and extemporaneous effusions of its teachers.

The Musselmans, whose erroneous devotion (at least in the lower orders) is most sincere, and therefore impressive, are accustomed to repeat their prescribed orisons and prayers wherever they may be at the stated hours – of course frequently in the open air, kneeling upon a light mat (which they carry for the purpose of a bed or cushion as required); the ceremony lasts some minutes, during which they are totally absorbed, and only living in their supplication. Nothing can disturb them. On me the simple and entire sincerity of these men, and the spirit which appeared to be within and upon them, made a far greater impression than any general rite which was ever performed in places of worship, of which I have seen those of almost every persuasion under the sun: including most of our own sectaries, and the Greek, the Catholic, the Armenian, the Lutheran, the Jewish, and the Mahometan. Many of the negroes, of whom there are numbers in the Turkish empire, are idolators, and have free exercise of their belief and its rites. Some of these I had a distant view of at Patras, and from what I could make out of them, they appeared to be of a truly pagan description, and not very agreeable to a spectator' (Byron's note).

[148] *Goth* one of a Germanic tribe, who, in the third, fourth and fifth centuries, invaded both the Eastern and Western empires, and founded kingdoms in Italy, France and Spain.

[149] *earth and air* once again, Byron is thinking of the pantheistic statement of faith in *Tintern Abbey*, in which Wordsworth seeks 'a sense sublime' in 'the round ocean, and the living air, / And the blue sky, and in the mind of man' (ll. 96–100).

[150] *fond* foolish.

[151] 'The thunder-storms to which these lines refer occurred on 13 June 1816 at midnight. I have seen among the Acroceraunian mountains of Chimari several more terrible, but none more beautiful' (Byron's note).

And Jura answers through her misty shroud
Back to the joyous Alps, who call to her aloud!

93

And this is in the night – most glorious night,
Thou wert not sent for slumber! Let me be   870
A sharer in thy fierce and far delight,
A portion of the tempest and of thee!
How the lit lake shines, a phosphoric sea,
And the big rain comes dancing to the earth!
And now again 'tis black, and now the glee   875
Of the loud hills shakes with its mountain-mirth,
As if they did rejoice o'er a young earthquake's birth.[152]

94

Now where the swift Rhone cleaves his way between
Heights which appear as lovers who have parted
In hate, whose mining depths so intervene   880
That they can meet no more, though broken-hearted,
Though in their souls (which thus each other thwarted)
Love was the very root of the fond rage
Which blighted their life's bloom, and then departed –
Itself expired, but leaving them an age   885
Of years all winters, war within themselves to wage;

95

Now where the quick Rhone thus hath cleft his way,
The mightiest of the storms hath ta'en his stand:
For here not one but many make their play,
And fling their thunderbolts from hand to hand,   890
Flashing and cast around; of all the band
The brightest through these parted hills hath forked
His lightnings, as if he did understand
That in such gaps as desolation worked,
There the hot shaft[153] should blast whatever therein lurked.   895

96

Sky, mountains, river, winds, lake, lightnings – ye
With night and clouds and thunder, and a soul
To make these felt and feeling, well may be
Things that have made me watchful; the far roll

---

[152]   *a young earthquake's birth* cf. Shelley, *Mont Blanc* 72–3.   [153]   *the hot shaft* i.e. of lightning.

Of your departing voices is the knoll[154]   900
Of what in me is sleepless – if I rest.
But where of ye, oh tempests, is the goal?
Are ye like those within the human breast?
Or do ye find, at length, like eagles, some high nest?

97

Could I embody and unbosom now   905
That which is most within me! Could I wreak[155]
My thoughts upon expression, and thus throw
Soul, heart, mind, passions, feelings (strong or weak),
All that I would have sought and all I seek,
Bear, know, feel, and yet breathe – into *one* word,   910
And that one word were lightning, I would speak!
But as it is, I live and die unheard
With a most voiceless thought, sheathing it as a sword.

98

The morn is up again, the dewy morn
With breath all incense, and with cheek all bloom,   915
Laughing the clouds away with playful scorn
And living as if earth contained no tomb,
And glowing into day: we may resume
The march of our existence. And thus I,
Still on thy shores, fair Leman, may find room   920
And food for meditation, nor pass by
Much that may give us pause, if pondered fittingly.

99

Clarens![156] Sweet Clarens, birthplace of deep Love!
Thine air is the young breath of passionate thought;
Thy trees take root in Love; the snows above,   925
The very glaciers have his colours caught,

---

154   *knoll* summit.
155   *wreak* vent.
156   Byron and Shelley sailed to Clarens, visiting the Castle
of Chillon, on 26 June 1816. Shelley had just been reading *La
Nouvelle Héloïse*; Byron had read it many times before.

And sunset into rose hues[157] sees them wrought
By rays which sleep there lovingly: the rocks,
The permanent crags, tell here of Love, who sought
In them a refuge from the worldly shocks,   930
Which stir and sting the soul with hope that woos, then mocks.

100

Clarens! By heavenly feet thy paths are trod –
Undying Love's, who here ascends a throne
To which the steps are mountains;[158] where the god
Is a pervading life and light – so shown   935
Not on those summits solely, nor alone
In the still cave and forest; o'er the flower
His eye is sparkling, and his breath hath blown,
His soft and summer breath, whose tender power
Passes the strength of storms in their most desolate hour.   940

---

[157] 'Rousseau's Héloïse, Letter 17, part 4, note. "Ces montagnes sont si hautes qu'une demi-heure après le soleil couché, leurs sommets sont encore éclairés de ses rayons; dont le rouge forme sur ces cimes blanches *une belle couleur de rose* qu'on apperçoit de fort loin."

This applies more particularly to the heights over Meillerie. "J'allai à Vevay loger à la Clef, et pendant deux jours que j'y restai sans voir personne, je pris pour cette ville un amour qui m'a suivi dans tous mes voyages, et qui m'y a fait établir enfin les héros de mon roman. Je dirois volontiers à ceux qui ont du goût et qui sont sensibles: allez à Vevay – visitez le pays, examinez les sites, promenez-vous sur le lac, et dites si la Nature n'a pas fait ce beau pays pour une Julie, pour une Claire et pour un St Preux; mais ne les y cherchez pas." *Les Confessions*, livre iv. Page 306. Lyons ed. 1796.

In July 1816, I made a voyage round the Lake of Geneva; and, as far as my own observations have led me in a not uninterested nor inattentive survey of all the scenes most celebrated by Rousseau in his *Héloïse*, I can safely say, that in this there is no exaggeration. It would be difficult to see Clarens (with the scenes around it, Vevay, Chillon, Bôveret, St Gingo, Meillerie, Evian, and the entrances of the Rhone), without being forcibly struck with its peculiar adaptation to the persons and events with which it has been peopled. But this is not all; the feeling with which all around Clarens, and the opposite rocks of Meillerie is invested, is of a still higher and more comprehensive order than the mere sympathy with individual passion; it is a sense of the existence of love in its most extended and sublime capacity, and of our own participation of its good and of its glory: it is the great principle of the universe, which is there more condensed, but not less manifested; and of which, though knowing ourselves a part, we lose our individuality, and mingle in the beauty of the whole.

If Rousseau had never written, nor lived, the same associations would not less have belonged to such scenes. He has added to the interest of his works by their adoption; he has shown his sense of their beauty by the selection; but they have done for him which no human being could do for them.

I had the fortune (good or evil as it might be) to sail from Meillerie (where we landed for some time), to St Gingo during a lake storm, which added to the magnificence of all around, although occasionally accompanied by danger to the boat, which was small and overloaded. It was over this very part of the lake that Rousseau has driven the boat of St Preux and Madame Wolmar to Meillerie for shelter during a tempest.

On gaining the shore at St Gingo, I found that the wind had been sufficiently strong to blow down some fine old chestnut trees on the lower part of the mountains. On the opposite height of Clarens is a chateau.

The hills are covered with vineyards, and interspersed with some small but beautiful woods; one of these was named the "Bosquet de Julie", and it is remarkable that, though long ago cut down by the brutal selfishness of the monks of St Bernard (to whom the land appertained), that the ground might be enclosed into a vineyard for the miserable drones of an execrable superstition, the inhabitants of Clarens still point out the spot where its trees stood, calling it by the name which consecrated and survived them.

Rousseau has not been particularly fortunate in the preservation of the "local habitations" he has given to "airy nothings". The Prior of Great St Bernard has cut down some of his woods for the sake of a few casks of wine, and Bonaparte has levelled part of the rocks of Meillerie in improving the road to the Simplon. The road is an excellent one, but I cannot quite agree with a remark which I heard made, that "La route vaut mieux que les souvenirs" ' (Byron's note).

[158] *a throne . . . mountains* this image is reworked at *Manfred* I i 60–2, and picked up by Shelley, *Mont Blanc* 15–17.

101

All things are here of *him*;[159] from the black pines,
Which are his shade on high, and the loud roar
Of torrents, where he listeneth, to the vines
Which slope his green path downward to the shore,
Where the bowed waters meet him, and adore,   945
Kissing his feet with murmurs; and the wood,
The covert of old trees, with trunks all hoar,
But light leaves, young as joy, stands where it stood,
Offering to him, and his, a populous solitude,

102

A populous solitude of bees and birds,   950
And fairy-formed and many-coloured things,
Who worship him with notes more sweet than words,
And innocently open their glad wings,
Fearless and full of life: the gush of springs,
And fall of lofty fountains, and the bend   955
Of stirring branches, and the bud which brings
The swiftest thought of beauty, here extend
Mingling, and made by Love, unto one mighty end.

103

He who hath loved not, here would learn that lore,
And make his heart a spirit; he who knows   960
That tender mystery, will love the more,
For this is Love's recess, where vain men's woes,
And the world's waste, have driven him far from those,
For 'tis his nature to advance or die;
He stands not still, but or decays, or grows   965
Into a boundless blessing, which may vie
With the immortal lights, in its eternity!

104

'Twas not for fiction chose Rousseau this spot,
Peopling it with affections; but he found
It was the scene which passion must allot   970
To the mind's purified beings; 'twas the ground
Where early Love his Psyche's zone unbound,[160]
And hallowed it with loveliness: 'tis lone,
And wonderful, and deep, and hath a sound,

---

[159] *him* i.e. Love.
[160] *Where early Love his Psyche's zone unbound* Love undid Psyche's girdle when he made love to her, disobeying the orders of Venus, who was jealous of Psyche's beauty. Byron's point is that Rousseau chose Clarens for setting his novel's love scenes because he wanted to project, through the novel, his own feelings for Madame d'Houdetot (one of the mind's 'purified beings').

And sense, and sight of sweetness; here the Rhone   975
Hath spread himself a couch, the Alps have reared a throne.[161]

105

Lausanne, and Ferney! Ye have been the abodes
Of names[162] which unto you bequeathed a name;
Mortals who sought and found, by dangerous roads,
A path to perpetuity of fame: 980
They were gigantic minds, and their steep aim
Was, Titan-like, on daring doubts to pile[163]
Thoughts which should call down thunder, and the flame
Of heaven again assailed – if heaven the while
On man, and man's research, could deign do more than smile.   985

106

The one[164] was fire and fickleness, a child
Most mutable in wishes, but in mind
A wit as various – gay, grave, sage, or wild –
Historian, bard, philosopher, combined;
He multiplied himself among mankind,   990
The Proteus[165] of their talents: but his own
Breathed most in ridicule – which, as the wind,
Blew where it listed,[166] laying all things prone –
Now to o'erthrow a fool, and now to shake a throne.[167]

107

The other,[168] deep and slow, exhausting thought,   995
And hiving[169] wisdom with each studious year,
In meditation dwelt, with learning wrought,[170]
And shaped his weapon with an edge severe,
Sapping a solemn creed with solemn sneer;
The lord of irony – that master-spell   1000
Which stung his foes to wrath, which grew from fear,
And doomed him to the zealot's ready hell,
Which answers to all doubts so eloquently well.[171]

---

[161]   *throne* in *Mont Blanc*, Shelley describes the mountain as
the 'secret throne' of Power (l. 17).
[162]   'Voltaire and Gibbon' (Byron's note). Edward Gibbon
(1737–94), author of *The Decline and Fall of the Roman Empire*,
lived at Lausanne 1783–93. Voltaire resided at his estate at
Ferney 1758–77. Both are examples of heroic freethinking.
[163]   *Titan-like . . . pile* the Titans and Giants piled Pelion
upon Ossa (mountains) in an attempt to gain heaven and over-
throw Jupiter.
[164]   *The one* i.e. Voltaire.
[165]   *Proteus* sea-god with the ability to change his shape;
Voltaire mastered different forms of intellectual endeavour.

[166]   *listed* wanted.
[167]   *now to shake a throne* i.e. Voltaire's writings helped bring
about the French Revolution.
[168]   *The other* i.e. Gibbon.
[169]   *hiving* hoarding.
[170]   *wrought* created (i.e. his history of the Roman Empire).
[171]   Gibbon's work was highly controversial in its day,
because it effectively demolished the traditional, religiously-
slanted views of the later Roman period. He said that his his-
tory recorded the triumph of superstition and barbarism over
culture and civilization.

108

Yet peace be with their ashes – for by them,
If merited, the penalty is paid;   1005
It is not ours to judge, far less condemn;
The hour must come when such things shall be made
Known unto all – or hope and dread allayed
By slumber, on one pillow, in the dust,
Which, thus much we are sure, must lie decayed;   1010
And when it shall revive, as is our trust,
'Twill be to be forgiven, or suffer what is just.

109

But let me quit man's works, again to read
His maker's,[172] spread around me, and suspend
This page, which from my reveries[173] I feed,   1015
Until it seems prolonging without end.
The clouds above me to the white Alps tend,
And I must pierce them, and survey whate'er
May be permitted, as my steps I bend
To their most great and growing region, where   1020
The earth to her embrace compels the powers of air.

110

Italia too, Italia! Looking on thee,
Full flashes on the soul the light of ages,
Since the fierce Carthaginian[174] almost won thee,
To the last halo of the chiefs and sages   1025
Who glorify thy consecrated pages;
Thou wert the throne and grave of empires;[175] still,
The fount at which the panting mind assuages
Her thirst of knowledge, quaffing there her fill,
Flows from the eternal source of Rome's imperial hill.[176]   1030

111

Thus far have I proceeded in a theme
Renewed with no kind auspices[177] – to feel

---

[172] *His maker's* i.e. nature.
[173] *reveries* i.e. his sublime experiences in the midst of natural things (which inspire him).
[174] *the fierce Carthaginian* Hannibal, Carthaginian general who attempted to conquer Italy in the third century BC, won many battles against the Romans, but finally failed.

[175] *Thou wert the throne and grave of empires* Rome conquered the Etruscan and Carthaginian civilizations, and incorporated the Greek and Persian empires.
[176] *Flows . . . hill* a reference to the founding of the Holy Roman Empire.
[177] *auspices* i.e. prospect of success.

We are not what we have been, and to deem
We are not what we should be; and to steel
The heart against itself; and to conceal,   1035
With a proud caution, love, or hate, or aught
(Passion or feeling, purpose, grief or zeal)
Which is the tyrant spirit of our thought,
Is a stern task of soul. No matter, it is taught.

112

And for these words, thus woven into song,   1040
It may be that they are a harmless wile,
The colouring of the scenes which fleet along,
Which I would seize, in passing, to beguile
My breast, or that of others, for a while.
Fame is the thirst of youth – but I am not   1045
So young as to regard men's frown or smile
As loss or guerdon[178] of a glorious lot;
I stood and stand alone, remembered or forgot.

113

I have not loved the world, nor the world me;
I have not flattered its rank breath, nor bowed   1050
To its idolatries a patient knee,
Nor coined[179] my cheek to smiles, nor cried aloud
In worship of an echo;[180] in the crowd
They could not deem me one of such.[181] I stood
Among them, but not of them, in a shroud   1055
Of thoughts which were not their thoughts, and still could,
Had I not filed[182] my mind,[183] which thus itself subdued.

114

I have not loved the world, nor the world me,
But let us part fair foes; I do believe,
Though I have found them not, that there may be   1060
Words which are things, hopes which will not deceive,
And virtues which are merciful, nor weave
Snares for the failing. I would also deem
O'er others' griefs that some sincerely grieve,[184]

---

178   *guerdon* reward.
179   *coined* counterfeited.
180   *In worship of an echo* to Byron, God is no more than an echo.
181   *such* i.e. a worshipper of God.
182   *filed* defiled.

183   *Had I not filed my mind* Byron notes the allusion to *Macbeth* III i 63–4: 'If't be so, / For Banquo's issue have I filed my mind'.
184   'It is said by Rochfoucault that "there is *always* something in the misfortunes of men's best friends not displeasing to them" ' (Byron's note).

That two, or one, are almost what they seem,   1065
That goodness is no name, and happiness no dream.

115

My daughter! with thy name this song begun!
My daughter! with thy name thus much shall end!
I see thee not – I hear thee not – but none
Can be so wrapped in thee; thou art the friend   1070
To whom the shadows of far years extend:
Albeit my brow thou never should'st behold,
My voice shall with thy future visions blend
And reach into thy heart – when mine is cold –
A token and a tone, even from thy father's mould.[185]   1075

116

To aid thy mind's development, to watch
Thy dawn of little joys, to sit and see
Almost thy very growth, to view thee catch
Knowledge of objects (wonders yet to thee!),
To hold thee lightly on a gentle knee,   1080
And print on thy soft cheek a parent's kiss –
This, it should seem, was not reserved for me,
Yet this was in my nature. As it is,
I know not what is there, yet something like to this.

117

Yet though dull hate as duty should be taught,   1085
I know that thou wilt love me, though my name
Should be shut from thee, as a spell still fraught[186]
With desolation, and a broken claim.
Though the grave closed between us, 'twere the same,
I know that thou wilt love me, though to drain   1090
My blood from out thy being were an aim
And an attainment, all would be in vain:
Still thou would'st love me, still that more than life retain.

118

The child of love, though born in bitterness
And nurtured in convulsion,[187] of thy sire   1095

---

[185] *mould* body.
[186] *fraught* loaded.

[187] *convulsion* i.e. Byron's rancorous separation from his wife.

These were the elements – and thine no less.
As yet such are around thee, but thy fire
Shall be more tempered, and thy hope far higher.
Sweet be thy cradled slumbers! O'er the sea
And from the mountains where I now respire,   1100
Fain would I waft such blessing upon thee,
As, with a sigh, I deem thou might'st have been to me!

Prometheus (composed July or early August 1816)[1]

From THE PRISONER OF CHILLON AND OTHER POEMS (1816)

I

Titan![2] to whose immortal eyes
    The sufferings of mortality
    Seen in their sad reality,
Were not as things that gods despise –
What was thy pity's recompense?   5
A silent suffering, and intense;
The rock, the vulture, and the chain,
All that the proud can feel of pain,
The agony they do not show,
The suffocating sense of woe   10
    Which speaks but in its loneliness,
And then is jealous lest the sky
Should have a listener, nor will sigh
    Until its voice is echoless.

II

Titan! to thee the strife was given   15
    Between the suffering and the will,
    Which torture where they cannot kill;
And the inexorable heaven,
And the deaf tyranny of fate,
The ruling principle of hate   20
Which for its pleasure doth create
The things it may annihilate,
Refused thee even the boon to die:
The wretched gift eternity

PROMETHEUS
[1] Prometheus was much on the minds of Shelley, Mary
Godwin and Byron in the summer of 1816. He inspired
Mary's *Frankenstein; or, the Modern Prometheus* (1818), and was
to inspire Shelley's *Prometheus Unbound* (pp. 864–930). When
Jupiter took fire away from earth, Prometheus stole replace-
ment fire from the chariot of the sun. In revenge, Jupiter had
Prometheus nailed to a rock for 30,000 years, with an eagle
incessantly devouring his liver. He was eventually freed, and
the bird killed, by Hercules. Byron uses the story to reprise
his concept of the Byronic overreacher.
[2] *Titan!* In classical literature, the Titans were the children
of Uranus (heaven) and Ge (earth); they were thrown out of
heaven by Jupiter (the aftermath of which is the subject of
Keats's *Hyperion* poems).

Was thine – and thou hast borne it well. 25
All that the thunderer[3] wrung from thee
Was but the menace which flung back
On him the torments of thy rack;[4]
The fate thou didst so well foresee
But would not to appease him tell; 30
And in thy silence was his sentence,
And in his soul a vain repentance,
And evil dread so ill dissembled
That in his hand the lightnings trembled.

III

Thy godlike crime was to be kind, 35
To render with thy precepts less
The sum of human wretchedness,
And strengthen man with his own mind;
But baffled[5] as thou wert from high,
Still in thy patient energy, 40
In the endurance and repulse
Of thine impenetrable spirit,
Which earth and heaven could not convulse,
A mighty lesson we inherit:
Thou art a symbol and a sign 45
To mortals of their fate and force;
Like thee, man is in part divine,
A troubled stream from a pure source;
And man in portions can foresee
His own funereal destiny; 50
His wretchedness and his resistance,
And his sad unallied existence:
To which his spirit may oppose
Itself – an equal to all woes,
And a firm will, and a deep sense, 55
Which even in torture can descry
Its own concentred recompense,
Triumphant where it dares defy,
And making death a victory.

---

3 *the thunderer* Jupiter, who was responsible for Prometheus's
punishment, used the thunderbolt as his instrument of war.
4 *rack* suffering.
5 *baffled* obstructed, prevented.

Stanzas to Augusta (composed 24 July 1816)[1]

From THE PRISONER OF CHILLON AND OTHER POEMS (1816)

I

Though the day of my destiny's over,
  And the star of my fate hath declined,
Thy soft heart refused to discover
  The faults which so many could find;
Though thy soul with my grief was acquainted,   5
  It shrunk not to share it with me,
And the love which my spirit hath painted
  It never hath found but in *thee*.

2

Then when nature around me is smiling
  The last smile which answers to mine,   10
I do not believe it beguiling
  Because it reminds me of thine;
And when winds are at war with the ocean,
  As the breasts I believed in with me,
If their billows excite an emotion   15
  It is that they bear me from *thee*.

3

Though the rock of my last hope is shivered[2]
  And its fragments are sunk in the wave,
Though I feel that my soul is delivered
  To pain – it shall not be its slave.   20
There is many a pang to pursue me –
  They may crush, but they shall not contemn;
They may torture, but shall not subdue me –
  'Tis of *thee* that I think, not of them.[3]

STANZAS TO AUGUSTA
[1] Originally published as *Stanzas to* ----------. Augusta
Leigh, Byron's half-sister, remained as close and affectionate as
ever despite the vilification directed at him in the wake of his
failed marriage; see pp. 662–3.
[2] *shivered* shattered.
[3] At this period Byron felt persecuted by the unfavourable
publicity arising from his separation from his wife; as he
told Thomas Moore on 29 February 1816: 'I am at war
"with all the world and his wife"; or, rather, "all the world
and *my* wife" are at war with me, and have not yet crushed
me – whatever they may do. I don't know that in the course
of a hair-breadth existence I was ever, at home or abroad,
in a situation so completely uprooting of present pleasure,
or rational hope for the future, as this same' (Marchand
v 35).

4

Though human, thou didst not deceive me; 25
    Though woman, thou didst not forsake;
Though loved, thou forborest to grieve me;
    Though slandered, thou never couldst shake;
Though trusted, thou didst not betray[4] me;
    Though parted, it was not to fly; 30
Though watchful, 'twas not to defame me,
    Nor, mute, that the world might belie.

5

Yet I blame not the world, nor despise it,
    Nor the war of the many with one –
If my soul was not fitted to prize it 35
    'Twas folly not sooner to shun:
And if dearly that error hath cost me,
    And more than I once could foresee,
I have found that, whatever it lost me,
    It could not deprive me of *thee*. 40

6

From the wreck of the past, which hath perished,
    Thus much I at least may recall,
It hath taught me that what I most cherished
    Deserved to be dearest of all:
In the desert a fountain is springing,[5] 45
    In the wide waste there still is a tree,
And a bird in the solitude singing,
    Which speaks to my spirit of *thee*.

Epistle to Augusta (composed August 1816; edited from MS)[1]

From THE PRISONER OF CHILLON AND OTHER POEMS (1816)

1

My sister, my sweet sister – if a name
    Dearer and purer were, it should be thine.

---

[4] *betray* All printed texts until McGann's Clarendon edition have 'disclaim'. McGann's emendation reinstates a reading attributable to Byron rather than his publisher.
[5] *In the desert a fountain is springing* the ultimate source is biblical (Judges 15:19), but Byron is probably recalling Milton, *Samson Agonistes* 581–2: 'But God who caused a fountain at thy prayer / From the dry ground to spring . . .'

EPISTLE TO AUGUSTA
[1] Originally published 1830, posthumously; this is Byron's first sustained composition in *ottava rima*.

Mountains and seas divide us,[2] but I claim
 No tears, but tenderness to answer mine:
Go where I will, to me thou art the same –   5
 A loved regret which I would not resign;
There yet are two things in my destiny:
 A world to roam through,[3] and a home with thee.

2

The first were nothing – had I still the last
 It were the haven of my happiness;   10
But other claims and other ties thou hast,[4]
 And mine is not the wish to make them less.
A strange doom[5] was thy father's son's,[6] and past
 Recalling, as it lies beyond redress,
Reversed for him our grandsire's fate of yore[7] –   15
He had no rest at sea, nor I on shore.

3

If my inheritance of storms hath been
 In other elements, and on the rocks
Of perils overlooked or unforeseen,
 I have sustained my share of worldly shocks;   20
The fault was mine – nor do I seek to screen
 My errors with defensive paradox:
I have been cunning in mine overthrow,[8]
The careful pilot of my proper woe.

4

Mine were my faults, and mine be their reward;   25
 My whole life was a contest, since the day
That gave me being gave me that which marred
 The gift – a fate or will that walked astray –
And I at times have found the struggle hard,
 And thought of shaking off my bonds of clay;[9]   30

---

[2] Byron was resident at the Villa Diodati on the shores of Lake Geneva (Lake Leman at l. 75).
[3] *A world to roam through* Byron had exiled himself from England in April 1816 after separating from his wife and daughter.
[4] *But other claims . . . hast* Augusta married Colonel George Leigh in 1807, and had by now given birth to three daughters.
[5] *doom* fate.
[6] *thy father's son's* i.e. Byron. They had the same father, Captain John (Mad Jack) Byron.
[7] The rough draft of the poem contains the following note in Byron's hand: 'Admiral Byron was remarkable for never making a voyage without a tempest: "But, though it were tempest-tossed, / Still his bark could not be lost." He returned safely from the wreck of the Wager (in Anson's voyage) and subsequently circumnavigated the world many years after, as commander of a similar expedition'. The quotation reworks *Macbeth* I iii 24–5.
[8] *overthrow* ruin; somewhat self-dramatizing, but Byron saw himself as having been ruined, at least in social terms, by his wife's campaign against him.
[9] *my bonds of clay* Byron felt more confined by the limits of his body than most, thanks to the club foot with which he was born; cf. Childe Harold, who spurns 'the clay-cold bonds which round our being cling' (*Childe Harold's Pilgrimage* iii 697).

But now I fain would for a time survive,
If but to see what next can well arrive.

5

Kingdoms and empires in my little day
   I have outlived and yet I am not old;
And when I look on this, the petty spray   35
   Of my own years of trouble, which have rolled
Like a wild bay of breakers, melts away:
   Something (I know not what) does still uphold
A spirit of slight patience; not in vain,
Even for its own sake, do we purchase pain.   40

6

Perhaps the workings of defiance stir
   Within me, or perhaps a cold despair
Brought on when ills habitually recur;
   Perhaps a harder clime or purer air –
For to all such may change of soul refer,   45
   And with light armour we may learn to bear –
Have taught me a strange quiet which was not
The chief companion of a calmer lot.

7

I feel almost at times as I have felt
   In happy childhood[10] – trees and flowers and brooks,   50
Which do remember me of where I dwelt
   Ere my young mind was sacrificed to books,
Come as of yore upon me, and can melt
   My heart with recognition of their looks –
And even at moments I could think I see   55
Some living things to love – but none like thee.

8

Here are the Alpine landscapes, which create
   A fund for contemplation – to admire
Is a brief feeling of a trivial date –
   But something worthier do such scenes inspire: 60
Here to be lonely is not desolate,
   For much I view which I could most desire,
And above all a lake I can behold –
Lovelier, not dearer, than our own of old.[11]

---

[10] *In happy childhood* Byron did not know Augusta as a child, when he was brought up by his mother in the Scottish countryside.

[11] *than our own of old* Byron refers to the lake at Newstead Abbey, where he had frolicked with Augusta in January and late August 1814.

9

Oh that thou wert but with me! – but I grow   65
        The fool of my own wishes, and forget;
The solitude which I have vaunted so
        Has lost its praise in this but one regret –
There may be others which I less may show;
        I am not of the plaintive mood – and yet   70
I feel an ebb in my philosophy
And the tide rising in my altered eye.

10

I did remind thee of our own dear lake
        By the old Hall which may be mine no more;[12]
Leman's is fair, but think not I forsake   75
        The sweet remembrance of a dearer shore:
Sad havoc time must with my memory make
        Ere *that* or *thou* can fade these eyes before –
Though like all things which I have loved, they[13] are
Resigned[14] for ever, or divided far.   80

11

The world is all before me[15] – I but ask
        Of Nature that with which she will comply:
It is but in her summer's sun to bask,
        To mingle in the quiet of her sky,[16]
To see her gentle face without a mask   85
        And never gaze on it with apathy.
She was my early friend, and now shall be
My sister – till I look again on thee.

12

I can reduce all feelings but this one,
        And that I would not – for at length I see   90
Such scenes as those wherein my life begun –
        The earliest – were the only paths for me.
Had I but sooner known the crowd to shun,
        I had been better than I now can be;
The passions which have torn me would have slept –   95
I had not suffered, and *thou* hadst not wept.

---

[12]   Byron needed to sell Newstead to pay off his debts. At
the time of writing, however, it was still on his hands; it was
sold in late 1817 to his Harrow schoolfriend Major Thomas
Wildman for £94,500.
[13]   *they* i.e. the lake at Newstead and Augusta.

[14]   *Resigned* surrendered.
[15]   A sardonic echo of the more optimistic context of Adam
and Eve leaving Eden, *Paradise Lost* xii 646.
[16]   *the quiet of her sky* a deliberate echo of Wordsworth, *Tintern Abbey* 8.

13

With false ambition what had I to do?
　　Little with love, and least of all with fame!
And yet they came unsought and with me grew,
　　And made me all which they can make – a name.　　　100
Yet this was not the end I did pursue –
　　Surely I once beheld a nobler aim.
But all is over – I am one the more
To baffled millions which have gone before.

14

And for the future – this world's future may　　　　　105
　　From me demand but little from my care;
I have outlived myself by many a day,
　　Having survived so many things that were;
My years have been no slumber – but the prey
　　Of ceaseless vigils; for I had the share　　　　　110
Of life which might have filled a century
Before its fourth in time had passed me by.

15

And for the remnants which may be to come
　　I am content – and for the past I feel
Not thankless, for within the crowded sum　　　　　115
　　Of struggles happiness at times would steal;
And for the present, I would not benumb
　　My feelings farther – nor shall I conceal
That with all this I still can look around
And worship nature with a thought profound.　　　　　120

16

For thee, my own sweet sister, in thy heart
　　I know myself secure – as thou in mine
We were and are – I am – even as thou art –
　　Beings who ne'er each other can resign,
It is the same together or apart:　　　　　　　　　125
　　From life's commencement to its slow decline
We are entwined – let death come slow or fast,
The tie[17] which bound the first endures the last.

---

[17]　*tie* As McGann indicates, Byron implicitly compares the
blood-tie to Augusta with the marriage-tie to Annabella.

Darkness (composed between 21 July and 25 August 1816)[1]

From THE PRISONER OF CHILLON AND OTHER POEMS (1816)

I had a dream, which was not all a dream.
The bright sun was extinguished, and the stars
Did wander darkling[2] in the eternal space,
Rayless, and pathless,[3] and the icy earth
Swung blind and blackening in the moonless air;   5
Morn came, and went – and came, and brought no day,
And men forgot their passions in the dread
Of this their desolation; and all hearts
Were chilled into a selfish prayer for light:
And they did live by watchfires – and the thrones,   10
The palaces of crowned kings – the huts,
The habitations of all things which dwell,
Were burnt for beacons;[4] cities were consumed,
And men were gathered round their blazing homes
To look once more into each other's face;   15
Happy were those who dwelt within the eye
Of the volcanoes, and their mountain-torch:
A fearful hope was all the world contained;
Forests were set on fire – but hour by hour
They fell and faded – and the crackling trunks   20
Extinguished with a crash – and all was black.
The brows of men by the despairing light
Wore an unearthly aspect, as by fits
The flashes fell upon them; some lay down
And hid their eyes and wept; and some did rest   25
Their chins upon their clenched hands, and smiled;
And others hurried to and fro, and fed
Their funeral piles with fuel, and looked up
With mad disquietude on the dull sky,
The pall of a past world; and then again   30
With curses cast them down upon the dust,
And gnashed their teeth and howled. The wild birds shrieked,
And, terrified, did flutter on the ground,[5]
And flap their useless wings; the wildest brutes
Came tame and tremulous;[6] and vipers crawled   35
And twined themselves among the multitude,
Hissing, but stingless – they were slain for food:

DARKNESS
1 The theme of apocalypse, like that of Prometheus, is distinctively a product of the intense exchanges that Byron enjoyed with Shelley and Mary Godwin in summer 1816. A later work on this theme is Mary's novel *The Last Man* (1826). The poem is indebted to various apocalyptic passages in the Bible, notably Jeremiah 4, Ezekiel 32 and 38, Joel 2:31, Matthew 25, and Revelation 6:12.
2 *darkling* in the dark.
3 *the stars . . . pathless* as McGann notes, there is an echo here of Milton's *Il Penseroso* (appropriately, as the poem was written at the Villa Diodati, where Milton resided), where the moon is compared with 'one that had been led astray / Through the heaven's wide pathless way' (ll. 69–70).
4 *beacons* signals – of continuing life.
5 *The wild birds . . . on the ground* a recollection of Coleridge's *Christabel*, where the sweet bird in Bracy's dream 'lay fluttering on the ground' (l. 532).
6 *The wildest brutes . . . tremulous* an allusion to the famous apocalyptic prophecy, when 'The wolf also shall dwell with the lamb, and the leopard shall lie down with the kid; and the calf and the young lion and the fatling together; and a little child shall lead them' (Isaiah 11:6).

And War, which for a moment was no more,
Did glut himself again; a meal was bought
With blood, and each sat sullenly apart   40
Gorging himself in gloom. No love was left;
All earth was but one thought – and that was death,
Immediate and inglorious; and the pang
Of famine fed upon all entrails – men
Died, and their bones were tombless as their flesh;   45
The meagre by the meagre were devoured,
Even dogs assailed their masters, all save one,
And he was faithful to a corpse, and kept
The birds and beasts and famished men at bay,
Till hunger clung[7] them, or the dropping dead   50
Lured their lank jaws; himself sought out no food,
But with a piteous and perpetual moan
And a quick desolate cry, licking the hand
Which answered not with a caress – he died.
The crowd was famished by degrees, but two   55
Of an enormous city did survive,
And they were enemies; they met beside
The dying embers of an altar-place
Where had been heaped a mass of holy things
For an unholy usage; they raked up,   60
And shivering scraped with their cold skeleton hands
The feeble ashes, and their feeble breath
Blew for a little life, and made a flame
Which was a mockery; then they lifted up
Their eyes as it grew lighter, and beheld   65
Each other's aspects – saw, and shrieked, and died –
Even of their mutual hideousness they died,
Unknowing who he was upon whose brow
Famine had written Fiend. The world was void,
The populous and the powerful – was a lump,   70
Seasonless, herbless, treeless, manless, lifeless –
A lump of death – a chaos of hard clay.
The rivers, lakes, and ocean all stood still,
And nothing stirred within their silent depths;
Ships sailorless lay rotting on the sea,   75
And their masts fell down piecemeal; as they dropped
They slept on the abyss without a surge –
The waves were dead; the tides were in their grave,
The moon their mistress had expired before;
The winds were withered in the stagnant air,   80
And the clouds perished; Darkness had no need
Of aid from them – she was the universe.

---

[7] *clung* shrivelled, as at *Macbeth* V v 39: 'Till famine cling
thee'.

Manfred, A Dramatic Poem (composed between September 1816 and 15 February 1817; published 1817)[1]

There are more things in heaven and earth, Horatio,
Than are dreamt of in your philosophy.[2]

Dramatis Personae

Manfred
Chamois Hunter
Abbot of St Maurice
Manuel
Herman
Witch of the Alps
Arimanes
Nemesis
The Destinies
Spirits, etc.

The scene of the drama is amongst the higher Alps – partly in the Castle of Manfred, and partly in the mountains.

ACT I, SCENE I[1]

Manfred alone. Scene: a Gothic gallery.[2] *Time: midnight.*

MANFRED The lamp must be replenished, but even then
It will not burn so long as I must watch;
My slumbers (if I slumber) are not sleep
But a continuance of enduring thought,
Which then I can resist not. In my heart   5
There is a vigil, and these eyes but close
To look within – and yet I live, and bear
The aspect and the form of breathing men.
But grief should be the instructor of the wise –
Sorrow is knowledge;[3] they who know the most   10
Must mourn the deepest o'er the fatal truth:
The tree of knowledge is not that of life.
Philosophy and science,[4] and the springs
Of wonder, and the wisdom of the world

MANFRED, A DRAMATIC POEM
[1] This verse drama is one of Byron's most explicit and earnest discussions of the concept of the overreacher; for further introductory comments see headnote, p. 664. See also Alan Richardson, '*Manfred*: "The Language of Another World"', *A Mental Theater: Poetic Drama and Consciousness in the Romantic Age* (Philadelphia, 1988), pp. 43–58.
[2] *Hamlet* I v 166–7. The epigraph underlines Byron's belief in the supernatural and metaphysical – of which he was, to put it mildly, highly sceptical by the time he published *Don Juan*, two years later.

ACT I SCENE I
[1] The first scene of the play most clearly betrays its source in Goethe's *Faust*, which M. G. Lewis (author of *The Monk* (1796)) translated for Byron, aloud, in August 1816. When Goethe read *Manfred*, he declared it 'a wonderful phenomenon'.
[2] *a Gothic gallery* Byron means a covered balcony designed in the gothic manner.
[3] *But grief . . . knowledge* Ecclesiastes 1:18: 'For in much wisdom is much grief: and he that increaseth knowledge increaseth sorrow.'
[4] *science* knowledge, although it includes subjects which today would be described as 'science' (physics, chemistry, and so forth).

I have essayed,[5] and in my mind there is 15
A power to make these subject to itself,
But they avail not. I have done men good,
And I have met with good even among men –
But this availed not. I have had my foes
And none have baffled,[6] many fallen before me – 20
But this availed not. Good or evil, life,
Powers, passions, all I see in other beings
Have been to me as rain unto the sands
Since that all-nameless hour. I have no dread,
And feel the curse to have no natural fear, 25
Nor fluttering throb that beats with hopes or wishes
Or lurking love of something on the earth.
Now to my task.
                    Mysterious agency![7]
Ye spirits of the unbounded universe
Whom I have sought in darkness and in light; 30
Ye who do compass earth about, and dwell
In subtler[8] essence; ye to whom the tops
Of mountains inaccessible are haunts,
And earth's and ocean's caves familiar things –
I call upon ye by the written charm 35
Which gives me power upon you: rise, appear! (*a pause*)
They come not yet. Now by the voice of him
Who is the first among you; by this sign
Which makes you tremble; by the claims of him
Who is undying[9] – rise, appear! Appear! (*a pause*) 40
If it be so. Spirits of earth and air,
Ye shall not thus elude me: by a power
Deeper than all yet urged, a tyrant-spell
Which had its birthplace in a star condemned,
The burning wreck of a demolished world, 45
A wandering hell in the eternal space;
By the strong curse which is upon my soul,
The thought which is within me and around me,
I do compel ye to my will. Appear!

A star is seen at the darker end of the gallery. It is stationary, and a voice is heard singing.

FIRST SPIRIT[10]

Mortal,[11] to thy bidding bowed 50
From my mansion in the cloud
Which the breath of twilight builds
And the summer's sunset gilds
With the azure and vermilion
Which is mixed for my pavilion, 55
Though thy quest may be forbidden,
On a starbeam I have ridden,

---

5   *essayed* attempted.
6   *baffled* confounded.
7   *Mysterious agency!* Significantly, Byron avoids the use of the word 'God'.
8   *subtler* i.e. more refined than human flesh.

9   *him / Who is undying* deliberately ambiguous – calculated to permit a reference to Satan as well as God.
10   The Spirit of the air.
11   *Mortal* the spirit puts Manfred in his place from the start.

To thine adjuration[12] bowed;
Mortal – be thy wish avowed!

Voice of the SECOND SPIRIT[13]
Mont Blanc[14] is the monarch of mountains,   60
    They crowned him long ago
On a throne of rocks,[15] in a robe of clouds
    With a diadem of snow.
Around his waist are forests braced,
    The avalanche in his hand;   65
But ere it fall that thundering ball[16]
    Must pause for my command.
The glacier's cold and restless mass
    Moves onward day by day,[17]
But I am he who bids it pass   70
    Or with its ice delay.
I am the spirit of the place,
    Could make the mountain bow
And quiver to his caverned base –
    And what with me wouldst *thou*?   75

Voice of the THIRD SPIRIT[18]
In the blue depth of the waters
    Where the wave hath no strife,
Where the wind is a stranger
    And the sea-snake hath life,
Where the mermaid is decking[19]   80
    Her green hair with shells,
Like the storm on the surface
    Came the sound of thy spells;
O'er my calm hall of coral
    The deep echo rolled –   85
To the spirit of ocean
    Thy wishes unfold!

FOURTH SPIRIT[20]
Where the slumbering earthquake
    Lies pillowed on fire,
And the lakes of bitumen   90
    Rise boilingly higher;
Where the roots of the Andes
    Strike deep in the earth,
As their summits to heaven
    Shoot soaringly forth;   95
I have quitted my birthplace,

---

[12] *adjuration* appeal.
[13] The Spirit of earth.
[14] Byron visited Mont Blanc with Hobhouse in late August–September 1816.
[15] *throne of rocks* an image stemming back to *Childe Harold* iii 932–4, and picked up by Shelley in *Mont Blanc* 15–17.
[16] *that thundering ball* i.e. the rock which starts the avalanche.

[17] *The glacier's . . . day by day* an observation made by Shelley on his visit to Mont Blanc and Chamounix; see p. 844.
[18] The Spirit of water.
[19] *decking* adorning.
[20] The Spirit of fire.

> Thy bidding to bide –
> Thy spell hath subdued me,
> Thy will be my guide!

FIFTH SPIRIT

> I am the rider of the wind,　　　　　　　　　　　　　100
> 　The stirrer of the storm;
> The hurricane I left behind
> 　Is yet with lightning warm;
> To speed to thee, o'er shore and sea
> 　I swept upon the blast;　　　　　　　　　　　　　105
> The fleet I met sailed well and yet
> 　'Twill sink ere night be passed.

SIXTH SPIRIT

> My dwelling is the shadow of the night,
> Why doth thy magic torture me with light?

SEVENTH SPIRIT

> The star which rules thy destiny　　　　　　　　　110
> Was ruled, ere earth began, by me;
> It was a world as fresh and fair
> As e'er revolved round sun in air;
> Its course was free and regular,
> Space bosomed not a lovelier star.　　　　　　　　115
> The hour arrived, and it became
> A wandering mass of shapeless flame,
> A pathless comet and a curse –
> The menace of the universe.
> Still rolling on with innate force,　　　　　　　　120
> Without a sphere, without a course,
> A bright deformity on high,
> The monster[21] of the upper sky!
> And thou beneath its influence born,
> Thou worm whom I obey and scorn!　　　　　　　125
> Forced by a power (which is not thine,
> And lent thee but to make thee mine)
> For this brief moment to descend,
> Where these weak spirits round thee bend
> And parley with a thing like thee –　　　　　　　130
> What wouldst thou, child of clay, with me?

THE SEVEN SPIRITS

> Earth, ocean, air, night, mountains, winds, thy star,
> 　Are at thy beck and bidding, child of clay!
> Before thee at thy quest their spirits are –
> 　What wouldst thou with us, son of mortals? Say!　135

---

[21] *monster* in the sense of an unnatural and extraordinary phenomenon.

MANFRED Forgetfulness —

FIRST SPIRIT   Of what, of whom, and why?

MANFRED Of that which is within me; read it there —
    Ye know it, and I cannot utter it.

SPIRIT We can but give thee that which we possess.
    Ask of us subjects, sovereignty, the power   140
    O'er earth, the whole or portion, or a sign
    Which shall control the elements whereof
    We are the dominators, each and all —
    These shall be thine.

MANFRED   Oblivion, self-oblivion —
    Can ye not wring from out the hidden realms   145
    Ye offer so profusely what I ask?

SPIRIT It is not in our essence, in our skill;
    But — thou mayst die.

MANFRED   Will death bestow it on me?

SPIRIT We are immortal and do not forget;
    We are eternal and to us the past   150
    Is, as the future, present. Art thou answered?

MANFRED Ye mock me — but the power which brought ye here
    Hath made you mine. Slaves, scoff not at my will!
    The mind, the spirit, the Promethean spark,
    The lightning of my being, is as bright,   155
    Pervading, and far-darting as your own —
    And shall not yield to yours, though cooped in clay!
    Answer, or I will teach ye what I am.

SPIRIT We answer as we answered; our reply
    Is even in thine own words.

MANFRED   Why say ye so?   160

SPIRIT If, as thou say'st, thine essence be as ours,
    We have replied in telling thee, the thing
    Mortals call death hath nought to do with us.

MANFRED I then have called ye from your realms in vain;
    Ye cannot, or ye will not, aid me.

SPIRIT   Say;   165
    What we possess we offer, it is thine.
    Bethink ere thou dismiss us, ask again;
    Kingdom, and sway, and strength, and length of days —

MANFRED Accursed! What have I to do with days?
    They are too long already. Hence! Begone!   170

SPIRIT Yet pause. Being here, our will would do thee service;
    Bethink thee, is there then no other gift
    Which we can make not worthless in thine eyes?

MANFRED No, none — yet stay one moment ere we part,
    I would behold ye face to face.[22] I hear   175
    Your voices, sweet and melancholy sounds,
    As music on the waters, and I see
    The steady aspect of a clear large star —
    But nothing more. Approach me as ye are,
    Or one, or all, in your accustomed forms.   180

---

[22]   *face to face* Exodus 33:11: 'And the Lord spake unto Moses
face to face, as a man speaketh unto his friend.'

SPIRIT We have no forms beyond the elements
 Of which we are the mind and principle.
 But choose a form – in that we will appear.
MANFRED I have no choice; there is no form on earth
 Hideous or beautiful to me. Let him   185
 Who is most powerful of ye, take such aspect
 As unto him may seem most fitting. Come!
SEVENTH SPIRIT (*appearing in the shape of a beautiful female figure*)[23]
 Behold!
MANFRED Oh God! If it be thus, and thou
 Art not a madness and a mockery,
 I yet might be most happy. I will clasp thee,   190
 And we again will be – (*the figure vanishes*)
     My heart is crushed!

Manfred falls senseless. A voice is heard in the incantation[24] *which follows.*
 When the moon is on the wave
  And the glow-worm in the grass,
 And the meteor on the grave
  And the wisp on the morass,[25]   195
 When the falling stars are shooting
 And the answered owls are hooting,
 And the silent leaves are still
 In the shadow of the hill,
 Shall my soul be upon thine   200
 With a power and with a sign.

 Though thy slumber may be deep
 Yet thy spirit shall not sleep;
 There are shades which will not vanish,
 There are thoughts thou canst not banish;   205
 By a power to thee unknown
 Thou canst never be alone;
 Thou art wrapped as with a shroud,
 Thou art gathered in a cloud –
 And forever shalt thou dwell   210
 In the spirit of this spell.

 Though thou seest me not pass by,
 Thou shalt feel me with thine eye
 As a thing that, though unseen,
 Must be near thee, and hath been;   215
 And when in that secret dread
 Thou hast turned around thy head,
 Thou shalt marvel I am not

---

23 The Spirit appears in the form of Astarte, but, as McGann observes, ll. 232–51 were written with Lady Byron in mind.
24 The incantation (ll. 192–261) was one of the earliest parts of *Manfred* to be composed, certainly by 14 August 1816, when Byron was resident at Villa Diodati in Geneva. Most of the remainder of the play was composed during Byron's tour of the Bernese Alps the following month, and during his residence in Venice, winter 1816–17.
25 *morass* bog, marsh. The 'wisp' is a phosphorescent light seen hovering or flitting over marshy ground, and supposed to be due to the spontaneous combustion of an inflammable gas (phosphuretted hydrogen) derived from decaying organic matter; popularly called *Will-o'-the-wisp*.

As thy shadow on the spot,
And the power which thou dost feel   220
Shall be what thou must conceal.

And a magic voice and verse
Hath baptized thee with a curse;
And a spirit of the air
Hath begirt thee with a snare;   225
In the wind there is a voice
Shall forbid thee to rejoice;
And to thee shall night deny
All the quiet of her sky;
And the day shall have a sun   230
Which shall make thee wish it done.

From thy false tears I did distill
An essence which hath strength to kill;
From thy own heart I then did wring
The black mood in its blackest spring;   235
From thy own smile I snatched the snake,
For there it coiled as in a brake;[26]
From thy own lip I drew the charm
Which gave all these their chiefest harm;
In proving every poison known,   240
I found the strongest was thine own.

By thy cold breast and serpent smile,
By thy unfathomed gulfs of guile,
By that most seeming virtuous eye,
By thy shut soul's hypocrisy,   245
By the perfection of thine art
Which passed for human thine own heart,
By thy delight in others' pain,
And by thy brotherhood of Cain,[27]
I call upon thee, and compel
Thyself to be thy proper[28] hell!   250

And on thy head I pour the vial
Which doth devote[29] thee to this trial;
Nor to slumber, nor to die,
Shall be in thy destiny;
Though thy death shall still seem near   255
To thy wish, but as a fear;
Lo! the spell now works around thee
And the clankless chain hath bound thee;
O'er thy heart and brain together
Hath the word been passed: now wither!   260

---

[26] *brake* thicket.
[27] Cain murdered his brother Abel, and was cast out, a fugitive and vagabond; Genesis 4:8–12. Manfred has been cursed in a similar manner to Cain.
[28] *proper* own.
[29] *devote* condemn.

ACT I, SCENE II[1]

The mountain of the Jungfrau.[2] *Time: morning. Manfred alone upon the cliffs.*

MANFRED The spirits I have raised abandon me,
The spells which I have studied baffle me,
The remedy I recked[3] of tortured me;
I lean no more on superhuman aid,
It hath no power upon the past, and for   5
The future, till the past be gulfed in darkness,
It is not of my search. My mother earth,
And thou fresh-breaking day, and you, ye mountains –
Why are ye beautiful? I cannot love ye.
And thou, the bright eye of the universe   10
That openest over all, and unto all
Art a delight – thou shin'st not on my heart.
And you, ye crags upon whose extreme edge
I stand, and on the torrent's brink beneath
Behold the tall pines dwindled as to shrubs   15
In dizziness of distance, when a leap,
A stir, a motion, even a breath would bring
My breast upon its rocky bosom's bed
To rest for ever – wherefore do I pause?
I feel the impulse, yet I do not plunge;   20
I see the peril, yet do not recede;
And my brain reels, and yet my foot is firm.
There is a power upon me which withholds
And makes it my fatality to live[4] –
If it be life to wear within myself   25
This barrenness of spirit, and to be
My own soul's sepulchre,[5] for I have ceased
To justify my deeds unto myself
(The last infirmity of evil).[6] (*An eagle passes*) Aye,
Thou winged and cloud cleaving minister,   30
Whose happy flight is highest into heaven,
Well may'st thou swoop so near me – I should be
Thy prey, and gorge thine eaglets. Thou art gone
Where the eye cannot follow thee, but thine
Yet pierces downward, onward, or above   35
With a pervading vision. Beautiful!
How beautiful is all this visible world,
How glorious in its action and itself!
But we who name ourselves its sovereigns, we
Half-dust, half-deity, alike unfit   40
To sink or soar,[7] with our mixed essence make

ACT I SCENE II
[1] As McGann notes, this scene reworks that of Prometheus bound on the rock of the Caucasus in Aeschylus's *Prometheus Bound*.
[2] Byron first saw the mountain of the Jungfrau 23 September 1816 (Marchand v 101–2).
[3] *recked* thought.
[4] *my fatality to live* a clever paradox that echoes Hamlet, who mentions the 'calamity of so long life' (*Hamlet* III i 68).

[5] *My own soul's sepulchre* cf. Milton's *Samson Agonistes* 102: 'Myself, my sepulchre, a moving grave'.
[6] *The last infirmity of evil* an echo of *Lycidas* 71, in which fame is 'That last infirmity of noble mind'.
[7] *How beautiful . . . sink or soar* There is a general recollection here of Hamlet's famous speech, *Hamlet* II ii 293–310.

A conflict of its elements, and breathe
The breath of degradation and of pride,
Contending with low wants and lofty will
Till our mortality predominates –   45
And men are what they name not to themselves,
And trust not to each other. (*The shepherd's pipe in the distance is heard*)
                          Hark! the note,
The natural music of the mountain reed
(For here the patriarchal days are not
A pastoral fable) pipes in the liberal[8] air,   50
Mixed with the sweet bells of the sauntering herd!
My soul would drink those echoes. Oh that I were
The viewless spirit of a lovely sound,
A living voice, a breathing harmony,
A bodiless enjoyment, born and dying   55
With the blessed tone which made me!

Enter from below a Chamois Hunter

CHAMOIS HUNTER   Even so
This way the chamois[9] leapt. Her nimble feet
Have baffled me; my gains today will scarce
Repay my breakneck travail. What is here
Who seems not of my trade, and yet hath reached   60
A height which none even of our mountaineers,
Save our best hunters, may attain? His garb
Is goodly, his mien manly, and his air
Proud as a freeborn peasant's, at this distance.
I will approach him nearer.

MANFRED (*not perceiving the other*) To be thus;   65
Grey-haired with anguish like these blasted pines,
Wrecks of a single winter, barkless, branchless,
A blighted trunk upon a cursed root,
Which but supplies a feeling to decay –
And to be thus, eternally but thus,   70
Having been otherwise! Now furrowed o'er
With wrinkles; ploughed by moments, not by years;
And hours all tortured into ages – hours
Which I outlive! Ye toppling crags of ice,
Ye avalanches whom a breath draws down   75
In mountainous o'erwhelming, come and crush me!
I hear ye momently above, beneath,
Crash with a frequent conflict, but ye pass
And only fall on things which still would live –
On the young flourishing forest, or the hut   80
And hamlet of the harmless villager.

CHAMOIS HUNTER The mists begin to rise from up the valley;
I'll warn him to descend, or he may chance
To lose at once his way and life together.

MANFRED The mists boil up around the glaciers; clouds   85
Rise curling fast beneath me, white and sulphury
Like foam from the roused ocean of deep hell

---

8 *liberal* abundant.   9 *chamois* antelope found in the highest parts of the Alps.

Whose every wave breaks on a living shore,
Heaped with the damned like pebbles.[10] I am giddy.
CHAMOIS HUNTER I must approach him cautiously; if near,   90
A sudden step will startle him, and he
Seems tottering already.
MANFRED   Mountains have fallen,
Leaving a gap in the clouds, and with the shock
Rocking their Alpine brethren, filling up
The ripe green valleys with destruction's splinters,   95
Damming the rivers with a sudden dash
Which crushed the waters into mist and made
Their fountains find another channel – thus,
Thus in its old age, did Mount Rosenberg;[11]
Why stood I not beneath it?
CHAMOIS HUNTER   Friend, have a care,   100
Your next step may be fatal! For the love
Of him who made you, stand not on that brink!
MANFRED (*not hearing him*) Such would have been for me a fitting tomb;
My bones had then been quiet in their depth;
They had not then been strewn upon the rocks   105
For the wind's pastime, as thus – thus they shall be,
In this one plunge. Farewell, ye opening heavens!
Look not upon me thus reproachfully,
Ye were not meant for me. Earth, take these atoms!
As Manfred is in act to spring from the cliff, the Chamois Hunter seizes and retains him with a sudden grasp.
CHAMOIS HUNTER Hold, madman! Though aweary of thy life,   110
Stain not our pure vales with thy guilty[12] blood!
Away with me – I will not quit my hold.
MANFRED I am most sick at heart – nay, grasp me not,
I am all feebleness; the mountains whirl
Spinning around me – I grow blind. What art thou?   115
CHAMOIS HUNTER I'll answer that anon. Away with me;
The clouds grow thicker – there, now lean on me;
Place your foot here – here, take this staff, and cling
A moment to that shrub. Now give me your hand
And hold fast by my girdle[13] – softly, well.   120
The chalet will be gained within an hour;
Come on, we'll quickly find a surer footing
And something like a pathway, which the torrent
Hath washed since winter. Come, 'tis bravely done –
You should have been a hunter! Follow me.   125
As they descend the rocks with difficulty, the scene closes

---

[10]   *The mists . . . pebbles* typically, Manfred sees everything in terms that reflect his sense of his own damnation.
[11]   On 2 September 1806 part of Mt Rossberg fell and buried four villages.

[12]   *guilty* i.e. guilty of suicide, although Manfred is guilty of other sins, which the Chamois Hunter knows nothing about.
[13]   *girdle* belt.

ACT II, SCENE I

A cottage amongst the Bernese Alps.[1] *Manfred and the Chamois Hunter.*

CHAMOIS HUNTER No, no – yet pause, thou must not yet go forth;
    Thy mind and body are alike unfit
    To trust each other for some hours, at least.
    When thou art better, I will be thy guide –
    But whither?
MANFRED   It imports not. I do know   5
    My route full well, and need no further guidance.
CHAMOIS HUNTER Thy garb and gait bespeak thee of high lineage –
    One of the many chiefs, whose castled crags
    Look o'er the lower valleys. Which of these
    May call thee lord? I only know their portals;[2]   10
    My way of life leads me but rarely down
    To bask by the huge hearths of those old halls,
    Carousing with the vassals; but the paths
    Which step from out our mountains to their doors
    I know from childhood – which of these is thine?   15
MANFRED No matter.
CHAMOIS HUNTER   Well sir, pardon me the question,
    And be of better cheer. Come taste my wine,
    'Tis of an ancient vintage – many a day
    'T has thawed my veins among our glaciers; now
    Let it do thus for thine. Come, pledge[3] me fairly.   20
MANFRED Away, away! There's blood upon the brim!
    Will it then never, never sink in the earth?
CHAMOIS HUNTER What dost thou mean? Thy senses wander from thee.
MANFRED I say 'tis blood – my blood! The pure warm stream
    Which ran in the veins of my fathers, and in ours   25
    When we were in our youth, and had one heart,
    And loved each other as we should not love,
    And this was shed.[4] But still it rises up,
    Colouring the clouds that shut me out from heaven,
    Where thou art not, and I shall never be.   30
CHAMOIS HUNTER Man of strange words and some half-maddening sin
    Which makes thee people vacancy, whate'er
    Thy dread and sufferance be, there's comfort yet –
    The aid of holy men, and heavenly patience –
MANFRED Patience and patience hence! That word was made   35
    For brutes of burden, not for birds of prey;
    Preach it to mortals of a dust like thine,
    I am not of thine order.
CHAMOIS HUNTER   Thanks to heaven!
    I would not be of thine for the free fame
    Of William Tell! But whatsoe'er thine ill,   40
    It must be borne, and these wild starts are useless.

ACT II SCENE I
[1] Byron toured the Bernese Alps with Hobhouse, 17–29 September 1816.
[2] *portals* gateways.

[3] *pledge* toast.
[4] *The pure warm stream . . . shed* the archetypal model of Manfred's sins is once again Cain, who killed his brother Abel.

MANFRED Do I not bear it? Look on me – I live.

CHAMOIS HUNTER This is convulsion, and no healthful life.

MANFRED I tell thee, man! I have lived many years,
    Many long years, but they are nothing now   45
    To those which I must number: ages, ages,
    Space and eternity – and consciousness
    With the fierce thirst of death – and still unslaked!

CHAMOIS HUNTER Why, on thy brow the seal of middle age
    Hath scarce been set; I am thine elder far.   50

MANFRED Think'st thou existence doth depend on time?
    It doth, but actions are our epochs. Mine
    Have made my days and nights imperishable,
    Endless, and all alike as sands on the shore,
    Innumerable atoms, and one desert,   55
    Barren and cold, on which the wild waves break
    But nothing rests save carcases and wrecks,
    Rocks, and salt-surf weeds of bitterness.

CHAMOIS HUNTER Alas, he's mad – but yet I must not leave him.

MANFRED I would I were, for then the things I see   60
    Would be but a distempered dream.

CHAMOIS HUNTER   What is it
    That thou dost see, or think thou look'st upon?

MANFRED Myself and thee, a peasant of the Alps;
    Thy humble virtues, hospitable home
    And spirit patient, pious, proud and free;   65
    Thy self-respect, grafted on innocent thoughts;
    Thy days of health and nights of sleep; thy toils
    By danger dignified, yet guiltless; hopes
    Of cheerful old age and a quiet grave
    With cross and garland over its green turf,   70
    And thy grandchildren's love for epitaph –
    This do I see, and then I look within –
    It matters not; my soul was scorched already.

CHAMOIS HUNTER And would'st thou then exchange thy lot for mine?

MANFRED No, friend! I would not wrong thee, nor exchange   75
    My lot with living being. I can bear –
    However wretchedly, 'tis still to bear –
    In life what others could not brook[5] to dream,
    But perish in their slumber.

CHAMOIS HUNTER   And with this,
    This cautious feeling for another's pain,   80
    Canst thou be black with evil? Say not so.
    Can one of gentle thoughts have wreaked revenge
    Upon his enemies?

MANFRED   Oh no, no, no!
    My injuries came down on those who loved me,
    On those whom I best loved. I never quelled   85
    An enemy, save in my just defence,
    My wrongs were all on those I should have cherished,
    But my embrace was fatal.

---

5 *brook* endure.

CHAMOIS HUNTER   Heaven give thee rest,
And penitence restore thee to thyself;
My prayers shall be for thee.
MANFRED   I need them not,   90
But can endure thy pity. I depart;
'Tis time, farewell! Here's gold, and thanks for thee –
No words, it is thy due. Follow me not.
I know my path, the mountain peril's past –
And once again I charge thee, follow not!   95
Exit Manfred

ACT II, SCENE II

A lower valley in the Alps. A cataract. Enter Manfred.
It is not noon. The sunbow's rays still arch
The torrent with the many hues of heaven,[1]
And roll the sheeted silver's waving column
O'er the crag's headlong perpendicular,
And fling its lines of foaming light along,   5
And to and fro, like the pale courser's tail,
The giant steed to be bestrode by death,
As told in the Apocalypse.[2] No eyes
But mine now drink this sight of loveliness;
I should be sole[3] in this sweet solitude,   10
And with the spirit of the place divide
The homage of these waters. I will call her.[4]

Manfred takes some of the water into the palm of his hand, and flings it in the air, muttering the adjuration. After a pause, the Witch of the Alps rises beneath the arch of the sunbow of the torrent
Beautiful spirit, with thy hair of light
And dazzling eyes of glory, in whose form
The charms of earth's least mortal daughters grow   15
To an unearthly stature in an essence
Of purer elements, while the hues of youth –
Carnationed like a sleeping infant's cheek,
Rocked by the beating of her mother's heart,
Or the rose tints, which summer's twilight leaves   20
Upon the lofty glacier's virgin snow,
The blush of earth embracing with her heaven –
Tinge thy celestial aspect, and make tame
The beauties of the sunbow which bends o'er thee;
Beautiful spirit, in thy calm clear brow   25
Wherein is glassed[5] serenity of soul,
Which of itself shows immortality,

ACT II SCENE II
[1] 'This iris is formed by the rays of the sun over the lower part of the Alpine torrents. It is exactly like a rainbow come down to pay a visit, and so close that you may walk into it. This effect lasts until noon' (Byron's note). Byron described the effect in his journal sent to Augusta Leigh, 23 September 1816: 'Before ascending the mountain went to the torrent . . . again – the sun upon it forming a rainbow of the lower part of all colours – but principally purple and gold' (Marchand v 101).

[2] *the Apocalypse* i.e. the Book of Revelation of St John the Divine 6:8. Lines 3–8 versify remarks made by Byron in his journal for his half-sister Augusta Leigh, 22 September 1816: 'the torrent is in shape curving over the rock – like the tail of a white horse streaming in the wind – such as it might be conceived would be that of the "pale horse" on which Death is mounted in the Apocalypse' (Marchand v 101).
[3] *sole* single, alone.
[4] *her* i.e. the spirit of the place, the Witch of the Alps.
[5] *glassed* reflected.

I read that thou wilt pardon to a son
Of earth, whom the abstruser[6] powers permit
At times to commune with them, if that he   30
Avail him of his spells, to call thee thus
And gaze on thee a moment.
WITCH   Son of earth!
I know thee and the powers which give thee power;
I know thee for a man of many thoughts
And deeds of good and ill (extreme in both),   35
Fatal and fated in thy sufferings.
I have expected this – what wouldst thou with me?
MANFRED To look upon thy beauty, nothing further.
The face of the earth hath maddened me, and I
Take refuge in her mysteries, and pierce   40
To the abodes of those who govern her,
But they can nothing aid me. I have sought
From them what they could not bestow, and now
I search no further.
WITCH   What could be the quest
Which is not in the power of the most powerful,   45
The rulers of the invisible?
MANFRED   A boon –
But why should I repeat it? 'Twere in vain.
WITCH I know not that; let thy lips utter it.
MANFRED Well, though it torture me, 'tis but the same;
My pang shall find a voice. From my youth upwards   50
My spirit walked not with the souls of men,
Nor looked upon the earth with human eyes;
The thirst of their ambition was not mine,
The aim of their existence was not mine;
My joys, my griefs, my passions and my powers   55
Made me a stranger; though I wore the form,
I had no sympathy with breathing flesh,
Nor midst the creatures of clay that girded me
Was there but one[7] who – but of her anon.
I said, with men, and with the thoughts of men   60
I held but slight communion, but instead
My joy was in the wilderness – to breathe
The difficult air of the iced mountain's top
Where the birds dare not build, nor insect's wing
Flit o'er the herbless granite; or to plunge   65
Into the torrent, and to roll along
On the swift whirl of the new-breaking wave
Of river-stream or ocean in their flow.
In these my early strength exulted – or
To follow through the night the moving moon,[8]   70
The stars and their development; or catch
The dazzling lightnings till my eyes grew dim;
Or to look, list'ning, on the scattered leaves

---

[6] *abstruser* hidden, concealed; i.e. not perceptible to the
senses.
[7] *one* i.e. Astarte, his sister.

[8] *the moving moon* borrowed from Coleridge, *The Ancient
Mariner* (1817) 263: 'The moving moon went up the sky'.

While autumn winds were at their evening song.
These were my pastimes, and to be alone; 75
For if the beings of whom I was one
(Hating to be so) crossed me in my path,
I felt myself degraded back to them
And was all clay again. And then I dived
In my lone wanderings to the caves of death, 80
Searching its cause in its effect, and drew
From withered bones and skulls and heaped-up dust
Conclusions most forbidden.⁹ Then I passed
The nights of years in sciences untaught,
Save in the old time, and with time and toil 85
And terrible ordeal, and such penance
As in itself hath power upon the air,
And spirits that do compass air and earth,
Space and the peopled infinite, I made
Mine eyes familiar with eternity, 90
Such as, before me, did the Magi¹⁰ and
He¹¹ who from out their fountain dwellings raised
Eros and Anteros at Gadara,
As I do thee. And with my knowledge grew
The thirst of knowledge, and the power and joy 95
Of this most bright intelligence, until –
WITCH Proceed.

MANFRED   Oh, I but thus prolonged my words,
Boasting these idle attributes,¹² because,
As I approach the core of my heart's grief –
But to my task. I have not named to thee 100
Father or mother, mistress, friend or being
With whom I wore the chain of human ties;
If I had such, they seemed not such to me.
Yet there was one¹³ –

WITCH   Spare not thyself; proceed.

MANFRED She was like me in lineaments – her eyes, 105
Her hair, her features, all, to the very tone
Even of her voice, they said were like to mine,
But softened all and tempered into beauty.
She had the same lone thoughts and wanderings,
The quest of hidden knowledge, and a mind 110
To comprehend the universe – nor these
Alone, but with them gentler powers than mine:
Pity and smiles and tears (which I had not)
And tenderness (but that I had for her),
Humility (and that I never had). 115
Her faults were mine; her virtues were her own –

---

⁹ *And then I dived . . . forbidden* Manfred's dabbling among corpses has much in common with the researches of Victor Frankenstein in Mary Godwin's novel, conceived at the same time as Byron's poem, summer 1816, though not published until 1818. Byron is probably thinking, however, of Shelley's *Alastor*, who 'made my bed / In charnels and on coffins' (ll. 23–4).

¹⁰ *the Magi* the ancient Persian priestly caste.

¹¹ *He* 'The philosopher Iamblicus. The story of the raising of Eros and Anteros may be found in his life, by Eunapius. It is well-told' (Byron's note). Iamblicus (died *c.* AD 330) summoned by magic Love and its opposite from fountains in Syria.

¹² *attributes* i.e. achievements.

¹³ *one* i.e. Astarte.

I loved her, and destroyed her!

WITCH   With thy hand?

MANFRED Not with my hand, but heart – which broke her heart:
It gazed on mine and withered. I have shed
Blood, but not hers, and yet her blood was shed –   120
I saw and could not staunch it.

WITCH   And for this,
A being of the race thou dost despise,
The order which thine own would rise above,
Mingling with us and ours, thou dost forego
The gifts of our great knowledge, and shrink'st back   125
To recreant mortality? Away!

MANFRED Daughter of air, I tell thee, since that hour –
But words are breath; look on me in my sleep
Or watch my watchings – come and sit by me!
My solitude is solitude no more,   130
But peopled with the Furies;[14] I have gnashed
My teeth in darkness till returning morn,
Then cursed myself till sunset; I have prayed
For madness as a blessing – 'tis denied me;
I have affronted death, but in the war   135
Of elements the waters shrunk from me,
And fatal things passed harmless – the cold hand
Of an all-pitiless demon held me back,
Back by a single hair which would not break.
In fantasy, imagination, all   140
The affluence of my soul (which one day was
A Croesus in creation),[15] I plunged deep,
But like an ebbing wave, it dashed me back
Into the gulf of my unfathomed thought.
I plunged amidst mankind; forgetfulness   145
I sought in all save where 'tis to be found,
And that I have to learn; my sciences,
My long-pursued and superhuman art
Is mortal here. I dwell in my despair
And live – and live for ever.   150

WITCH   It may be
That I can aid thee.

MANFRED   To do this thy power
Must wake the dead, or lay me low with them.
Do so, in any shape, in any hour,
With any torture – so it be the last.

WITCH That is not in my province, but if thou   155
Wilt swear obedience to my will and do
My bidding, it may help thee to thy wishes.

MANFRED I will not swear![16] Obey? And whom? The spirits
Whose presence I command – and be the slave
Of those who served me? Never!

---

[14] *Furies* avenging agents of the gods.
[15] *A Croesus in creation* i.e. endlessly creative. Croesus was the last king of Lydia, of fabulous wealth; Byron may be recalling the legend that when Croesus met Solon, Solon distinguished between the imagined happiness of being Croesus and the genuine happiness of being dead.
[16] Manfred's defiance of the supernatural powers is an important departure from the *Faust* legend.

WITCH   Is this all?   160
Hast thou no gentler answer? Yet bethink thee,
And pause ere thou rejectest.
MANFRED   I have said it.
WITCH Enough! I may retire then – say!
MANFRED   Retire!
The Witch disappears
MANFRED (*alone*) We are the fools of time and terror. Days
Steal on us and steal from us, yet we live,   165
Loathing our life, and dreading still to die.
In all the days of this detested yoke
(This heaving burden, this accursed breath,
This vital weight upon the struggling heart
Which sinks with sorrow or beats quick with pain,   170
Or joy that ends in agony or faintness);
In all the days of past and future – for
In life there is no present – we can number
How few, how less than few, wherein the soul
Forbears to pant for death and yet draws back   175
As from a stream in winter, though the chill
Be but a moment's. I have one resource
Still in my science; I can call the dead
And ask them what it is we dread to be.
The sternest answer can but be the grave,   180
And that is nothing; if they answer not . . .
The buried prophet answered to the hag
Of Endor,[17] and the Spartan monarch drew
From the Byzantine maid's unsleeping spirit
An answer and his destiny – he slew   185
That which he loved, unknowing what he slew,
And died unpardoned, though he called in aid
The Phyxian Jove, and in Phigalia roused
The Arcadian evocators[18] to compel
The indignant shadow[19] to depose[20] her wrath   190
Or fix her term of vengeance; she replied
In words of dubious import, but fulfilled.[21]
    If I had never lived, that which I love
Had still been living; had I never loved,
That which I loved would still be beautiful,   195
Happy and giving happiness. What is she,
What is she now? A sufferer for my sins,
A thing I dare not think upon – or nothing.
Within few hours I shall not call in vain,
Yet in this hour I dread the thing I dare.   200
Until this hour I never shrunk to gaze
On spirit, good or evil; now I tremble
And feel a strange cold thaw upon my heart.

---

[17] Samuel was raised from the dead by the Witch of Endor,
I Samuel 28:7.
[18] *evocators* those who invoke spirits.
[19] *shadow* ghost.
[20] *depose* lay aside.

[21] 'The story of Pausanias, King of Sparta (who commanded
the Greeks in the Battle of Platea, and afterwards perished for
an attempt to betray the Lacedemonians), and Cleonice, is told
in Plutarch's life of Cimon, and in the Laconics of Pausanias
the Sophist, in his description of Greece' (Byron's note).

But I can act even what I most abhor
And champion human fears. The night approaches.   205
    Exit

ACT II, SCENE III

The summit of the Jungfrau mountain. Enter First Destiny.

FIRST DESTINY The moon is rising broad and round and bright,
And here on snows where never human foot
Of common mortal trod,[1] we nightly tread
And leave no traces. O'er the savage sea,
The glassy ocean of the mountain ice,   5
We skim its rugged breakers, which put on
The aspect of a tumbling tempest's foam,
Frozen in a moment – a dead whirlpool's image;
And this most steep fantastic pinnacle,
The fretwork[2] of some earthquake where the clouds   10
Pause to repose themselves in passing by,
Is sacred to our revels or our vigils.
Here do I wait my sisters, on our way
To the Hall of Arimanes, for tonight
Is our great festival. 'Tis strange they come not.   15

A VOICE *without, singing*
    The captive usurper[3]
      Hurled down from the throne,[4]
    Lay buried in torpor,
      Forgotten and lone;
    I broke through his slumbers,   20
      I shivered[5] his chain,
    I leagued him with numbers[6] –
      He's tyrant again![7]
With the blood of a million he'll answer my care,
With a nation's destruction, his flight and despair.   25

SECOND VOICE *without*
    The ship sailed on, the ship sailed fast,
    But I left not a sail, and I left not a mast;
    There is not a plank of the hull or the deck,
    And there is not a wretch to lament o'er his wreck,
    Save one whom I held, as he swam, by the hair,   30
    And he was a subject well worthy my care –
    A traitor on land and a pirate at sea –
    But I saved him to wreak further havoc for me!

ACT II SCENE III

[1] The Jungfrau had been scaled in 1811.

[2] *fretwork* figurative; usually refers to carved, decorative woodwork.

[3] *The captive usurper* Napoleon Bonaparte who, at the time of writing, was in exile on St Helena. These lines should be read in the light of Byron's ambiguous admiration of Napoleon, expressed in *Childe Harold* iii, stanzas 36–42 (pp. 682–4).

[4] *Hurled down from the throne* Napoleon crowned himself Emperor in 1804, and abdicated in 1814. He was 'hurled down' when the combined might of the allies defeated him at Waterloo, 1815.

[5] *shivered* shattered.

[6] *numbers* i.e. of soldiers.

[7] The Spirit prophesies the return of Napoleon from St Helena. It was not to happen.

FIRST DESTINY (*answering*)
    The city lies sleeping;
      The morn, to deplore it,   35
    May dawn on it weeping;
      Sullenly, slowly,
    The black plague flew o'er it –
      Thousands lie lowly;
    Tens of thousands shall perish;   40
      The living shall fly from
    The sick they should cherish,
      But nothing can vanquish
    The touch that they die from.
      Sorrow and anguish
    And evil and dread   45
      Envelop a nation;
    The blessed are the dead
      Who see not the sight
    Of their own desolation.
      This work of a night,   50
    This wreck of a realm, this deed of my doing –
    For ages I've done and shall still be renewing!

Enter the Second and Third Destinies

THE THREE
    Our hands contain the hearts of men,
      Our footsteps are their graves;
    We only give to take again   55
      The spirits of our slaves!

FIRST DESTINY Welcome! Where's Nemesis?
SECOND DESTINY   At some great work,
    But what I know not, for my hands were full.
THIRD DESTINY   Behold, she cometh.
Enter Nemesis
FIRST DESTINY   Say, where hast thou been?   60
    My sisters and thyself are slow tonight.
NEMESIS I was detained repairing shattered thrones,[8]
    Marrying fools,[9] restoring dynasties,
    Avenging men upon their enemies,
    And making them repent their own revenge;   65
    Goading the wise to madness, from the dull
    Shaping out oracles[10] to rule the world
    Afresh – for they were waxing[11] out of date
    And mortals dared to ponder for themselves,
    To weigh kings in the balance,[12] and to speak   70

---

[8] *I was detained repairing shattered thrones* Byron has in mind the Treaty of Vienna in 1815, which restored to power the monarchies of Spain and France.

[9] *Marrying fools* perhaps a sardonic reference to Byron's own marriage to Annabella Milbanke, which had resulted in acrimonious separation and Byron's exile from England.

[10] *oracles* effectively, prophets and priests, empowered to utter the will of God. Byron may have in mind Joanna Southcott (1750–1814), who claimed to be pregnant by the Holy Ghost, with Shiloh, the saviour of the world. After her death the 'pregnancy' was diagnosed as dropsy.

[11] *waxing* growing.

[12] *To weigh kings in the balance* Daniel 5:27: 'Thou art weighed in the balances, and art found wanting.'

Of freedom, the forbidden fruit.[13] Away!
We have outstayed the hour; mount we our clouds!
Exeunt

ACT II, SCENE IV

The Hall of Arimanes,[1] *Arimanes on his throne, a globe of fire, surrounded by the spirits.*
    Hymn of the Spirits

Hail to our master, Prince of earth and air!
  Who walks the clouds and waters – in his hand
The sceptre of the elements, which tear
  Themselves to chaos at his high command!
He breatheth, and a tempest shakes the sea;   5
  He speaketh, and the clouds reply in thunder;
He gazeth – from his glance the sunbeams flee;
  He moveth – earthquakes rend the world asunder.
Beneath his footsteps the volcanoes rise;
  His shadow is the pestilence, his path   10
The comets herald through the crackling skies,
  And planets turn to ashes at his wrath.
To him war offers daily sacrifice,
  To him death pays his tribute; life is his,
With all its infinite of agonies,   15
  And his the spirit of whatever is!

Enter the Destinies and Nemesis

FIRST DESTINY Glory to Arimanes! On the earth
  His power increaseth; both my sisters did
  His bidding, nor did I neglect my duty.
SECOND DESTINY Glory to Arimanes! We who bow   20
  The necks of men, bow down before his throne.
THIRD DESTINY Glory to Arimanes! We await
  His nod.
NEMESIS   Sovereign of Sovereigns! We are thine,
  And all that liveth, more or less, is ours,
  And most things wholly so; still to increase   25
  Our power increasing thine, demands our care,
  And we are vigilant. Thy late commands
  Have been fulfilled to the utmost.
Enter Manfred
A SPIRIT   What is here?
  A mortal? Thou most rash and fatal wretch,
  Bow down and worship!
SECOND SPIRIT   I do know the man,   30
  A Magian[2] of great power and fearful skill.
THIRD SPIRIT Bow down and worship, slave! What, know'st thou not
  Thine and our sovereign? Tremble, and obey!

---

[13] Nemesis is effectively an anti-revolutionary force.

ACT II SCENE IV
[1] Arimanes derives his name from Ahriman, the principle of darkness and evil in Persian dualism.
[2] *Magian* magician, wizard.

ALL THE SPIRITS Prostrate thyself and thy condemned clay,
    Child of the earth, or dread the worst!
MANFRED   I know it,   35
    And yet ye see I kneel not.
FOURTH SPIRIT   'Twill be taught thee.
MANFRED 'Tis taught already; many a night on the earth,
    On the bare ground have I bowed down my face
    And strewed my head with ashes.[3] I have known
    The fullness of humiliation, for   40
    I sunk before my vain despair, and knelt
    To my own desolation.
FIFTH SPIRIT   Dost thou dare
    Refuse to Arimanes on his throne
    What the whole earth accords, beholding not
    The terror of his glory? Crouch, I say!   45
MANFRED Bid *him* bow down to that which is above him,
    The overruling Infinite, the Maker
    Who made him not for worship; let him kneel,
    And we will kneel together.
THE SPIRITS   Crush the worm!
    Tear him in pieces!
FIRST DESTINY   Hence! Avaunt! He's mine.   50
    Prince of the powers invisible! This man
    Is of no common order, as his port[4]
    And presence here denote. His sufferings
    Have been of an immortal nature like
    Our own; his knowledge and his powers and will,   55
    As far as is compatible with clay
    (Which clogs the ethereal essence), have been such
    As clay hath seldom borne; his aspirations
    Have been beyond the dwellers of the earth,
    And they have only taught him what we know –   60
    That knowledge is not happiness, and science
    But an exchange of ignorance for that
    Which is another kind of ignorance.
    This is not all. The passions, attributes
    Of earth and heaven, from which no power nor being   65
    Nor breath from the worm upwards is exempt,
    Have pierced his heart, and in their consequence
    Made him a thing which I, who pity not,
    Yet pardon those who pity. He is mine,
    And thine, it may be; be it so or not,   70
    No other spirit in this region hath
    A soul like his – or power upon his soul.
NEMESIS What doth he here then?
FIRST DESTINY   Let *him* answer that.
MANFRED Ye know what I have known, and without power
    I could not be amongst ye; but there are   75
    Powers deeper still beyond. I come in quest

---

[3] *strewed my head with ashes* expression of grief and repentance.   [4] *port* bearing, deportment.

Of such, to answer unto what I seek.

NEMESIS What wouldst *thou*?

MANFRED   Thou canst not reply to me.
Call up the dead – my question is for them.

NEMESIS Great Arimanes, doth thy will avouch   80
The wishes of this mortal?

ARIMANES   Yea.

NEMESIS   Whom would'st thou
Uncharnel?[5]

MANFRED   One without a tomb. Call up
Astarte.

NEMESIS

    Shadow or spirit,
      Whatever thou art,   85
    Which still doth inherit
      The whole or a part
    Of the form of thy birth,
      Of the mould of thy clay
    Which returned to the earth,   90
      Reappear to the day!
    Bear what thou borest,
      The heart and the form,
    And the aspect thou worest
      Redeem from the worm.   95
    Appear! Appear! Appear!
    Who sent thee there requires thee here!

The phantom of Astarte rises and stands in the midst

MANFRED Can this be death? There's bloom upon her cheek,
But now I see it is no living hue
But a strange hectic,[6] like the unnatural red   100
Which autumn plants upon the perished leaf.
It is the same! Oh God, that I should dread
To look upon the same – Astarte! No,
I cannot speak to her; but bid her speak –
Forgive me or condemn me.   105

NEMESIS

    By the power which hath broken
      The grave which enthralled[7] thee,
    Speak to him who hath spoken,
      Or those who have called thee!

MANFRED   She is silent,   110
And in that silence I am more than answered.

NEMESIS My power extends no further. Prince of air!
It rests with thee alone; command her voice.

ARIMANES Spirit – obey this sceptre!

NEMESIS   Silent still!
She is not of our order, but belongs   115
To the other powers. Mortal, thy quest is vain,

---

[5] *Uncharnel* i.e. raise from the dead. A charnel is a cemetery.   [7] *enthralled* imprisoned.
[6] *hectic* a flush or heightened colour on the cheek, often a
symptom of fever.

And we are baffled[8] also.

MANFRED   Hear me, hear me –
Astarte, my beloved, speak to me!
I have so much endured, so much endure –
Look on me! The grave hath not changed thee more   120
Than I am changed for thee. Thou lovedst me
Too much, as I loved thee; we were not made
To torture thus each other, though it were
The deadliest sin to love as we have loved.
Say that thou loath'st me not, that I do bear   125
This punishment for both, that thou wilt be
One of the blessed, and that I shall die,
For hitherto all hateful things conspire
To bind me in existence, in a life
Which makes me shrink from immortality –   130
A future like the past. I cannot rest.
I know not what I ask nor what I seek;
I feel but what thou art and what I am,
And I would hear yet once before I perish
The voice which was my music: speak to me!   135
For I have called on thee in the still night,
Startled the slumbering birds from the hushed boughs,
And woke the mountain wolves, and made the caves
Acquainted with thy vainly-echoed name,
Which answered me – many things answered me,   140
Spirits and men, but thou wert silent all.
Yet speak to me! I have outwatched the stars
And gazed o'er heaven in vain in search of thee.
Speak to me! I have wandered o'er the earth
And never found thy likeness – speak to me!   145
Look on the fiends around; they feel for me.
I fear them not, and feel for thee alone –
Speak to me, though it be in wrath, but say –
I reck[9] not what – but let me hear thee once –
This once – once more!

PHANTOM OF ASTARTE   Manfred!

MANFRED   Say on, say on;   150
I live but in the sound – it is thy voice!

PHANTOM OF ASTARTE Manfred! Tomorrow ends thine earthly ills.
Farewell!

MANFRED   Yet one word more: am I forgiven?

PHANTOM OF ASTARTE Farewell!

MANFRED   Say, shall we meet again?

PHANTOM OF ASTARTE   Farewell!

MANFRED One word for mercy; say thou lovest me.   155

PHANTOM OF ASTARTE   Manfred!

The spirit of Astarte disappears.

NEMESIS   She's gone and will not be recalled;
Her words will be fulfilled. Return to the earth.

A SPIRIT He is convulsed; this is to be a mortal

---

[8]   *baffled* defeated.   [9]   *reck* care.

And seek the things beyond mortality.

ANOTHER SPIRIT Yet see, he mastereth himself and makes   160
  His torture tributary to his will;
  Had he been one of us, he would have made
  An awful[10] spirit.

NEMESIS   Hast thou further question
  Of our great sovereign or his worshippers?

MANFRED None.

NEMESIS   Then for a time farewell.

MANFRED   We meet then –   165
  Where? On the earth?

NEMESIS   That will be seen hereafter.

MANFRED Even as thou wilt; and for the grace accorded
  I now depart a debtor. Fare ye well!

Exit Manfred

ACT III, SCENE I[1]

A hall in the castle of Manfred. Manfred and Herman.

MANFRED What is the hour?

HERMAN   It wants but one till sunset,
  And promises a lovely twilight.

MANFRED   Say,
  Are all things so disposed of[2] in the tower
  As I directed?

HERMAN   All, my lord, are ready;
  Here is the key and casket.

MANFRED   It is well;   5
  Thou mayst retire.

Exit Herman.

MANFRED (alone).   There is a calm upon me –
  Inexplicable stillness, which till now
  Did not belong to what I knew of life.
  If that I did not know philosophy
  To be of all our vanities the motliest,[3]   10
  The merest[4] word that ever fooled the ear
  From out the schoolman's[5] jargon, I should deem
  The golden secret, the sought kalon,[6] found
  And seated in my soul. It will not last,
  But it is well to have known it, though but once;   15
  It hath enlarged my thoughts with a new sense,
  And I within my tablets[7] would note down
  That there is such a feeling. Who is there?

Re-enter Herman

HERMAN   My lord, the Abbot of St Maurice craves
  To greet your presence.

Enter the Abbot of St Maurice

---

10   *awful* awe-inspiring.

ACT III SCENE I
1   This scene reworks Faust's meeting with an Old Man in
Faust V i.
2   *disposed of* arranged, prepared.

3   *motliest* most foolish.
4   *merest* most insignificant.
5   *schoolman's* scholar's.
6   *kalon* the ideal good, the morally beautiful.
7   *tablets* research documents.

ABBOT   Peace be with Count Manfred!⁸   20
MANFRED Thanks, holy father; welcome to these walls!
   Thy presence honours them, and blesseth those
   Who dwell within them.
ABBOT   Would it were so, Count;
   But I would fain confer with thee alone.
MANFRED Herman, retire. (*Exit Herman*) What would my reverend guest?   25
ABBOT   Thus, without prelude. Age and zeal, my office,
   And good intent, must plead my privilege;
   Our near, though not acquainted neighbourhood
   May also be my herald. Rumours strange
   And of unholy nature are abroad   30
   And busy with thy name – a noble name
   For centuries. May he who bears it now⁹
   Transmit it unimpaired!
MANFRED   Proceed, I listen.
ABBOT 'Tis said thou holdest converse with the things
   Which are forbidden to the search of man;   35
   That with the dwellers of the dark¹⁰ abodes,
   The many evil and unheavenly spirits
   Which walk the valley of the shade of death,¹¹
   Thou communest. I know that with mankind,
   Thy fellows in creation, thou dost rarely   40
   Exchange thy thoughts, and that thy solitude
   Is as an anchorite's, were it but holy.
MANFRED And what are they who do avouch these things?
ABBOT My pious brethren, the scared peasantry –
   Even thy own vassals, who do look on thee   45
   With most unquiet eyes. Thy life's in peril.
MANFRED Take it.
ABBOT   I come to save, and not destroy.¹²
   I would not pry into thy secret soul,
   But if these things be sooth,¹³ there still is time
   For penitence and pity: reconcile thee   50
   With the true church, and through the church to heaven.
MANFRED I hear thee. This is my reply: whate'er
   I may have been, or am, doth rest between
   Heaven and myself. I shall not choose a mortal
   To be my mediator. Have I sinned   55
   Against your ordinances?¹⁴ Prove and punish!
ABBOT My son, I did not speak of punishment,
   But penitence and pardon; with thyself
   The choice of such remains. And for the last,
   Our institutions and our strong belief   60
   Have given me power to smooth the path from sin
   To higher hope and better thoughts; the first

---

8   An ironic greeting, given the circumstances.
9   *he who bears it now* i.e. Manfred himself.
10 *dark* means both 'lacking in light' and 'evil'.
11 *the valley of the shade of death* Psalm 23:4: 'Yea, though I
walk through the valley of the shadow of death, I will fear no
evil . . .'

12 *I come to save, and not destroy* cf. Christ's words at Matthew
5:17: 'Think not that I am come to destroy the law, or the
prophets: I am not come to destroy, but to fulfil.'
13 *sooth* true.
14 *ordinances* laws.

I leave to heaven – 'Vengeance is mine alone!'[15]
So saith the Lord, and with all humbleness
His servant echoes back the awful word.   65

MANFRED Old man! There is no power in holy men,
Nor charm in prayer, nor purifying form
Of penitence, nor outward look, nor fast,
Nor agony – nor, greater than all these,
The innate tortures of that deep despair   70
Which is remorse without the fear of hell
But all in all sufficient to itself
Would make a hell of heaven, can exorcise
From out the unbounded spirit the quick[16] sense
Of its own sins, wrongs, sufferance, and revenge   75
Upon itself. There is no future pang
Can deal that justice on the self-condemned
He deals on his own soul.

ABBOT   All this is well –
For this will pass away, and be succeeded
By an auspicious hope which shall look up   80
With calm assurance to that blessed place[17]
Which all who seek may win, whatever be
Their earthly errors, so they be atoned;[18]
And the commencement of atonement is
The sense of its necessity. Say on,   85
And all our church can teach thee shall be taught,
And all we can absolve thee shall be pardoned.

MANFRED When Rome's sixth Emperor[19] was near his last,
The victim of a self-inflicted wound,
To shun the torments of a public death   90
From senates once his slaves, a certain soldier,
With show of loyal pity, would have staunched
The gushing throat with his officious[20] robe;
The dying Roman thrust him back and said
(Some empire[21] still in his expiring glance),   95
'It is too late – is this fidelity?'

ABBOT And what of this?

MANFRED   I answer with the Roman,
'It is too late!'

ABBOT   It never can be so,
To reconcile thyself with thy own soul,
And thy own soul with heaven. Hast thou no hope?   100
'Tis strange; even those who do despair above
Yet shape themselves some fantasy on earth
To which frail twig they cling like drowning men.

MANFRED Aye, father! I have had those earthly visions
And noble aspirations in my youth –   105
To make my own the mind of other men,

---

[15] See Romans 12:19.
[16] *quick* living, vital.
[17] *that blessed place* i.e. heaven.
[18] *atoned* reconciled (with God).

[19] Byron applies Suetonius's account of the death of Nero to
the suicide of Otho, the sixth Emperor of Rome.
[20] *officious* dutiful.
[21] *empire* i.e. some sense of his emperor-ship.

The enlightener[22] of nations, and to rise
I knew not whither; it might be to fall,
But fall even as the mountain-cataract
Which, having leaped from its more dazzling height,   110
Even in the foaming strength of its abyss
(Which casts up misty columns that become
Clouds raining from the reascended skies)
Lies low but mighty still. But this is passed;
My thoughts mistook themselves.   115

ABBOT   And wherefore so?

MANFRED I could not tame my nature down; for he
Must serve who fain would sway, and soothe, and sue,[23]
And watch all time, and pry into all place –
And be a living lie, who would become
A mighty thing amongst the mean (and such   120
The mass are). I disdained to mingle with
A herd, though to be leader – and of wolves.
The lion is alone, and so am I.

ABBOT And why not live and act with other men?

MANFRED Because my nature was averse from life,   125
And yet not cruel – for I would not make,
But find a desolation. Like the wind,
The red-hot breath of the most lone simoom,[24]
Which dwells but in the desert, and sweeps o'er
The barren sands which bear no shrubs to blast,   130
And revels o'er their wild and arid waves
And seeketh not, so that it is not sought,
But being met is deadly; such hath been
The course of my existence. But there came
Things in my path which are no more.   135

ABBOT   Alas,
I 'gin to fear that thou art past all aid
From me and from my calling; yet so young,
I still would –

MANFRED   Look on me! There is an order
Of mortals on the earth, who do become
Old in their youth, and die ere middle age   140
Without the violence of warlike death –
Some perishing of pleasure, some of study,
Some worn with toil, some of mere weariness,
Some of disease, and some insanity,
And some of withered or of broken hearts;   145
For this last is a malady which slays
More than are numbered in the lists of fate,
Taking all shapes, and bearing many names.
Look upon me! For even of all these things
Have I partaken, and of all these things   150
One were enough; then wonder not that I
Am what I am, but that I ever was,

---

22 *enlightener* guide, teacher.
23 *sue* follow.

24 *simoom* a hot, dry, suffocating sand wind which sweeps
across the African deserts at intervals during the spring and
summer.

Or, having been, that I am still on earth.

ABBOT Yet hear me still –

MANFRED   Old man! I do respect   155
Thine order, and revere thine years; I deem
Thy purpose pious, but it is in vain.
Think me not churlish;[25] I would spare thyself
Far more than me, in shunning at this time
All further colloquy[26] – and so farewell.

Exit Manfred

ABBOT This should have been a noble creature; he   160
Hath all the energy which would have made
A goodly frame of glorious elements,[27]
Had they been wisely mingled. As it is,
It is an awful[28] chaos – light and darkness,
And mind and dust, and passions and pure thoughts,   165
Mixed and contending without end or order,
All dormant or destructive: he will perish,
And yet he must not. I will try once more,
For such are worth redemption, and my duty
Is to dare all things for a righteous end.   170
I'll follow him – but cautiously, though surely.

Exit Abbot

ACT III, SCENE II

Another chamber. Manfred and Herman.

HERMAN My Lord, you bade me wait on you at sunset:
He[1] sinks behind the mountain.

MANFRED   Doth he so?
I will look on him.

Manfred advances to the window of the hall

                     Glorious orb![2] The idol
Of early nature, and the vigorous race
Of undiseased mankind, the giant sons   5
Of the embrace of angels, with a sex
More beautiful than they, which did draw down
The erring spirits who can ne'er return;[3]
Most glorious orb, that wert a worship ere
The mystery of thy making was revealed!   10
Thou earliest minister of the Almighty,
Which gladdened on their mountain-tops the hearts
Of the Chaldean shepherds,[4] till they poured
Themselves in orisons![5] Thou material god
And representative of the unknown,   15
Who chose thee for his shadow! Thou chief star,

---

[25] *churlish* ungracious.
[26] *colloquy* conversation.
[27] *A goodly frame of glorious elements* The Abbot echoes Hamlet's description of the earth as 'this goodly frame' (II ii 298), and there is a general recollection of Hamlet's comments on man's innate nobility, II ii 303–10.
[28] *awful* awesome.

ACT III SCENE II
[1] *He* the sun.
[2] This is a pagan address to the sun.
[3] See Genesis 6:1–4.
[4] *the Chaldean shepherds* renowned astronomers; see *Childe Harold* iii 118.
[5] Compare *Childe Harold's Pilgrimage* III stanza 91, above. *orisons* prayers.

Centre of many stars, which mak'st our earth
Endurable, and temperest the hues
And hearts of all who walk within thy rays!
Sire of the seasons! Monarch of the climes   20
And those who dwell in them (for near or far,
Our inborn spirits have a tint of thee,
Even as our outward aspects), thou dost rise
And shine and set in glory – fare thee well,
I ne'er shall see thee more! As my first glance   25
Of love and wonder was for thee, then take
My latest look: thou wilt not beam on one
To whom the gifts of life and warmth have been
Of a more fatal nature. He is gone;
I follow.   30
Exit Manfred

ACT III, SCENE III

The mountains. The castle of Manfred at some distance. A terrace before a tower. Time: twilight. Herman, Manuel, and other dependants of Manfred.

HERMAN 'Tis strange enough; night after night for years
He hath pursued long vigils in this tower
Without a witness. I have been within it –
So have we all been oft-times; but from it,
Or its contents, it were impossible   5
To draw conclusions absolute of aught
His studies tend to. To be sure, there is
One chamber where none enter; I would give
The fee of what I have to come these three years[1]
To pore upon its mysteries.

MANUEL   'Twere dangerous;   10
Content thyself with what thou knowest already.

HERMAN Ah, Manuel! Thou art elderly and wise,
And could'st say much; thou hast dwelt within the castle –
How many years is't?

MANUEL   Ere Count Manfred's birth
I served his father, whom he nought resembles.   15

HERMAN There be more sons in like predicament.
But wherein do they differ?

MANUEL   I speak not
Of features or of form, but mind and habits:
Count Sigismund was proud, but gay and free,
A warrior and a reveller; he dwelt not   20
With books and solitude, nor made the night
A gloomy vigil, but a festal time,
Merrier than day; he did not walk the rocks
And forests like a wolf, nor turn aside
From men and their delights.

HERMAN   Beshrew the hour,   25

ACT III SCENE III
[1]   *The fee of what I have to come these three years* i.e. his next
three years' salary.

But those were jocund times! I would that such
Would visit the old walls again; they look
As if they had forgotten them.

MANUEL   These walls
Must change their chieftain first – oh, I have seen
Some strange things in them, Herman!

HERMAN   Come, be friendly,   30
Relate me some to while away our watch;
I've heard thee darkly speak of an event
Which happened hereabouts, by this same tower.

MANUEL That was a night indeed. I do remember
'Twas twilight, as it may be now, and such   35
Another evening; yon red cloud, which rests
On Eiger's pinnacle,[2] so rested then,
So like that it might be the same; the wind
Was faint and gusty, and the mountain snows
Began to glitter with the climbing moon.   40
Count Manfred was, as now, within his tower,
How occupied we knew not, but with him
The sole companion of his wanderings
And watchings – her, whom of all earthly things
That lived, the only thing he seemed to love,   45
As he indeed by blood was bound to do,
The lady Astarte, his[3] –
                  Hush! Who comes here?

Enter the Abbot

ABBOT Where is your master?

HERMAN   Yonder, in the tower.

ABBOT I must speak with him.

MANUEL   'Tis impossible.
He is most private, and must not be thus   50
Intruded on.

ABBOT   Upon myself I take
The forfeit of my fault, if fault there be;
But I must see him.

HERMAN   Thou hast seen him once
This eve already.

ABBOT   Sirrah, I command thee
Knock and apprise the Count of my approach!   55

HERMAN We dare not.

ABBOT   Then it seems I must be herald
Of my own purpose.

MANUEL   Reverend father, stop,
I pray you pause.

ABBOT   Why so?

MANUEL   But step this way,
And I will tell you further.

Exeunt

---

[2] *Eiger's pinnacle* the Eiger is a mountain, east of the Jungfrau, which Byron first saw 22 September 1816.
[3] This is the closest anyone in the play gets to saying that Astarte was Manfred's sister, but the implication is clear enough.

ACT III, SCENE IV

Interior of the tower. Manfred alone.

MANFRED The stars are forth, the moon above the tops
Of the snow-shining mountains – beautiful!
I linger yet with nature, for the night
Hath been to me a more familiar face
Than that of man, and in her starry shade   5
Of dim and solitary loveliness
I learned the language of another world.
I do remember me that in my youth
When I was wandering, upon such a night[1]
I stood within the Colosseum's wall   10
Midst the chief relics of almighty Rome;[2]
The trees which grew along the broken arches
Waved dark in the blue midnight, and the stars
Shone through the rents of ruin; from afar
The watchdog bayed beyond the Tiber, and   15
More near from out the Caesars' palace came
The owl's long cry, and, interruptedly,
Of distant sentinels the fitful song
Begun and died upon the gentle wind.
Some cypresses beyond the time-worn breach[3]   20
Appeared to skirt the horizon, yet they stood
Within a bowshot,[4] where the Caesars dwelt,
And dwell the tuneless birds of night; amidst
A grove which springs through levelled battlements,
And twines its roots with the imperial hearths,   25
Ivy usurps the laurel's[5] place of growth;
But the gladiators' bloody circus[6] stands,
A noble wreck in ruinous perfection,[7]
While Caesar's chambers and the Augustan halls
Grovel on earth in indistinct decay.   30
And thou didst shine, thou rolling moon, upon
All this, and cast a wide and tender light
Which softened down the hoar austerity
Of rugged desolation, and filled up,
As 'twere, anew, the gaps of centuries,   35
Leaving that beautiful which still was so,
And making that which was not, till the place
Became religion, and the heart ran o'er
With silent worship of the great of old[8] –

ACT III SCENE IV

[1] *upon such a night* there is a general recollection, throughout this speech, of the exchange between Jessica and Lorenzo, *Merchant of Venice* V i 1–22, which uses the repeated tag, 'In such a night . . .'

[2] Byron first visited Rome in April 1817. This passage may have been inspired partly by Gibbon's *Decline and Fall of the Roman Empire*; Gibbon is celebrated as a freethinker at the conclusion of *Childe Harold* iii (see p. 704).

[3] *breach* break in the old city walls.

[4] *Within a bowshot* i.e. within about 300 yards.

[5] Ivy (a plant of death) has taken over where the laurel (plant of victory) once grew.

[6] *circus* oval arena.

[7] *A noble wreck in ruinous perfection* Manfred is effectively describing himself.

[8] *till the place . . . great of old* these lines prove that, even at this late stage, Manfred might still be redeemed to the cause of orthodox religion.

The dead but sceptred sovereigns who still rule   40
Our spirits from their urns.
                    'Twas such a night!
'Tis strange that I recall it at this time,
But I have found our thoughts take wildest flight
Even at the moment when they should array[9]
Themselves in pensive[10] order.

Enter the Abbot

ABBOT   My good Lord!   45
I crave a second grace for this approach,
But yet let not my humble zeal offend
By its abruptness; all it hath of ill
Recoils on me. Its good in the effect
May light upon your head – could I say *heart*,   50
Could I touch *that*, with words or prayers, I should
Recall a noble spirit which hath wandered
But is not yet all lost.

MANFRED   Thou know'st me not;
My days are numbered and my deeds recorded.
Retire, or 'twill be dangerous – away!   55

ABBOT Thou dost not mean to menace me?

MANFRED   Not I;
I simply tell thee peril is at hand
And would preserve thee.

ABBOT   What dost mean?

MANFRED   Look there –
What dost thou see?

ABBOT   Nothing.

MANFRED   Look there, I say,
And steadfastly; now tell me what thou seest?   60

ABBOT That which should shake me, but I fear it not;
I see a dusk and awful figure rise
Like an infernal god from out the earth,
His face wrapped in a mantle, and his form
Robed as with angry clouds. He stands between   65
Thyself and me, but I do fear him not.

MANFRED Thou hast no cause; he shall not harm thee, but
His sight may shock thine old limbs into palsy.[11]
I say to thee, retire!

ABBOT   And I reply
Never, till I have battled with this fiend.   70
What doth he here?

MANFRED   Why, aye, what doth he here?
I did not send for him, he is unbidden.

ABBOT Alas, lost mortal! What with guests like these
Hast thou to do? I tremble for thy sake;
Why doth he gaze on thee, and thou on him?   75
Ah! he unveils his aspect: on his brow
The thunder-scars are graven; from his eye
Glares forth the immortality of hell –

---

9   *array* arrange.   11   *palsy* paralysis.
10 *pensive* meditative, reflective.

    Avaunt!

MANFRED   Pronounce – what is thy mission?

SPIRIT   Come!

ABBOT What art thou, unknown being? Answer! Speak!   80

SPIRIT The genius[12] of this mortal. Come, 'tis time!

MANFRED I am prepared for all things, but deny

    The power which summons me. Who sent thee here?

SPIRIT Thou'lt know anon; come, come!

MANFRED   I have commanded

    Things of an essence greater far than thine,   85

    And striven with thy masters. Get thee hence!

SPIRIT Mortal, thine hour is come. Away, I say!

MANFRED I knew, and know my hour is come, but not

    To render up my soul to such as thee;

    Away! I'll die as I have lived – alone.   90

SPIRIT Then I must summon up my brethren. Rise!

Other spirits rise up

ABBOT Avaunt, ye evil ones! Avaunt I say!

    Ye have no power where piety hath power,

    And I do charge ye in the name –

SPIRIT   Old man!

    We know ourselves, our mission, and thine order;   95

    Waste not thy holy words on idle uses,

    It were in vain – this man is forfeited.

    Once more I summon him: away, away!

MANFRED I do defy ye, though I feel my soul

    Is ebbing from me, yet I do defy ye;   100

    Nor will I hence, while I have earthly breath

    To breathe my scorn upon ye, earthly strength

    To wrestle (though with spirits): what ye take

    Shall be ta'en limb by limb.

SPIRIT   Reluctant mortal!

    Is this the Magian who would so pervade   105

    The world invisible, and make himself

    Almost our equal? Can it be that thou

    Art thus in love with life – the very life

    Which made thee wretched?

MANFRED   Thou false fiend, thou liest!

    My life is in its last hour – *that* I know,   110

    Nor would redeem a moment of that hour;

    I do not combat against death, but thee

    And thy surrounding angels; my past power

    Was purchased by no compact with thy crew,

    But by superior science, penance, daring,   115

    And length of watching, strength of mind, and skill

    In knowledge of our fathers – when the earth

    Saw men and spirits walking side by side,

    And gave ye no supremacy. I stand

    Upon my strength: I do defy, deny,   120

    Spurn back, and scorn ye!

SPIRIT   But thy many crimes

---

[12] *genius* guardian spirit.

Have made thee –

MANFRED   What are they to such as thee?
Must crimes be punished but by other crimes
And greater criminals? Back to thy hell!
Thou hast no power upon me, *that* I feel;   125
Thou never shalt possess me, *that* I know.
What I have done is done; I bear within
A torture which could nothing gain from thine.
The mind which is immortal makes itself
Requital for its good or evil thoughts,[13]   130
Is its own origin of ill and end,
And its own place and time; its innate sense,
When stripped of this mortality, derives
No colour from the fleeting things without,
But is absorbed in sufferance or in joy,   135
Born from the knowledge of its own desert.
Thou didst not tempt me, and thou couldst not tempt me,
I have not been thy dupe nor am thy prey –
But was my own destroyer, and will be
My own hereafter. Back, ye baffled fiends,   140
The hand of death is on me – but not yours!

The demons disappear

ABBOT Alas, how pale thou art! Thy lips are white
And thy breast heaves, and in thy gasping throat
The accents rattle; give thy prayers to heaven;
Pray, albeit but in thought – but die not thus.   145

MANFRED 'Tis over; my dull eyes can fix thee not,
But all things swim around me, and the earth
Heaves as it were beneath me. Fare thee well;
Give me thy hand.

ABBOT   Cold, cold, even to the heart;
But yet one prayer – alas, how fares it with thee?

MANFRED Old man! 'Tis not so difficult to die. *) –§ Byron said that it*   150
Manfred expires   *was moral*

ABBOT He's gone; his soul hath ta'en its earthless flight –
Whither, I dread to think – but he is gone.

Letter from Lord Byron to Thomas Moore, 28 February 1817 (extract; including 'So we'll go no more a-roving')[1]

I feel anxious to hear from you, even more than usual, because your last indicated that you were unwell. At present, I am on the invalid regimen myself. The Carnival – that is, the latter part of it – and sitting up late o' nights, had knocked me up a little. But it is over, and it is now Lent, with all its abstinence and Sacred Music.

The mumming[2] closed with a masked ball at the Fenice,[3] where I went, as also to most of the ridottos,[4] etc., etc. And, though I did not dissipate much upon the whole, yet I find 'the sword wearing out the scabbard', though I have but just turned the corner of twenty-nine.

---

[13]   *The mind . . . thoughts* cf. *Paradise Lost* i 254–5: 'The mind is its own place, and in itself / Can make a heaven of hell, a hell of heaven.'

LETTER FROM LORD BYRON TO THOMAS MOORE
[1]   This important letter was written from Venice, and presents Byron's famous poem, '*So we'll go no more a-*

roving', in the context in which it was first composed.
[2]   *mumming* revelries conducted behind masks.
[3]   *the Fenice* Venetian opera theatre, principal venue for the carnival, which closed on the evening of 18 February. It was destroyed by fire in summer 1996.
[4]   *ridottos* entertainment or social assembly consisting of music and dancing.

So we'll go no more a-roving
   So late into the night,
Though the heart be still as loving,
   And the moon be still as bright.

For the sword outwears its sheath,   5
   And the soul wears out the breast,
And the heart must pause to breathe,
   And love itself have rest.

Though the night was made for loving,
   And the day returns too soon,   10
Yet we'll go no more a-roving
   By the light of the moon.

Don Juan (edited from MS)[1]

Dedication (composed between 3 July and 6 September 1818)

1

Bob Southey! You're a poet — Poet Laureate,[2]
   And representative of all the race;[3]
Although 'tis true that you turned out a Tory at
   Last, yours has lately been a common case;
And now, my epic renegade, what are ye at,   5
   With all the Lakers[4] in and out of place?
A nest of tuneful persons, to my eye
Like 'four and twenty blackbirds in a pie,

2

Which pie[5] being opened, they began to sing'
   (This old song and new simile holds good),   10
'A dainty dish to set before the King'
   Or Regent,[6] who admires such kind of food.
And Coleridge[7] too has lately taken wing,
   But like a hawk encumbered with his hood,
Explaining metaphysics to the nation;[8]   15
I wish he would explain his explanation.

DON JUAN

[1] *Don Juan* is probably Byron's greatest achievement. Cantos I and II appeared first, without the Dedication, in 1819; they are published here in their entirety. For introductory remarks see headnote, pp. 664–5.

[2] Southey was Poet Laureate 1813–43, a post that entailed the composition of occasional poems in honour of the king. For Byron and Shelley, this was conclusive proof, were any needed, that he had abandoned his early radicalism. In an unpublished Preface to *Don Juan*, Byron wrote that the Dedication 'may be further supposed to be produced by someone who may have a cause of aversion from the said Southey — for some personal reason — perhaps a gross calumny invented or circulated by this Pantisocratic apostle of apostasy, who is sometimes as unguarded in his assertions as atrocious in his conjectures, and feeds the cravings of his wretched vanity — disappointed in its nobler hopes, and reduced to prey upon such snatches of fame as his contributions to the *Quarterly Review*'. Byron's animus towards him was indeed personal: as he told Hobhouse on 11 November 1818, 'The son of a bitch on his return from Switzerland two years ago, said that Shelley and I "had formed a league of incest and practised our precepts with etc." He lied like a rascal, for *they were not sisters* — one being Godwin's daughter by Mary Wollstonecraft, and the other the daughter of the present Mrs Godwin by a *former* husband. The attack contains no allusion to the cause, but some good verses, and all political and poetical. He lied in another sense, for there was no promiscuous intercourse, my commerce being limited to the carnal knowledge of the Miss Clairmont' (Marchand vi 76). Having heard Byron read the Dedication, Shelley said of Southey that 'The poor wretch will writhe under the lash' (Jones ii 42); in the event, he did not, as Byron published *Don Juan* without the Dedication.

[3] *all the race* i.e. of poets.

[4] *Lakers* i.e. Southey, Wordsworth and Coleridge (who actually lived in London, rather than the Lake District).

[5] *pie* there is possibly a pun on the name of Henry James Pye (1745–1813), arch poetaster and Laureate prior to Southey.

[6] George, Prince of Wales, governed as Prince Regent 1810–20.

[7] As recently as 1816, Byron had given Coleridge £100 to help him through a bad patch; enmity developed because, as Byron told John Murray, 'Coleridge went about repeating Southey's lie with pleasure' (Marchand v 83). The lie is, of course, the rumour about the league of incest (see n. 2, above).

[8] Byron is thinking of Coleridge's recent prose discourses, *The Stateman's Manual* (1816), *Biographia Literaria* and *Lay Sermon* (1817), and *The Friend* (1818).

3

You, Bob, are rather insolent, you know,
    At being disappointed in your wish
To supersede all warblers here below,
    And be the only blackbird in the dish;   20
And then you overstrain yourself, or so,
    And tumble downward like the flying fish
Gasping on deck, because you soar too high, Bob,
And fall for lack of moisture, quite a dry-bob!⁹

4

And Wordsworth, in a rather long *Excursion*   25
    (I think the quarto holds five hundred pages¹⁰),
Has given a sample from the vasty¹¹ version
    Of his new system to perplex the sages;
'Tis poetry (at least by his assertion),
    And may appear so when the dog-star rages;¹²   30
And he who understands it would be able
To add a story¹³ to the Tower of Babel.¹⁴

5

You gentlemen, by dint of long seclusion
    From better company, have kept your own
At Keswick,¹⁵ and, through still-continued fusion   35
    Of one another's minds, at last have grown
To deem as a most logical conclusion
    That poesy has wreaths for you alone;
There is a narrowness in such a notion
Which makes me wish you'd change your lakes
                                for ocean.   40

6

I would not imitate the petty thought,
    Nor coin¹⁶ my self-love to so base a vice,
For all the glory your conversion¹⁷ brought,
    Since gold alone should not have been its price.
You have your salary – was't for that you
                                wrought?¹⁸   45
And Wordsworth has his place in the Excise.¹⁹
You're shabby fellows, true – but poets still,
And duly seated on the immortal hill.²⁰

7

Your bays²¹ may hide the baldness of your brows,
    Perhaps some virtuous blushes (let them go);   50
To you I envy neither fruit nor boughs,
    And for the fame you would engross²² below
The field is universal, and allows
    Scope to all such as feel the inherent glow –
Scott, Rogers, Campbell, Moore and Crabbe²³
                                will try   55
'Gainst you the question with posterity.

---

⁹ *dry bob* coition without emission.
¹⁰ Jeffrey criticized the length of *The Excursion* (1814), p. 556, above.
¹¹ *vasty* vast, enormous.
¹² *when the dog-star rages* The star Sirius, in the constellation of the Greater Dog, the brightest of the fixed stars, has been alleged to have all kinds of bad effects when its influence rises with the sun; the joke here is that it will distort everyone's judgement so much as to make *The Excursion* appear to be poetry. Cf. also Pope, *Epistle to Dr Arbuthnot* 3–4: 'The dog-star rages! Nay 'tis past a doubt, / All Bedlam, or Parnassus, is let out'.
¹³ *story* 'tale' as well as 'floor', 'level'.
¹⁴ *the Tower of Babel* the cause of God's decision to confound the language of men; Genesis 11:1–9.
¹⁵ In fact, only Southey lived at Keswick (as Byron well knew); Coleridge lived in London, and Wordsworth in Grasmere.
¹⁶ *coin* 'fashion', effectively, 'convert'. The implication is that Southey's vanity has led him to relinquish his ideals for the small pittance he is paid as Laureate.
¹⁷ *conversion* a pun, meaning: (i) conversion of vanity to the gold Southey is paid as Laureate, and (ii) conversion from radical to Tory.
¹⁸ *wrought* i.e. composed poetry.

¹⁹ An unpublished note appears in the proofs: 'Wordsworth's place may be in the Customs; it is, I think, in that of the Excise – besides another at Lord Lonsdale's table, where this poetical charlatan and political parasite picks up the crumbs with a hardened alacrity, the converted Jacobin having long subsided into the clownish sycophant of the worst prejudices of aristocracy'. William Lowther, 1st Earl of Lonsdale, was Wordsworth's patron; he procured Wordsworth's job as Distributor of Stamps and was the dedicatee of *The Excursion*.
²⁰ *the immortal hill* Parnassus, a mountain of Phocis (northwest of Athens), was sacred to the muses.
²¹ *bays* the leaves of the bay-tree or bay-laurel were, in classical times, the symbol of poetic ability.
²² *engross* monopolize. It could hardly have been said, however, that Byron was anything but famous himself; cf. Lady Caroline Lamb's opening stanzas of *A New Canto* (pp. 650–1).
²³ For Scott, Moore and Crabbe see pp. 428, 617–18, 36. Samuel Rogers (1763–1855) was the author of the couplet poem, *The Pleasures of Memory* (1792), and Thomas Campbell (1777–1844) the author of *The Pleasures of Hope* (1799). Byron saw them as working, broadly speaking, within the neo-classical tradition stemming from Pope; as such, they were vastly preferable to the Lakers.

8

For me who, wandering with pedestrian[24] muses,
   Contend not with you on the winged steed,
I wish your fate may yield ye, when she chooses,
   The fame you envy[25] and the skill you
                      need;[26]   60
And recollect a poet nothing loses
   In giving to his brethren their full meed
Of merit, and complaint of present days
Is not the *certain* path to future praise.[27]

9

He that reserves his laurels for posterity   65
   (Who does not often claim the bright reversion?)[28]
Has generally no great crop[29] to spare it, he
   Being only injured by his own assertion;
And although here and there some glorious rarity
   Arise like Titan from the sea's immersion,[30]   70
The major part of such appellants[31] go
To God knows where – for no one else can know.

10

If, fallen in evil days on evil tongues,[32]
   Milton appealed to the avenger, Time;
If Time, the avenger, execrates his wrongs,   75
   And makes the word 'Miltonic' mean 'sublime',
He deigned not to belie his soul in songs,
   Nor turn his very talent to a crime;
He did not loathe the sire to laud the son,[33]
But closed the tyrant-hater he begun.[34]   80

11

Think'st thou, could he, the blind old man,[35] arise
   Like Samuel from the grave,[36] to freeze once more
The blood of monarchs with his prophecies,
   Or be alive again, again all hoar
With time and trials, and those helpless eyes   85
   And heartless daughters,[37] worn and pale and
                             poor –
Would *he* adore a sultan? – *he* obey
The intellectual eunuch Castlereagh?[38]

12

Cold-blooded, smooth-faced, placid miscreant!
   Dabbling its sleek young hands in Erin's[39]
                        gore,   90
And thus for wider carnage taught to pant,
   Transferred to gorge upon a sister-shore;
The vulgarest tool that tyranny could want,
   With just enough of talent, and no more,
To lengthen fetters by another fixed,   95
And offer poison long already mixed.

13

An orator of such set trash of phrase[40]
   Ineffably, legitimately vile,
That even its grossest flatterers dare not praise,
   Nor foes (all nations) condescend to smile;   100
Not even a sprightly blunder's spark can blaze
   From that Ixion grindstone's[41] ceaseless toil,
That turns and turns, to give the world a notion
Of endless torments and perpetual motion.

---

[24] *pedestrian* by implication, less metaphysical and more down to earth.
[25] *The fame you envy* in the Proem to *Carmen Nuptiale* (1816), Southey had written: 'There was a time when all my youthful thought / Was of the muse; and of the poet's fame' (ll. 1–2).
[26] *need* i.e. lack.
[27] *And recollect . . . praise* in the Proem to *Carmen Nuptiale* (1816), Southey wrote that Fancy had told him to walk 'Far from the vain, the vicious, and the proud' (l.27). Byron seems to have taken this as a reference to himself.
[28] *the bright reversion* the right of succession (i.e. to posthumous fame).
[29] *no great crop* i.e. of praise for other poets.
[30] *Arise like Titan from the sea's immersion* Byron has in mind Helios, son of Hyperion, god of the sun.
[31] *appellants* challengers, i.e. those who reserve their laurels for posterity.
[32] *Paradise Lost* vii 25–6.
[33] *sire . . . son* Charles I and II. Byron's point is that Southey hated George III (in his radical youth) but has praised his son

(the Prince Regent). Milton remained a republican throughout his life.
[34] *But closed the tyrant-hater he begun* as far as Byron was concerned, both George III and the Prince Regent were tyrants. At that time, the monarch (an inherited post) had enormous political power.
[35] *the blind old man* Milton.
[36] *Like Samuel from the grave* Samuel was raised from the grave by the Witch of Endor; I Samuel 28:13–14.
[37] *heartless daughters* said to have robbed Milton of his books.
[38] Robert Stewart, Viscount Castlereagh (1769–1822), Foreign Secretary 1812–22. As Secretary to the Lord Lieutenant of Ireland (1797–1801), he had been responsible for imprisoning the leaders of the United Irish rebellion.
[39] *Erin's* Ireland's.
[40] *such set trash of phrase* Castlereagh was renowned as an incompetent speaker.
[41] *Ixion grindstone's* Ixion, king of Thessaly, was banished from heaven and sentenced to be tied to a burning and spinning wheel in Hades.

point of Ireland stuff?

14

A bungler even in its disgusting trade,   *105*
    And botching, patching, leaving still behind
Something of which its masters are afraid,
    States to be curbed[42] and thoughts to be confined,
Conspiracy or congress[43] to be made,
    Cobbling at manacles for all mankind –   *110*
A tinkering slavemaker who mends old chains,
With God and man's abhorrence for its gains.

15

Castlereagh

If we may judge of matter by the mind,
    Emasculated to the marrow, *It*
Hath but two objects: how to serve and bind,   *115*
    Deeming the chain it wears even men may fit;
Eutropius[44] of its many masters – blind
    To worth as freedom, wisdom as to wit –
Fearless, because *no* feeling dwells in ice,
Its very courage stagnates to a vice.   *120*

16

Where shall I turn me not to view its bonds
    (For I will never feel them)? Italy,
Thy late-reviving Roman soul desponds
    Beneath the lie this state-thing[45] breathed o'er thee;
Thy clanking chain and Erin's yet green wounds   *125*
    Have voices, tongues to cry aloud for me.
Europe has slaves, allies, kings, armies still –
And Southey lives to sing them very ill.[46]

17

Meantime, Sir Laureate,[47] I proceed to dedicate,
    In honest, simple verse, this song to you,   *130*
And if in flattering strains I do not predicate,[48]
    'Tis that I still retain my 'buff and blue'[49]
(My politics, as yet, are all to educate);
    Apostasy's so fashionable too,
To keep *one* creed's a task grown quite herculean –   *135*
Is it not so, my Tory ultra-Julian?[50]

Canto I

1

I want a hero[1] – an uncommon want
    When every year and month sends forth a new one,
Till after cloying the gazettes with cant,
    The age discovers he is not the true one;
Of such as these I should not care to vaunt,   *5*
    I'll therefore take our ancient friend Don Juan;[2]
We all have seen him in the pantomime[3]
Sent to the devil,[4] somewhat ere his time.

2

Vernon, the butcher Cumberland, Wolfe, Hawke,
    Prince Ferdinand, Granby, Burgoyne, Keppel,
                                        Howe,[5]   *10*
Evil and good, have had their tithe of talk,
    And filled their signposts then, like Wellesley now;[6]

---

[42] *States to be curbed* i.e. France under Napoleon; Castlereagh helped negotiate the alliance with Russia, Austria and Prussia that led to Napoleon's defeat.

[43] *congress* as Foreign Secretary, Castlereagh was instrumental in the Treaty of Paris (May 1814), which restored the Bourbon monarchy after Napoleon's abdication, and in the Congress of Vienna (1814–15), which reorganized Europe after the Napoleonic Wars.

[44] *Eutropius* Roman eunuch raised to high office.

[45] *this state-thing* i.e. Castlereagh.

[46] This stanza provides an overview of Castlereagh's misdeeds. In 1798 he had helped to defeat the Irish insurrection and establish the Union of 1801; as a chief negotiator of the Treaty of Vienna, 1814–15, he had been responsible for suppressing the revival of free Italian cities, instead placing Italy under Austrian rule. Southey celebrated his deeds in *Carmen Triumphale* (1814) and *The Poet's Pilgrimage to Waterloo* (1816).

[47] *Sir Laureate* Southey.

[48] *predicate* extol, commend (i.e. Southey and his poetry).

[49] *buff and blue* colours of the Whig Club. The comparison is with Southey, who has relinquished all his liberal credentials.

[50] 'I allude not to our friend Landor's hero, the traitor Count Julian, but to Gibbon's hero, vulgarly yclept "The Apostate"'

(Byron's note). Julian was brought up as a Christian, but secretly worshipped the Roman gods before he became Emperor in AD 361. During his brief reign he attempted to restore pagan worship (he died 363).

CANTO I

[1] *I want a hero* Byron's lack of a hero is a witty variation on the Virgilian epic opening, 'Of arms and the man I sing . . .'

[2] *Juan* pronounced with a hard 'j', to rhyme with 'new one' and 'true one'.

[3] *pantomime* musical drama without words. In London, only Drury Lane and Covent Garden were allowed to perform 'spoken drama'; all other theatres were confined to plays without words. Byron may well have seen Don Juan portrayed in Italian

[4] *Sent to the devil* by contrast, Byron's poem will humanize Juan, and redeem him from the accusations commonly levelled against him.

[5] *Vernon . . . Howe* all celebrated eighteenth-century military commanders.

[6] *And filled their signposts then, like Wellesley now* Wellington Street (named after Arthur Wellesley, Duke of Wellington) and Waterloo Bridge, were opened and dedicated on the anniversary of Wellington's victory at Waterloo in 1817.

Each in their turn like Banquo's monarchs stalk,[7]
   Followers of fame, 'nine farrow' of that sow;[8]
France, too, had Buonaparté and Dumourier,[9]   *15*
Recorded in the *Moniteur* and *Courier*.[10]

3

Barnave, Brissot, Condorcet, Mirabeau,
   Petion, Clootz, Danton, Marat, La Fayette
Were French, and famous people as we know;
   And there were others, scarce forgotten yet –   *20*
Joubert, Hoche, Marceau, Lannes, Dessaix, Moreau,[11]
   With many of the military set,
Exceedingly remarkable at times,
But not at all adapted to my rhymes.

4

Nelson[12] was once Britannia's god of war,   *25*
   And still should be so, but the tide is turned;
There's no more to be said of Trafalgar –
   'Tis with our hero quietly inurned
Because the army's grown more popular,[13]
   At which the naval people are concerned;   *30*
Besides, the Prince is all for the land-service,
Forgetting Duncan, Nelson, Howe, and Jervis.[14]

5

Brave men were living before Agamemnon[15]
   And since, exceeding valorous and sage –
A good deal like him too, though quite the same
                       none;   *35*
   But then they shone not on the poet's page,
And so have been forgotten. I condemn none,

But can't find any in the present age
Fit for my poem (that is, for my new one),
So as I said, I'll take my friend Don Juan.   *40*

6

Most epic poets plunge *in medias res*[16]
   (Horace makes this the heroic turnpike road[17]),
And then your hero tells, whene'er you please,
   What went before by way of episode,
While seated after dinner at his ease   *45*
   Beside his mistress in some soft abode –
Palace or garden, paradise or cavern,
Which serves the happy couple for a tavern.

7

That is the usual method, but not mine;
   My way is to begin with the beginning.   *50*
The regularity of my design
   Forbids all wandering as the worst of sinning,
And therefore I shall open with a line
   (Although it cost me half an hour in spinning)
Narrating somewhat of Don Juan's father   *55*
And also of his mother, if you'd rather.

8

In Seville was he born, a pleasant city
   Famous for oranges and women; he
Who has not seen it will be much to pity,
   So says the proverb – and I quite agree:[18]   *60*
Of all the Spanish towns is none more pretty
   (Cadiz perhaps, but that you soon may see).[19]
Don Juan's parents lived beside the river,
A noble stream, and called the Guadalquivir.

---

7 *like Banquo's monarchs stalk* an allusion to the vision granted Macbeth at *Macbeth* IV ii 112–24.
8 *'nine farrow' of that sow* an allusion to the witches' spell in *Macbeth* IV i 64–5: 'Pour in sow's blood, that hath eaten / Her nine farrow'.
9 Charles Dumouriez (1739–1823) defeated the Austrian army in 1792 at Jemappes.
10 *the Moniteur and Courier* French newspapers: *Gazette Nationale; ou le moniteur universel* and *Courier Républicain*.
11 These are politicians and military leaders involved with the French Revolution.
12 Horatio, Lord Nelson (1758–1805), killed at the Battle of Trafalgar, with Napoleon's forces, 21 October 1805.

13 *Because the army's grown more popular* i.e. since Waterloo.
14 These are all distinguished admirals.
15 Agamemnon commanded the Greeks in the Trojan wars.
16 *in medias res* in the middle of things; i.e. in mid-story. This is the recommendation of Horace, *Ars Poetica* 148.
17 *the heroic turnpike road* i.e. the initial step in the writing of an epic poem. A 'turnpike road' is one on which turnpikes are or were erected for the collection of tolls; hence, a main road or highway.
18 Byron was in Seville, 25–9 July 1809. The 'proverb' runs: 'Quien no ha visto Sevilla / No ha visto maravilla' ('Whoever has not seen Seville has not seen a marvel').
19 Byron was in Cadiz, 29 July–3 August 1809.

9

His father's name was Jóse (Don, of course) –   65
   A true hidalgo,[20] free from every stain
Of Moor or Hebrew blood, he traced his source
   Through the most Gothic gentlemen of Spain;
A better cavalier ne'er mounted horse
   (Or, being mounted, e'er got down again)   70
Than Jóse, who begot our hero, who
Begot – but that's to come. Well, to renew:

10

His mother was a learned lady famed
   For every branch of every science known,[21]
In every Christian language ever named,   75
   With virtues equalled by her wit alone;
She made the cleverest people quite ashamed,
   And even the good with inward envy groan,
Finding themselves so very much exceeded
In their own way by all the things that she did.   80

11

Her memory was a mine – she knew by heart
   All Calderon and greater part of Lopé,[22]
So that if any actor missed his part
   She could have served him for the prompter's copy;
For her Feinagle's[23] were an useless art,   85
   And he himself obliged to shut up shop – he
Could never make a memory so fine as
That which adorned the brain of Donna Inez.

12

Her favourite science was the mathematical,[24]
   Her noblest virtue was her magnanimity,   90
Her wit (she sometimes tried at wit) was Attic[25] all,
   Her serious sayings darkened to sublimity;

In short, in all things she was fairly what I call
   A prodigy – her morning dress was dimity,[26]
Her evening silk or, in the summer, muslin   95
(And other stuffs with which I won't stay puzzling).

13

She knew the Latin – that is, the Lord's prayer,
   And Greek – the alphabet, I'm nearly sure;
She read some French romances here and there,
   Although her mode of speaking was not pure;   100
For native Spanish she had no great care
   (At least her conversation was obscure);
Her thoughts were theorems, her words a problem,
As if she deemed that mystery would ennoble 'em.

14

She liked the English and the Hebrew tongue,   105
   And said there was analogy between 'em;
She proved it somehow out of sacred song,
   But I must leave the proofs to those who've
                 seen 'em;
But this I heard her say, and can't be wrong,
   And all may think which way their judgments
                 lean 'em,   110
"Tis strange; the Hebrew noun which means "I am",
The English always use to govern d——n.'[27]

15

Some women use their tongues, she looked a lecture,
   Each eye a sermon, and her brow a homily,
An all-in-all-sufficient self-director   115
   Like the lamented late Sir Samuel Romilly,[28]
The law's expounder and the state's corrector[29]
   Whose suicide was almost an anomaly –
One sad example more that 'All is vanity';[30]
The jury brought their verdict in: insanity.   120

---

20 *hidalgo* a gentleman by birth, one of the lower nobility.
21 *His mother . . . known* Byron always denied that Donna Inez was supposed to be a caricature of his wife, but friends recognized the similarities, and advised him not to publish the poem on that account. Lady Byron was renowned for her expertise at mathematics, classical literature, and philosophy.
22 Pedro Calderón de la Barca (1600–81) and Lopé de Vega (1562–1635) were Spanish playwrights.
23 Gregor von Feinagle (1765–1819) devised a system of mnemonics, on which he lectured in England and Scotland in 1811.
24 Byron used to call his wife the Princess of Parallelograms.
25 Attic wit is refined, delicate and poignant.

26 *dimity* stout cotton fabric; said by Moore to have been Lady Byron's favourite dress material.
27 Yahweh ('I am' in Hebrew) means God (as in 'God damn!'); see Exodus 3:13–14.
28 Romilly (1757–1818) sided with Lady Byron when she separated from her husband, earning Byron's lasting hatred. Even after his suicide, Byron was capable of writing of him: 'I still loathe him as much as we can hate dust – but that is nothing' (Marchand vi 150).
29 *the state's corrector* Romilly was a legal reformer whose chief efforts were devoted to lessening the severity of English criminal law.
30 Ecclesiastes 1:2: 'Vanity of vanities, saith the Preacher, vanity of vanities; all is vanity'.

16

In short, she was a walking calculation,
　　Miss Edgeworth's[31] novels stepping from their
　　　　　　　　　　　　　　　　covers,
Or Mrs Trimmer's books on education,[32]
　　Or 'Coeleb's Wife' set out in search of lovers,[33]
Morality's prim personification　　　　　　*125*
　　In which not envy's self a flaw discovers:
To others' share let 'female errors fall',[34]
For she had not even one – the worst of all.

17

Oh she was perfect past all parallel
　　Of any modern female saint's comparison;　　*130*
So far beyond the cunning powers of hell,
　　Her guardian angel had given up his garrison;
Even her minutest motions went as well
　　As those of the best timepiece made by Harrison;[35]
In virtues nothing earthly could surpass her,　　*135*
Save thine 'incomparable oil', Macassar![36]

18

Perfect she was, but as perfection is
　　Insipid in this naughty world of ours,
Where our first parents[37] never learned to kiss
　　Till they were exiled from their earlier
　　　　　　　　　　　　　　　　bowers,[38]　*140*
Where all was peace and innocence and bliss
　　(I wonder how they got through the twelve hours) –
Don Jóse, like a lineal son of Eve,
Went plucking various fruit without her leave.

19

He was a mortal of the careless kind　　　*145*
　　With no great love for learning or the learned,
Who chose to go where'er he had a mind,
　　And never dreamed his lady was concerned;
The world, as usual, wickedly inclined
　　To see a kingdom or a house o'erturned,　　*150*
Whispered he had a mistress, some said *two* –
But for domestic quarrels *one* will do.

20

Now Donna Inez had, with all her merit,
　　A great opinion of her own good qualities;
Neglect, indeed, requires a saint to bear it –　　*155*
　　And so indeed, she was in her moralities;
But then she had a devil of a spirit,
　　And sometimes mixed up fancies with realities,
And let few opportunities escape
Of getting her liege-lord into a scrape.　　*160*

21

This was an easy matter with a man
　　Oft in the wrong and never on his guard;
And even the wisest, do the best they can,
　　Have moments, hours, and days, so unprepared
That you might 'brain them with their lady's
　　　　　　　　　　　　　　　　fan',[39]　*165*
　　And sometimes ladies hit exceeding hard,
And fans turn into falchions[40] in fair hands,
And why and wherefore no one understands.

[31]　Maria Edgeworth (1767–1849) wrote educational volumes for children, including *The Parent's Assistant* (1796) and *Practical Education* (co-authored with her father, Richard Lovell Edgeworth) (1798). She was also a distinguished novelist.
[32]　Sarah Trimmer (1741–1810) wrote a number of exemplary tales and moral lessons for children, including *An Easy Introduction to the Knowledge of Nature* (1790) and *Instructive Tales* (1810).
[33]　Hannah More was famous in 1819 as the author of a monstrously successful didactic novel, *Coelebs in Search of a Wife* (1808), which had gone to a 12th edition by the end of 1809.
[34]　*female errors fall* an allusion to Pope, *The Rape of the Lock* ii 17–18: 'If to her share some female errors fall, / Look on her face, and you'll forget 'em all'.
[35]　John Harrison (1693–1776), eminent horologist of the day.
[36]　*thine 'incomparable oil', Macassar* early tonic for the follicles

advertised in hyperbolic terms that no doubt gave Byron and his cronies much amusement; see, for example, the front page of *The Courier*, 2 January 1809: 'Macassar oil, for the growth of HAIR. The virtues of this oil, extracted from a tree in the island of Macassar, are proudly pre-eminent to anything ever produced in this or any other country, for improving and accelerating the growth of hair, preventing it falling off, or turning grey, giving it an incomparable gloss, and producing wonderful effects on children's hair. Its virtues need only the test of experience to evince its extraordinary effects.' Byron was using Macassar oil as he composed *Don Juan* (Marchand vi 137).
[37]　*our first parents* Adam and Eve.
[38]　Adam and Eve had children only after being cast out of Paradise.
[39]　*1 Henry IV* II iii 23.
[40]　*falchions* broad swords.

22

'Tis pity learned virgins ever wed
    With persons of no sort of education,   *170*
Or gentlemen who, though well-born and bred,
    Grow tired of scientific conversation.
I don't choose to say much upon this head;
    I'm a plain man and in a single station,
But oh, ye lords of ladies intellectual,[41]   *175*
Inform us truly, have they not hen-pecked you all?

23

Don Jóse and his lady quarrelled – *why*
    Not any of the many could divine,
Though several thousand people chose to try,
    'Twas surely no concern of theirs nor mine;   *180*
I loathe that low vice curiosity,
    But if there's anything in which I shine,
'Tis in arranging all my friends' affairs –
Not having, of my own, domestic cares.

24

And so I interfered, and with the best   *185*
    Intentions, but their treatment was not kind;
I think the foolish people were possessed,
    For neither of them could I ever find,
Although their porter afterwards confessed –
    But that's no matter, and the worst's behind,   *190*
For little Juan o'er me threw, downstairs,
A pail of housemaid's water, unawares.

25

A little curly-headed, good-for-nothing,
    And mischief-making monkey from his birth;
His parents ne'er agreed except in doting   *195*
    Upon the most unquiet imp on earth;
Instead of quarrelling, had they been but both in
    Their senses, they'd have sent young master forth
To school, or had him soundly whipped at home
To teach him manners for the time to come.   *200*

26

Don Jóse and the Donna Inez led
    For some time an unhappy sort of life,
Wishing each other not divorced but dead;
    They lived respectably as man and wife,
Their conduct was exceedingly well-bred,   *205*
    And gave no outward signs of inward strife –
Until at length the smothered fire broke out,
And put the business past all kind of doubt.

27

For Inez called some druggists and physicians[42]
    And tried to prove her loving lord was mad,[43]   *210*
But as he had some lucid intermissions,
    She next decided he was only bad;
Yet when they asked her for her depositions,[44]
    No sort of explanation could be had,
Save that her duty both to man and God   *215*
Required this conduct (which seemed very odd).

28

She kept a journal where his faults were noted
    And opened certain trunks of books and letters –
All which might, if occasion served, be quoted;
    And then she had all Seville for abettors,   *220*
Besides her good old grandmother (who doted);
    The hearers of her case became repeaters,
Then advocates, inquisitors, and judges –
Some for amusement, others for old grudges.[45]

29

And then this best and meekest woman bore   *225*
    With such serenity her husband's woes,
Just as the Spartan ladies did of yore
    Who saw their spouses killed, and nobly chose
Never to say a word about them more;
    Calmly she heard each calumny that rose,   *230*
And saw his agonies with such sublimity
That all the world exclaimed 'What magnanimity!'

---

[41] *ladies intellectual* a reference to bluestocking circles of Byron's day, which included Lady Caroline Lamb, Lady Oxford, Annabella Milbanke.
[42] *druggists and physicians* chemists and doctors.

[43] Byron believed his wife had tried to prove him mad.
[44] *depositions* statements, testimony (that he was mad).
[45] This is a description of the whispering campaign conducted against Byron by his wife.

30

No doubt this patience, when the world is damning us,
 Is philosophic in our former friends;
'Tis also pleasant to be deemed magnanimous 235
 (The more so in obtaining our own ends);
And what the lawyers call a *malus animus*,[46]
 Conduct like this by no means comprehends:[47]
Revenge in person's certainly no virtue,
But then 'tis not *my* fault, if *others* hurt you. 240

31

And if our quarrels should rip up old stories
 And help them with a lie or two additional,
I'm not to blame, as you well know, no more is
 Anyone else – they were become traditional;
Besides, their resurrection aids our glories 245
 By contrast, which is what we just were wishing all:
And science profits by this resurrection –
Dead scandals form good subjects for dissection.

32

Their friends[48] had tried at reconciliation,
 Then their relations[49] who made matters
       worse 250
('Twere hard to say upon a like occasion
 To whom it may be best to have recourse;
I can't say much for friend or yet relation);
 The lawyers did their utmost for divorce
But scarce a fee was paid on either side 255
Before, unluckily, Don Jóse died.

33

He died – and most unluckily, because,
 According to all hints I could collect
From counsel[50] learned in those kinds of laws
 (Although their talk's obscure and
       circumspect), 260

His death contrived to spoil a charming cause:
 A thousand pities also with respect
To public feeling, which on this occasion
Was manifested in a great sensation.

34

But ah, he died – and buried with him lay 265
 The public feeling and the lawyers' fees;
His house was sold, his servants sent away,
 A Jew took one of his two mistresses,
A priest the other (at least so they say).
 I asked the doctors after his disease: 270
He died of the slow fever called the tertian[51]
And left his widow to her own aversion.

35

Yes, Jóse was an honourable man[52] –
 That I must say, who knew him very well;
Therefore his frailties I'll no further scan 275
 (Indeed there were not many more to tell),
And if his passions now and then outran
 Discretion, and were not so peaceable
As Numa's (who was also named Pompilius),[53]
He had been ill brought up, and was born
       bilious.[54] 280

36

Whate'er might be his worthlessness or worth,
 Poor fellow, he had many things to wound him,
Let's own, since it can do no good on earth;
 It was a trying moment that which found him
Standing alone beside his desolate hearth 285
 Where all his household gods lay shivered[55]
       round him;
No choice was left his feelings or his pride
Save death or Doctors' Commons[56] – so he died.

---

[46] *malus animus* bad intent.
[47] *comprehends* comprises.
[48] *friends* in Byron's case, Hobhouse, Rogers and Madame de Staël.
[49] *relations* in Byron's case, his sister Augusta, and cousin George Anson Byron (who ended up supporting Lady Byron, which Byron could not forgive).
[50] *counsel* body of legal advisers.

[51] *the slow fever called the tertian* tertian fever progresses slowly because it strikes only every other day.
[52] *an honourable man* an echo of Antony's attack on Brutus and the assassins of Caesar, *Julius Caesar* III ii 82–3.
[53] The forty-three-year reign of Numa, second king of Rome, was known for its peaceability.
[54] *bilious* ill-tempered.
[55] *shivered* shattered.
[56] *Doctors' Commons* divorce courts.

37

Dying intestate, Juan was sole heir
  To a chancery-suit[57] and messuages[58] and lands 290
Which, with a long minority and care,
  Promised to turn out well in proper hands;
Inez became sole guardian (which was fair)
  And answered but to nature's just demands;
An only son left with an only mother 295
Is brought up much more wisely than another.

38

Sagest of women, even of widows, she
  Resolved that Juan should be quite a paragon
And worthy of the noblest pedigree
  (His sire was of Castile, his dam from Aragon). 300
Then for accomplishments of chivalry,
  In case our lord the king should go to war again,
He learned the arts of riding, fencing, gunnery,
And how to scale a fortress – or a nunnery.

39

But that which Donna Inez most desired, 305
  And saw into herself each day before all
The learned tutors whom for him she hired,
  Was that his breeding should be strictly moral;
Much into all his studies she enquired,
  And so they were submitted first to her, all, 310
Arts, sciences – no branch was made a mystery
To Juan's eyes, excepting natural history.

40

The languages (especially the dead),[59]
  The sciences (and most of all the abstruse),
The arts (at least all such as could be said 315
  To be the most remote from common use) –
In all these he was much and deeply read;
  But not a page of anything that's loose[60]
Or hints continuation of the species
Was ever suffered, lest he should grow vicious.[61] 320

41

His classic studies made a little puzzle
  Because of filthy loves of gods and goddesses
Who in the earlier ages made a bustle,
  But never put on pantaloons or bodices;
His reverend tutors had at times a tussle, 325
  And for their *Aeneid*s, *Iliad*s, and *Odyssey*s,
Were forced to make an odd sort of apology –
For Donna Inez dreaded the mythology.

42

Ovid's a rake, as half his verses show him,
  Anacreon's morals are a still worse sample, 330
Catullus scarcely has a decent poem,
  I don't think Sappho's 'Ode' a good example,
Although Longinus tells us there is no hymn
  Where the sublime soars forth on wings more ample;
But Virgil's songs are pure, except that horrid
    one 335
Beginning with *Formosum pastor Corydon*.[62]

43

Lucretius' irreligion[63] is too strong
  For early stomachs, to prove wholesome food;
I can't help thinking Juvenal was wrong
  (Although no doubt his real intent was good) 340
For speaking out so plainly in his song –
  So much indeed as to be downright rude;[64]
And then what proper person can be partial
To all those nauseous epigrams of Martial?[65]

44

Juan was taught from out the best edition, 345
  Expurgated by learned men who place
Judiciously, from out the schoolboy's vision,
  The grosser parts; but fearful to deface
Too much their modest bard by this omission,
  And pitying sore his mutilated case, 350

---

57 *chancery-suit* legal claim for property.
58 *messuages* dwelling-place with adjoining lands.
59 *The languages (especially the dead)* i.e. Latin and Greek.
60 *loose* wanton, immoral.
61 *vicious* immoral, depraved.
62 *Ovid's a rake . . . Corydon* Byron lists erotic poets and poems, including Sappho's 'Ode to Aphrodite', Ovid's *Amores* and *Ars Amatoria*, the love songs of Anacreon and Catullus, and Virgil's *Eclogue* ii (dealing with pederastic love).

63 *Lucretius' irreligion* in *De rerum natura*, Lucretius attempted to show that the course of world history had taken place without divine intervention.
64 *downright rude* Juvenal portrayed the vices and depravities of Roman society.
65 *Martial* Roman epigrammatist, witty and rude.

They only add them all in an appendix[66] –
Which saves, in fact, the trouble of an index;

45

For there we have them all at one fell swoop,
   Instead of being scattered through the pages;
They stand forth marshalled in a handsome
                      troop   355
   To meet the ingenuous youth of future ages,
Till some less rigid editor shall stoop
   To call them back into their separate cages,
Instead of standing staring altogether
Like garden gods – and not so decent either.   360

46

The missal[67] too (it was the family missal)
   Was ornamented in a sort of way
Which ancient mass-books often are, and this all
   Kinds of grotesques illumined; and how they,
Who saw those figures on the margin kiss all,   365
   Could turn their optics[68] to the text and pray
Is more than I know – but Don Juan's mother
Kept this herself, and gave her son another.

47

Sermons he read and lectures he endured,
   And homilies and lives of all the saints;   370
To Jerome and to Chrysostom[69] inured,
   He did not take such studies for restraints;
But how faith is acquired and then insured,
   So well not one of the aforesaid paints
As St Augustine in his fine *Confessions* –   375
Which make the reader envy his transgressions.[70]

48

This too was a sealed book to little Juan –
   I can't but say that his mamma was right,
If such an education was the true one.
   She scarcely trusted him from out her sight;   380

Her maids were old, and if she took a new one
   You might be sure she was a perfect fright;
She did this during even her husband's life –
I recommend as much to every wife.

49

Young Juan waxed[71] in goodliness and grace;   385
   At six a charming child, and at eleven
With all the promise of as fine a face
   As e'er to man's maturer growth was given.
He studied steadily and grew apace
   And seemed, at least, in the right road to
                  heaven –   390
For half his days were passed at church, the other
Between his tutors, confessor, and mother.

50

At six, I said, he was a charming child,
   At twelve he was a fine but quiet boy;
Although in infancy a little wild,   395
   They tamed him down amongst them; to destroy
His natural spirit not in vain they toiled
   (At least it seemed so); and his mother's joy
Was to declare how sage and still and steady
Her young philosopher was grown already.   400

51

I had my doubts – perhaps I have them still,
   But what I say is neither here nor there;
I knew his father well, and have some skill
   In character, but it would not be fair
From sire to son to augur good or ill;   405
   He and his wife were an ill-sorted pair –
But scandal's my aversion, I protest
Against all evil speaking, even in jest.

52

For my part I say nothing – nothing – but
   This I will say (my reasons are my own):   410
That if I had an only son to put

---

[66] 'Fact. There is, or was, such an edition, with all the obnoxious epigrams of Martial placed by themselves at the end' (Byron's note).
[67] *missal* Roman Catholic prayer book containing Masses for each day of the year.
[68] *optics* eyes.

[69] Jerome and Chrysostom were apologists for Christianity.
[70] *his transgressions* i.e. as committed in his early life.
[71] *waxed* grew. There seems to be an echo of Christ: 'And the child grew, and waxed strong in spirit, filled with wisdom: and the grace of God was upon him' (Luke 2:40).

To school (as God be praised that I have none),
    'Tis not with Donna Inez I would shut
      Him up to learn his catechism alone –
No, no; I'd send him out betimes to college,   415
For there it was I picked up my own knowledge.

53

For there one learns – 'tis not for me to boast,
    Though I acquired – but I pass over *that*,
As well as all the Greek I since have lost;
    I say that there's the place – but *Verbum sat*;[72]   420
I think I picked up too, as well as most,
    Knowledge of matters – but no matter *what* –
I never married – but I think, I know,
That sons should not be educated so.

54

Young Juan now was sixteen years of age –   425
    Tall, handsome, slender, but well-knit; he seemed
Active, though not so sprightly, as a page,
    And everybody but his mother deemed
Him almost man. But she flew in a rage
    And bit her lips (for else she might have
                        screamed) 430
If any said so – for to be precocious
Was in her eyes a thing the most atrocious.

55

Amongst her numerous acquaintance, all
    Selected for discretion and devotion,
There was the Donna Julia, whom to call   435
    Pretty were but to give a feeble notion
Of many charms in her as natural
    As sweetness to the flower, or salt to ocean,
Her zone to Venus,[73] or his bow to Cupid
(But this last simile is trite and stupid).   440

56

The darkness of her oriental eye
    Accorded with her Moorish origin
(Her blood was not all Spanish, by the by –

In Spain, you know, this is a sort of sin);
When proud Granada fell and, forced to fly,   445
    Boabdil wept,[74] of Donna Julia's kin
Some went to Africa, some stayed in Spain;
Her great-great-grandmamma chose to remain.

57

She married (I forget the pedigree)
    With an hidalgo, who transmitted down   450
His blood less noble than such blood should be;
    At such alliances his sires would frown,
In that point so precise in each degree
    That they bred *in and in*, as might be shown,
Marrying their cousins – nay, their aunts and
                      nieces,   455
Which always spoils the breed, if it increases.

58

This heathenish cross restored the breed again,
    Ruined its blood, but much improved its flesh;
For from a root the ugliest in old Spain
    Sprung up a branch as beautiful as fresh –   460
The sons no more were short, the daughters plain
    (But there's a rumour which I fain would hush:
'Tis said that Donna Julia's grandmamma
Produced her Don more heirs at love than law).

59

However this might be, the race[75] went on   465
    Improving still through every generation
Until it centred in an only son
    Who left an only daughter; my narration
May have suggested that this single one
    Could be but Julia (whom on this occasion   470
I shall have much to speak about), and she
Was married, charming, chaste, and twenty-three.

60

Her eye (I'm very fond of handsome eyes)
    Was large and dark, suppressing half its fire

---

72   *Verbum sat* 'a word [to the wise] is enough'.
73   Venus's girdle ('zone') would make the wearer fall in love.
74   *Boabdil wept* Mohamed XI, last Moorish king of Granada,
wept when the city was besieged and surrendered to Spain, 1492.

75   *race* family.

Until she spoke, then through its soft disguise   475
    Flashed an expression more of pride than ire,
And love than either; and there would arise
    A something in them which was not desire,
But would have been, perhaps – but for the soul
Which struggled through and chastened down the
            whole.   480

61

Her glossy hair was clustered o'er a brow
    Bright with intelligence, and fair and smooth;
Her eyebrow's shape was like the aerial bow,[76]
    Her cheek all purple with the beam of youth
Mounting, at times, to a transparent glow   485
    As if her veins ran lightning; she, in sooth,
Possessed an air and grace by no means common,
Her stature tall – I hate a dumpy woman.

62

Wedded she was some years, and to a man
    Of fifty – and such husbands are in plenty;   490
And yet, I think, instead of such a ONE
    'Twere better to have TWO of five and twenty,
Especially in countries near the sun;
    And now I think on't, 'mi vien in mente',[77]
Ladies even of the most uneasy virtue   495
Prefer a spouse whose age is short of thirty.

63

'Tis a sad thing, I cannot choose but say,
    And all the fault of that indecent sun
Who cannot leave alone our helpless clay,[78]
    But will keep baking, broiling, burning on,   500
That howsoever people fast and pray
    The flesh is frail,[79] and so the soul undone;
What men call gallantry, and gods adultery,
Is much more common where the climate's sultry.

64

Happy the nations of the moral north!   505
    Where all is virtue, and the winter season

Sends sin, without a rag on, shivering forth
    ('Twas snow that brought St Francis back to
            reason);[80]
Where juries cast up what a wife is worth
    By laying whate'er sum, in mulct,[81] they
            please on   510
The lover, who must pay a handsome price,
Because it is a marketable vice.

65

Alfonso was the name of Julia's lord –
    A man well looking for his years and who
Was neither much beloved nor yet abhorred;   515
    They lived together as most people do,
Suffering each other's foibles by accord,
    And not exactly either *one* or *two*;
Yet he was jealous, though he did not show it,
For jealousy dislikes the world to know it.   520

66

Julia was (yet I never could see why)
    With Donna Inez quite a favourite friend;
Between their tastes there was small sympathy,
    For not a line had Julia ever penned;
Some people whisper (but no doubt they lie,   525
    For malice still imputes some private end)
That Inez had, ere Don Alfonso's marriage,
Forgot with him her very prudent carriage.[82]

67

And that still keeping up the old connection,
    Which time had lately rendered much more
            chaste,   530
She took his lady also in affection,
    And certainly this course was much the best.
She flattered Julia with her sage protection
    And complimented Don Alfonso's taste,
And if she could not (who can?) silence scandal,   535
At least she left it a more slender handle.

---

76   *the aerial bow* rainbow.
77   *mi vien in mente* 'it occurs to me'.
78   *clay* i.e. flesh.
79   *The flesh is frail* Matthew 26:41: 'the spirit indeed is willing, but the flesh is weak'.

80   St Francis had a 'wife of snow', according to Jacobus de Voragine's *Golden Legend*, which included the 'Life of St Francis'.
81   *mulct* penalty.
82   *carriage* social behaviour, conduct.

68

I can't tell whether Julia saw the affair
    With other people's eyes, or if her own
Discoveries made, but none could be aware
    Of this; at least no symptom e'er was shown.   540
Perhaps she did not know, or did not care,
    Indifferent from the first, or callous grown;
I'm really puzzled what to think or say –
She kept her counsel in so close a way.

69

Juan she saw and, as a pretty child,   545
    Caressed him often – such a thing might be
Quite innocently done, and harmless styled,
    When she had twenty years and thirteen he;
But I am not so sure I should have smiled
    When he was sixteen, Julia twenty-three   550
(These few short years make wondrous alterations,
Particularly amongst sunburnt nations).

70

Whate'er the cause might be, they had become
    Changed; for the dame grew distant, the youth shy,
Their looks cast down, their greetings almost
                         dumb,   555
    And much embarrassment in either eye.
There surely will be little doubt with some
    That Donna Julia knew the reason why;
But as for Juan, he had no more notion
Than he who never saw the sea of ocean.   560

71

Yet Julia's very coldness still was kind,
    And tremulously gentle her small hand
Withdrew itself from his, but left behind
    A little pressure, thrilling, and so bland[83]
And slight, so very slight, that to the mind   565
    'Twas but a doubt – but ne'er magician's wand
Wrought change with all Armida's[84] fairy art
Like what this light touch left on Juan's heart.

72

And if she met him, though she smiled no more,
    She looked a sadness sweeter than her smile,   570
As if her heart had deeper thoughts in store
    She must not own, but cherished more the while,
For that compression in its burning core;
    Even innocence itself has many a wile
And will not dare to trust itself with truth –   575
And love is taught hypocrisy from youth.

73

But passion most dissembles yet betrays
    Even by its darkness; as the blackest sky
Foretells the heaviest tempest, it displays
    Its workings through the vainly guarded eye,   580
And in whatever aspect it arrays
    Itself, 'tis still the same hypocrisy;
Coldness or anger, even disdain or hate
Are masks it often wears, and still too late.

74

Then there were sighs, the deeper for suppression,   585
    And stolen glances, sweeter for the theft,
And burning blushes, though for no transgression,
    Tremblings when met, and restlessness when left;
All these are little preludes to possession
    Of which young passion cannot be bereft,   590
And merely tend to show how greatly love is
Embarrassed at first starting with a novice.

75

Poor Julia's heart was in an awkward state –
    She felt it going, and resolved to make
The noblest efforts for herself and mate,   595
    For honour's, pride's, religion's, virtue's sake;
Her resolutions were most truly great
    And almost might have made a Tarquin quake;[85]
She prayed the Virgin Mary for her grace,
As being the best judge of a lady's case.   600

---

[83] *bland* soothing.
[84] Armida is the sorceress in Tasso, *Jerusalem Delivered*, who ensnares the hero, Rinaldo.

[85] *Her resolutions ... quake* the comparison is with Lucretia, legendary heroine of ancient Rome, the beautiful and virtuous wife of the nobleman Lucius Tarquinius Collatinus. She was raped by Sextus Tarquinius, and later stabbed herself to death.

76

She vowed she never would see Juan more
 And next day paid a visit to his mother,
And looked extremely at the opening door
 Which, by the Virgin's grace, let in another;
Grateful she was, and yet a little sore; 605
 Again it opens, it can be no other,
'Tis surely Juan now – no! I'm afraid
That night the Virgin was no further prayed.

77

She now determined that a virtuous woman
 Should rather face and overcome temptation, 610
That flight was base and dastardly, and no man
 Should ever give her heart the least sensation –
That is to say, a thought beyond the common
 Preference, that we must feel upon occasion
For people who are pleasanter than others, 615
But then they only seem so many brothers.

78

And even if by chance (and who can tell?
 The Devil's so very sly) she should discover
That all within was not so very well,
 And if still free, that such or such a lover 620
Might please perhaps, a virtuous wife can quell
 Such thoughts and be the better when they're over;
And if the man should ask, 'tis but denial:
I recommend young ladies to make trial.

79

And then there are things such as love divine, 625
 Bright and immaculate, unmixed and pure,
Such as the angels think so very fine,
 And matrons who would be no less secure,
Platonic, perfect, 'just such love as mine',
 Thus Julia said, and thought so, to be sure – 630
And so I'd have her think, were I the man
On whom her reveries celestial ran.

80

Such love is innocent, and may exist
 Between young persons without any danger;
A hand may first, and then a lip be kissed – 635
 For my part, to such doings I'm a stranger,
But *hear* these freedoms form the utmost list[86]
 Of all o'er which such love may be a ranger;
If people go beyond, 'tis quite a crime
But not my fault – I tell them all in time. 640

81

Love then, but love within its proper limits
 Was Julia's innocent determination
In young Don Juan's favour, and to him its
 Exertion might be useful on occasion;
And lighted at too pure a shrine to dim its 645
 Ethereal lustre, with what sweet persuasion
He might be taught by love and her together –
I really don't know what, nor Julia either.

82

Fraught with this fine intention, and well-fenced[87]
 In mail of proof[88] – her purity of soul, 650
She, for the future of her strength convinced,
 And that her honour was a rock, or mole,[89]
Exceeding sagely from that hour dispensed
 With any kind of troublesome control;
But whether Julia to the task was equal 655
Is that which must be mentioned in the sequel.[90]

83

Her plan she deemed both innocent and feasible,
 And surely with a stripling of sixteen
Not scandal's fangs could fix on much that's seizable,
 Or if they did so, satisfied to mean 660
Nothing but what was good, her breast was peaceable –
 A quiet conscience makes one so serene!
Christians have burnt each other, quite persuaded
That all the Apostles would have done as they did.

---

86 *list* territory.
87 *well-fenced* well-protected.
88 *mail of proof* good-quality chain mail; but the usage is metaphorical.

89 *mole* great immoveable mass.
90 *the sequel* i.e. what follows.

84

And if in the meantime her husband died –   665
    But heaven forbid that such a thought should cross
Her brain, though in a dream! And then she sighed;
    Never could she survive that common loss,
But just suppose that moment should betide –
    I only say suppose it, *inter nos*[91]   670
(This should be *entre nous*, for Julia thought
In French, but then the rhyme would go for nought),

85

I only say suppose this supposition:
    Juan being then grown up to man's estate[92]
Would fully suit a widow of condition[93] –   675
    Even seven years hence it would not be too late;
And in the interim (to pursue this vision)
    The mischief, after all, could not be great,
For he would learn the rudiments of love
(I mean the seraph[94] way of those above).   680

86

So much for Julia. Now we'll turn to Juan –
    Poor little fellow, he had no idea
Of his own case, and never hit the true one;
    In feelings quick as Ovid's Miss Medea[95]
He puzzled over what he found a new one,   685
    But not as yet imagined it could be a
Thing quite in course, and not at all alarming
Which, with a little patience, might grow charming.

87

Silent and pensive, idle, restless, slow,
    His home deserted for the lonely wood,   690
Tormented with a wound he could not know,
    His, like all deep grief, plunged in solitude;
I'm fond myself of solitude or so,
    But then I beg it may be understood –
By solitude I mean a sultan's, not   695
A hermit's, with a harem for a grot.

88

'Oh love, in such a wilderness as this,
    Where transport and security entwine,
Here is the empire of thy perfect bliss,
    And here thou art a god indeed divine!'[96]   700
The bard I quote from does not sing amiss,
    With the exception of the second line –
For that same twining 'transport and security'
Are twisted to a phrase of some obscurity.

89

The poet meant, no doubt (and thus appeals   705
    To the good sense and senses of mankind),
The very thing which everybody feels,
    As all have found on trial, or may find –
That no one likes to be disturbed at meals
    Or love. I won't say more about 'entwined'   710
Or 'transport', as we knew all that before,
But beg 'security' will bolt the door.

90

Young Juan wandered by the glassy brooks
    Thinking unutterable things; he threw
Himself at length within the leafy nooks   715
    Where the wild branch of the cork forest grew;
There poets find materials for their books,
    And every now and then we read them through
So that[97] their plan and prosody are eligible –
Unless, like Wordsworth, they prove unintelligible.   720

91

He, Juan (and not Wordsworth),[98] so pursued
    His self-communion with his own high soul,
Until his mighty heart[99] in its great mood
    Had mitigated part (though not the whole)

---

[91] *inter nos* between us.
[92] *man's estate* i.e. manhood.
[93] *of condition* of quality.
[94] Seraphs are angels whose purpose is to adore God.
[95] *Ovid's Miss Medea* Medea felt a sudden, overpowering love for Jason, leader of the famous Argonauts, in Ovid, *Metamorphoses* vii 9–10.
[96] Campbell, *Gertrude of Wyoming* iii 1–4.

[97] *So that* so long as.
[98] *and not Wordsworth* somewhat disingenuous, as Byron is using Juan's love-sickness to burlesque Wordsworthian responses to nature.
[99] *mighty heart* the phrase is borrowed from Wordsworth, *Composed upon Westminster Bridge, 3 September 1802* 14: 'And all that mighty heart is lying still'.

Of its disease; he did the best he could   725
    With things not very subject to control,
And turned, without perceiving his condition,
Like Coleridge, into a metaphysician.

                            92

He thought about himself, and the whole earth,
    Of man the wonderful, and of the stars,   730
And how the deuce they ever could have birth;
    And then he thought of earthquakes and of wars,
How many miles the moon might have in girth,
    Of air-balloons,[100] and of the many bars[101]
To perfect knowledge of the boundless skies –   735
And then he thought of Donna Julia's eyes.

                            93

In thoughts like these true wisdom may discern
    Longings sublime and aspirations high,
Which some are born with, but the most part learn
    To plague themselves withal, they know not
                                        why;   740
'Twas strange that one so young should thus concern
    His brain about the action of the sky:
If you think 'twas philosophy that this did,
I can't help thinking puberty assisted.

                            94

He pored upon the leaves and on the flowers,   745
    And heard a voice in all the winds; and then
He thought of wood-nymphs and immortal bowers,
    And how the goddesses came down to men:
He missed the pathway, he forgot the hours,
    And when he looked upon his watch again,   750
He found how much old Time had been a winner –
He also found that he had lost his dinner.

                            95

Sometimes he turned to gaze upon his book,
    Boscan or Garcilasso;[102] by the wind
Even as the page is rustled while we look,   755

So by the poesy of his own mind
Over the mystic leaf his soul was shook,
    As if 'twere one whereon magicians bind
Their spells, and give them to the passing gale,
According to some good old woman's tale.   760

                            96

Thus would he while his lonely hours away
    Dissatisfied, nor knowing what he wanted;
Nor[103] glowing reverie, nor poet's lay
    Could yield his spirit that for which it panted,
A bosom whereon he his head might lay,   765
    And hear the heart beat with the love it granted,
With – several other things which I forget,
Or which, at least, I need not mention yet.

                            97

Those lonely walks and lengthening reveries
    Could not escape the gentle Julia's eyes;   770
She saw that Juan was not at his ease;
    But that which chiefly may, and must surprise
Is that the Donna Inez did not tease
    Her only son with question or surmise –
Whether it was she did not see or would not,   775
Or like all very clever people, could not.

                            98

This may seem strange, but yet 'tis very common;
    For instance, gentlemen, whose ladies take
Leave to o'erstep the written rights of woman,
    And break the – which commandment is't
                                they break?[104]   780
I have forgot the number, and think no man
    Should rashly quote, for fear of a mistake.
I say, when these same gentlemen are jealous,
They make some blunder which their ladies tell us.

                            99

A real husband always is suspicious,   785
    But still no less suspects in the wrong place,

---

[100]   *air-balloons* hot-air balloons were the invention of Joseph
Michel Montgolfier, 1783. They were all the rage across Europe
at this time.
[101]   *bars* barriers.
[102]   *Boscan or Garcilasso* Juan Boscán Almogáver (d. *c.*1543) and
Garcilaso de la Vega, sixteenth-century Spanish poets who intro-

duced Italian features into their literature through their imita-
tions of Petrarch.
[103]   *Nor* neither.
[104]   *which commandment is't they break* 'Thou shalt not commit
adultery' (Exodus 20:14).

Jealous of someone who had no such wishes,[105]
   Or pandering blindly to his own disgrace
By harbouring some dear friend extremely vicious[106] –
   The last indeed's infallibly the case,   790
And when the spouse and friend are gone off wholly,[107]
He wonders at their vice, and not his folly.

100

Thus parents also are at times short-sighted;
   Though watchful as the lynx, they ne'er discover
(The while the wicked world beholds delighted)   795
   Young Hopeful's mistress or Miss Fanny's lover,
Till some confounded escapade has blighted
   The plan of twenty years, and all is over;
And then the mother cries, the father swears,
And wonders why the devil he got[108] heirs.   800

101

But Inez was so anxious and so clear
   Of sight, that I must think on this occasion
She had some other motive much more near
   For leaving Juan to this new temptation;
But what that motive was I shan't say here –   805
   Perhaps to finish Juan's education,
Perhaps to open Don Alfonso's eyes
In case he thought his wife too great a prize.

102

It was upon a day, a summer's day –
   Summer's indeed a very dangerous season,   810
And so is spring about the end of May;
   The sun, no doubt, is the prevailing reason;
But whatsoe'er the cause is, one may say
   (And stand convicted of more truth than treason),
That there are months which nature grows more
               merry in;   815
March has its hares, and May must have its heroine.

103

'Twas on a summer's day, the sixth of June –
   I like to be particular in dates,

Not only of the age and year, but moon;
   They are a sort of post-house[109] where the
               Fates[110]   820
Change horses, making history change its tune,
   Then spur away o'er empires and o'er states,
Leaving at last not much besides chronology,
Excepting the post-obits[111] of theology.

104

'Twas on the sixth of June, about the hour   825
   Of half-past six – perhaps still nearer seven,
When Julia sat within as pretty a bower
   As e'er held houri[112] in that heathenish heaven
Described by Mahomet and 'Anacreon' Moore –[113]
   To whom the lyre and laurels have been given   830
With all the trophies of triumphant song;
He won them well, and may he wear them long!

105

She sat, but not alone; I know not well
   How this same interview had taken place,
And even if I knew, I should not tell –   835
   People should hold their tongues in any case;
No matter how or why the thing befell,
   But there were she and Juan, face to face –
When two such faces are so, 'twould be wise
(But very difficult) to shut their eyes.   840

106

How beautiful she looked! Her conscious heart
   Glowed in her cheek, and yet she felt no wrong.
Oh love, how perfect is thy mystic art,
   Strengthening the weak, and trampling on the
               strong;
How self-deceitful is the sagest part   845
   Of mortals whom thy lure hath led along;
The precipice she stood on was immense –
So was her creed[114] in her own innocence.

---

[105] *no such wishes* i.e. to commit adultery.
[106] *vicious* immoral. The husband makes the mistake of unwittingly welcoming a friend who is having an affair with his wife.
[107] *are gone off wholly* i.e. have run away together.
[108] *got* begot.
[109] *post-house* inn where horses are kept for the use of travellers.
[110] In Greek myth, the Fates were three goddesses who determined the course of human life.

[111] *post-obits* legacies.
[112] *houri* nymph of the Muslim heaven.
[113] *'Anacreon' Moore* Thomas Moore translated Anacreon's *Odes* (1800). It was one of his most successful publications.
[114] *creed* belief.

107

She thought of her own strength,[115] and Juan's youth,
   And of the folly of all prudish fears,   850
Victorious virtue and domestic truth –
   And then of Don Alfonso's fifty years:
I wish these last had not occurred, in sooth,
   Because that number rarely much endears,
And through all climes, the snowy and the sunny,   855
Sounds ill in love, whate'er it may in money.

108

When people say, 'I've told you *fifty* times',
   They mean to scold, and very often do;
When poets say, 'I've written *fifty* rhymes',
   They make you dread that they'll recite them too;   860
In gangs of *fifty*, thieves commit their crimes;
   At *fifty* love for love is rare, 'tis true –
But then, no doubt, it equally as true is,
A good deal may be bought for *fifty* louis.[116]

109

Julia had honour, virtue, truth and love   865
   For Don Alfonso, and she inly swore
By all the vows below to powers above
   She never would disgrace the ring she wore,
Nor leave a wish which wisdom might reprove;
   And while she pondered this, besides much more,   870
One hand on Juan's carelessly was thrown
Quite by mistake – she thought it was her own;

110

Unconsciously she leaned upon the other
   Which played within the tangles of her hair;[117]
And to contend with thoughts she could not
                    smother, 875
   She seemed by the distraction of her air.
'Twas surely very wrong in Juan's mother
   To leave together this imprudent pair,
She who for many years had watched her son so –
I'm very certain *mine* would not have done so.   880

111

The hand which still held Juan's, by degrees
   Gently but palpably confirmed its grasp,
As if it said 'detain me, if you please';
   Yet there's no doubt she only meant to clasp
His fingers with a pure Platonic squeeze;   885
   She would have shrunk as from a toad or asp
Had she imagined such a thing could rouse
A feeling dangerous to a prudent spouse.

112

I cannot know what Juan thought of this,
   But what he did is much what you would do;   890
His young lip thanked it with a grateful kiss,
   And then, abashed at its own joy, withdrew
In deep despair lest he had done amiss –
   Love is so very timid when 'tis new;
She blushed and frowned not, but she strove to
                     speak 895
And held her tongue, her voice was grown so weak.

113

The sun set and uprose the yellow moon –
   The devil's in the moon for mischief; they
Who called her chaste, methinks began too soon
   Their nomenclature;[118] there is not a day,   900
The longest, not the twenty-first of June,
   Sees half the business in a wicked way
On which three single hours of moonshine smile –
And then she looks so modest all the while.

114

There is a dangerous silence in that hour,
   A stillness which leaves room for the full soul
To open all itself, without the power
   Of calling wholly back its self-control;
The silver light which, hallowing tree and tower,
   Sheds beauty and deep softness o'er the whole,   910
Breathes also to the heart, and o'er it throws
A loving languor which is not repose.

---

[115] *strength* i.e. moral strength.
[116] *louis* gold coin issued in the reign of Louis XIII and subsequently till the time of Louis XVI.

[117] *Which played . . . hair* cf. *Lycidas* 68–9: 'To sport with Amaryllis in the shade, / Or with the tangles of Neaera's hair?'
[118] *nomenclature* act of naming things.

115

And Julia sat with Juan, half-embraced
    And half-retiring from the glowing arm,
Which trembled like the bosom where 'twas
                    placed;   *915*
    Yet still she must have thought there was no harm,
Or else 'twere easy to withdraw her waist;
    But then the situation had its charm,
And then – God knows what next – I can't go on;
I'm almost sorry that I e'er begun.   *920*

116

Oh Plato! Plato! You have paved the way,
    With your confounded fantasies, to more
Immoral conduct by the fancied sway
    Your system feigns o'er the controlless core
Of human hearts, than all the long array   *925*
    Of poets and romancers – you're a bore,
A charlatan, a coxcomb, and have been
At best no better than a go-between.

117

And Julia's voice was lost except in sighs,
    Until too late for useful conversation;   *930*
The tears were gushing from her gentle eyes –
    I wish, indeed, they had not had occasion,
But who, alas, can love, and then be wise?
    Not that remorse did not oppose temptation,
A little still she strove, and much repented,   *935*
And whispering 'I will ne'er consent' – consented.

118

'Tis said that Xerxes[119] offered a reward
    To those who could invent him a new pleasure –
Methinks the requisition's rather hard
    And must have cost his majesty a treasure;   *940*
For my part, I'm a moderate-minded bard,
    Fond of a little love (which I call leisure);
I care not for new pleasures, as the old
Are quite enough for me, so they but hold.

119

Oh pleasure, you're indeed a pleasant thing,   *945*
    Although one must be damned for you, no doubt;
I make a resolution every spring
    Of reformation, ere the year run out;
But somehow, this my vestal vow[120] takes wing,
    Yet still, I trust, it may be kept throughout: *950*
I'm very sorry, very much ashamed,
And mean, next winter, to be quite reclaimed.

120

Here my chaste muse a liberty must take –
    Start not, still chaster reader! She'll be nice hence-
Forward, and there is no great cause to quake;   *955*
    This liberty is a poetic licence,
Which some irregularity may make
    In the design, and as I have a high sense
Of Aristotle and the rules,[121] 'tis fit
To beg his pardon when I err a bit.   *960*

121

This licence is to hope the reader will
    Suppose from June the sixth (the fatal day
Without whose epoch my poetic skill
    For want of facts would all be thrown away),
But keeping Julia and Don Juan still   *965*
    In sight, that several months have passed; we'll say
'Twas in November, but I'm not so sure
About the day – the era's more obscure.

122

We'll talk of that anon. 'Tis sweet to hear
    At midnight on the blue and moonlit deep   *970*
The song and oar of Adria's[122] gondolier
    By distance mellowed, o'er the waters sweep;
'Tis sweet to see the evening star appear;
    'Tis sweet to listen as the nightwinds creep
From leaf to leaf; 'tis sweet to view on high   *975*
The rainbow, based on ocean, span the sky;

---

[119] Xerxes I, king who fought in the Persian Wars, 485–80
BC. Montaigne wrote that he was 'wrapped in all human plea-
sures . . . [and] offered a prize to anyone who would find him
others' ('Of Experience').

[120]   *vestal vow* vow of chastity.
[121]   *the rules* i.e. of rhetoric.
[122]   *Adria* Venice.

123

'Tis sweet to hear the watchdog's honest bark
   Bay deep-mouthed welcome as we draw near home;
'Tis sweet to know there is an eye will mark
   Our coming, and look brighter when we come; 980
'Tis sweet to be awkened by the lark
   Or lulled by falling waters; sweet the hum
Of bees, the voice of girls, the song of birds,
The lisp of children and their earliest words;

124

Sweet is the vintage, when the showering grapes 985
   In Bacchanal profusion[123] reel to earth
Purple and gushing; sweet are our escapes
   From civic revelry to rural mirth;
Sweet to the miser are his glittering heaps;
   Sweet to the father is his first-born's birth; 990
Sweet is revenge – especially to women,
Pillage to soldiers, prize-money[124] to seamen;

125

Sweet is a legacy, and passing sweet
   The unexpected death of some old lady
Or gentleman of seventy years complete, 995
   Who've made 'us youth'[125] wait too too long already
For an estate or cash or country-seat,
   Still breaking, but with stamina so steady,
That all the Israelites[126] are fit to mob its
Next owner for their double-damned post-obits.[127] 1000

126

'Tis sweet to win (no matter how) one's laurels
   By blood or ink; 'tis sweet to put an end
To strife; 'tis sometimes sweet to have our quarrels,
   Particularly with a tiresome friend;
Sweet is old wine in bottles, ale in barrels; 1005
   Dear is the helpless creature we defend

Against the world; and dear the schoolboy spot
We ne'er forget, though there we are forgot.

127

But sweeter still than this, than these, than all,
   Is first and passionate love – it stands alone 1010
Like Adam's recollection of his fall;
   The tree of knowledge has been plucked, all's known,
And life yields nothing further to recall
   Worthy of this ambrosial[128] sin, so shown
No doubt in fable, as the unforgiven 1015
Fire which Prometheus filched for us from heaven.

128

Man's a strange animal, and makes strange use
   Of his own nature and the various arts,[129]
And likes particularly to produce
   Some new experiment to show his parts;[130] 1020
This is the age of oddities let loose,
   Where different talents find their different marts;
You'd best begin with truth, and when you've lost your
Labour, there's a sure market for imposture.

129

What opposite discoveries we have seen 1025
   (Signs of true genius, and of empty pockets)!
One makes new noses, one a guillotine,
   One breaks your bones, one sets them in their sockets;
But vaccination certainly has been
   A kind antithesis to Congreve's rockets, 1030
With which the doctor paid off an old pox
By borrowing a new one from an ox.[131]

130

Bread has been made (indifferent) from potatoes,
   And galvanism has set some corpses grinning,
But has not answered like the apparatus 1035

---

[123] *Bacchanal profusion* Bacchus was the Roman name for the god of wine. The individual grapes are, by implication, like drunken revellers.
[124] *prize-money* proceeds from the sale of a captured ship, distributed among the captors.
[125] 'They hate us youth'; Falstaff, *1 Henry IV* II ii 93.
[126] *Israelites* i.e. money-lenders.
[127] *post-obits* in this case, money owed to them by the deceased, for which the heir is liable.

[128] *ambrosial* divine; Prometheus was one of the Titans of Greek myth.
[129] *arts* skills, abilities.
[130] *parts* as McGann notes, an obscene pun.
[131] The American quack doctor Benjamin Charles Perkins made new noses; Sir William Congreve (1772–1828) invented an artillery shell, first used against the French in the Battle of Leipzig (1813); Edward Jenner (1749–1823) first vaccinated against smallpox in 1796.

Of the Humane Society's beginning,
By which men are unsuffocated gratis;
    What wondrous new machines have late been
                    spinning![132]
I said the smallpox has gone out of late,
Perhaps it may be followed by the great.[133]   1040

131

'Tis said the great came from America,
    Perhaps it may set out on its return;
The population there so spreads, they say,
    'Tis grown high time to thin it in its turn
With war or plague or famine, any way,   1045
    So that civilization they may learn,
And which in ravage the more loathsome evil is:
Their real lues,[134] or our pseudo-syphilis?

132

This is the patent-age of new inventions
    For killing bodies and for saving souls,[135]   1050
All propagated with the best intentions:
    Sir Humphry Davy's lantern,[136] by which coals
Are safely mined for in the mode he mentions;
    Tombuctoo travels, voyages to the Poles
Are ways to benefit mankind, as true,   1055
Perhaps, as shooting them at Waterloo.

133

Man's a phenomenon, one knows not what,
    And wonderful beyond all wondrous measure;
'Tis pity though, in this sublime world, that
    Pleasure's a sin, and sometimes sin's a pleasure; *1060*
Few mortals know what end[137] they would be at,
    But whether glory, power, or love or treasure,
The path is through perplexing ways, and when
The goal is gained, we die, you know – and then –

134

What then? I do not know, no more do you –   *1065*
    And so goodnight. Return we to our story:
'Twas in November when fine days are few,
    And the far mountains wax[138] a little hoary
And clap a white cape on their mantles blue;
    And the sea dashes round the promontory,   *1070*
And the loud breaker boils against the rock,
And sober suns must set at five o'clock.

135

'Twas, as the watchmen say, a cloudy night;
    No moon, no stars, the wind was low or loud
By gusts, and many a sparkling hearth was bright *1075*
    With the piled wood round which the family crowd;
There's something cheerful in that sort of light,
    Even as a summer sky's without a cloud –
I'm fond of fire and crickets, and all that,
A lobster-salad, and champagne, and chat.   *1080*

136

'Twas midnight; Donna Julia was in bed –
    Sleeping, most probably – when at her door
Arose a clatter might awake the dead
    (If they had never been awoke before,
And that they have been so we all have read,   *1085*
    And are to be so, at the least, once more);[139]
The door was fastened, but with voice and fist
First knocks were heard, then 'Madam, madam – hist!

137

For God's sake, madam – madam, here's my master
    With more than half the city at his back;   *1090*
Was ever heard of such a cursed disaster!
    'Tis not my fault, I kept good watch – alack!

---

[132] Luigi Galvani used electricity to attempt to restore corpses to life (an inspiration for Mary Shelley's *Frankenstein*), as well as for therapeutic purposes (first described 1792); the Humane Society was founded 1774, for the rescue of drowning persons (the 'apparatus' is a resuscitator); the spinning-jenny was patented by James Hargreaves, 1770.

[133] *the great* syphilis.

[134] *lues* syphilis.

[135] *saving souls* probably a reference to the British and Foreign Bible Society, founded 1804, which published and distributed cheap bibles around the world. It is still going strong.

[136] Davy (1778–1829), friend of Wordsworth, Coleridge, Scott and Byron, not only wrote poetry but invented the miner's safety-lamp, 1815.

[137] *end* an obscene pun.

[138] *wax* become.

[139] A reference to I Corinthians 15:51–2, which prophecies that 'the dead shall be raised incorruptible'. It is typical of Byron to belittle this notion by relegating it to a parenthesis.

Do pray undo the bolt a little faster;
    They're on the stair just now, and in a crack[140]
Will all be here – perhaps he yet may fly;   1095
Surely the window's not so *very* high!'

138

By this time Don Alfonso was arrived
    With torches, friends and servants in great number;
The major part of them had long been wived,
    And therefore paused not[141] to disturb the
                  slumber   1100
Of any wicked woman who contrived
    By stealth her husband's temples to encumber;[142]
Examples of this kind are so contagious,
Were *one* not punished, *all* would be outrageous.

139

I can't tell how or why or what suspicion   1105
    Could enter into Don Alfonso's head,
But for a cavalier of his condition[143]
    It surely was exceedingly ill-bred,
Without a word of previous admonition,
    To hold a levee[144] round his lady's bed   1110
And summon lackeys armed with fire and sword,
To prove himself the thing he most abhorred.[145]

140

Poor Donna Julia! Starting as from sleep
    (Mind that I do not say she had not slept)
Began at once to scream and yawn and weep;   1115
    Her maid Antonia, who was an adept,
Contrived to fling the bedclothes in a heap,
    As if she had just now from out them crept –
I can't tell why she should take all this trouble
To prove her mistress had been sleeping double.   1120

141

But Julia mistress, and Antonia maid,
    Appeared like two poor harmless women who

Of goblins, but still more of men afraid,
    Had thought one man might be deterred by two,
And therefore side by side were gently laid   1125
    Until the hours of absence should run through,
And truant husband should return and say,
'My dear, I was the first who came away.'

142

Now Julia found at length a voice, and cried,
    'In Heaven's name, Don Alfonso, what d'ye
                  mean?   1130
Has madness seized you? Would that I had died
    Ere such a monster's victim I had been!
What may this midnight violence betide?
    A sudden fit of drunkenness or spleen?
Dare you suspect me, whom the thought would
                  kill?   1135
Search then the room!' Alfonso said, 'I will.'

143

He searched, *they* searched, and rummaged everywhere,
    Closet and clothes-press, chest and window-seat,
And found much linen, lace, and several pair
    Of stockings, slippers, brushes, combs,
                  complete   1140
With other articles of ladies fair,
    To keep them beautiful or leave them neat;
Arras they pricked,[146] and curtains with their swords,
And wounded several shutters and some boards.

144

Under the bed they searched, and there they
                  found –   1145
    No matter what, it was not that they sought;
They opened windows, gazing if the ground
    Had signs or footmarks, but the earth said nought;
And then they stared each others' faces round:
    'Tis odd not one of all these seekers thought   1150
(And seems to me almost a sort of blunder)
Of looking *in* the bed as well as under.

---

[140] *in a crack* immediately.
[141] *paused not* did not hesitate.
[142] *her husband's temples to encumber* horns sprout on the foreheads of cuckolded husbands.
[143] *a cavalier of his condition* a gentleman of his rank.

[144] *levee* a social meeting held immediately on rising from bed; Don Alfonso has not even allowed his wife the opportunity to get up.
[145] *the thing he most abhorred* i.e. a cuckold.
[146] *Arras they pricked* i.e. they poked the hanging tapestry with their swords.

145

During this inquisition Julia's tongue
    Was not asleep: 'Yes, search and search', she
      cried,
'Insult on insult heap, and wrong on wrong!   *1155*
    It was for this that I became a bride!
For this in silence I have suffered long
    A husband like Alfonso at my side;
But now I'll bear no more, nor here remain,
If there be law or lawyers in all Spain.   *1160*

146

Yes, Don Alfonso, husband now no more
    (If ever you indeed deserved the name)!
Is't worthy of your years? You have threescore,
    Fifty or sixty (it is all the same),
Is't wise or fitting causeless to explore   *1165*
    For facts against a virtuous woman's fame?
Ungrateful, perjured, barbarous Don Alfonso –
How dare you think your lady would go on so?

147

Is it for this I have disdained to hold
    The common privileges of my sex? –[147]   *1170*
That I have chosen a confessor so old
    And deaf, that any other it would vex,
And never once he has had cause to scold,
    But found my very innocence perplex
So much, he always doubted I was married?   *1175*
How sorry you will be when I've miscarried![148]

148

Was it for this that no cortejo ere
    I yet have chosen from out the youth of Seville?

Is it for this I scarce went anywhere
    Except to bullfights, mass, play, rout[149] and
      revel?   *1180*
Is it for this, whate'er my suitors were,
    I favoured none – nay, was almost uncivil?
Is it for this that General Count O'Reilly,
Who took Algiers,[150] declares I used him vilely?

149

Did not the Italian musico Cazzani[151]   *1185*
    Sing at my heart six months at least in vain?
Did not his countryman, Count Corniani,[152]
    Call me the only virtuous wife in Spain?
Were there not also Russians, English, many?
    The Count Strongstroganoff[153] I put in pain,   *1190*
And Lord Mount Coffeehouse, the Irish peer,[154]
Who killed himself for love (with wine) last year.

150

Have I not had two bishops at my feet,
    The Duke of Ichar, and Don Fernan Nunez?
And is it thus a faithful wife you treat?   *1195*
    I wonder in what quarter now the moon is;[155]
I praise your vast forbearance not to beat
    Me also, since the time so opportune is –
Oh valiant man, with sword drawn and cocked trigger,
Now tell me, don't you cut a pretty figure?   *1200*

151

Was it for this you took your sudden journey
    Under pretence of business indispensable
With that sublime of rascals, your attorney,
    Whom I see standing there, and looking sensible[156]
Of having played the fool? Though both I spurn,
      he   *1205*

---

[147] *The common privileges of my sex* i.e. to take a lover (or 'cortejo').
[148] *when I've miscarried* i.e. when you've lost me.
[149] *rout* party.
[150] 'Donna Julia here made a mistake. Count O'Reilly did not take Algiers – but Algiers very nearly took him. He and his army and fleet retreated with great loss, and not much credit, from before that city in the year 1775' (Byron's note). The Irish-born Spanish general Alexander O'Reilly (?1722–94) was governor of Madrid and later Cadiz. The unsuccessful assault on Algiers was mounted in 1775.
[151] *musico* musician. Cazzani is an obscene pun on 'cazzo' (penis).

[152] Corniani derives from 'cornuto' (horned, cuckolded).
[153] *Count Strongstroganoff* Count Alexander Stroganov was a fellow reveller of Byron's in Venice.
[154] This is a disdainful reference to the peerages created by the Act of Union between Ireland and England in 1801, for which Byron's *bête noire*, Castlereagh, had been largely responsible. The Mount was a coffeehouse near Grosvenor Square, London.
[155] *I wonder in what quarter now the moon is* i.e. because a full moon would explain why Don Alfonso is behaving like a lunatic.
[156] *sensible* aware.

Deserves the worst, his conduct's less defensible,
Because, no doubt, 'twas for his dirty fee,
And not from any love to you nor me.

152

If he comes here to take a deposition,[157]
    By all means let the gentleman proceed –   *1210*
You've made the apartment in a fit condition!
    There's pen and ink for you, sir, when you need;
Let everything be noted with precision
    (I would not you for nothing should be feed);[158]
But as my maid's undressed, pray turn your spies
              out.' *1215*
'Oh!' sobbed Antonia, 'I could tear their eyes out!'

153

'There is the closet,[159] there the toilet,[160] there
    The antechamber[161] – search them under, over;
There is the sofa, there the great armchair,
    The chimney (which would really hold a
              lover). *1220*
I wish to sleep, and beg you will take care
    And make no further noise, till you discover
The secret cavern of this lurking treasure –
And when 'tis found, let me, too, have that pleasure.

154

And now, hidalgo, now that you have thrown *1225*
    Doubt upon me, confusion over all,[162]
Pray have the courtesy to make it known
    Who is the man you search for? How d'ye call
Him? What's his lineage? Let him but be shown;
    I hope he's young and handsome – is he tall? *1230*
Tell me, and be assured that since you stain
My honour thus, it shall not be in vain.

155

At least, perhaps, he has not sixty years –
    At that age he would be too old for slaughter
Or for so young a husband's jealous fears! *1235*

Antonia, let me have a glass of water;
I am ashamed of having shed these tears,
    They are unworthy of my father's daughter;
My mother dreamed not in my natal hour[163]
That I should fall into a monster's power. *1240*

156

Perhaps 'tis of Antonia you are jealous –
    You saw that she was sleeping by my side
When you broke in upon us with your fellows;
    Look where you please, we've nothing, sir, to hide;
Only another time, I trust, you'll tell us, *1245*
    Or for the sake of decency abide
A moment at the door, that we may be
Dressed to receive so much good company.

157

And now, sir, I have done, and say no more;
    The little I have said may serve to show *1250*
The guileless heart in silence may grieve o'er
    The wrongs to whose exposure it is slow;
I leave you to your conscience as before –
    'Twill one day ask you *why* you used me so?
God grant you feel not then the bitterest grief! *1255*
Antonia, where's my pocket-handkerchief?'

158

She ceased, and turned upon her pillow; pale
    She lay, her dark eyes flashing through their tears
Like skies that rain and lighten; as a veil,
    Waved and o'ershading her wan cheek, appears *1260*
Her streaming hair; the black curls strive but fail
    To hide the glossy shoulder, which uprears
Its snow through all; her soft lips lie apart,
And louder than her breathing beats her heart.

159

The *señor* Don Alfonso stood confused; *1265*
    Antonia bustled round the ransacked room
And, turning up her nose, with looks abused

---

[157] *deposition* statement for use as evidence.
[158] *I would not you for nothing should be feed* I would not want
you to be paid ('feed') for doing nothing.
[159] *closet* private apartment.
[160] *toilet* table on which toilet articles are placed.

[161] *antechamber* waiting-room.
[162] *confusion over all* an echo of the final line of Pope's *Dunciad*:
'And universal darkness buries all.'
[163] *my natal hour* hour of my birth.

Her master and his myrmidons,[164] of whom
Not one, except the attorney, was amused;
   He, like Achates,[165] faithful to the tomb,   *1270*
So[166] there were quarrels, cared not for the cause,
Knowing they must be settled by the laws.

160

With prying snubnose and small eyes he stood,
   Following Antonia's motions here and there
With much suspicion in his attitude;   *1275*
   For reputations he had little care,
So that a suit or action were made good;
   Small pity had he for the young and fair,
And ne'er believed in negatives, till these
Were proved by competent false witnesses.   *1280*

161

But Don Alfonso stood with downcast looks,
   And, truth to say, he made a foolish figure –
When after searching in five hundred nooks,
   And treating a young wife with so much rigour,
He gained no point except some self-rebukes,   *1285*
   Added to those his lady with such vigour
Had poured upon him for the last half-hour,
Quick, thick, and heavy, as a thunder-shower.

162

At first he tried to hammer an excuse
   To which the sole reply were tears and sobs   *1290*
And indications of hysterics, whose
   Prologue is always certain throes and throbs,
Gasps and whatever else the owners choose;
   Alfonso saw his wife and thought of Job's;[167]
He saw too, in perspective,[168] her relations,   *1295*
And then he tried to muster all his patience.

163

He stood in act to speak, or rather stammer,
   But sage Antonia cut him short before

The anvil of his speech received the hammer,
   With, 'Pray sir, leave the room, and say no
                       more,   *1300*
Or madam dies.' Alfonso muttered, 'D—n her!'
   But nothing else – the time of words was o'er;
He cast a rueful look or two, and did
(He knew not wherefore) that which he was bid.

164

With him retired his *posse comitatus* –[169]   *1305*
   The attorney last, who lingered near the door
Reluctantly, still tarrying there as late as
   Antonia let him, not a little sore
At this most strange and unexplained hiatus[170]
   In Don Alfonso's facts, which just now wore   *1310*
An awkward look; as he resolved the case
The door was fastened in his legal face.

165

No sooner was it bolted than – oh shame!
   Oh sin! Oh sorrow! And oh womankind!
How can you do such things and keep your fame,   *1315*
   Unless this world (and t'other too) be blind?
Nothing so dear as an unfilched good name![171]
   But to proceed, for there is more behind;
With much heartfelt reluctance be it said,
Young Juan slipped, half-smothered, from the bed   *1320*

166

He had been hid – I don't pretend to say
   How, nor can I indeed describe the where;
Young, slender, and packed easily, he lay
   No doubt, in little compass, round or square;
But pity him I neither must nor may   *1325*
   His suffocation by that pretty pair;
'Twere better, sure, to die so, than be shut
With maudlin Clarence in his Malmsey butt.[172]

167

And secondly, I pity not, because
   He had no business to commit a sin   *1330*

---

[164] *myrmidons* base unscrupulous henchmen.
[165] Achates was Aeneas's proverbially faithful companion on his travels through Libya.
[166] *So* if.
[167] Job's wife berated him: 'Dost thou still retain thine integrity? Curse God, and die' (Job 2:9).
[168] *in perspective* i.e. stretching into the distance.

[169] *posse comitatus* 'the force of the county'; armed posse.
[170] *hiatus* i.e. missing piece of evidence.
[171] *Nothing so dear as an unfilched good name* cf. *Othello* III iii 159: 'But he that filches from me my good name . . .'
[172] George, Duke of Clarence, brother of Richard III, is threatened with being drowned in a barrel of malmsey wine in Shakespeare's play (*Richard III* I iv 270).

Forbid by heavenly, fined by human laws
   (At least 'twas rather early to begin);
But at sixteen the conscience rarely gnaws
   So much as when we call our old debts in
At sixty years, and draw the accompts of evil,   *1335*
And find a deuced balance with the Devil.

168

Of his position I can give no notion;
   'Tis written in the Hebrew chronicle
How the physicians, leaving pill and potion,
   Prescribed by way of blister, a young belle,   *1340*
When old King David's blood grew dull in motion,
   And that the medicine answered very well;[173]
Perhaps 'twas in a different way applied,
For David lived, but Juan nearly died.

169

What's to be done? Alfonso will be back   *1345*
   The moment he has sent his fools away.
Antonia's skill was put upon the rack,
   But no device could be brought into play –
And how to parry the renewed attack?
   Besides, it wanted but few hours of day;   *1350*
Antonia puzzled, Julia did not speak
But pressed her bloodless lip to Juan's cheek.

170

He turned his lip to hers, and with his hand
   Called back the tangles of her wandering hair;
Even then their love they could not all command,   *1355*
   And half forgot their danger and despair.
Antonia's patience now was at a stand –[174]
   'Come, come, 'tis no time now for fooling there',
She whispered in great wrath, 'I must deposit
This pretty gentleman within the closet: *1360*

171

Pray keep your nonsense for some luckier night –
   Who can have put my master in this mood?
What will become on't? I'm in such a fright,
   The Devil's in the urchin, and no good –

Is this a time for giggling? this a plight?   *1365*
   Why, don't you know that it may end in blood?
You'll lose your life, and I shall lose my place,[175]
My mistress, all, for that half-girlish face.

172

Had it but been for a stout cavalier
   Of twenty-five or thirty (come, make haste!) –   *1370*
But for a child, what piece of work is here![176]
   I really, madam, wonder at your taste –
Come sir, get in; my master must be near.
   There for the present, at the least he's fast,
And if we can but till the morning keep
Our counsel – Juan, mind, you must not sleep!'   *1375*

173

Now Don Alfonso entering, but alone,
   Closed the oration of the trusty maid;
She loitered, and he told her to be gone –
   An order somewhat sullenly obeyed;   *1380*
However, present remedy was none,
   And no great good seemed answered if she stayed;
Regarding both with slow and sidelong view,
She snuffed the candle, curtsied and withdrew.

174

Alfonso paused a minute, then begun   *1385*
   Some strange excuses for his late proceeding;
He would not justify what he had done –
   To say the best, it was extreme ill-breeding;
But there were ample reasons for it, none
   Of which he specified in this his pleading: *1390*
His speech was a fine sample, on the whole,
Of rhetoric which the learned call *rigmarole*.

175

Julia said nought, though all the while there rose
   A ready answer – which at once enables
A matron (who her husband's foible knows)   *1395*
   By a few timely words to turn the tables,

---

[173] *'Tis written . . . very well* see I Kings 1:1–3. King David was revived by 'a young virgin'.
[174] *at a stand* i.e. at an end.

[175] *place* job.
[176] *what piece of work is here* an ironic reworking of *Hamlet* II ii 303–4: 'What a piece of work is a man . . .'

Which, if it does not silence, still must pose,
    Even if it should comprise a pack of fables;
'Tis to retort with firmness, and when he
Suspects with *one*, do you reproach with *three*.   *1400*

176

Julia in fact had tolerable grounds:
    Alfonso's loves with Inez were well-known;
But whether 'twas that one's own guilt confounds –
    But that can't be, as has been often shown,
A lady with apologies abounds;   *1405*
    It might be that her silence sprang alone
From delicacy to Don Juan's ear,
To whom she knew his mother's fame was dear.

177

There might be one more motive (which makes two):
    Alfonso ne'er to Juan had alluded –   *1410*
Mentioned his jealousy, but never who
    Had been the happy lover he concluded
Concealed amongst his premises; 'tis true
    His mind the more o'er this its mystery brooded;
To speak of Inez now were, one may say,   *1415*
Like throwing Juan in Alfonso's way.

178

A hint, in tender cases, is enough;
    Silence is best – besides there is a *tact*[177]
(That modern phrase appears to me sad stuff,
    But it will serve to keep my verse compact)   *1420*
Which keeps, when pushed by questions rather rough,
    A lady always distant from the fact –
The charming creatures lie with such a grace,
There's nothing so becoming to the face.

179

They blush, and we believe them – at least I   *1425*
    Have always done so; 'tis of no great use
In any case attempting a reply,

For then their eloquence grows quite profuse;
    And when at length they're out of breath, they sigh
And cast their languid eyes down, and let loose   *1430*
A tear or two, and then we make it up,
And then – and then – and then – sit down and sup.

180

Alfonso closed his speech and begged her pardon,
    Which Julia half-withheld, and then half-granted,
And laid conditions, he thought, very hard on,   *1435*
    Denying several little things he wanted;
He stood like Adam lingering near his garden,[178]
    With useless penitence perplexed and haunted,
Beseeching she no further would refuse –
When lo! he stumbled o'er a pair of shoes.   *1440*

181

A pair of shoes! What then? Not much, if they
    Are such as fit with lady's feet, but these
(No one can tell how much I grieve to say)
    Were masculine: to see them and to seize
Was but a moment's act – ah wel-a-day![179]   *1445*
    My teeth begin to chatter, my veins freeze;
Alfonso first examined well their fashion,
And then flew out into another passion.

182

He left the room for his relinquished sword
    And Julia instant to the closet flew,   *1450*
'Fly, Juan, fly! For Heaven's sake, not a word –
    The door is open, you may yet slip through
The passage you so often have explored;
    Here is the garden-key – fly – fly – adieu!
Haste, haste! I hear Alfonso's hurrying feet –   *1455*
Day has not broke; there's no one in the street.'

183

None can say that this was not good advice,
    The only mischief was it came too late;
Of all experience 'tis the usual price,

---

[177] *tact* a keen faculty of perception or discrimination likened to the sense of touch.
[178] *Adam lingering near his garden* while being cast out of Eden in Milton's poem, Adam and Eve lingered near the eastern gate (*Paradise Lost* xii 636–9).

[179] *ah wel-a-day* cf. Coleridge, *Christabel* 252.

A sort of income tax[180] laid on by fate: *1460*
Juan had reached the room-door in a trice
    And might have done so by the garden-gate,
But met Alfonso in his dressing-gown,
Who threatened death – so Juan knocked him down.

184

Dire was the scuffle, and out went the light,   *1465*
    Antonia cried out 'Rape!' and Julia, 'Fire!'
But not a servant stirred to aid the fight.
    Alfonso, pommelled to his heart's desire,
Swore lustily he'd be revenged this night;
    And Juan too blasphemed an octave higher,   *1470*
His blood was up – though young, he was a Tartar,[181]
And not at all disposed to prove a martyr.

185

Alfonso's sword had dropped ere he could draw it,
    And they continued battling hand to hand,
For Juan very luckily ne'er saw it;   *1475*
    His temper not being under great command,
If at that moment he had chanced to claw it,
    Alfonso's days had not been in the land
Much longer. Think of husbands', lovers', lives,
And how ye may be doubly widows, wives!   *1480*

186

Alfonso grappled to detain the foe
    And Juan throttled him to get away,
And blood ('twas from the nose) began to flow;
    At last, as they more faintly wrestling lay,
Juan contrived to give an awkward blow,   *1485*
    And then his only garment quite gave way;
He fled, like Joseph,[182] leaving it – but there,
I doubt, all likeness ends between the pair.

187

Lights came at length, and men and maids who found
    An awkward spectacle their eyes before: *1490*

Antonia in hysterics, Julia swooned,
    Alfonso leaning breathless by the door;
Some half-torn drapery scattered on the ground,
    Some blood and several footsteps, but no more –
Juan the gate gained, turned the key about,   *1495*
And liking not the inside, locked the out.

188

Here ends this canto. Need I sing, or say,
    How Juan, naked, favoured by the night
(Who favours what she should not), found his way,
    And reached his home in an unseemly plight?   *1500*
The pleasant scandal which arose next day,
    The nine days' wonder which was brought to light,
And how Alfonso sued for a divorce,
Were in the English newspapers, of course.

189

If you would like to see the whole proceedings,   *1505*
    The depositions, and the cause at full,
The names of all the witnesses, the pleadings
    Of counsel to nonsuit or to annul,[183]
There's more than one edition, and the readings
    Are various, but they none of them are dull;   *1510*
The best is that in shorthand ta'en by Gurney,[184]
Who to Madrid on purpose made a journey.

190

But Donna Inez, to divert the train[185]
    Of one of the most circulating scandals
That had for centuries been known in Spain   *1515*
    Since Roderic's Goths or older Genseric's Vandals,[186]
First vowed (and never had she vowed in vain)
    To Virgin Mary several pounds of candles;
And then by the advice of some old ladies,
She sent her son to be embarked[187] at Cadiz.   *1520*

---

180   *income tax* introduced in England as a war tax in 1799.
181   *a Tartar* i.e. a young savage.
182   *like Joseph* when Joseph refused to commit adultery with Potiphar's wife, she claimed that he had raped her, and that, 'when he heard that I lifted up my voice and cried, that he left his garment with me, and fled, and got him out' (Genesis 39:14).
183   *to nonsuit or to annul* i.e. to bring the case to an end through lack of sufficient evidence.

184   William Brodie Gurney (1777–1855), shorthand clerk in Parliament, famous for transcripts of trials and speeches of the day.
185   *train* progress.
186   Don Roderick was the last of Spain's Gothic kings, and ruled in the eighth century. In the year 455 the Vandal King Genseric led a marauding expedition against Rome, which he took and completely sacked.
187   *embarked* put on board ship.

191

She had resolved that he should travel through
　　All European climes by land or sea
To mend his former morals, or get new,
　　Especially in France and Italy –
At least this is the thing most people do.　　*1525*
　　Julia was sent into a nunnery,
And there perhaps her feelings may be better
Shown in the following copy of her letter:

192

'They tell me 'tis decided – you depart.
　　'Tis wise, 'tis well, but not the less a pain;　　*1530*
I have no further claim on your young heart –
　　Mine was the victim, and would be again;
To love too much has been the only art
　　I used; I write in haste, and if a stain
Be on this sheet, 'tis not what it appears –　　*1535*
My eyeballs burn and throb, but have no tears.

193

I loved, I love you, for that love have lost
　　State, station, heaven, mankind's, my own esteem,
And yet cannot regret what it hath cost,
　　So dear is still the memory of that dream;　　*1540*
Yet if I name my guilt, 'tis not to boast –
　　None can deem harshlier of me than I deem:
I trace this scrawl because I cannot rest,
I've nothing to reproach, nor to request.

194

Man's love is of his life a thing apart,　　*1545*
　　'Tis woman's whole existence; man may range
The court, camp, church, the vessel and the mart,
　　Sword, gown, gain, glory, offer in exchange
Pride, fame, ambition, to fill up his heart,
　　And few there are whom these cannot estrange; *1550*
Man has all these resources, we but one –
To love again, and be again undone.

195

My breast has been all weakness, is so yet;
　　I struggle, but cannot collect my mind;
My blood still rushes where my spirit's set　　*1555*
　　As roll the waves before the settled wind;
My brain is feminine, nor can forget –
　　To all, except your image, madly blind;
As turns the needle trembling to the pole
It ne'er can reach, so turns to you, my soul.　　*1560*

196

You will proceed in beauty and in pride,
　　Beloved and loving many; all is o'er
For me on earth, except some years to hide
　　My shame and sorrow deep in my heart's core;
These I could bear, but cannot cast aside　　*1565*
　　The passion which still rends it as before,
And so farewell; forgive me, love me – no,
That word is idle now, but let it go.

197

I have no more to say, but linger still,
　　And dare not set my seal upon this sheet,　　*1570*
And yet I may as well the task fulfil –
　　My misery can scarce be more complete;
I had not lived till now, could sorrow kill;
　　Death flies the wretch who fain the blow would meet,
And I must even survive this last adieu,　　*1575*
And bear with life, to love and pray for you!'

198

This note was written upon gilt-edged paper
　　With a neat crow-quill – rather hard, but new;
Her small white fingers scarce could reach the taper
　　But trembled as magnetic needles do,　　*1580*
And yet she did not let one tear escape her;
　　The seal a sunflower, 'Elle vous suit partout'[188]
The motto, cut upon a white cornelian;[189]
The wax was superfine, its hue vermilion.

---

[188] 'She follows you everywhere'. Byron owned a seal bearing this motto.

[189] *cornelian* stone used for making seals (for letters).

199

This was Don Juan's earliest scrape – but whether   *1585*
   I shall proceed with his adventures is
Dependent on the public altogether;
   We'll see, however, what they say to this;
Their favour in an author's cap's a feather,
   And no great mischief's done by their caprice;   *1590*
And if their approbation we experience,
Perhaps they'll have some more about a year hence.

200

My poem's epic, and is meant to be
   Divided in twelve books, each book containing,
With love and war, a heavy gale at sea,   *1595*
   A list of ships and captains, and kings reigning,
New characters; the episodes are three:
   A panorama view of hell's in training[190]
After the style of Virgil and of Homer,
So that my name of epic's no misnomer.   *1600*

201

All these things will be specified in time
   With strict regard to Aristotle's rules,
The vade-mecum[191] of the true sublime
   Which makes so many poets, and some fools;
Prose poets like blank verse, I'm fond of rhyme –   *1605*
   Good workmen never quarrel with their tools;
I've got new mythological machinery
And very handsome supernatural scenery.

202

There's only one slight difference between
   Me and my epic brethren gone before,   *1610*
And here the advantage is my own, I ween[192]
   (Not that I have no several merits more,
But this will more peculiarly be seen) –

They so embellish that 'tis quite a bore
Their labyrinth of fables to thread through,   *1615*
Whereas this story's actually true.

203

If any person doubt it, I appeal
   To history, tradition, and to facts,
To newspapers (whose truth all know and feel),
   To plays in five, and operas in three acts –   *1620*
All these confirm my statement a good deal,
   But that which more completely faith exacts
Is that myself, and several now in Seville,
Saw Juan's last elopement with the Devil.[193]

204

If ever I should condescend to prose,   *1625*
   I'll write poetical commandments[194] which
Shall supersede beyond all doubt all those
   That went before; in these I shall enrich
My text with many things that no one knows,
   And carry precept to the highest pitch: *1630*
I'll call the work 'Longinus o'er a bottle,
Or, Every poet his *own* Aristotle'.

205

Thou shalt believe in Milton, Dryden, Pope;
   Thou shalt not set up Wordsworth, Coleridge,
                        Southey,
Because the first is crazed beyond all hope,   *1635*
   The second drunk,[195] the third so quaint and
                        mouthy;[196]
With Crabbe it may be difficult to cope,
   And Campbell's Hippocrene[197] is somewhat
                        drouthy;[198]
Thou shalt not steal from Samuel Rogers, nor
Commit . . . flirtation with the muse of Moore.[199]   *1640*

---

[190] *training* preparation.
[191] *vade-mecum* handbook.
[192] *ween* believe.
[193] When in Seville in 1809, Byron saw a performance of *El Burlador de Sevilla o el Convidado de Piedra* ('The Trickster of Seville, or the Guest Made of Stone'), by Tirso de Molina (1583–1648).
[194] *poetical commandments* the parody of the ten commandments in the following stanzas caused uproar in England when *Don Juan* was first published.

[195] *drunk* stupefied by opium.
[196] *quaint and mouthy* affected and bombastic (in language).
[197] *Hippocrene* fountain of Mt Helicon, sacred to the muses.
[198] *drouthy* dry.
[199] For Crabbe, Rogers and Moore, see pp. 36, 753 n. 23, 617–18. Thomas Campbell, whom Byron also admired, was famous for *The Pleasures of Hope* (1799). Byron's comment about him here refers to the fact that Campbell had recently given up poetry for the writing of prose criticism.

206

Thou shalt not covet Mr Sotheby's[200] muse,
   His Pegasus,[201] nor anything that's his;
Thou shalt not bear false witness like the Blues[202]
   (There's one, at least, is very fond of this);
Thou shalt not write, in short, but what I choose: *1645*
   This is true criticism, and you may kiss
Exactly as you please, or not, the rod –
But if you don't, I'll lay it on, by G-d!

207

If any person should presume to assert
   This story is not moral, first I pray   *1650*
That they will not cry out before they're hurt,
   Then that they'll read it o'er again, and say
(But, doubtless, nobody will be so pert)
   That this is not a moral tale, though gay;
Besides, in Canto Twelfth I mean to show   *1655*
The very place where wicked people go.

208

If, after all, there should be some so blind
   To their own good this warning to despise,
Led by some tortuosity[203] of mind
   Not to believe my verse and their own eyes,   *1660*
And cry that they 'the moral cannot find',
   I tell him, if a clergyman, he lies;
Should captains the remark or critics make,
They also lie too – under a mistake.

209

The public approbation I expect,   *1665*
   And beg they'll take my word about the moral,
Which I with their amusement will connect

(So children cutting teeth receive a coral);
   Meantime, they'll doubtless please to recollect
My epical pretensions to the laurel: *1670*
For fear some prudish readers should grow skittish
I've bribed my grandmother's review – the *British*.[204]

210

I sent it in a letter to the editor
   Who thanked me duly by return of post –
I'm for a handsome article his creditor;   *1675*
   Yet if my gentle muse he please to roast,
And break a promise after having made it her,
   Denying the receipt of what it cost
And smear his page with gall[205] instead of honey,
All I can say is – that he had the money.   *1680*

211

I think that with this holy new alliance
   I may ensure the public, and defy
All other magazines of art or science –
   Daily or monthly or three-monthly; I
Have not essayed[206] to multiply their clients   *1685*
   Because they tell me 'twere in vain to try,
And that the *Edinburgh Review* and *Quarterly*
Treat a dissenting author very martyrly.

212

'Non ego hoc ferrem calida juventa
   Consule Planco',[207] Horace said, and so   *1690*
Say I; by which quotation there is meant a
   Hint that some six or seven good years ago
(Long ere I dreamt of dating from the Brenta)[208]
   I was most ready to return a blow,
And would not brook at all this sort of thing   *1695*
In my hot youth – when George the third was King.

---

[200] William Sotheby (1757–1833), most famous for his translation of Wieland's *Oberon* (1798), and for his plays, *The Death of Darnley* (1814) and *Ivan* (1816).

[201] Pegasus was the winged horse who created Hippocrene, the fountain of Mt Helicon, with his hoof; he is generally referred to as a symbol of poetic inspiration.

[202] *the Blues* i.e. the bluestockings, many of whom were acquainted with Byron (Lady Blessington, Lady Oxford, Lady Caroline Lamb).

[203] *tortuosity* crookedness.

[204] The *British Review* was outraged by *Don Juan*, and particularly by this line; its editor, William Roberts, in his review of

the poem, solemnly denied the 'accusation', provoking Byron's 'Letter to the Editor of my Grandmother's Review' in the *Liberal* (1822).

[205] *gall* i.e. bitterness.

[206] *essayed* attempted.

[207] Horace, *Odes* III xiv 27–8; translated (roughly) at lines 1695–6.

[208] *dating from the Brenta* i.e. to think in terms of how long he has been resident in Venice.

213

But now at thirty years my hair is gray
  (I wonder what it will be like at forty?
I thought of a peruke[209] the other day),
    My heart is not much greener, and, in short, I   *1700*
Have squandered my whole summer while 'twas May,
    And feel no more the spirit to retort; I
Have spent my life, both interest and principal,
And deem not what I deemed, my soul invincible.

214

No more, no more – oh never more on me   *1705*
    The freshness of the heart can fall like dew,
Which out of all the lovely things we see
    Extracts emotions beautiful and new,
Hived[210] in our bosoms like the bag o' the bee:
    Think'st thou the honey with those objects
                                                    grew?   *1710*
Alas, 'twas not in them, but in thy power
To double even the sweetness of a flower.

215

No more, no more – oh never more, my heart,
    Canst thou be my sole world, my universe!
Once all in all, but now a thing apart,   *1715*
    Thou canst not be my blessing or my curse;
The illusion's gone forever, and thou art
    Insensible, I trust, but none the worse,
And in thy stead I've got a deal of judgement –
Though heaven knows how it ever found a
                                                    lodgement.   *1720*

216

My days of love are over, me no more
    The charms of maid, wife, and still less of widow,
Can make the fool of which they made before; –
    In short, I must not lead the life I did do;
The credulous hope of mutual minds is o'er,   *1725*
    The copious use of claret is forbid too –

So, for a good old gentlemanly vice,
I think I must take up with avarice.

217

Ambition was my idol, which was broken
    Before the shrines of sorrow and of pleasure;   *1730*
And the two last have left me many a token
    O'er which reflection may be made at leisure;
Now like Friar Bacon's brazen[211] head I've spoken,
    'Time is, time was, time's past';[212] a chemic[213]
                                                    treasure
Is glittering youth, which I have spent betimes –   *1735*
My heart in passion, and my head on rhymes.

218

What is the end of fame?[214] 'Tis but to fill
    A certain portion of uncertain paper;
Some liken it to climbing up a hill
    Whose summit, like all hills', is lost in vapour;   *1740*
For this men write, speak, preach, and heroes kill,
    And bards burn what they call their 'midnight taper' –
To have, when the original is dust,
A name, a wretched picture, and worse bust.[215]

219

What are the hopes of man? Old Egypt's King   *1745*
    Cheops erected the first pyramid
And largest, thinking it was just the thing
    To keep his memory whole, and mummy hid;
But somebody or other rummaging,
    Burglariously broke his coffin's lid: *1750*
Let not a monument give you or me hopes,
Since not a pinch of dust remains of Cheops.

220

But I, being fond of true philosophy,
    Say very often to myself, 'Alas!

---

209   *peruke* wig.
210   *Hived* stored.
211   *brazen* brass.
212   The words of the brass head, Robert Greene, *Friar Bacon and Friar Bungay* (1594), IV i 1584, 1595, 1604.
213   *chemic* i.e. transforming; alchemists attempted to convert base metals into gold.

214   Literary fame was the sort of which Byron was disdainful; cf. his remarks about Southey, Dedication, l. 60.
215   Bertel Thorwaldsen, the Danish sculptor, made a bust of Byron during his stay in Rome, summer 1817. Byron found it embarrassing, and commented that 'It is not at all like me; my expression is more unhappy'.

All things that have been born were born to die,   *1755*
    And flesh (which death mows down to hay) is
                    grass;[216]
You've passed your youth not so unpleasantly,
    And if you had it o'er again, 'twould pass;
So thank your stars that matters are no worse
And read your Bible, sir, and mind your purse.'   *1760*

221

But for the present, gentle reader and
    Still gentler purchaser, the bard (that's I)
Must with permission shake you by the hand;
    And so your humble servant, and goodbye!
We meet again, if we should understand   *1765*
    Each other — and if not, I shall not try
Your patience further than by this short sample
('Twere well if others followed my example).

222

'Go, little book, from this my solitude!
    I cast thee on the waters, go thy ways!   *1770*
And if, as I believe, thy vein be good,
    The world will find thee after many days.'[217]
When Southey's read, and Wordsworth understood,
    I can't help putting in my claim to praise;
The four first rhymes are Southey's every line —   *1775*
For God's sake, reader, take them not for mine!

Canto II (composed between 13 December 1818 and mid
January 1819)

1

Oh ye who teach the ingenuous youth of nations —
    Holland, France, England, Germany, or Spain —
I pray ye flog them upon all occasions:
    It mends their morals, never mind the pain!
The best of mothers and of educations   5
    In Juan's case were but employed in vain,
Since, in a way that's rather of the oddest, he
Became divested of his native modesty.[1]

2

Had he but been placed at a public school,[2]
    In the third form, or even in the fourth,   10
His daily task had kept his fancy cool,
    At least, had he been nurtured in the north;
Spain may prove an exception to the rule,
    But then exceptions always prove its worth —
A lad of sixteen causing a divorce   15
Puzzled his tutors very much, of course.

3

I can't say that it puzzles me at all,
    If all things be considered: first there was
His lady-mother, mathematical,
    A — never mind; his tutor, an old ass;   20
A pretty woman (that's quite natural,
    Or else the thing had hardly come to pass);
A husband rather old, not much in unity
With his young wife; a time, and opportunity.

4

Well — well, the world must turn upon its axis,   25
    And all mankind turn with it, heads or tails,
And live and die, make love and pay our taxes,
    And, as the veering wind shifts, shift our sails;
The king commands us, and the doctor quacks us,[3]
    The priest instructs, and so our life exhales   30
A little breath, love, wine, ambition, fame,
Fighting, devotion, dust, perhaps a name.

5

I said that Juan had been sent to Cadiz —
    A pretty town, I recollect it well —
'Tis there the mart of the colonial trade is   35
    (Or was, before Peru learned to rebel);[4]
And such sweet girls — I mean, such graceful ladies,
    Their very walk would make your bosom swell;
I can't describe it, though so much it strike,
Nor liken it — I never saw the like: 40

---

216 *And flesh . . . is grass* cf. Isaiah 40:6.
217 Southey, 'L'Envoy', *Carmen Nuptiale* (1816).

CANTO II
1 *native modesty* i.e. the modesty he was born with.
2 *a public school* in England, one of the old established fee-paying

schools, like Eton and Harrow (where Byron was educated).
3 *quacks us* administers quack medicines to us.
4 The Peruvian struggle for independence had begun in 1813, and after many obstacles was won in 1824, under Bolivar's leadership.

6

An Arab horse, a stately stag, a barb[5]
   New broke, a cameleopard,[6] a gazelle –
No, none of these will do – and then their garb,
   Their veil and petticoat! (Alas, to dwell
Upon such things would very near absorb   45
   A canto!) Then their feet and ankles – well,
Thank heaven I've got no metaphor quite ready
(And so, my sober muse, come, let's be steady,

7

Chaste Muse! – Well, if you must, you must); the veil
   Thrown back a moment with the glancing
                     hand,   50
While the o'erpowering eye that turns you pale
   Flashes into the heart. All sunny land
Of love, when I forget you, may I fail
   To – say my prayers; but never was there planned
A dress through which the eyes give such a volley,   55
Excepting the Venetian fazzioli.[7]

8

But to our tale: the Donna Inez sent
   Her son to Cadiz only to embark;
To stay there had not answered her intent,
   But why? We leave the reader in the dark –   60
'Twas for a voyage that the young man was meant,
   As if a Spanish ship were Noah's ark,
To wean him from the wickedness of earth
And send him like a dove of promise forth.

9

Don Juan bade his valet pack his things   65
   According to direction, then received
A lecture and some money: for four springs
   He was to travel, and though Inez grieved
(As every kind of parting has its stings),
   She hoped he would improve – perhaps believed: 70

A letter, too, she gave (he never read it)
Of good advice – and two or three of credit.

10

In the meantime, to pass her hours away,
   Brave Inez now set up a Sunday school
For naughty children, who would rather play   75
   (Like truant rogues) the devil or the fool;
Infants of three years old were taught that day,
   Dunces were whipped, or set upon a stool:
The great success of Juan's education[8]
Spurred her to teach another generation.   80

11

Juan embarked, the ship got under way,
   The wind was fair, the water passing rough;
A devil of a sea rolls in that bay,
   As I, who've crossed it oft,[9] know well enough;
And, standing upon deck, the dashing spray   85
   Flies in one's face, and makes it weather-tough:
And there he stood to take, and take again,
His first, perhaps his last, farewell of Spain.

12

I can't but say it is an awkward sight
   To see one's native land receding through   90
The growing waters;[10] it unmans one quite,
   Especially when life is rather new.
I recollect Great Britain's coast looks white,
   But almost every other country's blue,
When gazing on them, mystified by distance,   95
We enter on our nautical existence.

13

So Juan stood, bewildered, on the deck:
   The wind sung, cordage[11] strained, and sailors swore,
And the ship creaked, the town became a speck,
   From which away so fair and fast they bore.   100

---

5 *barb* horse from the Barbary coast.
6 *cameleopard* giraffe.
7 *fazzioli* white kerchiefs used as a veil by the lower ranks.
8 *The great success of Juan's education* ironic, of course.
9 *As I, who've crossed it oft* Byron sailed from Cadiz on 3 August
1809, travelling to Gibraltar.

10 *I can't but say . . . waters* Byron draws on his own experience
of self-exile.
11 *cordage* the ship's rigging.

The best of remedies is a beefsteak
    Against seasickness; try it, sir, before
You sneer, and I assure you this is true,
For I have found it answer – so may you.

14

Don Juan stood and, gazing from the stern,   *105*
    Beheld his native Spain receding far.
First partings form a lesson hard to learn,
    Even nations feel this when they go to war;
There is a sort of unexpressed concern,
    A kind of shock that sets one's heart ajar:[12]   *110*
At leaving even the most unpleasant people
And places, one keeps looking at the steeple.

15

But Juan had got many things to leave,
    His mother, and a mistress, and no wife,
So that he had much better cause to grieve   *115*
    Than many persons more advanced in life;
And if we now and then a sigh must heave
    At quitting even those we quit in strife,
No doubt we weep for those the heart endears –
That is, till deeper griefs congeal our tears.   *120*

16

So Juan wept, as wept the captive Jews
    By Babel's waters, still remembering Zion:[13]
I'd weep, but mine is not a weeping muse,
    And such light griefs are not a thing to die on;
Young men should travel, if but to amuse   *125*
    Themselves – and the next time their servants tie on
Behind their carriages their new portmanteau,[14]
Perhaps it may be lined with this my canto.

17

And Juan wept, and much he sighed and thought,
    While his salt tears dropped into the salt sea, *130*
'Sweets to the sweet' (I like so much to quote;
    You must excuse this extract – 'tis where she,

The Queen of Denmark, for Ophelia brought
    Flowers to the grave),[15] and, sobbing often, he
Reflected on his present situation,   *135*
And seriously resolved on reformation.

18

'Farewell, my Spain, a long farewell!' he cried,
    'Perhaps I may revisit thee no more,
But die, as many an exiled heart hath died,
    Of its own thirst to see again thy shore;   *140*
Farewell, where Guadalquivir's waters glide!
    Farewell, my mother! And, since all is o'er,
Farewell, too dearest Julia!' (Here he drew
Her letter out again, and read it through.)

19

'And oh, if e'er I should forget, I swear –   *145*
    But that's impossible, and cannot be –
Sooner shall this blue ocean melt to air,
    Sooner shall earth resolve itself to sea,
Than I resign thine image, oh my fair!
    Or think of anything excepting thee;   *150*
A mind diseased no remedy can physic –'[16]
(Here the ship gave a lurch, and he grew seasick.)

20

'Sooner shall heaven kiss earth –' (Here he fell sicker)
    'Oh Julia, what is every other woe?
(For God's sake let me have a glass of liquor,   *155*
    Pedro, Battista,[17] help me down below!)
Julia, my love! – you rascal, Pedro, quicker –
    Oh Julia! – this cursed vessel pitches so –
Beloved Julia, hear me still beseeching!'
(Here he grew inarticulate with reaching.)[18]   *160*

21

He felt that chilling heaviness of heart,
    Or rather stomach – which, alas, attends,
Beyond the best apothecary's[19] art,
    The loss of love, the treachery of friends,

---

[12] *ajar* out of harmony.
[13] Psalm 137:1: 'By the rivers of Babylon, there we sat down, yea, we wept, when we remembered Zion'.
[14] *portmanteau* travelling bag.
[15] *Hamlet* V i 243.
[16] *physic* cure. The line recalls *Macbeth* V iii 40: 'Canst thou not minister to a mind diseased . . . ?'

[17] Byron's own servant was a former gondolier called Giovanni Battista Lusieri (1798–1874). He remained with him until his death at Missolonghi.
[18] *reaching* retching.
[19] *apothecary* one who prepared and sold drugs for medicinal purposes – the business now (since about 1800) conducted by a chemist.

Or death of those we dote on, when a part   *165*
    Of us dies with them as each fond hope ends:
No doubt he would have been much more pathetic,
But the sea acted as a strong emetic.[20]

22

Love's a capricious power; I've known it hold
    Out through a fever caused by its own heat,   *170*
But be much puzzled by a cough and cold,
    And find a quinsy[21] very hard to treat;
Against all noble maladies he's bold,
    But vulgar illnesses don't like to meet –
Nor that a sneeze should interrupt his sigh,   *175*
Nor inflammations redden his blind eye.

23

But worst of all is nausea, or a pain
    About the lower region of the bowels;
Love, who heroically breathes a vein,[22]
    Shrinks from the application of hot towels,   *180*
And purgatives are dangerous to his reign,
    Seasickness death: his love was perfect, how else
Could Juan's passion, while the billows roar,
Resist his stomach, ne'er at sea before?

24

The ship, called the most holy *Trinidada*,   *185*
    Was steering duly for the port Leghorn,
For there the Spanish family Moncada[23]
    Were settled long ere Juan's sire was born:
They were relations, and for them he had a
    Letter of introduction, which the morn   *190*
Of his departure had been sent him by
His Spanish friends for those in Italy.

25

His suite consisted of three servants and
    A tutor – the licentiate[24] Pedrillo,
Who several languages did understand,   *195*
    But now lay sick and speechless on his pillow,

And, rocking in his hammock, longed for land,
    His headache being increased by every billow;
And the waves oozing through the porthole made
His berth a little damp, and him afraid.   *200*

26

'Twas not without some reason, for the wind
    Increased at night until it blew a gale;
And though 'twas not much to a naval mind,
    Some landsmen would have looked a little pale –
For sailors are, in fact, a different kind.   *205*
    At sunset they began to take in sail,
For the sky showed it would come on to blow,
And carry away, perhaps, a mast or so.

27

At one o'clock the wind with sudden shift
    Threw the ship right into the trough of the
                    sea,[25]   *210*
Which struck her aft, and made an awkward rift,
    Started the stern-post,[26] also shattered the
Whole of her stern-frame, and ere she could lift
    Herself from out her present jeopardy
The rudder tore away: 'twas time to sound[27]   *215*
The pumps, and there were four feet water found.

28

One gang of people instantly was put
    Upon the pumps, and the remainder set
To get up part of the cargo, and what-not,
    But they could not come at the leak as yet;   *220*
At last they did get at it really, but
    Still their salvation was an even bet.
The water rushed through in a way quite puzzling,
While they thrust sheets, shirts, jackets, bales of muslin

29

Into the opening – but all such ingredients   *225*
    Would have been vain, and they must have gone
                    down,

---

[20]   *emetic* medicine designed to induce vomiting.
[21]   *a quinsy* tonsillitis.
[22]   *breathes a vein* lancing the veins was in Byron's day a frequently used method of treatment.
[23]   A family of this name lived next door to Byron at La Mira, Venice, in 1818.
[24]   *licentiate* Pedrillo was licensed in one or both of two ways: either he held a degree from the University of Salamanca (stanza 37), or was authorized to teach and perform religious rites.

[25]   *the trough of the sea* the hollow between waves.
[26]   *Started the stern-post* displaced or loosened the upright beam at the stern of the ship, which supported the rudder.
[27]   *sound* i.e. use the pumps to find out how much water the ship had taken in.

Despite of all their efforts and expedients,
    But for the pumps: I'm glad to make them known
To all the brother tars who may have need hence,
    For fifty tons of water were upthrown   230
By them per hour, and they had all been undone
But for their maker, Mr Mann, of London.[28]

30

As day advanced the weather seemed to abate,
    And then the leak they reckoned to reduce,
And keep the ship afloat, though three feet yet   235
    Kept two hand- and one chain-pump[29] still in use.
The wind blew fresh again: as it grew late
    A squall came on, and while some guns broke loose,
A gust, which all descriptive power transcends,
Laid with one blast the ship on her beam-ends.[30]   240

31

There she lay, motionless, and seemed upset;
    The water left the hold, and washed the decks,
And made a scene men do not soon forget;
    For they remember battles, fires, and wrecks,
Or any other thing that brings regret,   245
    Or breaks their hopes, or hearts, or heads, or necks:
Thus drownings are much talked of by the divers
And swimmers who may chance to be survivors.

32

Immediately the masts were cut away,
    Both main and mizen; first the mizen went,   250
The mainmast followed. But the ship still lay
    Like a mere log, and baffled our intent.
Foremast and bowsprit were cut down, and they
    Eased her at last (although we never meant
To part with all till every hope was blighted),   255
And then with violence the old ship righted.

33

It may be easily supposed, while this
    Was going on, some people were unquiet,

That passengers would find it much amiss
    To lose their lives as well as spoil their diet;   260
That even the able seaman, deeming his
    Days nearly o'er, might be disposed to riot,
As upon such occasions tars will ask
For grog, and sometimes drink rum from the cask.

34

There's nought, no doubt, so much the spirit calms   265
    As rum and true religion; thus it was
Some plundered, some drank spirits, some sung psalms,
    The high wind made the treble, and as bass
The hoarse harsh waves kept time; fright cured the qualms
    Of all the luckless landsmen's seasick maws: 270
Strange sounds of wailing, blasphemy, devotion,
Clamoured in chorus to the roaring ocean.

35

Perhaps more mischief had been done, but for
    Our Juan who, with sense beyond his years,
Got to the spirit-room,[31] and stood before   275
    It with a pair of pistols; and their fears,
As if Death were more dreadful by his door
    Of fire than water, spite of oaths and tears,
Kept still aloof the crew who, ere they sunk,
Thought it would be becoming to die drunk.   280

36

'Give us more grog', they cried, 'for it will be
    All one an hour hence.' Juan answered, 'No!
'Tis true that death awaits both you and me,
    But let us die like men, not sink below
Like brutes.' And thus his dangerous post kept he,   285
    And none liked to anticipate the blow;
And even Pedrillo, his most reverend tutor,
Was for some rum a disappointed suitor.

37

The good old gentleman was quite aghast
    And made a loud and a pious lamentation,   290

---

[28] *Mr Mann, of London* this detail derives from Byron's source, Sir John Graham Dalyell's *Shipwrecks and Disasters at Sea* (3 vols, 1812).
[29] *chain-pump* machine for raising water by means of an endless chain.

[30] *Laid . . . beam-ends* when the ends of a ship's beams touch the water, the vessel lies on its side, in imminent danger of capsizing.
[31] *spirit-room* cabin where alcohol was stored.

Repented all his sins, and made a last
  Irrevocable vow of reformation;
Nothing should tempt him more (this peril past)
  To quit his academic occupation
In cloisters of the classic Salamanca,[32]   295
To follow Juan's wake like Sancho Panza.[33]

38

But now there came a flash of hope once more:
  Day broke, and the wind lulled – the masts were
                                              gone,
The leak increased; shoals round her, but no shore,
  The vessel swam, yet still she held her own.   300
They tried the pumps again, and though before
  Their desperate efforts seemed all useless grown,
A glimpse of sunshine set some hands to bale –
The stronger pumped, the weaker thrummed a sail.[34]

39

Under the vessel's keel the sail was past,   305
  And for the moment it had some effect;
But with a leak, and not a stick of mast,
  Nor rag of canvas, what could they expect?
But still 'tis best to struggle to the last,
  'Tis never too late to be wholly wrecked –   310
And though 'tis true that man can only die once,
'Tis not so pleasant in the Gulf of Lyons.

40

There winds and waves had hurled them, and from
                                              thence,
  Without their will, they carried them away;
For they were forced with steering to dispense,   315
  And never had as yet a quiet day
On which they might repose, or even commence
  A jury-mast[35] or rudder, or could say
The ship would swim an hour, which, by good luck,
Still swam – though not exactly like a duck.   320

41

The wind, in fact, perhaps, was rather less,
  But the ship laboured so, they scarce could hope

To weather out much longer; the distress
  Was also great with which they had to cope
For want of water, and their solid mess   325
  Was scant enough: in vain the telescope
Was used – nor sail nor shore appeared in sight,
Nought but the heavy sea, and coming night.

42

Again the weather threatened; again blew
  A gale, and in the fore- and after-hold   330
Water appeared – yet, though the people knew
  All this, the most were patient, and some bold,
Until the chains and leathers were worn through
  Of all our pumps: a wreck complete she rolled
At mercy of the waves, whose mercies are   335
Like human beings during civil war.

43

Then came the carpenter at last, with tears
  In his rough eyes, and told the captain he
Could do no more; he was a man in years,
  And long had voyaged through many a stormy
                                              sea,   340
And if he wept at length, they were not fears
  That made his eyelids as a woman's be,
But he, poor fellow, had a wife and children,
Two things for dying people quite bewildering.

44

The ship was evidently settling now   345
  Fast by the head;[36] and, all distinction gone,
Some went to prayers again, and made a vow
  Of candles to their saints – but there were none
To pay them with; and some looked o'er the bow;
  Some hoisted out the boats; and there was one   350
That begged Pedrillo for an absolution,
Who told him to be damned – in his confusion.

45

Some lashed them in their hammocks, some put on
  Their best clothes, as if going to a fair;
Some cursed the day on which they saw the sun,[37] 355

---

32 *the classic Salamanca* Spanish university founded in the thirteenth century.
33 Sancho Panza was Don Quixote's sidekick in Cervantes' famous novel.
34 *thrummed a sail* they fastened bunches of rope-yarn over a sail so as to produce a shaggy surface, suitable to stop the leak.

35 *jury-mast* temporary replacement mast.
36 *head* the fore-part of the ship, the bow.
37 *Some cursed . . . the sun* as at Jeremiah 20:14: 'Cursed be the day wherein I was born'.

And gnashed their teeth and, howling, tore their hair;
   And others went on as they had begun,
      Getting the boats out, being well aware
That a tight boat will live in a rough sea,
Unless with breakers close beneath her lee.[38]   *360*

46

The worst of all was that, in their condition,
   Having been several days in great distress,
'Twas difficult to get out such provision
      As now might render their long suffering less –
Men, even when dying, dislike inanition.   *365*
      Their stock was damaged by the weather's stress:
Two casks of biscuit and a keg of butter
Were all that could be thrown into the cutter.[39]

47

But in the longboat they contrived to stow
   Some pounds of bread, though injured by the
                       wet;   *370*
Water, a twenty gallon cask or so;
   Six flasks of wine; and they contrived to get
A portion of their beef up from below,
      And with a piece of pork, moreover, met,
But scarce enough to serve them for a luncheon – *375*
Then there was rum, eight gallons in a puncheon.[40]

48

The other boats, the yawl and pinnace, had
   Been stove[41] in the beginning of the gale;
And the longboat's condition was but bad,
      As there were but two blankets for a sail   *380*
And one oar for a mast, which a young lad
      Threw in by good luck over the ship's rail –
And two boats could not hold, far less be stored,
To save one half the people then on board.

49

'Twas twilight, and the sunless day went down *385*
   Over the waste of waters, like a veil

Which, if withdrawn, would but disclose the frown
   Of one whose hate is masked but to assail;
Thus to their hopeless eyes the night was shown
      And grimly darkled o'er their faces pale,   *390*
And the dim desolate deep; twelve days had Fear
Been their familiar, and now Death was here.

50

Some trial had been making at a raft
   With little hope in such a rolling sea –
A sort of thing at which one would have laughed, *395*
      If any laughter at such times could be,
Unless with people who too much have quaffed,
      And have a kind of wild and horrid glee,
Half-epileptical, and half-hysterical:
Their preservation would have been a miracle.   *400*

51

At half-past eight o'clock, booms, hencoops, spars,
   And all things, for a chance, had been cast loose,
That still could keep afloat the struggling tars –
      For yet[42] they strove, although of no great use.
There was no light in heaven but a few stars,   *405*
      The boats put off o'ercrowded with their crews;
She gave a heel, and then a lurch to port,
And, going down head foremost – sunk, in short.

52

Then rose from sea to sky the wild farewell,
   Then shrieked the timid, and stood still the
                     brave, *410*
Then some leaped overboard with dreadful yell,
      As eager to anticipate their grave;
And the sea yawned around her like a hell,
      And down she sucked with her the whirling wave,
Like one who grapples with his enemy,   *415*
And strives to strangle him before he die.

53

And first one universal shriek there rushed,
   Louder than the loud ocean, like a crash

---

38   *lee* side of the boat sheltered from the wind. The line means 'unless the boat could be driven by the wind against breakers to the lee-side'.
39   *cutter* lifeboat.
40   *puncheon* large cask.
41   *had / Been stove* had a hole made in the side.
42   *yet* still.

Of echoing thunder; and then all was hushed
    Save the wild wind and the remorseless dash   *420*
Of billows; but at intervals there gushed,
    Accompanied with a convulsive splash,
A solitary shriek, the bubbling cry
Of some strong swimmer in his agony.

54

The boats, as stated, had got off before,   *425*
    And in them crowded several of the crew;
And yet their present hope was hardly more
    Than what it had been, for so strong it blew
There was slight chance of reaching any shore;
    And then they were too many, though so few –   *430*
Nine in the cutter, thirty in the boat
Were counted in them when they got afloat.

55

All the rest perished; near two hundred souls
    Had left their bodies – and, what's worse, alas!
When over Catholics the ocean rolls,   *435*
    They must wait several weeks before a mass
Takes off one peck[43] of purgatorial coals,
    Because, till people know what's come to pass,
They won't lay out their money on the dead:
It costs three francs for every mass that's said.   *440*

56

Juan got into the longboat, and there
    Contrived to help Pedrillo to a place;
It seemed as if they had exchanged their care,
    For Juan wore the magisterial face
Which courage gives, while poor Pedrillo's pair   *445*
    Of eyes were crying for their owner's case:
Battista, though (a name called shortly Tita),
Was lost by getting at some aqua vita.[44]

57

Pedro, his valet, too, he tried to save,
    But the same cause, conducive to his loss,   *450*
Left him so drunk, he jumped into the wave
    As o'er the cutter's edge he tried to cross,
And so he found a wine-and-watery grave;

They could not rescue him although so close,
    Because the sea ran higher every minute,   *455*
And for the boat – the crew kept crowding in it.

58

A small old spaniel which had been Don Jóse's,
    His father's, whom he loved, as ye may think
(For on such things the memory reposes
    With tenderness), stood howling on the brink,   *460*
Knowing (dogs have such intellectual noses!),
    No doubt, the vessel was about to sink;
And Juan caught him up, and ere he stepped
Off, threw him in, then after him he leapt.

59

He also stuffed his money where he could   *465*
    About his person, and Pedrillo's too –
Who let him do, in fact, whate'er he would,
    Not knowing what himself to say or do,
As every rising wave his dread renewed;
    But Juan, trusting they might still get through,   *470*
And deeming there were remedies for any ill,
Thus re-embarked[45] his tutor and his spaniel.

60

'Twas a rough night, and blew so stiffly yet,
    That the sail was becalmed between the seas,
Though on the wave's high top too much to set,   *475*
    They dared not take it in for all the breeze;
Each sea curled o'er the stern, and kept them wet,
    And made them bale without a moment's ease,
So that themselves as well as hopes were damped,
And the poor little cutter quickly swamped.   *480*

61

Nine souls more went in her: the longboat still
    Kept above water, with an oar for mast;
Two blankets stitched together, answering ill
    Instead of sail, were to the oar made fast –
Though every wave rolled menacing to fill,   *485*
    And present peril all before surpassed,
They grieved for those who perished with the cutter,
And also for the biscuit casks and butter.

---

43 *peck* small quantity (technically, the fourth part of a bushel, or two gallons).

44 *aqua vita* spirits (brandy, most probably).
45 *re-embarked* again put on board a boat.

62

The sun rose red and fiery, a sure sign
    Of the continuance of the gale: to run   *490*
Before the sea, until it should grow fine,
    Was all that for the present could be done.
A few teaspoonfuls of their rum and wine
    Was served out to the people, who begun
To faint, and damaged bread wet through the bags, *495*
And most of them had little clothes but rags.

63

They counted thirty, crowded in a space
    Which left scarce room for motion or exertion.
They did their best to modify their case:
    One half sat up, though numbed with the
                    immersion,   *500*
While t'other half were laid down in their place
    At watch and watch; thus, shivering like the tertian
Ague[46] in its cold fit, they filled their boat,
With nothing but the sky for a greatcoat.

64

'Tis very certain the desire of life   *505*
    Prolongs it; this is obvious to physicians
When patients, neither plagued with friends nor wife,
    Survive through very desperate conditions,
Because they still can hope, nor shines the knife
    Nor shears of Atropos[47] before their visions: *510*
Despair of all recovery spoils longevity,
And makes men's miseries of alarming brevity.

65

'Tis said that persons living on annuities
    Are longer lived than others – God knows why,
Unless to plague the grantors;[48] yet so true it is, *515*
    That some, I really think, *do* never die.
Of any creditors the worst a Jew it is,
    And *that's* their mode of furnishing supply:
In my young days they lent me cash that way,
Which I found very troublesome to pay.[49]   *520*

66

'Tis thus with people in an open boat,
    They live upon the love of life, and bear
More than can be believed, or even thought,
    And stand like rocks the tempest's wear and tear;
And hardship still has been the sailor's lot   *525*
    Since Noah's ark went cruising here and there;
She had a curious crew as well as cargo,
Like the first old Greek privateer, the Argo.[50]

67

But man is a carnivorous production
    And must have meals, at least one meal a day; *530*
He cannot live, like woodcocks, upon suction,[51]
    But, like the shark and tiger, must have prey –
Although his anatomical construction
    Bears vegetables in a grumbling way,
Your labouring people think beyond all question *535*
Beef, veal, and mutton, better for digestion.

68

And thus it was with this our hapless crew,
    For on the third day there came on a calm,
And though at first their strength it might renew,
    And lying on their weariness like balm,   *540*
Lulled them like turtles sleeping on the blue
    Of ocean, when they woke they felt a qualm,
And fell all ravenously on their provision,
Instead of hoarding it with due precision.

69

The consequence was easily foreseen: *545*
    They ate up all they had, and drank their wine
In spite of all remonstrances, and then –
    On what, in fact, next day were they to dine?
They hoped the wind would rise, these foolish men,
    And carry them to shore! These hopes were fine, *550*
But as they had but one oar, and that brittle,
It would have been more wise to save their victual.[52]

---

46   *the tertian / Ague* a fever that recurs every other day.
47   *shears of Atropos* Atropos, eldest of the three Fates, is
represented blind, with a pair of scissors with which she cuts the
thread of life.
48   *the grantors* those who set up the annuity.
49   *In my young days . . . to pay* by 1816, when he left England,
Byron had amassed £30,000 in debts.

50   *Argo* the ship (named after the city of Argos) which carried
Jason and his companions to capture the golden fleece.
51   *like woodcocks, upon suction* woodcocks appear to be sucking as
they probe with their long bills in the turf.
52   *victual* food (pronounced 'vittle').

70

The fourth day came, but not a breath of air,
　　And ocean slumbered like an unweaned child;
The fifth day, and their boat lay floatingthere,　555
　　The sea and sky were blue, and clear, and mild –
With their one oar (I wish they had had a pair)
　　What could they do? And hunger's rage grew wild;
So Juan's spaniel, spite of his entreating,
Was killed, and portioned out for present eating.　560

71

On the sixth day they fed upon his hide,
　　And Juan, who had still refused, because
The creature was his father's dog that died,
　　Now feeling all the vulture[53] in his jaws,
With some remorse received (though first denied)　565
　　As a great favour one of the forepaws,
Which he divided with Pedrillo, who
Devoured it, longing for the other too.

72

The seventh day, and no wind; the burning sun
　　Blistered and scorched, and, stagnant on the sea,　570
They lay like carcasses; and hope was none,
　　Save in the breeze that came not. Savagely
They glared upon each other – all was done,
　　Water, and wine, and food; and you might see
The longings of the cannibal arise　575
(Although they spoke not) in their wolfish eyes.

73

At length one whispered his companion, who
　　Whispered another, and thus it went round,
And then into a hoarser murmur grew –
　　An ominous, and wild, and desperate sound;　580
And when his comrade's thought each sufferer knew,
　　'Twas but his own, suppressed till now, he found.
And out they spoke of lots for flesh and blood,
And who should die to be his fellow's food.

74

But ere they came to this, they that day shared　585
　　Some leathern caps, and what remained of shoes;

And then they looked around them and despaired,
　　And none to be the sacrifice would choose;
At length the lots were torn up and prepared,
　　But of materials that much shock the muse –　590
Having no paper, for the want of better,
They took by force from Juan Julia's letter.

75

The lots were made, and marked, and mixed and handed
　　In silent horror, and their distribution
Lulled even the savage hunger which demanded,　595
　　Like the Promethean vulture,[54] this pollution;[55]
None in particular had sought or planned it,
　　'Twas nature gnawed them to this resolution
By which none were permitted to be neuter[56] –
And the lot fell on Juan's luckless tutor.　600

76

He but requested to be bled to death:
　　The surgeon had his instruments, and bled
Pedrillo, and so gently ebbed his breath,
　　You hardly could perceive when he was dead.
He died as born, a Catholic in faith,　605
　　Like most in the belief in which they're bred,
And first a little crucifix he kissed,
And then held out his jugular and wrist.

77

The surgeon, as there was no other fee,
　　Had his first choice of morsels for his pains;　610
But being thirstiest at the moment, he
　　Preferred a draught from the fast-flowing veins:
Part was divided, part thrown in the sea,
　　And such things as the entrails and the brains
Regaled two sharks, who followed o'er the billow –　615
The sailors ate the rest of poor Pedrillo.

78

The sailors ate him, all save three or four
　　Who were not quite so fond of animal food;
To these was added Juan who, before

---

[53]　*feeling all the vulture* i.e. feeling as hungry as a vulture.
[54]　*the Promethean vulture* Prometheus was nailed to the rock of
the Caucasus for 3,000 years while an eagle (in some versions a
vulture) feasted on his liver.

[55]　*pollution* defilement (of Julia's love letter). Nothing is sacred
in the face of starvation.
[56]　*neuter* exempt.

Refusing his own spaniel, hardly could   620
Feel now his appetite increased much more;
    'Twas not to be expected that he should,
Even in extremity of their disaster,
Dine with them on his pastor and his master.

79

'Twas better that he did not, for, in fact,   625
    The consequence was awful in the extreme;
For they who were most ravenous in the act
    Went raging mad – Lord, how they did blaspheme,
And foam and roll, with strange convulsions racked,
    Drinking salt-water like a mountain-stream, 630
Tearing and grinning, howling, screeching, swearing,
And, with hyena laughter, died despairing.

80

Their numbers were much thinned by this infliction,
    And all the rest were thin enough, Heaven knows;
And some of them had lost their recollection,   635
    Happier than they who still perceived their woes;
But others pondered on a new dissection,
    As if not warned sufficiently by those
Who had already perished, suffering madly,
For having used their appetites so sadly.   640

81

And next they thought upon the master's mate
    As fattest – but he saved himself because,
Besides being much averse from such a fate,
    There were some other reasons: the first was
He had been rather indisposed of late;   645
    And that which chiefly proved his saving clause
Was a small present made to him at Cadiz,
By general subscription of the ladies.[57]

82

Of poor Pedrillo something still remained,
    But was used sparingly – some were afraid, 650
And others still their appetites constrained,

Or but at times a little supper made;
All except Juan, who throughout abstained,
    Chewing a piece of bamboo, and some lead:
At length they caught two boobies and a noddy,[58] 655
And then they left off eating the dead body.

83

And if Pedrillo's fate should shocking be,
    Remember Ugolino condescends
To eat the head of his arch-enemy
    The moment after he politely ends   660
His tale;[59] if foes be food in hell, at sea
    'Tis surely fair to dine upon our friends
When shipwreck's short allowance grows too scanty,
Without being much more horrible than Dante.

84

And the same night there fell a shower of rain 665
    For which their mouths gaped, like the cracks of
                                   earth
When dried to summer dust; till taught by pain,
    Men really know not what good water's worth:
If you had been in Turkey or in Spain,
    Or with a famished boat's-crew had your berth, 670
Or in the desert heard the camel's bell,
You'd wish yourself where Truth is – in a well.

85

It poured down torrents, but they were no richer
    Until they found a ragged piece of sheet
Which served them as a sort of spongy pitcher, 675
    And when they deemed its moisture was complete,
They wrung it out, and though a thirsty ditcher[60]
    Might not have thought the scanty draught so sweet
As a full pot of porter, to their thinking
They ne'er till now had known the joys of drinking. 680

86

And their baked lips,[61] with many a bloody crack,
    Sucked in the moisture, which like nectar streamed;
Their throats were ovens, their swoln tongues were black

---

57 *a small present . . . ladies* i.e. he was suffering from syphilis.
58 *boobies . . . noddy* species of sea-bird.
59 *Remember Ugolino . . . His tale* In his *Inferno*, Dante relates how Count Ugolino was imprisoned with his two sons and two grandsons and starved to death with them. In Hell, Ugolino is

seen chewing on the skull of the man responsible for the atrocity (*Inferno* xxxiii 76–8).
60 *ditcher* one who makes and repairs ditches.
61 *baked lips* apparently an echo of Coleridge, *Ancient Mariner* (1817) 157: 'With throat unslaked, with black lips baked'.

As the rich man's in hell,[62] who vainly screamed
To beg the beggar, who could not rain back   685
   A drop of dew, when every drop had seemed
To taste of heaven (if this be true, indeed,
Some Christians have a comfortable creed).

87

There were two fathers in this ghastly crew,
   And with them their two sons, of whom the one 690
Was more robust and hardy to the view,
   But he died early; and when he was gone,
His nearest messmate[63] told his sire, who threw
   One glance on him, and said, 'Heaven's will be done!
I can do nothing', and he saw him thrown   695
Into the deep without a tear or groan.

88

The other father had a weaklier child,
   Of a soft cheek, and aspect delicate;
But the boy bore up long, and with a mild
   And patient spirit held aloof his fate;   700
Little he said, and now and then he smiled,
   As if to win a part from off the weight
He saw increasing on his father's heart,
With the deep deadly thought that they must part.

89

And o'er him bent his sire, and never raised   705
   His eyes from off his face, but wiped the foam
From his pale lips, and ever on him gazed,
   And when the wished-for shower at length was come,
And the boy's eyes, which the dull film half glazed,
   Brightened, and for a moment seemed to roam, 710
He squeezed from out a rag some drops of rain
Into his dying child's mouth – but in vain.

90

The boy expired; the father held the clay,[64]
   And looked upon it long, and when at last

Death left no doubt, and the dead burden lay   715
   Stiff on his heart, and pulse and hope were past,
He watched it wistfully, until away
   'Twas borne by the rude wave wherein 'twas cast.
Then he himself sunk down all dumb and shivering,
And gave no sign of life, save his limbs quivering.[65] 720

91

Now overhead a rainbow, bursting through
   The scattering clouds, shone, spanning the dark sea,
Resting its bright base on the quivering blue;
   And all within its arch appeared to be
Clearer than that without, and its wide hue   725
   Waxed[66] broad and waving, like a banner free,
Then changed like to a bow that's bent, and then
Forsook the dim eyes of these shipwrecked men.

92

It changed, of course; a heavenly chameleon,
   The airy child of vapour and the sun,   730
Brought forth in purple, cradled in vermilion,
   Baptized in molten gold, and swathed in dun,[67]
Glittering like crescents o'er a Turk's pavilion,
   And blending every colour into one,
Just like a black eye in a recent scuffle[68]   735
(For sometimes we must box without the muffle[69]).

93

Our shipwrecked seamen thought it a good omen –
   It is as well to think so, now and then;
'Twas an old custom of the Greek and Roman,
   And may become of great advantage when   740
Folks are discouraged; and most surely no men
   Had greater need to nerve themselves again
Than these, and so this rainbow looked like hope –
Quite a celestial kaleidoscope.[70]

94

About this time a beautiful white bird,   745
   Webfooted, not unlike a dove in size

---

[62] *As the rich man's in hell* an allusion to the parable of Dives and Lazarus, Luke 16:19–26.
[63] *messmate* companion at mealtimes; a sardonic joke.
[64] *clay* body.
[65] The relation between this episode and Dante's Ugolino is discussed by Ralph Pite, *The Circle of our Vision: Dante's Presence in English Romantic Poetry* (Oxford, 1994), pp. 222–4.
[66] *Waxed* became.

[67] *dun* dull brown.
[68] Byron is deliberately profaning the image celebrated in Wordsworth's *The Rainbow*.
[69] *muffle* boxing-glove. Bareknuckle boxing was commonplace throughout the nineteenth century.
[70] *kaleidoscope* invented as recently as 1817 by Sir David Brewster; Byron was sent one by John Murray in November 1818.

And plumage (probably it might have erred
    Upon its course), passed oft before their eyes
And tried to perch, although it saw and heard
    The men within the boat, and in this guise   750
It came and went, and fluttered round them till
Night fell – this seemed a better omen still.

95

But in this case I also must remark
    'Twas well this bird of promise did not perch,
Because the tackle of our shattered bark   755
    Was not so safe for roosting as a church;
And had it been the dove from Noah's ark,
    Returning there from her successful search,
Which in their way that moment chanced to fall,
They would have eat[71] her, olive-branch and all.[72]   760

96

With twilight it again came on to blow,
    But not with violence; the stars shone out,
The boat made way; yet now they were so low,
    They knew not where nor what they were about;
Some fancied they saw land, and some said 'No!'   765
    The frequent fog-banks gave them cause to doubt –
Some swore that they heard breakers,[73] others guns,
And all mistook about the latter once.

97

As morning broke the light wind died away,
    When he who had the watch sung out and swore   770
If 'twas not land that rose with the sun's ray,
    He wished that land he never might see more;
And the rest rubbed their eyes, and saw a bay,
    Or thought they saw, and shaped their course
                              for shore –
For shore it was,[74] and gradually grew   775
Distinct, and high, and palpable to view.

98

And then of these some part burst into tears,
    And others, looking with a stupid stare,
Could not yet separate their hopes from fears,
    And seemed as if they had no further care;   780
While a few prayed (the first time for some years),
    And at the bottom of the boat three were
Asleep; they shook them by the hand and head,
And tried to awaken them, but found them dead.

99

The day before, fast sleeping on the water,   785
    They found a turtle of the hawk's-bill kind,
And by good fortune gliding softly, caught her,
    Which yielded a day's life, and to their mind
Proved even still a more nutritious matter
    Because it left encouragement behind: 790
They thought that in such perils, more than chance
Had sent them this for their deliverance.

100

The land appeared a high and rocky coast,
    And higher grew the mountains as they drew,
Set by a current, toward it: they were lost   795
    In various conjectures, for none knew
To what part of the earth they had been tossed,
    So changeable had been the winds that blew;
Some thought it was Mount Etna, some the highlands
Of Candia,[75] Cyprus, Rhodes, or other islands.   800

101

Meantime the current, with a rising gale,
    Still set them onwards to the welcome shore
Like Charon's bark of spectres,[76] dull and pale.
    Their living freight was now reduced to four,
And three dead, whom their strength could not
                              avail   805
    To heave into the deep with those before –
Though the two sharks still followed them, and dashed
The spray into their faces as they splashed.

---

[71] *eat* pronounced 'ett' by Byron.
[72] See Genesis 8:6–11. In a useful note, Peter Cochran suggests that Byron has in mind a narrative of the shipwreck of the *Medusa*; see 'Byron's *Don Juan*, Canto II, Stanza 95: A Previously Unnoted Source in the *Medusa* Narrative', *N&Q* 39 (1992) 172–3.
[73] *breakers* waves breaking against the shore.
[74] *For shore it was* that of one of the smaller Cyclades (l.1010);

as the *Trinidada* went down near the Golfe du Lion, that would mean that the survivors had drifted an improbable 2,000 kilometers.
[75] *Candia* Crete.
[76] *Like Charon's bark of spectres* the grim ferryman Charon took the ghosts of the dead across the Acheron (river of woe) and the black Cocytus (river of wailing).

102

Famine, despair, cold, thirst and heat, had done
  Their work on them by turns, and thinned
            them to   810
Such things a mother had not known her son
  Amidst the skeletons of that gaunt crew;
By night chilled, by day scorched – thus one by one
  They perished, until withered to these few,
But chiefly by a species of self-slaughter,   815
In washing down Pedrillo with salt water.

103

As they drew nigh the land, which now was seen
  Unequal in its aspect here and there,
They felt the freshness of its growing green
  That waved in forest-tops and smoothed the air,   820
And fell upon their glazed eyes like a screen
  From glistening waves, and skies so hot and bare –
Lovely seemed any object that should sweep
Away the vast, salt, dread, eternal deep.

104

The shore looked wild, without a trace of man,   825
  And girt by formidable waves; but they
Were mad for land, and thus their course they ran,
  Though right ahead the roaring breakers lay;
A reef between them also now began
  To show its boiling surf and bounding spray –   830
But finding no place for their landing better,
They ran the boat for shore, and overset[77] her.

105

But in his native stream, the Guadalquivir,
  Juan to lave his youthful limbs was wont;
And having learnt to swim in that sweet river,   835
  Had often turned the art to some account:
A better swimmer you could scarce see ever,
  He could, perhaps, have passed the Hellespont,
As once (a feat on which ourselves we prided)
Leander, Mr Ekenhead, and I did.[78]   840

106

So here, though faint, emaciated, and stark,
  He buoyed his boyish limbs, and strove to ply
With the quick wave, and gain, ere it was dark,
  The beach which lay before him, high and dry:
The greatest danger here was from a shark   845
  That carried off his neighbour by the thigh;
As for the other two they could not swim,
So nobody arrived on shore but him.

107

Nor yet had he arrived but for the oar,
  Which, providentially for him, was washed   850
Just as his feeble arms could strike no more,
  And the hard wave o'erwhelmed him as 'twas dashed
Within his grasp; he clung to it, and sore
  The waters beat while he thereto was lashed;
At last, with swimming, wading, scrambling, he   855
Rolled on the beach, half-senseless, from the sea.

108

There, breathless, with his digging nails he clung
  Fast to the sand, lest the returning wave,
From whose reluctant[79] roar his life he wrung,
  Should suck him back to her insatiate grave: 860
And there he lay, full-length, where he was flung,
  Before the entrance of a cliff-worn cave,
With just enough of life to feel its pain,
And deem that it was saved, perhaps, in vain.

109

With slow and staggering effort he arose,   865
  But sunk again upon his bleeding knee
And quivering hand; and then he looked for those
  Who long had been his mates upon the sea,
But none of them appeared to share his woes
  Save one, a corpse from out the famished three,   870
Who died two days before, and now had found
An unknown barren beach for burial ground.

---

77 *overset* capsized.
78 A MS note by Byron reads: 'Mr Ekenhead, Lieutenant of Marines on board of the Salsette (then commanded by Capt Bathurst) swam across the Dardanelles May 10th (I think) 1810. See the account in Hobhouse's travels'. Byron actually swam the Hellespont on 3 May 1810, and it was described in detail in

'Extract from Lord Byron's Journal', *London Magazine* 1 (1820) 295–6.
79 *reluctant* opposing; Byron is also punning on the Latin root, '*reluctari*', 'to struggle against'.

110

And as he gazed, his dizzy brain spun fast,
    And down he sunk; and as he sunk, the sand
Swam round and round, and all his senses passed: *875*
    He fell upon his side, and his stretched hand
Drooped dripping on the oar (their jury-mast),[80]
    And, like a withered lily, on the land
His slender frame and pallid aspect lay,
As fair a thing as e'er was formed of clay.[81]   *880*

111

How long in his damp trance young Juan lay[82]
    He knew not, for the earth was gone for him,
And Time had nothing more of night nor day
    For his congealing blood, and senses dim;
And how this heavy faintness passed away   *885*
    He knew not, till each painful pulse and limb
And tingling vein seemed throbbing back to life –
For Death, though vanquished, still retired with strife.

112

His eyes he opened, shut, again unclosed,
    For all was doubt and dizziness; methought   *890*
He still was in the boat, and had but dozed,
    And felt again with his despair o'erwrought,
And wished it death in which he had reposed,
    And then once more his feelings back were brought;
And slowly by his swimming eyes was seen   *895*
A lovely female face of seventeen.

113

'Twas bending close o'er his, and the small mouth
    Seemed almost prying into his for breath;
And chafing him, the soft warm hand of youth
    Recalled his answering spirits back from death;   *900*
And, bathing his chill temples, tried to soothe
    Each pulse to animation, till beneath
Its gentle touch and trembling care, a sigh
To these kind efforts made a low reply.

114

Then was the cordial poured, and mantle flung   *905*
    Around his scarce-clad limbs; and the fair arm

Raised higher the faint head which o'er it hung;
    And her transparent cheek, all pure and warm,
Pillowed his death-like forehead; then she wrung
    His dewy curls, long drenched by every storm;   *910*
And watched with eagerness each throb that drew
A sigh from his heaved bosom – and hers too.

115

And lifting him with care into the cave,
    The gentle girl, and her attendant – one
Young, yet her elder, and of brow less grave,   *915*
    And more robust of figure – then begun
To kindle fire, and as the new flames gave
    Light to the rocks that roofed them, which the sun
Had never seen, the maid, or whatsoe'er
She was, appeared distinct, and tall, and fair.   *920*

116

Her brow was overhung with coins of gold
    That sparkled o'er the auburn of her hair,
Her clustering hair, whose longer locks were rolled
    In braids behind, and though her stature were
Even of the highest for a female mould,   *925*
    They nearly reached her heel; and in her air
There was a something which bespoke command,
As one who was a lady in the land.

117

Her hair, I said, was auburn, but her eyes
    Were black as death, their lashes the same hue,   *930*
Of downcast length, in whose silk shadow lies
    Deepest attraction – for when to the view
Forth from its raven fringe the full glance flies,
    Ne'er with such force the swiftest arrow flew;
'Tis as the snake late coiled, who pours his length,   *935*
And hurls at once his venom and his strength.

118

Her brow was white and low, her cheek's pure dye
    Like twilight rosy still with the set sun;
Short upper lip, sweet lips! – that make us sigh
    Ever to have seen such, for she was one   *940*
Fit for the model of a statuary

---

80   *jury-mast* replacement mast.
81   *clay* flesh.

82   *How long in his damp trance young Juan lay* an echo of
Coleridge, *Ancient Mariner* (1817) 393–4: 'How long in that
same fit I lay, / I have not to declare'.

(A race of mere impostors, when all's done;
I've seen much finer women, ripe and real,
Than all the nonsense of their stone [83] ideal).

119

I'll tell you why I say so, for 'tis just   945
    One should not rail without a decent cause:
There was an Irish lady,[84] to whose bust
    I ne'er saw justice done, and yet she was
A frequent model; and if e'er she must
    Yield to stern Time and Nature's wrinkling
                                    laws,   950
They will destroy a face which mortal thought
Ne'er compassed, nor less mortal chisel wrought.

120

And such was she, the lady of the cave:
    Her dress was very different from the Spanish –
Simpler, and yet of colours not so grave;   955
    For, as you know, the Spanish women banish
Bright hues when out of doors, and yet, while wave
    Around them (what I hope will never vanish)
The basquiña[85] and the mantilla,[86] they
Seem at the same time mystical[87] and gay.   960

121

But with our damsel this was not the case:
    Her dress was many-coloured, finely spun;
Her locks curled negligently round her face,
    But through them gold and gems profusely shone;
Her girdle sparkled, and the richest lace   965
    Flowed in her veil, and many a precious stone
Flashed on her little hand; but, what was shocking,
Her small snow feet had slippers, but no stocking.

122

The other female's dress was not unlike,
    But of inferior materials; she   970
Had not so many ornaments to strike[88] –
    Her hair had silver only, bound to be

Her dowry; and her veil, in form alike,
    Was coarser; and her air, though firm, less free;
Her hair was thicker, but less long; her eyes   975
As black, but quicker, and of smaller size.

123

And these two tended him, and cheered him both
    With food and raiment, and those soft attentions
Which are (as I must own) of female growth,
    And have ten thousand delicate inventions: 980
They made a most superior mess of broth,
    A thing which poesy but seldom mentions,
But the best dish that e'er was cooked since Homer's
Achilles ordered dinner for newcomers.[89]

124

I'll tell you who they were, this female pair,   985
    Lest they should seem princesses in disguise;
Besides, I hate all mystery, and that air
    Of claptrap, which your recent poets prize;
And so, in short, the girls they really were
    They shall appear before your curious eyes –   990
Mistress and maid; the first was only daughter
Of an old man, who lived upon the water.

125

A fisherman he had been in his youth,
    And still a sort of fisherman was he;
But other speculations were, in sooth,   995
    Added to his connection with the sea –
Perhaps not so respectable, in truth:
    A little smuggling, and some piracy
Left him, at last, the sole of many masters
Of an ill-gotten million of piastres.[90]   1000

126

A fisher, therefore, was he – though of men,
    Like Peter the Apostle[91] – and he fished
For wandering merchant vessels, now and then,

---

83   *stone* an early MS reading is 'damned'.
84   *an Irish lady* probably, as commentators have noted, Lady
Adelaide Forbes (1789–1858); 'The Apollo Belvidere is the
image of Lady Adelaide Forbes', he told Moore, 12 May 1817
(Marchand v 227).
85   *basquiña* outer skirt placed over indoor dress when going
out.
86   *mantilla* light cloak.

87   *mystical* solemn.
88   *strike* remove, take off.
89   *But the best dish . . . newcomers* Homer describes in *Iliad* ix
how Patroclus, Achilles and Automedon ate a sheep, a goat and
a pig.
90   *piastres* small Turkish coins.
91   *though of men . . . Apostle* see Matthew 4:18–19.

And sometimes caught as many as he wished;
   The cargoes he confiscated, and gain   1005
      He sought in the slave-market too, and dished
Full many a morsel for that Turkish trade,
By which, no doubt, a good deal may be made.

127

He was a Greek, and on his isle had built
   (One of the wild and smaller Cyclades)[92]   1010
A very handsome house from out his guilt,
   And there he lived exceedingly at ease;
Heaven knows what cash he got, or blood he spilt –
   A sad[93] old fellow was he, if you please,
But this I know: it was a spacious building,   1015
Full of barbaric carving, paint, and gilding.

128

He had an only daughter called Haidee,[94]
   The greatest heiress of the Eastern Isles;
Besides, so very beautiful was she,
   Her dowry was as nothing to her smiles: 1020
Still in her teens, and like a lovely tree
   She grew to womanhood, and between whiles
Rejected several suitors, just to learn
How to accept a better in his turn.

129

And walking out upon the beach below   1025
   The cliff, towards sunset, on that day she found,
Insensible – not dead, but nearly so –
   Don Juan, almost famished, and half-drowned;
But being naked, she was shocked, you know,
   Yet deemed herself in common pity bound,   1030
As far as in her lay, 'to take him in,
A stranger',[95] dying, with so white a skin.

130

But taking him into her father's house
   Was not exactly the best way to save,
But like conveying to the cat the mouse,   1035
   Or people in a trance into their grave;
Because the good old man had so much νοῦς,[96]
   Unlike the honest Arab thieves so brave,
He would have hospitably cured the stranger,
And sold him instantly when out of danger.   1040

131

And therefore, with her maid, she thought it best
   (A virgin always on her maid relies)
To place him in the cave for present rest;
   And when, at last, he opened his black eyes,
Their charity increased about their guest,   1045
   And their compassion grew to such a size,
It opened half the turnpike-gates to heaven
(St Paul says 'tis the toll which must be given).[97]

132

They made a fire, but such a fire as they
   Upon the moment could contrive with such   1050
Materials as were cast up round the bay –
   Some broken planks, and oars, that to the touch
Were nearly tinder, since so long they lay,
   A mast was almost crumbled to a crutch;
But, by God's grace, here wrecks were in such
                  plenty,   1055
That there was fuel to have furnished twenty.

133

He had a bed of furs, and a pelisse,[98]
   For Haidee stripped her sables off to make
His couch; and, that he might be more at ease
   And warm, in case by chance he should
                  awake,   1060
They also gave a petticoat apiece,
   She and her maid, and promised by daybreak
To pay him a fresh visit, with a dish
For breakfast, of eggs, coffee, bread, and fish.

---

92 *Cyclades* group of islands in the Aegean between the Pelopennesus and the Dodecanese.
93 *sad* appallingly bad.
94 *Haidee* 'a caress', or 'the carressed one'; Byron would have encountered the name in popular Greek songs of the time.
95 Matthew 25:35.

96 νοῦς pronounced 'nouse' (rhyme with 'mouse'); sense, intelligence.
97 'And above all these things put on charity, which is the bond of perfectness' (Colossians 3:14).
98 *pelisse* long cloak reaching the ankles, with sleeves or arm-holes.

134

And thus they left him to his lone repose.   *1065*
　　Juan slept like a top,[99] or like the dead
Who sleep at last, perhaps (God only knows),
　　Just for the present; and in his lulled head
Not even a vision of his former woes
　　Throbbed in accursed dreams, which some-
　　　　　　　　　　　　　times spread   *1070*
Unwelcome visions of our former years,
Till the eye, cheated, opens thick with tears.

135

Young Juan slept all dreamless, but the maid
　　Who smoothed his pillow as she left the den
Looked back upon him, and a moment stayed,   *1075*
　　And turned, believing that he called again.
He slumbered; yet she thought, at least she said
　　(The heart will slip even as the tongue and pen),
He had pronounced her name – but she forgot
That at this moment Juan knew it not.   *1080*

136

And pensive to her father's house she went,
　　Enjoining silence strict to Zoe,[100] who
Better than her knew what, in fact, she meant,
　　She being wiser by a year or two:
A year or two's an age when rightly spent,   *1085*
　　And Zoe spent hers, as most women do,
In gaining all that useful sort of knowledge
Which is acquired in nature's good old college.

137

The morn broke, and found Juan slumbering still
　　Fast in his cave, and nothing clashed upon   *1090*
His rest; the rushing of the neighbouring rill
　　And the young beams of the excluded sun
Troubled him not, and he might sleep his fill;
　　And need he had of slumber yet, for none
Had suffered more – his hardships were
　　　　　　　　　　　　　comparative   *1095*
To those related in my granddad's *Narrative*.[101]

138

Not so Haidee: she sadly tossed and tumbled,
　　And started from her sleep, and, turning o'er,
Dreamed of a thousand wrecks o'er which she stumbled,
　　And handsome corpses strewed upon the shore;   *1100*
And woke her maid so early that she grumbled,
　　And called her father's old slaves up, who swore
In several oaths – Armenian, Turk, and Greek;
They knew not what to think of such a freak.[102]

139

But up she got, and up she made them get   *1105*
　　With some pretence about the sun, that makes
Sweet skies just when he rises, or is set;
　　And 'tis, no doubt, a sight to see when breaks
Bright Phoebus, while the mountains still are wet
　　With mist, and every bird with him awakes,   *1110*
And night is flung off like a mourning suit
Worn for a husband, or some other brute.

140

I say, the sun is a most glorious sight;
　　I've seen him rise full oft, indeed of late
I have sat up on purpose all the night,   *1115*
　　Which hastens, as physicians say, one's fate –
And so all ye, who would be in the right
　　In health and purse, begin your day to date
From daybreak, and when coffined at fourscore,[103]
Engrave upon the plate, you rose at four.   *1120*

141

And Haidee met the morning face to face;
　　Her own was freshest, though a feverish flush
Had dyed it with the headlong blood, whose race
　　From heart to cheek is curbed into a blush,
Like to a torrent which a mountain's base,   *1125*
　　That overpowers some alpine river's rush,

---

99   *Juan slept like a top* a reference to the apparent stillness of a
spinning top when its axis of rotation is vertical.
100   *Zoe* 'animal life'.
101   *my granddad's Narrative* i.e. *A Narrative of the Hon. John
Byron, containing an account of the great distress suffered by himself
and his companions on the coast of Patagonia, from the year 1740, till*

their arrival in England, 1746 (1768) – a popular volume which
went through eleven editions before 1825, reprinted intermit-
tently until 1925.
102   *a freak* i.e. freakish behaviour.
103   *fourscore* eighty.

Checks to a lake, whose waves in circles spread,
Or the Red Sea – but the sea is not red.

142

And down the cliff the island virgin came,
    And near the cave her quick light footsteps
                                        drew,   *1130*
While the sun smiled on her with his first flame,
    And young Aurora[104] kissed her lips with dew,
Taking her for a sister; just the same
    Mistake you would have made on seeing the two,
Although the mortal, quite as fresh and fair,   *1135*
Had all the advantage too of not being air.

143

And when into the cavern Haidee stepped
    All timidly, yet rapidly, she saw
That like an infant Juan sweetly slept;
    And then she stopped, and stood as if in awe   *1140*
(For sleep is awful),[105] and on tiptoe crept
    And wrapped him closer, lest the air, too raw,
Should reach his blood, then o'er him still as death
Bent, with hushed lips, that drank his scarce-drawn
                                        breath.

144

And thus like to an angel o'er the dying   *1145*
    Who die in righteousness,[106] she leaned; and there
All tranquilly the shipwrecked boy was lying,
    As o'er him lay the calm and stirless air.
But Zoe the meantime some eggs was frying,
    Since, after all, no doubt the youthful pair   *1150*
Must breakfast, and betimes; lest they should ask it,
She drew out her provision from the basket.

145

She knew that the best feelings must have victual
    And that a shipwrecked youth would hungry be;
Besides, being less in love, she yawned a little,   *1155*

And felt her veins chilled by the neighbouring sea.
    And so she cooked their breakfast to a tittle;[107]
I can't say that she gave them any tea,
    But there were eggs, fruit, coffee, bread, fish, honey,
With Scio[108] wine – and all for love, not money.   *1160*

146

And Zoe, when the eggs were ready, and
    The coffee made, would fain have wakened Juan,
But Haidee stopped her with her quick small hand,
    And without a word, a sign her finger drew on
Her lip, which Zoe needs must understand;   *1165*
    And, the first breakfast spoilt, prepared a new one,
Because her mistress would not let her break
That sleep which seemed as it would ne'er awake.

147

For still he lay, and on his thin worn cheek
    A purple hectic[109] played like dying day   *1170*
On the snow-tops of distant hills; the streak
    Of sufferance yet upon his forehead lay,
Where the blue veins looked shadowy, shrunk, and weak;
    And his black curls were dewy with the spray
Which weighed upon them yet, all damp and salt,   *1175*
Mixed with the stony vapours of the vault.

148

And she bent o'er him, and he lay beneath,
    Hushed as the babe upon its mother's breast,
Drooped as the willow when no winds can breathe,
    Lulled like the depth of ocean when at rest,   *1180*
Fair as the crowning rose of the whole wreath,
    Soft as the callow cygnet[110] in its nest;
In short, he was a very pretty fellow,
Although his woes had turned him rather yellow.

149

He woke and gazed, and would have slept again,   *1185*
    But the fair face which met his eyes forbade

---

104   *Aurora* goddess of dawn and morning.
105   *awful* awe-inspiring.
106   *the dying . . . righteousness* a profane reference to Matthew 25:46.
107   *to a tittle* with minute exactness.

108   *Scio* Italian form of Chios (island off the Ionian coast between Lesbos and Samos, known for the high quality of its wines).
109   *purple hectic* purple flush.
110   *cygnet* young swan.

Those eyes to close, though weariness and pain
    Had further sleep a further pleasure made;
For woman's face was never formed in vain
    For Juan, so that, even when he prayed,   *1190*
He turned from grisly saints and martyrs hairy
To the sweet portraits of the Virgin Mary.

150

And thus upon his elbow he arose,
    And looked upon the lady, in whose cheek
The pale contended with the purple rose,   *1195*
    As with an effort she began to speak;
Her eyes were eloquent, her words would pose,[111]
    Although she told him, in good modern Greek,
With an Ionian accent, low and sweet,
That he was faint, and must not talk, but eat.   *1200*

151

Now Juan could not understand a word,
    Being no Grecian; but he had an ear,
And her voice was the warble of a bird,
    So soft, so sweet, so delicately clear,
That finer, simpler music ne'er was heard;   *1205*
    The sort of sound we echo with a tear
Without knowing why – an overpowering tone
Whence melody descends as from a throne.

152

And Juan gazed as one who is awoke
    By a distant organ, doubting if he be   *1210*
Not yet a dreamer, till the spell is broke
    By the watchman, or some such reality,
Or by one's early valet's cursed knock –
    At least it is a heavy sound to me
Who like a morning slumber, for the night   *1215*
Shows stars and women in a better light.

153

And Juan, too, was helped out from his dream
    Or sleep, or whatsoe'er it was, by feeling
A most prodigious appetite: the steam

Of Zoe's cookery no doubt was stealing   *1220*
Upon his senses, and the kindling beam
    Of the new fire, which Zoe kept up, kneeling,
To stir her viands, made him quite awake
And long for food, but chiefly a beefsteak.

154

But beef is rare within these oxless isles;   *1225*
    Goat's flesh there is, no doubt, and kid, and mutton;
And, when a holiday upon them smiles,
    A joint upon their barbarous spits they put on:
But this occurs but seldom, between whiles,
    For some of these are rocks with scarce a hut on; *1230*
Others are fair and fertile, among which
This, though not large, was one of the most rich.

155

I say that beef is rare, and can't help thinking
    That the old fable of the Minotaur –
From which our modern morals, rightly shrinking, *1235*
    Condemn the royal lady's taste who wore
A cow's shape for a mask – was only (sinking
    The allegory) a mere type, no more;
That Pasiphae promoted breeding cattle
To make the Cretans bloodier in battle.[112]   *1240*

156

For we all know that English people are
    Fed upon beef (I won't say much of beer
Because 'tis liquor only, and being far
    From this my subject, has no business here);
We know, too, they are very fond of war,   *1245*
    A pleasure (like all pleasures) rather dear;
So were the Cretans – from which I infer
That beef and battles both were owing to her.[113]

157

But to resume. The languid Juan raised
    His head upon his elbow, and he saw   *1250*
A sight on which he had not lately gazed,
    As all his latter meals had been quite raw –

---

[111]   *pose* puzzle, confuse.
[112]   Minos of Crete challenged Poseidon, god of the sea, to produce a bull from the ocean. So beautiful was it, that he could not sacrifice it, and substituted another, incurring Poseidon's wrath. After Minos's marriage to Pasiphae, Poseidon made her fall in love with the bull, with which she had intercourse, giving birth to the Minotaur – half bull, half man. It became a scourge,

devouring the Cretans, until Daedalus built a labyrinth to contain it.
[113]   *her* Pasiphae. As a result of the imprisonment of the Minotaur in the labyrinth, Minos waged war on Athens; having defeated it, he fed the Minotaur a yearly tribute of seven young men and seven maidens.

Three or four things, for which the Lord he praised,
    And, feeling still the famished vulture gnaw,
He fell upon whate'er was offered, like   *1255*
A priest, a shark, an alderman,[114] or pike.

158

He ate, and he was well supplied; and she
    Who watched him like a mother, would have fed
Him past all bounds, because she smiled to see
    Such an appetite in one she had deemed dead: *1260*
But Zoe, being older than Haidee,
    Knew (by tradition, for she ne'er had read)
That famished people must be slowly nursed,
And fed by spoonfuls, else they always burst.

159

And so she took the liberty to state,   *1265*
    Rather by deeds than words, because the case
Was urgent, that the gentleman whose fate
    Had made her mistress quit her bed to trace[115]
The seashore at this hour, must leave his plate
    Unless he wished to die upon the place –   *1270*
She snatched it and refused another morsel,
Saying he had gorged enough to make a horse ill.

160

Next they – he being naked, save a tattered
    Pair of scarce decent trousers – went to work,
And in the fire his recent rags they scattered   *1275*
    And dressed him, for the present, like a Turk
Or Greek; that is (although it not much mattered),
    Omitting turban, slippers, pistols, dirk,[116]
They furnished him, entire except some stitches,
With a clean shirt and very spacious breeches.   *1280*

161

And then fair Haidee tried her tongue at speaking,
    But not a word could Juan comprehend,
Although he listened so that the young Greek in
    Her earnestness would ne'er have made an end;
And, as he interrupted not, went ekeing   *1285*

Her speech out to her protégé and friend,
Till pausing at the last her breath to take,
She saw he did not understand Romaic.[117]

162

And then she had recourse to nods and signs,
    And smiles, and sparkles of the speaking eye,   *1290*
And read (the only book she could) the lines
    Of his fair face, and found, by sympathy,
The answer eloquent, where the soul shines
    And darts in one quick glance a long reply;
And thus in every look she saw expressed   *1295*
A world of words, and things at which she guessed.

163

And now, by dint of fingers and of eyes,
    And words repeated after her, he took
A lesson in her tongue – but by surmise,
    No doubt, less of her language than her look;   *1300*
As he who studies fervently the skies
    Turns oftener to the stars than to his book,
Thus Juan learned his alpha beta better
From Haidee's glance than any graven letter.

164

'Tis pleasing to be schooled in a strange tongue   *1305*
    By female lips and eyes;[118] that is, I mean,
When both the teacher and the taught are young,
    As was the case, at least, where I have been;
They smile so when one's right, and when one's wrong
    They smile still more, and then there
                       intervene   *1310*
Pressure of hands, perhaps even a chaste kiss;
I learned the little that I know by this –

165

That is, some words of Spanish, Turk, and Greek,
    Italian not at all, having no teachers;
Much English I cannot pretend to speak,   *1315*
    Learning that language chiefly from its preachers,
Barrow, South, Tillotson, whom every week

---

[114] *alderman* in London, the chief officer of a ward. They were a byword for greed, for the way they levied fines.
[115] *trace* tread.
[116] *dirk* dagger.
[117] *Romaic* modern Greek vernacular, some of which Byron

learnt on his visit to Athens in 1810–11.
[118] *'Tis pleasing . . . eyes* Byron learned Spanish in Seville from a female tutor, Greek from Teresa Macri in Athens, and Italian from Marianna Segati in Venice.

I study, also Blair[119] – the highest reachers
Of eloquence in piety and prose;
I hate your poets, so read none of those.[120]   *1320*

166

As for the ladies, I have nought to say,
    A wanderer from the British world of fashion,[121]
Where I, like other 'dogs, have had my day';[122]
    Like other men too, may have had my passion –
But that, like other things, has passed away,   *1325*
    And all her fools whom I *could* lay the lash on:
Foes, friends, men, women, now are nought to me
But dreams of what has been, no more to be.

167

Return we to Don Juan. He begun
    To hear new words, and to repeat them, but   *1330*
Some feelings, universal as the sun,
    Were such as could not in his breast be shut
More than within the bosom of a nun;
    He was in love – as you would be, no doubt,
With a young benefactress; so was she,   *1335*
Just in the way we very often see.

168

And every day by daybreak – rather early
    For Juan, who was somewhat fond of rest,
She came into the cave, but it was merely
    To see her bird reposing in his nest;   *1340*
And she would softly stir his locks so curly,
    Without disturbing her yet-slumbering guest,
Breathing all gently o'er his cheek and mouth,
As o'er a bed of roses the sweet south.[123]

169

And every morn his colour freshlier came,   *1345*
    And every day helped on his convalescence;

'Twas well, because health in the human frame
    Is pleasant, besides being true love's essence;
For health and idleness to passion's flame
    Are oil and gunpowder, and some good lessons   *1350*
Are also learnt from Ceres and from Bacchus,[124]
Without whom Venus will not long attack us.[125]

170

While Venus fills the heart (without heart really
    Love, though good always, is not quite so good),
Ceres presents a plate of vermicelli;[126]   *1355*
    For love must be sustained like flesh and blood,
While Bacchus pours out wine, or hands a jelly.[127]
    Eggs, oysters too, are amatory food;[128]
But who is their purveyor from above
Heaven knows – it may be Neptune, Pan, or Jove.   *1360*

171

When Juan woke he found some good things ready;
    A bath, a breakfast, and the finest eyes
That ever made a youthful heart less steady,
    Besides her maid's, as pretty for their size –
But I have spoken of all this already,   *1365*
    And repetition's tiresome and unwise;
Well, Juan, after bathing in the sea,
Came always back to coffee and Haidee.

172

Both were so young, and one so innocent,
    That bathing passed for nothing; Juan
                        seemed   *1370*
To her, as 'twere, the kind of being sent,
    Of whom these two years she had nightly dreamed:
A something to be loved, a creature meant
    To be her happiness, and whom she deemed
To render happy; all who joy would win   *1375*
Must share it – Happiness was born a twin.

---

[119]   Isaac Barrow (1630–77), Robert South (1634–1716), John Tillotson (1630–94), and Hugh Blair (1718–1800), distinguished sermonists.
[120]   *I hate your poets, so read none of those* an overstatement designed to emphasize Byron's dislike of the Lake poets and admiration of Pope.
[121]   *the British world of fashion* in which Byron was a very big fish, 1812–16.
[122]   *Hamlet* V i 292: 'The cat will mew, and dog will have his day'.

[123]   *the sweet south* i.e. the warm south wind.
[124]   *Ceres . . . Bacchus* corn (bread) and wine. Ceres is the goddess of corn and harvest; Bacchus the god of wine.
[125]   *Are also learnt . . . attack us* a reworking of Terence, *Eunuchus* iv 5,6: 'sine Cerere et Libero friget Venus' (without Ceres and Bacchus, Venus is frigid).
[126]   *vermicelli* pasta is made out of wheat.
[127]   *a jelly* partly made out of wine.
[128]   *amatory food* aphrodisiacs.

173

It was such pleasure to behold him, such
    Enlargement of existence to partake
Nature with him, to thrill beneath his touch,
    To watch him slumbering, and to see him
                   wake: *1380*
To live with him for ever were too much,
    But then the thought of parting made her quake;
He was her own, her ocean-treasure, cast
Like a rich wreck – her first love, and her last.[129]

174

And thus a moon rolled on, and fair Haidee   *1385*
    Paid daily visits to her boy, and took
Such plentiful precautions, that still he
    Remained unknown within his craggy nook;
At last her father's prows put out to sea,
    For certain merchantmen upon the look,   *1390*
Not as of yore to carry off an Io,[130]
But three Ragusan[131] vessels, bound for Scio.

175

Then came her freedom, for she had no mother,
    So that, her father being at sea, she was
Free as a married woman, or such other   *1395*
    Female, as where she likes may freely pass,
Without even the encumbrance of a brother –
    The freest she that ever gazed on glass
(I speak of Christian lands in this comparison,
Where wives, at least, are seldom kept in garrison). *1400*

176

Now she prolonged her visits and her talk
    (For they must talk), and he had learnt to say
So much as to propose to take a walk –
    For little had he wandered since the day
On which, like a young flower snapped from the
                   stalk, *1405*

Drooping and dewy on the beach he lay;
And thus they walked out in the afternoon,
And saw the sun set opposite the moon.

177

It was a wild and breaker-beaten coast,
    With cliffs above, and a broad sandy shore   *1410*
Guarded by shoals and rocks as by an host,[132]
    With here and there a creek whose aspect wore
A better welcome to the tempest-tossed;
    And rarely ceased the haughty billow's roar,
Save on the dead long summer days, which
                   make *1415*
The outstretched ocean glitter like a lake.

178

And the small ripple spilt upon the beach
    Scarcely o'erpassed the cream of your champagne,
When o'er the brim the sparkling bumpers reach,
    That spring-dew of the spirit, the heart's rain! *1420*
Few things surpass old wine – and they may preach
    Who please (the more because they preach in vain) –
Let us have wine and woman, mirth and laughter,
Sermons and soda-water the day after.

179

Man, being reasonable, must get drunk;   *1425*
    The best of life is but intoxication:
Glory, the grape, love, gold – in these are sunk
    The hopes of all men, and of every nation;
Without their sap, how branchless were the trunk
    Of life's strange tree, so fruitful on occasion. *1430*
But to return; get very drunk, and when
You wake with headache, you shall see what then.

180

Ring for your valet, bid him quickly bring
    Some hock[133] and soda-water[134] – then you'll know

---

[129] *her first love, and her last* a claim Byron himself made in a letter to Countess Teresa Guiccioli on 22 April 1819: 'You who are my only and last love, who are my only joy'.
[130] *Io* changed into a cow, Io, a priestess at Argos, went on protracted wanderings of the earth until it reached Memphis on the Nile, where Zeus restored it to human form.
[131] Ragusa was in Byron's day the name for Dubrovnik, an ancient seaport still flourishing on the Adriatic coast of the former Yugoslavia.
[132] *host* army.
[133] *hock* white German wine.

[134] *hock and soda-water* cf. the stanza used as a headpiece to the poem in editions from 1832 onwards. Byron never intended it as a headpiece, and in fact scribbled it in MS and then deleted it:

> I would to Heaven that I were so much clay –
>   As I am blood – bone – marrow, passion – feeling –
> Because at least the past were past away –
>   And for the future (but I write this reeling,
> Having got drunk exceedingly today
>   So that I seem to stand upon the ceiling)
> I say, the future is a serious matter –
> And so, for godsake, hock and soda-water.

A pleasure worthy Xerxes the great king;[135]   *1435*
 For not the blessed sherbet, sublimed[136] with snow,
Nor the first sparkle of the desert-spring,
 Nor Burgundy in all its sunset glow,
After long travel, ennui,[137] love, or slaughter,
Vie with that draught of hock and soda-water.   *1440*

181

The coast (I think it was the coast that I
 Was just describing; yes, it *was* the coast)
Lay at this period quiet as the sky,
 The sands untumbled, the blue waves untossed,
And all was stillness save the sea-bird's cry   *1445*
 And dolphin's leap, and little billow crossed
By some low rock or shelf, that made it fret[138]
Against the boundary it scarcely wet.

182

And forth they wandered, her sire being gone,
 As I have said, upon an expedition;   *1450*
And mother, brother, guardian, she had none,
 Save Zoe, who, although with due precision
She waited on her lady with the sun,
 Thought daily service was her only mission,
Bringing warm water, wreathing her long tresses,   *1455*
And asking now and then for cast-off dresses.

183

It was the cooling hour, just when the rounded
 Red sun sinks down behind the azure hill,
Which then seems as if the whole earth it bounded,
 Circling all nature, hushed, and dim, and still,   *1460*
With the far mountain-crescent half surrounded
 On one side, and the deep sea calm and chill
Upon the other, and the rosy sky,
With one star sparkling through it like an eye.

184

And thus they wandered forth, and, hand in hand,   *1465*
 Over the shining pebbles and the shells

Glided along the smooth and hardened sand,
 And in the worn and wild receptacles
Worked by the storms, yet worked as it were planned,
 In hollow halls, with sparry[139] roofs and cells,   *1470*
They turned to rest; and, each clasped by an arm,
Yielded to the deep twilight's purple charm.

185

They looked up to the sky, whose floating glow
 Spread like a rosy ocean, vast and bright;
They gazed upon the glittering sea below,   *1475*
 Whence the broad moon rose circling into sight;
They heard the wave's splash, and the wind so low,
 And saw each other's dark eyes darting light
Into each other; and, beholding this,
Their lips drew near, and clung into a kiss –   *1480*

186

A long, long kiss, a kiss of youth and love
 And beauty, all concentrating like rays
Into one focus, kindled from above;
 Such kisses as belong to early days
Where heart and soul and sense in concert[140]
       move,   *1485*
 And the blood's lava, and the pulse ablaze,
Each kiss a heartquake – for a kiss's strength,
I think, it must be reckoned by its length.

187

By length I mean duration; theirs endured
 Heaven knows how long – no doubt they never
      reckoned,   *1490*
And if they had, they could not have secured
 The sum of their sensations to a second:
They had not spoken, but they felt allured
 As if their souls and lips each other beckoned,
Which, being joined, like swarming bees they
      clung,   *1495*
Their hearts the flowers from whence the honey sprung.

---

[135] Xerxes I, Persian king who in 480 BC assembled a great navy and army to avenge his father Darius for the loss of the Battle of Marathon in 490 BC. He was eventually defeated at Salamis.
[136] *sherbet, sublimed* a cooling drink of the East, made of fruit juice and sweetened water, often cooled ('sublimed') with snow.

[137] *ennui* feeling of mental weariness and dissatisfaction produced by want of occupation.
[138] *fret* chafe.
[139] *spar* an opaque crystalline mineral, which is embedded in the roofs and cells of the rocks.
[140] *concert* unison.

188

They were alone, but not alone as they
    Who shut in chambers think it loneliness;
The silent ocean, and the starlight bay,
    The twilight glow, which momently grew
                  less, *1500*
The voiceless sands, and dropping caves that lay
    Around them, made them to each other press,
As if there were no life beneath the sky
Save theirs, and that their life could never die.

189

They feared no eyes nor ears on that lone beach, *1505*
    They felt no terrors from the night,[141] they were
All in all to each other; though their speech
    Was broken words, they *thought* a language there,
And all the burning tongues the passions teach
    Found in one sigh the best interpreter *1510*
Of nature's oracle – first love, that all
Which Eve has left her daughters since her fall.

190

Haidee spoke not of scruples, asked no vows,
    Nor offered any; she had never heard
Of plight and promises to be a spouse, *1515*
    Or perils by a loving maid incurred;
She was all which pure ignorance allows,
    And flew to her young mate like a young bird;
And, never having dreamt of falsehood, she
Had not one word to say of constancy. *1520*

191

She loved, and was beloved; she adored,
    And she was worshipped; after nature's fashion,
Their intense souls, into each other poured,
    If souls could die, had perished in that passion;
But by degrees their senses were restored, *1525*
    Again to be o'ercome, again to dash on;
And, beating 'gainst *his* bosom, Haidee's heart
Felt as if never more to beat apart.

192

Alas, they were so young, so beautiful,
    So lonely, loving, helpless, and the hour *1530*
Was that in which the heart is always full,
    And, having o'er itself no further power,
Prompts deeds eternity cannot annul,
    But pays off moments in an endless shower
Of hellfire – all prepared for people giving *1535*
Pleasure or pain to one another living.

193

Alas for Juan and Haidee! They were
    So loving and so lovely – till then never,
Excepting our first parents, such a pair
    Had run the risk of being damned for ever; *1540*
And Haidee, being devout as well as fair,
    Had doubtless heard about the Stygian river,[142]
And hell and purgatory – but forgot
Just in the very crisis she should not.

194

They look upon each other, and their eyes *1545*
    Gleam in the moonlight; and her white arm clasps
Round Juan's head, and his around hers lies
    Half-buried in the tresses which it grasps;
She sits upon his knee, and drinks his sighs,
    He hers, until they end in broken gasps; *1550*
And thus they form a group that's quite antique –
Half-naked, loving, natural, and Greek.

195

And when those deep and burning moments passed,
    And Juan sunk to sleep within her arms,
She slept not, but all tenderly, though fast, *1555*
    Sustained his head upon her bosom's charms;
And now and then her eye to heaven is cast,
    And then on the pale cheek her breast now warms,
Pillowed on her o'erflowing heart, which pants
With all it granted, and with all it grants. *1560*

---

[141] *They felt no terrors from the night* a profane allusion to Psalm 91:5, where the godly are told: 'Thou shalt not be afraid for the terror by night'.

[142] *the Stygian river* the river Styx circled Hades nine times; those seeking to enter Hades had to be ferried across it by Charon.

196

An infant when it gazes on a light,
 A child the moment when it drains the breast,
A devotee when soars the Host[143] in sight,
 An Arab with a stranger for a guest,
A sailor when the prize has struck in fight,[144] *1565*
 A miser filling his most hoarded chest,
Feel rapture; but not such true joy are reaping
As they who watch o'er what they love while sleeping.

197

For there it lies so tranquil, so beloved,
 All that it hath of life with us is living; *1570*
So gentle, stirless, helpless, and unmoved,
 And all unconscious of the joy 'tis giving;
All it hath felt, inflicted, passed, and proved,
 Hushed into depths beyond the watcher's diving;
There lies the thing we love with all its errors *1575*
And all its charms, like death without its terrors.

198

The lady watched her lover, and that hour
 Of love's, and night's, and ocean's solitude
O'erflowed her soul with their united power;
 Amidst the barren sand and rocks so rude *1580*
She and her wave-worn love had made their bower
 Where nought upon their passion could intrude,
And all the stars that crowded the blue space
Saw nothing happier than her glowing face.

199

Alas, the love of women! It is known *1585*
 To be a lovely and a fearful thing;
For all of theirs upon that die[145] is thrown,
 And if 'tis lost, life hath no more to bring
To them but mockeries of the past alone,
 And their revenge is as the tiger's spring, *1590*
Deadly, and quick, and crushing; yet as real
Torture is theirs – what they inflict they feel.

200

They are right; for man, to man so oft unjust,
 Is always so to women; one sole bond
Awaits them, treachery is all their trust; *1595*
 Taught to conceal, their bursting hearts despond
Over their idol, till some wealthier lust
 Buys them in marriage – and what rests beyond?
A thankless husband, next a faithless lover,
Then dressing, nursing, praying, and all's over. *1600*

201

Some take a lover, some take drams[146] or prayers,
 Some mind their household, others dissipation,
Some run away and but exchange their cares,
 Losing the advantage of a virtuous station;
Few changes e'er can better their affairs, *1605*
 Theirs being an unnatural situation
From the dull palace to the dirty hovel:
Some play the devil, and then write a novel.[147]

202

Haidee was Nature's bride, and knew not this;[148]
 Haidee was Passion's child, born where the sun *1610*
Showers triple light, and scorches even the kiss
 Of his gazelle-eyed daughters; she was one
Made but to love, to feel that she was his
 Who was her chosen: what was said or done
Elsewhere was nothing – she had nought to fear, *1615*
Hope, care, nor love beyond, her heart beat *here*.

203

And oh, that quickening of the heart, that beat!
 How much it costs us! Yet each rising throb
Is in its cause as its effect so sweet,
 That Wisdom, ever on the watch to rob *1620*
Joy of its alchemy,[149] and to repeat
 Fine truths, even Conscience, too, has a tough job
To make us understand each good old maxim,
So good – I wonder Castlereagh don't tax 'em.

---

[143] *Host* eucharistic wafer. The word 'soars' is distinctly comic.
[144] *when the prize has struck in fight* i.e. when the prize-ship (being attacked) has surrendered ('struck'). At this point it and its contents became booty, to be divided among the crew.
[145] *die* dice.
[146] *drams* a dram is a measure – in this case, of alcohol.
[147] *Some play the devil, and then write a novel* Lady Caroline Lamb, unceremoniously dumped by Byron after an affair of sev-eral months in 1812, took her revenge by fictionalizing their relationship in *Glenarvon* (1816). She went on to write a highly effective parody of *Don Juan*, called *A New Canto* (see pp. 650–7).
[148] *this* i.e. the sufferings of the woman of the world, related in the previous three stanzas.
[149] *alchemy* magic.

204

And now 'twas done – on the lone shore were
                              plighted   *1625*
    Their hearts; the stars, their nuptial torches, shed
Beauty upon the beautiful they lighted;
    Ocean their witness, and the cave their bed,
By their own feelings hallowed and united,
    Their priest was Solitude, and they were wed: *1630*
And they were happy, for to their young eyes
Each was an angel, and earth paradise.

205

Oh love, of whom great Caesar was the suitor,
    Titus the master, Antony the slave,[150]
Horace, Catullus scholars, Ovid tutor,[151]   *1635*
    Sappho the sage bluestocking, in whose grave
All those may leap who rather would be neuter
    (Leucadia's rock still overlooks the wave);[152]
Oh love, thou art the very god of evil –
For, after all, we cannot call thee devil.   *1640*

206

Thou mak'st the chaste connubial[153] state precarious,
    And jestest with the brows of mightiest men:
Caesar and Pompey, Mahomet, Belisarius,[154]
    Have much employed the muse of history's pen;
Their lives and fortunes were extremely various,   *1645*
    Such worthies Time will never see again;
Yet to these four in three things the same luck holds –
They all were heroes, conquerors, and cuckolds.

207

Thou mak'st philosophers; there's Epicurus
    And Aristippus,[155] a material crew!   *1650*
Who to immoral courses would allure us
    By theories quite practicable too;
If only from the devil they would insure us,
    How pleasant were the maxim (not quite new),

'Eat, drink, and love, what can the rest avail us?' –   *1655*
So said the royal sage Sardanapalus.[156]

208

But Juan! Had he quite forgotten Julia?
    And should he have forgotten her so soon?
I can't but say it seems to me most truly a
    Perplexing question; but, no doubt, the moon   *1660*
Does these things for us, and whenever newly a
    Strong palpitation rises, 'tis her boon;
Else how the devil is it that fresh features
Have such a charm for us poor human creatures?

209

I hate inconstancy – I loathe, detest,   *1665*
    Abhor, condemn, abjure the mortal made
Of such quicksilver[157] clay that in his breast
    No permanent foundation can be laid;
Love, constant love, has been my constant guest,
    And yet last night, being at a masquerade,   *1670*
I saw the prettiest creature, fresh from Milan,
Which gave me some sensations like a villain.

210

But soon Philosophy came to my aid
    And whispered, 'Think of every sacred tie!'
'I will, my dear Philosophy!' I said,   *1675*
    'But then her teeth, and then, oh heaven, her eye!
I'll just enquire if she be wife or maid,
    Or neither, out of curiosity'
'Stop!' cried Philosophy, with air so Grecian
(Though she was masked then as a fair Venetian).   *1680*

211

'Stop!' So I stopped. But to return: that which
    Men call inconstancy is nothing more
Than admiration due where nature's rich
    Profusion with young beauty covers o'er

---

[150]   Julius Caesar was Cleopatra's suitor; Mark Antony was her
slave. Titus 'mastered' his love of Berenice and sent her away.
[151]   Horace, Catullus and Ovid wrote about love.
[152]   Sappho was said to have thrown herself off the Leucadian
rock into the sea when her love for Phaon was unrequited.
[153]   *connubial* married.
[154]   *Caesar and Pompey, Mahomet, Belisarius* famous cuckolds:
Caesar was cuckolded by his first wife, Pompeia; Pompey by his
wife Mucia (who 'played the wanton' with Caesar); Mahomet by
his wife Ayesha; and Belisarius (famous Roman general) by his
wife Antonina (who seduced their adopted son).

[155]   Aristippus (*c.*370 BC) founded a hedonistic philosophy that
offered pleasure as the goal of life; he lived luxuriously. Epicurus
(342–270 BC) said that happiness was the aim of life, achieved
through virtuous living. Epicureanism was quickly devalued and
became associated with sensual pleasures.
[156]   Sardanapalus was an Assyrian of uncertain historical origin
and character, renowned for being effeminate, slothful, and
immersed in luxury and debauchery. He is the subject of a
tragedy written by Byron in 1821.
[157]   *quicksilver* fast-changing.

Some favoured object; and as in the niche   *1685*
    A lovely statue we almost adore,
This sort of adoration of the real
Is but a heightening of the *beau-ideal*.[158]

                    212

'Tis the perception of the beautiful,
    A fine extension of the faculties,   *1690*
Platonic, universal, wonderful,
    Drawn from the stars, and filtered through the skies,
Without which life would be extremely dull;
    In short, it is the use of our own eyes,
With one or two small senses added, just   *1695*
To hint that flesh is formed of fiery dust.

                    213

Yet 'tis a painful feeling, and unwilling,
    For surely if we always could perceive
In the same object graces quite as killing[159]
    As when she rose upon us like an Eve,   *1700*
'Twould save us many a heartache, many a shilling[160]
    (For we must get them anyhow, or grieve),
Whereas if one sole lady pleased for ever,
How pleasant for the heart, as well as liver![161]

                    214

The heart is like the sky, a part of heaven,   *1705*
    But changes night and day too, like the sky;

Now o'er it clouds and thunder must be driven,
    And darkness and destruction as on high:
But when it hath been scorched, and pierced, and riven,
    Its storms expire in water-drops; the eye   *1710*
Pours forth at last the heart's-blood turned to tears,
Which make the English climate of our years.

                    215

The liver is the lazaret[162] of bile,[163]
    But very rarely executes its function,
For the first passion stays there such a while,   *1715*
    That all the rest creep in and form a junction
Like knots of vipers on a dunghill's soil –
    Rage, fear, hate, jealousy, revenge, compunction –
So that all mischiefs spring up from this entrail[164]
Like earthquakes from the hidden fire called
                                'central'.   *1720*

                    216

In the meantime, without proceeding more
    In this anatomy, I've finished now
Two hundred and odd stanzas as before,
    That being about the number I'll allow
Each canto of the twelve, or twenty-four;   *1725*
    And laying down my pen, I make my bow,
Leaving Don Juan and Haidee to plead
For them and theirs with all who deign to read.

---

[158] *beau-ideal* ideal beauty. Byron's argument (deliberately specious) is that admiration of a beautiful woman is no different from that of a beautiful work of art.
[159] *killing* overpoweringly beautiful.
[160] *many a shilling* a typically Byronic twist, reducing everything to material terms. His point is that if he had loved only one woman, he would have saved the money he has spent on the many he has known in his life.
[161] *liver* seat of intense passion.
[162] *lazaret* lazaretto, hospital.
[163] *bile* intense passion, anger.
[164] *entrail* organ (i.e. the liver).

To the Po. *2 June 1819* (composed 1 or 2 June 1819; first published 1824; edited from MS)

River that rollest by the ancient walls
    Where dwells the lady of my love,[1] when she
Walks by thy brink and there perchance recalls
    A faint and fleeting memory of me –
What if thy deep and ample stream should be   5
    A mirror of my heart, where she may read
The thousand thoughts I now betray[2] to thee,
    Wild as thy wave and headlong as thy speed?
What do I say? 'A mirror of my heart'?
    Are not thy waters sweeping, dark and strong?   10
Such as my feelings were and are, thou art,
    And such as thou art were my passions long;
Time may have somewhat tamed them – not forever
    Thou overflow'st thy banks, and not for aye
The bosom overboils, congenial river!   15
    Thy floods subside, and mine have sunk away,
But left long wrecks behind us; yet again
    Borne on our old career unchanged we move,
Thou tendest wildly to the wilder main
    And I to loving one I should not love.   20
The current I behold will sweep beneath
    Her palace walls, and murmur at her feet,
Her eyes will look on thee when she shall breathe
    The twilight air unchained from summer's heat.
She will look on thee; I have looked on thee   25
    Full of that thought, and from this moment ne'er
Thy waters could I name, hear named, or see
    Without the inseparable sigh for her.
Her bright eyes will be imaged in thy stream –
    Yes, they will meet the wave I gaze on now,   30
But mine cannot even witness in a dream
    That happy wave repass me in its flow;
The wave that bears my tear returns no more –
    Will she return by whom that wave shall sweep?
Both tread thy bank, both wander by thy shore,   35
    I near thy source,[3] and she by the blue deep;
But that which keepeth us apart is not
    Distance, nor depth of wave, nor space of earth,
But the distractions of a various lot –
    Ah, various as the climates of our birth!   40
A stranger loves a lady of the land
    Born far beyond the mountains, but his blood
Is all meridian,[4] as if never fanned

TO THE PO. 2 JUNE 1819
[1] *the lady of my love* Contessa Teresa Guiccioli, whose relationship with Byron began April 1819, and lasted until Byron's death in 1824. At the time of writing he believed her to be with her husband at their estate Ca'Zen, on the Po. He was on his way to Bologna, and was 'passing the Po' (Marchand vii 76).

[2] *betray* reveal.
[3] *near thy source* the Po, Italy's major river, rises at Mt Viso, in Piedmont.
[4] *meridian* noon; at its most passionate.

By the bleak wind that chills the polar flood.
My heart is all meridian; were it not,   45
  I had not suffered now, nor should I be,
Despite of tortures ne'er to be forgot,
  The slave again, oh love, at least of thee!
'Tis vain to struggle – I have struggled long
  To love again no more as once I loved.   50
Oh time, why leave this earliest passion strong? –
  To tear a heart which pants to be unmoved?

Letter from Lord Byron to Douglas Kinnaird, 26 October 1819 (extract)

As to *Don Juan*, confess – confess, you dog (and be candid), that it is the sublime of *that there* sort of writing. It may be bawdy, but is it not good English? It may be profligate, but is it not *life*, is it not *the thing*? Could any man have written it who has not lived in the world? – and tooled in a post-chaise? In a hackney coach? In a gondola? Against a wall? In a court carriage? In a vis-à-vis?[1] On a table – and under it? I have written about a hundred stanzas of a third Canto, but it is damned modest – the outcry has frightened me.[2] I had such projects for the Don, but the *cant* is so much stronger than *cunt* nowadays, that the benefit of experience in a man who had well weighed the worth of both monosyllables must be lost to despairing posterity.[3]

Messalonghi, 22 January 1824. On This Day I Complete My Thirty-Sixth Year (first published 1824; edited from MS)

1

'Tis time this heart should be unmoved,
  Since others it hath ceased to move;
Yet though I cannot be beloved,
    Still let me love.

2

My days are in the yellow leaf,   5
  The flowers and fruits of love are gone,
The worm, the canker and the grief
    Are mine alone.

3

The fire that on my bosom preys
  Is lone as some volcanic isle,   10

LETTER FROM LORD BYRON TO DOUGLAS KINNAIRD
[1] *vis-à-vis* light carriage for two people sitting face to face.
[2] *Don Juan* I–II was strongly attacked for 'degrading debauchery' and 'shameless indecency'.

[3] All the same, *Don Juan* III–V was published August 1821.

No torch is kindled at its blaze –
    A funeral pile!

4

The hope, the fear, the jealous care,
    The exalted portion of the pain,
And power of love I cannot share   15
    But wear the chain.

5

But 'tis not thus, and 'tis not here
    Such thoughts should shake my soul, nor now
Where glory decks the hero's bier
    Or binds his brow.   20

6

The sword, the banner, and the field,
    Glory and Greece about us see –
The Spartan borne upon his shield[1]
    Was not more free!

7

Awake (not Greece – she *is* awake),[2]   25
    Awake my spirit – think through whom
Thy life-blood tracks its parent lake
    And then strike home!

8

Tread those reviving passions down,
    Unworthy manhood; unto thee   30
Indifferent should the smile or frown
    Of beauty be.

9

If thou regret'st thy youth, why live?
    The land of honourable death
Is here: up to the field, and give   35
    Away thy breath!

MESSALONGHI, 22 JANUARY 1824
[1] 'The slain were borne upon their shields' (Byron's MS note).

[2] The Greeks were waging a war of independence against the Turks.

10

Seek out (less often sought than found)
A soldier's grave, for thee the best,
Then look around and choose thy ground
And take thy rest.

Richard Woodhouse, Jr   (1788–1834)

Woodhouse was neither a poet, playwright, nor a novelist. He was not an artist of any kind. He was, in fact, the legal adviser to Keats's publishers, Taylor and Hessey, and one of the most far-sighted and perceptive of Keats's friends.

He was born in Bath, 11 December 1788, the eldest in a family of fourteen children. After being educated at Eton, he went to Spain and Portugal; when he returned, he decided not to go to university (although he was capable of doing so), instead turning to the law. He met the publishers John Taylor and James Augustus Hessey in March 1811 when he was working as a conveyancer, and quickly entered their intellectual circle. Taylor regarded him at this time as erudite, hardworking, self-effacing and strictly religious.

He met Keats at 93 Fleet Street soon after Keats himself had been introduced to Taylor and Hessey by John Hamilton Reynolds. Woodhouse's shrewd eye saw in the young Keats a genius equal to Shakespeare. He realized that there were faults in Keats's diction, but at the same time regarded him as potentially a great poet: 'Such a genius, I very much believe, has not appeared since Shakespeare and Milton'.[1] With equal shrewdness he realized that one day all 'Keatsiana' (a term he himself uses at least twice) would be invaluable. Thus, he copied every Keats manuscript, poem and letter on which he could lay his hands, with the result that today, a number of texts are known only through his transcriptions. The letters below reveal Woodhouse's skill as an interpreter and critic of Keats. The first outlines Keats's concept of the poetical character and negative capability; the second discusses his revision of *The Eve of St Agnes*.

After Keats's death, Woodhouse increased his efforts to gather materials that would be of use to scholars and biographers. He sought out acquaintances of the poet and spoke to them, jotting down detailed accounts of their conversations; he encouraged John Taylor to write a biography; he commissioned a portrait of the poet by Hilton, and a medallion by Giuseppe Girometti.

In due course, Woodhouse developed tuberculosis, the same disease that had killed Keats. Like the poet, he went south in search of improved health, visiting Madeira in 1829–30, and Italy two years later. Back in London, his health declined rapidly, and he died on 3 September 1834.

Letter from Richard Woodhouse to John Taylor, *c.* 27 October 1818
(extract)

I believe him to be right with regard to his own poetical character, and I perceive clearly the distinction he draws between himself and those of the Wordsworth school.[1]

There are gradations in poetry and in poets. One is purely descriptive, confining himself to external nature and visible objects; another describes, in addition, the effects of the thoughts of which he is conscious, and which others are affected by. Another will soar so far into the regions of imagination as to conceive of beings and substances in situations different from what he has ever seen them, but still such as either have actually occurred or may possibly occur. Another will reason in poetry; another be witty; another will imagine things that never did nor probably ever will occur, or such as cannot in nature occur, and yet he will describe them so that you recognize nothing very unnatural in the

---

RICHARD WOODHOUSE, JR
[1]   *The Keats Circle* ed. Hyder E. Rollins (2 vols, Cambridge, Mass., 1965), i p. cxlv.

LETTER FROM RICHARD WOODHOUSE TO JOHN TAYLOR
[1]   For Keats's comments on Wordsworth, see pp. 1020–2.

descriptions when certain principles or powers or conditions are admitted. Another will throw himself into various characters and make them speak as the passions would naturally incite them to do.

The highest order of poet will not only possess all the above powers but will have as high an imagination that he will be able to throw his own soul into any object he sees or imagines, so as to see, feel, be sensible of, and express all that the object itself would see, feel, be sensible of, or express – and he will speak out of that object, so that his own self will, with the exception of the mechanical part, be 'annihilated'.[2] And it is [of] the excess of this power that I suppose Keats to speak, when he says he has no identity. As a poet, and when the fit is upon him, this is true. And it is a fact that he does by the power of his imagination create ideal personages, substances, and powers – that he lives for a time in their souls or essences or ideas – and that occasionally so intensely as to lose consciousness of what is round him. We all do the same in a degree, when we fall into a reverie.[3]

If, then, his imagination has such power, and he is continually cultivating it and giving it play, it will acquire strength by the indulgence and exercise. This in excess is the case of mad persons. And this may be carried to that extent that he may lose sight of his identity so far as to give him a habit of speaking generally in an assumed character. So that what he says shall be tinged with the sentiments proper to the character which, at the time, has possessed itself of his imagination.

This being his idea of the poetical character, he may well say that a poet has no identity. As a man he must have identity, but as a poet he need not. And in this sense a poet is 'the most unpoetical of God's creatures',[4] for his soul has no distinctive characteristic – it cannot be itself made the subject of poetry, that is, another person's soul cannot be thrown into the poet's, for there is no identity (separatedness, distinctiveness) or personal impulse to be acted upon.

Shakespeare was a poet of the kind above mentioned, and he was perhaps the only one besides Keats who possessed this power in an extraordinary degree, so as to be a feature in his works. He gives a description of his idea of a poet:

> The poet's eye, in a fine frenzy rolling,
> Doth glance from heaven to earth, from earth to heaven;
> And as imagination bodies forth
> The forms of things unknown, the poet's pen
> Turns them to shapes, and gives to airy nothing
> A local habitation and a name.[5]

Lord Byron does not come up to this character. He can certainly conceive and describe a dark accomplished villain in love, and a female tender and kind who loves him; or a sated and palled sensualist, misanthrope, and deist[6] – but here his power ends. The true poet cannot only conceive this, but can assume any character, essence, idea, or substance at pleasure. And he has this imaginative faculty not in a limited manner, but in full universality.

Let us pursue speculation on these matters, and we shall soon be brought to believe in the truth of every syllable of Keats' letter, taken as a description of himself and his own ideas and feelings.

---

[2] *annihilated* Woodhouse is discussing negative capability; for Keats's account see p. 1019.
[3] 'The power of his imagination is apparent in every page of his *Endymion*. And he has affirmed that he can conceive of a billiard ball – that it may have a sense of delight from its own roundness, smoothness, volubility, and the rapidity of its motion' (Woodhouse's note).
[4] Woodhouse is quoting from a letter Keats had sent him

that day; see p. 1042.
[5] *A Midsummer Night's Dream* V i 12–17.
[6] Woodhouse has in mind a range of works by Byron. The latest hit of the moment was *Beppo*, published in the summer of 1818. Woodhouse seems also to be referring to *Manfred* (1816) and *Childe Harold's Pilgrimage*, the final Canto of which had been published in April 1818.

Letter from Richard Woodhouse to John Taylor, 19 September 1819
(extract)

He had 'The Eve of St Agnes' copied fair.[1] He has made trifling alterations, inserted an additional stanza early in the poem to make the *legend* more intelligible,[2] and correspondent[3] with what afterwards takes place, particularly with respect to the supper and the playing on the lute. He retains the name of Porphyro, has altered the last three lines to leave on the reader a sense of pettish disgust, by bringing Old Angela in (only) dead, stiff and ugly.[4] He says he likes that the poem should leave off with this change of sentiment – it was what he aimed at, and was glad to find from my objections to it that he had succeeded. I apprehend he had a fancy for trying his hand at an attempt to play with his reader, and fling him off[5] at last. I should have thought he affected the 'Don Juan'[6] style of mingling up sentiment and sneering, but that he had before asked Hessey[7] if he could procure him a sight of that work, as he had not met with it – and if 'The Eve of St Agnes' had not, in all probability, been altered before his Lordship[8] had thus flown in the face of the public.

There was another alteration, which I abused for 'a full hour by the Temple clock'.[9] You know, if a thing has a decent side, I generally look no further. As the poem was originally written, *we* innocent ones (ladies and myself) might very well have supposed that Porphyro, when acquainted with Madeline's love for him, and when 'he arose, / Ethereal, flushed'[10] etc. etc. (turn to it), set himself at once to persuade her to go off with him, and succeeded and went over the 'Dartmoor black' (now changed for some other place)[11] to be married, in right honest, chaste, and sober wise.[12] But as it is now altered, as soon as Madeline has confessed her love, Porphyro winds by degrees his arm round her, presses breast to breast, and acts all the acts of a bona fide husband, while she fancies she is only playing the part of a wife in a dream.[13]

This alteration is of about three stanzas, and though there are no improper expressions, but all is left to inference; and though, profanely speaking, the interest on the reader's imagination is greatly heightened – yet I do apprehend it will render the poem unfit for ladies, and indeed scarcely to be mentioned to them among the 'things that are'.[14] He says he does not want ladies to read his poetry; that he writes for men,[15] and that if in the former poem there was an opening for doubt what took place, it was his fault for not writing clearly and comprehensibly; that he should despise a man who would be such an eunuch in sentiment as to leave a maid, with that character about her, in such a situation;[16] and should despise himself to write about it, etc., etc., etc. – and all this sort of Keats-like rodomontade.[17]

LETTER FROM RICHARD WOODHOUSE TO JOHN TAYLOR

[1] *The Eve of St Agnes* was composed between 18 January and 2 February 1819, and revised the following September. Woodhouse is discussing Keats's revisions, not all of which were published in the 1820 text.

[2] *inserted . . . intelligible* The stanza was not included in the published text; I include it in a note, p. 1044 n. 10.

[3] *correspondent* consistent.

[4] See *The Eve of St Agnes* 375–8.

[5] *fling him off* i.e. Keats is trying deliberately to disgust the reader at the end of the poem.

[6] Byron's poem had been published anonymously on 15 July 1819.

[7] James Augustus Hessey (1785–1870), business partner of John Taylor (1781–1864); together they published Keats, Clare, Hazlitt and Lamb.

[8] *his Lordship* i.e. Byron.

[9] *1 Henry IV* V iv 148: 'fought a long hour by Shrewsbury clock'.

[10] *The Eve of St Agnes* 317–18.

[11] *now changed . . . place* 'the southern moors' (line 351).

[12] *wise* manner.

[13] *But as it is now altered . . . dream* see stanzas 35–6. The revised stanza did not appear in the 1820 text; I include it in a footnote, p. 1052 n. 66.

[14] An allusion that demonstrates how well read Woodhouse was; as Bob Cummings tells me, the quotation is from Shelley, *The Revolt of Islam* (1818), ix stanza 29: 'let sense and thought / Pass from our being, or be numbered not / Among the things that are' (ll. 4–6).

[15] *that he writes for men* this extraordinary statement may have been suggested by Keats's desire to resist the 'effeminate' influence of Leigh Hunt, and imitate the more 'manly' poetry of Byron; see my 'Keats and Byron: A Reassessment', *Byron Journal* 24 (1996) 12–32.

[16] *in such a situation* i.e. in bed, 'entoiled in woofed fantasies'.

[17] *rodomontade* vainglorious bragging.

Percy Bysshe Shelley (1792–1822)

In his important essay 'On Paradox and Common-Place', Hazlitt commented that Shelley

> has a fire in his eye, a fever in his blood, a mag-got in his brain, a hectic flutter in his speech, which mark out the philosophic fanatic. He is sanguine complexioned, and shrill-voiced. . . . He is clogged by no dull system of realities, no earth-bound feelings, no rooted prejudices, by nothing that belongs to the mighty trunk and hard husk of nature and habit, but is drawn up by irresistible levity to the regions of mere speculation and fancy, to the sphere of air and fire, where his delighted spirit floats in 'seas of pearl and clouds of amber'.[1]

Few descriptions are more evocative of the visionary, proselytizing energies of one of the greatest of the romantic poets.

Percy Bysshe Shelley was born 4 August 1792 at Field Place, near Horsham in Sussex, the eldest child and only son of a baronet and Whig MP. After two years at Syon House Academy in London, where he met his lifelong friend Thomas Medwin, he was sent to Eton, 1804–10. There he received a thorough ground-ing in the classics, became interested in science and radical politics, and wrote two gothic novels – *Zas-trozzi* and *St Irvyne* (both published 1810). Such promise might have been expected to blossom at Uni-versity College, Oxford, where he matriculated in October 1810 – and, in a sense, it did. His academic career came to an abrupt halt when he was expelled in March 1811, for refusing to answer questions concern-ing a pamphlet, *The Necessity of Atheism*, which he had written with his friend, Thomas Jefferson Hogg. It argued that God's existence can be proved only by ref-erence to the senses, reason and the testimony of oth-ers. Having denied the validity of any of these, it concluded: 'Truth has always been found to promote the best interests of mankind. Every reflecting mind must allow that there is no proof of the existence of a Deity. Q.E.D.'[2] After only two terms at Oxford they were both sent down; C. J. Ridley, who witnessed their expulsion, recorded: 'The aforesaid two had made themselves as conspicuous as possible by great singu-larity of dress, and by walking up and down the centre of the quadrangle, as if proud of their anticipated fate. I believe no one regretted their departure, for there are but few, if any, who are not afraid of Shelley's strange and fantastic pranks, and the still stranger opinions he was known to entertain.'

This, and his elopement with Harriet Westbrook to Edinburgh in August (where he married her at the end of the month), led to lasting estrangement from his father. He spent November–December in the Lake District, where he wanted to meet Wordsworth and Coleridge but met Southey instead. The two men (between whom there was twenty years difference in age) talked at considerable length, and Southey made the observation that, as Shelley reported to Elizabeth Hitchener, 'I am not an atheist but a pantheist' (Jones i 219). In February the following year he set off for Dublin, where he published and distributed another pamphlet, *An Address to the Irish People* (1812), which argued for Catholic emancipation and the repeal of the Act of Union. He distributed all 1,500 copies, often giving them out on street corners, within the month. After delivering a public speech at Fishamble Street Theatre, he came under the surveillance of Home Office spies, but continued to publish his political writings.

Godwin was Shelley's principal intellectual guru at this period and, having initiated a correspondence before leaving for Ireland, Shelley was pleased, on returning to England, to meet him in October 1812. Besides the moral support this provided, and Godwin's manifest influence on Shelley's first important poem, *Queen Mab* (1813), this encounter was crucial because it led to his meeting with Godwin's daughter, Mary Wollstonecraft Godwin (pp. 1094–5). In 1814, though still married to Harriet, he eloped with Mary to the continent, along with her step-sister, Claire Clairmont. Two months later, after a whirlwind tour of France, Switzerland and Germany, they were back in England, and in August 1815 set up house at Bishops-gate, near Windsor Great Park, where he began his first major work, *Alastor*. It was composed after an expedition up the Thames with Mary, Charles Clair-mont, and the novelist Thomas Love Peacock, and the river is a constant presence in the poem; as the central character pursues the winding of the cavern, travelling downstream to the sea, he is also engaged on another kind of journey towards the origins and longings of the human imagination. The river journey, Yeats wrote, as 'an image that has transcended particular time and place, becomes a symbol, passes beyond death, as it

PERCY BYSSHE SHELLEY
[1] Howe viii 148–9.

[2] P. B. Shelley (with T. J. Hogg), *The Necessity of Atheism* (1811), p. 13. Critics were particularly enraged by the final 'Q.E.D.'

were, and becomes a living soul'. In all this, Shelley was deeply influenced by Wordsworth, whose *Excursion* was published in 1814. Both he and Mary had read it on publication, but without enthusiasm. While they admired Wordsworth's insights into the human spirit, they regarded him in much the same light as Byron in the Dedication to *Don Juan* (pp. 752–5) – as a traitor to his earlier radicalism. 'He is a slave', Mary wrote in her journal on 14 September 1814, noting also that they were 'much disappointed' with *The Excursion*.[3]

Alastor was published in February 1816, with Shelley's important sonnet *To Wordsworth*. Claire Clairmont had an affair with Byron in March and April, and, carrying his child, she joined Percy and Mary for a second foray to the Continent in the summer. As they made their way through Switzerland, Percy amused himself by placing the word 'atheist' after his name in at least four hotel registers, and English tourists, including Southey, saw and made the most of the impropriety.[4] In truth, Percy's attitude to God was more complex than the word 'atheist' suggests. It is not surprising that the concept was inimical to someone so opposed to an established church not merely complicit, but deeply implicated, in the social and political oppression prevalent in England at the time. On the other hand, he was tremendously attracted to the pantheist life-force of *Tintern Abbey*, and could not resist pleading the existence of a similar 'Power' in his poetry. However, he stopped well short of believing in a benevolent deity capable of intervening in human affairs. Much of his poetry tacitly accepts the existence of a superhuman 'Power', but its moral character is not always clear. On one level, it is identified with the tyrannical Jupiter in *Prometheus Unbound*; on another, it is closer to the benevolent Demogorgon. Writing approvingly of Leigh Hunt's spiritual beliefs in 1811, Shelley noted Hunt's belief in a God 'by no means perfect, but composed of good and evil like man' (Jones i 77). From time to time this is what Shelley himself thought, but he could also contemplate the possibility of a universe without a creator. If any phrase were used to encapsulate his position, it might be 'awful doubt'[5] – a feeling of awe for the power (sometimes frighteningly destructive) evident in the natural world, mixed with scepticism as to whether it reveals a divine presence.

Shelley was introduced to Byron for the first time on the shore of Lake Geneva, 27 May 1816; on 10 June Byron moved into the Villa Diodati, where Milton had stayed in 1639. It was the beginning of a highly stimulating and productive summer, not dissimilar to the *annus mirabilis* of 1797–8, when Wordsworth, Dorothy and Coleridge had enjoyed a whole year of intellectual and creative collaboration (see pp. 189–90). Wordsworth had been the principal poetical inspiration behind *Alastor*; Shelley remained an enthusiastic, if critical, reader of his work, eagerly devouring the collected *Poems* of 1815 – especially *Tintern Abbey* and the *Ode*.[6] Byron later told Thomas Medwin that, during the summer of 1816, Shelley 'used to dose me with Wordsworth physic even to nausea'.[7] As a result of his ministrations, Byron composed most of *Childe Harold's Pilgrimage* Canto III, affecting, not always convincingly, a Wordsworthian enthusiasm for nature (see pp. 693–4), and would go on, toward the end of the summer, to write *Manfred*, which also betrays Wordsworth's influence (see pp. 718–51). As for Shelley, he composed two of his most important poems, also in response to ideas in *Tintern Abbey* – *Mont Blanc* and the *Hymn to Intellectual Beauty* (see pp. 841–3, 845–9). What Shelley no doubt enjoyed about *Tintern Abbey* was its refusal to subscribe to conventional notions of the deity; it is that 'sense sublime / Of something far more deeply interfused'[8] that flows straight into his poetry, which celebrates not God, but the beauty directly comparable to 'spirit that impels / All thinking things, all objects of all thought, / And rolls through all things' proclaimed by the young Wordsworth. But Shelley is capable of pulling back even from that, and suggesting that it is illusory – that, as he suggests in the *Hymn*, the grave might not be the gateway to life everlasting but, 'Like life and fear, a dark reality' (l. 48), or that, as the final line of *Mont Blanc* proposes, 'Silence and solitude were vacancy'. The association with Byron also produced one of the greatest novels of the period, *Frankenstein*, not published till 1818, but begun as a result of a ghost story competition proposed by Byron on 17 June. It was soon afterwards that Mary and Percy toured Mont Blanc, Chamounix and the Mer de Glace – locations vividly described both in *Frankenstein* and *Mont Blanc*.[9] The journal letter to Peacock of 22 and 25 July 1816 (pp. 843–4) describes the landscape, and anticipates *Mont Blanc* in a number of ideas and phrases.

A month after they returned to London in Septem-

---

3   *Shelley Journals* i 25.
4   For scholarly discussion see Peter Cochran, 'Robert Southey, the "Atheist" Inscription, and the "League of Incest"', *N&Q* 37 (1990) 415–18.
5   *Mont Blanc* 77.
6   Neither Shelley, Byron or Keats knew *The Prelude*, which remained unpublished until 1850, long after they had died.

7   Medwin 237.
8   *Tintern Abbey* 96–7.
9   Byron toured these locations with Hobhouse in September, on his way to Italy.

ber, Harriet drowned herself in the Serpentine. Mary and Percy were married on 30 December. Moving to Marlow, Buckinghamshire, they expanded their acquaintance, becoming friendly with Leigh Hunt (see p. 620) and John Keats, among others. It was in a competition with Horace Smith later that year that Shelley wrote his most intriguing sonnet, *Ozymandias* (see p. 849). But the year following Harriet's suicide was a difficult one; Percy suffered bad health and lost custody of their children, Charles and Ianthe. The repressive political situation exacerbated his feelings of despair, and he left the country for the last time in March 1818. He and his new family led a nomadic existence, living variously at Milan, Leghorn, Venice, Rome, Naples, Leghorn again, Florence and Pisa. During this time he suffered several severe blows, including the deaths of Clara and William, his children by Mary.

He had been travelling for about a year in Italy when a political event in England inspired a burst of intense creative activity that would result in the production of some of his greatest works. On 16 August 1819, at St Peter's Field, on the outskirts of Manchester, a political meeting of 60,000 working men and women was dispersed by mounted dragoons, with a brutality that left (according to the very conservative official figures) eleven people dead and 421 cases of serious injury (including more than 100 women and children, and 162 individual cases of sabre wounds). Unofficial figures were much higher. The events were widely reported, and news reached Shelley within the week. A fortnight later he told his publisher, Charles Ollier, that 'the torrent of my indignation has not yet done boiling in my veins. I wait anxiously to hear how the country will express its sense of this bloody murderous oppression of its destroyers' (Jones ii 117). His own response was swift: within twelve days he composed one of the greatest poems of political protest in the language. *The Mask of Anarchy* begins with vicious satire, depicting the ministers of Lord Liverpool's government riding the horses which trample the crowd; from stanzas 34 to 63, a maid who has risen up to halt Anarchy (the idol of both the government and the people) addresses the crowd, telling them of false freedom, and then of true freedom; and in the concluding section of the poem, she tells them to stand up for their rights using the technique of passive, non-violent demonstration:

> Rise like lions after slumber
> In unvanquishable number;
> Shake your chains to earth like dew

Which in sleep had fallen on you –
Ye are many, they are few. (ll. 368–72)

Shelley posted the poem to Leigh Hunt for publication in his journal, *The Examiner*; it had arrived by 23 September, only five weeks after the massacre itself. But these were repressive times; when Sir Francis Burdett protested about the government's handling of the massacre in a newspaper, he was fined £2,000 – no small sum. Not surprisingly, perhaps, Hunt realized how inflammatory Shelley's poem was, and decided not to publish it; he had already served a sentence in jail for libelling the Prince Regent, and had no desire to repeat the experience. As might be expected, Hunt put it slightly differently; when it was first published, he wrote that he did not publish it in 1819 'because I thought that the public at large had not become sufficiently discerning to do justice to the sincerity and kind-heartedness of the spirit that walked in this flaming robe of verse'.[10] It first appeared in 1832, after Shelley's death, to coincide with the passing of the Reform Bill.

Shelley wrote *Ode to the West Wind* around 25 October, just over a month later. Like the *Mask*, it is a statement of faith in the ability of human beings to resist the oppression of church and state, and to realize their power of self-determination; thus, the 'Pestilence-stricken multitudes' are bidden to participate in the millennial vision of 'a new birth'. But the poem goes further even than that. It insists on the primacy of the poet as the central agency, the saviour-like prophet, 'tameless, and swift, and proud', who will awaken the masses to their potential: 'Drive my dead thoughts over the universe / Like withered leaves to quicken a new birth!' (ll. 63–4).

The poet-figure had by this point become central to Shelley's poetic project, and it was reworked further in *Prometheus Unbound*. The Prometheus figure resounds through the writings of Shelley and Byron. According to classical sources, Prometheus was the son of Iapetus and Asia, renowned for his cunning, which led to his theft of fire from heaven for the benefit of mankind. When Jupiter took fire away from the earth, Prometheus stole replacement fire from the chariot of the sun. Enraged, Jupiter nailed him to the rock of the Caucasus for 3,000 years, with an eagle incessantly devouring his liver. He was finally freed, and the bird slaughtered, by Hercules. Byron once recalled how, at Harrow, he had read Aeschylus's *Prometheus Bound*, commenting that 'The Prometheus – if not exactly in my plan – has always been so much in my head – that I can easily conceive its influence over all or anything

---

10   Preface, *The Masque of Anarchy* (London, 1832).

that I have written'.[11] Prometheus had been a topic of discussion when Shelley met Byron at Geneva in 1816; one of Byron's poems of that moment was *Prometheus* (see pp. 708–9), and Mary Shelley's *Frankenstein* reinvents the myth. With *Prometheus Unbound*, Shelley gives the story a twist of his own. His Prometheus is a recognizable reworking of the poet-figure of the *Ode to the West Wind*, who in turn was an echo of Christ. The rebirth foreseen in the *Ode* is also much in evidence here, and it follows on from the moment Prometheus utters the Christ-like speech to Jupiter: 'Disdain? Ah no, I pity thee' (I 53). Shelley's Prometheus redeems the world from post-lapsarian hostilities, leading to the 'diviner day' of the millennium:

> Beyond the glassy gulfs we flee
> Of shadow-peopled Infancy,
> Through death and birth to a diviner day –
> A paradise of vaulted bowers
> Lit by downward-gazing flowers . . .
>   (II v 101–5)

The play is a remarkable achievement, and Shelley called it 'the most perfect of my productions' (Jones ii 127). Its most percipient and helpful critic was Mary Shelley, who expressed its central concern when she commented that 'The prominent feature of Shelley's theory of the destiny of the human species was that evil is not inherent in the system of the creation, but an accident that might be expelled'; see her exceedingly useful 'Note on the *Prometheus Unbound*', pp. 1098–1100.

In April 1821, Shelley heard of Keats's death. They had met at Leigh Hunt's in 1817, and although the result had not been a relationship as productive as that with Byron, Shelley had become an admirer of his work, particularly *Hyperion*. Keats's premature death resulted from consumption, which he caught while nursing his brother Tom, but it suited Shelley's purposes to argue that the disease had been exacerbated, and its progress accelerated, by a hostile review of *Endymion* published in the *Quarterly Review*. Why? Because it turned Keats into yet another version of the Christ-poet figure, the visionary prophet doomed to suffer for the benefit of art and the select few who will understand his work and use it to help bring about permanent and lasting change in the human condition.[12] But *Adonais*, Shelley's elegy for Keats, is also the occasion for some of the most persuasive neo-Platonic poetry ever composed:

> He is made one with Nature: there is heard
> His voice in all her music, from the moan
> Of thunder, to the song of night's sweet bird;
> He is a presence to be felt and known
> In darkness and in light, from herb and stone,
> Spreading itself where'er that Power may move
> Which has withdrawn his being to its own,
> Which wields the world with never-wearied love,
> Sustains it from beneath, and kindles it above.
>   (ll. 370–8)

This kind of writing is akin to the pantheist passages in *Tintern Abbey* (ll. 94–103); both poems speak of the indefinable 'presence' that transcends the limitations of the human condition, co-existent with a universal consciousness that runs throughout nature. Shelley sees Keats as absorbed into that larger entity, just as the nameless woman of Wordsworth's *A Slumber did my Spirit Seal* was incorporated into the 'earth's diurnal course / With rocks and stones and trees!' (ll. 7–8).

The poet in Shelley's work is always a suffering, Christ-like figure, doomed and neglected, and that, to a large extent, is how he perceived himself. Despite his best efforts, the literary world took little notice of him. In the essay 'On Love' he observed, 'I have found my language misunderstood like one in a distant and savage land' (see p. 849), and in a letter of April 1819 he expressed his cynicism as to the reviewers' opinions of *Rosalind and Helen* (1819): 'As to the reviews, I suppose there is nothing but abuse' (Jones ii 94). In stark contrast to those of Byron, his books appeared in small editions, often printed at his own expense, which did not sell.

Shelley died tragically early. He and Mary moved to San Terenzo near Lerici in April 1822, where he received his boat, the *Ariel*, on 22 May. He sailed to Livorno with a friend, Edward Williams, and drowned on the return voyage, 8 July.

His literary reputation has risen comparatively slowly; this is, in large part, thanks to the deplorable state of his texts. Most of his poems were printed incorrectly, often because, being out of England, he was unable to supervise their production. One of Mary Shelley's greatest achievements was to edit the first collection of her husband's poetry, in 1839, which remains the critical standard even today. But she did not have access to all the materials available to modern scholars, and a new edition is badly needed. The works presented here have been newly edited for this anthology from early printed texts and Shelley's manuscripts.

---

[11]   Marchand v 268.
[12]   This is discussed in detail by James A. W. Heffernan, '*Adonais*: Shelley's Consumption of Keats', *Romanticism: A Critical Reader* 173–91.

Further reading

Neville Rogers, *Shelley at Work: A Critical Inquiry* (2nd edn, Oxford, 1967)

Judith Chernaik, *The Lyrics of Shelley* (Cleveland and London, 1972)

Richard Holmes, *Shelley: The Pursuit* (London, 1974)

Timothy Webb, *Shelley: A Voice not Understood* (Manchester, 1977)

Richard Cronin, *Shelley's Poetic Thoughts* (London, 1981)

William Keach, *Shelley's Style* (London, 1984)

Shelley's Prose ed. David Lee Clark (London, 1988)

Stuart M. Sperry, *Shelley's Major Verse: The Narrative and Dramatic Poetry* (Cambridge, Mass., 1988)

Stephen C. Behrendt, *Shelley and his Audiences* (Lincoln, 1989)

Timothy Clark, *Embodying Revolution: The Figure of the Poet in Shelley* (Oxford, 1989)

Michael O'Neill, *The Human Mind's Imaginings: Conflict and Achievement in Shelley's Poetry* (Oxford, 1989)

David Pirie, *Percy Bysshe Shelley: A Literary Life* (Basingstoke, 1989)

John Lucas, 'Shelley and the Men of England', *England and Englishness* (London, 1990), pp. 119–34

Donald H. Reiman, *Percy Bysshe Shelley* (2nd edn, Boston, 1990)

Michael O'Neill, *Shelley* (London, 1993)

Susan J. Wolfson, 'Social Form: Shelley and the Determination of Reading', *Formal Charges: The Shaping of Poetry in British Romanticism* (Stanford, Calif., 1997), pp. 193–226

To Wordsworth (composed probably September–October 1815)[1]

From ALASTOR; OR, THE SPIRIT OF SOLITUDE, AND OTHER POEMS (1816)

> Poet of nature, thou hast wept to know
> That things depart which never may return;
> Childhood and youth, friendship and love's first glow
> Have fled like sweet dreams,[2] leaving thee to mourn.
> These common woes I feel. One loss is mine   5
> Which thou too feel'st, yet I alone deplore.[3]
> Thou wert as a lone star,[4] whose light did shine
> On some frail bark in winter's midnight roar;
> Thou hast like to a rock-built refuge stood
> Above the blind and battling multitude;   10
> In honoured poverty[5] thy voice did weave
> Songs consecrate to truth and liberty –
> Deserting these, thou leavest me to grieve,
> Thus having been, that thou shouldst cease to be.

[handwritten margin notes: "Tintern Abbey: feeling of loss overcome; ironic"; "dif. in tone b/t Shelley & Byron regarding Wordsworth?"]

TO WORDSWORTH

[1] Wordsworth was a tremendously important influence on Shelley's poetry, but Shelley did not feel unambiguously about him. He admired *Tintern Abbey* and the *Ode*, but was disappointed by *The Excursion* (1814), and despised Wordsworth for the conservatism of his middle age. He did not know *The Prelude*. See headnote for further discussion.

[2] *Poet of nature . . . dreams* a reference to Wordsworth's lament for the loss of his earlier intensity of vision in the *Ode* (pp. 375–80).

[3] *deplore* lament.

[4] *Thou wert as a lone star* cf. Wordsworth's praise of Milton, *London 1802* 9 (p. 374).

[5] *In honoured poverty* it cannot be said that Wordsworth was ever truly poor (although he and his siblings had known hard times after they were orphaned in 1783). Shelley is really lamenting Wordsworth's acceptance of the job of Distributor for Stamps in Westmorland, which brought him a yearly salary of £400 (no small sum in those days).

Alastor; or, The Spirit of Solitude (composed between 10 September and 14 December 1815)[1]

From ALASTOR; OR, THE SPIRIT OF SOLITUDE, AND OTHER POEMS (1816)

Preface

The poem entitled 'Alastor' may be considered as allegorical of one of the most interesting situations of the human mind. It represents a youth[2] of uncorrupted feelings and adventurous genius led forth by an imagination inflamed and purified through familiarity with all that is excellent and majestic, to the contemplation of the universe. He drinks deep of the fountains of knowledge and is still insatiate. The magnificence and beauty of the external world sinks profoundly into the frame of his conceptions, and affords to their modifications a variety not to be exhausted. So long as it is possible for his desires to point towards objects thus infinite and unmeasured, he is joyous and tranquil and self-possessed. But the period arrives when these objects cease to suffice. His mind is at length suddenly awakened and thirsts for intercourse with an intelligence similar to itself. He images to himself the being whom he loves. Conversant with speculations of the sublimest and most perfect natures, the vision in which he embodies his own imaginations unites all of wonderful, or wise, or beautiful, which the poet, the philosopher, or the lover could depicture. The intellectual faculties, the imagination, the functions of sense, have their respective requisitions[3] on the sympathy of corresponding powers in other human beings. The poet is represented as uniting these requisitions, and attaching them to a single image. He seeks in vain for a prototype of his conception.[4] Blasted by his disappointment, he descends to an untimely grave.

The picture is not barren of instruction to actual men. The poet's self-centred seclusion was avenged by the furies of an irresistible passion pursuing him to speedy ruin. But that power which strikes the luminaries of the world with sudden darkness and extinction, by awakening them to too exquisite a perception of its influences, dooms to a slow and poisonous decay those meaner spirits that dare to abjure its dominion. Their destiny is more abject and inglorious as their delinquency is more contemptible and pernicious. They who, deluded by no generous error, instigated by no sacred thirst of doubtful knowledge, duped by no illustrious superstition, loving nothing on this earth, and cherishing no hopes beyond, yet keep aloof from sympathies with their kind, rejoicing neither in human joy nor mourning with human grief; these, and such as they, have their apportioned curse. They languish because none feel with them their common nature. They are morally dead. They are neither friends, nor lovers, nor fathers, nor citizens of the world, nor benefactors of their country. Among those who attempt to exist without human sympathy, the pure and tender-hearted perish through the intensity and passion of their search after its communities, when the vacancy of their spirit suddenly makes itself felt. All else,[5] selfish, blind, and torpid, are those unforeseeing multitudes who constitute, together with their own, the lasting misery and loneliness of the world. Those who love not their fellow-beings live unfruitful lives, and prepare for their old age a miserable grave.

ALASTOR; OR, THE SPIRIT OF SOLITUDE

[1] For introductory remarks on this poem see pp. 819–20. Thomas Love Peacock recalled, in his Memoirs of Shelley: 'I proposed that [title] which he adopted: Alastor; or, the Spirit of Solitude. The Greek word Ἀλάστωρ is an evil genius, κακοδαίμων. . . . The poem treated the spirit of solitude as a spirit of evil. I mention the true meaning of the word because many have supposed Alastor to be the name of the hero of the poem'.

[2] a youth not named in the poem, though obviously a version of Shelley himself.

[3] requisitions claims.

[4] a prototype of his conception i.e. an ideal embodiment of his imaginings. The essay 'On Love' refers to 'the ideal prototype of everything excellent or lovely that we are capable of conceiving as belonging to the nature of man'; see p. 850. See also Shelley's letter to John Gisborne, 18 June 1822: 'I think one is always in love with something or other; the error (and I confess it is not easy for spirits cased in flesh and blood to avoid it) consists in seeking in a mortal image the likeness of what is perhaps eternal' (Jones ii 434). For more on ideal prototypes, see 'On Love', pp. 849–50.

[5] All else completely otherwise.

The good die first,
And those whose hearts are dry as summer dust,
Burn to the socket![6]   14 December 1815

Nondum amabam, et amare amabam, quaerebam quid amarem, amans amare.[7]

Earth, ocean, air, beloved brotherhood!
If our great mother[8] has imbued my soul
With aught of natural piety[9] to feel
Your love, and recompense the boon with mine;
If dewy morn, and odorous noon, and even,   5
With sunset and its gorgeous ministers,
And solemn midnight's tingling silentness;
If autumn's hollow sighs in the sere[10] wood,
And winter robing with pure snow and crowns
Of starry ice the grey grass and bare boughs;   10
If spring's voluptuous pantings when she breathes
Her first sweet kisses, have been dear to me;
If no bright bird, insect, or gentle beast
I consciously[11] have injured, but still loved
And cherished these my kindred – then forgive   15
This boast, beloved brethren, and withdraw
No portion of your wonted favour now.
     Mother of this unfathomable world![12]
Favour my solemn song, for I have loved
Thee ever, and thee only; I have watched   20
Thy shadow and the darkness of thy steps,
And my heart ever gazes on the depth
Of thy deep mysteries. I have made my bed
In charnels[13] and on coffins, where black death
Keeps record of the trophies won from thee,   25
Hoping to still these obstinate questionings[14]
Of thee and thine, by forcing some lone ghost,
Thy messenger, to render up the tale
Of what we are.[15] In lone and silent hours,
When night makes a weird sound of its own stillness,   30
Like an inspired and desperate alchemist[16]
Staking his very life on some dark hope,
Have I mixed awful talk[17] and asking looks
With my most innocent love, until strange tears,
Uniting with those breathless kisses, made   35
Such magic as compels the charmed night

---

[6] Shelley quoted these lines from Wordsworth, *The Excursion* i 500–2, but they had originally been composed as *The Ruined Cottage* 96–8 (p. 279).

[7] 'I was not yet in love, and I loved to be in love, I sought what I might love, in love with loving', St Augustine, *Confessions* III i.

[8] *our great mother* Cybele, goddess of the powers of nature.

[9] *natural piety* Wordsworth, *The Rainbow* 9.

[10] *sere* dry, withered.

[11] *consciously* i.e. conscious of his culpability.

[12] *Mother of this unfathomable world* Nature, as well as Necessity; compare *Queen Mab* vi 198: 'Necessity! Thou mother of the world!'

[13] *charnels* graveyards.

[14] *obstinate questionings* an allusion to Wordsworth, *Ode* 144.

[15] *I have made . . . what we are* Thomas Jefferson Hogg recalled that Shelley had, as a boy, frequented graveyards in the hope of meeting ghosts.

[16] *alchemist* alchemists sought to turn base metals to gold – an impossibility.

[17] *awful talk* awe-inspired discussion.

To render up thy charge – and though ne'er yet
Thou hast unveiled thy inmost sanctuary,
Enough from incommunicable dream,
And twilight phantasms, and deep noonday thought,   40
Has shone within me, that serenely now
And moveless, as a long-forgotten lyre[18]
Suspended in the solitary dome
Of some mysterious and deserted fane,[19]
I wait thy breath, Great Parent, that my strain   45
May modulate with murmurs of the air
And motions of the forests and the sea,
And voice of living beings, and woven hymns
Of night and day, and the deep heart of man.

    There was a poet whose untimely tomb   50
No human hands with pious reverence reared,
But the charmed eddies of autumnal winds
Built o'er his mouldering bones a pyramid
Of mouldering leaves in the waste wilderness;
A lovely youth – no mourning maiden decked   55
With weeping flowers or votive cypress[20] wreath
The lone couch of his everlasting sleep;
Gentle and brave and generous – no lorn[21] bard
Breathed o'er his dark fate one melodious sigh;
He lived, he died, he sung, in solitude.   60
Strangers have wept to hear his passionate notes,
And virgins, as unknown he passed, have pined
And wasted for fond love of his wild eyes.
The fire of those soft orbs has ceased to burn,
And silence, too enamoured of that voice,   65
Locks its mute music in her rugged cell.
    By solemn vision and bright silver dream
His infancy was nurtured;[22] every sight
And sound from the vast earth and ambient[23] air
Sent to his heart its choicest impulses.   70
The fountains of divine philosophy
Fled not his thirsting lips, and all of great
Or good or lovely, which the sacred past
In truth or fable consecrates, he felt
And knew. When early youth had passed, he left   75
His cold fireside and alienated home[24]
To seek strange truths in undiscovered lands:
Many a wide waste and tangled wilderness
Has lured his fearless steps, and he has bought
With his sweet voice and eyes, from savage men,   80
His rest and food. Nature's most secret steps

---

[18]   *a long-forgotten lyre* an Aeolian harp; with lines 42–9 compare Coleridge, *Eolian Harp* 36–40.
[19]   *fane* temple.
[20]   *cypress* symbol of death and mourning.
[21]   *lorn* lonesome.
[22]   *By solemn vision . . . nurtured* Shelley catches the tone of Wordsworth's account of the Wanderer's natural education in

The Excursion, originally composed as *The Pedlar* in 1798 (see pp. 289–98).
[23]   *ambient* surrounding.
[24]   *alienated home* like Victor Frankenstein, the poet alienates his family. Shelley's relationship with his own father became very strained during his undergraduate years, and ended with a complete break in January 1812.

He like her shadow has pursued, where'er
The red volcano overcanopies
Its fields of snow and pinnacles of ice
With burning smoke, or where bitumen lakes[25]   85
On black bare pointed islets ever beat
With sluggish surge, or where the secret caves
Rugged and dark, winding among the springs
Of fire and poison, inaccessible
To avarice or pride, their starry domes   90
Of diamond and of gold expand above
Numberless and immeasurable halls,
Frequent[26] with crystal column, and clear shrines
Of pearl, and thrones radiant with chrysolite.[27]
Nor had that scene of ampler majesty   95
Than gems or gold, the varying roof of heaven
And the green earth lost in his heart its claims
To love and wonder; he would linger long
In lonesome vales, making the wild his home,
Until the doves and squirrels would partake   100
From his innocuous hand his bloodless food,[28]
Lured by the gentle meaning of his looks,
And the wild antelope that starts whene'er
The dry leaf rustles in the brake, suspend
Her timid steps to gaze upon a form   105
More graceful than her own.

                 His wandering step,[29]
Obedient to high thoughts, has visited
The awful ruins of the days of old:
Athens, and Tyre, and Balbec,[30] and the waste
Where stood Jerusalem,[31] the fallen towers   110
Of Babylon,[32] the eternal pyramids,
Memphis and Thebes,[33] and whatsoe'er of strange
Sculptured on alabaster obelisk
Or jasper tomb, or mutilated sphinx,
Dark Ethiopia in her desert hills   115
Conceals. Among the ruined temples there,
Stupendous columns and wild images
Of more than man, where marble demons[34] watch
The Zodiac's brazen mystery[35] and dead men
Hang their mute thoughts on the mute walls around,   120

---

[25] *bitumen lakes* lakes of mineral pitch, used in ancient times as mortar. Cf. the 'lakes of bitumen' in Byron's *Manfred* I i 90.
[26] *Frequent* crowded.
[27] *chrysolite* the precious olivine, a silicate of magnesia and iron found in lava. Its colour varies from pale yellowish-green (the precious stone) to dark bottle-green.
[28] *his bloodless food* Shelley was a vegetarian; see his 'Essay on the Vegetable System of Diet'. This aspect of his life and work is discussed by Timothy Morton, *Shelley and the Revolution in Taste: The Body and the Natural World* (Cambridge, 1995).
[29] The poet's journey takes him back through human history to the birth of time (l. 128).
[30] *Tyre, and Balbec* ancient cities in the present-day Lebanon.

[31] Jerusalem was destroyed by the Emperor Titus in AD 70. In 1867 it still had a population of only 16,000.
[32] The ancient city of Babylon, home of the hanging gardens (one of the seven wonders of the ancient world), was in modern Iraq, south of Baghdad.
[33] *Memphis and Thebes* the youth goes up the Nile; these are ancient Egyptian cities.
[34] *demons* spirits, genii.
[35] *The Zodiac's brazen mystery* the Zodiac in the temple of Denderah, Upper Egypt, was renowned; mythological figures were arranged around the ceiling of its portico. The Zodiac was taken to Paris in 1822 and is now in the Bibliothèque Nationale.

He lingered, poring on memorials
Of the world's youth, through the long burning day
Gazed on those speechless shapes, nor, when the moon
Filled the mysterious halls with floating shades,
Suspended he that task, but ever gazed   125
And gazed, till meaning on his vacant mind
Flashed[36] like strong inspiration, and he saw
The thrilling secrets of the birth of time.

    Meanwhile an Arab maiden brought his food,
Her daily portion, from her father's tent,   130
And spread her matting for his couch, and stole
From duties and repose to tend his steps –
Enamoured, yet not daring for deep awe
To speak her love – and watched his nightly sleep,
Sleepless herself, to gaze upon his lips   135
Parted in slumber, whence the regular breath
Of innocent dreams arose. Then when red morn
Made paler the pale moon, to her cold home
Wildered, and wan, and panting, she returned.

    The poet wandering on, through Arabie   140
And Persia and the wild Carmanian waste,
And o'er the aerial mountains which pour down
Indus and Oxus from their icy caves,
In joy and exultation held his way;
Till in the Vale of Kashmir,[37] far within   145
Its loneliest dell, where odorous plants entwine
Beneath the hollow rocks a natural bower,
Beside a sparkling rivulet he stretched
His languid limbs.[38] A vision on his sleep
There came, a dream of hopes that never yet   150
Had flushed his cheek: he dreamed a veiled maid
Sat near him, talking in low solemn tones.
Her voice was like the voice of his own soul
Heard in the calm of thought;[39] its music long,[40]
Like woven sounds of streams and breezes, held   155
His inmost sense suspended in its web
Of many-coloured woof and shifting hues.
Knowledge and truth and virtue were her theme,
And lofty hopes of divine liberty,
Thoughts the most dear to him, and poesy,   160
Herself a poet. Soon the solemn mood
Of her pure mind kindled through all her frame
A permeating fire – wild numbers[41] then
She raised, with voice stifled in tremulous sobs
Subdued by its own pathos;[42] her fair hands   165

---

[36] *on his vacant mind / Flashed* as in Wordsworth's *Daffodils* 15–16: 'They flash upon that inward eye / Which is the bliss of solitude'.

[37] *through Arabie . . . Kashmir* the poet's journey takes him through Arabia, Persia (modern Iran), through the Kerman desert in eastern Persia, over the Hindu Kush mountains (the 'Indian Caucasus'), and into Kashmir in north-west India.

[38] *he stretched . . . limbs* a recollection of Gray, *Elegy* 103–4:

'His listless length at noontide would he stretch / And pore upon the brook that babbles by.'

[39] 'His mind . . . thirsts for intercourse with an intelligence similar to itself. He images to himself the being whom he loves', p. 824, above; see also 'On Love', pp. 849–50, below.

[40] *long* for a long time.

[41] *numbers* a song, with the accompaniment of a lute.

[42] *pathos* emotion.

Were bare alone, sweeping from some strange harp
Strange symphony,[43] and in their branching veins
The eloquent blood told an ineffable tale.
The beating of her heart was heard to fill
The pauses of her music, and her breath   170
Tumultuously accorded with those fits
Of intermitted song. Sudden she rose,
As if her heart impatiently endured
Its bursting burden: at the sound he turned,
And saw by the warm light of their own life   175
Her glowing limbs beneath the sinuous veil
Of woven wind, her outspread arms now bare,
Her dark locks floating in the breath of night,
Her beamy bending eyes, her parted lips
Outstretched and pale, and quivering eagerly.   180
His strong heart sunk and sickened with excess
Of love. He reared his shuddering limbs and quelled
His gasping breath, and spread his arms to meet
Her panting bosom; she drew back awhile,
Then, yielding to the irresistible joy,   185
With frantic gesture and short breathless cry
Folded his frame in her dissolving arms.
Now blackness veiled his dizzy eyes, and night
Involved[44] and swallowed up the vision; sleep,
Like a dark flood suspended in its course,   190
Rolled back its impulse on his vacant brain.
    Roused by the shock he started from his trance –
The cold white light of morning, the blue moon
Low in the west, the clear and garish[45] hills,
The distinct valley and the vacant woods,   195
Spread round him where he stood. Whither have fled
The hues of heaven that canopied his bower
Of yesternight? The sounds that soothed his sleep,
The mystery and the majesty of earth,
The joy, the exultation? His wan eyes   200
Gaze on the empty scene as vacantly
As ocean's moon looks on the moon in heaven.
The spirit of sweet human love has sent
A vision to the sleep of him who spurned
Her choicest gifts. He eagerly pursues   205
Beyond the realms of dream that fleeting shade;
He overleaps the bounds.[46] Alas, alas!
Were limbs and breath and being intertwined
Thus treacherously? Lost, lost, forever lost
In the wide pathless desert of dim sleep,   210
That beautiful shape! Does the dark gate of death

---

43 *Strange symphony* there is possibly an echo here of Coleridge's *Kubla Khan* 42–3: 'Could I revive within me / Her symphony and song'.
44 *Involved* wrapped around.
45 *garish* glaring.
46 *the bounds* i.e. between illusion and reality, in trying to pursue the dream-image into the real world. As Peter Butter suggests, there is a divergence here from the essay 'On Love' (pp. 849–50). There, the desire for love draws us to nature; here, the natural world appears vacant and dead to the poet, whose love is narcissistic, directed to an ideal conceived within his own mind.

Conduct to thy mysterious paradise,
Oh sleep? Does the bright arch of rainbow clouds
And pendent[47] mountains seen in the calm lake
Lead only to a black and watery depth,   215
While death's blue vault with loathliest[48] vapours hung,
Where every shade which the foul grave exhales
Hides its dead eye from the detested day,
Conducts, oh sleep, to thy delightful realms?[49]
This doubt with sudden tide flowed on his heart;   220
The insatiate hope which it awakened stung
His brain even like despair.[50]
                                    While daylight held
The sky, the poet kept mute conference[51]
With his still soul. At night the passion came
Like the fierce fiend of a distempered dream,   225
And shook him from his rest, and led him forth
Into the darkness. As an eagle grasped
In folds of the green serpent, feels her breast
Burn with the poison, and precipitates
Through night and day, tempest and calm and cloud,   230
Frantic with dizzying anguish, her blind flight
O'er the wide airy wilderness; thus driven
By the bright shadow[52] of that lovely dream,
Beneath the cold glare of the desolate night,
Through tangled swamps and deep precipitous dells,   235
Startling with careless step the moonlight snake,
He fled. Red morning dawned upon his flight,
Shedding the mockery of its vital hues
Upon his cheek of death. He wandered on
Till vast Aornos seen from Petra's steep[53]   240
Hung o'er the low horizon like a cloud;
Through Balk[54] and where the desolated tombs
Of Parthian kings scatter to every wind
Their wasting dust, wildly he wandered on
Day after day, a weary waste of hours,   245
Bearing within his life the brooding care
That ever fed on its decaying flame.
And now his limbs were lean: his scattered hair
Sered[55] by the autumn of strange suffering
Sung dirges in the wind; his listless hand   250
Hung like dead bone within its withered skin;
Life, and the lustre that consumed it, shone
As in a furnace burning secretly
From his dark eyes alone. The cottagers,

---

47   *pendent* overhanging.
48   *loathliest* obnoxious.
49   *Does the bright arch . . . delightful realms?* i.e. can it be that
nature in all its beauty leads to nothing, while death, in all its
horror, leads to the paradise revealed to the poet in sleep? The
question is not answered.
50   *despair* i.e. of ever being united with the ideal he has been
allowed to see.
51   *conference* communion; part of his inner being was at repose.

52   *shadow* memory.
53   *vast Aornos seen from Petra's steep* the poet returns from
India, where the great rock Aornos stands by the Indus. There
is no place called Petra in this area.
54   The ancient city of Balkh was in modern-day
Afghanistan. He is travelling through the area south-east of
the Caspian Sea, where the Parthian kingdom used to be.
55   *Sered* thinned, faded.

Who ministered with human charity 255
His human wants, beheld with wondering awe
Their fleeting visitant. The mountaineer,
Encountering on some dizzy precipice
That spectral form, deemed that the spirit of wind
With lightning eyes, and eager breath, and feet 260
Disturbing not the drifted snow, had paused
In its career; the infant would conceal
His troubled visage in his mother's robe
In terror at the glare of those wild eyes,
To remember their strange light in many a dream 265
Of after-times; but youthful maidens, taught
By nature, would interpret half the woe[56]
That wasted him, would call him with false names
Brother and friend, would press his pallid hand
At parting, and watch, dim through tears, the path 270
Of his departure from their father's door.
    At length upon the lone Chorasmian shore[57]
He paused, a wide and melancholy waste
Of putrid marshes. A strong impulse urged
His steps to the seashore; a swan[58] was there, 275
Beside a sluggish stream among the reeds.
It rose as he approached, and with strong wings
Scaling the upward sky, bent its bright course
High over the immeasurable main.
His eyes pursued its flight. 'Thou hast a home, 280
Beautiful bird; thou voyagest to thine home,
Where thy sweet mate will twine her downy neck
With thine, and welcome thy return with eyes
Bright in the lustre of their own fond joy.
And what am I that I should linger here, 285
With voice far sweeter than thy dying notes,
Spirit more vast than thine, frame more attuned
To beauty, wasting these surpassing powers
In the deaf air, to the blind earth, and heaven
That echoes not my thoughts?' A gloomy smile 290
Of desperate hope wrinkled his quivering lips –
For sleep, he knew, kept[59] most relentlessly
Its precious charge, and silent death exposed,
Faithless perhaps as sleep, a shadowy lure,[60]
With doubtful smile mocking its own strange charms.[61] 295
    Startled by his own thoughts he looked around.
There was no fair fiend near him, not a sight
Or sound of awe but in his own deep mind.
A little shallop[62] floating near the shore
Caught the impatient wandering of his gaze. 300
It had been long abandoned, for its sides

---

[56] *would interpret half the woe* i.e. they would guess that he was in love, but not that he was in love with an ideal.
[57] *Chorasmian shore* eastern shore of the Caspian Sea.
[58] *a swan* sacred to Apollo, god of poetry; it sang before dying.

[59] *kept* concealed, kept to itself.
[60] *lure* temptation.
[61] *For sleep . . . charms* the poet has not seen his vision in sleep; perhaps he will not see her in death.
[62] *shallop* small open boat.

Gaped wide with many a rift, and its frail joints
Swayed with the undulations of the tide.
A restless impulse urged him to embark
And meet lone death on the drear ocean's waste,   305
For well he knew that mighty shadow loves
The slimy caverns of the populous deep.
    The day was fair and sunny, sea and sky
Drank its inspiring radiance, and the wind
Swept strongly from the shore, blackening the waves.   310
Following his eager soul, the wanderer
Leaped in the boat, he spread his cloak aloft
On the bare mast and took his lonely seat,
And felt the boat speed o'er the tranquil sea
Like a torn cloud before the hurricane.   315
    As one that in a silver vision floats
Obedient to the sweep of odorous winds
Upon resplendent clouds, so rapidly
Along the dark and ruffled waters fled
The straining boat. A whirlwind swept it on   320
With fierce gusts and precipitating force
Through the white ridges of the chafed sea.
The waves arose; higher and higher still
Their fierce necks writhed beneath the tempest's scourge
Like serpents struggling in a vulture's grasp.   325
Calm and rejoicing in the fearful war
Of wave ruining[63] on wave, and blast on blast
Descending, and black flood on whirlpool driven
With dark obliterating course, he sat:
As if their genii were the ministers   330
Appointed to conduct him to the light
Of those beloved eyes, the poet sat
Holding the steady helm. Evening came on,
The beams of sunset hung their rainbow hues[64]
High mid the shifting domes of sheeted spray   335
That canopied his path o'er the waste deep;
Twilight, ascending slowly from the east,
Entwined in duskier wreaths her braided locks
O'er the fair front and radiant eyes of day;
Night followed, clad with stars. On every side   340
More horribly the multitudinous streams
Of ocean's mountainous waste to mutual war
Rushed in dark tumult thundering, as to mock
The calm and spangled sky. The little boat
Still fled before the storm, still fled like foam   345
Down the steep cataract of a wintry river –
Now pausing on the edge of the riven[65] wave,
Now leaving far behind the bursting mass
That fell, convulsing ocean; safely fled –
As if that frail and wasted human form   350
Had been an elemental god.[66]

---

[63] *ruining* tumbling violently, collapsing.
[64] *hung their rainbow hues* i.e. made rainbows in the spray.
[65] *riven* split, torn asunder.
[66] *an elemental god* a god of the elements.

                                  At midnight
The moon arose – and lo! the ethereal cliffs[67]
Of Caucasus,[68] whose icy summits shone
Among the stars like sunlight, and around
Whose caverned base the whirlpools and the waves,   355
Bursting and eddying irresistibly,
Rage and resound forever. Who shall save?
The boat fled on, the boiling torrent drove,
The crags closed round with black and jagged arms,
The shattered mountain overhung the sea,   360
And faster still, beyond all human speed,
Suspended on the sweep of the smooth wave,
The little boat was driven. A cavern there
Yawned, and amid its slant and winding depths
Engulfed the rushing sea. The boat fled on   365
With unrelaxing speed. 'Vision and love!'
The poet cried aloud, 'I have beheld
The path of thy departure. Sleep and death
Shall not divide us long!'
                                  The boat pursued
The windings of the cavern. Daylight shone   370
At length upon that gloomy river's flow;
Now, where the fiercest war among the waves
Is calm, on the unfathomable stream
The boat moved slowly. Where the mountain, riven,
Exposed those black depths to the azure sky,   375
Ere yet the flood's enormous volume fell
Even to the base of Caucasus, with sound
That shook the everlasting rocks, the mass
Filled with one whirlpool all that ample chasm;
Stair above stair the eddying waters rose,[69]   380
Circling immeasurably fast, and laved
With alternating dash the gnarled roots
Of mighty trees that stretched their giant arms
In darkness over it. I' the midst was left,
Reflecting yet distorting every cloud,   385
A pool of treacherous and tremendous calm.
Seized by the sway of the ascending stream,
With dizzy swiftness, round and round and round,
Ridge after ridge the straining boat arose,
Till on the verge of the extremest curve,   390
Where, through an opening of the rocky bank,
The waters overflow, and a smooth spot
Of glassy quiet mid those battling tides
Is left, the boat paused shuddering. Shall it sink
Down the abyss? Shall the reverting stress   395
Of that resistless gulf embosom it?
Now shall it fall? A wandering stream of wind,

---

[67] *the ethereal cliffs* the cliffs seem to reach into the sky.
[68] The boat has crossed the Caspian Sea to the mountains of the Caucasus, now in Russia, on the western shore. Prometheus was nailed to the Caucasus by Jupiter.

[69] *Stair above stair the eddying waters rose* as it spins, the whirlpool lifts the boat up at its outer edge higher and higher ('Stair above stair').

Breathed from the west, has caught the expanded sail,
And lo! with gentle motion, between banks
Of mossy slope, and on a placid stream,   400
Beneath a woven grove it sails – and hark!
The ghastly torrent mingles its far roar
With the breeze murmuring in the musical woods.
Where the embowering trees recede, and leave
A little space of green expanse, the cove   405
Is closed by meeting banks, whose yellow flowers[70]
Forever gaze on their own drooping eyes,
Reflected in the crystal calm. The wave
Of the boat's motion marred their pensive task
Which nought but vagrant bird, or wanton wind,   410
Or falling spear-grass, or their own decay
Had e'er disturbed before. The poet longed
To deck with their bright hues his withered hair,
But on his heart its solitude returned
And he forbore. Not the strong impulse hid   415
In those flushed cheeks, bent eyes, and shadowy frame
Had yet performed its ministry;[71] it hung
Upon his life, as lightning in a cloud
Gleams, hovering ere it vanish, ere the floods
Of night close over it.

        The noonday sun   420
Now shone upon the forest, one vast mass
Of mingling shade whose brown[72] magnificence
A narrow vale embosoms; there huge caves,
Scooped in the dark base of their airy[73] rocks,
Mocking its moans,[74] respond and roar forever.   425
The meeting boughs and implicated[75] leaves
Wove twilight o'er the poet's path as, led
By love, or dream, or god, or mightier death,
He sought in nature's dearest haunt some bank,
Her cradle,[76] and his sepulchre. More dark   430
And dark the shades accumulate. The oak,
Expanding its immense and knotty arms,
Embraces the light beech. The pyramids
Of the tall cedar overarching, frame
Most solemn domes within, and far below,   435
Like clouds suspended in an emerald sky,[77]
The ash and the acacia floating hang
Tremulous and pale. Like restless serpents clothed
In rainbow and in fire, the parasites,[78]
Starred with ten thousand blossoms, flow around   440

---

[70] *yellow flowers* Narcissus was a beautiful youth who mistook his own image, reflected in the water, for a nymph. He fell in love with it, committed suicide, and was changed into the flower today named after him (common name: 'daffodil').

[71] *performed its ministry* an allusion to Coleridge, *Frost at Midnight* 1: 'The frost performs its secret ministry'.

[72] *brown* dark.

[73] *airy* lofty, high.

[74] *Mocking its moans* echoing the moans of the wind in the forest.

[75] *implicated* intertwining.

[76] *Her cradle* the poet travels back to the source of life.

[77] *Most solemn domes . . . sky* perhaps a recollection of the 'Cloudscape New Jerusalem' passage from Wordsworth's *Excursion* (see pp. 410–11).

[78] *parasites* climbing plants.

The grey trunks, and, as gamesome[79] infants' eyes
With gentle meanings and most innocent wiles
Fold their beams round the hearts of those that love,
These twine their tendrils with the wedded boughs
Uniting their close union; the woven leaves   445
Make network of the dark blue light of day[80]
And the night's noontide clearness, mutable
As shapes in the weird clouds. Soft mossy lawns[81]
Beneath these canopies extend their swells,
Fragrant with perfumed herbs, and eyed with blooms   450
Minute yet beautiful. One darkest glen
Sends from its woods of musk-rose, twined with jasmine,
A soul-dissolving odour, to invite
To some more lovely mystery. Through the dell,
Silence and Twilight here, twin-sisters, keep   455
Their noonday watch, and sail among the shades
Like vaporous shapes half-seen; beyond, a well,
Dark, gleaming, and of most translucent wave,
Images[82] all the woven boughs above,
And each depending[83] leaf, and every speck   460
Of azure sky, darting between their chasms;
Nor aught else in the liquid mirror laves
Its portraiture,[84] but some inconstant star
Between one foliaged lattice[85] twinkling fair,
Or painted bird, sleeping beneath the moon,   465
Or gorgeous insect floating motionless,
Unconscious of the day ere yet his wings
Have spread their glories to the gaze of noon.[86]
        Hither the poet came. His eyes beheld
Their own wan light through the reflected lines   470
Of his thin hair, distinct in the dark depth
Of that still fountain; as the human heart,
Gazing in dreams over the gloomy grave,
Sees its own treacherous likeness there.[87] He heard
The motion of the leaves, the grass that sprung   475
Startled and glanced and trembled even to feel
An unaccustomed presence, and the sound
Of the sweet brook that from the secret springs
Of the dark fountain rose. A spirit[88] seemed
To stand beside him, clothed in no bright robes   480
Of shadowy silver or enshrining light
Borrowed from aught the visible world affords
Of grace, or majesty, or mystery –
But, undulating woods and silent well,
And leaping rivulet and evening gloom   485

---

79   *gamesome* playful.
80   *Make network of the dark blue light of day* daylight is seen as
if through netted threads.
81   *lawns* grassy clearings.
82   *Images* reflects.
83   *depending* hanging.
84   *laves / Its portraiture* there is nothing else reflected in the
well.

85   *one foliaged lattice* a mass of interlaced leaves.
86   *Or gorgeous insect . . . noon* the butterfly is unaware that
outside the forest it is noon.
87   *Gazing in dreams . . . there* i.e. imagines its continued but
uncertain (treacherous) life after death.
88   *A spirit* probably Nature.

Now deepening the dark shades, for speech assuming[89]
Held commune with him, as if he and it
Were all that was – only, when his regard
Was raised by intense pensiveness, two eyes,
Two starry eyes, hung in the gloom of thought   490
And seemed with their serene and azure smiles
To beckon him.
           Obedient to the light
That shone within his soul, he went pursuing
The windings of the dell. The rivulet
Wanton and wild, through many a green ravine   495
Beneath the forest flowed. Sometimes it fell
Among the moss with hollow harmony
Dark and profound; now on the polished stones
It danced, like childhood laughing as it went;
Then through the plain in tranquil wanderings crept,   500
Reflecting every herb and drooping bud
That overhung its quietness. 'Oh stream!
Whose source is inaccessibly profound,
Whither do thy mysterious waters tend?
Thou imagest my life: thy darksome stillness,   505
Thy dazzling waves, thy loud and hollow gulfs,
Thy searchless fountain[90] and invisible course
Have each their type[91] in me. And the wide sky
And measureless ocean may declare as soon
What oozy[92] cavern or what wandering cloud   510
Contains thy waters, as the universe
Tell where these living thoughts reside, when stretched
Upon thy flowers my bloodless limbs shall waste
I' the passing wind!'
             Beside the grassy shore
Of the small stream he went; he did impress   515
On the green moss his tremulous step that caught
Strong shuddering from his burning limbs. As one
Roused by some joyous madness from the couch
Of fever, he did move, yet not like him
Forgetful of the grave,[93] where, when the flame   520
Of his frail exultation shall be spent,
He must descend. With rapid steps he went
Beneath the shade of trees, beside the flow
Of the wild babbling rivulet – and now
The forest's solemn canopies were changed   525
For the uniform and lightsome evening sky.
Grey rocks did peep from the spare moss, and stemmed
The struggling brook; tall spires of windlestrae[94]
Threw their thin shadows down the rugged slope,
And nought but gnarled roots of ancient pines   530

---

[89]   *for speech assuming* Nature used woods, well, rivulet, and gloom as a means of communication.
[90]   *searchless fountain* undiscoverable source.
[91]   *type* i.e. corresponding idealized version.
[92]   *oozy* damp.

[93]   *Forgetful of the grave* it is the fever-stricken man who, in his delirium, forgets the grave; the poet is all too mindful of death.
[94]   *windlestrae* dry grass-stalks.

Branchless and blasted, clenched with grasping roots
The unwilling soil. A gradual change was here,
Yet ghastly. For, as fast years flow away,
The smooth brow gathers, and the hair grows thin
And white, and where irradiate[95] dewy eyes   535
Had shone, gleam stony orbs: so from his steps
Bright flowers departed, and the beautiful shade
Of the green groves, with all their odorous winds
And musical motions. Calm, he still pursued
The stream, that with a larger volume[96] now   540
Rolled through the labyrinthine dell; and there
Fretted[97] a path through its descending curves
With its wintry speed. On every side now rose
Rocks which, in unimaginable forms,
Lifted their black and barren pinnacles   545
In the light of evening, and, its precipice
Obscuring, the ravine disclosed above,
Mid toppling stones, black gulfs and yawning caves,
Whose windings gave ten thousand various tongues
To the loud stream. Lo! where the pass expands   550
Its stony jaws, the abrupt mountain breaks
And seems, with its accumulated crags,
To overhang the world – for wide expand,
Beneath the wan stars and descending moon,
Islanded seas, blue mountains, mighty streams,   555
Dim tracts and vast, robed in the lustrous gloom
Of leaden-coloured even,[98] and fiery hills
Mingling their flames with twilight, on the verge
Of the remote horizon. The near scene,
In naked and severe simplicity,   560
Made contrast with the universe. A pine,
Rock-rooted, stretched athwart the vacancy
Its swinging boughs, to each inconstant blast
Yielding one only response, at each pause
In most familiar cadence, with the howl,   565
The thunder and the hiss of homeless streams
Mingling its solemn song, whilst the broad river,
Foaming and hurrying o'er its rugged path,
Fell into that immeasurable void,
Scattering its waters to the passing winds.   570
    Yet the grey precipice and solemn pine
And torrent were not all; one silent nook
Was there. Even on the edge of that vast mountain,
Upheld by knotty roots and fallen rocks,
It overlooked in its serenity   575
The dark earth and the bending vault of stars.
It was a tranquil spot that seemed to smile
Even in the lap of horror. Ivy clasped

---

95   *irradiate* shining.
96   *volume* of water.

97   *Fretted* wore, ground.
98   *leaden-coloured even* dark grey evening.

The fissured stones with its entwining arms,
And did embower with leaves forever green,   580
And berries dark, the smooth and even space
Of its inviolated floor; and here
The children of the autumnal whirlwind[99] bore,
In wanton sport, those bright leaves whose decay,
Red, yellow, or ethereally pale,   585
Rivals the pride of summer. 'Tis the haunt
Of every gentle wind whose breath can teach
The wilds to love tranquillity. One step,[100]
One human step alone, has ever broken
The stillness of its solitude; one voice   590
Alone[101] inspired its echoes – even that voice
Which hither came floating among the winds,
And led the loveliest among human forms[102]
To make their[103] wild haunts the depository
Of all the grace and beauty that endued[104]   595
Its motions, render up its majesty,
Scatter its music on the unfeeling storm,
And to the damp leaves and blue cavern mould,
Nurses of rainbow flowers and branching moss,
Commit[105] the colours of that varying cheek,   600
That snowy breast, those dark and drooping eyes.
    The dim and horned moon hung low, and poured
A sea of lustre on the horizon's verge
That overflowed its mountains. Yellow mist
Filled the unbounded atmosphere, and drank   605
Wan moonlight even to fullness: not a star
Shone, not a sound was heard; the very winds,
Danger's grim playmates, on that precipice
Slept, clasped in his embrace. Oh storm of Death,
Whose sightless speed divides this sullen night,   610
And thou, colossal skeleton,[106] that, still
Guiding its irresistible career
In thy devastating omnipotence,
Art king of this frail world – from the red field
Of slaughter, from the reeking hospital,   615
The patriot's sacred couch, the snowy bed
Of innocence, the scaffold and the throne,
A mighty voice invokes thee: Ruin calls
His brother Death. A rare and regal prey[107]
He hath prepared, prowling around the world –   620
Glutted with which thou mayst repose, and men
Go to their graves like flowers or creeping worms,
Nor ever more offer at thy dark shrine
The unheeded tribute of a broken heart.

---

99   *The children of the autumnal whirlwind* i.e. gusts of wind.
100   *One step* i.e. that of the poet.
101   *one voice / Alone* i.e. that of the vision.
102   *the loveliest among human forms* the poet.
103   *their* i.e. the winds'.
104   *endued* invested.

105   *Commit* entrust.
106   *colossal skeleton* Death.
107   *A rare and regal prey* i.e. the world's rulers, who will glut
Death, so that their victims may die according to their worth.
It is worth remembering that this poem was written just after
Napoleon's defeat at Waterloo.

When on the threshold of the green recess 625
The wanderer's footsteps fell, he knew that death
Was on him. Yet a little, ere it fled,
Did he resign his high and holy soul
To images of the majestic past
That paused within his passive[108] being now, 630
Like winds that bear sweet music when they breathe
Through some dim latticed chamber. He did place
His pale lean hand upon the rugged trunk
Of the old pine; upon an ivied stone
Reclined his languid head; his limbs did rest, 635
Diffused and motionless, on the smooth brink
Of that obscurest chasm – and thus he lay,
Surrendering to their final impulses
The hovering powers of life. Hope and despair,
The torturers, slept;[109] no mortal pain or fear 640
Marred his repose, the influxes of sense[110]
And his own being unalloyed by pain,
Yet feebler and more feeble, calmly fed
The stream of thought, till he lay breathing there
At peace, and faintly smiling. His last sight 645
Was the great moon, which o'er the western line
Of the wide world her mighty horn suspended,
With those dun beams inwoven darkness seemed
To mingle. Now upon the jagged hills
It rests, and still as[111] the divided frame 650
Of the vast meteor[112] sunk, the poet's blood,
That ever beat in mystic sympathy
With nature's ebb and flow, grew feebler still;
And when two lessening points of light[113] alone
Gleamed through the darkness, the alternate gasp 655
Of his faint respiration scarce did stir
The stagnate[114] night – till the minutest ray
Was quenched, the pulse yet lingered in his heart.
It paused, it fluttered. But when heaven remained
Utterly black, the murky shades involved 660
An image, silent, cold, and motionless,
As their own voiceless earth and vacant air.
Even as a vapour[115] fed with golden beams
That ministered on sunlight ere the west
Eclipses it, was now that wondrous frame – 665
No sense, no motion,[116] no divinity –
A fragile lute[117] on whose harmonious strings
The breath of heaven did wander, a bright stream

---

[108] *passive* an important detail; compare *Mont Blanc* 37–8.

[109] *Hope and despair . . . slept* cf. Percy's journal entry for 28 July 1814: 'I hope – but my hopes are not unmixed with fear for what will befall this inestimable spirit when we appear to die' (*Shelley Journals* i 7).

[110] *the influxes of sense* his perceptions.

[111] *still as* i.e. as still as.

[112] *the vast meteor* the moon.

[113] *two lessening points of light* from the moon. Cf. ll. 179, 489–92.

[114] *stagnate* stagnant.

[115] *vapour* cloud.

[116] *No sense, no motion* echoes Wordsworth, *A slumber did my spirit seal* 5: 'No motion has she now, no force'.

[117] *A fragile lute* once again, Shelley has in mind an Aeolian harp.

Once fed with many-voiced[118] waves, a dream
Of youth, which night and time have quenched for ever –   670
Still, dark, and dry, and unremembered now.
    Oh for Medea's wondrous alchemy,
Which wheresoe'er it fell made the earth gleam
With bright flowers, and the wintry boughs exhale
From vernal blooms fresh fragrance![119] Oh that God,   675
Profuse[120] of poisons, would concede the chalice
Which but one living man[121] has drained – who now,
Vessel of deathless wrath, a slave that feels
No proud exemption in the blighting curse
He bears, over the world wanders for ever,   680
Lone as incarnate death! Oh that the dream
Of dark magician[122] in his visioned cave,
Raking the cinders of a crucible
For life and power, even when his feeble hand
Shakes in its last decay, were the true law   685
Of this so lovely world! But thou art fled
Like some frail exhalation which the dawn
Robes in its golden beams – ah, thou hast fled! –
The brave, the gentle, and the beautiful,
The child of grace and genius. Heartless things   690
Are done and said i' the world, and many worms
And beasts and men live on, and mighty earth
From sea and mountain, city and wilderness,
In vesper low or joyous orison,[123]
Lifts still its solemn voice – but thou art fled;   695
Thou canst no longer know or love the shapes
Of this phantasmal scene,[124] who have to thee
Been purest ministers – who are, alas,
Now thou art not! Upon those pallid lips,
So sweet even in their silence, on those eyes   700
That image sleep in death, upon that form
Yet safe from the worm's outrage, let no tear
Be shed, not even in thought; nor – when those hues
Are gone, and those divinest lineaments
Worn by the senseless[125] wind – shall live alone   705
In the frail pauses of this simple strain.
Let not high verse, mourning the memory
Of that which is no more, or painting's woe
Or sculpture, speak in feeble imagery
Their own cold powers. Art and eloquence   710
And all the shows o' the world are frail and vain
To weep a loss that turns their lights to shade.

---

[118]   *many-voiced* compare *Mont Blanc* 13.
[119]   *Oh for . . . fragrance* Medea, an enchantress in Greek mythology, brewed a potion to restore youth to Aeson, the father of her lover Jason; when spilt on the ground it had the effects described here.
[120]   *Profuse* productive.
[121]   *one living man* Ahasuerus, the wandering Jew, doomed to eternal life.

[122]   *dark magician* the alchemist who, besides seeking to turn base metals into gold, seeks the elixir of eternal life.
[123]   *vesper . . . orison* evensong . . . prayer – uttered, figuratively, by the earth.
[124]   *this phantasmal scene* i.e. the transcendent, visionary world.
[125]   *senseless* oblivious.

It is a woe too 'deep for tears',[126] when all
Is reft at once, when some surpassing spirit,
Whose light adorned the world around it, leaves   715
Those who remain behind not sobs or groans,
The passionate tumult of a clinging hope,
But pale despair and cold tranquillity,
Nature's vast frame, the web of human things,
Birth and the grave, that are not as they were.   720

Hymn to Intellectual Beauty (composed between 22 June and 29 August 1816; edited from printed text corrected by Shelley)[1]

From THE EXAMINER No. 473 (19 January 1817, p. 41)

1

The awful[2] shadow of some unseen Power
   Floats though unseen amongst us, visiting
   This various world with as inconstant wing[3]
As summer winds that creep from flower to flower;
Like moonbeams that behind some piny mountain shower,[4]   5
     It visits with inconstant glance
     Each human heart and countenance;
Like hues and harmonies of evening,
     Like clouds in starlight widely spread,
     Like memory of music fled,   10
     Like aught that for its grace may be
Dear, and yet dearer for its mystery.

2

Spirit of Beauty, that doth consecrate
   With thine own hues all thou dost shine upon
   Of human thought or form – where art thou gone?   15
Why dost thou pass away and leave our state,
This dim vast vale of tears, vacant and desolate?
     Ask why the sunlight not forever
     Weaves rainbows o'er yon mountain river,
Why aught should fail and fade that once is shown,   20
     Why fear and dream, and death and birth
     Cast on the daylight of this earth

---

[126] *It is a woe too 'deep for tears'* Wordsworth, *Ode* 206: 'Thoughts that do often lie too deep for tears.'

HYMN TO INTELLECTUAL BEAUTY
[1] This important poem should be read in the light of Wordsworth's *Ode* (pp. 375–80), by which it was inspired, which is also about the 'inconstancy' of the kind of intense vision that Shelley celebrates.

[2] *awful* awesome.

[3] *with as inconstant wing* Shelley's point is that the 'awful Power' is not always perceptible.

[4] *some piny mountain shower* rainfall among the pine trees on a mountain slope. This poem was composed during Shelley's residence in Switzerland.

Such gloom, why man has such a scope
For love and hate, despondency and hope?

3

No voice from some sublimer world hath ever   25
   To sage or poet these responses given;
   Therefore the name of God, and ghosts, and heaven
Remain the records of their vain endeavour,
Frail spells, whose uttered charm might not avail to sever,
   From all we hear and all we see,   30
   Doubt, chance, and mutability.
Thy light alone, like mist o'er mountains driven,
   Or music by the night wind sent
   Through strings of some still instrument,[5]
   Or moonlight on a midnight stream,   35
Gives grace and truth to life's unquiet dream.

4

Love, hope, and self-esteem, like clouds depart
   And come, for some uncertain moments lent.
   Man were immortal and omnipotent,
Didst thou,[6] unknown and awful as thou art,   40
Keep with thy glorious train firm state within his heart.
   Thou messenger of sympathies
   That wax and wane in lovers' eyes;
Thou that to human thought art nourishment,
   Like darkness to a dying flame![7]   45
   Depart not as thy shadow came,
   Depart not lest the grave should be,
Like life and fear, a dark reality.

5

While yet a boy I sought for ghosts, and sped
   Through many a listening chamber, cave and ruin   50
   And starlight wood, with fearful steps pursuing
Hopes of high talk with the departed dead.[8]
I called on poisonous names[9] with which our youth is fed –
   I was not heard, I saw them not
   When musing deeply on the lot   55
Of life, at that sweet time when winds are wooing

---

5 *some still instrument* an Aeolian harp.
6 *Man were . . . Didst thou* man would be . . . if thou didst . . .
7 *nourishment, / Like darkness to a dying flame* strong light was believed to stifle candlelight; conversely, darkness would feed it.

8 As a boy, Shelley did go to cemeteries and woods at night, in the hope of meeting ghosts.
9 *poisonous names* presumably those of God and Christ. In earlier years Shelley did try prayer.

All vital things that wake to bring
 News of buds and blossoming.
 Sudden thy shadow fell on me –
I shrieked, and clasped my hands in ecstasy!   60

6

I vowed that I would dedicate my powers
  To thee and thine; have I not kept the vow?
  With beating heart and streaming eyes, even now
I call the phantoms of a thousand hours
Each from his voiceless grave: they have in visioned bowers   65
  Of studious zeal or love's delight
  Outwatched with me the envious night;
They know that never joy illumed my brow
  Unlinked with hope that thou wouldst free
  This world from its dark slavery,   70
  That thou, oh awful loveliness,
Wouldst give whate'er these words cannot express.

7

The day becomes more solemn and serene
  When noon is past; there is a harmony
  In autumn, and a lustre in its sky,   75
Which through the summer is not heard or seen,
As if it could not be, as if it had not been!
  Thus let thy power, which like the truth
  Of nature on my passive youth
Descended,[10] to my onward life supply   80
  Its calm – to one who worships thee,
  And every form containing thee,
  Whom, spirit fair, thy spells did bind
To fear[11] himself, and love all humankind.

---

[10] *the truth / Of nature . . . Descended* the passivity of the mind is equivalent to the psychological relaxation mentioned by De Quincey in his discussion of Wordsworth's *There was a boy* (pp. 640–2). Shelley discusses it in his 'Essay on Christianity', written between 1813 and 1819: 'All that it [i.e. human life] contains of pure or of divine visits the passive mind in some serenest mood' (*Shelley's Prose* 205).

[11] *fear* revere.

Journal-Letter from Percy Bysshe Shelley to Thomas Love Peacock, 22 July to 2 August 1876 (extract)[1]

22 July 1816. From Servox, three leagues remain to Chamounix. Mont Blanc was before us. The Alps with their innumerable glaciers on high, all around, closing in the complicated windings of the single vale; forests inexpressibly beautiful, but majestic in their beauty; interwoven beech and pine and oak overshadowed our road or receded whilst lawns of such verdure as I had never seen before occupied these openings, and, extending gradually, becoming darker into their recesses.

Mont Blanc was before us but was covered with cloud, and its base furrowed with dreadful gaps was seen alone. Pinnacles of snow, intolerably bright, part of the chain connected with Mont Blanc, shone though the clouds at intervals on high. I never knew, I never imagined what mountains were before. The immensity of these aerial[2] summits excited, when they suddenly burst upon the sight, a sentiment of ecstatic wonder not unallied to madness. And remember this was all one scene. It all pressed home to our regard and to our imagination. Though it embraced a great number of miles, the snowy pyramids which shot into the bright blue sky seemed to overhang our path; the ravine, clothed with gigantic pines and black with its depth below (so deep that the very roaring of the untameable Arve which rolled through it could not be heard above), was close to our very footsteps. All was as much our own as if we had been the creators of such impressions in the minds of others, as now occupied our own. Nature was the poet whose harmony held our spirits more breathless than that of the divinest.

25 July 1816. We have returned from visiting this glacier – a scene, in truth, of dizzying wonder. The path that winds to it along the side of a mountain, now clothed with pines, now intersected with snowy hollows, is wide and steep. The cabin of Montanvert is three leagues from Chamounix, half of which distance is performed on mules – not so sure-footed but that, on the first day, the one which I rode fell in what the guides call a 'mauvais pas', so that I narrowly escaped being precipitated down the mountain. The guide continually held that which Mary rode.

We passed over a hollow covered with snow down which vast stones, detached from the rock above, are accustomed to roll. One had fallen the preceding day, a little time after we had returned. The guides desired us to pass quickly, for it is said that sometimes the least sound will accelerate their fall. We arrived at Montanvert, however, safe.

On all sides precipitous mountains, the abodes of unrelenting frost, surround this vale. Their sides are banked up with ice and snow, broken and heaped-up, and exhibiting terrific chasms. The summits are sharp and naked pinnacles whose overhanging steepness will not even permit snow to rest there. They pierce the clouds like things not belonging to this earth. The vale itself is filled with a mass of undulating ice, and has an ascent sufficiently gradual even to the remotest abysses of these horrible deserts. It is only half a league (about two miles) in breadth, and seems much less. It exhibits an appearance as if frost had suddenly bound up the waves and whirlpools of a mighty torrent.

We walked to some distance upon its surface. The waves are elevated about 12 or 15 feet from the surface of the mass, which is intersected with long gaps of unfathomable depth, the ice of whose sides is more beautifully azure than the sky. In these regions, everything changes and is in motion. This vast mass of ice has one general progress which ceases neither day nor night. It breaks and rises forever; its undulations sink whilst others rise. From the precipices which surround it, the echo of rocks which fall from their aerial summits, or of the ice and snow, scarcely ceases for one moment. One would think that Mont Blanc was a living being, and that the frozen blood forever circulated slowly through his stony veins.

JOURNAL-LETTER FROM PERCY BYSSHE SHELLEY TO THOMAS LOVE PEACOCK

[1] This important letter describes Shelley's initial response to the landscape which later provided an important setting for *Mont Blanc* and *Frankenstein*. He had set off, with Mary Godwin and Claire Clairmont, on a tour of the vale of Chamounix, on 21 July; they would return to Maison Chappuis a week later.

[2] *aerial* lofty.

Mont Blanc. Lines written in the Vale of Chamouni (composed between 22 July and 29 August 1816)[1]

From HISTORY OF A SIX WEEKS' TOUR THROUGH A PART OF FRANCE, SWITZERLAND, GERMANY AND HOLLAND *by* Percy Bysshe AND Mary Shelley (1817)

I

The everlasting universe of things
Flows through the mind, and rolls its rapid waves,
Now dark, now glittering, now reflecting gloom,
Now lending splendour, where from secret springs
The source of human thought its tribute[2] brings   5
Of waters, with a sound but half its own,[3]
Such as a feeble brook will oft assume
In the wild woods, among the mountains lone,
Where waterfalls around it leap forever,
Where woods and winds contend, and a vast river   10
Over its rocks ceaselessly bursts and raves.

II

Thus thou, ravine of Arve – dark, deep ravine –
Thou many-coloured, many-voicéd vale,
Over whose pines, and crags, and caverns sail
Fast cloud-shadows and sunbeams: awful[4] scene,   15
Where Power in likeness of the Arve comes down
From the ice gulfs that gird his secret throne,
Bursting through these dark mountains like the flame
Of lightning through the tempest; thou dost lie,
Thy giant brood of pines around thee clinging,   20
Children of elder time, in whose devotion
The chainless winds still come and ever came
To drink their odours, and their mighty swinging
To hear – an old and solemn harmony;
Thine earthly rainbows stretched across the sweep   25
Of the ethereal waterfall, whose veil
Robes some unsculptured image;[5] the strange sleep

MONT BLANC
[1] This is Shelley's exploration of the nature of imaginative thought, and its relation to the natural world; as such, it should be read in the light of Wordsworth's *Tintern Abbey*, to which it is a response (see pp. 265–9). It has been seen as a defiant reaction to the religious certainties of Coleridge's *Chamouny; the Hour Before Sunrise. A Hymn* (pp. 505–7), which Shelley may have read in *The Friend* (1809). Jonathan Wordsworth provides a useful commentary in 'The Secret Strength of Things', *TWC* 18 (1987) 99–107. Mary Shelley wrote that the poem 'was composed under the immediate impression of the deep and powerful feelings excited by the objects which it attempts to describe; and, as an undisciplined overflowing of the soul, rests its claim to approbation on an attempt to imitate the untamable wilderness and inaccessible solemnity from which those feelings sprang.'
[2] *tribute* tributary. In Shelley's metaphor the human mind is like a mountain spring feeding into a large river (the 'everlasting universe of things' – effectively, the perceived world).
[3] *with a sound but half its own* cf. *Tintern Abbey*, in which Wordsworth refers to 'what they [the senses] half-create / And what perceive' (ll. 107–8).
[4] *awful* awe-inspiring.
[5] *some unsculptured image* artistic potential.

Which, when the voices of the desert fail,
Wraps all in its own deep eternity;
Thy caverns echoing to the Arve's commotion –   30
A loud, lone sound no other sound can tame;
Thou art pervaded with that ceaseless motion,
Thou art the path of that unresting sound,
Dizzy ravine! – and when I gaze on thee
I seem as in a trance sublime and strange   35
To muse on my own separate fantasy,
My own, my human mind, which passively[6]
Now renders and receives fast influencings,
Holding an unremitting interchange[7]
With the clear universe of things around;   40
One legion of wild thoughts, whose wandering wings
Now float above thy darkness, and now rest
Where that[8] or thou[9] art no unbidden guest,
In the still cave of the witch Poesy,
Seeking among the shadows that pass by,   45
Ghosts of all things that are, some shade of thee,
Some phantom, some faint image;[10] till the breast
From which they[11] fled recalls them, thou art there![12]

III

Some say that gleams of a remoter world
Visit the soul in sleep, that death is slumber,   50
And that its shapes the busy thoughts outnumber
Of those who wake and live.[13] I look on high;
Has some unknown omnipotence unfurled[14]
The veil of life and death? Or do I lie
In dream, and does the mightier world of sleep   55
Spread far around and inaccessibly
Its circles?[15] For the very spirit fails,
Driven like a homeless cloud from steep to steep
That vanishes among the viewless gales!
Far, far above, piercing the infinite sky,   60
Mont Blanc appears, still, snowy, and serene.
Its subject mountains their unearthly forms
Pile around it, ice and rock; broad vales between
Of frozen floods, unfathomable deeps

---

[6] *passively* the mind is receptive to outside stimuli, not willing itself to do, or be, anything.

[7] *an unremitting interchange* the 'interchange' takes place because the mind does not merely perceive; it works on its perceptions, transforming them imaginatively.

[8] *that* the darkness of line 42.

[9] *thou* the ravine.

[10] Shelley claims that his art bears the same relation to truth as do the shadows, in Plato's allegory of the cave, to a metaphysical reality; see Plato, *Republic* vii, summarized by Rogers, *Shelley at Work* (Oxford, 1967), pp. 148–7.

[11] *they* the 'legion of wild thoughts' (l. 41).

[12] Until Shelley recalls the 'wild thoughts' (line 41) by coming out of his reverie, the ravine he has been addressing, and the mystery that surrounds it, are to be found within Poesy's cave (i.e. subject to the imagination, and perhaps half-created by it).

[13] *Some say . . . live* Some say (i) that the soul is visited in sleep by 'gleams' of otherworldly truth; (ii) that death is an extreme form of this visionary sleep, and (iii) that it is more active and imaginative than anything experienced by the living mind. Shelley has in mind Wordsworth's *Ode*: 'The winds come to me from the fields of sleep' (l. 28).

[14] *unfurled* drawn aside.

[15] *Or do I lie . . . circles* Shelley suggests that the ecstatic vision he enjoys is a kind of sleep.

Blue as the overhanging heaven, that spread 65
And wind among the accumulated steeps;
A desert peopled by the storms alone,
Save when the eagle brings some hunter's bone,
And the wolf tracks her there. How hideously
Its shapes are heaped around! – rude, bare, and high, 70
Ghastly, and scarred, and riven. Is this the scene
Where the old earthquake-demon[16] taught her young
Ruin? Were these their toys?[17] Or did a sea
Of fire envelop once this silent snow?
None can reply – all seems eternal now. 75
The wilderness has a mysterious tongue
Which teaches awful doubt,[18] or faith so mild,
So solemn, so serene, that man may be
But for such faith with nature reconciled.[19]
Thou hast a voice, great mountain, to repeal 80
Large codes[20] of fraud and woe – not understood
By all, but which the wise, and great, and good
Interpret, or make felt, or deeply feel.[21]

IV

The fields, the lakes, the forests, and the streams,
Ocean, and all the living things that dwell 85
Within the daedal[22] earth; lightning, and rain,
Earthquake, and fiery flood, and hurricane,
The torpor of the year[23] when feeble dreams
Visit the hidden buds, or dreamless sleep
Holds every future leaf and flower; the bound 90
With which from that detested trance they leap;
The works and ways of man, their death and birth,
And that of him and all that his may be;
All things that move and breathe[24] with toil and sound
Are born and die; revolve, subside and swell. 95
Power dwells apart in its tranquillity
Remote, serene, and inaccessible:[25]
And *this*, the naked countenance of earth

---

[16] *earthquake-demon* spirit of earthquake, which gives rise to destructive tremors (its 'young').

[17] Shelley replaces Christian theology with pagan caprice. With the children of the old earthquake-demon, compare Byron, *Childe Harold's Pilgrimage* iii 877.

[18] *awful doubt* awe-inspired scepticism – effectively Shelley's own position.

[19] *But for . . . reconciled* Only by ('But for') a Wordsworthian faith in nature can man be reconciled to the mysterious indifference and violence of nature; otherwise, one must adopt Shelley's respectful open-mindedness ('awful doubt').

[20] *codes* laws.

[21] *Thou hast a voice . . . feel* Enlightened witnesses to nature's Power will defy the codes of fraud and woe made by the church and the state. The imaginative perception of nature therefore has the ability to liberate the individual from politi-cal oppression. Shelley's argument that the voice of the mountain is deeply felt is highly Wordsworthian; cf. *Pedlar* 217–18 (which Shelley knew from *The Excursion*): 'in all things / He saw one life, and felt that it was joy'.

[22] *daedal* variously adorned.

[23] *The torpor of the year* i.e. winter.

[24] *All things that move and breathe* an echo of Wordsworth's pantheist statement of faith (much admired by Shelley) in *Tintern Abbey* 101–3:
   A motion and a spirit that impels
   All thinking things, all objects of all thought,
   And rolls through all things.

[25] *inaccessible* at 4810 metres, Mont Blanc is the highest mountain in Europe; it had been climbed only three times by 1816.

On which I gaze, even these primeval mountains
Teach the adverting[26] mind. The glaciers creep   100
Like snakes that watch their prey, from their far fountains
Slow rolling on; there, many a precipice,
Frost and the sun in scorn of mortal power
Have piled: dome, pyramid, and pinnacle,
A city of death, distinct[27] with many a tower   105
And wall impregnable of beaming ice.[28]
Yet not a city, but a flood of ruin
Is there, that from the boundaries of the sky
Rolls its perpetual stream; vast pines are strewing
Its destined path, or in the mangled soil   110
Branchless and shattered stand; the rocks, drawn down
From yon remotest waste, have overthrown
The limits of the dead and living world,
Never to be reclaimed. The dwelling-place
Of insects, beasts, and birds, becomes its spoil;   115
Their food and their retreat for ever gone,
So much of life and joy is lost. The race
Of man flies far in dread; his work and dwelling
Vanish like smoke before the tempest's stream,
And their place is not known. Below, vast caves   120
Shine in the rushing torrents' restless gleam,
Which from those secret chasms in tumult welling[29]
Meet in the vale; and one majestic river,
The breath and blood of distant lands, forever
Rolls its loud waters to the ocean waves,[30]   125
Breathes its swift vapours to the circling air.

V

Mont Blanc yet gleams on high: the Power is there,
The still and solemn Power of many sights
And many sounds, and much of life and death.
In the calm darkness of the moonless nights,   130
In the lone glare of day, the snows descend
Upon that mountain; none beholds them there,
Nor when the flakes burn in the sinking sun,
Or the starbeams dart through them; winds contend
Silently there, and heap the snow with breath   135
Rapid and strong, but silently! Its home
The voiceless lightning in these solitudes
Keeps innocently, and like vapour broods
Over the snow. The secret strength of things
Which governs thought, and to the infinite dome   140

---

[26] *adverting* heedful, observant, thoughtful.
[27] *distinct* adorned.
[28] *A city of death . . . ice* probably a recollection of the 'Cloudscape New Jerusalem' passage from Wordsworth's *Excursion* (pp. 410–11).
[29] *Which from those secret chasms in tumult welling* an echo of

Coleridge's recently-published *Kubla Khan* 17: 'And from this chasm, with ceaseless turmoil seething'. Shelley had seen Byron's copy of the printed text, brought from England in April 1816.
[30] *Rolls . . . ocean waves* the Arve flows into Lake Geneva, which in turn flows through France into the Mediterranean.

Of heaven is as a law, inhabits thee!
And what were thou, and earth, and stars, and sea,
If to the human mind's imaginings
Silence and solitude were vacancy?[31]

Ozymandias (composed *c*. December 1817)[1]

From The Examiner No. 524 (11 January 1818, p. 24)

I met a traveller from an antique land
Who said, 'Two vast and trunkless legs of stone
Stand in the desert. Near them, on the sand
Half-sunk, a shattered visage lies, whose frown
And wrinkled lip, and sneer of cold command,   5
Tell that its sculptor well those passions read
Which yet survive, stamped on these lifeless things,
The hand that mocked them, and the heart that fed;
And on the pedestal these words appear:
"My name is Ozymandias, King of Kings,   10
Look on my works, ye mighty, and despair!"
Nothing beside remains. Round the decay
Of that colossal wreck, boundless and bare,
The lone and level sands stretch far away.'

[handwritten annotation: The hand = the artist / them = the passions]

On Love (composed probably 20–5 July 1818; edited from MS)[1]

What is love? Ask him who lives, what is life; ask him who adores, what is God.

I know not the internal constitution of other men, or even of thine whom I now address. I see that in some external attributes they resemble me, but, when misled by that appearance I have thought to appeal to something in common and unburden my inmost soul to them, I have found my language misunderstood like one in a distant and savage land. The more opportunities they have afforded me for experience, the wider has appeared the interval between us, and to a greater distance have the points of sympathy been withdrawn. With a spirit ill-fitted to sustain such proof, trembling and feeble through its tenderness, I have everywhere sought, and have found only repulse and disappointment.

---

[31]   Shelley's concluding expression of doubt stands in stark contrast to the certainty of Coleridge's *Chamouny; the Hour Before Sunrise. A Hymn* (see pp. 505–7).

Ozymandias
[1]   Horace Smith (1779–1849), a banker and writer of light verse, met Shelley in London in December 1816. Shelley and Smith often visited the British Museum together, and their admiration of the newly-acquired statue of Rameses II (thirteenth century BC, also known as Ozymandias) in 1817 prompted Smith to propose a sonnet competition on the subject. Smith's sonnet was published on 1 February 1818 in *The Examiner*, and reads as follows:

  In Egypt's sandy silence, all alone,
    Stands a gigantic leg, which far off throws
      The only shadow that the desert knows.
  'I am great Ozymandias', saith the stone,

  'The King of Kings; this mighty city shows
  The wonders of my hand.' The city's gone;
    Nought but the leg remaining to disclose
  The site of this forgotten Babylon.
  We wonder, and some hunter may express
  Wonder like ours, when through the wilderness
    Where London stood, holding the wolf in chase,
  He meets some fragment huge, and stops to guess
    What powerful but unrecorded race
    Once dwelt in that annihilated place.

On Love
[1]   This essay, Reiman suggests, is 'Shelley's response to Plato's *Symposium* and may possibly be the false start of an essay introductory to his translation' (*SC* vi 639). Shelley translated the *Symposium* 7–20 July 1818.

Thou demandest what is love. It is that powerful attraction towards all that we conceive, or fear, or hope beyond ourselves, when we find within our own thoughts the chasm of an insufficient void, and seek to awaken in all things that are, a community with what we experience within ourselves. If we reason, we would be understood; if we imagine, we would that the airy children of our brain were born anew within another's; if we feel, we would that another's nerves should vibrate to our own, that the beams of their eyes should kindle at once and mix and melt into our own, that lips of motionless ice should not reply to lips quivering and burning with the heart's best blood. This is love. This is the bond and the sanction which connects not only man with man, but with everything which exists. We are born into the world and there is something within us which, from the instant that we live and move, thirsts after its likeness; it is probably in correspondence with this law that the infant drains milk from the bosom of its mother. This propensity develops itself with the development of our nature.

We see dimly[2] within our intellectual nature a miniature, as it were, of our entire self, yet deprived of all that we condemn or despise: the ideal prototype of everything excellent or lovely that we are capable of conceiving as belonging to the nature of man – not only the portrait of our external being, but an assemblage of the minutest particulars of which our nature is composed; a mirror whose surface reflects only the forms of purity and brightness; a soul within our soul that describes a circle around its proper paradise which pain and sorrow and evil dare not overleap. To this we eagerly refer all sensations, thirsting that they should resemble or correspond with it.

The discovery of its antitype – the meeting with an understanding capable of clearly estimating the deductions of our own, an imagination which should enter into and seize upon the subtle and delicate peculiarities which we have delighted to cherish and unfold in secret, with a frame whose nerves, like the chords of two exquisite lyres strung to the accompaniment of one delightful voice, vibrate with the vibrations of our own, and of a combination of all these in such proportion as the type within demands: this is the invisible and unattainable point to which love tends, and to attain which it urges forth the powers of man to arrest the faintest shadow of that without the possession of which there is no rest or respite to the heart over which it rules.

Hence in solitude, or in that deserted state when we are surrounded by human beings and yet they sympathize not with us, we love the flowers, the grass, and the waters and the sky. In the motion of the very leaves of spring in the blue air there is then found a secret correspondence with our heart. There is eloquence in the tongueless wind and a melody in the flowing of brooks and the rustling of the reeds beside them, which by their inconceivable relation to something within the soul, awaken the spirits to a dance of breathless rapture, and bring tears of mysterious tenderness to the eyes like the enthusiasm of patriotic success or the voice of one beloved singing to you alone. Sterne says that if he were in a desert he would love some cypress[3] . . . So soon as this want or power is dead, man becomes the living sepulchre of himself, and what yet survives is the mere husk of what once he was.

Lines Written among the Euganean Hills, October 1818[1]

From ROSALIND AND HELEN (1819)

Many a green isle needs must be
In the deep wide sea of misery,
Or the mariner, worn and wan,

---

[2] 'These words inefficient and metaphorical. Most words so. No help' (Shelley's note).

[3] 'I declare, said I, clapping my hands cheerily together, that was I in a desert, I would find out wherewith in it to call forth my affections. If I could not do better, I would fasten them upon some sweet myrtle, or seek some melancholy cypress to connect myself to' (Sterne, *A Sentimental Journey*, ed. Gardner D. Stout, Jr, Berkeley CA, 1967, pp. 115–16).

LINES WRITTEN AMONG THE EUGANEAN HILLS
[1] This meditative poem was written at a difficult moment in Shelley's life. His baby daughter Clara had died at Venice in late September (barely a year old), and on their return to Byron's villa at Este, I Capuccini, a deep gloom had pervaded the household. Clara's death depressed Mary, and Percy found himself in bad health.

Never thus could voyage on
Day and night, and night and day,   5
Drifting on his dreary way,
With the solid darkness black
Closing round his vessel's track;
Whilst above, the sunless sky,
Big with clouds, hangs heavily,   10
And behind the tempest fleet
Hurries on with lightning feet,
Riving[2] sail and cord and plank
Till the ship has almost drank
Death from the o'er-brimming deep,   15
And sinks down, down, like that sleep
When the dreamer seems to be
Weltering[3] through eternity;
And the dim low line before
Of a dark and distant shore   20
Still recedes, as ever still
Longing with divided will,
But no power to seek or shun,
He is ever drifted on
O'er the unreposing wave   25
To the haven of the grave.
What if there no friends will greet?[4]
What if there no heart will meet
His with love's impatient beat?
Wander wheresoe'er he may,   30
Can he dream before that day
To find refuge from distress
In friendship's smile, in love's caress?
Then 'twill wreak[5] him little woe
Whether such there be or no: 35
Senseless[6] is the breast, and cold,
Which relenting love would fold;
Bloodless are the veins and chill
Which the pulse of pain did fill;
Every little living nerve   40
That from bitter words did swerve
Round the tortured lips and brow,
Are like sapless leaflets now
Frozen upon December's bough.
On the beach of a northern sea[7]   45
Which tempests shake eternally,
As once the wretch there lay to sleep,
Lies a solitary heap:
One white skull and seven dry bones,
On the margin of the stones   50

---

2   *Riving* tearing.
3   *Weltering* tumbling.
4   *What if there no friends will greet?* In Greek myth, friends were supposed to be reunited after death in the Elysian fields, where they would revel for eternity.
5   *wreak* give.
6   *Senseless* i.e. unperceiving (because dead).
7   Shelley's daughter Clara was buried on the Lido, by the northern Adriatic.

Where a few grey rushes stand,
Boundaries of the sea and land.
Nor is heard one voice of wail
But the sea-mews, as they sail
O'er the billows of the gale;   55
Or the whirlwind up and down
Howling like a slaughtered town,
When a king in glory rides
Through the pomp of fratricides.[8]
Those unburied bones around   60
There is many a mournful sound;
There is no lament for him
Like a sunless vapour, dim,
Who once clothed with life and thought
What now moves nor murmurs not.   65

Aye, many flowering islands lie
In the waters of wide agony;
To such a one this morn was led
My bark, by soft winds piloted.
Mid the mountains Euganean[9]   70
I stood listening to the paean
With which the legioned rooks[10] did hail
The sun's uprise majestical;
Gathering round with wings all hoar,
Through the dewy mist they soar   75
Like grey shades, till th' eastern heaven
Bursts,[11] and then, as clouds of even[12]
Flecked with fire and azure lie
In the unfathomable sky,
So their plumes of purple grain,[13]   80
Starred with drops of golden rain,
Gleam above the sunlight woods,
As in silent multitudes
On the morning's fitful gale
Through the broken mist they sail,   85
And the vapours cloven and gleaming
Follow down the dark steep streaming,
Till all is bright and clear and still
Round the solitary hill.

Beneath is spread like a green sea   90
The waveless plain of Lombardy,[14]
Bounded by the vaporous air,

---

[8] *fratricides* the king is responsible for the death of his
brother man (in the 'slaughtered town').
[9] Shelley began this poem while resident at Este, in the
Euganean Hills near Padua, October 1818.
[10] *rooks* no doubt Shelley presents these none too attractive
birds in such a favourable light because Coleridge had done so
in *This Lime-Tree Bower My Prison* (pp. 551–3).
[11] *Bursts* i.e. into light – the sun rises in the east.
[12] *even* i.e. night.

[13] *their plumes of purple grain* their feathers were dyed purple
by the light of the rising sun.
[14] *Beneath . . . Lombardy* in a letter to Peacock of 8 October
1818 Shelley described the view from his villa in the
Euganean Hills: 'We see before us the wide flat plains of Lom-
bardy, in which we see the sun and moon rise and set, and the
evening star, and all the golden magnificence of autumnal
clouds' (Jones ii 43).

Islanded by cities fair;
Underneath day's azure eyes
Ocean's nursling, Venice,[15] lies,   95
A peopled labyrinth of walls,
Amphitrite's[16] destined halls
Which her hoary sire now paves
With his blue and beaming waves.
Lo! the sun upsprings behind,   100
Broad, red, radiant, half-reclined
On the level quivering line
Of the waters crystalline;
And before that chasm of light,
As within a furnace bright,   105
Column, tower, and dome, and spire,
Shine like obelisks of fire,
Pointing with inconstant motion
From the altar of dark ocean
To the sapphire-tinted skies;   110
As the flames of sacrifice
From the marble shrines did rise,
As to pierce the dome of gold[17]
Where Apollo spoke of old.

Sun-girt city, thou hast been   115
Ocean's child, and then his queen;
Now is come a darker day,[18]
And thou soon must be his prey,
If the power that raised thee here
Hallow so thy watery bier.   120
A less drear ruin then than now,
With thy conquest-branded brow
Stooping to the slave of slaves
From thy throne, among the waves
Wilt thou be, when the sea-mew   125
Flies, as once before it flew,
O'er thine isles depopulate,[19]
And all is in its ancient state,
Save where many a palace gate
With green sea-flowers overgrown   130
Like a rock of ocean's own,
Topples o'er the abandoned sea
As the tides change sullenly.
The fisher on his watery way,
Wandering at the close of day,   135
Will spread his sail and seize his oar
Till he pass the gloomy shore,

[15]   Shelley was at Venice for a few days at the end of September 1818.
[16]   Amphitrite was the daughter of Oceanus, god of the sea (her 'sire', line 98), and the wife of Poseidon.
[17]   *dome of gold* the Delphic oracle, through which Apollo (god of youth, poetry, and music) was believed to speak.

[18]   *Now is come a darker day* Shelley's sorrow for Venice was due partly to the fact that, by the terms of the Congress of Vienna, 1815, it had been handed over to Austria; as he told Peacock on 8 October 1818: 'Venice, which was once a tyrant, is now the next worse thing – a slave' (Jones ii 43).
[19]   *depopulate* laid waste.

Lest thy dead should, from their sleep
Bursting o'er the starlight deep,
Lead a rapid masque[20] of death   140
O'er the waters of his path.

Those who alone thy towers behold
Quivering through aerial gold,
As I now behold them here,
Would imagine not they were   145
Sepulchres where human forms,
Like pollution-nourished worms,
To the corpse of greatness cling,
Murdered and now mouldering;[21]
But if Freedom should awake   150
In her omnipotence, and shake
From the Celtic Anarch's[22] hold
All the keys of dungeons[23] cold,
Where a hundred cities lie
Chained like thee, ingloriously,   155
Thou and all thy sister band
Might adorn this sunny land,
Twining memories of old time
With new virtues more sublime:
If not, perish thou and they! –   160
Clouds which stain truth's rising day
By her sun consumed away,
Earth can spare ye, while like flowers
In the waste of years and hours,
From your dust new nations spring   165
With more kindly blossoming.

Perish! let there only be
Floating o'er thy hearthless sea,
As the garment of thy sky
Clothes the world immortally,   170
One remembrance more sublime
Than the tattered pall of time,
Which scarce hides thy visage wan –
That a tempest-cleaving swan[24]
Of the songs of Albion,[25]   175
Driven from his ancestral streams
By the might of evil dreams,[26]
Found a nest in thee; and Ocean

---

[20] *masque* procession.
[21] Shelley was shocked by the degraded state of Venice
under Austrian occupation: 'I had no conception of the excess
to which avarice, cowardice, superstition, ignorance, passion-
less lust, and all the inexpressible brutalities which degrade
human nature could be carried, until I had lived a few days
among the Venetians' (Jones ii 43).
[22] *Celtic Anarch* Austrian tyrant, as at line 223.
[23] *dungeons* on his visit to Venice in September 1818 Shelley
visited the dungeons in the Doges' palace 'where the prisoners

were confined sometimes half up to their middles in stinking
water' (Jones ii 43).
[24] *a tempest-cleaving swan* Byron, then living at the Palazzo
Mocenigo, Venice, where Shelley had met him the previous
month.
[25] *Albion* England.
[26] *Driven . . . dreams* Byron was in self-exile, regarding him-
self as driven out of England by his wife's campaign against
him after their separation (see p. 663).

Welcomed him with such emotion
That its joy grew his,[27] and sprung   180
From his lips[28] like music flung
O'er a mighty thunder-fit,
Chastening terror. What though yet
Poesy's unfailing river,
Which through Albion winds forever,   185
Lashing with melodious wave
Many a sacred poet's grave,
Mourn its latest nursling fled?
What though thou with all thy dead
Scarce can for this fame repay   190
Aught thine own?[29] Oh rather say,
Though[30] thy sins and slaveries foul
Overcloud a sunlike soul?
As the ghost of Homer clings
Round Scamander's[31] wasting springs;   195
As divinest Shakespeare's might
Fills Avon and the world with light,
Like omniscient power which he
Imaged mid mortality;
As the love from Petrarch's urn   200
Yet amid yon hills doth burn,[32]
A quenchless lamp by which the heart
Sees things unearthly – so thou art,
Mighty spirit;[33] so shall be
The city that did refuge thee.   205

Lo, the sun floats up the sky
Like thought-winged liberty,
Till the universal light
Seems to level plain and height;
From the sea a mist has spread,   210
And the beams of morn lie dead
On the towers of Venice now,
Like its glory long ago.
By the skirts of that grey cloud
Many-domed Padua[34] proud   215
Stands, a peopled solitude
Mid the harvest-shining plain,
Where the peasant heaps his grain
In the garner of his foe,[35]
And the milk-white oxen slow   220
With the purple vintage strain,

---

27 *its joy grew his* as Shelley reported to Peacock on 8 October 1818: '[Byron] is changed into the liveliest, and happiest looking man I ever met' (Jones ii 42).
28 *sprung / From his lips* a reference to *Don Juan* Canto I, which Byron had read to Shelley in late September 1818.
29 *What though . . . own* Venice lacks a poet of its own as famous as Byron.
30 *Though* i.e. '[What] Though thy sins . . . ?'
31 Scamander, river near Troy, the site of the wars described by Homer in *The Iliad*.

32 *As the love . . . burn* the house and grave of the great Italian poet Petrarch (1304–74) are at Arqua in the Euganean Hills.
33 *Mighty spirit* Byron.
34 Shelley was in Padua August 1818.
35 *his foe* i.e. the Austrians. As Shelley told Peacock, 'The Austrians take sixty percent in taxes' (Jones ii 43).

Heaped upon the creaking wain,
That the brutal Celt[36] may swill
Drunken sleep with savage will;
And the sickle to the sword   225
Lies unchanged, though many a lord,
Like a weed whose shade is poison,
Overgrows this region's foison,[37]
Sheaves of whom are ripe to come
To destruction's harvest home: 230
Men must reap the things they sow,
Force from force must ever flow
Or worse – but 'tis a bitter woe
That love or reason cannot change
The despot's rage, the slave's revenge.   235

Padua, thou within whose walls
Those mute guests at festivals,
Son and mother, Death and Sin,
Played at dice for Ezzelin,[38]
Till Death cried, 'I win, I win!'   240
And Sin cursed to lose the wager,
But Death promised, to assuage her,
That he would petition for
Her to be made Vice-Emperor,
When the destined years were o'er,   245
Over all between the Po
And the eastern Alpine snow,
Under the mighty Austrian.
Sin smiled so as Sin only can,
And since that time, aye, long before,   250
Both have ruled from shore to shore –
That incestuous pair who follow
Tyrants as the sun the swallow,
As repentance follows crime,
And as changes follow time.   255

In thine halls the lamp of learning,
Padua, now no more is burning;[39]
Like a meteor, whose wild way
Is lost over the grave of day,
It gleams betrayed and to betray.   260
Once remotest nations came
To adore that sacred flame,
When it lit not many a hearth
On this cold and gloomy earth;
Now new fires from antique light   265
Spring beneath the wide world's might,
But their spark lies dead in thee,

---

[36]   *Celt* Austrian.
[37]   *foison* plenty.
[38]   Ezzelino da Romano, thirteenth-century despot of Padua.
Shelley is probably recalling Coleridge's *Ancient Mariner*, where Death and Life-in-Death cast dice for the mariner's soul.
[39]   *In thine halls . . . burning* Padua University is one of the oldest in Europe.

Trampled out by tyranny.
As the Norway woodman quells,
In the depth of piny dells,[40]   270
One light flame among the brakes,[41]
While the boundless forest shakes,
And its mighty trunks are torn
By the fire thus lowly born;
The spark beneath his feet is dead,   275
He starts to see the flames it fed
Howling through the darkened sky
With a myriad tongues victoriously,
And sinks down in fear: so thou,
Oh tyranny, beholdest now   280
Light around thee, and thou hearest
The loud flames ascend, and fearest –
Grovel on the earth! Aye, hide
In the dust thy purple[42] pride!

Noon descends around me now;   285
'Tis the noon of autumn's glow
When a soft and purple mist,
Like a vaporous amethyst,
Or an air-dissolved star
Mingling light and fragrance, far   290
From the curved horizon's bound
To the point of heaven's profound,
Fills the overflowing sky;
And the plains that silent lie
Underneath, the leaves unsodden   295
Where the infant frost has trodden
With his morning-winged feet,
Whose bright print is gleaming yet;
And the red and golden vines,
Piercing with their trellised lines   300
The rough, dark-skirted wilderness;
The dun and bladed grass no less,
Pointing from this hoary tower
In the windless air; the flower
Glimmering at my feet; the line   305
Of the olive-sandalled Apennine
In the south dimly islanded;
And the Alps, whose snows are spread
High between the clouds and sun;
And of living things each one;   310
And my spirit which so long
Darkened this swift stream of song –
Interpenetrated lie
By the glory of the sky:
Be it love, light, harmony,   315
Odour, or the soul of all

---

[40] *piny dells* dells of pine-trees.
[41] *brakes* thick branches.

[42] *purple* colour of imperial triumph.

Which from heaven like dew doth fall,
Or the mind which feeds this verse
Peopling the lone universe.

Noon descends, and after noon   320
Autumn's evening meets me soon,
Leading the infantine moon
And that one star,[43] which to her
Almost seems to minister
Half the crimson light she brings   325
From the sunset's radiant springs;
And the soft dreams of the morn
(Which like winged winds had borne
To that silent isle, which lies
Mid remembered agonies,   330
The frail bark of this lone being)
Pass, to other sufferers fleeing,
And its ancient pilot, Pain,
Sits beside the helm again.

Other flowering isles must be   335
In the sea of life and agony;
Other spirits float and flee
O'er that gulf – even now, perhaps,
On some rock the wild wave wraps,
With folding wings they waiting sit   340
For my bark, to pilot it
To some calm and blooming cove,
Where for me and those I love,
May a windless bower be built
Far from passion, pain, and guilt,[44]   345
In a dell mid lawny hills
Which the wild sea-murmur fills,
And soft sunshine, and the sound
Of old forests echoing round,
And the light and smell divine   350
Of all flowers that breathe and shine.
We may live so happy there
That the spirits of the air,
Envying us, may even entice
To our healing paradise   355
The polluting multitude;
But their rage would be subdued
By that clime divine and calm,
And the winds whose wings rain balm
On the uplifted soul, and leaves   360
Under which the bright sea heaves;
While each breathless interval
In their whisperings musical
The inspired soul supplies

---

43   *that one star* Hesperus, the evening star.
44   *guilt* this poem is inspired partly by guilt. His daughter,
Clara's death was due in part to his own negligence.

With its own deep melodies, 365
And the love which heals all strife
Circling like the breath of life,
All things in that sweet abode
With its own mild brotherhood:
They, not it, would change, and soon 370
Every sprite beneath the moon
Would repent its envy vain,
And the earth grow young again.

Ode to the West Wind (composed *c.* 25 October 1819)[1]

From PROMETHEUS UNBOUND[2] (1820)

I

Oh wild west wind, thou breath of autumn's being;
Thou from whose unseen presence the leaves dead
Are driven, like ghosts from an enchanter fleeing,

Yellow, and black, and pale, and hectic red,
Pestilence-stricken multitudes; oh thou 5
Who chariotest to their dark wintry bed

The winged seeds, where they lie cold and low,
Each like a corpse within its grave, until
Thine azure sister of the spring shall blow

Her clarion[3] o'er the dreaming earth, and fill 10
(Driving sweet buds like flocks to feed in air)
With living hues and odours plain and hill –

Wild spirit, which art moving everywhere,
Destroyer and preserver, hear, oh hear!

II

Thou on whose stream, mid the steep sky's commotion, 15
Loose clouds like earth's decaying leaves are shed,
Shook from the tangled boughs of heaven and ocean,

ODE TO THE WEST WIND

[1] 'This poem was conceived and chiefly written in a wood that skirts the Arno, near Florence, and on a day when that tempestuous wind, whose temperature is at once mild and animating, was collecting the vapours which pour down the autumnal rains. They began, as I foresaw, at sunset, with a violent tempest of hail and rain, attended by that magnificent thunder and lightning peculiar to the Cisalpine regions' (Shel-

ley's note). This important poem contains Shelley's clearest and most powerful statement of faith in the millennial future to come, and in the role of the poet as prophet (see headnote, pp. 821–2).
[2] In addition to *Prometheus Unbound*, Shelley's 1820 volume contained a number of shorter works composed in Italy.
[3] *clarion* trumpet.

Angels[4] of rain and lightning; there are spread
On the blue surface of thine airy surge,
Like the bright hair uplifted from the head   20

Of some fierce maenad,[5] even from the dim verge
Of the horizon to the zenith's height,
The locks of the approaching storm. Thou dirge[6]

Of the dying year, to which this closing night
Will be the dome of a vast sepulchre,   25
Vaulted with all thy congregated might

Of vapours, from whose solid atmosphere
Black rain, and fire, and hail will burst – oh hear!

III

Thou who didst waken from his summer dreams
The blue Mediterranean, where he lay,   30
Lulled by the coil of his crystalline streams,

Beside a pumice isle in Baiae's bay,
And saw in sleep old palaces and towers
Quivering within the wave's intenser day,[7]

All overgrown with azure moss and flowers   35
So sweet, the sense faints picturing them! Thou
For whose path the Atlantic's level powers

Cleave themselves into chasms, while far below
The sea-blooms and the oozy woods which wear
The sapless foliage of the ocean, know   40

Thy voice, and suddenly grow grey with fear,
And tremble and despoil themselves[8] – oh hear!

IV

If I were a dead leaf thou mightest bear; ⟨¹|
If I were a swift cloud to fly with thee; (²|
A wave to pant beneath thy power, and share (³)   45

---

4   *Angels* messengers.
5   *maenad* Bacchante, inspired votary of Bacchus, god of wine.
6   *dirge* lament for the dead.
7   *Beside a pumice isle . . . day* In a letter to Peacock of 17 or 18 December 1818, Shelley described 'passing the Bay of Baiae and observing the ruins of its antique grandeur standing like rocks in the transparent sea under our boat' (Jones ii 61). In Roman times Baiae was the resort of Emperors.
8   'The phenomenon alluded to at the conclusion of the third stanza is well known to naturalists. The vegetation at the bottom of the sea, of rivers, and of lakes, sympathizes with that of the land in the change of seasons, and is consequently influenced by the winds which announce it' (Shelley's note).

The impulse of thy strength, only less free
Than thou, oh uncontrollable! If even
I were as in my boyhood, and could be

The comrade of thy wanderings over heaven,
As then, when to outstrip thy skyey speed
Scarce seemed a vision; I would ne'er have striven   50

As thus with thee in prayer in my sore need.
Oh lift me as a wave, a leaf, a cloud!
I fall upon the thorns of life! I bleed!

A heavy weight of hours has chained and bowed   55
One too like thee[9] – tameless, and swift, and proud.

V

Make me thy lyre, even as the forest is:
What if my leaves are falling like its own?
The tumult of thy mighty harmonies

Will take from both a deep autumnal tone,   60
Sweet though in sadness. Be thou, spirit fierce,
My spirit! Be thou me, impetuous one!

Drive my dead thoughts over the universe
Like withered leaves to quicken a new birth!
And, by the incantation of this verse,   65

Scatter, as from an unextinguished hearth
Ashes and sparks, my words among mankind!
Be through my lips to unawakened earth

The trumpet of a prophecy! Oh wind,
If winter comes, can spring be far behind?   70

On Life (composed late 1819) (vol. i pp. 176–81)

From Essays, Letters from Abroad, Translations and Fragments (2 vols, Philadelphia, 1840)

Life and the world, or whatever we call that which we are and feel, is an astonishing thing. The mist of familiarity[1] obscures from us the wonder of our being. We are struck with admiration at some of its transient modifications, but it is itself the great miracle. What are changes of empires, the wreck of dynasties, with the opinions which supported them; what is the birth and the extinction of religious and of political systems, to life? What are the revolutions of the globe which we inhabit, and the operations of the elements of which it is composed, compared with life? What is the universe of

---

9   *One too like thee* i.e. the poet.

On Life
1   *mist of familiarity* compare Coleridge's 'film of familiarity', *Biographia Literaria*, p. 526, above.

stars and suns (of which this inhabited earth is one), and their motions and their destiny, compared with life? Life, the great miracle, we admire not because it is so miraculous. It is well that we are so shielded by the familiarity of what is at once so certain and so unfathomable, from an astonishment which would otherwise absorb and overawe the functions of that which is its object.

If any artist, I do not say had executed, but had merely conceived in his mind the system of the sun, and the stars and planets, they not existing, and had painted to us in words or upon canvas the spectacle now afforded by the nightly cope of heaven, and illustrated it by the wisdom of astronomy, great would be our admiration. Or had he imagined the scenery of this earth, the mountains, the seas and the rivers, the grass and the flowers, and the variety of the forms and masses of the leaves of the woods, and the colours which attend the setting and the rising sun, and the hues of the atmosphere, turbid or serene, these things not before existing, truly we should have been astonished – and it would not have been a vain boast to have said of such a man, 'Non merita nome di creatore, sennon Iddio ed il Poeta'.[2] But now these things are looked on with little wonder, and to be conscious of them with intense delight is esteemed to be the distinguishing mark of a refined and extraordinary person. The multitude of men care not for them; it is thus with life – that which includes all.

What is life? Thoughts and feelings arise, with or without our will, and we employ words to express them. We are born, and our birth is unremembered, and our infancy remembered but in fragments. We live on, and in living we lose the apprehension of life. How vain is it to think that words can penetrate the mystery of our being! Rightly used they may make evident our ignorance to ourselves, and this is much. For what are we? Whence do we come, and whither do we go? Is birth the commencement, is death the conclusion of our being? What is birth and death?

The most refined abstractions of logic conduct to a view of life which, though startling to the apprehension, is in fact that which the habitual sense of its repeated combinations has extinguished in us. It strips, as it were, the painted curtain from this scene of things. I confess that I am one of those who am unable to refuse my assent to the conclusions of those philosophers who assert that nothing exists but as it is perceived.

It is a decision against which all our persuasions struggle, and we must be long convicted before we can be convinced that the solid universe of external things is 'such stuff as dreams are made of'.[3] The shocking absurdities of the popular philosophy of mind and matter, and its fatal consequences in morals, their violent dogmatism concerning the source of all things, had early conducted me to materialism.[4] This materialism is a seducing system to young and superficial minds; it allows its disciples to talk, and dispenses them from thinking. But I was discontented with such a view of things as it afforded; man is a being of high aspirations 'looking both before and after',[5] whose 'thoughts wander through eternity',[6] disclaiming alliance with transience and decay, incapable of imagining to himself annihilation, existing but in the future and the past, being not what he is, but what he has been and shall be. Whatever may be his true and final destination, there is a spirit within him at enmity with nothingness and dissolution. This is the character of all life and being. Each is at once the centre and the circumference, the point to which all things are referred, and the line in which all things are contained. Such contemplations as these, materialism and the popular philosophy of mind and matter alike forbid; they are only consistent with the intellectual system.

It is absurd to enter into a long recapitulation of arguments sufficiently familiar to those enquiring minds whom alone a writer on abstruse subjects can be conceived to address. Perhaps the most clear and vigorous statement of the intellectual system is to be found in Sir William Drummond's *Academical Questions*; after such an exposition it would be idle to translate into other words what could only lose its energy and fitness by the change. Examined point by point and word by word, the most discriminating intellects have been able to discern no train of thoughts in the process of reasoning, which does not conduct inevitably to the conclusion which has been stated.

What follows from the admission? It establishes no new truth, it gives us no additional insight

---

[2] 'None deserves the name of creator except God and the poet'; from Pierantonio Serassi's *Life of Torquato Tasso* (1785).
[3] *The Tempest* IV i 156–7.
[4] *materialism* i.e. the philosophy of Locke, Hartley, Priestley, and of the French Enlightenment, particularly Holbach.
[5] *Hamlet* IV iv 37.
[6] *Paradise Lost* ii 148: 'Those thoughts that wander through eternity'.

into our hidden nature, neither its action, nor itself. Philosophy, impatient as it may be to build, has much work yet remaining as pioneer for the overgrowth of ages. It makes one step towards this object; it destroys error and the roots of error. It leaves what is too often the duty of the reformer in political and ethical questions to leave – a vacancy. It reduces the mind to that freedom in which it would have acted, but for the misuse of words and signs, the instruments of its own creation. By signs, I would be understood in a wide sense, including what is properly meant by that term, and what I peculiarly mean. In this latter sense, almost all familiar objects are signs, standing not for themselves but for others, in their capacity of suggesting one thought which shall lead to a train of thoughts. Our whole life is thus an education of error.

Let us recollect our sensations as children. What a distinct and intense apprehension had we of the world and of ourselves. Many of the circumstances of social life were then important to us, which are now no longer so. But that is not the point of comparison on which I mean to insist. We less habitually distinguished all that we saw and felt from ourselves. They seemed as it were to constitute one mass. There are some persons who in this respect are always children. Those who are subject to the state called reverie feel as if their nature were dissolved into the surrounding universe, or as if the surrounding universe were absorbed into their being.[7] They are conscious of no distinction. And these are states which precede or accompany or follow an unusually intense and vivid apprehension of life. As men grow up, this power commonly decays, and they become mechanical and habitual agents. Thus feelings and then reasonings are the combined result of a multitude of entangled thoughts, and of a series of what are called impressions, planted by reiteration.

The view of life presented by the most refined deductions of the intellectual philosophy, is that of unity. Nothing exists but as it is perceived. The difference is merely nominal between those two classes of thought which are vulgarly distinguished by the names of ideas and of external objects.[8] Pursuing the same thread of reasoning, the existence of distinct individual minds, similar to that which is employed in now questioning its own nature, is likewise found to be a delusion. The words, *I, you, they* are not signs of any actual difference subsisting between the assemblage of thoughts thus indicated, but are merely marks employed to denote the different modifications of the one mind.

Let it not be supposed that this doctrine conducts to the monstrous presumption that I, the person who now write and think, am that one mind. I am but a portion of it. The words *I*, and *you* and *they* are grammatical devices invented simply for arrangement and totally devoid of the intense and exclusive sense usually attached to them. It is difficult to find terms adequate to express so subtle a conception as that to which the intellectual philosophy has conducted us. We are on that verge where words abandon us, and what wonder if we grow dizzy to look down the dark abyss of how little we know!

The relations of *things* remain unchanged by whatever system. By the word *things* is to be understood any object of thought; that is, any thought upon which any other thought is employed, with an apprehension of distinction. The relations of these remain unchanged – and such is the material of our knowledge.

What is the cause of life? That is, how was it produced, or what agencies distinct from life, have acted or act upon life? All recorded generations of mankind have wearily busied themselves in inventing answers to this question. And the result has been religion. Yet that the basis of all things cannot be (as the popular philosophy alleges) mind, is sufficiently evident. Mind (as far as we have any experience of its properties, and, beyond that experience how vain is argument) cannot create, it can only perceive. It is said also to be the cause; but cause is only a word expressing a certain state of the human mind with regard to the manner in which two thoughts are apprehended to be related to each other. If anyone desires to know how unsatisfactorily the popular philosophy employs itself upon this great question, they need only impartially reflect upon the manner in which thoughts develop themselves in their minds. It is infinitely improbable that the cause of mind – that is, of existence – is similar to mind.

7 *as if . . . being* Compare Wordsworth's 'abyss of idealism', p. 418, above. This paragraph is reminiscent of the *Ode*.
8 This is essentially the argument put forward by George Berkeley, to whose ideas the young Coleridge subscribed (see p. 459 n. 17); it was a means of justifying Coleridge's hope that thoughts and things were essentially the same – that they were 'Parts and proportions of one wondrous whole' (*Religious Musings* 142).

Prometheus Unbound; A Lyrical Drama in Four Acts (composed between September 1818 and December 1819; edited from printed and MS sources)[1]

From PROMETHEUS UNBOUND (1820)

Audisne haec Amphiarae, sub terram abdite?[2]

Preface

The Greek tragic writers, in selecting as their subject any portion of their national history or mythology, employed in their treatment of it a certain arbitrary discretion. They by no means conceived themselves bound to adhere to the common interpretation, or to imitate in story (as in title) their rivals and predecessors. Such a system would have amounted to a resignation of those claims to preference over their competitors which incited the composition: the Agamemnonian story[3] was exhibited on the Athenian theatre with as many variations as dramas.

I have presumed to employ a similar licence. The *Prometheus Unbound* of Aeschylus supposed the reconciliation of Jupiter with his victim[4] as the price of the disclosure of the danger threatened to his empire by the consummation of his marriage with Thetis. Thetis, according to this view of the subject, was given in marriage to Peleus;[5] and Prometheus, by the permission of Jupiter, delivered from his captivity by Hercules. Had I framed my story on this model, I should have done no more than have attempted to restore the lost drama of Aeschylus[6] – an ambition which, if my preference to this mode of treating the subject had incited me to cherish, the recollection of the high comparison such an attempt would challenge might well abate. But in truth, I was averse from a catastrophe so feeble as that of reconciling the champion with the oppressor of mankind. The moral interest of the fable, which is so powerfully sustained by the sufferings and endurance of Prometheus, would be annihilated if we could conceive of him as unsaying his high language and quailing before his successful and perfidious adversary.[7] The only imaginary being resembling in any degree Prometheus, is Satan; and Prometheus is, in my judgement, a more poetical character than Satan, because, in addition to courage and majesty, and firm and patient opposition to omnipotent force, he is susceptible of being described as exempt from the taints of ambition, envy, revenge, and a desire for personal aggrandizement[8] – which, in the hero of *Paradise Lost*, interfere with the interest. The character of Satan engenders in the mind a pernicious casuistry which leads us to weigh his faults with his wrongs, and to excuse the former because the latter exceed all measure. In the minds of those who consider that magnificent fiction with a religious feeling, it engenders something worse. But Prometheus is, as it were, the type of the highest perfection of moral and intellectual nature, impelled by the purest and the truest motives to the best and noblest ends.

PROMETHEUS UNBOUND; A LYRICAL DRAMA IN FOUR ACTS

[1]   This important work should be read in the light of Mary Shelley's note, pp. 1098–1100; for introductory remarks see pp. 821–2. See also M. H. Abrams, 'Shelley's "Prometheus Unbound"', *Natural Supernaturalism: Tradition and Revolution in Romantic Literature* (New York, 1971), pp. 299–307.

[2]   'Do you hear this, Amphiaraus, in your home beneath the earth?' (Cicero, *Tusculan Disputations* II xxv 59). Amphiaraus was a prophet, saved by Jupiter from pursuers by being miraculously swallowed by the earth, after which he became an oracular god. Shelley directs the comment to Aeschylus (see note 3), asking him to hear this reworking of the Prometheus myth.

[3]   *the Agamemnonian story* most famously related by Aeschylus in the *Agamemnon*, the first play in his Oresteian trilogy (458 BC), that tells of the tragic homecoming of the Greek commander Agamemnon from the Trojan wars.

[4]   *his victim* Prometheus, who he nailed to the rock of the Caucasus for 3,000 years.

[5]   Thetis, a goddess of the sea, married Peleus, King of Thessaly, after a long courtship.

[6]   *the lost drama of Aeschylus* i.e. Aeschylus's *Prometheus Unbound*, the lost sequel to *Prometheus Bound*. It is not known how Aeschylus effected the reconciliation between Prometheus and Jupiter. Fragments show that it opened with Prometheus restored to light after 3,000 years, and that the chorus was composed of Titans. The Titans were a godlike race expelled from heaven by Jupiter in Greek myth.

[7]   Shelley points to a crucial distinction between his work and Aeschylus's. He refused to accept the idea of Prometheus's submission to Jupiter; in his poem it is Jupiter who succumbs.

[8]   *Prometheus is . . . aggrandizement* Prometheus returned fire to man after it was taken away by Jupiter.

This poem was chiefly written upon the mountainous ruins of the Baths of Caracalla,[9] among the flowery glades, and thickets of odoriferous blossoming trees, which are extended in ever-winding labyrinths upon its immense platforms and dizzy arches suspended in the air. The bright blue sky of Rome, and the effect of the vigorous awakening spring in that divinest climate, and the new life with which it drenches the spirits even to intoxication, were the inspiration of this drama.

The imagery which I have employed will be found, in many instances, to have been drawn from the operations of the human mind, or from those external actions by which they are expressed. This is unusual in modern poetry, although Dante and Shakespeare are full of instances of the same kind – Dante indeed more than any other poet, and with greater success. But the Greek poets, as writers to whom no resource of awakening the sympathy of their contemporaries was unknown, were in the habitual use of this power; and it is the study of their works (since a higher merit would probably be denied me) to which I am willing that my readers should impute this singularity.

One word is due in candour to the degree in which the study of contemporary writings may have tinged my composition, for such has been a topic of censure with regard to poems far more popular (and indeed more deservedly popular) than mine.[10] It is impossible that anyone who inhabits the same age with such writers[11] as those who stand in the foremost ranks of our own, can conscientiously assure himself that his language and tone of thought may not have been modified by the study of the productions of those extraordinary intellects. It is true that, not the spirit of their genius, but the forms in which it has manifested itself, are due less to the peculiarities of their own minds than to the peculiarity of the moral and intellectual condition of the minds among which they have been produced. Thus a number of writers possess the form, whilst they want the spirit, of those whom (it is alleged) they imitate; because the former is the endowment of the age in which they live, and the latter must be the uncommunicated lightning of their own mind.

The peculiar style of intense and comprehensive imagery which distinguishes the modern literature of England has not been, as a general power, the product of the imitation of any particular writer. The mass of capabilities remains at every period materially the same; the circumstances which awaken it to action perpetually change. If England were divided into forty republics, each equal in population and extent to Athens, there is no reason to suppose but that, under institutions not more perfect than those of Athens, each would produce philosophers and poets equal to those who (if we except Shakespeare) have never been surpassed. We owe the great writers of the golden age of our literature[12] to that fervid awakening of the public mind which shook to dust the oldest and most oppressive form of the Christian religion.[13] We owe Milton to the progress and development of the same spirit – the sacred Milton was, let it ever be remembered, a republican, and a bold enquirer into morals and religion. The great writers of our own age are, we have reason to suppose, the companions and forerunners of some unimagined change in our social condition, or the opinions which cement it. The cloud of mind is discharging its collected lightning, and the equilibrium between institutions and opinions is now restoring, or is about to be restored.

As to imitation, poetry is a mimetic art. It creates, but it creates by combination and representation. Poetical abstractions are beautiful and new, not because the portions of which they are composed had no previous existence in the mind of man or in nature, but because the whole produced by their combination has some intelligible and beautiful analogy with those sources of emotion and thought, and with the contemporary condition of them. One great poet is a masterpiece of nature which another not only ought to study but must study. He might as wisely and as easily determine that his

---

9 *the Baths of Caracalla* ancient baths in Rome, named after Emperor Caracalla (188–217 AD). In fact Shelley began *Prometheus Unbound* in Este near Venice, September 1818, and completed it in Rome in December 1819.

10 *One word . . . than mine* the remainder of the Preface is a response to John Taylor Coleridge who, in an anonymous review of *The Revolt of Islam* (1818) in the *Quarterly Review* 21 (1819) 460–71, had described Shelley as 'an unsparing imitator' of Wordsworth, 'to whose religious mind it must be matter, we think, of perpetual sorrow to see the philosophy which

comes pure and holy from his pen, degraded and perverted, as it continually is, by this miserable crew of atheists or pantheists'.

11 *such writers* identified in the MS as Wordsworth, Coleridge and Byron.

12 *the golden age of our literature* Shelley means the Elizabethan age – that of Spenser and Sidney.

13 *the oldest and most oppressive form of the Christian religion* Roman Catholicism.

mind should no longer be the mirror of all that is lovely in the visible universe, as exclude from his contemplation the beautiful which exists in the writings of a great contemporary. The pretence of doing it would be a presumption in any but the greatest; the effect, even in him, would be strained, unnatural, and ineffectual. A poet is the combined product of such internal powers as modify the nature of others, and of such external influences as excite and sustain these powers; he is not one, but both. Every man's mind is, in this respect, modified by all the objects of nature and art; by every word and every suggestion which he ever admitted to act upon his consciousness; it is the mirror upon which all forms are reflected,[14] and in which they compose one form. Poets, not otherwise than philosophers, painters, sculptors and musicians, are in one sense the creators, and in another the creations, of their age. From this subjection the loftiest do not escape. There is a similarity between Homer and Hesiod, between Aeschylus and Euripides, between Virgil and Horace, between Dante and Petrarch, between Shakespeare and Fletcher, between Dryden and Pope: each has a generic resemblance under which their specific distinctions are arranged. If this similarity be the result of imitation, I am willing to confess that I have imitated.

Let this opportunity be conceded to me of acknowledging that I have what a Scotch philosopher[15] characteristically terms, 'a passion for reforming the world'. What passion incited him to write and publish his book, he omits to explain. For my part, I had rather be damned with Plato and Lord Bacon,[16] than go to heaven with Paley and Malthus.[17] But it is a mistake to suppose that I dedicate my poetical compositions solely to the direct enforcement of reform, or that I consider them in any degree as containing a reasoned system on the theory of human life. Didactic poetry is my abhorrence; nothing can be equally well expressed in prose that is not tedious and supererogatory in verse. My purpose has hitherto been simply to familiarize the highly-refined imagination of the more select classes of poetical readers with beautiful idealisms of moral excellence, aware that until the mind can love, and admire, and trust, and hope, and endure, reasoned principles of moral conduct are seeds cast upon the highway of life, which the unconscious passenger tramples into dust although they would bear the harvest of his happiness. Should I live to accomplish what I purpose (that is, produce a systematical history of what appear to me to be the genuine elements of human society), let not the advocates of injustice and superstition flatter themselves that I should take Aeschylus rather than Plato as my model.[18]

The having spoken of myself with unaffected freedom will need little apology with the candid, and let the uncandid consider that they injure me less than their own hearts and minds by misrepresentation. Whatever talents a person may possess to amuse and instruct others (be they ever so inconsiderable), he is yet bound to exert them. If his attempt be ineffectual, let the punishment of an unaccomplished purpose have been sufficient; let none trouble themselves to heap the dust of oblivion upon his efforts. The pile they raise will betray his grave which might otherwise have been unknown.

---

[14]   *the mirror . . . reflected* cf. Coleridge's 'convex mirror', p. 450, above.

[15]   *a Scotch philosopher* Robert Forsyth in *The Principles of Moral Science* (1805).

[16]   *Plato and Lord Bacon* in the MS, Shelley adds Rousseau and Milton to this group. Francis Bacon (1561–1626), Lord Chancellor of England, philosopher and essayist, appealed to Shelley because he was a neo-Platonist. Neo-Platonism is an essentially non-materialist, metaphysical school of philosophy deriving from Plotinus and Plato.

[17]   William Paley (1743–1805) argued the usefulness of hell as a means of controlling morals; Thomas Robert Malthus (1776–1834) argued that famine, war and disease were necessary as means of controlling population growth. Shelley regarded Paley and Malthus as essentially conservative.

[18]   Plato's hero is a man leading others towards the light.

Dramatis Personae

Prometheus
Demogorgon
Jupiter
The Earth
Ocean
Apollo
Mercury
Hercules
Asia ⎫
Panthea ⎬ Oceanides
Ione ⎭
The Phantasm of Jupiter
The Spirit of the Earth
The Spirit of the Moon
Spirits of the Hours
Echoes
Fauns
Furies
Spirits

ACT I

Scene: a ravine of icy rocks in the Indian Caucasus.[1] Prometheus[2] is discovered bound to the precipice. Panthea and Ione are seated at his feet. Time: night. During the scene, morning slowly breaks.

PROMETHEUS Monarch of Gods and Demons,[3] and all spirits
But One,[4] who throng those bright and rolling worlds
Which thou and I alone of living things
Behold with sleepless eyes! Regard this earth
Made multitudinous with thy slaves, whom thou   5
Requitest for knee-worship, prayer, and praise,
And toil, and hecatombs[5] of broken hearts,
With fear and self-contempt and barren hope;
Whilst me, who am thy foe, eyeless in hate,[6]
Hast thou made reign and triumph, to thy scorn,   10
O'er mine own misery and thy vain revenge.
Three thousand years of sleep-unsheltered hours
And moments, aye[7] divided by keen pangs
Till they seemed years, torture and solitude,
Scorn and despair – these are mine empire: 15
More glorious far than that which thou surveyest
From thine unenvied throne, oh mighty God!

ACT I
[1] Shelley moves the location from the Caucasus mountains near the Caspian, to the Indian Caucasus, the Hindu Kush mountains in north India and Afghanistan. It was believed to have been the original home of the human race, and was associated with the golden age; it was thus appropriate as the location for the birth of a second golden age.
[2] *Prometheus* 'forethinker' in Greek.
[3] *Monarch of Gods and Demons* Jupiter (Jove). In Shelley's terms, a symbol of political and religious tyranny. The 'demons' are spirits.
[4] *One* Prometheus, who is in much the same position that Shelley felt himself to be.
[5] *hecatombs* numerous sacrifices.
[6] *eyeless in hate* blind with hatred; for a moment Prometheus becomes Samson, 'Eyeless in Gaza at the mill with slaves' (Milton, *Samson Agonistes* 41).
[7] *aye* continually.

Almighty, had I deigned to share the shame
Of thine ill tyranny, and hung not here
Nailed to this wall of eagle-baffling mountain,   20
Black, wintry, dead, unmeasured; without herb,
Insect, or beast, or shape or sound of life –
Ah me, alas! Pain, pain ever, forever!
　　No change, no pause, no hope; yet I endure.
I ask the Earth, have not the mountains felt?   25
I ask yon Heaven, the all-beholding Sun,
Has it not seen? The Sea, in storm or calm,
Heaven's ever-changing shadow, spread below,
Have its deaf waves not heard my agony?
Ah me, alas! Pain, pain ever, forever!   30
　　The crawling glaciers[8] pierce me with the spears
Of their moon-freezing crystals; the bright chains
Eat with their burning cold into my bones;
Heaven's winged hound,[9] polluting from thy lips
His beak in poison not his own, tears up   35
My heart; and shapeless sights come wandering by,
The ghastly people of the realm of dream,
Mocking me; and the Earthquake-fiends are charged
To wrench the rivets from my quivering wounds
When the rocks split and close again behind;   40
While from their loud abysses howling throng
The genii of the storm, urging the rage
Of whirlwind, and afflict me with keen hail.
　　And yet to me welcome is Day and Night,
Whether one breaks the hoar-frost of the morn,   45
Or starry, dim, and slow, the other climbs
The leaden-coloured east – for then they lead
The wingless, crawling Hours,[10] one among whom
(As some dark priest hales[11] the reluctant victim)
Shall drag thee, cruel King, to kiss the blood   50
From these pale feet, which then might trample thee
If they disdained not such a prostrate slave.
Disdain? Ah no, I pity thee.[12] What Ruin
Will hunt thee undefended through wide Heaven!
How will thy soul, cloven to its depth with terror,   55
Gape like a hell within! I speak in grief,
Not exultation, for I hate no more
As then, ere misery made me wise. The curse
Once breathed on thee I would recall.[13] Ye Mountains,
Whose many-voiced Echoes, through the mist   60
Of cataracts, flung the thunder of that spell;
Ye icy Springs, stagnant with wrinkling frost,
Which vibrated to hear me, and then crept

---

[8]   *crawling glaciers* observed by Shelley in Switzerland; see his
letter to Peacock (p. 844), and the creeping glaciers at *Mont
Blanc* 100.
[9]   *Heaven's winged hound* Prometheus was nailed to a rock by
Jupiter for 3,000 years with an eagle incessantly devouring his
liver.

[10] *Hours* Latin 'Horae', female divinities supposed to preside
over the changing of the seasons.
[11] *hales* drags.
[12] *Ah no, I pity thee* the pivotal statement of the play.
Prometheus's Christ-like pity for his torturer is his redemption.
[13] *recall* revoke.

Shuddering through India; thou serenest Air,
Through which the Sun walks burning without beams;   65
And ye swift Whirlwinds, who on poised wings
Hung mute and moveless o'er yon hushed abyss,
As thunder, louder than your own, made rock
The orbed world – if then my words had power
(Though I am changed so that aught evil wish   70
Is dead within, although no memory be
Of what is hate), let them not lose it now!
What was that curse, for ye all heard me speak?

FIRST VOICE (*from the mountains*)
Thrice three hundred thousand years[14]
   O'er the Earthquake's couch we stood;   75
Oft, as men convulsed with fears,
   We trembled in our multitude.

SECOND VOICE (*from the springs*)
Thunderbolts had parched our water,
   We had been stained with bitter blood,
And had run mute, mid shrieks of slaughter,   80
   Through a city and a solitude.

THIRD VOICE (*from the air*)
I had clothed, since Earth uprose,
   Its wastes in colours not their own,
And oft had my serene repose
   Been cloven by many a rending groan.   85

FOURTH VOICE (*from the whirlwinds*)
We had soared beneath these mountains
   Unresting ages; nor had thunder,
Nor yon volcano's flaming fountains,
   Nor any power above or under
   Ever made us mute with wonder.   90

FIRST VOICE
But never bowed our snowy crest
As at the voice of thine unrest.[15]

SECOND VOICE
Never such a sound before
To the Indian waves we bore.
A pilot asleep on the howling sea   95
Leaped up from the deck in agony,
And heard, and cried, 'Ah, woe is me!'
And died as mad as the wild waves be.

---

[14] ll. 74–106 describe the effects of the curse of Prometheus   [15] *the voice of thine unrest* i.e. Prometheus's curse.
on Jupiter, which he has now revoked.

THIRD VOICE

By such dread words from Earth to Heaven
My still realm was never riven;   100
When its wound was closed, there stood
Darkness o'er the day like blood.

FOURTH VOICE

And we shrank back; for dreams of ruin
To frozen caves our flight pursuing
Made us keep silence thus, and thus,   105
Though silence is as hell to us.

THE EARTH The tongueless caverns of the craggy hills
Cried, 'Misery!' then; the hollow Heaven replied
'Misery!' And the Ocean's purple waves,
Climbing the land, howled to the lashing winds,   110
And the pale nations heard it, 'Misery!'
PROMETHEUS I heard a sound of voices – not the voice
Which I gave forth. Mother,[16] thy sons and thou
Scorn him, without whose all-enduring will
Beneath the fierce omnipotence of Jove   115
Both they and thou had vanished, like thin mist
Unrolled on the morning wind. Know ye not me,
The Titan?[17] He who made his agony
The barrier to your else all-conquering foe?
Oh rock-embosomed lawns and snow-fed streams   120
Now seen athwart frore[18] vapours, deep below,
Through whose o'ershadowing woods I wandered once
With Asia,[19] drinking life from her loved eyes,
Why scorns the spirit which informs ye, now
To commune with me? Me alone, who checked,   125
As one who checks a fiend-drawn charioteer,
The falsehood and the force of him who reigns
Supreme, and with the groans of pining slaves
Fills your dim glens and liquid wildernesses?
Why answer ye not still, brethren?[20]
THE EARTH   They dare not.   130
PROMETHEUS Who dares? For I would hear that curse again.
Ha, what an awful whisper rises up!
'Tis scarce like sound; it tingles through the frame
As lightning tingles, hovering ere it strike.
Speak, Spirit! From thine inorganic voice   135
I only know that thou art moving near
And love. How cursed I him?
THE EARTH   How canst thou hear,
Who knowest not the language of the dead?
PROMETHEUS Thou art a living spirit; speak as they.

---

[16]   *Mother* Earth, mother of the Titans and of all things that spring from the earth.
[17]   *The Titan* Prometheus was one of the Titans.
[18]   *frore* frosty.

[19]   *Asia* daughter of Oceanus and bride of Prometheus, from whom she is now separated.
[20]   *brethren* Prometheus is the sibling of forests and streams, as they are all children of Earth.

THE EARTH I dare not speak like life, lest Heaven's fell King 140
Should hear, and link me to some wheel of pain[21]
More torturing than the one whereon I roll.
Subtle thou art and good, and though the Gods
Hear not this voice, yet thou art more than God,
Being wise and kind. Earnestly hearken now. 145
PROMETHEUS Obscurely through my brain, like shadows dim,
Sweep awful thoughts, rapid and thick. I feel
Faint, like one mingled in entwining love;
Yet 'tis not pleasure.
THE EARTH   No, thou canst not hear;
Thou art immortal, and this tongue is known 150
Only to those who die.
PROMETHEUS   And what art thou,
Oh melancholy Voice?
THE EARTH   I am the Earth,
Thy mother; she within whose stony veins,[22]
To the last fibre of the loftiest tree
Whose thin leaves trembled in the frozen air, 155
Joy ran, as blood within a living frame,
When thou didst from her bosom, like a cloud
Of glory,[23] arise – a spirit of keen joy![24]
And at thy voice her pining sons uplifted
Their prostrate brows from the polluting dust, 160
And our almighty Tyrant[25] with fierce dread
Grew pale, until his thunder chained thee here.
Then – see those million worlds which burn and roll
Around us; their inhabitants beheld
My sphered light wane in wide heaven; the sea 165
Was lifted by strange tempest, and new fire
From earthquake-rifted mountains of bright snow
Shook its portentous hair beneath Heaven's frown;
Lightning and inundation vexed the plains;
Blue thistles bloomed in cities; foodless toads 170
Within voluptuous chambers panting crawled,
When plague had fallen on man and beast and worm,
And famine and black blight on herb and tree;
And in the corn and vines and meadow-grass
Teemed ineradicable poisonous weeds 175
Draining their growth – for my wan breast was dry
With grief, and the thin air, my breath, was stained
With the contagion of a mother's hate
Breathed on her child's destroyer. Aye, I heard
Thy curse, the which, if thou rememberest not, 180
Yet my innumerable seas and streams,
Mountains, and caves, and winds, and yon wide air,

---

[21] *some wheel of pain* Ixion's punishment was to be banished from heaven and tied to a burning and spinning wheel in Hades.
[22] *stony veins* in his letter to Peacock, Shelley had referred to the blood circulating through the 'stony veins' of Mont Blanc (see p. 844).

[23] *a cloud / Of glory* compare Wordsworth, *Ode*: 'But trailing clouds of glory do we come / From God, who is our home' (ll. 64–5).
[24] This refers to Prometheus's rebellion against Jupiter.
[25] *our almighty Tyrant* Jupiter.

And the inarticulate people of the dead,
Preserve, a treasured spell. We meditate
In secret joy and hope those dreadful words,   185
But dare not speak them.

PROMETHEUS   Venerable mother!
All else who live and suffer take from thee
Some comfort: flowers, and fruits, and happy sounds,
And love, though fleeting. These may not be mine;
But mine own words, I pray, deny me not.   190

THE EARTH They shall be told. Ere Babylon was dust,
The magus Zoroaster,[26] my dead child,
Met his own image walking in the garden;
That apparition, sole of men, he saw.
For know there are two worlds of life and death;   195
One that which thou beholdest – but the other
Is underneath the grave, where do inhabit
The shadows of all forms that think and live
Till death unite them and they part no more,
Dreams and the light imaginings of men,   200
And all that faith creates or love desires,
Terrible, strange, sublime and beauteous shapes.
There thou art, and dost hang, a writhing shade
Mid whirlwind-peopled mountains; all the gods
Are there, and all the powers of nameless worlds –   205
Vast, sceptred phantoms, heroes, men, and beasts,
And Demogorgon,[27] a tremendous gloom –
And he, the supreme Tyrant,[28] on his throne
Of burning gold. Son, one of these shall utter
The curse which all remember. Call at will   210
Thine own ghost, or the ghost of Jupiter,
Hades or Typhon,[29] or what mightier Gods
From all-prolific Evil since thy ruin
Have sprung and trampled on my prostrate sons.
Ask, and they must reply; so the revenge   215
Of the Supreme may sweep through vacant shades,
As rainy wind through the abandoned gate
Of a fallen palace.

PROMETHEUS   Mother, let not aught
Of that which may be evil pass again
My lips, or those of aught resembling me.   220
Phantasm of Jupiter, arise, appear!

IONE[30]

My wings are folded o'er mine ears;
My wings are crossed over mine eyes;

---

[26] *Zoroaster* Persian religious leader, King of Bactria (sixth
or seventh century BC), who taught that the universe is ruled
by two powers, but that the eventual victory of the good spirit
(Ahura Mazda or Ormuzd) over the evil (Ahriman) is guaran-
teed. The encounter with his double is apocryphal; Shelley
apparently has in mind Zoroaster's formative meeting with
the angel Vohu Manah ('good thought'), who introduced him
to Ahura Mazda.
[27] *Demogorgon* important deity described by Mary Shelley as

'the primal power of the world'.
[28] *the supreme Tyrant* Jupiter.
[29] *Hades or Typhon* in Greek myth, Hades was the brother of
Jupiter and king of the underworld; Typhon was a monster
with a hundred serpentine heads, each of which emitted
flames.
[30] Ione and Panthea are daughters of Oceanus and younger
sisters of Asia. They are a chorus, describing and commenting
on the events.

Yet through their silver shade appears,
    And through their lulling plumes arise   225
A shape, a throng of sounds:
    May it be no ill to thee,
Oh thou of many wounds,[31]
Near whom, for our sweet sister's sake,
Ever thus we watch and wake.   230

PANTHEA
The sound is of whirlwind underground,
    Earthquake, and fire, and mountains cloven;[32]
The shape is awful like the sound,
    Clothed in dark purple, star-inwoven.
A sceptre of pale gold,   235
    To stay[33] steps proud, o'er the slow cloud
His veined hand doth hold.[34]
Cruel he looks, but calm and strong,
Like one who does, not suffers wrong.

PHANTASM OF JUPITER Why have the secret powers of this strange world   240
Driven me, a frail and empty phantom, hither
On direst storms? What unaccustomed sounds
Are hovering on my lips, unlike the voice
With which our pallid race hold ghastly talk
In darkness? And, proud sufferer, who art thou?   245
PROMETHEUS Tremendous Image, as thou art must be
He whom thou shadowest forth. I am his foe,
The Titan. Speak the words which I would hear
Although no thought inform thine empty voice.
THE EARTH Listen, and though your echoes must be mute,   250
Grey mountains, and old woods, and haunted springs,
Prophetic caves, and isle-surrounding streams,
Rejoice to hear what yet ye cannot speak.
PHANTASM A spirit seizes me and speaks within:
It tears me as fire tears a thunder-cloud!   255
PANTHEA See how he lifts his mighty looks; the heaven
Darkens above.
IONE   He speaks; oh shelter me!
PROMETHEUS I see the curse on gestures proud and cold,
And looks of firm defiance and calm hate,
And such despair as mocks itself with smiles,   260
Written as on a scroll – yet speak, oh speak!

PHANTASM
Fiend, I defy thee! With a calm, fixed mind,
    All that thou canst inflict I bid thee do;
Foul tyrant both of Gods and humankind,
    One only being shalt thou not subdue.   265
Rain then thy plagues upon me here,

---

[31] *Oh thou of many wounds* Prometheus.
[32] *cloven* split asunder.
[33] *stay* steady.

[34] *A sceptre . . . hold* the Phantasm of Jupiter holds a sceptre
as he approaches over the cloud.

Ghastly disease, and frenzying fear;
And let alternate frost and fire
Eat into me, and be thine ire
Lightning, and cutting hail, and legioned forms   270
Of furies, driving by upon the wounding storms.

Aye, do thy worst. Thou art omnipotent.
   O'er all things but thyself I gave thee power,
And my own will.[35] Be thy swift mischiefs sent
   To blast mankind, from yon ethereal tower.   275
Let thy malignant spirit move
Its darkness over those I love;
On me and mine I imprecate[36]
The utmost torture of thy hate,
And thus devote[37] to sleepless agony   280
This undeclining head, while thou must reign on high.

But thou, who art the God and Lord – oh thou
   Who fillest with thy soul this world of woe;
To whom all things of Earth and Heaven do bow
   In fear and worship; all-prevailing foe!   285
I curse thee! Let a sufferer's curse
Clasp thee, his torturer, like remorse;
Till thine infinity shall be
A robe of envenomed agony,[38]
And thine omnipotence a crown of pain   290
To cling like burning gold round thy dissolving brain.

Heap on thy soul, by virtue of this curse,
   Ill deeds; then be thou damned, beholding good,
Both infinite as is the universe,
   And thou, and thy self-torturing solitude.[39]   295
An awful image of calm power
Though now thou sittest, let the hour
Come when thou must appear to be
That which thou art internally;
And after many a false and fruitless crime   300
Scorn track thy lagging fall through boundless space and time.
The Phantasm vanishes

PROMETHEUS Were these my words, oh Parent?
THE EARTH   They were thine.
PROMETHEUS It doth repent me; words are quick and vain –
Grief for awhile is blind, and so was mine.
I wish no living thing to suffer pain.[40]   305

---

[35]   *O'er all things . . . will* Prometheus empowered Jupiter; in the same way mankind has empowered the tyrants who rule over humanity.
[36]   *imprecate* invoke, call down.
[37]   *devote* condemn, doom.
[38]   *A robe of envenomed agony* there is a recollection here of Nessus's poisoned shirt which, when worn by Hercules, burned his skin, and tore off his flesh when he attempted to remove it.
[39]   *Both infinite . . . solitude* '. . . both good and evil being infinite as the universe is, and as thou art, and as thy solitude is.'
[40]   A deleted stage-direction in the MS reveals at this point that Prometheus 'bends his head as in pain'.

THE EARTH.

    Misery, oh misery to me,
    That Jove at length should vanquish thee.
    Wail, howl aloud, Land and Sea;
    The Earth's rent heart shall answer ye.
    Howl, spirits of the living and the dead,   310
    Your refuge, your defence lies fallen and vanquished.

FIRST ECHO Lies fallen and vanquished?

SECOND ECHO   Fallen and vanquished!

IONE

    Fear not, 'tis but some passing spasm –
      The Titan is unvanquished still.   315
    But see, where through the azure chasm
      Of yon forked and snowy hill,
    Trampling the slant winds on high
      With golden-sandalled feet that glow
    Under plumes of purple dye   320
    Like rose-ensanguined ivory –
      A shape comes now,
    Stretching on high from his right hand
    A serpent-cinctured[41] wand.

PANTHEA 'Tis Jove's world-wandering herald, Mercury.[42]   325

IONE

    And who are those with hydra tresses[43]
      And iron wings that climb the wind,
    Whom the frowning God represses
      Like vapours steaming up behind,
    Clanging loud, an endless crowd?   330

PANTHEA

    These are Jove's tempest-walking hounds[44]
    Whom he gluts with groans and blood,
    When charioted on sulphurous cloud
      He bursts Heaven's bounds.

IONE

    Are they now led from the thin dead   335
    On new pangs to be fed?

PANTHEA. The Titan looks as ever – firm, not proud.

FIRST FURY Ha! I scent life!

SECOND FURY   Let me but look into his eyes.

THIRD FURY The hope of torturing him smells like a heap

Of corpses to a death-bird after battle.   340

FIRST FURY Darest thou delay, oh Herald? Take cheer, hounds

---

[41] *cinctured* entwined.
[42] *Mercury* son of Maia and Zeus, messenger of the gods. He is the unwilling servant of tyranny.

[43] *hydra tresses* hair of snakes.
[44] *Jove's tempest-walking hounds* i.e. the Furies, avenging spirits.

Of hell; what if the Son of Maia[45] soon
Should make us food and sport? Who can please long
The Omnipotent?

MERCURY   Back to your towers of iron
And gnash, beside the streams of fire and wail,   345
Your foodless teeth![46] Geryon, arise! And Gorgon,
Chimera, and thou Sphinx,[47] subtlest of fiends,
Who ministered to Thebes Heaven's poisoned wine:
Unnatural love and more unnatural hate[48] –
These shall perform your task.

FIRST FURY   Oh mercy, mercy!   350
We die with our desire; drive us not back.

MERCURY Crouch then in silence.

                                    Awful sufferer!
To thee unwilling, most unwillingly
I come, by the great Father's will driven down,
To execute a doom[49] of new revenge.   355
Alas, I pity thee, and hate myself
That I can do no more. Aye from thy sight
Returning, for a season, Heaven seems Hell,
So thy worn form pursues me night and day,
Smiling reproach. Wise art thou, firm and good,   360
But vainly wouldst stand forth alone in strife
Against the Omnipotent, as yon clear lamps
That measure and divide the weary years
From which there is no refuge, long have taught
And long must teach. Even now thy torturer arms   365
With the strange might of unimagined pains
The powers who scheme slow agonies in Hell,
And my commission is to lead them here,
Or what more subtle, foul or savage fiends
People the abyss, and leave them to their task.   370
Be it not so! There is a secret[50] known
To thee, and to none else of living things,
Which may transfer the sceptre of wide Heaven,
The fear of which perplexes the Supreme.
Clothe it in words, and bid it clasp his throne   375
In intercession; bend thy soul in prayer,
And like a suppliant in some gorgeous fane
Let the will kneel within thy haughty heart;
For benefits and meek submission tame
The fiercest and the mightiest.

PROMETHEUS   Evil minds   380
Change good to their own nature. I gave all
He has, and in return he chains me here

---

45 *the Son of Maia* Mercury.
46 *Back to your towers . . . teeth* Mercury threatens to drive the Furies back to Hades, where flow the rivers Phlegethon and Cocytus ('streams of fire and wail' – 'wail' is a noun).
47 Geryon, Gorgon, Chimera and Sphinx are all monsters of classical legend.
48 *Unnatural love and more unnatural hate* By solving the riddle of the Sphinx, Oedipus, King of Thebes, was led to an 'Unnatural love' for his mother, and to kill his father ('more unnatural hate').
49 *doom* judgement.
50 *a secret* i.e. that the children of Thetis, a sea-goddess, will be greater than their father, so that if Jupiter unites with her he will be overthrown by his own son.

Years, ages, night and day – whether the sun
Split my parched skin, or in the moony night
The crystal-winged snow cling round my hair –   385
Whilst my beloved race is trampled down
By his thought-executing[51] ministers.
Such is the Tyrant's recompense – 'tis just;
He who is evil can receive no good;
And for a world bestowed, or a friend lost,   390
He can feel hate, fear, shame – not gratitude.
He but requites me for his own misdeed.
Kindness to such is keen reproach, which breaks
With bitter stings the light sleep of Revenge.
Submission, thou dost know I cannot try;   395
For what submission but that fatal word,
The death-seal of mankind's captivity –
Like the Sicilian's hair-suspended sword
Which trembles o'er his crown[52] – would he accept;
Or could I yield? Which yet I will not yield.   400
Let others flatter Crime, where it sits throned
In brief omnipotence; secure are they,
For Justice, when triumphant, will weep down
Pity, not punishment, on her own wrongs,
Too much avenged by those who err.[53] I wait,   405
Enduring thus the retributive hour
Which since we spake is even nearer now.
But hark, the hell-hounds clamour; fear delay!
Behold – Heaven lours[54] under thy Father's frown!
MERCURY Oh that we might be spared – I to inflict   410
And thou to suffer. Once more answer me:
Thou knowest not the period[55] of Jove's power?
PROMETHEUS I know but this, that it must come.
MERCURY   Alas!
Thou canst not count thy years to come of pain?
PROMETHEUS They last while Jove must reign – nor more nor less   415
Do I desire or fear.
MERCURY   Yet pause, and plunge
Into eternity, where recorded time,
Even all that we imagine, age on age,
Seems but a point, and the reluctant mind
Flags wearily in its unending flight,   420
Till it sink, dizzy, blind, lost, shelterless.
Perchance it has not numbered the slow years
Which thou must spend in torture, unreprieved.
PROMETHEUS Perchance no thought can count them – yet they pass.
MERCURY If thou might'st dwell among the Gods the while,   425
Lapped in voluptuous joy?
PROMETHEUS   I would not quit

---

51 *thought-executing* i.e. acting out one's will as quickly as it
is conceived; cf. *King Lear* III ii 4: 'Yon sulph'rous and
thought-executing fires'.
52 *Like the Sicilian's . . . crown* Damocles was a court flatterer
exposed by Dionysius I of Syracuse who, to show him the tri-
als of monarchy, seated Damocles on a throne beneath a sword
suspended by a hair.

53 *For Justice . . . err* Justice will take pity on those who com-
mit crimes against her, evil-doers having already punished
themselves by the misery of being what they are.
54 *lours* cowers.
55 *period* end.

This bleak ravine, these unrepentant pains.
MERCURY Alas! I wonder at, yet pity thee.
PROMETHEUS Pity the self-despising slaves of Heaven –
Not me, within whose mind sits peace serene   430
As light in the sun, throned. How vain is talk!
Call up the fiends.
IONE   Oh sister, look! White fire
Has cloven to the roots yon huge snow-loaded cedar;
How fearfully God's thunder howls behind!
MERCURY I must obey his words and thine, alas;   435
Most heavily remorse hangs at my heart.[56]
PANTHEA See where the child of Heaven,[57] with winged feet
Runs down the slanted sunlight of the dawn.
IONE Dear sister, close thy plumes over thine eyes
Lest thou behold and die; they come – they come   440
Blackening the birth of day with countless wings,
And hollow underneath, like death.
FIRST FURY   Prometheus!
SECOND FURY Immortal Titan!
THIRD FURY   Champion of Heaven's slaves!
PROMETHEUS He whom some dreadful voice invokes is here –
Prometheus, the chained Titan. Horrible forms,   445
What and who are ye? Never yet there came
Phantasms so foul through monster-teeming Hell
From the all-miscreative[58] brain of Jove.
Whilst I behold such execrable shapes,
Methinks I grow like what I contemplate,   450
And laugh and stare in loathsome sympathy.
FIRST FURY We are the ministers of pain and fear,
And disappointment, and mistrust, and hate,
And clinging crime; and as lean dogs pursue
Through wood and lake some struck and sobbing fawn,[59]   455
We track all things that weep and bleed and live,
When the great King betrays them to our will.
PROMETHEUS Oh many fearful natures in one name,
I know ye; and these lakes and echoes know
The darkness and the clangour of your wings.   460
But why more hideous than your loathed selves
Gather ye up in legions from the deep?
SECOND FURY We knew not that; sisters, rejoice, rejoice!
PROMETHEUS Can aught exult in its deformity?
SECOND FURY The beauty of delight makes lovers glad,   465
Gazing on one another; so are we.
As from the rose which the pale priestess kneels
To gather for her festal crown of flowers
The aerial crimson falls, flushing her cheek –
So from our victim's destined agony   470

---

[56] Shelley is implicitly critical of Mercury. Although he sympathizes with Prometheus, he continues to obey Jupiter. He is like those who detest the tyrants who govern them, but do nothing to bring them down.
[57] *the child of Heaven* Mercury.

[58] *all-miscreative* Jupiter is infinitely capable of creating bad or horrible things – like the Furies.
[59] *as lean dogs . . . fawn* cf. Wordsworth's *Hart-Leap Well* and *Twelfth Night* I i 21–2: 'And my desires, like fell and cruel hounds, / E'er since pursue me'.

The shade which is our form invests us round,
Else are we shapeless as our mother Night.
PROMETHEUS I laugh your power, and his who sent you here,
To lowest scorn. Pour forth the cup of pain.
FIRST FURY Thou thinkest we will rend thee bone from bone,   475
And nerve from nerve, working like fire within?
PROMETHEUS Pain is my element, as hate is thine;
Ye rend me now — I care not.
SECOND FURY   Dost imagine
We will but laugh into thy lidless[60] eyes?
PROMETHEUS I weigh not what ye do, but what ye suffer,   480
Being evil. Cruel was the Power which called
You, or aught else so wretched, into light.
THIRD FURY Thou think'st we will live through thee, one by one,
Like animal life, and though we can obscure not
The soul which burns within, that we will dwell   485
Beside it, like a vain loud multitude
Vexing the self-content of wisest men;
That we will be dread thought beneath thy brain,
And foul desire round thine astonished heart,
And blood within thy labyrinthine veins   490
Crawling like agony.[61]
PROMETHEUS   Why, ye are thus now;
Yet am I king over myself, and rule
The torturing and conflicting throngs within,
As Jove rules you when Hell grows mutinous.

CHORUS OF FURIES
From the ends of the earth, from the ends of the earth,   495
Where the night has its grave and the morning its birth,
       Come, come, come!
Oh ye who shake hills with the scream of your mirth
When cities sink howling in ruin, and ye
Who with wingless footsteps trample the sea,   500
And close upon shipwreck and famine's track
Sit chattering with joy on the foodless wreck —
       Come, come, come!
   Leave the bed, low, cold, and red,
   Strewed beneath a nation dead;   505
   Leave the hatred, as in ashes
      Fire is left for future burning:
   It will burst in bloodier flashes
      When ye stir it, soon returning;
   Leave the self-contempt implanted   510
   In young spirits, sense-enchanted,
      Misery's yet unkindled fuel;
   Leave Hell's secrets half unchanted
      To the maniac dreamer — cruel
   More than ye can be with hate,   515
      Is he with fear.

---

[60] *lidless* unclosing.
[61] Evils thoughts and desires will be as intimately present to
Prometheus as the blood in his body.

Come, come, come!
We are steaming up from Hell's wide gate,
  And we burden the blasts of the atmosphere,
  But vainly we toil till ye come here.   520

IONE Sister, I hear the thunder of new wings.[62]
PANTHEA These solid mountains quiver with the sound
Even as the tremulous air; their shadows make
The space within my plumes more black than night.

FIRST FURY
  Your call was as a winged car   525
  Driven on whirlwinds fast and far;
  It rapt[63] us from red gulfs of war;

SECOND FURY
  From wide cities, famine-wasted;

THIRD FURY
  Groans half-heard, and blood untasted;

FOURTH FURY
  Kingly conclaves[64] stern and cold,   530
  Where blood with gold is bought and sold;

FIFTH FURY
  From the furnace, white and hot,
  In which –

A FURY
          Speak not, whisper not!
  I know all that ye would tell,
  But to speak might break the spell[65]   535
  Which must bend the Invincible,
  The stern of thought;
  He yet defies the deepest power of Hell.

A FURY Tear the veil![66]
ANOTHER FURY   It is torn!
CHORUS   The pale stars of the morn
Shine on a misery dire to be borne.   540
Dost thou faint, mighty Titan? We laugh thee to scorn.
Dost thou boast the clear knowledge thou wakenedst for man?
Then was kindled within him a thirst which outran
Those perishing waters; a thirst of fierce fever,

---

[62] *new wings* a second group of Furies which are to show
Prometheus visions of external evils (the first have shown him
internal ones).
[63] *rapt* carried.
[64] *Kingly conclaves* secret meetings where important decisions
are taken.
[65] *to speak might break the spell* to speak might weaken the
force of that which is shown.
[66] A deleted stage direction in the MS reveals that at this
point 'The Furies, having mingled in a strange dance, divide,
and in the background is seen a plain covered with burning
cities'. The events Prometheus is shown are in the past: the
Crucifixion, the French Revolution, and their consequences.

Hope, love, doubt, desire – which consume him forever. 545
 One[67] came forth of gentle worth
 Smiling on the sanguine earth;
 His words outlived him, like swift poison
  Withering up truth, peace, and pity.
 Look, where round the wide horizon 550
  Many a million-peopled city
 Vomits smoke in the bright air.
 Hark that outcry of despair!
 'Tis his mild and gentle ghost
  Wailing for the faith he kindled. 555
 Look again, the flames almost
  To a glow-worm's lamp have dwindled;
 The survivors round the embers
  Gather in dread.
   Joy, joy, joy! 560
Past ages crowd on thee,[68] but each one remembers,
And the future is dark, and the present is spread
Like a pillow of thorns for thy slumberless head.

SEMICHORUS I
 Drops of bloody agony flow
 From his white and quivering brow.[69] 565
 Grant a little respite now –
 See, a disenchanted nation[70]
 Springs like day from desolation;
 To Truth its state is dedicate,
 And Freedom leads it forth, her mate; 570
 A legioned band of linked brothers
 Whom Love calls children –

SEMICHORUS II
     'Tis another's:[71]
 See how kindred murder kin![72]
 'Tis the vintage-time for Death and Sin;
 Blood, like new wine, bubbles within, 575
  Till Despair smothers
The struggling world, which slaves and tyrants win.
All the Furies vanish, except one
IONE Hark, sister! What a low yet dreadful groan
Quite unsuppressed is tearing up the heart
Of the good Titan, as storms tear the deep, 580
And beasts hear the sea moan in inland caves.
Darest thou observe how the fiends torture him?
PANTHEA Alas, I looked forth twice, but will no more.
IONE What didst thou see?
PANTHEA   A woeful sight; a youth[73]

---

67 *One* Jesus Christ.
68 *thee* Prometheus, rather than Christ.
69 ll. 564–5 describe Prometheus as if he were Christ.
70 *a disenchanted nation* France during the Revolution.
71 *'Tis another's* the revolutionaries are no longer children of Love, but of Hatred.

72 *See how kindred murder kin!* During the Reign of Terror (July 1793–July 1794), Robespierre and his henchmen were responsible for the guillotining of many innocent people.
73 *a youth* Christ.

With patient looks nailed to a crucifix.   585
IONE What next?
PANTHEA   The Heaven around, the earth below
Was peopled with thick shapes of human death,
All horrible, and wrought by human hands;
And some appeared the work of human hearts,
For men were slowly killed by frowns and smiles.   590
And other sights too foul to speak and live
Were wandering by. Let us not tempt worse fear
By looking forth; those groans are grief enough.
FURY Behold an emblem: those who do endure
Deep wrongs for man, and scorn, and chains, but heap   595
Thousandfold torment on themselves and him.
PROMETHEUS Remit the anguish of that lighted stare;
Close those wan lips; let that thorn-wounded brow
Stream not with blood – it mingles with thy tears!
Fix, fix those tortured orbs[74] in peace and death,   600
So thy sick throes shake not that crucifix,
So those pale fingers play not with thy gore.
Oh horrible! Thy name I will not speak –
It hath become a curse. I see, I see
The wise, the mild, the lofty, and the just,   605
Whom thy slaves hate for being like to thee;[75]
Some hunted by foul lies from their heart's home,
An early-chosen, late-lamented home,
As hooded ounces[76] cling to the driven hind;[77]
Some linked to corpses in unwholesome cells;   610
Some (hear I not the multitude laugh loud?)
Impaled in lingering fire. And mighty realms
Float by my feet, like sea-uprooted isles,
Whose sons are kneaded down in common blood
By the red light of their own burning homes.   615
FURY Blood thou canst see, and fire – and canst hear groans;
Worse things, unheard, unseen, remain behind.
PROMETHEUS Worse?
FURY   In each human heart terror survives
The ravin[78] it has gorged; the loftiest fear
All that they would disdain to think were true.[79]   620
Hypocrisy and custom make their minds
The fanes of many a worship, now outworn.
They dare not devise good for man's estate,
And yet they know not that they do not dare.
The good want power, but to weep barren tears;   625

---

74 *tortured orbs* eyes, tormented by the appalling sights they have witnessed.
75 *Whom thy slaves hate for being like to thee* cf. Shelley's note to *Hellas* 1090–1: 'The sublime human character of Jesus Christ was deformed by an imputed identification with a Power, who tempted, betrayed, and punished the innocent beings who were called into existence by His sole will; and for the period of a thousand years, the spirit of this most just, wise, and benevolent of men has been propitiated with myri-

ads of hecatombs of those who approached the nearest to His innocence and wisdom'.
76 *hooded ounces* hunting leopards, hooded until released at their prey.
77 *hind* female deer.
78 *ravin* prey.
79 *In each human heart . . . true* 'Superstitious fear lingers in every man's mind after he has stopped believing in the cause of it'.

The powerful goodness want – worse need for them;
The wise want love, and those who love want wisdom;
And all best things are thus confused to ill.
Many are strong and rich, and would be just,
But live among their suffering fellow-men   630
As if none felt: they know not what they do.[80]
PROMETHEUS Thy words are like a cloud of winged snakes;
And yet I pity those they torture not.[81]
FURY Thou pitiest them? I speak no more. (*vanishes*)
PROMETHEUS   Ah woe!
Ah woe! Alas, pain, pain ever, forever!   635
I close my tearless eyes, but see more clear
Thy works within my woe-illumed mind,
Thou subtle[82] Tyrant! Peace is in the grave.
The grave hides all things beautiful and good:
I am a God and cannot find it there –   640
Nor would I seek it. For, though dread revenge,
This is defeat, fierce King, not victory.
The sights with which thou torturest gird my soul
With new endurance, till the hour arrives
When they shall be no types of things which are.   645
PANTHEA Alas! What sawest thou more?
PROMETHEUS   There are two woes:
To speak, and to behold; thou spare me one.
Names are there, nature's sacred watchwords: they
Were borne aloft in bright emblazonry.
The nations thronged around, and cried aloud   650
As with one voice, 'Truth, Liberty, and Love!'[83]
Suddenly fierce confusion fell from Heaven
Among them – there was strife, deceit, and fear;
Tyrants rushed in, and did divide the spoil.
This was the shadow[84] of the truth I saw.   655
THE EARTH I felt thy torture, son, with such mixed joy
As pain and virtue give. To cheer thy state
I bid ascend[85] those subtle and fair spirits
Whose homes are the dim caves of human thought,
And who inhabit, as birds wing the wind,   660
Its world-surrounding ether; they behold
Beyond that twilight realm, as in a glass,[86]
The future: may they speak comfort to thee!
PANTHEA Look, sister, where a troop of spirits gather,
Like flocks of clouds in spring's delightful weather,   665
Thronging in the blue air!
IONE   And see, more come,

---

[80]   ll. 618–31 comprise the climax of the temptation. The
temptation is to despair, because it seems impossible to
improve things. Prometheus silences the Fury by saying that
he would prefer any amount of suffering to acquiescence. *they
know not what they do* an allusion to Christ on the cross, Luke
23:34: 'Father, forgive them; for they know not what they do'.
[81]   *And yet I pity those they torture not* a transcendental act of
pity; Prometheus pities those who do not recognize the mis-
eries of the world for what they are.

[82]   *subtle* cunning.
[83]   *'Truth, Liberty, and Love!'* a reference to the motto of the
French Revolution: *liberté, egalité, fraternité*.
[84]   *shadow* image.
[85]   *ascend* the spirits, which are like angels, ascend from
within, rather than descend from without.
[86]   *glass* fortune-teller's glass ball.

Like fountain-vapours when the winds are dumb,
That climb up the ravine in scattered lines.
And hark — is it the music of the pines?
Is it the lake? Is it the waterfall?   670
PANTHEA 'Tis something sadder, sweeter far than all.

CHORUS OF SPIRITS
    From unremembered ages we
    Gentle guides and guardians be
    Of Heaven-oppressed mortality;
    And we breathe, and sicken not,   675
    The atmosphere of human thought:
    Be it dim, and dank, and grey,
    Like a storm-extinguished day
    Travelled o'er by dying gleams;
        Be it bright as all between   680
    Cloudless skies and windless streams,
        Silent, liquid, and serene;
    As the birds within the wind,
        As the fish within the wave,
    As the thoughts of man's own mind   685
        Float through all above the grave,
    We make there our liquid lair,
    Voyaging cloudlike and unpent[87]
    Through the boundless element:
    Thence we bear the prophecy   690
    Which begins and ends in thee.

IONE More yet come, one by one: the air around them
Looks radiant as the air around a star.

FIRST SPIRIT
    On a battle-trumpet's blast
    I fled hither, fast, fast, fast,   695
    Mid the darkness upward cast.
    From the dust of creeds outworn,[88]
    From the tyrant's banner torn,
    Gathering round me, onward borne,
    There was mingled many a cry —   700
    'Freedom! Hope! Death! Victory!'
    Till they faded through the sky;
    And one sound above, around,
    One sound beneath, around, above,
    Was moving — 'twas the soul of love;   705
    'Twas the hope, the prophecy
    Which begins and ends in thee.

SECOND SPIRIT
    A rainbow's arch stood on the sea,
    Which rocked beneath, immovably;
    And the triumphant storm did flee,   710

---

[87] *unpent* free, unconfined.   [88] *creeds outworn* Wordsworth, *The world is too much with us* 10.

Like a conqueror swift and proud,
Between, with many a captive cloud,
A shapeless, dark and rapid crowd,
Each by lightning riven in half.
I heard the thunder hoarsely laugh.   715
Mighty fleets were strewn like chaff
And spread beneath a hell of death[89]
O'er the white waters. I alit
On a great ship lightning-split,
And speeded hither on the sigh   720
Of one who gave an enemy
His plank, then plunged aside to die.

THIRD SPIRIT
I sat beside a sage's bed,
And the lamp was burning red
Near the book where he had fed,[90]   725
When a dream with plumes of flame
To his pillow hovering came,
And I knew it was the same
Which had kindled long ago
Pity, eloquence, and woe;   730
And the world awhile below
Wore the shade its lustre made.
It has borne me here as fleet
As Desire's lightning feet:
I must ride it back ere morrow,   735
Or the sage will wake in sorrow.

FOURTH SPIRIT
On a poet's lips I slept
Dreaming like a love-adept[91]
In the sound his breathing kept;
Nor seeks nor finds he mortal blisses,   740
But feeds on the aerial kisses
Of shapes that haunt thought's wildernesses.
He will watch from dawn to gloom
The lake-reflected sun illume
The yellow bees in the ivy-bloom,   745
Nor heed nor see what things they be;
But from these create he can
Forms more real than living man,
Nurslings of immortality!
One of these awakened me,   750
And I sped to succour thee.

IONE Behold'st thou not two shapes from the east and west
Come, as two doves to one beloved nest,
Twin nurslings of the all-sustaining air

---

[89]   *Mighty fleets . . . death* Spread beneath the wrecked fleets
was a hell of death.

[90]   *where he had fed* i.e. his mind.

[91]   *love-adept* one skilled in love.

On swift still wings glide down the atmosphere?   755
And hark, their sweet, sad voices! 'Tis despair
Mingled with love, and then dissolved in sound.
PANTHEA Canst thou speak, sister? All my words are drowned.
IONE Their beauty gives me voice. See how they float
On their sustaining wings of skyey grain,[92]   760
Orange and azure deepening into gold;
Their soft smiles light the air like a star's fire.
CHORUS OF SPIRITS Hast thou beheld the form of Love?
FIFTH SPIRIT   As over wide dominions
I sped, like some swift cloud that wings the wide air's wildernesses,
That planet-crested shape swept by on lightning-braided pinions,[93]   765
Scattering the liquid joy of life[94] from his ambrosial[95] tresses:
His footsteps paved the world with light, but as I passed 'twas fading,
And hollow Ruin yawned behind. Great sages bound in madness,
And headless patriots and pale youths who perished, unupbraiding,
Gleamed in the night I wandered o'er; till thou, oh King of sadness,   770
Turned by thy smile the worst I saw to recollected gladness.
SIXTH SPIRIT Ah sister! Desolation is a delicate thing:
It walks not on the earth, it floats not on the air,
But treads with lulling footstep, and fans with silent wing
The tender hopes which in their hearts the best and gentlest bear,   775
Who, soothed to false repose by the fanning plumes above,
And the music-stirring motion of its soft and busy feet,
Dream visions of aerial joy, and call the monster, Love,
And wake, and find the shadow Pain, as he whom now we greet.

CHORUS
    Though Ruin now Love's shadow be,   780
    Following him destroyingly
      On Death's white and winged steed,[96]
    Which the fleetest cannot flee –
      Trampling down both flower and weed,
    Man and beast, and foul and fair,   785
    Like a tempest through the air;
    Thou shalt quell this horseman grim,
    Woundless though in heart or limb.
PROMETHEUS Spirits, how know ye this shall be?

CHORUS
    In the atmosphere we breathe –   790
    As buds grow red when snowstorms flee
      From spring gathering up beneath,
    Whose mild winds shake the elder brake,[97]
    And the wandering herdsmen know
    That the whitethorn[98] soon will blow –   795
    Wisdom, Justice, Love, and Peace,

---

[92]   *skyey grain* the colour of the sky.
[93]   *pinions* wings.
[94]   *the liquid joy of life* love; for Shelley, love is a liquid energy (just as electricity, heat, and light were believed to be forms of liquid energy in his day).
[95]   *ambrosial* divine, celestial.

[96]   *On Death's white and winged steed* Revelation 6:8: 'And I looked, and behold a pale horse: and his name that sat on him was Death, and Hell followed with him'.
[97]   *brake* bushes.
[98]   *whitethorn* hawthorn; compare Milton, *Lycidas* 48.

When they struggle to increase,
    Are to us as soft winds be
    To shepherd-boys — the prophecy
    Which begins and ends in thee.   800

IONE Where are the spirits fled?

PANTHEA   Only a sense
Remains of them, like the omnipotence
Of music, when the inspired voice and lute
Languish, ere yet the responses are mute
Which, through the deep and labyrinthine soul,   805
Like echoes through long caverns, wind and roll.

PROMETHEUS How fair these airborne shapes! And yet I feel
Most vain all hope but love — and thou art far,
Asia, who, when my being overflowed,
Wert like a golden chalice to bright wine   810
Which else had sunk into the thirsty dust.
All things are still. Alas, how heavily
This quiet morning weighs upon my heart.
Though I should dream, I could even sleep with grief
If slumber were denied not. I would fain   815
Be what it is my destiny to be,
The saviour and the strength of suffering man,
Or sink into the original gulf of things.
There is no agony and no solace left;
Earth can console, Heaven can torment no more.   820

PANTHEA Hast thou forgotten one who watches thee
The cold dark night, and never sleeps but when
The shadow of thy spirit falls on her?

PROMETHEUS I said all hope was vain but love; thou lovest.

PANTHEA Deeply in truth; but the eastern star looks white,   825
And Asia waits in that far Indian vale,
The scene of her sad exile — rugged once,
And desolate and frozen, like this ravine,
But now invested with fair flowers and herbs,
And haunted by sweet airs and sounds, which flow   830
Among the woods and waters, from the ether[99]
Of her transforming presence, which would fade
If it were mingled not with thine. Farewell!

ACT II, SCENE I

Morning. A lovely vale in the Indian Caucasus. Asia[1] *alone.*

ASIA From all the blasts of Heaven thou hast descended —
Yes, like a spirit, like a thought which makes
Unwonted tears throng to the horny eyes,[2]
And beatings haunt the desolated heart
Which should have learnt repose; thou hast descended   5
Cradled in tempests; thou dost wake, oh Spring,
Oh child of many winds! As suddenly

---

99 *ether* a more refined substance than air, believed in the
nineteenth century to be the medium which transmitted heat,
light and electricity.

ACT II, SCENE I
1 *Asia* daughter of Oceanus and bride of Prometheus.
2 *horny eyes* the eyes have the appearance of horn.

Thou comest as the memory of a dream,
Which now is sad because it hath been sweet;
Like genius, or like joy which riseth up   10
As from the earth, clothing with golden clouds
The desert of our life.
This is the season, this the day, the hour;
At sunrise thou shouldst come, sweet sister mine,
Too long desired, too long delaying, come!   15
How like death-worms the wingless moments crawl!
The point of one white star[3] is quivering still
Deep in the orange light of widening morn
Beyond the purple mountains; through a chasm
Of wind-divided mist the darker lake   20
Reflects it: now it wanes – it gleams again
As the waves fade, and as the burning threads
Of woven cloud unravel in pale air.
'Tis lost! And through yon peaks of cloudlike snow
The roseate sunlight quivers – hear I not   25
The Aeolian music of her[4] sea-green plumes
Winnowing the crimson dawn? (*Panthea enters*)
                              I feel, I see
Those eyes which burn through smiles that fade in tears,
Like stars half-quenched in mists of silver dew.
Beloved and most beautiful, who wearest   30
The shadow of that soul by which I live,
How late thou art! The sphered sun had climbed
The sea, my heart was sick with hope, before
The printless air felt thy belated plumes.
PANTHEA Pardon, great sister; but my wings were faint   35
With the delight of a remembered dream,
As are the noontide plumes of summer winds
Satiate with sweet flowers. I was wont to sleep
Peacefully, and awake refreshed and calm
Before the sacred Titan's fall and thy   40
Unhappy love had made, through use and pity,
Both love and woe familiar to my heart
As they had grown to thine. Erewhile[5] I slept
Under the glaucous[6] caverns of old Ocean
Within dim bowers of green and purple moss,   45
Our young Ione's soft and milky arms
Locked then, as now, behind my dark moist hair,
While my shut eyes and cheek were pressed within
The folded depth of her life-breathing bosom –
But not as now, since I am made the wind   50
Which fails beneath the music that I bear
Of thy most wordless converse; since dissolved
Into the sense with which love talks, my rest
Was troubled and yet sweet, my waking hours
Too full of care and pain.
ASIA   Lift up thine eyes   55

---

[3]   *one white star* Venus, the morning star.
[4]   *her* i.e. Panthea's.

[5]   *Erewhile* before Prometheus's fall.
[6]   *glaucous* pale green.

And let me read thy dream.
PANTHEA   As I have said,
With our sea-sister at his feet I slept.[7]
The mountain mists, condensing at our voice
Under the moon, had spread their snowy flakes,
From the keen ice shielding our linked sleep.   60
Then two dreams came.[8] One I remember not.
But in the other his pale, wound-worn limbs
Fell from Prometheus, and the azure night
Grew radiant with the glory of that form
Which lives unchanged within, and his voice fell   65
Like music which makes giddy the dim brain,
Faint with intoxication of keen joy:
'Sister of her whose footsteps pave the world
With loveliness – more fair than aught but her,
Whose shadow thou art – lift thine eyes on me!'   70
I lifted them: the overpowering light
Of that immortal shape was shadowed o'er
By love, which, from his soft and flowing limbs,
And passion-parted lips, and keen, faint eyes,
Steamed forth like vaporous fire – an atmosphere   75
Which wrapped me in its all-dissolving power
As the warm ether of the morning sun
Wraps ere it drinks some cloud of wandering dew.
I saw not, heard not, moved not, only felt
His presence flow and mingle through my blood   80
Till it became his life, and his grew mine,
And I was thus absorbed until it passed,
And like the vapours when the sun sinks down,
Gathering again in drops upon the pines,
And tremulous as they, in the deep night   85
My being was condensed; and as the rays
Of thought were slowly gathered, I could hear
His voice, whose accents lingered ere they died
Like footsteps of far melody. Thy name
Among the many sounds, alone I heard   90
Of what might be articulate; though still
I listened through the night when sound was none.
Ione wakened then, and said to me,
'Canst thou divine what troubles me tonight?
I always knew what I desired before,   95
Nor ever found delight to wish in vain.
But now I cannot tell thee what I seek,
I know not – something sweet, since it is sweet
Even to desire. It is thy sport, false sister;
Thou hast discovered some enchantment old,   100
Whose spells have stolen my spirit as I slept
And mingled it with thine[9] – for when just now

---

7 *I slept* in Act I, we saw Panthea leaving Prometheus after
seeing his ordeal and sympathizing with it. Now we hear of
her sleep and dreams before departing for Asia.
8 The relation of the dreams is the main action of the scene.

9 *Whose spells . . . thine* both Ione and Panthea have experi-
enced a loss of their sense of separate identity, in favour of a
spiritual co-mingling.

We kissed, I felt within thy parted lips
The sweet air that sustained me, and the warmth
Of the life-blood, for loss of which I faint,   105
Quivered between our intertwining arms.'
I answered not, for the eastern star grew pale,
But fled to thee.

ASIA   Thou speakest, but thy words
Are as the air; I feel them not. Oh lift
Thine eyes, that I may read his written soul!   110

PANTHEA I lift them, though they droop beneath the load
Of that they would express: what canst thou see
But thine own fairest shadow imaged there?

ASIA Thine eyes are like the deep, blue, boundless Heaven
Contracted to two circles underneath   115
Their long, fine lashes; dark, far, measureless,
Orb within orb, and line through line inwoven.

PANTHEA Why lookest thou as if a spirit passed?

ASIA There is a change; beyond their inmost depth
I see a shade, a shape – 'tis he, arrayed   120
In the soft light of his own smiles, which spread
Like radiance from the cloud-surrounded moon.
Prometheus, it is thou – depart not yet!
Say not those smiles that we shall meet again
Within that bright pavilion which their beams   125
Shall build o'er the waste world? The dream is told.
What shape is that between us?[10] Its rude hair
Roughens the wind that lifts it, its regard
Is wild and quick, yet 'tis a thing of air –
For through its grey robe gleams the golden dew   130
Whose stars the noon has quenched not.

DREAM   Follow, follow!

PANTHEA It is mine other dream.

ASIA   It disappears.

PANTHEA It passes now into my mind. Methought
As we sat here, the flower-enfolding buds
Burst[11] on yon lightning-blasted almond tree,   135
When swift from the white Scythian wilderness
A wind swept forth, wrinkling the earth with frost.
I looked, and all the blossoms were blown down;[12]
But on each leaf was stamped – as the blue-bells
Of Hyacinth tell Apollo's written grief[13] –   140
'Oh follow, follow!'

ASIA   As you speak, your words
Fill, pause by pause, my own forgotten sleep
With shapes. Methought among these lawns together
We wandered, underneath the young grey dawn,
And multitudes of dense white fleecy clouds   145
Were wandering in thick flocks along the mountains,

---

[10]   *What shape is that between us?* It is the second dream.
[11]   *Burst* blossomed.
[12]   The almond tree blossoms early, in anticipation of the
spring. Panthea and Asia must not be discouraged by the fall
of the blossoms, but must follow the dream.

[13]   *as the blue-bells . . . grief* After Hyacinthus was killed by
Zephyrus, Apollo changed his blood into a flower and wrote
his lament, 'Ai', on the petals.

Shepherded by the slow, unwilling wind;
And the white dew on the new-bladed grass,
Just piercing the dark earth, hung silently.
And there was more which I remember not,   150
But on the shadows of the morning clouds,
Athwart the purple mountain slope, was written
'Follow, oh follow!' as they vanished by;
And on each herb from which heaven's dew had fallen
The like was stamped, as with a withering fire.   155
A wind arose among the pines; it shook
The clinging music from their boughs, and then
Low, sweet, faint sounds like the farewell of ghosts,
Were heard: 'Oh follow, follow, follow me!'
And then I said, 'Panthea, look on me.'   160
But in the depth of those beloved eyes
Still I saw, 'Follow, follow!'
ECHO   Follow, follow!
PANTHEA The crags, this clear spring morning, mock our voices
As they were spirit-tongued.
ASIA   It is some being
Around the crags. What fine clear sounds, oh list!   165

ECHOES (*unseen*)
    Echoes we; listen!
      We cannot stay:
    As dew-stars glisten
      Then fade away,
        Child of Ocean![14]   170
ASIA Hark! Spirits speak! The liquid responses
Of their aerial tongues yet sound.
PANTHEA   I hear.

ECHOES
    Oh follow, follow,
      As our voice recedeth
    Through the caverns hollow   175
      Where the forest spreadeth; (*more distant*)
    Oh follow, follow,
    Through the caverns hollow;
As the song floats, thou pursue,
Where the wild bee never flew,   180
Through the noontide darkness deep,
By the odour-breathing sleep
Of faint night-flowers, and the waves
At the fountain-lighted caves,
While our music, wild and sweet,   185
Mocks thy gently-falling feet,
        Child of Ocean!
ASIA Shall we pursue the sound? It grows more faint
And distant.

---

[14] *Child of Ocean* Asia, Panthea and Ione are daughters of Ocean.

PANTHEA   List, the strain floats nearer now.

ECHOES

In the world unknown   190

  Sleeps a voice unspoken;

By thy step alone

  Can its rest be broken,

    Child of Ocean!

ASIA How the notes sink upon the ebbing wind!   195

ECHOES

Oh follow, follow,

  Through the caverns hollow;

As the song floats thou pursue,

By the woodland noontide dew,

By the forest, lakes, and fountains,   200

Through the many-folded mountains,

To the rents, and gulfs, and chasms,

Where the Earth reposed from spasms,

On the day when he and thou

Parted, to commingle now,   205

  Child of Ocean!

ASIA Come, sweet Panthea, link thy hand in mine,

And follow ere the voices fade away.

ACT II, SCENE II

A forest, intermingled with rocks and caverns. Asia and Panthea pass into it. Two young fauns[1] *are sitting on a rock, listening.*

SEMICHORUS 1 OF SPIRITS

The path through which that lovely twain[2]

  Have passed, by cedar, pine, and yew,

  And each dark tree that ever grew,

  Is curtained out from Heaven's wide blue;

Nor sun, nor moon, nor wind, nor rain,   5

    Can pierce its interwoven bowers;

  Nor aught, save when some cloud of dew,

Drifted along the earth-creeping breeze

Between the trunks of the hoar trees,

    Hangs each a pearl in the pale flowers[3]   10

  Of the green laurel, blown anew,

And bends, and then fades silently,

One frail and fair anemone;

Or when some star of many a one

That climbs and wanders through steep night,   15

Has found the cleft through which alone

Beams fall from high those depths upon,

Ere it is borne away, away,

ACT II, SCENE II

[1] *fauns* minor Roman deities, usually depicted as men with the ears, horns, tail and feet of goats.

[2] *that lovely twain* Asia and Panthea.

[3] *Hangs each a pearl in the pale flowers* hangs a pearl in each pale flower.

By the swift Heavens that cannot stay —
It scatters drops of golden light,   20
Like lines of rain that ne'er unite;
And the gloom divine is all around,
And underneath is the mossy ground.

SEMICHORUS II
There the voluptuous nightingales
 Are awake through all the broad noonday.   25
When one with bliss or sadness fails
  (And through the windless ivy-boughs,
 Sick with sweet love, droops dying away
On its mate's music-panting bosom),
Another from the swinging blossom,   30
  Watching to catch the languid close
 Of the last strain, then lifts on high
 The wings of the weak melody,
Till some new strain of feeling bear
 The song, and all the woods are mute;   35
When there is heard through the dim air
The rush of wings, and rising there
 Like many a lake-surrounded flute,
Sounds overflow the listener's brain
So sweet that joy is almost pain.   40

SEMICHORUS I
There those enchanted eddies play
 Of echoes, music-tongued, which draw,
 By Demogorgon's mighty law,
 With melting rapture or deep awe,
All spirits on that secret way,   45
 As inland boats are driven to ocean
Down streams made strong with mountain-thaw;
  And first there comes a gentle sound
  To those in talk or slumber bound,
 And wakes the destined; soft emotion   50
Attracts, impels them. Those who saw
 Say from the breathing earth behind
 There steams a plume-uplifting wind
Which drives them on their path, while they
 Believe their own swift wings and feet   55
The sweet desires within obey;
And so they float upon their way
Until, still sweet, but loud and strong,
The storm of sound is driven along,
 Sucked up and hurrying — as they fleet   60
 Behind, its gathering billows meet
And to the fatal mountain bear[4]
Like clouds amid the yielding air.

---

[4] The 'destined' spirits (Asia and Panthea) are borne by the
gathering 'storm of sound' to the 'fatal' (i.e. fated, destined)
mountain of Demogorgon.

FIRST FAUN Canst thou imagine where those spirits live
Which make such delicate music in the woods?   65
We haunt within the least frequented caves
And closest coverts, and we know these wilds,
Yet never meet them, though we hear them oft:
Where may they hide themselves?
SECOND FAUN   'Tis hard to tell.
I have heard those more skilled in spirits say,   70
The bubbles, which the enchantment of the sun
Sucks from the pale faint water-flowers that pave
The oozy bottom of clear lakes and pools,
Are the pavilions where such dwell and float
Under the green and golden atmosphere   75
Which noontide kindles through the woven leaves;
And when these burst, and the thin fiery air,
The which they breathed within those lucent[5] domes,
Ascends to flow like meteors through the night,
They ride on it, and rein their headlong speed,   80
And bow their burning crests, and glide in fire
Under the waters of the earth again.[6]
FIRST FAUN If such live thus, have others other lives,
Under pink blossoms or within the bells
Of meadow flowers, or folded violets deep,   85
Or on their dying odours, when they die,
Or in the sunlight of the sphered dew?
SECOND FAUN Aye, many more which we may well divine.
But should we stay to speak, noontide would come,
And thwart[7] Silenus find his goats undrawn,[8]   90
And grudge to sing those wise and lovely songs
Of fate, and chance, and God, and Chaos old,
And love, and the chained Titan's woeful doom,
And how he shall be loosed, and make the earth
One brotherhood: delightful strains which cheer   95
Our solitary twilights, and which charm
To silence the unenvying nightingales.

ACT II, SCENE III

A pinnacle of rock among mountains. Asia and Panthea.

PANTHEA Hither the sound has borne us – to the realm
Of Demogorgon, and the mighty portal,[1]
Like a volcano's meteor-breathing[2] chasm,
Whence the oracular vapour[3] is hurled up
Which lonely men drink wandering in their youth,   5

---

[5] *lucent* shining.
[6] *I have heard those . . . again* in Shelley's day it was believed
that hydrogen was released by pond-plants in hot weather,
and that it ascended to the upper atmosphere, where it
became charged with electricity, ignited, and appeared as
meteors or falling stars. ll.81–2 describe the return of atmos-
pheric electricity to the earth.
[7] *thwart* obstinate, difficult.
[8] *undrawn* unmilked; Silenus was a demigod and attendant
of Bacchus.

ACT II, SCENE III
[1] *portal* gateway.
[2] *meteor-breathing* meteors were believed to be exhalations
from the earth.
[3] *the oracular vapour* anyone inhaling the vapour of Demogor-
gon's volcano-like residence is likely to be inspired with the
power of prophecy.

And call truth, virtue, love, genius, or joy;
That maddening wine of life, whose dregs they drain
To deep intoxication, and uplift,
Like maenads[4] who cry loud, 'Evoe! Evoe!' –
The voice which is contagion to the world.   10

ASIA Fit throne for such a Power – magnificent!
How glorious art thou, Earth! And if thou be
The shadow of some spirit lovelier still,[5]
Though evil stain its work, and it should be
Like its creation, weak yet beautiful,   15
I could fall down and worship that and thee.
Even now my heart adoreth – wonderful!
Look, sister, ere the vapour dim thy brain:
Beneath is a wide plain of billowy mist,
As a lake, paving in the morning sky,   20
With azure waves which burst in silver light,
Some Indian vale. Behold it, rolling on
Under the curdling winds, and islanding
The peak whereon we stand; midway, around,
Encinctured[6] by the dark and blooming forests,   25
Dim twilight-lawns, and stream-illumed caves,
And wind-enchanted shapes of wandering mist;
And far on high the keen sky-cleaving mountains
From icy spires of sunlike radiance fling
The dawn, as lifted Ocean's dazzling spray,   30
From some Atlantic islet scattered up,
Spangles the wind with lamp-like water-drops.
The vale is girdled with their walls; a howl
Of cataracts from their thaw-cloven ravines
Satiates the listening wind, continuous, vast,   35
Awful as silence. Hark, the rushing snow!
The sun-awakened avalanche! whose mass,
Thrice sifted by the storm, had gathered there
Flake after flake, in Heaven-defying minds
As thought by thought is piled, till some great truth   40
Is loosened, and the nations echo round,
Shaken to their roots, as do the mountains now.

PANTHEA Look how the gusty sea of mist is breaking
In crimson foam, even at our feet! It rises
As Ocean at the enchantment of the moon   45
Round foodless men wrecked on some oozy isle.

ASIA The fragments of the cloud are scattered up;
The wind that lifts them disentwines my hair;
Its billows now sweep o'er mine eyes; my brain
Grows dizzy; seest those shapes within the mist?   50

PANTHEA A countenance with beckoning smiles: there burns
An azure fire within its golden locks!
Another and another – hark, they speak!

---

4 *maenads* drunken female worshippers of Bacchus who slaughtered everything in their path.
5 *And if thou be . . . still* a similar thought occurs in *Paradise Lost* v 574–6: 'though what if earth / Be but the shadow of heaven, and things therein / Each to other like, more than on earth is thought?'
6 *Encinctured* surrounded.

SONG OF SPIRITS

To the deep, to the deep,
    Down, down!   55
Through the shade of sleep,
Through the cloudy strife
Of Death and of Life;
Through the veil and the bar[7]
Of things which seem and are,   60
Even to the steps of the remotest throne,
    Down, down!

While the sound whirls around,
    Down, down!
As the fawn draws the hound,   65
As the lightning the vapour,
As a weak moth the taper;
Death, despair; love, sorrow;
Time both; today, tomorrow;
As steel obeys the spirit of the stone,[8]   70
    Down, down!

Through the grey, void abysm,
    Down, down!
Where the air is no prism,[9]
And the moon and stars are not,   75
And the cavern-crags wear not
The radiance of Heaven,
Nor the gloom to Earth given;
Where there is One pervading, One alone,
    Down, down!   80

In the depth of the deep,
    Down, down!
Like veiled lightning asleep,
Like that spark nursed in embers,
The last look Love remembers,   85
Like a diamond which shines
On the dark wealth of mines,[10]
A spell is treasured but for thee alone.
    Down, down!

We have bound thee, we guide thee   90
    Down, down![11]
With the bright form beside thee;
Resist not the weakness;
Such strength is in meekness,

---

[7] *bar* barrier. Asia and Panthea are passing through the barrier dividing earthly appearance from the higher, transcendental reality.
[8] *the stone* i.e. a magnet.
[9] *Where the air is no prism* Shelley believed that white light in its purest form was that of heaven, and that its breaking down into different colours was characteristic of the fallen world.

[10] *Like a diamond . . . mines* eighteenth-century scientists believed that diamonds glowed in the dark.
[11] *We have bound thee . . . down* Asia and Panthea have been bound, and are being led by the spirits. Asia has to submit so that Demogorgon (the Eternal) can permit the destined downfall of Jupiter.

That the Eternal, the Immortal,   95
Must unloose through life's portal
The snake-like Doom coiled underneath his throne
    By that alone.

ACT II, SCENE IV

The Cave of Demogorgon. Asia and Panthea.

PANTHEA What veiled form sits on that ebon throne?
ASIA The veil has fallen.
PANTHEA   I see a mighty darkness
Filling the seat of power, and rays of gloom
Dart round, as light from the meridian sun,[1]
Ungazed upon and shapeless; neither limb,   5
Nor form, nor outline[2] – yet we feel it is
A living spirit.
DEMOGORGON   Ask what thou wouldst know.
ASIA What canst thou tell?
DEMOGORGON   All things thou dar'st demand.
ASIA Who made the living world?
DEMOGORGON   God.
ASIA   Who made all
That it contains – thought, passion, reason, will,   10
Imagination?
DEMOGORGON   God. Almighty God.
ASIA Who made that sense which, when the winds of spring
In rarest visitation, or the voice
Of one beloved heard in youth alone,
Fills the faint eyes with falling tears which dim   15
The radiant looks of unbewailing flowers,
And leaves this peopled earth a solitude
When it returns no more?
DEMOGORGON   Merciful God.
ASIA And who made terror, madness, crime, remorse,
Which from the links of the great chain of things,   20
To every thought within the mind of man
Sway and drag heavily, and each one reels
Under the load towards the pit of death;[3]
Abandoned hope, and love that turns to hate;
And self-contempt, bitterer to drink than blood;   25
Pain, whose unheeded and familiar speech
Is howling, and keen shrieks, day after day;
And Hell, or the sharp fear of Hell?
DEMOGORGON   He reigns.[4]

ACT II, SCENE IV
[1] *the meridian sun* the noonday sun.
[2] *neither limb . . . outline* cf. Milton's description of Death, *Paradise Lost* ii 668–9 (p. 5).
[3] *Which from the links . . . death* the great chain of being was the doctrine by which England justified its monarchy and its rigidly hierarchical social system for centuries. The image may, as Peter Butter suggests, have been inspired by the sight of convicts chained together in Rome, which Shelley described to Peacock on 6 April 1819: 'In the square of St Peter's there are about 300 fettered criminals at work, hoeing out the weeds that grow between the stones of the pavement. Their legs are heavily ironed, and some are chained two by two. They sit in long rows hoeing out the weeds. . . . Near them sit or saunter groups of soldiers armed with loaded muskets' (Jones ii 93).
[4] *He reigns* a statement that fails to identify the force that has taken over a world created by a benevolent deity. It could be Jupiter, or 'Almighty God', or some other force entirely.

ASIA Utter his name. A world pining in pain
Asks but his name; curses shall drag him down.   30
DEMOGORGON He reigns.
ASIA   I feel, I know it – who?
DEMOGORGON   He reigns.
ASIA Who reigns? There was the Heaven and Earth[5] at first,
And Light and Love; then Saturn,[6] from whose throne
Time fell, an envious shadow; such the state
Of the earth's primal spirits beneath his sway,   35
As the calm joy of flowers and living leaves
Before the wind or sun has withered them,
And semivital worms; but he[7] refused
The birthright of their being – knowledge, power,
The skill which wields the elements, the thought   40
Which pierces this dim universe like light,
Self-empire and the majesty of love –
For thirst of which they fainted. Then Prometheus
Gave wisdom, which is strength, to Jupiter,
And with this law alone, 'Let man be free',   45
Clothed him with the dominion of wide Heaven.
To know nor faith, nor love, nor law; to be
Omnipotent but friendless is to reign –
And Jove now reigned; for on the race of man
First famine, and then toil, and then disease,   50
Strife, wounds, and ghastly death unseen before,
Fell; and the unseasonable seasons[8] drove,
With alternating shafts of frost and fire,
Their shelterless, pale tribes to mountain caves;
And in their desert[9] hearts fierce wants[10] he sent,   55
And mad disquietudes, and shadows idle
Of unreal good, which levied[11] mutual war,
So ruining the lair wherein they raged.
Prometheus saw, and waked the legioned hopes
Which sleep within folded Elysian[12] flowers,   60
Nepenthe, moly, amaranth,[13] fadeless blooms,
That they might hide with thin and rainbow wings
The shape of Death; and Love he sent to bind
The disunited tendrils of that vine
Which bears the wine of life, the human heart;   65
And he tamed fire which, like some beast of chase
Most terrible, but lovely, played beneath
The frown of man; and tortured to his will
Iron and gold, the slaves and signs of power,
And gems and poisons, and all subtlest forms   70
Hidden beneath the mountains and the waves.

---

[5] *Heaven and Earth* Ouranos and Gaia, parents of Saturn and the other Titans.
[6] *Saturn* (or Kronos, time) the origin of evil.
[7] *he* Saturn.
[8] *unseasonable seasons* in the golden age perpetual spring reigned.
[9] *desert* abandoned, desolate.

[10] *fierce wants* desperate needs.
[11] *levied* undertook.
[12] *Elysian* heavenly; from the Elysian fields, where Greek heroes were believed to spend an afterlife in revelry.
[13] Nepenthe is a grief-banishing drug; moly is the magic herb given by Hermes to Odysseus to counteract the poison of Circe; amaranth is an unfading flower.

He gave man speech, and speech created thought,
Which is the measure of the universe;
And Science struck the thrones of Earth and Heaven,
Which shook but fell not; and the harmonious mind   75
Poured itself forth in all-prophetic song,
And music lifted up the listening spirit
Until it walked, exempt from mortal care,
Godlike, o'er the clear billows of sweet sound;
And human hands first mimicked and then mocked,[14]   80
With moulded limbs more lovely than its own,
The human form, till marble grew divine,
And mothers, gazing, drank the love men see
Reflected in their race,[15] behold, and perish.
He told the hidden power of herbs and springs,   85
And Disease drank and slept. Death grew like sleep.
He taught the implicated[16] orbits woven
Of the wide-wandering stars,[17] and how the sun
Changes his lair,[18] and by what secret spell
The pale moon is transformed, when her broad eye   90
Gazes not on the interlunar[19] sea.
He taught to rule, as life directs the limbs,
The tempest-winged chariots of the Ocean,[20]
And the Celt knew the Indian. Cities then
Were built, and through their snow-like columns flowed   95
The warm winds, and the azure ether shone,
And the blue sea and shadowy hills were seen.
Such the alleviations of his state
Prometheus gave to man, for which he hangs
Withering in destined pain; but who rains down   100
Evil, the immedicable plague, which, while
Man looks on his creation like a God
And sees that it is glorious, drives him on,
The wreck of his own will, the scorn of earth,
The outcast, the abandoned, the alone?   105
Not Jove; while yet his frown shook Heaven – aye, when
His adversary from adamantine chains
Cursed him – he trembled like a slave. Declare
Who is his master? Is he too a slave?
DEMOGORGON All spirits are enslaved which serve things evil;   110
Thou knowest if Jupiter be such or no.
ASIA Whom calledst thou God?
DEMOGORGON   I spoke but as ye speak,
For Jove is the supreme of living things.
ASIA Who is the master of the slave?
DEMOGORGON   If the abysm
Could vomit forth its secrets – but a voice   115

---

[14] *mimicked . . . mocked* imitated . . . created forms more beautiful than the merely natural (i.e. idealized).
[15] *And mothers . . . race* pregnant women, gazing at the statues, gave birth to children like them, whose features reflect the passion with which the statues were made. Yeats reworks this idea in his poem, *The Statues*.

[16] *implicated* intertwined.
[17] *stars* planets or comets.
[18] *lair* position in the Zodiac.
[19] *interlunar* between the old and the new moon.
[20] *chariots of the Ocean* boats.

Is wanting, the deep truth is imageless;[21]
For what would it avail to bid thee gaze
On the revolving world? What to bid speak
Fate, Time, Occasion, Chance, and Change? To these
All things are subject but eternal Love.   120
ASIA So much I asked before, and my heart gave
The response thou hast given; and of such truths
Each to itself must be the oracle.
One more demand; and do thou answer me
As my own soul would answer, did it know   125
That which I ask. Prometheus shall arise
Henceforth the Sun of this rejoicing world:
When shall the destined hour arrive?
DEMOGORGON   Behold![22]
ASIA The rocks are cloven, and through the purple night
I see cars[23] drawn by rainbow-winged steeds   130
Which trample the dim winds; in each there stands
A wild-eyed charioteer urging their flight.
Some look behind, as fiends pursued them there,
And yet I see no shapes but the keen stars;
Others, with burning eyes, lean forth, and drink   135
With eager lips the wind of their own speed,
As if the thing they loved fled on before,
And now, even now, they clasped it. Their bright locks
Stream like a comet's flashing hair – they all
Sweep onward.
DEMOGORGON   These are the immortal Hours,   140
Of whom thou didst demand. One waits for thee.
ASIA A spirit with a dreadful countenance
Checks its dark chariot by the craggy gulf.
Unlike thy brethren, ghastly charioteer,
What art thou? Whither wouldst thou bear me? Speak!   145
SPIRIT I am the shadow of a destiny
More dread than is my aspect; ere yon planet
Has set, the Darkness which ascends with me
Shall wrap in lasting night Heaven's kingless throne.
ASIA What meanest thou?
PANTHEA   The terrible shadow[24] floats   150
Up from its throne, as may the lurid smoke
Of earthquake-ruined cities o'er the sea.
Lo! it ascends the car; the coursers fly
Terrified. Watch its path among the stars
Blackening the night!
ASIA   Thus I am answered; strange!   155
PANTHEA See, near the verge,[25] another chariot stays;
An ivory shell inlaid with crimson fire
Which comes and goes within its sculptured rim
Of delicate strange tracery; the young spirit

---

[21] *the deep truth is imageless* Neville Rogers offers a useful Platonic reading; see *Shelley at Work* (2nd edn, Oxford, 1967), pp. 160–1.
[22] *Behold* i.e. the destined hour *has* arrived.
[23] *cars* chariots.
[24] *The terrible shadow* Demogorgon.
[25] *verge* horizon.

That guides it has the dove-like eyes of hope;   160
How its soft smiles attract the soul! as light
Lures winged insects through the lampless air.

SPIRIT
My coursers are fed with the lightning,
    They drink of the whirlwind's stream,
And when the red morning is bright'ning   165
    They bathe in the fresh sunbeam;
    They have strength for their swiftness, I deem –
Then ascend with me, Daughter of Ocean.

I desire – and their speed makes night kindle;
    I fear – they outstrip the typhoon;   170
Ere the cloud piled on Atlas can dwindle
    We encircle the earth and the moon;
    We shall rest from long labours ere noon –
Then ascend with me, Daughter of Ocean.

ACT II, SCENE V

The car pauses within a cloud on the top of a snowy mountain. Asia, Panthea, and the Spirit of the Hour.

SPIRIT
On the brink of the night and the morning
    My coursers are wont to respire;[1]
But the Earth has just whispered a warning
    That their flight must be swifter than fire –
    They shall drink the hot speed of desire!   5

ASIA Thou breathest on their nostrils, but my breath
Would give them swifter speed.
SPIRIT   Alas, it could not.
PANTHEA Oh Spirit, pause and tell whence is the light
Which fills the cloud? The sun is yet unrisen.
SPIRIT The sun will rise not until noon. Apollo   10
Is held in Heaven by wonder; and the light
Which fills this vapour, as the aerial hue
Of fountain-gazing roses fills the water,
Flows from thy mighty sister.[2]
PANTHEA   Yes, I feel –
ASIA What is it with thee, sister? Thou art pale.   15
PANTHEA How thou art changed! I dare not look on thee;
I feel, but see thee not. I scarce endure
The radiance of thy beauty. Some good change
Is working in the elements, which suffer
Thy presence thus unveiled. The Nereids[3] tell   20
That on the day when the clear hyaline[4]
Was cloven at thine uprise, and thou didst stand

ACT II, SCENE V
[1] *respire* rest.
[2] *the light . . . sister* Asia emanates light, as a revelation of
what she essentially is.

[3] *Nereids* sea-nymphs, daughters of Nereus.
[4] *hyaline* glassy, transparent sea.

Within a veined shell,[5] which floated on
Over the calm floor of the crystal sea,
Among the Aegean isles, and by the shores   25
Which bear thy name – love, like the atmosphere
Of the sun's fire filling the living world,
Burst from thee, and illumined Earth and Heaven
And the deep Ocean and the sunless caves
And all that dwells within them; till grief cast   30
Eclipse upon the soul from which it came:
Such art thou now; nor is it I alone,
Thy sister, thy companion, thine own chosen one,
But the whole world which seeks thy sympathy.
Hearest thou not sounds i' the air which speak the love   35
Of all articulate beings? Feelest thou not
The inanimate winds enamoured of thee? List!
(*Music*)
ASIA Thy words are sweeter than aught else but his
Whose echoes they are – yet all love is sweet,
Given or returned. Common as light is love,   40
And its familiar voice wearies not ever.
Like the wide Heaven, the all-sustaining air,
It makes the reptile equal to the God:
They who inspire it most are fortunate,
As I am now; but those who feel it most   45
Are happier still, after long sufferings,
As I shall soon become.
PANTHEA   List! Spirits speak.
VOICE (*in the air, singing*)[6]
    Life of Life! thy lips enkindle
        With their love the breath between them;
    And thy smiles before they dwindle   50
        Make the cold air fire; then screen them
    In those looks, where whoso gazes
    Faints, entangled in their mazes.

    Child of Light! thy limbs are burning
        Through the vest which seems to hide them,   55
    As the radiant lines of morning
        Through the clouds ere they divide them;
    And this atmosphere divinest
    Shrouds thee wheresoe'er thou shinest.

    Fair are others; none beholds thee,   60
        But thy voice sounds low and tender
    Like the fairest, for it folds thee
        From the sight, that liquid splendour,
    And all feel, yet see thee never,
    As I feel now, lost forever!   65

---

5   *thou didst stand . . . shell* Asia is identified with Aphrodite,   6   This is the voice of Prometheus.
the goddess of love, who came to land on the island of Cythera
floating on a shell.

Lamp of Earth! where'er thou movest
    Its dim shapes are clad with brightness,
And the souls of whom thou lovest
    Walk upon the winds with lightness,
Till they fail, as I am failing,   70
Dizzy, lost, yet unbewailing!

ASIA
My soul is an enchanted boat,
    Which, like a sleeping swan, doth float
Upon the silver waves of thy sweet singing;
    And thine doth like an angel sit   75
    Beside the helm conducting it,
Whilst all the winds with melody are ringing.
    It seems to float ever, forever,
    Upon that many-winding river,
    Between mountains, woods, abysses,   80
    A paradise of wildernesses!
Till, like one in slumber bound,
Borne to the ocean, I float down, around,
Into a sea profound of ever-spreading sound.

    Meanwhile thy spirit lifts its pinions   85
    In music's most serene dominions,
Catching the winds that fan that happy Heaven.
    And we sail on, away, afar,
    Without a course, without a star,
But by the instinct of sweet music driven,   90
    Till through Elysian garden islets
    By thee, most beautiful of pilots,
    Where never mortal pinnace glided,
    The boat of my desire is guided:
Realms where the air we breathe is love,   95
Which in the winds and on the waves doth move,
Harmonizing this earth with what we feel above.

    We have passed Age's icy caves,
    And Manhood's dark and tossing waves,
And Youth's smooth ocean, smiling to betray: 100
    Beyond the glassy gulfs we flee
    Of shadow-peopled Infancy,
Through death and birth to a diviner day[7] –
    A paradise of vaulted bowers
    Lit by downward-gazing flowers,   105
    And watery paths that wind between
    Wildernesses calm and green,
Peopled by shapes too bright to see,
And rest, having beheld – somewhat like thee,
Which walk upon the sea and chaunt melodiously![8]   110

---

[7] *Beyond the glassy gulfs . . . day* Asia and Prometheus travel into the world of pre-existence, described by Wordsworth in his *Ode* (pp. 375–80).
[8] *Peopled by shapes . . . melodiously* the inhabitants of the realm of pre-existence are too bright to see at first, but now that Asia and Prometheus have got used to it, Asia sees that Prometheus is the same kind of being as the others, and that they both belong there.

ACT III, SCENE I

Heaven. Jupiter on his throne; Thetis and the other deities assembled.

JUPITER Ye congregated powers of Heaven, who share
The glory and the strength of him ye serve,
Rejoice! Henceforth I am omnipotent.
All else had been subdued to me; alone
The soul of man, like unextinguished fire,   5
Yet burns towards Heaven with fierce reproach, and doubt,
And lamentation, and reluctant prayer –
Hurling up insurrection, which might make
Our antique empire insecure, though built
On eldest faith, and Hell's coeval,[1] fear.   10
And though my curses through the pendulous air,[2]
Like snow on herbless peaks, fall flake by flake
And cling to it;[3] though under my wrath's night
It climb the crags of life, step after step,
Which wound it, as ice wounds unsandalled feet,   15
It yet remains supreme o'er misery,
Aspiring, unrepressed, yet soon to fall.
Even now have I begotten a strange wonder,
That fatal child, the terror of the earth,[4]
Who waits but till the destined Hour arrive,   20
Bearing from Demogorgon's vacant throne
The dreadful might of ever-living limbs
Which clothed that awful spirit unbeheld,
To redescend and trample out the spark.
    Pour forth Heaven's wine, Idaean Ganymede,[5]   25
And let it fill the daedal[6] cups like fire;
And from the flower-inwoven soil divine
Ye all-triumphant harmonies arise,
As dew from earth under the twilight stars.
Drink! Be the nectar circling through your veins   30
The soul of joy, ye ever-living Gods,
Till exultation burst in one wide voice
Like music from Elysian winds!
                     And thou
Ascend beside me, veiled in the light
Of the desire which makes thee one with me,   35
Thetis,[7] bright image of eternity!
When thou didst cry, 'Insufferable might!
God! Spare me! I sustain not the quick flames,
The penetrating presence;[8] all my being
(Like him whom the Numidian seps did thaw   40
Into a dew with poison)[9] is dissolved,

ACT III, SCENE I
[1] *coeval* contemporary. Fear and faith allow Jupiter to retain power.
[2] *pendulous air* the air hangs; cf. *King Lear* III iv 69.
[3] *it* i.e. the soul of man, as in line 16.
[4] *That fatal child, the terror of the earth* Jupiter's rape of Thetis produced Demogorgon.
[5] A shepherd-boy from Mt Ida, Ganymede was abducted to serve as Zeus's cup-bearer.
[6] *daedal* beautifully crafted.
[7] Thetis was the daughter of Nereus, a sea-god.
[8] Thetis was consumed by fire when tricked into lying with Jupiter.
[9] Sabellus dissolved when bitten by a seps (legendary snake) in the Numidian desert.

Sinking through its foundations' – even then
Two mighty spirits, mingling, made a third
Mightier than either, which unbodied now
Between us floats, felt although unbeheld,   45
Waiting the incarnation which ascends
(Hear ye the thunder of the fiery wheels
Griding[10] the winds?) from Demogorgon's throne.
Victory! Victory! Feel'st thou not, oh World,
The earthquake of his chariot thundering up   50
Olympus?

(The car of the Hour arrives. Demogorgon descends, and moves towards the throne of Jupiter.)
        Awful shape, what art thou? Speak!
DEMOGORGON Eternity. Demand no direr name.
Descend, and follow me down the abyss.
I am thy child, as thou wert Saturn's child,
Mightier than thee: and we must dwell together   55
Henceforth in darkness. Lift thy lightnings not.
The tyranny of Heaven none may retain,
Or reassume, or hold, succeeding thee;
Yet if thou wilt (as 'tis the destiny
Of trodden worms to writhe till they are dead),   60
Put forth thy might.
JUPITER   Detested prodigy!
Even thus beneath the deep Titanian prisons[11]
I trample thee! Thou lingerest?
               Mercy! Mercy!
No pity, no release, no respite! Oh,
That thou wouldst make mine enemy my judge,   65
Even where he hangs, seared by my long revenge,
On Caucasus! He would not doom me thus.
Gentle, and just, and dreadless, is he not
The monarch of the world? What then art thou?
No refuge! No appeal!
          Sink with me then;   70
We two will sink on the wide waves of ruin,
Even as a vulture and a snake outspent
Drop, twisted in inextricable fight,
Into a shoreless sea. Let Hell unlock
Its mounded oceans of tempestuous fire,   75
And whelm[12] on them into the bottomless void
The desolated world, and thee, and me,
The conqueror and the conquered, and the wreck
Of that for which they combated.
              Ai! Ai!
The elements obey me not. I sink   80
Dizzily down – ever, forever, down –
And, like a cloud, mine enemy above
Darkens my fall with victory! Ai! Ai!

---

[10] *Griding* cutting through.
[11] *the deep Titanian prisons* after their overthrow by Jupiter,
the Titans were imprisoned in Tartarus, far below the earth.
[12] *whelm* throw violently.

ACT III, SCENE II

The mouth of a great river in the island Atlantis.[1] *Ocean*[2] *is discovered reclining near the shore; Apollo stands beside him.*

OCEAN He fell, thou sayest, beneath his conqueror's frown?

APOLLO Aye, when the strife was ended which made dim
The orb I rule,[3] and shook the solid stars.[4]
The terrors of his eye illumined Heaven
With sanguine light through the thick ragged skirts   5
Of the victorious Darkness, as he fell,
Like the last glare of day's red agony,
Which from a rent among the fiery clouds
Burns far along the tempest-wrinkled deep.

OCEAN He sunk to the abyss? To the dark void?   10

APOLLO An eagle so,[5] caught in some bursting cloud
On Caucasus, his thunder-baffled wings
Entangled in the whirlwind, and his eyes,
Which gazed on the undazzling sun, now blinded
By the white lightning, while the ponderous hail   15
Beats on his struggling form, which sinks at length
Prone, and the aerial ice clings over it.

OCEAN Henceforth the fields of Heaven-reflecting sea
Which are my realm, will heave, unstained with blood,
Beneath the uplifting winds, like plains of corn   20
Swayed by the summer air; my streams will flow
Round many-peopled continents, and round
Fortunate isles; and from their glassy thrones
Blue Proteus[6] and his humid nymphs shall mark
The shadow of fair ships – as mortals see   25
The floating bark of the light-laden moon[7]
With that white star,[8] its sightless pilot's crest,
Borne down the rapid sunset's ebbing sea –
Tracking their path no more by blood and groans,
And desolation, and the mingled voice   30
Of slavery and command, but by the light
Of wave-reflected flowers, and floating odours,
And music soft, and mild, free, gentle voices,
That sweetest music, such as spirits love.

APOLLO And I shall gaze not on the deeds which make   35
My mind obscure with sorrow, as eclipse
Darkens the sphere I guide; but list, I hear
The small, clear, silver lute of the young spirit
That sits in the morning star.[9]

OCEAN   Thou must away?
Thy steeds will pause at even, till when farewell.   40
The loud deep calls me home even now, to feed it

ACT III, SCENE II

[1] *Atlantis* legendary sunken city west of the straits of Gibraltar, believed by Plato to be the home of an ideal commonwealth.
[2] Ocean was god of the sea.
[3] *The orb I rule* Apollo was the Greek god of the sun.
[4] *solid stars* fixed stars.

[5] *An eagle so* i.e. 'Yes, he sank like an eagle . . .'
[6] *Blue Proteus* elusive sea-god, able to change his shape at will.
[7] *the light-laden moon* the new moon (full of light).
[8] *that white star* Venus, the evening star.
[9] *I hear . . . star* it is time for the sun to rise. All the events thus far have taken place during a single dawn.

With azure calm out of the emerald urns
Which stand forever full beside my throne.
Behold the Nereids under the green sea –
Their wavering limbs borne on the wind-like streams,   45
Their white arms lifted o'er their streaming hair
With garlands pied and starry sea-flower crowns –
Hastening to grace their mighty sister's joy. (*A sound of waves is heard*)
It is the unpastured[10] sea hungering for calm.
Peace, monster; I come now. Farewell.
APOLLO   Farewell.   50

ACT III, SCENE III

Caucasus. Prometheus, Hercules, Ione, the Earth, Spirits, Asia, and Panthea, borne in the car with the Spirit of the Hour. Hercules unbinds Prometheus, who descends.[1]

HERCULES Most glorious among spirits, thus doth strength
To wisdom, courage, and long-suffering love,
And thee, who art the form they animate,
Minister like a slave.
PROMETHEUS   Thy gentle words
Are sweeter even than freedom long desired   5
And long delayed.
                    Asia, thou light of life,
Shadow of beauty unbeheld; and ye,
Fair sister nymphs, who made long years of pain
Sweet to remember, through your love and care –
Henceforth we will not part. There is a cave,   10
All overgrown with trailing odorous[2] plants
Which curtain out the day with leaves and flowers,
And paved with veined emerald; and a fountain
Leaps in the midst with an awakening sound.
From its curved roof the mountain's frozen tears,   15
Like snow, or silver, or long diamond spires,
Hang downward, raining forth a doubtful light;
And there is heard the ever-moving air
Whispering without from tree to tree, and birds
And bees; and all around are mossy seats,   20
And the rough walls are clothed with long soft grass –
A simple dwelling which shall be our own,
Where we will sit and talk of time and change
As the world ebbs and flows, ourselves unchanged.
What can hide man from mutability?   25
And if ye sigh, then I will smile; and thou,
Ione, shall chant fragments of sea-music
Until I weep, when ye shall smile away
The tears she brought, which yet were sweet to shed.
We will entangle buds and flowers and beams   30
Which twinkle on the fountain's brim, and make

---

[10] *unpastured* unfed.

ACT III, SCENE III
[1] According to legend, Hercules killed the eagle torturing
Prometheus and freed him after Prometheus had made his
peace with Jupiter.
[2] *odorous* fragrant.

Strange combinations out of common things,
Like human babes in their brief innocence;
And we will search, with looks and words of love,
For hidden thoughts, each lovelier than the last,   35
Our unexhausted spirits, and, like lutes
Touched by the skill of the enamoured wind,
Weave harmonies divine, yet ever new,
From difference sweet where discord cannot be.
And hither come – sped on the charmed winds   40
Which meet from all the points of Heaven, as bees
From every flower aerial Enna[3] feeds
At their known island-homes in Himera[4] –
The echoes of the human world, which tell
Of the low voice of love, almost unheard,   45
And dove-eyed pity's murmured pain, and music,
Itself the echo of the heart, and all
That tempers or improves man's life, now free.
And lovely apparitions, dim at first,
Then radiant – as the mind, arising bright   50
From the embrace of beauty (whence the forms
Of which these are the phantoms) casts on them
The gathered rays which are reality –
Shall visit us, the progeny immortal
Of Painting, Sculpture, and rapt Poesy,   55
And arts, though unimagined, yet to be.
The wandering voices and the shadows these
Of all that man becomes, the mediators[5]
Of that best worship, Love, by him and us
Given and returned; swift shapes and sounds which grow   60
More fair and soft as man grows wise and kind,
And veil by veil, evil and error fall:[6]
Such virtue has the cave and place around. (*Turning to the Spirit of the Hour*)
For thee, fair Spirit, one toil remains. Ione,
Give her that curved shell which Proteus old   65
Made Asia's nuptial boon, breathing within it
A voice to be accomplished, and which thou
Didst hide in grass under the hollow rock.
IONE Thou most desired Hour, more loved and lovely
Than all thy sisters, this is the mystic shell;   70
See the pale azure fading into silver,
Lining it with a soft yet glowing light –
Looks it not like lulled music sleeping there?
SPIRIT It seems in truth the fairest shell of Ocean;
Its sound must be at once both sweet and strange.   75
PROMETHEUS Go, borne over the cities of mankind
On whirlwind-footed coursers – once again
Outspeed the sun around the orbed world;
And as thy chariot cleaves the kindling air,

---

3   *Enna* plain in the middle of Sicily often regarded as an earthly paradise.
4   *Himera* river which nearly bisects Sicily.
5   *mediators* man's works of art are the mediators of love between him and Prometheus.

6   *evil and error fall* Shelley regards human nature as progressive.

Thou breathe into the many-folded shell,   80
Loosening its mighty music; it shall be
As thunder mingled with clear echoes. Then
Return, and thou shalt dwell beside our cave.
And thou, oh Mother Earth –
THE EARTH   I hear, I feel;
Thy lips are on me, and their touch runs down   85
Even to the adamantine central gloom
Along these marble nerves – 'tis life, 'tis joy,
And through my withered, old, and icy frame
The warmth of an immortal youth shoots down,
Circling. Henceforth the many children fair   90
Folded in my sustaining arms – all plants
And creeping forms, and insects rainbow-winged,
And birds, and beasts, and fish, and human shapes,
Which drew disease and pain from my wan bosom,
Draining the poison of despair – shall take   95
And interchange sweet nutriment; to me
Shall they become like sister-antelopes
By one fair dam, snow-white and swift as wind,
Nursed among lilies near a brimming stream.
The dew-mists of my sunless sleep shall float   100
Under the stars like balm; night-folded flowers
Shall suck unwithering hues in their repose;
And men and beasts in happy dreams shall gather
Strength for the coming day and all its joy;
And death shall be the last embrace of her   105
Who takes the life she gave, even as a mother
Folding her child, says, 'Leave me not again.'
ASIA Oh mother, wherefore speak the name of death?
Cease they to love, and move, and breathe, and speak,
Who die?
THE EARTH   It would avail not to reply: 110
Thou art immortal, and this tongue is known
But to the uncommunicating dead.
Death is the veil which those who live call life:
They sleep, and it is lifted;[7] and meanwhile
In mild variety the seasons mild –   115
With rainbow-skirted showers, and odorous winds,
And long blue meteors cleansing the dull night,
And the life-kindling shafts of the keen sun's
All-piercing bow, and the dew-mingled rain
Of the calm moonbeams, a soft influence mild –   120
Shall clothe the forests and the fields, aye, even
The crag-built deserts of the barren deep
With ever-living leaves, and fruits, and flowers.
And thou![8] There is a cavern where my spirit
Was panted forth in anguish whilst thy pain   125
Made my heart mad, and those who did inhale it
Became mad too, and built a temple there,

---

7   *They sleep . . . lifted* cf. *Mont Blanc* 50: 'death is slumber'.   8   *And thou!* Earth turns from Asia to Prometheus.

And spoke, and were oracular,[9] and lured
The erring nations round to mutual war
And faithless faith, such as Jove kept with thee —   130
Which breath now rises, as among tall weeds
A violet's exhalation, and it fills
With a serener light and crimson air
Intense, yet soft, the rocks and woods around;
It feeds the quick growth of the serpent vine,   135
And the dark linked ivy tangling wild,
And budding, blown, or odour-faded blooms
Which star the winds with points of coloured light
As they rain through them, and bright golden globes
Of fruit, suspended in their own green heaven,   140
And, through their veined leaves and amber stems
The flowers whose purple and translucid bowls
Stand ever mantling with aerial dew,
The drink of spirits. And it circles round,
Like the soft waving wings of noonday dreams,   145
Inspiring calm and happy thoughts like mine,
Now thou art thus restored. This cave is thine.
Arise, appear! (*A spirit rises in the likeness of a winged child*)
          This is my torch-bearer,
Who let his lamp out in old time with gazing
On eyes from which he kindled it anew   150
With love, which is as fire, sweet daughter mine,
For such is that within thine own. Run, wayward!
And guide this company beyond the peak
Of Bacchic Nysa,[10] maenad-haunted mountain,
And beyond Indus and its tribute rivers,   155
Trampling the torrent streams and glassy lakes
With feet unwet, unwearied, undelaying;
And up the green ravine, across the vale,
Beside the windless and crystalline pool,
Where ever lies, on unerasing waves,   160
The image of a temple,[11] built above,
Distinct with column, arch, and architrave,
And palm-like capital, and over-wrought,
And populous with most living imagery —
Praxitelean shapes,[12] whose marble smiles   165
Fill the hushed air with everlasting love.
It is deserted now, but once it bore
Thy name, Prometheus; there the emulous youths
Bore to thy honour through the divine gloom
The lamp which was thine emblem[13] – even as those   170

---

9   *a temple . . . oracular* perhaps the temple at Delphi, where
the priestess uttered prophecies in a state of ecstasy – although
Shelley's meaning could be metaphorical.
10   They are to be guided from the Indian Caucasus to Greece,
passing Nysa (a city in India), where Bacchus was born.
11   *a temple* the Academy outside Athens, where Plato once
taught.
12   *Praxitelean shapes* i.e. statues carved by Praxiteles, Greek
sculptor of the fourth century BC, famous for his depictions of

Artemis and Aphrodite. In Rome, March 1819, Shelley saw
the statues of Castor and Pollux believed to have been made
by Praxiteles: 'These figures combine the irresistible energy
with the sublime and perfect loveliness supposed to have
belonged to the divine nature' (Jones ii 88–9).
13   *there the . . . emblem* in the Athenian festival in honour of
the fire-gods, young men raced from the altar of Prometheus to
the city, carrying lighted torches, without letting them go out.

Who bear the untransmitted torch of hope
Into the grave, across the night of life,
As thou hast borne it most triumphantly
To this far goal of time. Depart – farewell.
Beside that temple is the destined cave.   175

ACT III, SCENE IV

A forest. In the background a cave. Prometheus, Asia, Panthea, Ione, and the Spirit of the Earth.

IONE Sister, it is not earthly: how it glides
Under the leaves! How on its head there burns
A light, like a green star whose emerald beams
Are twined with its fair hair! How, as it moves,
The splendour drops in flakes upon the grass!   5
Knowest thou it?
PANTHEA   It is the delicate spirit
That guides the earth through Heaven. From afar
The populous constellations call that light
The loveliest of the planets; and sometimes
It floats along the spray of the salt sea,   10
Or makes its chariot of a foggy cloud,
Or walks through fields or cities while men sleep,
Or o'er the mountain-tops, or down the rivers,
Or through the green waste wilderness, as now,
Wondering at all it sees. Before Jove reigned   15
It loved our sister Asia, and it came
Each leisure hour to drink the liquid light
Out of her eyes, for which it said it thirsted
As one bit by a dipsas;[1] and with her
It made its childish confidence, and told her   20
All it had known or seen, for it saw much,
Yet idly reasoned what it saw; and called her
(For whence it sprung it knew not, nor do I)
'Mother, dear mother'.
THE SPIRIT OF THE EARTH (*running to Asia*) Mother, dearest mother;
May I then talk with thee as I was wont?   25
May I then hide my eyes in thy soft arms
After thy looks have made them tired of joy?
May I then play beside thee the long noons
When work is none in the bright silent air?
ASIA I love thee, gentlest being, and henceforth   30
Can cherish thee unenvied; speak, I pray –
Thy simple talk once solaced, now delights.
SPIRIT OF THE EARTH Mother, I am grown wiser, though a child
Cannot be wise like thee, within this day,
And happier too – happier and wiser both.   35
Thou knowest that toads, and snakes, and loathly worms,
And venomous and malicious beasts, and boughs
That bore ill berries in the woods, were ever
An hindrance to my walks o'er the green world;

ACT III, SCENE IV
[1] *dipsas* serpent which induced an unquenchable thirst in
those it bit.

And that, among the haunts of humankind, 40
Hard-featured men, or with proud, angry looks,
Or cold, staid gait, or false and hollow smiles,
Or the dull sneer of self-loved ignorance,
Or other such foul masks, with which ill thoughts
Hide that fair being whom we spirits call man; 45
And women too, ugliest of all things evil
(Though fair, even in a world where thou art fair
When good and kind, free and sincere like thee),
When false or frowning made me sick at heart
To pass them, though they slept, and I unseen. 50
Well, my path lately lay through a great city
Into the woody hills surrounding it.
A sentinel was sleeping at the gate,
When there was heard a sound so loud, it shook
The towers amid the moonlight, yet more sweet 55
Than any voice but thine, sweetest of all;
A long, long sound, as it would never end –
And all the inhabitants leapt suddenly
Out of their rest, and gathered in the streets,
Looking in wonder up to Heaven, while yet 60
The music pealed along. I hid myself
Within a fountain in the public square,
Where I lay like the reflex[2] of the moon
Seen in a wave under green leaves – and soon
Those ugly human shapes and visages 65
Of which I spoke as having wrought me pain,
Passed floating through the air, and fading still
Into the winds that scattered them; and those
From whom they passed seemed mild and lovely forms
After some foul disguise had fallen, and all 70
Were somewhat changed, and after brief surprise
And greetings of delighted wonder, all
Went to their sleep again; and when the dawn
Came – wouldst thou think that toads, and snakes, and efts,[3]
Could e'er be beautiful? Yet so they were, 75
And that with little change of shape or hue:
All things had put their evil nature off.
I cannot tell my joy, when o'er a lake,
Upon a drooping bough with nightshade twined,
I saw two azure halcyons clinging downward 80
And thinning one bright bunch of amber berries
With quick long beaks,[4] and in the deep there lay
Those lovely forms imaged as in a sky.
So with my thoughts full of these happy changes,
We meet again, the happiest change of all. 85
ASIA And never will we part, till thy chaste sister[5]
Who guides the frozen and inconstant moon,

---

2   *reflex* reflection.
3   *efts* small lizards. Everything is returning to a pre-lapsarian state.
4   *Upon a drooping bough . . . beaks* In the regenerated, purified world, deadly nightshade is no longer poisonous, and king-fishers turn vegetarian rather than eat fish. (Shelley was a vegetarian.)
5   *thy chaste sister* Selene, Greek goddess of the moon.

Will look on thy more warm and equal light
Till her heart thaw like flakes of April snow,
And love thee.
SPIRIT OF THE EARTH What? As Asia loves Prometheus?   90
ASIA Peace, wanton![6] Thou are yet not old enough.
Think ye by gazing on each other's eyes
To multiply your lovely selves, and fill
With sphered fires the interlunar air?
Spirit of the Earth Nay, mother, while my sister trims her lamp[7]   95
'Tis hard I should go darkling.[8]
ASIA   Listen, look! (*The Spirit of the Hour enters*)
PROMETHEUS We feel what thou hast heard and seen — yet speak.
SPIRIT OF THE HOUR Soon as the sound had ceased whose thunder filled
The abysses of the sky and the wide earth
There was a change: the impalpable thin air   100
And the all-circling sunlight were transformed,
As if the sense of love dissolved in them
Had folded itself round the sphered world.
My vision then grew clear, and I could see
Into the mysteries of the universe: 105
Dizzy as with delight I floated down;
Winnowing[9] the lightsome air with languid plumes
My coursers sought their birthplace in the sun,
Where they henceforth will live exempt from toil,
Pasturing flowers of vegetable fire,   110
And where my moonlike car will stand within
A temple — gazed upon by Phidian forms[10]
Of thee, and Asia, and the Earth, and me,
And you fair nymphs, looking the love we feel,
In memory of the tidings it has borne —   115
Beneath a dome fretted[11] with graven flowers,[12]
Poised on twelve columns of resplendent stone,
And open to the bright and liquid sky.
Yoked to it by an amphisbaenic snake
The likeness of those winged steeds will mock   120
The flight from which they find repose. Alas!
Whither has wandered now my partial tongue
When all remains untold which ye would hear?
As I have said, I floated to the earth:
It was, as it is still, the pain of bliss   125
To move, to breathe, to be; I wandering went
Among the haunts and dwellings of mankind,
And first was disappointed not to see
Such mighty change as I had felt within
Expressed in outward things. But soon I looked,   130
And behold! thrones were kingless, and men walked

---

6 *wanton* spoiled child.
7 *trims her lamp* when trimming a lamp, one prepares the wick for fresh burning.
8 *darkling* in the dark.
9 *Winnowing* beating.
10 *Phidian forms* statues carved by Phidias, Greek sculptor of the fifth century BC, famous for his portrayal of Jupiter at Olympia.

11 *fretted* decorated.
12 The scene described is based on the Pantheon at Rome and the Sala della Biga in the Vatican, both of which Shelley visited. The Biga is a two-horse chariot, the emblem of the moon. Its yoke was a snake with a head at both ends, the amphisbaena.

One with the other even as spirits do –
None fawned, none trampled; hate, disdain, or fear,
Self-love or self-contempt, on human brows
No more inscribed, as o'er the gate of Hell,   135
'All hope abandon, ye who enter here';[13]
None frowned, none trembled, none with eager fear
Gazed on another's eye of cold command
Until the subject of a tyrant's will
Became, worse fate, the abject of his own,[14]   140
Which spurred him, like an outspent horse, to death;
None wrought his lips in truth-entangling lines
Which smiled the lie his tongue disdained to speak;
None, with firm sneer, trod out in his own heart
The sparks of love and hope, till there remained   145
Those bitter ashes, a soul self-consumed,
And the wretch crept, a vampire among men,
Infecting all with his own hideous ill;
None talked that common, false, cold, hollow talk
Which makes the heart deny the 'yes' it breathes,   150
Yet question that unmeant hypocrisy
Which such a self-mistrust as has no name.
And women, too – frank, beautiful, and kind
As the free Heaven which rains fresh light and dew
On the wide earth, passed – gentle radiant forms,   155
From custom's evil taint exempt and pure,
Speaking the wisdom once they could not think,
Looking emotions once they feared to feel,
And changed to all which once they dared not be,
Yet being now, made earth like Heaven; nor pride,   160
Nor jealousy, nor envy, nor ill shame,
The bitterest of those drops of treasured gall,
Spoilt the sweet taste of the nepenthe,[15] love.
    Thrones, altars, judgement-seats[16] and prisons (wherein,
And beside which, by wretched men were borne   165
Sceptres, tiaras, swords and chains, and tomes
Of reasoned wrong glozed on[17] by ignorance)
Were like those monstrous and barbaric shapes,[18]
The ghosts of a no more remembered fame
Which, from their unworn obelisks,[19] look forth   170
In triumph o'er the palaces and tombs
Of those who were their conquerors, mouldering round.
These[20] imaged to the pride of kings and priests
A dark yet mighty faith, a power as wide
As is the world it wasted, and are now   175
But an astonishment; even so the tools
And emblems of its last captivity,
Amid the dwellings of the peopled earth,

---

[13] Dante, *Inferno* iii 9.
[14] *the abject of his own* the outcast of his own will.
[15] *nepenthe* grief-banishing drink.
[16] *judgement-seats* tribunals.
[17] *glozed on* explained.

[18] *monstrous and barbaric shapes* i.e. of Egyptian deities, carved into the obelisks.
[19] *obelisks* Egyptian obelisks had been brought to Rome in ancient times and erected in the main piazzas, where Shelley saw them.
[20] *These* i.e. the 'monstrous and barbaric shapes' (l. 168).

Stand, not o'erthrown, but unregarded now.
And those foul shapes,[21] abhorred by God and man –   180
Which, under many a name and many a form
Strange, savage, ghastly, dark and execrable,
Were Jupiter, the tyrant of the world;
And which the nations, panic-stricken, served
With blood, and hearts broken by long hope, and love   185
Dragged to his altars soiled and garlandless,
And slain amid men's unreclaiming tears,
Flattering the thing they feared, which fear was hate –
Frown,[22] mouldering fast, o'er their abandoned shrines.
The painted veil, by those who were, called life,   190
Which mimicked, as with colours idly spread,
All men believed and hoped, is torn aside;
The loathsome mask has fallen, the man remains
Sceptreless, free, uncircumscribed – but man:
Equal, unclassed, tribeless, and nationless,   195
Exempt from awe, worship, degree; the king
Over himself; just, gentle, wise – but man.
Passionless? No, yet free from guilt or pain,
Which were, for his will made, or suffered them;
Nor yet exempt, though ruling them like slaves,   200
From chance, and death, and mutability,
The clogs[23] of that which else might oversoar
The loftiest star of unascended Heaven,
Pinnacled dim in the intense inane.[24]

ACT IV

Scene: a part of the forest near the Cave of Prometheus. Panthea and Ione are sleeping; they awaken gradually during the first song.

VOICE OF UNSEEN SPIRITS.
        The pale stars are gone!
        For the sun, their swift shepherd,
        To their folds them compelling
        In the depths of the dawn,
Hastes, in meteor-eclipsing array, and they flee   5
        Beyond his blue dwelling,
        As fawns flee the leopard.
        But where are ye?
(A *train of dark forms and shadows passes by confusedly, singing*)
        Here, oh, here;
        We bear the bier   10
Of the father of many a cancelled year!
        Spectres we
        Of the dead Hours be,
We bear Time to his tomb in eternity.

---

[21] *those foul shapes* i.e. of false religions associated with the tyranny of Jupiter.
[22] *Frown* the subject governing this verb is 'shapes' (l. 180).
[23] *clogs* hindrances.
[24] *intense inane* deep space.

Strew, oh strew 15
Hair, not yew!
Wet the dusty pall with tears, not dew!
Be the faded flowers
Of Death's bare bowers
Spread on the corpse of the King of Hours! 20

Haste, oh haste!
As shades are chased,
Trembling, by day, from heaven's blue waste,
We melt away,
Like dissolving spray, 25
From the children of a diviner day,
With the lullaby
Of winds that die
On the bosom of their own harmony.

IONE What dark forms were they?
PANTHEA The past Hours weak and grey, 30
With the spoil which their toil
Raked together
From the conquest but One[1] could foil.
IONE Have they passed?
PANTHEA   They have passed; 35
They outspeeded the blast,
While 'tis said, they are fled –
IONE Whither, oh whither?
PANTHEA To the dark, to the past, to the dead.

VOICE OF UNSEEN SPIRITS
Bright clouds float in Heaven,
Dew-stars gleam on earth, 40
Waves assemble on ocean –
They are gathered and driven
By the storm of delight, by the panic of glee!
They shake with emotion,
They dance in their mirth – 45
But where are ye?[2]

The pine boughs are singing
Old songs with new gladness,
The billows and fountains
Fresh music are flinging, 50
Like the notes of a spirit from land and from sea;
The storms mock the mountains
With the thunder of gladness –
But where are ye?
IONE What charioteers are these? 55
PANTHEA   Where are their chariots?

ACT IV
[1] *One* Prometheus.
[2] *ye* the new Hours.

SEMICHORUS OF HOURS I
The voice of the Spirits of Air and of Earth
Has drawn back the figured[3] curtain of sleep
Which covered our being and darkened our birth
In the deep —

A VOICE
        In the deep?
SEMICHORUS II
           Oh, below the deep.   60
SEMICHORUS I
A hundred ages[4] we had been kept
Cradled in visions of hate and care,
And each one who waked as his brother slept,
Found the truth —
SEMICHORUS II
           Worse than his visions were!
SEMICHORUS I
We have heard the lute of Hope in sleep;   65
We have known the voice of Love in dreams;
We have felt the wand of Power, and leap —

SEMICHORUS II
As the billows leap in the morning beams!

CHORUS
Weave the dance on the floor of the breeze,
   Pierce with song heaven's silent light,   70
Enchant the Day that too swiftly flees,
   To check its flight ere the cave of Night.

Once the hungry Hours were hounds
   Which chased the Day like a bleeding deer,
And it limped and stumbled with many wounds   75
   Through the nightly dells of the desert year.

But now, oh weave the mystic measure
   Of music and dance and shapes of light;
Let the Hours, and the spirits of might and pleasure,
   Like the clouds and sunbeams, unite.

A VOICE
             Unite!   80

PANTHEA See, where the Spirits of the human mind[5]
Wrapped in sweet sounds, as in bright veils, approach.

CHORUS OF SPIRITS
      We join the throng
      Of the dance and the song,

---

3 *figured* patterned.
4 *A hundred ages* i.e. for the duration of Saturn's very long
reign.

5 *the Spirits of the human mind* presumably the same spirits
who comforted Prometheus in Act I.

By the whirlwind of gladness borne along –   85
    As the flying-fish leap
    From the Indian deep,
And mix with the sea-birds, half asleep.

CHORUS OF HOURS
Whence come ye, so wild and so fleet,
For sandals of lightning are on your feet,   90
And your wings are soft and swift as thought,
And your eyes are as love which is veiled not?

CHORUS OF SPIRITS
    We come from the mind
    Of humankind,
Which was late so dusk,[6] and obscene, and blind;   95
    Now 'tis an ocean
    Of clear emotion,
A Heaven of serene and mighty motion;

    From that deep abyss
    Of wonder and bliss,   100
Whose caverns are crystal palaces;
    From those skyey towers
    Where Thought's crowned powers
Sit watching your dance, ye happy Hours;

    From the dim recesses   105
    Of woven caresses,
Where lovers catch ye by your loose tresses;
    From the azure isles
    Where sweet Wisdom smiles,
Delaying your ships with her siren wiles;   110

    From the temples high
    Of man's ear and eye,
Roofed over Sculpture and Poesy;
    From the murmurings
    Of the unsealed springs,   115
Where Science[7] bedews her daedal[8] wings.

    Years after years,
    Through blood and tears
And a thick hell of hatreds, and hopes, and fears,
    We waded and flew,   120
    And the islets were few
Where the bud-blighted flowers of happiness grew.

    Our feet now, every palm,
    Are sandalled with calm,
And the dew of our wings is a rain of balm;   125

---

[6] *dusk* gloomy.   [8] *daedal* skilful.
[7] *Science* knowledge.

And beyond our eyes[9]
The human love lies
Which makes all it gazes on paradise.

CHORUS OF SPIRITS AND HOURS
    Then weave the web of the mystic measure;
From the depths of the sky and the ends of the earth,   130
    Come, swift Spirits of might and of pleasure,
Fill the dance and the music of mirth –
    As the waves of a thousand streams rush by
    To an ocean of splendour and harmony!

CHORUS OF SPIRITS
        Our spoil is won,   135
        Our task is done,
    We are free to dive, or soar, or run
        Beyond and around,
        Or within the bound[10]
Which clips[11] the world with darkness round.   140

        We'll pass the eyes
        Of the starry skies
    Into the hoar deep to colonize;
        Death, Chaos, and Night,
        From the sound of our flight   145
Shall flee, like mist from a tempest's might;

        And Earth, Air, and Light,
        And the Spirit of Might
    Which drives round the stars in their fiery flight;
        And Love, Thought, and Breath,   150
        The powers that quell Death,
Wherever we soar shall assemble beneath;

        And our singing shall build,
        In the void's loose field,
    A world for the Spirit of Wisdom to wield;   155
        We will take our plan
        From the new world of man,
And our work shall be called the Promethean.

CHORUS OF HOURS
Break the dance, and scatter the song;
Let some depart and some remain.   160

SEMICHORUS I
We, beyond Heaven, are driven along –

SEMICHORUS II
Us the enchantments of earth retain –

---

[9] *beyond our eyes* beyond our range of vision.   [11] *clips* embraces.
[10] *the bound* i.e. of the earth's atmosphere.

SEMICHORUS I

Ceaseless, and rapid, and fierce, and free,
With the Spirits which build a new earth and sea,
And a Heaven where yet Heaven could never be.   165

SEMICHORUS II

Solemn, and slow, and serene, and bright,
Leading the Day and outspeeding the Night
With the powers of a world of perfect light.

SEMICHORUS I

We whirl, singing loud, round the gathering sphere,
Till the trees, and the beasts, and the clouds appear   170
From its chaos made calm by love, not fear.

SEMICHORUS II

We encircle the oceans and mountains of earth,
And the happy forms of its death and birth
Change to the music of our sweet mirth.

CHORUS OF HOURS AND SPIRITS

Break the dance, and scatter the song;   175
    Let some depart, and some remain;
Wherever we fly we lead along
In leashes, like starbeams, soft yet strong,
    The clouds that are heavy with love's sweet rain.

PANTHEA Ha! They are gone!
IONE   Yet feel you no delight   180
From the past sweetness?
PANTHEA   As the bare green hill
When some soft cloud vanishes into rain,
Laughs with a thousand drops of sunny water
To the unpavilioned sky![12]
IONE   Even whilst we speak
New notes arise. What is that awful sound?   185
PANTHEA 'Tis the deep music of the rolling world,
Kindling within the strings of the waved air
Aeolian modulations.
IONE   Listen too,
How every pause is filled with under-notes,
Clear, silver, icy, keen, awakening tones,   190
Which pierce the sense, and live within the soul,
As the sharp stars pierce winter's crystal air
And gaze upon themselves within the sea.
PANTHEA But see where, through two openings in the forest
Which hanging branches overcanopy,   195
And where two runnels[13] of a rivulet,
Between the close moss, violet-inwoven,

---

[12] *the unpavilioned sky* the sky is not separated from the earth   [13] *runnels* streamlets.
by a pavilion.

Have made their path of melody – like sisters
Who part with sighs that they may meet in smiles,
Turning their dear disunion to an isle   200
Of lovely grief, a wood of sweet sad thoughts –
Two visions of strange radiance float upon
The ocean-like enchantment of strong sound,
Which flows intenser, keener, deeper yet
Under the ground and through the windless air.   205
IONE I see a chariot – like that thinnest boat
In which the mother of the months[14] is borne
By ebbing light into her western cave
When she upsprings from interlunar dreams –
O'er which is curved an orblike canopy   210
Of gentle darkness, and the hills and woods,
Distinctly seen through that dusk[15] airy veil,
Regard[16] like shapes in an enchanter's glass;
Its wheels are solid clouds, azure and gold,
Such as the genii of the thunderstorm   215
Pile on the floor of the illumined sea
When the sun rushes under it; they roll
And move and grow as with an inward wind.
Within it sits a winged infant: white
Its countenance, like the whiteness of bright snow;   220
Its plumes are as feathers of sunny frost;
Its limbs gleam white through the wind-flowing folds
Of its white robe, woof of ethereal pearl;
Its hair is white – the brightness of white light[17]
Scattered in strings; yet its two eyes are heavens   225
Of liquid darkness, which the Deity
Within seems pouring, as a storm is poured
From jagged clouds, out of their arrowy lashes,
Tempering the cold and radiant air around
With fire that is not brightness;[18] in its hand   230
It sways a quivering moonbeam, from whose point
A guiding power directs the chariot's prow
Over its wheeled clouds, which, as they roll
Over the grass, and flowers, and waves, wake sounds
Sweet as a singing rain of silver dew.   235
PANTHEA And from the other opening in the wood
Rushes, with loud and whirlwind harmony,
A sphere, which is as many thousand spheres,
Solid as crystal, yet through all its mass
Flow, as through empty space, music and light: 240
Ten thousand orbs involving and involved,[19]
Purple and azure, white, and green, and golden,
Sphere within sphere; and every space between
Peopled with unimaginable shapes,

---

[14] *the mother of the months* the moon.
[15] *dusk* dark, dusk-like.
[16] *Regard* appear.
[17] *the brightness of white light* in other words, the brilliant, unrefracted light of 'pure', transcendental vision.
[18] *fire that is not brightness* contemporary scientific thought indicated that there were 'dark rays' – infrared emanations that produced heat but no light. Humphry Davy had suggested that these were emitted by the moon.
[19] *involving and involved* entwined and entwining; inextricably intertwined.

Such as ghosts dream dwell in the lampless deep,   245
Yet each intertranspicuous;[20] and they whirl
Over each other with a thousand motions,
Upon a thousand sightless[21] axles spinning,
And, with the force of self-destroying swiftness,
Intensely, slowly, solemnly roll on,   250
Kindling with mingled sounds, and many tones,
Intelligible words and music wild.
With mighty whirl the multitudinous[22] orb
Grinds the bright brook into an azure mist
Of elemental subtlety, like light;   255
And the wild odour of the forest flowers,
The music of the living grass and air,
The emerald light of leaf-entangled beams
Round its intense yet self-conflicting speed,
Seem kneaded into one aerial mass   260
Which drowns the sense. Within the orb itself,
Pillowed upon its alabaster arms
Like to a child o'erwearied with sweet toil,
On its own folded wings and wavy hair
The Spirit of the Earth is laid asleep,   265
And you can see its little lips are moving
Amid the changing light of their own smiles,
Like one who talks of what he loves in dream –
IONE 'Tis only mocking[23] the orb's harmony.
PANTHEA And from a star upon its forehead, shoot –   270
Like swords of azure fire, or golden spears
With tyrant-quelling myrtle[24] overtwined,
Embleming Heaven and Earth united now –
Vast beams like spokes of some invisible wheel
Which whirl as the orb whirls, swifter than thought,   275
Filling the abyss with sunlike lightenings;
And perpendicular now, and now transverse,
Pierce the dark soil, and, as they pierce and pass,
Make bare the secrets of the earth's deep heart:
Infinite mines of adamant and gold,   280
Valueless[25] stones, and unimagined gems,
And caverns on crystalline columns poised
With vegetable silver[26] overspread;
Wells of unfathomed fire, and water-springs
Whence the great sea, even as a child, is fed,   285
Whose vapours clothe earth's monarch mountain-tops
With kingly, ermine snow. The beams flash on
And make appear the melancholy ruins
Of cancelled cycles[27] – anchors, beaks of ships,
Planks turned to marble, quivers, helms,[28] and spears,   290

---

[20] *intertranspicuous* transparent between and through each
other.
[21] *sightless* invisible.
[22] *multitudinous* thronging with multitudes.
[23] *mocking* imitating.
[24] *tyrant-quelling myrtle* Greek warriors were crowned with
myrtle.

[25] *Valueless* precious beyond price.
[26] *vegetable silver* like the 'vegetable gold' at *Paradise Lost* iv
220, this is a reference to the philosophers' stone believed to
preserve health.
[27] *cycles* i.e. eras of time.
[28] *helms* helmets.

And gorgon-headed targes,[29] and the wheels
Of scythed chariots,[30] and the emblazonry
Of trophies, standards, and armorial beasts –
Round which Death laughed: sepulchred emblems
Of dead Destruction, ruin within ruin!   295
The wrecks beside of many a city vast,
Whose population which the earth grew over
Was mortal, but not human – see, they lie,
Their monstrous works and uncouth skeletons,
Their statues, homes and fanes;[31] prodigious[32] shapes   300
Huddled in grey annihilation, split,
Jammed in the hard black deep; and over[33] these
The anatomies of unknown winged things,
And fishes which were isles of living scale,
And serpents, bony chains, twisted around   305
The iron crags, or within heaps of dust
To which the tortuous strength of their last pangs
Had crushed the iron crags; and over[34] these
The jagged alligator, and the might
Of earth-convulsing behemoth,[35] which once   310
Were monarch beasts, and on the slimy shores
And weed-overgrown continents of earth
Increased and multiplied like summer worms
On an abandoned corpse, till the blue globe
Wrapped deluge round it like a cloak, and they   315
Yelled, gasped, and were abolished – or some God
Whose throne was in a comet, passed, and cried,
'Be not!' – and like my words they were no more.

THE EARTH[36]
The joy, the triumph, the delight, the madness!
The boundless, overflowing, bursting gladness!   320
The vaporous exultation not to be confined!
    Ha! Ha! the animation of delight
    Which wraps me, like an atmosphere of light,
And bears me as a cloud is borne by its own wind!

THE MOON
    Brother mine, calm wanderer,   325
    Happy globe of land and air,
Some spirit is darted like a beam from thee,
    Which penetrates my frozen frame,
    And passes with the warmth of flame,
With love, and odour, and deep melody   330
    Through me, through me!

---

[29] *targes* shields.
[30] *scythed chariots* the Saxon queen Boadicea used to put blades on the axles of her chariots.
[31] *fanes* temples.
[32] *prodigious* fantastic.
[33] *over* i.e. under. Shelley is burrowing ever further into the mists of time.

[34] *over* i.e. under.
[35] *behemoth* either the elephant or the hippopotamus – probably, as in Milton, the former: 'Behemoth biggest born of earth upheaved / His vastness' (*Paradise Lost* vii 471–2).
[36] Where the Earth of Acts I and III iv was a Hellenic goddess and earth-mother, that which appears here is brother and lover of the moon.

THE EARTH

Ha! Ha! the caverns of my hollow mountains,
My cloven fire-crags,[37] sound-exulting fountains,
Laugh with a vast and inextinguishable laughter:
    The oceans, and the deserts, and the abysses
    Of the deep air's unmeasured wildernesses,
Answer from all their clouds and billows, echoing after.   335

    They cry aloud as I do: 'Sceptred Curse,[38]
    Who all our green and azure universe
Threatenedst to muffle round with black destruction, sending   340
    A solid cloud to rain hot thunderstones,
    And splinter and knead down my children's bones,
All I bring forth, to one void mass battering and blending;

    Until each crag-like tower, and storied column,
    Palace, and obelisk, and temple solemn,   345
My imperial mountains crowned with cloud, and snow, and fire,
    My sea-like forests, every blade and blossom
    Which finds a grave or cradle in my bosom,
Were stamped by thy strong hate into a lifeless mire:

    How art thou sunk, withdrawn, covered, drunk up   350
    By thirsty nothing, as the brackish cup[39]
Drained by a desert-troop, a little drop for all;
    And from beneath, around, within, above,
    Filling thy void annihilation, love
Burst in like light on caves cloven by the thunderball.   355

THE MOON

    The snow upon my lifeless mountains
    Is loosened into living fountains,
My solid oceans flow, and sing, and shine;
    A spirit from my heart bursts forth,
    It clothes with unexpected birth
My cold bare bosom – oh, it must be thine   360
        On mine, on mine!

    Gazing on thee I feel, I know
    Green stalks burst forth, and bright flowers grow,
And living shapes upon my bosom move;   365
    Music is in the sea and air,
    Winged clouds soar here and there,
Dark with the rain new buds are dreaming of –
        'Tis love, all love!

THE EARTH

    It interpenetrates my granite mass,   370
    Through tangled roots and trodden clay doth pass
Into the utmost leaves and delicatest flowers;

---

37   *My cloven fire-crags* volcanoes.
38   *Sceptred Curse* Jupiter.
39   *the brackish cup* i.e. the salty water in the cup.

Upon the winds, among the clouds 'tis spread;
It wakes a life in the forgotten dead –
They breathe a spirit up from their obscurest bowers – 375

And like a storm, bursting its cloudy prison
With thunder and with whirlwind, has arisen[40]
Out of the lampless caves of unimagined being,
With earthquake shock and swiftness making shiver
Thought's stagnant chaos, unremoved for ever,[41] 380
Till hate, and fear, and pain, light-vanquished shadows, fleeing,

Leave Man – who was a many-sided mirror
Which could distort to many a shape of error
This true fair world of things – a sea reflecting love;
Which[42] over all his kind,[43] as the sun's Heaven 385
Gliding o'er ocean, smooth, serene, and even,
Darting from starry depths radiance and life, doth move:

Leave Man, even as a leprous child is left
Who follows a sick beast to some warm cleft
Of rocks, through which the might of healing springs is poured; 390
Then when it wanders home with rosy smile,
Unconscious, and its mother fears awhile
It is a spirit, then weeps on her child restored:[44]

Man, oh not men! a chain of linked thought,
Of love and might to be divided not, 395
Compelling the elements with adamantine stress,
As the sun rules, even with a tyrant's gaze,
The unquiet republic of the maze
Of planets, struggling fierce toward Heaven's free wilderness:

Man, one harmonious soul of many a soul, 400
Whose nature is its own divine control,
Where all things flow to all, as rivers to the sea;
Familiar acts are beautiful through love;
Labour, and Pain, and Grief, in life's green grove
Sport like tame beasts – none knew how gentle they could be! 405

His will – with all mean passions, bad delights,
And selfish cares, its trembling satellites,
A spirit ill to guide, but mighty to obey –
Is as a tempest-winged ship, whose helm
Love rules through waves which dare not overwhelm, 410
Forcing life's wildest shores to own its sovereign sway:

All things confess his strength. Through the cold mass
Of marble and of colour his dreams pass –

---

[40] *has arisen* Love is the subject that governs this verb.
[41] *unremoved for ever* i.e. hitherto not removed.
[42] *Which* i.e. Love.
[43] *his kind* i.e. mankind.

[44] *Leave man . . . restored* Shelley refers to the legend of King Bladud of Britain, a leper who followed a lost pig to the hot springs of Bath, by which he was cured.

Bright threads whence mothers weave the robes their children wear;
   Language is a perpetual Orphic song,[45]
   Which rules with daedal harmony a throng
Of thoughts and forms, which else senseless and shapeless were:

   The lightning is his slave;[46] Heaven's utmost deep
   Gives up her stars, and like a flock of sheep
They pass before his eye, are numbered, and roll on!
   The tempest is his steed, he strides the air;[47]
   And the abyss shouts from her depth laid bare,
'Heaven, hast thou secrets? Man unveils me; I have none.'

THE MOON
   The shadow of white Death has passed
   From my path in heaven at last,
A clinging shroud of solid frost and sleep;
   And through my newly-woven bowers
   Wander happy paramours
Less mighty, but as mild as those who keep
   Thy vales more deep.

THE EARTH
   As the dissolving warmth of dawn may fold
   A half-unfrozen dew-globe, green and gold
And crystalline, till it becomes a winged mist,
   And wanders up the vault of the blue day,
   Outlives the noon, and on the sun's last ray
Hangs o'er the sea, a fleece of fire and amethyst –

THE MOON
   Thou art folded, thou art lying
   In the light which is undying
Of thine own joy, and Heaven's smile divine;
   All suns and constellations shower
   On thee a light, a life, a power
Which doth array thy sphere; thou pourest thine
   On mine, on mine!

THE EARTH
   I spin beneath my pyramid of night,[48]
   Which points into the heavens, dreaming delight,
Murmuring victorious joy in my enchanted sleep –
   As a youth lulled in love-dreams, faintly sighing,
   Under the shadow of his beauty lying,[49]
Which round his rest a watch of light and warmth doth keep.

415

420

425

430

435

440

445

---

[45] *Language is a perpetual Orphic song* i.e. it governs our morals and actions. Orpheus tamed wild beasts and stopped the tortures of Hades with his music.

[46] *The lightning is his slave* in the sense that man was discovering how electricity could be harnessed to his purposes.

[47] *he strides the air* Ballooning became all the rage in London only months after the Montgolfier brothers made the first flight in 1783. Shelley had used balloons as a means of distributing his broadside, 'A Declaration of Rights', in the summer of 1812.

[48] *my pyramid of night* as with the 'shadowy cone' at *Paradise Lost* iv 776, Shelley refers to the idea that the earth's shadow is a cone or pyramid of darkness that circles round it in diametrical opposition to the sun.

[49] *As a youth . . . lying* The youth lies under the halo ('shadow') cast by the light of his beauty into the air above him.

THE MOON

As in the soft and sweet eclipse   450
When soul meets soul on lovers' lips,
High hearts are calm, and brightest eyes are dull –
So when thy shadow falls on me,
Then am I mute and still, by thee
Covered; of thy love, Orb most beautiful,   455
Full, oh too full!

Thou art speeding round the sun,
Brightest world of many a one,
Green and azure sphere, which shinest
With a light which is divinest   460
Among all the lamps of Heaven
To whom life and light is given;
I, thy crystal paramour
Borne beside thee by a power
Like the polar paradise,   465
Magnet-like, of lovers' eyes;
I, a most enamoured maiden,
Whose weak brain is overladen
With the pleasure of her love,
Maniac-like around thee move,   470
Gazing, an insatiate bride,
On thy form from every side
Like a maenad round the cup
Which Agave lifted up
In the weird Cadmaean forest.⁵⁰   475
Brother, wheresoe'er thou soarest
I must hurry, whirl and follow
Through the heavens wide and hollow,
Sheltered, by the warm embrace
Of thy soul, from hungry space;   480
Drinking from thy sense and sight
Beauty, majesty, and might,
As a lover or chameleon
Grows like what it looks upon;
As a violet's gentle eye   485
Gazes on the azure sky
Until its hue grows like what it beholds;
As a grey and watery mist
Glows like solid amethyst
Athwart the western mountain it enfolds,   490
When the sunset sleeps
Upon its snow.

THE EARTH
And the weak day weeps

---

⁵⁰   *Like a maenad . . . forest* Agave, daughter of Cadmus,
became a maenad and killed her own son, Pentheus.

That it should be so.
Oh gentle Moon, the voice of thy delight   495
Falls on me like thy clear and tender light
Soothing the seaman, borne the summer night
    Through isles forever calm;
Oh gentle Moon, thy crystal accents pierce
The caverns of my pride's deep universe,   500
Charming the tiger joy, whose tramplings fierce
    Made wounds which need thy balm.

PANTHEA I rise as from a bath of sparkling water,
A bath of azure light, among dark rocks,
Out of the stream of sound.
IONE   Ah me! sweet sister,   505
The stream of sound has ebbed away from us,
And you pretend to rise out of its wave
Because your words fall like the clear soft dew
Shaken from a bathing wood-nymph's limbs and hair.
PANTHEA Peace, peace! A mighty Power, which is as darkness,   510
Is rising out of Earth, and from the sky
Is showered like night, and from within the air
Bursts, like eclipse which had been gathered up
Into the pores of sunlight: the bright visions,
Wherein the singing spirits rode and shone,   515
Gleam like pale meteors through a watery night.
IONE There is a sense of words upon mine ear —
PANTHEA A universal sound like words — oh list!

DEMOGORGON
Thou Earth, calm empire of a happy soul,
    Sphere of divinest shapes and harmonies;   520
Beautiful orb! gathering as thou dost roll
    The love which paves thy path along the skies:

THE EARTH
I hear! I am as a drop of dew that dies.

DEMOGORGON
Thou Moon, which gazest on the nightly Earth
    With wonder, as it gazes upon thee,   525
Whilst each to men, and beasts, and the swift birth[51]
    Of birds, is beauty, love, calm, harmony:

THE MOON
I hear! I am a leaf shaken by thee.

DEMOGORGON
Ye kings of suns and stars, Daemons and Gods,
    Ethereal Dominations,[52] who possess   530
Elysian, windless, fortunate abodes
    Beyond Heaven's constellated wilderness:

---

[51] *birth* race.
[52] *Dominations* the fourth of the nine orders of angels, as at
Paradise Lost iii 392.

A VOICE (*from above*)
    Our great Republic hears: we are blessed, and bless.

DEMOGORGON
Ye happy dead, whom beams of brightest verse
    Are clouds to hide, not colours to portray, 535
Whether your nature is that universe
    Which once ye saw and suffered –

A VOICE (*from beneath*)
                    Or as they
    Whom we have left, we change and pass away.

DEMOGORGON
Ye elemental Genii,[53] who have homes
    From man's high mind even to the central stone 540
Of sullen lead; from Heaven's star-fretted domes
    To the dull weed some sea-worm battens[54] on:

A CONFUSED VOICE
    We hear: thy words waken Oblivion.

DEMOGORGON
Spirits, whose homes are flesh; ye beasts and birds;
    Ye worms and fish; ye living leaves and buds; 545
Lightning and wind; and ye untameable herds,
    Meteors and mists, which throng air's solitudes:

A VOICE
    Thy voice to us is wind among still woods.

DEMOGORGON
Man, who wert once a despot and a slave;
    A dupe and a deceiver; a decay; 550
A traveller from the cradle to the grave
    Through the dim night[55] of this immortal day:

ALL
    Speak: thy strong words may never pass away.

DEMOGORGON
This is the day, which down the void abysm
    At the Earth-born's spell[56] yawns for Heaven's despotism, 555
    And Conquest is dragged captive through the deep:
Love, from its awful throne of patient power
In the wise heart, from the last giddy hour
    Of dread endurance, from the slippery, steep,

---

53 *elemental Genii* the elements.
54 *battens* feeds gluttonously.
55 *the dim night* i.e. the period preceding the eternal day.

56 *the Earth-born's spell* i.e. Prometheus' revocation of his curse.

And narrow verge of crag-like agony, springs   560
And folds over the world its healing wings.

Gentleness, Virtue, Wisdom, and Endurance:
These are the seals of that most firm assurance
    Which bars the pit over Destruction's strength;
And if, with infirm hand, Eternity,   565
Mother of many acts and hours, should free
    The serpent that would clasp her with his length,
These are the spells by which to reassume
An empire o'er the disentangled Doom.

To suffer woes which Hope thinks infinite;   570
To forgive wrongs darker than death or night;
    To defy Power which seems omnipotent;
To love, and bear; to hope, till Hope creates
From its own wreck the thing it contemplates;
    Neither to change, nor falter, nor repent: 575
This, like thy glory, Titan, is to be
Good, great and joyous, beautiful and free;
This is alone Life, Joy, Empire, and Victory.

The Mask of Anarchy. Written on the Occasion of the Massacre at Manchester (composed 5–23 September 1819; edited from MS)[1]

As I lay asleep in Italy[2]
There came a voice from over the Sea,
And with great power it forth led me
To walk in the visions of Poesy.

I met Murder on the way –   5
He had a mask like Castlereagh[3] –
Very smooth he looked, yet grim;
Seven bloodhounds followed him.[4]

All were fat; and well they might
Be in admirable plight,   10
For one by one, and two by two,
He tossed them human hearts to chew,
Which from his wide cloak he drew.

THE MASK OF ANARCHY
[1] On 16 August 1819, at St Peter's Field, on the outskirts of Manchester, a political meeting of 60,000 working men and women was dispersed by mounted dragoons, with a brutality that left eleven people dead and 421 cases of serious injury. The news reached Shelley within about the week, and he began meditating this poetic response to the event. For further comment see headnote, p. 821 above. A helpful reading is provided by Morton D. Paley, 'Apocapolitics: Allusion and Structure in Shelley's *Mask of Anarchy*', *Huntington Library Quarterly* 54 (1991) 91–109.
[2] Shelley was in Leghorn when he heard of the Peterloo Massacre, 'and the torrent of my indignation has not yet done boiling in my veins', as he told Charles Ollier on 5 September 1819 (Jones ii 117).
[3] Robert Stewart, Viscount Castlereagh (1769–1822), Foreign Secretary 1812–22. As Secretary to the Lord Lieutenant of Ireland (1797–1801), he had been responsible for imprisoning the leaders of the United Irish rebellion. Shelley would have been aware of Byron's stanzas attacking him, *Don Juan* Dedication, stanzas 12–15 (pp. 754–5).
[4] In 1815, Britain joined an alliance of seven other nations (Austria, France, Russia, Prussia, Portugal, Spain and Sweden) in an agreement to postpone final abolition of the slave trade.

Next came Fraud, and he had on,
Like Eldon,[5] an ermined gown;
His big tears, for he wept well,
Turned to millstones as they fell.

15

And the little children, who
Round his feet played to and fro,
Thinking every tear a gem,
Had their brains knocked out by them.

20

Clothed with the Bible, as with light,
And the shadows of the night,
Like Sidmouth,[6] next Hypocrisy
On a crocodile[7] rode by.

25

And many more Destructions played
In this ghastly masquerade,
All disguised, even to the eyes,
Like Bishops, lawyers, peers, or spies.

Last came Anarchy[8]: he rode
On a white horse, splashed with blood;
He was pale even to the lips,
Like Death in the Apocalypse.[9]

30

And he wore a kingly crown,
And in his grasp a sceptre shone;
On his brow this mark I saw –
'I am God, and King, and Law.'[10]

35

With a pace stately and fast,
Over English land he passed,
Trampling to a mire of blood
The adoring multitude.[11]

40

And a mighty troop around,
With their trampling shook the ground,

---

5   John Scott, Baron Eldon, Lord Chancellor, who, on 27 March 1817, was responsible for depriving Shelley of access to his children (Ianthe and Charles) by Harriet Westbrook. Shelley did not see Ianthe again, and Charles he never saw. In *Spirit of the Age* (1825) Hazlitt described Eldon as 'an exceedingly good-natured man' (p. 345).
6   Henry Addington (1757–1844), created Viscount Sidmouth in 1805, had been Prime Minister and Chancellor of the Exchequer, and was in 1819 Home Secretary. He was distinguished for having applauded the Peterloo Massacre in the House of Commons, as reported by Hazlitt (Howe xx 142).
7   *a crocodile* crocodiles were believed to weep so as to attract their prey, and 'crocodile tears' are still a byword for hypocrisy.
8   *Anarchy* In Shelley's distinctive usage 'anarchy' means the breakdown of order due to bad or corrupt government.
9   *He was pale . . . Apocalypse* Revelation 6:8: 'And I looked,

and behold a pale horse: and his name that sat on him was Death, and Hell followed with him'. Possible pictorial influences include Benjamin West's painting *Death on the Pale Horse*, exhibited in London in 1817, and John Hamilton Mortimer, *Death on a Pale Horse*.
10   *On his brow . . . Law* a parody of the inscription borne by the messianic rider of Revelation: 'And he hath on his vesture and on his thigh a name written, KING OF KINGS, AND LORD OF LORDS' (Revelation 19:16).
11   *The adoring multitude* significantly, the people are complicit in the empowering of these corrupt politicians. In April 1819 Shelley had been enraged to see Italians turn out in the streets of Rome to applaud, the Austrian royal family: 'The Emperor of Austria is here, and Maria Louisa is coming. On the journey through the other cities of Italy she was greeted with loud acclamations and vivas of Napoleon. Idiots and slaves!' (Jones ii 93).

Waving each a bloody sword,
For the service of their Lord.[12]   45

And with glorious triumph, they
Rode through England proud and gay,
Drunk as with intoxication
Of the wine of desolation.

O'er fields and towns, from sea to sea,   50
Passed the Pageant[13] swift and free,
Tearing up, and trampling down,
Till they came to London town.

And each dweller, panic-stricken,
Felt his heart with terror sicken   55
Hearing the tempestuous cry
Of the triumph of Anarchy.

For with pomp to meet him came
Clothed in arms like blood and flame,
The hired murderers, who did sing   60
'Thou art God, and Law, and King.

We have waited, weak and lone,
For thy coming, Mighty One!
Our purses are empty, our swords are cold,
Give us glory, and blood, and gold.'   65

Lawyers and priests, a motley crowd,
To the earth their pale brows bowed;
Like a bad prayer, not overloud,
Whispering, 'Thou art Law and God.'

Then all cried with one accord,   70
'Thou art King, and God, and Lord;
Anarchy, to thee we bow,
By thy name made holy now!'

And Anarchy, the Skeleton,
Bowed and grinned to everyone,   75
As well as if his education
Had cost ten millions to the nation.

For he knew the Palaces
Of our Kings were rightly his;
His the sceptre, crown, and globe,[14]   80
And the gold-inwoven robe.

---

[12] *their Lord* George III, the 'old, mad, blind, despised, and dying king' of *England in 1819* (p. 940).

[13] *Pageant* tableau, allegorical procession.
[14] *globe* golden orb, symbol of kingly power.

So he sent his slaves before
To seize upon the Bank and Tower,[15]
And was proceeding with intent
To meet his pensioned Parliament;[16]   85

When one fled past, a maniac maid,
And her name was Hope, she said;
But she looked more like Despair,
And she cried out in the air:

'My father Time is weak and grey   90
With waiting for a better day;
She how idiot-like he stands,
Fumbling with his palsied hands!

He has had child after child
And the dust of death is piled   95
Over everyone but me –
Misery, oh, misery!'

Then she lay down in the street,
Right before the horses' feet,
Expecting, with a patient eye,   100
Murder, Fraud and Anarchy.

When between her and her foes
A mist, a light, an image rose,
Small at first, and weak, and frail,
Like the vapour of a vale;   105

Till as clouds grow on the blast,
Like tower-crowned giants striding fast,
And glare with lightnings as they fly,
And speak in thunder to the sky,

It grew – a Shape arrayed in mail   110
Brighter than the viper's scale,
And upborne on wings whose grain[17]
Was as the light of sunny rain.

On its helm,[18] seen far away,
A planet, like the morning's,[19] lay;   115
And those plumes[20] its light rained through
Like a shower of crimson dew.

---

[15] *the Bank and Tower* strongholds of power: the Bank of England, in Threadneedle Street since 1734, and the Tower of London, the most perfect medieval fortress in Britain, on Tower Hill since around 1066. They had been the objects of an alleged plot in 1817, providing an excuse for the suspension of Habeas Corpus.

[16] *his pensioned Parliament* the politicians are in the pay of Anarchy.

[17] *grain* colour.
[18] *helm* helmet.
[19] *A planet, like the morning's* i.e. a star, like Venus (the morning star).
[20] *plumes* feathers in the helmet.

With step as soft as wind it passed
O'er the heads of men – so fast
That they knew the presence there,   120
And looked – and all was empty air.

As flowers beneath May's footstep waken,
As stars from night's loose hair are shaken,
As waves arise when loud winds call,
Thoughts sprung where'er that step did fall.   125

And the prostrate multitude
Looked – and ankle-deep in blood,
Hope, that maiden most serene,
Was walking with a quiet mien.

And Anarchy, the ghastly birth,   130
Lay dead earth upon the earth;
The Horse of Death, tameless as wind,
Fled, and with his hoofs did grind
To dust the murderers thronged behind.

A rushing light of clouds and splendour,   135
A sense awakening and yet tender,
Was heard and felt – and at its close
These words of joy and fear arose

(As if their own indignant Earth
Which gave the sons of England birth   140
Had felt their blood upon her brow,
And shuddering with a mother's throe

Had turned every drop of blood
By which her face had been bedewed
To an accent unwithstood;   145
As if her heart had cried aloud):

'Men of England, heirs of Glory,
Heroes of unwritten story,
Nurslings of one mighty Mother,
Hopes of her, and one another,   150

Rise like lions after slumber
In unvanquishable number,
Shake your chains to Earth like dew
Which in sleep had fallen on you –
Ye are many; they are few.   155

What is Freedom? Ye can tell
That which slavery is, too well –
For its very name has grown
To an echo of your own.

'Tis to work and have such pay   160
As just keeps life from day to day
In your limbs, as in a cell
For the tyrants' use to dwell.

So that ye for them are made
Loom, and plough, and sword, and spade,   165
With or without your own will bent
To their defence and nourishment.

'Tis to see your children weak
With their mothers pine and peak,[21]
When the winter winds are bleak –   170
They are dying whilst I speak.

'Tis to hunger for such diet
As the rich man in his riot[22]
Casts to the fat dogs that lie
Surfeiting beneath his eye.   175

'Tis to let the Ghost of Gold[23]
Take from toil a thousandfold –
More than ere its substance could
In the tyrannies of old.

Paper coin – that forgery   180
Of the title-deeds, which ye
Hold to something of the worth
Of the inheritance of Earth.

'Tis to be a slave in soul
And to hold no strong control   185
Over your own wills, but be
All that others make of ye.

And at length when ye complain
With a murmur weak and vain,
'Tis to see the Tyrant's crew   190
Ride over your wives and you –
Blood is on the grass like dew.

Then it is to feel revenge
Fiercely thirsting to exchange
Blood for blood and wrong for wrong –   195
Do not thus when ye are strong.

Birds find rest in narrow nest
When weary of their winged quest;
Beasts find fare in woody lair
When storm and snow are in the air.   200

---

[21] *pine and peak* grow thin and emaciated; cf. *Macbeth* I iii 23.
[22] *riot* extravagance.
[23] *the Ghost of Gold* paper money, which Shelley regarded as a trick to inflate the currency and depress the cost of labour.

Asses, swine, have litter spread
And with fitting food are fed;
All things have a home but one –
Thou, oh, Englishman, hast none![24]

This is slavery – savage men   205
Or wild beasts within a den
Would endure not as ye do;
But such ills they never knew.

What art thou Freedom? Oh, could slaves
Answer from their living graves   210
This demand, tyrants would flee
Like a dream's dim imagery.

Thou art not, as impostors say,
A shadow soon to pass away,
A superstition, and a name   215
Echoing from the cave of Fame.[25]

For the labourer thou art bread,
And a comely table spread
From his daily labour come
To a neat and happy home.   220

Thou art clothes, and fire, and food
For the trampled multitude;
No – in countries that are free
Such starvation cannot be
As in England now we see.   225

To the rich thou art a check,
When his foot is on the neck
Of his victim, thou dost make
That he treads upon a snake.

Thou art Justice; ne'er for gold   230
May thy righteous laws be sold
As laws are in England – thou
Shieldst alike the high and low.

Thou art Wisdom – Freemen never
Dream that God will damn for ever   235
All who think those things untrue
Of which Priests make such ado.

Thou art Peace – never by thee
Would blood and treasure wasted be,

---

[24]   *Asses, swine . . . hast none* a reworking of Christ's words: [25]   *Fame* rumour, gossip.
'The foxes have holes, and the birds of the air have nests; but
the Son of man hath not where to lay his head' (Matthew
8:20).

As tyrants wasted them, when all 240
Leagued to quench thy flame in Gaul.[26]

What if English toil and blood
Was poured forth, even as a flood?
It availed, oh Liberty!
To dim, but not extinguish thee. 245

Thou art Love — the rich[27] have kissed
Thy feet, and like him following Christ,[28]
Give their substance to the free
And through the rough world follow thee;

Or turn their wealth to arms, and make 250
War for thy beloved sake
On wealth, and war, and fraud — whence they
Drew the power which is their prey.

Science,[29] Poetry, and Thought
Are thy lamps; they make the lot 255
Of the dwellers in a cot[30]
So serene, they curse it not.

Spirit, Patience, Gentleness,
All that can adorn and bless
Art thou — let deeds, not words, express 260
Thine exceeding loveliness.

Let a great Assembly be
Of the fearless and the free
On some spot of English ground
Where the plains stretch wide around. 265

Let the blue sky overhead
The green earth on which ye tread,
All that must eternal be
Witness the solemnity.

From the corners uttermost 270
Of the bounds of English coast;
From every hut, village and town
Where those who live and suffer moan
For others' misery or their own;

From the workhouse and the prison 275
Where pale as corpses newly risen,
Women, children, young and old,
Groan for pain, and weep for cold;

---

26 *Gaul* Revolutionary France. England was at war with France from February 1793 (shortly after the execution of Louis XVI) until the Napoleonic Wars ended in 1815.
27 *the rich* i.e. those dedicated to liberty.
28 *like him following Christ* Shelley appears to have in mind the three disciples of Christ described at Luke 9:57–62.
29 *Science* knowledge.
30 *cot* cottage.

From the haunts of daily life
Where is waged the daily strife   280
With common wants and common cares
Which sows the human heart with tares;[31]

Lastly from the palaces
Where the murmur of distress
Echoes, like the distant sound   285
Of a wind alive around,

Those prison halls of wealth and fashion,
Where some few feel such compassion
For those who groan, and toil, and wail
As must make their brethren pale –   290

Ye who suffer woes untold,
Or to feel, or[32] to behold
Your lost country bought and sold
With a price of blood and gold –

Let a vast Assembly be,   295
And with great solemnity
Declare with measured words that ye
Are, as God has made ye, free.

Be your strong and simple words
Keen to wound as sharpened swords,   300
And wide as targes[33] let them be
With their shade to cover ye.

Let the tyrants pour around
With a quick and startling sound,
Like the loosening of a sea,   305
Troops of armed emblazonry.

Let the charged artillery drive
Till the dead air seems alive
With the clash of clanging wheels,
And the tramp of horses' heels.   310

Let the fixed bayonet
Gleam with sharp desire to wet
Its bright point in English blood,
Looking keen as one for food.

Let the horsemen's scimitars[34]   315
Wheel and flash, like sphereless stars
Thirsting to eclipse their burning
In a sea of death and mourning.

---

[31] *tares* weeds – i.e. anxieties.
[32] *or . . . or* either . . . or.
[33] *targes* shields.

[34] *the horsemen's scimitars* most of the wounded at Peterloo suffered from sabre cuts.

Stand ye calm and resolute,
Like a forest close and mute,   320
With folded arms and looks which are
Weapons of an unvanquished war;

And let Panic, who outspeeds
The career of armed steeds
Pass, a disregarded shade   325
Through your phalanx undismayed.

Let the laws of your own land,
Good or ill, between ye stand
Hand to hand, and foot to foot,
Arbiters of the dispute,   330

The old laws of England – they
Whose reverend heads with age are grey,
Children of a wiser day;
And whose solemn voice must be
Thine own echo – Liberty!   335

On those who first should violate
Such sacred heralds in their state,
Rest the blood that must ensue,
And it will not rest on you.

And if then the tyrants dare,   340
Let them ride among you there,
Slash, and stab, and maim, and hew –
What they like, that let them do.

With folded arms and steady eyes,
And little fear, and less surprise,   345
Look upon them as they slay,
Till their rage has died away.

Then they will return with shame
To the place from which they came,
And the blood thus shed will speak   350
In hot blushes on their cheek.

Every woman in the land
Will point at them as they stand –
They will hardly dare to greet
Their acquaintance in the Street.   355

And the bold, true warriors
Who have hugged Danger in wars
Will turn to those who would be free,
Ashamed of such base company.

And that slaughter to the nation   360
Shall steam up like inspiration,

Eloquent, oracular –
A volcano heard afar.[35]

And these words shall then become
Like oppression's thundered doom   365
Ringing through each heart and brain,
Heard again – again – again.

Rise like lions after slumber
In unvanquishable number;
Shake your chains to earth like dew   370
Which in sleep had fallen on you –
Ye are many, they are few.'

England in 1819 (composed by 23 December 1819; published 1839; edited from MS)

An old, mad, blind, despised, and dying king;[1]
Princes,[2] the dregs of their dull race, who flow
Through public scorn – mud from a muddy spring;
Rulers who neither see, nor feel, nor know,
But leech-like to their fainting country cling,   5
Till they drop, blind in blood, without a blow.
A people starved and stabbed in th' untilled field;[3]
An army, which liberticide[4] and prey
Makes as a two-edged sword to all who wield;[5]
Golden and sanguine laws which tempt and slay;   10
Religion Christless, Godless – a book sealed;
A senate, time's worst statute, unrepealed[6] –
Are graves from which a glorious phantom may
Burst, to illumine our tempestuous day.

Sonnet (composed 1819; first published 1824; edited from MS)

Lift not the painted veil which those who live
Call Life; though unreal shapes be pictured there
And it but mimic all we would believe
With colours idly spread – behind lurk Fear
And Hope, twin destinies, who ever weave   5
Their shadows o'er the chasm, sightless and drear.[1]

---

35   *And that slaughter . . . afar* this image of revolution is comparable to the image of 'a volcano's meteor-breathing chasm, / Whence the oracular vapour is hurled up' (*Prometheus Unbound* II iii 3–4).

ENGLAND IN 1819
1   George III, on the throne since 1760, was old and ill, and had been insane for years. He died 29 January 1820.
2   *Princes* George III's sons were prodigal, profligate, and unstable to the point of madness.

3   *A people . . . field* a reference to the Peterloo Massacre, 16 August 1819 (see p. 821).
4   *liberticide* the liberty of the people is being killed.
5   *Makes . . . wield* the soldiers destroy their own freedom as they cut down the crowd.
6   An early, deleted version of this line in MS reads: 'A cloak of lies worn on Power's holiday'.

SONNET
1   *sightless and drear* invisible and dark.

I knew one who had lifted it. He sought,
For his lost heart was tender, things to love
But found them not, alas; nor was there aught
The world contains, the which he could approve.   10
Through the unheeding many[2] he did move,
A splendour among shadows, a bright blot
Upon this gloomy scene, a Spirit that strove
For truth, and like the preacher, found it not.

To a Skylark (composed late June 1820)[1]

From PROMETHEUS UNBOUND[2] (1820)

Hail to thee, blithe spirit!
    Bird thou never wert –
That from heaven, or near it,
    Pourest thy full heart
In profuse strains of unpremeditated art.   5

Higher still and higher
    From the earth thou springest
Like a cloud of fire;
    The blue deep thou wingest,
And singing still dost soar, and soaring ever singest.   10

In the golden lightning
    Of the sunken sun
O'er which clouds are brightning,
    Thou dost float and run
Like an unbodied joy whose race is just begun.   15

The pale purple even
    Melts around thy flight;
Like a star of heaven
    In the broad daylight
Thou art unseen[3] – but yet I hear thy shrill delight,   20

Keen as are the arrows
    Of that silver sphere,[4]
Whose intense lamp narrows
    In the white dawn clear,
Until we hardly see – we feel that it is there.   25

---

[2] *many* i.e. crowds, multitudes.

To A SKYLARK
[1] As Mary Shelley recalled, this poem was written at the
Gisbornes' house at Leghorn: 'It was on a beautiful summer
evening, while wandering among the lanes whose myrtle
hedges were the bowers of the fireflies, that we heard the car-
olling of the skylark which inspired one of the most beautiful
of his poems'.
[2] In addition to *Prometheus Unbound*, Shelley's 1820 volume
contained a number of shorter works composed in Italy.

[3] *Thou art unseen* John Gisborne recalled how he and Shelley
used to listen to the skylarks, which flew 'to a height at which
the straining eye could scarcely ken the stationary and
diminutive specks into which their soft and still receding
forms had at length vanished' (journal of John Gisborne, 20
October 1827).
[4] *that silver sphere* the morning star (Venus) is so bright that
it can be seen even after sunrise.

All the earth and air
   With thy voice is loud,
As when night is bare
   From one lonely cloud
The moon rains out her beams – and heaven is overflowed.   30

What thou art we know not;
   What is most like thee?
From rainbow clouds there flow not
   Drops so bright to see
As from thy presence showers a rain of melody.   35

Like a poet hidden
   In the light of thought,
Singing hymns unbidden,[5]
   Till the world is wrought
To sympathy with hopes and fears it heeded not;   40

Like a high-born maiden
   In a palace-tower,
Soothing her love-laden
   Soul in secret hour,
With music sweet as love, which overflows her bower;   45

Like a glow-worm golden
   In a dell of dew,
Scattering unbeholden
   Its aerial hue
Among the flowers and grass which screen it from the view;   50

Like a rose embowered
   In its own green leaves,
By warm winds deflowered
   Till the scent it gives
Makes faint with too much sweet these heavy-winged thieves;   55

Sound of vernal showers
   On the twinkling grass,
Rain-awakened flowers,
   All that ever was
Joyous and clear and fresh, thy music doth surpass.   60

Teach us, sprite or bird,
   What sweet thoughts are thine;
I have never heard
   Praise of love or wine
That panted forth a flood of rapture so divine: 65

Chorus Hymeneal[6]
   Or triumphal chaunt

---

[5] *hymns unbidden* i.e. poems that are the direct result of inspiration.

[6] *Chorus Hymeneal* wedding-song. Hymen was the Greek god of marriage.

Matched with thine would be all
    But an empty vaunt,[7]
A thing wherein we feel there is some hidden want.   70

    What objects are the fountains
      Of thy happy strain?[8]
    What fields or waves or mountains?
      What shapes of sky or plain?
What love of thine own kind? What ignorance of pain?   75

    With thy clear keen joyance
      Languor cannot be –
    Shadow of annoyance
      Never came near thee;
Thou lovest, but ne'er knew love's sad satiety.   80

    Waking or asleep,
      Thou of death must deem
    Things more true and deep
      Than we mortals dream,
Or how could thy notes flow in such a crystal stream?   85

    We look before and after,[9]
      And pine for what is not;
    Our sincerest laughter
      With some pain is fraught –
Our sweetest songs are those that tell of saddest thought.   90

    Yet if we could scorn
      Hate and pride and fear;
    If we were things born
      Not to shed a tear,
I know not how thy joy we ever should come near.   95

    Better than all measures
      Of delightful sound;
    Better than all treasures
      That in books are found –
Thy skill to poet were, thou scorner of the ground!   100

    Teach me half the gladness
      That thy brain must know,
    Such harmonious madness[10]
      From my lips would flow
The world should listen then, as I am listening now.   105

[handwritten annotation: compare to (eat)]

---

7 *vaunt* boast.
8 *strain* song.
9 *We look before and after* Hamlet speaks of how human beings were created 'with such large discourse, / Looking before and after' (*Hamlet* IV iv 36–7).
10 *harmonious madness* inspiration to write beautiful poetry.

A Defence of Poetry; or, Remarks Suggested by an Essay Entitled 'The Four Ages of Poetry' (extracts) (composed February–March 1821; first published 1840; edited from MS)[1]

According to one mode of regarding those two classes of mental action which are called reason and imagination, the former may be considered as mind contemplating the relations borne by one thought to another, however produced; and the latter, as mind acting upon those thoughts so as to colour them with its own light, and composing from them, as from elements, other thoughts, each containing within itself the principle of its own integrity. The one is the τὸ ποιεῖν,[2] or the principle of synthesis, and has for its objects those forms which are common to universal nature and existence itself; the other is the τὸ λογίζειν,[3] or principle of analysis, and its action regards the relations of things simply as relations, considering thoughts not in their integral unity but as the algebraical representations which conduct to certain general results. Reason is the enumeration of quantities already known; imagination the perception of the value of those quantities, both separately and as a whole. Reason respects the differences, and imagination the similitudes of things. Reason is to imagination as the instrument to the agent, as the body to the spirit, as the shadow to the substance.

Poetry, in a general sense, may be defined to be 'the expression of the imagination'; and poetry is connate[4] with the origin of man. Man is an instrument over which a series of external and internal impressions are driven, like the alternations of an ever-changing wind over an Aeolian lyre, which move it, by their motion, to ever-changing melody.[5] But there is a principle within the human being (and perhaps within all sentient beings) which acts otherwise than in the lyre, and produces not melody alone, but harmony, by an internal adjustment of the sounds or motions thus excited to the impressions which excite them. It is as if the lyre could accommodate its chords to the motions of that which strikes them, in a determined proportion of sound – even as the musician can accommodate his voice to the sound of the lyre. A child at play by itself will express its delight by its voice and motions, and every inflection of tone and every gesture will bear exact relation to a corresponding antitype[6] in the pleasurable impressions which awakened it. It will be the reflected image of that impression – and as the lyre trembles and sounds after the wind has died away, so the child seeks, by prolonging in its voice and motions the duration of the effect, to prolong also a consciousness of the cause. In relation to the objects which delight a child, these expressions are what poetry is to higher objects.

The savage (for the savage is to ages what the child is to years) expresses the emotions produced in him by surrounding objects in a similar manner – and language and gesture, together with plastic or pictorial imitation, become the image of the combined effect of those objects, and of his apprehension of them. Man in society, with all his passions and his pleasures, next becomes the object of the pas-

---

A DEFENCE OF POETRY

1   Inspired by Thomas Love Peacock's essay, 'The Four Ages of Poetry', published in *Ollier's Literary Miscellany* (1820). His argument was that classical poetry passed through four ages: (1) an iron age of warriors, heroes and gods; (2) a golden age of recollection (Homeric); (3) a silver age in which poetry took new forms and recreated itself (Virgilian); and (4) the brass age, a second childhood in which it regressed to the crudities of the iron age. Then came the dark ages, and then the 'four ages' of modern poetry. The romantic age, Peacock argued, is that of brass, in which the poet is half-barbarian, living in the past, with an outmoded way of thinking. Shelley had read his friend's essay by 20 January 1821, and told Ollier (his and Peacock's publisher) that it 'has excited my polemical faculties so violently, that the moment I get rid of ophthalmia I mean to set about an answer to it, which I will send you, if you please. It is very clever, but, I think, very false' (Jones ii 258). Shelley began work on his response in late February, Part I of

which was finished by 20 March. He sent it to Ollier, promising another two Parts after its publication. Unfortunately, the *Literary Miscellany* failed, and Part I of the 'Defence' did not appear; Shelley was drowned in 1822 without completing it or seeing Part I into print. It was published in 1840. There are two central influences on the 'Defence': Wordsworth's Preface to *Lyrical Ballads* and Sir Philip Sidney's *Apologie for Poetrie*.

2   'making something'. The Greek word is the source of the word 'poet'.

3   'discussing its structure'.

4   *connate* coeval, as old as.

5   *Man is an instrument . . . melody* cf. Shelley's 'Essay on Christianity': 'There is a power by which we are surrounded, like the atmosphere in which some motionless lyre is suspended, which visits with its breath our silent chords at will'.

6   *antitype* 'that which is shadowed forth or represented by the "type" or symbol' (*OED*).

sions and pleasures of man; an additional class of emotions produces an augmented treasure of expressions; and language, gesture, and the imitative arts become at once the representation and the medium, the pencil and the picture, the chisel and the statue, the chord and the harmony. The social sympathies (or those laws from which as from its elements society results) begin to develop themselves from the moment that two human beings coexist; the future is contained within the present as the plant within the seed; and equality, diversity, unity, contrast, mutual dependence, become the principles alone capable of affording the motives according to which the will of a social being is determined to action (inasmuch as he is social), and constitute pleasure in sensation, virtue in sentiment, beauty in art, truth in reasoning, and love in the intercourse of kind. Hence men, even in the infancy of society, observe a certain order in their words and actions distinct from that of the objects and the impressions represented by them, all expression being subject to the laws of that from which it proceeds.

But let us dismiss those more general considerations which might involve an enquiry into the principles of society itself, and restrict our view to the manner in which the imagination is expressed upon its forms.

In the youth of the world, men dance and sing and imitate natural objects, observing in these actions (as in all others) a certain rhythm or order. And although all men observe a similar, they observe not the same order in the motions of the dance, in the melody of the song, in the combinations of language, in the series of their imitations of natural objects. For there is a certain order or rhythm belonging to each of these classes of mimetic representation, from which the hearer and the spectator receive an intenser and a purer pleasure than from any other. The sense of an approximation to this order has been called taste by modern writers.[7] Every man in the infancy of art observes an order which approximates more or less closely to that from which this highest delight results. But the diversity is not sufficiently marked as that its gradations should be sensible,[8] except in those instances where the predominance of this faculty of approximation to the beautiful (for so we may be permitted to name the relation between this highest pleasure and its cause) is very great. Those in whom it exists in excess are poets, in the most universal sense of the word – and the pleasure resulting from the manner in which they express the influence of society or nature upon their own minds, communicates itself to others, and gathers a sort of reduplication from that community. Their language is vitally metaphorical; that is, it marks the before unapprehended relations of things, and perpetuates their apprehension, until the words which represent them become through time signs for portions or classes of thoughts, instead of pictures of integral thoughts; and then if no new poets should arise to create afresh the associations which have been thus disorganized, language will be dead to all the nobler purposes of human intercourse.

These similitudes or relations are finely said by Lord Bacon[9] to be 'the same footsteps of nature impressed upon the various subjects of the world'[10] – and he considers the faculty which perceives them as the storehouse of axioms common to all knowledge. In the infancy of society every author is necessarily a poet, because language itself is poetry; and to be a poet is to apprehend the true and the beautiful, in a word the good which exists in the relation subsisting first between existence and perception, and secondly between perception and expression. Every original language near to its source is in itself the chaos of a cyclic poem: the copiousness of lexicography and the distinctions of grammar are the works of a later age, and are merely the catalogue and the form of the creations of poetry.

But poets, or those who imagine and express this indestructible order, are not only the authors of language and of music, of the dance and architecture and statuary and painting; they are the institu-

---

7   *has been called taste by modern writers* most notably Hazlitt, who, in his 'Essay on Taste' (1818), wrote: 'Genius is the power of producing excellence: taste is the power of perceiving the excellence thus produced in its several sorts and degrees, with all their force, refinement, distinctions, and connections' (Howe xvii 57). Other writers on the subject include Coleridge (in *Biographia Literaria*), Burke and Hume.
8   *sensible* perceptible.
9   Francis Bacon, Baron Verulam, Viscount St Albans

(1561–1626), Lord Chancellor of England, philosopher and essayist. His work appealed to Shelley because he was a neo-Platonist.
10   *Of the Advancement of Learning* (1605), Book II, Chapter 5: 'Are not the organs of the senses of one kind with the organs of reflection, the eye with a glass. . . ? Neither are these only similitudes, as men of narrow observation may conceive them to be, but the same footsteps of Nature, treading or printing upon several subjects or matters'.

tors of laws, and the founders of civil society, and the inventors of the arts of life, and the teachers who draw into a certain propinquity with the beautiful and the true that partial apprehension of the agencies of the invisible world which is called religion. Hence all original religions are allegorical, or susceptible of allegory, and like Janus have a double face of false and true. Poets, according to the circumstances of the age and nation in which they appeared, were called in the earlier epochs of the world legislators or prophets.[11] A poet essentially comprises and unites both these characters. For he not only beholds intensely the present as it is, and discovers those laws according to which present things ought to be ordered, but he beholds the future in the present, and his thoughts are the germs of the flower and the fruit of latest time. Not that I assert poets to be prophets in the gross sense of the word, or that they can foretell the form as surely as they foreknow the spirit of events – such is the pretence of superstition which would make poetry an attribute of prophecy, rather than prophecy an attribute of poetry.

A poet participates in the eternal, the infinite, and the one; as far as relates to his conceptions, time and place and number are not. The grammatical forms which express the moods of time, and the difference of persons and the distinction of place are convertible with respect to the highest poetry without injuring it as poetry, and the choruses of Aeschylus, and the Book of Job, and Dante's *Paradise* would afford, more than any other writings, examples of this fact, if the limits of this paper did not forbid citation. The creations of sculpture, painting, and music, are illustrations still more decisive.

Language, colour, form, and religious and civil habits of action are all the instruments and the materials of poetry; they may be called poetry by that figure of speech which considers the effect as a synonym of the cause. But poetry in a more restricted sense expresses those arrangements of language, and especially metrical language, which are created by that imperial faculty whose throne is curtained within the invisible nature of man. And this springs from the nature itself of language, which is a more direct representation of the actions and passions of our internal being, and is susceptible of more various and delicate combinations, than colour, form, or motion, and is more plastic[12] and obedient to the control of that faculty of which it is the creation. For language is arbitrarily produced by the imagination and has relation to thoughts alone; but all other materials, instruments and conditions of art, have relations among each other which limit and interpose between conception and expression. The former is as a mirror which reflects, the latter as a cloud which enfeebles, the light of which both are mediums of communication. Hence the fame of sculptors, painters and musicians (although the intrinsic powers of the great masters of these arts may yield in no degree to that of those who have employed language as the hieroglyphic of their thoughts) has never equalled that of poets in the restricted sense of the term, as two performers of equal skill will produce unequal effects from a guitar and a harp. The fame of legislators and founders of religions (so long as their institutions last) alone seems to exceed that of poets in the restricted sense – but it can scarcely be a question whether, if we deduct the celebrity which their flattery of the gross opinions of the vulgar usually conciliates, together with that which belonged to them in their higher character of poets, any excess will remain.

We have thus circumscribed the word 'poetry' within the limits of that art which is the most familiar and the most perfect expression of the faculty itself. It is necessary however to make the circle still narrower, and to determine the distinction between measured and unmeasured language,[13] for the popular division into prose and verse is inadmissible in accurate philosophy.

Sounds as well as thoughts have relation both between each other and towards that which they represent, and a perception of the order of those relations has always been found connected with a perception of the order of the relations of thoughts. Hence the language of poets has ever affected a certain uniform and harmonious recurrence of sound, without which it were not poetry, and which is scarcely less indispensable to the communication of its influence than the words themselves, without reference to that peculiar order. Hence the vanity of translation: it were as wise to cast a violet into a crucible

---

[11] *prophets* in his *Apologie for Poetrie*, Sir Philip Sidney had observed: 'Among the Romans a poet was called "Vates", which is as much as a diviner, foreseer, or prophet . . . so heavenly a title did that excellent people bestow upon this heart-ravishing knowledge'.

[12] *plastic* susceptible to the artist's creative power.
[13] *measured and unmeasured language* Shelley is looking for a more accurate definition of poetry and prose than that popularly conceived.

that you might discover the formal principle of its colour and odour, as seek to transfuse from one language into another the creations of a poet. The plant must spring again from its seed or it will bear no flower – and this is the burden of the curse of Babel.

An observation of the regular mode of the recurrence of this harmony in the language of poetical minds, together with its relation to music, produced metre, or a certain system of traditional forms of harmony and language. Yet it is by no means essential that a poet should accommodate his language to this traditional form, so that the harmony which is its spirit be observed. The practice is indeed convenient and popular, and to be preferred, especially in such composition as includes much action: but every great poet must inevitably innovate upon the example of his predecessors in the exact structure of his peculiar versification.

The distinction between poets and prose writers is a vulgar error. The distinction between philosophers and poets has been anticipated. Plato was essentially a poet[14] – the truth and splendour of his imagery and the melody of his language is the most intense that it is possible to conceive. He rejected the measure of the epic, dramatic, and lyrical forms, because he sought to kindle a harmony in thoughts divested of shape and action, and he forbore to invent any regular plan of rhythm which would include, under determinate forms, the varied pauses of his style. Cicero[15] sought to imitate the cadence of his periods but with little success. Lord Bacon was a poet.[16] His language has a sweet and majestic rhythm which satisfies the sense no less than the almost superhuman wisdom of his philosophy satisfies the intellect; it is a strain which distends,[17] and then bursts the circumference of the reader's mind, and pours itself forth together with it into the universal element with which it has perpetual sympathy. All the authors of revolutions in opinion are not only necessarily poets as they are inventors, nor even as their words unveil the permanent analogy of things by images which participate in the life of truth – but as their periods[18] are harmonious and rhythmical and contain in themselves the elements of verse, being the echo of the eternal music. Nor are those supreme poets who have employed traditional forms of rhythm on account of the form and action of their subjects, less capable of perceiving and teaching the truth of things, than those who have omitted that form. Shakespeare, Dante and Milton (to confine ourselves to modern writers) are philosophers of the very loftiest power.

A poem is the very image of life expressed in its eternal truth. There is this difference between a story and a poem: that a story is a catalogue of detached facts which have no other bond of connection than time, place, circumstance, cause and effect; the other is the creation of actions according to the unchangeable forms of human nature, as existing in the mind of the creator, which is itself the image of all other minds. The one is partial, and applies only to a definite period of time, and a certain combination of events which can never again recur; the other is universal, and contains within itself the germ of a relation to whatever motives or actions have place in the possible varieties of human nature. Time, which destroys the beauty and the use of the story of particular facts, stripped of the poetry which should invest them, augments that of poetry, and forever develops new and wonderful applications of the eternal truth which it contains. Hence epitomes[19] have been called the moths of just history;[20] they eat out the poetry of it. The story of particular facts is as a mirror which obscures and distorts that which should be beautiful: poetry is a mirror which makes beautiful that which is distorted.

The parts of a composition may be poetical, without the composition as a whole being a poem. A single sentence may be considered as a whole though it may be found in the midst of a series of unassimilated portions; a single word even may be a spark of inextinguishable thought. And thus all the

---

[14] *Plato was essentially a poet* again, Shelley follows Sidney, who wrote in his *Apologie*: 'Of all philosophers he [Plato] is the most poetical'.

[15] Marcus Tullius Cicero (106–43 BC), Roman statesman and man of letters.

[16] 'See the Filium Labyrinthi, and the Essay on Death particularly' (Shelley's note).

[17] *distends* expands.

[18] *periods* sentences.

[19] *epitomes* summary accounts.

[20] Bacon, *Of the Advancement of Learning* Book II, chapter 2: 'As for the corruptions and moths of history, which are epitomes, the use of them deserveth to be banished, as all men of sound judgment have confessed, as those that have fretted and corroded the sound bodies of many excellent histories, and wrought them into base and unprofitable dregs'.

great historians – Herodotus, Plutarch, Livy[21] – were poets; and although the plan of these writers, especially that of Livy, restrained them from developing this faculty in its highest degree, they make copious and ample amends for their subjection, by filling all the interstices of their subject with living images.

Having determined what is poetry and who are poets, let us proceed to estimate its effects upon society.

Poetry is ever accompanied with pleasure: all spirits on which it falls, open themselves to receive the wisdom which is mingled with its delight.[22] In the infancy of the world, neither poets themselves nor their auditors are fully aware of the excellency of poetry, for it acts in a divine and unapprehended manner, beyond and above consciousness – and it is reserved for future generations to contemplate and measure the mighty cause and effect in all the strength and splendour of their union. Even in modern times, no living poet ever arrived at the fullness of his fame. The jury which sits in judgement upon a poet, belonging as he does to all time, must be composed of his peers; it must be impanelled[23] by Time from the selectest of the wise of many generations. A poet is a nightingale who sits in darkness and sings to cheer its own solitude with sweet sounds; his auditors are as men entranced by the melody of an unseen musician, who feel that they are moved and softened, yet know not whence or why.[24] The poems of Homer and his contemporaries were the delight of infant Greece; they were the elements of that social system which is the column upon which all succeeding civilization has reposed. Homer embodied the ideal perfection of his age in human character – nor can we doubt that those who read his verses were awakened to an ambition of becoming like to Achilles, Hector and Ulysses.[25] The truth and beauty of friendship, patriotism and persevering devotion to an object, were unveiled to the depths in these immortal creations; the sentiments of the auditors must have been refined and enlarged by a sympathy with such great and lovely impersonations, until from admiring they imitated, and from imitation they identified themselves with the objects of their admiration. Nor let it be objected that these characters are remote from moral perfection, and that they can by no means be considered as edifying patterns for general imitation. Every epoch under names more or less specious has deified its peculiar errors; revenge is the naked idol of the worship of a semi-barbarous age, and self-deceit is the veiled image of unknown evil before which luxury and satiety[26] lie prostrate.

But a poet considers the vices of his contemporaries as the temporary dress in which his creations must be arrayed, and which cover without concealing the eternal proportions of their beauty.[27] An epic or dramatic personage is understood to wear them around his soul, as he may the ancient armour or the modern uniform around his body – whilst it is easy to conceive a dress more graceful than either. The beauty of the internal nature cannot be so far concealed by its accidental vesture,[28] but that the spirit of its form shall communicate itself to the very disguise, and indicate the shape it hides from the manner in which it is worn. A majestic form and graceful motions will express themselves through the most barbarous and tasteless costume. Few poets of the highest class have chosen to exhibit the beauty of their conceptions in its naked truth and splendour, and it is doubtful whether the alloy of costume, habit, etc., be not necessary to temper this planetary music for mortal ears.

---

[21] *Herodotus, Plutarch, Livy* historians of ancient Greece and Rome: Herodotus (*c.*480–*c.*425 BC) wrote the first Greek history in 9 Books about the struggle between Asia and Greece, from Croesus to Xerxes; Plutarch (*c.* AD 46–*c.*120) wrote the *Parallel Lives* of eminent Romans and Greeks; Titus Livius (59 BC–AD 17) wrote a history of Rome in 142 books, 35 of which are extant.

[22] *Poetry . . . delight* Shelley echoes Sidney's remark that the poet 'cometh to you with words set in delightful proportion, either accompanied with, or prepared for the well enchanting skill of music; and with a tale forsooth he cometh unto you, with a tale which holdeth children from play, and old men from the chimney corner; and, pretending no more, doth intend the winning of the mind from wickedness to virtue'.

[23] *impanelled* summoned, chosen.

[24] *A poet . . . or why* cf. *To a Skylark* 36–40.

[25] *Achilles, Hector and Ulysses* heroes in the Trojan war.

[26] *luxury and satiety* lust and excessive gratification.

[27] *But a poet . . . beauty* cf. Shelley's remark in a letter to the Gisbornes of 13 July 1821: 'Poets, the best of them, are a very chameleonic race: they take the colour not only of what they feed on, but of the very leaves under which they pass' (Jones ii 308). This is close to Keats's notion of negative capability, which also uses the metaphor of a chameleon; see his letter to Woodhouse of 27 October 1818 (p. 1042).

[28] *accidental vesture* i.e. outward appearance.

The whole objection however of the immorality of poetry rests upon a misconception of the manner in which poetry acts to produce the moral improvement of man. Ethical science[29] arranges the elements which poetry has created, and propounds schemes and proposes examples of civil and domestic life. Nor is it for want of admirable doctrines that men hate, and despise, and censure, and deceive, and subjugate one another. But poetry acts in another and a diviner manner. It awakens and enlarges the mind itself by rendering it the receptacle of a thousand unapprehended combinations of thought. Poetry lifts the veil from the hidden beauty of the world, and makes familiar objects be as if they were not familiar; it re-produces all that it represents, and the impersonations clothed in its Elysian[30] light stand thenceforward in the minds of those who have once contemplated them as memorials of that gentle and exalted content which extends itself over all thoughts and actions with which it coexists. The great secret of morals is love, or a going out of our own nature, and an identification of ourselves with the beautiful which exists in thought, action, or person not our own. A man, to be greatly good, must imagine intensely and comprehensively; he must put himself in the place of another and of many others; the pains and pleasures of his species must become his own. The great instrument of moral good is the imagination – and poetry administers to the effect by acting upon the cause.[31]

Poetry enlarges the circumference of the imagination by replenishing it with thoughts of ever-new delight which have the power of attracting and assimilating to their own nature all other thoughts, and which form new intervals and interstices whose void forever craves fresh food. Poetry strengthens the faculty which is the organ of the moral nature of man, in the same manner as exercise strengthens a limb. A poet therefore would do ill to embody his own conceptions of right and wrong (which are usually those of his place and time) in his poetical creations (which participate in neither). By this assumption of the inferior office of interpreting the effect, in which perhaps after all he might acquit himself but imperfectly, he would resign a glory in a participation in the cause. There was little danger that Homer, or any of the eternal poets, should have so far misunderstood themselves as to have abdicated this throne of their widest dominion. Those in whom the poetical faculty, though great, is less intense (as Euripides, Lucan, Tasso, Spenser)[32] have frequently affected a moral aim, and the effect of their poetry is diminished in exact proportion to the degree in which they compel us to advert to[33] this purpose. . . .

The poetry of Dante[34] may be considered as the bridge thrown over the stream of time, which unites the modern and the ancient world. The distorted notions of invisible things which Dante and his rival Milton have idealised, are merely the mask and the mantle in which these great poets walk through eternity enveloped and disguised. It is a difficult question to determine how far they were conscious of the distinction which must have subsisted[35] in their minds between their own creed and that of the people. Dante at least appears to wish to mark the full extent of it by placing Riphaeus (whom Virgil calls 'justissimus unus')[36] in Paradise, and observing a most heretical caprice in his distribution of rewards and punishments. And Milton's poem contains within itself a philosophical refutation of that system of which, by a strange but natural antithesis, it has been a chief popular support.

Nothing can exceed the energy and magnificence of the character of Satan as expressed in *Paradise Lost*. It is a mistake to suppose that he could ever have been intended for the popular personification of evil. Implacable hate, patient cunning, and a sleepless refinement of device to inflict the extremest anguish on an enemy – these things are evil; and, although venial[37] in a slave, are not to be forgiven in a tyrant; although redeemed by much that ennobles his defeat in one subdued, are marked by all

---

29 *Ethical science* i.e. those who seek to use knowledge in a morally responsible manner.
30 *Elysian* divine.
31 *A man . . . upon the cause* a fundamental principal in Shelley's philosophy.
32 *Euripides, Lucan, Tasso, Spenser* Euripides (c.480–406 BC), one of the three great Attic tragedians, author of *Orestes*, *Medea*, *Bacchae*, among others; Marcus Annaeus Lucanus (AD 39–65), whose one surviving poem is the *Pharsalia*, the greatest Latin epic after the *Aeneid*; Torquato Tasso (1544–95) was the author of the epic *Gerusalemme Liberata* (1575).

33 *advert to* take notice of.
34 *The poetry of Dante* Shelley read Dante in the original and in the blank verse translation of H. F. Cary (1775–1844), which began with the *Inferno* (1805), and continued in 1812 with *Purgatorio* and *Paradiso*. He visited Dante's tomb at Ravenna in August 1821 (Jones ii 335).
35 *subsisted* existed.
36 'The one man who was most just' (*Aeneid* ii 426). Dante places the Trojan Rhipheus in Paradise, even though he died before Christ's birth (*Paradiso* xx).
37 *venial* pardonable.

that dishonours his conquest in the victor. Milton's Devil as a moral being is as far superior to his God as one who perseveres in some purpose which he has conceived to be excellent in spite of adversity and torture, is to one who in the cold security of undoubted triumph inflicts the most horrible revenge upon his enemy, not from any mistaken notion of inducing him to repent of a perseverance in enmity, but with the alleged design of exasperating him to deserve new torments. Milton has so far violated the popular creed (if this shall be judged to be a violation) as to have alleged no superiority of moral virtue to his God over his Devil. And this bold neglect of a direct moral purpose is the most decisive proof of the supremacy of Milton's genius. He mingled, as it were, the elements of human nature as colours upon a single palette, and arranged them into the composition of his great picture according to the laws of epic truth; that is, according to the laws of that principle by which a series of actions of the external universe and of intelligent and ethical beings is calculated to excite the sympathy of succeeding generations of mankind. The *Divina Commedia* and *Paradise Lost* have conferred upon modern mythology a systematic form; and when change and time shall have added one more superstition to the mass of those which have arisen and decayed upon the earth, commentators will be learnedly employed in elucidating the religion of ancestral Europe, only not utterly forgotten because it will have been stamped with the eternity of genius.

Homer was the first, and Dante the second, epic poet – that is, the second poet the series of whose creations bore a defined and intelligible relation to the knowledge, and sentiment, and religion, and political conditions of the age in which he lived, and of the ages which followed it, developing itself in correspondence with their development. For Lucretius had limed[38] the wings of his swift spirit in the dregs of the sensible[39] world; and Virgil, with a modesty which ill became his genius, had affected the fame of an imitator even whilst he created anew all that he copied; and none among the flock of mock-birds, though their notes were sweet (Apollonius Rhodius, Quintus Calaber Smyrnaeus, Nonnus, Lucan, Statius, or Claudian),[40] have sought even to fulfil a single condition of epic truth. Milton was the third epic poet. For, if the title of epic in its highest sense is to be refused to the *Aeneid*, still less can it be conceded to the *Orlando Furioso*,[41] the *Gerusalemme Liberata*, *The Lusiad*,[42] or *The Faerie Queene*.

Dante and Milton were both deeply penetrated with the ancient religion of the civilised world – and its spirit exists in their poetry probably in the same proportion as its forms survived in the unreformed worship of modern Europe.[43] The one preceded and the other followed the Reformation at almost equal intervals. Dante was the first religious reformer, and Luther surpassed him rather in the rudeness and acrimony, than in the boldness of his censures of papal usurpation.[44] Dante was the first awakener of entranced Europe; he created a language in itself music and persuasion out of a chaos of inharmonious barbarisms; he was the congregator of those great spirits who presided over the resurrection of learning, the Lucifer[45] of that starry flock which in the thirteenth century shone forth from republican Italy, as from a heaven, into the darkness of the benighted world. His very words are instinct[46] with spirit – each is as a spark, a burning atom of inextinguishable thought, and many yet lie covered in the ashes of their birth, and pregnant with a lightning which has yet found no conductor. All high poetry is infinite; it is as the first acorn, which contained all oaks potentially. Veil after veil may be undrawn, and the inmost naked beauty of the meaning never exposed. A great poem is a fountain forever overflowing with the waters of wisdom and delight – and after one person or one age

---

38   *limed* birds were caught by smearing bird-lime, a sticky substance, on twigs where they perched.
39   *sensible* perceived.
40   *Apollonius Rhodius . . . Claudian* minor classical poets: Apollonius Rhodius (*c*.295–215 BC), author of *Argonautica*; Quintus Smyrnaeus (fourth century AD), called Calaber because of the discovery in Calabria of the only known MS of his *Posthomerica*, a fourteen-volume sequel to Homer; Nonnus (*c*. AD 400), author of a Greek epic in forty-eight books on the adventures of the god Dionysus, *Dionysiaca*; Marcus Annaeus Lucanus (AD 39–65), whose one surviving poem is the *Pharsalia*, the greatest Latin epic after the *Aeneid*; Publius

Papinius Statius (*c*. AD 40–*c*.96), author of the *Thebaid*; Claudius Claudianus, Roman poet of the fourth century AD, author of the epic *Rape of Proserpine*.
41   *Orlando Furioso* epic by Ariosto.
42   the *Gerusalemme Liberata* see note 31 above; *The Lusiad* epic by Luiz de Camoëns.
43   the *unreformed worship of modern Europe* i.e. domination of the Roman Catholic church.
44   *papal usurpation* wrongful assumption of supreme authority of the Pope.
45   *Lucifer* i.e. light-bearer.
46   *instinct* imbued.

has exhausted all its divine effluence[47] which its peculiar relations enable them to share, another and yet another succeeds, and new relations are ever developed, the source of an unforeseen and an unconceived delight.

The age immediately succeeding to that of Dante, Petrarch, and Boccaccio, was characterized by a revival of painting, sculpture, music, and architecture. Chaucer caught the sacred inspiration, and the superstructure of English literature is based upon the materials of Italian invention.

But let us not be betrayed from a defence into a critical history of poetry and its influence on society. Be it enough to have pointed out the effects of poetry (in the large and true sense of the word) upon their own and all succeeding times, and to revert to the partial instances cited as illustrations of an opinion the reverse of that attempted to be established by the author of 'The Four Ages of Poetry'.[48]

But poets have been challenged to resign the civic crown[49] to reasoners and mechanists on another plea. It is admitted that the exercise of the imagination is more delightful, but it is alleged that that of the reason is more useful. Let us examine as the grounds of this distinction what is here meant by utility. Pleasure or good in a general sense is that which the consciousness of a sensitive and intelligent being seeks, and in which, when found, it acquiesces. There are two modes or degrees of pleasure – one durable, universal, and permanent; the other transitory and particular. Utility may either express the means of producing the former or the latter. In the former sense, whatever strengthens and purifies the affections, enlarges the imagination, and adds a spirit to sense, is useful. But the meaning in which the author of 'The Four Ages of Poetry' seems to have employed the word utility is the narrower one of banishing the importunity of the wants of our animal nature, the surrounding men with security of life, the dispersing the grosser delusions of superstition, and the conciliating such a degree of mutual forbearance among men as may consist with the motives of personal advantage.

Undoubtedly the promoters of utility in this limited sense have their appointed office in society. They follow the footsteps of poets, and copy the sketches of their creations into the book of common life. They make space, and give time. Their exertions are of the highest value so long as they confine their administration of the concerns of the inferior powers of our nature within the limits of what is due to the superior ones. But whilst the sceptic destroys gross superstitions, let him spare to deface, as some of the French writers have defaced, the eternal truths charactered[50] upon the imaginations of men. Whilst the mechanist abridges,[51] and the political economist combines labour,[52] let them beware that their speculations, for want of a correspondence with those first principles which belong to the imagination, do not tend, as they have in modern England, to exasperate at once the extremes of luxury[53] and want. They have exemplified the saying, 'To him that hath, more shall be given; and from him that hath not, the little that he hath shall be taken away'.[54] The rich have become richer, and the poor have become poorer; and the vessel of the state is driven between the Scylla and Charybdis[55] of anarchy and despotism. Such are the effects which must ever flow from an unmitigated exercise of the calculating faculty.

It is difficult to define pleasure in its highest sense, the definition involving a number of apparent paradoxes. For, from an inexplicable defect of harmony in the constitution of human nature, the pain of the inferior is frequently connected with the pleasure of the superior portions of our being. Sorrow, terror, anguish, despair itself are often the chosen expressions of an approximation to the highest good. Our sympathy in tragic fiction depends on this principle; tragedy delights by affording a shadow of the pleasure which exists in pain. This is the source also of the melancholy which is inseparable from the sweetest melody.[56] The pleasure that is in sorrow is sweeter than the pleasure of plea-

---

47   *effluence* emanations.
48   *the author of 'The Four Ages of Poetry'* Thomas Love Peacock (see note 1, p. 944).
49   *civic crown* (*corona civica*) a garland of oak leaves and acorns, bestowed as a much-prized distinction upon one that saved the life of a fellow citizen in war, here meant as the emblem of public utility.
50   *charactered* represented.
51   *the mechanist abridges* by inventing machines that reduce the need for labour.

52   *the political economist combines labour* by organizing workers in the most efficient manner.
53   *luxury and want* excessive over-indulgence and desperate poverty.
54   Matthew 25:29.
55   *Scylla and Charybdis* dangerous cave of the monster Scylla, and whirlpool, which demolished part of Ulysses' fleet in the *Odyssey*.
56   *This is the source . . . melody* cf. *To a Skylark* 90: 'Our sweetest songs are those that tell of saddest thought'.

sure itself – and hence the saying, 'It is better to go to the house of mourning than to the house of mirth'.[57] Not that this highest species of pleasure is necessarily linked with pain. The delight of love and friendship, the ecstasy of the admiration of nature, the joy of the perception and still more of the creation of poetry is often wholly unalloyed.

The production and assurance of pleasure in this highest sense is true utility; those who produce and preserve this pleasure are poets or poetical philosophers.

The exertions of Locke, Hume, Gibbon, Voltaire, Rousseau,[58] and their disciples, in favour of oppressed and deluded humanity, are entitled to the gratitude of mankind. Yet it is easy to calculate the degree of moral and intellectual improvement which the world would have exhibited had they never lived. A little more nonsense would have been talked for a century or two, and perhaps a few more men, women and children burnt as heretics. We might not at this moment have been congratulating each other on the abolition of the Inquisition in Spain.[59] But it exceeds all imagination to conceive what would have been the moral condition of the world if neither Dante, Petrarch, Boccaccio, Chaucer, Shakespeare, Calderón,[60] Lord Bacon, nor Milton, had ever existed; if Raphael and Michelangelo had never been born; if the Hebrew poetry had never been translated; if a revival of a study of Greek literature had never taken place; if no monuments of ancient sculpture had been handed down to us; and if the poetry of the religion of the ancient world had been extinguished together with its belief. The human mind could never, except by the intervention of these excitements, have been awakened to the invention of those grosser[61] sciences, and that application of analytical reasoning to the aberrations of society, which it is now attempted to exalt over the direct expression of the inventive and creative faculty itself.

We have more moral, political and historical wisdom than we know how to reduce into practice; we have more scientific and economical knowledge than can be accommodated to the just distribution of the produce which they multiply. The poetry in these systems of thought is concealed by the accumulation of facts and calculating processes. There is no want of knowledge respecting what is wisest and best in morals, government, and political economy – or at least, what is wiser and better than what men now practise and endure. But we let '*I dare not* wait upon *I would*, like the poor cat i' the adage'.[62] We want the creative faculty to imagine that which we know; we want the generous impulse to act that which we imagine; we want the poetry of life – our calculations have outrun conception; we have eaten more than we can digest. The cultivation of those sciences which have enlarged the limits of the empire of man over the external world, has, for want of the poetical faculty, proportionally circumscribed those of the internal world – and man, having enslaved the elements, remains himself a slave. To what but to a cultivation of the mechanical arts in a degree disproportioned to the presence of the creative faculty (which is the basis of all knowledge) is to be attributed the abuse of all inventions for abridging and combining labour, to the exasperation of the inequality of mankind? From what other cause has it arisen that these inventions which should have lightened, have added a weight to the curse imposed on Adam?[63] Thus, poetry, and the principle of self (of which money is the visible incarnation) are the God and the Mammon of the world.[64]

The functions of the poetical faculty are twofold: by one it creates new materials for knowledge and power and pleasure; by the other it engenders in the mind a desire to reproduce and arrange them according to a certain rhythm and order which may be called the beautiful and the good. The cultivation of poetry is never more to be desired than at periods when, from an excess of the selfish and calculating principle, the accumulation of the materials of external life exceed the quantity of the power

57   Ecclesiastes 7:2.
58   'I follow the classification adopted by the author of "The Four Ages of Poetry", but Rousseau was essentially a poet. The others, even Voltaire, were mere reasoners' (Shelley's note).
59   *We might not . . . Spain* The Spanish Inquisition was suppressed in 1820, restored 1823, and abolished finally in 1834.
60   Pedro Calderón de la Barca (1600–81), whose plays Shelley was reading in Spanish in August 1819; as he told Peacock: 'A kind of Shakespeare is this Calderon, and I have some

thoughts, if I find that I cannot do anything better, of translating some of his plays' (Jones ii 115).
61   *grosser* more materialistic, to do with the physical world.
62   *Macbeth* I vii 44–5.
63   *the curse imposed on Adam* at Genesis 3:17–19.
64   *the God and the Mammon of the world* 'No man can serve two masters: for either he will hate the one, and love the other; or else he will hold to the one, and despise the other. Ye cannot serve God and mammon' (Matthew 6:24).

of assimilating them to the internal laws of human nature. The body has then become too unwieldy for that which animates it.

Poetry is indeed something divine. It is at once the centre and the circumference of knowledge; it is that which comprehends all science, and that to which all science must be referred. It is at the same time the root and the blossom of all other systems of thought. It is that from which all spring, and that which adorns all – and that which, if blighted, denies the fruit and the seed, and withholds from the barren world the nourishment and the succession of the scions[65] of the tree of life. It is the perfect and consummate[66] surface and bloom of things; it is as the odour and the colour of the rose to the texture of the elements which compose it, as the form and the splendour of unfaded beauty to the secrets of anatomy and corruption. What were virtue, love, patriotism, friendship etc.; what were the scenery of this beautiful universe which we inhabit; what were our consolations on this side of the grave; and what were our aspirations beyond it – if poetry did not ascend to bring light and fire from those eternal regions where the owl-winged faculty of calculation dare not ever soar? Poetry is not like reasoning, a power to be exerted according to the determination of the will. A man cannot say, 'I will compose poetry'. The greatest poet even cannot say it: for the mind in creation is as a fading coal which some invisible influence, like an inconstant wind, awakens to transitory brightness. This power arises from within, like the colour of a flower which fades and changes as it is developed, and the conscious portions of our natures are unprophetic either of its approach or its departure. Could this influence be durable in its original purity and force, it is impossible to predict the greatness of the results – but when composition begins, inspiration is already on the decline, and the most glorious poetry that has ever been communicated to the world is probably a feeble shadow of the original conception of the poet. I appeal to the greatest poets of the present day, whether it be not an error to assert that the finest passages of poetry are produced by labour and study. The toil and the delay recommended by critics can be justly interpreted to mean no more than a careful observation of the inspired moments, and an artificial connection of the spaces between them by the intertexture of conventional expressions; a necessity only imposed by a limitedness of the poetical faculty itself. For Milton conceived the *Paradise Lost* as a whole before he executed it in portions. We have his own authority also for the muse having 'dictated' to him the 'unpremeditated song',[67] and let this be an answer to those who would allege the fifty-six various readings of the first line of the *Orlando Furioso*. Compositions so produced are to poetry what mosaic is to painting. This instinct and intuition of the poetical faculty is still more observable in the plastic and pictorial arts:[68] a great statue or picture grows under the power of the artist as a child in the mother's womb, and the very mind which directs the hands in formation is incapable of accounting to itself for the origin, the gradations, or the media of the process.

Poetry is the record of the best and happiest moments of the happiest and best minds. We are aware of evanescent visitations of thought and feeling sometimes associated with place or person, sometimes regarding our own mind alone, and always arising unforeseen and departing unbidden, but elevating and delightful beyond all expression – so that even in the desire and the regret they leave, there cannot but be pleasure, participating as it does in the nature of its object. It is, as it were, the interpenetration of a diviner nature through our own, but its footsteps are like those of a wind over a sea, which the coming calm erases, and whose traces remain only as on the wrinkled sand which paves it.

These, and corresponding conditions of being, are experienced principally by those of the most delicate sensibility and the most enlarged imagination – and the state of mind produced by them is at war with every base desire. The enthusiasm of virtue, love, patriotism and friendship, is essentially linked with these emotions; and whilst they last, self appears as what it is – an atom to a universe. Poets are not only subject to these experiences as spirits of the most refined organization, but they can colour all that they combine with the evanescent hues of this ethereal world; a word or a trait in the representation of a scene or a passion, will touch the enchanted chord, and reanimate, in those who have ever experienced these emotions, the sleeping, the cold, the buried image of the past. Poetry thus

---

[65] *scions* shoots, buds.
[66] *consummate* complete.
[67] *We have . . . song* a reference to *Paradise Lost* ix 21–4, where Milton says that Urania, his 'celestial patroness', 'dic-

tates to me slumbering, or inspires / Easy my unpremeditated verse'.
[68] *the plastic and pictorial arts* sculpture and painting.

makes immortal all that which is best and most beautiful in the world; it arrests the vanishing apparitions which haunt the interlunations[69] of life, and veiling them in language or in form sends them forth among mankind, bearing sweet news of kindred joy to those with whom their sisters abide – abide, because there is no portal of expression from the caverns of the spirit which they inhabit, into the universe of things. Poetry redeems from decay the visitations of the divinity in man.

Poetry turns all things to loveliness: it exalts the beauty of that which is most beautiful, and it adds beauty to that which is most deformed; it marries exultation and horror, grief and pleasure, eternity and change; it subdues to union under its light yoke all irreconcilable things. It transmutes all that it touches, and every form moving within the radiance of its presence is changed by wondrous sympathy to an incarnation of the spirit which it breathes; its secret alchemy turns to potable gold[70] the poisonous waters which flow from death through life; it strips the veil of familiarity from the world, and lays bare the naked and sleeping beauty which is the spirit of its forms.[71]

All things exist as they are perceived, at least in relation to the percipient: 'The mind is its own place, and of itself can make a heaven of hell, a hell of heaven'.[72] But poetry defeats the curse which binds us to be subjected to the accident of surrounding impressions. And whether it spreads its own figured[73] curtain or withdraws life's dark veil from before the scene of things, it equally creates for us a being within our being. It makes us the inhabitants of a world to which the familiar world is a chaos. It reproduces the common universe of which we are portions and percipients, and it purges from our inward sight the film of familiarity which obscures from us the wonder of our being. It compels us to feel that which we perceive, and to imagine that which we know. It creates anew the universe after it has been annihilated in our minds by the recurrence of impressions blunted by reiteration. It justifies that bold and true word of Tasso: 'Non merita nome di creatore, sennon Iddio ed il Poeta'.[74]

A poet, as he is the author to others of the highest wisdom, pleasure, virtue and glory, so he ought personally to be the happiest, the best, the wisest, and the most illustrious of men. As to his glory, let time be challenged to declare whether the fame of any other institutor of human life be comparable to that of a poet. That he is the wisest, the happiest, and the best, inasmuch as he is a poet, is equally incontrovertible: the greatest poets have been men of the most spotless virtue, of the most consummate prudence, and (if we could look into the interior of their lives) the most fortunate of men. And the exceptions, as they regard those who possessed the imaginative faculty in a high yet an inferior degree, will be found on consideration to confirm rather than destroy the rule. Let us for a moment stoop to the arbitration[75] of popular breath, and usurping and uniting in our own persons the incompatible characters of accuser, witness, judge and executioner, let us without trial, testimony, or form, determine that certain motives of those who are 'there sitting where we dare not soar'[76] are reprehensible. Let us assume that Homer was a drunkard, that Virgil was a flatterer, that Horace was a coward, that Tasso was a madman, that Lord Bacon was a peculator,[77] that Raphael was a libertine, that Spenser was a Poet Laureate.[78] It is inconsistent with this division of our subject to cite living poets, but posterity has done ample justice to the great names now referred to. Their errors have been weighed and have been found as dust in the balance – if their sins 'were as scarlet, they are now white as snow';[79] they have been washed in the blood of the mediator and the redeemer Time. Observe in what a ludicrous chaos the imputations of real and of fictitious crime have been confused in the contemporary calumnies against poetry and poets; consider how little is as it appears – or appears as it is; look to your own motives, and judge not lest ye be judged.[80]

---

69 *interlunations* dark intervals.

70 *potable gold* the elixir of life, potable (drinkable) gold, was the goal of the alchemist. There are rivers of it at *Paradise Lost* iii 608–9.

71 *it strips . . . forms* probably a recollection of *Biographia Literaria* chapter 14, where Coleridge says that Wordsworth aimed to remove 'the film of familiarity' from 'the wonders of the world before us' (see p. 526).

72 *Paradise Lost* i 254–5.

73 *figured* patterned.

74 'None deserves the name of creator except God and the poet'; from Pierantonio Serassi's *Life of Torquato Tasso* (1785).

75 *arbitration* judgement.

76 *Paradise Lost* iv 829.

77 *peculator* embezzler of public money.

78 *Poet Laureate* Shelley thought much the same as Byron of Southey, who had been Laureate since 1813; see *Don Juan*, Dedication (pp. 752–5).

79 A paraphrase of Isaiah 1:18.

80 *judge not lest ye be judged* There are a number of scriptural echoes; see Daniel 5:27; Isaiah 40:15; Revelation 7:14; Hebrews 9:15; and Matthew 7:1.

Poetry, as has been said, in this respect differs from logic: that it is not subject to the control of the active powers of the mind, and that its birth and recurrence has no necessary connection with consciousness or will. It is presumptuous to determine that these are the necessary conditions of all mental causation, when mental effects are experienced insusceptible of being referred to them. The frequent recurrence of the poetical power, it is obvious to suppose, may produce in the mind an habit of order and harmony correlative with its own nature and with its effects upon other minds. But in the intervals of inspiration (and they may be frequent without being durable) a poet becomes a man, and is abandoned to the sudden reflux[81] of the influences under which others habitually live. But as he is more delicately organized than other men, and sensible to pain and pleasure (both his own and that of others) in a degree unknown to them, he will avoid the one and pursue the other with an ardour proportioned to this difference. And he renders himself obnoxious to calumny, when he neglects to observe the circumstances under which these objects of universal pursuit and flight have disguised themselves in one another's garments.

But there is nothing necessarily evil in this error, and thus cruelty, envy, revenge, avarice, and the passions purely evil, have never formed any portion of the popular imputations on the lives of poets.

I have thought it most favourable to the cause of truth to set down these remarks according to the order in which they were suggested to my mind by a consideration of the subject itself, instead of following that of the treatise which excited me to make them public. Thus, although devoid of the formality of a polemical reply, if the views which they contain be just, they will be found to involve a refutation of the doctrines of 'The Four Ages of Poetry', so far at least as regards the first division of the subject. I can readily conjecture what should have moved the gall[82] of the learned and intelligent author of that paper; I confess myself, like him, unwilling to be stunned by the *Theseids* of the hoarse Codri of the day.[83] Bavius and Maevius undoubtedly are, as they ever were, insufferable persons.[84] But it belongs to a philosophical critic to distinguish rather than confound.

The first part of these remarks has related to poetry in its elements and principles; and it has been shown, as well as the narrow limits assigned them would permit, that what is called poetry in a restricted sense has a common source with all other forms of order and of beauty according to which the materials of human life are susceptible of being arranged, and which is poetry in an universal sense.

The second part[85] will have for its object an application of these principles to the present state of the cultivation of poetry, and a defence of the attempt to idealize the modern forms of manners and opinion, and compel them into a subordination to the imaginative and creative faculty. For the literature of England, an energetic development of which has ever preceded or accompanied a great and free development of the national will, has arisen, as it were, from a new birth. In spite of the low-thoughted envy which would undervalue contemporary merit, our own will be a memorable age in intellectual achievements, and we live among such philosophers and poets as surpass beyond comparison any who have appeared since the last national struggle for civil and religious liberty. The most unfailing herald, companion, or follower of the awakening of a great people to work a beneficial change in opinion or institution, is poetry. At such periods there is an accumulation of the power of communicating and receiving intense and impassioned conceptions respecting man and nature. The persons in whom this power resides may often (as far as regards many portions of their nature) have little apparent correspondence with that spirit of good of which they are the ministers.[86] But even

---

[81] *reflux* flowing back.

[82] *gall* bitterness. Peacock had argued that the poets of the present day were barbarians.

[83] *unwilling to be stunned . . . day* Juvenal had criticized Codrus's *Theseid* in the first of his satires.

[84] *Bavius and Maevius . . . persons* Bavius and Maevius were mediocre poets mocked by Virgil (*Eclogues* iii 90–1) and (Maevius only) Horace (*Epode* x). William Gifford was the author of *The Baviad* (1794) and *The Maeviad* (1795) in which he had lampooned the Della Cruscans (mannered popular versifiers of the 1780s and 90s) and their ilk. Shelley refers to the prolifer-

ation of bad poetry in his own day; as he told Peacock, 21 March 1821: 'The Bavii and Maevii of the day are very fertile' (Jones ii 276).

[85] *The second part* never written by Shelley (see note 1, p. 944).

[86] *The persons . . . ministers* Shelley may be thinking of Southey and Wordsworth, who had both, in Shelley's eyes, betrayed the cause of 'civil and religious liberty'; like Byron, he regarded both as traitors to the radical cause.

whilst they deny and abjure,[87] they are yet compelled to serve the power which is seated upon the throne of their own soul. It is impossible to read the compositions of the most celebrated writers of the present day without being startled with the electric life which burns within their words. They measure the circumference and sound the depths of human nature with a comprehensive and all-penetrating spirit, and they are themselves perhaps the most sincerely astonished at its manifestations, for it is less their own spirit than the spirit of the age. Poets are the hierophants[88] of an unapprehended inspiration, the mirrors of the gigantic shadows which futurity casts upon the present, the words which express what they understand not; the trumpets which sing to battle, and feel not what they inspire; the influence which is moved not, but moves. Poets are the unacknowledged legislators of the world.

Adonais: An Elegy on the Death of John Keats, author of Endymion, Hyperion, etc. (1821; composed between 11 April and 8 June 1821)[1]

[Ἀστὴρ πρὶν μὲν ἔλαμπες ἐνὶ ζωοῖσιν Ἑῷος.
  Νῦν δὲ θανὼν, λάμπεις Ἕσπερος ἐν φθιμένοις]

Plato[2]

Preface

[Φάρμακον ἦλθε, Βίων, ποτὶ σὸν στόμα, φάρμακον εἶδες·
  Πῶς τευ τοῖς χείλεσσι ποτέδραμε, κοὐκ ἐγλυκάνθη;
  Τίς δὲ βροτὸς τοσσοῦτον ἀνάμερος, ἢ κεράσαι τοι,
  Ἢ δοῦναι λαλέοντι τὸ φάρμακον; ἔκφυγεν ᾠδάν.]

Moschus, Lament for Bion[3]

It is my intention to subjoin to the London edition of this poem,[4] a criticism upon the claims of its lamented object to be classed among the writers of the highest genius who have adorned our age. My known repugnance to the narrow principles of taste on which several of his earlier compositions were modelled, prove at least that I am an impartial judge. I consider the fragment of *Hyperion*[5] as second to nothing that was ever produced by a writer of the same years.

John Keats died at Rome of a consumption in his twenty-fourth year, on the — of — 1821,[6] and was buried in the romantic and lonely cemetery of the protestants in that city, under the pyramid which is the tomb of Cestius, and the massy walls and towers, now mouldering and desolate, which formed the circuit of ancient Rome. The cemetery is an open space among the ruins covered in winter

---

87   *abjure* recant.
88   *hierophants* expounders.

ADONAIS: AN ELEGY ON THE DEATH OF JOHN KEATS
1   For introductory comments, see headnote, p. 822. See also James A. W. Heffernan, '*Adonais*: Shelley's Consumption of Keats', *Romanticism: A Critical Reader* 173–91. Shelley adapted the name from Adonis, the beautiful youth with whom Aphrodite, Greek goddess of fertility, fell in love. He was killed by a wild boar, and from his blood sprang the rose, or from Aphrodite's tears the anemone. The poem was completed by 11 June 1821, and five days later Shelley told John Gisborne: 'this day I send it to the press at Pisa. . . . I think it will please you: I have dipped my pen in consuming fire for his destroyers, otherwise the style is calm and solemn' (Jones ii 300).
2   Shortly before composing *Adonais*, Shelley translated Plato's *Epigram on Aster*:
    Thou wert the morning star among the living,
    Ere thy fair light had fled;

Now, having died, thou art as Hesperus, giving
    New splendour to the dead.
3   'Poison came, Bion, to thy mouth, thou didst know poison. To such lips as thine did it come, and was not sweetened? What mortal was so cruel that could mix poison for thee, or who could give thee the venom that heard thy voice? Surely, he had not music in his soul'.
4   *the London edition of this poem* Shelley supervised the first publication of this poem in Pisa, 1821, but died before it could appear in London. The first English edition was published at Cambridge, 1829.
5   *the fragment of Hyperion* i.e. *Hyperion: A Fragment*, published 1820 (see pp. 1022–41), rather than *The Fall of Hyperion* (pp. 1081–92), not published during Shelley's lifetime. When Shelley first received Keats's 1820 volume, he commented: 'the fragment called Hyperion promises for him that he is destined to become one of the first writers of the age' (letter of 29 October 1820, Jones ii 239).
6   Keats died 23 February 1821, aged twenty-five.

with violets and daisies. It might make one in love with death[7] to think that one should be buried in so sweet a place.[8]

The genius[9] of the lamented person to whose memory I have dedicated these unworthy verses was not less delicate and fragile than it was beautiful; and where canker-worms abound, what wonder if its young flower was blighted in the bud? The savage criticism on his *Endymion*, which appeared in the *Quarterly Review*, produced the most violent effect on his susceptible mind; the agitation thus originated ended in the rupture of a blood-vessel in the lungs; a rapid consumption ensued, and the succeeding acknowledgements from more candid critics of the true greatness of his powers, were ineffectual to heal the wound thus wantonly inflicted.[10]

It may be well said that these wretched men know not what they do.[11] They scatter their insults and their slanders without heed as to whether the poisoned shaft lights on a heart made callous by many blows, or one like Keats', composed of more penetrable stuff.[12] One of their associates is, to my knowledge, a most base and unprincipled calumniator.[13] As to *Endymion* — was it a poem (whatever might be its defects) to be treated contemptuously by those who had celebrated with various degrees of complacency and panegyric, *Paris*, and *Woman*, and *A Syrian Tale*, and Mrs. Lefanu, and Mr. Barrett, and Mr Howard Payne,[14] and a long list of the illustrious obscure? Are these the men who, in their venal good nature, presumed to draw a parallel between the Revd Mr Milman and Lord Byron?[15] What gnat did they strain at here, after having swallowed all those camels?[16] Against what woman taken in adultery, dares the foremost of these literary prostitutes to cast his opprobrious stone?[17] Miserable man! You, one of the meanest, have wantonly defaced one of the noblest specimens of the workmanship of God. Nor shall it be your excuse that, murderer as you are, you have spoken daggers but used none.[18]

The circumstances of the closing scene of poor Keats' life were not made known to me until the *Elegy* was ready for the press. I am given to understand that the wound which his sensitive spirit had received from the criticism of *Endymion*, was exasperated by the bitter sense of unrequited benefits; the poor fellow seems to have been hooted from the stage of life, no less by those on whom he had wasted the promise of his genius, than those on whom he had lavished his fortune and his care. He was accompanied to Rome, and attended in his last illness by Mr Severn,[19] a young artist of the highest promise, who, I have been informed, 'almost risked his own life, and sacrificed every prospect to unwearied attendance upon his dying friend.'[20] Had I known these circumstances before the completion of my poem, I should have been tempted to add my feeble tribute of applause to the more solid recompense which the virtuous man finds in the recollection of his own motives. Mr Severn can dispense with a reward from 'such stuff as dreams are made of.'[21] His conduct is a golden augury of the success of his future career; may the unextinguished spirit of his illustrious friend animate the creations of his pencil, and plead against oblivion for his name!

---

[7] *in love with death* Compare Keats, *Ode to a Nightingale* 52.

[8] Shelley visited the non-Catholic Cemetery in Rome (Il Cimitero Acattolico) in late November 1818; his son William was buried there in 1819.

[9] *genius* spirit.

[10] *The savage criticism . . . inflicted* this remark helped perpetuate the myth that Keats was 'killed' by a review — that of *Endymion* in the *Quarterly* for April 1818, by Croker.

[11] *these wretched men know not what they do* an echo of Christ's comment on those who crucified him: 'Father, forgive them; for they know not what they do' (Luke 23:34).

[12] *penetrable stuff* cf. *Hamlet* III iv 35–6: 'And let me wring your heart, for so I shall / If it be made of penetrable stuff'.

[13] *One of their associates . . . calumniator* Robert Southey, who Shelley thought had attacked his poem, *The Revolt of Islam*, in the *Quarterly* in 1817; the actual author was John Taylor Coleridge. Shelley has in mind Southey's part in the spreading of rumours about the 'league of incest'; see pp. 752 n. 2.

[14] Revd George Croly, *Paris in 1815* (1817); Eaton Stannard Barrett, *Woman* (1810); H. Galley Knight, *Ilderim: A Syrian*

Tale (1816): all these works were reviewed in the *Quarterly*, 1817–20. Mrs Alicia Lefanu (*c.*1795–*c.*1826) was the author of *The Flowers* (1809). John Howard Payne was an American dramatist, whose *Brutus* was reviewed harshly by the *Quarterly*.

[15] Revd Henry Hart Milman's *Saviour*, *Lord of the Bright City* and *Fall of Jerusalem* were praised by the *Quarterly*, 1818–20.

[16] *What gnat . . . camels* cf. Christ's criticism of the pharisees, Matthew 23:24: 'Ye blind guides, which strain at a gnat, and swallow a camel.'

[17] *Against what woman . . . stone* John 8:7.

[18] *you have spoken daggers but used none* cf. *Hamlet* III ii 396: 'I will speak daggers to her, but use none'.

[19] Joseph Severn (1793–1879), who accompanied Keats to Rome, and nursed him to his death. Severn remained in Rome, became British Consul there in 1860, and was buried next to Keats.

[20] This information was in a letter from the Revd Robert Finch to John Gisborne, and was passed on to Shelley on 13 June 1821.

[21] *The Tempest* IV i 156–7.

I

I weep for Adonais – he is dead!
Oh weep for Adonais, though our tears
Thaw not the frost which binds so dear a head!
And thou, sad Hour, selected from all years
To mourn our loss, rouse thy obscure compeers,   5
And teach them thine own sorrow, say: 'With me
Died Adonais; till the Future dares
Forget the Past, his fate and fame shall be
An echo and a light unto eternity!'

II

Where wert thou, mighty Mother,[1] when he lay,   10
When thy Son lay, pierced by the shaft[2] which flies
In darkness?[3] Where was lorn Urania
When Adonais died? With veiled eyes,
Mid listening Echoes, in her Paradise
She sat, while one, with soft enamoured breath,   15
Rekindled all the fading melodies,
With which, like flowers that mock the corpse beneath,
He had adorned and hid the coming bulk of death.

III

Oh weep for Adonais – he is dead!
Wake, melancholy Mother, wake and weep!   20
Yet wherefore? Quench within their burning bed
Thy fiery tears, and let thy loud heart keep,
Like his, a mute and uncomplaining sleep;
For he is gone, where all things wise and fair
Descend. Oh dream not that the amorous Deep   25
Will yet restore him to the vital air –
Death feeds on his mute voice, and laughs at our despair.

IV

Most musical of mourners, weep again!
Lament anew, Urania! He died,[4]
Who was the Sire of an immortal strain,   30
Blind, old, and lonely, when his country's pride,
The priest, the slave, and the liberticide,[5]

---

[1] *mighty Mother* Urania, muse of astronomy, who Shelley makes the mother of Adonais.
[2] *the shaft* i.e. of an arrow. Shelley is writing figuratively of Croker's hostile review of *Endymion* in the *Quarterly*.
[3] *Where wert thou . . . darkness* the appeal is an essential part of formal elegy; cf. Milton's *Lycidas* 50–1: 'Where were ye

nymphs when the remorseless deep / Closed o'er the head of your loved Lycidas?'
[4] *He died* Milton, whose muse was also Urania. He died 8 November 1674 in Bunhill House, London.
[5] *liberticide* destroyer of liberty.

Trampled and mocked with many a loathed rite
Of lust and blood;[6] he went, unterrified,
Into the gulf of death, but his clear Sprite   35
Yet reigns o'er earth – the third among the sons of light.[7]

V

Most musical of mourners, weep anew!
Not all to that bright station dared to climb –
And happier they their happiness who knew,
Whose tapers yet burn through that night of time   40
In which suns perished;[8] others more sublime,
Struck by the envious wrath of man or God,
Have sunk, extinct in their refulgent[9] prime;
And some yet live, treading the thorny road
Which leads, through toil and hate, to Fame's serene abode.   45

VI

But now, thy youngest, dearest one, has perished
The nursling of thy widowhood, who grew,
Like a pale flower by some sad maiden cherished,
And fed with true love tears instead of dew[10] –
Most musical of mourners, weep anew!   50
Thy extreme hope, the loveliest and the last,
The bloom, whose petals nipped before they blew[11]
Died on the promise of the fruit, is waste;
The broken lily lies – the storm is overpast.

VII

To that high Capital,[12] where kingly Death   55
Keeps his pale court[13] in beauty and decay,
He came; and bought, with price of purest breath,
A grave among the eternal.[14] Come away![15]
Haste, while the vault of blue Italian day
Is yet his fitting charnel-roof![16] while still   60

---

[6] When the Stuart monarchy was restored with Charles II in 1660, those responsible for the execution of Charles I were executed.

[7] *the third among the sons of light* a reference to Shelley's discussion of epic poets in 'A Defence of Poetry', where Milton is ranked alongside Homer and Dante. In a MS note, Shelley lists the poets who would mourn Keats: 'It is difficult to assign any order of precedence except that founded on fame; thence (why the Scriptures excepted), Virgil, Anacreon, Petrarch, Homer, Sophocles, Aeschylus, Dante, Lucretius, Calderon, Shakespeare, Milton.'

[8] *And happier they . . . perished* minor poets ('tapers') whose works survive are happier than major poets ('suns') whose work is lost.

[9] *refulgent* glorious, radiant.

[10] Lines 48–9 recall Keats's *Isabella* 424.

[11] *blew* blossomed.

[12] *that high Capital* Rome.

[13] *Death . . . court* an echo of *Richard II* III ii 160–2:
for within the hollow crown
That rounds the mortal temples of a king
Keeps Death his court . . .

[14] *the eternal* i.e. both Rome, the eternal city, and the many illustrious people buried there.

[15] *Come away!* addressed to those gathered round the body of Adonais.

[16] *charnel-roof* the roof of a tomb.

He lies, as if in dewy sleep he lay;
Awake him not! surely he takes his fill
Of deep and liquid[17] rest, forgetful of all ill.

VIII

He will awake no more, oh never more!
Within the twilight chamber spreads apace   65
The shadow of white Death, and at the door
Invisible Corruption waits to trace
His extreme way to her dim dwelling-place;
The eternal Hunger sits, but pity and awe
Soothe her pale rage, nor dares she to deface   70
So fair a prey, till darkness, and the law
Of mortal change, shall fill the grave which is her maw.

IX

Oh weep for Adonais! The quick Dreams,[18]
The passion-winged Ministers of thought
Who were his flocks, whom near the living streams   75
Of his young spirit he fed, and whom he taught
The love which was its music, wander not –
Wander no more from kindling brain to brain,
But droop there, whence they sprung; and mourn their lot
Round the cold heart, where, after their sweet pain,   80
They ne'er will gather strength, or find a home again.

X

And one with trembling hands clasps his cold head,
And fans him with his moonlight wings, and cries,
'Our love, our hope, our sorrow, is not dead;[19]
See, on the silken fringe of his faint eyes,   85
Like dew upon a sleeping flower, there lies
A tear some Dream has loosened from his brain.'
Lost Angel of a ruined Paradise![20]
She knew not 'twas her own; as with no stain
She faded, like a cloud which had outwept its rain.[21]   90

XI

One from a lucid urn of starry dew
Washed his light limbs as if embalming them;

---

17 *liquid* undisturbed, perfect.
18 *quick Dreams* Keats's poems, which grieve his death.
19 *our sorrow, is not dead* cf. *Lycidas* 166: 'For Lycidas your
sorrow is not dead'.

20 *a ruined Paradise* Adonais's creative imagination.
21 *like a cloud that had outwept its rain* i.e. like a cloud that
had more grief than it could express through its available
moisture.

Another clipped her profuse locks, and threw
The wreath upon him, like an anadem,[22]
Which frozen tears instead of pearls begem;   95
Another in her wilful grief would break
Her bow and winged reeds,[23] as if to stem
A greater loss with one which was more weak,
And dull the barbed fire[24] against his frozen cheek.

XII

Another Splendour on his mouth alit[25] –   100
That mouth, whence it was wont to draw the breath
Which gave it strength to pierce the guarded wit,
And pass into the panting heart beneath
With lightning and with music: the damp death
Quenched its caress upon his icy lips,   105
And, as a dying meteor stains a wreath
Of moonlight vapour, which the cold night clips,[26]
It flushed through his pale limbs, and passed to its eclipse.

XIII

And others came – Desires and Adorations,
Winged Persuasions and veiled Destinies,   110
Splendours, and Glooms, and glimmering Incarnations
Of hopes and fears, and twilight Fantasies;
And Sorrow, with her family of Sighs,
And Pleasure, blind with tears, led by the gleam
Of her own dying smile instead of eyes,   115
Came in slow pomp – the moving pomp might seem
Like pageantry of mist on an autumnal stream.

XIV

All he had loved, and moulded into thought,
From shape, and hue, and odour, and sweet sound,
Lamented Adonais. Morning sought   120
Her eastern watchtower, and her hair unbound,
Wet with the tears which should adorn the ground,
Dimmed the aerial eyes that kindle day;
Afar the melancholy thunder moaned,
Pale Ocean in unquiet slumber lay,   125
And the wild winds flew round, sobbing in their dismay.

---

[22] *anadem* garland of flowers.
[23] *winged reeds* arrows.
[24] *barbed fire* a peculiar image that refers to the hooks or
barbs on arrows that makes them difficult to remove from the
wound. Shelley is almost certainly thinking of the 'storm of
arrows barbed with fire' at *Paradise Lost* vi 546.

[25] *alit* alighted.
[26] *clips* means both 'embraces' and 'cuts off'.

XV

Lost Echo[27] sits amid the voiceless mountains
And feeds her grief with his remembered lay,[28]
And will no more reply to winds or fountains,
Or amorous birds perched on the young green spray,   130
Or herdsman's horn, or bell at closing day;
Since she can mimic not his lips, more dear
Than those for whose disdain she pined away
Into a shadow of all sounds – a drear
Murmur, between their songs, is all the woodmen hear.   135

XVI

Grief made the young Spring wild, and she threw down
Her kindling buds, as if she Autumn were,
Or they dead leaves; since her delight is flown
For whom should she have waked the sullen year?
To Phoebus was not Hyacinth so dear[29]   140
Nor to himself Narcissus, as to both
Thou Adonais: wan they stand and sere[30]
Amid the drooping comrades of their youth,
With dew all turned to tears; odour, to sighing ruth.[31]

XVII

Thy spirit's sister, the lorn nightingale,[32]   145
Mourns not her mate with such melodious pain;
Not so the eagle, who like thee could scale
Heaven, and could nourish in the sun's domain
Her mighty youth with morning,[33] doth complain,
Soaring and screaming round her empty nest,   150
As Albion[34] wails for thee: the curse of Cain[35]
Light on his head[36] who pierced thy innocent breast,
And scared the angel soul that was its earthly guest!

XVIII

Ah woe is me! Winter is come and gone,
But grief returns with the revolving year;   155

[27]   The nymph Echo faded into an echo of sound when Narcissus rejected her; Narcissus fell in love with his own reflection and was transformed into a flower.
[28]   *lay* Keats's poetry.
[29]   Hyacinth, loved by Phoebus Apollo, was killed out of jealousy by Zephyrus and then turned into a flower by Apollo.
[30]   *sere* withered.
[31]   *ruth* pity.
[32]   *the lorn nightingale* a reference to Keats's *Ode to a Nightingale*, which Shelley read in Keats's 1820 volume.
[33]   The eagle was believed to be able to replenish its youth-
ful vision by flying into the sun and then diving into a fountain.
[34]   *Albion* England.
[35]   *the curse of Cain* Cain, who killed his brother Abel and brought murder into the world, was cursed as 'a fugitive and a vagabond . . . in the earth' (Genesis 4:12, 14).
[36]   *his head* i.e. that of the critic held responsible by Shelley for Keats's death – John Wilson Croker (although Shelley suspected it was Southey, the review having been published anonymously).

The airs and streams renew their joyous tone;
The ants, the bees, the swallows reappear;
Fresh leaves and flowers deck the dead Seasons' bier;
The amorous birds now pair in every brake,[37]
And build their mossy homes in field and brere;[38]   160
And the green lizard, and the golden snake,
Like unimprisoned flames, out of their trance awake.

XIX

Through wood and stream and field and hill and Ocean
A quickening life from the Earth's heart has burst
As it has ever done, with change and motion,   165
From the great morning of the world when first
God dawned on Chaos; in its steam immersed
The lamps of Heaven flash with a softer light;
All baser things pant with life's sacred thirst,
Diffuse themselves, and spend in love's delight,   170
The beauty and the joy of their renewed might.

XX

The leprous corpse touched by this spirit tender
Exhales itself in flowers of gentle breath;[39]
Like incarnations of the stars, when splendour
Is changed to fragrance, they illumine death   175
And mock the merry worm that wakes beneath;
Nought we know, dies. Shall that alone which knows[40]
Be as a sword consumed before the sheath[41]
By sightless[42] lightning? – th' intense atom glows
A moment, then is quenched in a most cold repose.   180

XXI

Alas! that all we loved of him should be,
But for our grief, as if it had not been,
And grief itself be mortal! Woe is me!
Whence are we, and why are we? Of what scene
The actors or spectators? Great and mean   185
Meet massed in death, who lends what life must borrow.
As long as skies are blue, and fields are green,
Evening must usher night, night urge the morrow,
Month follow month with woe, and year wake year to sorrow.

---

37 *brake* thicket.
38 *brere* archaic spelling of 'briar'.
39 *flowers of gentle breath* anemones, thought to have sprung
from Adonis's blood when he was killed by a boar.
40 *that alone which knows* the human mind.

41 *a sword consumed before the sheath* Shelley would have
known Byron's variations on this image: *Childe Harold's Pil-
grimage* iii 911–13 (p. 701), and 'So we'll go no more a-roving'
5: 'For the sword outwears its sheath'.
42 *sightless* invisible.

XXII

He will awake no more, oh never more!   190
'Wake thou', cried Misery, 'childless Mother, rise
Out of thy sleep, and slake, in thy heart's core,
A wound more fierce than his with tears and sighs.
And all the Dreams that watched Urania's eyes,
And all the Echoes whom their sister's song[43]   195
Had held in holy silence, cried: 'Arise!'
Swift as a Thought by the snake Memory stung,
From her ambrosial[44] rest the fading Splendour sprung.[45]

XXIII

She rose like an autumnal Night, that springs
Out of the East, and follows wild and drear   200
The golden Day, which, on eternal wings,
Even as a ghost abandoning a bier,
Had left the Earth a corpse. Sorrow and fear
So struck, so roused, so rapt[46] Urania;
So saddened round her like an atmosphere   205
Of stormy mist; so swept her on her way
Even to the mournful place where Adonais lay.

XXIV

Out of her secret Paradise she sped,
Through camps and cities rough with stone, and steel,
And human hearts, which to her airy tread   210
Yielding not, wounded the invisible
Palms of her tender feet where'er they fell:
And barbed tongues,[47] and thoughts more sharp than they
Rent the soft Form they never could repel,
Whose sacred blood, like the young tears of May,   215
Paved with eternal flowers that undeserving way.

XXV

In the death-chamber for a moment Death,
Shamed by the presence of that living Might,
Blushed to annihilation, and the breath
Revisited those lips, and life's pale light   220
Flashed through those limbs, so late her dear delight.
'Leave me not wild and drear and comfortless,
As silent lightning leaves the starless night!

---

[43] *And all the Echoes . . . song* Echo repeated Keats's poem at
line 15.
[44] *ambrosial* heavenly.
[45] *the fading Splendour sprung* the Splendour was fading from
grief.

[46] *rapt* enchanted.
[47] *barbed tongues* i.e. barbed commentators.

Leave me not!' cried Urania. Her distress
Roused Death: Death rose and smiled, and met her vain caress.   225

XXVI

'Stay yet awhile! speak to me once again;
Kiss me, so long but as a kiss may live;
And in my heartless[48] breast and burning brain
That word, that kiss shall all thoughts else survive,
With food of saddest memory kept alive,   230
Now thou art dead, as if it were a part
Of thee, my Adonais! I would give
All that I am to be as thou now art!
But I am chained to Time, and cannot thence depart!

XXVII

Oh gentle child, beautiful as thou wert,   235
Why didst thou leave the trodden paths of men
Too soon, and with weak hands[49] though mighty heart
Dare the unpastured dragon[50] in his den?
Defenceless as thou wert, oh where was then
Wisdom the mirrored shield,[51] or scorn the spear?   240
Or hadst thou waited the full cycle, when
Thy spirit should have filled its crescent sphere,
The monsters of life's waste had fled from thee like deer.

XXVIII

The herded wolves, bold only to pursue;
The obscene ravens, clamorous o'er the dead;   245
The vultures to the conqueror's banner true
Who feed where Desolation first has fed,
And whose wings rain contagion – how they fled,
When, like Apollo, from his golden bow,
The Pythian of the age one arrow sped   250
And smiled![52] The spoilers[53] tempt no second blow,
They fawn on the proud feet that spurn them as they go.

---

[48] *heartless* disheartened, dejected.
[49] *with weak hands* a reference to the weakness of Keats's early verse. Keats wrote to Shelley, 16 August 1820: 'I remember you advising me not to publish my first-blights, on Hampstead Heath' (Rollins ii 323). In fact, Keats's first volume, *Poems* (1817) received generally favourable reviews; it was *Endymion* (1818) that attracted criticism.
[50] *the unpastured dragon* the critic blamed by Shelley for Keats's death.

[51] *the mirrored shield* Perseus used a mirrored shield to slay the Medusa.
[52] *The Pythian . . . smiled* Byron's *English Bards and Scotch Reviewers* (1809) attacked those responsible for the harsh review of his *Hours of Idleness*; see pp. 661–2. Apollo killed a python with an arrow and established the Pythian games in celebration.
[53] *spoilers* ravagers, barbarians (i.e. the reviewers).

XXIX

The sun comes forth, and many reptiles spawn;
He sets, and each ephemeral insect then
Is gathered into death without a dawn,   255
And the immortal stars awake again;[54]
So is it in the world of living men:
A godlike mind soars forth, in its delight
Making earth bare and veiling heaven, and when
It sinks, the swarms that dimmed or shared its light   260
Leave to its kindred lamps the spirit's awful night.'

XXX

Thus ceased she: and the mountain shepherds came
Their garlands sere, their magic mantles rent;
The Pilgrim of Eternity[55] (whose fame
Over his living head like Heaven is bent,   265
An early but enduring monument)
Came, veiling all the lightnings of his song
In sorrow; from her wilds Ierne sent
The sweetest lyrist[56] of her saddest wrong,
And love taught grief to fall like music from his tongue.   270

literary history

but Byron didn't like Keats

XXXI

Midst others of less note came one frail Form,[57]
A phantom among men, companionless
As the last cloud of an expiring storm
Whose thunder is its knell. He, as I guess,
Had gazed on Nature's naked loveliness,   275
Actaeon-like,[58] and now he fled astray
With feeble steps o'er the world's wilderness,
And his own thoughts, along that rugged way,
Pursued, like raging hounds, their father and their prey.

XXXII

Shelley

A pardlike[59] Spirit beautiful and swift,   280
A Love in desolation masked, a Power
Girt round with weakness – it can scarce uplift
The weight of the superincumbent hour:[60]

---

54   *The sun . . . awake again* in Shelley's metaphor, the sun is the great poet during his lifetime; the reptiles are the critics; the ephemeral insects imitate the great poet's works; the stars are great poets of the past.
55   *The Pilgrim of Eternity* Byron; the reference is to *Childe Harold's Pilgrimage*.
56   *Ierne sent . . . lyrist* Thomas Moore, from Ireland (Ierne); for more on whom, see pp. 617–18. Shelley forwarded a copy of *Adonais* to Moore through Horace Smith, who reported, 3

October 1821: 'I gave Moore your copy of *Adonais* and he was very much pleased with it, particularly with the allusion to himself' (Jones ii 351).
57   *one frail Form* Shelley.
58   Actaeon, seeing Diana bathing, was turned into a stag and torn to pieces by his own dogs.
59   *pardlike* in an early draft, Shelley has 'Pantherlike'.
60   *the superincumbent hour* The overhanging ('superincumbent') hour is that of Adonais's death.

It is a dying lamp, a falling shower,
A breaking billow; even whilst we speak,   285
Is it not broken? On the withering flower
The killing sun smiles brightly: on a cheek
The life can burn in blood, even while the heart may break.

XXXIII

His head was bound with pansies overblown,
And faded violets, white, and pied, and blue;   290
And a light spear topped with a cypress cone,
Round whose rude shaft dark ivy tresses grew[61]
Yet dripping with the forest's noonday dew,
Vibrated, as the ever-beating heart
Shook the weak hand that grasped it: of that crew   295
He came the last, neglected and apart –
A herd-abandoned deer struck by the hunter's dart.

XXXIV

All stood aloof, and at his partial moan
Smiled through their tears; well knew that gentle band
Who in another's fate now wept his own;   300
As in the accents of an unknown land,
He sung new sorrow; sad Urania scanned
The Stranger's mien, and murmured, 'Who art thou?'
He answered not, but with a sudden hand
Made bare his branded and ensanguined brow,   305
Which was like Cain's or Christ's[62] – oh that it should be so!

XXXV

What softer voice is hushed over the dead?
Athwart what brow is that dark mantle thrown?
What form leans sadly o'er the white deathbed
In mockery of monumental stone,   310
The heavy heart heaving without a moan?
If it be He[63] who, gentlest of the wise,
Taught, soothed, loved, honoured the departed one,
Let me not vex, with inharmonious sighs,
The silence of that heart's accepted sacrifice.   315

---

[61] *a light spear . . . grew* a thyrsus, a staff or spear tipped with an ornament like a pine-cone, and sometimes wreathed with ivy or vine branches, was carried, in Greek myth, by Dionysus (Bacchus) and his votaries. Ivy was the emblem of the poet in Latin poetry.
[62] Shelley's comparison of himself with Christ enraged early reviewers, although it had already been made, implicitly at least, in *Ode to the West Wind*. In particular, the Revd George Croly, in *Blackwood's Edinburgh Magazine* (December 1821), quoted this line and remarked: 'We have heard it mentioned as the only apology for the predominant irreligion and nonsense of this person's works, that his understanding is unsettled.'
[63] *He* Leigh Hunt, a crucial influence on Keats (p. 620).

XXXVI

Our Adonais has drunk poison – oh
What deaf and viperous murderer could crown
Life's early cup with such a draught of woe?[64]
The nameless worm would now itself disown:
It felt, yet could escape the magic tone   320
Whose prelude held all envy, hate, and wrong,
But what was howling in one breast alone,
Silent with expectation of the song,
Whose master's hand is cold, whose silver lyre unstrung.

XXXVII

Live thou whose infamy is not thy fame!   325
Live! Fear no heavier chastisement from me,
Thou noteless[65] blot on a remembered name! *Keats*
But be thyself, and know thyself to be!
And ever at thy season[66] be thou free
To spill the venom when thy fangs o'erflow –   330
Remorse and self-contempt shall cling to thee;
Hot Shame shall burn upon thy secret brow,
And like a beaten hound tremble thou shalt – as now.

intestines of reviewer

XXXVIII

Nor let us weep that our delight is fled
Far from these carrion kites that scream below –   335
He wakes or sleeps with the enduring dead;
Thou canst not soar where he is sitting now.
Dust to the dust! But the pure spirit shall flow
Back to the burning fountain whence it came,
A portion of the Eternal, which must glow   340
Through time and change, unquenchably the same,
Whilst thy cold embers choke the sordid hearth of shame.

XXXIX

Peace, peace! He is not dead, he doth not sleep –
He hath awakened from the dream of life –
'Tis we who, lost in stormy visions, keep   345
With phantoms an unprofitable strife,
And in mad trance, strike with our spirit's knife
Invulnerable nothings. *We* decay
Like corpses in a charnel;[67] fear and grief
Convulse us and consume us day by day,   350
And cold hopes swarm like worms within our living clay.

immortality allows us to conquer death

---

[64] *What deaf . . . woe* Stanzas 36–7 attack the reviewer
responsible for Keats's death. Shelley thought him to be
Southey, although the actual culprit was John Wilson Croker.
[65] *noteless* not worth noting, undistinguished.

[66] *at thy season* every quarter, when the *Quarterly Review* was
published.
[67] *charnel* tomb.

XL

He has outsoared the shadow of our night;[68]
Envy and calumny and hate and pain,
And that unrest which men miscall delight,
Can touch him not and torture not again;   355
From the contagion of the world's slow stain
He is secure, and now can never mourn
A heart grown cold, a head grown grey in vain;
Nor, when the spirit's self has ceased to burn,
With sparkless ashes load an unlamented urn.   360

[handwritten marginalia:] his heart a the heart of another direct allusion to wordsworth

XLI

He lives, he wakes – 'tis Death is dead, not he;
Mourn not for Adonais. Thou young Dawn
Turn all thy dew to splendour, for from thee
The spirit thou lamentest is not gone;
Ye caverns and ye forests, cease to moan!   365
Cease ye faint flowers and fountains, and thou Air
Which like a mourning veil thy scarf hadst thrown
O'er the abandoned Earth, now leave it bare
Even to the joyous stars which smile on its despair!

XLII

He is made one with Nature: there is heard   370
His voice in all her music, from the moan
Of thunder, to the song of night's sweet bird;[69]
He is a presence to be felt and known
In darkness and in light, from herb and stone,
Spreading itself where'er that Power[70] may move   375
Which has withdrawn his being to its own,
Which wields the world with never-wearied love,
Sustains it from beneath, and kindles it above.[71]

XLIII

He is a portion of the loveliness
Which once he made more lovely: he doth bear   380
His part, while the one Spirit's plastic stress[72]
Sweeps through the dull dense world, compelling there
All new successions to the forms they wear;
Torturing th' unwilling dross that checks its flight
To its own likeness, as each mass may bear;   385
And bursting in its beauty and its might
From trees and beasts and men into the Heaven's light.

---

[68] *the shadow of our night* the shadow cast by the earth away from the sun.
[69] *night's sweet bird* the nightingale. Shelley refers, again, to Keats's *Ode to a Nightingale*.
[70] *Power* cf. *Mont Blanc* and *Hymn to Intellectual Beauty*.
[71] On the neo-Platonism of this stanza see headnote, p. 822.

[72] *plastic stress* shaping, moulding power. Shelley is almost certainly thinking of the pantheism of Coleridge's *Eolian Harp*, where the divine 'intellectual breeze' is 'Plastic and vast' (l. 39).

XLIV

The splendours of the firmament of time[73]
May be eclipsed, but are extinguished not;
Like stars to their appointed height they climb,   390
And death is a low mist which cannot blot
The brightness it may veil. When lofty thought
Lifts a young heart above its mortal lair,
And love and life contend in it for what
Shall be its earthly doom, the dead live there   395
And move like winds of light on dark and stormy air.[74]

XLV

The inheritors of unfulfilled renown[75]
Rose from their thrones, built beyond mortal thought,
Far in the Unapparent. Chatterton
Rose pale, his solemn agony had not   400
Yet faded from him; Sidney, as he fought
And as he fell and as he lived and loved
Sublimely mild, a Spirit without spot,
Arose; and Lucan, by his death approved:
Oblivion as they rose shrank like a thing reproved.   405

XLVI

And many more whose names on Earth are dark,
But whose transmitted effluence[76] cannot die
So long as fire outlives the parent spark,
Rose, robed in dazzling immortality.
'Thou art become as one of us', they cry,   410
'It was for thee yon kingless sphere has long
Swung blind in unascended majesty,
Silent alone amid an Heaven of song.
Assume thy winged throne, thou Vesper of our throng!'[77]

XLVII

Who mourns for Adonais? Oh come forth   415
Fond[78] wretch, and know thyself and him aright!
Clasp with thy panting soul the pendulous Earth;[79]
As from a centre, dart thy spirit's light
Beyond all worlds, until its spacious might

---

73   *The splendours . . . time* i.e. the works of Keats and other poets.
74   *When lofty thought . . . air* The creative minds of the dead influence the hearts of the young.
75   *inheritors of unfulfilled renown* poets who died before they could realize their full potential. Shelley goes on to specify Thomas Chatterton, who committed suicide at the age of seventeen in 1770; Sir Philip Sidney, who died in 1586 at the age of thirty-two, from a wound sustained in the Netherlands in their fight against Spain; and Lucan, who committed suicide in AD 65 at the age of twenty-six.

76   *effluence* i.e. power.
77   In the Ptolemaic system of astronomy, the songs of concentric whirling spheres around the earth blended into a harmony. Adonais is to be the genius of the third sphere of Venus.
78   *Fond* it is foolish ('Fond') to mourn Adonais.
79   *the pendulous Earth* an allusion to 'The pendulous round earth' of *Paradise Lost* iv 1000, where 'pendulous' means 'suspended' (i.e. in space).

Satiate the void circumference; then shrink   420
Even to a point within our day and night –
And keep thy heart light lest it make thee sink
When hope has kindled hope, and lured thee to the brink.[80]

XLVIII

Or go to Rome, which is the sepulchre
Oh not of him, but of our joy: 'tis nought   425
That ages, empires, and religions there
Lie buried in the ravage they have wrought;
For such as he[81] can lend – they borrow not
Glory from those who made the world their prey;[82]
And he is gathered to the kings of thought[83]   430
Who waged contention with their time's decay,
And of the past are all that cannot pass away.

XLIX

Go thou to Rome – at once the Paradise,
The grave, the city, and the wilderness;
And where its wrecks like shattered mountains rise,   435
And flowering weeds, and fragrant copses dress
The bones of Desolation's nakedness,
Pass, till the Spirit of the spot shall lead
Thy footsteps to a slope of green access[84]
Where, like an infant's smile,[85] over the dead,   440
A light of laughing flowers along the grass is spread.

L

And grey walls[86] moulder round, on which dull Time
Feeds, like slow fire upon a hoary brand;[87]
And one keen pyramid with wedge sublime,[88]
Pavilioning the dust of him who planned   445
This refuge for his memory, doth stand
Like flame transformed to marble; and beneath,
A field is spread, on which a newer band
Have pitched in Heaven's smile their camp of death
Welcoming him we lose with scarce extinguished breath.   450

---

[80] *And keep . . . brink* Shelley tells the 'Fond wretch' to keep his heart light so that when death is near, he has not built too much hope on his own immortality.

[81] *he* Adonais.

[82] *they borrow not . . . prey* Adonais lends his glory to his Roman surroundings; the ruins of empires pass away, while the influence of creative minds endures. Those who have made the world their prey would include the likes of Ozymandias (see p. 849).

[83] *kings of thought* including Chatterton, Sidney and Lucan.

[84] *a slope of green access* the non-Catholic Cemetery in Rome (Il Cimitero Acattolico), where Keats was buried.

[85] *like an infant's smile* Shelley's son William died suddenly at the age of three in June 1819; he was too buried in the non-Catholic Cemetery in Rome.

[86] *grey walls* of Rome, begun by Aurelian, which bound one side of the cemetery.

[87] *a hoary brand* a log in the fireplace, nearly burnt up.

[88] The pyramid is a monument to a Roman tribune, Caius Cestius, who died about 30 BC.

LI

Here pause: these graves are all too young as yet
To have outgrown the sorrow which consigned
Its charge to each; and if the seal is set,
Here, on one fountain of a mourning mind,
Break it not thou![89] Too surely shalt thou find   455
Thine own well full, if thou returnest home,
Of tears and gall.[90] From the world's bitter wind
Seek shelter in the shadow of the tomb.
What Adonais is, why fear we to become?

LII

The One remains, the many change and pass;   460
Heaven's light forever shines, Earth's shadows fly;
Life, like a dome of many-coloured glass,
Stains the white radiance of Eternity,[91]
Until Death tramples it to fragments. Die,
If thou wouldst be with that which thou dost seek!   465
Follow where all is fled! Rome's azure sky,
Flowers, ruins, statues, music, words, are weak
The glory they transfuse with fitting truth to speak.

LIII

Why linger, why turn back, why shrink, my Heart?[92]
Thy hopes are gone before: from all things here   470
They have departed – thou shouldst now depart!
A light is passed from the revolving year,
And man, and woman; and what still is dear
Attracts to crush, repels to make thee wither.
The soft sky smiles, the low wind whispers near: 475
'Tis Adonais calls! Oh, hasten thither,
No more let Life divide what Death can join together.

LIV

That Light whose smile kindles the Universe,
That Beauty in which all things work and move,
That Benediction which the eclipsing Curse   480
Of birth can quench not, that sustaining Love
Which through the web of being blindly wove
By man and beast and earth and air and sea,
Burns bright or dim, as each are mirrors of
The fire for which all thirst – now beams on me,   485
Consuming the last clouds of cold mortality.

---

[89] *on one fountain . . . thou* The mourner is told not to break
the seal on the fountain of Shelley's grief for his son William.
[90] *gall* bitter grief.

[91] *Life . . . Eternity* Shelley thought white light was pure,
and its breakdown into colours a symbol of humanity's frac-
tured life.
[92] Shelley is addressing himself.

The West Wind [handwritten]

LV

The breath whose might I have invoked in song
Descends on me; my spirit's bark is <u>driven</u> → *used in Ode to W.W.* [handwritten]
Far from the shore, far from the trembling throng — *romantic individual not* [handwritten]
Whose sails were never to the tempest given; *w/ the crowd* [handwritten]
The massy earth and sphered skies are riven! — *effect of the storm* [handwritten]   490
I am borne darkly, fearfully, afar;
Whilst burning through the inmost veil of Heaven,
The soul of Adonais, like a star,
Beacons from the abode where the Eternal are.[93]   495

John Clare   (1793–1864)

Clare was born on 13 July 1793 in the village of Help-ston, Northamptonshire. His father, Parker Clare, was a thresher, but, as the illegitimate son of a Scottish schoolmaster, he wanted to give his son the best education he could, and sent him to school for at least three months a year until he was twelve. John met Mary Joyce at school, who was four years younger; she was his girlfriend until their relationship ended at around the time of her father's death. She was the subject of many of his later poems; in later life he believed that she was his wife.

He became a labourer while still a boy, and began to write poetry for pleasure, scribbling on any scrap he could find. With the encouragement of Edward Drury, a local businessman, he found a supporter (and editor)[1] in the London publisher, John Taylor. *Poems Descriptive of Rural Life and Scenery* went into print in January 1820; its success made him a literary celebrity, the 'Northamptonshire Peasant Poet', and he began mixing with the likes of Lamb,[2] Hazlitt, De Quincey and Coleridge.[3] Another volume, *The Village Minstrel*, was published in 1821, but sales were disappointing; it had sold only 1,250 copies by the end of the decade. Clare had to continue working as a labourer, and suffered increasing bouts of ill health; six years passed before *The Shepherd's Calendar* (1827), which sold only

425 copies in the next two years. When he asked for an accounting of the proceeds from his publications in 1829, Clare learnt that he was actually £140 in debt.

His attempt to set himself up as an independent farmer at Northborough in 1831 was blighted by bouts of bad physical and mental health. He was committed to Matthew Allen's asylum by John Taylor in June 1837, from which he escaped in 1841, believing that when he returned to Northborough he would find his childhood sweetheart, Mary Joyce, waiting for him. Six months later he was taken to the General Lunatic Asylum at Northampton, where he remained until his death on 20 May 1864.

Clare appears to have written incessantly throughout his life, even during his insanity. Obsessed with Byron, and believing that he was the noble Lord, he composed two poems, *Child Harold* and *Don Juan*, which adapt the Byronic manner and concerns in his own idiosyncratic way. The vast majority of Clare's poems remained unpublished, existing only in manuscript, until very recently; as a result, it is only during the last decade that the scale of his achievement has become evident. In the selection that follows I have concentrated on Clare's lyrics – of which *First Love*, '*I am*', *Oh could I be as I have been*, *The Flitting*, and *Silent Love* are among his finest.

---

[93]   *The soul of Adonais . . . are* an allusion to Plato's epigram (p. 956 n. 2).

JOHN CLARE
[1]   Much has been written about Clare's relationship with Taylor; for different viewpoints, see Tim Chilcott, *A Publisher and his Circle: The Life and Work of John Taylor, Keats's Publisher* (London, 1972), and Zachary Leader, 'John Taylor and the Poems of Clare', *Revision and Romantic Authorship* (Oxford, 1996), pp. 206–61.
[2]   See Scott McEathron, 'John Clare and Charles Lamb: Friends in the Past', *Charles Lamb Bulletin* NS 95 (1996) 98–109.
[3]   For more on Clare and London, see James C. McKusick, 'John Clare's London Journal: A Peasant Poet Encounters the Metropolis', *TWC* 23 (1992) 172–5.

Further reading

The Late Poems of John Clare 1837–1864 ed. Eric Robinson and David Powell (2 vols, Oxford, 1984)

The Early Poems of John Clare 1804–22 ed. Eric Robinson and David Powell (2 vols, Oxford, 1989)

John Lucas, 'Peasants and Outlaws: John Clare', *England and Englishness* (London, 1990), pp. 135–60

John Clare: A Bicentenary Celebration ed. Richard Foulkes (Leicester, 1994)

The Independent Spirit: John Clare and the Self-Taught Tradition ed. John Goodridge (n.p., 1994)

John Clare in Context ed. Hugh Haughton, Adam Phillips, and Geoffrey Summerfield (Cambridge, 1994)

John Lucas, *John Clare* (Plymouth, 1994)

Tom Paulin, 'John Clare in Babylon', *Romanticism: A Critical Reader* 401–7

John Clare: The Poems of the Middle Period 1822–1837 ed. Eric Robinson, David Powell, and P. M. S. Dawson (2 vols, Oxford, 1996)

The *John Clare Journal* is published annually by the John Clare Society.

To Elia (unsigned)[1]

From THE LONDON MAGAZINE 6 (1822, p. 151)

Elia, thy reveries and visioned themes
    To care's lorn heart a luscious pleasure prove,
Wild as the mystery of delightful dreams,
    Soft as the anguish of remembered love;
Like records of past days their memory dances   5
    Mid the cool feelings manhood's reason brings,
As the unearthly visions of romances
    Peopled with sweet and uncreated things;
And yet thy themes thy gentle worth enhances!
    Then wake again thy wild harp's tenderest strings –   10
Sing on, sweet bard, let fairy loves again
    Smile in thy dreams with angel ecstasies;
Bright o'er our souls will break the heavenly strain
    Through the dull gloom of earth's realities.

Sonnet (first published *London Magazine* 6 (1822, p. 272; edited from MS)

Ere I had known the world and understood
Those many follys wisdom names its own
Distinguishing things evil from things good
The dreads of sin and death ere I had known
Knowledge the root of evil – had I been   5
Left in some lone place where the world is wild
And trace of troubling man was never seen
Brought up by nature as her favoured child
As born for nought but joy where all rejoice
Emparadised in ignorance of sin   10
Where nature trys with never chiding voice
Like tender nurse nought but our smiles to win
The future dreamless – beautiful would be
The present – foretaste of eternity

To Elia
[1]　Elia was the pen-name of Charles Lamb (pp. 577–8).

January (A Cottage Evening) (extract)

From THE SHEPHERD'S CALENDAR (first published 1827; edited from MS)

Oh spirit of the days gone bye
Sweet childhoods fearful extacy
The witching[1] spells of winter nights   235
Where are they fled wi their delights
When listning on the corner seat
The winter evenings length to cheat
I heard my mothers memory tell
Tales superstition loves so well   240
Things said or sung a thousand times
In simple prose or simpler ryhmes
Ah where is page of poesy
So sweet as theirs was wont to be
The majic wonders that decievd   245
When fictions were as truths believd
The fairey feats that once prevaild
Told to delight and never faild
Where are they now their fears and sighs
And tears from founts of happy eyes   250
Breathless suspense and all their crew
To what wild dwelling have they flew
I read in books but find them not
For poesy hath its youth forgot
I hear them told to childern still   255
But fear ne'er numbs my spirits chill
I still see faces pale wi dread
While mine coud laugh at what is said
See tears imagind woes supply
While mine wi real cares are dry   260
Where are they gone the joys and fears
The links the life of other years
I thought they bound around my heart
So close that we coud never part
Till reason like a winters day   265
Nipt childhoods visions all away
Nor left behind one withering flower
To cherish in a lonly hour
Memory may yet the themes repeat
But childhoods heart doth cease to beat   270
At storys reasons sterner lore
Turneth like gossips from her door

JANUARY (A COTTAGE EVENING)
[1]   *witching* bewitching.

June (extract)

From THE SHEPHERD'S CALENDAR (first published 1827; edited from MS)

And now when sheering of the flocks are done 105
Some ancient customs mixd wi harmless fun
Crowns the swains merry toils – the timid maid
Pleasd to be praisd and yet of praise affraid
Seeks her best flowers not those of woods and fields
But such as every farmers garden yields 110
Fine cabbage roses[1] painted like her face
And shining pansys trimd in golden lace
And tall tuft larkheels[2] featherd thick wi flowers
And woodbines[3] climbing oer the door in bowers
And London tufts[4] of many a mottld hue 115
And pale pink pea and monkshood[5] darkly blue
And white and purple jiliflowers[6] that stay
Lingering in blossom summer half away
And single blood walls[7] of a lucious smell
Old fashiond flowers which hus wives love so well 120
And columbines stone blue or deep night brown
Their honey-comb-like blossoms hanging down
Each cottage-gardens fond adopted child
Tho heaths still claim them where they yet grow wild
Mong their old wild companions summer blooms 125
Furze brake and mozzling ling[8] and golden broom
Snap dragons gaping like to sleeping clowns[9]
And 'clipping pinks'[10] (which maidens sunday gowns
Full often wear catched at by toying chaps)
Pink as the ribbons round their snowy caps 130
'Bess in her bravery'[11] too of glowing dyes
As deep as sunsets crimson pillowd skyes
And marjoram notts sweet briar and ribbon grass
And lavender the choice of every lass
And sprigs of lads love[12] all familiar names 135
Which every garden thro the village claims
These the maid gathers wi a coy delight
And tyes them up in readiness for night
Giving to every swain tween love and shame
Her 'clipping poseys'[13] as their yearly claim 140
And turning as he claims the custom kiss
Wi stifld smiles half ankering after bliss
She shrinks away and blushing calls it rude
But turns to smile and hopes to be pursued

JUNE
1   *cabbage rose* the Provins rose, *rosa centifolia.*
2   *larkheels* larkspurs, *delphinium ambiguum.*
3   *woodbines* honeysuckles, *lonicera periclymenum.*
4   *London tuft* London pride, *saxifraga ambrosa.*
5   *monkshood* poisonous plant, *aconitum napelus.*
6   *jiliflowers* gillyflowers, wallflowers, *cheiranthus cheiri.*
7   *blood walls* dark, double wallflower.

8   *mozzling ling* mottled heather.
9   *clowns* peasants.
10   *clipping pinks* common garden carnation.
11   *Bess in her bravery* probably the double-flowered garden daisy with a mass of crimson-tipped white petals.
12   *lads love* southernwood, *artemisia abrotanum.*
13   *clipping poseys* nosegays given to sheep-shearers.

While one to whom the seeming hint applied 145
Follows to claim it and is not denyd
No doubt a lover for within his coat
His nosgay owns each flower of better sort
And when the envious mutter oer their beer
And nodd the secret to his neighbor near 150
Raising the laugh to make the matter known
She blushes silent and will not disown
And ale and songs and healths and merry ways
Keeps up a shadow of old farmers days
But the old beachen bowl that once supplyd 155
Its feast of frumity[14] is thrown aside
And the old freedom that was living then
When masters made them merry wi their men
Whose coat was like his neighbors russet brown
And whose rude speech was vulgar as his clown 160
Who in the same hour drank the rest among
And joind the chorus while a labourer sung
All this is past – and soon may pass away
The time torn remnant of the holiday
As proud distinction makes a wider space 165
Between the genteel and the vulgar race
Then must they fade as pride oer custom showers
Its blighting mildew on her feeble flowers

To the Snipe (composed before 1831)

Lover of swamps
The quagmire[1] overgrown
With hassock[2] tufts of sedge – where fear encamps
Around thy home alone

The trembling grass 5
Quakes from the human foot
Nor bears the weight of man to let him pass
Where he alone and mute

Sitteth at rest
In safety neath[3] the clump 10
Of hugh flag-forrest[4] that thy haunts invest
Or some old sallow[5] stump

Thriving on seams
That tiney islands swell

---

[14] *frumity* frumenty, a dish of hulled wheat boiled in milk, seasoned with cinnamon and sugar.

TO THE SNIPE
[1] *quagmire* bog, marsh. Clare is thinking of Whittlesey Mere, the habitat of snipes and other water birds, which extended to 2,000 acres; it was drained in 1850.

[2] *hassock* firm tuft or clump of matted vegetation, especially of coarse grass or sedge, such as occurs in boggy ground.
[3] *neath* underneath.
[4] *hugh flag-forrest* a forest of huge marsh-reeds.
[5] *sallow* willow.

Just hilling from the mud and rancid streams   15
Suiting thy nature well

For here thy bill
Suited by wisdom good
Of rude unseemly length doth delve and drill
The gelid mass for food   20

And here may hap
When summer suns hath drest
The moors rude desolate and spungy lap
May hide thy mystic nest

Mystic indeed   25
For isles that ocean make
Are scarcely more secure for birds to build
Then this flag-hidden lake

Boys thread the woods
To their remotest shades   30
But in these marshy flats these stagnant floods
Security pervades

From year to year
Places untrodden lye
Where man nor boy nor stock[6] hath ventured near   35
– Nought gazed on but the sky

And fowl that dread
The very breath of man
Hiding in spots that never knew his tread
A wild and timid clan   40

Wigeon and teal[7]
And wild duck – restless lot
That from mans dreaded sight will ever steal
To the most dreary spot

Here tempests howl   45
Around each flaggy plot[8]
Where they who dread mans sight the water fowl
Hide and are frighted not

Tis power divine
That heartens them to brave
The roughest tempest and at ease recline   50
On marshes or the wave

Yet instinct knows
Not safetys bounds to shun

---

6   *stock* livestock, cattle.
7   *Wigeon and teal* wigeon is a species of duck; teal is a small
freshwater bird.

8   *flaggy plot* the plot is overgrown with wild irises.

The firmer ground where skulking fowler goes   55
With searching dogs and gun

By tepid springs
Scarcely one stride across
Though brambles from its edge a shelter flings
Thy safety is at loss   60

And never chuse
The little sinky foss[9]
Streaking the moores whence spa-red water[10] spews
From puddles fringed with moss

Free booters[11] there   65
Intent to kill and slay
Startle with cracking guns the trepid[12] air
And dogs thy haunts betray

From dangers reach
Here thou art safe to roam   70
Far as these washy flag-worn marshes stretch
A still and quiet home

In these thy haunts
Ive gleaned habitual love
From the vague world where pride and folly taunts   75
I muse and look above

Thy solitudes
The unbounded heaven esteems
And here my heart warms into higher moods
And dignifying dreams   80

I see the sky
Smile on the meanest spot
Giving to all that creep or walk or flye
A calm and cordial lot

Thine teaches me   85
Right feelings to employ
That in the dreariest places peace will be
A dweller and a joy

The Flitting (composed 1832; edited from MS)[1]

Ive left my own old home of homes[2]
Green fields and every pleasant place
The summer like a stranger comes

---

9   *sinky foss* yielding ditch.
10 *spa-red water* the water is red with iron oxide.
11 *Free booters* plunderers, poachers.
12 *trepid* agitated, fearful.

THE FLITTING
1   The valedictory tone of this remarkable poem owes much
to the fact that it was composed shortly after Clare had moved
to a cottage in Northborough from Helpston.
2   Clare was born at Helpston in 1793; he moved three miles
down the road to Northborough in 1832.

I pause and hardly know her face
I miss the hazels happy green   5
The blue bells quiet hanging blooms
Where envys sneer was never seen
Where staring malice never comes

I miss the heath its yellow furze
Molehills and rabbit tracks that lead   10
Through beesom ling[3] and teazel burrs
That spread a wilderness indeed
The woodland oaks and all below
That their white powdered branches shield
The mossy pads[4] – the very crow   15
Croaked music in my native fields

I sit me in my corner chair
That seems to feel itself from home
I hear bird music here and there
From awthorn hedge and orchard come   20
I hear but all is strange and new
– I sat on my old bench in June
The sailing puddocks[5] shrill 'peelew'
Oer royce wood[6] seemed a sweeter tune

I walk adown the narrow lane   25
The nightingale is singing now
But like to me she seems at loss
For royce wood and its shielding bough
I lean upon the window sill
The trees and summer happy seem   30
Green sunny green they shine – but still
My heart goes far away to dream

Of happiness and thoughts arise
With home bred pictures many a one
Green lanes that shut out burning skies   35
And old crooked stiles to rest upon
Above them hangs the maple tree
Below grass swells a velvet hill
And little footpads[7] sweet to see
Goes seeking sweeter places still   40

With bye and bye a brook to cross
Oer which a little arch is thrown
No brook is here I feel the loss
From home and friends and all alone
– The stone pit with its shelvey sides   45
Seemed hanging rocks in my esteem

---

3   *beesom ling* besom (heath and broom), and heather ('ling').
4   *pads* paths.
5   *puddocks* kites.

6   *royce wood* As Eric Robinson and David Powell have noted, Royce Wood was a favourite haunt of Clare's, and provided a home to many nightingales.
7   *footpads* footpaths.

I miss the prospect far and wide
From Langley bush[8] and so I seem

Alone and in a stranger scene
Far far from spots my heart esteems   50
The closen with their ancient green
Heath woods and pastures sunny streams
The hawthorns here were hung with may
But still they seem in deader green
The sun e'en seems to loose its way   55
Nor knows the quarter[9] it is in

I dwell on trifles like a child
I feel as ill becomes a man
And still my thoughts like weedlings wild
Grow up to blossom where they can   60
They turn to places known so long
And feel that joy was dwelling there
So homebred pleasure fills the song
That has no present joys to heir

I read in books for happiness   65
But books mistake the way to joy
They change as well give age the glass
To hunt its visage when a boy
For books they follow fashions new
And throw all old esteems away   70
In crowded streets flowers never grew
But many there hath died away

Some sing the pomps of chivalry[10]
As legends of the ancient time
Where gold and pearls and mystery   75
Are shadows painted for sublime
But passions of sublimity
Belong to plain and simpler things
And David underneath a tree
Sought when a shepherd Salems[11] springs[12]   80

Where moss did unto cushions spring
Forming a seat of velvet hue
A small unnoticed trifling thing
To all but heavens daily dew
And Davids crown hath passed away   85
Yet poesy breaths his shepherd-skill
His palace lost – and to this day
The little moss is blooming still[13]

---

8   *Langley bush* an old whitethorn bush that was a favourite
spot for gypsies in Clare's youth. Clare's journal records its
destruction in 1823.
9   *the quarter* i.e. which part of the sky.
10   *Some sing the pomps of chivalry* John Lucas, *John Clare* (1994),
p. 61, suggests that Clare has Byron in mind at this point.
11   *Salems* Jerusalem's.
12   *And David . . . springs* Clare could have any number of the
Psalms in mind.

13   John Lucas comments on lines 79–88: 'Clare is saying not
merely that true poetry is "nature" poetry, but that it has its
roots in ordinary living, the lives of commoners. "Salems
springs" can after all be linked not merely to the life of the
fields but to the sermons of the radical Methodists who spoke
to and for the people. . . . Methodist chapels were often named
"Salem" ' (*John Clare* (1994), p. 61).

Strange scenes mere shadows are to me
Vague unpersonifying things   90
I love with my old haunts to be
By quiet woods and gravel springs
Where little pebbles wear as smooth
As hermits beads by gentle floods
Whose noises doth my spirits sooth   95
And warms them into singing moods

Here every tree is strange to me
All foreign things where ere I go
Theres none where boyhood made a swee[14]
Or clambered up to rob a crow   100
No hollow tree or woodland bower
Well known when joy was beating high
Where beauty ran to shun a shower
And love took pains to keep her dry

And laid the shoaf[15] upon the ground   105
To keep her from the dripping grass
And ran for stowks[16] and set them round
Till scarse a drop of rain could pass
Through – where the maidens they reclined
And sung sweet ballads now forgot   110
Which brought sweet memorys to the mind
But here a memory knows them not

There have I sat by many a tree
And leaned oer many a rural stile
And conned[17] my thoughts as joys to me   115
Nought heeding who might frown or smile
Twas natures beautys that inspired
My heart with rapture not its own
And shes a fame that never tires
How could I feel myself alone   120

No – pasture molehills used to lie
And talk to me of sunny days
And then the glad sheep listing bye
And still in ruminating praise
Of summer and the pleasant place   125
And every weed and blossom too
Was looking upward in my face
With friendships welcome 'how do ye do'

All tennants of an ancient place
And heirs of noble heritage   130
Coeval they with adams race
And blest with more substantial age
For when the world first saw the sun

---

[14] *swee* swing.   [16] *stowk* stook (of wheat or barley).
[15] *shoaf* sheaf.   [17] *conned* examined.

These little flowers beheld him too
And when his love for earth begun   135
They were the first his smiles to woo

These little lambtoe[18] bunches springs
In red tinged and begolden dye
For ever and like china kings
They come but never seem to die   140
These may-blooms with its little threads
Still comes upon the thorny bowers
And ne'er forgets those pinky heads
Like fairy pins amid the flowers

And still they bloom as in the day   145
They first crowned wilderness and rock
When abel haply crowned with may
The firstlings of his little flock
And Eve might from the matted thorn
To deck her lone and lovely brow   150
Reach that same rose that heedless scorn
Misnames as the dog rosey[19] now

Give me no high flown fangled things
No haughty pomp in marching chime
Where muses play on golden strings   155
And splendour passes for sublime
Where citys stretch as far as fame
And fancys straining eye can go
And piled untill the sky for shame
Is stooping far away below   160

I love the verse that mild and bland
Breaths of green fields and open sky[20]
I love the muse that in her hand
Bears wreaths of native poesy
Who walks nor skips the pasture brook   165
In scorn – but by the drinking horse
Leans oer its little brig[21] to look
How far the sallows[22] lean accross

And feels a rapture in her breast
Upon their root-fringed grains to mark   170
A hermit morehens sedgy nest
Just like a naiads[23] summer bark
She counts the eggs she cannot reach
Admires the spot and loves it well

---

[18] *lambtoe* common bird's-foot-trefoil, a wild flower.
[19] *dog rosey* dog-rose, a common species of wild rose (*rosa canina*), with pale red flowers, frequent in hedges.
[20] *green fields and open sky* possibly an echo of Wordsworth, *Composed Upon Westminster Bridge, 3 September 1802* 6–7:

'Ships, towers, domes, theatres, and temples lie / Open unto the fields, and to the sky'.
[21] *brig* bridge.
[22] *sallows* willows.
[23] *naiad* water-nymph.

And yearns so natures lessons teach   175
Amid such neighbourhoods to dwell

I love the muse who sits her down
Upon the molehills little lap
Who feels no fear to stain her gown
And pauses by the hedgerow gap   180
Not with that affectation praise
Of song to sing and never see
A field flower grown in all her days
Or e'en a forests aged tree

E'en here my simple feelings nurse   185
A love for every simple weed
And e'en this little shepherds purse[24]
Grieves me to cut it up – Indeed
I feel at times a love and joy
For every weed and every thing   190
A feeling kindred from a boy
A feeling brought with every spring

And why – this 'shepherds purse' that grows
In this strange spot in days gone bye
Grew in the little garden rows   195
Of that old hut[25] now left – and I
Feel what I never felt before
This weed an ancient neighbour here
And though I own the spot no more
Its every trifle makes it dear   200

The ivy at the parlour end
The woodbine[26] at the garden gate
Are all and each affections friend
That renders parting desolate
But times will change and friends must part   205
And nature still can make amends
Their memory lingers round the heart
Like life whose essence is its friends

Time looks on pomp with careless moods
Or killing apathys disdain   210
– So where old marble citys stood
Poor persecuted weeds remain
She feels a love for little things
That very few can feel beside
And still the grass eternal springs   215
Where castles stood and grandeur died[27]

---

[24] *shepherds purse* common cruciferous weed.
[25] *hut* cottage – presumably the one he had just moved out of in Helpston.
[26] *woodbine* honeysuckle.
[27] The poem ends on a note of defiance: the grass is like the poor because no matter how often you cut it down it grows back up. Lucas commends Clare's 'exultant insistence on the "grass eternal" as an invading army which will finally overwhelm its apparently irresistible enemies' (*John Clare* (1994), p. 62).

The Badger (composed between 1835 and 1837; edited from MS)

The badger grunting on his woodland track
With shaggy hide and sharp nose scrowed[1] with black
Roots in the bushes and the woods and makes
A great hugh[2] burrow in the ferns and brakes[3]
With nose on ground he runs a awkard pace   5
And anything will beat him in the race
The shepherds dog will run him to his den
Followed and hooted by the dogs and men
The woodman when the hunting comes about
Go round at night to stop the foxes out   10
And hurrying through the bushes ferns and brakes
Nor sees the many holes the badger makes
And often through the bushes to the chin
Breaks the old holes and tumbles headlong in

When midnight comes a host of dogs and men   15
Go out and track the badger to his den
And put a sack within the hole and lye
Till the old grunting badger passes bye
He comes and hears they let the strongest loose
The old fox hears the noise and drops the goose   20
The poacher shoots and hurrys from the cry
And the old hare half wounded buzzes bye
They get a forked stick to bear him down
And clapt[4] the dogs and bore him to the town
And bait him all the day with many dogs   25
And laugh and shout and fright the scampering hogs
He runs along and bites at all he meets
They shout and hollo down the noisey streets
He turns about to face the loud uproar
And drives the rebels to their very doors   30
The frequent stone is hurled where ere they go
When badgers fight and every ones a foe
The dogs are clapt and urged to join the fray
The badger turns and drives them all away
Though scarcely half as big dimute[5] and small   35
He fights with dogs for hours and beats them all
The heavy mastiff savage in the fray
Lies down and licks his feet and turns away
The bull dog knows his match and waxes[6] cold
The badger grins and never leaves his hold   40
He drives the crowd and follows at their heels
And bites them through the drunkard swears and reels

THE BADGER
[1] *scrowed* marked.
[2] *hugh* huge.
[3] *brakes* bracken.
[4] *clapt* set on.
[5] *dimute* diminutive.
[6] *waxes* becomes.

The frighted women takes the boys away
The blackguard laughs and hurrys on the fray
He trys to reach the woods a awkard race   45
But sticks and cudgels quickly stop the chace
He turns agen and drives the noisey crowd
And beats the many dogs in noises loud
He drives away and beats them every one
And then they loose them all and set them on   50
He falls as dead and kicked by boys and men
Then starts and grins and drives the crowd agen
Till kicked and torn and beaten out he lies
And leaves his hold and cackles groans and dies

Some keep a baited badger tame as hog   55
And tame him till he follows like the dog
They urge him on like dogs and show fair play
He beats and scarcely wounded goes away
Lapt[7] up as if asleep he scorns to fly
And siezes any dog that ventures nigh   60
Clapt like a dog he never bites the men
But worrys dogs and hurrys to his den
They let him out and turn a barrow down
And there he fights the pack of all the town
He licks the patting hand and trys to play   65
And never trys to bite or run away
And runs away from noise in hollow trees
Burnt by the boys to get a swarm of bees

A Vision (composed 2 August 1844; edited from MS)[1]

1

I lost the love, of heaven above;
I spurn'd the lust, of earth below;
I felt the sweets of fancied love, –
And hell itself my only foe.

2

I lost earths joys, but felt the glow,   5
Of heaven's flame abound in me:
'Till loveliness, and I did grow,
The bard of immortality.

3

I loved, but woman fell away;
I hid me, from her faded fame: 10
I snatched the sun's eternal ray, –
And wrote 'till earth was but a name.

---

[7]   *Lapt* curled.

A VISION
[1]   For a useful discussion of this poem within the context of
Clare's confinement in the Northamptionshire Asylum, 1844,

see Edward Strickland, 'Approaching "A Vision"', *Victorian Poetry* 22 (1984) 229–45.

4
In every language upon earth,
On every shore, o'er every sea;
I gave my name immortal birth,   15
And kep't my spirit with the free.

[*I am*] (composed by 20 December 1846; edited from MS)

1
I am – yet what I am, none cares or knows;
    My friends forsake me like a memory lost: –
I am the self-consumer of my woes; –
    They rise and vanish in oblivion's host,
Like shadows in love's frenzied stifled throes: –   5
And yet I am, and live – like vapours tost

2
Into the nothingness of scorn and noise, –
    Into the living sea of waking dreams,
Where there is neither sense of life or joys,
    But the vast shipwreck of my lifes esteems;   10
Even the dearest, that I love the best
Are strange – nay, rather stranger than the rest.

3
I long for scenes where man hath never trod
    A place where woman never smiled or wept
There to abide with my Creator, God;
    And sleep as I in childhood, sweetly slept,   15
Untroubling, and untroubled where I lie,
The grass below – above the vaulted sky.

An Invite to Eternity (composed by July 1847; edited from MS)

1
Wilt thou go with me sweet maid
Say maiden wilt thou go with me
Through the valley depths of shade
Of night and dark obscurity
Where the path hath lost its way   5
Where the sun forgets the day
Where there's nor life nor light to see
Sweet maiden wilt thou go with me

2
Where stones will turn to flooding streams
Where plains will rise like ocean waves   10
Where life will fade like visioned dreams
And mountains darken into caves
Say maiden wilt thou go with me

Through this sad non-identity
Where parents live and are forgot   15
And sisters live and know us not

3

Say maiden wilt thou go with me
In this strange death of life to be
To live in death and be the same
Without this life, or home, or name   20
At once to be, and not to be
That was, and is not – yet to see
Things pass like shadows – and the sky
Above, below, around us lie

4

The land of shadows wilt thou trace   25
And look – nor know each others face
The present mixed with reasons gone
And past, and present all as one
Say maiden can thy life be led
To join the living with the dead   30
Then trace thy footsteps on with me
We're wed to one eternity

Little Trotty Wagtail (composed 9 August 1849; edited from MS)

1

Little trotty wagtail he went in the rain
And tittering tottering sideways he near got straight again
He stooped to get a worm and look'd up to catch a fly
And then he flew away e're his feathers they were dry

2

Little trotty wagtail he waddled in the mud
And left his little foot marks trample where he would   5
He waddled in the water pudge and waggle went his tail
And chirrupt up his wings to dry upon the garden rail

3

Little trotty wagtail you nimble all about
And in the dimpling water pudge you waddle in and out   10
Your home is nigh at hand and in the warm pigsty
So little Master Wagtail I'll bid you a 'Good bye'

Silent Love (composed between 1842 and 1864; edited from MS)

1

The dew it trembles on the thorn
Then vanishes so love is born
Young love that speaks in silent thought
'Till scorned, then withers and is nought

2

The pleasure of a single hour   5
The blooming of a single flower
The glitter of the morning dew
Such is young love when it is new

3

The twitter of the wild birds wing
The murmur of the bees   10
Lays of hay crickets when they sing
Or other things more frail than these

4

Such is young love when silence speaks
Till weary with the joy it seeks
Then fancy shapes supplies   15
'Till sick of its own heart it dies

5

The dew drop falls at mornings hour
When none are standing by
And noiseless fades the broken flower
So lovers in their silence die   20

['*O could I be as I have been*'] (composed between 1842 and 1864; edited
from MS)

1

O could I be as I have been
    And ne'er can be no more
A harmless thing in meadows green
    Or on the wild sea shore

2

Oh could I be what once I was   5
    In heaths and valleys green
A dweller in the summer grass
    Green fields and places green

3

A tennant of the happy fields
    By grounds of wheat and beans   10
By gipseys' camps and milking bield[1]
    Where lussious woodbine[2] leans

4

To sit on the deserted plough
    Left when the corn was sown

'O COULD I BE AS I HAVE BEEN'   [2]   *woodbine* honeysuckle.
[1]   *bield* shelter.

In corn and wild weeds buried now   15
   In quiet peace unknown

5

The harrows resting by the hedge
   The roll[3] within the Dyke[4]
Hid in the Ariff[5] and the sedge[6]
   Are things I used to like.   20

6

I used to tread through fallow lands
   And wade through paths of grain
When wheat ears pattered on the hands
   And head-aches[7] left a stain

7

I wish I was what I have been   25
   And what I was could be
As when I roved in shadows green
   And loved my willow tree

8

To gaze upon the starry sky
   And higher fancies build   30
And make in solitary joy
   Loves temple in the field

Felicia Dorothea Hemans (*née* Browne)   (1793–1835)

Felicia Dorothea Browne was born at 118 Duke Street, Liverpool, on 25 September 1793,[1] the daughter of George Browne, merchant, and Felicity Wagner (of mingled German, Italian and Lancashire descent). She had three brothers: Sir Thomas Henry Browne, KCH (1787–1855), distinguished in the Peninsular Wars; Lt.-Col. George Baxter Browne, CB, also distinguished in the Peninsular, and later Chief Commissioner of Police in Ireland; and Claude Scott Browne, Deputy Assistant Commissary-General in Upper Canada. Her father suffered business problems in 1800, and moved his family to Gwyrch, near Abergele, North Wales, where Felicia was largely brought up, her education being supervised by her mother. She learned Latin, modern languages and drawing, and is said to have had a phenomenal memory. Her sister recalled that 'She could repeat pages of poetry from her favourite authors, after having read them but once over. . . . One of her earliest tastes was a passion for Shakespeare, which she read, as her choicest recreation, at six years old'.[2]

She began writing poetry at an early age, and published her first volume of poems by subscription, when she was still only fourteen, in 1808. One of the subscribers was the young Thomas Medwin, who had met its author in North Wales. He showed them to his friend, Percy Bysshe Shelley, who in turn wrote to Thomas Jefferson Hogg, 28 July 1811: 'Now there is Miss F. D. Browne (certainly a tyger); yet she surpasses my sister in poetical talents, this your dispassionate criticism *must* allow'.[3] Shelley scholarship has it that the young man bombarded Miss F. D. Browne with

---

3   *roll* large wooden roller for breaking clods of earth.
4   *Dyke* ditch.
5   *Ariff* goose-grass.
6   *sedge* various coarse grassy, rush-like or flag-like plants growing in wet places.
7   *head-aches* poppies.

FELICIA DOROTHEA HEMANS
1   The year of her birth is variously given as 1793, 1794 and 1795. I have followed the dating given by her sister, Harriet Hughes, in her memoir in *The Works of Mrs Hemans* (7 vols, Edinburgh and London, 1839).
2   *The Works of Mrs Hemans*, i 6.
3   Jones i 129.

letters but that, recognizing trouble when she saw it, Felicia's mother forbade her from replying.[4]

The family was not much happier with Captain Alfred Hemans, whom she had met when she was fifteen. He was a soldier, and fought in the Peninsular campaign with her brothers. In 1811 he returned to her, carrying scars sustained in the British withdrawal from Corunna in 1809, and a fever contracted during the Walcheren expedition. While still Felicia Dorothea Browne, she published *The Domestic Affections* in 1812, shortly before marrying him. For a while they lived at Daventry, the sort of suburban hell-hole she detested, before returning to her maternal home in Wales. They were evidently ill-suited; Captain Hemans is reported to have said that 'it was the curse of having a literary wife that he could never get a pair of stockings mended'.[5] After having no less than five children they separated in 1818, when Hemans went to live in Rome, in search of improved health, never to see her again.

Although her mother and sister helped her raise her children, the need to provide for them meant that she had to keep publishing. She was caught in a trap from which she was never to escape. 'Her poetry was often written with a readiness approaching improvisation', W. M. Rossetti wrote many years later, 'this she felt as in some degree a blemish, and towards the close of her life she regretted having often had to write in a haphazard way, so as to supply means for the education of her sons.'[6] The rush in which her poems were composed is clearly seen in her manuscripts;[7] few carry corrections, revisions, or even deletions. Her working life was one of furious productivity, undertaken in spare moments from household chores; works included *Tales, and Historic Scenes in Verse* (1819); *Stanzas to the Memory of the Late King* (1820); *Welsh Melodies* (1822); *The Siege of Valencia, and Other Poems* (1823); *The Forest Sanctuary* (1825); *Lays of Many Lands* (1826); *Records of Woman* (1828), and *Songs of the Affections* (1830) – an astonishing publication record. She also contributed poems and essays to a wide range of periodicals and magazines; in 1823 she became a regular contributor to the *New Monthly Magazine*. Her usual practice was to publish poems first in periodicals, and then collect them in volume form. By this means she maximized her income, and became well known to readers of annuals. By the 1820s she was tremendously popular, and critics tended to acknowledge this when commenting on

her work. Reviewing *The Siege of Valencia* in 1823, the *British Critic* remarked: 'When a woman can write like this, she *ought* to write. Her mind is national property. In the grand scheme of a popular literature, there are many departments which can alone be filled by the emanations of female genius.'[8] In 1826 the *Literary Chronicle* called her 'the first poetess of the day'.[9]

Her mother's death in 1827 was a terrible blow, by which time her own health, ravaged by years of unrelenting hard work, was beginning to fail. She moved to Liverpool, where she found her celebrity wearisome, but still managed to compose. In need of a break, she toured Scotland and the Lakes in 1830, meeting Sir Walter Scott and Wordsworth along the way. Felicia was always an admirer of Wordsworth. His poems, she once wrote, 'quite haunt me, and I have a strange feeling as if I must have known them in my childhood, they come over me so like old melodies'.[10] They got on, and it was on this basis that Wordsworth lamented her death in the 1837 text of his *Extempore Effusion on the Death of James Hogg* (see pp. 417 n. 13). She moved to Dublin to be closer to her brother, George, in 1831. In spite of her declining health, she continued to write, and to educate her sons. She died 16 May 1835, of tuberculosis, and was buried in St Anne's Church, Dublin.

Felicia spent the first two decades of her life in a country waging war with Napoleon. There were two ways of reacting to this: you could denounce the war, like Anna Laetitia Barbauld in her poem, *Eighteen Hundred and Eleven*; or if your brothers and husband had seen service, as was true of Felicia, you were more likely to strike an appropriately patriotic attitude. This was partly the cause of her popularity, and explains why she was acceptable to Tory critics like Croker, who attacked Barbauld, Keats, Owenson and Wordsworth for ideological reasons. But it would be a mistake to dismiss Felicia as merely jingoistic; even her early work is concerned with more than love of her country. Pride, defiance, courage in the face of inevitable defeat, even love: these are the virtues that pervade her poems. *Records of Woman* (1828), probably her most important single volume, concentrated on the hardships faced specifically by women. She had a good deal to say on the subject, having been under pressure to support her large family from the moment her husband abandoned her. 'My life after eighteen became so painfully, laboriously domestic, that it was an absolute

4   See Newman Ivey White, *Shelley* (2 vols, London, 1947), i 61.
5   *A Short Sketch of the Life of Mrs Hemans* (1835), p. 32.
6   *The Poetical Works of Mrs Felicia Hemans* ed. W. M. Rossetti (London, 1873), p. xxv.
7   Her MSS can be found in the British Library and the Buffalo and Erie County Public Library, among other repositories.

8   *British Critic* 20 (1823) 50–61, p. 53.
9   *Literary Chronicle* 379 (19 August 1826) 518–19, p. 518.
10 Henry F. Chorley, *Memorials of Mrs Hemans* (2 vols, 1836), i 175.

duty to crush intellectual tastes', she once confided, 'I could neither read nor write legitimately till the day was over'.[11] Many of the *Records of Woman* are concerned with the plight of those lumbered with feckless, unreliable, weak or ineffectual men: Properzia Rossi lavishes her love and art on a man not worthy of her; the Indian Woman is deserted by her husband for another woman, and so forth. But it would be a mistake to describe Felicia as having feminist designs; the other side to these poems is the high value their author places on the relationship between the sexes. It is easy now to laugh at the sentimentality of the boy on the burning deck – *Casabianca* has lost much of its power through the philistine over-familiarity with which the English, in their embarrassment, have treated it. But if read without readiness to scoff, it emerges as a moving story of someone who remains true to their word, even if it means the ultimate sacrifice (pp. 998–9). None of this, it seems to me, is at all 'feminine', which is how she was categorized – and to a large extent patronized – by contemporary reviewers. The moral questions at the heart of her work are not gender-specific; they extend beyond those barriers into areas of life that concern everyone.

A much larger selection of her work is available in my *Romantic Women Poets: An Anthology*, including all of the *Records of Woman* poems, and a complete text of *Stanzas to the Memory of the Late King* (1820).

Further reading

Peter W. Trinder, *Mrs Hemans* (Wales, 1984)

Norma Clarke, *Ambitious Heights: Writing, Friendship, Love – The Jewsbury Sisters, Felicia Hemans, and Jane Welsh Carlyle* (London, 1990)

Nanora Sweet, 'History, Imperialism, and the Aesthetics of the Beautiful: Hemans and the Post-Napoleonic Moment', in Mary A. Favret and Nicola J. Watson eds., *At the Limits of Romanticism* (Bloomington, 1994)

Jerome J. McGann, *The Poetics of Sensibility: A Revolution in Literary Style* (Oxford, 1996), pp. 174–94

Anthony John Harding, 'Felicia Hemans and the Effacement of Woman', *RWW* 138–49

Susan J. Wolfson, ' "Domestic Affections" and "the spear of Minerva": Felicia Hemans and the Dilemma of Gender', *RR* 128–66

Properzia Rossi

From RECORDS OF WOMAN: WITH OTHER POEMS (1828)

Properzia Rossi, a celebrated female sculptor of Bologna,[1] possessed also of talents for poetry and music, died in consequence of an unrequited attachment. A painting by Ducis[2] represents her showing her last work, a basso-relievo of Ariadne,[3] to a Roman knight, the object of her affection, who regards it with indifference.

> *Tell me no more, no more*
> *Of my soul's lofty gifts! Are they not vain*
> *To quench its haunting thirst for happiness?*
> *Have I not loved, and striven, and failed to bind*
> *One true heart unto me, whereon my own*
> *Might find a resting-place, a home for all*
> *Its burden of affections? I depart*
> *Unknown, though Fame goes with me; I must leave*
> *The earth unknown. Yet it may be that death*
> *Shall give my name a power to win such tears*
> *As would have made life precious.*[4]

---

[11] Ibid., i 166, 175.

PROPERZIA ROSSI

[1] Properzia Rossi (?1491–1530) specialized in bas-relief sculptures, usually in stone or wood.

[2] Louis Ducis (1775–1847), painter of historical subjects and portraits.

[3] An appropriate subject: Ariadne helped Theseus to escape the minotaur's labyrinth. Afterwards she married him and had his child, but he abandoned her at Naxos and married her sister, Phaedra.

[4] This epigraph, like so many of those in Felicia's poems, was composed especially for this poem by Felicia herself.

I

One dream of passion and of beauty more,
And in its bright fulfilment let me pour
My soul away! Let earth retain a trace
Of that which lit my being, though its race
Might have been loftier far – yet one more dream!   5
From my deep spirit one victorious gleam
Ere I depart – for thee alone, for thee!
May this last work, this farewell triumph be –
Thou, loved so vainly! I would leave enshrined
Something immortal of my heart and mind   10
That yet may speak to thee when I am gone,
Shaking thine inmost bosom with a tone
Of lost affection – something that may prove
What she hath been whose melancholy love
On thee was lavished; silent pang and tear,   15
And fervent song that gushed when none were near,
And dream by night, and weary thought by day,
Stealing the brightness from her life away,
While thou – awake, not yet within me die
Under the burden and the agony   20
Of this vain tenderness; my spirit, wake!
Ev'n for thy sorrowful affection's sake,
Live! In thy work breathe out, that he may yet,
Feeling sad mastery there, perchance regret
Thine unrequited gift.

II

           It comes – the power   25
Within me born flows back, my fruitless dower
That could not win me love. Yet once again
I greet it proudly, with its rushing train
Of glorious images: they throng, they press;
A sudden joy lights up my loneliness –   30
I shall not perish all!
           The bright work grows
Beneath my hand, unfolding, as a rose,
Leaf after leaf, to beauty; line by line
I fix my thought, heart, soul, to burn, to shine
Through the pale marble's veins. It grows – and now   35
I give my own life's history to thy brow,
Forsaken Ariadne! Thou shalt wear
My form, my lineaments – but oh, more fair,
Touched into lovelier being by the glow
   Which in me dwells, as by the summer light   40
All things are glorified! From thee my woe
   Shall yet look beautiful to meet his sight
When I am passed away. Thou art the mould
Wherein I pour the fervent thoughts, th' untold,
The self-consuming! Speak to him of me,   45

Thou, the deserted by the lonely sea,
With the soft sadness of thine earnest eye;
Speak to him, lorn one, deeply, mournfully,
Of all my love and grief! Oh could I throw
Into thy frame a voice, a sweet and low   50
And thrilling voice of song – when he came nigh,
To send the passion of its melody
Through his pierced bosom – on its tones to bear
My life's deep feeling, as the southern air
Wafts the faint myrtle's breath – to rise, to swell,   55
To sink away in accents of farewell,
Winning but one, *one* gush of tears, whose flow
Surely my parted spirit yet might know,
If love be strong as death!

III

            Now fair thou art,
Thou form whose life is of my burning heart!   60
Yet all the vision that within me wrought,
    I cannot make thee! Oh, I might have given
Birth to creations of far nobler thought;
    I might have kindled, with the fire of heaven,
Things not of such as die! But I have been   65
Too much alone; a heart whereon to lean,
With all these deep affections that o'erflow
My aching soul, and find no shore below,
An eye to be my star, a voice to bring
Hope o'er my path, like sounds that breathe of spring,   70
These are denied me – dreamt of still in vain,
Therefore my brief aspirings from the chain
Are ever but as some wild fitful song,
Rising triumphantly to die erelong
In dirge-like echoes.

IV

            Yet the world will see   75
Little of this, my parting work, in thee;
    Thou shalt have fame – oh mockery! Give the reed
From storms a shelter, give the drooping vine
Something round which its tendrils may entwine;
    Give the parched flower a raindrop, and the meed   80
Of love's kind words to woman! Worthless fame,
That in *his* bosom wins not for my name
Th' abiding place it asked! Yet how my heart,
In its own fairy world of song and art,
Once beat for praise! Are those high longings o'er?   85
That which I have been can I be no more?
Never, oh never more – though still thy sky
Be blue as then, my glorious Italy!

And though the music, whose rich breathings fill
Thine air with soul, be wandering past me still,   90
And though the mantle of thy sunlight streams
Unchanged on forms instinct with poet-dreams –
Never, oh never more! Where'er I move,
The shadow of this broken-hearted love   95
Is on me and around! Too well *they* know,
   Whose life is all within, too soon and well,
When there the blight hath settled – but I go
   Under the silent wings of peace to dwell;
From the slow wasting, from the lonely pain,   100
The inward burning of those words 'in vain'
   Seared on the heart – I go. 'Twill soon be past.
Sunshine, and song, and bright Italian heaven,
   And thou, oh thou on whom my spirit cast
Unvalued wealth, who know'st not what was given   105
In that devotedness – the sad and deep
And unrepaid, farewell! If I could weep
Once, only once, beloved one, on thy breast,
Pouring my heart forth ere I sink to rest!
But that were happiness, and unto me   110
Earth's gift is *fame*. Yet I was formed to be
So richly blessed! With thee to watch the sky,
Speaking not, feeling but that thou wert nigh;
With thee to listen, while the tones of song
Swept ev'n as part of our sweet air along,   115
To listen silently – with thee to gaze
On forms, the deified of olden days –
This had been joy enough, and hour by hour,
From its glad wellsprings drinking life and power,
How had my spirit soared, and made its fame   120
   A glory for thy brow. Dreams, dreams! The fire
Burns faint within me. Yet I leave my name –
   As a deep thrill may linger on the lyre
When its full chords are hushed – awhile to live,
And one day haply in thy heart revive   125
Sad thoughts of me; I leave it with a sound,
A spell o'er memory, mournfully profound,
I leave it on my country's air to dwell –
Say proudly yet, ''Twas hers who loved me well!'

Indian Woman's Death Song

From RECORDS OF WOMAN: WITH OTHER POEMS (1828)

An Indian woman, driven to despair by her husband's desertion of her for another wife, entered a
canoe with her children, and rowed it down the Mississippi towards a cataract. Her voice was heard
from the shore singing a mournful death-song until overpowered by the sound of the waters in which
she perished. The tale is related in Long's *Expedition to the Source of St Peter's River*.[1]

INDIAN WOMAN'S DEATH SONG
[1] William H. Keating, *Narrative of an Expedition to the source
of the St Peter's River ... under the command of S. H. Long* was
first published in two volumes in Philadelphia, 1824; it was
published in London the following year.

[*Non, je ne puis vivre avec un coeur brisé. Il faut que je retrouve la joie, et que je m'unisse aux esprits libres de l'air.*[2]]

Bride of Messina, *translated by Madame de Staël* [3]

[*Let not my child be a girl, for very sad is the life of a woman.*]
The Prairie [4]

Down a broad river of the western wilds,
Piercing thick forest glooms, a light canoe
Swept with the current: fearful was the speed
Of the frail bark, as by a tempest's wing
Borne leaf-like on to where the mist of spray   5
Rose with the cataract's thunder. Yet within,
Proudly, and dauntlessly, and all alone,
Save that a babe lay sleeping at her breast,
A woman stood. Upon her Indian brow
Sat a strange gladness, and her dark hair waved   10
As if triumphantly. She pressed her child,
In its bright slumber, to her beating heart,
And lifted her sweet voice that rose awhile
Above the sound of waters, high and clear,
Wafting a wild proud strain, her song of death.   15

Roll swiftly to the spirit's land, thou mighty stream and free!
Father of ancient waters, roll, and bear our lives with thee!
The weary bird that storms have tossed would seek the sunshine's calm,
And the deer that hath the arrow's hurt flies to the woods of balm.

Roll on! My warrior's eye hath looked upon another's face,   20
And mine hath faded from his soul, as fades a moonbeam's trace;
My shadow comes not o'er his path, my whisper to his dream,
He flings away the broken reed – roll swifter yet, thou stream!

The voice that spoke of other days is hushed within *his* breast,
But *mine* its lonely music haunts, and will not let me rest;   25
It sings a low and mournful song of gladness that is gone;
I cannot live without that light – father of waves, roll on!

Will he not miss the bounding step that met him from the chase?
The heart of love that made his home an ever-sunny place?
The hand that spread the hunter's board, and decked his couch of yore? 30
He will not! Roll, dark foaming stream, on to the better shore!

Some blessed fount amidst the woods of that bright land must flow
Whose waters from my soul may lave the memory of this woe;
Some gentle wind must whisper there, whose breath may waft away
The burden of the heavy night, the sadness of the day.   35

---

[2]   'No, I can't live with a broken heart. I must retrieve my happiness, and be reunited with the free spirits of the air'.
[3]   Schiller's *Die Braut von Messina* was first published in 1803, and not translated into English in full until 1837. Anne-Louise-Germaine Necker, Madame de Staël (1766–1817), published her translation in chapter 19 of *De l'Allemagne*, in 1807, in which she also gives a summary of the play. I am grateful to Susan Wolfson for this information.
[4]   James Fenimore Cooper's popular book was first published in London, 1827.

And thou, my babe, though born, like me, for woman's weary lot,
Smile – to that wasting of the heart, my own! I leave thee not;
Too bright a thing art *thou* to pine in aching love away,
Thy mother bears thee far, young fawn, from sorrow and decay.

She bears thee to the glorious bowers where none are heard to weep,   40
And where th' unkind one hath no power again to trouble sleep;
And where the soul shall find its youth, as wakening from a dream –
One moment, and that realm is ours: on, on, dark rolling stream!

The Grave of a Poetess[1]

From RECORDS OF WOMAN: WITH OTHER POEMS (1828)

Ne me plaignez pas – si vous saviez
Combien de peines ce tombeau m'a épargnées![2]

I stood beside thy lowly grave,
    Spring odours breathed around,
And music in the river-wave
    Passed with a lulling sound.

All happy things that love the sun[3]   5
    In the bright air glanced by,
And a glad murmur seemed to run
    Through the soft azure sky.

Fresh leaves were on the ivy-bough
    That fringed the ruins near;   10
Young voices were abroad, but thou
    Their sweetness couldst not hear.

And mournful grew my heart for thee,
    Thou in whose woman's mind
The ray that brightens earth and sea,   15
    The light of song was shrined;[4]

THE GRAVE OF A POETESS
[1] 'Extrinsic interest has lately attached to the fine scenery of Woodstock, near Kilkenny, on account of its having been the last residence of the author of *Psyche* [Mary Tighe]. Her grave is one of many in the churchyard of the village. The river runs smoothly by. The ruins of an ancient abbey that have been partially converted into a church reverently throw their mantle of tender shadow over it. (*Tales by the O'Hara Family*)' (Hemans's note). John Banim (1798–1842) and Michael Banim (1796–1874) published *Tales by the O'Hara Family* in 1825–7. Felicia managed to visit Mary Tighe's grave only in April 1831, when she described it as follows: 'We went to the tomb, "the grave of a poetess", where there is a monument by Flaxman. It consists of a recumbent female figure, with much of the repose, the mysterious sweetness of happy death, which is to me so affecting in monumental sculpture. There is, however, a very small Titania-looking sort of figure with wings, sitting at the head of the sleeper, which I thought interfered with the singleness of effect which the tomb would have produced. Unfortunately, too, the monument is carved in very rough stone, which allows no delicacy of touch. That place of rest made me very thoughtful; I could not but reflect on the many changes which had brought me to the spot I had commemorated three years since, without the slightest idea of ever visiting it; and, though surrounded by attention and the appearance of interest, my heart was envying the repose of her who slept there' (*The Works of Mrs Hemans* (7 vols, Edinburgh and London, 1839), i 238–9).
[2] 'Don't pity me; if only you knew how much suffering this tomb has spared me!'
[3] *All happy things that love the sun* an echo of Wordsworth, *Resolution and Independence* 8: 'All things that love the sun are out of doors'.
[4] *shrined* enshrined.

Mournful that thou wert slumbering low
  With a dread curtain drawn
Between thee and the golden glow
  Of this world's vernal dawn.   20

Parted from all the song and bloom
  Thou wouldst have loved so well,
To thee the sunshine round thy tomb
  Was but a broken spell.

The bird, the insect on the wing,   25
  In their bright reckless play,
Might feel the flush and life of spring,
  And thou wert passed away!

But then, ev'n then, a nobler thought
  O'er my vain sadness came;   30
Th' immortal spirit woke, and wrought
  Within my thrilling frame.

Surely on lovelier things, I said,
  Thou must have looked ere now,
Than all that round our pathway shed   35
  Odours and hues below,

The shadows of the tomb are here,
  Yet beautiful is earth!
What seest thou then where no dim fear,
  No haunting dream hath birth?   40

Here a vain love to passing flowers
  Thou gav'st, but where thou art
The sway is not with changeful hours –
  There love and death must part.

Thou hast left sorrow in thy song,   45
  A voice not loud, but deep!
The glorious bowers of earth among,
  How often didst thou weep!

Where couldst thou fix on mortal ground
  Thy tender thoughts and high?   50
Now peace the woman's heart hath found,
  And joy the poet's eye.

CASABIANCA
[1] 'Young Casabianca, a boy about thirteen years old, son to
the Admiral of the Orient, remained at his post (in the Battle
of the Nile) after the ship had taken fire, and all the guns had
been abandoned, and perished in the explosion of the vessel,
when the flames had reached the powder' (Hemans's note).

Casabianca[1]

From THE FOREST SANCTUARY: WITH OTHER POEMS (2nd edn, 1829)

The boy stood on the burning deck
 Whence all but he had fled;
The flame that lit the battle's wreck
 Shone round him o'er the dead.

Yet beautiful and bright he stood,   5
 As born to rule the storm –
A creature of heroic blood,
 A proud though childlike form.

The flames rolled on, he would not go
 Without his father's word;   10
That father, faint in death below,
 His voice no longer heard.

He called aloud, 'Say, father, say
 If yet my task is done?'
He knew not that the chieftain lay   15
 Unconscious of his son.

'Speak, father!' once again he cried,
 'If I may yet be gone!
And –'. But the booming shots replied,
 And fast the flames rolled on.   20

Upon his brow he felt their breath
 And in his waving hair,
And looked from that lone post of death
 In still yet brave despair,

And shouted but once more aloud,   25
 'My father, must I stay?'
While o'er him fast, through sail and shroud,
 The wreathing fires made way.

They wrapped the ship in splendour wild,
 They caught the flag on high,   30
And streamed above the gallant child
 Like banners in the sky.

There came a burst of thunder sound;
 The boy – oh, where was he?
Ask of the winds that far around   35
 With fragments strewed the sea.

With mast, and helm, and pennon fair
 That well had borne their part,
But the noblest thing which perished there
 Was that young faithful heart!   40

The Land of Dreams

From SONGS OF THE AFFECTIONS, WITH OTHER POEMS (1830)

> *And dreams, in their development, have breath*
> *And tears, and tortures, and the touch of joy;*
> *They leave a weight upon our waking thoughts. . . .*
> *They make us what we were not – what they will,*
> *And shake us with the vision that's gone by . . .*[1]

Oh spirit land, thou land of dreams!
A world thou art of mysterious gleams,
Of startling voices, and sounds at strife –
A world of the dead in the hues of life.

Like a wizard's magic-glass thou art   5
When the wavy shadows float by, and part –
Visions of aspects, now loved, now strange,
Glimmering and mingling in ceaseless change.

Thou art like a city of the past
With its gorgeous halls into fragments cast,   10
Amidst whose ruins there glide and play
Familiar forms of the world's today.

Thou art like the depths where the seas have birth,
Rich with the wealth that is lost from earth –
All the sere flowers of our days gone by,   15
And the buried gems in thy bosom lie.

Yes, thou art like those dim sea-caves,
A realm of treasures, a realm of graves!
And the shapes through thy mysteries that come and go,
Are of beauty and terror, of power and woe.   20

But for *me*, oh thou picture-land of sleep,
Thou art all one world of affections deep –
And wrung from my heart is each flushing dye
That sweeps o'er thy chambers of imagery.

And thy bowers are fair – even as Eden fair;   25
All the beloved of my soul are there!
The forms my spirit most pines to see,
The eyes whose love hath been life to me –

They are there, and each blessed voice I hear,
Kindly, and joyous, and silvery clear;   30
But undertones are in each, that say,
'It is but a dream; it will melt away!'

THE LAND OF DREAMS
[1] Byron, *The Dream* 5–7, 15–16.

I walk with sweet friends in the sunset's glow;
I listen to music of long ago;
But one thought, like an omen, breathes faint through the lay –   35
'It is but a dream; it will melt away!'

I sit by the hearth of my early days;
All the home-faces are met by the blaze,
And the eyes of the mother shine soft, yet say,
'It is but a dream; it will melt away!'   40

And away, like a flower's passing breath, 'tis gone,
And I wake more sadly, more deeply lone –
Oh, a haunted heart is a weight to bear!
Bright faces, kind voices, where are ye, where?

Shadow not forth, oh thou land of dreams,   45
The past, as it fled by my own blue streams!
Make not my spirit within me burn
For the scenes and the hours that may ne'er return!

Call out from the *future* thy visions bright,
From the world o'er the grave, take thy solemn light,   50
And oh! with the loved, whom no more I see,
Show me my home as it yet may be!

As it yet may be in some purer sphere –
No cloud, no parting, no sleepless fear;
So my soul may bear on through the long, long day,   55
Till I go where the beautiful melts not away!

Nature's Farewell

From SONGS OF THE AFFECTIONS, WITH OTHER POEMS (1830)

The beautiful is vanished, and returns not. [1]

A youth rode forth from his childhood's home,
Through the crowded paths of the world to roam,
And the green leaves whispered as he passed:
'Wherefore, thou dreamer, away so fast?

Knew'st thou with what thou art parting here,   5
Long wouldst thou linger in doubt and fear;
Thy heart's light laughter, thy sunny hours,
Thou hast left in our shades with the spring's wild-flowers.

Under the arch by our mingling made,
Thou and thy brother have gaily played;   10
Ye may meet again where ye roved of yore,
But as ye *have* met there – oh, never more!'

NATURE'S FAREWELL
[1] Coleridge, *The Death of Wallenstein*, V i 68.

On rode the youth – and the boughs among,
Thus the free birds o'er his pathway sung:
'Wherefore so fast unto life away?   15
Thou art leaving for ever thy joy in our lay!'[2]

Thou mayst come to the summer woods again,
And thy heart have no echo to greet their strain;
Afar from the foliage its love will dwell –
A change must pass o'er thee – farewell, farewell!'   20

On rode the youth, and the founts and streams
Thus mingled a voice with his joyous dreams:
'We have been thy playmates through many a day,
Wherefore thus leave us? Oh yet delay!

Listen but once to the sound of our mirth!   25
For thee 'tis a melody passing from earth.[3]
Never again wilt thou find in its flow
The peace it could once on thy heart bestow.

Thou wilt visit the scenes of thy childhood's glee
With the breath of the world on thy spirit free;   30
Passion and sorrow its depth will have stirred,
And the singing of waters be vainly heard.

Thou wilt bear in our gladsome laugh no part –
What should it do for a burning heart?
Thou wilt bring to the banks of our freshest rill   35
Thirst which no fountain on earth may still.

Farewell! When thou comest again to thine own,
Thou wilt miss from our music its loveliest tone;
Mournfully true is the tale we tell –
Yet on, fiery dreamer! Farewell, farewell!'   40

And a something of gloom on his spirit weighed
As he caught the last sounds of his native shade;
But he knew not, till many a bright spell broke,
How deep were the oracles nature spoke!

Second Sight

From SONGS OF THE AFFECTIONS, WITH OTHER POEMS (1830)

*Ne'er erred the prophet heart that grief inspired,
Though joy's illusions mock their votarist.*

Maturin[1]

---

2   *lay* song.
3   *'tis a melody passing from earth* Felicia echoes Wordsworth,
Ode 18: 'there hath passed away a glory from the earth'.

SECOND SIGHT
1   Charles Robert Maturin (1782–1824), *Bertram* IV ii
144–5. Maturin's play was produced by Kean at Drury Lane
in 1816, with great success.

A mournful gift is mine, oh friends,
   A mournful gift is mine!
A murmur of the soul which blends
   With the flow of song and wine.

An eye that through the triumph's hour   5
   Beholds the coming woe,
And dwells upon the faded flower
   Midst the rich summer's glow.

Ye smile to view fair faces bloom
   Where the father's board is spread;   10
I see the stillness and the gloom
   Of a home whence all are fled.

I see the withered garlands lie
   Forsaken on the earth,
While the lamps yet burn and the dancers fly   15
   Through the ringing hall of mirth.

I see the blood-red future stain
   On the warrior's gorgeous crest,
And the bier amidst the bridal train
   When they come with roses dressed.   20

I hear the still small moan of time[2]
   Through the ivy branches made,
Where the palace in its glory's prime
   With the sunshine stands arrayed.

The thunder of the seas I hear,   25
   The shriek along the wave,
When the bark sweeps forth, and song and cheer
   Salute the parting brave.

With every breeze a spirit sends
   To me some warning sign –
A mournful gift is mine, oh friends,   30
   A mournful gift is mine!

Oh, prophet heart, thy grief, thy power
   To all deep souls belong;
The shadow in the sunny hour,   35
   The wail in the mirthful song.

Their sight is all too sadly clear –
   For them a veil is riven;
Their piercing thoughts repose not here,
   Their home is but in heaven.   40

---

[2]   *the still small moan of time* an echo of I Kings 19:12: 'And
after the earthquake a fire; but the Lord was not in the fire:
and after the fire a *still small voice*.'

Thoughts During Sickness: II. Sickness Like Night

From THE NEW MONTHLY MAGAZINE 43 (1835, p. 329)

> Thou art like night, oh sickness, deeply stilling
> Within my heart the world's disturbing sound,
> And the dim quiet of my chamber filling
> With low, sweet voices, by life's tumult drowned.
> Thou art like awful night! Thou gatherest round   5
> The things that are unseen, though close they lie,
> And with a truth, clear, startling, and profound,
> Giv'st their dread presence to our mortal eye.
> Thou art like starry, spiritual night!
> High and immortal thoughts attend thy way,   10
> And revelations, which the common light
> Brings not, though wakening with its rosy ray
> All outward life: be welcome, then, thy rod,
> Before whose touch my soul unfolds itself to God!

John Gibson Lockhart (1794–1854)

A graduate of the University of Glasgow, Lockhart went to Balliol College, Oxford, where he graduated in 1813. He became a lawyer in Edinburgh, but always nutured literary ambitions, which found an outlet in *Blackwood's Edinburgh Magazine*, as editors of which he and John Wilson (see pp. 625–6) were appointed in 1817. The journal was Tory in its politics, and its opposition to Leigh Hunt was inspired partly by Hunt's vaunted radicalism. Lockhart was the mastermind behind a series of articles entitled 'The Cockney School of Poetry', published under the initial 'Z', which commenced in *Blackwood's* for October 1817. The primary target was Hunt, and it concentrated on his alleged immorality, taking the line that ethics are directly related to art:

> Every man is, according to Mr Hunt, a dull potato-eating blockhead – of no greater value to God or man than any ox or dray-horse – who is not an admirer of Voltaire's *romans*, a worshipper of Lord Holland and Mr Haydon, and a quoter of John Buncle and Chaucer's Flower and Leaf. Every woman is useful only as a breeding machine, unless she is fond of reading Launcelot of the Lake, in an antique summerhouse.

How such a profligate creature as Mr Hunt can pretend to be an admirer of Mr Wordsworth, is to us a thing altogether inexplicable. One great charm of Wordsworth's noble compositions consists in the dignified purity of thought, and the patriarchal simplicity of feeling, with which they are throughout penetrated and imbued. We can conceive a vicious man admiring with distant awe the spectacle of virtue and purity; but if he does so sincerely, he must also do so with the profoundest feeling of the error of his own ways, and the resolution to amend them. His admiration must be humble and silent, not pert and loquacious. Mr Hunt praises the purity of Wordsworth as if he himself were pure, his dignity as if he also were dignified.[1]

The most important feature of Lockhart's case is that it is ideologically motivated. The main reason for targeting Hunt was his radicalism, and the adjectives used to describe him – 'profligate', 'vicious', 'humble' – are calculated to appeal to the class prejudices of *Blackwood's* Tory readership; at the same time, Wordsworth's 'patriarchal' simplicity of feeling elevates him to the same level as the politicians whose

JOHN GIBSON LOCKHART
[1] 'On the Cockney School of Poetry No. 1', *Blackwood's Edinburgh Magazine* 2 (1817) 38–41, p. 40.

fear of revolution led to the Peterloo massacre. The paragraph thus plays out a drama – that of the patrician poet besieged by the dissolute imitator of a lower class, desperate for a share of his fame. Hunt is alleged to worship Lord Holland[2] and Haydon (see p. 658) in much the same way that he sullies the purity of Wordsworth; it is simply another example of a social reprobate getting above himself. But behind the snobbery, Lockhart is worrying away at an aesthetic matter, for the clues to Hunt's alleged depravity are literary: Voltaire, Chaucer, *John Buncle*, Launcelot of the Lake. For Lockhart, they are examples of either radical (in the case of Voltaire) or 'low' culture (as with Thomas Amory's novel, *John Buncle*). And why should *The Flower and the Leaf* be included in this list – at the time thought to have been written by Chaucer, but now ascribed to an anonymous female poet of the last quarter of the fifteenth century? Because, only months before, on 16 March, *The Examiner* had published Keats's sonnet *Written on a Blank Space at the end of Chaucer's Tale of 'The Floure and the Lefe'*. Hunt had published it under a brief introductory note: 'The following exquisite Sonnet, as well as one or two others that have lately appeared under the same signature, is from the pen of the young poet (KEATS), who was mentioned not long since in this paper, and who may already lay true claim to that title: – "The youngest he, / That sits in shadow of Apollo's tree." '[3] The inclusion of *The Flower and the Leaf* in Lockhart's list reveals that he had noted Keats's poem and Hunt's proprietorial note, and, for those in the know, it suggests that Keats's strategy is no different from Hunt's – that of contaminating other writers by pretending to understand and admire them. More disturbing, Lockhart signals to Keats that he is next. Such was Keats's interpretation when, still in shock, he reported the article to Bailey on 3 November: 'There has been a flaming attack upon Hunt in the Edinburgh Magazine[4] – I never read any thing so virulent – accusing him of the greatest Crimes ... I have no doubt that the second Number was intended for me'.[5]

Keats was right on both counts; Hunt also found the attack 'virulent', and in *The Examiner* for 16 November he challenged 'Z' to 'avow himself; which he cannot fail to do, unless to an utter disregard of all Truth and Decency, he adds the height of Meanness and COWARDICE.' There were no less than three appeals in the *Examiner* to 'Z' to disclose his identity, none of which were heeded. Keats was correct also in believing that he was one of Lockhart's targets, and the fourth of the 'Cockney School of Poetry' articles singles him out for special treatment. In particular, Lockhart takes exception to Keats's lack of classical learning and his social class. This was the harshest of the reviews which Keats received, worse than Croker's review of *Endymion* in the *Quarterly* (April 1818), which Shelley claimed precipitated Keats's demise (see p. 957). Shelley apparently did not know about Lockhart's review – but then, he was in Italy when it was published. It stands as a monument to the factionalism that seems perennially to reign in the British literary world. As for Keats, he was confident enough to take a lofty view of such matters, when writing to George and Georgiana Keats on 19 February 1819:

> I have no doubt of success in a course of years if I persevere. But it must be patience, for the reviews have enervated and made indolent men's minds; few think for themselves. These reviews too are getting more and more powerful and especially the *Quarterly*. They are like a superstition which, the more it prostrates the crowd, and the longer it continues, the more powerful it becomes just in proportion to their increasing weakness. (Rollins ii 65)

Lockhart got into real trouble with another review, which led to a challenge from John Scott, editor of the *London Magazine*. They did not actually fight a duel, but Scott ended up fighting Lockhart's friend Jonathan Christie and lost his life. Lockhart found it a sobering experience; his arrogance and intolerance were further tempered by marriage to Walter Scott's daughter, Sophia. In later years he became editor of the *Quarterly Review* (1825–53). His masterpiece was the seven-volume *Life of Sir Walter Scott* (1837–8), an enormous success for years after his death.

Further reading

Andrew Lang, *The Life and Letters of John Gibson Lockhart* (2 vols, London, 1897)

John Gibson Lockhart, *Peter's Letters to his Kinsfolk* ed. William Ruddick (Edinburgh, 1977)

---

[2] Henry Richard Vassall Fox, third Baron Holland (1773–1840), statesman and man of letters, a nephew of Charles James Fox.

[3] *The Examiner*, 16 March 1817, p. 173.

[4] Keats meant *Blackwood's Edinburgh Magazine*.

[5] Rollins i 180.

The Cockney School of Poetry No. IV (signed 'Z.') (extracts)

From BLACKWOOD'S EDINBURGH MAGAZINE 3 (1818, pp. 519–24)

Of Keats,
The muses' son of promise, and what feats
He yet may do, etc.

Cornelius Webb[1]

Of all the manias of this mad age, the most incurable, as well as the most common, seems to be no other than the *metromanie*.[2] The just celebrity of Robert Burns and Miss Baillie[3] has had the melancholy effect of turning the heads of we know not how many farm-servants and unmarried ladies; our very footmen compose tragedies, and there is scarcely a superannuated governess in the island that does not leave a roll of lyrics behind her in her bandbox.[4]

To witness the disease of any human understanding, however feeble, is distressing – but the spectacle of an able mind reduced to a state of insanity is of course ten times more afflicting. It is with such sorrow as this that we have contemplated the case of Mr John Keats. This young man appears to have received from nature talents of an excellent, perhaps even of a superior order – talents which, devoted to the purposes of any useful profession, must have rendered him a respectable, if not an eminent citizen. His friends, we understand, destined him to the career of medicine, and he was bound apprentice some years ago to a worthy apothecary in town.[5]

But all has been undone by a sudden attack of the malady to which we have alluded. Whether Mr John had been sent home with a diuretic or composing draught[6] to some patient far gone in the poetical mania, we have not heard. This much is certain: that he has caught the infection, and that thoroughly. For some time we were in hopes that he might get off with a violent fit or two, but of late the symptoms are terrible. The frenzy of the *Poems* was bad enough in its way,[7] but it did not alarm us half so seriously as the calm, settled, imperturbable drivelling idiocy of *Endymion*.[8] We hope, however, that in so young a person, and with a constitution originally so good, even now the disease is not utterly incurable. Time, firm treatment, and rational restraint, do much for many apparently hopeless invalids – and if Mr Keats should happen, at some interval of reason, to cast his eye upon our pages, he may perhaps be convinced of the existence of his malady, which in such cases is often all that is necessary to put the patient in a fair way of being cured.

The readers of the *Examiner* newspaper were informed, some time ago, by a solemn paragraph, in Mr Hunt's best style, of the appearance of two new stars of glorious magnitude and splendour in the poetical horizon of the land of Cockaigne.[9] One of these turned out, by and by, to be no other than Mr John Keats. This precocious adulation confirmed the wavering apprentice in his desire to quit the gallipots, and at the same time excited in his too susceptible mind a fatal admiration for the character and talents of the most worthless and affected[10] of all the versifiers of our time. One of his first productions was the following sonnet, 'written on the day when Mr Leigh Hunt left prison'. It will be

---

THE COCKNEY SCHOOL OF POETRY NO. IV

[1] Cornelius Francis Webb, or Webbe (*c*.1790–*c*.1848) published widely in the *New Monthly Magazine* and the *London Magazine*. The poem from which Lockhart quotes was entitled *Epistle to a Friend*, and is now, apparently, lost. The phrase, 'The muses' son of promise', was quoted in ridicule of Keats for years afterwards.

[2] *metromanie* mania for writing poetry.

[3] Joanna Baillie (1762–1851), dramatist; see p. 153.

[4] *bandbox* cardboard box for caps, hats, millinery.

[5] *His friends . . . town* Keats entered Guy's Hospital as a student in October 1815, and qualified at Apothecaries' Hall in July 1816. Apothecaries were the forerunners of the modern-day chemist.

[6] *a diuretic or composing draught* a diuretic is a drug designed to promote the production of urine; a 'composing draught' is a sedative.

[7] *The frenzy . . . way* Keats's *Poems* (1817) had a reasonable press from the reviewers; of the six notices, three were by friends, and the remainder were favourable.

[8] *the calm, settled . . . Endymion* by the time Lockhart's essay appeared, *Endymion* (1818) had been given short shrift by a number of reviewers, including *The British Critic* and the *Quarterly Review*.

[9] *The readers . . . Cockaigne* Lockhart refers to Hunt's article, 'Young Poets', in the *Examiner* for 1 December 1817, in which he presented to his readers the work of Shelley, John Hamilton Reynolds and Keats. It is true that this article confirmed Keats in his desire to be a poet. 'Cockaigne' is an imaginary land of idleness and luxury, but here it also contains an ironical reference to Cockney London.

[10] *affected* mannered.

recollected that the cause of Hunt's confinement was a series of libels against his sovereign, and that its fruit was the odious and incestuous *Story of Rimini*.

[Quotes all of Keats's *Written on the Day that Mr Leigh Hunt left Prison* ('What though, for showing truth to flattered state'), published *Poems* (1817). Lockhart italicizes the phrases 'Kind Hunt', 'In Spenser's walls', and 'With daring Milton'.]

The absurdity of the thought in this sonnet is, however, if possible, surpassed in another, 'addressed to Haydon'[11] the painter, that clever, but most affected artist, who as little resembles Raphael in genius as he does in person, notwithstanding the foppery of having his hair curled over his shoulders in the old Italian fashion. In this exquisite piece it will be observed that Mr Keats classes together Wordsworth, Hunt, and Haydon as the three greatest spirits of the age, and that he alludes to himself, and some others of the rising brood of Cockneys, as likely to attain hereafter an equally honourable elevation. Wordsworth and Hunt! What a juxtaposition! The purest, the loftiest, and, we do not fear to say it, the most classical of living English poets, joined together in the same compliment with the meanest, the filthiest, and the most vulgar of Cockney poetasters. No wonder that he who could be guilty of this should class Haydon with Raphael, and himself with Spenser.

[Quotes *Addressed to Haydon*, italicizing ll. 5–6 and 13–14.]

The nations are to listen and be dumb! And why, good Johnny Keats? Because Leigh Hunt is editor of the *Examiner*, and Haydon has painted the judgement of Solomon,[12] and you and Cornelius Webb, and a few more city sparks, are pleased to look upon yourselves as so many future Shakespeares and Miltons! The world has really some reason to look to its foundations! Here is a *tempestas in matulâ*[13] with a vengeance. At the period when these sonnets were published, Mr Keats had no hesitation in saying that he looked on himself as 'not yet a glorious denizen of the wide heaven of poetry', but he had many fine soothing visions of coming greatness, and many rare plans of study to prepare him for it. The following we think is very pretty raving.

[Quotes ll. 98–121 of *Sleep and Poetry*.]

Having cooled a little from this 'fine passion', our youthful poet passes very naturally into a long strain of foaming abuse against a certain class of English poets, whom, with Pope at their head, it is much the fashion with the ignorant unsettled pretenders of the present time to undervalue.[14] Begging these gentlemen's pardon, although Pope was not a poet of the same high order with some who are now living, yet, to deny his genius, is just about as absurd as to dispute that of Wordsworth, or to believe in that of Hunt. Above all things, it is pitiably ridiculous to hear men, of whom their country will always have reason to be proud, reviled by uneducated and flimsy striplings, who are not capable of understanding either merits, or those of any other *men of power* – fanciful dreaming tea-drinkers, who, without logic enough to analyse a single idea, or imagination enough to form one original image, or learning enough to distinguish between the written language of Englishmen and the spoken jargon of Cockneys, presume to talk with contempt of some of the most exquisite spirits the world ever produced, merely because they did not happen to exert their faculties in laborious affected descriptions of flowers seen in window-pots, or cascades heard at Vauxhall;[15] in short, because they chose to be wits, philosophers, patriots, and poets, rather than to found the Cockney school of versification, morality, and politics, a century before its time. . . .

So much for the opening bud; now for the expanded flower. It is time to pass from the juvenile *Poems* to the mature and elaborate *Endymion: A Poetic Romance*. The old story of the moon falling in love with a shepherd, so prettily told by a Roman classic,[16] and so exquisitely enlarged and adorned by one of

---

11 See p. 658.

12 Haydon painted *The Judgement of Solomon* 1812–14. It is now at Plymouth Museum and Art Gallery.

13 *tempestas in matulâ* storm in a pisspot.

14 Wordsworth was regularly criticized by the likes of Byron and Jeffrey for his alleged disdain of Pope.

15 The Vauxhall pleasure gardens on the south bank of the Thames contained ruins, arches, statues, a cascade, a music room, Chinese pavilions, and a Gothic orchestra accommodating fifty musicians.

16 *The old story . . . classic* Endymion was a shepherd king of Elis who asked Jupiter to make him ever young. Diana, virgin goddess of the moon, saw him lying naked on Mt Latmus and fell in love with him. In time she bore him fifty daughters. His story had been told by the Greek writers Apollodorus and Pausanias, but Lockhart must have in mind the retelling by Ovid, who was in fact one of Keats's sources.

the most elegant of German poets,[17] has been seized upon by Mr John Keats, to be done with as might seem good unto the sickly fancy of one who never read a single line either of Ovid or of Wieland. If the quantity, not the quality, of the verses dedicated to the story is to be taken into account, there can be no doubt that Mr John Keats may now claim Endymion entirely to himself.

To say the truth, we do not suppose either the Latin or the German poet would be very anxious to dispute about the property of the hero of the 'Poetic Romance'. Mr Keats has thoroughly appropriated the character, if not the name. His Endymion is not a Greek shepherd loved by a Grecian goddess; he is merely a young Cockney[18] rhymester dreaming a fantastic dream at the full of the moon. Costume, were it worthwhile to notice such a trifle, is violated in every page of this goodly octavo.[19] From his prototype Hunt,[20] John Keats has acquired a sort of vague idea that the Greeks were a most tasteful people, and that no mythology can be so finely adapted for the purposes of poetry as theirs. It is amusing to see what a hand the two Cockneys make of this mythology: the one confesses that he never read the Greek tragedians, and the other knows Homer only from Chapman[21] – and both of them write about Apollo, Pan, nymphs, muses and mysteries as might be expected from persons of their education. We shall not, however, enlarge at present upon this subject, as we mean to dedicate an entire paper to the classical attainments and attempts of the Cockney poets.

As for Mr Keats' Endymion, it has just as much to do with Greece as it has with 'old Tartary the fierce'.[22] No man whose mind has ever been imbued with the smallest knowledge or feeling of classical poetry or classical history, could have stooped to profane and vulgarize every association in the manner which has been adopted by this 'son of promise'. Before giving any extracts, we must inform our readers that this romance is meant to be written in English heroic rhyme. To those who have read any of Hunt's poems, this hint might indeed be needless; Mr Keats has adopted the loose, nerveless versification and Cockney rhymes of the poet of Rimini.[23] But in fairness to that gentleman, we must add that the defects of the system are tenfold more conspicuous in his disciple's work than in his own. Mr Hunt is a small poet, but he is a clever man. Mr Keats is a still smaller poet, and he is only a boy of pretty[24] abilities, which he has done everything in his power to spoil. . . .

We had almost forgot to mention that Keats belongs to the Cockney School of Politics, as well as the Cockney School of Poetry.

It is fit that he who holds Rimini to be the first poem should believe The Examiner[25] to be the first politician of the day. We admire consistency, even in folly. Hear how their bantling[26] has already learned to lisp sedition.

[Quotes Endymion iii 1–23]

And now good morrow to 'the muses' son of promise'; as for 'the feats he yet may do', as we do not pretend to say, like himself, 'Muse of my native land am I inspired',[27] we shall adhere to the safe old rule of pauca verba.[28] We venture to make one small prophecy: that his bookseller[29] will not a second time venture £50 upon anything he can write. It is a better and a wiser thing to be a starved apothecary than a starved poet; so back to the shop Mr John, back to 'plasters, pills, and ointment boxes',

---

[17]   Christoph Martin Wieland (1733–1813), whose Oberon incorporated the story of Endymion and gained tremendous popularity in England through William Sotheby's translation (1798).

[18]   Cockney although this word is usually applied to anyone born within the sound of Bow bells, it had a specific meaning for Lockhart. Through his attacks on Hunt and Keats he redefined it to apply to lower-middle-class vulgarity, lasciviousness, radicalism and aesthetic lack of taste (see headnote, pp. 1004–5).

[19]   octavo the format in which the book was published, taken from the fact that its pages were made from a folio sheet folded three times, so as to create eight leaves.

[20]   his prototype Hunt Lockhart's point is that Keats is a pale imitation of Hunt.

[21]   know Homer only from Chapman a sarcastic reference to Keats's On First Looking into Chapman's Homer (pp. 1012–13).

[22]   old Tartary the fierce a quotation from Endymion iv 262.

[23]   Leigh Hunt, The Story of Rimini was published in February 1816.

[24]   pretty satisfactory. Not a compliment.

[25]   Radical journal edited by Leigh Hunt and his brother John, 1808–21.

[26]   bantling brat.

[27]   Endymion iv 354. Lockhart deliberately omits the questionmark at the end of this line in Keats's text.

[28]   pauca verba few words.

[29]   bookseller publishers – i.e. John Taylor (1781–1864) and James Augustus Hessey (1785–1870).

etc. But for heaven's sake, young Sangrado,[30] be a little more sparing of extenuatives and soporifics[31] in your practice than you have been in your poetry.

[*When youthful faith has fled*] (composed 21 June 1841)[1]

From Andrew Lang, THE LIFE AND LETTERS OF JOHN GIBSON LOCKHART (1897)

When youthful faith has fled,
  Of loving take thy leave;
Be constant to the dead –
  The dead cannot deceive.

Sweet modest flowers of spring,   5
  How fleet your balmy day!
And man's brief year can bring
  No secondary May.

No earthly burst again
  Of gladness out of gloom;   10
Fond hope and vision vain,
  Ungrateful to the tomb!

But 'tis an old belief,
  That on some solemn shore,
Beyond the sphere of grief,   15
  Dear friends will meet once more.

Beyond the sphere of time,
  And sin, and fate's control,
Serene in changeless prime
  Of body and of soul.   20

That creed I fain would keep,
  That hope I'll not forego;
Eternal be the sleep,
  Unless to waken so.

John Keats   (1795–1821)

Of the six major poets of the romantic period, Keats was the last to be born and the first to die – at the early age of twenty-five. Had most of the other writers in this volume died so young, we would probably regard them as no more than promising; Keats was amazingly precocious. Perhaps suspecting that he had little time to live,[1] he worked hard at his craft, and in the little time available to him wrote some of the finest poetry of his day.

He was born 31 October 1795, at Finsbury, the eldest child of Thomas Keats, head ostler at the Swan and Hoop, and Frances Jennings. They were not working class, as has sometimes been supposed, but were a fairly well-to-do lower-middle-class family. His brothers George and Tom were born in 1797 and 1799, and his sister Fanny in 1803. Like Wordsworth, Keats and

---

[30] *Sangrado* name of a character in Le Sage's *Gil Blas*, a physician whose sole remedies were bleeding and the drinking of hot water; often applied to quack doctors of any kind.
[31] *extenuatives and soporifics* diet- and sleeping-pills.

WHEN YOUTHFUL FAITH HAS FLED
[1] This poem was written after the death of Lockhart's wife Sophia in 1837.

JOHN KEATS
[1] The sore throat that plagued him through early 1819 was, he realized, the harbinger of far worse to come.

his siblings were orphaned early; in 1804 their father died after falling from his horse, and in 1810 their mother died from consumption. He attended the Revd John Clarke's school in Enfield, 1803–11, whose son, Charles Cowden Clarke, became a lifelong friend. From the very beginning Keats knew he wanted to be a poet, declaring as much from the moment he could speak.[2]

But he knew he had to make a living, and left school in 1811, intending, having nursed his mother through her final illness, to become a physician. He began as an apprentice to Thomas Hammond, a surgeon in Edmonton, and in October 1815 registered as a student at Guy's Hospital in the City. By July the following year he was licensed to practise as an apothecary and surgeon. Throughout these years he did not renounce his desire to write poetry; a fellow student at Guy's later recalled that in the lecture room, 'I have seen Keats in a deep poetic dream: his mind was on Parnassus with the muses'.[3] He had begun reading *The Examiner*, the radical journal Leigh Hunt edited with his brother John (see p. 620), while still at school. Among other things, the Hunts published poetry, and his first published work, *O Solitude*, appeared in *The Examiner* for 5 May 1816. Cowden Clarke introduced Keats to Hunt in early October; Hunt later recalled: 'I shall never forget the impression made upon me by the exuberant specimens of genuine though young poetry that were laid before me, and the promise of which was seconded by the fine fervid countenance of the writer.'[4] Among the poems Hunt would have seen at their first meeting was *On First Looking into Chapman's Homer* (pp. 1012–3). He was so impressed that he wrote a sonnet of praise to Keats, which he published in *Foliage* (1818).[5]

This was a vitally important friendship, as Hunt provided him with the encouragement he needed to relinquish medicine and pursue a literary career. At the same time, Keats absorbed many of the extravagances of Hunt's style. Hunt believed that literature was primarily a vehicle of pleasure, and for this reason favoured the use of excessively lush and sensuous images and words, and was unafraid of eroticized sentiment. What with his vaunted radical opinions, this made him an easy target for the Tory critics, and Keats quickly became one too. The worst review of Keats's poems was probably that by Lockhart (see pp. 1006–9), but other critics like Croker, in the *Quarterly Review*, were unbridled in their contempt for Keats's 'Cockney' manner. Shelley believed, and made it

generally known, that Croker's review had led directly to the disease from which Keats was to die. This was not true, and such claims tended to obscure the fact that this was not purely a matter of ideological difference. To take an extreme example, *Sleep and Poetry*, which appeared in the 1817 volume, begins:

> What is more gentle than a wind in summer?
> What is more soothing than the pretty hum-
> mer
> That stays one moment in an open flower
> And buzzes cheerily from bower to bower?
>
> (ll. 1–4)

The feminine rhyme endings, diction such as 'hummer' ('bee'), and the unrestrained use of weak adjectives like 'pretty', were characteristic of what Lockhart called 'Cockney' versification, and, with or without Hunt's influence, they would be evidence enough of artistic immaturity. Keats had little time in which to grow out of this; he published three volumes in his lifetime – *Poems* (1817), *Endymion* (1818), and *Lamia, Isabella, The Eve of St Agnes, and Other Poems* (1820) – and all contain Huntian solecisms. But Keats was aware of the limitations of the school in which he had been coached, and sought, in the little time he had, to outgrow them.

One feature of this was his attitude towards Wordsworth. From his reading of *Tintern Abbey*, he admired the way in which Wordsworth incorporated the hardships and vicissitudes of the world into a transcendent vision; or, as he told John Hamilton Reynolds on 3 May 1818:

> We no sooner get into the second chamber, which I shall call the chamber of maiden thought, than we become intoxicated with the light and the atmosphere, we see nothing but pleasant wonders, and think of delaying there forever in delight. However, among the effects this breathing is father of, is that tremendous one of sharpening one's vision into the heart and nature of man, of convincing one's nerves that the world is full of misery and heartbreak, pain, sickness, and oppression – whereby this chamber of maiden thought becomes gradually darkened and, at the same time, on all sides of it many doors are set open – but all dark, all leading to dark passages. We see not the balance of good and evil. We are in a mist. *We are*

---

[2] According to Benjamin Robert Haydon, *The Diary of Benjamin Robert Haydon* ed. Willard Bissell Pope (5 vols, Cambridge, Mass., 1960–3), ii 107.

[3] W. C. Dendy, *The Philosophy of Mystery* (1841), p. 99.

[4] Leigh Hunt, *Lord Byron and Some of his Contemporaries* (2 vols, London, 1828), pp. 409–10.

[5] See pp. 622.

now in that state. We feel the 'burden of the mystery'. To this point was Wordsworth come, as far as I can conceive, when he wrote 'Tintern Abbey', and it seems to me that his genius is explorative of those dark passages. (pp. 1021–2)

Tintern Abbey is the poem of Wordsworth's artistic coming of age. It looked back to the time when nature 'To me was all in all', in favour of the present of July 1798, when the poet's perceptions are qualified by 'The still sad music of humanity'. That matured vision, tempered by 'misery and heartbreak, pain, sickness, and oppression', is precisely what Keats envies.[6] With this in mind, he was determined, by 1819, to eliminate the 'smokeability'[7] of his early works. It informed his reworking of *The Eve of St Agnes*, into which he introduced several details that his friend Richard Woodhouse found distasteful. The last stanza was revised so as to bring in Old Angela, as Woodhouse complained, 'dead, stiff and ugly', and, more notably, the climax of the poem was altered so as to leave no doubt that Porphyro 'acts all the acts of a *bona fide* husband'. When told by Woodhouse that ladies would not want to read such erotic material (an important matter, as the vast majority of poetry readers were women), Keats replied that he wrote only for men.[8] It was not that he sought to be disgusting or offensive for its own sake; he wanted to bring his poetry out of the luxurious unreality cultivated under Hunt's tutelage, and into the real world, with all its daily horrors and vices.

And yet Keats was suspicious of Wordsworth's 'egotistical sublime' (see p. 1042) – the tendency of Wordsworth to focus his attention on his own imaginative processes.[9] Why? Because Hunt had taught him one important lesson which he was never to relinquish – that it is not the poet's task to impose a vision or interpretation on the outside world, but to immerse, and lose, the self in what is perceived. Where Wordsworth and Coleridge had placed all the emphasis on 'the conferring, the abstracting, and the modifying powers of the imagination' (p. 413) – in other words, on a sustained analysis of the poet's mental processes, Keats insisted that the imaginative experience was more like a kind of dream: 'A poet is the most unpoetical of any thing in existence, because he has no identity, he is continually in for – and filling – some other body. The sun, the moon, the sea, and men and women who are creatures of impulse, are poetical,

and have about them an unchangeable attribute; the poet has none, no identity – he is certainly the most unpoetical of all God's creatures' (p. 1042). In other words, the poet is capable of losing all sense of self in the contemplation of external reality, making it possible for him to 'be' anything he wants. And he goes even further:

> What the imagination seizes as beauty must be truth, whether it existed before or not. For I have the same idea of all our passions as of love: they are all in their sublime, creative of essential beauty.... The imagination may be compared to Adam's dream: he awoke and found it truth. (p. 1018)

Emerging from an imaginative experience in which he has 'lost' awareness of the self, the poet 'awakens' to an apprehension that he would not otherwise have been granted – that of the 'essential beauty' of the object with which he has been merged. The terms Keats uses are unhelpfully vague, and are not susceptible to the analysis of the aesthetician (*Lamia* is all about the antithesis of philosophy and poetry). But it is clear that by 'beauty', Keats means the sensation shared by the poet with the external object into which his consciousness is merged. It is to do with the hitherto unknown reality of what it is to share in the existence of the nightingale or the Grecian urn; an imaginative involvement with those things is inherently beautiful, and true – in the sense that it is real, rooted in the world of 'misery and heartbreak, pain, sickness, and oppression'. There is nothing escapist about any of this; indeed, the great Odes of summer 1819 are permeated with an awareness of death. The important point is that, to Keats, the imaginative mind was diametrically opposed to the intellect; it was 'capable of being in uncertainties, mysteries, doubts, without any irritable reaching after fact and reason'.[10] He called this negative capability. If he had any reservations about Wordsworth and Coleridge, it was that they seemed constantly to be following rational, logical trains of thought ('consequitive reasoning', as Keats calls it). On the one occasion when he met Coleridge, the elder statesman of English letters bore out Keats's suspicions by discoursing at length on 'a thousand things' with barely a glance in his direction: 'I heard his voice as he came towards me – I heard it as he moved away – I had heard it all the interval' (p. 1054).

Keats's increased resistance to Hunt was inspired

---

[6] For more on Keats's reading of Wordsworth, see Beth Lau, *Keats's Reading of the Romantic Poets* (Ann Arbor, Mich., 1991), chapter 1.

[7] 'smokeability' Keats's own word for susceptibility to ridicule.

[8] For Woodhouse's important account see p. 818.

[9] It would be interesting to know what Keats would have made of *The Prelude*, which remained unpublished until 1850.

[10] See his letter to George and Tom Keats, 21 December 1817, p. 1019.

partly by ambition. He always wanted to be a great poet, and the composition of *Endymion* was his first attempt at epic. Turning away from Hunt, toward Wordsworth and Milton, he attempted another: *Hyperion: A Fragment*, later reworked as *The Fall of Hyperion*. It is about loss and suffering, that most Wordsworthian of subjects, and treats the Titans and gods of myth as if they were human. In its incomplete state, both versions of the poem appear to be about failure, but it was originally designed as a very different kind of work. Its central figure is Apollo, who represents the negatively-capable poet. In its completed state, it would have shown the dethronement of Hyperion, the former God of the Sun, by Apollo, and climaxed with his apotheosis. *Hyperion: A Fragment* was an attempt to rewrite *Paradise Lost* in non-Christian terms, and that, as much as anything else, was why Shelley so admired it. On 29 October 1820 Shelley told Marianne Hunt that 'the fragment called "Hyperion" promises for him that he is destined to become one of the first writers of the age' (Jones ii 239).

Keats's enemy was time. He did not have enough fully to mature; the two 'Hyperions' and the Odes provide a hint of the poet he might have been. He may already have been infected with tuberculosis when he went on the walking tour of the Lakes and Scotland with Charles Brown in summer 1818. By spring 1820 he was suffering occasional haemorrhages and in September he set out for Italy in the hope that its climate would be conducive to better health. But the journey was rough, and his condition declined drastically. He died in Rome on 23 February 1821, and was buried in the non-Catholic Cemetery (Il Cimitero Acattolico) three days later. He immediately became the subject of myth, when Shelley composed *Adonais*, which portrayed him as a poet 'killed' by unsympathetic reviews (see pp. 956–7). At home, his old cronies further fuelled the legend with their various recollections, some of which, like this one by William Hone,

appealed to the sentimental tastes of the Victorians:

In the neighbourhood of Hampstead church, and between that edifice and the heath, there are several old groves. Winding southwardly from the heath, there is a charming little grove in Well Walk, with a bench at the end; whereon I last saw poor Keats, the poet of the 'Pot of Basil', sitting and sobbing his dying breath into a handkerchief, – gleaning parting looks towards the quiet landscape he had delighted in – musing, as in his 'Ode to a Nightingale'.[11]

Further reading

Cleanth Brooks, 'History Without Footnotes: An Account of Keats' Urn', *The Well Wrought Urn* (New York, 1947)

Ian Jack, *Keats and the Mirror of Art* (Oxford, 1967)

John Jones, *John Keats's Dream of Truth* (London, 1969)

Jack Stillinger, *The Hoodwinking of Madeline and Other Essays on Keats's Poetry* (Urbana, Illinois, 1971)

Christopher Ricks, *Keats and Embarrassment* (Oxford, 1974)

Stuart M. Sperry, *Keats the Poet* (Princeton, 1974)

John Bayley, *The Uses of Division: Unity and Disharmony in Literature* (London, 1976), pp. 107–56

Walter Jackson Bate, *John Keats* (London, 1979)

Helen Vendler, *The Odes of John Keats* (Cambridge, Mass., 1983)

John Barnard, *John Keats* (Cambridge, 1987)

Andrew Bennett, *Keats, Narrative and Audience: The Posthumous Life of Writing* (Cambridge, 1994)

Keats and History ed. Nicholas Roe (Cambridge, 1995)

Robert Woof and Stephen Hebron, *John Keats* (Grasmere, 1995)

Nicholas Roe, *John Keats and the Culture of Dissent* (Oxford, 1997)

On First Looking into Chapman's Homer (composed October 1816)[1]

From POEMS (1817)

Much have I travelled in the realms of gold,
And many goodly states and kingdoms seen;
Round many western islands have I been
Which bards in fealty to Apollo[2] hold.

---

[11]   William Hone, *The Every-day Book and Table Book* (3 vols, London, 1830–1), iii 810.

ON FIRST LOOKING INTO CHAPMAN'S HOMER
[1]   George Chapman (1559–1634) translated *The Whole Works of Homer* (1614). In October Charles Cowden Clarke was

lent a copy, and read through it with Keats. Keats returned to his lodgings in Dean Street late at night and composed this poem, first published in *The Examiner*, 1 December 1816.
[2]   Apollo is the god of poetry.

Oft of one wide expanse had I been told   5
  That deep-browed Homer ruled as his demesne,[3]
  Yet did I never breathe its pure serene[4]
Till I heard Chapman speak out loud and bold:
Then felt I like some watcher of the skies
  When a new planet swims into his ken;   10
Or like stout Cortez[5] when with eagle eyes
  He stared at the Pacific, and all his men
Looked at each other with a wild surmise –
  Silent, upon a peak in Darien.[6]

Addressed to Haydon[1] (composed 19 or 20 November 1816)

From POEMS (1817)

Great spirits now on earth are sojourning:[2]
  He of the cloud, the cataract, the lake,
  Who on Helvellyn's[3] summit, wide awake,
Catches his freshness from archangel's wing;
He of the rose, the violet, the spring,   5
  The social smile, the chain for freedom's sake;[4]
  And lo! whose steadfastness would never take
A meaner sound than Raphael's whispering.[5]
And other spirits there are standing apart
  Upon the forehead of the age to come;   10
These, these will give the world another heart
  And other pulses: hear ye not the hum
Of mighty workings?[6] —
  Listen awhile ye nations, and be dumb.

From *Endymion: A Poetic Romance Book I* (extracts) (composed April–November 1817; published 1818)

[*A thing of beauty is a joy for ever*]

A thing of beauty is a joy for ever:
  Its loveliness increases; it will never
  Pass into nothingness, but still will keep

---

3 *demesne* domain, kingdom.
4 *serene* clear, bright sky.
5 *Cortez* it was in fact Vasco Nunez de Balboa (1475–1519) who was the first European to stand, in 1513, on that peak and see the Pacific (which he claimed for Spain). In 1519 Hernan Cortes (1485–1547) conquered Mexico for Spain and entered Mexico City for the first time.
6 *Darien* region south and east of the Panama canal between Darien, a town in the middle of the isthmus (founded by Balboa, 1510), and Colombia.

ADDRESSED TO HAYDON
1 See p. 658.

2 Keats celebrates the achievement of Wordsworth (lines 2–4), Leigh Hunt (lines 5–6) and Haydon (lines 7–8). For Lockhart's highly critical remarks on this sonnet, see p. 1007.
3 Helvellyn mountain towers over Grasmere (3116 ft).
4 *the chain for freedom's sake* a reference to Hunt's spell in jail for libelling the Prince Regent (p. 620).
5 *whose steadfastness ... Raphael's whispering* Obscurity is an element of Keats's early manner, and this is certainly obscure. His overall meaning is that Haydon's artistic ability rivals that of Raphael.
6 The incompleteness of the line is deliberate, and was suggested by Haydon. It originally read: 'Of mighty workings in a distant mart?'

A bower quiet for us, and a sleep
Full of sweet dreams, and health, and quiet breathing. 5
Therefore, on every morrow, are we wreathing
A flowery band to bind us to the earth,
Spite of despondence, of the inhuman dearth
Of noble natures, of the gloomy days,
Of all the unhealthy and o'er-darkened ways 10
Made for our searching – yes, in spite of all,
Some shape of beauty moves away the pall
From our dark spirits. Such the sun, the moon,
Trees old and young, sprouting a shady boon
For simple sheep; and such are daffodils 15
With the green world they live in; and clear rills
That for themselves a cooling covert make
'Gainst the hot season; the mid-forest brake,
Rich with a sprinkling of fair musk-rose¹ blooms;
And such too is the grandeur of the dooms² 20
We have imagined for the mighty dead,
All lovely tales that we have heard or read –
An endless fountain of immortal drink,
Pouring unto us from the heaven's brink.

[Hymn to Pan]¹

Oh thou, whose mighty palace roof doth hang
From jagged trunks, and overshadoweth
Eternal whispers, glooms, the birth, life, death
Of unseen flowers in heavy peacefulness;
Who lov'st to see the hamadryads² dress 235
Their ruffled locks where meeting hazels darken,
And through whole solemn hours dost sit, and hearken
The dreary melody of bedded reeds
In desolate places, where dank moisture breeds 240
The pipy hemlock³ to strange overgrowth;
Bethinking thee, how melancholy loath
Thou wast to lose fair Syrinx⁴ – do thou now,
By thy love's milky brow,
By all the trembling mazes that she ran, 245
Hear us, great Pan!

Oh thou, for whose soul-soothing quiet, turtles⁵
Passion their voices⁶ cooingly 'mong myrtles,⁷
What time thou wanderest at eventide
Through sunny meadows that outskirt the side 250

A THING OF BEAUTY IS A JOY FOR EVER
¹ *musk-rose* rambling rose with white flowers.
² *dooms* destinies.

HYMN TO PAN
¹ In spite of the fact that Wordsworth disparagingly told Keats that the *Hymn to Pan* was 'a very pretty piece of paganism', it looks forward to the mature style of the major 1819 Odes. Pan is the god of universal nature.

² *hamadryads* wood-nymphs fabled to live and die with the tree which they inhabited.
³ *pipy hemlock* poison hemlock has tall hollow stems.
⁴ When Pan pursued Syrinx, she was changed into a reed.
⁵ *turtles* turtle-doves.
⁶ *Passion their voices* fill their voices with passion.
⁷ *myrtles* shrub with shiny evergreen leaves and white sweet-scented flowers, sacred to Venus and used as an emblem of love.

Of thine enmossed realms; oh thou, to whom
Broad-leaved fig trees even now foredoom[8]
Their ripened fruitage, yellow-girted bees
Their golden honeycombs, our village leas
Their fairest-blossomed beans and poppied corn,   255
The chuckling[9] linnet its five young unborn
To sing for thee, low-creeping strawberries
Their summer coolness, pent-up butterflies[10]
Their freckled wings – yea, the fresh-budding year
All its completions; be quickly near,   260
By every wind that nods the mountain pine,[11]
Oh forester divine!

    Thou, to whom every faun and satyr flies
For willing service, whether to surprise
The squatted hare[12] while in half-sleeping fit;   265
Or upward ragged precipices flit
To save poor lambkins from the eagle's maw;
Or by mysterious enticement draw
Bewildered shepherds to their path again;
Or to tread breathless round the frothy main,   270
And gather up all fancifullest shells
For thee to tumble into naiads'[13] cells,
And, being hidden, laugh at their out-peeping;
Or to delight thee with fantastic leaping,
The while they pelt each other on the crown   275
With silvery oak-apples, and fir-cones brown –
By all the echoes that about thee ring,
Hear us, oh satyr king!

    Oh hearkener to the loud-clapping shears,
While ever and anon to his shorn peers   280
A ram goes bleating; winder of the horn,[14]
When snouted wild-boars routing[15] tender corn
Anger our huntsmen; breather round our farms,
To keep off mildews and all weather harms;
Strange ministrant of undescribed sounds,   285
That come a-swooning over hollow grounds
And wither drearily on barren moors;
Dread opener of the mysterious doors
Leading to universal knowledge – see,
Great son of Dryope,[16]   290
The many that are come to pay their vows
With leaves about their brows!

    Be still the unimaginable lodge
For solitary thinkings; such as dodge

---

8 *foredoom* anticipate.
9 *chuckling* clucking.
10 *pent-up butterflies* butterflies still in chrysalis.
11 *pine* emblem of Pan.
12 *squatted hare* the hare in its 'form', the hollow where it nests.

13 *naiad* water-nymph.
14 *winder of the horn* one who blows the horn.
15 *routing* digging up (with the snout).
16 Homer claimed Dryope to have been Pan's mother.

Conception to the very bourne[17] of heaven,   295
Then leave the naked brain; be still the leaven
That spreading in this dull and clodded earth
Gives it a touch ethereal,[18] a new birth;[19]
Be still a symbol of immensity,
A firmament reflected in a sea,   300
An element filling the space between,
An unknown – but no more. We humbly screen
With uplift hands our foreheads, lowly bending,
And giving out a shout most heaven-rending,
Conjure thee to receive our humble paean,[20]   305
Upon thy Mount Lycean![21]

[*The Pleasure Thermometer*][1]

Wherein lies happiness? In that which becks[2]
Our ready minds to fellowship divine,
A fellowship with essence,[3] till we shine
Full alchemized,[4] and free of space. Behold   780
The clear religion[5] of heaven! Fold
A rose-leaf round thy finger's taperness
And soothe thy lips; hist, when the airy stress
Of music's kiss impregnates the free winds,
And with a sympathetic touch unbinds   785
Aeolian magic from their lucid wombs;[6]
Then old songs waken from enclouded[7] tombs,
Old ditties sigh above their father's grave,
Ghosts of melodious prophesyings rave
Round every spot where trod Apollo's foot;   790
Bronze clarions awake and faintly bruit[8]
Where long ago a giant battle[9] was;
And from the turf, a lullaby doth pass
In every place where infant Orpheus[10] slept.
Feel we these things? That moment have we stepped   795
Into a sort of oneness, and our state
Is like a floating spirit's. But there are

---

[17]   *bourne* boundary.
[18]   *ethereal* divine.
[19]   *Be still the unimaginable lodge ... new birth* in his hostile
review of *Endymion* in the *Quarterly Review* (April 1818), John
Wilson Croker quoted these lines to support his charge that
Keats 'seems to us to write a line at random, and then he fol-
lows not the thought excited by this line, but that suggested
by the *rhyme* with which it concludes. . . . *Lodge, dodge – heaven,
leaven – earth, birth*; such, in six words, is the sum and sub-
stance of six lines'.
[20]   *paean* hymn of praise.
[21]   Lycaeus was a mountain of Arcadia sacred to Pan.

THE PLEASURE THERMOMETER
[1]   The 'thermometer' measures happiness by its intensity and
selfless involvement; the four 'degrees', in ascending order, are
(i) sensual enjoyment of nature (line 782); (ii) music (lines
783–94); (iii) friendship (lines 803–5); (iv) passion (lines
805–42). This passage is spoken by Endymion. Keats com-
mented on it in his letter to John Taylor of 30 January 1818:

'The whole thing must, I think, have appeared to you, who are
a consequitive man, as a thing almost of mere words. But I
assure you that when I wrote it, it was a regular stepping of the
Imagination towards a Truth. My having written that argu-
ment will perhaps be of the greatest service to me of anything I
ever did. It set before me at once the gradations of happiness
even like a kind of Pleasure Thermometer' (Rollins i 218).
[2]   *becks* beckons.
[3]   *essence* used as a synonym for 'a thing of beauty'.
[4]   *alchemized* transformed, spiritualized.
[5]   *religion* pronounced as four syllables.
[6]   *when the airy stress ... wombs* Keats is thinking of an Aeo-
lian harp.
[7]   *enclouded* dim, obscure.
[8]   *bruit* proclaim.
[9]   *a giant battle* between the Titans and the gods of Olympus,
the background to *Hyperion*.
[10]   Orpheus was taught to play the lyre by Apollo, his father,
and reached such skill that he could influence animate and
inanimate nature by his music.

Richer entanglements, enthralments far
More self-destroying,[11] leading, by degrees,
To the chief intensity: the crown of these   800
Is made of love and friendship, and sits high
Upon the forehead of humanity.
All its more ponderous and bulky worth
Is friendship, whence there ever issues forth
A steady splendour; but at the tip-top   805
There hangs by unseen film an orbed drop
Of light, and that is love. Its influence,
Thrown in our eyes, genders[12] a novel sense
At which we start and fret; till in the end,
Melting into its radiance, we blend,   810
Mingle, and so become a part of it —
Nor with aught else can our souls interknit
So wingedly. When we combine therewith,
Life's self is nourished by its proper pith,[13]
And we are nurtured like a pelican brood.[14]   815
Aye, so delicious is the unsating[15] food,
That men who might have towered in the van[16]
Of all the congregated world, to fan
And winnow from the coming step of time
All chaff of custom, wipe away all slime   820
Left by men-slugs and human serpentry,
Have been content to let occasion[17] die
Whilst they did sleep in love's Elysium.
And truly, I would rather be struck dumb
Than speak against this ardent listlessness;[18]   825
For I have ever thought that it might bless
The world with benefits unknowingly,
As does the nightingale, up-perched high,
And cloistered among cool and bunched leaves —
She sings but to her love, nor e'er conceives   830
How tiptoe night holds back her dark-grey hood.
Just so may love, although 'tis understood
The mere commingling[19] of passionate breath,
Produce more than our searching witnesseth:
What I know not — but who of men can tell   835
That flowers would bloom, or that green fruit would swell
To melting pulp, that fish would have bright mail,[20]
The earth its dower[21] of river, wood, and vale,
The meadows runnels,[22] runnels pebble-stones,
The seed its harvest, or the lute its tones,   840
Tones ravishment, or ravishment its sweet,
If human souls did never kiss and greet?

---

[11] *self-destroying* capable of negating our sense of self (a good thing in Keats; see headnote, p. 1011).
[12] *genders* creates.
[13] *proper pith* own substance.
[14] *a pelican brood* the pelican was said to feed its young with its own blood.
[15] *unsating* uncloying.
[16] *towered in the van* a military metaphor; been foremost at the front of an attacking army.

[17] *occasion* ephemeral circumstance.
[18] *ardent listlessness* passionate suspension of self-consciousness, mystic trance.
[19] *commingling* intermingling.
[20] *bright mail* i.e. scales.
[21] *dower* gift.
[22] *runnels* streams.

Letter from John Keats to Benjamin Bailey, 22 November 1817
(extract)[1]

I wish you knew all that I think about genius and the heart – and yet I think you are thoroughly acquainted with my innermost breast in that respect, or you could not have known me even thus long and still hold me worthy to be your dear friend. In passing, however, I must say of one thing that has pressed upon me lately and increased my humility and capability of submission, and that is this truth: men of genius are great as certain ethereal chemicals operating on the mass of neutral intellect – but they have not any individuality, any determined character. I would call the top and head of those who have a proper self, men of power.

But I am running my head into a subject which I am certain I could not do justice to under five years' study and 3 vols. octavo – and moreover long to be talking about the imagination. So, my dear Bailey, do not think of this unpleasant affair if possible – do not – I defy any harm to come of it – I defy – I shall write to Crips this week and request him to tell me all his goings-on from time to time by letter whererever I may be – it will all go on well. So don't, because you have suddenly discovered a coldness in Haydon,[2] suffer yourself to be teased. Do not, my dear fellow.

Oh, I wish I was as certain of the end of all your troubles as that of your momentary start about the authenticity of the imagination. I am certain of nothing but of the holiness of the heart's affections[3] and the truth of imagination. What the imagination seizes as beauty must be truth, whether it existed before or not. For I have the same idea of all our passions as of love: they are all in their sublime, creative of essential beauty.[4] In a word, you may know my favourite speculation by my first book and the little song I sent in my last – which is a representation from the fancy of the probable mode of operating in these matters. The imagination may be compared to Adam's dream: he awoke and found it truth.[5] I am the more zealous in this affair because I have never yet been able to perceive how anything can be known for truth by consequitive[6] reasoning – and yet it must be. Can it be that even the greatest philosopher ever arrived at his goal without putting aside numerous objections? However it may be, oh for a life of sensations rather than of thoughts! It is 'a vision in the form of youth', a shadow of reality to come. And this consideration has further convinced me, for it has come as auxiliary to another favourite speculation of mine – that we shall enjoy ourselves hereafter by having what we called happiness on earth repeated in a finer tone and so repeated. And yet such a fate can only befall those who delight in sensation, rather than hunger as you do after truth; Adam's dream will do here, and seems to be a conviction that imagination and its empyreal reflection is the same as human life and its spiritual repetition. But as I was saying, the simple imaginative mind may have its rewards in the repetition of its own silent working coming continually on the spirit with a fine suddenness. To compare great things with small, have you never, by being surprised with an old melody in a delicious place by a delicious voice, felt over again your very speculations and surmises at the time it first operated on your soul? Do you not remember forming to yourself the singer's face more beautiful than it was possible, and yet with the elevation of the moment you did not think so? Even then, you were mounted on the wings of imagination so high that the prototype must be hereafter – that delicious face you will see! What a time!

I am continually running away from the subject. Sure this cannot be exactly the case with a complex mind, one that is imaginative and at the same time careful of its fruits, who would exist partly

---

LETTER FROM JOHN KEATS TO BENJAMIN BAILEY
[1] This letter contains one of Keats's earliest, and most important, statements on the imagination. Benjamin Bailey (1791–1853) was an undergraduate at Oxford when John Hamilton Reynolds introduced him to Keats (spring 1817). Throughout September 1817 Keats had shared Bailey's college quarters, and composed *Endymion* Book III there.
[2] Benjamin Robert Haydon, artist and friend of Keats; see p. 658.
[3] *affections* feelings.

[4] *For I have ... beauty* at their most sublime (i.e. intense and powerful), human emotions ('passions') apprehend the inherent beauty of the 'essences' they perceive.
[5] *The imagination ... truth* Genesis 2:21–2: 'And the Lord God caused a deep sleep to fall upon Adam, and he slept: and he took one of his ribs, and closed up the flesh instead thereof; And the rib, which the Lord God had taken from man, made he a woman, and brought her unto the man'. This episode was reworked in one of the most impressive passages of *Paradise Lost* viii 452–86.
[6] *consequitive* consecutive, logical, rational.

on sensation, partly on thought – to whom it is necessary that years should bring the philosophic mind.[7] Such an one I consider yours and therefore it is <u>necessary to your eternal happiness</u> that you not only drink this old wine of heaven, which I shall call the redigestion of our most ethereal musings on earth, but also increase in knowledge and know all things.

Letter from John Keats to George and Tom Keats, 21 December 1817 (extract)

I spent Friday evening with Wells[1] and went the next morning to see 'Death on the Pale Horse'.[2] It is a wonderful picture when West's age is considered, but there is nothing to be intense upon – no women one feels mad to kiss, no face swelling into reality.[3] The excellence of every art is its intensity, capable of making all disagreeables evaporate, from their being in close relationship with beauty and truth. Examine *King Lear* and you will find this exemplified throughout, but in this picture we have unpleasantness without any momentous depth of speculation excited, in which to bury its repulsiveness. The picture is larger than 'Christ Rejected'.[4]

I dined with Haydon the Sunday after you left, and had a very pleasant day. I dined too (for I have been out too much lately) with Horace Smith, and met his two brothers[5] with Hill and Kingston and one Dubois. They only served to convince me how superior humour is to wit in respect to enjoyment. These men say things which make one start without making one feel. They are all alike; their manners are alike; they all know fashionables; they have a mannerism in their very eating and drinking, in their mere handling a decanter. They talked of Kean[6] and his low company. Would I were with that company instead of yours, said I to myself! I know suchlike acquaintance will never do for me, and yet I am going to Reynolds[7] on Wednesday.

Brown and Dilke[8] walked with me and back from the Christmas pantomime. I had not a dispute but a disquisition with Dilke, on various subjects. Several things dovetailed in my mind, and at once it struck me what quality went to form a man of achievement, especially in literature, and which Shakespeare possessed so enormously [I mean *negative capability*; that is, when man is capable of being in uncertainties, mysteries, doubts, without any irritable reaching after fact and reason.] Coleridge, for instance, would let go by a fine isolated verisimilitude[9] caught from the penetralium[10] of mystery, from being incapable of remaining content with half-knowledge. This pursued through volumes would perhaps take us no further than this: that with <u>a great poet the sense of beauty overcomes every other consideration, or rather obliterates all consideration.</u>

---

[7]   *the philosophic mind* Wordsworth, *Ode* 189.

LETTER FROM JOHN KEATS TO GEORGE AND TOM KEATS
[1]   Charles Jeremiah Wells (1800–79), a schoolfriend of Tom Keats.
[2]   Painting by Benjamin West (1738–1820), President of the Royal Academy. His exhibition was at 125 Pall Mall.
[3]   *It is ... reality* Keats follows the opinions expressed by Hazlitt in his article, 'West's Picture of Death on the Pale Horse', in the *Edinburgh Magazine* for December 1817: 'There is no gusto, no imagination in Mr West's colouring' (Howe xviii 138).
[4]   West painted *Christ Rejected* 1812–14; it had been exhibited in the autumn of 1814 in Pall Mall, and attracted almost a quarter of a million visitors.

[5]   Horace (1779–1849) and James Smith (1775–1839) were responsible for the parodic *Rejected Addresses* (1812). Their brother was Leonard Smith (1778–1837).
[6]   Edmund Kean (1787–1833), after Kemble the most celebrated Shakespearean actor of his day.
[7]   John Hamilton Reynolds (1794–1852), friend of Keats, and poet.
[8]   Charles Armitage Brown (1786–1842), one of Keats's closest friends; Charles Wentworth Dilke (1789–1864), with whose family Keats was close, and who introduced Keats to the love of his life, Fanny Brawne.
[9]   *verisimilitude* revelation.
[10] *penetralium* interior, depth.

On Sitting Down to Read King Lear Once Again (composed 22 January 1818; published 1838; edited from MS)

Oh golden-tongued Romance, with serene lute!
 Fair plumed siren,[1] queen of far away!
Leave melodizing on this wintry day,
Shut up thine olden pages, and be mute.
Adieu! for, once again, the fierce dispute   5
 Betwixt damnation and impassioned clay[2]
 Must I burn through; once more humbly assay[3]
The bitter-sweet of this Shakespearian fruit.
Chief poet, and ye clouds of Albion,[4]
 Begetters of our deep eternal theme!   10
When through the old oak forest I am gone,[5]
 Let me not wander in a barren dream;
But when I am consumed in the fire,
Give me new phoenix wings to fly at my desire.

Sonnet (composed 22–31 January 1818; edited from MS)

When I have fears that I may cease to be
Before my pen has gleaned my teeming brain,
Before high-piled books, in charact'ry,[1]
Hold like rich garners[2] the full-ripened grain;
When I behold, upon the night's starred face,   5
Huge cloudy symbols of a high romance,
And think that I may never live to trace
Their shadows, with the magic hand of chance;
And when I feel, fair creature of an hour,[3]
That I shall never look upon thee more,   10
Never have relish in the fairy power
Of unreflecting love – then on the shore
Of the wide world I stand alone and think,
Till love and fame to nothingness do sink.

Letter from John Keats to John Hamilton Reynolds, 3 February 1818 (extract)

It may be said that we ought to read our contemporaries, that Wordsworth etc. should have their due from us. But, for the sake of a few fine imaginative or domestic passages, are we to be bullied into a certain philosophy engendered in the whims of an egotist?[1] Every man has his speculations, but every

---

ON SITTING DOWN TO READ KING LEAR ONCE AGAIN
[1] *Fair plumed siren* Romance is imagined as a fair-haired heroine.
[2] *clay* i.e. flesh.
[3] *assay* test.
[4] *Albion* England.
[5] *When through the old oak forest I am gone* i.e. when I have finished reading this play . . .

SONNET
[1] *charact'ry* words.
[2] *garners* storehouses for grain.
[3] *fair creature of an hour* according to Woodhouse (p. 816), Keats was remembering a beautiful woman he had seen at Vauxhall pleasure garden.

LETTER FROM JOHN KEATS TO JOHN HAMILTON REYNOLDS
[1] Keats, like Hazlitt, regarded Wordsworth as too preoccupied with the workings of his own mind.

man does not brood and peacock[2] over them till he makes a false coinage and deceives himself. Many a man can travel to the very bourne of heaven,[3] and yet want confidence to put down his half-seeing. Sancho[4] will invent a journey heavenward as well as anybody. We hate poetry that has a palpable design upon us – and if we do not agree, seems to put its hand in its breeches' pocket.[5] Poetry should be great and unobtrusive, a thing which enters into one's soul, and does not startle it or amaze it with itself but with its subject. How beautiful are the retired flowers! How would they lose their beauty were they to throng into the highway crying out, 'Admire me, I am a violet!', 'Dote upon me, I am a primrose!' Modern poets differ from the Elizabethans in this: each of the moderns, like an Elector[6] of Hanover, governs his petty state, and knows how many straws are swept daily from the causeways in all his dominions, and has a continual itching that all the housewives should have their coppers[7] well-scoured. The ancients were emperors of vast provinces – they had only heard of the remote ones and scarcely cared to visit them. I will cut all this – I will have no more of Wordsworth or Hunt in particular. Why should we be of the tribe of Manasseh, when we can wander with Esau?[8] Why should we kick against the pricks,[9] when we can walk on roses? Why should we be owls, when we can be eagles? Why be teased with 'nice-eyed wagtails',[10] when we have in sight 'The cherub Contemplation'?[11] Why with Wordsworth's Matthew, 'with a bough of wilding in his hand',[12] when we can have Jaques 'under an oak',[13] etc. The secret of the bough of wilding will run through your head faster than I can write it. Old Matthew spoke to him some years ago on some nothing, and because he happens in an evening walk to imagine the figure of the old man, he must stamp it down in black and white, and it is henceforth sacred. I don't mean to deny Wordsworth's grandeur and Hunt's merit, but I mean to say we need not be teased with grandeur and merit, when we can have them uncontaminated and unobtrusive. Let us have the old poets and Robin Hood!

Letter from John Keats to John Hamilton Reynolds, 3 May 1818 (extract)

I will return to Wordsworth, whether or no he has an extended vision or a circumscribed grandeur, whether he is an eagle in his nest or on the wing. And to be more explicit and to show you how tall I stand by the giant, I will put down a simile of human life as far as I now perceive it – that is, to the point to which I say we both have arrived at. Well, I compare human life to a large mansion of many apartments,[1] two of which I can only describe, the doors of the rest being as yet shut upon me. The first we step into we call the infant or thoughtless chamber, in which we remain as long as we do not think. We remain there a long while, and, notwithstanding the doors of the second chamber remain wide open, showing a bright appearance, we care not to hasten to it, but are at length imperceptibly impelled by the awakening of the thinking principle within us. We no sooner get into the second chamber, which I shall call the chamber of maiden thought, than we become intoxicated with the light and the atmosphere, we see nothing but pleasant wonders, and think of delaying there forever in

[2] *peacock* preen himself.

[3] *the very bourne of heaven* the gateway to heaven; Keats alludes to himself, *Endymion* i 295.

[4] Sancho Panza, comic buffoon who accompanies Don Quixote on his adventures.

[5] *seems to put its hand . . . pocket* apparently a gesture of defiant hostility.

[6] *Elector* one of the Princes of Germany formerly entitled to take part in the election of the Emperor.

[7] *coppers* copper fittings (on their front doors, etc.).

[8] *Why should we . . . Esau* Keats may be thinking of Gideon's comment, 'my family is poor in Manasseh, and I am the least in my father's house' (Judges 6:15).

[9] *Why should we . . . pricks* Keats alludes to Acts 9:5: 'I am Jesus whom thou persecutest: it is hard for thee to kick against the pricks'.

[10] *nice-eyed wagtails* an allusion to Leigh Hunt, 'The Nymphs' (1818) ii 169–71:

> little ponds that hold the rains,
> Where the nice-eyed wagtails glance,
> Sipping 'twixt their jerking dance.

[11] Milton, *Il Penseroso* 54.

[12] Wordsworth, *The Two April Mornings* 59–60.

[13] In *As You Like It*, Jaques is described 'Under an oak, whose antique root peeps out / Upon the brook that brawls along this wood' (II i 31–2).

LETTER FROM JOHN KEATS TO JOHN HAMILTON REYNOLDS

[1] *a large mansion . . . apartments* cf. John 14:2: 'In my Father's house are many mansions'.

delight. However, among the effects this breathing[2] is father of, is that tremendous one of sharpening one's vision into the heart and nature of man, of convincing one's nerves that the world is full of misery and heartbreak, pain, sickness, and oppression – whereby this chamber of maiden thought becomes gradually darkened and, at the same time, on all sides of it many doors are set open – but all dark, all leading to dark passages. We see not the balance of good and evil. We are in a mist. *We* are now in that state. We feel the 'burden of the mystery'.[3] To this point was Wordsworth come, as far as I can conceive, when he wrote 'Tintern Abbey', and it seems to me that his genius is explorative of those dark passages. Now if we live, and go on thinking, we too shall explore them. He is a genius and superior to us, insofar as he can, more than we, make discoveries, and shed a light in them. Here I must think Wordsworth is deeper than Milton, though I think it has depended more upon the general and gregarious advance of intellect, than individual greatness of mind. From the *Paradise Lost* and the other works of Milton, I hope it is not too presuming (even between ourselves) to say, his philosophy, human and divine, may be tolerably understood by one not much advanced in years. In his time, Englishmen were just emancipated from a great superstition[4] – and men had got hold of certain points and resting-places in reasoning which were too newly born to be doubted, and too much opposed by the mass of Europe not to be thought ethereal and authentically divine. Who could gainsay his ideas on virtue, vice, and chastity in *Comus*, just at the time of the dismissal of codpieces,[5] and a hundred other disgraces? Who would not rest satisfied with his hintings at good and evil in the *Paradise Lost*, when just free from the Inquisition[6] and burning in Smithfield?[7] The Reformation produced such immediate and great benefits, that Protestantism was considered under the immediate eye of heaven, and its own remaining dogmas and superstitions then, as it were, regenerated, constituted those resting-places and seeming sure points of reasoning. From that I have mentioned, Milton, whatever he may have thought in the sequel, appears to have been content with these by his writings. ⟨He did not think into the human heart, as Wordsworth has done; yet Milton as a philosopher had sure as great powers as Wordsworth. What is then to be inferred? Oh, many things. It proves there is really a grand march of intellect; it proves that a mighty providence subdues the mightiest minds to the service of the time being, whether it be in human knowledge or religion.⟩

Hyperion: A Fragment (composed between late September and 1 December 1818; abandoned April 1819)

From LAMIA, ISABELLA, THE EVE OF ST AGNES, AND OTHER POEMS (1820)

Book I

Deep in the shady sadness of a vale
Far sunken from the healthy breath of morn,
Far from the fiery noon, and eve's one star,
Sat grey-haired Saturn,[1] quiet as a stone,
Still as the silence round about his lair;   5

---

[2] *breathing* influence.
[3] *Tintern Abbey* 39.
[4] *a great superstition* the Roman Catholic Church.
[5] *the dismissal of codpieces* codpieces (bagged appendages, often highly ornamented, worn by men on the front of the breeches) went out of fashion in the last half of the 17th century. Milton's *Comus* was written in 1634.
[6] *the Inquisition* ecclesiastical tribunal (officially styled the Holy Office) for the suppression of heresy and punishment of heretics, organized in the thirteenth century under Pope Innocent III, under a central governing body at Rome called the Congregation of the Holy Office. The Inquisition existed in Italy, France, the Netherlands, Spain, Portugal, and the Spanish and Portuguese colonies. The Spanish Inquisition, reorga-

nized 1478–83, became notorious in the sixteenth century for its severities. It was abolished in France in 1772, and in Spain finally in 1834. The Congregation of the Holy Office still exists, but is chiefly concerned with heretical literature.
[7] *burning in Smithfield* many witches and heretics were burned, roasted or boiled alive in Smithfield in the City of London for about 400 years.

HYPERION: A FRAGMENT (BOOK I)
[1] *grey-haired Saturn* Hyperion's brother, leader of the Titans and father of the rebellious Jupiter (Jove). As the poem opens Saturn and the Titans are defeated. The Titans were a godlike race expelled from heaven by Jupiter in Greek myth.

Forest on forest hung about his head
Like cloud on cloud. No stir of air was there,
Not so much life as on a summer's day
Robs not one light seed from the feathered grass,
But where the dead leaf fell, there did it rest.   10
A stream went voiceless by, still deadened more
By reason of his fallen divinity
Spreading a shade; the naiad[2] mid her reeds
Pressed her cold finger closer to her lips.

    Along the margin-sand large footmarks went,   15
No further than to where his feet had strayed,
And slept there since. Upon the sodden ground
His old right hand lay nerveless,[3] listless, dead,
Unsceptred; and his realmless eyes were closed,
While his bowed head seemed list'ning to the earth,   20
His ancient mother, for some comfort yet.

    It seemed no force could wake him from his place;
But there came one who, with a kindred hand
Touched his wide shoulders, after bending low
With reverence, though to one who knew it not.   25
She was a goddess of the infant world;
By her in stature the tall Amazon
Had stood a pigmy's height – she would have ta'en
Achilles by the hair and bent his neck,
Or with a finger stayed Ixion's wheel.[4]   30
Her face was large as that of Memphian sphinx,[5]
Pedestalled haply in a palace court
When sages looked to Egypt for their lore.
But oh, how unlike marble was that face!
How beautiful, if sorrow had not made   35
Sorrow more beautiful than Beauty's self.
There was a listening fear in her regard,
As if calamity had but begun;
As if the vanward clouds of evil days
Had spent their malice, and the sullen rear   40
Was with its stored thunder labouring up.[6]
One hand she pressed upon that aching spot
Where beats the human heart, as if just there,
Though an immortal, she felt cruel pain;
The other upon Saturn's bended neck   45
She laid, and to the level of his ear
Leaning with parted lips, some words she spake
In solemn tenor and deep organ tone,
Some mourning words which in our feeble tongue
Would come in these like accents (oh how frail   50
To[7] that large utterance of the early gods!),
'Saturn, look up! – though wherefore, poor old King?

---

2   *naiad* water-nymph.
3   *nerveless* weak.
4   *Ixion's wheel* Ixion was banished from heaven and sentenced to be tied to a burning and spinning wheel in Hades for eternity.
5   *Memphian sphinx* Memphis was a city in Egypt. Keats saw a sphinx in the British Museum, early 1819.

6   *As if the vanward clouds . . . up* calamity is compared to clouds building up before a storm, followed by the cloud mass; the storm itself is compared with the artillery moving in the wake of advancing troops.
7   *To* i.e. compared with.

I have no comfort for thee, no, not one;
I cannot say, "Oh wherefore sleepest thou?"
For heaven is parted from thee, and the earth   55
Knows thee not, thus afflicted, for a god;
And ocean too, with all its solemn noise,
Has from thy sceptre passed, and all the air
Is emptied of thine hoary majesty.
Thy thunder, conscious of the new command,[8]   60
Rumbles reluctant o'er our fallen house,
And thy sharp lightning in unpractised hands
Scorches and burns our once serene domain.[9]
Oh aching time! Oh moments big as years!
All as ye pass swell out the monstrous truth,   65
And press it so upon our weary griefs
That unbelief has not a space to breathe.
Saturn, sleep on! Oh thoughtless, why did I
Thus violate thy slumbrous solitude?
Why should I ope thy melancholy eyes?   70
Saturn, sleep on, while at thy feet I weep!'
      As when, upon a tranced summer night,
Those green-robed senators of mighty woods,
Tall oaks, branch-charmed by the earnest stars,
Dream, and so dream all night without a stir,   75
Save from one gradual solitary gust
Which comes upon the silence, and dies off
As if the ebbing air had but one wave;
So came these words and went, the while in tears
She touched her fair large forehead to the ground,   80
Just where her falling hair might be outspread,
A soft and silken mat for Saturn's feet.
One moon, with alteration slow, had shed
Her silver seasons four upon the night,
And still these two were postured motionless,   85
Like natural sculpture in cathedral cavern[10] –
The frozen god still couchant[11] on the earth,
And the sad goddess weeping at his feet.
Until at length old Saturn lifted up
His faded eyes, and saw his kingdom gone,   90
And all the gloom and sorrow of the place,
And that fair kneeling goddess, and then spake
As with a palsied tongue, and while his beard
Shook horrid[12] with such aspen[13] malady:
'Oh tender spouse of gold Hyperion,[14]   95
Thea, I feel thee ere I see thy face;
Look up, and let me see our doom in it,
Look up, and tell me if this feeble shape
Is Saturn's; tell me if thou hear'st the voice
Of Saturn; tell me if this wrinkling brow,   100

---

[8]   *conscious of the new command* Jupiter is the new thunderer.
[9]   *our once serene domain* the Saturnian Golden Age.
[10]   *Like natural sculpture in cathedral cavern* the motionless
gods are compared to huge rock formations.
[11]   *couchant* lying down.

[12]   *horrid* bristling.
[13]   *aspen* the leaves of the aspen tremble in the slightest
breeze.
[14]   Thea is the sister and wife of Hyperion.

Naked and bare of its great diadem,
Peers like the front[15] of Saturn. Who had power
To make me desolate? Whence came the strength?
How was it nurtured to such bursting forth,
While Fate seemed strangled in my nervous[16] grasp?   105
But it is so, and I am smothered up
And buried from all godlike exercise
Of influence benign on planets pale,[17]
Of admonitions to the winds and seas,
Of peaceful sway above man's harvesting,   110
And all those acts which deity supreme
Doth ease its heart of love in. I am gone
Away from my own bosom; I have left
My strong identity, my real self,[18]
Somewhere between the throne and where I sit   115
Here on this spot of earth. Search, Thea, search!
Open thine eyes eterne, and sphere them round
Upon all space – space starred, and lorn of light;
Space regioned with life-air, and barren void;
Spaces of fire, and all the yawn of hell.   120
Search, Thea, search! And tell me if thou seest
A certain shape or shadow, making way
With wings or chariot fierce to repossess
A heaven he lost erewhile: it must – it must
Be of ripe progress; Saturn must be King.   125
Yes, there must be a golden victory;
There must be gods thrown down, and trumpets blown
Of triumph calm, and hymns of festival
Upon the gold clouds metropolitan,[19]
Voices of soft proclaim, and silver stir   130
Of strings in hollow shells; and there shall be
Beautiful things made new, for the surprise
Of the sky-children. I will give command:
Thea! Thea! Thea! Where is Saturn?'
    This passion lifted him upon his feet,   135
And made his hands to struggle in the air,
His Druid locks[20] to shake and ooze with sweat,
His eyes to fever out, his voice to cease.
He stood, and heard not Thea's sobbing deep;
A little time, and then again he snatched   140
Utterance thus: 'But cannot I create?
Cannot I form? Cannot I fashion forth
Another world, another universe,
To overbear and crumble this to naught?
Where is another chaos? Where?' That word   145
Found way unto Olympus,[21] and made quake

---

[15] *front* forehead.
[16] *nervous* muscular.
[17] *And buried . . . pale* Jupiter has taken control of the planets.
[18] *My strong identity, my real self* Titans depend on their identity for their power.

[19] *the gold clouds metropolitan* the clouds are the gods' metropolis.
[20] *Druid locks* i.e. long hair.
[21] *Olympus* mountain that provided Jupiter with his seat of power.

The rebel three.[22] Thea was startled up,
And in her bearing was a sort of hope
As thus she quick-voiced spake, yet full of awe:
'This cheers our fallen house; come to our friends,[23]   150
Oh Saturn, come away and give them heart!
I know the covert,[24] for thence came I hither.'
Thus brief, then with beseeching eyes she went
With backward footing through the shade a space;
He followed, and she turned to lead the way   155
Through aged boughs that yielded like the mist
Which eagles cleave upmounting from their nest.
    Meanwhile in other realms big tears were shed,
More sorrow like to this, and suchlike woe
Too huge for mortal tongue or pen of scribe.   160
The Titans fierce, self-hid, or prison-bound,
Groaned for the old allegiance once more,
And listened in sharp pain for Saturn's voice.
But one of the whole mammoth-brood still kept
His sov'reignty, and rule, and majesty: 165
Blazing Hyperion on his orbed fire[25]
Still sat, still snuffed the incense, teeming up
From man to the sun's god – yet unsecure.
For as among us mortals omens drear
Fright and perplex, so also shuddered he –   170
Not at dog's howl, or gloom-bird's[26] hated screech,
Or the familiar visiting of one
Upon the first toll of his passing-bell,[27]
Or prophesyings of the midnight lamp,
But horrors portioned[28] to a giant nerve   175
Oft made Hyperion ache. His palace bright,
Bastioned with pyramids of glowing gold,
And touched with shade of bronzed obelisks,
Glared a blood-red through all its thousand courts,
Arches, and domes, and fiery galleries;   180
And all its curtains of aurorean[29] clouds
Flushed angerly,[30] while sometimes eagle's wings
(Unseen before by gods or wondering men)
Darkened the place; and neighing steeds were heard,
Not heard before by gods or wondering men.   185
Also, when he would taste the spicy wreaths
Of incense, breathed aloft from sacred hills,
Instead of sweets, his ample palate took
Savour of poisonous brass and metal sick.
And so, when harboured in the sleepy west   190
After the full completion of fair day,
For rest divine upon exalted couch

---

22 *The rebel three* Saturn's sons, Jupiter, Neptune and Pluto.
23 *our friends* the rest of the Titans.
24 *covert* hiding-place.
25 *orbed fire* the sun, of which Hyperion is god.
26 *gloom-bird* owl.
27 *passing-bell* death-bell.

28 *portioned* proportioned.
29 *aurorean* roseate.
30 *His palace . . . angerly* Hyperion's palace is part Greek, part Byzantine and part Egyptian. The model for this description is probably the 'Cloudscape New Jerusalem' passage in Wordsworth's *Excursion* (see pp. 410–11).

And slumber in the arms of melody,
He paced away the pleasant hours of ease
With stride colossal on from hall to hall;   195
While far within each aisle and deep recess
His winged minions in close clusters stood,
Amazed and full of fear, like anxious men
Who on wide plains gather in panting troops
When earthquakes jar their battlements and towers.   200
Even now, while Saturn, roused from icy trance,
Went step for step with Thea through the woods,
Hyperion, leaving twilight in the rear,
Came slope[31] upon the threshold of the west;
Then, as was wont, his palace-door flew ope   205
In smoothest silence, save what solemn tubes[32]
Blown by the serious zephyrs[33] gave of sweet
And wandering sounds, slow-breathed melodies;
And like a rose in vermeil[34] tint and shape,
In fragrance soft, and coolness to the eye,   210
That inlet to severe magnificence
Stood full-blown, for the god to enter in.
    He entered, but he entered full of wrath;
His flaming robes streamed out beyond his heels
And gave a roar as if of earthly fire,   215
That scared away the meek ethereal Hours[35]
And made their dove-wings tremble. On he flared,
From stately nave to nave, from vault to vault,
Through bowers of fragrant and enwreathed light
And diamond-paved lustrous long arcades,   220
Until he reached the great main cupola.[36]
There standing fierce beneath, he stamped his foot,
And from the basements deep to the high towers
Jarred his own golden region; and before
The quavering thunder thereupon had ceased,   225
His voice leaped out, despite of godlike curb,
To this result: 'Oh dreams of day and night!
Oh monstrous forms! Oh effigies of pain!
Oh spectres busy in a cold, cold gloom!
Oh lank-eared phantoms of black-weeded pools!   230
Why do I know ye? Why have I seen ye? Why
Is my eternal essence[37] thus distraught
To see and to behold these horrors new?
Saturn is fallen, am I too to fall?
Am I to leave this haven of my rest,   235
This cradle of my glory, this soft clime,
This calm luxuriance of blissful light,
These crystalline pavilions and pure fanes[38]
Of all my lucent[39] empire? It is left

---

[31] *slope* sloping downward.
[32] *solemn tubes* of a musical instrument, such as an organ.
[33] *zephyrs* breezes.
[34] *vermeil* scarlet.
[35] *Hours* 'Horae', attendant nymphs of the sun.

[36] *cupola* dome.
[37] *essence* being.
[38] *fanes* temples.
[39] *lucent* shining.

Deserted, void, nor any haunt of mine.   240
The blaze, the splendour, and the symmetry,
I cannot see – but darkness, death and darkness.
Even here, into my centre of repose,
The shady visions come to domineer,
Insult, and blind, and stifle up my pomp.   245
Fall? No, by Tellus[40] and her briny robes!
Over the fiery frontier of my realms
I will advance a terrible right arm
Shall scare that infant thunderer, rebel Jove,
And bid old Saturn take his throne again.'   250
He spake, and ceased, the while a heavier threat
Held struggle with his throat but came not forth;
For as in theatres of crowded men
Hubbub increases more they call out 'Hush!'
So at Hyperion's words the phantoms pale   255
Bestirred themselves, thrice horrible and cold,
And from the mirrored level where he stood
A mist arose as from a scummy marsh.
At this, through all his bulk an agony
Crept gradual from the feet unto the crown,   260
Like a lithe serpent vast and muscular
Making slow way, with head and neck convulsed
From over-strained might. Released, he fled
To the eastern gates, and full six dewy hours
Before the dawn in season due should blush,   265
He breathed fierce breath against the sleepy portals,[41]
Cleared them of heavy vapours, burst them wide
Suddenly on the ocean's chilly streams.
The planet orb of fire whereon he rode
Each day from east to west the heavens through,   270
Spun round in sable curtaining of clouds;
Not therefore veiled quite, blindfold and hid,
But ever and anon the glancing spheres,
Circles, and arcs, and broad-belting colure,[42]
Glowed through, and wrought upon the muffling dark   275
Sweet-shaped lightnings from the nadir deep
Up to the zenith – hieroglyphics old[43]
Which sages and keen-eyed astrologers
Then living on the earth, with labouring thought
Won from the gaze of many centuries –   280
Now lost, save what we find on remnants huge
Of stone, or marble swart,[44] their import gone,
Their wisdom long since fled. Two wings this orb
Possessed for glory, two fair argent[45] wings
Ever exalted at the god's approach;   285
And now from forth the gloom their plumes immense

---

40   *Tellus* mother of the Titans, married to her brother Sat-
urn.
41   *portals* gateways.
42   *colure* technical term for 'each of two great circles which
intersect each other at right angles at the poles, and divide the
equinoctial and the ecliptic into four equal parts' (*OED*).

43   *hieroglyphics old* signs of the zodiac.
44   *swart* black.
45   *argent* silver.

Rose one by one, till all outspreaded were,
While still the dazzling globe maintained eclipse,
Awaiting for Hyperion's command.
Fain would he have commanded, fain took throne   290
And bid the day begin, if but for change.
He might not – no, though a primeval god;
The sacred seasons might not be disturbed.
Therefore the operations of the dawn
Stayed in their birth, even as here 'tis told.   295
Those silver wings expanded sisterly,
Eager to sail their orb; the porches wide
Opened upon the dusk demesnes[46] of night;
And the bright Titan, frenzied with new woes,
Unused to bend, by hard compulsion bent   300
His spirit to the sorrow of the time;
And all along a dismal rack of clouds,[47]
Upon the boundaries of day and night,
He stretched himself in grief and radiance faint.
There as he lay, the heaven with its stars   305
Looked down on him with pity, and the voice
Of Coelus,[48] from the universal space,
Thus whispered low and solemn in his ear:
'Oh brightest of my children dear, earth-born
And sky-engendered, son of mysteries   310
All unrevealed even to the powers[49]
Which met at thy creating; at whose joys
And palpitations sweet, and pleasures soft,
I, Coelus, wonder how they came and whence,
And at the fruits thereof what shapes they be,   315
Distinct and visible – symbols divine,
Manifestations of that beauteous life
Diffused unseen throughout eternal space.
Of these new-formed art thou, oh brightest child!
Of these, thy brethren and the goddesses!   320
There is sad feud among ye, and rebellion
Of son against his sire.[50] I saw him fall,
I saw my first-born[51] tumbled from his throne!
To me his arms were spread, to me his voice
Found way from forth the thunders round his head!   325
Pale wox[52] I, and in vapours hid my face.
Art thou, too, near such doom? Vague fear there is,
For I have seen my sons most unlike gods.
Divine ye were created, and divine
In sad demeanour, solemn, undisturbed,   330
Unruffled, like high gods, ye lived and ruled.
Now I behold in you fear, hope, and wrath,
Actions of rage and passion – even as
I see them on the mortal world beneath,

---

46 *demesnes* domains, regions.
47 *rack of clouds* cloud-mass.
48 *Coelus* father of the Titans.
49 *the powers* Coelus and Tellus (parents of the Titans).

50 *son against his sire* i.e. Jupiter's rebellion against Saturn.
51 *my first-born* Saturn.
52 *wox* became.

In men who die. This is the grief, oh son;   335
Sad sign of ruin, sudden dismay, and fall!
Yet do thou strive; as thou art capable,
As thou canst move about, an evident god,[53]
And canst oppose to each malignant hour
Ethereal presence. I am but a voice;   340
My life is but the life of winds and tides,
No more than winds and tides can I avail –
But thou canst. Be thou therefore in the van
Of circumstance;[54] yea, seize the arrow's barb
Before the tense string murmur.[55] To the earth!   345
For there thou wilt find Saturn and his woes.
Meantime I will keep watch on thy bright sun,
And of thy seasons be a careful nurse.'
Ere half this region-whisper had come down,
Hyperion arose, and on the stars   350
Lifted his curved lids, and kept them wide
Until it ceased, and still he kept them wide,
And still they were the same bright, patient stars.
Then with a slow incline of his broad breast,
Like to a diver in the pearly seas,   355
Forward he stooped over the airy shore
And plunged all noiseless into the deep night.

Book II

Just at the self-same beat of Time's wide wings
Hyperion slid into the rustled air,
And Saturn gained with Thea that sad place
Where Cybele and the bruised Titans mourned.
It was a den where no insulting[1] light   5
Could glimmer on their tears; where their own groans
They felt, but heard not, for the solid roar
Of thunderous waterfalls and torrents hoarse,
Pouring a constant bulk, uncertain where.[2]
Crag jutting forth to crag, and rocks that seemed   10
Ever as if just rising from a sleep,
Forehead to forehead held their monstrous horns;
And thus in thousand hugest fantasies
Made a fit roofing to this nest of woe.
Instead of thrones, hard flint they sat upon,   15
Couches of rugged stone, and slaty ridge
Stubborned with iron. All were not assembled,
Some chained in torture and some wandering.
Coeus, and Gyges, and Briareus,
Typhon, and Dolor, and Porphyrion,   20
With many more, the brawniest in assault,

---

[53] *an evident god* Saturn has being; Coelus is the sky, and is just a place – he cannot move around and has no 'essence'.
[54] *the van / Of circumstance* i.e. act, take the initiative.
[55] *seize . . . murmur* i.e. seize the arrow even before it has been fired.

BOOK II
[1] *insulting* the light would be an insulting reminder of their loss of power.
[2] *for the solid roar . . . where* Keats recollects the waterfalls he had seen on his walking tour of the Lake District and Scotland, summer 1818.

Were pent in regions of laborious breath,
Dungeoned in opaque element to keep
Their clenched teeth still clenched, and all their limbs
Locked up like veins of metal, cramped and screwed;   25
Without a motion, save of their big hearts
Heaving in pain, and horribly convulsed
With sanguine feverous boiling gurge[3] of pulse.[4]
Mnemosyne[5] was straying in the world;
Far from her moon had Phoebe[6] wandered;   30
And many else were free to roam abroad,
But for the main, here found they covert[7] drear.
Scarce images of life, one here, one there,
Lay vast and edgeways; like a dismal cirque
Of Druid stones upon a forlorn moor,[8]   35
When the chill rain begins at shut of eve
In dull November, and their chancel vault,[9]
The heaven itself, is blinded throughout night.
Each one kept shroud,[10] nor to his neighbour gave
Or word, or look, or action of despair.   40
Creus was one; his ponderous iron mace
Lay by him, and a shattered rib of rock
Told of his rage ere he thus sank and pined.
Iapetus another – in his grasp
A serpent's plashy[11] neck, its barbed tongue   45
Squeezed from the gorge,[12] and all its uncurled length
Dead, and because[13] the creature could not spit
Its poison in the eyes of conquering Jove.
Next Cottus; prone he lay, chin uppermost
As though in pain, for still upon the flint   50
He ground severe his skull, with open mouth
And eyes at horrid working.[14] Nearest him
Asia, born of most enormous Caf,
Who cost her mother Tellus keener pangs,
Though feminine, than any of her sons.   55
More thought than woe was in her dusky face,
For she was prophesying of her glory,
And in her wide imagination stood
Palm-shaded temples and high rival fanes
By Oxus or in Ganges' sacred isles.[15]   60
Even as Hope upon her anchor[16] leans,
So leant she, not so fair, upon a tusk
Shed from the broadest of her elephants.
Above her, on a crag's uneasy shelve,[17]

---

[3] *gurge* whirlpool.
[4] *pulse* i.e. that of blood in the heart.
[5] *Mnemosyne* mother of the muses by Jupiter, included among the Titans. She is seeking Apollo.
[6] *Phoebe* goddess of the moon.
[7] *covert* shelter.
[8] *Druid stones upon a forlorn moor* Keats visited the Castlerigg Stone Circle near Keswick in June 1818.
[9] *their chancel vault* the stones and the darkness evoke the atmosphere of a church.

[10] *shroud* shrouded.
[11] *plashy* crushed.
[12] *gorge* throat.
[13] *and because* i.e. and all this because.
[14] *at horrid working* looking round in a frightening manner.
[15] *For she was ... sacred isles* Asia will become the goddess of a future cult.
[16] *anchor* traditional emblem of hope.
[17] *shelve* slope.

Upon his elbow raised, all prostrate else,   65
Shadowed Enceladus – once tame and mild
As grazing ox unworried in the meads,
Now tiger-passioned, lion-thoughted, wroth,
He meditated, plotted, and even now[18]
Was hurling mountains in that second war[19]   70
Not long delayed, that scared the younger gods
To hide themselves in forms of beast and bird.
Not far hence Atlas; and beside him prone
Phorcus, the sire of Gorgons. Neighboured close
Oceanus, and Tethys, in whose lap   75
Sobbed Clymene among her tangled hair.[20]
In midst of all lay Themis, at the feet
Of Ops the queen, all clouded round from sight;
No shape distinguishable, more than when
Thick night confounds the pine-tops with the clouds: 80
And many else whose names may not be told.
For when the muse's wings are air-ward spread
Who shall delay her flight? And she must chaunt
Of Saturn and his guide, who now had climbed
With damp and slippery footing from a depth   85
More horrid[21] still. Above a sombre cliff
Their heads appeared, and up their stature grew
Till on the level height their steps found ease;
Then Thea spread abroad her trembling arms
Upon the precincts of this nest of pain,   90
And sidelong fixed her eye on Saturn's face.
There saw she direst strife, the supreme god
At war with all the frailty of grief,
Of rage, of fear, anxiety, revenge,
Remorse, spleen, hope, but most of all despair.   95
Against these plagues he strove in vain, for Fate
Had poured a mortal oil upon his head,
A disanointing poison,[22] so that Thea,
Affrighted, kept her still, and let him pass
First onwards in, among the fallen tribe.   100
      As with us mortal men, the laden heart
Is persecuted more, and fevered more,
When it is nighing to the mournful house
Where other hearts are sick of the same bruise;
So Saturn, as he walked into the midst,   105
Felt faint, and would have sunk among the rest,
But that he met Enceladus' eye,
Whose mightiness and awe of him, at once
Came like an inspiration – and he shouted,
'Titans, behold your god!' At which some groaned,   110
Some started on their feet, some also shouted,
Some wept, some wailed, all bowed with reverence;

---

[18] *even now* i.e. in his imagination.
[19] *that second war* presumably to have been the subject of a
further book of the poem, never written.
[20] *her tangled hair* a recollection of *Lycidas* 69: 'the tangles of
Naeara's hair'.

[21] *horrid* frightening.
[22] *A disanointing poison* the ointment deprives Saturn of his
godhead.

And Ops, uplifting her black folded veil,
Showed her pale cheeks and all her forehead wan,
Her eyebrows thin and jet, and hollow eyes. 115
There is a roaring in the bleak-grown pines
When winter lifts his voice; there is a noise
Among immortals when a god gives sign,
With hushing finger, how he means to load
His tongue with the full weight of utterless[23] thought, 120
With thunder, and with music, and with pomp:
Such noise is like the roar of bleak-grown pines,
Which, when it ceases in this mountained world,
No other sound succeeds; but ceasing here,
Among these fallen, Saturn's voice therefrom 125
Grew up like organ, that begins anew
Its strain, when other harmonies, stopped short,
Leave the dinned air vibrating silverly.[24]
Thus grew it up: 'Not in my own sad breast,
Which is its own great judge and searcher-out, 130
Can I find reason why ye should be thus;
Not in the legends of the first of days,
Studied from that old spirit-leaved book[25]
Which starry Uranus with finger bright
Saved from the shores of darkness, when the waves 135
Low-ebbed still hid it up in shallow gloom,
And the which book ye know I ever kept
For my firm-based footstool – ah, infirm!
Not there, nor in sign, symbol, or portent
Of element, earth, water, air, and fire, 140
At war, at peace, or inter-quarrelling
One against one, or two, or three, or all
Each several one against the other three,
As fire with air loud warring when rainfloods
Drown both, and press them both against earth's face, 145
Where, finding sulphur, a quadruple wrath
Unhinges the poor world – not in that strife,
Wherefrom I take strange lore and read it deep,
Can I find reason why ye should be thus.
No, nowhere can unriddle, though I search 150
And pore on nature's universal scroll
Even to swooning, why ye divinities,
The first-born of all shaped and palpable gods,
Should cower beneath what, in comparison,
Is untremendous might. Yet ye are here, 155
O'erwhelmed, and spurned, and battered – ye are here!
Oh Titans, shall I say "Arise"? Ye groan;
Shall I say "Crouch"? Ye groan. What can I then?
Oh heaven wide! Oh unseen parent dear!
What can I? Tell me, all ye brethren gods, 160

---

[23] *utterless* unutterable.
[24] *silverly* with a silvery sound.
[25] *that old spirit-leaved book* imaginary book dating from the
beginning of time, recording the first stages of the evolution
of the world

How we can war, how engine our great wrath;[26]
Oh speak your counsel now, for Saturn's ear
Is all a-hungered. Thou, Oceanus,
Ponderest high and deep, and in thy face
I see, astonied,[27] that severe content   165
Which comes of thought and musing – give us help!'
  So ended Saturn, and the god of the sea,[28]
Sophist and sage from no Athenian grove,[29]
But cogitation in his watery shades,
Arose, with locks not oozy,[30] and began,   170
In murmurs, which his first-endeavouring tongue
Caught infant-like from the far-foamed sands:
'Oh ye, whom wrath consumes, who, passion-stung,
Writhe at defeat, and nurse your agonies!
Shut up your senses, stifle up your ears,   175
My voice is not a bellows unto ire.
Yet listen, ye who will, whilst I bring proof
How ye, perforce, must be content to stoop;
And in the proof much comfort will I give,
If ye will take that comfort in its truth.   180
We fall by course of nature's law, not force
Of thunder, or of Jove. Great Saturn, thou
Hast sifted well the atom-universe;[31]
But for this reason, that thou art the King,
And only blind from sheer supremacy,   185
One avenue was shaded from thine eyes
Through which I wandered to eternal truth.
And first, as thou wast not the first of powers,
So art thou not the last; it cannot be.
Thou art not the beginning nor the end.[32]   190
From chaos and parental darkness came
Light, the first fruits of that intestine broil,[33]
That sullen ferment which for wondrous ends
Was ripening in itself. The ripe hour came,
And with it light, and light, engendering   195
Upon its own producer,[34] forthwith touched
The whole enormous matter into life.
Upon that very hour, our parentage,
The heavens and the earth, were manifest;
Then thou first-born, and we the giant-race,   200
Found ourselves ruling new and beauteous realms.
Now comes the pain of truth, to whom 'tis pain;[35]
Oh folly! for to bear all naked truths,

---

[26] *engine our great wrath* turn our wrath into an instrument of war.
[27] *astonied* astonished; an archaism used by Spenser and Milton.
[28] *the god of the sea* Oceanus, father of all the gods.
[29] *no Athenian grove* Oceanus did not gain his wisdom from an academy in Athens.
[30] *locks not oozy* Oceanus is not in the sea; Keats is also alluding to *Lycidas* 175: 'With nectar pure his oozy locks he laves'.
[31] *atom-universe* although Keats may be echoing Milton (see *Paradise Lost* ii 900), he was aware that John Dalton

(1766–1844) had proposed in 1801 that all elements are composed of fundamental units, or 'atoms', that are specific to that element.
[32] *Thou art not the beginning nor the end* Revelation 1:8: 'I am Alpha and Omega, the beginning and the ending, saith the Lord'.
[33] *intestine broil* civil war.
[34] *its own producer* the darkness of chaos.
[35] *to whom 'tis pain* for those to whom it is pain.

And to envisage circumstance, all calm,
That is the top of sovereignty. Mark well!   205
As heaven and earth are fairer, fairer far
Than chaos and blank darkness, though once chiefs;
And as we show beyond[36] that heaven and earth
In form and shape compact and beautiful,
In will, in action free, companionship,   210
And thousand other signs of purer life –
So on our heels a fresh perfection treads,
A power more strong in beauty, born of us
And fated to excel us, as we pass
In glory that old darkness. Nor are we   215
Thereby more conquered than by us the rule
Of shapeless chaos. Say, doth the dull soil
Quarrel with the proud forests it hath fed,
And feedeth still, more comely than itself?
Can it deny the chiefdom of green groves?   220
Or shall the tree be envious of the dove
Because it cooeth, and hath snowy wings
To wander wherewithal and find its joys?
We are such forest trees, and our fair boughs
Have bred forth not pale solitary doves   225
But eagles golden-feathered, who do tower
Above us in their beauty, and must reign
In right thereof; for 'tis the eternal law
That first in beauty should be first in might –
Yea, by that law another race may drive   230
Our conquerors to mourn as we do now.
Have ye beheld the young god of the seas,[37]
My dispossessor? Have ye seen his face?
Have ye beheld his chariot, foamed along
By noble winged creatures he hath made?   235
I saw him on the calmed waters scud,
With such a glow of beauty in his eyes
That it enforced me to bid sad farewell
To all my empire; farewell sad I took,
And hither came to see how dolorous fate   240
Had wrought upon ye, and how I might best
Give consolation in this woe extreme.
Receive the truth, and let it be your balm.'

    Whether through posed[38] conviction, or disdain,
They guarded silence when Oceanus   245
Left murmuring, what deepest thought can tell?
But so it was; none answered for a space,
Save one whom none regarded, Clymene.[39]
And yet she answered not, only complained
With hectic[40] lips, and eyes up-looking mild,   250
Thus wording timidly among the fierce:

---

[36] *show beyond* are manifestly superior to.
[37] *the young god of the seas* Neptune, traditionally depicted as riding a chariot over the sea.

[38] *posed* feigned.
[39] *Clymene* daughter of Oceanus and Tethys.
[40] *hectic* feverish.

'Oh father, I am here the simplest voice,
And all my knowledge is that joy is gone,
And this thing woe crept in among our hearts,
There to remain for ever, as I fear.   255
I would not bode of evil, if I thought
So weak a creature could turn off the help
Which by just right should come of mighty gods;
Yet let me tell my sorrow, let me tell
Of what I heard, and how it made we weep,   260
And know that we had parted from all hope.
I stood upon a shore, a pleasant shore
Where a sweet clime was breathed from a land
Of fragrance, quietness, and trees, and flowers.
Full of calm joy it was, as I of grief,   265
Too full of joy and soft delicious warmth —
So that I felt a movement in my heart
To chide, and to reproach that solitude
With songs of misery, music of our woes;
And sat me down, and took a mouthed shell   270
And murmured into it, and made melody.
Oh melody no more! For while I sang,
And with poor skill let pass into the breeze
The dull shell's echo, from a bowery strand[41]
Just opposite, an island of the sea,   275
There came enchantment with the shifting wind,
That did both drown and keep alive my ears.
I threw my shell away upon the sand
And a wave filled it, as my sense was filled
With that new blissful golden melody.   280
A living death was in each gush of sounds,
Each family of rapturous hurried notes
That fell, one after one, yet all at once,
Like pearl beads dropping sudden from their string;
And then another, then another strain,   285
Each like a dove leaving its olive perch,
With music winged instead of silent plumes,
To hover round my head, and make me sick
Of joy and grief at once.[42] Grief overcame,
And I was stopping up my frantic ears,   290
When, past all hindrance of my trembling hands,
A voice came sweeter, sweeter than all tune,
And still it cried, "Apollo! Young Apollo!
The morning-bright Apollo! Young Apollo!"
I fled, it followed me, and cried "Apollo!"   295
Oh father and oh brethren, had ye felt
Those pains of mine — oh Saturn, hadst thou felt,
Ye would not call this too indulged tongue
Presumptous in thus venturing to be heard.'
    So far her voice flowed on, like timorous brook   300
That, lingering along[43] a pebbled coast,

---

[41] *bowery strand* sheltered sea shore.   [43] *lingering along* meandering towards.
[42] *Of joy and grief at once* joy at the music; grief that her music is surpassed.

Doth fear to meet the sea – but sea it met
And shuddered; for the overwhelming voice
Of huge Enceladus[44] swallowed it in wrath –
The ponderous syllables, like sullen waves   305
In the half-glutted[45] hollows of reef-rocks,
Came booming thus, while still upon his arm
He leaned (not rising, from supreme contempt):
'Or shall we listen to the over-wise,
Or to the over-foolish, giant gods?   310
Not thunderbolt on thunderbolt, till all
That rebel Jove's whole armoury were spent,
Not world on world upon these shoulders piled
Could agonize me more than baby-words
In midst of this dethronement horrible.   315
Speak! Roar! Shout! Yell, ye sleepy Titans all!
Do ye forget the blows, the buffets vile?
Are ye not smitten by a youngling arm?[46]
Dost thou forget, sham monarch of the waves,
Thy scalding in the seas? What, have I roused   320
Your spleens with so few simple words as these?
Oh joy, for now I see ye are not lost!
Oh joy, for now I see a thousand eyes
Wide glaring for revenge!' As this he said,
He lifted up his stature vast, and stood,   325
Still without intermission speaking thus:
'Now ye are flames, I'll tell you how to burn
And purge the ether of our enemies;[47]
How to feed fierce the crooked stings of fire[48]
And singe away the swollen clouds of Jove,   330
Stifling that puny essence in its tent.
Oh let him feel the evil he hath done –
For though I scorn Oceanus' lore,
Much pain have I for more than loss of realms.
The days of peace and slumberous calm are fled;   335
Those days, all innocent of scathing war,
When all the fair Existences of heaven
Came open-eyed to guess what we would speak –
That was before our brows were taught to frown,
Before our lips knew else but solemn sounds;   340
That was before we knew the winged thing,
Victory, might be lost, or might be won.
And be ye mindful that Hyperion,
Our brightest brother, still is undisgraced –
Hyperion, lo! His radiance is here!'   345
      All eyes were on Enceladus' face,
And they beheld, while still Hyperion's name
Flew from his lips up to the vaulted rocks,[49]
A pallid gleam across his features stern –
Not savage, for he saw full many a god   350

---

44   *Enceladus* one of the most powerful of the Titans.
45   *half-glutted* half-filled.
46   *youngling arm* inexperienced arm.

47   *the ether of our enemies* the air our enemies breathe.
48   *the crooked stings of fire* flashes of lightning.
49   *the vaulted rocks* the rocks form a roof above them.

Wroth as himself. He looked upon them all,
And in each face he saw a gleam of light,
But splendider in Saturn's, whose hoar locks
Shone like the bubbling foam about a keel
When the prow sweeps into a midnight cove.   355
In pale and silver silence they remained,
Till suddenly a splendour, like the morn,
Pervaded all the beetling[50] gloomy steeps,
All the sad spaces of oblivion,
And every gulf, and every chasm old,   360
And every height, and every sullen depth,
Voiceless, or hoarse with loud tormented streams,
And all the everlasting cataracts,
And all the headlong torrents far and near,
Mantled[51] before in darkness and huge shade,   365
Now saw the light and made it terrible.
It was Hyperion: a granite peak
His bright feet touched, and there he stayed to view
The misery his brillance had betrayed
To the most hateful seeing of itself.[52]   370
Golden his hair of short Numidian curl,
Regal his shape majestic, a vast shade
In midst of his own brightness, like the bulk
Of Memnon's image at the set of sun
To one who travels from the dusking east;[53]   375
Sighs, too, as mournful as that Memnon's harp
He uttered, while his hands contemplative
He pressed together, and in silence stood.
Despondence seized again the fallen gods
At sight of the dejected King of Day,   380
And many hid their faces from the light.
But fierce Enceladus sent forth his eyes
Among the brotherhood, and at their glare
Uprose Iapetus, and Creus too,
And Phorcus, sea-born, and together strode   385
To where he towered on his eminence.[54]
There those four shouted forth old Saturn's name;
Hyperion from the peak loud answered, 'Saturn!'
Saturn sat near the mother of the gods,
In whose face was no joy, though all the gods   390
Gave from their hollow throats the name of 'Saturn!'

Book III

Thus in alternate uproar and sad peace,
Amazed were those Titans utterly.

---

[50]   *beetling* overhanging.
[51]   *Mantled* cloaked, obscured.
[52]   *The misery . . . itself* Hyperion's radiance throws the misery
of the Titans into sharper relief.
[53]   *Memnon's image . . . east* the statue was in fact one of a pair
representing the Egyptian King Amenhotep III, outside his
funerary temple on the west bank at Thebes, mentioned by

Juvenal in his fifteenth satire. The eighteenth- and early nine-
teenth-century English poets believed that the statue held a
lyre which, when struck by the sun at dawn or sunset,
sounded forth. See Robin C. Dix, 'The Harps of Memnon and
Aeolus: A Study in the Propagation of an Error', *Modern
Philology* 85 (1988) 288–93.
[54]   *eminence* mountain.

Oh leave them, muse! Oh leave them to their woes,
For thou art weak to sing such tumults dire;
A solitary sorrow best befits   5
Thy lips, and antheming a lonely grief.
Leave them, oh muse! For thou anon wilt find
Many a fallen old divinity[1]
Wandering in vain about bewildered shores.
Meantime touch piously the Delphic harp,[2]   10
And not a wind of heaven but will breathe
In aid soft warble from the Dorian flute;[3]
For lo! 'tis for the father of all verse.[4]
Flush everything that hath a vermeil[5] hue,
Let the rose glow intense and warm the air,   15
And let the clouds of even and of morn
Float in voluptuous fleeces o'er the hills;
Let the red wine within the goblet boil,
Cold as a bubbling well; let faint-lipped shells
On sands or in great deeps, vermilion turn   20
Through all their labyrinths; and let the maid
Blush keenly, as with some warm kiss surprised.
Chief isle of the embowered Cyclades,[6]
Rejoice, oh Delos,[7] with thine olives green,
And poplars, and lawn-shading palms, and beech   25
In which the zephyr breathes the loudest song,
And hazels thick, dark-stemmed beneath the shade.
Apollo is once more the golden theme!
Where was he when the giant of the sun[8]
Stood bright amid the sorrow of his peers?   30
Together had he left his mother fair
And his twin-sister[9] sleeping in their bower,
And in the morning twilight wandered forth
Beside the osiers of a rivulet,
Full ankle-deep in lilies of the vale.   35
The nightingale had ceased, and a few stars
Were lingering in the heavens, while the thrush
Began calm-throated. Throughout all the isle
There was no covert,[10] no retired cave
Unhaunted by the murmurous noise of waves,   40
Though scarcely heard in many a green recess.
He listened and he wept, and his bright tears
Went trickling down the golden bow he held.
Thus with half-shut suffused[11] eyes he stood,
While from beneath some cumbrous boughs hard by   45
With solemn step an awful goddess[12] came,
And there was purport in her looks for him,

BOOK III
[1] *divinity* god.
[2] *the Delphic harp* i.e. the divinely-inspired harp.
[3] *the Dorian flute* flute of classical Greece. Keats echoes *Paradise Lost* i 550–1: 'the Dorian mood/Of flutes and soft recorders'. He marked the lines in his copy of Milton with the comment: 'The light and shade . . . the sorrow, the pain, the sad-sweet melody'.
[4] *the father of all verse* Apollo, god of the sun and poetry.
[5] *vermeil* bright scarlet.

[6] *Cyclades* cluster of islands in the Aegean.
[7] *Delos* island in the centre of the Cyclades, sacred to Apollo as it was his birthplace.
[8] *the giant of the sun* Hyperion.
[9] *mother . . . twin-sister* Latona and Diana.
[10] *covert* hiding-place.
[11] *suffused* tearful.
[12] *an awful goddess* the awe-inspiring goddess is Mnemosyne, mother of the muses by Jupiter, and another Titan. She has abandoned the Titans and joined Apollo.

Which he with eager guess began to read
Perplexed, the while melodiously he said:
'How cam'st thou over the unfooted sea?   50
Or hath that antique mien and robed form
Moved in these vales invisible till now?
Sure I have heard those vestments[13] sweeping o'er
The fallen leaves, when I have sat alone
In cool mid-forest. Surely I have traced   55
The rustle of those ample skirts about
These grassy solitudes, and seen the flowers
Lift up their heads, as still the whisper passed.
Goddess! I have beheld those eyes before,
And their eternal calm, and all that face,   60
Or I have dreamed.' 'Yes', said the supreme shape,
'Thou hast dreamed of me; and awaking up
Didst find a lyre all golden by thy side,
Whose strings touched by thy fingers, all the vast
Unwearied ear of the whole universe   65
Listened in pain and pleasure at the birth
Of such new tuneful wonder. Is't not strange
That thou shouldst weep, so gifted? Tell me, youth,
What sorrow thou canst feel – for I am sad
When thou dost shed a tear. Explain thy griefs   70
To one who in this lonely isle hath been
The watcher of thy sleep and hours of life,
From the young day when first thy infant hand
Plucked witless the weak flowers, till thine arm
Could bend that bow heroic to all times.   75
Show thy heart's secret to an ancient power
Who hath forsaken old and sacred thrones
For prophecies of thee, and for the sake
Of loveliness new born.' Apollo then,
With sudden scrutiny and gloomless eyes,[14]   80
Thus answered, while his white melodious throat
Throbbed with the syllables: 'Mnemosyne!
Thy name is on my tongue I know not how;
Why should I tell thee what thou so well seest?
Why should I strive to show what from thy lips   85
Would come no mystery? For me, dark, dark
And painful, vile oblivion seals my eyes.
I strive to search wherefore I am so sad
Until a melancholy numbs my limbs;
And then upon the grass I sit and moan   90
Like one who once had wings. Oh why should I
Feel cursed and thwarted, when the liegeless air[15]
Yields to my step aspirant? Why should I
Spurn the green turf as hateful to my feet?
Goddess benign, point forth some unknown thing.   95
Are there not other regions than this isle?
What are the stars? There is the sun, the sun!

---

[13] *vestments* clothes.
[14] *gloomless eyes* Apollo's gloom lifts at hearing Mnemosyne.

[15] *the liegeless air* the air owes allegiance to no master.

And the most patient brilliance of the moon!
And stars by thousands! Point me out the way
To any one particular beauteous star,   100
And I will flit into it with my lyre
And make its silvery splendour pant with bliss.
I have heard the cloudy thunder. Where is power?
Whose hand, whose essence, what divinity
Makes this alarum[16] in the elements   105
While I here idle listen on the shores
In fearless yet in aching[17] ignorance?
Oh tell me, lonely goddess, by thy harp
That waileth every morn and eventide,
Tell me why thus I rave about these groves!   110
Mute thou remainest, mute! Yet I can read
A wondrous lesson in thy silent face:
Knowledge enormous[18] makes a god of me.
Names, deeds, grey legends, dire events, rebellions,
Majesties, sovran[19] voices, agonies,   115
Creations and destroyings, all at once
Pour into the wide hollows of my brain
And deify me, as if some blithe wine
Or bright elixir peerless I had drunk,
And so become immortal.' Thus the god,   120
While his enkindled eyes, with level glance
Beneath his white soft temples, steadfast kept
Trembling with light upon Mnemosyne.
Soon wild commotions shook him, and made flush
All the immortal fairness of his limbs,   125
Most like the struggle at the gate of death;
Or liker still to one who should take leave
Of pale immortal death, and with a pang
As hot as death's is chill, with fierce convulse[20]
Die into life. So young Apollo anguished;   130
His very hair, his golden tresses famed
Kept undulation round his eager neck.
During the pain Mnemosyne upheld
Her arms as one who prophesied. At length
Apollo shrieked – and lo! from all his limbs   135
Celestial[21] . . .

---

[16] *alarum* turmoil.
[17] *aching* longing.
[18] *Knowledge enormous* knowledge of suffering has made a god
of Apollo. See Keats's admiring comments on Wordsworth for
his ability to portray a world 'full of misery and heartbreak,
pain, sickness, and oppression' (p. 1022).
[19] *sovran* sovereign.
[20] *convulse* convulsion.

[21] In his annotated copy of *Endymion* (1818), Richard
Woodhouse (see p. 816) recorded that this poem, 'if com-
pleted, would have treated of the dethronement of Hyperion,
the former god of the sun, by Apollo (and incidentally of those
of Oceanus by Neptune, of Saturn by Jupiter, etc., and of the
war of the giants for Saturn's re-establishment), with other
events of which we have but very dark hints in the mythologi-
cal poets of Greece and Rome. In fact, the incidents would
have been pure creations of the poet's brain' (p. 426).

Letter from John Keats to Richard Woodhouse, 27 October 1818[1]

My dear Woodhouse,

Your letter gave me a great satisfaction, more on account of its friendliness than any relish of that matter in it which is accounted so acceptable in the 'genus irritabile'.[2] The best answer I can give you is, in a clerk-like manner, to make some observations on two principal points, which seem to point like indices into the midst of the whole pro and con, about genius, and views, and achievements, and ambition, etc.

First: as to the poetical character itself (I mean that sort of which, if I am anything, I am a member – that sort distinguished from the Wordsworthian or egotistical sublime, which is a thing *per se* and stands alone),[3] it is not itself – it has no self – it is everything and nothing – it has no character – it enjoys light and shade – it lives in gusto,[4] be it foul or fair, high or low, rich or poor, mean or elevated. It has as much delight in conceiving an Iago as an Imogen.[5] What shocks the virtuous philosopher delights the chameleon poet. It does no harm from its relish of the dark side of things, any more than from its taste for the bright one – because they both end in speculation. A poet is the most unpoetical of any thing in existence, because he has no identity, he is continually in for – and filling – some other body. The sun, the moon, the sea, and men and women who are creatures of impulse, are poetical, and have about them an unchangeable attribute; the poet has none, no identity – he is certainly the most unpoetical of all God's creatures. If, then, he has no self, and if I am a poet, where is the wonder that I should say I would write no more? Might I not at that very instant have been cogitating on the characters of Saturn and Ops?[6] It is a wretched thing to confess, but is a very fact that not one word I ever utter can be taken for granted as an opinion growing out of my identical nature – how can it, when I have no nature? When I am in a room with people, if I ever am free from speculating on creations of my own brain, then not myself goes home to myself: but the identity of everyone in the room begins so to press upon me, that I am, in a very little time, annihilated – not only among men; it would be the same in a nursery of children. I know not whether I make myself wholly understood. I hope enough so to let you see that no dependence is to be placed on what I said that day.

In the second place I will speak of my views, and of the life I purpose to myself. I am ambitious of doing the world some good – if I should be spared, that may be the work of maturer years. In the interval I will assay to reach to as high a summit in poetry as the nerve bestowed upon me will suffer. The faint conceptions I have of poems to come brings the blood frequently into my forehead. All I hope is that I may not lose all interest in human affairs, that the solitary indifference I feel for applause, even from the finest spirits, will not blunt any acuteness of vision I may have. I do not think it will – I feel assured I should write from the mere yearning and fondness I have for the beautiful, even if my night's labours should be burnt every morning and no eye ever shine upon them.

But even now I am perhaps not speaking from myself, but from some character in whose soul I now live. I am sure, however, that this next sentence is from myself. I feel your anxiety, good opinion, and friendliness, in the highest degree, and am

Yours most sincerely

John Keats

LETTER FROM JOHN KEATS TO RICHARD WOODHOUSE

[1] This important letter about negative capability was the occasion for Woodhouse's equally important summary of it in correspondence with John Taylor on the same day; see pp. 816–17.

[2] Horace, *Epistles* II ii 102.

[3] *Troilus and Cressida* I ii 15–16: 'he is a very man *per se*, / And stands alone'.

[4] *gusto* as an admirer of Hazlitt, Keats uses this word in its Hazlittian sense (see pp. 597–9).

[5] Iago is the villain of *Othello*, Imogen the virtuous daughter to Cymbeline by a former Queen in *Cymbeline*.

[6] Saturn and Ops are characters in *Hyperion*. Ops is usually identified with Cybele, wife of Saturn.

The Eve of St Agnes (composed between 18 January and 2 February 1819; revised September 1819)[1]

I

St Agnes' Eve – ah, bitter chill it was!
The owl, for all his feathers, was a-cold;
The hare limped trembling through the frozen grass,
And silent was the flock in woolly fold.
Numb were the beadsman's[2] fingers, while he told[3]   5
His rosary, and while his frosted breath,
Like pious incense from a censer old,
Seemed taking flight for heaven, without a death,
Past the sweet Virgin's picture, while his prayer he saith.

II

His prayer he saith, this patient, holy man;   10
Then takes his lamp and riseth from his knees,
And back returneth, meagre,[4] barefoot, wan,
Along the chapel aisle by slow degrees.
The sculptured dead on each side seem to freeze,
Imprisoned in black, purgatorial rails;   15
Knights, ladies, praying in dumb orat'ries,[5]
He passeth by; and his weak spirit fails
To think how they may ache in icy hoods and mails.

III

Northward he turneth through a little door,
And scarce three steps ere music's golden tongue   20
Flattered to tears this aged man and poor;
But no – already had his deathbell rung,
The joys of all his life were said and sung –
His was harsh penance on St Agnes' Eve:
Another way he went, and soon among   25
Rough ashes sat he for his soul's reprieve,[6]
And all night kept awake, for sinners' sake to grieve.

IV

That ancient beadsman heard the prelude[7] soft,
And so it chanced, for many a door was wide
From hurry to and fro. Soon, up aloft,   30

THE EVE OF ST AGNES
[1] The inspiration for this poem was the superstition that on St Agnes' Eve (20 January) virgins might use various means of divination to see an image of their future husbands. Keats originally composed the poem between 18 January and 2 February 1819; he revised it in September, much to the dismay of Woodhouse, who communicated his feelings to Keats's publishers, Taylor and Hessey (see p. 818). Although Woodhouse later noted that 'Keats left it to his publishers to adopt which [alterations] they pleased,' Keats went through the proofs of the poem as printed in 1820, and insisted that some of the revisions be included. Some of the more controversial revisions, not included in 1820, are given in footnotes, below.
[2] *beadsman* one paid to pray for others.
[3] *told* counted.
[4] *meagre* thin.
[5] *Knights . . . orat'ries* Keats probably saw the sculptured effigies on the tombstones in Chichester cathedral, January 1819. An oratory is a small chapel.
[6] *reprieve* redemption.
[7] *prelude* introductory music.

The silver, snarling trumpets 'gan to chide;
The level chambers, ready with their pride,
Were glowing to receive a thousand guests;
The carved angels, ever eager-eyed,
Stared, where upon their heads the cornice[8] rests,   35
With hair blown back, and wings put crosswise on their breasts.

V

At length burst in the argent[9] revelry,
With plume, tiara, and all rich array,
Numerous as shadows haunting fairily
The brain, new stuffed in youth, with triumphs gay   40
Of old romance. These let us wish away,
And turn, sole-thoughted, to one lady there,
Whose heart had brooded all that wintry day
On love, and winged St Agnes' saintly care,
As she had heard old dames full many times declare.   45

VI

They told her how, upon St Agnes' Eve,
Young virgins might have visions of delight,
And soft adorings from their loves receive
Upon the honeyed middle of the night,
If ceremonies due they did aright –   50
As, supperless to bed they must retire,
And couch supine their beauties, lily-white;
Nor look behind, nor sideways, but require
Of heaven with upward eyes for all that they desire.[10]

VII

Full of this whim was thoughtful Madeline.   55
The music, yearning like a god in pain,
She scarcely heard; her maiden eyes divine,
Fixed on the floor, saw many a sweeping train[11]
Pass by – she heeded not at all; in vain
Came many a tiptoe, amorous cavalier,   60
And back retired, not cooled by high disdain,
But she saw not; her heart was otherwhere.
She sighed for Agnes' dreams, the sweetest of the year.

VIII

She danced along with vague, regardless eyes;
Anxious her lips, her breathing quick and short.   65

---

8   *cornice* ornamental moulding between the wall and ceiling.
9   *argent* silver.
10   At this point in his revised version of the poem, Keats
inserted an additional stanza, intended to clarify the narrative:
     'Twas said her future lord would there appear
     Offering, as sacrifice (all in the dream),
     Delicious food, even to her lips brought near,

Viands, and wine, and fruit, and sugared cream,
To touch her palate with the fine extreme
Of relish; then soft music heard, and then
More pleasures followed in a dizzy stream,
Palpable almost; then to wake again
Warm in the virgin morn, no weeping Magdalen.
11   *train* long skirts and robes sweeping along the floor.

The hallowed hour was near at hand: she sighs
Amid the timbrels[12] and the thronged resort
Of whisperers in anger, or in sport,
Mid looks of love, defiance, hate, and scorn,
Hoodwinked with fairy fancy – all amort,[13]   70
Save to St Agnes and her lambs unshorn,[14]
And all the bliss to be before tomorrow morn.

IX

So, purposing each moment to retire,
She lingered still. Meantime, across the moors
Had come young Porphyro, with heart on fire   75
For Madeline. Beside the portal doors,
Buttressed from moonlight,[15] stands he, and implores
All saints to give him sight of Madeline
But for one moment in the tedious hours,
That he might gaze and worship all unseen,   80
Perchance speak, kneel, touch, kiss – in sooth such things have been.

X

He ventures in – let no buzzed whisper tell;
All eyes be muffled, or a hundred swords
Will storm his heart, love's fev'rous citadel.
For him those chambers held barbarian hordes,[16]   85
Hyena foemen, and hot-blooded lords
Whose very dogs would execrations howl
Against his lineage;[17] not one breast affords
Him any mercy in that mansion foul,
Save one old beldame,[18] weak in body and in soul.   90

XI

Ah, happy chance! The aged creature came,
Shuffling along with ivory-headed wand
To where he stood, hid from the torch's flame
Behind a broad hall-pillar, far beyond
The sound of merriment and chorus bland.[19]   95
He startled her; but soon she knew his face,
And grasped his fingers in her palsied hand,
Saying, 'Mercy, Porphyro! Hie thee from this place;
They are all here tonight, the whole bloodthirsty race!

XII

Get hence! Get hence! There's dwarfish Hildebrand –   100
He had a fever late, and in the fit

---

[12] *timbrels* tambourines.
[13] *amort* listless, inanimate.
[14] *her lambs unshorn* The Feast of St Agnes is celebrated, 21 January, at the basilica of St Agnes in Rome by the presentation and blessing of two unshorn lambs.
[15] *Buttressed from moonlight* Porphyro stands in the shade of a buttress.

[16] *barbarian hordes* the barbarians who attacked Rome.
[17] *Against his lineage* Madeline's and Porphyro's families are at war.
[18] *beldame* old lady.
[19] *bland* soothing.

He cursed thee and thine, both house and land;
Then there's that old Lord Maurice, not a whit
More tame for his grey hairs. Alas me! Flit,
Flit like a ghost away!' 'Ah, gossip[20] dear,   105
We're safe enough; here in this armchair sit
And tell me how –' 'Good Saints! Not here, not here;
Follow me, child, or else these stones will be thy bier.'

XIII

He followed through a lowly arched way,
Brushing the cobwebs with his lofty plume,   110
And as she muttered, 'Wel-a – wel-a-day!'[21]
He found him in a little moonlight room,
Pale, latticed, chill, and silent as a tomb.
'Now tell me where is Madeline', said he,
'Oh tell me, Angela, by the holy loom   115
Which none but secret sisterhood may see,
When they St Agnes' wool are weaving piously.'[22]

XIV

'St Agnes! Ah! It is St Agnes' Eve –
Yet men will murder upon holy days!
Thou must hold water in a witch's sieve   120
And be liege-lord[23] of all the elves and fays
To venture so; it fills me with amaze
To see thee, Porphyro! St Agnes' Eve!
God's help! My lady fair the conjuror plays[24]
This very night. Good angels her deceive![25]   125
But let me laugh awhile, I've mickle[26] time to grieve.'

XV

Feebly she laugheth in the languid moon,
While Porphyro upon her face doth look
Like puzzled urchin on an aged crone
Who keepeth closed a wondrous riddle-book,   130
As spectacled she sits in chimney nook.
But soon his eyes grew brilliant, when she told
His lady's purpose; and he scarce could brook[27]
Tears, at the thought of those enchantments cold,[28]
And Madeline asleep in lap of legends old.   135

---

[20]   *gossip* talkative old lady.
[21]   *Wel-a – wel-a-day* Keats is probably recalling Coleridge, *Christabel* 252.
[22]   *by the holy loom . . . piously* The Feast of St Agnes is celebrated by the presentation and blessing of two unshorn sheep, whose wool is woven by nuns.
[23]   *liege-lord* master.
[24]   *the conjuror plays* Madeline is attempting to conjure visions of her future husband.

[25]   *Good angels her deceive* let angels send her instead good dreams.
[26]   *mickle* much.
[27]   *brook* restrain.
[28]   *enchantments cold* if Madeline is successful she will see only cold visions, not a living being.

XVI

Sudden a thought came like a full-blown rose,
Flushing his brow, and in his pained heart
Made purple riot;[29] then doth he propose
A stratagem that makes the beldame start:
'A cruel man and impious thou art –   140
Sweet lady, let her pray, and sleep, and dream
Alone with her good angels, far apart
From wicked men like thee. Go, go! I deem
Thou canst not surely be the same that thou didst seem.'

XVII

'I will not harm her, by all saints I swear',   145
Quoth Porphyro, 'Oh may I ne'er find grace
When my weak voice shall whisper its last prayer,
If one of her soft ringlets I displace,
Or look with ruffian passion in her face;
Good Angela, believe me by these tears,   150
Or I will, even in a moment's space,
Awake, with horrid shout, my foemen's ears,
And beard[30] them, though they be more fanged than wolves and bears.'

XVIII

'Ah, why wilt thou affright a feeble soul?
A poor, weak, palsy-stricken, churchyard thing,   155
Whose passing-bell[31] may ere the midnight toll;
Whose prayers for thee, each morn and evening,
Were never missed!' Thus plaining, doth she bring
A gentler speech from burning Porphyro;
So woeful, and of such deep sorrowing,   160
That Angela gives promise she will do
Whatever he shall wish, betide her weal or woe[32] –

XIX

Which was to lead him, in close secrecy,
Even to Madeline's chamber, and there hide
Him in a closet, of such privacy   165
That he might see her beauty unespied,
And win perhaps that night a peerless bride,
While legioned fairies paced the coverlet
And pale enchantment held her sleepy-eyed.
Never on such a night have lovers met,   170
Since Merlin paid his Demon all the monstrous debt.[33]

---

29 *Made purple riot* i.e. made his heart beat excitedly.
30 *beard* defy.
31 *passing-bell* death-bell.
32 *betide her weal or woe* whether good or ill befalls her.

33 *Since Merlin . . . debt* the precise reference of this line has puzzled commentators. Merlin was the son of a Welsh princess and a demon-father, from whom he inherited his magical powers.

XX

'It shall be as thou wishest', said the Dame,
'All cates[34] and dainties shall be stored there
Quickly on this feast-night; by the tambour frame[35]
Her own lute thou wilt see. No time to spare,   175
For I am slow and feeble, and scarce dare
On such a catering trust my dizzy head.
Wait here, my child, with patience; kneel in prayer
The while. Ah! Thou must needs the lady wed,
Or may I never leave my grave among the dead.'   180

XXI

So saying, she hobbled off with busy fear.
The lover's endless minutes slowly passed;
The dame returned, and whispered in his ear
To follow her, with aged eyes aghast
From fright of dim espial.[36] Safe at last,   185
Through many a dusky gallery, they gain
The maiden's chamber, silken, hushed, and chaste,
Where Porphyro took covert,[37] pleased amain.
His poor guide hurried back with agues in her brain.

XXII

Her falt'ring hand upon the balustrade,   190
Old Angela was feeling for the stair,
When Madeline, St Agnes' charmed maid,[38]
Rose, like a missioned spirit, unaware.
With silver taper's light, and pious care,
She turned, and down the aged gossip led   195
To a safe level matting. Now prepare,
Young Porphyro, for gazing on that bed:
She comes, she comes again, like ring-dove frayed[39] and fled.

XXIII

Out went the taper as she hurried in;
Its little smoke, in pallid moonshine, died.   200
She closed the door, she panted, all akin
To spirits of the air, and visions wide –
No uttered syllable, or woe betide![40]
But to her heart, her heart was voluble,[41]
Paining with eloquence her balmy[42] side,   205
As though a tongueless nightingale should swell
Her throat in vain, and die, heart-stifled, in her dell.

---

[34] *cates* delicacies.
[35] *tambour frame* embroidery frame.
[36] *aghast / From fright of dim espial* terrified of not being able
to see the dangers around them.
[37] *took covert* hid himself.
[38] *maid* maiden.

[39] *frayed* frightened.
[40] *No uttered syllable, or woe betide* if she speaks she will break
the spell.
[41] *voluble* beating fast with excitement.
[42] *balmy* soft and fragrant.

XXIV

A casement high and triple-arched there was,
All garlanded with carven imag'ries[43]
Of fruits, and flowers, and bunches of knot-grass,   210
And diamonded with panes of quaint device,
Innumerable of stains and splendid dyes,
As are the tiger-moth's deep-damasked wings;
And in the midst, 'mong thousand heraldries,
And twilight saints, and dim emblazonings,   215
A shielded scutcheon[44] blushed with blood of queens and kings.

XXV

Full on this casement[45] shone the wintry moon,
And threw warm gules[46] on Madeline's fair breast,
As down she knelt for heaven's grace and boon;[47]
Rose-bloom fell on her hands, together pressed,   220
And on her silver cross soft amethyst,
And on her hair a glory,[48] like a saint:
She seemed a splendid angel, newly dressed,
Save wings, for heaven. Porphyro grew faint;
She knelt, so pure a thing, so free from mortal taint.   225

XXVI

Anon his heart revives; her vespers[49] done,
Of all its wreathed pearls her hair she frees,
Unclasps her warmed jewels one by one,
Loosens her fragrant bodice – by degrees
Her rich attire creeps rustling to her knees.   230
Half-hidden, like a mermaid in seaweed,
Pensive awhile she dreams awake, and sees
In fancy, fair St Agnes in her bed,
But dares not look behind, or all the charm is fled.

XXVII

Soon, trembling in her soft and chilly nest,   235
In sort of wakeful swoon, perplexed she lay,
Until the poppied warmth of sleep oppressed
Her soothed limbs, and soul fatigued away –
Flown like a thought, until the morrow-day,
Blissfully havened both from joy and pain,   240
Clasped like a missal where swart paynims pray;[50]
Blinded alike from sunshine and from rain,
As though a rose should shut, and be a bud again.

---

43 *imag'ries* designs.
44 *shielded scutcheon* coat-of-arms with royal quarterings on a field of gules.
45 *casement* window.
46 *gules* red light.

47 *boon* blessing.
48 *glory* halo.
49 *vespers* evening prayers.
50 *Clasped like a missal where swart paynims pray* clasped like a prayer-book carried by a believer through a pagan country.

XXVIII

Stol'n to this paradise, and so entranced,
Porphyro gazed upon her empty dress,   245
And listened to her breathing, if it chanced
To wake into a slumberous tenderness;
Which when he heard, that minute did he bless,
And breathed himself, then from the closet crept,
Noiseless as fear in a wide wilderness –   250
And over the hushed carpet, silent stepped
And 'tween the curtains peeped, where lo! – how fast she slept.

XXIX

Then by the bedside, where the faded moon
Made a dim, silver twilight, soft he set
A table, and, half anguished, threw thereon   255
A cloth of woven crimson, gold, and jet.
Oh for some drowsy Morphean amulet![51]
The boisterous, midnight, festive clarion,[52]
The kettle-drum, and far-heard clarionet,
Affray his ears, though but in dying tone;   260
The hall door shuts again, and all the noise is gone.

XXX

And still she slept an azure-lidded sleep
In blanched linen, smooth and lavendered,
While he from forth the closet brought a heap
Of candied apple, quince, and plum, and gourd;[53]   265
With jellies soother[54] than the creamy curd,
And lucent syrups tinct with cinnamon;[55]
Manna[56] and dates, in argosy[57] transferred
From Fez;[58] and spiced dainties, every one
From silken Samarcand to cedared Lebanon.   270

XXXI

These delicates he heaped with glowing hand
On golden dishes and in baskets bright
Of wreathed silver; sumptuous they stand
In the retired quiet of the night,
Filling the chilly room with perfume light.   275
'And now, my love, my seraph fair, awake!
Thou art my heaven, and I thine eremite.[59]
Open thine eyes, for meek St Agnes' sake,
Or I shall drowse beside thee, so my soul doth ache.'

---

[51] *Morphean amulet* sleeping pill.
[52] *clarion* trumpet.
[53] *gourd* melon.
[54] *soother* more soothing.
[55] *lucent syrups tinct with cinnamon* clear syrups flavoured with cinnamon.

[56] *Manna* probably an exotic fruit.
[57] *argosy* large merchant ship.
[58] *Fez* in northern Morocco.
[59] *eremite* hermit.

XXXII

Thus whispering, his warm, unnerved[60] arm   280
Sank in her pillow. Shaded was her dream
By the dusk curtains; 'twas a midnight charm
Impossible to melt as iced stream.
The lustrous salvers in the moonlight gleam,
Broad golden fringe[61] upon the carpet lies;   285
It seemed he never, never could redeem
From such a steadfast spell his lady's eyes;
So mused awhile, entoiled in woofed[62] fantasies.

XXXIII

Awakening up, he took her hollow lute;
Tumultuous, and, in chords that tenderest be,   290
He played an ancient ditty, long since mute,
In Provence called, 'La belle dame sans mercy',[63]
Close to her ear touching the melody –
Wherewith disturbed, she uttered a soft moan.
He ceased – she panted quick – and suddenly   295
Her blue affrayed[64] eyes wide open shone;
Upon his knees he sank, pale as smooth-sculptured stone.

XXXIV

Her eyes were open, but she still beheld,
Now wide awake, the vision of her sleep –
There was a painful change, that nigh expelled   300
The blisses of her dream so pure and deep.
At which fair Madeline began to weep
And moan forth witless words with many a sigh,
While still her gaze on Porphyro would keep;
Who knelt, with joined hands and piteous eye,   305
Fearing to move or speak, she looked so dreamingly.

XXXV

'Ah, Porphyro!' said she, 'but even now
Thy voice was at sweet tremble in mine ear,
Made tuneable with every sweetest vow,
And those sad eyes were spiritual[65] and clear.   310
How changed thou art! How pallid, chill, and drear!
Give me that voice again, my Porphyro,
Those looks immortal, those complainings dear!
Oh leave me not in this eternal woe,
For if thou diest, my love, I know not where to go.'   315

---

60 *unnerved* weak.
61 *golden fringe* of the tablecloth.
62 *woofed* woven.
63 *La belle dame sans mercy* title of a poem by Alain Chartier,
1424. Keats's poem of the same name is on pp. 1054–6.
64 *affrayed* startled.
65 *spiritual* lacking bodily substance.

XXXVI

Beyond a mortal man impassioned far
At these voluptuous accents, he arose
Ethereal, flushed, and like a throbbing star
Seen mid the sapphire heaven's deep repose;
Into her dream he melted, as the rose   320
Blendeth its odour with the violet –
Solution sweet.[66] Meantime the frost-wind blows
Like love's alarum pattering the sharp sleet
Against the window-panes; St Agnes' moon hath set.

XXXVII

'Tis dark; quick pattereth the flaw-blown sleet.[67]   325
'This is no dream, my bride, my Madeline!'
'Tis dark; the iced gusts still rave and beat.
'No dream, alas! Alas, and woe is mine!
Porphyro will leave me here to fade and pine.
Cruel! What traitor could thee hither bring?   330
I curse not, for my heart is lost in thine,
Though thou forsakest a deceived thing,
A dove forlorn and lost with sick unpruned[68] wing.'

XXXVIII

'My Madeline! Sweet dreamer! Lovely bride!
Say, may I be for aye thy vassal blessed?   335
Thy beauty's shield, heart-shaped and vermeil dyed?
Ah, silver shrine, here will I take my rest
After so many hours of toil and quest,
A famished pilgrim, saved by miracle.
Though I have found, I will not rob thy nest,   340
Saving of thy sweet self – if thou think'st well
To trust, fair Madeline, to no rude infidel.

XXXIX

Hark! 'Tis an elfin-storm from fairy land,
Of haggard seeming,[69] but a boon[70] indeed.
Arise, arise! The morning is at hand;   345
The bloated wassaillers will never heed.
Let us away, my love, with happy speed;
There are no ears to hear, or eyes to see,
Drowned all in Rhenish[71] and the sleepy mead.

---

[66] The revised version of lines 314–22 reads:
See, while she speaks, his arms encroaching slow,
Have zoned her, heart to heart – loud, loud the dark
                                              winds blow!

For on the midnight came a tempest fell;
More sooth, for that his quick rejoinder flows
Into her burning ear – and still the spell
Unbroken guards her in serene repose.
With her wild dream he mingled, as a rose

Marryeth its odour to a violet.
Still, still she dreams; louder the frost-wind blows . . .
For Woodhouse's comment on the stanza, see p. 818, above.
[67] *flaw-blown sleet* sleet blown by a sudden, tempestuous gust of wind.
[68] *unpruned* unpreened.
[69] *haggard seeming* wild appearance.
[70] *boon* blessing.
[71] *Rhenish* wine from the Rhine valley.

Awake! Arise, my love, and fearless be,   350
For o'er the southern moors I have a home for thee.'

XL

She hurried at his words, beset with fears,
For there were sleeping dragons[72] all around,
At glaring watch, perhaps, with ready spears;
Down the wide stairs a darkling[73] way they found.   355
In all the house was heard no human sound;
A chain-drooped lamp was flickering by each door;
The arras,[74] rich with horseman, hawk, and hound
Fluttered in the besieging wind's uproar,
And the long carpets rose along the gusty floor.   360

XLI

They glide, like phantoms, into the wide hall;
Like phantoms to the iron porch they glide,
Where lay the porter, in uneasy sprawl,
With a huge empty flagon by his side;
The wakeful bloodhound rose and shook his hide,   365
But his sagacious eye an inmate owns.
By one, and one, the bolts full easy slide,
The chains lie silent on the footworn stones –
The key turns, and the door upon its hinges groans.

XLII

And they are gone – aye, ages long ago   370
These lovers fled away into the storm.
That night the Baron dreamt of many a woe,
And all his warrior-guests, with shade and form
Of witch and demon, and large coffin-worm,
Were long be-nightmared. Angela the old   375
Died palsy-twitched,[75] with meagre face deform;
The beadsman, after thousand aves told,
For aye unsought for, slept among his ashes cold.

Journal-Letter from John Keats to George and Georgiana Keats, 14 February to 3 May 1819 (extracts)[1]

[16 April 1819] Last Sunday I took a walk towards Highgate and, in the lane that winds by the side of Lord Mansfield's park, I met Mr Green, our demonstrator at Guy's, in conversation with Coleridge.[2] I joined them, after enquiring by a look whether it would be agreeable. I walked with

---

72 *dragons* dragoons.
73 *darkling* dark.
74 *arras* tapestry.
75 *Angela ... palsy-twitched* for Woodhouse's view of this, see
p. 818.

JOURNAL-LETTER FROM JOHN KEATS TO GEORGE AND GEORGIANA
KEATS
1   The lengthy journal-letter from which these two extracts
are taken is one of Keats's most entertaining and illuminating.
2   Coleridge's account of this meeting can be found on p.
549. It took place in the grounds of Kenwood House, seat of
William Murray, Lord Mansfield (1705–93). Joseph Henry
Green (1791–1863) was Coleridge's literary executor, and had
been Keats's demonstrator at Guy's Hospital, 1815–16.

him at his alderman[3]-after-dinner pace for near two miles, I suppose. In those two miles he broached a thousand things; let me see if I can give you a list. Nightingales, poetry – on poetical sensation – metaphysics – different genera and species of dreams – nightmare – a dream accompanied by a sense of touch – single and double touch – a dream related – first and second consciousness – the difference explained between will and volition – so many metaphysicians from a want of smoking – the second consciousness – monsters – the kraken[4] – mermaids – Southey believes in them – Southey's belief too much diluted – a ghost story – Good morning – I heard his voice as he came towards me – I heard it as he moved away – I had heard it all the interval (if it may be called so). He was civil enough to ask me to call on him at Highgate[5] goodnight! It looks so much like rain I shall not go to town to day, but put it off till tomorrow. . . .

[21 April 1819][1] Do you not see how necessary a world of pains and troubles is to school an intelligence and make it a soul, a place where the heart must feel and suffer in a thousand diverse ways? Not merely is the heart a horn-book,[2] it is the mind's Bible, it is the mind's experience, it is the teat from which the mind or intelligence sucks its identity. As various as the lives of men are, so various become their souls, and thus does God make individual beings, souls, identical souls of the sparks of his own essence. This appears to me a faint sketch of a system of salvation which does not affront our reason and humanity; I am convinced that many difficulties which Christians labour under would vanish before it.

There is one which even now strikes me: the salvation of children. In them the spark or intelligence returns to God without any identity, it having had no time to learn of, and be altered by, the heart – or seat of the human passions. It is pretty generally suspected that the Christian scheme has been copied from the ancient Persian and Greek philosophers. Why may they not have made this simple thing even more simple for common apprehension, by introducing mediators and personages in the same manner as in the heathen mythology abstractions are personified? Seriously, I think it probable that this system of soul-making may have been the parent of all the more palpable and personal schemes of redemption, among the Zoroastrians, the Christians, and the Hindus. For as one part of the human species must have their carved Jupiter, so another part must have the palpable and named mediator and saviour – their Christ, their Oromanes, and their Vishnu.

If what I have said should not be plain enough, as I fear it may not be, I will put you in the place where I began in this series of thoughts. I mean, I began by seeing how man was formed by circumstances – and what are circumstances, but touchstones[3] of his heart? And what are touchstones, but provings of his heart? And what are provings of his heart, but fortifiers or alterers of his nature? And what is his altered nature, but his soul? And what was his soul before it came into the world and had these provings and alterations and perfectionings? An intelligence without identity – and how is this identity to be made? Through the medium of the heart? And how is the heart to become this medium, but in a world of circumstances?

La Belle Dame Sans Merci: A Ballad (composed 21 or 28 April 1819; edited from MS)

I

Oh what can ail thee, knight-at-arms,
Alone and palely loitering?
The sedge has withered from the lake,
And no birds sing.

---

[3] *alderman* in London, the chief officer of a ward. Keats's point is that aldermen tend to obesity from too many City banquets; cf. p. 805 n. 114.
[4] *kraken* mythical sea-monster of enormous size.
[5] Coleridge was at this time resident at Highgate in north London, at the home of Dr James Gillman.

21 APRIL 1819
[1] For useful comment on this important letter see John Barnard, *John Keats* (Cambridge, 1987), pp. 134–5.

[2] *horn-book* a leaf of paper containing the alphabet (often with the addition of the ten digits, some elements of spelling, and the Lord's Prayer) protected by a thin plate of translucent horn, and mounted on a tablet of wood with a projecting piece for a handle.
[3] *touchstone* anything that can be used to test the authenticity of something else.

2

Oh what can ail thee, knight-at-arms,   5
    So haggard and so woe-begone?
The squirrel's granary is full,
    And the harvest's done.

3

I see a lily on thy brow
    With anguish moist and fever dew,   10
And on thy cheeks a fading rose
    Fast withereth too.

4

I met a lady in the meads,
    Full beautiful – a fairy's child;
Her hair was long, her foot was light,   15
    And her eyes were wild.

5

I made a garland for her head,
    And bracelets too, and fragrant zone;[1]
She looked at me as she did love,
    And made sweet moan.   20

6

I set her on my pacing steed,
    And nothing else saw all day long,
For sidelong would she bend, and sing
    A fairy's song.

7

She found me roots of relish sweet,   25
    And honey wild and manna dew,
And sure in language strange she said,
    'I love thee true'.

8

She took me to her elfin grot
    And there she wept, and sighed full sore,   30
And there I shut her wild wild eyes
    With kisses four.

9

And there she lulled me asleep,
    And there I dreamed – ah, woe betide! –
The latest dream I ever dreamed   35
    On the cold hill's side.

La Belle Dame Sans Merci: A Ballad
[1] *fragrant zone* belt made out of flowers.

10

I saw pale kings and princes too,
  Pale warriors, death-pale were they all;
They cried, 'La belle dame sans merci
  Hath thee in thrall!'   40

11

I saw their starved lips in the gloam
  With horrid warning gaped wide,
And I awoke and found me here
  On the cold hill's side.

12

And this is why I sojourn here,   45
  Alone and palely loitering,
Though the sedge is withered from the lake,
  And no birds sing.

Ode to Psyche (composed 21–30 April 1819)[1]

From LAMIA, ISABELLA, THE EVE OF ST AGNES, AND OTHER POEMS (1820)

Oh goddess! Hear these tuneless numbers,[2] wrung
  By sweet enforcement and remembrance dear,
And pardon that thy secrets should be sung
  Even into thine own soft-conchèd[3] ear.
Surely I dreamt today, or did I see   5
  The winged Psyche with awakened eyes?
    I wandered in a forest thoughtlessly,[4]
  And, on the sudden, fainting with surprise,
Saw two fair creatures, couched side by side
  In deepest grass, beneath the whisp'ring roof   10
  Of leaves and trembled blossoms, where there ran
    A brooklet, scarce espied.
Mid hushed, cool-rooted flowers, fragrant-eyed,
  Blue, silver-white, and budded Tyrian,[5]
They lay calm-breathing on the bedded grass;   15
  Their arms embraced, and their pinions[6] too;
    Their lips touched not, but had not bade adieu,
  As if disjoined by soft-handed slumber,
  And ready still past kisses to outnumber
    At tender eye-dawn of aurorean love.   20

ODE TO PSYCHE

[1] According to Keats's source, Lemprière's *Bibliotheca Classica* (1788), Psyche was 'a nymph whom Cupid [Eros] married and carried to a place of bliss, where he long enjoyed her company. Venus put her to death because she had robbed the world of her son; but Jupiter, at the request of Cupid, granted immortality to Psyche. The word signifies *the soul*, and this personification of Psyche is posterior to the Augustan age, though still it is connected with ancient mythology. Psyche is generally represented with the wings of a butterfly, to intimate the lightness of the soul, of which the butterfly is the symbol, and on that account, among the ancients, when a man has just expired, a butterfly appeared fluttering above, as if rising from the mouth of the deceased.' Keats was an admirer of Mary Tighe's *Psyche* (1805), and Claude Lorrain's famous painting, 'Landscape with Psyche outside the Palace of Cupid' (1664, now at the National Gallery, London).

[2] *tuneless numbers* his poetry.

[3] *soft-conched* her ear is shaped like a conch-shell.

[4] *thoughtlessly* in a carefree manner.

[5] *Tyrian* purple, after the dye made at Tyre.

[6] *pinions* wings.

The winged boy[7] I knew;
But who wast thou, oh happy, happy dove?
His Psyche true!
Oh latest born and loveliest vision far
Of all Olympus' faded hierarchy![8]   25
Fairer than Phoebe's sapphire-regioned star,[9]
Or Vesper,[10] amorous glow-worm of the sky;
Fairer than these, though temple thou hast none,
 Nor altar heaped with flowers;
Nor virgin-choir to make delicious moan   30
 Upon the midnight hours;
No voice, no lute, no pipe, no incense sweet
 From chain-swung censer teeming;
No shrine, no grove, no oracle, no heat
 Of pale-mouthed prophet dreaming.[11]   35

Oh brightest! though too late for antique vows,
 Too, too late for the fond believing lyre,[12]
When holy were the haunted forest boughs,
 Holy the air, the water and the fire;
Yet even in these days so far retired   40
 From happy pieties, thy lucent fans,[13]
 Fluttering among the faint Olympians,
I see, and sing, by my own eyes inspired.
So let me be thy choir, and make a moan
 Upon the midnight hours;   45
Thy voice, thy lute, thy pipe, thy incense sweet
 From swinged censer teeming;
Thy shrine, thy grove, thy oracle, thy heat
 Of pale-mouthed prophet dreaming.

Yes, I will be thy priest, and build a fane[14]   50
 In some untrodden region of my mind,
Where branched thoughts, new grown with pleasant pain,
 Instead of pines shall murmur in the wind;
Far, far around shall those dark-clustered trees
 Fledge the wild-ridged mountains steep by steep;   55
And there by zephyrs, streams, and birds, and bees,
 The moss-lain dryads[15] shall be lulled to sleep;
And in the midst of this wide quietness
A rosy sanctuary will I dress
With the wreathed trellis of a working brain,   60
 With buds, and bells, and stars without a name,
 With all the gardener Fancy e'er could feign,[16]

---

7 *The winged boy* Cupid.
8 *Olympus' faded hierarchy* the gods of Olympus are faded by comparison with the beauty of Psyche.
9 *Phoebe's sapphire-regioned star* the moon, of which Phoebe is goddess.
10 *Vesper* evening star.
11 *No heat . . . dreaming* there are no prophets inspired to speak on Psyche's behalf.
12 *fond believing lyre* hymns sung by the unquestioningly devoted.
13 *lucent fans* shining wings.
14 *fane* temple.
15 *dryads* wood-nymphs.
16 *feign* invent.

Who, breeding flowers, will never breed the same:
And there shall be for thee all soft delight
    That shadowy thought can win –   65
A bright torch, and a casement[17] ope at night,
    To let the warm love in!

Ode to a Nightingale (composed May 1819)[1]

From LAMIA, ISABELLA, THE EVE OF ST AGNES, AND OTHER POEMS (1820)

1

My heart aches, and a drowsy numbness pains
    My sense, as though of hemlock[2] I had drunk,
Or emptied some dull opiate to the drains[3]
    One minute past,[4] and Lethe-wards[5] had sunk;
'Tis not through envy of thy happy lot,   5
    But being too happy in thine happiness,
        That thou, light-winged dryad[6] of the trees,
            In some melodious plot
Of beechen green, and shadows numberless,
    Singest of summer in full-throated ease.   10

[handwritten margin note: Socrates reference → death]

2

Oh for a draught of vintage![7] that hath been
    Cooled a long age in the deep-delved earth,
Tasting of flora and the country green,
    Dance, and Provençal song, and sunburnt mirth!
Oh for a beaker full of the warm south,[8]   15
    Full of the true, the blushful Hippocrene,[9]
        With beaded bubbles winking at the brim,
            And purple-stained mouth;
That I might drink, and leave the world unseen,
    And with thee fade away into the forest dim –   20

3

Fade far away, dissolve, and quite forget
    What thou among the leaves hast never known,
The weariness,[10] the fever, and the fret

---

[17]   *casement* window.

ODE TO A NIGHTINGALE

[1]   Twenty years after the event Keats's friend Charles Brown
recorded how this poem was composed: 'In the spring of 1819
a nightingale had built her nest near my house. Keats felt a
tranquil and continual joy in her song; and one morning he
took his chair from the breakfast-table to the grass-plot under
a plum-tree, where he sat for two or three hours. When he
came into the house, I perceived he had some scraps of paper
in his hand, and these he was quietly thrusting behind the
books. On enquiry, I found those scraps, four or five in num-
ber, contained his poetic feeling on the song of our nightin-
gale. The writing was not well legible; and it was difficult to
arrange the stanzas on so many scraps. With his assistance I

succeeded, and this was his "Ode to a Nightingale", a poem
which has been the delight of everyone' (*Keats Circle* ii 65).
[2]   *hemlock* can be used as a sedative; it should be noted that
Keats is not saying that he has actually taken hemlock.
[3]   *drains* dregs.
[4]   *past* ago.
[5]   *Lethe-wards* towards Lethe, river of forgetfulness in Hades,
from which souls drank to forget their past lives.
[6]   *dryad* wood-nymph.
[7]   *vintage* wine.
[8]   *warm south* wine from the Mediterranean.
[9]   *Hippocrene* spring sacred to the muses on Mt Helicon.
Keats means wine.
[10]   *weariness* Wordsworth had written of 'hours of weariness'
amid the 'din / Of towns and cities' in *Tintern Abbey* 26–8.

Here, where men sit and hear each other groan;
　Where palsy shakes a few, sad, last grey hairs,　　　　　　　　25
　　Where youth grows pale, and spectre-thin, and dies;[11]
　　　Where but to think is to be full of sorrow
　　　　And leaden-eyed despairs;
　　Where Beauty cannot keep her lustrous eyes,
　　　Or new Love pine at them beyond tomorrow.　　　　　　　　30

4

Away! Away! For I will fly to thee,
　Not charioted by Bacchus and his pards,[12]
But on the viewless[13] wings of Poesy,
　Though the dull brain perplexes and retards;
Already with thee! Tender is the night,　　　　　　　　　　　35
　And haply[14] the Queen Moon is on her throne,
　　Clustered around by all her starry fays;[15]
　　　But here there is no light　*nerc - in the shiny*
Save what from heaven is with the breezes blown　　　*world*
　　Through verdurous glooms and winding mossy ways.　　　40

5

I cannot see what flowers are at my feet,
　Nor what soft incense hangs upon the boughs,
But, in embalmed darkness,[16] guess each sweet
　Wherewith the seasonable month[17] endows
The grass, the thicket, and the fruit-tree wild,　　　　　　　45
　White hawthorn, and the pastoral eglantine,
　　Fast-fading violets covered up in leaves,
　　　And mid-May's eldest child,
　The coming musk-rose,[18] full of dewy wine,
　　The murmurous haunt of flies on summer eves.　　　　　　50

6

Darkling[19] I listen; and for many a time
　I have been half in love with easeful Death,
Called him soft names in many a mused rhyme,
　To take into the air my quiet breath;
Now more than ever seems it rich to die,　　　　　　　　　55
　To cease upon the midnight with no pain,
　　While thou art pouring forth thy soul abroad
　　　In such an ecstasy!
　Still wouldst thou sing, and I have ears in vain –
　　To thy high requiem become a sod.　　　　　　　　　　60

---

[11] *Where youth . . . dies* often interpreted as a reference to the death of Tom Keats from consumption, 1 December 1818. Cf. Wordsworth, *Excursion* iv 760: 'While man grows old, and dwindles, and decays'.
[12] *Not charioted by Bacchus and his pards* Keats's source, Lemprière's *Bibliotheca Classica* (1788), recorded that when Bacchus (god of wine) travelled east, he 'was drawn in a chariot by a lion and a tyger and was accompanied by Pan and Silenus and all the satyrs'.

[13] *viewless* invisible.
[14] *haply* perhaps.
[15] *fays* fairies.
[16] *embalmed darkness* the night is full of the scent of plants.
[17] *the seasonable month* May.
[18] *The coming musk-rose* usually flowers in June.
[19] *Darkling* in darkness.

7

Thou wast not born for death, immortal bird!
    No hungry generations tread thee down;
The voice I hear this passing night was heard
    In ancient days by emperor and clown:[20]
Perhaps the self-same song that found a path   65
    Through the sad heart of Ruth, when, sick for home,
        She stood in tears amid the alien corn;[21]
            The same that oft-times hath
    Charmed magic casements, opening on the foam
        Of perilous seas, in fairy lands forlorn.   70

8

Forlorn! The very word is like a bell
    To toll me back from thee to my sole self!
Adieu! The fancy cannot cheat so well
    As she is famed to do, deceiving elf.
Adieu! Adieu! Thy plaintive anthem fades   75
    Past the near meadows, over the still stream,
        Up the hillside, and now 'tis buried deep
            In the next valley-glades:
    Was it a vision, or a waking dream?
        Fled is that music – do I wake or sleep?   80

Ode on a Grecian Urn (composed *c.* May 1819)[1]

From LAMIA, ISABELLA, THE EVE OF ST AGNES, AND OTHER POEMS (1820)

1

Thou still unravished bride of quietness,
    Thou foster-child of silence and slow time,[2]
Sylvan historian,[3] who canst thus express
    A flowery tale more sweetly than our rhyme –
What leaf-fringed legend haunts about thy shape   5
    Of deities or mortals, or of both,
        In Tempe or the dales of Arcady?[4]
    What men or gods are these? What maidens loath?
What mad pursuit? What struggle to escape?
        What pipes and timbrels?[5] What wild ecstasy?   10

2

Heard melodies are sweet, but those unheard
    Are sweeter; therefore, ye soft pipes, play on –

---

[20] *clown* peasant.
[21] *Through the . . . corn* Ruth was forced, by famine, to leave
home and labour in the fields of her kinsman, Boaz (Ruth
2:1–2).

ODE ON A GRECIAN URN
[1] The inspiration for this poem came from a variety of
sources, including the Townley Vase at the British Museum
and the Elgin Marbles (reproduced Woof and Hebron, *John
Keats* (Grasmere, 1995), pp. 128–30).

[2] *foster-child of silence and slow time* the potter who made the
vase is dead, leaving it to be fostered by time and silence.
[3] *Sylvan historian* the vase is a historian because it tells a
story; 'sylvan' refers to the pastoral scenes it depicts.
[4] Tempe and Arcadia, places known in classical times for
their beauty and the happiness of their inhabitants.
[5] *timbrels* tambourines.

Not to the sensual ear,[6] but, more endeared,
    Pipe to the spirit ditties of no tone:
Fair youth, beneath the trees, thou canst not leave   15
    Thy song, nor ever can those trees be bare;
        Bold lover, never, never canst thou kiss,
Though winning near the goal – yet do not grieve;
    She cannot fade, though thou hast not thy bliss,
        For ever wilt thou love, and she be fair!   20

3

Ah, happy, happy boughs! that cannot shed
    Your leaves, nor ever bid the spring adieu;
And, happy melodist, unwearied,
    For ever piping songs for ever new;
More happy love, more happy, happy love!   25
    For ever warm and still to be enjoyed,
    For ever panting and for ever young;
All breathing human passion far above,[7]
    That leaves a heart high-sorrowful and cloyed,
        A burning forehead, and a parching tongue.   30

4

Who are these coming to the sacrifice?
    To what green altar, oh mysterious priest,
Lead'st thou that heifer lowing at the skies,
    And all her silken flanks with garlands dressed?
What little town by river or seashore,   35
    Or mountain-built with peaceful citadel,
        Is emptied of this folk, this pious morn?
And, little town, thy streets for evermore
    Will silent be, and not a soul to tell
        Why thou art desolate, can e'er return.   40

5

Oh Attic[8] shape! Fair attitude! With brede[9]
    Of marble men and maidens overwrought,[10]
With forest branches and the trodden weed;
    Thou, silent form, dost tease us out of thought
As doth eternity. Cold Pastoral!   45
    When old age shall this generation waste,
        Thou shalt remain, in midst of other woe
Than ours, a friend to man, to whom thou say'st,
    Beauty is truth, truth beauty'; that is all
        Ye know on earth, and all ye need to know.   50

---

[6] *sensual ear* physical ear.
[7] *All breathing . . . above* Compare Hazlitt's remarks on Greek statuary, 'On Gusto', p. 599.
[8] *Attic* Grecian.
[9] *brede* braid.
[10] *overwrought* fashioned over the surface of the urn.

Ode on Melancholy (composed *c.* May 1819)[1]

From LAMIA, ISABELLA, THE EVE OF ST AGNES, AND OTHER POEMS (1820)

1

No, no, go not to Lethe, neither twist
    Wolfsbane,[2] tight-rooted, for its poisonous wine;
Nor suffer thy pale forehead to be kissed
    By nightshade,[3] ruby grape of Proserpine;[4]
Make not your rosary of yew-berries,[5]   5
    Nor let the beetle, nor the death-moth[6] be
        Your mournful Psyche, nor the downy owl
A partner in your sorrow's mysteries;
    For shade to shade will come too drowsily,
        And drown the wakeful anguish of the soul.   10

2

But when the melancholy fit shall fall
    Sudden from heaven like a weeping cloud,
That fosters the droop-headed flowers all,
    And hides the green hill in an April shroud;
Then glut thy sorrow on[7] a morning rose,   15
    Or on the rainbow of the salt sand-wave,
        Or on the wealth of globed peonies;
Or if thy mistress some rich anger shows,
    Imprison her soft hand, and let her rave,
        And feed deep, deep upon her peerless eyes.   20

3

She dwells with Beauty – Beauty that must die;
    And Joy, whose hand is ever at his lips
Bidding adieu; and aching Pleasure nigh,
    Turning to poison while the bee-mouth sips.
Aye, in the very temple of Delight   25
    Veiled Melancholy has her sovran shrine,
        Though seen of none save him whose strenuous tongue
Can burst Joy's grape against his palate fine;
    His soul shall taste the sadness of her might,
        And be among her cloudy trophies hung.   30

ODE ON MELANCHOLY
1 A cancelled opening stanza in MS reads:
    Though you should build a bark of dead men's bones,
    And rear a phantom gibbet for a mast,
    Stitch creeds together for a sail, with groans
    To fill it out, bloodstained and aghast;
    Although your rudder be a dragon's tail,
    Long severed, yet still hard with agony,
    Your cordage large uprootings from the skull
    Of bald Medusa, certes you would fail
    To find the Melancholy – whether she
    Dreameth in any isle of Lethe dull.

2 *Wolfsbane* aconite, a poisonous plant.
3 *nightshade* poisonous plant with bright red berries.
4 *Proserpine* Queen of the Underworld.
5 *yew-berries* yew-trees have small red berries which are poisonous.
6 *death-moth* the death's head moth has markings which resemble a human skull.
7 *glut . . . on* enjoy to the full . . . by thinking of.

Ode on Indolence (composed between 19 March and 9 June 1819; edited from MS)[1]

They toil not, neither do they spin.[2]

1

One morn before me were three figures seen,
    With bowed necks and joined hands, side-faced;
And one behind the other stepped serene,
    In placid sandals and in white robes graced;
They passed, like figures on a marble urn,   5
    When shifted round to see the other side;
        They came again, as when the urn once more
Is shifted round, the first-seen shades return –
    And they were strange to me, as may betide
        With vases, to one deep in Phidian lore.[3]   10

2

How is it, shadows, that I knew ye not?
    How came ye muffled in so hush[4] a masque?[5]
Was it a silent deep-disguised plot
    To steal away, and leave without a task
My idle days? Ripe was the drowsy hour;   15
    The blissful cloud of summer indolence
        Benumbed my eyes; my pulse grew less and less;
Pain had no sting, and pleasure's wreath no flower –
    Oh why did ye not melt, and leave my sense
        Unhaunted quite of all but – nothingness?   20

3

A third time passed they by, and, passing, turned
    Each one the face a moment whiles to me;
Then faded, and to follow them I burned
    And ached for wings, because I knew the three:
The first was a fair maid, and Love her name;   25
    The second was Ambition, pale of cheek
        And ever watchful with fatigued eye;
The last, whom I love more, the more of blame
    Is heaped upon her, maiden most unmeek,
        I knew to be my demon Poesy.   30

4

They faded, and, forsooth, I wanted wings!
    Oh folly! What is love? And where is it?
And, for that poor ambition – it springs
    From a man's little heart's short fever-fit;[6]
For Poesy! No, she has not a joy –   35

ODE ON INDOLENCE

1 This poem was not included in Keats's 1820 volume.
2 Matthew 6:28: 'Consider the lilies of the field, how they grow; they toil not, neither do they spin.'
3 *Phidian lore* sculpture; Phidias (born *c*.500 BC) may have designed and probably supervised construction of the Elgin marbles.

4 *hush* silent.
5 *masque* procession.
6 *fever-fit* an echo of *Macbeth* III ii 23: 'After life's fitful fever he sleeps well'.

At least for me – so sweet as drowsy noons,
    And evenings steeped in honeyed indolence.
Oh for an age so sheltered from annoy,[7]
    That I may never know how change the moons,
    Or hear the voice of busy common sense!   40

5

A third time came they by – alas, wherefore?
    My sleep had been embroidered with dim dreams;
My soul had been a lawn besprinkled o'er
    With flowers, and stirring shades, and baffled beams;
The morn was clouded, but no shower fell,   45
    Though in her lids hung the sweet tears of May;
    The open casement pressed a new-leaved vine,
    Let in the budding warmth and throstle's lay –
Oh shadows, 'twas a time to bid farewell!
    Upon your skirts had fallen no tears of mine.   50

6

So ye three ghosts, adieu! Ye cannot raise
    My head cool-bedded in the flowery grass,
For I would not be dieted with praise –
    A pet-lamb in a sentimental farce![8]
Fade softly from my eyes, and be once more   55
    In masque-like figures on the dreamy urn;
    Farewell! I yet have visions for the night,
And for the day faint visions there is store.
    Vanish, ye phantoms, from my idle sprite,
    Into the clouds, and never more return!   60

Lamia (Part I written *c.* 28 June and 11 July 1819, whole poem completed between 12 August and *c.* 5 September 1819, revised March 1820)[1]

From LAMIA, ISABELLA, THE EVE OF ST AGNES, AND OTHER POEMS (1820)

Part I

Upon a time, before the fairy broods
Drove nymph and satyr from the prosperous woods,[2]

---

[7] *annoy* harm.

[8] *For I would not ... farce* Keats is saying that praise from reviewers is worthless – as patronizing as the stroking of a lamb.

LAMIA (PART I)

[1] When the poem was printed in 1820, Keats added a note providing the source for this poem: ' "Philostratus, in his fourth book *de Vita Apollonii*, hath a memorable instance in this kind, which I may not omit, of one Menippus Lycius, a young man twenty-five years of age, that going betwixt Cenchreas and Corinth, met such a phantasm in the habit of a fair gentlewoman, which taking him by the hand, carried him home to her house in the suburbs of Corinth, and told him she was a Phoenician by birth, and if he would tarry with her, he should hear her sing and play, and drink such wine as never any drank, and no man should molest him; but she, being fair and lovely, would live and die with him, that was fair and lovely to behold. The young man, a philosopher, otherwise staid and discreet, able to moderate his passions, though not this of love, tarried with her a while to his great content, and at last married her, to whose wedding, amongst other guests, came Apollonius; who, by some probable conjectures, found her out to be a serpent, a lamia; and that all her furniture was, like Tantalus' gold, described by Homer, no substance but mere illusions. When she saw herself descried, she wept, and desired Apollonius to be silent, but he would not be moved, and thereupon she, plate, house, and all that was in it, vanished in an instant: many thousands took notice of this fact, for it was done in the midst of Greece." Burton's *Anatomy of Melancholy* Part 3. Sect. 2. Memb. 1. Subs. 1'.

[2] *prosperous woods* the woods were more widespread than now.

Before King Oberon's bright diadem,
Sceptre, and mantle, clasped with dewy gem,
Frighted away the dryads[3] and the fauns   5
From rushes green, and brakes, and cowslipped lawns,[4]
The ever-smitten Hermes[5] empty left
His golden throne, bent warm on amorous theft.
From high Olympus had he stolen light
On this side of Jove's clouds, to escape the sight   10
Of his great summoner, and made retreat
Into a forest on the shores of Crete,
For somewhere in that sacred island[6] dwelt
A nymph to whom all hoofed satyrs knelt,
At whose white feet the languid Tritons[7] poured   15
Pearls, while on land they withered and adored.
Fast by the springs where she to bathe was wont,
And in those meads where sometime she might haunt,
Were strewn rich gifts, unknown to any muse,[8]
Though fancy's casket were unlocked to choose.   20
'Ah, what a world of love was at her feet!'
So Hermes thought, and a celestial heat
Burnt from his winged heels to either ear,
That from a whiteness, as the lily clear,
Blushed into roses mid his golden hair,   25
Fallen in jealous curls about his shoulders bare.
    From vale to vale, from wood to wood, he flew,
Breathing upon the flowers his passion new,
And wound with many a river to its head
To find where this sweet nymph prepared her secret bed –   30
In vain; the sweet nymph might nowhere be found.
And so he rested on the lonely ground,
Pensive, and full of painful jealousies
Of the wood-gods, and even the very trees.
There as he stood, he heard a mournful voice,   35
Such as once heard, in gentle heart, destroys
All pain but pity. Thus the lone voice spake:
'When from this wreathed tomb shall I awake?
When move in a sweet body fit for life
And love and pleasure, and the ruddy strife   40
Of hearts and lips? Ah, miserable me!'
The god, dove-footed, glided silently
Round bush and tree, soft-brushing, in his speed,
The taller grasses and full-flowering weed,
Until he found a palpitating snake,   45
Bright, and cirque-couchant[9] in a dusky brake.
    She was a gordian[10] shape of dazzling hue,
Vermilion-spotted, golden, green, and blue;
Striped like a zebra, freckled like a pard,[11]

---

[3] *dryads* wood-nymphs.
[4] *before the fairy broods ... lawns* i.e. before medieval fairy-lore had superseded classical myth.
[5] *The ever-smitten Hermes* or Mercury, messenger of the gods, celebrated for his numerous love affairs.
[6] *sacred island* Crete was sacred as the birthplace of Zeus.

[7] *Tritons* sea-gods – half-man, half-fish.
[8] *unknown to any muse* beyond the imagination of any poet.
[9] *cirque-couchant* lying in circular coils.
[10] *gordian* intricately knotted.
[11] *pard* leopard.

Eyed like a peacock, and all crimson barred;   50
And full of silver moons that, as she breathed,
Dissolved, or brighter shone, or interwreathed
Their lustres with the gloomier tapestries –
So rainbow-sided, touched with miseries,
She seemed at once some penanced lady elf,   55
Some demon's mistress, or the demon's self.
Upon her crest she wore a wannish fire
Sprinkled with stars, like Ariadne's tiar;[12]
Her head was serpent but – ah, bitter-sweet! –
She had a woman's mouth with all its pearls complete.   60
And for her eyes: what could such eyes do there
But weep and weep, that they were born so fair? –
As Proserpine[13] still weeps for her Sicilian air.
Her throat was serpent, but the words she spake
Came, as through bubbling honey, for love's sake,   65
And thus; while Hermes on his pinions lay,
Like a stooped falcon ere he takes his prey.

 'Fair Hermes, crowned with feathers, fluttering light,
I had a splendid dream of thee last night:
I saw thee sitting on a throne of gold   70
Among the gods upon Olympus old,
The only sad one – for thou didst not hear
The soft, lute-fingered Muses chaunting clear,
Nor even Apollo when he sang alone,
Deaf to his throbbing throat's long, long melodious moan.   75
I dreamt I saw thee, robed in purple flakes,[14]
Break amorous through the clouds, as morning breaks,
And, swiftly as a bright Phoebean dart,[15]
Strike for the Cretan isle – and here thou art!
Too gentle Hermes, hast thou found the maid?'   80
Whereat the star of Lethe[16] not delayed
His rosy eloquence, and thus enquired:
'Thou smooth-lipped serpent, surely high inspired!
Thou beauteous wreath, with melancholy eyes,
Possess whatever bliss thou canst devise,   85
Telling me only where my nymph is fled –
Where she doth breathe!' 'Bright planet, thou hast said',
Returned the snake, 'but seal with oaths, fair God!'
'I swear', said Hermes, 'by my serpent rod,
And by thine eyes, and by thy starry crown!'   90
Light flew his earnest words among the blossoms blown.
Then thus again the brilliance feminine:
'Too frail of heart! for this lost nymph of thine,
Free as the air, invisibly she strays
About these thornless wilds; her pleasant days   95

---

[12]   *Ariadne's tiar* Ariadne was a nymph loved by Bacchus, god of wine. He gave her a crown of seven stars which, after her death, was made into a constellation. Keats probably has in mind Titian's painting, *Bacchus and Ariadne*, in the National Gallery.

[13]   Proserpine, gathering flowers in the Vale of Enna in Sicily, was carried off by Pluto, king of the underworld, to be his queen.

[14]   *purple flakes* fleecy clouds, coloured by the sun.

[15]   *Phoebean dart* a ray of the sun, Phoebus being god of the sun.

[16]   *the star of Lethe* Hermes, so-called because he led the souls of the dead to Hades over Lethe, the river of forgetfulness.

She tastes unseen; unseen her nimble feet
Leave traces in the grass and flowers sweet;
From weary tendrils and bowed branches green
She plucks the fruit unseen, she bathes unseen:
And by my power is her beauty veiled   100
To keep it unaffronted, unassailed
By the love-glances of unlovely eyes,
Of satyrs, fauns, and bleared Silenus'[17] sighs.
Pale grew her immortality, for woe
Of all these lovers, and she grieved so   105
I took compassion on her, bade her steep
Her hair in weird syrups that would keep
Her loveliness invisible, yet free
To wander as she loves, in liberty.
Thou shalt behold her, Hermes, thou alone,   110
If thou wilt, as thou swearest, grant my boon!'
　　　Then once again, the charmed god began
An oath, and through the serpent's ears it ran
Warm, tremulous, devout, psalterian.[18]
Ravished, she lifted her Circean[19] head,   115
Blushed a live damask, and swift-lisping said:
'I was a woman, let me have once more
A woman's shape, and charming as before.
I love a youth of Corinth – oh the bliss!
Give me my woman's form, and place me where he is.   120
Stoop, Hermes, let me breathe upon thy brow,
And thou shalt see thy sweet nymph even now.'
The god on half-shut feathers sank serene,
She breathed upon his eyes, and swift was seen
Of both the guarded nymph near-smiling[20] on the green.   125
It was no dream – or say a dream it was,
Real are the dreams of gods, and smoothly pass
Their pleasures in a long immortal dream.
One warm, flushed moment, hovering, it might seem
Dashed by the wood-nymph's beauty, so he burned;   130
Then, lighting on the printless verdure, turned
To the swooned[21] serpent, and with languid arm
Delicate, put to proof the lithe caducean charm.[22]
　　　So done, upon the nymph his eyes he bent
Full of adoring tears and blandishment,   135
And towards her stepped; she, like a moon in wane,
Faded before him, cowered, nor could restrain
Her fearful sobs, self-folding like a flower
That faints into itself at evening hour.
But the god fostering her chilled hand,   140
She felt the warmth, her eyelids opened bland,
And, like new flowers at morning song of bees,

---

[17] Silenus, a demi-god of the woods, was the foster-father of Bacchus.
[18] *psalterian* like the sound of a psalter, an antique stringed instrument.
[19] *Circean* Circe was the enchantress who was capable of turning men into animals.

[20] *near-smiling* smiling nearby.
[21] *swooned* with love.
[22] *lithe caducean charm* an olive staff wound about with two intertwined ('lithe') snakes at one end.

Bloomed, and gave up her honey to the lees;[23]
Into the green-recessed woods they flew,
Nor grew they pale, as mortal lovers do.   145
        Left to herself, the serpent now began
To change; her elfin blood in madness ran,
Her mouth foamed, and the grass, therewith besprent,[24]
Withered at dew so sweet and virulent.
Her eyes in torture fixed, and anguish drear,   150
Hot, glazed, and wide, with lid-lashes all sear,[25]
Flashed phosphor and sharp sparks, without one cooling tear.
The colours all inflamed throughout her train,
She writhed about, convulsed with scarlet pain;
A deep volcanian yellow took the place   155
Of all her milder-mooned body's grace,
And, as the lava ravishes the mead,[26]
Spoilt all her silver mail, and golden brede,
Made gloom of all her frecklings, streaks and bars,
Eclipsed her crescents, and licked up her stars.   160
So that in moments few she was undressed
Of all her sapphires, greens, and amethyst,
And rubious-argent;[27] of all these bereft,
Nothing but pain and ugliness were left.
Still shone her crown – that vanished, also she   165
Melted and disappeared as suddenly,
And in the air, her new voice luting soft,
Cried, 'Lycius! Gentle Lycius!' Borne aloft
With the bright mists about the mountains hoar
These words dissolved – Crete's forests heard no more.   170
        Whither fled Lamia, now a lady bright,
A full-born beauty new and exquisite?
She fled into that valley they pass o'er
Who go to Corinth from Cenchreas' shore,
And rested at the foot of those wild hills,   175
The rugged founts of the Peraean rills,
And of that other ridge whose barren back
Stretches, with all its mist and cloudy rack,
South-westward to Cleone. There she stood
About a young bird's flutter from a wood,   180
Fair on a sloping green of mossy tread,
By a clear pool, wherein she passioned
To see herself escaped from so sore ills,
While her robes flaunted[28] with the daffodils.
        Ah, happy Lycius! For she was a maid   185
More beautiful than ever twisted braid,
Or sighed, or blushed, or on spring-flowered lea
Spread a green kirtle[29] to the minstrelsy –
A virgin purest lipped, yet in the lore
Of love deep learned to the red heart's core;   190

---

[23] *gave up her honey to the lees* surrendered totally.
[24] *besprent* sprinkled – an archaism even in Keats's day.
[25] *sear* scorched.
[26] *lava ravishes the mead* lava buries and burns the grass.

[27] *rubious-argent* silver embedded with rubies.
[28] *flaunted* waved vigorously.
[29] *kirtle* woman's gown.

Not one hour old, yet of sciential[30] brain
To unperplex bliss from its neighbour pain;
Define their pettish limits, and estrange
Their points of contact, and swift counterchange;
Intrigue with the specious chaos, and dispart   195
Its most ambiguous atoms with sure art,
As though in Cupid's college she had spent
Sweet days a lovely graduate, still unshent,[31]
And kept his rosy terms in idle languishment.

Why this fair creature chose so fairily   200
By the wayside to linger, we shall see;
But first 'tis fit to tell how she could muse
And dream, when in the serpent prison-house,
Of all she list, strange or magnificent;
How, ever, where she willed, her spirit went –   205
Whether to faint Elysium,[32] or where
Down through tress-lifting waves the nereids[33] fair
Wind into Thetis'[34] bower by many a pearly stair,
Or where god Bacchus drains his cups divine,
Stretched out at ease beneath a glutinous[35] pine,   210
Or where in Pluto's[36] gardens palatine[37]
Mulciber's columns gleam in far piazzian line.[38]
And sometimes into cities she would send
Her dream, with feast and rioting to blend;
And once, while among mortals dreaming thus,   215
She saw the young Corinthian Lycius
Charioting foremost in the envious race
Like a young Jove with calm uneager face
And fell into a swooning love of him.
Now on the moth-time[39] of that evening dim   220
He would return that way, as well she knew,
To Corinth from the shore – for freshly blew
The eastern soft wind, and his galley now
Grated the quaystones with her brazen prow
In port Cenchreas, from Egina isle   225
Fresh anchored, whither he had been awhile
To sacrifice to Jove, whose temple there
Waits with high marble doors for blood and incense rare.
Jove heard his vows, and bettered his desire;
For by some freakful chance he made retire   230
From his companions, and set forth to walk,
Perhaps grown wearied of their Corinth talk.
Over the solitary hills he fared,
Thoughtless at first, but ere eve's star appeared
His fantasy was lost where reason fades,   235

---

[30] *sciental* wise.
[31] *unshent* unspoilt.
[32] *Elysium* paradisal place of rest where Greek heroes were believed to spend an afterlife revelling and sporting in the sunshine.
[33] *nereids* water-nymphs.
[34] *Thetis* a sea-deity, daughter of Nereus and Doris.
[35] *glutinous* resinous.

[36] Pluto was King of the underworld.
[37] *palatine* palatial.
[38] *in far piazzian line* the construction resembles a piazza – a square or colonnaded walkway surrounded by buildings. Keats is recalling the construction of Pandemonium by Mulciber (Vulcan) in *Paradise Lost* i 713–15.
[39] *moth-time* early evening.

In the calmed twilight of Platonic shades.[40]
    Lamia beheld him coming, near, more near –
Close to her passing, in indifference drear,
His silent sandals swept the mossy green;
So neighboured to him, and yet so unseen   240
She stood. He passed, shut up in mysteries,
His mind wrapped like his mantle, while her eyes
Followed his steps, and her neck regal white
Turned, syllabling thus: 'Ah, Lycius bright,
And will you leave me on the hills alone?   245
Lycius, look back, and be some pity shown!'
He did, not with cold wonder fearingly,
But Orpheus-like at an Eurydice[41] –
For so delicious were the words she sung,
It seemed he had loved them a whole summer long.   250
And soon his eyes had drunk her beauty up,
Leaving no drop in the bewildering cup,
And still the cup was full – while he, afraid
Lest she should vanish ere his lip had paid
Due adoration, thus began to adore;   255
Her soft look growing coy, she saw his chain[42] so sure.
'Leave thee alone! Look back! Ah, goddess, see
Whether my eyes can ever turn from thee!
For pity do not this sad heart belie –
Even as thou vanishest so I shall die.   260
Stay, though a Naiad of the rivers, stay!
To thy far wishes will thy streams obey;
Stay, though the greenest woods be thy domain,
Alone they can drink up the morning rain!
Though a descended Pleiad,[43] will not one   265
Of thine harmonious sisters keep in tune
Thy spheres,[44] and as thy silver proxy shine?
So sweetly to these ravished ears of mine
Came thy sweet greeting, that if thou shouldst fade
Thy memory will waste me to a shade: 270
For pity do not melt!'
                 'If I should stay',
Said Lamia, 'here, upon this floor of clay,
And pain my steps upon these flowers too rough,
What canst thou say or do of charm enough
To dull the nice remembrance of my home?   275
Thou canst not ask me with thee here to roam
Over these hills and vales, where no joy is –
Empty of immortality and bliss!
Thou art a scholar, Lycius, and must know
That finer spirits cannot breathe below   280
In human climes, and live. Alas, poor youth,

---

[40] *In the calm . . . shades* Lycius begins his walk unthinkingly, but starts to meditate on Plato's mystic philosophy.

[41] Orpheus nearly managed to reclaim his lover, Eurydice, from Hades, but lost her forever when he looked back at her out of curiosity.

[42] *chain* the metaphorical 'chain' of love.

[43] The Pleiads were the seven daughters of Atlas, who became a constellation after death.

[44] *Thy spheres* reference to the music which the heavenly bodies were believed to make as they circled the earth.

What taste of purer air hast thou to soothe
My essence? What serener palaces,
Where I may all my many senses please,
And by mysterious sleights a hundred thirsts appease?   285
It cannot be. Adieu!'
                     So said, she rose
Tiptoe with white arms spread. He, sick to lose
The amorous promise of her lone complain,[45]
Swooned, murmuring of love, and pale with pain.
The cruel lady, without any show   290
Of sorrow for her tender favourite's woe —
But rather, if her eyes could brighter be,
With brighter eyes and slow amenity,
Put her new lips to his, and gave afresh
The life she had so tangled in her mesh;   295
And as he from one trance was wakening
Into another, she began to sing,
Happy in beauty, life, and love, and everything,
A song of love, too sweet for earthly lyres,
While, like held breath, the stars drew in their panting fires.   300
    And then she whispered in such trembling tone,
As those who, safe together met alone
For the first time through many anguished days,
Use other speech than looks — bidding him raise
His drooping head, and clear his soul of doubt,   305
For that she was a woman, and without
Any more subtle[46] fluid in her veins
Than throbbing blood, and that the self-same pains
Inhabited her frail-strung heart as his.
And next she wondered how his eyes could miss   310
Her face so long in Corinth, where, she said,
She dwelt but half retired, and there had led
Days happy as the gold coin could invent
Without the aid of love — yet in content
Till she saw him, as once she passed him by,   315
Where 'gainst a column he leant thoughtfully
At Venus' temple porch, mid baskets heaped
Of amorous herbs and flowers, newly reaped
Late on that eve, as 'twas the night before
The Adonian feast;[47] whereof she saw no more,   320
But wept alone those days, for why should she adore?
    Lycius from death awoke into amaze
To see her still, and singing so sweet lays;
Then from amaze into delight he fell
To hear her whisper woman's lore so well;   325
And every word she spake enticed him on
To unperplexed delight and pleasure known.
Let the mad poets say whate'er they please

---

[45] *complain* complaint.
[46] *subtle* rarefied.
[47] *The Adonian feast* a fertility ritual held annually in
Venus's temple. Adonis was the beautiful young man in love
with Venus, who was killed by a boar while hunting.

Of the sweets of fairies, peris,[48] goddesses;
There is not such a treat among them all,   330
Haunters of cavern, lake, and waterfall,
As a real woman, lineal indeed
From Pyrrha's pebbles[49] or old Adam's seed.
Thus gentle Lamia judged, and judged aright,
That Lycius could not love in half a fright,   335
So threw the goddess off, and won his heart
More pleasantly by playing woman's part
With no more awe than what her beauty gave,
That, while it smote, still guaranteed to save.
Lycius to all made eloquent reply,   340
Marrying to every word a twinborn sigh;
And last, pointing to Corinth, asked her sweet,
If 'twas too far that night for her soft feet.
The way was short, for Lamia's eagerness
Made, by a spell, the triple league decrease   345
To a few paces – not at all surmised
By blinded Lycius, so in her comprised.[50]
They passed the city gates, he knew not how,
So noiseless, and he never thought to know.

      As men talk in a dream, so Corinth all,   350
Throughout her palaces imperial,
And all her populous streets and temples lewd[51]
Muttered like tempest in the distance brewed
To the wide-spreaded night above her towers.
Men, women, rich and poor, in the cool hours,   355
Shuffled their sandals o'er the pavement white,
Companioned or alone, while many a light
Flared here and there from wealthy festivals,
And threw their moving shadows on the walls,
Or found them clustered in the corniced shade   360
Of some arched temple door or dusky colonnade.

      Muffling his face, of greeting friends in fear,
Her fingers he pressed hard, as one came near
With curled gray beard, sharp eyes, and smooth bald crown,
Slow-stepped, and robed in philosophic gown.   365
Lycius shrank closer as they met and passed
Into his mantle, adding wings to haste,
While hurried Lamia trembled. 'Ah', said he,
'Why do you shudder, love, so ruefully?
Why does your tender palm dissolve in dew?'   370
'I'm wearied', said fair Lamia. 'Tell me who
Is that old man? I cannot bring to mind
His features. Lycius, wherefore did you blind
Yourself from his quick eyes?' Lycius replied,

---

[48] *peris* superhuman beings or good genii from Persian myth.
[49] Exasperated by the crimes of humanity, Jupiter is said to have sent a flood that covered the world. The only ones to be saved, Deucalion and Pyrrha, repopulated the world by throwing stones behind them which turned into men and women.

[50] *comprised* absorbed.
[51] *lewd* see Burton's description of Corinth: 'every day strangers came in, at each gate, from all quarters. In that one temple of Venus a thousand whores did prostitute themselves ... all nations resorted thither as to a school of Venus' (*Anatomy of Melancholy*).

"Tis Apollonius[52] sage, my trusty guide   375
And good instructor. But tonight he seems
The ghost of folly haunting my sweet dreams.'
    While yet he spake they had arrived before
A pillared porch with lofty portal door,
Where hung a silver lamp, whose phosphor[53] glow   380
Reflected in the slabbed steps below,
Mild as a star in water – for so new
And so unsullied was the marble hue,
So through the crystal polish, liquid fine,
Ran the dark veins, that none but feet divine   385
Could e'er have touched there. Sounds Aeolian[54]
Breathed from the hinges, as the ample span
Of the wide doors disclosed a place unknown
Some time to any, but those two alone,
And a few Persian mutes, who that same year   390
Were seen about the markets; none knew where
They could inhabit – the most curious
Were foiled, who watched to trace them to their house.
And but the flitter-winged verse must tell,
For truth's sake, what woe afterwards befell;   395
'Twould humour many a heart to leave them thus,
Shut from the busy world of more incredulous.

Part II

Love in a hut,[1] with water and a crust,
Is (Love forgive us!) cinders, ashes, dust;
Love in a palace is perhaps at last
More grievous torment than a hermit's fast:
That is a doubtful tale from fairyland,   5
Hard for the non-elect to understand.
Had Lycius lived to hand his story down
He might have given the moral a fresh frown
Or clenched it quite[2] – but too short was their bliss
To breed distrust and hate, that make the soft voice hiss.   10
Besides, there, nightly, with terrific glare,
Love, jealous[3] grown of so complete a pair,
Hovered and buzzed his wings with fearful roar
Above the lintel of their chamber door,
And down the passage cast a glow upon the floor.[4]   15
    For all[5] this came a ruin: side by side
They were enthroned in the eventide,
Upon a couch, near to a curtaining
Whose airy texture, from a golden string,
Floated into the room, and let appear   20

---

[52] Apollonius of Tyana, philosopher of the first century AD, whose life was recorded by Philostratus. He advocated strict moral and religious reform, and was credited with magic powers.
[53] *phosphor* phosphorescent.
[54] *Sounds Aeolian* i.e. like the sounds of an Aeolian harp.

PART II
[1] *hut* cottage.
[2] *clenched it quite* proved it conclusively.
[3] *jealous* protective.
[4] *Love . . . floor* Cupid guards perfect love from intrusion.
[5] *For all* In spite of.

Unveiled the summer heaven, blue and clear,
Betwixt two marble shafts.[6] There they reposed
Where use had made it sweet, with eyelids closed,
Saving a tithe[7] which love still open kept,
That they might see each other while they almost slept —   25
When, from the slope side of a suburb hill,
Deafening the swallow's twitter, came a thrill
Of trumpets. Lycius started — the sounds fled,
But left a thought, a buzzing in his head.
For the first time, since first he harboured in   30
That purple-lined palace of sweet sin,
His spirit passed beyond its golden bourn[8]
Into the noisy world almost forsworn.
The lady, ever watchful, penetrant,[9]
Saw this with pain, so arguing a want   35
Of something more, more than her empery[10]
Of joys; and she began to moan and sigh
Because he mused beyond her, knowing well
That but a moment's thought is passion's passing-bell.
'Why do you sigh, fair creature?' whispered he.   40
'Why do you think?' returned she tenderly;
'You have deserted me; where am I now?
Not in your heart while care weighs on your brow.
No, no, you have dismissed me, and I go
From your breast houseless — aye, it must be so.'   45
    He answered, bending to her open eyes,
Where he was mirrored small in paradise:
'My silver planet,[11] both of eve and morn!
Why will you plead yourself so sad forlorn
While I am striving how to fill my heart   50
With deeper crimson and a double smart?
How to entangle, trammel up[12] and snare
Your soul in mine, and labyrinth you there
Like the hid scent in an unbudded rose?
Aye, a sweet kiss — you see your mighty woes.   55
My thoughts! Shall I unveil them? Listen then!
What mortal hath a prize, that other men
May be confounded and abashed withal,
But lets it sometimes pace abroad majestical
And triumph, as in thee I should rejoice   60
Amid the hoarse alarm of Corinth's voice?
Let my foes choke, and my friends shout afar,
While through the thronged streets your bridal car
Wheels round its dazzling spokes!'
                                    The lady's cheek
Trembled; she nothing said but, pale and meek,   65
Arose and knelt before him, wept a rain
Of sorrows at his words; at last with pain

---

6   *marble shafts* two marble pillars supporting the lintel of the
window.
7   *tithe* a small part.
8   *bourn* realm, domain.

9   *penetrant* perceptive, acute.
10   *empery* empire.
11   *silver planet* Venus, star of morning and evening.
12   *trammel up* enmesh.

Beseeching him, the while his hand she wrung
To change his purpose. He thereat was stung,
Perverse, with stronger fancy to reclaim   70
Her wild and timid nature to his aim –
Besides, for all his love, in self-despite,
Against his better self, he took delight
Luxurious in her sorrows, soft and new.
His passion, cruel grown, took on a hue   75
Fierce and sanguineous[13] as 'twas possible
In one whose brow had no dark veins to swell.
Fine was the mitigated[14] fury, like
Apollo's presence when in act to strike
The serpent[15] – ha, the serpent! Certes[16] she   80
Was none. She burnt, she loved the tyranny,
And, all subdued, consented to the hour
When to the bridal he should lead his paramour.
       Whispering in midnight silence, said the youth:
'Sure some sweet name thou hast, though, by my truth,   85
I have not asked it, ever thinking thee
Not mortal, but of heavenly progeny,
As still I do. Hast any mortal name,
Fit appellation for this dazzling frame?
Or friends or kinsfolk on the citied earth,   90
To share our marriage feast and nuptial mirth?'
'I have no friends', said Lamia, 'no, not one;
My presence in wide Corinth hardly known.
My parents' bones are in their dusty urns
Sepulchred, where no kindled incense burns,   95
Seeing all their luckless race are dead, save me –
And I neglect the holy rite for thee.
Even as you list invite your many guests;
But if, as now it seems, your vision rests
With any pleasure on me, do not bid   100
Old Apollonius – from him keep me hid.'
Lycius, perplexed at words so blind and blank,
Made close enquiry, from whose touch she shrank,
Feigning a sleep – and he to the dull shade
Of deep sleep in a moment was betrayed.[17]   105
       It was the custom then to bring away
The bride from home at blushing shut of day
Veiled in a chariot, heralded along
By strewn flowers, torches, and a marriage song,
With other pageants – but this fair unknown   110
Had not a friend. So being left alone
(Lycius was gone to summon all his kin)
And knowing surely she could never win
His foolish heart from its mad pompousness,[18]
She set herself, high-thoughted, how to dress   115

---

[13] *sanguineous* red with anger.
[14] *mitigated* moderated.
[15] Apollo killed a huge dragon (called Python) at Delphi,
where he established his shrine.

[16] *Certes* certainly.
[17] *to the dull shade ... betrayed* Lycius is tricked into a deep
sleep by Lamia's magic spell.
[18] *pompousness* love of display.

The misery in fit magnificence.
She did so, but 'tis doubtful how and whence
Came, and who were her subtle[19] servitors.
About the halls, and to and from the doors
There was a noise of wings, till in short space   120
The glowing banquet-room shone with wide-arched grace.
A haunting music, sole perhaps and lone
Supportress of the fairy-roof, made moan
Throughout, as fearful the whole charm might fade.
Fresh carved cedar, mimicking a glade   125
Of palm and plantain,[20] met from either side
High in the midst, in honour of the bride –
Two palms and then two plantains, and so on,
From either side their stems branched one to one
All down the aisled place; and beneath all   130
There ran a stream of lamps straight on from wall to wall.
　　So canopied, lay an untasted feast
Teeming with odours. Lamia, regal dressed,
Silently paced about, and as she went,
In pale contented sort of discontent,   135
Missioned her viewless[21] servants to enrich
The fretted[22] splendour of each nook and niche.
Between the tree-stems, marbled plain at first,
Came jasper panels; then anon there burst
Forth creeping imagery of slighter trees,   140
And with the larger wove in small intricacies.
Approving all, she faded[23] at self-will,
And shut the chamber up, close, hushed and still,
Complete and ready for the revels rude,
When dreadful guests would come to spoil her solitude.   145
　　The day appeared, and all the gossip rout.
Oh senseless Lycius! Madman! Wherefore flout
The silent-blessing fate, warm cloistered hours,
And show to common eyes these secret bowers?
The herd approached – each guest, with busy brain,   150
Arriving at the portal, gazed amain,
And entered marvelling, for they knew the street,
Remembered it from childhood all complete
Without a gap, yet ne'er before had seen
That royal porch, that high-built fair demesne.[24]   155
So in they hurried all, mazed, curious and keen,
Save one who looked thereon with eye severe,
And with calm-planted steps walked in austere;
'Twas Apollonius; something too he laughed,
As though some knotty problem, that had daffed[25]   160
His patient thought, had now begun to thaw
And solve and melt – 'twas just as he foresaw.
　　He met within the murmurous vestibule

---

19 *subtle* invisible.
20 *plantain* a tropical tree-like plant.
21 *viewless* invisible.
22 *fretted* carved.

23 *faded* disappeared, as if by magic.
24 *demesne* palace.
25 *daffed* toyed with, baffled.

His young disciple. ''Tis no common rule,
Lycius', said he, 'for uninvited guest   165
To force himself upon you, and infest
With an unbidden presence the bright throng
Of younger friends – yet must I do this wrong,
And you forgive me.' Lycius blushed, and led
The old man through the inner doors broad-spread;   170
With reconciling words and courteous mien
Turning into sweet milk the sophist's[26] spleen.

   Of wealthy lustre was the banquet-room,
Filled with pervading brilliance and perfume;
Before each lucid[27] panel fuming stood   175
A censer fed with myrrh and spiced wood,
Each by a sacred tripod held aloft
Whose slender feet wide-swerved upon the soft
Wool-woofed carpets; fifty wreaths of smoke
From fifty censers their light voyage took   180
To the high roof, still mimicked as they rose
Along the mirrored walls by twin-clouds odorous.
Twelve sphered tables, by silk seats ensphered,
High as the level of a man's breast reared
On libbard's[28] paws, upheld the heavy gold   185
Of cups and goblets, and the store thrice told
Of Ceres' horn,[29] and, in huge vessels, wine
Come from the gloomy tun[30] with merry shine.
Thus loaded with a feast the tables stood,
Each shrining in the midst the image of a god.   190
   When in an ante-chamber every guest
Had felt the cold full sponge to pleasure pressed
By minist'ring slaves upon his hands and feet,
And fragrant oils with ceremony meet
Poured on his hair, they all moved to the feast   195
In white robes, and themselves in order placed
Around the silken couches, wondering
Whence all this mighty cost and blaze of wealth could spring.
   Soft went the music the soft air along,
While fluent Greek a vowelled undersong   200
Kept up among the guests, discoursing low
At first, for scarcely was the wine at flow;
But when the happy vintage touched their brains,
Louder they talk, and louder come the strains
Of powerful instruments. The gorgeous dyes,   205
The space, the splendour of the draperies,
The roof of awful richness, nectarous cheer,
Beautiful slaves and Lamia's self appear,
Now, when the wine has done its rosy deed,
And every soul from human trammels freed,   210
No more so strange – for merry wine, sweet wine,
Will make Elysian shades not too fair, too divine.[31]

---

[26] *sophist* learned man.
[27] *lucid* shining.
[28] *libbard's* leopard's.
[29] *Ceres' horn* the horn of plenty.

[30] *tun* cask.
[31] Wine makes the idyllic world of the Elysian fields seem less remote.

Soon was god Bacchus at meridian height;
Flushed were their cheeks, and bright eyes double bright.
Garlands of every green, and every scent   215
From vales deflowered, or forest-trees branch-rent,
In baskets of bright osiered[32] gold were brought
High as the handles heaped, to suit the thought
Of every guest – that each, as he did please,
Might fancy-fit his brows, silk-pillowed at his ease.   220
      What wreath for Lamia? What for Lycius?
What for the sage, old Apollonius?
Upon her aching forehead be there hung
The leaves of willow and of adder's tongue;[33]
And for the youth – quick, let us strip for him   225
The thyrsus,[34] that his watching eyes may swim
Into forgetfulness; and, for the sage,
Let spear-grass and the spiteful thistle wage
War on his temples. Do not all charms fly
At the mere touch of cold philosophy?   230
There was an awful[35] rainbow once in heaven:
We know her woof, her texture – she is given
In the dull catalogue of common things.
Philosophy will clip an angel's wings,
Conquer all mysteries by rule and line,   235
Empty the haunted air, and gnomed mine,
Unweave a rainbow, as it erewhile made
The tender-personed Lamia melt into a shade.
      By her glad Lycius sitting in chief place
Scarce saw in all the room another face   240
Till, checking his love trance, a cup he took
Full brimmed, and opposite sent forth a look
'Cross the broad table, to beseech a glance
From his old teacher's wrinkled countenance,
And pledge him. The bald-head philosopher   245
Had fixed his eye without a twinkle or stir
Full on the alarmed beauty of the bride,
Brow-beating her fair form, and troubling her sweet pride.
Lycius then pressed her hand, with devout touch,
As pale it lay upon the rosy couch: 250
'Twas icy, and the cold ran through his veins –
Then sudden it grew hot, and all the pains
Of an unnatural heat shot to his heart.
'Lamia, what means this? Wherefore dost thou start?
Know'st thou that man?' Poor Lamia answered not.   255
He gazed into her eyes, and not a jot
Owned they the lovelorn piteous appeal;
More, more he gazed; his human senses reel;
Some hungry spell that loveliness absorbs –
There was no recognition in those orbs.   260

---

32 *osiered* woven.
33 *The leaves of willow and of adder's tongue* emblems of grief;
adder's tongue is a fern once used as a medicine for its sooth-
ing properties.

34 Lycius's wreath is made from the ivy and vine-leaves
wrapped round Bacchus's thyrsus (wand).
35 *awful* awe-inspiring.

'Lamia!' he cried – and no soft-toned reply.
The many heard, and the loud revelry
Grew hush; the stately music no more breathes;
The myrtle sickened in a thousand wreaths.
By faint degrees, voice, lute, and pleasure ceased;   265
A deadly silence step by step increased
Until it seemed a horrid presence there,
And not a man but felt the terror in his hair.
'Lamia!' he shrieked – and nothing but the shriek
With its sad echo did the silence break.   270
'Begone, foul dream!' he cried, gazing again
In the bride's face, where now no azure vein
Wandered on fair-spaced temples; no soft bloom
Misted the cheek; no passion to illume
The deep-recessed vision – all was blight.   275
Lamia, no longer fair, there sat a deadly white.
  'Shut, shut those juggling[36] eyes, thou ruthless man!
Turn them aside, wretch, or the righteous ban
Of all the gods, whose dreadful images
Here represent their shadowy presences,   280
May pierce them on the sudden with the thorn
Of painful blindness – leaving thee forlorn,
In trembling dotage to the feeblest fright
Of conscience, for their long offended might,
For all thine impious proud-heart sophistries,   285
Unlawful magic, and enticing lies.
Corinthians, look upon that gray-beard wretch!
Mark how, possessed, his lashless eyelids stretch
Around his demon eyes! Corinthians, see!
My sweet bride withers at their potency.'   290
  'Fool!' said the sophist, in an undertone
Gruff with contempt; which a death-nighing moan
From Lycius answered, as heart-struck and lost,
He sank supine beside the aching ghost.
'Fool! Fool!' repeated he, while his eyes still   295
Relented not, nor moved. 'From every ill
Of life have I preserved thee to this day,
And shall I see thee made a serpent's prey?'
Then Lamia breathed death breath; the sophist's eye,
Like a sharp spear, went through her utterly,   300
Keen, cruel, perceant,[37] stinging; she, as well
As her weak hand could any meaning tell,
Motioned him to be silent – vainly so,
He looked and looked again a level 'No!'
  'A serpent!' echoed he – no sooner said,   305
Than with a frightful scream she vanished,
And Lycius' arms were empty of delight,
As were his limbs of life from that same night.[38]
On the high couch he lay – his friends came round,
Supported him; no pulse or breath they found,   310
And, in its marriage robe, the heavy body wound.

---

[36] *juggling* conjuring.
[37] *perceant* piercing.

[38] Apollonius saves Lycius from Lamia, killing them both in the process.

To Autumn (composed *c.* 19 September 1819)

From LAMIA, ISABELLA, THE EVE OF ST AGNES, AND OTHER POEMS (1820)

I

Season of mists and mellow fruitfulness,
   Close bosom-friend of the maturing sun,
Conspiring with him how to load and bless
   With fruit the vines that round the thatch-eaves run;
To bend with apples the mossed cottage-trees,   5
   And fill all fruit with ripeness to the core;
      To swell the gourd,[1] and plump the hazel shells
With a sweet kernel; to set budding more,
   And still more, later flowers for the bees,
   Until they think warm days will never cease,   10
      For summer has o'er-brimmed their clammy cells.

2

Who hath not seen thee oft amid thy store?
   Sometimes whoever seeks abroad may find
Thee sitting careless[2] on a granary floor,
   Thy hair soft-lifted by the winnowing wind;   15
Or on a half-reaped furrow sound asleep,
   Drowsed with the fume of poppies,[3] while thy hook[4]
      Spares the next swath[5] and all its twined flowers;
And sometimes like a gleaner[6] thou dost keep
   Steady thy laden head across a brook;   20
   Or by a cider-press, with patient look,
      Thou watchest the last oozings hours by hours.

3

Where are the songs of spring? Aye, where are they?
   Think not of them, thou hast thy music too –
While barred clouds bloom the soft-dying day,   25
   And touch the stubble-plains with rosy hue;
Then in a wailful choir the small gnats mourn
   Among the river sallows,[7] borne aloft
      Or sinking as the light wind lives or dies;
And full-grown lambs loud bleat from hilly bourn,   30
   Hedge-crickets sing, and now with treble soft
   The redbreast whistles from a garden-croft,
      And gathering swallows twitter in the skies.

TO AUTUMN
[1] *gourd* thick-skinned fruit of squashes, and other plants, that can be used as a drinking vessel.
[2] *careless* without care.
[3] *Drowsed . . . poppies* poppies are associated with sleep.
[4] *hook* blade used for reaping corn.
[5] *swath* width of corn cut by a hook.
[6] *gleaner* one who gathers stray ears of corn missed by the reapers.
[7] *sallows* willows.

The Fall of Hyperion: A Dream (composed July–September 1819; edited from MS)[1]

Canto I

Fanatics[2] have their dreams, wherewith they weave
A paradise for a sect; the savage too
From forth the loftiest fashion of his sleep[3]
Guesses at heaven; pity these have not
Traced upon vellum or wild Indian leaf   5
The shadows of melodious utterance.
But bare of laurel they live, dream and die;
For Poesy alone can tell her dreams,
With the fine spell of words alone can save
Imagination from the sable charm   10
And dumb enchantment. Who alive can say
'Thou art no poet; may'st not tell thy dreams'?
Since every man whose soul is not a clod
Hath visions, and would speak, if he had loved
And been well nurtured in his mother tongue.   15
Whether the dream now purposed to rehearse
Be poet's or fanatic's will be known
When this warm scribe my hand is in the grave.

    Methought I stood where trees of every clime,
Palm, myrtle, oak, and sycamore, and beech,   20
With plantain,[4] and spice-blossoms, made a screen;
In neighbourhood of fountains, by the noise
Soft-showering in mine ears, and, by the touch
Of scent, not far from roses. Turning round,
I saw an arbour with a drooping roof   25
Of trellis vines, and bells, and larger blooms,
Like floral censers swinging light in air;
Before its wreathed doorway, on a mound
Of moss, was spread a feast of summer fruits,
Which nearer seen, seemed refuse of a meal   30
By angel tasted, or our mother Eve;
For empty shells were scattered on the grass,
And grape-stalks but half bare, and remnants more,
Sweet smelling, whose pure kinds I could not know.
Still was more plenty than the fabled horn[5]   35
Thrice emptied could pour forth, at banqueting
For Proserpine[6] returned to her own fields,
Where the white heifers low. And appetite
More yearning than on earth I ever felt
Growing within, I ate deliciously;   40
And, after not long, thirsted, for thereby

THE FALL OF HYPERION: A DREAM
[1] This much revised version of *Hyperion* was first published in 1857.
[2] *Fanatics* religious fanatics.
[3] *the loftiest fashion of his sleep* the depths of his dreams.
[4] *plantain* tropical tree-like plant.

[5] *the fabled horn* the cornucopia of plenty.
[6] Proserpine was Ceres's daughter; she was carried off to hell by Pluto. To soothe Ceres's grief, Jupiter decided that Proserpine should spend half the year in hell, and the other half on earth.

Stood a cool vessel of transparent juice
Sipped by the wandered bee, the which I took,
And, pledging all the mortals of the world,
And all the dead whose names are in our lips,   45
Drank. That full draught is parent of my theme.
No Asian poppy nor elixir fine
Of the soon-fading jealous Caliphat,[7]
No poison gendered in close monkish cell
To thin the scarlet conclave of old men,[8]   50
Could so have rapt[9] unwilling life away.
Among the fragrant husks and berries crushed,
Upon the grass I struggled hard against
The domineering potion, but in vain –
The cloudy swoon came on, and down I sunk   55
Like a Silenus[10] on an antique vase.
How long I slumbered 'tis a chance to guess.
When sense of life returned, I started up
As if with wings; but the fair trees were gone,
The mossy mound and arbour were no more.   60
I looked around upon the carved sides
Of an old sanctuary with roof august,
Builded so high, it seemed that filmed clouds
Might spread beneath, as o'er the stars of heaven.
So old the place was, I remembered none   65
The like upon the earth – what I had seen
Of grey cathedrals, buttressed walls, rent towers,
The superannuations[11] of sunk realms,
Or nature's rocks toiled hard in waves and winds,
Seemed but the faulture[12] of decrepit things   70
To that eternal domed monument.
Upon the marble at my feet there lay
Store of strange vessels, and large draperies
Which needs had been of dyed asbestos wove,
Or in that place the moth could not corrupt,[13]   75
So white the linen; so, in some, distinct
Ran imageries[14] from a sombre loom.
All in a mingled heap confused there lay
Robes, golden tongs, censer and chafing-dish,
Girdles, and chains, and holy jewelleries.   80
    Turning from these with awe, once more I raised
My eyes to fathom the space every way;
The embossed roof, the silent massy range
Of columns north and south, ending in mist
Of nothing; then to eastward, where black gates   85
Were shut against the sunrise evermore.

---

[7] *No Asian poppy ... Caliphat* the Caliphs ruled the Muslim world after the death of Mohammed. They were believed to use poison as a means of political intrigue.
[8] *the scarlet conclave of old men* Cardinals elect a Pope in 'scarlet conclave'.
[9] *rapt* taken.
[10] *Silenus* attendant of Bacchus, who would sink down in a drunken stupor.

[11] *superannuations* ruins.
[12] *faulture* weakness.
[13] *Or in ... corrupt* heaven; Matthew 6:19–20: 'Lay not up for yourselves treasures upon earth, where moth and rust doth corrupt and where thieves break through and steal'.
[14] *imageries* patterns in the cloth.

Then to the west I looked, and saw far off
An image,[15] huge of feature as a cloud,
At level of whose feet an altar slept,
To be approached on either side by steps,   90
And marble balustrade, and patient travail
To count with toil the innumerable degrees.
Towards the altar sober-paced I went,
Repressing haste as too unholy there;
And, coming nearer, saw beside the shrine   95
One minist'ring;[16] and there arose a flame.
When in mid-May the sickening east wind
Shifts sudden to the south, the small warm rain
Melts out the frozen incense from all flowers,
And fills the air with so much pleasant health   100
That even the dying man forgets his shroud;
Even so that lofty sacrificial fire,
Sending forth Maian incense,[17] spread around
Forgetfulness of everything but bliss,
And clouded all the altar with soft smoke,   105
From whose white fragrant curtains thus I heard
Language pronounced: 'If thou canst not ascend
These steps, die on that marble where thou art.
Thy flesh, near cousin to the common dust,
Will parch for lack of nutriment; thy bones   110
Will wither in few years, and vanish so
That not the quickest eye could find a grain
Of what thou now art on that pavement cold.
The sands of thy short life are spent this hour,
And no hand in the universe can turn   115
Thy hourglass, if these gummed leaves[18] be burnt
Ere thou canst mount up these immortal steps.'
    I heard, I looked – two senses both at once,
So fine, so subtle, felt the tyranny
Of that fierce threat and the hard task proposed.   120
Prodigious seemed the toil; the leaves were yet
Burning, when suddenly a palsied chill
Struck from the paved level up my limbs,
And was ascending quick to put cold grasp
Upon those streams that pulse beside the throat.   125
I shrieked, and the sharp anguish of my shriek
Stung my own ears – I strove hard to escape
The numbness, strove to gain the lowest step.
Slow, heavy, deadly was my pace; the cold
Grew stifling, suffocating, at the heart;   130
And when I clasped my hands I felt them not.
One minute before death, my iced foot touched
The lowest stair; and as it touched, life seemed
To pour in at the toes. I mounted up,
As once fair angels on a ladder flew   135

---

[15] *An image* of Saturn.
[16] *One minist'ring* Moneta, the priestess of the temple.
[17] *Maian incense* flowery scent.
[18] *gummed leaves* leaves of a gum-tree.

From the green turf to heaven. 'Holy Power',
Cried I, approaching near the horned shrine,
'What am I that should so be saved from death?
What am I, that another death come not
To choke my utterance sacrilegious here?'   140
Then said the veiled shadow:[19] 'Thou hast felt
What 'tis to die and live again before
Thy fated hour. That thou hadst power to do so
Is thy own safety; thou hast dated on
Thy doom.'[20] 'High Prophetess', said I, 'purge off   145
Benign, if so it please thee, my mind's film.'[21]
'None can usurp this height', returned that shade,
'But those to whom the miseries of the world
Are misery, and will not let them rest.
All else who find a haven in the world,   150
Where they may thoughtless sleep away their days,
If by a chance into this fane[22] they come,
Rot on the pavement where thou rotted'st half.'
'Are there not thousands in the world', said I,
Encouraged by the sooth[23] voice of the shade,   155
'Who love their fellows even to the death;
Who feel the giant agony of the world;
And more, like slaves to poor humanity,
Labour for mortal good? I sure should see
Other men here – but I am here alone.'   160
'They whom thou spak'st of are no vision'ries',
Rejoined that voice, 'They are no dreamers weak,
They seek no wonder but the human face,
No music but a happy-noted voice,
They come not here, they have no thought to come –   165
And thou art here, for thou art less than they.
What benefit canst thou do, or all thy tribe,
To the great world? Thou art a dreaming thing,
A fever of thyself.[24] Think of the earth;
What bliss even in hope is there for thee?   170
What haven? Every creature hath its home;
Every sole[25] man hath days of joy and pain,
Whether his labours be sublime or low –
The pain alone; the joy alone; distinct.
Only the dreamer venoms all his days,[26]   175
Bearing more woe than all his sins deserve.
Therefore, that happiness be somewhat shared,
Such things as thou art are admitted oft
Into like gardens thou didst pass erewhile,
And suffered in these temples; for that cause   180
Thou standest safe beneath this statue's knees.'
'That I am favoured for unworthiness,

---

19   *veiled shadow* Moneta.
20   *dated on / Thy doom* postponed your death.
21   *purge off . . . film* help me to understand clearly.
22   *fane* temple.
23   *sooth* smooth.

24   *A fever of thyself* i.e. he is prone to feverish fits of poetic inspiration.
25   *sole* single.
26   *Only the dreamer venoms all his days* with the awareness of human misery.

By such propitious parley medicined
In sickness not ignoble, I rejoice –
Aye, and could weep for love of such award.'   185
So answered I, continuing, 'If it please,
Majestic shadow, tell me – sure not all
Those melodies sung into the world's ear
Are useless? Sure a poet is a sage,
A humanist,[27] physician to all men.   190
That I am none I feel, as vultures feel
They are no birds when eagles are abroad.
What am I then? Thou spakest of my tribe –
What tribe?' The tall shade veiled in drooping white
Then spake, so much more earnest, that the breath   195
Moved the thin linen folds that drooping hung
About a golden censer from the hand
Pendent: 'Art thou not of the dreamer tribe?
The poet and the dreamer are distinct,
Diverse, sheer opposite, antipodes.   200
The one pours out a balm upon the world,
The other vexes it.' Then shouted I
Spite of myself, and with a Pythia's spleen:[28]
'Apollo! Faded, far-flown Apollo![29]
Where is thy misty pestilence to creep   205
Into the dwellings, through the door crannies,
Of all mock lyrists, large self-worshippers,
And careless hectorers in proud bad verse?[30]
Though I breathe death with them it will be life
To see them sprawl before me into graves.   210
Majestic shadow, tell me where I am;
Whose altar this; for whom this incense curls;
What image this, whose face I cannot see,
For the broad marble knees; and who thou art,
Of accent feminine, so courteous.'   215
      Then the tall shade, in drooping linens veiled,
Spake out, so much more earnest, that her breath
Stirred the thin folds of gauze that drooping hung
About a golden censer from her hand
Pendent – and by her voice I knew she shed   220
Long-treasured tears: 'This temple sad and lone
Is all spared[31] from the thunder of a war[32]
Foughten long since by giant hierarchy
Against rebellion. This old image here,
Whose carved features wrinkled as he fell,   225
Is Saturn's; I, Moneta,[33] left supreme,
Sole priestess of his desolation.'
I had no words to answer, for my tongue,
Useless, could find about its roofed home

---

[27] *humanist* humanitarian.
[28] *a Pythia's spleen* Oracles in the temple of Apollo, god of poetry and prophecy, at Delphi were delivered by a priestess called 'the Pythia' whose wild and incoherent speeches were recorded by the priest.
[29] *Apollo* son of Jupiter.
[30] *careless hectorers in proud bad verse* suggested candidates include Byron, Wordsworth and Moore.
[31] *Is all spared* is all that is spared.
[32] *war* that of the Titans against the Olympians.
[33] *Moneta* Mnemosyne, mother of the muses.

No syllable of a fit majesty   230
To make rejoinder to Moneta's mourn.
There was a silence while the altar's blaze
Was fainting for sweet food. I looked thereon,
And on the paved floor, where nigh were piled
Faggots of cinnamon, and many heaps   235
Of other crisped spice-wood – then again
I looked upon the altar, and its horns
Whitened with ashes, and its lang'rous flame,
And then upon the offerings again;
And so by turns, till sad Moneta cried,   240
'The sacrifice is done, but not the less
Will I be kind to thee for thy good will.
My power, which to me is still a curse,
Shall be to thee a wonder; for the scenes
Still swooning vivid through my globed brain[34]   245
With an electral[35] changing misery,
Thou shalt with those dull mortal eyes behold,
Free from all pain, if wonder pain thee not.'
As near as an immortal's sphered words
Could to a mother's soften, were these last.   250
But yet I had a terror of her robes,
And chiefly of the veils, that from her brow
Hung pale, and curtained her in mysteries,
That made my heart too small to hold its blood.
This saw that goddess, and with sacred hand   255
Parted the veils. Then saw I a wan face,
Not pined by human sorrows, but bright-blanched
By an immortal sickness which kills not;
It works a constant change, which happy death
Can put no end to; deathwards progressing   260
To no death was that visage; it had passed
The lily and the snow; and beyond these
I must not think now, though I saw that face –
But for her eyes I should have fled away.
They held me back with a benignant light,   265
Soft-mitigated by divinest lids
Half-closed, and visionless[36] entire they seemed
Of all external things – they saw me not,
But in blank splendour beamed like the mild moon,
Who comforts those she sees not, who knows not   270
What eyes are upward cast. As I had found
A grain of gold upon a mountain's side,
And twinged with avarice strained out my eyes
To search its sullen entrails rich with ore,
So at the view of sad Moneta's brow   275
I ached to see what things the hollow brain
Behind enwombed, what high tragedy
In the dark secret chambers of her skull

---

34 *the scenes ... brain* the scenes are vivid enough in her
memory to make her swoon.
35 *electral* charged as if by electricity.

36 *visionless* the eyes do not see the outside world, but are
directed on inner visions.

Was acting, that could give so dread a stress
To her cold lips, and fill with such a light   280
Her planetary eyes, and touch her voice
With such a sorrow. 'Shade of Memory!'[37]
Cried I, with act adorant at her feet,
'By all the gloom hung round thy fallen house,
By this last temple, by the golden age,[38]   285
By great Apollo, thy dear foster child,[39]
And by thyself, forlorn divinity,
The pale omega[40] of a withered race,
Let me behold, according as thou said'st,
What in thy brain so ferments to and fro.'   290
No sooner had this conjuration passed
My devout lips, than side by side we stood,
Like a stunt bramble by a solemn pine,
Deep in the shady sadness of a vale,
Far sunken from the healthy breath of morn,   295
Far from the fiery noon and eve's one star.
Onward I looked beneath the gloomy boughs,
And saw what first I thought an image huge,
Like to the image pedestalled so high
In Saturn's temple. Then Moneta's voice   300
Came brief upon mine ear: 'So Saturn sat
When he had lost his realms.' Whereon there grew
A power within me of enormous ken[41]
To see as a god sees, and take the depth
Of things as nimbly as the outward eye   305
Can size and shape pervade. The lofty theme
At those few words hung vast before my mind,
With half-unravelled web. I set myself
Upon an eagle's watch, that I might see,
And seeing ne'er forget. No stir of life   310
Was in this shrouded vale, not so much air
As in the zoning[42] of a summer's day
Robs not one light seed from the feathered grass,
But where the dead leaf fell there did it rest.
A stream went voiceless by, still deadened more   315
By reason of the fallen divinity
Spreading more shade; the naiad[43] mid her reeds
Pressed her cold finger closer to her lips.
Along the margin sand large footmarks went
No farther than to where old Saturn's feet   320
Had rested, and there slept – how long a sleep!
Degraded, cold, upon the sodden ground
His old right hand lay nerveless,[44] listless, dead,
Unsceptred; and his realmless eyes were closed,
While his bowed head seemed listening to the earth,   325

---

37 *Shade of Memory* Moneta.

38 *the golden age* of Saturn's rule.

39 *Apollo, thy dear foster child* Apollo was the son of Jupiter
by Latona. Moneta was Jupiter's wife at the time.

40 *omega* survivor (omega is the final letter of the Greek
alphabet).

41 *ken* sight.

42 *zoning* duration.

43 *naiad* water-nymph.

44 *nerveless* weak.

His ancient mother,[45] for some comfort yet.
  It seemed no force could wake him from his place;
But there came one who, with a kindred hand
Touched his wide shoulders, after bending low
With reverence, though to one who knew it not.   330
Then came the grieved voice of Mnemosyne,
And grieved I hearkened: 'That divinity
Whom thou saw'st step from yon forlornest wood,
And with slow pace approach our fallen King,
Is Thea,[46] softest-natured of our brood.'   335
I marked the goddess in fair statuary[47]
Surpassing wan Moneta by the head,
And in her sorrow nearer woman's tears.
There was a listening fear in her regard,
As if calamity had but begun;   340
As if the vanward clouds of evil days
Had spent their malice, and the sullen rear
Was with its stored thunder labouring up.[48]
One hand she pressed upon that aching spot
Where beats the human heart, as if just there,   345
Though an immortal, she felt cruel pain;
The other upon Saturn's bended neck
She laid, and to the level of his hollow ear,
Leaning with parted lips, some words she spake
In solemn tenor and deep organ tune –   350
Some mourning words, which in our feeble tongue
Would come in this-like accenting (how frail
To that large utterance of the early gods!):
'Saturn, look up! And for what, poor lost King?
I have no comfort for thee – no, not one;   355
I cannot cry, "Wherefore thus sleepest thou?"
For heaven is parted from thee, and the earth
Knows thee not, so afflicted, for a god;
And ocean too, with all its solemn noise,
Has from thy sceptre passed, and all the air   360
Is emptied of thine hoary majesty.
Thy thunder, captious[49] at the new command,
Rumbles reluctant o'er our fallen house;
And thy sharp lightning in unpractised hands
Scorches and burns our once serene domain.[50]   365
With such remorseless speed still come new woes
That unbelief has not a space to breathe.
Saturn, sleep on. Me thoughtless, why should I
Thus violate thy slumbrous solitude?
Why should I ope thy melancholy eyes?   370
Saturn, sleep on, while at thy feet I weep.'

45   *His ancient mother* Tellus (earth).
46   *Thea* daughter of Uranus and Terra.
47   *statuary* stature.
48   *As if the vanward clouds ... up* calamity is compared to clouds building up before a storm, followed by the cloud mass; the storm itself is compared with artillery moving in the wake of advancing troops.
49   *captious* objecting querulously.
50   *our once serene domain* the Saturnian Golden Age.

As when, upon a tranced summer night,
Forests, branch-charmed by the earnest stars,
Dream, and so dream all night, without a noise,
Save from one gradual solitary gust   375
Swelling upon the silence, dying off,
As if the ebbing air had but one wave;
So came these words, and went, the while in tears
She pressed her fair large forehead to the earth,
Just where her fallen hair might spread in curls,   380
A soft and silken mat for Saturn's feet.
Long, long those two were postured motionless,
Like sculpture builded up upon the grave
Of their own power. A long awful time
I looked upon them; still they were the same,   385
The frozen god still bending to the earth,
And the sad goddess weeping at his feet;
Moneta silent. Without stay or prop
But my own weak mortality, I bore
The load of this eternal quietude,   390
The unchanging gloom, and the three fixed shapes
Ponderous upon my senses a whole moon.
For by my burning brain I measured sure
Her silver seasons shedded on the night,
And every day by day methought I grew   395
More gaunt and ghostly; oftentimes I prayed
Intense, that death would take me from the vale
And all its burdens; gasping with despair
Of change, hour after hour I cursed myself –
Until old Saturn raised his faded eyes,   400
And looked around and saw his kingdom gone,
And all the gloom and sorrow of the place,
And that fair kneeling goddess at his feet.
As the moist scent of flowers, and grass, and leaves
Fills forest dells with a pervading air   405
Known to the woodland nostril, so the words
Of Saturn filled the mossy glooms around,
Even to the hollows of time-eaten oaks,
And to the windings in the foxes' hole,
With sad low tones, while thus he spake, and sent   410
Strange musings to the solitary Pan:[51]
'Moan, brethren, moan, for we are swallowed up
And buried from all godlike exercise
Of influence benign on planets pale,
And peaceful sway above man's harvesting,   415
And all those acts which deity supreme
Doth ease its heart of love in. Moan and wail.
Moan, brethren, moan, for lo! the rebel spheres
Spin round, the stars their ancient courses keep,
Clouds still with shadowy moisture haunt the earth,   420
Still suck their fill of light from sun and moon,
Still buds the tree, and still the seashores murmur.

---

[51] Pan is the natural world, solitary after the passing of the
golden age.

There is no death in all the universe,
No smell of death – there shall be death. Moan, moan,
Moan, Cybele,[52] moan, for thy pernicious babes   425
Have changed a god into a shaking palsy.
Moan, brethren, moan, for I have no strength left,
Weak as the reed – weak – feeble as my voice –
Oh, oh, the pain, the pain of feebleness.
Moan, moan, for still I thaw – or give me help: 430
Throw down those imps,[53] and give me victory.
Let me hear other groans, and trumpets blown
Of triumph calm, and hymns of festival
From the gold peaks of heaven's high-piled clouds;
Voices of soft proclaim, and silver stir   435
Of strings in hollow shells; and let there be
Beautiful things made new, for the surprise
Of the sky-children.' So he feebly ceased,
With such a poor and sickly sounding pause,
Methought I heard some old man of the earth   440
Bewailing earthly loss; nor could my eyes
And ears act with that pleasant unison of sense
Which marries sweet sound with the grace of form,
And dolorous accent from a tragic harp
With large-limbed visions. More I scrutinized: 445
Still fixed he sat beneath the sable trees,
Whose arms spread straggling in wild serpent forms,
With leaves all hushed; his awful presence there,
Now all was silent, gave a deadly lie
To what I erewhile heard – only his lips   450
Trembled amid the white curls of his beard.
They told the truth, though, round the snowy locks
Hung nobly, as upon the face of heaven
A midday fleece of clouds. Thea arose
And stretched her white arm through the hollow dark,   455
Pointing some whither, whereat he too rose
Like a vast giant seen by men at sea
To grow pale from the waves at dull midnight.
They melted from my sight into the woods;
Ere I could turn, Moneta cried, 'These twain   460
Are speeding to the families of grief,
Where roofed in by black rocks they waste in pain
And darkness for no hope.' And she spake on,
As ye may read who can unwearied pass
Onward from the antechamber of this dream,   465
Where even at the open doors awhile
I must delay, and glean my memory
Of her high phrase – perhaps no further dare.

----

52   *Cybele* mother of all the gods.
53   *those imps* his own children, the Olympians, by whom he
has been usurped.

Canto II

'Mortal, that thou may'st understand aright,
I humanize my sayings to thine ear,
Making comparisons of earthly things;
Or thou might'st better listen to the wind,
Whose language is to thee a barren noise,   5
Though it blows legend-laden through the trees.
In melancholy realms big tears are shed,
More sorrow like to this, and suchlike woe
Too huge for mortal tongue, or pen of scribe.
The Titans[1] fierce, self-hid or prison-bound,   10
Groan for the old allegiance once more,
Listening in their doom for Saturn's voice.
But one of our whole eagle-brood still keeps
His sov'reignty, and rule, and majesty;
Blazing Hyperion on his orbed fire[2]   15
Still sits, still snuffs the incense teeming up
From man to the sun's god – yet unsecure.
For as upon the earth dire prodigies[3]
Fright and perplex, so also shudders he;
Nor at dog's howl, or gloom-bird's even screech,[4]   20
Or the familiar visitings of one
Upon the first toll of his passing-bell,[5]
But horrors, portioned[6] to a giant nerve,
Make great Hyperion ache. His palace bright,
Bastioned with pyramids of glowing gold,   25
And touched with shade of bronzed obelisks,
Glares a blood-red through all the thousand courts,
Arches, and domes, and fiery galleries;
And all its curtains of aurorean[7] clouds
Flush angerly[8] – when he would taste the wreaths   30
Of incense breathed aloft from sacred hills,
Instead of sweets, his ample palate takes
Savour of poisonous brass and metals sick.
Wherefore, when harboured in the sleepy west,
After the full completion of fair day,   35
For rest divine upon exalted couch
And slumber in the arms of melody,
He paces through the pleasant hours of ease
With strides colossal, on from hall to hall,
While far within each aisle and deep recess   40
His winged minions in close clusters stand
Amazed, and full of fear; like anxious men
Who on a wide plain gather in sad troops
When earthquakes jar their battlements and towers.

CANTO II
[1] *The Titans* a godlike race expelled from heaven by Jupiter in Greek myth.
[2] *orbed fire* the sun; Hyperion is god of the sun.
[3] *prodigies* unnatural events.
[4] *gloom-bird's even screech* owl's hooting in the evening.
[5] *passing-bell* death-bell.
[6] *portioned* proportioned.
[7] *aurorean* roseate.
[8] *His palace . . . angerly* Hyperion's palace is part Greek, part Byzantine and part Egyptian. The model for this description is probably the 'Cloudscape New Jerusalem' passage in Wordsworth's *Excursion* (see pp. 410–11).

Even now, while Saturn, roused from icy trance,   45
Goes step for step with Thea from yon woods,
Hyperion, leaving twilight in the rear,
Is sloping to the threshold of the west.
Thither we tend.' Now in clear light I stood,
Relieved from the dusk vale. Mnemosyne   50
Was sitting on a square-edged polished stone,
That in its lucid depth reflected pure
Her priestess-garments. My quick eyes ran on
From stately nave to nave, from vault to vault,
Through bowers of fragrant and enwreathed light   55
And diamond-paved lustrous long arcades.
Anon rushed by the bright Hyperion;
His flaming robes streamed out beyond his heels,
And gave a roar, as if of earthly fire,
That scared away the meek ethereal hours[9]   60
And made their dove-wings tremble. On he flared . . .

[Bright star, would I were steadfast as thou art] (composed October–December 1819; edited from MS)[1]

Bright star, would I were steadfast as thou art –
    Not in lone splendour hung aloft the night
And watching, with eternal lids apart,
    Like nature's patient, sleepless eremite,[2]
The moving waters at their priestlike task   5
    Of pure ablution[3] round earth's human shores,
Or gazing on the new soft-fallen mask
    Of snow upon the mountains and the moors;
No – yet still steadfast, still unchangeable,
    Pillowed upon my fair love's ripening breast,   10
To feel for ever its soft swell and fall,
    Awake for ever in a sweet unrest,
Still, still to hear her tender-taken breath,
And so live ever – or else swoon to death.

[This living hand, now warm and capable] (composed towards the end of 1819)[1]

This living hand, now warm and capable
Of earnest grasping, would, if it were cold
And in the icy silence of the tomb,
So haunt thy days and chill thy dreaming nights
That thou would wish thine own heart dry of blood,
So in my veins red life might stream again,
And thou be conscience-calmed. See, here it is –
I hold it towards you.

---

[9] *hours* Latin 'Horae', attendant nymphs of the sun.

[3] *ablution* cleansing.

BRIGHT STAR, WOULD I WERE STEADFAST AS THOU ART
[1] This sonnet was published first in 1838.
[2] *eremite* anchorite, hermit.

THIS LIVING HAND, NOW WARM AND CAPABLE
[1] First published 1898. This is probably a jotting for use in a play or poem.

Hartley Coleridge   (1796–1849)

Thoroughly mythologized by some of the greatest poetry of the age (see Coleridge's *The Nightingale*, *Frost at Midnight*, conclusion to *Christabel*, and Wordsworth's *To H. C., Six Years Old*, and *Ode*), Hartley no doubt felt he had a great deal to live up to. Born 19 September 1796, he was gifted with a prodigious intelligence, but, thanks partly to his father's abandonment of his family, his early education was erratic and irregular. He was elected to a Fellowship at Oriel College, Oxford, 16 April 1819, but his academic career was blighted from the start by his drunkenness. After the College Dean found him lying in the gutter of Oriel Lane one evening, Hartley was asked to resign.

He went to London to pursue a journalistic career, but his best works were his poems. His first published verses appeared in the *London Magazine* in 1823. As a journalist his main problem was that he was unproductive. By the summer of 1823 he was in Ambleside, working as a schoolteacher. That lasted only a short time, and he moved to Leeds where he published

Biographia Borealis; or, Lives of Distinguished Northerns in 1833. In the same year he published a volume of *Poems*. In *Long time a child*, he addressed the mythologized self of *Frost at Midnight*; there is pathos in the reckoning, more pronounced in *When I review the course that I have run*, posthumously published in 1851. *To Wordsworth*, however, is a moving tribute to the poet who first described him as a 'Seer blessed' (*Ode* 114).

Hartley never lived up to the tremendous hopes that had burdened him, and died, hopeless and destitute in 1849. He was buried in Grasmere churchyard.

Further reading

Sister Mary Joseph Pomeroy, *The Poetry of Hartley Coleridge* (Washington, D.C., 1927)

Herbert Hartman, *Hartley Coleridge: Poet's Son and Poet* (Oxford, 1931)

Letters of Hartley Coleridge ed. Grace Evelyn Griggs and Earl Leslie Griggs (Oxford, 1937)

Sonnet IX

From POEMS (1833)

Long time a child, and still a child, when years
Had painted manhood on my cheek, was I;
For yet I lived like one not born to die;
A thriftless prodigal of smiles and tears,
No hope I needed, and I knew no fears.   5
But sleep, though sweet, is only sleep, and waking,
I waked to sleep no more, at once o'ertaking
The vanguard of my age, with all arrears
Of duty on my back. Nor child, nor man,
Nor youth, nor sage, I find my head is grey,   10
For I have lost the race I never ran,
A rathe[1] December blights my lagging May;
And still I am a child, though I be old –
Time is my debtor for my years untold.

VII

From ESSAYS AND MARGINALIA ed. Derwent Coleridge (1851)

When I review the course that I have run,
And count the loss of all my wasted days,
I find no argument for joy or praise

SONNET IX
[1]   *rathe* early.

In whatsoe'er my soul hath thought or done.
I am a desert, and the kindly sun   5
On me hath vainly spent his fertile rays.
Then wherefore do I tune my idle lays,
Or dream that haply I may be the one
Of the vain thousands, that shall win a place
Among the poets – that a single rhyme   10
Of my poor wit's devising may find grace
To breed high memories in the womb of time?
But to confound the time the muse I woo;
Then 'tis but just that time confound me too.

XV. To Wordsworth

From ESSAYS AND MARGINALIA ed. Derwent Coleridge (1851)

There have been poets that in verse display
The elemental forms of human passions;
Poets have been, to whom the fickle fashions
And all the wilful humours of the day
Have furnished matter for a polished lay;   5
And many are the smooth elaborate tribe
Who, emulous of thee, the shape describe,
And fain would every shifting hue portray
Of restless nature. But, thou mighty seer!
'Tis thine to celebrate the thoughts that make   10
The life of souls, the truths for whose sweet sake
We to ourselves and to our God are dear.
Of nature's inner shrine thou art the priest,
Where most she works when we perceive her least.

Mary Wollstonecraft Shelley (*née* Godwin) (1797–1851)

Born 30 August 1797, Mary Wollstonecraft Godwin could hardly have had two more distinguished parents – William Godwin (pp. 47–8) and Mary Wollstonecraft (pp. 140–1). Her mother died of post-natal septicaemia ten days later. She was raised by her father and stepmother, Mary Jane Clairmont, who had two children, Charles and Jane (later known as Claire).

Her father had been conducting a mutually admiring correspondence with the young Percy Bysshe Shelley for almost two years when she met him at dinner on 11 November 1812. Shelley was married to Harriet Westbrook at the time, but over the next eighteen months unresolvable strains developed between them; Mary and Percy began seeing a good deal of each other in June and July 1814, and the emotional pressure cul-

minated in their flight to the continent, with Claire Clairmont, on 28 July. They toured France and Switzerland, returning to England in the autumn. In 1816 they set out for the continent again, with Claire once again in tow, and spent the summer in Geneva, where they made the acquaintance of Byron. This was one of those remarkable moments in literary history where the unique chemistry of the various personalities was conducive to the production of great literature: under Shelley's influence, Byron composed *Childe Harold's Pilgrimage*, Canto III (pp. 672–708) and *Manfred*, and Shelley composed two of his greatest poems, *Mont Blanc* and *Hymn to Intellectual Beauty* (pp. 840–3, 845–9). But perhaps the most enduringly popular work of that summer was Mary's great novel *Franken-*

stein, inspired by a ghost-story competition.[1] Something of the flavour of the summer of 1816 is captured in the first of the journal entries, below.

In December 1816 Harriet Shelley committed suicide, and Percy and Mary were married, 30 December. Mary completed *Frankenstein* in Mary 1817, and it was published the following year. The Shelleys lived a nomadic and difficult life, residing successively in Venice, Rome, Naples, Florence and Pisa. In May 1822 they settled in Lerici, and Percy was drowned in July when sailing in a storm in a dangerously unstable boat. Mary was almost as devastated by Byron's death two years later, as her journal entry, reproduced below, shows.

She published more novels, including *Mathilda* (1819), *Valperga* (1823), *The Last Man* (1826), *Perkin Warbeck* (1830), *Lodore* (1835), and *Falkner* (1837). And in 1839 she supervised the production of what remains the definitive edition of her husband's *Poetical Works*, which included her own commentary. It was an extraordinary act of scholarship, and her note on

Prometheus Unbound, below, remains an essential tool in the study of that challenging work.

Her life after Percy's death was difficult. She was often impoverished, ostracized from society, and encountered much opposition from her late husband's father over the maintenance and custody of Percy Florence Shelley (her only surviving child). However, she persevered and established herself, at least in Bohemian circles, as a novelist and reviewer. Her health was never good, and in 1846 she fell seriously ill. She died 1 February 1851 at the age of fifty-three.

Further reading

R. Glynn Grylls, *Mary Shelley: A Biography* (London, 1938)
Muriel Spark, *Mary Shelley* (London, 1988)
The Mary Shelley Reader ed. Betty T. Bennett and Charles E. Robinson (New York, 1990)
The Novels and Selected Works of Mary Shelley, general editor Nora Crook with Pamela Clemit (8 vols, London, 1996)

From Journals (edited from MS) 28 May 1817

I am melancholy with reading the third Canto of *Childe Harold*. Do you not remember, Shelley, when you first read it to me, one evening after returning from Diodati?[1] It was in our little room at Chapuis;[2] the lake was before us and the mighty Jura. That time is past and this will also pass, when I may weep to read these words and again moralize on the flight of time.

Dear Lake! I shall ever love thee. How a powerful mind[3] can sanctify past scenes and recollections! His is a powerful mind, one that fills me with melancholy yet mixed with pleasure, as is always the case when intellectual energy is displayed. To think of our excursions on the Lake; how we saw him when he came down to us or welcomed our arrival with a good-humoured smile.[4] How very vividly does each verse of his poem recall some scene of this kind to my memory. This time will soon also be a recollection. We may see him again and again, enjoy his society, but the time will also arrive when that which is now an anticipation will be only in the memory Death will at length come and in the last moment all will be a dream.

From Journals (edited from MS) 15 May 1824

This then was the 'coming event' that cast its shadow on my last night's miserable thoughts. Byron has become one of the people of the grave[1] – that innumerable conclave to which the beings I best

MARY WOLLSTONECRAFT SHELLEY
[1] See Mary's Preface to the 1831 edition of the novel. For a thorough account of *Frankenstein* see John Beer's article in *A Companion to Romanticism* ed. Duncan Wu (Oxford, 1998).

FROM JOURNALS (EDITED FROM MS) 28 MAY 1817
[1] Byron was resident at Villa Diodati, on the shores of Lake Geneva, during the summer of 1816.
[2] On 3 June 1816 the Shelleys moved into a small cottage near Cologny in the region of Montalègre, known as Campagne Chappuis; they moved out on 29 August. Their reading of *Childe Harold* III is likely to have taken place between *c.* 14

August (when Claire Clairmont produced a fair copy) and the end of the month. Percy took a copy of the poem to Byron's publisher in London the following month.
[3] *a powerful mind* Mary is thinking of Byron's comments on Lake Geneva in *Childe Harold* III stanza 68ff.
[4] Shelley's cottage was a mere 8-minute walk down the slope from Diodati.

FROM JOURNALS (EDITED FROM MS) 15 MAY 1824
[1] *Byron . . . grave* news of Byron's death on 19 April 1824 at Missolonghi reached England 14 May.

loved belong. I knew him in the bright days of youth, when neither care or fear had visited me; before death had made me feel my mortality and the earth was the scene of my hopes. Can I forget our evening visits to Diodati, our excursions of the lake when he sang the Tyrolese hymn, and his voice was harmonized with winds and waves? Can I forget his attentions and consolations to me during my deepest misery? Never. Beauty sat on his countenance and power beamed from his eye; his faults being for the most part weaknesses, induced one readily to pardon them. Albe,[2] the dear capricious fascinating Albe has left this desert world.

What do I do here? Why am I doomed to live on seeing all expire before me? God grant I may die young. A new race is springing about me. At the age of twenty six I am in the condition of an aged person. All my friends are gone; I have no wish to form new. I cling to the few remaining, but they slide away and my heart fails when I think by how few ties I hold to the world. Albe, dearest Albe, was knit by long associations. Each day I repeat with bitterer feelings, 'Life is the desert and the solitude, how populous the grave'[3] – and that region, to the dearer and best beloved beings which it has torn from me, now adds that resplendent spirit, whose departure leaves the dull earth dark as midnight.

On Reading Wordsworth's Lines on Peele Castle (composed 8 December 1825; edited from MS)

It is with me, as erst with you,
   Oh poet, nature's chronicler,
The summer seas have lost their hue
   And storm sits brooding everywhere.

The gentlest rustling of the deep   5
   Is but the dirge of him I lost,
And when waves raise their furrows steep,
   And bring foam in which is tossed

A voice I hear upon the wind
   Which bids me haste to join him there,   10
And woo the tempest's breath unkind
   Which gives to me a kindred bier.

And when all smooth are ocean's plains
   And sails afar are glittering,
The fairest skiff his form contains   15
   To my poor heart's fond picturing.

Then wildly to the beach I rush,
   And fain would seize the frailest boat,
And from dull earth the slight hull push,
   On dancing waves towards him to float.   20

'Nor may I e'er again behold
   The sea, and be as I have been;
My bitter grief will ne'er grow old,
   Nor say I this with mind serene.'[1]

---

[2] Albe i.e. 'LB', a familiar name for Byron in the Shelley circle.
[3] Young, Night Thoughts i 115–16.

ON READING WORDSWORTH'S LINES ON PEELE CASTLE
[1] See Wordsworth, Elegiac Stanzas Suggested by a Picture of Peele Castle 37–40.

For oft I weep in solitude   25
   And shed so many bitter tears,
While on past joys I vainly brood
   And shrink in fear from coming years.

A Dirge (composed November 1827; edited from MS)

To the air of 'My Phillida, adieu, love!'

This morn thy gallant bark, love,
   Sailed on a sunny sea;
'Tis noon, and tempests dark, love,
   Have wrecked it on the lee.
     Ah woe! Ah woe! Ah woe!   5
    By spirits of the deep
    He's cradled on the billow
    To his unwaking sleep.

Thou liest upon the shore, love,
   Beside the knelling surge,   10
But sea-nymphs evermore, love,
   Shall sadly chaunt thy dirge.
     Oh come! Oh come! Oh come!
    Ye spirits of the deep,
    While near his seaweed pillow   15
    My lonely watch I keep.

From far across the sea, love,
   I hear a wild lament,
By Echo's voice for thee, love,
   From ocean's caverns sent: 20
     Oh list! Oh list! Oh list!
    The spirits of the deep –
    Loud sounds their wail of sorrow,
    While I for ever weep.

[Oh listen while I sing to thee] (composed 12 March 1838; edited from MS)

Oh listen while I sing to thee,
   My song is meant for thee alone;
My thought imparts its melody,
   And gives the soft impassioned tone.

I sing of joy, and see thy smile   5
   That to the swelling note replies;
I sing of love, and feel the while
   The gaze of thy love-beaming eyes.

If thou wert far, my voice would die
   In murmurs faint and sorrowing;   10
If thou wert fake – in agony
   My heart would break, I could not sing.

> Then listen while I sing to thee,
>   My song is meant for thee alone;
> And now that thou art near to me
>   I pour a full impassioned tone.

15

Note on the 'Prometheus Unbound' (extracts) (ii 132–6, 137–40)

From THE POETICAL WORKS OF PERCY BYSSHE SHELLEY ed. Mary Shelley
(4 vols, 1839)

The prominent feature of Shelley's theory of the destiny of the human species was that evil is not inherent in the system of the creation, but an accident that might be expelled. This also forms a portion of Christianity: God made earth and man perfect, till he, by his fall, 'Brought death into the world, and all our woe'.[1] Shelley believed that mankind had only to will that there should be no evil, and there would be none. It is not my part in these notes to notice the arguments that have been urged against this opinion, but to mention the fact that he entertained it, and was indeed attached to it with fervent enthusiasm. That man could be so perfectionized as to be able to expel evil from his own nature and from the greater part of the creation, was the cardinal point of his system. And the subject he loved best to dwell on, was the image of One warring with the Evil Principle, oppressed not only by it, but by all – even the good who were deluded into considering evil a necessary portion of humanity.

A victim full of fortitude and hope, and the spirit of triumph emanating from a reliance in the ultimate omnipotence of good: such he had depicted in his last poem,[2] when he made Laon the enemy and the victim of tyrants. He now took a more idealized image of the same subject. He followed certain classical authorities in figuring Saturn as the good principle, Jupiter the usurping evil one, and Prometheus as the regenerator, who, unable to bring mankind back to primitive innocence, used knowledge as a weapon to defeat evil, by leading mankind beyond the state wherein they are sinless through ignorance, to that in which they are virtuous through wisdom. Jupiter punished the temerity of the Titan by chaining him to a rock of Caucasus, and causing a vulture to devour his still renewed heart. There was a prophecy afloat in heaven portending the fall of Jove, the secret of averting which was known only to Prometheus – and the god offered freedom from torture on condition of its being communicated to him. According to the mythological story, this referred to the offspring of Thetis, who was destined to be greater than his father. Prometheus at last bought pardon for his crime of enriching mankind with his gifts, by revealing the prophecy. Hercules killed the vulture and set him free, and Thetis was married to Peleus, the father of Achilles.

Shelley adapted the catastrophe of this story to his peculiar views. The son, greater than his father, born of the nuptials of Jupiter and Thetis, was to dethrone Evil, and bring back a happier reign than that of Saturn. Prometheus defies the power of his enemy, and endures centuries of torture till the hour arrives when Jove, blind to the real event, but darkly guessing that some great good to himself will flow, espouses Thetis. At the moment, the primal power of the world drives him from his usurped throne, and strength, in the person of Hercules, liberates humanity, typified in Prometheus, from the tortures generated by evil done or suffered. Asia, one of the Oceanides, is the wife of Prometheus (she was, according to other mythological interpretations, the same as Venus and nature). When the benefactor of mankind is liberated, nature resumes the beauty of her prime, and is united to her husband, the emblem of the human race, in perfect and happy union. In the fourth Act, the poet gives further scope to his imagination and idealizes the forms of creation, such as we know them,

---

NOTE ON THE 'PROMETHEUS UNBOUND'
[1]   *Paradise Lost* i 3.
[2]   *his last poem* i.e. his previous poem, *Laon and Cythna*, later retitled *The Revolt of Islam*, composed March–September 1817, published December 1817.

instead of such as they appeared to the Greeks. Maternal Earth, the mighty parent, is superseded by the Spirit of the Earth – the guide of our planet through the realms of sky – while his fair and weaker companion and attendant, the Spirit of the Moon, receives bliss from the annihilation of Evil in the superior sphere.

Shelley develops (more particularly in the lyrics of this drama) his abstruse and imaginative theories with regard to the creation. It requires a mind as subtle and penetrating as his own to understand the mystic meanings scattered throughout the poem. They elude the ordinary reader by their abstraction and delicacy of distinction, but they are far from vague. It was his design to write prose metaphysical essays on the nature of man, which would have served to explain much of what is obscure in his poetry; a few scattered fragments of observations and remarks alone remain. He considered these philosophical views of mind and nature to be instinct with the intensest spirit of poetry.

More popular poets clothe the ideal with familiar and sensible imagery. Shelley loved to idealize the real – to gift the mechanism of the material universe with a soul and a voice, and to bestow such also on the most delicate and abstract emotions and thoughts of the mind. Sophocles was his great master in this species of imagery. . . .

In the 'Prometheus Unbound', Shelley fulfils the promise quoted from a letter in the note on *The Revolt of Islam*. The tone of the composition is calmer and more majestic, the poetry more perfect as a whole, and the imagination displayed at once more pleasingly beautiful and more varied and daring. The description of the Hours as they are seen in the cave of Demogorgon, is an instance of this – it fills the mind as the most charming picture; we long to see an artist at work to bring to our view the

> cars drawn by rainbow-winged steeds
> Which trample the dim winds; in each there stands
> A wild-eyed charioteer urging their flight.
> Some look behind, as fiends pursued them there,
> And yet I see no shapes but the keen stars;
> Others, with burning eyes, lean forth, and drink
> With eager lips the wind of their own speed,
> As if the thing they loved fled on before,
> And now, even now, they clasped it. Their bright locks
> Stream like a comet's flashing hair – they all
> Sweep onward.[3]

Through the whole poem there reigns a sort of calm and holy spirit of love; it soothes the tortured, and is hope to the expectant, till the prophecy is fulfilled, and love, untainted by any evil, becomes the law of the world.

England had been rendered a painful residence to Shelley, as much by the sort of persecution with which in those days all men of liberal opinions were visited, and by the injustice he had lately endured in the Court of Chancery,[4] as by the symptoms of disease which made him regard a visit to Italy as necessary to prolong his life. An exile, and strongly impressed with the feeling that the majority of his countrymen regarded him with sentiments of aversion (such as his own heart could experience towards none), he sheltered himself from such disgusting and painful thoughts in the calm retreats of poetry, and built up a world of his own, with the more pleasure, since he hoped to induce some one or two to believe that the earth might become such, did mankind themselves consent. The charm of the Roman climate helped to clothe his thoughts in greater beauty than they had ever worn before. And as he wandered among the ruins, made one with nature in their decay, or gazed on the Praxitelean shapes[5] that throng the Vatican, the Capitol, and the palaces of Rome, his soul imbibed

---

3 *Prometheus Unbound* II iv 130–40.

4 *the injustice . . . Chancery* Shelley lost his battle for custody of Charles and Ianthe, his two children by his first wife, Harriet Westbrook, on 17 March 1816. Shelley departed for the continent on 3 May.

5 *Praxitelean shapes* statues like those by Praxiteles, one of the most famous Greek sculptors, born at Athens, *c.*390 BC. Mary is recalling *Prometheus Unbound* III iii 165 (p. 910).

forms of loveliness which became a portion of itself.[6] There are many passages in the 'Prometheus' which show the intense delight he received from such studies, and give back the impression with a beauty of poetical description peculiarly his own. He felt this, as a poet must feel when he satisfies himself by the result of his labours, and he wrote from Rome: 'My "Prometheus Unbound" is just finished, and in a month or two I shall send it. It is a drama, with characters and mechanism of a kind yet unattempted, and I think the execution is better than any of my former attempts.'

Letitia Elizabeth Landon (L.E.L.)   (1802–1838)

Letitia was born on 14 August 1802 at 25 Hans Place, Chelsea. Her education was fragmented and unsystematic; she was taught to read by an invalid neighbour, and at five sent to Miss Rowden's Chelsea school where Lady Caroline Lamb and Mary Russell Mitford had been pupils. But this was only for a few months. She was a voracious reader, at an early age having memorized Scott's *Lady of the Lake*, and read between 100 and 150 volumes of Cooke's *Poets and Novelists*, in addition to 'Rollin's Ancient History, Hume and Smollett; then come Plutarch's Lives, the Fables of Gay and Aesop, Life of Josephus, Montesquieu's Spirit of the Laws, Dobson's Life of Petrarch, and many others, more or less adapted to the young reader.'[1] Also by this time she was composing poetry.

When she was thirteen the family moved to Fulham and then Old Brompton, largely because of her father's troubled finances. It was in Old Brompton, while still a teenager, that she first came to the notice of William Jerdan, editor of the *Literary Gazette*. She began contributing to the *Literary Gazette* under the initials 'L.E.L.', and quickly attracted a following. At first she had great difficulty finding a publisher for a long poem she had written, *The Improvisatrice*; it was, she later recalled, rejected by every publisher in London. But the notoriety of her work for the *Literary Gazette* made it comparatively easy for her to find a publisher in 1824. She later told Alaric Watts that 'I wrote the *Improvisatrice* in less than five weeks, and during that time I often was for two or three days without touching it. I never saw the MS till in proof-sheets a year afterwards, and I made no additions, only verbal alterations.'[2] Her publishers paid her £300 for it, and it was an instant success, going through six editions within the year. Reviews were generally favourable,

and among the first was an outrageous puff by Jerdan in the *Literary Gazette*, describing Letitia as 'the English Sappho'.

This was, of course, business. By 1824 women poets were not just acceptable to the literary marketplace – they were positively fashionable. Always hungry for new talent, publishers were willing to take anything saleable and feed it to the ever-open maw of the reading public. Felicia Hemans had colluded with the process because, as a single parent with five children, she had little choice; she burned herself out and died young. In a recent essay on Landon, Germaine Greer remarks: 'The reality of her life was daily work, endless deadlines, poor pay and no power whatsoever, even to express what she really believed. Grub Street destroyed her personal integrity, worked her to exhaustion and then turned on her.'[3] Like Felicia Hemans, Landon was strongly influenced by Wordsworth, as she admits in her tribute, *On Wordsworth's Cottage, near Grasmere Lake*. Landon's verse at its best embodies the Wordsworthian virtue of being able to address deeply-felt emotions without the sentimentality favoured by many poets at the end of the eighteenth century. This is evident in her discussion of the lot of the female poet in the elegant *Stanzas on the Death of Mrs Hemans*, which provoked a response from the young Elizabeth Barrett (pp. 1109–10). *A Poet's Love* laments, among other things, the loss of imaginative vision; it was published only after her death.

William Jerdan calculated that Letitia earned £2,585 in total from her work, about £250 a year.[4] Besides *The Improvisatrice*, she published *The Troubadour* (1825), *The Golden Violet* (1827) and *The Venetian Bracelet* (1829), among other titles. But the real hardship in her literary life was her embroilment in scandal

---

[6]   See Shelley's letter of 23 March 1819 to Peacock: 'Rome is yet the capital of the world. It is a city of palaces and temples more glorious than those which any other city contains, and of ruins more glorious than they' (Jones ii 87).

LETITIA ELIZABETH LANDON
[1]   Lamon Blanchard, *Life and Literary Remains of L.E.L.*, (2 vols, London, 184), i 10.
[2]   Alaric Alfred Watts, *Alaric Watts: A Narrative of his Life* (2 vols, London, 1884), ii 21.
[3]   *Slip-Shod Sibyls* (London, 1995), p. 259.
[4]   *The Autobiography of William Jerdan* (4 vols, London, 1853), iii 185.

– first through her association with the dissolute William Maginn, and then through her friendship with Daniel Maclise, the artist. Rumours about her can only have intensified the desire for domestic stability, and on 7 June 1838 at St Mary's, Bryanston Square, she married George Maclean, governor of Cape Coast Castle in Africa. She sailed for Africa on 5 July, and arrived on 15 August. Two months later she was found dead, a bottle of prussic acid in her hand. She was only thirty-six. Suspicions about her husband, and the failure of the coroner to perform a post-mortem, led to much speculation about the causes and means of her death.

Further reading

Germaine Greer, *Slip-Shod Sibyls: Recognition, Rejection and the Woman Poet* (London, 1995), chapter 10

Letitia Elizabeth Landon, *The Improvisatrice, 1825* Introduction by Jonathan Wordsworth (Poole, 1996)

F. J. Sypher, 'The Magical Letters of L.E.L.', *Columbia Library Columns* 39 (1990) 3–9

Glennis Stephenson, 'Letitia Landon and the Victorian Improvisatrice: The Construction of L.E.L.', *Victorian Poetry* 30 (1992) 1–17

Virginia Blain, 'Letitia Elizabeth Landon, Eliza Mary Hamilton, and the Genealogy of the Victorian Poetess', *Victorian Poetry* 33 (1995) 31–52

[*When should lovers breathe their vows?*]

From THE IMPROVISATRICE AND OTHER POEMS (1824)

When should lovers breathe their vows?
　　When should ladies hear them?
When the dew is on the boughs,
　　When none else are near them;
When the moon shines cold and pale,　　　　　　5
　　When the birds are sleeping,
When no voice is on the gale,
　　When the rose is weeping;
When the stars are bright on high,
　　Like hopes in young love's dreaming,　　　　10
And glancing round the light clouds fly,
　　Like soft fears to shade their beaming.
The fairest smiles are those that live
　　On the brow by starlight wreathing;
And the lips their richest incense give　　　　　15
　　When the sigh is at midnight breathing.
Oh softest is the cheek's love-ray
　　When seen by moonlight hours,
Other roses seek the day,
　　But blushes are night-flowers.　　　　　　20
Oh when the moon and stars are bright,
　　When the dew-drops glisten,
Then their vows should lovers plight,
　　Then should ladies listen!

Stanzas on the Death of Mrs Hemans

From NEW MONTHLY MAGAZINE 44 (1835, pp. 286–8)

> *The rose – the glorious rose is gone.*
> *Felicia Hemans,* Lays of Many Lands[1]

Bring flowers to crown the cup and lute,
    Bring flowers, the bride is near;
Bring flowers to soothe the captive's cell,
    Bring flowers to strew the bier!
Bring flowers! – thus said the lovely song;[2]   5
    And shall they not be brought
To her who linked the offering
    With feeling and with thought?

Bring flowers, the perfumed and the pure,
    Those with the morning dew,   10
A sigh in every fragrant leaf,
    A tear on every hue.
So pure, so sweet thy life has been,
    So filling earth and air
With odours and with loveliness   15
    Till common scenes grew fair.

Thy song around our daily path
    Flung beauty born of dreams,
That shadows on the actual world
    The spirit's sunny gleams.   20
Mysterious influence, that to earth
    Brings down the heaven above,
And fills the universal heart
    With universal love.

Such gifts were thine – as from the block,   25
    The unformed and the cold,
The sculptor calls to breathing life
    Some shape of perfect mould;
So thou from common thoughts and things
    Didst call a charmed song,   30
Which on a sweet and swelling tide
    Bore the full soul along.

And thou from far and foreign lands
    Didst bring back many a tone,
And giving such new music still,   35
    A music of thine own.
A lofty strain of generous thoughts,
    And yet subdued and sweet –

STANZAS ON THE DEATH OF MRS HEMANS
[1] The quotation is from *The Nightingale's Death-Song* 3–4:
'The rose, the glorious rose is gone, / And I, too, will depart.'

[2] *Bring Flowers*, one of the miscellaneous poems included in
Hemans's *Lays of Many Lands* (1825).

An angel's song, who sings of earth,
    Whose cares are at his feet.   40

And yet thy song is sorrowful,
    Its beauty is not bloom;
The hopes of which it breathes are hopes
    That look beyond the tomb.
Thy song is sorrowful as winds   45
    That wander o'er the plain,
And ask for summer's vanished flowers,
    And ask for them in vain.

Ah, dearly purchased is the gift,
    The gift of song like thine;   50
A fated doom is hers who stands
    The priestess of the shrine.
The crowd – they only see the crown,
    They only hear the hymn –
They mark not that the cheek is pale,   55
    And that the eye is dim.

Wound to a pitch too exquisite,
    The soul's fine chords are wrung;
With misery and melody
    They are too highly strung.   60
The heart is made too sensitive
    Life's daily pain to bear;
It beats in music, but it beats
    Beneath a deep despair.

It never meets the love it paints,   65
    The love for which it pines;
Too much of heaven is in the faith
    That such a heart enshrines.
The meteor wreath the poet wears
    Must make a lonely lot;   70
It dazzles only to divide
    From those who wear it not.

Didst thou not tremble at thy fame
    And loathe its bitter prize,
While what to others triumph seemed,   75
    To thee was sacrifice?
Oh flower brought from paradise
    To this cold world of ours,
Shadows of beauty such as thine
    Recall thy native bowers.   80

Let others thank thee – 'twas for them
    Thy soft leaves thou didst wreathe;
The red rose wastes itself in sighs
    Whose sweetness others breathe!
And they have thanked thee – many a lip   85

Has asked of thine for words,
When thoughts, life's finer thoughts, have touched
   The spirit's inmost chords.

How many loved and honoured thee
   Who only knew thy name;   90
Which o'er the weary working world
   Like starry music came!
With what still hours of calm delight
   Thy songs and image blend;
I cannot choose but think thou wert   95
   An old familiar friend.

The charm that dwelt in songs of thine
   My inmost spirit moved;
And yet I feel as thou hadst been
   Not half enough beloved.   100
They say that thou wert faint and worn
   With suffering and with care;
What music must have filled the soul
   That had so much to spare!

Oh weary one! since thou art laid   105
   Within thy mother's breast —
The green, the quiet mother earth —
   Thrice blessed be thy rest!
Thy heart is left within our hearts
   Although life's pang is o'er;   110
But the quick tears are in my eyes,
   And I can write no more.

On Wordsworth's Cottage, near Grasmere Lake

From THE ZENANA, AND MINOR POEMS OF L.E.L. (1839)

Not for the glory on their heads
   Those stately hilltops wear,
Although the summer sunset sheds
   Its constant crimson there;
Not for the gleaming lights that break   5
The purple of the twilight lake,
   Half dusky and half fair,
Does that sweet valley seem to be
A sacred place on earth to me.

The influence of a moral spell   10
   Is found around the scene,
Giving new shadows to the dell,
   New verdure to the green.
With every mountain-top is wrought
The presence of associate thought,   15
   A music that has been;

Calling that loveliness to life,
With which the inward world is rife.

His home, our English poet's home,
    Amid these hills is made;   20
Here with the morning hath he come,
    There, with the night delayed.
On all things is his memory cast,
For every place wherein he passed
    Is with his mind arrayed –   25
That, wandering in a summer hour,
Asked wisdom of the leaf and flower.

Great poet, if I dare to throw
    My homage at thy feet,
'Tis thankfulness for hours which thou   30
    Hast made serene and sweet;
As wayfarers have incense thrown
Upon some mighty altar-stone
    Unworthy, and yet meet –
The human spirit longs to prove   35
The truth of its uplooking love.

Until thy hand unlocked its store,
    What glorious music slept!
Music that can be hushed no more
    Was from our knowledge kept.   40
But the great Mother[1] gave to thee
The poet's universal key,
    And forth the fountains swept –
A gushing melody for ever,
The witness of thy high endeavour.   45

Rough is the road which we are sent,
    Rough with long toil and pain;
And when upon the steep ascent,
    A little way we gain,
Vexed with our own perpetual care,   50
Little we heed what sweet things are
    Around our pathway blent;[2]
With anxious steps we hurry on,
The very sense of pleasure gone.

But thou dost in this feverish dream   55
    Awake a better mood,
With voices from the mountain stream,
    With voices from the wood.
And with their music dost impart
Their freshness to the world-worn heart,   60
    Whose fever is subdued

On Wordsworth's Cottage, near Grasmere Lake   [2] *blent* mingled.
[1] *the great Mother* earth.

By memories sweet with other years,
By gentle hopes, and soothing tears.

A solemn creed is thine, and high,
      Yet simple as a child,   65
Who looketh hopeful to yon sky
      With eyes yet undefiled
By all the glitter and the glare
This life's deceits and follies wear,
      Exalted, and yet mild,   70
Conscious of those diviner powers
Brought from a better world than ours.

Thou hast not chosen to rehearse
      The old heroic themes;
Thou hast not given to thy verse   75
      The heart's impassioned dreams.
Forth flows thy song as waters flow,
So bright above – so calm below,
      Wherein the heaven seems
Eternal as the golden shade   80
Its sunshine on the stream hath laid.

The glory which thy spirit hath
      Is round life's common things,
And flingeth round our common path,
      As from an angel's wings,   85
A light that is not of our sphere,
Yet lovelier for being here,
      Beneath whose presence springs
A beauty never marked before,
Yet once known, vanishing no more.   90

How often with the present sad,
      And weary with the past,
A sunny respite have we had,
      By but a chance look cast
Upon some word of thine that made   95
The sullenness forsake the shade,
      Till shade itself was past:
For hope divine, serene and strong,
Perpetual lives within thy song.

Eternal as the hills thy name,   100
      Eternal as thy strain;
So long as ministers of fame
      Shall love and hope remain.
The crowded city in its streets,
The valley, in its green retreats,   105
      Alike thy words retain.
What need hast thou of sculptured stone?
Thy temple is thy name alone.

A Poet's Love

From LIFE AND LITERARY REMAINS OF L.E.L. (1841)

Faint and more faint amid the world of dreams,
That which was once my all, thy image, seems
Pale as a star that in the morning gleams.

Long time that sweet face was my guiding star,
Bringing me visions of the fair and far, 5
Remote from this world's toil and this world's jar.

Around it was an atmosphere of light,
Deep with the tranquil loveliness of night,
Subdued and shadowy, yet serenely bright.

Like to a spirit did it dwell apart, 10
Hushed in the sweetest silence of my heart,
Lifting me to the heaven from whence thou art.

Too soon the day broke on that haunted hour,
Loosing its spell, and weakening its power,
All that had been imagination's dower. 15

The noontide quenched that once enchanted ray;
Care, labour, sorrow, gathered on the day –
Toil was upon my steps, dust on my way.

They melted down to earth my upward wings;
I half forgot the higher, better things, 20
The hope which yet again thy image brings.

Would I were worthier of thee? I am fain,
Amid my life of bitterness and pain,
To dream once more my early dreams again.

Elizabeth Barrett Browning   (1806–1861)

Elizabeth Barrett was the eldest of eleven children born to Edward and Mary Moulton Barrett, at Coxhoe Hall, Durham, 6 March 1806. As a child, she was a precocious scholar, sharing her brother's lessons, and overtaking him in the study of Greek and Latin. She later taught herself Hebrew. An illness in her teens (still not adequately diagnosed or explained) left her a semi-invalid for the rest of her life, and led to her frequent use of laudanum.

She was composing poetry by eleven, when she wrote *The Battle of Marathon*, privately printed three years later. Her first published poem appeared in a magazine when she was fifteen, and in 1826 she published a second volume, *An Essay on Mind, with Other Poems*. Further books, *Prometheus Bound* (1833) and *The Seraphim, and Other Poems* (1838), were fairly well received and led to her collected poems in 1844. Her courtship with Robert Browning began a year later, and they married clandestinely, against her father's wishes, 12 September 1845. A week later they eloped to Italy.

For most of her life she remained there, returning to London for occasional visits. Her major poetical works are *Casa Guidi Windows* (1851) and *Aurora Leigh* (1857). She died in Florence on 29 June 1861, and was buried in the Protestant Cemetery in Florence.

Although Elizabeth's best work marks her as an important Victorian writer, she grew up a romantic. One of her first idols was Byron, and as a teenager she enjoyed dressing up as his page. Her *Stanzas on the Death of Lord Byron*, among her earliest published poems, shows a deft control of the Spenserian stanza, the essentially slow tempo of which was suited to elegy (more so, perhaps, than to *Childe Harold's Pilgrimage*). It can be read as a farewell to romanticism itself. Another elegy, *Stanzas Addressed to Miss Landon*, responds to Landon's lament for Felicia Hemans, advising her to take comfort from Christian consolation. It is underpinned in part by Barrett's reservations about Landon's verse; as she told Lady Margaret Cocks on 9 December 1835, Landon 'is deficient in energy and condensation, as well as in variety.... There is a vividness and a naturalness, both in the ideas and the expression of them – yes! And a pathos too! She is like a bird of few notes. They are few – but nature gave them!'[1] Barrett's concerns are sharply focused in the elegy she composed a year later for Landon, *L.E.L.'s Last Question*, which deals with Landon's mysterious death, apparently by prussic acid poisoning. Barrett's best work was yet to come, but her originality and unique abilities are evident even here.

For a fuller account of her life and work, see *Victorian Women Poets: An Anthology* ed. Angela Leighton and Margaret Reynolds (Oxford, 1995), pp. 63–129.

Further reading

Alethea Hayter, *Mrs Browning: A Poet's Work and its Setting* (London, 1962)

Angela Leighton, *Elizabeth Barrett Browning* (Brighton, 1986)

Stanzas on the Death of Lord Byron (composed shortly after 14 May 1824)

From THE GLOBE AND TRAVELLER No. 6733 (30 June 1824)

> λέγε πασιν ἀπώλετο.[1]
> *I am not what I have been.*[2]

He *was*, and *is* not! Graecia's trembling shore,
    Sighing through all her palmy groves, shall tell
That Harold's pilgrimage at last is o'er;
    Mute the impassioned tongue, and tuneful shell,
    That erst was wont in noblest strains to swell!   5
Hushed the proud shouts that rode th' Aegean wave,
    For lo! the great deliv'rer breathes farewell!
Gives to the world his mem'ry, and a grave –
And dies amidst the land he lived and fought to save!

Mourn, Hellas,[3] mourn! and o'er thy widowed brow,   10
    For aye the cypress wreath of sorrow twine;
And in thy new-formed beauty, desolate, throw
    The fresh-culled flowers on *his* sepulchral shrine.
    Yes, let that heart, whose fervour was all thine,
In consecrated urn lamented be!   15
    That generous heart whose genius thrilled divine
Hath spent its last most glorious throb for thee –
Then sank amidst the storm that made thy children free.

Britannia's poet, Graecia's hero, sleeps!
    And Freedom, bending o'er the breathless clay,   20

ELIZABETH BARRETT BROWNING
[1] *The Brownings' Correspondence* iii 159.

STANZAS ON THE DEATH OF LORD BYRON
[1] Bion, *Lament for Adonis* 5: '... tell everyone he is utterly lost ...'
[2] Byron, *Childe Harold's Pilgrimage* iv 1662–3.
[3] *Hellas* Greece.

Lifts up her voice, and in her wildness weeps!
 For *us*, a night hath clouded o'er our day
 And hushed the lips that breathed our fairest lay.
Alas! and must the British lyre resound
 A requiem, while the spirit wings away   25
Of *him* who on her strings such music found,
 And taught her startling chords to breathe so sweet a sound?

The theme grows sadder – and my soul shall find
 A language in these tears. No more, no more!
Soon, midst the shrieking of the tossing wind,   30
 The 'dark blue depths'[4] he sang of shall have bore
 Our *all* of Byron to his native shore![5]
His grave is thick with voices, murm'ring here
 The awful tale of greatness swiftly o'er;
But mem'ry strives with death and, ling'ring near,   35
Shall consecrate the dust of Harold's lonely bier!

Stanzas Addressed to Miss Landon, and Suggested by her 'Stanzas on the Death of Mrs Hemans' (signed 'B.')

From NEW MONTHLY MAGAZINE 45 (1838, p. 82)

Thou bay-crowned living one,[1] who o'er
 The bay-crowned dead[2] art bowing,
And o'er the shadeless, moveless brow
 Thy human shadow throwing;
And o'er the sighless, songless lips   5
 The wail and music wedding,
Dropping o'er the tranquil eyes
 Tears not of *their* shedding[3] –

Go take thy music from the dead,
 Whose silentness is sweeter;   10
Reserve thy tears for living brows,
 For whom such tears are meeter;
And leave the violets in the grass
 To brighten where thou treadest –
No flowers for her – oh, bring no flowers,   15
 Albeit 'Bring flowers',[4] thou saidest.

But bring not near her solemn corse
 A type of human seeming;
Lay only dust's stern verity
 Upon her dust undreaming.   20
And while the calm perpetual stars

---

4 Byron *Manfred* I i 76.
5 Byron's remains arrived in London 5 July 1824.

STANZAS ADDRESSED TO MISS LANDON
1 Letitia Landon, who died in the year in which this poem

was published. Bay was used to crown distinguished poets in ancient times.
2 Felicia Hemans (see pp. 990–2).
3 See Landon, *Stanzas on the Death of Mrs Hemans* 111.
4 See Landon, *Stanzas on the Death of Mrs Hemans* 1–5.

Shall look upon it solely,
Her sphered soul shall look on *them*
With eyes more bright and holy.

Nor mourn, oh living one, because   25
Her part in life was mourning:
Would she have lost the poet's flame
For anguish of the burning?
The minstrel harp, for the strained string?
The tripod,[5] for th' afflated[6]   30
Woe? Or the vision, for those tears
Through which it shone dilated?

Perhaps she shuddered while the world's
Cold hand her brow was wreathing,
But wronged she ne'er that mystic breath   35
Which breathed in all her breathing;
Which drew from rocky earth and man
Abstractions high and moving –
Beauty, if not the beautiful,
And love, if not the loving.   40

Such visionings have paled in sight
The Saviour she descrieth,
And little recks who wreathed the brow
That on His bosom lieth.
The whiteness of His innocence   45
O'er all her garments flowing –
There learneth she that sweet 'new song'
She will not mourn in knowing.

Be blessed, crowned and living one,
And when thy dust decayeth,   50
May thine own England say for thee
What now for her it sayeth –
'Albeit softly in our ears
Her silver song was ringing,
The footsteps of her parting soul   55
Were softer than her singing.'

L.E.L.'s Last Question

From THE ATHENAEUM No. 587 (26 January 1839, p. 69)

'Do you think of me as I think of you,
My friends, my friends?'[1] She said it from the sea,

---

5   *tripod* the priestess at Delphi usually sat on a three-legged
stool when delivering her prophecies.
6   *afflated* inspired.

L.E.L.'s LAST QUESTION
1   Barrett's sister, Arabella, explained to Hugh Stuart Boyd
on 28 January 1839: 'I daresay you heard of Miss Landon's last
letter that she wrote to some friend in England, a day or two
before her death.... the question upon which these lines are
written were the last words of her letter.'

The English minstrel in her minstrelsy,
While under brighter skies than erst she knew[2]
Her heart grew dark, and gropèd as the blind,   5
To touch, across the waves, friends left behind –
'Do you think of me as I think of you?'

It seemed not much to ask – 'as I of you?'
We all do ask the same – no eyelids cover
Within the meekest eyes that question over;   10
And little in this world the loving do
But sit (among the rocks?) and listen for
The echo of their own love evermore;
Do you think of me as I think of you?

Love-learned, she had sung of only love,   15
And as a child asleep (with weary head
Dropped on the fairy book he lately read),
Whatever household noises round him move,
Hears in his dream some elfin turbulence –
Even so, suggestive to her inward sense,   20
All sounds of life assumed one tune of love.

And when the glory of her dream withdrew,
When knightly gestes[3] and courtly pageantries
Were broken in her visionary eyes
By tears, the solemn seas attested true –   25
Forgetting that sweet lute beside her hand,
She asked not, 'Do you praise me, oh my land?'
But 'Think ye of me, friends, as I of you?'

True heart to love, that pourèd many a year
Love's oracles for England, smooth and well –   30
Would God thou hadst an inward oracle
In that lone moment, to confirm thee dear!
For when thy questioned friends in agony
Made passionate response, 'We think of thee',
Thy place was in the dust – too deep to hear!   35

Could she not wait to catch the answering breath?
Was she content with that drear ocean's sound,
Dashing his mocking infinite around
The craver of a little love, beneath
Those stars, content – where last her song had gone?   40
They, mute and cold in radiant life, as soon
Their singer was to be, in darksome death!

Bring your vain answers, cry, 'We think of thee!'
How think ye of her? In the long ago
Delights, or crowned by new bays? Not so;   45
None smile, and none are crowned where lyeth she,

---

[2]   *under brighter skies ... knew* Landon died on the Gold
Coast, where she resided with her husband, George Maclean,
Governor of Cape Coast Castle.
[3]   *gestes* brave deeds.

With all her visions unfulfilled – save one,
Her childhood's, of the palm-trees in the sun:
And lo, their shadow on her sepulchre!

Do you think of me as I think of you?   50
Oh friends, oh kindred, oh dear brotherhood
Of the whole world, what are we that we should
For covenants of long affection sue?
Why press so near each other, when the touch
Is barred by graves? Not much, and yet too much,   55
This 'Think upon me as I think of you.'

But while on mortal lips I shape anew
A sigh to mortal issues, verily
Above th' unshaken stars that see us die,
A vocal pathos rolls – and He who drew   60
All life from dust, and *for* all tasted death,
By death, and life, and love appealing, saith,
'Do you think of me as I think of you?'

Sonnet on Mr Haydon's Portrait of Mr Wordsworth[1]

From THE ATHENAEUM No. 783 (29 October 1842, p. 932)

Wordsworth upon Helvellyn! Let the cloud
Ebb audibly along the mountain wind,
Then break against the rock, and show behind
The lowland valleys floating up to crowd
The sense with beauty. *He* with forehead bowed   5
And humble-lidded eyes, as one inclined
Before the sovran thoughts of his own mind,
And very meek with inspirations proud,
Takes here his rightful place as poet-priest,
By the high altar, singing prayer and prayer   10
To the yet higher heav'ns. A vision free
And noble, Haydon, hath thine art released[2] –
No portrait this, with academic air!
This is the poet and his poetry.

SONNET ON MR HAYDON'S PORTRAIT OF MR WORDSWORTH
[1]   Haydon's painting, *Wordsworth on Helvellyn*, was completed in 1842 and is now at the National Gallery, London. It is reproduced by Gill, *William Wordsworth: A Life* (Oxford, 1989), plate 17. Haydon and Barrett enjoyed a warm and friendly correspondence, but never met; they were brought together by a mutual admiration for Wordsworth.
[2]   Haydon forwarded a copy of the sonnet to Wordsworth on 19 October 1842. In an appreciative letter to her of 26 October, Wordsworth suggested a revision to lines 11–12: 'By a vision free / And noble, Haydon, is thine art released' (*LY* iv 384–5).

Index of Titles and First Lines

This index lists titles and first lines of verse only. Extracts from poems are listed by the name of the work only (as opposed to the title of the extract); dramatic works are listed by title only.

Index to Headnotes and Notes

descriptions when certain principles or powers or conditions are admitted. Another will throw himself into various characters and make them speak as the passions would naturally incite them to do.

The highest order of poet will not only possess all the above powers but will have as high an imagination that he will be able to throw his own soul into any object he sees or imagines, so as to see, feel, be sensible of, and express all that the object itself would see, feel, be sensible of, or express – and he will speak out of that object, so that his own self will, with the exception of the mechanical part, be 'annihilated'.[2] And it is [of] the excess of this power that I suppose Keats to speak, when he says he has no identity. As a poet, and when the fit is upon him, this is true. And it is a fact that he does by the power of his imagination create ideal personages, substances, and powers – that he lives for a time in their souls or essences or ideas – and that occasionally so intensely as to lose consciousness of what is round him. We all do the same in a degree, when we fall into a reverie.[3]

If, then, his imagination has such power, and he is continually cultivating it and giving it play, it will acquire strength by the indulgence and exercise. This in excess is the case of mad persons. And this may be carried to that extent that he may lose sight of his identity so far as to give him a habit of speaking generally in an assumed character. So that what he says shall be tinged with the sentiments proper to the character which, at the time, has possessed itself of his imagination.

This being his idea of the poetical character, he may well say that a poet has no identity. As a man he must have identity, but as a poet he need not. And in this sense a poet is 'the most unpoetical of God's creatures',[4] for his soul has no distinctive characteristic – it cannot be itself made the subject of poetry, that is, another person's soul cannot be thrown into the poet's, for there is no identity (separatedness, distinctiveness) or personal impulse to be acted upon.

Shakespeare was a poet of the kind above mentioned, and he was perhaps the only one besides Keats who possessed this power in an extraordinary degree, so as to be a feature in his works. He gives a description of his idea of a poet:

> The poet's eye, in a fine frenzy rolling,
> Doth glance from heaven to earth, from earth to heaven;
> And as imagination bodies forth
> The forms of things unknown, the poet's pen
> Turns them to shapes, and gives to airy nothing
> A local habitation and a name.[5]

Lord Byron does not come up to this character. He can certainly conceive and describe a dark accomplished villain in love, and a female tender and kind who loves him; or a sated and palled sensualist, misanthrope, and deist[6] – but here his power ends. The true poet cannot only conceive this, but can assume any character, essence, idea, or substance at pleasure. And he has this imaginative faculty not in a limited manner, but in full universality.

Let us pursue speculation on these matters, and we shall soon be brought to believe in the truth of every syllable of Keats' letter, taken as a description of himself and his own ideas and feelings.

---

[2] *annihilated* Woodhouse is discussing negative capability; for Keats's account see p. 1019.

[3] 'The power of his imagination is apparent in every page of his *Endymion*. And he has affirmed that he can conceive of a billiard ball – that it may have a sense of delight from its own roundness, smoothness, volubility, and the rapidity of its motion' (Woodhouse's note).

[4] Woodhouse is quoting from a letter Keats had sent him that day; see p. 1042.

[5] *A Midsummer Night's Dream* V i 12–17.

[6] Woodhouse has in mind a range of works by Byron. The latest hit of the moment was *Beppo*, published in the summer of 1818. Woodhouse seems also to be referring to *Manfred* (1816) and *Childe Harold's Pilgrimage*, the final Canto of which had been published in April 1818.

Letter from Richard Woodhouse to John Taylor, 19 September 1819
(extract)

He had 'The Eve of St Agnes' copied fair.[1] He has made trifling alterations, inserted an additional stanza early in the poem to make the *legend* more intelligible,[2] and correspondent[3] with what afterwards takes place, particularly with respect to the supper and the playing on the lute. He retains the name of Porphyro, has altered the last three lines to leave on the reader a sense of pettish disgust, by bringing Old Angela in (only) dead, stiff and ugly.[4] He says he likes that the poem should leave off with this change of sentiment – it was what he aimed at, and was glad to find from my objections to it that he had succeeded. I apprehend he had a fancy for trying his hand at an attempt to play with his reader, and fling him off[5] at last. I should have thought he affected the 'Don Juan'[6] style of mingling up sentiment and sneering, but that he had before asked Hessey[7] if he could procure him a sight of that work, as he had not met with it – and if 'The Eve of St Agnes' had not, in all probability, been altered before his Lordship[8] had thus flown in the face of the public.

There was another alteration, which I abused for 'a full hour by the Temple clock'.[9] You know, if a thing has a decent side, I generally look no further. As the poem was originally written, *we* innocent ones (ladies and myself) might very well have supposed that Porphyro, when acquainted with Madeline's love for him, and when 'he arose, / Ethereal, flushed'[10] etc. etc. (turn to it), set himself at once to persuade her to go off with him, and succeeded and went over the 'Dartmoor black' (now changed for some other place)[11] to be married, in right honest, chaste, and sober wise.[12] But as it is now altered, as soon as Madeline has confessed her love, Porphyro winds by degrees his arm round her, presses breast to breast, and acts all the acts of a bona fide husband, while she fancies she is only playing the part of a wife in a dream.[13]

This alteration is of about three stanzas, and though there are no improper expressions, but all is left to inference; and though, profanely speaking, the interest on the reader's imagination is greatly heightened – yet I do apprehend it will render the poem unfit for ladies, and indeed scarcely to be mentioned to them among the 'things that are'.[14] He says he does not want ladies to read his poetry; that he writes for men,[15] and that if in the former poem there was an opening for doubt what took place, it was his fault for not writing clearly and comprehensibly; that he should despise a man who would be such an eunuch in sentiment as to leave a maid, with that character about her, in such a situation;[16] and should despise himself to write about it, etc., etc., etc. – and all this sort of Keats-like rodomontade.[17]

LETTER FROM RICHARD WOODHOUSE TO JOHN TAYLOR

[1]   *The Eve of St Agnes* was composed between 18 January and 2 February 1819, and revised the following September. Woodhouse is discussing Keats's revisions, not all of which were published in the 1820 text.

[2]   *inserted . . . intelligible* The stanza was not included in the published text; I include it in a note, p. 1044 n. 10.

[3]   *correspondent* consistent.

[4]   See *The Eve of St Agnes* 375–8.

[5]   *fling him off* i.e. Keats is trying deliberately to disgust the reader at the end of the poem.

[6]   Byron's poem had been published anonymously on 15 July 1819.

[7]   James Augustus Hessey (1785–1870), business partner of John Taylor (1781–1864); together they published Keats, Clare, Hazlitt and Lamb.

[8]   *his Lordship* i.e. Byron.

[9]   *1 Henry IV* V iv 148: 'fought a long hour by Shrewsbury clock'.

[10]   *The Eve of St Agnes* 317–18.

[11]   *now changed . . . place* 'the southern moors' (line 351).

[12]   *wise* manner.

[13]   *But as it is now altered . . . dream* see stanzas 35–6. The revised stanza did not appear in the 1820 text; I include it in a footnote, p. 1052 n. 66.

[14]   An allusion that demonstrates how well read Woodhouse was; as Bob Cummings tells me, the quotation is from Shelley, *The Revolt of Islam* (1818), ix stanza 29: 'let sense and thought / Pass from our being, or be numbered not / Among the things that are' (ll. 4–6).

[15]   *that he writes for men* this extraordinary statement may have been suggested by Keats's desire to resist the 'effeminate' influence of Leigh Hunt, and imitate the more 'manly' poetry of Byron; see my 'Keats and Byron: A Reassessment', *Byron Journal* 24 (1996) 12–32.

[16]   *in such a situation* i.e. in bed, 'entoiled in woofed fantasies'.

[17]   *rodomontade* vainglorious bragging.